Oxford
Thesaurus of
Current English

Compiled by
Alan Spooner

OXFORD
UNIVERSITY PRESS

OXFORD
UNIVERSITY PRESS

Great Clarendon Street, Oxford OX2 6DP

Oxford University Press is a department of the University of Oxford.
It furthers the University's objective of excellence in research, scholarship,
and education by publishing worldwide in

Oxford New York

Auckland Bangkok Buenos Aires Cape Town Chennai
Dar es Salaam Delhi Hong Kong Istanbul Karachi Kolkata
Kuala Lumpur Madrid Melbourne Mexico City Mumbai
Nairobi São Paulo Singapore Taipei Tokyo Toronto

Oxford is a registered trade mark of Oxford University Press
in the UK and in certain other countries

© Alan Spooner 1992, 1997, 1998, 2003

First published as the *Oxford Quick Reference Thesaurus* 1997
Published as the *Oxford Thesaurus of Current English* 1992, 2003

British Library Cataloguing in Publication Data
Data available

Library of Congress Cataloging in Publication Data
Data available

ISBN 0-19-860746-6
ISBN 0-19-5419162 (Canadian edition)

10 9 8 7 6 5 4 3 2 1

Printed in Great Britain by
Clays Ltd. Bungay, Suffolk

Contents

Preface

A thesaurus helps you find the words you need to express yourself more effectively and more interestingly. This thesaurus is designed to combine maximum ease of use with maximum helpfulness. It includes a larger range of synonyms and other information than might be expected in a book of this size. Headwords are arranged in a simple alphabetical sequence, and the organization of each entry is straightforward and largely self-explanatory. Normally, you will find what you want under the headword you look up, though cross-references may be necessary if you need opposites, or if you want a larger range of words to choose from.

A thesaurus should be used with caution. Firstly, no synonym list should be regarded as 'complete'. Many could be extended, some almost indefinitely. Consider, for example, the variety of words we might substitute for (say) *good* or *pleasant*. Secondly, seldom in English are two words completely interchangeable. So-called synonyms may convey distinct nuances of meaning, or belong to different contexts, or carry different signals about the writer or intended reader—and so on. I hope, therefore, that this volume will be a useful resource, but not just as a lifeless repository of 'words to use': my main hope is that a thesaurus will prompt us to *think* about language, and enable us to exploit more fully our own knowledge and understanding of its complex processes.

ALAN SPOONER

Using the thesaurus

In this thesaurus you will find

Headwords

The words you want to look up are printed in bold and arranged in a single alphabetical sequence. In addition, there may be sub-heads in bold at the end of main entries for derived forms and phrases.

Synonyms

Synonyms are listed alphabetically, except that distinct senses of a headword are numbered and treated separately.

Under some headwords, in addition to the lists of synonyms given there, a cross-reference printed in SMALL CAPITALS takes you to another entry to provide an extended range of synonyms. These cross-references are marked by the arrowhead symbol ▷.

Related words

Lists of words which are not synonyms but which have a common relationship to the headword (eg, kinds of vehicle listed under *vehicle*) are printed in italic, flagged by the symbol □.

Antonyms

Cross-references printed in SMALL CAPITALS introduce you to lists of opposites. These cross-references are preceded by the abbreviation Opp.

Part-of-speech labels

Part-of-speech labels are given throughout. (See list of abbreviations.) Under each headword, uses as adjective, adverb, noun, and verb are separated by the symbol ●.

Illustrative phrases

Meanings of less obvious senses are indicated by illustrative phrases printed in *italic*.

Usage warnings

Usage markers in *italic* precede words which are normally informal, derogatory, etc. (See list of abbreviations.)

Abbreviations

Parts of speech

adj	adjective
adv	adverb
int	interjection
n	noun
prep	preposition
vb	verb

Other abbreviations

derog	normally used in a derogatory, negative, or uncomplimentary sense
fem	feminine
inf	normally used informally
joc	normally jocular or joking
old use	old-fashioned or obsolete
opp	opposites, antonyms
plur	plural
poet	poetic
sl	slang
Amer	word or phrase usually regarded as American usage
Fr	word or phrase common in English contexts, but still identifiably French
Ger	ditto German
Gr	ditto Greek
It	ditto Italian
Lat	ditto Latin
Scot	word or phrase usually regarded as Scottish usage
▷	This symbol shows that you will find relevant information if you go to the word indicated.

A

abandon *v* **1** evacuate, leave, quit, vacate, withdraw from. **2** break with, desert, *inf* dump, forsake, jilt, leave behind, *inf* leave in the lurch, maroon, renounce, strand, *inf* throw over, *inf* wash your hands of. **3** *abandon a claim.* abdicate, cancel, cede, *sl* chuck in, discontinue, disown, *inf* ditch, drop, forfeit, forgo, give up, relinquish, resign, surrender, waive, yield.

abbey *n* cathedral, church, convent, friary, monastery, nunnery, priory.

abbreviate *v* abridge, compress, condense, cut, digest, edit, précis, reduce, shorten, summarize, truncate. *Opp* LENGTHEN.

abdicate *v* renounce the throne, *inf* step down. ▷ ABANDON, RESIGN.

abduct *v* carry off, kidnap, *inf* make away with, seize.

abhor *v* detest, execrate, loathe, shudder at. ▷ HATE.

abhorrent *adj* abominable, detestable, execrable, loathsome, nauseating, obnoxious, repellent, revolting. ▷ HATEFUL. *Opp* ATTRACTIVE.

abide *v* **1** accept, bear, endure, put up with, stand, *inf* stomach, suffer, tolerate. **2** ▷ STAY. **abide by** ▷ OBEY.

ability *n* aptitude, bent, brains, capability, capacity, cleverness, competence, expertise, flair, genius, gift, intelligence, knack, *inf* know-how, knowledge, means, power, proficiency, prowess, resources, scope, skill, strength, talent, training, wit.

ablaze *adj* afire, aflame, aglow, alight, blazing, burning, flaming, lit up, on fire, raging.

able *adj* **1** accomplished, adept, capable, clever, competent, effective, efficient, experienced, expert, *inf* handy, intelligent, masterly, practised, proficient, skilful, skilled, talented. *Opp* INCOMPETENT. **2** allowed, at liberty, authorized, available, eligible, fit, free, permitted, willing. *Opp* UNABLE.

abnormal *adj* aberrant, anomalous, atypical, *inf* bent, bizarre, curious, deformed, deviant, distorted, eccentric, exceptional, extraordinary, freak, funny, idiosyncratic, irregular, *inf* kinky, malformed, odd, peculiar, perverted, queer, singular, strange, uncharacteristic, unnatural, unorthodox, unrepresentative, untypical, unusual, wayward, weird. *Opp* NORMAL.

abolish *v* abrogate, annul, delete, destroy, dispense with, do away with, eliminate, end, eradicate, finish, get rid of, liquidate, nullify, overturn, put an end to, quash, remove, suppress, terminate, withdraw. *Opp* CREATE.

abominable *adj* abhorrent, appalling, atrocious, awful, base, beastly, brutal, cruel, despicable, detestable, disgusting, dreadful, execrable, foul, hateful, heinous, horrible, inhuman, inhumane, loathsome, nasty, obnoxious, odious, repellent, repugnant, repulsive, revolting, terrible, vile. ▷ UNPLEASANT. *Opp* PLEASANT.

abort *v* **1** be born prematurely, die, miscarry. **2** *abort take-off.* call off, end, halt, nullify, stop, terminate.

abortion *n* **1** miscarriage, premature birth, termination of pregnancy. **2** ▷ MONSTER.

abortive *adj* fruitless, futile, ineffective, pointless, stillborn, unfruitful, unsuccessful, vain. *Opp* SUCCESSFUL.

abound *v* be plentiful, flourish, prevail, swarm, teem, thrive.

abrasive *adj* biting, caustic, galling, grating, harsh, hurtful, irritating, rough, sharp. ▷ UNKIND. *Opp* KIND.

abridge *v* abbreviate, compress, condense, cut, edit, précis, reduce, shorten, summarize, truncate. *Opp* EXPAND.

abridged *adj* abbreviated, bowdlerized, censored, compact, concise, cut, edited, *inf* potted, shortened.

abrupt *adj* **1** hasty, headlong, hurried, precipitate, quick, rapid, sudden, unexpected, unforeseen. **2** *an abrupt drop.* precipitous, sharp, sheer, steep. **3** *an abrupt manner.* blunt, brisk, brusque, curt, discourteous, rude, snappy, terse, uncivil, ungracious *Opp* GENTLE, GRADUAL.

absent *adj* **1** away, *sl* bunking off, gone, missing, off, out, playing truant, *inf* skiving. *Opp* PRESENT. **2** ▷ ABSENT-MINDED.

absent-minded *adj* absent, absorbed, abstracted, careless, distracted, dreamy, forgetful, inattentive, oblivious, preoccupied, scatterbrained, unaware, unthinking, vague, withdrawn, wool-gathering. *Opp* ALERT.

absolute *adj* **1** categorical, certain, complete, conclusive, decided, definite, downright, genuine, implicit, inalienable, indubitable, *inf* out-and-out, perfect, positive, pure, sheer, sure, thorough, total, unadulterated, unambiguous, unconditional, unequivocal, unmitigated, unqualified, unreserved, unrestricted, utter. **2** *absolute ruler.* autocratic, despotic, dictatorial, omnipotent, totalitarian, tyrannical. **3** *absolute opposites.* *inf* dead, diametrical, exact.

absorb *v* **1** assimilate, consume, digest, drink in, hold, imbibe, incorporate, ingest, mop up, soak up, suck up, take in. *Opp* EMIT. **2** *absorb a blow.* cushion, deaden, lessen, soften. **3** *absorb a person.* captivate, engage,

engross, enthral, fascinate, occupy, preoccupy. ▷ INTEREST. **absorbed** ▷ INTERESTED.

absorbent *adj* absorptive, permeable, pervious, porous, spongy. *Opp* IMPERVIOUS.

absorbing *adj* engrossing, fascinating, gripping, spellbinding. ▷ INTERESTING.

abstain *v* **abstain from** avoid, cease, deny yourself, desist from, eschew, forgo, give up, go without, refrain from, refuse, resist, shun, withhold from.

abstemious *adj* ascetic, frugal, moderate, restrained, self-denying, sparing, temperate. *Opp* SELF-INDULGENT.

abstract *adj* **1** academic, hypothetical, indefinite, intangible, intellectual, metaphysical, notional, philosophical, theoretical, unreal. *Opp* CONCRETE. **2** *abstract art.* non-pictorial, non-representational, symbolic. ● *n* outline, précis, résumé, summary, synopsis.

abstruse *adj* complex, cryptic, deep, devious, difficult, enigmatic, esoteric, hard, incomprehensible, mysterious, obscure, perplexing, problematical, profound, unfathomable. *Opp* OBVIOUS.

absurd *adj* crazy, daft, eccentric, farcical, foolish, grotesque, illogical, incongruous, irrational, laughable, ludicrous, nonsensical, outlandish, paradoxical, preposterous, ridiculous, senseless, silly, stupid, surreal, unreasonable, zany. ▷ FUNNY, MAD. *Opp* RATIONAL.

abundant *adj* ample, bountiful, copious, excessive, flourishing, generous, lavish, liberal, luxuriant, overflowing, plentiful, profuse, rampant, rank, rich, well-supplied. *Opp* SCARCE.

abuse *n* **1** assault, ill-treatment, maltreatment, misappropriation, misuse, perversion. **2** *verbal abuse.* curse, execration, imprecation, insult, invective, obscenity, slander, vilification, vituperation. ● *v* **1** damage, exploit, harm, hurt, ill-treat, injure, maltreat, misuse, molest, rape, spoil, treat roughly. **2** *abuse verbally*. affront, berate, be rude to, *inf* call names, castigate, curse, defame, denigrate, insult, inveigh against, libel, malign, revile, slander, *inf* smear, sneer at, swear at, vilify, vituperate, wrong.

abusive *adj* acrimonious, angry, censorious, critical, cruel, defamatory, denigrating, derogatory, disparaging, hurtful, impolite, injurious, insulting, libellous, offensive, opprobrious, pejorative, rude, scathing, scornful, scurrilous, slanderous, vituperative. *Opp* POLITE.

abysmal *adj* **1** bottomless, boundless, deep, immeasurable, incalculable, infinite, profound, vast. **2** ▷ BAD.

abyss *n inf* bottomless pit, chasm, crater, fissure, gap, gulf, hole, pit, rift, void.

academic *adj* **1** educational, pedagogical, scholastic. **2** bookish, brainy, clever, erudite, highbrow, intelligent, learned, scholarly, studious. **3** *academic study*. abstract, conjectural, hypothetical, impractical, intellectual, speculative, theoretical. ● *n inf* egghead, highbrow, intellectual, scholar, thinker.

accelerate *v* **1** *inf* get a move on, go faster, hasten, pick up speed, quicken, speed up. **2** bring on, expedite, spur on, step up, stimulate.

accent *n* **1** brogue, cadence, dialect, enunciation, intonation, pronunciation, speech pattern, tone. **2** accentuation, beat, emphasis, pulse, rhythm, stress.

accept *v* **1** get, *inf* jump at, receive, take, welcome. **2** acknowledge, admit, bear, put up with, reconcile yourself to, resign yourself to, submit to, suffer, tolerate, undertake. **3** *accept an argument*. abide by, accede to, acquiesce in, agree to, believe in, be reconciled to, consent to, defer to, grant, recognize, *inf* stomach, *inf* swallow, take in. *Opp* REJECT.

acceptable *adj* **1** agreeable, gratifying, pleasant, pleasing, worthwhile. **2** adequate, admissible, moderate, passable, satisfactory, suitable, tolerable. *Opp* UNACCEPTABLE.

acceptance *n* acquiescence, agreement, approval, consent. *Opp* REFUSAL.

accepted *adj* acknowledged, agreed, axiomatic, common, indisputable, recognized, standard, undisputed, unquestioned. *Opp* CONTROVERSIAL.

accessible *adj* approachable, at hand, attainable, available, close, convenient, *inf* handy, within reach. *Opp* INACCESSIBLE.

accessory *n* **1** addition, appendage, attachment, component, extra. **2** ▷ ACCOMPLICE.

accident *n* **1** blunder, chance, coincidence, fate, fluke, fortune, luck, misadventure, mischance, mishap, mistake, *inf* pot luck, serendipity. **2** catastrophe, collision, crash, disaster, *inf* pile-up, wreck.

accidental *adj* arbitrary, casual, chance, coincidental, *inf* fluky, fortuitous, fortunate, haphazard, inadvertent, lucky, random, unexpected, unforeseen, unintended, unintentional, unlucky, unplanned, unpremeditated. *Opp* INTENTIONAL.

acclaim *v* applaud, celebrate, cheer, clap, commend, extol, hail, honour, praise, salute, welcome.

accommodate *v* **1** assist, equip, fit, furnish, help, provide, serve, supply. **2** *accommodate guests*. billet, board, cater for, harbour, house, lodge, provide for, *inf* put up, quarter, shelter, take in. **3** *accommodate yourself to new surroundings*. accustom, adapt, reconcile. **accommodating** ▷ CONSIDERATE.

accommodation *n* board, home, housing, lodgings, pied-à-terre, premises, shelter. □ *apartment, inf bedsit, boarding house, inf digs, flat, guest house, hall of residence, hostel, hotel, inn, motel, pension, rooms, self-catering, timeshare, youth hostel.* ▷ HOUSE.

accompany *v* **1** attend, chaperon, conduct, escort, follow, go with, guard, guide, look after, partner, *inf* tag along with. **2** be associated with, be linked with, belong with, complement, occur with, supplement.

accompanying *adj* associated, attached, attendant, complementary, related.

accomplice *n* abettor, accessory, associate, collaborator, colleague, confederate, conspirator, helper, partner.

accomplish *v* achieve, attain, *inf* bring off, carry out, carry through, complete, consummate, discharge, do successfully, effect, finish, fulfil, realize, succeed in.

accomplished *adj* adept, expert, gifted, polished, proficient, skilful, talented.

accomplishment *n* ability, attainment, expertise, gift, skill, talent.

accord *n* agreement, concord, harmony, rapport, understanding.

account *n* **1** bill, calculation, check, computation, invoice, receipt, reckoning, *inf* score, statement. **2** commentary, description, diary, explanation, history, log, memoir, narrative, record, report, statement, story, tale, *inf* write-up. **3** *of no account.* advantage, benefit, concern, consequence, importance, interest, significance, use, value, worth. **account for** ▷ EXPLAIN.

accumulate *v* accrue, aggregate, amass, assemble, bring together, build up, collect, come together, gather, grow, heap up, hoard, increase, multiply, pile up, stockpile, store up. *Opp* DISPERSE.

accumulation *n* *inf* build-up, collection, conglomeration, gathering, heap, hoard, mass, stockpile, store.

accurate *adj* authentic, careful, correct, exact, factual, faultless, meticulous, minute, nice, perfect, precise, reliable, scrupulous, sound, *inf* spot-on, true, truthful, unerring, veracious. *Opp* INACCURATE.

accusation *n* allegation, charge, citation, complaint, impeachment, indictment, summons.

accuse *v* attack, blame, bring charges against, censure, charge, condemn, denounce, impeach, impugn, indict, *inf* point the finger at, prosecute, summons, tax. *Opp* DEFEND.

accustomed *adj* common, customary, established, expected, familiar, habitual, normal, ordinary, prevailing, routine, traditional, usual. **get accustomed** ▷ ADAPT.

ache *n* anguish, discomfort, hurt, pain, pang, smart, soreness, throbbing, twinge. ● *v* **1** be painful, be sore, hurt, smart, sting, throb. **2** ▷ DESIRE.

achieve *v* **1** accomplish, attain, bring off, carry out, complete, conclude, do successfully, effect, engineer, execute, finish, fulfil, manage, succeed in. **2** *achieve fame.* acquire, earn, gain, get, obtain, reach, win.

acid *adj* sharp, sour, stinging, tangy, tart, vinegary. *Opp* SWEET.

acknowledge *v* **1** accede, accept, acquiesce, admit, allow, concede, confess, confirm, endorse, grant, own up to, profess. *Opp* DENY. **2** *acknowledge a greeting.* answer, react to, reply to, respond to, return. **3** *acknowledge a friend.* greet, hail, recognize, *inf* say hello to. *Opp* IGNORE.

acme *n* apex, crown, height, highest point, peak, pinnacle, summit, top, zenith. *Opp* NADIR.

acquaint *v* announce, apprise, brief, enlighten, inform, make aware, make familiar, notify, reveal, tell.

acquaintance *n* **1** awareness, familiarity, knowledge, understanding. **2** ▷ FRIEND.

acquire *v* buy, come by, earn, get, obtain, procure, purchase.

acquisition *n* accession, addition, *inf* buy, gain, possession, purchase.

acquit *v* absolve, clear, declare innocent, discharge, excuse, exonerate, find innocent, free, *inf* let off, release, reprieve, set free, vindicate. *Opp* CONDEMN. **acquit yourself** ▷ BEHAVE.

acrid *adj* bitter, caustic, pungent, sharp, unpleasant.

acrimonious *adj* abusive, acerbic, angry, bad-tempered, bitter, caustic, hostile, hot-tempered, ill-natured, ill-tempered, irascible, quarrelsome, rancorous, sarcastic, sharp, spiteful, tart, testy, venomous, virulent, waspish. *Opp* PEACEABLE.

act *n* **1** deed, exploit, feat, operation, undertaking. ▷ ACTION. **2** *act of parliament*. bill [= *draft act*], decree, edict, law, regulation, statute. **3** *a stage act*. performance, routine, sketch, turn. ● *v* **1** behave, carry on, conduct yourself, deport yourself. **2** function, operate, serve, take effect, work. **3** *Act now!* do something, get involved, take steps. ▷ BEGIN. **4** *act a role*. appear (as), *derog* camp it up, characterize, dramatize, enact, *derog* ham it up, impersonate, mime, mimic, *derog* overact, perform, personify, play, portray, pose as, represent. ▷ PRETEND.

acting *adj* deputy, interim, standby, stopgap, substitute, temporary, vice-.

action *n* **1** act, deed, enterprise, exploit, feat, measure, performance, proceeding, step, undertaking, work. **2** activity, drama, energy, enterprise, excitement, exertion, liveliness, movement, vigour, vitality. **3** *action of a play*. events, happenings, story. **4** *action of a watch*. mechanism, operation, working, works. **5** *military action*. ▷ BATTLE.

activate *v* actuate, energize, excite, fire, galvanize, initiate, mobilize, rouse, set in motion, set off, start, stimulate, trigger.

active *adj* **1** animated, brisk, bustling, busy, dynamic, energetic, enthusiastic, functioning, hyperactive, live, lively, militant, nimble, *inf* on the go, restless, sprightly, strenuous, vigorous, vivacious, working. **2** *active support*. committed, dedicated, devoted, diligent, hard-working, industrious, involved, occupied, sedulous, staunch, zealous. *Opp* INACTIVE.

activity *n* **1** action, animation, bustle, commotion, energy, hurly-burly, hustle, industry, life, movement, stir. **2** hobby, interest, job, occupation, pastime, pursuit, task, venture. ▷ WORK.

actor, actress *ns* artist, artiste, lead, leading lady, performer, player, star, supporting actor. ▷ ENTERTAINER. **actors** cast, company, troupe.

actual *adj* authentic, bona fide, confirmed, corporeal, definite, existing, factual, genuine, indisputable, in existence, legitimate, living, material, real, tangible, true, verifiable. *Opp* IMAGINARY.

acute *adj* **1** narrow, pointed, sharp. **2** *acute pain*. excruciating, exquisite, extreme, intense, keen, piercing, racking, severe, sharp, shooting, violent. **3** *an acute mind*. alert, analytical, astute, *inf* cute, discerning, incisive, intelligent, keen, penetrating, perceptive, sharp, subtle. ▷ CLEVER. **4** *an acute problem*. crucial, immediate, important, overwhelming, pressing, serious, urgent. **5** *an acute illness*. critical, sudden. *Opp* CHRONIC, STUPID.

adapt *v* **1** acclimatize, accustom, adjust, attune, become conditioned, become hardened, fit, get accustomed (to), get used (to), habituate, reconcile, suit, tailor, turn. **2** *adapt to a new use*. alter, amend, change, convert, modify, process, rearrange, rebuild, reconstruct, refashion, remake, reorganize, transform. ▷ EDIT.

add *v* annex, append, attach, combine, integrate, join, *inf* tack on, unite. *Opp* DEDUCT. **add to** ▷ INCREASE. **add up (to)** ▷ TOTAL.

addict *n* **1** alcoholic, *sl* junkie, *inf* user. **2** ▷ ENTHUSIAST.

addiction *n* compulsion, craving, dependence, fixation, habit, obsession.

addition *n* **1** adding up, calculation, computation, reckoning, totalling, *inf* totting up. **2** accession, accessory, accretion, addendum, additive, adjunct, admixture, annexe, appendage, appendix, appurtenance, attachment, continuation, development, expansion, extension, extra, increase, increment, postscript, supplement.

additional *adj* added, extra, further, increased, more, new, other, spare, supplementary.

address *n* **1** directions, location, whereabouts. **2** *deliver an address*. discourse, harangue, homily, lecture, sermon, speech, talk. ● *v* **1** accost, approach, *inf* buttonhole, greet, hail, salute, speak to, talk to. **2** *address an audience*. give a speech to, harangue, lecture. **address yourself to** ▷ TACKLE.

adept *adj* clever, competent, gifted, practised, proficient. ▷ SKILFUL. *Opp* UNSKILFUL.

adequate *adj* acceptable, all right, average, competent, fair, fitting, middling, *inf* OK, passable, presentable, satisfactory, *inf* so-so, sufficient, tolerable. *Opp* INADEQUATE.

adhere *v* bind, bond, cement, cling, glue, gum, paste. ▷ STICK.

adherent *n* aficionado, devotee, fan, follower, *inf* hanger-on, supporter.

adhesive *adj* glued, gluey, gummed. ▷ STICKY.

adjoining *adj* abutting, adjacent, bordering, contiguous, juxtaposed, neighbouring, next, touching. *Opp* DISTANT.

adjourn *v* break off, defer, discontinue, interrupt, postpone, put off, suspend.

adjournment *n* break, interruption, pause, postponement, recess, stay, suspension.

adjust *v* **1** adapt, alter, amend, balance, change, convert, correct, modify, put right, rectify, regulate, remake, remodel, reorganize, reshape, set, tailor, temper, tune. **2** acclimatize, accommodate, accustom, fit, habituate, reconcile yourself.

administer *v* **1** administrate, conduct affairs, control, direct, govern, lead, manage, organize, oversee, preside over, regulate, rule, run, supervise. **2** *administer justice*. carry out, execute, implement, prosecute. **3** *administer medicine*. dispense, distribute, give, hand out, measure out, mete out, provide, supply.

administrator *n* bureaucrat, civil servant, controller, director, executive, manager, *derog* mandarin, organizer. ▷ CHIEF.

admirable *adj* awe-inspiring, commendable, creditable, deserving, estimable, excellent, exemplary, great, honourable, laudable, marvellous, meritorious, pleasing, praiseworthy, wonderful, worthy. *Opp* CONTEMPTIBLE.

admiration *n* appreciation, awe, commendation, esteem, hero-worship, high regard, honour, praise, respect. *Opp* CONTEMPT.

admire *v* applaud, appreciate, approve of, be delighted by, commend, esteem, have a high opinion of, hero-worship, honour, idolize, laud, look up to, marvel at, praise, respect, revere, think highly of, value, venerate, wonder at. ▷ LOVE. **admiring** ▷ COMPLIMENTARY, RESPECTFUL.

admission *n* **1** access, admittance, entrance, entry. **2** acceptance, acknowledgement, affirmation, concession, confession, declaration, disclosure, revelation. *Opp* DENIAL.

admit *v* **1** accept, allow in, let in, provide a place (in), receive, take in. **2** *admit guilt*. accept, acknowledge, allow, concede, confess, declare, disclose, own up, recognize, reveal, say reluctantly. *Opp* DENY.

adolescence *n* boyhood, girlhood, growing up, puberty, *inf* your teens, youth.

adolescent *adj* boyish, girlish, immature, juvenile, pubescent, teenage, youthful. ● *n* boy, girl, juvenile, minor, *inf* teenager, youngster, youth.

adopt v **1** appropriate, approve, back, choose, embrace, endorse, follow, inf go for, patronize, support, take on, take up. **2** befriend, foster, stand by, take in.

adore v adulate, dote on, glorify, honour, love, revere, venerate, worship. ▷ ADMIRE. Opp HATE.

adorn v beautify, decorate, embellish, garnish, ornament, trim.

adrift adj **1** afloat, anchorless, drifting, floating. **2** aimless, astray, directionless, lost, purposeless.

adult adj full-grown, full-size, grown-up, marriageable, mature, of age. Opp IMMATURE.

adulterate v alloy, contaminate, corrupt, debase, dilute, inf doctor, pollute, taint, weaken.

advance n development, evolution, forward movement, growth, headway, improvement, progress. ● v **1** approach, bear down, come near, forge ahead, gain ground, go forward, make headway, make progress, move forward, press on, progress, inf push on. Opp RETREAT. **2** science advances. develop, evolve, improve, prosper, thrive. **3** advance your career. accelerate, assist, benefit, boost, further, help the progress of, promote. Opp HINDER. **4** advance a theory. adduce, give, present, propose, submit, suggest. **5** advance money. lend, offer, pay, provide, supply. Opp WITHHOLD.

advanced adj **1** latest, modern, sophisticated, up-to-date. **2** advanced ideas. avant-garde, contemporary, experimental, forward-looking, futuristic, imaginative, innovative, new, novel, original, pioneering, progressive, revolutionary, trend-setting, inf way-out. **3** advanced maths. complex, difficult, hard, higher. **4** advanced for her age. grown-up, mature, precocious, sophisticated, well-developed. Opp BACKWARD, BASIC.

advantage n **1** aid, asset, assistance, benefit, boon, gain, help, profit, usefulness. **2** have an advantage. dominance, edge, inf head start, superiority. **take advantage of** ▷ EXPLOIT.

advantageous adj beneficial, favourable, helpful, positive, profitable, salutary, useful, valuable, worthwhile. ▷ GOOD. Opp USELESS.

adventure n **1** chance, escapade, exploit, feat, gamble, occurrence, risk, undertaking, venture. **2** danger, excitement, hazard.

adventurous adj **1** audacious, bold, brave, courageous, daredevil, daring, derog foolhardy, intrepid, derog reckless, venturesome. **2** an adventurous trip. challenging, dangerous, difficult, exciting, hazardous, risky. Opp UNADVENTUROUS.

adversary n antagonist, attacker, enemy, foe, opponent.

adverse adj **1** attacking, censorious, critical, derogatory, hostile, hurtful, inimical, negative, uncomplimentary, unfavourable, unkind, unsympathetic. **2** adverse conditions. deleterious, detrimental, disadvantageous, harmful, inappropriate, opposing, prejudicial, uncongenial, unpropitious. Opp FAVOURABLE.

advertise v announce, broadcast, display, flaunt, make known, market, merchandise, inf plug, proclaim, promote, publicize, inf push, show off, tout.

advertisement n inf advert, bill, inf blurb, circular, commercial, handout, leaflet, notice, placard, inf plug, poster, promotion, publicity, sign, inf small ad.

advice n **1** admonition, counsel, guidance, help, opinion, recommendation, tip, view, warning. **2** ▷ NEWS.

advisable adj expedient, judicious, politic, prudent, recommended, sensible. ▷ WISE.

advise v **1** admonish, caution, counsel, enjoin, exhort, guide, instruct, recommend, suggest, urge, warn. **2** ▷ INFORM.

adviser n confidant(e), consultant, counsellor, guide, mentor.

advocate n **1** apologist, backer, champion, proponent, supporter. **2** ▷ LAWYER. ● v argue for, back, champion, favour, recommend, speak for, uphold.

aesthetic adj artistic, beautiful, cultivated, sensitive, tasteful. Opp UGLY.

affair n **1** activity, business, concern, interest, issue, matter, project, subject, topic, undertaking. **2** circumstance, episode, event, happening, incident, occurrence, thing. **3** love affair. amour, attachment, intrigue, involvement, liaison, relationship, romance.

affect v **1** act on, agitate, alter, attack, change, concern, disturb, have an effect on, have an impact on, impinge on, impress, influence, move, perturb, relate to, stir, touch, trouble, upset. **2** affect an accent. adopt, assume, feign, inf put on. ▷ PRETEND.

affectation n artificiality, insincerity, mannerism, posturing. ▷ PRETENCE.

affected adj **1** artificial, contrived, insincere, inf put on, studied, unnatural. ▷ PRETENTIOUS. **2** affected by disease. afflicted, damaged, infected, injured, poisoned, stricken, troubled.

affection n attachment, fondness, friendliness, friendship, liking, partiality, inf soft spot, tenderness, warmth. ▷ LOVE.

affectionate adj caring, doting, fond, kind, tender. ▷ LOVING. Opp ALOOF.

affinity n closeness, compatibility, kinship, like-mindedness, likeness, rapport, relationship, similarity, sympathy.

affirm v assert, aver, avow, declare, maintain, state, swear, testify.

affirmation n assertion, avowal, declaration, oath, promise, statement, testimony.

affirmative adj agreeing, assenting, concurring, confirming, positive. Opp NEGATIVE.

afflict v affect, annoy, beset, bother, burden, cause suffering to, distress, harass, harm, hurt, oppress, pain, plague, torment, torture, trouble, try, worry, wound.

affluent adj **1** inf flush, sl loaded, moneyed, prosperous, rich, wealthy, inf well-heeled, well-off, well-to-do. **2** affluent life-style. expensive, gracious, lavish, opulent, self-indulgent, sumptuous. Opp POOR.

afford v **1** be rich enough, have the means, manage to give, sacrifice, inf stand. **2** ▷ PROVIDE.

afloat adj aboard, adrift, floating, on board ship, under sail.

afraid adj **1** aghast, agitated, alarmed, anxious, apprehensive, cowardly, cowed, daunted, diffident, faint-hearted, fearful, frightened, hesitant, horrified, intimidated, jittery, nervous, panicky, panic-stricken, reluctant, scared, terrified, timid, timorous, trembling, unheroic, inf windy. Opp FEARLESS. **2** [inf] I'm afraid I'm late. apologetic, regretful, sorry. **be afraid** ▷ FEAR.

afterthought n addendum, addition, extra, postscript.

age n **1** advancing years, decrepitude, dotage, old age, senility. **2** a bygone age. days, epoch, era, time. **3** [inf] ages ago. lifetime, long time. ● v degenerate, grow older, look older, mature, mellow, ripen. **aged** ▷ OLD.

agenda n list, plan, programme, schedule, timetable.

agent n broker, delegate, envoy, executor, old use functionary, go-between, intermediary, mediator, middleman, negotiator, proxy, representative, surrogate, trustee.

aggravate v **1** add to, augment, compound, exacerbate, exaggerate, increase, inflame, intensify, make worse, worsen. Opp ALLEVIATE. **2** [Some think this use wrong.] ▷ ANNOY.

aggressive adj antagonistic, assertive, bellicose, belligerent, bullying, sl butch, destructive, hostile, sl macho, militant, offensive, pugnacious, pushful, inf pushy, quarrelsome, violent, warlike. *Opp* DEFENSIVE, PEACEABLE.

aggressor *n* assailant, attacker, instigator, invader.

agile *adj* acrobatic, adroit, deft, fleet, graceful, lissom, lithe, mobile, nimble, quick-moving, sprightly, spry, supple. *Opp* CLUMSY.

agitate *v* **1** beat, churn, froth up, ruffle, shake, stimulate, stir, toss, work up. **2** alarm, arouse, confuse, discomfit, disconcert, excite, fluster, incite, perturb, stir up, trouble, unsettle, upset, worry. *Opp* CALM. **agitated** ▷ EXCITED, NERVOUS.

agitator *n* firebrand, rabblerouser, revolutionary, troublemaker.

agonize *v* hurt, labour, suffer, worry, wrestle.

agony *n* anguish, distress, suffering, torment, torture. ▷ PAIN.

agree *v* **1** accede, acquiesce, admit, allow, assent, be willing, concede, consent, grant, make a contract, pledge yourself, promise, undertake. **2** accord, be unanimous, be united, concur, correspond, fit, get on, harmonize, match, *inf* see eye to eye. *Opp* DISAGREE. **agree on** ▷ CHOOSE. **agree with** ▷ ENDORSE.

agreeable *adj* acceptable, delightful, enjoyable, nice. ▷ PLEASANT. *Opp* DISAGREEABLE.

agreement *n* **1** accord, compatibility, concord, conformity, consensus, consent, consistency, correspondence, harmony, similarity, sympathy, unanimity, unity. **2** alliance, armistice, arrangement, bargain, compact, contract, convention, covenant, deal, *Fr* entente, pact, settlement, treaty, truce, understanding. *Opp* DISAGREEMENT.

agricultural *adj* **1** agrarian, bucolic, pastoral, rural. **2** *agricultural land.* cultivated, farmed, productive, tilled.

agriculture *n* agronomy, crofting, cultivation, farming, husbandry, tilling.

aground *adj* beached, grounded, helpless, marooned, shipwrecked, stranded.

aid *n* assistance, avail, backing, benefit, cooperation, donation, funding, grant, guidance, help, loan, patronage, relief, sponsorship, subsidy, succour, support. ● *v* abet, assist, back, benefit, collaborate with, cooperate with, encourage, facilitate, help, *inf* lend a hand, promote, prop up, *inf* rally round, relieve, subsidize, succour, support.

ailing *adj* feeble, infirm, poorly, sick, unwell, weak. ▷ ILL.

ailment *n* affliction, disorder, infirmity, sickness. ▷ ILLNESS.

aim *n* ambition, cause, design, destination, direction, dream, focus, goal, hope, intent, intention, mark, object, objective, plan, purpose, wish. ● *v* **1** address, beam, direct, fire at, line up, point, sight, take aim, train, turn, zero in on. **2** *aim to win.* aspire, design, endeavour, essay, intend, plan, propose, resolve, strive, try, want, wish.

aimless *adj* chance, directionless, purposeless, rambling, random, undisciplined, unfocused. *Opp* PURPOSEFUL.

air *n* **1** airspace, atmosphere, ether, heavens, sky. **2** *fresh air.* breath, breeze, draught, wind, *poet* zephyr. **3** *air of authority.* ambience, appearance, aspect, aura, bearing, character, demeanour, feeling, impression, look, manner, mood, style. ● *v* **1** aerate, dry off, freshen, ventilate. **2** *air opinions.* articulate, display, exhibit, express, give vent to, make known, make public, vent, voice.

aircraft *n old use* flying-machine. □ aeroplane, airliner, airship, balloon, biplane, bomber, dirigible, fighter, glider, gunship, hang-glider, helicopter, jet, jumbo, jump-jet, monoplane, plane, seaplane.

airman *n* aviator, flier, pilot.

airport *n* aerodrome, airfield, air strip, heliport, landing-strip, runway.

airy *adj* breezy, draughty, fresh, open, ventilated. *Opp* STUFFY.

aisle *n* corridor, passage, passageway.

akin *adj* allied, related, similar.

alarm *n* 1 alert, signal, warning. □ *alarm-clock*, *bell*, *fire-alarm*, *siren*, *whistle*. 2 anxiety, consternation, dismay, fright, nervousness, panic, uneasiness. ▷ FEAR. ● *v* agitate, dismay, distress, panic, *inf* put the wind up, shock, startle, unnerve, worry. ▷ FRIGHTEN. *Opp* REASSURE.

alcohol *n sl* bevvy, *inf* booze, drink, intoxicant, liquor, spirits, wine.

alcoholic *adj* brewed, distilled, fermented, intoxicating, *inf* strong. ● *n* addict, dipsomaniac, drunkard, inebriate. *Opp* TEETOTALLER.

alert *adj* active, alive (to), attentive, awake, careful, eagle-eyed, heedful, lively, observant, on the lookout, on the watch, on your guard, on your toes, perceptive, ready, sensitive, sharp-eyed, vigilant, watchful, wide-awake. *Opp* ABSENT-MINDED, INATTENTIVE. ● *v* advise, alarm, forewarn, make aware, notify, signal, tip off, warn.

alibi *n* excuse, explanation.

alien *adj* extra-terrestrial, foreign, outlandish, strange, unfamiliar. ● *n* foreigner, newcomer, outsider, stranger.

alight *adj* ablaze, aflame, blazing, burning, fiery, ignited, illuminated, lit up, live, on fire. ● *v* come down, come to rest, disembark, dismount, get down, get off, land, touch down.

align *v* 1 arrange in line, line up, straighten up. 2 *align with the opposition.* affiliate, ally, associate, join, side, sympathize.

alike *adj* analogous, cognate, comparable, equivalent, identical, indistinguishable, like, matching, parallel, resembling, similar, twin, uniform. *Opp* DISSIMILAR.

alive *adj* 1 animate, breathing, existing, extant, flourishing, in existence, live, living, *old use* quick. 2 *alive to new ideas.* ▷ ALERT. *Opp* DEAD.

allay *v* calm, check, diminish, ease, mollify, pacify, quell, quench, quieten, reduce, slake (*thirst*), subdue. ▷ ALLEVIATE. *Opp* STIMULATE.

allegation *n* accusation, assertion, charge, claim, declaration, statement, testimony.

allege *v* assert, asseverate, attest, aver, avow, claim, declare, depose, maintain, make a charge, plead, state.

allegiance *n* devotion, duty, faithfulness, fidelity, loyalty.

allergic *adj* antipathetic, averse, hostile, incompatible (with), opposed.

alleviate *v* abate, allay, ameliorate, assuage, check, diminish, ease, lessen, lighten, mitigate, moderate, quell, quench, reduce, relieve, slake (*thirst*), soften, subdue, temper. *Opp* AGGRAVATE.

alliance *n* affiliation, agreement, bloc, cartel, coalition, compact, concordat, confederation, connection, consortium, covenant, entente, federation, guild, marriage, pact, partnership, relationship, treaty, union.

allot *v* allocate, allow, assign, deal out, *inf* dish out, dispense, distribute, *inf* dole out, give out, grant, provide, ration, share out.

allow *v* 1 approve, authorize, consent to, enable, grant permission for, let, license, permit, sanction, *inf* stand, tolerate. *Opp* FORBID. 2 acknowledge, admit, concede, grant, own. 3 ▷ ALLOT. *Opp* DENY.

allowance *n* 1 allocation, measure, portion, quota, ration, share. 2 alimony, annuity, grant, payment, pension, pocket money. 3 *allowance on the full price.* deduction, discount, rebate, reduction. **make allowances for** ▷ TOLERATE.

alloy *n* admixture, aggregate, amalgam, blend, compound, fusion, mixture.

allude *v* **allude to** make an allusion to, mention, refer to, speak of, touch on.

amazing

allure v attract, beguile, cajole, charm, decoy, draw, entice, fascinate, lead on, lure, magnetize, seduce, tempt.

allusion n mention, reference, suggestion.

ally n abettor, accessory, accomplice, associate, backer, collaborator, colleague, companion, comrade, confederate, friend, helper, helpmate, inf mate, partner, supporter. Opp ENEMY. • v affiliate, amalgamate, associate, band together, collaborate, combine, confederate, cooperate, form an alliance, fraternize, join, join forces, league, inf link up, marry, merge, side, inf team up, unite.

almighty adj 1 all-powerful, omnipotent, supreme. 2 ▷ BIG.

almost adv about, all but, approximately, around, as good as, just about, nearly, not quite, practically, virtually.

alone adj apart, by yourself, deserted, desolate, forlorn, friendless, isolated, lonely, lonesome, on your own, separate, single, solitary, solo, unaccompanied, unassisted.

aloof adj chilly, cold, cool, detached, disinterested, dispassionate, distant, formal, frigid, haughty, impassive, inaccessible, indifferent, remote, reserved, reticent, self-contained, self-possessed, inf standoffish, supercilious, unapproachable, unconcerned, undemonstrative, unemotional, unforthcoming, unfriendly, uninvolved, unresponsive, unsociable, unsympathetic. Opp FRIENDLY, SOCIABLE.

aloud adv audibly, clearly, distinctly, out loud.

also adv additionally, besides, furthermore, in addition, moreover, joc to boot, too.

alter v adapt, adjust, amend, change, convert, edit, emend, enlarge, modify, reconstruct, reduce, reform, remake, remodel, reorganize, reshape, revise, transform, vary.

alteration n adaptation, adjustment, amendment, change, conversion, difference, modification, reorganization, revision, transformation.

alternate v come alternately, follow each other, interchange, oscillate, replace each other, rotate, inf seesaw, substitute for each other, take turns.

alternative n 1 choice, option, selection. 2 back-up, replacement, substitute.

altitude n elevation, height.

altogether adv absolutely, completely, entirely, fully, perfectly, quite, thoroughly, totally, utterly, wholly.

always adv consistently, constantly, continually, continuously, endlessly, eternally, everlastingly, evermore, forever, invariably, perpetually, persistently, regularly, repeatedly, unceasingly, unfailingly, unremittingly.

amalgamate v affiliate, ally, associate, band together, blend, coalesce, combine, come together, compound, confederate, form an alliance, fuse, integrate, join, join forces, league, inf link up, marry, merge, mix, put together, synthesize, inf team up, unite. Opp SPLIT.

amateur adj inexperienced, lay, unpaid, unqualified. ▷ AMATEURISH. • n dabbler, dilettante, enthusiast, layman, non-professional. Opp PROFESSIONAL.

amateurish adj clumsy, crude, inf do-it-yourself, incompetent, inept, inexpert, inf roughand-ready, second-rate, shoddy, unpolished, unprofessional, unskilful, unskilled, untrained. Opp SKILLED.

amaze v astonish, astound, awe, bewilder, confound, confuse, daze, disconcert, dumbfound, inf flabbergast, perplex, inf rock, shock, stagger, startle, stun, stupefy, surprise. **amazed** ▷ SURPRISED.

amazing adj astonishing, astounding, awe-inspiring, breathtaking, exceptional, exciting, extraordinary, inf fantastic, incredible, miraculous, notable, phenomenal, prodigious, remarkable, *inf* sensational, shocking, special, staggering, startling, stunning, stupendous, unusual, *inf* wonderful. *Opp* ORDINARY.

ambassador *n* agent, attaché, *Fr* chargé d'affaires, consul, diplomat, emissary, envoy, legate, nuncio, plenipotentiary, representative.

ambiguous *adj* ambivalent, confusing, enigmatic, equivocal, indefinite, indeterminate, puzzling, uncertain, unclear, vague, woolly. ▷ UNCERTAIN. *Opp* DEFINITE.

ambition *n* **1** commitment, drive, energy, enterprise, enthusiasm, *inf* go, initiative, *inf* push, pushfulness, self-assertion, thrust, zeal. **2** aim, aspiration, desire, dream, goal, hope, ideal, intention, object, objective, target, wish.

ambitious *adj* **1** assertive, committed, eager, energetic, enterprising, enthusiastic, go-ahead, *inf* go-getting, hard-working, industrious, keen, *inf* pushy, zealous. **2** *ambitious ideas. inf* big, far-reaching, grand, grandiose, large-scale, unrealistic. *Opp* APATHETIC.

ambivalent *adj* ambiguous, backhanded (*compliment*), confusing, doubtful, equivocal, inconclusive, inconsistent, indefinite, self-contradictory, *inf* two-faced, unclear, uncommitted, unresolved, unsettled. ▷ UNCERTAIN.

ambush *n* ambuscade, attack, snare, surprise attack, trap. ● *v* attack, ensnare, entrap, intercept, lie in wait for, pounce on, surprise, swoop on, trap, waylay.

amenable *adj* accommodating, acquiescent, adaptable, agreeable, biddable, complaisant, compliant, cooperative, deferential, docile, open-minded, persuadable, responsive, submissive, tractable, willing. *Opp* OBSTINATE.

amend *v* adapt, adjust, alter, ameliorate, change, convert, correct, edit, emend, improve, make better, mend, modify, put right, rectify, reform, remedy, reorganize, reshape, revise, transform, vary.

amiable *adj* affable, agreeable, amicable, friendly, genial, good-natured, kind-hearted, kindly, likeable, well-disposed. *Opp* UNFRIENDLY.

ammunition *n* buckshot, bullet, cartridge, grenade, missile, projectile, round, shell, shrapnel.

amoral *adj* lax, loose, unethical, unprincipled, without standards. ▷ IMMORAL. *Opp* MORAL.

amorous *adj* affectionate, ardent, carnal, doting, enamoured, erotic, fond, impassioned, loving, lustful, passionate, *sl* randy, sexual, *inf* sexy. *Opp* COLD.

amount *n* aggregate, bulk, entirety, extent, lot, mass, measure, quantity, quantum, reckoning, size, sum, supply, total, value, volume, whole. ● *v* **amount to** add up to, aggregate, be equivalent to, come to, equal, make, mean, total.

ample *adj* abundant, bountiful, broad, capacious, commodious, considerable, copious, extensive, fruitful, generous, great, large, lavish, liberal, munificent, plentiful, profuse, roomy, spacious, substantial, unstinting, voluminous. ▷ BIG, PLENTY. *Opp* INSUFFICIENT.

amplify *v* **1** add to, augment, broaden, develop, dilate upon, elaborate, enlarge, expand, expatiate on, extend, fill out, lengthen, make fuller, make longer, supplement. **2** *amplify sound.* boost, heighten, increase, intensify, magnify, make louder, raise the volume. *Opp* DECREASE.

amputate *v* chop off, cut off, dock, lop off, poll, pollard, remove, sever, truncate. ▷ CUT.

amuse *v* absorb, beguile, cheer (up), delight, divert, engross, enliven, entertain, gladden, interest, involve, make laugh, occupy, please, raise a smile, *inf* tickle. *Opp* BORE. **amusing** ▷ ENJOYABLE, FUNNY.

amusement *n* **1** delight, enjoyment, fun, hilarity, laughter, mirth. ▷ MERRIMENT. **2** distraction, diversion, entertainment, game, hobby, interest, joke, leisure activity, pastime, play, pleasure, recreation, sport.

anaemic *adj* bloodless, colourless, feeble, frail, pale, pallid, pasty, sallow, sickly, unhealthy, wan, weak.

analogy *n* comparison, likeness, metaphor, parallel, resemblance, similarity, simile.

analyse *v* anatomize, assay, break down, criticize, dissect, evaluate, examine, interpret, investigate, scrutinize, separate out, take apart, test.

analysis *n* breakdown, critique, dissection, enquiry, evaluation, examination, interpretation, investigation, *inf* post-mortem, scrutiny, study, test. *Opp* SYNTHESIS.

analytical *adj* analytic, critical, *inf* in-depth, inquiring, investigative, logical, methodical, penetrating, questioning, rational, searching, systematic. *Opp* SUPERFICIAL.

anarchy *n* bedlam, chaos, confusion, disorder, disorganization, insurrection, lawlessness, misgovernment, misrule, mutiny, pandemonium, riot. *Opp* ORDER.

ancestor *n* antecedent, forebear, forefather, forerunner, precursor, predecessor, progenitor.

ancestry *n* blood, derivation, descent, extraction, family, genealogy, heredity, line, lineage, origin, parentage, pedigree, roots, stock, strain.

anchor *v* berth, make fast, moor, secure, tie up. ▷ FASTEN.

anchorage *n* harbour, haven, marina, moorings, port, refuge, sanctuary, shelter.

ancient *adj* **1** aged, antediluvian, antiquated, antique, archaic, elderly, fossilized, obsolete, old, old-fashioned, outmoded, out-of-date, passé, superannuated, time-worn, venerable. **2** *ancient times.* bygone, earlier, early, former, *poet* immemorial, *inf* olden, past, prehistoric, primeval, primitive, primordial, remote, *old use* of yore. *Opp* MODERN.

angel *n* archangel, cherub, divine messenger, seraph.

angelic *adj* **1** beatific, blessed, celestial, cherubic, divine, ethereal, heavenly, holy, seraphic, spiritual. **2** *angelic behaviour.* exemplary, innocent, pious, pure, saintly, unworldly, virtuous. ▷ GOOD. *Opp* DEVILISH.

anger *n* angry feelings, annoyance, antagonism, bitterness, choler, displeasure, exasperation, fury, hostility, indignation, ire, irritability, outrage, passion, pique, rage, rancour, resentment, spleen, tantrum, temper, vexation, wrath. ● *v inf* aggravate, antagonize, *sl* bug, displease, *inf* drive mad, enrage, exasperate, incense, incite, inflame, infuriate, irritate, madden, make angry, *inf* make someone's blood boil, *inf* needle, outrage, pique, provoke, *inf* rile, vex. ▷ ANNOY. *Opp* PACIFY.

angle *n* **1** bend, corner, crook, nook, point. **2** *a new angle.* approach, outlook, perspective, point of view, position, slant, standpoint, viewpoint. ● *v* bend, bevel, chamfer, slant, turn, twist.

angry *adj inf* aerated, apoplectic, bad-tempered, bitter, *inf* bristling, *inf* choked, choleric, cross, disgruntled, enraged, exasperated, excited, fiery, fuming, furious, heated, hostile, *inf* hot under the collar, ill-tempered, incensed, indignant, infuriated, *inf* in high dudgeon, irascible, irate, livid, mad, outraged, provoked, raging, *inf* ratty, raving, resentful, riled, seething, smouldering, *inf* sore, splenetic, *sl* steamed up, stormy, tempestuous, vexed, *inf* ugly, *inf* up in arms, wild, wrathful. ▷ ANNOYED. *Opp* CALM. **be angry, become angry** *inf* be in a paddy, *inf* blow up, boil, bridle, bristle, flare up, *inf* fly off the handle, fulminate, fume, *inf* get steamed up, lose your temper, rage, rant, rave, *inf* see red, seethe, snap, storm. **make angry** ▷ ANGER.

anguish *n* agony, anxiety, distress, grief, heartache, misery, pain, sorrow, suffering, torment, torture, tribulation, woe.

angular *adj* bent, crooked, indented, jagged, sharp-cornered, zigzag. *Opp* STRAIGHT.

animal *adj* beastly, bestial, brutish, carnal, fleshly, inhuman, instinctive, physical, savage, sensual, subhuman, wild. ● *n* beast, being, brute, creature, *pl* fauna, organism, *pl* wildlife. □ amphibian, arachnid, biped, carnivore, herbivore, insect, invertebrate, mammal, marsupial, mollusc, monster, omnivore, pet, quadruped, reptile, rodent, scavenger, vertebrate. ▷ BIRD, FISH, INSECT. □ aardvark, antelope, ape, armadillo, baboon, badger, bear, beaver, bison, buffalo, camel, caribou, cat, chamois, cheetah, chimpanzee, chinchilla, chipmunk, coypu, deer, dog, dolphin, donkey, dormouse, dromedary, elephant, elk, ermine, ferret, fox, frog, gazelle, gerbil, gibbon, giraffe, gnu, goat, gorilla, grizzly bear, guinea-pig, hamster, hare, hedgehog, hippopotamus, horse, hyena, ibex, impala, jackal, jaguar, jerboa, kangaroo, koala, lemming, lemur, leopard, lion, llama, lynx, marmoset, marmot, marten, mink, mongoose, monkey, moose, mouse, musquash, ocelot, octopus, opossum, orang-utan, otter, panda, panther, pig, platypus, polar bear, pole-cat, porcupine, porpoise, rabbit, rat, reindeer, rhinoceros, roe, salamander, scorpion, seal, sea-lion, sheep, shrew, skunk, snake, spider, squirrel, stoat, tapir, tiger, toad, vole, wallaby, walrus, weasel, whale, wildebeest, wolf, wolverine, wombat, yak, zebra.

animate *adj* alive, breathing, conscious, feeling, live, living, sentient. ▷ ANIMATED. *Opp* INANIMATE. ● *v* activate, arouse, brighten up, *inf* buck up, cheer up, encourage, energize, enliven, excite, exhilarate, fire, galvanize, incite, inspire, invigorate, kindle, liven up, make lively, move, *inf* pep up, *inf* perk up, quicken, rejuvenate, revitalize, revive, rouse, spark, spur, stimulate, stir, urge, vitalize.

animated *adj* active, alive, bright, brisk, bubbling, busy, cheerful, eager, ebullient, energetic, enthusiastic, excited, exuberant, gay, impassioned, lively, passionate, quick, spirited, sprightly, vibrant, vigorous, vivacious, zestful. *Opp* LETHARGIC.

animation *n* activity, briskness, eagerness, ebullience, energy, enthusiasm, excitement, exhilaration, gaiety, high spirits, life, liveliness, *inf* pep, sparkle, spirit, sprightliness, verve, vigour, vitality, vivacity, zest. *Opp* LETHARGY.

animosity *n* acerbity, acrimony, animus, antagonism, antipathy, asperity, aversion, bad blood, bitterness, dislike, enmity, grudge, hate, hatred, hostility, ill will, loathing, malevolence, malice, malignancy, malignity, odium, rancour, resentment, sarcasm, sharpness, sourness, spite, unfriendliness, venom, vindictiveness, virulence. *Opp* FRIENDLINESS.

annex *v* acquire, appropriate, conquer, occupy, purloin, seize, take over, usurp.

annihilate *v* abolish, destroy, eliminate, eradicate, erase, exterminate, extinguish, extirpate, *inf* finish off, *inf* kill off, *inf* liquidate, nullify, obliterate, raze, slaughter, wipe out.

annotation *n* comment, commentary, elucidation, explanation, footnote, gloss, interpretation, note.

announce *v* **1** advertise, broadcast, declare, disclose, divulge, give notice of, intimate, make public, notify, proclaim, promulgate, propound, publicize, publish, put out, report, reveal, state. **2** *announce a speaker.* introduce, lead into, preface, present.

announcement *n* advertisement, bulletin, communiqué, declaration, disclosure, intimation, notification, proclamation, promulgation, publication, report, revelation, statement.

announcer *n* anchorman, anchorwoman, broadcaster, commentator, compère, disc jockey, DJ, *poet* harbinger, herald, master of ceremonies, *inf* MC, messenger, newscaster, newsreader, reporter, town crier.

annoy *v* *inf* aggravate, antagonize, *inf* badger, be an annoyance to, bother, *sl* bug, chagrin, displease, distress, drive mad, exasperate, fret, gall, *inf* get at, *inf* get on your nerves, grate, harass, harry, infuriate, irk, irritate, jar, madden, make cross, molest, *inf* needle, *inf* nettle, offend, peeve, pester, pique, *inf* plague, provoke, put out, rankle, rile, *inf* rub up the wrong way, ruffle, *inf* spite, tease, trouble, try (someone's patience), upset, vex, worry. ▷ ANGER. *Opp* PLEASE.

annoyance *n* **1** chagrin, crossness, displeasure, exasperation, irritation, pique, vexation. ▷ ANGER. **2** *Noise is an annoyance.* inf aggravation, bother, harassment, irritant, nuisance, offence, *inf* pain in the neck, pest, provocation, worry.

annoyed *adj* chagrined, cross, displeased, exasperated, *inf* huffy, irritated, jaundiced, *inf* miffed, *inf* needled, *inf* nettled, offended, *inf* peeved, piqued, *inf* put out, *inf* riled, *inf* shirty, *inf* sore, upset, vexed. ▷ ANGRY. *Opp* PLEASED. **be annoyed** *inf* go off in a huff, take offence, *inf* take umbrage.

annoying *adj inf* aggravating, bothersome, displeasing, exasperating, galling, grating, inconvenient, infuriating, irksome, irritating, jarring, maddening, offensive, provocative, provoking, tiresome, troublesome, trying, upsetting, vexatious, vexing, wearisome, worrying.

anoint *v* **1** embrocate, grease, lubricate, oil, rub, smear. **2** bless, consecrate, dedicate, hallow, sanctify.

anonymous *adj* **1** incognito, nameless, unacknowledged, unidentified, unknown, unnamed, unspecified, unsung. **2** *anonymous letters.* unattributed, unsigned. **3** *anonymous style.* characterless, impersonal, nondescript, unidentifiable, unrecognizable, unremarkable.

answer *n* **1** acknowledgement, *inf* comeback, reaction, rejoinder, reply, response, retort, riposte. **2** explanation, outcome, solution. **3** *answer to a charge.* countercharge, defence, plea, rebuttal, refutation, vindication. ● *v* **1** acknowledge, give an answer, react, rejoin, reply, respond, retort,

return. **2** explain, resolve, solve. **3** *answer a charge.* counter, defend yourself against, disprove, rebut, refute. **4** *answer a need.* correspond to, echo, fit, match up to, meet, satisfy, serve, suffice, suit. **answer back** ▷ ARGUE.

antagonism *n* antipathy, dissension, enmity, friction, opposition, rancour, rivalry, strife. ▷ HOSTILITY.

antagonize *v* alienate, anger, annoy, embitter, estrange, irritate, make an enemy of, offend, provoke, *inf* put off, upset.

anthem *n* canticle, chant, chorale, hymn, introit, paean, psalm.

anthology *n* collection, compendium, compilation, digest, miscellany, selection, treasury.

anticipate *v* **1** forestall, obviate, preclude, pre-empt, prevent. **2** [Many think this use incorrect.] ▷ FORESEE.

anticlimax *n* bathos, *inf* comedown, *inf* damp squib, disappointment, *inf* let-down.

antics *plur n* buffoonery, capers, clowning, escapades, foolery, fooling, *inf* larking-about, pranks, *inf* skylarking, tomfoolery, tricks.

antidote *n* antitoxin, corrective, countermeasure, cure, drug, neutralizing agent, remedy.

antiquarian *n* antiquary, antiques expert, collector, dealer.

antiquated *adj* aged, anachronistic, ancient, antediluvian, archaic, dated, medieval, obsolete, old, old-fashioned, *inf* out, out-dated, outmoded, out-of-date, passé, *inf* past it, *inf* prehistoric, *inf* primeval, primitive, quaint, superannuated, unfashionable. ▷ ANTIQUE. *Opp* NEW.

antique *adj* antiquarian, collectible, historic, old-fashioned, traditional, veteran, vintage. ▷ ANTIQUATED. ● *n* collectible, collector's item, curio, curiosity, Fr objet d'art, rarity.

antiquity *n* classical times, days gone by, former times, *inf* olden days, the past.

antiseptic adj aseptic, clean, disinfectant, disinfected, germ free, germicidal, hygienic, medicated, sanitized, sterile, sterilized, sterilizing, unpolluted.

antisocial adj alienated, anarchic, disagreeable, disorderly, disruptive, misanthropic, nasty, obnoxious, offensive, rebellious, rude, troublesome, uncooperative, undisciplined, unruly, unsociable. ▷ UNFRIENDLY. Opp SOCIABLE.

anxiety n **1** angst, apprehension, concern, disquiet, distress, doubt, dread, fear, foreboding, fretfulness, misgiving, nervousness, qualm, scruple, strain, stress, tension, uncertainty, unease, worry. **2** anxiety to succeed. desire, eagerness, enthusiasm, impatience, keenness, longing, solicitude, willingness.

anxious adj **1** afraid, agitated, alarmed, apprehensive, concerned, distracted, distraught, distressed, disturbed, edgy, fearful, inf fraught, fretful, inf jittery, nervous, inf nervy, inf on edge, overwrought, perturbed, restless, tense, troubled, uneasy, upset, watchful, worried. **2** anxious to succeed. avid, careful, desirous, inf desperate, inf dying, eager, impatient, intent, inf itching, keen, longing, solicitous, willing, yearning. **be anxious** ▷ WORRY.

apathetic adj casual, cool, dispassionate, dull, emotionless, half-hearted, impassive, inactive, indifferent, indolent, languid, lethargic, listless, passive, phlegmatic, slow, sluggish, tepid, torpid, unambitious, uncommitted, unconcerned, unenterprising, unenthusiastic, unfeeling, uninterested, uninvolved, unmotivated, unresponsive. Opp ENTHUSIASTIC.

apathy n coolness, inactivity, indifference, lassitude, lethargy, listlessness, passivity, torpor. Opp ENTHUSIASM.

apex n **1** crest, crown, head, peak, pinnacle, point, summit, tip, top, vertex. **2** apex of your career. acme, apogee, climax, consummation, crowning moment, culmination, height, high point, zenith. Opp NADIR.

aphrodisiac adj arousing, erotic, inf sexy, stimulating.

apologetic adj ashamed, blushing, conscience-stricken, contrite, penitent, red-faced, regretful, remorseful, repentant, rueful, sorry. Opp UNREPENTANT.

apologize v ask pardon, be apologetic, express regret, make an apology, repent, say sorry.

apology n acknowledgement, confession, defence, excuse, explanation, justification, plea.

apostle n crusader, disciple, evangelist, follower, messenger, missionary, preacher, propagandist, proselytizer, teacher.

appal v alarm, disgust, dismay, distress, harrow, horrify, nauseate, outrage, revolt, shock, sicken, terrify, unnerve. ▷ FRIGHTEN. **appalling** ▷ ATROCIOUS, BAD, FRIGHTENING.

apparatus n appliance, inf contraption, device, equipment, gadget, inf gear, implement, instrument, machine, machinery, mechanism, inf set-up, system, inf tackle, tool, utensil.

apparent adj blatant, clear, conspicuous, detectable, discernible, evident, manifest, noticeable, observable, obvious, ostensible, overt, patent, perceptible, recognizable, self-explanatory, unconcealed, unmistakable, visible. Opp HIDDEN.

apparition n chimera, ghost, hallucination, illusion, manifestation, phantasm, phantom, presence, shade, spectre, spirit, inf spook, vision, wraith.

appeal n **1** application, call, Fr cri de coeur, cry, entreaty, petition, plea, prayer, request, solicitation, supplication. **2** allure, attractiveness, charisma, charm, inf pull, seductiveness. ● v ask earnestly, beg, beseech, call, canvass, cry out, entreat, implore, invoke, petition, plead, pray, request, solicit, supplicate. **appeal to** ▷ ATTRACT.

appear v **1** arise, arrive, attend, begin, be published, be revealed, be seen, *inf* bob up, come, come into view, come out, *inf* crop up, enter, develop, emerge, *inf* heave into sight, loom, materialize, occur, originate, show, *inf* show up, spring up, surface, turn up. **2** *I appear to be wrong.* look, seem, turn out. **3** *appear in a play.* ▷ PERFORM.

appearance n **1** arrival, advent, emergence, presence, rise. **2** *a smart appearance.* air, aspect, bearing, demeanour, exterior, impression, likeness, look, mien, semblance.

appease v assuage, calm, conciliate, humour, mollify, pacify, placate, propitiate, quiet, reconcile, satisfy, soothe, *inf* sweeten, tranquillize, win over. *Opp* ANGER.

appendix n addendum, addition, annexe, codicil, epilogue, postscript, rider, supplement.

appetite n craving, demand, desire, eagerness, fondness, greed, hankering, hunger, keenness, longing, lust, passion, predilection, proclivity, relish, *inf* stomach, taste, thirst, urge, willingness, wish, yearning, *inf* yen, zeal, zest.

appetizing adj delicious, *inf* moreish, mouthwatering, tasty, tempting.

applaud v acclaim, approve, *inf* bring the house down, cheer, clap, commend, compliment, congratulate, eulogize, extol, *inf* give someone a hand, give someone an ovation, hail, laud, praise, salute. *Opp* CRITICIZE.

applause n acclaim, acclamation, approval, cheering, clapping, éclat, ovation, plaudits. ▷ PRAISE.

appliance n apparatus, contraption, device, gadget, implement, instrument, machine, mechanism, tool, utensil.

applicant n aspirant, candidate, competitor, entrant, interviewee, participant, postulant.

apply v **1** administer, affix, bring into contact, lay on, put on, rub on, spread, stick. ▷ FASTEN. **2** *rules apply to all.* appertain, be relevant, have a bearing (on), pertain, refer, relate. **3** *apply common sense.* bring into use, employ, exercise, implement, practise, use, utilize, wield. **apply for** ▷ REQUEST. **apply yourself** ▷ CONCENTRATE.

appoint v **1** arrange, authorize, decide on, determine, establish, fix, ordain, prescribe, settle. **2** *appoint you to do a job.* assign, choose, co-opt, delegate, depute, designate, detail, elect, make an appointment, name, nominate, *inf* plump for, select, settle on, vote for.

appointment n **1** arrangement, assignation, consultation, date, engagement, fixture, interview, meeting, rendezvous, session, *old use* tryst. **2** choice, choosing, commissioning, election, naming, nomination, selection. **3** job, office, place, position, post, situation.

appreciate v **1** admire, applaud, approve of, be grateful for, be sensitive to, cherish, commend, enjoy, esteem, favour, find worthwhile, like, praise, prize, rate highly, regard highly, respect, sympathize with, treasure, value, welcome. **2** *appreciate the facts.* acknowledge, apprehend, comprehend, know, realize, recognize, see, understand. **3** *value appreciates.* build up, escalate, gain, go up, grow, improve, increase, inflate, mount, rise, soar, strengthen. *Opp* DEPRECIATE, DESPISE, DISREGARD.

apprehensive adj afraid, concerned, disturbed, edgy, fearful, *inf* jittery, nervous, *inf* nervy, *inf* on edge, troubled, uneasy, worried. ▷ ANXIOUS. *Opp* FEARLESS.

apprentice n beginner, learner, novice, probationer, pupil, starter, tiro, trainee.

approach n **1** advance, advent, arrival, coming, movement, nearing. **2** access, doorway, entrance, entry, passage, road, way in. **3** *your approach to work.* attitude, course, manner, means, method, mode, *Lat* modus operandi, procedure, style, system, technique, way. **4** *an approach for help.* appeal, application, invitation, offer,

overture, proposal, proposition. ● v
1 advance, bear down, catch up,
come near, draw near, gain (on),
loom, move towards, near, progress.
Opp RETREAT. **2** *approach a task*. ▷ BEGIN.
3 *approach someone for help*. ▷ CONTACT.

approachable adj accessible, affable, informal, kind, open, relaxed,
sympathetic, *inf* unstuffy, well-disposed. ▷ FRIENDLY. *Opp* ALOOF.

appropriate adj applicable, apposite, apropos, apt, becoming, befitting,
compatible, correct, decorous,
deserved, due, felicitous, fit, fitting,
germane, happy, just, *old use* meet,
opportune, pertinent, proper, relevant, right, seasonable, seemly,
suitable, tactful, tasteful, timely,
well-judged, well-suited, well-timed.
Opp INAPPROPRIATE. ● v annex, arrogate,
commandeer, confiscate, expropriate, gain control of, *inf* hijack, requisition, seize, take, take over,
usurp. ▷ STEAL.

approval n **1** acclaim, acclamation,
admiration, applause, appreciation,
approbation, commendation, esteem, favour, liking, plaudits, praise,
regard, respect, support. *Opp* DISAP-
PROVAL. **2** acceptance, acquiescence,
agreement, assent, authorization, *inf*
blessing, confirmation, consent,
endorsement, *inf* go-ahead, *inf* green
light, licence, mandate, *inf* OK, permission, ratification, sanction, seal,
stamp, support, *inf* thumbs up, validation. *Opp* REFUSAL.

approve v accede to, accept, affirm,
agree to, allow, assent to, authorize,
inf back, *inf* bless, confirm, consent
to, countenance, endorse, *inf* give
your blessing to, *inf* go along with,
pass, permit, ratify, *inf* rubber-stamp,
sanction, sign, subscribe to, support,
tolerate, uphold, validate. *Opp* REFUSE,
VETO. **approve of** ▷ ADMIRE.

approximate adj close, estimated,
imprecise, inexact, loose, near,
rough. *Opp* EXACT. ● v **approximate to**
approach, be close to, be similar to,
border on, come near to, equal,
roughly, look like, resemble, simulate, verge on.

approximately adv about,
approaching, around, *Lat* circa, close
to, just about, loosely, more or less,
nearly, *inf* nigh on, *inf* pushing,
roughly, round about.

aptitude n ability, bent, capability,
facility, fitness, flair, gift, suitability,
talent. ▷ SKILL.

arbitrary adj **1** capricious, casual,
chance, erratic, fanciful, illogical,
indiscriminate, irrational, random,
subjective, unplanned, unpredictable, unreasonable, whimsical, wilful. *Opp* METHODICAL. **2** *arbitrary rule*.
absolute, autocratic, despotic, dictatorial, high-handed, imperious,
summary, tyrannical, tyrannous,
uncompromising.

arbitrate v adjudicate, decide the
outcome, intercede, judge, make
peace, mediate, negotiate, pass
judgement, referee, settle, umpire.

arbitration n adjudication, *inf* good
offices, intercession, judgement,
mediation, negotiation, settlement.

arbitrator n adjudicator, arbiter,
go-between, intermediary, judge,
mediator, middleman, negotiator,
ombudsman, peacemaker, referee,
inf trouble-shooter, umpire.

arch n arc, archway, bridge, vault.
● v arc, bend, bow. ▷ CURVE.

archetype n classic, example, ideal,
model, original, paradigm, pattern,
precursor, prototype, standard.

archives plur n annals, chronicles,
documents, history, libraries, me-
morials, museums, papers, records,
registers.

ardent adj eager, enthusiastic, fervent, hot, impassioned, intense,
keen, passionate, warm, zealous. *Opp*
APATHETIC.

arduous adj backbreaking, demanding, exhausting, gruelling, heavy,
herculean, laborious, onerous, punishing, rigorous, severe, strenuous,
taxing, tiring, tough, uphill. ▷ DIFFI-
CULT. *Opp* EASY.

area n **1** acreage, breadth, expanse,
extent, patch, sheet, size, space,

square-footage, stretch, surface, tract, width. **2** district, environment, environs, locality, neighbourhood, part, precinct, province, quarter, region, sector, terrain, territory, vicinity, zone. **3** *an area of study.* field, sphere, subject.

argue *v* **1** answer back, *inf* bandy words, bargain, bicker, debate, deliberate, demur, differ, disagree, discuss, dispute, dissent, expostulate, fall out, feud, fight, haggle, have an argument, *inf* have words, object, protest, quarrel, remonstrate, *inf* row, spar, squabble, take exception, wrangle. **2** *argue a case.* assert, claim, contend, demonstrate, hold, maintain, make a case, plead, prove, reason, show, suggest.

argument *n* **1** altercation, bickering, clash, conflict, controversy, difference (of opinion), disagreement, dispute, expostulation, feud, fight, protest, quarrel, remonstration, row, *inf* set-to, squabble, *inf* tiff, wrangle. **2** consultation, debate, defence, deliberation, dialectic, discussion, exposition, polemic. **3** *argument of a lecture.* abstract, case, contention, gist, hypothesis, idea, outline, plot, reasoning, summary, synopsis, theme, thesis, view.

arid *adj* **1** barren, desert, dry, fruitless, infertile, lifeless, parched, sterile, torrid, unproductive, waste, waterless. *Opp* FRUITFUL. **2** *arid work.* boring, dreary, dull, pointless, tedious, uninspired, uninteresting, vapid.

arise *v* come up, crop up, get up, rise. ▷ APPEAR.

aristocrat *n* grandee, lady, lord, noble, nobleman, noblewoman, patrician. ▷ PEER.

aristocratic *adj inf* blueblooded, courtly, élite, gentle, highborn, lordly, noble, patrician, princely, royal, thoroughbred, titled, upper class.

arm *n* appendage, bough, branch, extension, limb, offshoot, projection.

● *v* equip, fortify, furnish, provide, supply. **arms** ▷ WEAPON(S).

armed services *pl n* force, forces, troops. □ *air force, army, militia, navy.* □ *cavalry, infantry.* □ *battalion, brigade, cohort, company, corps, foreign legion, garrison, legion, patrol, platoon, rearguard, regiment, reinforcements, squad, squadron, task-force, vanguard.* ▷ FIGHTER, RANK, SOLDIER.

armistice *n* agreement, cease-fire, peace, treaty, truce.

armoury *n* ammunition-dump, arsenal, depot, magazine, ordnance depot, stockpile.

aroma *n* bouquet, fragrance, odour, perfume, redolence, savour, scent, smell, whiff.

arouse *v* awaken, call forth, encourage, foment, foster, kindle, provoke, quicken, stimulate, stir up, *inf* whip up. ▷ CAUSE. *Opp* ALLAY.

arrange *v* **1** adjust, align, array, categorize, classify, collate, display, dispose, distribute, grade, group, lay out, line up, marshal, order, organize, *inf* pigeon-hole, position, put in order, range, rank, set out, sift, sort (out), space out, systematize, tabulate, tidy up. **2** *arrange a party.* bring about, contrive, coordinate, devise, manage, organize, plan, prepare, see to, settle, set up. **3** *arrange music.* adapt, harmonize, orchestrate, score, set.

arrangement *n* **1** adjustment, alignment, design, disposition, distribution, grouping, layout, marshalling, organization, planning, positioning, setting out, spacing, tabulation. ▷ ARRAY. **2** agreement, bargain, compact, contract, deal, pact, scheme, settlement, terms, understanding. **3** *musical arrangement.* adaptation, harmonization, orchestration, setting, version.

array *n* arrangement, assemblage, collection, demonstration, display, exhibition, formation, *inf* line-up, muster, panoply, parade, presentation, show, spectacle. ● *v* **1** adorn, apparel, attire, clothe, deck, decorate,

arrest

dress, equip, fit out, garb, rig out, robe, wrap. **2** ▷ ARRANGE.

arrest *n* apprehension, capture, detention, seizure. ● *v* **1** bar, block, check, delay, end, halt, hinder, impede, inhibit, interrupt, obstruct, prevent, restrain, retard, slow, stem, stop. **2** *arrest a suspect.* apprehend, *inf* book, capture, catch, *inf* collar, detain, have up, hold, *inf* nab, *inf* nick, *inf* pinch, *inf* run in, seize, take into custody, take prisoner.

arrival *n* **1** advent, appearance, approach, coming, entrance, homecoming, landing, return, touchdown. **2** *new arrivals.* caller, newcomer, visitor.

arrive *v* **1** appear, come, disembark, drive up, drop in, enter, get in, land, make an entrance, *inf* roll in, *inf* roll up, show up, touch down, turn up. **2** ▷ SUCCEED. **arrive at** ▷ REACH.

arrogant *adj* boastful, brash, brazen, bumptious, cavalier, *inf* cocky, conceited, condescending, disdainful, egotistical, haughty, *inf* high and mighty, high-handed, imperious, impudent, insolent, lofty, lordly, overbearing, patronizing, pompous, presumptuous, proud, scornful, self-admiring, self-important, smug, snobbish, *inf* snooty, *inf* stuck-up, supercilious, superior, vain. *Opp* MODEST.

arsonist *n* fire-raiser, incendiary, pyromaniac.

art *n* **1** aptitude, artistry, cleverness, craft, craftsmanship, dexterity, expertise, facility, knack, proficiency, skilfulness, skill, talent, technique, touch, trick. **2** artwork, craft, fine art. □ *architecture, batik, carpentry, cloisonné, collage, crochet, drawing, embroidery, enamelling, engraving, etching, fashion design, graphics, handicraft, illustration, jewellery, knitting, linocut, lithography, marquetry, metalwork, modelling, monoprint, needlework, origami, painting, patchwork, photography, pottery, printmaking, sculpture, sewing, sketching, spinning, weaving, woodcut, woodwork.*

artful *adj* astute, canny, clever, crafty, cunning, deceitful, designing, devious, *inf* fly, *inf* foxy, ingenious, knowing, scheming, shrewd, skilful, sly, smart, sophisticated, subtle, tricky, wily. *Opp* NAÏVE.

article *n* **1** item, object, thing. **2** *magazine article.* ▷ WRITING.

articulate *adj* clear, coherent, comprehensible, distinct, eloquent, expressive, fluent, *derog* glib, intelligible, lucid, understandable, vocal. *Opp* INARTICULATE. ● *v* ▷ SPEAK.

articulated *adj* bending, flexible, hinged, jointed.

artificial *adj* **1** fabricated, made-up, man-made, manufactured, synthetic, unnatural. **2** *artificial style.* affected, assumed, bogus, concocted, contrived, counterfeit, factitious, fake, false, feigned, forced, imitation, insincere, laboured, mock, *inf* phoney, pretended, pseudo, *inf* put on, sham, simulated, spurious, unreal. *Opp* NATURAL.

artist *n* craftsman, craftswoman. □ *architect, carpenter, cartoonist, commercial artist, designer, draughtsman, draughtswoman, engraver, goldsmith, graphic designer, illustrator, mason, painter, photographer, potter, printer, sculptor, silversmith, smith, weaver.* ▷ ENTERTAINER, MUSICIAN, PERFORMER.

artistic *adj* aesthetic, attractive, beautiful, creative, cultured, decorative, *inf* designer, imaginative, ornamental, tasteful. *Opp* UGLY.

ascend *v* climb, come up, defy gravity, fly, go up, levitate, lift off, make an ascent, mount, move up, rise, scale, slope up, soar, take off. *Opp* DESCEND.

ascent *n* ascension, climb, gradient, hill, incline, ramp, rise, slope. *Opp* DESCENT.

ascertain *v* confirm, determine, discover, establish, find out, identify, learn, make certain, make sure, settle, verify.

ascetic *adj* abstemious, austere, celibate, chaste, frugal, harsh, hermit-like, plain, puritanical, restrained, rigorous, selfcontrolled, self-denying, selfdisciplined, severe, spartan, strict, temperate. *Opp* SELF-INDULGENT.

ash *n* burnt remains, cinders, clinker, embers.

ashamed *adj* **1** abashed, apologetic, chagrined, chastened, conscience-stricken, contrite, discomfited, distressed, guilty, humbled, humiliated, mortified, penitent, red-faced, remorseful, repentant, rueful, shamefaced, sorry, upset. **2** *ashamed of your nakedness.* bashful, blushing, demure, diffident, embarrassed, modest, prudish, self-conscious, sheepish, shy. *Opp* SHAMELESS.

ask *v* appeal, apply, badger, beg, beseech, catechize, crave, demand, enquire, entreat, implore, importune, inquire, interrogate, invite, petition, plead, pose a question, pray, press, query, question, quiz, request, require, seek, solicit, sue, supplicate. **ask for** ▷ ATTRACT.

asleep *adj* comatose, *inf* dead to the world, dormant, dozing, *inf* fast off, hibernating, inactive, inattentive, *inf* in the land of nod, *sl* kipping, napping, *inf* off, *inf* out like a light, resting, sedated, sleeping, slumbering, snoozing, *inf* sound off, unconscious, under sedation. ▷ NUMB. *Opp* AWAKE.

aspect *n* **1** angle, attribute, characteristic, circumstance, detail, element, facet, feature, quality, side, standpoint, viewpoint. **2** air, appearance, attitude, bearing, countenance, demeanour, expression, face, look, manner, mien, visage. **3** *a southern aspect.* direction, orientation, outlook, position, prospect, situation, view.

asperity *n* abrasiveness, acerbity, acidity, acrimony, astringency, bitterness, churlishness, crossness, harshness, hostility, irascibility, irritability, peevishness, rancour, roughness, severity, sharpness, sourness, venom, virulence. *Opp* MILDNESS.

aspiration *n* aim, ambition, craving, desire, dream, goal, hope, longing, objective, purpose, wish, yearning.

aspire *v* **aspire to** aim for, crave, desire, dream of, hope for, long for, pursue, seek, set your sights on, strive after, want, wish for, yearn for. **aspiring** ▷ POTENTIAL.

assail *v* assault, bombard, pelt, set on. ▷ ATTACK.

assault *n* battery, *inf* GBH, mugging, rape. ▷ ATTACK. ● *v* abuse, assail, *inf* beat up, *inf* do over, fall on, fight, fly at, jump on, lash out at, *inf* lay into, mob, molest, mug, *inf* pitch into, pounce on, rape, rush at, set about, set on, strike at, violate, *inf* wade into. ▷ ATTACK.

assemble *v* **1** come together, congregate, convene, converge, crowd, flock, gather, group, herd, join up, meet, rally round, swarm, throng round. **2** accumulate, amass, bring together, collect, gather, get together, marshal, mobilize, muster, pile up, rally, round up. **3** build, construct, erect, fabricate, fit together, make, manufacture, piece together, produce, put together. *Opp* DISMANTLE, DISPERSE.

assembly *n* assemblage, conclave, conference, congregation, congress, convention, convocation, council, gathering, meeting, parliament, rally, synod. ▷ CROWD.

assent *n* acceptance, accord, acquiescence, agreement, approbation, approval, compliance, consent, *inf* go-ahead, permission, sanction, willingness. *Opp* REFUSAL. ● *v* accede, accept, acquiesce, agree, approve, be willing, comply, concede, concur, consent, express agreement, give assent, say 'yes', submit, yield. *Opp* REFUSE.

assert *v* affirm, allege, argue, asseverate, attest, claim, contend, declare, emphasize, insist, maintain, proclaim, profess, protest, state, stress, swear, testify. **assert yourself** ▷ INSIST.

assertive *adj* aggressive, assured, authoritative, bold, *inf* bossy, certain, confident, decided, decisive, definite, dogmatic, domineering, emphatic, firm, forceful, insistent, peremptory, *derog* opinionated, positive, *derog* pushy, self-assured, strong, strong-willed, *derog* stubborn, uncompromising. *Opp* SUBMISSIVE.

assess v appraise, assay (*metal*), calculate, compute, consider, determine, estimate, evaluate, fix, gauge, judge, price, reckon, review, *inf* size up, value, weigh up, work out.

asset n advantage, aid, benefit, blessing, boon, *inf* godsend, good, help, profit, resource, strength, support. **assets** capital, effects, estate, funds, goods, holdings, means, money, possessions, property, resources, savings, securities, valuables, wealth, *inf* worldly goods.

assign v **1** allocate, allot, apportion, consign, dispense, distribute, give, hand over, share out. **2** *assign to a job.* appoint, authorize, delegate, designate, nominate, ordain, prescribe, put down, select, specify, stipulate. **3** *assign my success to luck.* accredit, ascribe, attribute, credit.

assignment n chore, duty, errand, job, mission, obligation, post, project, responsibility, task. ▷ WORK.

assist v abet, advance, aid, back, benefit, boost, collaborate, co-operate, facilitate, further, help, *inf* lend a hand, promote, *inf* rally round, reinforce, relieve, second, serve, succour, support, sustain, work with. *Opp* HINDER.

assistance n aid, backing, benefit, collaboration, contribution, co-operation, encouragement, help, patronage, reinforcement, relief, sponsorship, subsidy, succour, support. *Opp* HINDRANCE.

assistant n abettor, accessory, accomplice, acolyte, aide, ally, associate, auxiliary, backer, collaborator, colleague, companion, comrade, confederate, deputy, helper, helpmate, *inf* henchman, mainstay, *derog* minion, partner, *inf* right-hand man, *inf* right-hand woman, second, second-in-command, stand-by, subordinate, supporter.

associate n ▷ ASSISTANT, FRIEND. ● v **1** ally yourself, be friends, combine, consort, fraternize, *inf* gang up, *inf* go around (with), *sl* hang out (with), *inf* hob nob (with), join up, keep company, link up, make friends, mingle, mix, side, socialize. *Opp* DISSOCIATE. **2** *associate snow with winter.* bracket together, connect, put together, relate, *inf* tie up.

association n affiliation, alliance, amalgamation, body, brotherhood, cartel, clique, club, coalition, combination, company, confederation, consortium, cooperative, corporation, federation, fellowship, group, league, marriage, merger, organization, partnership, party, society, syndicate, trust, union. ▷ FRIENDSHIP.

assorted adj different, differing, *old use* divers, diverse, heterogeneous, manifold, miscellaneous, mixed, motley, multifarious, sundry, varied, various.

assortment n agglomeration, array, choice, collection, diversity, farrago, jumble, medley, mélange, miscellany, *inf* mishmash, *inf* mixed bag, mixture, pot-pourri, range, selection, variety.

assume v **1** believe, deduce, expect, guess, *inf* have a hunch, have no doubt, imagine, infer, presume, presuppose, suppose, surmise, suspect, take for granted, think, understand. **2** *assume duties.* accept, embrace, take on, undertake. **3** *assume an air of.* acquire, adopt, affect, don, dress up in, fake, feign, pretend, put on, simulate, try on, wear.

assumption n belief, conjecture, expectation, guess, hypothesis, premise, premiss, supposition, surmise, theory.

assurance n commitment, guarantee, oath, pledge, promise, vow, undertaking, word (of honour).

assure v convince, give a promise, guarantee, make sure, persuade, pledge, promise, reassure, swear, vow. **assured** ▷ CONFIDENT.

astonish v amaze, astound, baffle, bewilder, confound, daze, *inf* dazzle, dumbfound, electrify, *inf* flabbergast, leave speechless, nonplus, shock, stagger, startle, stun, stupefy, surprise, take aback, take by surprise, *inf* take your breath away, *sl* wow. **astonishing** ▷ AMAZING.

astound v ▷ ASTONISH.

astray adv adrift, amiss, awry, lost, off course, *inf* off the rails, wide of the mark, wrong.

astute adj acute, adroit, artful, canny, clever, crafty, cunning, discerning, *inf* fly, *inf* foxy, guileful, ingenious, intelligent, knowing, observant, perceptive, perspicacious, sagacious, sharp, shrewd, sly, subtle, wily. *Opp* STUPID.

asylum n cover, haven, refuge, retreat, safety, sanctuary, shelter.

asymmetrical adj awry, crooked, distorted, irregular, lop-sided, unbalanced, uneven, *inf* wonky. *Opp* SYMMETRICAL.

atheist n heathen, pagan, sceptic, unbeliever.

athletic adj acrobatic, active, energetic, fit, muscular, powerful, robust, sinewy, *inf* sporty, *inf* strapping, strong, sturdy, vigorous, well-built, wiry. *Opp* WEAK.

athletics n field events, track events. □ cross-country, *decathlon*, *discus*, high jump, hurdles, *javelin*, long jump, marathon, pentathlon, pole-vault, relay, running, shot, sprint, triple jump.

atmosphere n 1 aerospace, air, ether, heavens, ionosphere, sky, stratosphere, troposphere. 2 ambience, aura, character, climate, environment, feeling, mood, spirit, tone, *inf* vibes, vibrations.

atom n *inf* bit, crumb, grain, iota, jot, molecule, morsel, particle, scrap, speck, spot, trace.

atone v answer, be punished, compensate, do penance, expiate, make amends, make reparation, make up (for), pay the penalty, pay the price, recompense, redeem yourself, redress.

atrocious adj abominable, appalling, barbaric, bloodthirsty, brutal, brutish, callous, cruel, diabolical, dreadful, evil, execrable, fiendish, frightful, grim, gruesome, hateful, heartless, heinous, hideous, horrendous, horrible, horrific, horrifying, inhuman, merciless, monstrous, nauseating, revolting, sadistic, savage, shocking, sickening, terrible, vicious, vile, villainous, wicked.

atrocity n crime, cruelty, enormity, offence, outrage. ▷ EVIL.

attach v 1 add, affix, anchor, append, bind, combine, connect, couple, fix, join, link, secure, stick, tie, unite, weld. ▷ FASTEN. *Opp* DETACH. 2 ascribe, assign, associate, attribute, impute, place, relate to. **attached** ▷ LOVING.

attack n 1 aggression, ambush, assault, battery, blitz, bombardment, broadside, cannonade, charge, counter-attack, foray, incursion, invasion, offensive, onset, onslaught, pre-emptive strike, raid, rush, sortie, strike. 2 *verbal attack*. abuse, censure, criticism, diatribe, impugnment, invective, outburst, tirade. 3 *attack of coughing*. bout, convulsion, fit, outbreak, paroxysm, seizure, spasm, stroke, *inf* turn. ● v 1 ambush, assail, assault, *inf* beat up, *inf* blast, bombard, charge, counterattack, descend on, *inf* do over, engage, fall on, fight, fly at, invade, jump on, lash out at, *inf* lay into, mob, mug, *inf* pitch into, pounce on, raid, rush, set about, set on, storm, strike at, *inf* wade into. 2 *attack verbally*. abuse, censure, criticize, denounce, impugn, inveigh against, libel, malign, round on, slander, snipe at, traduce, vilify. *Opp* DEFEND. 3 *attack a task*. ▷ BEGIN.

attacker n aggressor, assailant, critic, detractor, enemy, intruder, invader, mugger, opponent, persecutor, raider, slanderer. ▷ FIGHTER.

attain

attain *v* accomplish, achieve, acquire, arrive at, complete, earn, fulfil, gain, get, grasp, *inf* make, obtain, *inf* pull off, procure, reach, realize, secure, touch, win.

attempt *n* assault, bid, effort, endeavour, *inf* go, start, try, undertaking. ● *v* aim, aspire, do your best, endeavour, essay, exert yourself, *inf* have a crack, *inf* have a go, make a bid, make an assault, make an effort, put yourself out, seek, *inf* spare no effort, strive, *inf* sweat blood, tackle, try, undertake, venture.

attend *v* **1** appear, be present, go (to), frequent, present yourself, *inf* put in an appearance, visit. **2** accompany, chaperon, conduct, escort, follow, guard, usher. **3** *attend carefully*. concentrate, follow, hear, heed, listen, mark, mind, note, notice, observe, pay attention, think, watch. **attend to** assist, care for, help, look after, mind, minister to, nurse, see to, take care of, tend, wait on.

attendant *n* assistant, escort, helper, usher. ▷ SERVANT.

attention *n* **1** alertness, awareness, care, concentration, concern, diligence, heed, notice, recognition, thought, vigilance. **2** *kind attention*. attentiveness, civility, consideration, courtesy, gallantry, good manners, kindness, politeness, regard, respect, thoughtfulness.

attentive *adj* **1** alert, awake, concentrating, heedful, intent, observant, watchful. *Opp* INATTENTIVE. **2** ▷ POLITE. *Opp* RUDE.

attire *n* accoutrements, apparel, array, clothes, clothing, costume, dress, finery, garb, garments, *inf* gear, *old use* habit, outfit, raiment, wear, *old use* weeds. ● *v* ▷ DRESS.

attitude *n* **1** air, approach, aspect, bearing, behaviour, carriage, demeanour, disposition, frame of mind, manner, mien, mood, posture, stance. **2** *political attitudes*. approach, belief, feeling, opinion, orientation, outlook, position, standpoint, thought, view, viewpoint.

attract *v* **1** allure, appeal to, beguile, bewitch, bring in, captivate, charm, decoy, enchant, entice, fascinate, *sl* get someone going, interest, inveigle, lure, magnetize, seduce, tempt, *sl* turn someone on. **2** *a magnet attracts iron*. drag, draw, pull, tug at. **3** *attract attention*. ask for, cause, court, encourage, generate, incite, induce, invite, provoke, seek out, *inf* stir up. *Opp* REPEL.

attractive *adj* adorable, alluring, appealing, appetizing, becoming, bewitching, captivating, *inf* catchy (*tune*), charming, *inf* cute, delightful, desirable, disarming, enchanting, endearing, engaging, enticing, enviable, fascinating, fetching, flattering, glamorous, good-looking, gorgeous, handsome, hypnotic, interesting, inviting, irresistible, lovable, lovely, magnetic, personable, pleasing, prepossessing, pretty, quaint, seductive, sought-after, stunning, *inf* taking, tasteful, tempting, winning, winsome. ▷ BEAUTIFUL. *Opp* REPULSIVE.

attribute *n* characteristic, feature, property, quality, trait. ● *v* accredit, ascribe, assign, blame, charge, credit, impute, put down, refer, trace back.

audacious *adj* adventurous, courageous, daring, fearless, *derog* foolhardy, intrepid, *derog* rash, *derog* reckless, venturesome. ▷ BOLD. *Opp* TIMID.

audacity *n* boldness, *inf* cheek, effrontery, forwardness, impertinence, impudence, presumptuousness, rashness, *inf* sauce, temerity. ▷ COURAGE.

audible *adj* clear, detectable, distinct, high, loud, noisy, recognizable. *Opp* INAUDIBLE.

audience *n* assembly, congregation, crowd, gathering, house, listeners, meeting, onlookers, *TV* ratings, spectators, *inf* turn-out, viewers.

auditorium *n* assembly room, concert-hall, hall, theatre.

augment v add to, amplify, boost, eke out, enlarge, expand, extend, fill out, grow, increase, intensify, magnify, make larger, multiply, raise, reinforce, strengthen, supplement, swell. *Opp* DECREASE.

augur v bode, forebode, foreshadow, forewarn, give an omen, herald, portend, predict, promise, prophesy, signal.

augury n forecast, forewarning, omen, portent, prophecy, sign, warning.

auspicious adj favourable, *inf* hopeful, lucky, positive, promising, propitious. *Opp* OMINOUS.

austere adj **1** abstemious, ascetic, chaste, cold, economical, exacting, forbidding, formal, frugal, grave, hard, harsh, hermit-like, parsimonious, puritanical, restrained, rigorous, self-denying, selfdisciplined, serious, severe, sober, spartan, stern, *inf* strait-laced, strict, thrifty, unpampered. **2** *austere dress.* modest, plain, simple, unadorned, unfussy. *Opp* LUXURIOUS, ORNATE.

authentic adj accurate, actual, bona fide, certain, dependable, factual, genuine, honest, legitimate, original, real, reliable, true, trustworthy, truthful, undisputed, valid, veracious. ▷ AUTHORITATIVE. *Opp* FALSE.

authenticate v certify, confirm, corroborate, endorse, substantiate, validate, verify.

author n **1** composer, dramatist, novelist, playwright, poet, scriptwriter. ▷ WRITER. **2** architect, begetter, creator, designer, father, founder, initiator, inventor, maker, mover, organizer, originator, parent, planner, prime mover, producer.

authoritarian adj autocratic, *inf* bossy, despotic, dictatorial, dogmatic, domineering, strict, tyrannical.

authoritative adj approved, certified, definitive, dependable, official, recognized, sanctioned, scholarly. ▷ AUTHENTIC.

authority n **1** approval, authorization, consent, licence, mandate, permission, permit, sanction, warrant. **2** charge, command, control, domination, force, influence, jurisdiction, might, power, prerogative, right, sovereignty, supremacy, sway, weight. **3** *authority on wine.* *inf* boffin, *inf* buff, connoisseur, expert, scholar, specialist. **the authorities** administration, government, management, officialdom, *inf* powers that be.

authorize v accede to, agree to, allow, approve, *inf* back, commission, consent to, empower, endorse, entitle, legalize, license, make official, mandate, *inf* OK, pass, permit, ratify, *inf* rubber-stamp, sanction, sign the order, sign the warrant, validate. **authorized** ▷ OFFICIAL.

automatic adj **1** conditioned, habitual, impulsive, instinctive, involuntary, natural, reflex, spontaneous, unconscious, unintentional, unthinking. **2** automated, computerized, electronic, mechanical, programmable, programmed, robotic, self-regulating, unmanned.

autonomous adj free, independent, self-determining, selfgoverning, sovereign.

auxiliary adj additional, ancillary, assisting, *inf* back-up, emergency, extra, helping, reserve, secondary, spare, subordinate, subsidiary, substitute, supplementary, supporting, supportive.

available adj accessible, at hand, convenient, disposable, free, handy, obtainable, procurable, ready, to hand, uncommitted, unengaged, unused, usable. *Opp* INACCESSIBLE.

avaricious adj acquisitive, covetous, grasping, greedy, mercenary, miserly.

avenge v exact punishment, *inf* get your own back, repay, requite, take revenge.

average adj common, commonplace, everyday, mediocre, medium, middling, moderate, normal, regular, *inf* run of the mill, typical, unexceptional, usual. ▷ ORDINARY. *Opp* EXCEPTIONAL. ● n mean, mid-point, norm, standard. ● v equalize, even out, normalize, standardize.

averse adj antipathetic, disinclined, hostile, opposed, reluctant, resistant, unwilling.

aversion n antagonism, antipathy, dislike, distaste, hostility, reluctance, repugnance, unwillingness. ▷ HATRED.

avert v change the course of, deflect, draw off, fend off, parry, prevent, stave off, turn aside, turn away, ward off.

avoid v abstain from, be absent from, inf beg the question, inf bypass, circumvent, dodge, inf duck, elude, escape, eschew, evade, fend off, find a way round, get out of the way of, inf get round, inf give a wide berth to, help (can't help it), ignore, keep away from, keep clear of, refrain from, run away from, shirk, shun, side-step, skirt round, inf skive off, steer clear of. Opp SEEK.

await v be ready for, expect, hope for, lie in wait for, look out for, wait for.

awake adj 1 aware, conscious, insomniac, open-eyed, restless, sleepless, inf tossing and turning, wakeful, wide awake. 2 ▷ ALERT. Opp ASLEEP.

awaken v alert, animate, arouse, awake, call, excite, kindle, revive, rouse, stimulate, stir up, wake, waken.

award n badge, cap, cup, decoration, endowment, grant, medal, prize, reward, scholarship, trophy. ● v accord, allot, assign, bestow, confer, decorate with, endow, give, grant, hand over, present.

aware adj acquainted, alive (to), appreciative, attentive, cognizant, conscious, conversant, familiar, heedful, informed, knowledgeable, mindful, observant, responsive, sensible, sensitive, versed. Opp IGNORANT, INSENSITIVE.

awe n admiration, amazement, apprehension, dread, fear, respect, reverence, terror, veneration, wonder.

awe-inspiring adj awesome, old use awful, breathtaking, dramatic, grand, imposing, impressive, magnificent, marvellous, overwhelming, solemn, inf stunning, stupendous, sublime, wondrous. ▷ FRIGHTENING, WONDERFUL. Opp INSIGNIFICANT.

awful adj 1 ▷ AWE-INSPIRING. 2 awful weather. ▷ BAD.

awkward adj 1 blundering, bungling, clumsy, gauche, gawky, inf ham-fisted, inelegant, inept, inexpert, maladroit, uncoordinated, ungainly, ungraceful, unskilful, wooden. 2 an awkward load. bulky, cumbersome, inconvenient, unmanageable, unwieldy. 3 an awkward problem. annoying, difficult, perplexing, thorny, inf ticklish, troublesome, trying, vexatious, vexing. 4 an awkward silence. embarrassing, touchy, tricky, uncomfortable, uneasy. 5 awkward children. inf bloodyminded, sl bolshie, defiant, disobedient, disobliging, exasperating, intractable, misbehaving, naughty, obstinate, perverse, inf prickly, rebellious, refractory, rude, stubborn, touchy, uncooperative, undisciplined, unruly, wayward. Opp COOPERATIVE, EASY, NEAT.

awning n canopy, flysheet, screen, shade, shelter, tarpaulin.

axe n battleaxe, chopper, cleaver, hatchet, tomahawk. ● v cancel, cut, discharge, discontinue, dismiss, eliminate, get rid of, inf give the chop to, make redundant, rationalize, remove, sack, terminate, withdraw.

axle n rod, shaft, spindle.

B

baby *n* babe, child, infant, newborn, toddler.

babyish *adj* childish, immature, infantile, juvenile, puerile, simple. *Opp* MATURE.

back *adj* dorsal, end, hind, hinder, hindmost, last, rear, rearmost. ● *n* **1** end, hindquarters, posterior, rear, stern, tail, tail-end. **2** reverse, verso. *Opp* FRONT. ● *v* **1** back away, back off, back-pedal, backtrack, *inf* beat a retreat, give way, go backwards, move back, recede, recoil, retire, retreat, reverse. *Opp* ADVANCE. **2** ▷ SUPPORT. **back down** ▷ RETREAT. **back out** ▷ WITHDRAW.

backer *n* advocate, *inf* angel, benefactor, patron, promoter, sponsor, supporter.

background *n* **1** circumstances, context, history, *inf* lead-up, setting, surroundings. **2** breeding, culture, education, experience, grounding, milieu, tradition, training, upbringing.

backing *n* **1** aid, approval, assistance, encouragement, endorsement, funding, grant, help, investment, loan, patronage, sponsorship, subsidy, support. **2** *musical backing.* accompaniment, orchestration, scoring.

backward *adj* **1** regressive, retreating, retrograde, retrogressive, reverse. **2** afraid, bashful, coy, diffident, hesitant, inhibited, modest, reluctant, reserved, reticent, self-effacing, shy, timid, unassertive, unforthcoming. **3** *a backward pupil.* disadvantaged, handicapped, immature, late-starting, retarded, slow, subnormal, underdeveloped, undeveloped. *Opp* FORWARD.

bad *adj* [*Bad* describes anything we don't like. Possible synonyms are almost limitless.] **1** *bad men, deeds.* abhorrent, base, beastly, blameworthy, corrupt, criminal, cruel, dangerous, delinquent, deplorable, depraved, detestable, evil, guilty, immoral, infamous, malevolent, malicious, malignant, mean, mischievous, nasty, naughty, offensive, regrettable, reprehensible, rotten, shameful, sinful, unworthy, vicious, vile, villainous, wicked, wrong. **2** *a bad accident.* appalling, awful, calamitous, dire, disastrous, distressing, dreadful, frightful, ghastly, grave, hair-raising, hideous, horrible, painful, serious, severe, shocking, terrible, unfortunate, unpleasant, violent. **3** *bad driving, work.* abominable, abysmal, appalling, atrocious, awful, cheap, *inf* chronic, defective, deficient, diabolical, disgraceful, dreadful, egregious, execrable, faulty, feeble, *inf* grotty, hopeless, imperfect, inadequate, incompetent, incorrect, ineffective, inefficient, inferior, *inf* lousy, pitiful, poor, *inf* ropy, shoddy, *inf* sorry, substandard, unsound, unsatisfactory, useless, weak, worthless. **4** *bad conditions.* adverse, deleterious, detrimental, discouraging, *inf* frightful, harmful, harsh, hostile, inappropriate, inauspicious, prejudicial, uncongenial, unfortunate, unhelpful, unpropitious. **5** *bad smell.* decayed, decomposing, diseased, foul, loathsome, mildewed, mouldy, nauseating, noxious, objectionable, obnoxious, odious, offensive, polluted, putrid, rancid, repellent, repulsive, revolting, rotten, sickening, smelly, sour, spoiled, tainted, vile. **6** *I feel bad.* ▷ ILL. *Opp* GOOD.

badge *n* chevron, crest, device, emblem, insignia, logo, mark, medal, sign, symbol, token.

bad-tempered *adj* acrimonious, angry, bilious, cantankerous, churlish, crabbed, cross, *inf* crotchety, disgruntled, disobliging, dyspeptic, fretful, gruff, grumbling, grumpy, hostile, hot-humoured, ill-humoured, ill-tempered, irascible, irritable, malevolent, malign, moody, morose, peevish, petulant, quarrelsome, querulous, rude, scowling, short-tempered, shrewish, snappy, *inf* stroppy, sulky, sullen, testy, truculent, unfriendly, unsympathetic. *Opp* GOOD-TEMPERED.

baffle *v inf* bamboozle, bemuse, bewilder, confound, confuse, defeat, *inf* floor, *inf* flummox, foil, frustrate, mystify, perplex, puzzle, *inf* stump, thwart. **baffling** ▷ INEXPLICABLE.

bag *n* basket, carrier, carrier-bag, case, handbag, haversack, holdall, reticule, rucksack, sack, satchel, shopping-bag, shoulder-bag. ▷ BAGGAGE. ● *v* capture, catch, ensnare, snare.

baggage *n* accoutrements, bags, belongings, *inf* gear, impedimenta, paraphernalia. ▷ LUGGAGE.

bait *n* allurement, attraction, bribe, carrot, decoy, enticement, inducement, lure, temptation. ● *v* annoy, goad, harass, hound, jeer at, *inf* needle, persecute, pester, provoke, tease, torment.

balance *n* **1** scales, weighing-machine. **2** equilibrium, equipoise, poise, stability, steadiness. **3** correspondence, equality, equivalence, evenness, parity, symmetry. **4** *spend a bit & save the balance*. difference, excess, remainder, residue, rest, surplus. ● *v* **1** cancel out, compensate for, counteract, counterbalance, counterpoise, equalize, even up, level, make steady, match, neutralize, offset, parallel, stabilize, steady. **2** keep balanced, keep in equilibrium, poise, steady, support. **balanced** ▷ EVEN, IMPARTIAL, STABLE.

bald *adj* **1** baldheaded, bare, hairless, smooth, thin on top. **2** *bald truth*. direct, forthright, plain, simple, stark, straightforward, unadorned, uncompromising.

bale *n* bunch, bundle, pack, package, truss. ● *v* **bale out** eject, escape, jump out, parachute down.

ball *n* **1** drop, globe, globule, orb, shot, sphere, spheroid. **2** dance, disco, party, social.

balloon *n* airship, dirigible, hot-air balloon. ● *v* ▷ BILLOW.

ballot *n* election, plebiscite, poll, referendum, vote.

ban *n* boycott, embargo, interdiction, moratorium, prohibition, proscription, taboo, veto. ● *v* banish, bar, debar, disallow, exclude, forbid, interdict, make illegal, ostracize, outlaw, prevent, prohibit, proscribe, put a ban on, restrict, stop, suppress, veto. *Opp* PERMIT.

banal *adj* boring, clichéd, cliché-ridden, commonplace, *inf* corny, dull, hackneyed, humdrum, obvious, *inf* old hat, ordinary, over-used, pedestrian, platitudinous, predictable, stereotyped, trite, unimaginative, uninteresting, unoriginal, vapid. *Opp* INTERESTING.

band *n* **1** belt, border, fillet, hoop, line, loop, ribbon, ring, strip, stripe, swathe. **2** association, body, clique, club, company, crew, flock, gang, herd, horde, party, society, troop. ▷ GROUP. **3** [*music*] ensemble, group, orchestra.

bandage *n* dressing, gauze, lint, plaster.

bandit *n* brigand, buccaneer, desperado, footpad, gangster, gunman, highwayman, hijacker, marauder, outlaw, pirate, robber, thief.

bandy *adj* bandy-legged, bowed, bow-legged. ● *v* *bandy words*. exchange, interchange, pass, swap, throw, toss. ▷ ARGUE.

bang *n* **1** blow, *inf* box, bump, collision, cuff, knock, punch, slam, smack, stroke, thump, wallop, whack. ▷ HIT. **2** blast, boom, clap, crash, explosion, pop, report, thud, thump. ▷ SOUND.

banish v **1** deport, drive out, eject, evict, excommunicate, exile, expatriate, expel, ostracize, oust, outlaw, rusticate, send away, ship away, transport. **2** ban, bar, *inf* black, debar, eliminate, exclude, forbid, get rid of, make illegal, prohibit, proscribe, put an embargo on, remove, restrict, stop, suppress, veto.

bank n **1** camber, declivity, dike, earthwork, embankment, gradient, incline, mound, ramp, rampart, ridge, rise, slope, tilt. **2** *river bank*. brink, edge, margin, shore, side. **3** *bank of controls*. array, collection, display, file, group, line, panel, rank, row, series. ● v **1** cant, heel, incline, lean, list, pitch, slant, slope, tilt, tip. **2** *bank money*. deposit, save.

bankrupt adj *inf* broke, failed, *sl* gone bust, gone into liquida-tion, insolvent, ruined, spent up, wound up. ▷ POOR. *Opp* SOLVENT.

banner n banderole, colours, ensign, flag, pennant, pennon, standard, streamer.

banquet n *inf* binge, *sl* blow-out, dinner, feast, repast, *inf* spread. ▷ MEAL.

banter n badinage, chaffing, joking, persiflage, pleasantry, raillery, repartee, ribbing, ridicule, teasing, wordplay.

bar n **1** beam, girder, pole, rail, railing, rod, shaft, stake, stick, strut. **2** barricade, barrier, check, deterrent, hindrance, impediment, obstacle, obstruction. **3** band, belt, line, streak, strip, stripe. **4** *bar of soap*. block, cake, chunk, hunk, ingot, lump, nugget, piece, slab, wedge. **5** *drink in a bar*. café, canteen, counter, inn, lounge, pub, public house, saloon, taproom, tavern, wine bar. ● v **1** ban, banish, debar, exclude, forbid to enter, keep out, ostracize, outlaw, prevent from entering, prohibit, proscribe. **2** *bar the way*. arrest, block, check, deter, halt, hinder, impede, obstruct, prevent, stop, thwart.

barbarian adj ▷ BARBARIC. ● n boor, churl, heathen, hun, ignoramus, lout, pagan, philistine, savage, vandal, *sl* yob.

barbaric adj barbarous, brutal, brutish, crude, inhuman, primitive, rough, savage, uncivil, uncivilized, uncultivated, wild. ▷ CRUEL. *Opp* CIVILIZED.

bare adj **1** bald, denuded, exposed, naked, nude, stark-naked, stripped, unclad, unclothed, uncovered, undressed. **2** *bare moor*. barren, bleak, desolate, featureless, open, treeless, unwooded, windswept. **3** *bare trees*. defoliated, leafless, shorn. **4** *a bare room*. austere, empty, plain, simple, unadorned, undecorated, unfurnished, vacant. **5** *a bare wall*. blank, clean, unmarked. **6** *bare facts*. direct, explicit, hard, honest, literal, open, plain, straightforward, unconcealed, undisguised, unembellished. **7** *the bare minimum*. basic, essential, just adequate, just sufficient, minimal, minimum. ● v betray, bring to light, disclose, expose, lay bare, make known, publish, reveal, show, uncover, undress, unmask, unveil.

bargain n **1** agreement, arrangement, compact, contract, covenant, deal, negotiation, pact, pledge, promise, settlement, transaction, treaty, understanding. **2** *bargain in the sales*. *inf* give-away, good buy, good deal, loss-leader, reduced item, *inf* snip, special offer. ● v argue, barter, discuss terms, do a deal, haggle, negotiate. **bargain for** ▷ EXPECT.

bark v **1** growl, yap. **2** *bark your shin*. abrade, chafe, graze, rub, score, scrape, scratch.

barmaid,

barman ns attendant, server, steward, stewardess, waiter, waitress.

barracks *plur n* accommodation, billet, camp, garrison, lodging, quarters.

barrage n **1** ▷ BARRIER. **2** *barrage of gunfire*. assault, attack, battery, bombardment, cannonade, fusillade, gunfire, onslaught, salvo, storm, volley.

barrel n butt, cask, churn, cistern, drum, hogshead, keg, tank, tub, tun, water-butt.

barren adj **1** arid, bare, desert, desolate, dried-up, dry, empty, infertile, lifeless, non-productive, treeless, uncultivated, unproductive, unprofitable, untilled, useless, waste. **2** childless, fruitless, infertile, sterile, sterilized, unfruitful. Opp FERTILE.

barricade n ▷ BARRIER. ● v bar, block off, defend, obstruct.

barrier n **1** bar, barrage, barricade, blockade, boom, bulwark, dam, earthwork, embankment, fence, fortification, frontier, hurdle, obstacle, obstruction, palisade, railing, rampart, stockade, wall. **2** barrier to progress. check, drawback, handicap, hindrance, impediment, limitation, restriction, stumbling-block.

barter v bargain, deal, exchange, negotiate, swap, trade, traffic.

base adj contemptible, cowardly, degrading, depraved, despicable, detestable, dishonourable, evil, ignoble, immoral, inferior, low, mean, scandalous, selfish, shabby, shameful, sordid, undignified, unworthy, vulgar, vile. ▷ WICKED. ● n **1** basis, bed, bedrock, bottom, core, essentials, foot, footing, foundation, fundamentals, groundwork, infrastructure, pedestal, plinth, rest, root, stand, substructure, support, underpinning. **2** camp, centre, depot, headquarters, post, starting-point, station. ● v build, construct, establish, found, ground, locate, position, post, secure, set up, station.

basement n cellar, crypt, vault.

bashful adj abashed, backward, blushing, coy, demure, diffident, embarrassed, faint-hearted, inhibited, meek, modest, nervous, reserved, reticent, retiring, self-conscious, self-effacing, shamefaced, sheepish, shy, timid, timorous, uneasy, unforthcoming. Opp ASSERTIVE.

basic adj central, chief, crucial, elementary, essential, foremost, fundamental, important, intrinsic, key, main, necessary, primary, principal, radical, underlying, vital. Opp UNIMPORTANT.

basin n bath, bowl, container, dish, pool, sink, stoup.

basis n base, core, footing, foundation, ground, infrastructure, premise, principle, starting-point, support, underpinning.

bask v enjoy, feel pleasure, glory, lie, lounge, luxuriate, relax, sunbathe, wallow.

basket n bag, hamper, pannier, punnet, skip, trug.

bastard n illegitimate child, old use love-child, natural child.

bat n club, racket, racquet.

bath n douche, jacuzzi, pool, sauna, shower, inf soak, inf tub, wash.

bathe v **1** clean, cleanse, immerse, moisten, rinse, soak, steep, swill, wash. **2** bathe in the sea. go swimming, paddle, plunge, splash about, swim, inf take a dip.

bathos n anticlimax, inf come-down, disappointment, inf let-down. Opp CLIMAX.

baton n cane, club, cudgel, rod, staff, stick, truncheon.

batter v beat, bludgeon, cudgel, keep hitting, pound. ▷ HIT.

battery n **1** artillery-unit, emplacement. **2** electric battery. accumulator, cell. **3** assault and battery. assault, attack, inf beating-up, blows, mugging, onslaught, thrashing, violence.

battle n action, air-raid, Armageddon, attack, blitz, brush, campaign, clash, combat, conflict, confrontation, contest, crusade, inf dogfight, encounter, engagement, fight, fray, hostilities, offensive, pitched battle, pre-emptive strike, quarrel, inf shootout, siege, skirmish, strife, struggle, war, warfare. ● v ▷ FIGHT.

battlefield n arena, battleground, theatre of war.

bawdy adj broad, earthy, erotic, lusty, inf naughty, racy, inf raunchy, ribald, inf sexy, inf spicy. [derog synonyms] *inf* blue, coarse, dirty, immoral, improper, indecent, indecorous, indelicate, lascivious, lecherous, lewd, licentious, obscene, pornographic, prurient, risqué, rude, salacious, smutty, suggestive, titillating, vulgar. *Opp* PROPER.

bawl *v* cry, roar, shout, thunder, wail, yell, yelp.

bay *n* **1** bight, cove, creek, estuary, fjord, gulf, harbour, indentation, inlet, ria, sound. **2** alcove, booth, compartment, niche, nook, opening, recess.

bazaar *n* auction, boot-sale, bring-and-buy, fair, fête, jumble sale, market, sale.

be *v* **1** be alive, breathe, endure, exist, live. **2** *be here all day*. continue, dwell, inhabit, keep going, last, occupy a position, persist, remain, stay, survive. **3** *the next event will be tomorrow*. arise, befall, come about, happen, occur, take place. **4** *want to be a writer*. become, develop into.

beach *n* bank, coast, coastline, foreshore, littoral, sand, sands, seashore, seaside, shore, *poet* strand.

beacon *n* bonfire, fire, flare, light, lighthouse, pharos, signal.

bead *n* blob, drip, drop, droplet, globule, jewel, pearl.

beaker *n* cup, glass, goblet, jar, mug, tankard, tumbler.

beam *n* **1** bar, board, boom, brace, girder, joist, plank, post, rafter, spar, stanchion, stud, support, timber. **2** *beam of light*. gleam, pencil, ray, shaft, stream. ● *v* **1** aim, broadcast, direct, emit, radiate, send out, shine, transmit. **2** *beam happily*. grin, laugh, look radiant, radiate happiness, smile.

bear *v* **1** carry, hold, prop up, shoulder, support, sustain, take. **2** *bear an inscription*. display, exhibit, have, possess, show. **3** *bear gifts*. bring, carry, convey, deliver, fetch, move, take, transfer, transport. **4** *bear pain*. abide, accept, brook, cope with, endure, live with, permit, *inf* put up with, reconcile yourself to, *inf* stand, *inf* stom-

ach, suffer, sustain, tolerate, undergo. **5** *bear children, fruit*. breed, *old use* bring forth, develop, engender, generate, give birth to, produce, spawn, yield. **bear out** ▷ CONFIRM. **bear up** ▷ SURVIVE. **bear witness** ▷ TESTIFY.

bearable *adj* acceptable, endurable, supportable, survivable, sustainable, tolerable.

bearing *n* **1** air, appearance, aspect, attitude, behaviour, carriage, demeanour, deportment, look, manner, mien, poise, posture, presence, stance, style. **2** *evidence had no bearing*. applicability, application, connection, import, pertinence, reference, relation, relationship, relevance, significance. **bearings** aim, course, direction, line, location, orientation, path, position, road, sense of direction, tack, track, way, whereabouts.

beast *n* brute, creature, monster, savage. ▷ ANIMAL.

beastly *adj* abominable, barbaric, bestial, brutal, cruel, savage. ▷ VILE.

beat *n* **1** accent, pulse, rhythm, stress, tempo, throb. **2** *policeman's beat*. course, itinerary, journey, path, rounds, route, way. ● *v* **1** batter, bludgeon, buffet, cane, clout, cudgel, flail, flog, hammer, knock about, lash, *inf* lay into, manhandle, pound, punch, scourge, strike, *inf* tan, thrash, thump, trounce, *inf* wallop, whack, whip. ▷ HIT. **2** *beat eggs*. agitate, blend, froth up, knead, mix, pound, stir, whip, whisk. **3** *heart was beating*. flutter, palpitate, pound, pulsate, race, throb, thump. **4** *beat an opponent*. best, conquer, crush, defeat, excel, get the better of, *inf* lick, master, outclass, outdistance, outdo, outpace, outrun, outwit, overcome, overpower, overthrow, overwhelm, rout, subdue, surpass, *inf* thrash, trounce, vanquish, win against, worst. **beat up** ▷ ATTACK.

beautiful *adj* admirable, aesthetic, alluring, appealing, artistic, attractive, becoming, bewitching, brilliant, captivating, charming, *old use* comely, dainty, decorative, delightful, elegant, enjoyable, exquisite, *old use* fair, fascinating, fetching, fine, good-looking, glamorous, glorious, gorgeous, graceful, handsome, irresistible, lovely, magnificent, neat, picturesque, pleasing, pretty, pulchritudinous, quaint, radiant, ravishing, scenic, seductive, sensuous, sexy, spectacular, splendid, stunning, superb, tasteful, tempting. *Opp* UGLY.

beautify *v* adorn, bedeck, deck, decorate, embellish, garnish, make beautiful, ornament, prettify, *derog* tart up, *inf* titivate. *Opp* DISFIGURE.

beauty *n* allure, appeal, attractiveness, charm, elegance, fascination, glamour, glory, grace, handsomeness, loveliness, magnificence, picturesqueness, prettiness, pulchritude, radiance, splendour.

becalmed *adj* helpless, idle, motionless, still, unmoving.

beckon *v* gesture, motion, signal, summon, wave.

become *v* **1** be transformed into, change into, develop into, grow into, mature into, metamorphose into, turn into. **2** *Red becomes you.* be appropriate to, be becoming to, befit, enhance, fit, flatter, harmonize with, set off, suit. **becoming** ▷ ATTRACTIVE, SUITABLE.

bed *n* **1** resting-place. □ *air-bed, berth, bunk, cot, couch, couchette, cradle, crib, divan, four-poster, hammock, pallet, palliasse, truckle bed, waterbed.* **2** *bed of concrete.* base, foundation, groundwork, layer, substratum. **3** *river bed.* bottom, channel, course, watercourse. **4** *flower bed.* border, garden, patch, plot.

bedclothes *plur n* bedding, bed linen. □ *bedspread, blanket, bolster, continental quilt, counterpane, coverlet, duvet, eiderdown, electric-blanket, mattress, pillow, pillowcase, pillowslip, quilt, sheet, sleeping-bag.*

bedraggled *adj* dirty, dishevelled, drenched, messy, muddy, scruffy, sodden, soiled, stained, unkempt, untidy, wet, wringing. *Opp* SMART.

beer *n* ale, bitter, lager, mild, porter, stout.

befall *v* be the outcome, *old use* betide, chance, come about, *inf* crop up, eventuate, happen, occur, take place, *inf* transpire.

before *adv* already, earlier, in advance, previously, sooner.

befriend *v inf* chat up, *inf* gang up with, get to know, make friends with, make the acquaintance of, *inf* pal up with.

beg *v* **1** *inf* cadge, scrounge, solicit, sponge. **2** *beg a favour.* ask, beseech, cajole, crave, entreat, implore, importune, petition, plead, pray, request, supplicate, wheedle.

beget *v* breed, bring about, cause, create, engender, father, generate, give rise to, procreate, produce, propagate, result in, sire, spawn.

beggar *n* cadger, destitute person, down-and-out, homeless person, mendicant, pauper, ragamuffin, scrounger, sponger, tramp, vagrant. ▷ POOR.

begin *v* **1** activate, approach, attack, be first, broach, commence, conceive, create, embark on, enter into, found, *inf* get cracking, *inf* get going, inaugurate, initiate, inspire, instigate, introduce, kindle, launch, lay the foundations, lead off, move into, move off, open, originate, pioneer, precipitate, provoke, set about, set in motion, set off, set out, set up, *inf* spark off, start, *inf* take steps, take the initiative, take up, touch off, trigger off, undertake. **2** *Spring begins gradually.* appear, arise, break out, come into existence, crop up, emerge, get going, happen, materialize, originate, spring up. *Opp* END.

beginner *n* **1** creator, founder, initiator, inspiration, instigator, originator, pioneer. **2** *only a beginner.* apprentice, fresher, greenhorn, inexperienced person, initiate, learner, novice, recruit, starter, tiro, trainee.

beginning *n* **1** birth, commencement, conception, creation, dawn, embryo, emergence, establishment, foundation, genesis, germ, inauguration, inception, initiation, instigation, introduction, launch, onset, opening, origin, outset, point of departure, rise, source, start, starting-point, threshold. **2** *beginning of a book*. preface, prelude, prologue. *Opp* END.

begrudge *v* be bitter about, covet, envy, grudge, mind, object to, resent.

behave *v* **1** acquit yourself, act, *inf* carry on, comport yourself, conduct yourself, function, operate, perform, react, respond, run, work. **2** *told to behave*. act properly, be good, be on best behaviour.

behaviour *n* actions, attitude, bearing, comportment, conduct, courtesy, dealings, demeanour, deportment, manners, performance, reaction, response, ways.

behead *v* decapitate, guillotine.

behold *v* descry, discern, espy, look at, note, notice, see, set eyes on, view.

being *n* **1** actuality, essence, existence, life, living, reality, solidity, substance. **2** animal, creature, individual, person, spirit, soul.

belated *adj* behindhand, delayed, last-minute, late, overdue, posthumous, tardy, unpunctual.

belch *v* **1** *inf* burp, emit wind. **2** *belch smoke*. discharge, emit, erupt, fume, gush, send out, smoke, spew out, vomit.

belief *n* **1** acceptance, assent, assurance, certainty, confidence, credence, reliance, security, sureness, trust. **2** *religious belief*. attitude, conviction, creed, doctrine, dogma, ethos, faith, feeling, ideology, morality, notion, opinion, persuasion, principles, religion, standards, tenets, theories, views. *Opp* SCEPTICISM.

believe *v* **1** accept, be certain of, count on, credit, depend on, endorse, have faith in, reckon on, rely on, subscribe to, *inf* swallow, swear by, trust. *Opp* DISBELIEVE. **2** assume, consider, *inf* dare say, feel, gather, guess, hold, imagine, judge, know, maintain, postulate, presume, speculate, suppose, take it for granted, think. **make believe** ▷ IMAGINE.

believer *n* adherent, devotee, disciple, fanatic, follower, proselyte, supporter, upholder, zealot. *Opp* ATHEIST.

belittle *v* be unimpressed by, criticize, decry, denigrate, deprecate, depreciate, detract from, disparage, minimize, *inf* play down, slight, speak slightingly of, underrate, undervalue. *Opp* EXAGGERATE, FLATTER, PRAISE.

bell *n* alarm, carillon, chime, knell, peal, signal. ▷ RING.

belligerent *adj* aggressive, antagonistic, argumentative, bellicose, bullying, combative, contentious, defiant, disputatious, fierce, hawkish, hostile, jingoistic, martial, militant, militaristic, provocative, pugnacious, quarrelsome, violent, warlike, warmongering, warring. ▷ UNFRIENDLY. *Opp* PEACEABLE.

belong *v* **1** be owned (by), go (with), pertain (to), relate (to). **2** be at home, feel welcome, have a place. **3** *belong to a club*. be affiliated with, be a member of, be connected with, *inf* be in with.

belongings *plur n* chattels, effects, *inf* gear, goods, impedimenta, possessions, property, things.

belt *n* **1** band, circle, loop. **2** *belt round the waist*. cincture, cummerbund, girdle, girth, sash, strap, waistband, *old use* zone. **3** *green belt*. area, district, line, stretch, strip, swathe, tract, zone.

bemuse *v* befuddle, bewilder, confuse, mix up, muddle, perplex, puzzle, stupefy.

bench *n* **1** form, pew, seat, settle. **2** counter, table, work-bench, work-table. **3** *magistrate's bench*. court, courtroom, judge, magistrate, tribunal.

bend *n* angle, arc, bow, corner, crank, crook, curvature, curve, flexure, loop, turn, turning, twist, zigzag. ● *v* **1** arch, be flexible, bow, buckle, coil, contort, crook, curl, curve, deflect, distort, divert, flex, fold, *inf* give, loop, mould, refract, shape, turn, twist, warp, wind, yield. **2** bow, crouch, curtsy, duck, genuflect, kneel, lean, stoop.

benefactor *n inf* angel, backer, *derog* do-gooder, donor, *inf* fairy godmother, patron, philanthropist, promoter, sponsor, supporter, well-wisher.

beneficial *adj* advantageous, benign, constructive, favourable, fruitful, good, health-giving, healthy, helpful, improving, nourishing, nutritious, positive, productive, profitable, rewarding, salubrious, salutary, supportive, useful, valuable, wholesome. *Opp* HARMFUL.

beneficiary *n* heir, heiress, inheritor, legatee, recipient, successor (*to title*).

benefit *n* **1** advantage, asset, blessing, boon, convenience, gain, good thing, help, privilege, prize, profit, service, use. *Opp* DISADVANTAGE. **2** *unemployment benefit.* aid, allowance, assistance, *inf* dole, *inf* hand-out, grant, payment, social security, welfare. ● *v* advance, advantage, aid, assist, better, boost, do good to, enhance, further, help, improve, profit, promote, serve.

benevolent *adj* altruistic, beneficent, benign, caring, charitable, compassionate, considerate, friendly, generous, helpful, humane, humanitarian, kind-hearted, kindly, liberal, magnanimous, merciful, philanthropic, supportive, sympathetic, unselfish, warm-hearted. ▷ KIND. *Opp* UNKIND.

benign *adj* gentle, harmless, kind. ▷ BENEFICIAL, BENEVOLENT.

bent *adj* **1** angled, arched, bowed, buckled, coiled, contorted, crooked, curved, distorted, folded, hunched, looped, twisted, warped. **2** [*inf*] *a bent dealer.* corrupt, criminal, dishonest, illegal, immoral, untrustworthy, wicked. *Opp* HONEST, STRAIGHT. ● *n* ▷ APTITUDE, BIAS.

bequeath *v* endow, hand down, leave, make over, pass on, settle, will.

bequest *n* endowment, gift, inheritance, legacy, settlement.

bereavement *n* death, loss.

bereft *adj* deprived, destitute, devoid, lacking, robbed, wanting.

berserk *adj inf* beside yourself, crazed, crazy, demented, deranged, frantic, frenetic, frenzied, furious, infuriated, insane, mad, maniacal, rabid, violent, wild. *Opp* CALM. **go berserk** ▷ RAGE, RAMPAGE.

berth *n* **1** bed, bunk, hammock. **2** *berth for ships.* anchorage, dock, harbour, haven, landing-stage, moorings, pier, port, quay, slipway, wharf. ● *v* anchor, dock, drop anchor, land, moor, tie up. **give a wide berth to** ▷ AVOID.

beseech *v* ask, beg, entreat, implore, importune, plead, supplicate.

besiege *v* beleaguer, beset, blockade, cut off, encircle, encompass, hem in, isolate, pester, plague, siege, surround.

best *adj* choicest, excellent, finest, first-class, foremost, incomparable, leading, matchless, optimum, outstanding, pre-eminent, superlative, supreme, top, unequalled, unrivalled, unsurpassed.

bestial *adj* animal, beast-like, beastly, brutal, brutish, inhuman, subhuman. ▷ SAVAGE.

bestow *v* award, confer, donate, give, grant, present.

bet *n inf* flutter, gamble, *inf* punt, speculation, stake, wager. ● *v* bid, chance, do the pools, enter a lottery, gamble, *inf* have a flutter, hazard, lay bets, *inf* punt, risk, speculate, stake, venture, wager.

betray *v* **1** be a Judas to, be a traitor to, be false to, cheat, conspire against, deceive, denounce, desert, double-cross, give away, *inf* grass on, incriminate, inform against, inform on, jilt, let down, *inf* rat on, report, *inf* sell down the river, sell out, *inf* shop, *inf* tell tales about, *inf* turn Queen's evidence on. **2** *betray secrets.* disclose, divulge, expose, give away, indicate, let out, let slip, manifest, reveal, show, tell.

better *adj* **1** preferable, recommended, superior. **2** convalescent, cured, fitter, healed, healthier, improved, *inf* on the mend, progressing, recovered, recovering, restored. ● *v* ▷ IMPROVE, SURPASS.

beware *v* avoid, be alert, be careful, be cautious, be on your guard, guard (against), heed, keep clear (of), look out, mind, shun, steer away (from), take care, take heed, take precautions, watch out, *inf* watch your step.

bewilder *v* baffle, *inf* bamboozle, bemuse, confound, confuse, daze, disconcert, disorientate, distract, floor, *inf* flummox, mislead, muddle, mystify, perplex, puzzle, stump.

bewitch *v* captivate, cast a spell on, charm, enchant, enrapture, fascinate, spellbind.

bias *n* **1** aptitude, bent, inclination, leaning, liking, partiality, penchant, predilection, predisposition, preference, proclivity, proneness, propensity, tendency. **2** [*derog*] bigotry, chauvinism, favouritism, imbalance, injustice, nepotism, one-sidedness, partiality, partisanship, prejudice, racism, sexism, unfairness. ● *v* ▷ INFLUENCE.

biased *adj* bigoted, blinkered, chauvinistic, distorted, emotive, influenced, interested, jaundiced, loaded, one-sided, partial, partisan, prejudiced, racist, sexist, slanted, tendentious, unfair, unjust, warped. *Opp* UNBIASED.

bicycle *n inf* bike, cycle, penny-farthing, *inf* push-bike, racer, tandem, *inf* two-wheeler.

bid *n* **1** offer, price, proposal, proposition, tender. **2** *a bid to win.* attempt, *inf* crack, effort, endeavour, *inf* go, try, venture. ● *v* **1** make an offer, offer, proffer, propose, tender. **2** ▷ COMMAND.

big *adj* **1** above average, *inf* almighty, ample, astronomical, bold, broad, Brobdingnagian, bulky, burly, capacious, colossal, commodious, considerable, elephantine, enormous, extensive, fat, formidable, gargantuan, generous, giant, gigantic, grand, great, gross, heavy, hefty, high, huge, *inf* hulking, husky, immeasurable, immense, impressive, *inf* jumbo, *inf* king-sized, large, largish, lofty, long, mammoth, massive, mighty, monstrous, monumental, mountainous, overgrown, oversized, prodigious, roomy, sizeable, spacious, stupendous, substantial, swingeing (*increase*), tall, *inf* terrific, thick, *inf* thumping, tidy (*sum*), titanic, towering, *inf* tremendous, vast, voluminous, weighty, *inf* whacking, *inf* whopping, wide. **2** *a big decision.* grave, important, influential, leading, main, major, momentous, notable, powerful, prime, principal, prominent, serious, significant. **3** *a big number.* ▷ INFINITE. **4** *a big name.* ▷ FAMOUS. **5** *a big noise.* ▷ LOUD. *Opp* SMALL.

bigot *n* chauvinist, fanatic, prejudiced person, racist, sexist, zealot.

bigoted *adj* intolerant, one-sided, partial, prejudiced. ▷ BIASED.

bill *n* **1** account, invoice, receipt, statement, tally. **2** advertisement, broadsheet, bulletin, circular, handbill, handout, leaflet, notice, placard, poster, sheet. **3** *a Parliamentary bill.* draft law, proposed law. **4** *a bird's bill.* beak, mandible.

billow *v* balloon, belly, bulge, fill out, heave, puff out, rise, roll, surge, swell, undulate.

bind *v* **1** attach, clamp, combine, connect, fuse, hitch, hold together, join, lash, link, rope, secure, strap, tie, truss, unify, unite, weld. ▷ FASTEN. **2** *bind a wound.* bandage, cover, dress, encase, swathe, wrap. **3** *bound to obey.* compel, constrain, force, necessitate, oblige, require. **binding** ▷ COMPULSORY, FORMAL.

biography n autobiography, life, life-story, memoirs, recollections. ▷ WRITING.

bird n inf birdie, chick, cock, joc feathered friend, fledgling, fowl, hen, nestling. ☐ gamebird, plur poultry, seabird, wader, waterfowl, wildfowl. ☐ albatross, auk, bittern, blackbird, budgerigar, bullfinch, bunting, bustard, buzzard, canary, cassowary, chaffinch, chiff-chaff, chough, cockatoo, coot, cormorant, corncrake, crane, crow, cuckoo, curlew, dabchick, dipper, dove, duck, dunnock, eagle, egret, emu, falcon, finch, flamingo, flycatcher, fulmar, goldcrest, goldfinch, goose, grebe, greenfinch, grouse, gull, hawk, heron, hoopoe, hornbill, humming bird, ibis, jackdaw, jay, kingfisher, kestrel, kite, kiwi, kookaburra, lapwing, lark, linnet, macaw, magpie, martin, mina bird, moorhen, nightingale, nightjar, nuthatch, oriole, osprey, ostrich, ousel, owl, parakeet, parrot, partridge, peacock, peewit, pelican, penguin, peregrine, petrel, pheasant, pigeon, pipit, plover, ptarmigan, puffin, quail, raven, redbreast, redstart, robin, rook, sandpiper, seagull, shearwater, shelduck, shrike, skua, skylark, snipe, sparrow, sparrowhawk, spoonbill, starling, stonechat, stork, swallow, swan, swift, teal, tern, thrush, tit, toucan, turkey, turtle-dove, vulture, wagtail, warbler, waxwing, wheatear, woodcock, woodpecker, wren, yellowhammer.

birth n **1** childbirth, confinement, delivery, labour, nativity, parturition. **2** ancestry, background, blood, breeding, derivation, descent, extraction, family, genealogy, line, lineage, parentage, pedigree, race, stock, strain. **3** ▷ BEGINNING. **give birth** bear, calve, farrow, foal. ▷ BEGIN.

bisect v cross, cut in half, divide, halve, intersect.

bit n **1** atom, bite, block, chip, chunk, crumb, division, dollop, fraction, fragment, gobbet, grain, helping, hunk, iota, lump, modicum, morsel, mouthful, part, particle, piece, portion, sample, scrap, section, segment, share, slab, slice, snippet, soupçon, speck, spot, taste, titbit, trace. **2** Wait

a bit. flash, instant, inf jiffy, minute, moment, second, inf tick, time, while.

bite n **1** nip, pinch, sting. **2** a bite to eat. morsel, mouthful, nibble, snack, taste. ▷ BIT. ● v **1** champ, chew, crunch, cut into, gnaw, masticate, munch, nibble, nip, rend, snap, tear at, wound. **2** An insect bit me. pierce, sting. **3** The screw won't bite. grip, hold.

bitter adj **1** acid, acrid, harsh, sharp, sour, unpleasant. **2** a bitter experience. calamitous, dire, distasteful, distressing, galling, hateful, heartbreaking, painful, poignant, sorrowful, unhappy, unwelcome, upsetting. **3** bitter remarks. acrimonious, acerbic, angry, cruel, cynical, embittered, envious, hostile, jaundiced, jealous, malicious, rancorous, resentful, savage, sharp, spiteful, stinging, vicious, violent, waspish. **4** a bitter wind. biting, cold, fierce, freezing, perishing, piercing, raw. Opp KIND, MILD, PLEASANT.

bizarre adj curious, eccentric, fantastic, freakish, grotesque, odd, outlandish, outré, surreal, weird. ▷ STRANGE. Opp ORDINARY.

black adj blackish, coal-black, dark, dusky, ebony, funereal, gloomy, inky, jet, jet-black, moonless, murky, pitch-black, pitch-dark, raven, sable, sooty, starless, unlit. ● v **1** blacken, polish. **2** ▷ BLACKLIST.

blackleg n sl scab, strikebreaker, traitor.

blacklist v ban, bar, blackball, boycott, debar, disallow, exclude, ostracize, preclude, proscribe, put an embargo on, refuse to handle, repudiate, snub, veto.

blade n dagger, edge, knife, razor, scalpel, vane. ▷ SWORD.

blame n accountability, accusation, castigation, censure, charge, complaint, condemnation, criticism, culpability, fault, guilt, imputation, incrimination, liability, onus, inf rap, recrimination, reprimand, reproach, reproof, responsibility, inf stick, stricture. ● v accuse, admonish, censure, charge, chide, condemn, criticize, denounce, *inf* get at, hold responsible, incriminate, rebuke, reprehend, reprimand, reproach, reprove, round on, scold, tax, upbraid. *Opp* EXCUSE.

blameless *adj* faultless, guiltless, innocent, irreproachable, moral, unimpeachable, upright. *Opp* GUILTY.

bland *adj* affable, amiable, banal, boring, calm, characterless, dull, flat, gentle, insipid, mild, nondescript, smooth, soft, soothing, suave, tasteless, trite, unappetizing, unexciting, uninspiring, uninteresting, vapid, watery, weak, *inf* wishy-washy. *Opp* INTERESTING.

blank *adj* 1 bare, clean, clear, empty, plain, spotless, unadorned, unmarked, unused, void. 2 *a blank look.* apathetic, baffled, baffling, dead, *inf* deadpan, emotionless, expressionless, featureless, glazed, immobile, impassive, inane, inscrutable, lifeless, poker-faced, uncomprehending, unresponsive, vacant, vacuous. • *n* 1 emptiness, nothingness, vacuity, vacuum, void. 2 *blanks on a form.* box, break, gap, line, space.

blaspheme *v* curse, execrate, imprecate, profane, swear.

blasphemous *adj* disrespectful, godless, impious, irreligious, irreverent, profane, sacrilegious, sinful, ungodly, wicked. *Opp* REVERENT.

blast *n* 1 gale, gust, wind. 2 blare, din, noise, racket, roar, sound. 3 ▷ EXPLOSION. • *v* ▷ ATTACK, EXPLODE. **blast off** ▷ LAUNCH.

blatant *adj* apparent, barefaced, bold, brazen, conspicuous, evident, flagrant, glaring, obtrusive, obvious, open, overt, shameless, stark, unconcealed, undisguised, unmistakable, visible. *Opp* HIDDEN.

blaze *n* conflagration, fire, flame, flare-up, holocaust, inferno, outburst. • *v* burn, erupt, flame, flare.

bleach *v* blanch, discolour, etiolate, fade, lighten, pale, peroxide (*hair*), whiten.

bleak *adj* bare, barren, blasted, cheerless, chilly, cold, comfortless, depressing, desolate, dismal, dreary, exposed, grim, hopeless, joyless, sombre, uncomfortable, unpromising, windswept, wintry. *Opp* COMFORTABLE, WARM.

bleary *adj* blurred, *inf* blurry, cloudy, dim, filmy, fogged, foggy, fuzzy, hazy, indistinct, misty, murky, obscured, smeary, unclear, watery. *Opp* CLEAR.

blemish *n* blot, blotch, chip, crack, defect, deformity, disfigurement, eyesore, fault, flaw, imperfection, mark, mess, smudge, speck, stain, ugliness. □ *birthmark, blackhead, blister, callus, corn, freckle, mole, naevus, pimple, pustule, scar, spot, verruca, wart, whitlow, sl zit.* • *v* deface, disfigure, flaw, mar, mark, scar, spoil, stain, tarnish.

blend *n* alloy, amalgam, amalgamation, combination, composite, compound, concoction, fusion, mélange, mix, mixture, synthesis, union. • *v* 1 amalgamate, coalesce, combine, commingle, compound, fuse, harmonize, integrate, intermingle, intermix, meld, merge, mingle, synthesize, unite. 2 *blend in a bowl.* beat, mix, stir together, whip, whisk.

bless *v* 1 anoint, consecrate, dedicate, grace, hallow, make sacred, ordain, sanctify. 2 *bless God's name.* adore, exalt, extol, glorify, magnify, praise. *Opp* CURSE.

blessed *adj* 1 adored, divine, hallowed, holy, revered, sacred, sanctified. 2 ▷ HAPPY.

blessing *n* 1 benediction, consecration, grace, prayer. 2 approbation, approval, backing, concurrence, consent, leave, permission, sanction, support. 3 *Warmth is a blessing.* advantage, asset, benefit, boon, comfort, convenience, *inf* godsend, help. *Opp* CURSE, MISFORTUNE.

blight *n* affliction, ailment, *old use* bane, cancer, canker, curse, decay, disease, evil, illness, infestation, misfortune, *old use* pestilence, plague, pollution, rot, scourge, sickness, trouble. • *v* ▷ SPOIL.

blind adj **1** blinded, eyeless, sightless, unseeing. □ astigmatic, colour-blind, long-sighted, myopic, near-sighted, short-sighted, suffering from cataract, suffering from glaucoma, visually handicapped. **2** blind devotion. blinkered, heedless, ignorant, inattentive, indifferent, indiscriminate, insensible, insensitive, irrational, mindless, oblivious, prejudiced, unaware, unobservant, unreasoning. ● n awning, cover, curtain, screen, shade, shutters. ● v **1** dazzle, make blind. **2** ▷ DECEIVE.

blink v coruscate, flash, flicker, flutter, gleam, glimmer, shimmer, sparkle, twinkle, wink.

bliss n blessedness, delight, ecstasy, euphoria, felicity, gladness, glee, happiness, heaven, joy, paradise, rapture. ▷ PLEASURE. Opp MISERY.

bloated adj dilated, distended, enlarged, inflated, puffy, swollen.

block n **1** bar, brick, cake, chock, chunk, hunk, ingot, lump, mass, piece, slab. **2** ▷ BLOCKAGE. ● v **1** bar, barricade, inf bung up, choke, clog, close, congest, constrict, dam, fill, impede, jam, obstruct, plug, stop up. **2** block a plan. deter, halt, hamper, hinder, hold back, prevent, prohibit, resist, inf scotch, inf stonewall, stop, thwart.

blockage n barrier, block, bottleneck, congestion, constriction, hindrance, impediment, jam, obstacle, obstruction, resistance, stoppage.

blond,

blonde adjs bleached, fair, flaxen, golden, light, platinum, silvery, yellow.

bloodshed n bloodletting, butchery, carnage, killing, massacre, murder, slaughter, slaying, violence.

bloodthirsty adj barbaric, brutal, feral, ferocious, fierce, homicidal, inhuman, murderous, pitiless, ruthless, sadistic, sanguinary, savage, vicious, violent, warlike. ▷ CRUEL. Opp HUMANE.

bloody adj **1** bleeding, bloodstained, raw. **2** a bloody battle. cruel, gory, sanguinary. ▷ BLOODTHIRSTY.

bloom n **1** blossom, bud, floret, flower. **2** bloom of youth. beauty, blush, flush, glow, prime. ● v be healthy, blossom, poet blow, bud, burgeon, inf come out, develop, flourish, flower, grow, open, prosper, sprout, thrive. Opp FADE.

blot n **1** blob, blotch, mark, smear, smirch, smudge, inf splodge, spot, stain. **2** blot on the landscape. blemish, defect, eyesore, fault, flaw, ugliness. ● v bespatter, blemish, blotch, blur, disfigure, mar, mark, smudge, spoil, spot, stain. **blot out** ▷ OBLITERATE. **blot your copybook** ▷ MISBEHAVE.

blotchy adj blemished, brindled, discoloured, inflamed, marked, patchy, smudged, spotty, streaked, uneven.

blow n **1** bang, bash, inf belt, inf biff, box (ears), buffet, bump, clip, clout, clump, concussion, hit, jolt, knock, punch, rap, slap, inf slosh, smack, inf sock, stroke, swat, swipe, thump, thwack, wallop, welt, whack, whop. **2** a sad blow. affliction, inf bombshell, calamity, disappointment, disaster, misfortune, shock, surprise, upset. ● v blast, breathe, exhale, fan, puff, waft, whine, whirl, whistle. **blow up** **1** dilate, enlarge, expand, fill, inflate, pump up. **2** exaggerate, magnify, make worse, overstate. **3** blast, bomb, burst, detonate, dynamite, erupt, explode, go off, set off, shatter. **4** [inf] erupt, get angry, lose your temper, rage.

blue adj **1** aquamarine, azure, cerulean, cobalt, indigo, navy, sapphire, sky-blue, turquoise, ultramarine. **2** ▷ BAWDY. **3** ▷ SAD. ● v ▷ SQUANDER.

blueprint n basis, design, draft, model, outline, pattern, pilot, plan, project, proposal, prototype, scheme.

bluff v cozen, deceive, delude, dupe, fool, hoodwink, mislead.

blunder n inf boob, inf botch, inf clanger, sl cock-up, error, fault, Fr faux pas, gaffe, howler, indiscretion, miscalculation, misjudgement, mistake, slip, slip-up, solecism. ● v be clumsy, inf botch up, bumble, bungle, inf drop a clanger, err, flounder, inf foul up, sl goof, go wrong, inf make a hash of something, make a mistake, mess up, miscalculate, misjudge, inf put your foot in it, slip up, stumble.

blunt adj **1** dull, rounded, thick, unpointed, unsharpened, worn. Opp SHARP. **2** blunt criticism. abrupt, bluff, brusque, candid, curt, direct, downright, forthright, frank, honest, insensitive, outspoken, plain-spoken, rude, straightforward, tactless, unceremonious, undiplomatic. Opp TACTFUL. ● v abate, allay, anaesthetize, dampen, deaden, desensitize, dull, lessen, numb, soften, take the edge off, weaken. Opp SHARPEN.

blur v bedim, befog, blear, cloud, conceal, confuse, darken, dim, fog, mask, muddle, obscure, smear, unfocus.

blurred adj bleary, blurry, clouded, cloudy, confused, dim, faint, foggy, fuzzy, hazy, ill-defined, indefinite, indistinct, misty, nebulous, out of focus, smoky, unclear, unfocused, vague. Opp CLEAR.

blurt v **blurt out** be indiscreet, inf blab, burst out with, come out with, cry out, disclose, divulge, exclaim, inf give the game away, let out, let slip, reveal, inf spill the beans, tell, utter.

blush v be ashamed, colour, flush, glow, go red, redden.

blustering adj angry, boasting, boisterous, bragging, bullying, crowing, defiant, domineering, hectoring, noisy, ranting, selfassertive, showing-off, storming, swaggering, threatening, vaunting, violent. Opp MODEST.

blustery adj gusty, squally, unsettled, windy.

board n **1** blockboard, chipboard, clapboard, panel, plank, plywood, scantling, sheet, slab, slat, timber, weatherboard. **2** board of directors. cabinet, committee, council, direct-orate, jury, panel. ● v **1** accommodate, billet, feed, house, lodge, put up, quarter, stay. **2** board a bus. catch, embark (on), enter, get on, go on board.

boast v sl be all mouth, inf blow your own trumpet, bluster, brag, crow, exaggerate, gloat, praise yourself, sl shoot a line, show off, inf sing your own praises, swagger, inf swank, inf talk big, vaunt.

boaster n inf big-head, inf big mouth, braggadocio, braggart, inf loudmouth, inf poser, show-off, swaggerer, swank.

boastful adj inf big-headed, bragging, inf cocky, conceited, egotistical, ostentatious, proud, puffed up, swaggering, swanky, swollen-headed, vain, vainglorious. Opp MODEST.

boat n craft, ship. ▷ VESSEL.

boatman n bargee, coxswain, ferryman, gondolier, lighterman, oarsman, rower, waterman, yachtsman. ▷ SAILOR.

bob v be agitated, bounce, dance, hop, jerk, jig about, jolt, jump, leap, move about, nod, oscillate, shake, toss about, twitch. **bob up** ▷ APPEAR.

body n **1** anatomy, being, build, figure, form, frame, individual, physique, shape, substance, torso, trunk. **2** cadaver, carcass, corpse, mortal remains, mummy, relics, remains, sl stiff. **3** association, band, committee, company, corporation, society. ▷ GROUP. **4** body of material. accumulation, agglomeration, collection, corpus, mass.

bodyguard n defender, guard, minder, protector.

bog n fen, marsh, marshland, mire, morass, mudflats, peat bog, quagmire, quicksands, salt-marsh, old use slough, swamp, wetlands. **get bogged down** be hindered, get into difficulties, get stuck, grind to a halt, sink.

bogus adj counterfeit, fake, false, fictitious, fraudulent, imitation, inf phoney, sham, spurious. Opp GENUINE.

Bohemian *adj inf* arty, *old use* beatnik, bizarre, eccentric, hippie, informal, nonconformist, off-beat, unconventional, unorthodox, *inf* way-out, weird.

boil *n* abscess, blister, carbuncle, chilblain, eruption, gathering, gumboil, inflammation, pimple, pock, pustule, sore, spot, tumour, ulcer, *sl* zit. ● *v* **1** cook, heat, simmer, stew. **2** bubble, effervesce, foam, seethe, steam. **3** ▷ RAGE.

boisterous *adj* animated, disorderly, exuberant, irrepressible, lively, loud, noisy, obstreperous, riotous, rollicking, rough, rowdy, stormy, tempestuous, tumultuous, undisciplined, unrestrained, unruly, uproarious, wild. *Opp* CALM.

bold *adj* **1** adventurous, audacious, brave, confident, courageous, daredevil, daring, dauntless, enterprising, fearless, *derog* foolhardy, forceful, gallant, hardy, heroic, intrepid, *inf* plucky, *derog* rash, *derog* reckless, resolute, self-confident, unafraid, valiant, valorous, venturesome. **2** [*derog*] *a bold request.* brash, brazen, *inf* cheeky, forward, fresh, impertinent, impudent, insolent, pert, presumptuous, rude, saucy, shameless, unashamed. **3** *bold colours, writing.* big, bright, clear, conspicuous, eye-catching, large, obvious, prominent, pronounced, showy, striking, strong, vivid. *Opp* FAINT, TIMID.

bolster *n* cushion, pillow. ● *v* ▷ SUPPORT.

bolt *n* **1** arrow, dart, missile, projectile. **2** peg, pin, rivet, rod, screw. **3** *bolt on a door.* bar, catch, fastening, latch, lock. ● *v* **1** bar, close, fasten, latch, lock, secure. **2** *The animals bolted.* abscond, dart away, dash away, escape, flee, fly, run off, rush off. **3** *bolt food.* ▷ EAT. **bolt from the blue** ▷ SURPRISE.

bomb *n* bombshell, explosive. ▷ WEAPON. ● *v* ▷ BOMBARD.

bombard *v* **1** assail, assault, attack, batter, blast, blitz, bomb, fire at, pelt, pound, shell, shoot at, strafe. **2** badger, beset, harass, importune, pester, plague.

bombardment *n* attack, barrage, blast, blitz, broadside, burst, cannonade, discharge, fusillade, hail, salvo, volley.

bombastic *adj* extravagant, grandiloquent, grandiose, high-flown, inflated, magniloquent, pompous, turgid.

bond *n* **1** chain, cord, fastening, fetters, handcuffs, manacles, restraints, rope, shackles. **2** *bond of friendship.* affiliation, affinity, attachment, connection, link, relationship, tie, unity. **3** *a legal bond.* agreement, compact, contract, covenant, guarantee, legal document, pledge, promise, word. ● *v* ▷ STICK.

bondage *n* enslavement, serfdom, servitude, slavery, subjection, thraldom, vassalage.

bonus *n* **1** bounty, commission, dividend, gift, gratuity, hand-out, honorarium, largesse, payment, *inf* perk, reward, supplement, tip. **2** addition, advantage, benefit, extra, *inf* plus.

bony *adj* angular, emaciated, gangling, gawky, lanky, lean, scraggy, scrawny, skinny, thin, ungainly. *Opp* GRACEFUL, PLUMP.

book *n* booklet, copy, edition, hardback, paperback, publication, tome, volume, work. □ *album, annual, anthology, atlas, bestiary, old use chap-book, compendium, concordance, diary, dictionary, digest, directory, encyclopaedia, fiction, gazetteer, guidebook, handbook, hymnal, hymn-book, jotter, ledger, lexicon, libretto, manual, manuscript, missal, notebook, omnibus, picture-book, prayer-book, primer, psalter, reading book, reference book,* music *score, scrap-book, scroll, sketch-book, textbook, thesaurus, vade mecum.* ▷ WRITING. ● *v* **1** *book for speeding.* arrest, take your name, write down details. **2** *book in advance.* arrange, buy, engage, order, organize, reserve, sign up.

booklet *n* brochure, leaflet, pamphlet, paperback.

boom n **1** bang, blast, crash, explosion, reverberation, roar, rumble. ▷ SOUND. **2** *boom in trade.* bonanza, boost, expansion, growth, improvement, increase, spurt, upsurge, upturn. ▷ PROSPERITY. **3** *boom across a river.* ▷ BARRIER. ● v **1** ▷ SOUND. **2** ▷ PROSPER.

boorish adj barbarian, ignorant, ill-bred, ill-mannered, loutish, oafish, philistine, uncultured, vulgar. *Opp* CULTURED.

boost n aid, encouragement, fillip, impetus, help, lift, push, stimulus. ● v advance, aid, assist, augment, bolster, build up, buoy up, encourage, enhance, enlarge, expand, foster, further, give an impetus to, heighten, help, improve, increase, inspire, lift, promote, push up, raise, support, sustain. *Opp* DEPRESS.

booth n box, carrel, compartment, cubicle, hut, kiosk, stall, stand.

booty n contraband, gains, haul, loot, pickings, pillage, plunder, spoils, *inf* swag, takings, trophies, winnings.

border n **1** brim, brink, edge, edging, frame, frieze, frill, fringe, hem, margin, perimeter, periphery, rim, surround, verge. **2** borderline, boundary, frontier, limit. **3** *flower border.* bed, herbaceous border. ● v abut on, adjoin, be adjacent to, be alongside, join, share a border with, touch.

bore v **1** burrow, drill, mine, penetrate, sink, tunnel. ▷ PIERCE. **2** *bore listeners.* alienate, depress, jade, *inf* leave cold, tire, *inf* turn off, weary. *Opp* INTEREST.

boring adj arid, commonplace, dead, dreary, dry, dull, flat, humdrum, long-winded, monotonous, prolix, repetitious, repetitive, soporific, stale, tedious, tiresome, trite, uneventful, unexciting, uninspiring, uninteresting, vapid, wearisome, wordy. *Opp* INTERESTING.

born adj congenital, genuine, instinctive, natural, untaught.

borrow v adopt, appropriate, be lent, *inf* cadge, copy, crib, make use of, obtain, pirate, plagiarize, *inf* scrounge, *inf* sponge, take, use, usurp. *Opp* LEND.

boss n employer, head. ▷ CHIEF.

bossy adj aggressive, assertive, authoritarian, autocratic, bullying, despotic, dictatorial, domineering, exacting, hectoring, high-handed, imperious, lordly, magisterial, masterful, officious, oppressive, overbearing, peremptory, *inf* pushy, self-assertive, tyrannical. *Opp* SERVILE.

bother n **1** ado, difficulty, disorder, disturbance, fuss, *inf* hassle, problem, *inf* to-do. **2** annoyance, inconvenience, irritation, nuisance, pest, trouble, worry. ● v **1** annoy, bewilder, concern, confuse, disconcert, dismay, disturb, exasperate, harass, *inf* hassle, inconvenience, irk, irritate, molest, nag, perturb, pester, plague, trouble, upset, vex, worry. **2** be concerned, be worried, care, mind, take trouble. ▷ TROUBLE.

bottle n flask. □ *carafe, carboy, decanter, flagon, jar, jeroboam, magnum, phial, pitcher, vial, wine-bottle.* **bottle up** ▷ SUPPRESS.

bottom adj deepest, least, lowest, minimum. ● n **1** base, bed, depth, floor, foot, foundation, lowest point, nadir, pedestal, substructure, underneath, underside. *Opp* TOP. **2** basis, essence, grounds, heart, origin, root, source. **3** *your bottom.* vulg arse, backside, behind, *inf* bum, buttocks, *joc* posterior, rear, rump, seat, *inf* sit-upon.

bottomless adj deep, immeasurable, unfathomable, unplumbable.

bounce v bob, bound, bump, jump, leap, move about, rebound, recoil, ricochet, spring.

bound adj **1** certain, committed, compelled, constrained, destined, doomed, duty-bound, fated, forced, obligated, obliged, pledged, required, sure. **2** *bound with rope.* ▷ BIND. ● v bob, bounce, caper, frisk, frolic, gambol, hop, hurdle, jump, leap, pounce, romp, skip, spring, vault. **bound for** aimed at, directed towards, going to, heading for, making for, off to, travelling towards.

boundary n border, borderline, bounds, brink, circumference, confines, demarcation, edge, end, extremity, fringe, frontier, interface, limit, margin, perimeter, threshold, verge.

boundless adj endless, everlasting, immeasurable, incalculable, inexhaustible, infinite, limitless, unbounded, unconfined, unflagging, unlimited, unrestricted, untold. ▷ VAST. Opp FINITE.

bounty n alms, altruism, beneficence, benevolence, charity, generosity, giving, goodness, kindness, largesse, liberality, munificence, philanthropy, unselfishness.

bouquet n 1 arrangement, bunch, buttonhole, corsage, garland, nosegay, posy, spray, wreath. 2 bouquet of wine. ▷ SMELL.

bout n 1 attack, fit, period, run, spell, stint, stretch, time, turn. 2 battle, combat, competition, contest, encounter, engagement, fight, match, round, inf set-to, struggle.

bow v 1 bend, bob, curtsy, genuflect, incline, kowtow, nod, prostrate yourself, salaam, stoop. 2 ▷ SUBMIT.

bowels plur n 1 entrails, guts, inf innards, insides, intestines, viscera, vitals. 2 core, depths, heart, inside.

bower n alcove, arbour, bay, gazebo, grotto, hideaway, pavilion, pergola, recess, retreat, sanctuary, shelter, summer-house.

bowl n basin, bath, casserole, container, dish, pan, pie-dish, tureen. ● v fling, hurl, lob, pitch, throw, toss.

box n carton, case, chest, container, crate. □ bin, caddy, canister, cartridge, casket, coffer, coffin, pack, package, punnet, tea-chest, tin, trunk. ● v inf engage in fisticuffs, fight, punch, scrap, spar. ▷ HIT.

boxer n prize-fighter, sparring partner. □ bantamweight, cruiserweight, featherweight, flyweight, heavyweight, lightweight, middleweight, welterweight.

boy n derog brat, inf kid, lad, schoolboy, son, derog stripling, derog urchin, youngster, youth.

boycott n ban, blacklist, embargo, prohibition. ● v avoid, black, blackball, blacklist, exclude, inf give the cold-shoulder to, ignore, make unwelcome, ostracize, outlaw, prohibit, spurn, stay away from.

bracing adj crisp, exhilarating, health-giving, invigorating, refreshing, restorative, stimulating, tonic.

brag v crow, gloat, show off. ▷ BOAST.

brain n cerebrum, inf grey matter, intellect, intelligence, mind, inf nous, reason, sense, understanding, wisdom, wit.

brainwash v condition, indoctrinate, re-educate.

branch n 1 arm, bough, limb, prong, shoot, sprig, stem, twig. 2 department, division, office, offshoot, part, ramification, section, subdivision, wing. ● v diverge, divide, fork, ramify, split, subdivide. **branch out** ▷ DIVERSIFY.

brand n kind, label, line, make, sort, trademark, type, variety. ● v 1 burn, identify, label, mark, scar, stamp, tag. 2 censure, characterize, denounce, discredit, stigmatize, vilify.

brash adj brazen, bumptious, insolent, rash, reckless, rude, self-assertive. ▷ ARROGANT.

bravado n arrogance, bluster, braggadocio, machismo, swagger.

brave adj adventurous, audacious, bold, chivalrous, cool, courageous, daring, dauntless, determined, fearless, gallant, game, sl gutsy, heroic, indomitable, intrepid, lion-hearted, derog macho, noble, inf plucky, resolute, spirited, stalwart, stoical, stout-hearted, tough, unafraid, uncomplaining, undaunted, unshrinking, valiant, valorous, venturesome. Opp COWARDLY.

bravery n audacity, boldness, sl bottle, courage, daring, dauntlessness, determination, fearlessness, fibre, firmness, fortitude, gallantry, *inf* grit, *inf* guts, heroism, intrepidity, mettle, *inf* nerve, *inf* pluck, prowess, resolution, spirit, *sl* spunk, stoicism, tenacity, valour, will-power. *Opp* COWARDICE.

brawl *n* affray, altercation, *inf* bust-up, clash, *inf* dust-up, fracas, fray, *inf* free-for-all, mêlée, *inf* punch-up, quarrel, row, scrap, scuffle, *inf* set-to, tussle. ● *v* ▷ FIGHT.

brazen *adj* barefaced, blatant, cheeky, defiant, flagrant, impertinent, impudent, insolent, rude, shameless, unabashed, unashamed. *Opp* SHAMEFACED.

breach *n* **1** aperture, break, chasm, crack, fissure, gap, hole, opening, rent, space, split. **2** alienation, difference, disagreement, divorce, drifting apart, estrangement, quarrel, rift, rupture, schism, separation, split. **3** *breach of law.* contravention, failure, infringement, offence, transgression, violation.

bread *n* □ brioche, cob, croissant, French bread, loaf, roll, stick of bread, toast. ▷ FOOD.

break *n* **1** breach, breakage, burst, chink, cleft, crack, crevice, cut, fissure, fracture, gap, gash, hole, leak, opening, rent, rift, rupture, slit, split, tear. **2** *break from work.* *inf* breather, breathing-space, hiatus, interlude, intermission, interval, *inf* let-up, lull, pause, respite, rest, tea-break. **3** *break in service.* disruption, halt, interruption, lapse, suspension. ● *v* **1** breach, burst, *inf* bust, chip, crack, crumple, crush, damage, demolish, fracture, fragment, knock down, ruin, shatter, shiver, smash, *inf* smash to smithereens, snap, splinter, split, squash, wreck. ▷ DESTROY. **2** *break the law.* contravene, defy, disobey, disregard, fail to observe, flout, go back on, infringe, transgress, violate. **3** *break a record.* beat, better, do more than, exceed, excel, go beyond, outdo, outstrip, pass, surpass. **break down** ▷ ANALYSE, DEMOLISH. **break in** ▷ INTERRUPT, INTRUDE. **break off** ▷ FINISH. **break out** ▷ ESCAPE. **break through** ▷ PENETRATE. **break up** ▷ DISINTEGRATE.

breakdown *n* **1** collapse, destruction, disintegration, downfall, failure, fault, hitch, malfunction, ruin, stoppage. **2** analysis, classification, detailing, dissection, itemization, *inf* rundown.

breakthrough *n* advance, development, discovery, find, improvement, innovation, invention, leap forward, progress, revolution, success.

breakwater *n* groyne, jetty, mole, pier, sea-defence.

breath *n* breeze, gust, murmur, pant, puff, sigh, stir, waft, whiff, whisper.

breathe *vb* **1** exhale, inhale, pant, puff, respire, suspire. **2** hint, let out, tell, whisper.

breathless *adj* exhausted, gasping, out of breath, panting, *inf* puffed, *inf* puffing and blowing, tired out, wheezy, winded.

breed *n* ancestry, clan, family, kind, line, lineage, nation, pedigree, progeny, race, sort, species, stock, strain, type, variety. ● *vb* **1** bear young ones, beget young ones, increase, multiply, procreate, produce young, propagate (*plants*), raise young ones, reproduce. **2** *breed contempt.* arouse, cause, create, cultivate, develop, engender, foster, generate, induce, nourish, nurture, occasion.

breeze *n* air-current, breath, draught, waft, wind, *poet* zephyr.

breezy *adj* airy, *inf* blowy, draughty, fresh, gusty, windy.

brevity *n* briefness, compactness, compression, conciseness, concision, curtness, economy, incisiveness, pithiness, shortness, succinctness, terseness.

brew *n* blend, compound, concoction, drink, hash, infusion, liquor, mixture, potion, preparation, punch, stew. ● *vb* **1** boil, cook, ferment, infuse, make, simmer, steep, stew. **2** *brew mischief.* concoct, contrive, *inf* cook up, develop, devise, foment, hatch, plan, plot, prepare, scheme, stir up.

bribe n sl backhander, bribery, inf carrot, enticement, sl graft, gratuity, incentive, inducement, inf payola, protection money, inf sweetener, tip. ● vb buy off, corrupt, entice, inf grease your palm, influence, offer a bribe, pervert, reward, suborn, tempt, tip.

brick n block, breeze-block, cube, set, sett, stone.

bridge n arch, connection, crossing, link, span, way over. □ aqueduct, Bailey bridge, drawbridge, flyover, footbridge, overpass, pontoon bridge, suspension bridge, swing bridge, viaduct. ● vb connect, cross, fill, join, link, pass over, span, straddle, tie together, traverse, unite.

bridle vb check, control, curb, restrain.

brief adj 1 cursory, ephemeral, evanescent, fast, fleeting, hasty, limited, little, momentary, passing, quick, sharp, short, short-lived, temporary, transient, transitory. 2 brief comment. abbreviated, abridged, compact, compendious, compressed, concise, condensed, crisp, curt, curtailed, incisive, laconic, pithy, shortened, succinct, terse, thumbnail, to the point. Opp LONG. ● n 1 advice, briefing, data, description, directions, information, instructions, orders, outline, plan. 2 a barrister's brief. argument, case, defence, dossier, summary. ● vb advise, coach, direct, enlighten, inf fill someone in, give someone the facts, guide, inform, instruct, prepare, prime, inf put someone in the picture.

briefs n camiknickers, knickers, panties, pants, shorts, trunks, underpants.

brigand n bandit, buccaneer, desperado, footpad, gangster, highwayman, marauder, outlaw, pirate, robber, ruffian, thief.

bright adj 1 ablaze, aglow, alight, beaming, blazing, burnished, colourful, dazzling, flashing, derog flashy, fresh, derog gaudy, glaring, gleaming, glistening, glittering, glossy, glowing, incandescent, lambent, light, luminous, lustrous, pellucid, polished, radiant, refulgent, resplendent, scintillating, shimmering, shining, shiny, showy, sparkling, twinkling, vivid. 2 bright sky. clear, cloudless, fair, sunny. 3 bright prospects. auspicious, favourable, good, hopeful, optimistic, rosy. 4 a bright smile. ▷ CHEERFUL. 5 bright ideas. ▷ CLEVER. Opp DULL.

brighten vb 1 cheer (up), enliven, gladden, illuminate, light up, liven up, inf perk up, revitalize, smarten up. 2 The sky brightened. become sunny, clear up, lighten.

brilliant adj 1 coruscating, dazzling, glaring, glittering, glorious, intense, resplendent, scintillating, shining, showy, sparkling, splendid, vivid. ▷ BRIGHT. Opp DULL. 2 [inf] a brilliant game. ▷ EXCELLENT.

brim n brink, circumference, edge, limit, lip, margin, peri-meter, periphery, rim, top, verge.

bring vb 1 bear, carry, convey, deliver, fetch, take, transfer, transport. 2 bring a friend. accompany, conduct, escort, guide, lead, usher. 3 The play brought great applause. attract, cause, create, draw, earn, engender, generate, get, give rise to, induce, lead to, occasion, produce, prompt, provoke, result in. **bring about** ▷ CREATE. **bring in** ▷ EARN, INTRODUCE. **bring off** ▷ ACHIEVE. **bring on** ▷ ACCELERATE, CAUSE. **bring out** ▷ EMPHASIZE, PRODUCE. **bring up** ▷ EDUCATE, RAISE.

brink n bank, border, boundary, brim, circumference, edge, fringe, limit, lip, margin, perimeter, periphery, rim, skirt, threshold, verge.

brisk adj 1 active, alert, animated, bright, businesslike, bustling, busy, crisp, decisive, energetic, fast, keen, lively, nimble, quick, rapid, inf snappy, inf spanking (pace), speedy, spirited, sprightly, spry, vigorous. Opp LEISURELY. 2 a brisk wind. bracing, enlivening, fresh, invigorating, refreshing, stimulating.

bristle n barb, hair, prickle, quill, spine, stubble, thorn, whisker, wire. ● vb become angry, become defensive, become indignant, bridle, flare up.

brittle adj breakable, crackly, crisp, crumbling, delicate, easily broken, fragile, frail, frangible, weak. Opp FLEXIBLE, RESILIENT.

broad adj **1** ample, capacious, expansive, extensive, great, large, open, roomy, spacious, sweeping, vast, wide. **2** broad daylight. clear, full, open, plain, undisguised. **3** broad outline. general, imprecise, indefinite, inexact, non-specific, sweeping, undetailed, vague. **4** broad tastes. all-embracing, catholic, comprehensive, eclectic, encyclopaedic, universal, wide-ranging. **5** broad humour. bawdy, sl blue, coarse, earthy, improper, impure, indecent, indelicate, racy, ribald, suggestive, vulgar. ▷ BROAD-MINDED. Opp FINITE, NARROW.

broadcast n programme, relay, show, telecast, transmission. ● vb **1** advertise, announce, circulate, disseminate, make known, make public, proclaim, promulgate, publish, relay, report, send out, spread about, televise, transmit. **2** broadcast seed. scatter, sow at random.

broadcaster n anchor-man, announcer, commentator, compère, disc jockey, DJ, linkman, newsreader, presenter. ▷ ENTERTAINER.

broaden vb branch out, build up, develop, diversify, enlarge, expand, extend, increase, open up, spread, widen. Opp LIMIT.

broad-minded adj all-embracing, balanced, broad, catholic, comprehensive, cosmopolitan, eclectic, enlightened, liberal, open-minded, permissive, tolerant, unbiased, unbigoted, unprejudiced, unshockable. Opp NARROW-MINDED.

brochure n booklet, broadsheet, catalogue, circular, folder, handbill, leaflet, pamphlet, prospectus, tract.

brooch n badge, clasp, clip, fastening.

brood n children, clutch (of eggs), family, issue, litter, offspring, progeny, young. ● vb **1** hatch, incubate, sit on. **2** brood over mistakes. agonize, dwell (on), inf eat your heart out, fret, mope, sulk, worry. ▷ THINK.

brook n beck, burn, channel, poet rill, rivulet, runnel, stream, watercourse. ● vb ▷ TOLERATE.

browbeat vb badger, bully, coerce, cow, hector, intimidate, tyrannize. ▷ FRIGHTEN.

brown adj beige, bronze, buff, chestnut, chocolate, dun, fawn, khaki, ochre, russet, sepia, tan, tawny, terracotta, umber. ● vb bronze, burn, colour, grill, tan, toast.

browse vb **1** crop grass, eat, feed, graze, pasture. **2** browse in a book. dip in, flick through, leaf through, look through, peruse, read here and there, scan, skim, thumb through.

bruise n black eye, bump, contusion, discoloration, inf shiner, welt. ● vb blacken, crush, damage, discolour, injure, knock, mark. ▷ WOUND.

brush n **1** besom, broom. **2** brush with police. ▷ CONFLICT. ● vb **1** comb, groom, scrub, sweep, tidy, whisk. **2** just brushed the gatepost. graze, touch.
brush aside ▷ DISMISS, DISREGARD.
brush-off ▷ REBUFF. **brush up** ▷ REVISE.

brutal adj atrocious, barbaric, barbarous, beastly, bestial, bloodthirsty, bloody, brutish, callous, cold-blooded, cruel, dehumanized, ferocious, hard-hearted, heartless, inhuman, inhumane, merciless, murderous, pitiless, remorseless, ruthless, sadistic, savage, uncivilized, unfeeling, vicious, violent, wild. ▷ UNKIND. Opp HUMANE.

brutalize vb dehumanize, harden, inure, make brutal.

brute adj crude, irrational, mindless, physical, rough, stupid, unfeeling, unthinking. ▷ BRUTISH. ● n **1** beast, creature, dumb animal. ▷ ANIMAL. **2** [inf] a cruel brute. barbarian, bully, devil, lout, monster, ruffian, sadist, savage, swine.

brutish *adj* animal, barbaric, barbarous, beastly, bestial, boorish, brutal, coarse, cold-blooded, crude, cruel, *inf* gross, inhuman, insensitive, loutish, mindless, savage, senseless, stupid, subhuman, uncouth, unintelligent, unthinking. *Opp* HUMANE.

bubble *n* air-pocket, blister, hollow, vesicle. ● *vb* boil, effervesce, fizz, fizzle, foam, froth, gurgle, seethe, sparkle. **bubbles** effervescence, fizz, foam, froth, head, lather, suds.

bubbly *adj* carbonated, effervescent, fizzy, foaming, seething, sparkling. ▷ LIVELY.

buccaneer *n* adventurer, bandit, brigand, corsair, marauder, pirate, privateer, robber.

bucket *n* can, pail, scuttle, tub.

buckle *n* catch, clasp, clip, fastener, fastening, hasp. ● *vb* **1** clasp, clip, do up, fasten, hitch up, hook up, secure. **2** bend, bulge, cave in, collapse, contort, crumple, curve, dent, distort, fold, twist, warp.

bud *n* shoot, sprout. ● *vb* begin to grow, burgeon, develop, shoot, sprout. **budding** ▷ POTENTIAL, PROMISING.

budge *vb* **1** change position, give way, move, shift, stir, yield. **2** *can't budge him.* alter, change, dislodge, influence, move, persuade, propel, push, remove, shift, sway.

budget *n* accounts, allocation of funds, allowance, estimate, financial planning, funds, means, resources. ● *vb* allocate money, allot resources, allow (for), estimate expenditure, plan your spending, provide (for), ration your spending.

buff *n* ▷ ENTHUSIAST. ● *vb* burnish, clean, polish, rub, shine, smooth.

buffer *n* bulwark, bumper, cushion, fender, pad, safeguard, screen, shield, shock-absorber.

buffet *n* **1** bar, café, cafeteria, counter, snack-bar. **2** *a stand-up buffet.* ▷ MEAL. ● *vb* ▷ HIT.

bug *n* **1** ▷ INSECT, MICROBE. **2** *bug in a computer program.* breakdown, defect, error, failing, fault, flaw, *inf* gremlin, imperfection, malfunction, mistake, *inf* snarl-up, virus. ● *vb* **1** intercept, interfere with, listen in to, spy on, tap. **2** [*sl*] *Untidiness bugs me.* ▷ ANNOY.

build *vb* assemble, construct, develop, erect, fabricate, form, found, *inf* knock together, make, put together, put up, raise, rear, set up. **build up** ▷ INTENSIFY.

builder *n* bricklayer, construction worker, labourer.

building *n* construction, edifice, erection, piece of architecture, *inf* pile, premises, structure. □ *arcade, barn, barracks, basilica, boat-house, bungalow, cabin, castle, cathedral, chapel, chateau, church, cinema, college, complex, cottage, dovecote, factory, farmhouse, flats, fort, fortress, garage, gazebo, gymnasium, hall, hangar, hotel, house, inn, library, lighthouse, mansion, mausoleum, mill, monastery, monument, mosque, museum, observatory, outbuilding, outhouse, pagoda, palace, pavilion, pier, powerstation, prison, pub, public house, restaurant, school, shed, shop, silo, skyscraper, stable, storehouse, studio, summer-house, synagogue, temple, theatre, tower, villa, warehouse, windmill.*

bulb *n* **1** corm, tuber. □ *amaryllis, bluebell, crocus, daffodil, freesia, hyacinth, lily, narcissus, snowdrop, tulip.* **2** *electric bulb.* lamp, light.

bulbous *adj* bloated, bulging, convex, distended, ovoid, pear-shaped, pot-bellied, rotund, rounded, spherical, swollen, tuberous.

bulge *n* bump, distension, hump, knob, lump, projection, protrusion, protuberance, rise, swelling. ● *vb* belly, billow, dilate, distend, enlarge, expand, project, protrude, stick out, swell.

bulk *n* **1** amplitude, bigness, body, dimensions, extent, immensity, largeness, magnitude, mass, size, substance, volume, weight. **2** *the bulk* *of the work. inf* best part, greater part, majority, preponderance.

bulky *adj* awkward, chunky, cumbersome, large, unwieldy. ▷ BIG.

bulletin *n* account, announcement, communication, communiqué, dispatch, message, newsflash, notice, proclamation, report, statement.

bullion *n* bar, ingot, nugget, solid gold, solid silver.

bull's-eye *n* bull, centre, mark, middle, target.

bully *vb* bludgeon, browbeat, coerce, cow, domineer, frighten, harass, hector, intimidate, oppress, persecute, *inf* pick on, *inf* push around, terrorize, threaten, torment, tyrannize.

bulwark *n* defence, earthwork, fortification, parapet, protection, rampart, redoubt, wall. ▷ BARRIER.

bump *n* **1** bang, blow, buffet, collision, crash, knock, smash, thud, thump. **2** bulge, distension, hump, knob, lump, projection, protrusion, protuberance, rise, swelling, tumescence, welt. ● *vb* **1** bang, collide with, crash into, jar, knock, ram, slam, smash into, strike, thump, wallop. ▷ HIT. **2** bounce, jerk, jolt, shake. **bump into** ▷ MEET. **bump off** ▷ KILL.

bumptious *adj* arrogant, *inf* bigheaded, boastful, brash, *inf* cocky, conceited, egotistic, forward, immodest, officious, overbearing, over-confident, pompous, presumptuous, pretentious, *inf* pushy, self-assertive, self-important, smug, *inf* snooty, *inf* stuck-up, swaggering, vain, vainglorious, vaunting. *Opp* MODEST.

bumpy *adj* **1** bouncy, jarring, jerky, jolting. **2** *a bumpy road.* broken, irregular, jagged, knobbly, lumpy, pitted, rocky, rough, rutted, stony, uneven. *Opp* SMOOTH.

bunch *n* **1** batch, bundle, clump, cluster, collection, heap, lot, number, pack, quantity, set, sheaf, tuft. **2** *bunch of flowers.* bouquet, posy, spray. **3** *[inf] bunch of friends.* band, crowd, gang, gathering, mob, party, team, troop. ▷ GROUP. ● *vb* assemble, cluster, collect, congregate, crowd, flock, gather, group, herd, huddle, mass, pack. *Opp* DISPERSE.

bundle *n* bag, bale, bunch, carton, collection, pack, package, packet, parcel, sheaf, truss. ● *vb* bale, bind, enclose, fasten, pack, package, roll, tie, truss, wrap. **bundle out** ▷ EJECT.

bung *n* cork, plug, stopper. ● *vb* ▷ THROW.

bungle *vb* blunder, botch, *sl* cock up, *inf* foul up, fluff, *inf* make a hash of, *inf* make a mess of, *inf* mess up, mismanage, *inf* muck up, *inf* muff, ruin, *inf* screw up, spoil.

buoy *n* beacon, float, marker, mooring buoy, signal. ● *vb* **buoy up** ▷ RAISE.

buoyant *adj* **1** floating, light. **2** *a buoyant mood.* ▷ CHEERFUL.

burden *n* **1** cargo, encumbrance, load, weight. **2** *burden of guilt.* affliction, albatross, anxiety, care, cross, duty, handicap, millstone, obligation, onus, problem, responsibility, sorrow, trial, trouble, worry. ● *vb* afflict, bother, encumber, hamper, handicap, impose on, load (with), *inf* lumber (with), oppress, overload (with), *inf* saddle (with), strain, tax, trouble, weigh down, worry.

burdensome *adj* bothersome, difficult, exacting, hard, heavy, onerous, oppressive, taxing, tiring, troublesome, trying, wearisome, wearying, weighty, worrying. *Opp* EASY.

bureau *n* **1** desk, writing-desk. **2** *travel bureau.* agency, counter, department, office, service.

bureaucracy *n* administration, government, officialdom, paperwork, *inf* red tape, regulations.

burglar *n* cat-burglar, housebreaker, intruder, robber. ▷ THIEF.

burglary *n* break-in, forcible entry, house-breaking, larceny, pilfering, robbery, stealing, theft, thieving.

burgle *vb* break in, pilfer, rob. ▷ STEAL.

burial *n* entombment, funeral, interment, obsequies.

burlesque n caricature, imitation, mockery, parody, pastiche, satire, *inf* send-up, spoof, *inf* take-off, travesty.

burly adj athletic, beefy, brawny, heavy, hefty, hulking, husky, muscular, powerful, stocky, stout, *inf* strapping, strong, sturdy, thickset, tough, well-built. *Opp* THIN.

burn n blister, charring. ● vb **1** be alight, blaze, flame, flare, flash, flicker, glow, smoke, smoulder, spark, sparkle. **2** carbonize, consume, cremate, destroy by fire, ignite, incinerate, kindle, light, reduce to ashes, set fire to, set on fire. **3** *burn your skin*. blister, brand, char, scald, scorch, sear, shrivel, singe, sting, toast. ▷ FIRE, HEAT.

burning adj **1** ablaze, afire, aflame, alight, blazing, flaming, glowing, incandescent, lit up, on fire, raging, smouldering. **2** *burning pain*. biting, blistering, boiling, fiery, hot, inflamed, scalding, scorching, searing, smarting, stinging. **3** *burning chemicals*. acid, caustic, corrosive. **4** *a burning smell*. acrid, pungent, reeking, scorching, smoky. **5** *a burning desire*. acute, ardent, consuming, eager, fervent, flaming, frenzied, heated, impassioned, intense, passionate, red-hot, vehement. **6** *a burning issue*. crucial, important, pertinent, pressing, relevant, urgent, vital.

burrow n earth, excavation, hole, retreat, set, shelter, tunnel, warren. ● vb delve, dig, excavate, mine, tunnel.

burst vb **1** break, crack, disintegrate, erupt, explode, force open, give way, open suddenly, part suddenly, puncture, rupture, shatter, split, tear. **2** ▷ RUSH.

bury vb cover, embed, enclose, engulf, entomb, immerse, implant, insert, inter, lay to rest, plant, put away, secrete, sink, submerge. ▷ HIDE.

bus n *old use* charabanc, coach, double-decker, minibus, *old use* omnibus.

bushy adj bristling, bristly, dense, fluffy, fuzzy, hairy, luxuriant, rough, shaggy, spreading, sticking out, tangled, thick, thick-growing, unruly, untidy.

business n **1** affair, concern, duty, function, issue, matter, obligation, problem, question, responsibility, subject, task, topic. **2** calling, career, craft, employment, industry, job, line of work, occupation, profession, pursuit, trade, vocation, work. **3** buying and selling, commerce, dealings, industry, marketing, merchandising, selling, trade, trading, transactions. **4** company, concern, corporation, enterprise, establishment, firm, organization, *inf* outfit, partnership, practice, *inf* set-up, venture.

businesslike adj careful, efficient, hard-headed, logical, methodical, neat, orderly, practical, professional, prompt, systematic, well-organized. *Opp* DISORGANIZED.

businessman,

businesswoman ns dealer, entrepreneur, executive, financier, industrialist, magnate, manager, merchant, trader, tycoon.

bustle n activity, agitation, commotion, excitement, flurry, fuss, haste, hurly-burly, hurry, hustle, movement, restlessness, scurry, stir, *inf* to-do, *inf* toing and froing. ● vb dart, dash, fuss, hasten, hurry, hustle, make haste, move busily, rush, scamper, scramble, scurry, scuttle, *inf* tear, whirl.

busy adj **1** active, assiduous, bustling about, committed, dedicated, diligent, employed, energetic, engaged, engrossed, *inf* hard at it, immersed, industrious, involved, keen, occupied, *inf* on the go, pottering, preoccupied, slaving, *inf* tied up, tireless, *inf* up to your eyes, working. *Opp* IDLE. **2** *busy shops*. bustling, frantic, full, hectic, lively.

busybody n gossip, meddler, *inf* Nosey Parker, scandalmonger, snooper, spy. **be a busybody** ▷ INTERFERE.

butt *n* **1** haft, handle, shaft, stock. **2** barrel, cask, water-butt. **3** *cigar butt.* end, remains, remnant, stub. **4** *butt of ridicule.* end, mark, object, subject, target, victim. ● *vb* buffet, bump, jab, knock, poke, prod, punch, push, ram, shove, strike, thump. ▷ HIT. **butt in** ▷ INTERRUPT.

buttocks *n* vulg arse, backside, behind, bottom, *vulg* bum, *Amer* butt, *Fr* derrière, fundament, haunches, hindquarters, *joc* posterior, rear, rump, seat.

buttress *n* pier, prop, support. ● *vb* brace, prop up, reinforce, shore up, strengthen, support.

buxom *adj* ample, bosomy, *vulg* chesty, full-figured, healthy-looking, plump, robust, rounded, voluptuous. *Opp* THIN.

buy *vb* acquire, come by, gain, get, get on hire purchase, *inf* invest in, obtain, pay for, procure, purchase. *Opp* SELL.

buyer *n* client, consumer, customer, purchaser, shopper.

bypass *vb* avoid, circumvent, dodge, evade, find a way round, get out of, go round, ignore, neglect, omit, side-step, skirt.

by-product *n* adjunct, complement, consequence, corollary, repercussion, result, side-effect.

bystander *n* eyewitness, looker-on, observer, onlooker, passer-by, spectator, watcher, witness.

C

cabin n **1** bothy, chalet, cottage, hut, lodge, shack, shanty, shed, shelter. **2** *cabin on a ship.* berth, compartment, deck-house, quarters.

cable n **1** chain, cord, flex, guy, hawser, lead, line, mooring, rope, wire. **2** *news by cable.* message, telegram, wire.

cacophonous adj atonal, discordant, dissonant, harsh, noisy, unmusical. *Opp* HARMONIOUS.

cacophony n atonality, caterwauling, din, discord, disharmony, dissonance, harshness, jangle, noise, racket, row, rumpus, tumult. *Opp* HARMONY.

cadence n accent, beat, inflection, intonation, lilt, metre, pattern, rhythm, rise and fall, sound, stress, tune.

cadet n beginner, learner, recruit, tiro, trainee.

cadge vb ask, beg, scrounge, sponge.

café n bar, bistro, brasserie, buffet, cafeteria, canteen, coffee bar, coffee house, coffee shop, diner, restaurant, snack-bar, take-away, tea-room, tea-shop.

cage n aviary, coop, enclosure, hutch, pen, pound. ● vb ▷ CONFINE.

cajole vb inf butter up, coax, flatter, inveigle, persuade, seduce.

cake n **1** bun, gateau. **2** *cake of soap.* bar, block, chunk, cube, loaf, lump, mass, piece, slab. ● vb **1** coat, clog, cover, encrust, make dirty, make muddy. **2** coagulate, congeal, consolidate, dry, harden, solidify, thicken.

calamitous adj awful, cataclysmic, catastrophic, deadly, devastating, dire, disastrous, distressful, dreadful, fatal, ghastly, ruinous, serious, terrible, tragic, unfortunate, unlucky, woeful.

calamity n accident, affliction, cataclysm, catastrophe, disaster, misadventure, mischance, misfortune, mishap, tragedy, tribulation.

calculate vb add up, ascertain, assess, compute, count, determine, do sums, enumerate, estimate, evaluate, figure out, find out, gauge, judge, reckon, total, value, weigh, work out. **calculated** ▷ DELIBERATE. **calculating** ▷ CRAFTY.

calibre n **1** bore, diameter, gauge, measure, size. **2** ability, capability, capacity, character, competence, distinction, excellence, genius, gifts, importance, merit, proficiency, quality, skill, stature, talent, worth.

call n **1** bellow, cry, exclamation, roar, scream, shout, yell. **2** bidding, invitation, signal, summons. **3** *social call.* stay, stop, visit. **4** *no call for it.* cause, demand, excuse, justification, need, occasion, request, requirement. ● vb **1** bellow, clamour, cry out, exclaim, hail, roar, shout, yell. **2** *call on friends.* drop in, socialize, visit. **3** *called her 'Jane'.* baptize, christen, dub, name. **4** *play called 'Lear'.* entitle, title. **5** *call me at 7.* arouse, awaken, get someone up, rouse, wake, waken. **6** *call a meeting.* convene, gather, invite, order, summon. **7** *call by phone.* contact, dial, phone, ring, telephone. **call for** ▷ FETCH, REQUEST. **call off** ▷ CANCEL. **call someone names** ▷ INSULT.

calligraphy n copperplate, handwriting, illumination, lettering, penmanship, script.

calling n business, career, employment, job, line of work, métier, occupation, profession, pursuit, trade, vocation, work.

callous adj apathetic, cold, cold-hearted, cool, dispassionate, hard-bitten, *inf* hard-boiled, hardened, hard-hearted, *inf* hard-nosed, heartless, inhuman, insensitive, merciless, pitiless, ruthless, *inf* thick-skinned, uncaring, unconcerned, unemotional, unfeeling, unsympathetic. ▷ CRUEL. *Opp* SENSITIVE.

callow *adj* adolescent, *inf* born yesterday, *inf* green, immature, inexperienced, innocent, juvenile, naïve, raw, unsophisticated, *inf* wet behind the ears, young. *Opp* MATURE.

calm *adj* **1** airless, even, flat, glassy, *poet* halcyon (*days*), like a millpond, motionless, placid, quiet, slow-moving, smooth, still, unclouded, unwrinkled, windless. **2** collected, *derog* complacent, composed, controlled, cool, dispassionate, equable, impassive, imperturbable, *inf* laid-back, level-headed, moderate, pacific, passionless, patient, peaceful, poised, quiet, relaxed, restful, restrained, sedate, self-possessed, sensible, serene, tranquil, undemonstrative, unemotional, unexcitable, *inf* unflappable, unhurried, unperturbed, unruffled, untroubled. *Opp* EXCITABLE, STORMY. ● *n* flat sea, peace, quietness, stillness, tranquillity. ▷ CALMNESS. ● *vb* appease, compose, control, cool, lull, mollify, pacify, placate, quieten, sedate, settle down, smooth, sober down, soothe, tranquillize. *Opp* DISTURB.

calmness *n derog* complacency, composure, equability, equanimity, imperturbability, level-headedness, peace of mind, sang-froid, self-possession, serenity, *inf* unflappability. *Opp* ANXIETY, EXCITEMENT.

camouflage *n* blind, cloak, concealment, cover, disguise, façade, front, guise, mask, pretence, protective colouring, screen, veil. ● *vb* cloak, conceal, cover up, disguise, hide, mask, obscure, screen, veil.

camp *n* bivouac, camping-ground, campsite, encampment, settlement.

campaign *n* action, battle, crusade, drive, effort, fight, manoeuvre, movement, offensive, operation, push, struggle, war.

campus *n* grounds, setting, site.

canal *n* channel, waterway.

cancel *vb* abandon, abolish, abort, abrogate, annul, call off, countermand, cross out, delete, drop, eliminate, erase, expunge, frank (*stamps*), give up, invalidate, override, overrule, postpone, quash, repeal, repudiate, rescind, revoke, scrap, *inf* scrub, wipe out, write off. **cancel out** ▷ NEUTRALIZE.

cancer *n* canker, carcinoma, growth, malignancy, melanoma, tumour.

candid *adj* blunt, direct, fair, forthright, frank, honest, ingen-uous, just, *inf* no-nonsense, objective, open, outspoken, plain, sincere, straight, straightforward, transparent, true, truthful, unbiased, undisguised, unequivocal, unflattering, unprejudiced. *Opp* INSINCERE.

candidate *n* applicant, aspirant, competitor, contender, contestant, entrant, nominee, *inf* possibility, pretender (*to throne*), runner, suitor.

cane *n* bamboo, rod, stick. ● *vb* THRASH.

canoe *n* dug-out, kayak.

canopy *n* awning, cover, covering, shade, shelter, umbrella.

canvass *n* campaign, census, enquiry, examination, investigation, market research, opinion poll, poll, probe, scrutiny, survey. ● *vb* ask for, campaign, *inf* drum up support, electioneer, seek, solicit.

canyon *n* defile, gap, gorge, gulch, pass, ravine, valley.

cap *n* covering, lid, top. ▷ HAT. ● *vb* ▷ COVER.

capable *adj* able, accomplished, adept, clever, competent, effective, effectual, efficient, experienced, expert, gifted, *inf* handy, intelligent, masterly, practised, proficient, qualified, skilful, skilled, talented, trained. *Opp* INCAPABLE. **capable of** apt to, disposed to, equal to, liable to.

capacity *n* **1** content, dimensions, magnitude, room, size, volume. **2** ability, acumen, capability, cleverness, competence, intelligence, potential, power, skill, talent, wit. **3** *in an official capacity.* appointment, duty, function, job, office, place, position, post, province, responsibility, role.

cape n 1 cloak, coat, cope, mantle, robe, shawl, wrap. 2 head, headland, peninsula, point, promontory.

caper vb bound, cavort, dance, frisk, frolic, gambol, hop, jig about, jump, leap, play, prance, romp, skip, spring.

capital adj 1 chief, controlling, first, foremost, important, leading, main, paramount, pre-eminent, primary, principal. 2 capital letters. big, block, initial, large, upper-case. 3 ▷ EXCELLENT. ● n 1 chief city, centre of government. 2 assets, cash, finance, funds, investments, money, principal, property, sl (the) ready, resources, riches, savings, stock, wealth, inf the wherewithal.

capitulate vb acquiesce, be defeated, concede, desist, fall, give in, relent, submit, succumb, surrender, inf throw in the towel, yield.

capricious adj changeable, erratic, fanciful, fickle, fitful, flighty, impulsive, inconstant, mercurial, moody, quirky, uncertain, unpredictable, unreliable, unstable, variable, wayward, whimsical. Opp STEADY.

capsize vb flip over, invert, keel over, overturn, tip over, turn over, inf turn turtle, turn upside down.

capsule n lozenge, medicine, pill, tablet.

captain n 1 boss, chief, head, leader. 2 commander, master, officer in charge, pilot, skipper.

caption n description, explanation, heading, headline, superscription, title.

captivate vb attract, beguile, bewitch, charm, delight, enamour, enchant, enrapture, enslave, ensnare, enthral, entrance, fascinate, hypnotize, infatuate, mesmerize, seduce, inf steal your heart, inf turn your head, win. Opp DISGUST.

captive adj caged, captured, chained, confined, detained, enslaved, ensnared, fettered, gaoled, imprisoned, incarcerated, jailed, restricted, secure, taken prisoner, inf under lock and key. Opp FREE. ● n convict, detainee, hostage, internee, prisoner, slave.

captivity n bondage, confinement, custody, detention, duress, imprisonment, incarceration, internment, protective custody, remand, restraint, servitude, slavery. ▷ PRISON. Opp FREEDOM.

capture n apprehension, arrest, seizure. ● vb apprehend, arrest, inf bag, bind, catch, inf collar, corner, ensnare, entrap, inf get, inf nab, net, inf nick, overpower, secure, seize, snare, take prisoner, trap. ▷ CONQUER. Opp LIBERATE.

car n automobile, inf banger, joc bus, joc jalopy, motor, motor car, sl wheels. □ cab, convertible, coupé, Dormobile, estate, fastback, hatchback, jeep, Land Rover, limousine, Mini, panda car, patrol car, police car, saloon, shooting brake, sports car, taxi, tourer. ▷ VEHICLE.

carcass n 1 body, cadaver, corpse, meat, remains. 2 carcass of a car. framework, hulk, remains, shell, skeleton, structure.

card n cardboard, pasteboard. □ bank card, birthday card, business card, calling card, credit card, get-well card, greetings card, identity card, invitation, membership card, notelet, picture postcard, playing-card, postcard, union card, Valentine, visiting card.

care n 1 attention, carefulness, caution, circumspection, concentration, concern, diligence, exactness, forethought, heed, interest, meticulousness, pains, prudence, solicitude, thoroughness, thought, vigilance, watchfulness. 2 anxiety, burden, concern, difficulty, hardship, problem, responsibility, sorrow, stress, tribulation, vexation, woe, worry. ▷ TROUBLE. 3 left in my care. charge, control, custody, guardianship, keeping, management, protection, safe-keeping, ward. ● vb be troubled, bother, concern yourself, mind, worry. **care for** ▷ LOVE, TEND.

career n business, calling, craft, employment, job, livelihood, living, métier, occupation, profession, trade, vocation, work. ● vb ▷ RUSH.

cartridge

carefree adj **1** blasé, casual, cheery, contented, debonair, easy, easy-going, happy-go-lucky, indifferent, insouciant, inf laid-back, light-hearted, nonchalant, relaxed, unconcerned, unworried. ▷ HAPPY. **2** carefree holiday. leisured, peaceful, quiet, relaxing, restful, trouble-free, untroubled. Opp ANXIOUS.

careful adj **1** alert, attentive, cautious, chary, circumspect, heedful, mindful, observant, prudent, solicitous, thoughtful, vigilant, wary, watchful. **2** careful work. accurate, conscientious, deliberate, diligent, exhaustive, fastidious, derog fussy, judicious, methodical, meticulous, neat, orderly, organized, painstaking, particular, precise, punctilious, responsible, rigorous, scrupulous, systematic, thorough, well-organized. Opp CARELESS. **be careful** ▷ BEWARE.

careless adj **1** absent-minded, heedless, ill-considered, imprudent, inattentive, incautious, inconsiderate, irresponsible, negligent, rash, reckless, thoughtless, uncaring, unguarded, unthinking, unwary. **2** careless work. casual, confused, cursory, disorganized, hasty, imprecise, inaccurate, jumbled, messy, perfunctory, scatter-brained, shoddy, slapdash, slipshod, inf sloppy, slovenly, thoughtless, untidy. Opp CAREFUL.

carelessness n haste, inattention, irresponsibility, negligence, recklessness, inf sloppiness, slovenliness, thoughtlessness, untidiness. Opp CARE.

caress vb cuddle, embrace, fondle, hug, kiss, make love to, sl neck with, nuzzle, pat, pet, rub against, smooth, stroke, touch.

caretaker n custodian, janitor, keeper, porter, superintendent, warden, watchman.

careworn adj gaunt, grim, haggard. ▷ WEARY.

cargo n consignment, freight, goods, lading (bill of lading), load, merchandise, payload, shipment.

caricature n burlesque, cartoon, parody, satire, inf send-up, spoof, inf take-off, travesty. ● vb burlesque, distort, exaggerate, imitate, lampoon, make fun of, mimic, mock, overact, overdo, parody, ridicule, satirize, inf send up, inf take off.

caring n concern, kindness, nursing, solicitude.

carnage n blood-bath, bloodshed, butchery, havoc, holocaust, killing, massacre, pogrom, shambles, slaughter.

carnal adj animal, bodily, erotic, fleshly, natural, physical, sensual, sexual. ▷ LUSTFUL. Opp SPIRITUAL.

carnival n celebration, fair, festival, festivity, fête, fiesta, fun and games, gala, jamboree, merrymaking, pageant, parade, procession, revelry, show, spectacle.

carp vb cavil, find fault, inf go on, inf gripe, grumble, object, pick holes, quibble, inf split hairs, whinge. ▷ COMPLAIN.

carpentry n joinery, woodwork.

carriage n **1** coach. ▷ VEHICLE. **2** bearing, comportment, demeanour, gait, manner, mien, posture, presence, stance.

carrier n **1** bearer, conveyor, courier, delivery-man, delivery-woman, dispatch rider, errand-boy, errand-girl, haulier, messenger, porter, postman, runner. **2** carrier of a disease. contact, host, transmitter.

carry vb **1** bring, inf cart, communicate, ferry, fetch, haul, lead, lift, inf lug, manhandle, move, relay, remove, ship, shoulder, take, transfer, transmit, transport. ▷ CONVEY. **2** carry weight. bear, hold up, maintain, support. **3** carry a penalty. demand, entail, involve, lead to, occasion, require, result in. **carry on** ▷ CONTINUE. **carry out** ▷ DO.

cart n barrow, dray, truck, wagon, wheelbarrow. ● vb ▷ CARRY.

carton n box, cartridge, case, container, pack, package, packet.

cartoon n animation, caricature, comic strip, drawing, sketch.

cartridge n **1** canister, capsule, case, cassette, container, cylinder, tube.

2 *cartridge for a gun.* magazine, round, shell.

carve *vb* **1** slice. ▷ CUT. **2** *carve stone.* *inf* chip away at, chisel, engrave, fashion, hew, incise, sculpture, shape.

cascade *n* cataract, deluge, flood, gush, torrent, waterfall. ● *vb* ▷ POUR.

case *n* **1** box, cabinet, carton, casket, chest, container, crate, pack, packaging, suitcase, trunk. ▷ LUGGAGE. **2** *case of mistaken identity.* example, illustration, instance, occurrence, specimen, state of affairs. **3** *rules don't apply in his case.* circumstances, condition, context, plight, predicament, situation, state. **4** *a legal case.* action, argument, cause, dispute, inquiry, investigation, lawsuit, suit.

cash *n* banknotes, bills, change, coins, currency, *inf* dough, funds, hard money, legal tender, money, notes, *inf* (the) ready, *inf* the wherewithal. ● *vb* exchange for cash, realize, sell. **cash in on** ▷ PROFIT.

cashier *n* accountant, banker, check-out person, clerk, teller, treasurer. ● *vb* ▷ DISMISS.

cask *n* barrel, butt, hogshead, tub, tun, vat.

cast *n* **1** ▷ SCULPTURE. **2** *cast of a play.* characters, company, dramatis personae, performers, players, troupe. ● *vb* **1** bowl, chuck, drop, fling, hurl, impel, launch, lob, pelt, pitch, project, scatter, shy, sling, throw, toss. **2** *cast a sculpture.* form, found, mould, shape. ▷ SCULPTURE. **cast off** ▷ SHED, UNTIE.

castaway *adj* abandoned, deserted, exiled, marooned, rejected, shipwrecked, stranded.

caste *n* class, degree, estate, grade, level, position, rank, standing, station, status, stratum.

castigate *vb* censure, chasten, chastise, *old use* chide, correct, discipline, lash, punish, rebuke, reprimand, scold, *inf* tell off. ▷ CRITICIZE.

castle *n* château, citadel, fort, fortress, mansion, palace, stately home, stronghold, tower.

castrate *vb* emasculate, geld, neuter, spay, sterilize, unsex.

casual *adj* **1** accidental, chance, erratic, fortuitous, incidental, irregular, promiscuous, random, serendipitous, sporadic, unexpected, unforeseen, unintentional, unplanned, unpremeditated, unstructured, unsystematic. *Opp* DELIBERATE. **2** *casual attitude.* apathetic, blasé, careless, *inf* couldn't-care-less, easygoing, *inf* free-and-easy, lackadaisical, *inf* laid-back, lax, negligent, nonchalant, offhand, relaxed, *inf* slap-happy, *inf* throwaway, unconcerned, unenthusiastic, unimportant, unprofessional. *Opp* ENTHUSIASTIC. **3** *casual clothes.* comfortable, informal. *Opp* FORMAL.

casualty *n* dead person, death, fatality, injured person, injury, loss, victim, wounded person.

cat *n* kitten, *inf* moggy, *inf* pussy, tabby, tom, tomcat.

catacomb *n* crypt, sepulchre, tomb, underground passage, vault.

catalogue *n* brochure, directory, index, inventory, list, record, register, roll, schedule, table. ● *vb* classify, codify, file, index, list, make an inventory of, record, register, tabulate.

catapult *vb* fire, fling, hurl, launch. ▷ THROW.

cataract *n* cascade, falls, rapids, torrent, waterfall.

catastrophe *n* blow, calamity, cataclysm, crushing blow, débâcle, devastation, disaster, fiasco, holocaust, mischance, mishap, ruin, ruination, tragedy, upheaval. ▷ MISFORTUNE.

catch *n* **1** bag, booty, capture, haul, net, prey, prize, take. **2** *suspected a catch.* difficulty, disadvantage, drawback, obstacle, problem, snag, trap, trick. **3** *catch on a door.* bolt, clasp, clip, fastener, fastening, hasp, hook, latch, lock. ● *vb* **1** clutch, ensnare, entrap, grab, grasp, grip, hang on to, hold, hook, net, seize, snare, snatch, take, tangle, trap. **2** *catch a thief.* apprehend, arrest, capture, *inf* cop, corner, detect, discover, expose, intercept, *inf* nab, *inf* nobble, stop, surprise, take by surprise, unmask. **3** *caught me unawares.* come upon, discover, find, surprise. **4** *catch a bus.* be in time for, get on. **5** *catch a cold.* become infected by, contract, get. **catch on** ▷ SUCCEED, UNDERSTAND. **catch-phrase** ▷ SAYING. **catch-22** ▷ DILEMMA. **catch up** ▷ OVERTAKE.

catching *adj* communicable, contagious, infectious, spreading, transmissible, transmittable.

catchy *adj* attractive, haunting, memorable, popular, singable, tuneful.

categorical *adj* absolute, authoritative, certain, complete, decided, decisive, definite, direct, dogmatic, downright, emphatic, explicit, express, firm, forceful, *inf* out-and-out, positive, strong, total, unambiguous, unconditional, unequivocal, unmitigated, unqualified, unreserved, utter, vigorous. *Opp* TENTATIVE.

category *n* class, classification, division, grade, group, head, heading, kind, order, rank, ranking, section, sector, set, sort, type, variety.

cater *vb* cook, make arrangements, minister, provide, provision, serve, supply.

catholic *adj* all-embracing, all inclusive, broad, broad-minded, comprehensive, cosmopolitan, eclectic, general, liberal, universal, varied, wide, wide-ranging.

cattle *plur n* beef, bullocks, bulls, calves, cows, heifers, livestock, oxen, steers, stock.

catty *adj inf* bitchy, ill-natured, malevolent, malicious, mean, nasty, rancorous, sly, spiteful, venomous, vicious. ▷ UNKIND. *Opp* KIND.

cause *n* **1** basis, beginning, genesis, grounds, motivation, motive, occasion, origin, reason, root, source, spring, stimulus. **2** agent, author, *old use* begetter, creator, initiator, inspiration, inventor, originator, producer. **3** *cause of his lateness.* excuse, explanation, pretext, reason. **4** *a good cause.* aim, belief, concern, end, ideal, object, purpose, undertaking. ● *vb* **1** arouse, awaken, begin, bring about, bring on, create, effect, effectuate, engender, foment, generate, give rise to, incite, kindle, lead to,

occasion, precipitate, produce, provoke, result in, set off, spark off, stimulate, trigger off, *inf* whip up. **2** compel, force, induce, motivate.

caustic *adj* **1** acid, astringent, burning, corrosive, destructive. **2** *caustic criticism.* acidulous, acrimonious, biting, bitter, critical, cutting, mordant, pungent, sarcastic, scathing, severe, sharp, stinging, trenchant, virulent, waspish. *Opp* MILD.

caution *n* **1** alertness, attentiveness, care, carefulness, circumspection, discretion, forethought, heed, heedfulness, prudence, vigilance, wariness, watchfulness. **2** *let off with a caution.* admonition, caveat, *inf* dressing-down, injunction, reprimand, *inf* talkingto, *inf* ticking-off, warning. ● *vb* **1** advise, alert, counsel, forewarn, inform, *inf* tip off, warn. **2** *cautioned by the police.* admonish, censure, give a warning, reprehend, reprimand, *inf* tell off, *inf* tick off.

cautious *adj* **1** alert, attentive, careful, heedful, prudent, scrupulous, vigilant, watchful. **2** *cautious comments.* *inf* cagey, calculating, chary, circumspect, deliberate, discreet, gingerly, grudging, guarded, hesitant, judicious, non-committal, restrained, suspicious, tactful, tentative, unadventurous, wary, watchful. *Opp* RECKLESS.

cavalcade *n* march-past, parade, procession, spectacle, troop.

cave *n* cavern, cavity, den, grotto, hole, pothole, underground chamber. ● *vb* **cave in** ▷ COLLAPSE, SURRENDER.

cavity *n* cave, crater, dent, hole, hollow, pit.

cease *vb* break off, call a halt, conclude, cut off, desist, discontinue, end, finish, halt, *inf* kick in (*a habit*), *inf* knock off, *inf* lay off, leave off, *inf* pack in, *inf* pack up, refrain, stop, terminate. *Opp* BEGIN.

ceaseless *adj* chronic, constant, continual, continuous, endless, everlasting, incessant, interminable, never-ending, non-stop, permanent, perpetual, persistent, relentless, unending, unremitting, untiring. *Opp* INTERMITTENT, TEMPORARY.

celebrate *vb* **1** be happy, have a celebration, let yourself go, *inf* live it up, make merry, *inf* paint the town red, rejoice, revel, *old use* wassail. **2** *celebrate an anniversary.* commemorate, hold, honour, keep, observe, remember. **3** *celebrate a wedding.* officiate at, solemnize. **celebrated** ▷ FAMOUS.

celebration *n* banquet, binge, carnival, commemoration, feast, festivity, *inf* jamboree, *joc* jollification, merry-making, observance, *inf* orgy, party, *inf* rave-up, revelry, *church* service, *inf* shindig, solemnization. □ *anniversary, birthday, festival, fête, gala, jubilee, remembrance, reunion, wedding.*

celebrity *n* **1** ▷ FAME. **2** big name, *inf* bigwig, dignitary, famous person, idol, notability, personality, public figure, star, superstar, VIP, worthy.

celestial *adj* **1** astronomical, cosmic, galactic, interplanetary, interstellar, starry, stellar, universal. **2** *celestial beings.* angelic, blissful, divine, ethereal, godlike, heavenly, seraphic, spiritual, sublime, supernatural, transcendental, visionary.

celibacy *n* bachelorhood, chastity, continence, purity, self-restraint, spinsterhood, virginity.

celibate *adj* abstinent, chaste, continent, immaculate, single, unmarried, unwedded, virgin. ● *n* bachelor, spinster, virgin.

cell *n* cavity, chamber, compartment, cubicle, den, enclosure, living space, prison, room, space, unit.

cellar *n* basement, crypt, vault, wine-cellar.

cemetery *n* burial-ground, churchyard, graveyard, necropolis.

censor *vb* amend, ban, bowdlerize, *inf* clean up, cut, edit, exclude, expurgate, forbid, prohibit, remove.

censorious *adj* fault-finding, *inf* holier-than-thou, judgemental, moralistic, Pharisaical, selfrighteous. ▷ CRITICAL.

censure *n* accusation, admonition, blame, castigation, condemnation, criticism, denunciation, diatribe, disapproval, *inf* dressing-down, harangue, rebuke, reprimand, reproach, reprobation, reproof, *inf* slating, stricture, *inf* talking-to, *inf* telling-off, tirade, verbal attack, vituperation. ● *vb* admonish, berate, blame, *inf* carpet, castigate, caution, chide, condemn, criticize, denounce, lecture, rebuke, reproach, reprove, scold, take to task, *sl* tear (someone) off a strip, *inf* tell off, *inf* tick off, upbraid.

census *n* count, survey, tally.

central *adj* **1** focal, inner, innermost, interior, medial, middle. **2** *central facts.* chief, crucial, essential, fundamental, important, key, main, major, overriding, pivotal, primary, principal, vital. *Opp* PERIPHERAL.

centralize *vb* amalgamate, bring together, concentrate, rationalize, streamline, unify. *Opp* DISPERSE.

centre *n* bull's-eye, core, focal point, focus, heart, hub, inside, interior, kernel, middle, mid-point, nucleus, pivot. *Opp* PERIMETER. ● *vb* concentrate, converge, focus.

centrifugal *adj* dispersing, diverging, moving outwards, scattering, spreading. *Opp* CENTRIPETAL.

centripetal *adj* converging. *Opp* CENTRIFUGAL.

cereal *n* corn, grain. □ *barley, corn on the cob, maize, millet, oats, rice, rye, sweet corn, wheat.*

ceremonial *adj* celebratory, dignified, liturgical, majestic, official, ritual, ritualistic, solemn, stately. ▷ FORMAL. *Opp* INFORMAL.

ceremonious *adj* civil, courteous, courtly, dignified, formal, grand, *derog* pompous, proper, punctilious, *derog* starchy. ▷ POLITE. *Opp* CASUAL.

ceremony *n* **1** celebration, commemoration, *inf* do, event, formal occasion, function, occasion, parade, reception, rite, ritual, service, solemnity. **2** ceremonial, decorum, etiquette, formality, grandeur, pageantry, pomp, pomp and circumstance, protocol, ritual, spectacle.

certain *adj* **1** adamant, assured, confident, constant, convinced, decided, determined, firm, invariable, positive, resolved, satisfied, settled, stable, steady, sure, undoubting, unshakable, unwavering. **2** *certain proof*. absolute, authenticated, categorical, certified, clear, clear-cut, conclusive, convincing, definite, dependable, established, genuine, guaranteed, incontestable, incontrovertible, indubitable, infallible, irrefutable, known, official, plain, reliable, settled, sure, true, trustworthy, unarguable, undeniable, undisputed, undoubted, unmistakable, unquestionable, valid, verifiable. **3** *certain disaster*. destined, fated, guaranteed, imminent, inescapable, inevitable, inexorable, predestined, predictable, unavoidable. **4** *certain to pay up*. bound, compelled, obliged, required, sure. **5** *certain people*. individual, particular, some, specific, unnamed, unspecified. *Opp* UNCERTAIN. **be certain** ▷ KNOW. **for certain** ▷ DEFINITELY. **make certain** ▷ ENSURE.

certainty *n* **1** actuality, certain fact, *inf* foregone conclusion, foreseeable outcome, inevitability, necessity, *inf* sure thing. **2** assertiveness, assurance, authority, certitude, confidence, conviction, knowledge, positiveness, proof, sureness, truth, validity. *Opp* DOUBT.

certificate *n* authorization, award, credentials, degree, diploma, document, guarantee, licence, pass, permit, qualification, warrant.

certify *vb* **1** affirm, asseverate, attest, authenticate, aver, avow, bear witness, confirm, declare, endorse, guarantee, notify, sign, swear, testify, verify, vouch, vouchsafe, warrant, witness. **2** *certify as competent*. authorize, charter, commission, franchise, license, recognize, validate.

chain *n* **1** bonds, coupling, fetters, handcuffs, irons, links, manacles, shackles. **2** *chain of events*. column, combination, concatenation, cordon, line, progression, row, sequence, series, set, string, succession, train. ● *vb* bind, clap in irons, fetter, handcuff, link, manacle, shackle, tether, tie. ▷ FASTEN.

chair *n* armchair, carver, deckchair, dining-chair, easy chair, recliner, rocking-chair, throne. ▷ SEAT. ● *vb* ▷ PRESIDE.

chairperson *n* chair, chairman, chairwoman, convenor, director, leader, moderator, organizer, president, speaker.

challenge *vb* **1** accost, confront, *inf* have a go at, take on, tax. **2** *challenge to duel*. dare, defy, *old use* demand satisfaction, provoke, summon. **3** *challenge a decision*. argue against, call in doubt, contest, dispute, dissent from, impugn, object to, oppose, protest against, query, question, take exception to.

challenging *adj* inspiring, stimulating, testing, thought-provoking, worthwhile. ▷ DIFFICULT. *Opp* EASY.

chamber *n* cavity, cell, compartment, niche, nook, space. ▷ ROOM.

champion *adj* great, leading, record-breaking, supreme, top, unrivalled, victorious, winning, world-beating. ● *n* **1** conqueror, hero, medallist, prize-winner, record-breaker, superman, superwoman, titleholder, victor, winner. **2** *champion of the poor*. backer, defender, guardian, patron, protector, supporter, upholder, vindicator. **3** [*old use*] *champion in lists*. challenger, contender, contestant, fighter, knight, warrior. ● *vb* ▷ SUPPORT.

championship *n* competition, contest, series, tournament.

chance *adj* accidental, adventitious, casual, coincidental, *inf* fluky, fortuitous, fortunate, haphazard, inadvertent, incidental, lucky, random, unexpected, unforeseen, unfortunate, unlooked-for, unplanned, unpremeditated. *Opp* DELIBERATE. ● *n* **1** accident, coincidence, destiny, fate, fluke, fortune, gamble, hazard, luck, misfortune, serendipity. **2** *chance of rain*. danger, liability, likelihood, possibility, probability, prospect, risk. **3** occasion, opportunity, time, turn. ● *vb* **1** ▷ RISK. **2** ▷ HAPPEN.

chancy *adj* dangerous, *inf* dicey, *inf* dodgy, hazardous, *inf* iffy, insecure, precarious, risky, speculative, ticklish, tricky, uncertain, unpredictable, unsafe. *Opp* SAFE.

change *n* **1** adaptation, adjustment, alteration, break, conversion, deterioration, development, difference, diversion, improvement, innovation, metamorphosis, modification, modulation, mutation, new look, rearrangement, refinement, reformation, reorganization, revolution, shift, substitution, swing, transfiguration, transformation, transition, translation, transmogrification, transmutation, transposition, *inf* turn-about, U-turn, variation, variety, vicissitude. **2** *small change.* ▷ CASH. ● *vb* **1** acclimatize, accommodate, accustom, adapt, adjust, affect, alter, amend, convert, diversify, influence, modify, process, rearrange, reconstruct, refashion, reform, remodel, reorganize, reshape, restyle, tailor, transfigure, transform, translate, transmogrify, transmute, vary. **2** *opinions change.* alter, be transformed, *inf* chop and change, develop, fluctuate, metamorphose, move on, mutate, shift, vary. **3** *change one thing for another.* alternate, displace, exchange, replace, substitute, switch, swop, transpose. **4** *change money.* barter, convert, trade in. **change into** ▷ BECOME. **change someone's mind** ▷ CONVERT. **change your mind** ▷ RECONSIDER.

changeable *adj* capricious, chequered (*career*), erratic, fickle, fitful, fluctuating, fluid, inconsistent, inconstant, irregular, mercurial, mutable, protean, shifting, temperamental, uncertain, unpredictable, unreliable, unsettled, unstable, unsteady, *inf* up and down, vacillating, variable, varying, volatile, wavering. *Opp* CONSTANT.

channel *n* **1** aqueduct, canal, conduit, course, dike, ditch, duct, groove, gully, gutter, moat, overflow, pipe, sluice, sound, strait, trench, trough, watercourse, waterway. ▷ STREAM. **2** avenue, means, medium, path, route, way. **3** *TV channel.* *inf* side, station, waveband, wavelength.

● *vb* conduct, convey, direct, guide, lead, pass on, route, send, transmit.

chant *n* hymn, plainsong, psalm. ▷ SONG. ● *vb* intone. ▷ SING.

chaos *n* anarchy, bedlam, confusion, disorder, disorganization, lawlessness, mayhem, muddle, pandemonium, shambles, tumult, turmoil. *Opp* ORDER.

chaotic *adj* anarchic, confused, deranged, disordered, disorderly, disorganized, haphazard, *inf* haywire, *inf* higgledy-piggledy, jumbled, lawless, muddled, rebellious, riotous, *inf* shambolic, *inf* topsy-turvy, tumultuous, uncontrolled, ungovernable, unruly, untidy, *inf* upside-down. *Opp* ORDERLY.

char *vb* blacken, brown, burn, carbonize, scorch, sear, singe.

character *n* **1** distinctiveness, flavour, idiosyncrasy, individuality, integrity, peculiarity, quality, stamp, taste, uniqueness. ▷ CHARACTERISTIC. **2** *a forceful character.* attitude, constitution, disposition, individuality, make-up, manner, nature, personality, reputation, temper, temperament. **3** *a famous character.* figure, human being, individual, person, personality, *inf* type. **4** *She's a character!* *inf* case, comedian, comic, eccentric, *inf* nut-case, oddity, *derog* weirdo. **5** *character in a play.* part, persona, portrayal, role. **6** *written characters.* cipher, figure, hieroglyphic, ideogram, letter, mark, rune, sign, symbol, type.

characteristic *adj* **1** [*of an individual*] distinctive, distinguishing, essential, idiosyncratic, individual, particular, peculiar, recognizable, singular, special, specific, symptomatic, unique. **2** [*of a kind*] representative, typical. ● *n* attribute, distinguishing feature, feature, hallmark, idiosyncrasy, mark, peculiarity, property, quality, symptom, trait.

characterize *vb* brand, delineate, depict, describe, differentiate, distinguish, draw, identify, individualize, mark, portray, present, recognize, typify.

charade n absurdity, deceit, deception, fabrication, farce, make-believe, masquerade, mockery, *inf* play-acting, pose, pretence, *inf* put-up job, sham.

charge n 1 cost, expenditure, expense, fare, fee, payment, postage, price, rate, terms, toll, value. 2 *in my charge*. care, command, control, custody, guardianship, jurisdiction, keeping, protection, responsibility, safe-keeping, supervision, trust. 3 *criminal charges*. accusation, allegation, imputa-tion, indictment. 4 *cavalry charge*. action, assault, attack, drive, incursion, invasion, offensive, onslaught, raid, rush, sally, sortie, strike. ● vb 1 ask for, debit, exact, levy, make you pay, require. 2 accuse, blame, impeach, indict, prosecute, tax. 3 *charge with a duty*. burden, commit, empower, entrust, give, impose on. 4 *charged us to do our best*. ask, command, direct, enjoin, exhort, instruct. 5 *charge an enemy*. assail, assault, attack, *inf* fall on, rush, set on, storm, *inf* wade into.

charitable adj bountiful, generous, humanitarian, liberal, munificent, open-handed, philanthropic, unsparing. ▷ KIND. *Opp* MEAN.

charity n 1 affection, altruism, benevolence, bounty, caring, compassion, consideration, generosity, goodness, helpfulness, humanity, kindness, love, mercy, philanthropy, self-sacrifice, sympathy, tender-heartedness, unselfishness, warm-heartedness. 2 *old use* alms, alms-giving, bounty, donation, financial support, gift, *inf* handout, largesse, offering, patronage, poor relief. 3 good cause, the needy, the poor.

charm n 1 allure, appeal, attractiveness, charisma, fascination, hypnotic power, lovable nature, lure, magic, magnetism, power, pull, seductiveness. ▷ BEAUTY. 2 *magic charm*. curse, enchantment, incantation, magic, mumbo-jumbo, sorcery, spell, witchcraft, wizardry. 3 *charm on a bracelet*. amulet, lucky charm, mascot, ornament, talisman, trinket. ● vb allure, attract, beguile, bewitch, cajole, captivate, cast a spell on, decoy, delight, disarm, enchant, enrapture, enthral, entrance, fascinate, hold spellbound, hypnotize, intrigue, lure, mesmerize, please, seduce, soothe, win over.

charming ▷ ATTRACTIVE.

chart n diagram, graph, map, plan, sketch-map, table.

charter vb 1 employ, engage, hire, lease, rent. 2 ▷ CERTIFY.

chase vb drive, follow, go after, hound, hunt, pursue, run after, track, trail.

chasm n abyss, canyon, cleft, crater, crevasse, drop, fissure, gap, gulf, hole, hollow, opening, pit, ravine, rift, split, void.

chaste adj 1 abstinent, celibate, *inf* clean, continent, good, immaculate, inexperienced, innocent, moral, pure, sinless, uncorrupted, undefiled, unmarried, virgin, virginal, virtuous. *Opp* IMMORAL 2 *chaste dress*. austere, becoming, decent, decorous, maidenly, modest, plain, restrained, severe, simple, tasteful, unadorned. *Opp* INDECENT.

chasten vb 1 restrain, subdue. ▷ HUMILIATE. 2 ▷ CHASTISE.

chastise vb castigate, chasten, correct, discipline, penalize, rebuke, scold. ▷ PUNISH, REPRIMAND.

chastity n abstinence, celibacy, continence, innocence, integrity, maidenhood, morality, purity, restraint, sinlessness, virginity, virtue. *Opp* LUST.

chat n chatter, *inf* chin-wag, *inf* chitchat, conversation, gossip, *inf* heart-to-heart. ● vb chatter, converse, gossip, *inf* natter, prattle. ▷ TALK.

chat up ▷ WOO.

chauvinist n bigot, *inf* MCP (= *male chauvinist pig*), patriot, sexist, xenophobe.

cheap adj 1 bargain, budget, cutprice, *inf* dirt-cheap, discount, economical, economy, fair, inexpensive, *inf* knock-down, low-priced, reasonable, reduced, *inf* rockbottom, sale, under-priced. 2 *cheap quality*. base, inferior, poor, second-rate, shoddy, *inf* tatty, tawdry, *inf* tinny, *inf* trashy, worthless. 3 *a cheap insult*. contemptible, crude, despicable, facile, glib, ill-bred, ill-mannered, mean, silly, tasteless, unworthy, vulgar. *Opp* EXPENSIVE, WORTHY.

cheapen *vb* belittle, debase, degrade, demean, devalue, discredit, downgrade, lower the tone (of), popularize, prostitute, vulgarize.

cheat *n* **1** charlatan, cheater, *inf* conman, counterfeiter, deceiver, doublecrosser, extortioner, forger, fraud, hoaxer, impersonator, impostor, mountebank, *inf* phoney, *inf* quack, racketeer, rogue, *inf* shark, swindler, trickster, *inf* twister. **2** artifice, bluff, chicanery, *inf* con, confidence trick, deceit, deception, *sl* fiddle, fraud, hoax, imposture, lie, misrepresentation, pretence, *inf* put-up job, *inf* racket, *inf* ripoff, ruse, sham, swindle, *inf* swizz, treachery, trick. ● *vb* **1** bamboozle, beguile, bilk, *inf* con, deceive, defraud, *sl* diddle, *inf* do, double-cross, dupe, *sl* fiddle, *inf* fleece, fool, hoax, hoodwink, outwit, *inf* rip off, rob, *inf* short-change, swindle, take in, trick. **2** *cheat in an exam.* copy, crib, plagiarize.

check *adj* ▷ CHEQUERED. ● *n* **1** break, delay, halt, hesitation, hiatus, interruption, pause, stop, stoppage, suspension. **2** *medical check.* check-up, examination, *inf* going-over, inspection, investigation, *inf* once-over, scrutiny, test. ● *vb* **1** arrest, bar, block, bridle, control, curb, delay, foil, govern, halt, hamper, hinder, hold back, impede, inhibit, keep in check, obstruct, regulate, rein, repress, restrain, retard, slow down, stem, stop, stunt (*growth*), thwart. **2** *check answers.* *Amer* check out, compare, cross-check, examine, inspect, investigate, monitor, research, scrutinize, test, verify.

cheek *n* audacity, boldness, brazenness, effrontery, impertinence, impudence, insolence, presumptuousness, rudeness, shamelessness, temerity.

cheeky *adj* arrogant, audacious, bold, brazen, cool, discourteous, disrespectful, flippant, forward, impertinent, impolite, impudent, insolent, insulting, irreverent, mocking, pert,

presumptuous, rude, *inf* saucy, shameless, *inf* tongue-in-cheek. *Opp* RESPECTFUL.

cheer *n* **1** acclamation, applause, cry of approval, encouragement, hurrah, ovation, shout of approval. **2** ▷ HAPPINESS. ● *vb* **1** acclaim, applaud, clap, encourage, shout, yell. *Opp* JEER. **2** comfort, console, delight, encourage, exhilarate, gladden, make cheerful, please, solace, uplift. *Opp* SADDEN. **cheer someone up** ▷ COMFORT, ENTERTAIN. **cheer up** ▷ BRIGHTEN. **Cheer up!** *inf* buck up, look happy, *inf* perk up, smile, *sl* snap out of it, take heart.

cheerful *adj* animated, bouncy, bright, buoyant, cheery, *inf* chirpy, contented, convivial, delighted, elated, festive, gay, genial, glad, gleeful, good-humoured, hearty, hopeful, jaunty, jocund, jolly, jovial, joyful, joyous, jubilant, laughing, light, light-hearted, lively, merry, optimistic, *inf* perky, pleased, positive, rapturous, sparkling, spirited, sprightly, sunny, warm-hearted. ▷ HAPPY. *Opp* BAD-TEMPERED, CHEERLESS.

cheerless *adj* bleak, comfortless, dark, depressing, desolate, dingy, disconsolate, dismal, drab, dreary, dull, forbidding, forlorn, frowning, funereal, gloomy, grim, joyless, lacklustre, melancholy, miserable, mournful, sober, sombre, sullen, sunless, uncongenial, unhappy, uninviting, unpleasant, unpromising, woeful, wretched. ▷ SAD. *Opp* CHEERFUL.

chemical *n* compound, element, substance.

chemist *n old use* apothecary, *Amer* drug-store, pharmacist, pharmacy.

chequered *adj* **1** check, crisscross, in squares, like a chessboard, patchwork, tartan, tessellated. **2** *chequered career.* ▷ CHANGEABLE.

cherish *vb* be fond of, care for, cosset, foster, hold dear, keep safe, look after, love, nourish, nurse, nurture, prize, protect, treasure, value.

chest *n* **1** box, caddy, case, casket, coffer, crate, strongbox, trunk. **2** breast, rib-cage, thorax.

chew *vb* bite, champ, crunch, gnaw, grind, masticate, munch, nibble. ▷ EAT. **chew over** ▷ CONSIDER.

chick *n* fledgling, nestling.

chicken *n* bantam, broiler, cockerel, fowl, hen, pullet, rooster.

chief *adj* **1** arch, best, first, greatest, head, highest, in charge, leading, major, most experienced, most honoured, most important, oldest, outstanding, premier, principal, senior, supreme, top, unequalled, unrivalled. **2** *chief facts.* basic, cardinal, central, dominant, especial, essential, foremost, fundamental, high-priority, indispensable, key, main, necessary, overriding, paramount, predominant, primary, prime, salient, significant, substantial, uppermost, vital, weighty. *Opp* UNIMPORTANT. ● *n* administrator, authority-figure, *inf* bigwig, *inf* boss, captain, chairperson, chieftain, commander, commanding officer, commissioner, controller, director, employer, executive, foreman, forewoman, *inf* gaffer, *Amer inf* godfather, governor, head, king, leader, manager, managing director, master, mistress, *inf* number one, officer, organizer, overseer, owner, president, principal, proprietor, ringleader, ruler, superintendent, supervisor, *inf* supremo.

chiefly *adv* especially, essentially, generally, in particular, mainly, mostly, particularly, predominantly, primarily, principally, usually.

child *n* **1** adolescent, *inf* babe, baby, *Scot* bairn, *inf* bambino, boy, *derog* brat, girl, *derog* guttersnipe, infant, juvenile, *inf* kid, lad, lass, minor, newborn, *inf* nipper, offspring, *inf* stripling, toddler, *inf* tot, *derog* urchin, youngster, youth. **2** daughter, descendant, heir, issue, offspring, progeny, son.

childhood *n* adolescence, babyhood, boyhood, girlhood, infancy, minority, schooldays, *inf* teens, youth.

childish *adj* babyish, credulous, foolish, immature, infantile, juvenile, puerile. ▷ SILLY. *Opp* MATURE.

childlike *adj* artless, frank, *inf* green, guileless, ingenuous, innocent, naïve, natural, simple, trustful, unaffected, unsophisticated. *Opp* ARTFUL.

chill *n* ▷ COLD. ● *vb* cool, freeze, keep cold, make cold, refrigerate. *Opp* WARM.

chilly *adj* **1** cold, cool, crisp, fresh, frosty, icy, *inf* nippy, *inf* parky, raw, sharp, wintry. **2** *a chilly greeting.* aloof, cool, dispassionate, frigid, hostile, ill-disposed, remote, reserved, *inf* standoffish, unforthcoming, unfriendly, unresponsive, unsympathetic, unwelcoming. *Opp* WARM.

chime *n* carillon, peal, striking, tintinnabulation, tolling. ● *vb* ▷ RING.

chimney *n* flue, funnel, smokestack.

china *n* porcelain. ▷ CROCKERY.

chink *n* **1** cleft, crack, cranny, crevice, cut, fissure, gap, opening, rift, slit, slot, space, split. **2** ▷ SOUND.

chip *n* **1** bit, flake, fleck, fragment, piece, scrap, shard, shaving, shiver, slice, sliver, splinter, wedge. **2** *a chip in a cup.* crack, damage, flaw, gash, nick, notch, scratch, snick. ● *vb* break, crack, damage, gash, nick, notch, scratch, splinter. **chip away** ▷ CHISEL. **chip in** ▷ CONTRIBUTE, INTERRUPT.

chisel *vb* carve, *inf* chip away, cut, engrave, fashion, model, sculpture, shape.

chivalrous *adj* bold, brave, chivalric, courageous, courteous, courtly, gallant, generous, gentlemanly, heroic, honourable, knightly, noble, polite, respectable, true, trustworthy, valiant, valorous, worthy. *Opp* COWARDLY, RUDE.

choice *adj* ▷ EXCELLENT. ● *n* **1** alternative, dilemma, need to choose, option. **2** *make your choice.* choosing, decision, election, liking, nomination, pick, preference, say, vote. **3** *a choice of food.* array, assortment, diversity, miscellany, mixture, range, selection, variety.

choke *vb* **1** asphyxiate, garrotte, smother, stifle, strangle, suffocate, throttle. **2** *choke in smoke.* cough, gag, gasp, retch. **3** *choked with traffic.* block, *inf* bung up, clog, close, congest, constrict, dam, fill, jam, obstruct, smother, stop up. **choke back** ▷ SUPPRESS.

choose vb adopt, agree on, appoint, decide on, determine on, distinguish, draw lots for, elect, establish, fix on, identify, isolate, name, nominate, opt for, pick out, inf plump for, prefer, select, settle on, show a preference for, single out, vote for.

choosy adj dainty, discerning, discriminating, exacting, fastidious, finical, finicky, fussy, inf hard to please, nice, particular, pernickety, inf picky, selective. Opp INDIFFERENT.

chop vb cleave, cut, hack, hew, lop, slash, split. ▷ CUT. **chop and change** ▷ CHANGE.

chopper n axe, cleaver.

choppy adj roughish, ruffled, turbulent, uneven, wavy. Opp SMOOTH.

chore n burden, drudgery, duty, errand, job, task, work.

chorus n 1 choir, choral society, vocal ensemble. 2 join in the chorus. refrain, response.

christen vb anoint, baptize, call, dub, name.

chronic adj 1 ceaseless, constant, continuing, deep-rooted, habitual, incessant, incurable, ineradicable, ingrained, lasting, lifelong, lingering, long-lasting, long-lived, long-standing, never-ending, non-stop, permanent, persistent, unending. Opp ACUTE, TEMPORARY. 2 [inf] chronic driving. ▷ BAD.

chronicle n account, annals, archive, chronology, description, diary, history, journal, narrative, record, register, saga, story.

chronological adj consecutive, in order, sequential.

chronology n 1 almanac, calendar, diary, journal, log, schedule, timetable. 2 establish the chronology. dating, order, sequence, timing.

chubby adj buxom, dumpy, plump, podgy, portly, rotund, round, stout, tubby. ▷ FAT. Opp THIN.

chunk n bar, block, brick, chuck, inf dollop, hunk, lump, mass, piece, portion, slab, wad, wedge, inf wodge.

church n abbey, basilica, cathedral, chapel, convent, monastery, nunnery, parish church, priory.

churchyard n burial-ground, cemetery, graveyard.

chute n channel, incline, ramp, rapid, slide, slope.

cinema n films, old use flicks, Amer motion pictures, inf movies, inf pictures.

circle n 1 annulus, band, circlet, disc, hoop, ring. □ belt, circuit, circulation, circumference, circumnavigation, coil, cordon, curl, curve, cycle, ellipse, girdle, globe, gyration, lap, loop, orb, orbit, oval, revolution, rotation, round, sphere, spiral, tour, turn, wheel, whirl, whorl. 2 circle of friends. association, band, body, clique, club, company, fellowship, fraternity, gang, party, set, society. ▷ GROUP. ● vb 1 circulate, circumnavigate, circumscribe, coil, compass, corkscrew, curl, curve, go round, gyrate, loop, orbit, pirouette, pivot, reel, revolve, rotate, spin, spiral, swirl, swivel, tour, turn, wheel, whirl, wind. 2 trees circle the lawn. encircle, enclose, encompass, girdle, hem in, ring, skirt, surround.

circuit n journey round, lap, orbit, revolution, tour.

circuitous adj curving, devious, indirect, labyrinthine, mean-dering, oblique, rambling, roundabout, serpentine, tortuous, twisting, winding, zigzag. Opp DIRECT.

circular adj 1 annular, discoid, ringlike, round. 2 circular conversation. circumlocutory, cyclic, periphrastic, repeating, repetitive, roundabout, tautologous. ● n advertisement, leaflet, letter, notice, pamphlet.

circulate vb 1 go round, move about, move round, orbit. ▷ CIRCLE. 2 circulate gossip. advertise, disseminate, distribute, issue, make known, noise abroad, promulgate, publicize, publish, inf put about, send round, spread about.

circulation n 1 flow, movement, pumping, recycling. 2 broadcasting, diffusion, dissemination, distribution, promulgation, publication, spreading, transmission. 3 newspaper circulation. distribution, sales-figures.

circumference n border, boundary, circuit, edge, exterior, fringe,

class

limit, margin, outline, outside, perimeter, periphery, rim, verge.

circumstance n affair, event, happening, incident, occasion, occurrence. **circumstances 1** background, causes, conditions, considerations, context, contingencies, details, factors, facts, influences, particulars, position, situation, state of affairs, surroundings. **2** finances, income, resources.

circumstantial adj conjectural, deduced, inferred, unprovable. Opp PROVABLE.

cistern n bath, container, reservoir, tank.

citadel n acropolis, bastion, castle, fort, fortification, fortress, garrison, stronghold, tower.

cite vb adduce, advance, inf bring up, enumerate, mention, name, quote, inf reel off, refer to, specify.

citizen n burgess, commoner, denizen, dweller, freeman, householder, inhabitant, national, native, passport-holder, ratepayer, resident, subject, taxpayer, voter.

city n capital, conurbation, metropolis, town, urban district.

civil adj **1** affable, civilized, considerate, courteous, obliging, respectful, urbane, well-bred, well-mannered. ▷ POLITE. Opp IMPOLITE. **2** civil administration. civilian, domestic, internal, national. Opp MILITARY. **3** civil liberties. communal, public, social, state. **civil rights** freedom, human rights, legal rights, liberty, political rights. **civil servant** administrator, bureaucrat, derog mandarin.

civilization n achievements, attainments, culture, customs, mores, organization, refinement, sophistication, urbanity, urbanization.

civilize vb cultivate, domesticate, educate, enlighten, humanize, improve, make better, organize, refine, socialize, urbanize.

civilized adj advanced, cultivated, cultured, democratic, developed, domesticated, educated, enlightened, humane, orderly, polite, refined, sociable, social, sophisticated, urbane, urbanized, well-behaved, well-run. Opp UNCIVILIZED.

claim vb **1** ask for, collect, command, demand, exact, insist on, request, require, take. **2** affirm, allege, argue, assert, attest, contend, declare, insist, maintain, pretend, profess, state.

clairvoyant adj extra-sensory, oracular, prophetic, psychic, telepathic. ● n fortune-teller, oracle, prophet, seer, sibyl, soothsayer.

clamber vb climb, crawl, move awkwardly, scramble.

clammy adj close, damp, dank, humid, moist, muggy, slimy, sticky, sweaty, wet.

clamour n babel, commotion, din, hubbub, hullabaloo, noise, outcry, racket, row, screeching, shouting, storm, uproar. ● vb call out, cry out, exclaim, shout, yell.

clan n family, house, tribe.

clannish adj derog cliquish, close, close-knit, insular, isolated, narrow, united.

clap n bang, crack, crash, report, smack. ▷ SOUND. ● vb **1** applaud, sl put your hands together, show approval. **2** clap on the back. ▷ HIT.

clarify vb **1** clear up, define, elucidate, explain, explicate, gloss, illuminate, make clear, simplify, inf spell out, throw light on. Opp CONFUSE. **2** clarify wine. cleanse, clear, filter, purify, refine. Opp CLOUD.

clash vb **1** bang, clang, clank, crash, resonate, ring. ▷ SOUND. **2** ▷ CONFLICT. **3** The events clashed. ▷ COINCIDE.

clasp n **1** brooch, buckle, catch, clip, fastener, fastening, hasp, hook, pin. **2** cuddle, embrace, grasp, grip, hold, hug. ● vb **1** ▷ FASTEN. **2** cling to, clutch, embrace, enfold, grasp, grip, hold, hug, squeeze. **3** clasp your hands. hold together, wring.

class n **1** category, classification, division, domain, genre, genus, grade, group, kind, league, order, quality, rank, set, sort, species, sphere, type. **2** social class. caste, degree, descent, extraction, grouping, lineage, pedigree, standing, station, status. □ aristocracy, bourgeoisie, commoners, (the) commons, gentry, lower *class, middle class, nobility, proletariat, ruling class, serfs, upper class, upper-middle class, (the) workers, working class.* **3** *class in school.* band, form, *Amer* grade, group, set, stream, year. ● *vb* ▷ CLASSIFY.

classic *adj* **1** abiding, ageless, deathless, enduring, established, exemplary, flawless, ideal, immortal, lasting, legendary, masterly, memorable, notable, outstanding, perfect, time-honoured, undying, unforgettable, *inf* vintage. ▷ EXCELLENT. *Opp* COMMONPLACE, EPHEMERAL. **2** *a classic case.* archetypal, characteristic, copybook, definitive, model, paradigmatic, regular, standard, typical, usual. *Opp* UNUSUAL. ● *n* masterpiece, masterwork, model.

classical *adj* **1** ancient, Attic, Greek, Hellenic, Latin, Roman. **2** *classical style.* austere, dignified, elegant, pure, restrained, simple, symmetrical, well-proportioned. **3** *classical music.* established, harmonious, highbrow, serious.

classification *n* categorization, codification, ordering, organization, systematization, tabulation, taxonomy. ▷ CLASS.

classify *vb* arrange, bracket together, catalogue, categorize, class, grade, group, order, organize, *inf* pigeon-hole, put into sets, sort, systematize, tabulate. **classified** ▷ SECRET.

clause *n* article, condition, item, paragraph, part, passage, provision, proviso, section, subsection.

claw *n* nail, talon. ● *vb* graze, injure, lacerate, maul, rip, scrape, scratch, slash, tear.

clean *adj* **1** decontaminated, dirt-free, disinfected, hygienic, immaculate, laundered, perfect, polished, sanitary, scrubbed, spotless, sterile, sterilized, tidy, unadulterated, unsoiled, unstained, unsullied, washed, wholesome. **2** *clean water.* clarified, clear, distilled, fresh, pure, purified, unpolluted. **3** *clean paper.* blank, new, plain, uncreased, unmarked, untouched, unused. **4** *a clean edge.* neat, regular, smooth,

straight, tidy. **5** *a clean fight.* chivalrous, fair, honest, honourable, sporting, sportsmanlike. **6** *clean fun.* chaste, decent, good, innocent, moral, respectable, upright, virtuous. *Opp* DIRTY. ● *vb* cleanse, clear up, tidy up, wash. □ *bath, bathe, brush, buff, decontaminate, deodorize, disinfect, dry-clean, dust, filter, flush, groom, hoover, launder, mop, polish, purge, purify, rinse, sand-blast, sanitize, scour, scrape, scrub, shampoo, shower, soap, sponge, spring-clean, spruce up, sterilize, swab, sweep, swill, vacuum, wipe, wring out.* Opp CONTAMINATE. **make a clean breast of** ▷ CONFESS.

clean-shaven *adj* beardless, shaved, shaven, shorn, smooth.

clear *adj* **1** clean, colourless, crystalline, glassy, limpid, pellucid, pure, transparent. **2** *clear weather.* cloudless, fair, fine, sunny, starlit, unclouded. *Opp* CLOUDY. **3** *clear colours.* bright, lustrous, shining, sparkling, strong, vivid. **4** *clear conscience.* blameless, easy, guiltless, innocent, quiet, satisfied, sinless, undisturbed, untarnished, untroubled, unworried. **5** *clear handwriting.* bold, clean, definite, distinct, explicit, focused, legible, positive, recognizable, sharp, simple, visible, well-defined. **6** *clear sound.* audible, clarion (*call*), distinct, penetrating, sharp. **7** *clear instructions.* clear-cut, coherent, comprehensible, explicit, intelligible, lucid, perspicuous, precise, specific, straightforward, unambiguous, understandable, unequivocal, well-presented. **8** *clear case of cheating.* apparent, blatant, clear-cut, conspicuous, evident, glaring, indisputable, manifest, noticeable, obvious, palpable, perceptible, plain, pronounced, straightforward, unconcealed, undisguised, unmistakable. *Opp* UNCERTAIN. **9** *clear space.* empty, free, open, passable, uncluttered, uncrowded, unhampered, unhindered, unimpeded, unobstructed. ● *vb* **1** disappear, evaporate, fade, melt away, vanish. **2** become clear, brighten, clarify, lighten, uncloud. **3** clean, make clean, make transparent, polish, wipe. **4** *clear weeds*. disentangle, eliminate, get rid of, remove, strip. **5** *clear a drain*. clean out, free, loosen, open up, unblock, unclog. **6** *clear of blame*. absolve, acquit, exculpate, excuse, exonerate, free, *inf* let off, liberate, release, vindicate. **7** *clear a building*. empty, evacuate. **8** *clear a fence*. bound over, jump, leap over, pass over, spring over, vault. **clear away** ▷ REMOVE. **clear off** ▷ DEPART. **clear up** ▷ CLEAN, EXPLAIN.

clearing *n* gap, glade, opening, space.

cleave *vb* divide, halve, rive, slit, split. ▷ CUT.

clench *vb* **1** clamp up, close tightly, double up, grit (*your teeth*), squeeze tightly. **2** clasp, grasp, grip, hold.

clergyman *n* archbishop, ayatollah, bishop, canon, cardinal, chaplain, churchman, cleric, curate, deacon, *fem* deaconess, dean, divine, ecclesiastic, evangelist, friar, guru, imam, *inf* man of the cloth, minister, missionary, monk, padre, parson, pastor, preacher, prebend, prelate, priest, rabbi, rector, vicar. *Opp* LAYMAN.

clerical *adj* **1** *clerical and administrative work*. office, secretarial, *inf* white-collar. **2** *a clerical collar*. canonical, ecclesiastical, episcopal, ministerial, monastic, pastoral, priestly, rabbinical, sacerdotal, spiritual.

clerk *n* assistant, bookkeeper, computer operator, copyist, filing clerk, office boy, office girl, office worker, *inf* pen-pusher, receptionist, recorder, scribe, secretary, shorthand-typist, stenographer, typist, word-processor operator.

clever *adj* able, academic, accomplished, acute, adept, adroit, apt, artful, artistic, astute, *inf* brainy, bright, brilliant, canny, capable, *derog* crafty, creative, *derog* cunning, *inf* cute, *inf* deep, deft, dextrous, discerning, expert, *derog* foxy, gifted, guileful, *inf* handy, imaginative, ingenious, intellectual, intelligent, inventive, judicious, keen, knowing, knowledgeable, observant, penetrating, perceptive, percipient, perspica-cious, precocious, quick, quick-witted, rational, resourceful, sagacious, sensible, sharp, shrewd, skilful, skilled, slick, *derog* sly, smart, subtle, talented, *derog* wily, wise, witty. *Opp* STUPID, UNSKILFUL. **clever person** *inf* egghead, expert, genius, *derog* know-all, mastermind, prodigy, sage, *derog* smart alec, *derog* smartarse, virtuoso, wizard.

cleverness *n* ability, acuteness, astuteness, brilliance, *derog* cunning, expertise, ingenuity, intellect, intelligence, mastery, quickness, sagacity, sharpness, shrewdness, skill, subtlety, talent, wisdom, wit. *Opp* STUPIDITY.

cliché *n* banality, *inf* chestnut, commonplace, hackneyed phrase, platitude, stereotype, truism, well-worn phrase.

client *n plur* clientele, consumer, customer, patient, patron, shopper, user.

cliff *n* bluff, crag, escarpment, precipice, rock-face, scar, sheer drop.

climate *n* **1** ▷ WEATHER. **2** *climate of opinion*. ambience, atmosphere, aura, disposition, environment, feeling, mood, spirit, temper, trend.

climax *n* **1** acme, apex, apogee, crisis, culmination, head, highlight, high point, peak, summit, zenith. *Opp* BATHOS. **2** *sexual climax*. orgasm.

climb *n* ascent, grade, gradient, hill, incline, pitch, rise, slope. ● *vb* **1** ascend, clamber up, defy gravity, go up, levitate, lift off, mount, move up, scale, shin up, soar, swarm up, take off. **2** incline, rise, slope up. **3** *climb a mountain*. conquer, reach the top of. **climb down** ▷ DESCEND.

clinch *vb* agree, close, complete, conclude, confirm, decide, determine, finalize, make certain of, ratify, secure, settle, shake hands on, sign, verify.

cling *vb* adhere, attach, fasten, fix, hold fast, stick. **cling to** ▷ EMBRACE.

clinic *n* health centre, infirmary, medical centre, sick-bay, surgery.

clip *n* **1** ▷ FASTENER. **2** *clip from a film*. bit, cutting, excerpt, extract, fragment, part, passage, portion, quotation, section, snippet, trailer. ● vb 1 pin, staple. ▷ FASTEN. 2 crop, dock, prune, shear, snip, trim. ▷ CUT.

cloak n 1 cape, cope, mantle, poncho, robe, wrap. ▷ COAT. 2 ▷ COVER. ● vb cover, disguise, mantle, mask, screen, shroud, veil, wrap. ▷ HIDE.

clock n time-piece. □ alarm-clock, chronometer, dial, digital clock, grandfather clock, hourglass, pendulum clock, sundial, watch.

clog vb block, inf bung up, choke, close, congest, dam, fill, impede, jam, obstruct, plug, stop up.

close adj 1 accessible, adjacent, adjoining, at hand, convenient, handy, near, neighbouring, point-blank. 2 close friends. affectionate, attached, dear, devoted, familiar, fond, friendly, intimate, loving, inf thick. 3 close comparison. alike, analogous, comparable, compatible, corresponding, related, resembling, similar. 4 a close crowd. compact, compressed, congested, cramped, crowded, dense, inf jam-packed, packed, thick. 5 close scrutiny. attentive, careful, concentrated, detailed, minute, painstaking, precise, rigorous, searching, thorough. 6 close with information. confidential, private, reserved, reticent, secretive, taciturn. 7 close with money. illiberal, mean, inf mingy, miserly, niggardly, parsimonious, penurious, stingy, tight, tight-fisted, ungenerous. 8 close atmosphere. airless, confined, fuggy, humid, muggy, oppressive, stale, stifling, stuffy, suffocating, sweltering, unventilated, warm. Opp DISTANT, OPEN. ● n 1 cessation, completion, conclusion, culmination, end, finish, stop, termination. 2 cadence, coda, finale. 3 close of a play. denouement, last act. ● vb 1 bolt, fasten, lock, make inaccessible, padlock, put out of bounds, seal, secure, shut. 2 close a road. bar, barricade, block, make impassable, obstruct, seal off, stop up. 3 close proceedings. complete, conclude, culminate, discontinue, end, finish, stop, terminate, inf wind up. 4 close a gap. fill, join up, make smaller, reduce, shorten. Opp OPEN.

closed adj 1 fastened, locked, sealed, shut. 2 completed, concluded, done with, ended, finished, over, resolved, settled, tied up.

clot n embolism, lump, mass, thrombosis. ● vb coagulate, coalesce, congeal, curdle, make lumps, set, solidify, stiffen, thicken.

cloth n fabric, material, stuff, textile. □ astrakhan, bouclé, brocade, broderie anglaise, buckram, calico, cambric, candlewick, canvas, cashmere, cheesecloth, chenille, chiffon, chintz, corduroy, cotton, crepe, cretonne, damask, denim, dimity, drill, drugget, elastic, felt, flannel, flannelette, gabardine, gauze, georgette, gingham, hessian, holland, lace, lamé, lawn, linen, lint, mohair, moiré, moquette, muslin, nankeen, nylon, oilcloth, oilskin, organdie, organza, patchwork, piqué, plaid, plissé, plush, polycotton, polyester, poplin, rayon, sackcloth, sacking, sailcloth, sarsenet, sateen, satin, satinette, seersucker, serge, silk, stockinet, taffeta, tapestry, tartan, terry, ticking, tulle, tussore, tweed, velour, velvet, velveteen, viscose, voile, winceyette, wool, worsted.

clothe vb accoutre, apparel, array, attire, cover, deck, drape, dress, fit out, garb, inf kit out, outfit, robe, swathe, wrap up. Opp STRIP. **clothe yourself in** ▷ WEAR.

clothes plur n apparel, attire, inf clobber, clothing, costume, dress, ensemble, finery, garb, garments, inf gear, inf get-up, outfit, old use raiment, inf rig-out, sl togs, trousseau, underclothes, uniform, vestments, wardrobe, wear, weeds. □ anorak, apron, blazer, blouse, bodice, breeches, caftan, cagoule, cape, cardigan, cassock, chemise, chuddar, cloak, coat, crinoline, culottes, décolletage, doublet, dress, dressing-gown, duffel coat, dungarees, frock, gaiters, gauntlet, glove, gown, greatcoat, gym-slip, habit, housecoat, jacket, jeans, jerkin, jersey, jodhpurs, jumper, kilt, knickers, leg-warmers, leotard, livery, loincloth, lounge suit, mackintosh, mantle, miniskirt, muffler, neck-tie, négligé, nightclothes, nightdress, oilskins, overalls, overcoat, pants, parka, pinafore, poncho, pullover, pyjamas, raincoat,

*robe, rompers, sari, sarong, scarf, shawl,
shirt, shorts, singlet, skirt, slacks, smock,
sock, sou'wester, spats, stocking, stole,
suit, surplice, sweater, sweatshirt, tail-
coat, tie, tights, trousers, trunks, t-shirt,
tunic, tutu, uniform, waistcoat, wet-suit,
wind-cheater, wrap, yashmak.* ▷ HAT,
SHOE, UNDERCLOTHES.

cloud *n* billow, haze, mist, rain
cloud, storm cloud. ● *vb* blur, conceal, cover, darken, dull, eclipse,
enshroud, hide, mantle, mist up,
obfuscate, obscure, screen, shroud,
veil.

cloudless *adj* bright, clear, starlit,
sunny, unclouded. *Opp* CLOUDY.

cloudy *adj* **1** dark, dismal, dull,
gloomy, grey, leaden, lowering, overcast, sullen, sunless. *Opp* CLOUDLESS.
2 *cloudy windows.* blurred, blurry,
dim, misty, opaque, steamy, unclear.
3 *cloudy liquid.* hazy, milky, muddy,
murky. *Opp* CLEAR.

clown *n* buffoon, comedian, comic,
fool, funnyman, jester, joker. ▷ IDIOT.

club *n* **1** bat, baton, bludgeon, cosh,
cudgel, mace, staff, stick, truncheon.
2 association, brotherhood, circle,
company, federation, fellowship, fraternity, group, guild, league, order,
organization, party, set, sisterhood,
society, sorority, union. ● *vb* ▷ HIT.
club together ▷ COMBINE.

clue *n* hint, idea, indication, indicator, inkling, key, lead, pointer, sign,
suggestion, suspicion, tip, tip-off,
trace.

clump *n* bunch, bundle, cluster, collection, mass, shock (*of hair*), thicket,
tuft. ▷ GROUP.

clumsy *adj* **1** awkward, blundering, bumbling, bungling, fumbling,
gangling, gawky, graceless, *inf*
ham-fisted, heavy-handed, hulking,
inelegant, lumbering, maladroit,
shambling, uncoordinated, ungainly,
ungraceful, unskilful. *Opp* SKILFUL.
2 amateurish, badly-made, bulky,
cumbersome, heavy, inconvenient,
inelegant, large, ponderous, rough,
shapeless, unmanageable, unwieldy.
Opp NEAT. **3** *a clumsy remark.* boorish,
gauche, ill-judged, inappropriate,
indelicate, indiscreet, inept, insens-

itive, tactless, uncouth, undiplomatic, unsubtle, unsuitable.

cluster *n* assembly, batch, bunch,
clump, collection, crowd, gathering,
knot. ▷ GROUP. ● *vb* ▷ GATHER.

clutch *n* clasp, control, evil embrace,
grasp, grip, hold, possession, power.
● *vb* catch, clasp, cling to, grab,
grasp, grip, hang on to, hold on to,
seize, snatch, take hold of.

clutter *n* chaos, confusion, disorder,
jumble, junk, litter, lumber, mess,
mix-up, muddle, odds and ends, rubbish, tangle, untidiness. ● *vb* be scattered about, fill, lie about, litter,
make untidy, *inf* mess up, muddle,
strew.

coach *n* **1** bus, carriage, *old use*
charabanc. **2** *games coach.* instructor,
teacher, trainer, tutor. ● *vb* direct,
drill, exercise, guide, instruct, prepare, teach, train, tutor.

coagulate *vb* clot, congeal, curdle,
inf jell, set, solidify, stiffen, thicken.

coarse *adj* **1** bristly, gritty, hairy,
harsh, lumpy, prickly, rough,
scratchy, sharp, stony, uneven,
unfinished. *Opp* FINE, SOFT. **2** *coarse language.* bawdy, blasphemous, boorish,
common, crude, earthy, foul, immodest, impolite, improper, impure,
indecent, indelicate, offensive, ribald, rude, smutty, uncouth, unrefined, vulgar. *Opp* REFINED.

coast *n* beach, coastline, littoral,
seaboard, seashore, seaside, shore.
● *vb* cruise, drift, free-wheel, glide,
sail, skim, slide, slip.

coastal *adj* maritime, nautical,
naval, seaside.

coat *n* **1** □ *anorak, blazer, cagoule,
cardigan, dinner-jacket, doublet, duffel
coat, greatcoat, jacket, jerkin, mackintosh, overcoat, raincoat, tail-coat, tunic,
tuxedo, waistcoat, wind-cheater.* **2** *an
animal's coat.* fleece, fur, hair, hide,
pelt, skin. **3** *coat of paint.* coating,
cover, film, finish, glaze, layer, membrane, overlay, patina, sheet, veneer,
wash. ▷ COVERING. ● *vb* ▷ COVER. **coat
of arms** ▷ CREST.

coax *vb* allure, beguile, cajole,
charm, decoy, entice, induce, in-

veigle, manipulate, persuade, tempt, urge, wheedle.

cobble *vb* **cobble together** botch, knock up, make, mend, patch up, put together.

code *n* **1** etiquette, laws, manners, regulations, rule-book, rules, system. **2** *message in code.* cipher, secret language, signals, sign-system.

coerce *vb* bludgeon, browbeat, bully, compel, constrain, dragoon, force, frighten, intimidate, press-gang, pressurize, terrorize.

coercion *n* browbeating, brute force, bullying, compulsion, conscription, constraint, duress, force, intimidation, physical force, pressure, *inf* strong-arm tactics, threats.

coffer *n* box, cabinet, case, casket, chest, crate, trunk.

cog *n* ratchet, sprocket, tooth.

cogent *adj* compelling, conclusive, convincing, effective, forceful, forcible, indisputable, irresistible, logical, persuasive, potent, powerful, rational, sound, strong, unanswerable, weighty, well-argued. ▷ COHERENT. *Opp* IRRATIONAL.

cohere *vb* bind, cake, cling together, coalesce, combine, consolidate, fuse, hang together, hold together, join, stick together, unite.

coherent *adj* articulate, cohering, cohesive, connected, consistent, integrated, logical, lucid, orderly, organized, rational, reasonable, reasoned, sound, structured, systematic, unified, united, well-ordered, well-structured. ▷ COGENT. *Opp* INCOHERENT.

coil *n* circle, convolution, corkscrew, curl, helix, kink, loop, ring, roll, screw, spiral, twirl, twist, vortex, whirl, whorl. ● *vb* bend, curl, entwine, loop, roll, snake, spiral, turn, twine, twirl, twist, wind, writhe.

coin *n* **1** bit, piece. **2** [*plur*] cash, change, coppers, loose change, silver, small change. ▷ MONEY. ● *vb* **1** forge, make, mint, mould, stamp. **2** *coin a name.* conceive, concoct, create, devise, dream up, fabricate, hatch, introduce, invent, make up, originate, produce, think up.

coincide *vb* accord, agree, be congruent, be identical, be in unison, be the same, clash, coexist, come together, concur, correspond, fall together, happen together, harmonize, line up, match, square, synchronize, tally.

coincidence *n* **1** accord, agreement, coexistence, concurrence, conformity, congruence, congruity, correspondence, harmony, similarity. **2** *meet by coincidence.* accident, chance, fluke, luck.

cold *adj* **1** arctic, biting, bitter, bleak, chill, chilly, cool, crisp, cutting, draughty, freezing, fresh, frosty, glacial, heatless, ice-cold, icy, inclement, keen, *inf* nippy, numbing, *inf* parky, penetrating, perishing, piercing, polar, raw, shivery, Siberian, snowy, unheated, wintry. **2** *cold hands.* blue with cold, chilled, dead, frostbitten, frozen, numbed, shivering, shivery. **3** *a cold heart.* aloof, apathetic, callous, cold-blooded, cool, cruel, distant, frigid, hard, hardhearted, heartless, indifferent, inhospitable, inhuman, insensitive, passionless, phlegmatic, reserved, standoffish, stony, uncaring, unconcerned, undemonstrative, unemotional, unenthusiastic, unfeeling, unkind, unresponsive, unsympathetic. ▷ UNFRIENDLY. *Opp* HOT, KIND. ● *n* **1** chill, coldness, coolness, freshness, iciness, low temperature, wintriness. *Opp* HEAT. **2** *cold in the head.* catarrh, *inf* flu, influenza, *inf* the sniffles. **feel the cold** freeze, quiver, shake, shiver, shudder, suffer from hypothermia, tremble.

cold-blooded *adj* barbaric, brutal, callous, hard-hearted, inhuman, inhumane, merciless, pitiless, ruthless, savage. ▷ CRUEL. *Opp* HUMANE.

cold-hearted *adj* apathetic, cool, dispassionate, frigid, heartless, impassive, impersonal, indifferent, insensitive, thick-skinned, uncaring, unemotional, unfeeling, unkind, unresponsive, unsympathetic. ▷ UNFRIENDLY. *Opp* FRIENDLY.

collaborate *vb* **1** band together, cooperate, join forces, *inf* pull

colour

together, team up, work together. **2** [*derog*] collude, connive, conspire, join the opposition, *inf* rat, turn traitor.

collaboration *n* **1** association, concerted effort, cooperation, partnership, tandem, teamwork. **2** [*derog*] collusion, connivance, conspiracy, treachery.

collaborator *n* **1** accomplice, ally, assistant, associate, co-author, colleague, confederate, fellow-worker, helper, helpmate, partner, *joc* partner-in-crime, teammate. **2** *collaborator with an enemy.* blackleg, *inf* Judas, quisling, *inf* scab, traitor, turncoat.

collapse *n* break-down, break-up, cave-in, destruction, downfall, end, fall, ruin, ruination, subsidence, wreck. ● *vb* **1** break down, break up, buckle, cave in, crumble, crumple, deflate, disintegrate, double up, fall apart, fall down, fall in, fold up, give way, *inf* go west, sink, subside, tumble down. **2** *collapse in the heat.* become ill, *inf* bite the dust, black out, *inf* crack up, faint, founder, *inf* go under, *inf* keel over, pass out, *old use* swoon. **3** *sales collapsed.* become less, crash, deteriorate, diminish, drop, fail, slump, worsen.

collapsible *adj* adjustable, folding, retractable, telescopic.

colleague *n* associate, business partner, fellow-worker. ▷ COLLABORATOR.

collect *vb* **1** accumulate, agglomerate, aggregate, amass, assemble, bring together, cluster, come together, concentrate, congregate, convene, converge, crowd, forgather, garner, gather, group, harvest, heap, hoard, lay up, muster, pile up, put by, rally, reserve, save, scrape together, stack up, stockpile, store. *Opp* DISPERSE. **2** *collect money for charity.* be given, raise, secure, take. **3** *collect goods from a shop.* acquire, bring, fetch, get, load up, obtain, pick up. **collected** ▷ CALM.

collection *n* **1** accumulation, array, assemblage, assortment, cluster, conglomeration, heap, hoard, mass, pile, set, stack, store. ▷ GROUP. **2** *old use*

alms-giving, flag-day, free-will offering, offertory, voluntary contributions, *inf* whip-round.

collective *adj* combined, common, composite, co-operative, corporate, democratic, group, joint, shared, unified, united. *Opp* INDIVIDUAL.

college *n* academy, conservatory, institute, polytechnic, school, university.

collide *vb* **collide with** bump into, cannon into, crash into, knock, meet, run into, slam into, smash into, strike, touch. ▷ HIT.

collision *n* accident, bump, clash, crash, head-on collision, impact, knock, pile-up, scrape, smash, wreck.

colloquial *adj* chatty, conversational, everyday, informal, slangy, vernacular. *Opp* FORMAL.

colonist *n* colonizer, explorer, pioneer, settler. *Opp* NATIVE.

colonize *vb* occupy, people, populate, settle in, subjugate.

colony *n* **1** dependency, dominion, possession, protectorate, province, settlement, territory. **2** ▷ GROUP.

colossal *adj* Brobdingnagian, elephantine, enormous, gargantuan, giant, gigantic, herculean, huge, immense, *inf* jumbo, mammoth, massive, mighty, monstrous, monumental, prodigious, titanic, towering, vast. *Opp* SMALL.

colour *n* **1** coloration, colouring, hue, pigment, pigmentation, shade, tincture, tinge, tint, tone. □ *amber, azure, beige, black, blue, bronze, brown, buff, carroty, cherry, chestnut, chocolate, cobalt, cream, crimson, dun, fawn, gilt, gold, golden, green, grey, indigo, ivory, jet-black, khaki, lavender, maroon, mauve, navy blue, ochre, olive, orange, pink, puce, purple, red, rosy, russet, sandy, scarlet, silver, tan, tawny, turquoise, vermilion, violet, white, yellow.* **2** *colour in your cheeks.* bloom, blush, flush, glow, rosiness, ruddiness. ● *vb* **1** colour-wash, crayon, dye, paint, pigment, shade, stain, tinge, tint. **2** blush, bronze, brown, burn, flush, redden, tan. *Opp* FADE. **3** *coloured by prejudice.* affect, bias, distort,

colourful 70

impinge on, influence, pervert, prejudice, slant, sway. **colours** ▷ FLAG.

colourful adj **1** bright, brilliant, chromatic, gaudy, iridescent, multicoloured, psychedelic, showy, vibrant. **2** *colourful personality*. dashing, distinctive, dynamic, eccentric, energetic, exciting, flamboyant, flashy, florid, glamorous, unusual, vigorous. **3** *colourful description*. graphic, interesting, lively, picturesque, rich, stimulating, striking, telling, vivid. *Opp* COLOURLESS.

colouring n colourant, dye, pigment, pigmentation, stain, tincture. ▷ COLOUR.

colourless adj **1** albino, ashen, blanched, faded, grey, monochrome, neutral, pale, pallid, sickly, wan, *inf* washed out, waxen. ▷ WHITE. **2** bland, boring, characterless, dingy, dismal, dowdy, drab, dreary, dull, insipid, lacklustre, lifeless, ordinary, tame, uninspiring, uninteresting, vacuous, vapid. *Opp* COLOURFUL.

column n **1** pilaster, pile, pillar, pole, post, prop, shaft, support, upright. **2** *newspaper column*. article, feature, leader, leading article, piece. **3** *column of soldiers*. cavalcade, file, line, procession, queue, rank, row, string, train.

comb vb **1** arrange, groom, neaten, smarten up, spruce up, tidy, untangle. **2** *comb the house*. hunt through, ransack, rummage through, scour, search thoroughly.

combat n action, battle, bout, clash, conflict, contest, duel, encounter, engagement, fight, skirmish, struggle, war, warfare. ● vb battle against, contend against, contest, counter, defy, face up to, grapple with, oppose, resist, stand up to, strive against, struggle against, tackle, withstand. ▷ FIGHT.

combination n aggregate, alloy, amalgam, blend, compound, concoction, concurrence, conjunction, fusion, marriage, mix, mixture, synthesis, unification. **2** alliance, amalgamation, association, coalition, confederacy, confederation, consortium, conspiracy, federation, grouping, link-up, merger, partnership, syndicate, union.

combine vb **1** add together, amalgamate, bind, blend, bring together, compound, fuse, incorporate, integrate, intertwine, interweave, join, link, *inf* lump together, marry, merge, mingle, mix, pool, put together, synthesize, unify, unite. *Opp* DIVIDE. **2** *combine as a team*. ally, associate, band together, club together, coalesce, connect, cooperate, form an alliance, gang together, gang up, join forces, team up. *Opp* DISPERSE.

combustible adj flammable, inflammable. *Opp* INCOMBUSTIBLE.

come vb **1** advance, appear, approach, arrive, draw near, enter, get to, move (towards), near, reach, visit. **2** *take what comes*. happen, materialize, occur, put in an appearance, show up. **come about** ▷ HAPPEN. **come across** ▷ FIND. **come apart** ▷ DISINTEGRATE. **come clean** ▷ CONFESS. **come out with** ▷ SAY. **come round** ▷ RECOVER. **come up** ▷ ARISE. **come upon** ▷ FIND.

comedian n buffoon, clown, comic, fool, humorist, jester, joker, wag. ▷ ENTERTAINER.

comedy n buffoonery, clowning, facetiousness, farce, hilarity, humour, jesting, joking, satire, slapstick, wit.

comfort n **1** aid, cheer, consolation, encouragement, help, moral support, reassurance, relief, solace, succour, sympathy. **2** *living in comfort*. abundance, affluence, contentment, cosiness, ease, luxury, opulence, plenty, relaxation, well-being. *Opp* DISCOMFORT, POVERTY. ● vb assuage, calm, cheer up, console, ease, encourage, gladden, hearten, help, reassure, relieve, solace, soothe, succour, sympathize with.

comfortable adj **1** *inf* comfy, convenient, cosy, easy, padded, reassuring, relaxing, roomy, snug, soft, upholstered, warm. **2** *comfortable clothes*. informal, loose-fitting, well-fitting, well-made. **3** *a comfortable life*. affluent, agreeable, contented, happy, homely, luxurious, pleasant, prosperous, relaxed, restful, serene, tranquil, untroubled, well-off. *Opp* UNCOMFORTABLE.

comic *adj* absurd, amusing, comical, diverting, droll, facetious, farcical, funny, hilarious, humorous, hysterical, jocular, joking, laughable, ludicrous, *inf* priceless, *inf* rich, ridiculous, sarcastic, sardonic, satirical, side-splitting, silly, uproarious, waggish, witty. *Opp* SERIOUS. ● *n* **1** ▷ COMEDIAN. **2** ▷ MAGAZINE.

command *n* **1** behest, bidding, commandment, decree, directive, edict, injunction, instruction, mandate, order, requirement, ultimatum, writ. **2** authority, charge, control, direction, government, jurisdiction, management, oversight, power, rule, sovereignty, supervision, sway. **3** *command of a language.* grasp, knowledge, mastery. ● *vb* **1** adjure, *old use* bid, charge, compel, decree, demand, direct, enjoin, instruct, ordain, order, prescribe, request, require. **2** *command a ship.* administer, be in charge of, control, direct, govern, have authority over, head, lead, manage, reign over, rule, supervise.

commandeer *vb* appropriate, confiscate, hijack, impound, requisition, seize, sequester, take over.

commander *n* captain, commandant, commanding-officer, general, head, leader, officer-in-charge. ▷ CHIEF.

commemorate *vb* be a memorial to, be a reminder of, celebrate, honour, immortalize, keep alive the memory of, memorialize, pay your respects to, pay homage to, pay tribute to, remember, salute, solemnize.

commence *vb* embark on, enter on, inaugurate, initiate, launch, open, set off, set out, set up, start. ▷ BEGIN. *Opp* FINISH.

commend *vb* acclaim, applaud, approve of, compliment, congratulate, eulogize, extol, praise, recommend. *Opp* CRITICIZE.

commendable *adj* admirable, creditable, deserving, laudable, meritorious, praiseworthy, worthwhile. ▷ GOOD. *Opp* DEPLORABLE.

comment *n* animadversion, annotation, clarification, commentary, criticism, elucidation, explanation, footnote, gloss, interjection, interpolation, mention, note, observation, opinion, reaction, reference, remark, statement. ● *vb* animadvert, criticize, elucidate, explain, interject, interpolate, interpose, mention, note, observe, opine, remark, say, state.

commentary *n* **1** account, broadcast, description, report. **2** *commentary on a poem.* analysis, criticism, critique, discourse, elucidation, explanation, interpretation, notes, review.

commentator *n* announcer, broadcaster, journalist, reporter.

commerce *n* business, buying and selling, dealings, financial transactions, marketing, merchandising, trade, trading, traffic, trafficking.

commercial *adj* business, economic, financial, mercantile, monetary, money-making, pecuniary, profitable, profit-making, trading. ● *n inf* advert, advertisement, *inf* break, *inf* plug.

commiserate *vb* be sorry (for), be sympathetic, comfort, condole, console, feel (for), grieve, mourn, show sympathy (for), sympathize. *Opp* CONGRATULATE.

commission *n* **1** appointment, promotion, warrant. **2** *commission to do a job.* booking, order, request. **3** *commission on a sale.* allowance, *inf* cut, fee, percentage, *inf* rake-off, reward. **4** ▷ COMMITTEE.

commit *vb* **1** be guilty of, carry out, do, enact, execute, perform, perpetrate. **2** *commit to safe-keeping.* consign, deliver, deposit, entrust, give, hand over, put away, transfer. **commit yourself** ▷ PROMISE.

commitment *n* **1** assurance, duty, guarantee, liability, pledge, promise, undertaking, vow, word. **2** *commitment to a cause.* adherence, dedication, determination, devotion, involvement, loyalty, zeal. **3** *social* *commitments.* appointment, arrangement, engagement.

committed *adj* active, ardent, *inf* card-carrying, dedicated, devoted, earnest, enthusiastic, fervent, firm, keen, passionate, resolute, single-minded, staunch, unwavering, wholehearted, zealous. *Opp* APATHETIC.

committee *n* body, council, panel. □ *assembly, board, cabinet, caucus, commission, convention, junta, jury, parliament, quango, synod, think-tank, working party.* ▷ GROUP, MEETING.

common *adj* **1** average, *inf* common or garden, conventional, customary, daily, everyday, familiar, frequent, habitual, normal, ordinary, plain, popular, prevalent, regular, routine, *inf* run-of-the-mill, standard, stock, traditional, typical, undistinguished, unexceptional, unsurprising, usual, well-known, widespread, workaday. ▷ COMMONPLACE. **2** *common knowledge.* accepted, collective, communal, general, joint, mutual, open, popular, public, shared, universal. **3** *the common people.* lower class, lowly, plebeian, proletarian. **4** [*inf*] *Don't be common!* boorish, churlish, coarse, crude, disreputable, ill-bred, inferior, loutish, low, rude, uncouth, unrefined, vulgar, *inf* yobbish. *Opp* ARISTOCRATIC, DISTINCTIVE, UNUSUAL. ● *n* heath, park, parkland.

commonplace *adj* banal, boring, forgettable, hackneyed, humdrum, mediocre, obvious, ordinary, pedestrian, plain, platitudinous, predictable, prosaic, routine, standard, trite, unexciting, unremarkable. ▷ COMMON. *Opp* MEMORABLE. ● *n* ▷ PLATITUDE.

commotion *n inf* ado, agitation, *inf* bedlam, bother, brawl, *inf* brouhaha, *inf* bust-up, chaos, clamour, confusion, contretemps, din, disorder, disturbance, excitement, ferment, flurry, fracas, fray, furore, fuss, hubbub, hullabaloo, incident, *inf* kerfuffle, noise, *inf* palaver, pandemonium, *inf* punch-up, quarrel, racket, riot, row, rumpus, sensation, *inf* shemozzle, *inf* stir, *inf* to-do, tumult,

turbulence, turmoil, unrest, upheaval, uproar, upset.

communal *adj* collective, common, general, joint, mutual, open, public, shared. *Opp* PRIVATE.

communicate *vb* **1** commune, confer, converse, correspond, discuss, get in touch, interrelate, make contact, speak, talk, write (to). **2** *communicate information.* advise, announce, broadcast, convey, declare, disclose, disseminate, divulge, express, get across, impart, indicate, inform, intimate, make known, mention, network, notify, pass on, proclaim, promulgate, publish, put across, put over, relay, report, reveal, say, show, speak, spread, state, transfer, transmit, write. **3** *communicate a disease.* give, infect someone with, pass on, spread, transfer, transmit. **4** *The passage communicates with the kitchen.* be connected, lead (to).

communication *n* **1** communicating, communion, contact, interaction, *old use* intercourse. □ *announcement, bulletin, cable, card, communiqué, conversation, correspondence, dialogue, directive, dispatch, document, fax, gossip, inf grapevine, information, intelligence, intimation, letter, inf memo, memorandum, message, news, note, notice, proclamation, report, rumour, signal, statement, talk, telegram, transmission, wire, word of mouth, writing.* □ *CB, computer, intercom, radar, telegraph, telephone, teleprinter, walkie-talkie.* **2** *mass communication.* mass media, the media. □ *advertising, broadcasting, cable television, magazines, newspapers, the press, radio, satellite, telecommunication, television.*

communicative *adj* articulate, *inf* chatty, frank, informative, open, outgoing, responsive, sociable. ▷ TALKATIVE. *Opp* SECRETIVE.

community *n* colony, commonwealth, commune, country, kibbutz, nation, society, state. ▷ GROUP.

commute *vb* **1** adjust, alter, curtail, decrease, lessen, lighten, mitigate, reduce, shorten. **2** ▷ TRAVEL.

compact *adj* **1** close-packed, compacted, compressed, consolidated, dense, firm, heavy, packed, solid, tight-packed. *Opp* LOOSE. **2** handy, neat, portable, small. **3** abbreviated, abridged, brief, compendious, compressed, concentrated, condensed, short, small, succinct, terse. ▷ CONCISE. *Opp* LARGE. ● *n* ▷ AGREEMENT.

companion *n* accomplice, assistant, associate, chaperone, colleague, comrade, confederate, confidant(e), consort, *inf* crony, escort, fellow, follower, *inf* henchman, mate, partner, stalwart. ▷ FRIEND, HELPER.

company *n* **1** companionship, fellowship, friendship, society. **2** [*inf*] *company for tea*. callers, guests, visitors. **3** *mixed company*. assemblage, association, band, body, circle, club, community, coterie, crew, crowd, ensemble, entourage, gang, gathering, society, throng, troop, troupe (*of actors*). **4** *trading company*. business, cartel, concern, conglomerate, consortium, corporation, establishment, firm, house, line, organization, partnership, *inf* set-up, syndicate, union. ▷ GROUP.

comparable *adj* analogous, cognate, commensurate, compatible, corresponding, equal, equivalent, matching, parallel, proportionate, related, similar, twin. *Opp* DISSIMILAR.

compare *vb* check, contrast, correlate, draw parallels (between), equate, juxtapose, liken, make comparisons, make connections (between), measure (against), relate (to), set side by side, weigh (against). **compare with** ▷ EQUAL.

comparison *n* analogy, comparability, contrast, correlation, difference, distinction, juxtaposition, likeness, parallel, relationship, resemblance, similarity.

compartment *n* alcove, area, bay, berth, booth, cell, chamber, *inf* cubbyhole, cubicle, division, hole, kiosk, locker, niche, nook, partition, pigeonhole, section, slot, space, subdivision.

compatible *adj* **1** harmonious, like-minded, similar, well-matched. ▷

FRIENDLY. **2** *compatible claims*. accordant, congruent, consistent, consonant, matching, reconcilable. *Opp* INCOMPATIBLE.

compel *vb* bind, bully, coerce, constrain, dragoon, drive, exact, force, impel, make, necessitate, oblige, order, press, press-gang, pressurize, require, *inf* shanghai, urge.

compendium *n* abridgement, abstract, anthology, collection, condensation, digest, handbook, summary.

compensate *vb* **1** atone, *inf* cough up, expiate, indemnify, make amends, make good, make reparation, make restitution, make up for, pay back, pay compensation, recompense, redress, reimburse, remunerate, repay, requite. **2** counterbalance, counterpoise, even up, neutralize, offset.

compensation *n* amends, damages, indemnity, recompense, refund, reimbursement, reparation, repayment, restitution.

compère *n* anchor-man, announcer, disc jockey, host, hostess, linkman, Master of Ceremonies, MC, presenter.

compete *vb* **1** be a contestant, enter, participate, perform, take part, take up the challenge. **2** be in competition, conflict, contend, emulate, oppose, rival, strive, struggle, undercut, vie. ▷ FIGHT. *Opp* COOPERATE. **compete with** ▷ RIVAL.

competent *adj* able, acceptable, accomplished, adept, adequate, capable, clever, effective, effectual, efficient, experienced, expert, fit, *inf* handy, practical, proficient, qualified, satisfactory, skilful, skilled, trained, workmanlike, worthwhile. *Opp* INCOMPETENT.

competition *n* **1** competitiveness, conflict, contention, emulation, rivalry, struggle. **2** challenge, championship, contest, event, game, heat, match, quiz, race, rally, series, tournament, trial.

competitive *adj* **1** aggressive, antagonistic, combative, contentious, cutthroat, hard-fought, keen, lively, sporting, well-fought. **2** *competitive prices.* average, comparable with others, fair, moderate, reasonable, similar to others.

competitor *n* adversary, antagonist, candidate, challenger, contender, contestant, entrant, finalist, opponent, participant, rival.

compile *vb* accumulate, amass, arrange, assemble, collate, collect, compose, edit, gather, marshal, organize, put together.

complain *vb inf* beef, *inf* bellyache, *sl* bind, carp, cavil, find fault, fuss, *inf* gripe, groan, *inf* grouch, grouse, grumble, lament, moan, object, protest, wail, whine, *inf* whinge. *Opp* PRAISE. **complain about** ▷ CRITICIZE.

complaint *n* **1** accusation, *inf* beef, charge, condemnation, criticism, grievance, *inf* gripe, grouse, grumble, moan, objection, protest, stricture, whine, whinge. **2** *a medical complaint.* affliction, ailment, disease, disorder, infection, malady, malaise, sickness, upset. ▷ ILLNESS.

complaisant *adj* accommodating, acquiescent, amenable, biddable, compliant, cooperative, deferential, docile, obedient, obliging, pliant, polite, submissive, tractable, willing. *Opp* OBSTINATE.

complement *n* **1** completion, *inf* finishing touch, perfection. **2** *a full complement.* aggregate, capacity, quota, sum, total. ● *vb* add to, complete, make whole, perfect, round off, top up.

complementary *adj* interdependent, matching, reciprocal, toning, twin.

complete *adj* **1** comprehensive, entire, exhaustive, full, intact, total, unabbreviated, unabridged, uncut, unedited, unexpurgated, whole. **2** accomplished, achieved, completed, concluded, done, ended, finished, over. ▷ PERFECT. **3** *a complete disaster.* absolute, arrant, downright, extreme, *inf* out-and-out, outright, pure, rank, sheer, thorough, thoroughgoing, total, unmitigated, unmixed, unqualified, utter, *inf* wholesale. *Opp* INCOMPLETE. ● *vb*

1 accomplish, achieve, carry out, clinch, close, conclude, crown, do, end, finalize, finish, fulfil, perfect, perform, round off, terminate, *inf* top off, *inf* wind up. **2** *complete forms.* answer, fill in.

complex *adj* complicated, composite, compound, convoluted, elaborate, *inf* fiddly, heterogeneous, intricate, involved, *inf* knotty (*problem*), labyrinthine, manifold, mixed, multifarious, multiple, multiplex, ornate, perplexing, problematical, sophisticated, tortuous, *inf* tricky. *Opp* SIMPLE.

complexion *n* appearance, colour, colouring, look, pigmentation, skin, texture.

complicate *vb* compound, confound, confuse, elaborate, entangle, make complicated, mix up, muddle, *inf* screw up, *inf* snarl up, tangle, twist. *Opp* SIMPLIFY. **complicated** ▷ COMPLEX.

complication *n* complexity, confusion, convolution, difficulty, dilemma, intricacy, *inf* mix-up, obstacle, problem, ramification, setback, snag, tangle.

compliment *n* accolade, admiration, appreciation, approval, commendation, congratulations, encomium, eulogy, felicitations, flattery, honour, panegyric, plaudits, praise, testimonial, tribute. ● *vb* applaud, commend, congratulate, *inf* crack up, eulogize, extol, felicitate, flatter, give credit, laud, pay homage to, praise, salute, speak highly of. *Opp* INSULT.

complimentary *adj* admiring, appreciative, approving, commendatory, congratulatory, encomiastic, eulogistic, favourable, flattering, *derog* fulsome, generous, laudatory, panegyrical, rapturous, supportive. *Opp* ABUSIVE, CONTEMPTUOUS, CRITICAL.

comply *vb* abide (by), accede, accord, acquiesce, adhere (to), agree, assent, be in accordance, coincide, concur, consent, correspond (to), defer, fall in (with), fit in, follow, fulfil, harmonize, keep (to), match, meet, obey, observe, perform, respect, satisfy, square (with), submit, suit, yield. ▷ CONFORM. *Opp* DEFY.

component *n* bit, constituent, element, essential part, ingredient, item, part, piece, *inf* spare, spare part, unit.

compose *vb* **1** build, compile, constitute, construct, fashion, form, frame, make, put together. **2** *compose music.* arrange, create, devise, imagine, make up, produce, write. **3** *compose yourself.* calm, control, pacify, quieten, soothe, tranquillize. **be composed of** ▷ COMPRISE. **composed** ▷ CALM.

composition *n* **1** assembly, constitution, creation, establishment, formation, formulation, *inf* make-up, setting up. **2** balance, configuration, layout, organization, structure. **3** *a literary composition.* article, essay, story. ▷ WRITING. **4** *a musical composition.* opus, piece, work. ▷ MUSIC.

compound *adj* complex, complicated, composite, intricate, involved, multiple. *Opp* SIMPLE. ● *n* **1** alloy, amalgam, blend, combination, composite, composition, fusion, mixture, synthesis. **2** *compound for cattle.* Amer corral, enclosure, pen, run. ● *vb* ▷ COMBINE, COMPLICATE.

comprehend *vb* appreciate, apprehend, conceive, discern, fathom, follow, grasp, know, perceive, realize, see, take in, *inf* twig, understand.

comprehensible *adj* clear, easy, intelligible, lucid, meaningful, plain, self-explanatory, simple, straightforward, understandable. *Opp* INCOMPREHENSIBLE.

comprehensive *adj* allembracing, broad, catholic, compendious, complete, detailed, encyclopaedic, exhaustive, extensive, far-reaching, full, inclusive, indiscriminate, sweeping, thorough, total, universal, wholesale, wide-ranging. *Opp* SELECTIVE.

compress *vb* abbreviate, abridge, compact, concentrate, condense, constrict, contract, cram, crush, flatten, *inf* jam, précis, press, shorten, squash, squeeze, stuff, summarize,

telescope, truncate. *Opp* EXPAND. **compressed** ▷ COMPACT, CONCISE.

comprise *vb* be composed of, comprehend, consist of, contain, cover, embody, embrace, include, incorporate, involve.

compromise *n* bargain, concession, *inf* give-and-take, *inf* halfway house, middle course, middle way, settlement. ● *vb* **1** concede a point, go to arbitration, make concessions, meet halfway, negotiate a settlement, reach a formula, settle, *inf* split the difference, strike a balance. **2** *compromise your reputation.* damage, discredit, disgrace, dishonour, imperil, jeopardize, prejudice, risk, undermine, weaken. **compromising** ▷ SHAMEFUL.

compulsion *n* **1** coercion, duress, force, necessity, restraint, restriction. **2** *compulsion to smoke.* addiction, drive, habit, impulse, pressure, urge.

compulsive *adj* **1** besetting, compelling, driving, instinctive, involuntary, irresistible, overpowering, overwhelming, powerful, uncontrollable, urgent. **2** *compulsive drinker.* addicted, habitual, incorrigible, incurable, obsessive, persistent.

compulsory *adj* binding, contractual, *Fr* de rigueur, enforceable, essential, imperative, imposed, incumbent, indispensable, inescapable, mandatory, necessary, obligatory, official, prescribed, required, requisite, set, statutory, stipulated, unavoidable. *Opp* OPTIONAL.

compunction *n* contrition, hesitation, pang of conscience, qualm, regret, remorse, scruple, self-reproach.

compute *vb* add up, ascertain, assess, calculate, count, determine, estimate, evaluate, measure, reckon, total, work out.

computer *n* mainframe, micro, microcomputer, mini-computer, PC, personal computer, robot, word-processor.

comrade *n* associate, colleague, companion. ▷ FRIEND.

conceal *vb* blot out, bury, camouflage, cloak, cover up, disguise, envelop, gloss over, hide, hush up, keep dark, keep quiet, keep secret, mask, obscure, screen, secrete, suppress, veil. *Opp* REVEAL. **concealed** ▷ HIDDEN.

concede *vb* accept, acknowledge, admit, agree, allow, confess, grant, make a concession, own, profess, recognize. **concede defeat** capitulate, *inf* cave in, cede, give in, resign, submit, surrender, yield.

conceit *n* arrogance, boastfulness, egotism, self-admiration, self-esteem, self-love, vanity. ▷ PRIDE.

conceited *adj* arrogant, *inf* bigheaded, boastful, bumptious, *inf* cocksure, *inf* cocky, egocentric, egotistic(al), grand, haughty, *inf* high and mighty, immodest, narcissistic, overweening, pleased with yourself, proud, self-centred, self-important, self-satisfied, smug, snobbish, *inf* snooty, *inf* stuck-up, supercilious, *inf* swollen-headed, *inf* toffee-nosed, vain, vainglorious. *Opp* MODEST.

conceive *vb* **1** become pregnant. **2** *conceive a plan.* conjure up, contrive, create, design, devise, *inf* dream up, envisage, evolve, form, formulate, frame, germinate, hatch, imagine, initiate, invent, make up, originate, plan, plot, produce, realize, suggest, think up, visualize, work out. ▷ THINK.

concentrate *n* distillation, essence, extract. ● *vb* **1** apply yourself, attend, be absorbed, be attentive, engross yourself, think, work hard. **2** accumulate, centralize, centre, cluster, collect, congregate, converge, crowd, focus, gather, mass. *Opp* DISPERSE. **3** *concentrate a liquid.* condense, reduce, thicken. *Opp* DILUTE. **concentrated 1** ▷ INTENSIVE. **2** condensed, evaporated, reduced, strong, thick, undiluted.

conception *n* **1** begetting, conceiving, fathering, fertilization, genesis, impregnation, initiation, origin. ▷ BEGINNING. **2** ▷ IDEA.

concern *n* **1** attention, care, charge, consideration, heed, interest, regard. **2** *no concern of yours.* affair, business, involvement, matter, problem,

responsibility, task. **3** *matter for concern.* anxiety, burden, disquiet, distress, fear, malaise, solicitude, worry. **4** *business concern.* business, company, corporation, enterprise, establishment, firm, organization. ● *vb* affect, be important to, be relevant to, interest, involve, matter to, pertain to, refer to, relate to.

concerned *adj* **1** *concerned parents.* bothered, caring, distressed, disturbed, fearful, perturbed, solicitous, touched, troubled, uneasy, unhappy, upset, worried. ▷ ANXIOUS. **2** *the people concerned.* connected, implicated, interested, involved, referred to, relevant. ▷ RESPONSIBLE.

concerning *prep* about, apropos of, germane to, involving, re, regarding, relating to, relevant to, with reference to, with regard to.

concert *n* performance, programme, show. ▷ ENTERTAINMENT, MUSIC.

concerted *adj* collaborative, collective, combined, cooperative, joint, mutual, shared, united.

concession *n* adjustment, allowance, reduction.

concise *adj* brief, compact, compendious, compressed, concentrated, condensed, epigrammatic, laconic, pithy, short, small, succinct, terse. ▷ ABRIDGED. *Opp* DIFFUSE.

conclude *vb* **1** cease, close, complete, culminate, end, finish, round off, stop, terminate. **2** assume, decide, deduce, gather, infer, judge, reckon, suppose, surmise. ▷ THINK.

conclusion *n* **1** close, completion, culmination, end, epilogue, finale, finish, peroration, rounding-off, termination. **2** answer, belief, decision, deduction, inference, interpretation, judgement, opinion, outcome, resolution, result, solution, upshot, verdict.

conclusive *adj* certain, convincing, decisive, definite, persuasive, unambiguous, unanswerable, unequivocal, unquestionable. *Opp* INCONCLUSIVE.

concoct *vb* contrive, cook up, counterfeit, devise, fabricate, feign, formulate, hatch, invent, make up, plan, prepare, put together, think up.

concord n agreement, euphony, harmony, peace.

concrete adj actual, definite, existing, factual, firm, material, objective, palpable, physical, real, solid, substantial, tactile, tangible, touchable, visible. Opp ABSTRACT.

concur vb accede, accord, agree, assent. ▷ COMPLY.

concurrent adj coexisting, coinciding, concomitant, contemporaneous, contemporary, overlapping, parallel, simultaneous, synchronous.

condemn vb 1 blame, castigate, censure, criticize, damn, decry, denounce, deplore, deprecate, disapprove of, disparage, execrate, rebuke, reprehend, reprove, revile, inf slam, inf slate, upbraid. Opp COMMEND. 2 convict, find guilty, judge, pass judgement, prove guilty, punish, sentence. Opp ACQUIT.

condensation n haze, mist, precipitation, inf steam, water-drops.

condense vb 1 abbreviate, abridge, compress, contract, curtail, précis, reduce, shorten, summarize, synopsize. Opp EXPAND. 2 condense a liquid. concentrate, distil, reduce, solidify, thicken. Opp DILUTE.

condescend vb deign, demean yourself, humble yourself, lower yourself, stoop. **condescending** ▷ HAUGHTY.

condition n 1 case, circumstance, inf fettle, fitness, form, health, inf nick, order, shape, situation, state, inf trim, working order. 2 limitation, obligation, prerequisite, proviso, qualification, requirement, requisite, restriction, stipulation, terms. 3 medical condition. ▷ ILLNESS. ● vb acclimatize, accustom, brainwash, educate, mould, prepare, re-educate, inf soften up, teach, train.

conditional adj dependent, limited, provisional, qualified, restricted, safeguarded, inf with strings attached. Opp UNCONDITIONAL.

condone vb allow, connive at, disregard, endorse, excuse, forgive, ignore, let someone off, overlook, pardon, tolerate.

conducive adj advantageous, beneficial, encouraging, favourable, helpful, supportive. **be conducive to** ▷ ENCOURAGE.

conduct n 1 actions, attitude, bearing, behaviour, comportment, demeanour, deportment, manners, ways. 2 conduct of affairs. administration, control, direction, discharge, government, guidance, handling, leading, management, operation, organization, regulation, running, supervision. ● vb 1 administer, be in charge of, chair, command, control, direct, escort, govern, handle, head, look after, manage, organize, oversee, preside over, regulate, rule, run, steer, superintend, supervise, usher. 2 conduct me home. accompany, escort, guide, lead, pilot, take, usher. 3 conduct electricity. carry, channel, convey, transmit. **conduct yourself** ▷ BEHAVE.

confer vb 1 accord, award, bestow, give, grant, honour with, impart, invest, present. 2 compare notes, consult, converse, debate, deliberate, discourse, discuss, exchange ideas, inf put your heads together, seek advice. ▷ TALK.

conference n colloquium, congress, consultation, convention, council, deliberation, discussion, forum, seminar, symposium. ▷ MEETING.

confess vb acknowledge, admit, be truthful, inf come clean, concede, disclose, divulge, inf make a clean breast (of), own up, unbosom yourself, unburden yourself.

confession n acknowledgement, admission, declaration, disclosure, expression, profession, revelation.

confide vb consult, open your heart, speak confidentially, inf spill the beans, inf tell all, tell secrets, unbosom yourself, trust.

confidence n 1 belief, certainty, credence, faith, hope, optimism, positiveness, reliance, trust. 2 aplomb, assurance, boldness, composure, conviction, firmness, nerve, panache, self-assurance, self-confidence, self-possession, self-reliance, spirit, verve.

Opp DOUBT, HESITATION. **have confidence in** ▷ TRUST.

confident *adj* **1** certain, convinced, hopeful, optimistic, positive, sanguine, sure, trusting. **2** *a confident person*. assertive, assured, bold, *derog* cocksure, composed, cool, definite, fearless, secure, self-assured, self-confident, self-possessed, self-reliant, unafraid. *Opp* DOUBTFUL.

confidential *adj* **1** classified, *inf* hush-hush, intimate, *inf* off the record, personal, private, restricted, secret, suppressed, top secret. **2** *confidential secretary*. personal, private, trusted.

confine *vb* bind, box in, cage, circumscribe, constrain, *inf* coop up, cordon off, cramp, curb, detain, enclose, gaol, hedge in, hem in, *inf* hold down, immure, incarcerate, isolate, keep in, limit, localize, restrain, restrict, rope off, shut in, shut up, surround, wall up. ▷ IMPRISON. *Opp* FREE.

confirm *vb* **1** authenticate, back up, bear out, corroborate, demonstrate, endorse, establish, fortify, give credence to, justify, lend force to, prove, reinforce, settle, show, strengthen, substantiate, support, underline, vindicate, witness to. **2** *confirm a deal*. authorize, *inf* clinch, formalize, guarantee, make legal, make official, ratify, sanction, validate, verify.

confiscate *vb* appropriate, commandeer, expropriate, impound, remove, seize, sequester, sequestrate, take away, take possession of.

conflict *n* **1** antagonism, antipathy, contention, contradiction, difference, disagreement, discord, dissension, friction, hostility, incompatibility, inconsistency, opposition, strife. **2** altercation, battle, *inf* brush, clash, combat, confrontation, contest, dispute, encounter, engagement, feud, fight, quarrel, row, *inf* set-to, skirmish, struggle, war, warfare, wrangle. ● *vb* *inf* be at odds, be at variance, be incompatible, clash, compete, contend, contradict, contrast, *inf* cross swords, differ, disagree, oppose each other. ▷ FIGHT, QUARREL.

conform *vb* acquiesce, agree, be good, behave conventionally, blend in, *inf* do what you are told, fit in, *inf* keep in step, obey, *inf* see eye to eye, *inf* toe the line. ▷ COMPLY.

conformist *n* conventional person, traditionalist, yes-man. *Opp* REBEL.

conformity *n* complaisance, compliance, conventionality, obedience, orthodoxy, submission, uniformity.

confront *vb* accost, argue with, attack, brave, challenge, defy, encounter, face up to, meet, oppose, resist, stand up to, take on, withstand. *Opp* AVOID.

confuse *vb* **1** disarrange, disorder, distort, entangle, garble, jumble, *inf* mess up, mingle, mix up, muddle, tangle, *inf* throw into disarray, upset. **2** *rules confuse me*. agitate, baffle, befuddle, bemuse, bewilder, confound, disconcert, disorientate, distract, *inf* flummox, fluster, mislead, mystify, perplex, puzzle, *inf* rattle, *inf* throw. **3** *confuse twins*. fail to distinguish. **confusing** ▷ PUZZLING.

confused *adj* **1** chaotic, disordered, disorderly, disorganized, *inf* higgledy-piggledy, jumbled, messy, mixed up, muddled, *inf* screwed-up, *sl* shambolic, *inf* topsy-turvy, twisted. **2** *confused ideas*. aimless, contradictory, disconnected, disjointed, garbled, incoherent, inconsistent, irrational, misleading, obscure, rambling, unclear, unsound, unstructured, woolly. **3** *confused mind*. addled, addleheaded, baffled, bewildered, dazed, disorientated, distracted, flustered, fuddled, *inf* in a tizzy, inebriated, muddle-headed, *inf* muzzy, mystified, non-plussed, perplexed, puzzled. ▷ MAD. *Opp* ORDERLY.

confusion *n* **1** *inf* ado, anarchy, bedlam, bother, chaos, clutter, commotion, confusion, din, disorder, disorganization, disturbance, fuss, hubbub, hullabaloo, jumble, maelstrom, *inf* mayhem, mêlée, mess, *inf* mix-up, muddle, pandemonium, racket, riot, rumpus, shambles, tumult, turbulence, turmoil, upheaval, uproar, welter, whirl. **2** *mental confusion.* bemusement, bewilderment, disorientation, distraction, mystification, perplexity, puzzlement. *Opp* ORDER.

congeal *vb* clot, coagulate, coalesce, condense, curdle, freeze, harden, *inf* jell, set, solidify, stiffen, thicken.

congenial *adj* acceptable, agreeable, amicable, companionable, compatible, genial, kindly, suitable, sympathetic, understanding, well-suited. ▷ FRIENDLY. *Opp* UNCONGENIAL.

congenital *adj* hereditary, inborn, inbred, inherent, inherited, innate, natural.

congested *adj* blocked, choked, clogged, crammed, crowded, full, jammed, obstructed, overcrowded, stuffed. *Opp* CLEAR.

congratulate *vb* applaud, compliment, felicitate, praise.

congregate *vb* assemble, cluster, collect, come together, convene, converge, crowd, forgather, gather, get together, mass, meet, muster, rally, rendezvous, swarm, throng. ▷ GROUP.

conjure *vb* bewitch, charm, compel, enchant, invoke, raise, rouse, summon. **conjure up** ▷ PRODUCE.

conjuring *n* illusions, legerdemain, magic, sleight of hand, tricks, wizardry.

connect *vb* **1** attach, combine, couple, engage, fix, interlock, join, link, put on, switch on, tie, turn on, unite. ▷ FASTEN. **2** associate, bracket together, compare, make a connection between, put together, relate, tie up. *Opp* SEPARATE.

connection *n* affinity, association, bond, coherence, contact, correlation, correspondence, interrelationship, link, relationship, relevance, tie, *inf* tie-up, unity. *Opp* SEPARATION.

conquer *vb* **1** annex, beat, best, capture, checkmate, crush, defeat, get the better of, humble, *inf* lick, master, occupy, outdo, overcome, overpower, overrun, overthrow, overwhelm, possess, prevail over, quell, rout, seize, silence, subdue, subject, subjugate, succeed against, surmount, take, *inf* thrash, triumph over, vanquish, worst. ▷ WIN. **2** *conquer a mountain.* climb, reach the top of.

conquest *n* annexation, appropriation, capture, defeat, domination, invasion, occupation, overthrow, subjection, subjugation, *inf* takeover. ▷ VICTORY.

conscience *n* compunction, ethics, honour, fairness, misgivings, morality, morals, principles, qualms, reservations, scruples, standards.

conscientious *adj* accurate, attentive, careful, diligent, dutiful, exact, hard-working, high-minded, honest, meticulous, painstaking, particular, punctilious, responsible, rigorous, scrupulous, serious, thorough. *Opp* CARELESS.

conscious *adj* **1** alert, awake, aware, compos mentis, sensible. **2** *a conscious act.* calculated, deliberate, intended, intentional, knowing, planned, premeditated, self-conscious, studied, voluntary, waking, wilful. *Opp* UNCONSCIOUS.

consecrate *vb* bless, dedicate, devote, hallow, make sacred, sanctify. *Opp* DESECRATE.

consecutive *adj* continuous, following, one after the other, running (*3 days running*), sequential, succeeding, successive.

consent *n* acquiescence, agreement, approval, assent, concurrence, imprimatur, permission, seal of approval. ● *vb* accede, acquiesce, agree, approve, comply, concede, concur, conform, submit, undertake, yield. *Opp* REFUSE. **consent to** ▷ ALLOW.

consequence *n* **1** aftermath, byproduct, corollary, effect, end, *inf* follow-up, issue, outcome, repercussion, result, sequel, side-effect, upshot. **2** *of no consequence.* account, concern, importance, moment, note, significance, value, weight.

consequent *adj* consequential, ensuing, following, resultant, resulting, subsequent.

conservation *n* careful management, economy, good husbandry, maintenance, preservation, protection, safeguarding, saving, upkeep. *Opp* DESTRUCTION.

conservationist *n* ecologist, environmentalist, *inf* green, preservationist.

conservative *adj* 1 conventional, die-hard, hidebound, moderate, narrow-minded, old-fashioned, reactionary, sober, traditional, unadventurous. 2 *conservative estimate.* cautious, moderate, reasonable, understated, unexaggerated. 3 *conservative politics.* right-of-centre, right-wing, Tory. *Opp* PROGRESSIVE. ● *n* conformist, die-hard, reactionary, right-winger, Tory, traditionalist.

conserve *vb* be economical with, hold in reserve, keep, look after, maintain, preserve, protect, safeguard, save, store up, use sparingly. *Opp* DESTROY, WASTE.

consider *vb* 1 *inf* chew over, cogitate, contemplate, deliberate, discuss, examine, meditate, mull over, muse, ponder, puzzle over, reflect, ruminate, study, *inf* turn over, weigh up. ▷ THINK. 2 believe, deem, judge, reckon.

considerable *adj* appreciable, big, biggish, comfortable, fairly important, fairly large, noteworthy, noticeable, perceptible, reasonable, respectable, significant, sizeable, substantial, *inf* tidy (amount), tolerable, worthwhile. *Opp* NEGLIGIBLE.

considerate *adj* accommodating, altruistic, attentive, caring, charitable, cooperative, friendly, generous, gracious, helpful, kind, kind-hearted, kindly, neighbourly, obliging, polite, sensitive, solicitous, sympathetic, tactful, thoughtful, unselfish. *Opp* SELFISH.

consign *vb* commit, convey, deliver, devote, entrust, give, hand over, pass on, relegate, send, ship, transfer.

consignment *n* batch, cargo, delivery, load, lorry-load, shipment, van-load.

consist *vb* **consist of** add up to, amount to, be composed of, be made of, comprise, contain, embody, include, incorporate, involve.

consistent *adj* 1 constant, dependable, faithful, predictable, regular, reliable, stable, steadfast, steady, unchanging, undeviating, unfailing, uniform, unvarying. 2 *The stories are consistent.* accordant, compatible, congruous, conso-nant, in accordance, in agreement, in harmony, of a piece. *Opp* INCONSISTENT.

console *vb* calm, cheer, comfort, ease, encourage, hearten, relieve, solace, soothe, succour, sympathize with.

consolidate *vb* make secure, make strong, reinforce, stabilize, strengthen. *Opp* WEAKEN.

consort *vb* **consort with** accompany, associate with, befriend, be friends with, be seen with, fraternize with, *inf* gang up with, keep company with, mix with.

conspicuous *adj* apparent, blatant, clear, discernible, distinguished, dominant, eminent, evident, flagrant, glaring, impressive, manifest, marked, notable, noticeable, obtrusive, obvious, ostentatious, outstanding, patent, perceptible, plain, prominent, pronounced, self-evident, shining (*example*), showy, striking, unconcealed, unmistakable, visible. *Opp* INCONSPICUOUS.

conspiracy *n* cabal, collusion, connivance, *inf* frame-up, insider dealing, intrigue, machinations, plot, *inf* racket, scheme, stratagem, treason.

conspirator *n* plotter, schemer, traitor, *inf* wheeler-dealer.

conspire *vb* be in league, collude, combine, connive, cooperate, hatch a plot, have designs, intrigue, plot, scheme.

constant *adj* 1 ceaseless, chronic, consistent, continual, continuous, endless, eternal, everlasting, fixed, immutable, incessant, invariable, neverending, non-stop, permanent, perpetual, persistent, predictable, regular, relentless, repeated, stable, steady, sustained, unbroken, unchanging, unending, unflagging, uniform, uninterrupted, unremitting, unvarying. 2 *a constant friend.* dedicated, dependable, determined, devoted, faithful, firm, indefatigable, loyal, reliable, resolute, staunch, steadfast, tireless, true, trustworthy, trusty, unswerving, unwavering. *Opp* CHANGEABLE.

constitute *vb* appoint, bring together, compose, comprise, create, establish, form, found, inaugurate, make (up), set up.

construct *vb* assemble, build, create, engineer, erect, fabricate, fashion, fit together, form, *inf* knock together, make, manufacture, pitch (*tent*), produce, put together, put up, set up. *Opp* DEMOLISH.

construction *n* **1** assembly, building, creation, erecting, erection, manufacture, production, putting-up, setting-up. **2** building, edifice, erection, structure.

constructive *adj* advantageous, beneficial, cooperative, creative, helpful, positive, practical, productive, useful, valuable, worthwhile. *Opp* DESTRUCTIVE.

consult *vb* confer, debate, discuss, exchange views, *inf* put your heads together, refer (to), seek advice, speak (to), *inf* talk things over. ▷ QUESTION.

consume *vb* **1** devour, digest, drink, eat, *inf* gobble up, *inf* guzzle, *inf* put away, swallow. **2** *consume energy.* absorb, deplete, drain, eat into, employ, exhaust, expend, swallow up, use up, utilize.

contact *n* connection, join, junction, touch, union. ▷ COMMUNICATION. ● *vb* apply to, approach, call on, communicate with, correspond with, *inf* drop a line to, get hold of, get in touch with, make overtures to, notify, phone, ring, sound out, speak to, talk to, telephone.

contagious *adj* catching, communicable, infectious, spreading, transmittable.

contain *vb* **1** accommodate, enclose, hold. **2** be composed of, comprise, consist of, embody, embrace, include, incorporate, involve. **3** *contain your anger.* check, control, curb, hold back, keep back, limit, repress, restrain, stifle.

container *n* holder, receptacle, repository, vessel. ▷ BAG, BARREL, BOTTLE, BOWL, BOX, CUP, DISH, GLASS, LUGGAGE, POT.

contaminate *vb* adulterate, befoul, corrupt, debase, defile, dirty, foul, infect, poison, pollute, soil, spoil, stain, sully, taint. *Opp* PURIFY.

contemplate *vb* **1** eye, gaze at, look at, observe, regard, stare at, survey, view, watch. ▷ SEE. **2** cogitate, consider, day-dream, deliberate, examine, meditate, mull over, muse, plan, ponder, reflect, ruminate, study, work out. ▷ THINK. **3** envisage, expect, intend, propose.

contemporary *adj* **1** *contemporary with me at school.* coeval, coexistent, coinciding, concurrent, contemporaneous, simultaneous, synchronous. **2** *contemporary music.* current, fashionable, the latest, modern, newest, novel, present-day, topical, *inf* trendy, up-to-date, *inf* with-it.

contempt *n* abhorrence, contumely, derision, detestation, disdain, disgust, dislike, disrespect, loathing, ridicule, scorn. ▷ HATRED. *Opp* ADMIRATION. **feel contempt for** ▷ DESPISE.

contemptible *adj* base, beneath contempt, despicable, detestable, discreditable, disgraceful, dishonourable, disreputable, ignominious, inferior, loathsome, low-down, mean, odious, pitiful, *inf* shabby, shameful, worthless, wretched. ▷ HATEFUL. *Opp* ADMIRABLE.

contemptuous *adj* arrogant, belittling, condescending, derisive, disdainful, dismissive, disrespectful, haughty, *inf* holier-than-thou, imperious, insolent, insulting, jeering, lofty, patronizing, sarcastic, scathing, scornful, sneering, *sl* snide, snobbish, *inf* snooty, *sl* snotty, supercilious, superior, withering. *Opp* RESPECTFUL. **be contemptuous of** ▷ DESPISE.

contend *vb* **1** compete, contest, cope, dispute, grapple, oppose, rival, strive, struggle, vie. ▷ FIGHT, QUARREL. **2** *contend that you're innocent.* affirm, allege, argue, assert, claim, declare, maintain, plead.

content adj ▷ CONTENTED. ● n **1** constituent, element, ingredient, part. **2** ▷ CONTENTMENT. ● vb ▷ SATISFY.

contented adj cheerful, comfortable, derog complacent, content, fulfilled, gratified, peaceful, pleased, relaxed, satisfied, serene, smiling, smug, uncomplaining, untroubled, well-fed. ▷ HAPPY. Opp DISSATISFIED.

contentment n comfort, content, contentedness, ease, fulfilment, relaxation, satisfaction, serenity, smugness, tranquillity, well-being. ▷ HAPPINESS. Opp DISSATISFACTION.

contest n ▷ COMPETITION, FIGHT. ● vb **1** compete for, contend for, fight for, inf make a bid for, strive for, struggle for, take up the challenge of, vie for. **2** contest a decision. argue against, challenge, debate, dispute, doubt, oppose, query, question, refute, resist.

contestant n candidate, competitor, contender, entrant, opponent, participant, player, rival.

context n background, environment, frame of reference, framework, milieu, position, setting, situation, surroundings.

continual adj eternal, everlasting, frequent, limitless, ongoing, perennial, perpetual, recurrent, regular, repeated. ▷ CONTINUOUS. Opp OCCASIONAL.

continuation n **1** continuance, extension, maintenance, prolongation, protraction, resumption. **2** addition, appendix, postscript, sequel, supplement.

continue vb **1** carry on, endure, go on, keep on, last, linger, persevere, persist, proceed, pursue, remain, stay, inf stick at, survive, sustain. **2** continue after lunch. inf pick up the threads, recommence, restart, resume. **3** continue a series. extend, keep going, keep up, lengthen, maintain, prolong.

continuous adj ceaseless, constant, continuing, endless, incessant, interminable, lasting, never-ending, nonstop, permanent, persistent, relentless, inf round-the-clock, inf solid, sustained, unbroken, unceasing,

unending, uninterrupted, unremitting. ▷ CHRONIC, CONTINUAL. Opp INTERMITTENT.

contour n curve, form, outline, relief, shape.

contract n agreement, bargain, bond, commitment, compact, concordat, covenant, deal, indenture, lease, pact, settlement, treaty, understanding, undertaking. ● vb **1** become denser, become smaller, close up, condense, decrease, diminish, draw together, dwindle, fall away, lessen, narrow, reduce, shrink, shrivel, slim down, thin out, wither. Opp EXPAND. **2** agree, arrange, close a deal, covenant, negotiate a deal, promise, sign an agreement, undertake. **3** contract a disease. become infected by, catch, develop, get.

contraction n **1** diminution, narrowing, shortening, shrinkage, shrivelling. **2** abbreviation, diminutive, shortened form.

contradict vb argue with, challenge, confute, controvert, deny, disagree with, dispute, gainsay, impugn, oppose, speak against.

contradictory adj antithetical, conflicting, contrary, different, discrepant, incompatible, inconsistent, irreconcilable, opposed, opposite. Opp COMPATIBLE.

contraption n apparatus, contrivance, device, gadget, invention, machine, mechanism.

contrary adj **1** conflicting, contradictory, converse, different, opposed, opposite, other, reverse. **2** contrary winds. adverse, hostile, inimical, opposing, unfavourable. **3** a contrary child. awkward, cantankerous, defiant, difficult, disobedient, disobliging, disruptive, intractable, obstinate, perverse, rebellious, inf stroppy, stubborn, subversive, uncooperative, unhelpful, wayward, wilful. Opp HELPFUL.

contrast n antithesis, comparison, difference, differentiation, disparity, dissimilarity, distinction, divergence, foil, opposition. Opp SIMILARITY. ● vb **1** compare, differentiate, discriminate, distinguish, emphasize differences, make a distinction, set one against the other. **2** be set off (by), clash, conflict, deviate (from), differ (from). **contrasting** ▷ DISSIMILAR.

contribute vb add, bestow, inf chip in, donate, inf fork out, furnish, give, present, provide, put up, subscribe, supply. **contribute to** ▷ SUPPORT.

contribution n **1** donation, fee, gift, grant, inf hand-out, offering, payment, sponsorship, subscription. **2** addition, encouragement, input, support. ▷ HELP.

contributor n **1** backer, benefactor, donor, giver, helper, patron, sponsor, subscriber, supporter. **2** ▷ WRITER.

control n **1** administration, authority, charge, command, curb, direction, discipline, government, grip, guidance, influence, jurisdiction, leadership, management, mastery, orderliness, organization, oversight, power, regulation, restraint, rule, strictness, supervision, supremacy, sway. **2** button, dial, handle, key, lever, switch. ● vb **1** administer, inf be at the helm, be in charge, inf boss, command, conduct, cope with, deal with, direct, dominate, engineer, govern, guide, handle, have control of, lead, look after, manage, manipulate, order about, oversee, regiment, regulate, rule, run, superintend, supervise. **2** control animals. check, confine, contain, curb, hold back, keep in check, master, repress, restrain, subdue, suppress.

controversial adj **1** arguable, controvertible, debatable, disputable, doubtful, problematical, questionable. Opp ACCEPTED. **2** argumentative, contentious, dialectic, litigious, polemical, provocative.

controversy n altercation, argument, confrontation, contention, debate, disagreement, dispute, dissension, issue, polemic, quarrel, war of words, wrangle.

convalesce vb get better, improve, make progress, mend, recover, recuperate, regain strength.

convalescent adj getting better, healing, improving, making progress, inf on the mend, recovering, recuperating.

convene vb bring together, call, convoke, summon. ▷ GATHER.

convenient adj accessible, appropriate, at hand, available, commodious, expedient, handy, helpful, labour-saving, nearby, neat, opportune, serviceable, suitable, timely, usable, useful. Opp INCONVENIENT.

convention n **1** custom, etiquette, formality, matter of form, practice, rule, tradition. **2** ▷ ASSEMBLY.

conventional adj **1** accepted, accustomed, commonplace, correct, customary, decorous, expected, formal, habitual, mainstream, orthodox, prevalent, received, inf run-of-the-mill, standard, straight, traditional, unadventurous, unimaginative, unoriginal, unsurprising. ▷ ORDINARY. **2** [derog] bourgeois, conservative, hidebound, pedestrian, reactionary, rigid, stereotyped, inf stuffy. Opp UNCONVENTIONAL.

converge vb coincide, combine, come together, join, link up, meet, merge, unite. Opp DIVERGE.

conversation n inf chat, inf chinwag, colloquy, communication, conference, dialogue, discourse, discussion, exchange of views, gossip, inf heart-to-heart, intercourse, inf natter, palaver, phone-call, inf powwow, tête-à-tête. ▷ TALK.

convert vb change someone's mind, convince, persuade, re-educate, reform, regenerate, rehabilitate, save, win over. ▷ CHANGE.

convey vb **1** bear, bring, carry, conduct, deliver, export, ferry, fetch, forward, import, move, send, shift, ship, shuttle, take, taxi, transfer, transport. **2** convey a message. communicate, disclose, impart, imply, indicate, mean, relay, reveal, signify, tell, transmit.

convict n condemned person, criminal, culprit, felon, malefactor, prisoner, wrongdoer. ● vb condemn, declare guilty, prove guilty, sentence. Opp ACQUIT.

conviction n **1** assurance, certainty, confidence, firmness. **2** religious con-

viction. belief, creed, faith, opinion, persuasion, position, principle, tenet, view.

convince *vb* assure, *inf* bring round, convert, persuade, prove to, reassure, satisfy, sway, win over. **convincing** ▷ PERSUASIVE.

convulsion *n* **1** disturbance, eruption, outburst, tremor, turbulence, upheaval. **2** [*medical*] attack, fit, paroxysm, seizure, spasm.

convulsive *adj* jerky, shaking, spasmodic, *inf* twitchy, uncontrolled, uncoordinated, violent, wrenching.

cook *vb* concoct, heat up, make, prepare, warm up. □ *bake, barbecue, boil, braise, brew, broil, casserole, coddle, fry, grill, pickle, poach, roast, sauté, scramble, simmer, steam, stew, toast.* **cook up** ▷ PLOT.

cooking *n* baking, catering, cookery, cuisine.

cool *adj* **1** chilled, chilly, coldish, iced, refreshing, unheated. ▷ COLD. *Opp* HOT. **2** calm, collected, composed, dignified, elegant, *inf* laid-back, level-headed, phlegmatic, quiet, relaxed, self-possessed, sensible, serene, unexcited, unflustered, unruffled, urbane. ▷ BRAVE. **3** [*derog*] aloof, apathetic, cold-blooded, dispassionate, distant, frigid, half-hearted, indifferent, luke-warm, negative, offhand, reserved, *inf* stand-offish, unconcerned, unemotional, unenthusiastic, un-friendly, uninvolved, unrespons-ive, unsociable, unwelcoming. *Opp* PASSIONATE. **4** [*inf*] *cool customer.* ▷ INSOL-ENT. ● *vb* **1** chill, freeze, ice, refriger-ate. *Opp* HEAT. **2** *cool your enthusiasm.* abate, allay, assuage, calm, dampen, diminish, lessen, moderate, *inf* pour cold water on, quiet, temper. *Opp* INFLAME.

cooperate *vb* act in concert, collab-orate, combine, conspire, help each other, *inf* join forces, *inf* pitch in, *inf* play along, *inf* play ball, *inf* pull together, support each other, unite, work as a team, work together. *Opp* COMPETE.

cooperation *n* assistance, collab-oration, cooperative effort, coordi-nation, help, joint action, mutual support, teamwork. *Opp* COMPETITION.

cooperative *adj* **1** accommodating, comradely, constructive, hard-work-ing, helpful to each other, keen, obliging, supportive, united, willing, working as a team. **2** *cooperative effort.* collective, combined, communal, concerted, coordinated, corporate, joint, shared.

cope *vb* get by, make do, manage, survive, win through. **cope with** ▷ ENDURE, MANAGE.

copious *adj* abundant, ample, boun-tiful, extravagant, generous, great, huge, inexhaustible, large, lavish, lib-eral, luxuriant, overflowing, plenti-ful, profuse, unsparing, unstinting. *Opp* SCARCE.

copy *n* **1** carbon copy, clone, coun-terfeit, double, duplicate, facsimile, fake, forgery, imitation, likeness, model, pattern, photocopy, print, replica, representation, reproduction, tracing, transcript, twin, Xerox. **2** *copy of a book.* edition, volume. ● *vb* **1** borrow, counterfeit, crib, duplicate, emulate, follow, forge, imitate, pho-tocopy, plagiarize, print, repeat, reproduce, simulate, transcribe. **2** ape, imitate, impersonate, mimic, parrot.

cord *n* cable, catgut, lace, line, rope, strand, string, twine, wire.

cordon *n* barrier, chain, fence, line, ring, row. **cordon off** ▷ ISOLATE.

core *n* **1** centre, heart, inside, middle, nucleus. **2** *core of a problem.* central issue, crux, essence, gist, heart, ker-nel, *sl* nitty-gritty, nub.

cork *n* bung, plug, stopper.

corner *n* **1** angle, crook, joint. **2** bend, crossroads, intersection, junction, turn, turning. **3** *a quiet cor-ner.* hideaway, hiding-place, hole, niche, nook, recess, retreat. ● *vb* cap-ture, catch, trap.

corporation *n* **1** company, concern, enterprise, firm, organization. **2** council, local government.

corpse *n* body, cadaver, carcass, mortal remains, remains, skeleton, *sl* stiff.

counterfeit

correct adj **1** accurate, authentic, confirmed, exact, factual, faithful, faultless, flawless, genuine, literal, precise, reliable, right, strict, true, truthful, verified. **2** *correct manners.* acceptable, appropriate, fitting, just, normal, proper, regular, standard, suitable, tactful, unexceptionable, well-mannered. *Opp* WRONG. ● vb **1** adjust, alter, cure, *inf* debug, put right, rectify, redress, remedy, repair. **2** *correct pupils' work.* assess, mark. **3** ▷ REPRIMAND.

correspond vb accord, agree, be congruous, be consistent, coincide, concur, conform, correlate, fit, harmonize, match, parallel, square, tally. **corresponding** ▷ EQUIVALENT. **correspond with** communicate with, send letters to, write to.

correspondence n letters, memoranda, *inf* memos, messages, notes, writings.

correspondent n contributor, journalist, reporter. ▷ WRITER.

corridor n hall, hallway, passage, passageway.

corrode vb **1** consume, eat into, erode, oxidize, rot, rust, tarnish. **2** crumble, deteriorate, disintegrate, tarnish.

corrugated adj creased, *inf* crinkly, fluted, furrowed, lined, puckered, ribbed, ridged, wrinkled.

corrupt adj *inf* bent, bribable, criminal, crooked, debauched, decadent, degenerate, depraved, *inf* dirty, dishonest, dishonourable, dissolute, evil, false, fraudulent, illegal, immoral, iniquitous, low, perverted, profligate, rotten, sinful, unethical, unprincipled, unscrupulous, unsound, untrustworthy, venal, vicious, wicked. *Opp* HONEST. ● vb **1** bribe, divert, *inf* fix, influence, pervert, suborn, subvert. **2** *corrupt the innocent.* debauch, deprave, lead astray, make corrupt, seduce, tempt.

cosmetics plur n make-up, toiletries.

cosmic adj boundless, endless, infinite, limitless, universal.

cosmopolitan adj international, multicultural, sophisticated, urbane. *Opp* PROVINCIAL.

cost n amount, charge, expenditure, expense, fare, figure, outlay, payment, price, rate, tariff, value. ● vb be valued at, be worth, fetch, go for, realize, sell for, *inf* set you back.

costume n apparel, attire, clothing, dress, fancy-dress, garb, garments, *inf* get-up, livery, outfit, period dress, raiment, robes, uniform, vestments. ▷ CLOTHES.

cosy adj comfortable, *inf* comfy, easy, homely, intimate, reassuring, relaxing, restful, secure, snug, soft, warm. *Opp* UNCOMFORTABLE.

council n committee, conclave, convention, convocation, corporation, gathering, meeting. ▷ ASSEMBLY.

counsel n ▷ LAWYER. ● vb advise, discuss (with), give help, guide, listen to your views.

count vb **1** add up, calculate, check, compute, enumerate, estimate, figure out, keep account of, *inf* notch up, number, reckon, score, take stock of, tell, total, *inf* tot up, work out. **2** be important, have significance, matter, signify. **count on** ▷ EXPECT.

countenance n air, appearance, aspect, demeanour, expression, face, features, look, visage. ● vb ▷ APPROVE.

counter n **1** bar, sales-point, service-point, table. **2** chip, disc, marker, piece, token. ● vb answer, *inf* come back at, contradict, defend yourself against, hit back at, parry, react to, rebut, refute, reply to, resist, ward off.

counteract vb act against, annul, be an antidote to, cancel out, counterbalance, fight against, foil, invalidate, militate against, negate, neutralize, offset, oppose, resist, thwart, withstand, work against.

counterbalance vb balance, compensate for, counteract, counterpoise, counterweight, equalize.

counterfeit adj artificial, bogus, copied, ersatz, fake, false, feigned, forged, fraudulent, imitation, make-believe, meretricious, pastiche, *inf* phoney, *inf* pretend, *inf* pseudo, sham, simulated, spurious, synthetic. *Opp* GENUINE. ● *vb* copy, fake, falsify, feign, forge, imitate, pretend, *inf* put on, sham, simulate.

countless *adj* endless, immeasurable, incalculable, infinite, innumerable, limitless, many, measureless, myriad, numberless, numerous, unnumbered, untold. *Opp* FINITE.

country *n* **1** canton, commonwealth, domain, empire, kingdom, land, nation, people, power, principality, realm, state, territory. **2** *open country*. countryside, green belt, landscape, scenery.

couple *n* brace, duo, pair, twosome. ● *vb* **1** combine, connect, fasten, hitch, join, link, match, pair, unite, yoke. **2** ▷ MATE.

coupon *n* tear-off slip, ticket, token, voucher.

courage *n* audacity, boldness, *sl* bottle, bravery, daring, dauntlessness, determination, fearlessness, fibre, firmness, fortitude, gallantry, *inf* grit, *inf* guts, heroism, indomitability, intrepidity, mettle, *inf* nerve, patience, *inf* pluck, prowess, resolution, spirit, *sl* spunk, stoicism, tenacity, valour, will-power. *Opp* COWARDICE.

courageous *adj* audacious, bold, brave, cool, daring, dauntless, determined, fearless, gallant, game, *sl* gutsy, heroic, indomitable, intrepid, lion-hearted, noble, *inf* plucky, resolute, spirited, stalwart, stoical, stout-hearted, tough, unafraid, uncomplaining, undaunted, unshrinking, valiant, valorous. *Opp* COWARDLY.

course *n* **1** bearings, circuit, direction, line, orbit, path, route, track, way. **2** *course of events*. advance, continuation, development, movement, passage, passing, progress, progression, succession. **3** *course of lectures*. curriculum, programme, schedule, sequence, series, syllabus.

court *n* **1** assizes, bench, court martial, high court, lawcourt, magistrates' court. **2** entourage, followers, palace, retinue. **3** ▷ COURTYARD. ● *vb* **1** *inf* ask for, attract, invite, provoke,

seek, solicit. **2** date, *inf* go out with, make advances to, make love to, try to win, woo.

courteous *adj* civil, considerate, gentlemanly, ladylike, urbane, well-bred, well-mannered. ▷ POLITE.

courtier *n* attendant, follower, lady, lord, noble, page, steward.

courtyard *n* court, enclosure, forecourt, patio, *inf* quad, quadrangle, yard.

cover *n* **1** ▷ COVERING. **2** binding, case, dust-jacket, envelope, file, folder, portfolio, wrapper. **3** camouflage, cloak, concealment, cover-up, deception, disguise, façade, front, hiding-place, mask, pretence, refuge, sanctuary, shelter, smokescreen. **4** *air cover*. defence, guard, protection, support. ● *vb* **1** blot out, bury, camouflage, cap, carpet, cloak, clothe, cloud, coat, conceal, curtain, disguise, drape, dress, encase, enclose, enshroud, envelop, face, hide, hood, mantle, mask, obscure, overlay, overspread, plaster, protect, screen, shade, sheathe, shield, shroud, spread over, surface, tile, veil, veneer, wrap up. **2** *cover expenses*. be enough for, match, meet, pay for, suffice for. **3** *talk covered many subjects*. comprise, contain, deal with, embrace, encompass, include, incorporate, involve, treat.

covering *n* blanket, canopy, cap, carpet, casing, cladding, cloak, coat, coating, cocoon, cover, crust, facing, film, incrustation, layer, lid, mantle, outside, pall, rind, roof, screen, sheath, sheet, shell, shield, shroud, skin, surface, tarpaulin, top, veil, veneer, wrapping. ▷ BEDCLOTHES.

coward *n* *inf* chicken, craven, deserter, runaway, *inf* wimp.

cowardice *n* cowardliness, desertion, evasion, faint-heartedness, *inf* funk, shirking, spinelessness, timidity. ▷ FEAR. *Opp* COURAGE.

cowardly *adj* abject, afraid, base, chicken-hearted, cowering, craven, dastardly, faint-hearted, fearful, *inf* gutless, *inf* lily-livered, pusillanimous, spineless, submissive, timid, timorous, unchivalrous, ungallant,

creation

unheroic, *inf* wimpish, *sl* yellow. ▷ FRIGHTENED. *Opp* COURAGEOUS.

cower *vb* cringe, crouch, flinch, grovel, hide, quail, shiver, shrink, skulk, tremble.

coy *adj* arch, bashful, coquettish, demure, diffident, embarrassed, evasive, hesitant, modest, reserved, reticent, retiring, self-conscious, sheepish, shy, timid, unforthcoming. *Opp* BOLD.

crack *n* **1** breach, break, chink, chip, cleavage, cleft, cranny, craze, crevice, fissure, flaw, fracture, gap, opening, rift, rupture, slit, split. **2** ▷ JOKE. ● *vb* **1** break, chip, fracture, snap, splinter, split. **2** ▷ HIT, SOUND. **crack up** ▷ DISINTEGRATE.

craft *n* **1** handicraft, job, skilled work, technique, trade. ▷ CRAFTSMANSHIP, CUNNING. **2** *a sea-going craft.* ▷ VESSEL. ● *vb* ▷ MAKE.

craftsmanship *n* art, artistry, cleverness, craft, dexterity, expertise, handiwork, knack, *inf* know-how, workmanship. ▷ SKILL.

crafty *adj* artful, astute, calculating, canny, cheating, clever, conniving, cunning, deceitful, designing, devious, *inf* dodgy, *inf* foxy, furtive, guileful, ingenious, knowing, machiavellian, manipulative, scheming, shifty, shrewd, sly, *inf* sneaky, tricky, wily. *Opp* HONEST, NAÏVE.

craggy *adj* jagged, rocky, rough, rugged, steep, uneven.

cram *vb* **1** compress, crowd, crush, fill, force, jam, overcrowd, overfill, pack, press, squeeze, stuff. **2** ▷ STUDY.

cramped *adj* close, crowded, narrow, restricted, tight, uncomfortable. *Opp* ROOMY.

crane *n* davit, derrick, hoist.

crash *n* **1** bang, boom, clash, explosion. ▷ SOUND. **2** accident, bump, collision, derailment, disaster, impact, knock, pile-up, smash, wreck. **3** *crash on the stock market.* collapse, depression, failure, fall. ● *vb* **1** bump, collide, knock, lurch, pitch, smash. ▷ HIT. **2** collapse, crash-dive, dive, fall, plummet, plunge, topple.

crate *n* box, carton, case, packing-case, tea-chest.

crater *n* abyss, cavity, chasm, hole, hollow, opening, pit.

crawl *vb* **1** clamber, creep, edge, inch, slither, squirm, worm, wriggle. **2** [*inf*] be obsequious, cringe, fawn, flatter, grovel, *sl* suck up, toady.

craze *n* diversion, enthusiasm, fad, fashion, infatuation, mania, novelty, obsession, passion, pastime, rage, *inf* thing, trend, vogue.

crazy *adj* **1** berserk, crazed, delirious, demented, deranged, frantic, frenzied, hysterical, insane, lunatic, *inf* potty, *inf* scatty, unbalanced, unhinged, wild. ▷ MAD. **2** *crazy comedy.* daft, eccentric, farcical, idiotic, *inf* knockabout, ludicrous, ridiculous, *sl* wacky, zany. ▷ ABSURD. **3** *crazy ideas.* confused, foolish, ill-considered, illogical, impractical, irrational, senseless, silly, unrealistic, unreasonable, unwise. ▷ STUPID. **4** ▷ ENTHUSIASTIC. *Opp* SENSIBLE.

creamy *adj* milky, oily, rich, smooth, thick, velvety.

crease *n* corrugation, crinkle, fold, furrow, groove, line, pleat, pucker, ridge, ruck, tuck, wrinkle. ● *vb* crimp, crinkle, crumple, crush, fold, furrow, pleat, pucker, ridge, ruck, rumple, wrinkle.

create *vb* *old use* beget, begin, be the creator of, breed, bring about, bring into existence, build, cause, compose, conceive, concoct, constitute, construct, design, devise, *inf* dream up, engender, engineer, establish, father, forge, form, found, generate, give rise to, hatch, imagine, institute, invent, make up, manufacture, occasion, originate, produce, set up, shape, sire, think up. ▷ MAKE. *Opp* DESTROY.

creation *n* **1** beginning, birth, building, conception, constitution, construction, establishing, formation, foundation, generation, genesis, inception, institution, making, origin, procreation, production, shaping. **2** achievement, brainchild, concept, effort, handiwork, invention, product, work of art. *Opp* DESTRUCTION.

creative adj artistic, clever, fecund, fertile, imaginative, ingenious, inspired, inventive, original, positive, productive, resourceful, talented. Opp DESTRUCTIVE.

creator n architect, artist, author, begetter, builder, composer, craftsman, designer, deviser, discoverer, initiator, inventor, maker, manufacturer, originator, painter, parent, photographer, potter, producer, sculptor, smith, weaver, writer.

creature n beast, being, brute, mortal being, organism. ▷ ANIMAL.

credentials n authorization, documents, identity card, licence, passport, permit, proof of identity, warrant.

credible adj believable, conceivable, convincing, imaginable, likely, persuasive, plausible, possible, reasonable, tenable, thinkable, trustworthy. Opp INCREDIBLE.

credit n approval, commendation, distinction, esteem, fame, glory, honour, inf kudos, merit, praise, prestige, recognition, reputation, status, tribute. ● vb 1 accept, believe, inf buy, count on, depend on, endorse, have faith in, reckon on, rely on, subscribe to, inf swallow, swear by, trust. Opp DOUBT. 2 credit you with sense. ascribe to, assign to, attach to, attribute to. 3 credit £10 to my account. add, enter. Opp DEBIT.

creditable adj admirable, commendable, estimable, good, honourable, laudable, meritorious, praiseworthy, respectable, well thought of, worthy. Opp UNWORTHY.

credulous adj easily taken in, inf green, gullible, inf soft, trusting, unsuspecting. ▷ NAÏVE. Opp SCEPTICAL.

creed n belief, conviction, doctrine, dogma, faith, principle, teaching, tenet.

creek n bay, cove, estuary, harbour, inlet.

creep vb crawl, edge, inch, move quietly, move slowly, pussyfoot, slink, slip, slither, sneak, steal, tiptoe, worm, wriggle, writhe.

creepy adj disturbing, eerie, frightening, ghostly, hair-raising, macabre, ominous, scary, sinister, spine-chilling, inf spooky, supernatural, threatening, uncanny, unearthly, weird.

crest n 1 comb, plume, tuft. 2 crest of a hill. apex, brow, crown, head, peak, pinnacle, ridge, summit, top. 3 badge, coat of arms, design, device, emblem, heraldic device, insignia, seal, shield, sign, symbol.

crevice n break, chink, cleft, crack, cranny, fissure, furrow, groove, rift, slit, split.

crew n band, company, gang, party, team. ▷ GROUP.

crime n delinquency, dishonesty, old use felony, illegality, law-breaking, lawlessness, misconduct, misdeed, misdemeanour, offence, inf racket, sin, transgression of the law, violation, wrongdoing. □ abduction, arson, assassination, blackmail, burglary, extortion, hijacking, hooliganism, kidnapping, manslaughter, misappropriation, mugging, murder, pilfering, piracy, poaching, rape, robbery, shop-lifting, smuggling, stealing, terrorism, theft, treason, vandalism.

criminal adj inf bent, corrupt, inf crooked, culpable, dishonest, felonious, illegal, illicit, indictable, lawless, nefarious, inf shady, unlawful. ▷ WICKED, WRONG. Opp LAWFUL. ● n inf baddy, convict, inf crook, culprit, delinquent, desperado, felon, gangster, knave, lawbreaker, malefactor, miscreant, offender, outlaw, recidivist, ruffian, scoundrel, old use transgressor, villain, wrongdoer. □ bandit, brigand, buccaneer, defaulter, gunman, highwayman, sl hoodlum, hooligan, pickpocket, racketeer, receiver, swindler, thug, ▷ CRIME.

cringe vb blench, cower, crouch, dodge, duck, flinch, grovel, quail, quiver, recoil, shrink back, shy away, tremble, wince.

cripple vb 1 disable, dislocate, fracture, hamper, hamstring, incapacitate, lame, maim, mutilate, paralyse, weaken. 2 damage, make useless, put out of action, sabotage, spoil. **crippled** ▷ HANDICAPPED.

crisis n calamity, catastrophe, climax, critical moment, danger, diffi-

crowd

culty, disaster, emergency, predicament, problem, turning point.

crisp *adj* 1 breakable, brittle, crackly, crispy, crunchy, fragile, friable, hard and dry. 2 ▷ BRACING, BRISK.

criterion *n* measure, principle, standard, touchstone, yardstick.

critic *n* 1 analyst, authority, commentator, judge, pundit, reviewer. 2 attacker, detractor.

critical *adj* 1 captious, carping, censorious, criticizing, deprecatory, depreciatory, derogatory, disapproving, disparaging, faultfinding, hypercritical, judgemental, *inf* nit-picking, *derog* Pharisaical, scathing, slighting, uncomplimentary, unfavourable. *Opp* COMPLIMENTARY. 2 analytical, discerning, discriminating, intelligent, judicious, perceptive, probing, sharp. 3 *critical moment.* basic, crucial, dangerous, decisive, important, key, momentous, pivotal, vital. *Opp* UNIMPORTANT.

criticism *n* 1 censure, condemnation, diatribe, disapproval, disparagement, reprimand, reproach, stricture, tirade, verbal attack. 2 *literary criticism.* analysis, appraisal, appreciation, assessment, commentary, critique, elucidation, evaluation, judgement, valuation.

criticize *vb* 1 belittle, berate, blame, carp, *inf* cast aspersions on, castigate, censure, *old use* chide, condemn, complain about, decry, disapprove of, disparage, fault, find fault with, *inf* flay, *inf* get at, impugn, *inf* knock, *inf* lash, *inf* pan, *inf* pick holes in, *inf* pitch into, *inf* rap, rate, rebuke, reprimand, satirize, scold, *inf* slam, *inf* slate, snipe at. *Opp* PRAISE. 2 analyse, appraise, assess, evaluate, discuss, judge, review.

crockery *n* ceramics, china, crocks, dishes, earthenware, porcelain, pottery, tableware. □ *basin, bowl, coffee-cup, coffee-pot, cup, dinner plate, dish, jug, milk-jug, mug, plate, Amer platter, pot, sauceboat, saucer, serving dish, side plate, soup bowl, sugar-bowl, teacup, teapot, old use trencher, tureen.*

crook *n* 1 angle, bend, corner, hook. 2 ▷ CRIMINAL.

crooked *adj* 1 angled, askew, awry, bendy, bent, bowed, contorted, curved, curving, deformed, gnarled, lopsided, misshapen, off-centre, tortuous, twisted, twisty, warped, winding, zigzag. ▷ INDIRECT. 2 ▷ CRIMINAL.

crop *n* gathering, harvest, produce, sowing, vintage, yield. ● *vb* bite off, browse, clip, graze, nibble, shear, snip, trim. ▷ CUT. **crop up** ▷ ARISE.

cross *adj* bad-tempered, cantankerous, crotchety, *inf* grumpy, ill-tempered, irascible, irate, irritable, peevish, short-tempered, testy, tetchy, upset, vexed. ▷ ANGRY, ANNOYED. *Opp* GOOD-TEMPERED. ● *n* 1 intersection, X. 2 *a cross to bear.* affliction, burden, difficulty, grief, misfortune, problem, sorrow, trial, tribulation, trouble, worry. 3 *cross of breeds.* amalgam, blend, combination, cross-breed, half-way house, hybrid, mixture, mongrel. ● *vb* 1 criss-cross, intersect, meet, zigzag. 2 *cross a river.* bridge, ford, go across, pass over, span, traverse. 3 *cross someone.* annoy, block, frustrate, hinder, impede, interfere with, oppose, stand in the way of, thwart. **cross out** ▷ CANCEL. **cross swords** ▷ CONFLICT.

crossing *vb* 1 bridge, causeway, flyover, ford, level-crossing, overpass, pedestrian crossing, pelican crossing, stepping-stones, subway, underpass, zebra crossing. 2 *sea crossing.* ▷ JOURNEY.

crossroads *n* interchange, intersection, junction.

crouch *vb* bend, bow, cower, cringe, duck, kneel, squat, stoop.

crowd *n* 1 army, assemblage, assembly, bunch, circle, cluster, collection, company, crush, flock, gathering, horde, host, mass, mob, multitude, pack, press, rabble, swarm, throng. ▷ GROUP. 2 *a football crowd.* audience, gate, spectators. ● *vb* assemble, bundle, cluster, collect, compress, congregate, cram, crush, flock, gather, get together, herd, huddle, jam, jostle, mass, muster, overcrowd, pack, *inf* pile, press, push, squeeze, swarm, throng.

crowded adj congested, cramped, full, jammed, inf jam-packed, jostling, overcrowded, overflowing, packed, swarming, teeming, thronging. Opp EMPTY.

crown n 1 circlet, coronet, diadem, tiara. 2 crown of a hill. apex, brow, head, peak, ridge, summit, top. ● vb 1 anoint, appoint, enthrone, install. 2 cap, complete, conclude, consummate, culminate, finish off, perfect, round off, top.

crucial adj central, critical, decisive, essential, important, major, momentous, pivotal, serious. Opp UNIMPORTANT.

crude adj 1 natural, raw, unprocessed, unrefined. 2 crude work. amateurish, awkward, bungling, clumsy, inartistic, incompetent, inelegant, inept, makeshift, primitive, rough, rudimentary, unpolished, unskilful, unworkmanlike. Opp REFINED. 3 ▷ VULGAR.

cruel adj atrocious, barbaric, barbarous, beastly, bestial, bloodthirsty, bloody, brutal, callous, cold-blooded, cold-hearted, diabolical, ferocious, fiendish, fierce, flinty, grim, hard, hard-hearted, harsh, heartless, hellish, implacable, inexorable, inhuman, inhumane, malevolent, merciless, murderous, pitiless, relentless, remorseless, ruthless, sadistic, savage, severe, sharp, spiteful, stern, stony-hearted, tyrannical, unfeeling, unjust, unkind, unmerciful, unrelenting, vengeful, venomous, vicious, violent. Opp KIND.

cruelty n barbarity, bestiality, bloodthirstiness, brutality, callousness, cold-bloodedness, ferocity, hardheartedness, heartlessness, inhumanity, malevolence, ruthlessness, sadism, savagery, unkindness, viciousness, violence.

cruise n sail, voyage. ▷ TRAVEL.

crumb n bit, bite, fragment, grain, morsel, particle, scrap, shred, sliver, speck.

crumble vb break into pieces, break up, crush, decay, decompose, deteriorate, disintegrate, fall apart, fragment, grind, perish, pound, powder, pulverize.

crumbly adj friable, granular, powdery. Opp SOLID.

crumple vb crease, crinkle, crush, dent, fold, mangle, pucker, rumple, wrinkle.

crunch vb break, champ, chew, crush, grind, masticate, munch, scrunch, smash, squash.

crusade n campaign, drive, holy war, jehad, movement, struggle, war.

crush n congestion, jam. ▷ CROWD. ● vb 1 break, bruise, compress, crumple, crunch, grind, mangle, mash, pound, press, pulp, pulverize, shiver, smash, splinter, squash, squeeze. 2 crush opponents. humiliate, mortify, overwhelm, quash, rout, thrash, vanquish. ▷ CONQUER.

crust n incrustation, outer layer, outside, rind, scab, shell, skin, surface. ▷ COVERING.

crux n centre, core, crucial issue, essence, heart, nub.

cry n battle-cry, bellow, call, caterwaul, ejaculation, exclamation, hoot, howl, outcry, roar, scream, screech, shout, shriek, whoop, yell, yelp, yowl. ● vb bawl, blubber, grizzle, howl, keen, shed tears, snivel, sob, wail, weep, whimper, whinge. **cry off** ▷ WITHDRAW. **cry out** ▷ SHOUT.

crypt n basement, catacomb, cellar, grave, sepulchre, tomb, undercroft, vault.

cryptic adj arcane, cabbalistic, coded, concealed, enigmatic, esoteric, hidden, mysterious, mystical, obscure, occult, perplexing, puzzling, recondite, secret, unclear, unintelligible, veiled. Opp INTELLIGIBLE.

cuddle vb caress, clasp lovingly, dandle, embrace, fondle, hold closely, huddle against, hug, kiss, make love, nestle against, nurse, pet, snuggle up to.

cudgel n baton, bludgeon, cane, club, cosh, stick, truncheon. ● vb batter, beat, bludgeon, cane, inf clobber, cosh, pound, pummel, thrash, thump, inf thwack. ▷ HIT.

cue n hint, prompt, reminder, sign, signal.

culminate vb build up to, climax, conclude, reach a finale, rise to a peak. ▷ END.

culpable adj blameworthy, criminal, guilty, knowing, liable, punishable, reprehensible, wrong. ▷ DELIBERATE. Opp INNOCENT.

culprit n delinquent, malefactor, miscreant, offender, troublemaker, wrongdoer. ▷ CRIMINAL.

cult n **1** craze, fan-club, fashion, following, devotees, party, school, trend, vogue. **2** religious cult. ▷ DENOMINATION.

cultivate vb **1** dig, farm, fertilize, hoe, manure, mulch, plough, prepare, rake, till, turn, work. **2** grow, plant, produce, raise, sow, take cuttings, tend. **3** cultivate a friendship. court, develop, encourage, foster, further, improve, promote, pursue, try to achieve.

cultivated adj **1** agricultural, farmed, planted, prepared, tilled. **2** ▷ CULTURED.

cultivation n agriculture, agronomy, breeding, culture, farming, gardening, growing, horticulture, husbandry, nurturing.

cultural adj aesthetic, artistic, civilized, civilizing, educational, elevating, enlightening, highbrow, improving, intellectual.

culture n **1** art, background, civilization, customs, education, learning, mores, traditions, way of life. **2** ▷ CULTIVATION.

cultured adj artistic, civilized, cultivated, discriminating, educated, elegant, erudite, highbrow, knowledgeable, polished, refined, scholarly, sophisticated, wellbred, well-educated, well-read. Opp IGNORANT.

cunning adj **1** artful, devious, dodgy, guileful, insidious, knowing, machiavellian, sly, subtle, tricky, wily. ▷ CRAFTY. **2** adroit, astute, ingenious, skilful. ▷ CLEVER. ● n **1** artfulness, chicanery, craft, craftiness, deceit, deception, deviousness, duplicity, guile, slyness, trickery. **2** cleverness, expertise, ingenuity, skill.

cup n **1** beaker, bowl, chalice, glass, goblet, mug, tankard, teacup, tumbler, wine-glass. **2** award, prize, trophy.

cupboard n cabinet, chiffonier, closet, dresser, filing-cabinet, foodcupboard, larder, locker, sideboard, wardrobe.

curable adj operable, remediable, treatable. Opp INCURABLE.

curb vb bridle, check, contain, control, deter, hamper, hinder, hold back, impede, inhibit, limit, moderate, repress, restrain, restrict, subdue, suppress. Opp ENCOURAGE.

curdle vb clot, coagulate, congeal, go lumpy, go sour, thicken.

cure n **1** antidote, corrective, medication, nostrum, palliative, panacea, prescription, remedy, restorative, solution, therapy, treatment. ▷ MEDICINE. **2** deliverance, healing, recovery, recuperation, restoration, revival. ● vb alleviate, correct, counteract, ease, inf fix, heal, help, mend, palliate, put right, rectify, relieve, remedy, repair, restore, solve, treat. Opp AGGRAVATE.

curiosity n inquisitiveness, interest, interference, meddling, nosiness, prying, snooping.

curious adj **1** inquiring, inquisitive, interested, probing, puzzled, questioning, searching. **2** interfering, intrusive, meddlesome, inf nosy, prying. **3** ▷ STRANGE. **be curious** ▷ PRY.

curl n bend, coil, curve, kink, loop, ringlet, scroll, spiral, swirl, turn, twist, wave, whorl. ● vb **1** bend, coil, corkscrew, curve, entwine, loop, spiral, turn, twine, twist, wind, wreathe, writhe. **2** curl your hair. crimp, frizz, perm.

curly adj crimped, curled, curling, frizzy, fuzzy, kinky, permed, wavy. Opp STRAIGHT.

current adj **1** alive, contemporary, continuing, existing, extant, fashionable, living, modern, ongoing, present, present-day, prevailing, prevalent, reigning, remaining, surviving, inf trendy, up-to-date. **2** current passport. usable, valid. Opp OLD. ● n course, draught, drift, flow, jet, river, stream, tide, trend, undercurrent, undertow.

curriculum *n* course, programme of study, syllabus.

curse *n* blasphemy, exclamation, expletive, imprecation, malediction, oath, obscenity, profanity, swearword. ▷ EVIL. *Opp* BLESSING. ● *vb* blaspheme, damn, fulminate, swear, utter curses. *Opp* BLESS. **cursed** ▷ HATEFUL.

cursory *adj* brief, careless, casual, desultory, fleeting, hasty, hurried, perfunctory, quick, slapdash, superficial. *Opp* THOROUGH.

curt *adj* abrupt, blunt, brief, brusque, concise, crusty, gruff, laconic, monosyllabic, offhand, rude, sharp, short, snappy, succinct, tart, terse, unceremonious, uncommunicative, ungracious. ▷ RUDE. *Opp* EXPANSIVE.

curtail *vb* abbreviate, abridge, break off, contract, cut short, decrease, diminish, *inf* dock, guillotine, halt, lessen, lop, prune, reduce, restrict, shorten, stop, terminate, trim, truncate. *Opp* EXTEND.

curtain *n* blind, drape, drapery, hanging, screen. ● *vb* drape, mask, screen, shroud, veil. ▷ HIDE.

curtsy *vb* bend the knee, bow, genuflect, salaam.

curve *n* arc, arch, bend, bow, bulge, camber, circle, convolution, corkscrew, crescent, curl, curvature, cycloid, loop, meander, spiral, swirl, trajectory, turn, twist, undulation, whorl. ● *vb* arc, arch, bend, bow, bulge, camber, coil, corkscrew, curl, loop, meander, snake, spiral, swerve, swirl, turn, twist, wind. ▷ CIRCLE.

curved *adj* concave, convex, convoluted, crescent, crooked, curvilinear, curving, curvy, rounded, serpentine, shaped, sinuous, sweeping, swelling, tortuous, turned, undulating, whorled.

cushion *n* bean-bag, bolster, hassock, headrest, pad, pillow. ● *vb* absorb, bolster, deaden, lessen, mitigate, muffle, protect from, reduce the effect of, soften, support.

custodian *n* caretaker, curator, guardian, keeper, overseer, superin-tendent, warden, warder, *inf* watchdog, watchman.

custody *n* **1** care, charge, guardianship, keeping, observation, possession, preservation, protection, safekeeping. **2** *in police custody*. captivity, confinement, detention, imprisonment, incarceration, remand.

custom *n* **1** convention, etiquette, fashion, form, formality, habit, institution, manner, observance, policy, practice, procedure, routine, tradition, usage, way, wont. **2** *A shop needs custom*. business, buyers, customers, patronage, support, trade.

customary *adj* accepted, accustomed, common, commonplace, conventional, established, everyday, expected, fashionable, general, habitual, normal, ordinary, popular, prevailing, regular, routine, traditional, typical, usual, wonted. *Opp* UNUSUAL.

customer *n* buyer, client, consumer, patron, purchaser, shopper. *Opp* SELLER.

cut *n* **1** gash, graze, groove, incision, laceration, nick, notch, opening, rent, rip, slash, slice, slit, snick, snip, split, stab, tear. ▷ INJURY. **2** *cut in prices*. cut-back, decrease, fall, lowering, reduction, saving. ● *vb* **1** amputate, axe, carve, chip, chisel, chop, cleave, clip, crop, dice, dissect, divide, dock, engrave, fell, gash, gouge, grate, graze, guillotine, hack, halve, hew, incise, knife, lacerate, lance, lop, mince, mow, nick, notch, open, pare, pierce, poll, pollard, prune, reap, rive, saw, scalp, score, sever, share, shave, shear, shred, slash, slice, slit, snick, snip, split, stab, subdivide, trim, whittle, wound. **2** abbreviate, abridge, bowdlerize, censor, condense, curtail, digest, edit, précis, shorten, summarize, truncate. ▷ REDUCE. **cut and dried** ▷ DEFINITE. **cut in** ▷ INTERRUPT. **cut off** ▷ REMOVE, STOP. **cut short** ▷ CURTAIL.

cutlery *n inf* eating irons. □ *bread-knife, butter-knife, carving knife, cheese knife, dessert-spoon, fish knife, fish fork, fork, knife, ladle, salad servers, spoon, steak knife, tablespoon, teaspoon*.

cutter *n* □ *axe, billhook, chisel, chopper, clippers, harvester, guillotine, lawnmower, mower, saw, scalpel, scissors, scythe, secateurs, shears, sickle.* ▷ KNIFE.

cutting *adj* acute, biting, caustic, incisive, keen, mordant, sarcastic, satirical, sharp, trenchant. ▷ HURTFUL.

cycle *n* **1** circle, repetition, revolution, rotation, round, sequence, series. **2** bicycle, *inf* bike, moped, *inf* motor bike, motor cycle, pennyfarthing, scooter, tandem, tricycle. ● *vb* ▷ TRAVEL.

cyclic *adj* circular, recurring, repeating, repetitive, rotating.

cynical *adj* doubting, *inf* hard, incredulous, misanthropic, mocking, negative, pessimistic, questioning, sceptical, sneering. *Opp* OPTIMISTIC.

D

dabble *vb* **1** dip, paddle, splash, wet. **2** *dabble in a hobby.* potter about, tinker, work casually.

dabbler *n* amateur, dilettante, potterer.

dagger *n* bayonet, blade, *old use* dirk, knife, kris, poniard, stiletto.

daily *adj* diurnal, everyday, quotidian, regular.

dainty *adj* **1** charming, delicate, exquisite, fine, graceful, meticulous, neat, nice, pretty, skilful. **2** choosy, discriminating, fastidious, finicky, fussy, genteel, mincing, sensitive, squeamish, well-mannered. **3** *a dainty morsel.* appealing, appetizing, choice, delectable, delicious. *Opp* CLUMSY, GROSS.

dally *vb* dawdle, delay, *inf* dillydally, hang about, idle, linger, loaf, loiter, play about, procrastinate, saunter, *old use* tarry, waste time.

dam *n* bank, barrage, barrier, dike, embankment, wall, weir. ● *vb* block, check, hold back, obstruct, restrict, stanch, stem, stop.

damage *n* destruction, devastation, harm, havoc, hurt, injury, loss, mutilation, sabotage. ● *vb* **1** blemish, break, buckle, burst, *inf* bust, chip, crack, cripple, deface, destroy, disable, disfigure, *inf* do mischief to, flaw, fracture, harm, hurt, immobilize, impair, incapacitate, injure, make inoperative, make useless, mar, mark, mutilate, *inf* play havoc with, ruin, rupture, sabotage, scar, scratch, spoil, strain, vandalize, warp, weaken, wound, wreck. **damaged** ▷ FAULTY. **damages** ▷ COMPENSATION. **damaging** ▷ HARMFUL.

damn *vb* attack, berate, castigate, censure, condemn, criticize, curse, denounce, doom, execrate, sentence, swear at.

damnation *n* doom, everlasting fire, hell, perdition, ruin. *Opp* SALVATION.

damp *adj* clammy, dank, dewy, dripping, drizzly, foggy, humid, misty, moist, muggy, perspiring, rainy, soggy, steamy, sticky, sweaty, unaired, unventilated, wet, wettish. *Opp* DRY. ● *vb* **1** dampen, humidify, moisten, sprinkle. **2** ▷ DISCOURAGE.

dance *n* choreography, dancing. □ *ball, barn-dance, ceilidh, disco, discothèque, inf hop, inf knees-up, party, inf shindy, social, square dance.* □ *ballet, ballroom dancing, break-dancing, country dancing, disco dancing, flamenco dancing, folk dancing, Latin-American dancing, limbo dancing, morris dancing, old-time dancing, tap-dancing.* □ *bolero, cancan, conga, fandango, fling, foxtrot, gavotte, hornpipe, jig, mazurka, minuet, polka, polonaise, quadrille, quickstep, reel, rumba, square dance, tango, waltz.* ● *vb* caper, cavort, frisk, frolic, gambol, hop about, jig, jive, jump, leap, prance, rock, skip, *joc* trip the light fantastic, whirl.

danger *n* **1** crisis, distress, hazard, insecurity, jeopardy, menace, peril, pitfall, trouble, uncertainty. **2** *danger of frost.* chance, liability, possibility, risk, threat.

dangerous *adj* **1** alarming, breakneck, *inf* chancy, critical, destructive, explosive, grave, *sl* hairy, harmful, hazardous, insecure, menacing, *inf* nasty, noxious, perilous, precarious, reckless, risky, threatening, toxic, uncertain, unsafe. **2** *dangerous men.* desperate, ruthless, treacherous, unmanageable, unpredictable, violent, volatile, wild. *Opp* HARMLESS.

dangle vb be suspended, depend, droop, flap, hang, sway, swing, trail, wave about.

dank adj chilly, clammy, damp, moist, unaired.

dappled adj blotchy, brindled, dotted, flecked, freckled, marbled, motley, mottled, particoloured, patchy, pied, speckled, spotted, stippled, streaked, varicoloured, variegated.

dare vb **1** gamble, have the courage, risk, take a chance, venture. **2** challenge, defy, provoke, taunt. **daring** ▷ BOLD.

dark adj **1** black, blackish, cheerless, clouded, cloudy, coal-black, dim, dingy, dismal, drab, dreary, dull, dusky, funereal, gloomy, glowering, glum, grim, inky, moonless, murky, overcast, pitch-black, pitch-dark, poet sable, shadowy, shady, sombre, starless, stygian, sullen, sunless, tenebrous, unilluminated, unlighted, unlit. **2** dark colours. dense, heavy, strong. **3** dark complexion. black, brown, dark-skinned, dusky, swarthy, tanned. **4** ▷ HIDDEN, MYSTERIOUS. Opp LIGHT, PALE.

darken vb **1** become overcast, cloud over. **2** blacken, dim, eclipse, obscure, overshadow, shade. Opp LIGHTEN.

darling n inf apple of your eye, beloved, inf blue-eyed boy, dear, dearest, favourite, honey, love, loved one, pet, sweet, sweetheart, true love.

dart n arrow, bolt, missile, shaft. ● vb bound, fling, flit, fly, hurtle, leap, move suddenly, shoot, spring, inf whiz, inf zip. ▷ DASH.

dash n **1** chase, race, run, rush, sprint, spurt. ● vb **1** bolt, chase, dart, fly, hasten, hurry, move quickly, race, run, rush, speed, sprint, tear, inf zoom. **2** ▷ HIT.

dashing adj animated, dapper, dynamic, elegant, lively, smart, spirited, stylish, vigorous.

data plur n details, evidence, facts, figures, information, statistics.

date n **1** day. ▷ TIME. **2** date with a friend. appointment, assignation, engagement, fixture, meeting, rendezvous. **out-of-date** ▷ OBSOLETE. **up-to-date** ▷ MODERN.

daunt vb alarm, depress, deter, discourage, dishearten, dismay, intimidate, overawe, put off, unnerve. ▷ FRIGHTEN. Opp ENCOURAGE.

dawdle vb be slow, dally, delay, inf dilly-dally, hang about, idle, lag behind, linger, loaf about, loiter, move slowly, straggle, inf take it easy, inf take your time, trail behind. Opp HURRY.

dawn n day-break, first light, inf peep of day, sunrise. ▷ BEGINNING.

day n **1** daylight, daytime, light. **2** age, epoch, era, period, time.

day-dream n dream, fantasy, hope, illusion, meditation, pipe-dream, reverie, vision, woolgathering. ● vb dream, fantasize, imagine, meditate.

daze vb benumb, paralyse, shock, stun, stupefy. ▷ AMAZE.

dazzle vb blind, confuse, disorientate. **dazzling** ▷ BRILLIANT.

dead adj **1** cold, dead and buried, deceased, departed, inf done for, inanimate, inert, killed, late, lifeless, perished, rigid, stiff. Opp ALIVE. **2** dead language. died out, extinct, obsolete. **3** dead with cold. deadened, insensitive, numb, paralysed, without feeling. **4** dead battery, engine. burnt out, defunct, flat, inoperative, not going, not working, no use, out of order, unresponsive, used up, useless, worn out. **5** a dead party. boring, dull, moribund, slow, uninteresting. Opp LIVELY. **6** dead centre. ▷ EXACT. **dead person** ▷ CORPSE. **dead to the world** ▷ ASLEEP.

deaden vb **1** anaesthetize, desensitize, dull, numb, paralyse. **2** blunt, check, cushion, damp, diminish, hush, lessen, mitigate, muffle, mute, quieten, reduce, smother, soften, stifle, suppress, weaken.

deadlock n halt, impasse, stalemate, standstill, stop, stoppage, tie.

deadly adj dangerous, destructive, fatal, lethal, mortal, noxious, terminal. ▷ HARMFUL. Opp HARMLESS.

deafen vb make deaf, overwhelm. **deafening** ▷ LOUD.

deal n **1** agreement, arrangement, bargain, contract, pact, settlement, transaction, understanding. **2** amount, quantity, volume. ● vb **1** allot, apportion, assign, dispense, distribute, divide, inf dole out, give out, share out. **2** deal someone a blow. administer, apply, deliver, give, inflict, mete out. **3** deal in stocks and shares. buy and sell, do business, trade, traffic. **deal with** ▷ MANAGE, TREAT.

dealer n agent, broker, distributor, merchant, retailer, shopkeeper, stockist, supplier, trader, tradesman, vendor, wholesaler.

dear adj **1** adored, beloved, close, darling, intimate, loved, precious, treasured, valued, venerated. ▷ LOVABLE. Opp HATEFUL. **2** costly, exorbitant, expensive, high-priced, over-priced, inf pricey. Opp CHEAP. ● n ▷ DARLING.

death n **1** decease, demise, dying, loss, passing. ▷ END. **2** casualty, fatality. **put to death** ▷ EXECUTE.

debase vb belittle, commercialize, degrade, demean, depreciate, devalue, diminish, lower the tone of, pollute, reduce the value of, ruin, soil, spoil, sully, vulgarize.

debatable adj arguable, contentious, controversial, controvertible, disputable, doubtful, dubious, moot (point), open to doubt, open to question, problematical, questionable, uncertain, unsettled, unsure. Opp CERTAIN.

debate n argument, conference, consultation, controversy, deliberation, dialectic, discussion, disputation, dispute, polemic. ● vb argue, inf chew over, consider, deliberate, discuss, dispute, inf mull over, question, reflect on, weigh up, wrangle.

debit vb cancel, remove, subtract, take away. Opp CREDIT.

debris n bits, detritus, flotsam, fragments, litter, pieces, remains, rubbish, rubble, ruins, waste, wreckage.

debt n account, arrears, bill, debit, dues, indebtedness, liability, obligation, score, what you owe. **in debt** bankrupt, defaulting, insolvent. ▷ POOR.

decadent adj corrupt, debased, debauched, declining, degenerate, dissolute, immoral, self-indulgent. Opp MORAL.

decay vb atrophy, break down, corrode, crumble, decompose, degenerate, deteriorate, disintegrate, dissolve, fall apart, fester, go bad, go off, mortify, moulder, oxidize, perish, putrefy, rot, shrivel, spoil, waste away, weaken, wither.

deceit n artifice, cheating, chicanery, craftiness, cunning, deceitfulness, dishonesty, dissimulation, double-dealing, duplicity, guile, hypocrisy, insincerity, lying, misrepresentation, pretence, sham, slyness, treachery, trickery, underhandedness, untruthfulness. ▷ DECEPTION. Opp HONESTY.

deceitful adj cheating, crafty, cunning, deceiving, deceptive, designing, dishonest, double-dealing, duplicitous, false, fraudulent, furtive, hypocritical, insincere, lying, secretive, shifty, sneaky, treacherous, inf tricky, inf two-faced, underhand, unfaithful, untrustworthy, wily. Opp HONEST.

deceive vb inf bamboozle, be an impostor, beguile, betray, blind, bluff, cheat, inf con, defraud, delude, inf diddle, double-cross, dupe, fool, inf fox, inf have on, hoax, hoodwink, inf kid, inf lead on, lie, mislead, mystify, inf outsmart, outwit, pretend, swindle, inf take for a ride, inf take in, trick.

decelerate vb brake, decrease speed, go slower, lose speed, slow down. Opp ACCELERATE.

decent adj **1** acceptable, appropriate, becoming, befitting, chaste, courteous, decorous, delicate, fitting, honourable, modest, polite, presentable, proper, pure, respectable, seemly, sensitive, suitable, tasteful. *Opp* INDECENT. **2** [*inf*] *a decent meal.* agreeable, nice, pleasant, satisfactory. ▷ GOOD. *Opp* BAD.

deception *n* bluff, cheat, *inf* con, confidence trick, cover-up, deceit, fake, feint, *inf* fiddle, fraud, hoax, imposture, lie, pretence, ruse, sham, stratagem, subterfuge, swindle, trick, wile. ▷ DECEIT.

deceptive *adj* ambiguous, deceiving, delusive, dishonest, distorted, equivocal, evasive, fallacious, false, fraudulent, illusory, insincere, lying, mendacious, misleading, specious, spurious, treacherous, unreliable, wrong. *Opp* GENUINE.

decide *vb* adjudicate, arbitrate, choose, conclude, determine, elect, fix on, judge, make up your mind, opt for, pick, reach a decision, resolve, select, settle. **decided** ▷ DEFINITE.

decipher *vb* disentangle, *inf* figure out, read, work out. ▷ DECODE.

decision *n* conclusion, decree, finding, judgement, outcome, result, ruling, verdict.

decisive *adj* **1** conclusive, convincing, crucial, final, influential, positive, significant. **2** *decisive action.* certain, confident, decided, definite, determined, firm, forceful, forthright, incisive, resolute, strongminded, sure, unhesitating. *Opp* TENTATIVE.

declaration *n* affirmation, announcement, assertion, avowal, confirmation, deposition, disclosure, edict, manifesto, notice, proclamation, profession, promulgation, pronouncement, protestation, revelation, statement, testimony.

declare *vb* affirm, announce, assert, attest, avow, broadcast, certify, claim, confirm, contend, disclose, emphasize, insist, maintain, make known, proclaim, profess, pronounce, protest, report, reveal, show, state, swear, testify, *inf* trumpet forth, witness. ▷ SAY.

decline *n* decrease, degeneration, deterioration, diminuendo, downturn, drop, fall, falling off, loss, recession, reduction, slump, worsening. ● *vb* **1** decrease, degenerate, deteriorate, die away, diminish, drop away, dwindle, ebb, fail, fall off, flag, lessen, peter out, reduce, shrink, sink, slacken, subside, tail off, taper off, wane, weaken, wilt, worsen. *Opp* IMPROVE. **2** *decline an invitation.* abstain from, forgo, refuse, reject, *inf* turn down, veto. *Opp* ACCEPT.

decode *vb* *inf* crack, decipher, explain, figure out, interpret, make out, read, solve, understand, unravel, unscramble.

decompose *vb* break down, decay, disintegrate, go off, moulder, putrefy, rot.

decorate *vb* **1** adorn, array, beautify, *old use* bedeck, colour, deck, *inf* do up, embellish, embroider, festoon, garnish, make beautiful, ornament, paint, paper, *derog* prettify, refurbish, renovate, smarten up, spruce up, *derog* tart up, trim, wallpaper. **2** give a medal to, honour, reward.

decoration *n* **1** accessories, adornment, arabesque, elaboration, embellishment, finery, flourishes, ornament, ornamentation, trappings, trimmings. **2** award, badge, colours, medal, order, ribbon, star.

decorative *adj* elaborate, fancy, non-functional, ornamental, ornate. *Opp* FUNCTIONAL.

decorous *adj* appropriate, becoming, befitting, correct, dignified, fitting, genteel, polite, presentable, proper, refined, respectable, sedate, seemly, staid, suitable, well-behaved. ▷ DECENT. *Opp* INDECOROUS.

decorum *n* correctness, decency, dignity, etiquette, good form, good manners, gravity, modesty, politeness, propriety, protocol, respectability, seemliness.

decoy *n* bait, distraction, diversion, enticement, inducement, lure, red herring, stool-pigeon, trap. ● *vb* allure, attract, bait, draw, entice, inveigle, lead, lure, seduce, tempt, trick.

decrease n abatement, contraction, curtailment, cut, cut-back, decline, de-escalation, diminuendo, diminution, downturn, drop, dwindling, easing-off, ebb, fall, falling off, lessening, lowering, reduction, shrinkage, wane. *Opp* INCREASE. ● vb **1** abate, curtail, cut, ease off, lower, reduce, slim down, turn down. **2** condense, contract, decline, die away, diminish, dwindle, fall off, lessen, peter out, shrink, slacken, subside, *inf* tail off, taper off, wane. *Opp* INCREASE.

decree n act, command, declaration, dictate, dictum, directive, edict, enactment, fiat, injunction, judgement, law, mandate, order, ordinance, proclamation, promulgation, regulation, ruling, statute. ● vb command, decide, declare, determine, dictate, direct, ordain, order, prescribe, proclaim, promulgate, pronounce, rule.

decrepit adj battered, broken down, derelict, dilapidated, feeble, frail, infirm, ramshackle, tumbledown, weak, worn out. ▷ OLD.

dedicate vb **1** commit, consecrate, devote, give, hallow, pledge, sanctify, set apart. **2** *dedicate a book*. address, inscribe. **dedicated** ▷ KEEN, LOYAL.

dedication n **1** adherence, allegiance, commitment, devotion, enthusiasm, faithfulness, fidelity, loyalty, single-mindedness, zeal. **2** inscription.

deduce vb conclude, divine, draw the conclusion, extrapolate, gather, glean, infer, *inf* put two and two together, reason, surmise, *sl* suss out, understand, work out.

deduct vb *inf* knock off, subtract, take away. *Opp* ADD.

deduction n **1** allowance, decrease, diminution, discount, reduction, removal, subtraction, withdrawal. **2** conclusion, finding, inference, reasoning, result.

deed n **1** accomplishment, achievement, act, action, adventure, effort, endeavour, enterprise, exploit, feat, performance, stunt, undertaking. **2** ▷ DOCUMENT.

deep adj **1** abyssal, bottomless, chasmic, fathomless, profound, unfathomable, unplumbed, yawning. **2** *deep feelings*. earnest, extreme, genuine, heartfelt, intense, serious, sincere. **3** *deep in thought*. absorbed, concentrating, engrossed, immersed, lost, preoccupied, rapt, thoughtful. **4** *deep matters*. abstruse, arcane, esoteric, intellectual, learned, obscure, recondite. ▷ DIFFICULT. **5** *deep sleep*. heavy, sound. **6** *deep colour*. dark, rich, strong, vivid. **7** *deep sound*. bass, booming, growling, low, low-pitched, resonant, reverberating, sonorous. *Opp* SHALLOW, SUPERFICIAL, THIN.

deface vb blemish, damage, disfigure, harm, impair, injure, mar, mutilate, ruin, spoil, vandalize.

defeat n beating, conquest, downfall, *inf* drubbing, failure, humiliation, *inf* licking, overthrow, *inf* put-down, rebuff, repulse, reverse, rout, setback, subjugation, thrashing, trouncing. *Opp* VICTORY. ● vb baulk, beat, best, be victorious over, check, checkmate, *inf* clobber, confound, conquer, crush, destroy, *inf* flatten, foil, frustrate, get the better of, *sl* hammer, *inf* lay low, *inf* lick, master, outdo, outvote, outwit, overcome, overpower, overthrow, overwhelm, prevail over, put down, quell, repulse, rout, ruin, *inf* smash, stop, subdue, subjugate, suppress, *inf* thrash, thwart, triumph over, trounce, vanquish, whip, win a victory over. *Opp* LOSE. **be defeated** ▷ LOSE. **defeated** ▷ UNSUCCESSFUL.

defect n blemish, *computing* bug, deficiency, error, failing, fault, flaw, imperfection, inadequacy, irregularity, lack, mark, mistake, shortcoming, shortfall, spot, stain, want, weakness, weak point. ● vb change sides, desert, go over.

defective adj broken, deficient, faulty, flawed, *inf* gone wrong, imper-

defy

fect, incomplete, *inf* on the blink, unsatisfactory, wanting, weak. *Opp* PERFECT.

defence *n* **1** cover, deterrence, guard, protection, safeguard, security, shelter, shield. ▷ BARRIER. **2** alibi, apologia, apology, case, excuse, explanation, justification, plea, testimony, vindication.

defenceless *adj* exposed, helpless, impotent, insecure, powerless, unguarded, unprotected, vulnerable, weak.

defend *vb* **1** cover, fight for, fortify, guard, keep safe, preserve, protect, safeguard, screen, secure, shelter, shield, *inf* stick up for, watch over. **2** argue for, champion, justify, plead for, speak up for, stand by, stand up for, support, uphold, vindicate. *Opp* ATTACK.

defendant *n* accused, appellant, offender, prisoner.

defensive *adj* **1** cautious, defending, protective, wary, watchful. **2** apologetic, faint-hearted, self-justifying. *Opp* AGGRESSIVE.

defer *vb* **1** adjourn, delay, hold over, lay aside, postpone, prorogue (*parliament*), put off, *inf* shelve, suspend. **2** ▷ YIELD.

deference *n* acquiescence, compliance, obedience, submission. ▷ RESPECT.

defiant *adj* aggressive, antagonistic, belligerent, bold, brazen, challenging, daring, disobedient, headstrong, insolent, insubordinate, mutinous, obstinate, rebellious, recalcitrant, refractory, self-willed, stubborn, truculent, uncooperative, unruly, unyielding. *Opp* COOPERATIVE.

deficient *adj* defective, inadequate, insufficient, lacking, meagre, scanty, scarce, short, sketchy, unsatisfactory, wanting, weak. *Opp* ADEQUATE, EXCESSIVE.

defile *vb* contaminate, corrupt, degrade, desecrate, dirty, dishonour, foul, infect, make dirty, poison, pollute, soil, stain, sully, taint, tarnish.

define *vb* **1** be the boundary of, bound, circumscribe, delineate, demarcate, describe, determine, fix, limit, mark off, mark out, outline, specify. **2** *define a word.* clarify, explain, formulate, give the meaning of, interpret, spell out.

definite *adj* apparent, assured, categorical, certain, clear, clear-cut, confident, confirmed, cut-and-dried, decided, determined, discernible, distinct, emphatic, exact, explicit, express, fixed, incisive, marked, noticeable, obvious, particular, perceptible, plain, positive, precise, pronounced, settled, specific, sure, unambiguous, unequivocal, unmistakable, well-defined. *Opp* VAGUE.

definitely *adv* beyond doubt, certainly, doubtless, for certain, indubitably, positively, surely, unquestionably, without doubt, without fail.

definition *n* **1** clarification, elucidation, explanation, interpretation. **2** clarity, clearness, focus, precision, sharpness.

definitive *adj* agreed, authoritative, complete, conclusive, correct, decisive, final, last (*word*), official, permanent, reliable, settled, standard, ultimate, unconditional. *Opp* PROVISIONAL.

deflect *vb* avert, deviate, divert, fend off, head off, intercept, parry, prevent, sidetrack, swerve, switch, turn aside, veer, ward off.

deformed *adj* bent, buckled, contorted, crippled, crooked, defaced, disfigured, distorted, gnarled, grotesque, malformed, mangled, misshapen, mutilated, twisted, ugly, warped.

defraud *vb* *inf* con, *inf* diddle, embezzle, *inf* fleece, rob, swindle. ▷ CHEAT.

deft *adj* adept, adroit, agile, clever, dextrous, expert, handy, neat, *inf* nifty, nimble, proficient, quick, skilful. *Opp* CLUMSY.

defy *vb* **1** challenge, confront, dare, disobey, face up to, flout, *inf* kick against, rebel against, refuse to obey,

resist, stand up to, withstand. **2**
baffle, beat, defeat, elude, foil, frustrate, repel, repulse, resist, thwart,
withstand.

degenerate *adj* ▷ CORRUPT. ● *vb*
become worse, decline, deteriorate,
inf go to the dogs, regress, retrogress,
sink, slip, weaken, worsen. *Opp*
IMPROVE.

degrade *vb* **1** cashier, demote,
depose, downgrade. **2** abase, brutalize, cheapen, corrupt, debase, dehumanize, deprave, desensitize,
dishonour, harden, humiliate, mortify. **degrading** ▷ SHAMEFUL.

degree *n* **1** calibre, class, grade,
order, position, rank, standard,
standing, station, status. **2** extent,
intensity, level, measure.

deify *vb* idolize, treat as a god, venerate, worship.

deign *vb* concede, condescend,
demean yourself, lower yourself,
stoop, vouchsafe.

deity *n* creator, divinity, god, goddess, godhead, idol, immortal,
power, spirit, supreme being.

dejected *adj* depressed, disconsolate, dispirited, down, downcast,
downhearted, heavy-hearted, in low
spirits. ▷ SAD.

delay *n* check, deferment, deferral,
filibuster, hiatus, hitch, hold-up,
interruption, moratorium, pause,
postponement, setback, stay (*of execution*), stoppage, wait. ● *vb* **1** check,
defer, detain, halt, hinder, hold over,
hold up, impede, keep back, keep
waiting, make late, obstruct, postpone, put back, put off, retard, set
back, slow down, stay, stop, suspend.
2 be late, be slow, *inf* bide your time,
dally, dawdle, *inf* dilly-dally, *inf* drag
your feet, *inf* get bogged down, hang
about, hang back, hang fire, hesitate,
lag, linger, loiter, mark time, pause,
inf play for time, procrastinate, stall,
old use tarry, temporize, vacillate,
wait. *Opp* HURRY.

delegate *n* agent, ambassador,
emissary, envoy, go-between, legate,
messenger, nuncio, plenipotentiary,

representative, spokesperson. ● *vb*
appoint, assign, authorize, charge,
commission, depute, designate,
empower, entrust, mandate, nominate.

delegation *n* commission, deputation, mission.

delete *vb* blot out, cancel, cross out,
cut out, edit out, efface, eliminate,
eradicate, erase, expunge, obliterate,
remove, rub out, strike out, wipe out.

deliberate *adj* **1** arranged, calculated, cold-blooded, conscious, contrived, culpable, designed, intended,
intentional, knowing, malicious,
organized, planned, prearranged,
preconceived, premeditated, prepared, purposeful, studied, thought
out, wilful, worked out. **2** careful,
cautious, circumspect, considered,
diligent, measured, methodical,
orderly, painstaking, regular, slow,
thoughtful, unhurried, watchful. *Opp*
HASTY, INSTINCTIVE. ● *vb* ▷ THINK.

delicacy *n* **1** accuracy, care, cleverness, daintiness, discrimination,
exquisiteness, fineness, finesse,
fragility, intricacy, precision, sensitivity, subtlety, tact. **2** *delicacies to
eat.* rarity, speciality, treat.

delicate *adj* **1** dainty, diaphanous,
easily broken, easily damaged, elegant, exquisite, feathery, fine, flimsy,
fragile, frail, gauzy, gentle, intricate,
light, sensitive, slender, soft, tender.
Opp TOUGH. **2** *delicate work.* accurate,
careful, clever, deft, precise, skilled.
Opp CLUMSY. **3** *delicate flavour, colour.*
faint, mild, muted, pale, slight,
subtle. **4** *delicate health.* feeble, puny,
sickly, squeamish, unhealthy, weak.
5 *delicate problem.* awkward, confidential, embarrassing, private,
problematical, prudish, *inf* sticky,
ticklish, touchy. **6** *delicate handling.*
considerate, diplomatic, discreet,
judicious, prudent, sensitive, tactful.
Opp CRUDE.

delicious *adj* appetizing, choice,
delectable, enjoyable, luscious, *inf*
mouth-watering, *inf* nice, palatable,
savoury, *inf* scrumptious, succulent,

tasty, tempting, toothsome, *sl* yummy.

delight *n* bliss, delectation, ecstasy, enchantment, enjoyment, felicity, gratification, happiness, joy, paradise, pleasure, rapture, satisfaction. ● *vb* amuse, bewitch, captivate, charm, cheer, divert, enchant, enrapture, entertain, enthral, entrance, fascinate, gladden, gratify, please, ravish, thrill, transport. *Opp* DISMAY. **delighted** ▷ HAPPY, PLEASED.

delightful *adj* agreeable, attractive, captivating, charming, congenial, delectable, diverting, enjoyable, *inf* nice, pleasant, pleasing, pleasurable, rewarding, satisfying, spell-binding. ▷ BEAUTIFUL.

delinquent *n* culprit, defaulter, hooligan, lawbreaker, malefactor, miscreant, offender, roughneck, ruffian, *inf* tear-away, vandal, wrongdoer, young offender. ▷ CRIMINAL.

delirious *adj inf* beside yourself, crazy, demented, deranged, distracted, ecstatic, excited, feverish, frantic, frenzied, hysterical, incoherent, irrational, light-headed, rambling, wild. ▷ DRUNK, MAD. *Opp* SANE, SOBER.

deliver *vb* **1** bear, bring, carry, cart, convey, distribute, give out, hand over, make over, present, purvey, supply, surrender, take round, transfer, transport, turn over. **2** *deliver a lecture.* announce, broadcast, express, give, make, read. ▷ SPEAK. **3** *deliver a blow.* administer, aim, deal, direct, fire, inflict, launch, strike, throw. ▷ HIT. **4** ▷ RESCUE.

delivery *n* **1** conveyance, dispatch, distribution, shipment, transmission, transportation. **2** *a delivery of goods.* batch, consignment. **3** *delivery of a speech.* enunciation, execution, implementation, performance, presentation. **4** childbirth, confinement, parturition.

deluge *n* downpour, flood, inundation, rainfall, rainstorm, rush, spate. ● *vb* drown, engulf, flood, inundate, overwhelm, submerge, swamp.

delusion *n* dream, fantasy, hallucination, illusion, mirage, misconception, mistake, self-deception.

delve *vb* burrow, dig, explore, investigate, probe, research, search.

demand *n old use* behest, claim, command, desire, expectation, importunity, insistence, need, order, request, requirement, requisition, want. ● *vb* call for, claim, cry out for, exact, expect, insist on, necessitate, order, request, require, requisition, want. ▷ ASK. **demanding** ▷ DIFFICULT, IMPORTUNATE. **in demand** ▷ POPULAR.

demean *vb* abase, cheapen, debase, degrade, disgrace, humble, humiliate, lower, make (yourself) cheap, *inf* put (yourself) down, sacrifice (your) pride, undervalue. **demeaning** ▷ SHAMEFUL.

democratic *adj* **1** classless, egalitarian. **2** chosen, elected, elective, popular, representative. *Opp* TOTALITARIAN.

demolish *vb* break down, bulldoze, dismantle, flatten, knock down, level, pull down, raze, tear down, topple, undo, wreck. ▷ DESTROY. *Opp* BUILD.

demon *n* devil, evil spirit, fiend, goblin, imp, spirit.

demonstrable *adj* conclusive, confirmable, evident, incontrovertible, indisputable, irrefutable, palpable, positive, provable, undeniable, unquestionable, verifiable.

demonstrate *vb* **1** confirm, describe, display, embody, establish, evince, exemplify, exhibit, explain, expound, express, illustrate, indicate, manifest, prove, represent, show, substantiate, teach, typify, verify. **2** lobby, march, parade, picket, protest, rally.

demonstration *n* **1** confirmation, description, display, evidence, exhibition, experiment, expression, illustration, indication, manifestation, presentation, proof, representation, show, substantiation, test, trial, verification. **2** *inf* demo, march, parade, picket, protest, rally, sit-in, vigil.

demonstrative adj affectionate, effusive, emotional, fulsome, loving, open, uninhibited, unreserved, unrestrained. Opp RETICENT.

demote vb downgrade, put down, reduce, relegate. Opp PROMOTE.

demure adj bashful, coy, diffident, modest, prim, quiet, reserved, reticent, retiring, sedate, shy, sober, staid. Opp CONCEITED.

den n hideaway, hide-out, hiding-place, hole, lair, private place, retreat, sanctuary, secret place, shelter.

denial n abnegation, contradiction, disavowal, disclaimer, negation, refusal, refutation, rejection, renunciation, repudiation, veto. Opp ADMISSION.

denigrate vb belittle, blacken the reputation of, criticize, decry, disparage, impugn, malign, inf put down, inf run down, sneer at, speak slightingly of, traduce, inf turn your nose up, vilify. ▷ DESPISE. Opp PRAISE.

denomination n 1 category, class, classification, designation, kind, size, sort, species, type, value. 2 church, communion, creed, cult, order, persuasion, schism, school, sect.

denote vb be the sign for, designate, express, indicate, mean, represent, signal, signify, stand for, symbolize.

denouement n climax, inf pay-off, resolution, solution, inf sorting out, inf tidying up, unravelling. ▷ END.

denounce vb accuse, attack verbally, betray, blame, brand, censure, complain about, condemn, criticize, declaim against, decry, fulminate against, inf hold forth against, impugn, incriminate, inform against, inveigh against, pillory, report, reveal, stigmatize, inf tell off, vilify, vituperate. Opp PRAISE.

dense adj 1 close, compact, concentrated, heavy, impassable, impenetrable, inf jam-packed, lush, massed, packed, solid, thick, tight, viscous. Opp THIN. 2 ▷ STUPID.

dent n concavity, depression, dimple, dint, dip, hollow, indentation, pit. ● vb bend, buckle, crumple, knock in.

denude vb bare, defoliate, deforest, expose, remove, strip, unclothe, uncover. Opp CLOTHE.

deny vb 1 contradict, controvert, disagree with, disclaim, disown, dispute, gainsay, negate, oppose, rebuff, refute, reject, repudiate. Opp AGREE. 2 begrudge, deprive of, disallow, refuse, withhold. Opp GRANT. **deny yourself** ▷ ABSTAIN.

depart vb 1 abscond, begin a journey, inf check out, inf clear off, decamp, disappear, embark, emigrate, escape, exit, go away, sl hit the road, leave, make off, inf make tracks, inf make yourself scarce, migrate, move away, move off, inf push off, quit, retire, retreat, run away, run off, sl scarper, sl scram, set forth, set off, set out, start, take your leave, vanish, withdraw. 2 ▷ DEVIATE. **departed** ▷ DEAD.

department n 1 branch, division, office, part, section, sector, subdivision, unit. 2 [inf] not my department. area, concern, domain, field, function, job, line, province, responsibility, specialism, sphere.

departure n disappearance, embarkation, escape, exit, exodus, going, retirement, retreat, withdrawal. Opp ARRIVAL.

depend vb **depend on** inf bank on, be dependent on, count on, hinge on, need, pivot on, put your faith in, inf reckon on, rely on, rest on, trust.

dependable adj conscientious, consistent, faithful, honest, regular, reliable, safe, sound, steady, true, trustworthy, unfailing. Opp UNRELIABLE.

dependence n 1 confidence, need, reliance, trust. 2 ▷ ADDICTION.

dependent adj **dependent on 1** conditional on, connected with, controlled by, determined by, liable to, relative to, subject to, vulnerable to. Opp INDEPENDENT. **2** dependent on *drugs*. addicted to, enslaved by, *inf* hooked on, reliant on.

depict *vb* delineate, describe, draw, illustrate, narrate, outline, paint, picture, portray, represent, reproduce, show, sketch.

deplete *vb* consume, cut, decrease, drain, lessen, reduce, use up. *Opp* INCREASE.

deplorable *adj* awful, blameworthy, discreditable, disgraceful, disreputable, dreadful, execrable, lamentable, regrettable, reprehensible, scandalous, shameful, shocking, unfortunate, unworthy. ▷ BAD. *Opp* COMMENDABLE.

deplore *vb* **1** grieve over, lament, mourn, regret. **2** ▷ CONDEMN.

deploy *vb* arrange, bring into action, distribute, manage, position, use systematically, utilize.

deport *vb* banish, exile, expatriate, expel, remove, send abroad, transport.

depose *vb* demote, dethrone, dismiss, displace, get rid of, oust, remove, *inf* topple.

deposit *n* **1** advance payment, downpayment, initial payment, part-payment, retainer, security, stake. **2** accumulation, alluvium, dregs, layer, lees, precipitate, sediment, silt, sludge. ● *vb* **1** drop, *inf* dump, lay down, leave, *inf* park, place, precipitate, put down, set down. **2** *deposit money*. bank, pay in, save.

depot *n* **1** arsenal, base, cache, depository, dump, hoard, store, storehouse. **2** *bus depot*. garage, headquarters, station, terminus.

deprave *vb* brutalize, corrupt, debase, degrade, influence, pervert. **depraved** ▷ CORRUPT.

depreciate *vb* **1** become less, decrease, deflate, drop, fall, go down, lessen, lower, reduce, slump, weaken. *Opp* APPRECIATE. **2** ▷ DISPARAGE.

depress *vb* **1** burden, cast down, discourage, dishearten, dismay, dispirit, enervate, grieve, lower the spirits of, make sad, oppress, sadden, tire,

upset, weary. *Opp* CHEER. **2** *depress the market*. bring down, deflate, make less active, push down, undermine, weaken. *Opp* BOOST. **depressed**, **depressing** ▷ SAD.

depression *n* **1** *inf* blues, dejection, desolation, despair, despondency, gloom, glumness, heaviness, hopelessness, low spirits, melancholy, misery, pessimism, sadness, weariness. *Opp* HAPPINESS. **2** cavity, concavity, dent, dimple, dip, excavation, hole, hollow, impression, indentation, pit, recess, rut, sunken area. *Opp* BUMP. **3** *economic depression*. decline, hard times, recession, slump. *Opp* BOOM, HIGH.

deprive *vb* deprive of deny, dispossess of, prevent from using, refuse, rob of, starve of, strip of, take away, withdraw, withhold. **deprived** ▷ POOR.

deputize *vb* deputize for act as deputy, act as stand-in for, cover for, do the job of, replace, represent, stand in for, substitute for, take over from, understudy.

deputy *n* agent, ambassador, assistant, delegate, emissary, *inf* fill-in, locum, proxy, relief, replacement, representative, reserve, second-in-command, spokesperson, *inf* stand-in, substitute, supply, surrogate, understudy, vice-captain, vice-president.

derelict *adj* abandoned, broken down, decrepit, deserted, desolate, dilapidated, forgotten, forlorn, forsaken, neglected, overgrown, ruined, run-down, tumbledown, uncared-for, untended.

derivation *n* ancestry, descent, etymology, extraction, origin, root. ▷ BEGINNING.

derive *vb* acquire, borrow, collect, crib, draw, extract, gain, gather, get, glean, *inf* lift, obtain, pick up, procure, receive, secure, take. **be derived** ▷ ORIGINATE.

descend *vb* **1** climb down, come down, drop, fall, go down, move down, plummet, plunge, sink, swoop down. **2** decline, dip, incline, slant, slope. **3** alight, disembark, dismount, get down, get off. *Opp* ASCEND. **be descended** ▷ ORIGINATE. **descend on** ▷ ATTACK.

descendant *n* child, heir, scion, successor. *Opp* ANCESTOR. **descendants** family, issue, line, lineage, offspring, posterity, progeny, *old use* seed.

descent *n* **1** declivity, dip, drop, fall, incline, slant, slope, way down. *Opp* ASCENT. **2** *aristocratic descent*. ancestry, background, blood, derivation, extraction, family, genealogy, heredity, lineage, origin, parentage, pedigree, stock, strain.

describe *vb* **1** characterize, define, delineate, depict, detail, explain, express, give an account of, narrate, outline, portray, present, recount, relate, report, represent, sketch, speak of, tell about. **2** *describe a circle*. draw, mark out, trace.

description *n* account, characterization, commentary, definition, delineation, depiction, explanation, narration, outline, portrait, portrayal, report, representation, sketch, story, word-picture.

descriptive *adj* colourful, detailed, explanatory, expressive, graphic, illustrative, pictorial, vivid.

desecrate *vb* abuse, contaminate, corrupt, debase, defile, degrade, dishonour, pervert, pollute, profane, treat blasphemously, treat disrespectfully, treat irreverently, vandalize, violate, vitiate. *Opp* REVERE.

desert *adj* arid, barren, desolate, dry, infertile, isolated, lonely, sterile, uncultivated, unfrequented, uninhabited, waterless, wild. *Opp* FERTILE. ● *n* dust bowl, wasteland, wilderness. ● *vb* **1** abandon, betray, forsake, give up, jilt, leave, *inf* leave in the lurch, maroon, quit, *inf* rat on, renounce, strand, vacate, *inf* walk out on, *inf* wash your hands of. **2** abscond, decamp, defect, go absent, run away. **deserted** ▷ EMPTY, LONELY.

deserter *n* absconder, absentee, apostate, backslider, betrayer, defector, escapee, fugitive, outlaw, renegade, runaway, traitor, truant, turncoat.

deserve *vb* be good enough for, be worthy of, earn, justify, merit, rate, warrant. **deserving** ▷ WORTHY.

design *n* **1** blueprint, conception, draft, drawing, model, pattern, plan, proposal, prototype, sketch. **2** mark, style, type, version. **3** arrangement, composition, configuration, form, pattern, shape. **4** *wander without design*. aim, end, goal, intention, object, objective, purpose, scheme. ● *vb* conceive, construct, contrive, create, delineate, devise, draft, draw, draw up, fashion, form, intend, invent, lay out, make, map out, originate, outline, plan, plot, project, propose, scheme, shape, sketch, think up. **designing** ▷ CRAFTY. **have designs** ▷ PLOT.

designer *n* architect, artist, author, contriver, creator, deviser, inventor, originator.

desire *n* **1** ache, ambition, appetite, craving, fancy, hankering, hunger, *inf* itch, longing, requirement, thirst, urge, want, wish, yearning, *inf* yen. **2** avarice, covetousness, cupidity, greed, miserliness, rapacity. **3** *sexual desire*. ardour, libido, love, lust, passion. ● *vb* ache for, ask for, aspire to, covet, crave, dream of, fancy, hanker after, *inf* have a yen for, hope for, hunger for, *inf* itch for, like, long for, lust after, need, pine for, prefer, pursue, *inf* set your heart on, set your sights on, strive after, thirst for, want, wish for, yearn for.

desolate *adj* **1** abandoned, bare, barren, benighted, bleak, cheerless, depressing, deserted, dismal, dreary, empty, forsaken, gloomy, *inf* god-forsaken, inhospitable, isolated, lonely, remote, unfrequented, uninhabited, wild, windswept. **2** bereft, companionless, dejected, depressed, despairing, disconsolate, distressed, forlorn, forsaken, inconsolable, lonely, melancholy, miserable, neglected, solitary, suicidal, wretched. ▷ SAD. *Opp* CHEERFUL.

despair n anguish, dejection, depression, desperation, despondency, hopelessness, pessimism, resignation, wretchedness. ▷ MISERY. ● vb give in, give up, lose heart, lose hope, quit, surrender. Opp HOPE.

desperate adj 1 inf at your wits' end, beyond hope, despairing, inconsolable, wretched. 2 desperate situation. acute, bad, critical, dangerous, drastic, grave, hopeless, irretrievable, pressing, serious, severe, urgent. 3 desperate criminals. dangerous, foolhardy, impetuous, rash, reckless, violent, wild. 4 ▷ ANXIOUS.

despise vb be contemptuous of, condemn, deride, disapprove of, disdain, feel contempt for, hate, have a low opinion of, look down on, inf put down, scorn, sneer at, spurn, undervalue. ▷ DENIGRATE. Opp ADMIRE.

despondent adj dejected, depressed, discouraged, disheartened, down, downcast, inf down in the mouth, melancholy, morose, pessimistic, sad, sorrowful. ▷ MISERABLE.

despotic adj absolute, arbitrary, authoritarian, autocratic, dictatorial, domineering, oppressive, totalitarian, tyrannical. Opp DEMOCRATIC.

destination n goal, objective, purpose, stopping-place, target, terminus.

destined adj 1 foreordained, ineluctable, inescapable, inevitable, intended, ordained, predestined, predetermined, preordained, unavoidable. 2 destined to fail. bound, certain, doomed, fated, meant.

destiny n chance, doom, fate, fortune, karma, kismet, lot, luck, providence.

destitute adj bankrupt, deprived, down-and-out, homeless, impecunious, impoverished, indigent, insolvent, needy, penniless, poverty-stricken, inf skint. ▷ POOR. Opp WEALTHY.

destroy vb abolish, annihilate, blast, break down, burst, inf bust, crush, inf decimate, demolish, devastate, devour, dismantle, dispose of, do away with, eliminate, eradicate, erase, exterminate, extinguish, extirpate, finish off, flatten, fragment, get rid of, knock down, lay waste, level, liquidate, make useless, nullify, pull down, pulverize, put out of existence, raze, root out, ruin, sabotage, sack, scuttle, shatter, smash, stamp out, undo, uproot, vaporize, wipe out, wreck, write off. ▷ DEFEAT, END, KILL. Opp CONSERVE, CREATE.

destruction n annihilation, damage, inf decimation, demolition, depredation, devastation, elimination, end, eradication, erasure, extermination, extinction, extirpation, havoc, holocaust, liquidation, overthrow, pulling down, ruin, ruination, shattering, smashing, undoing, uprooting, wiping out, wrecking. ▷ KILLING. Opp CONSERVATION, CREATION.

destructive adj adverse, antagonistic, baleful, baneful, calamitous, catastrophic, damaging, dangerous, deadly, deleterious, detrimental, devastating, disastrous, fatal, harmful, injurious, internecine, lethal, malignant, negative, pernicious, pestilential, ruinous, violent. Opp CONSTRUCTIVE.

detach vb cut loose, cut off, disconnect, disengage, disentangle, divide, free, isolate, part, pull off, release, remove, segregate, separate, sever, take off, tear off, uncouple, undo, unfasten, unfix, unhitch. Opp ATTACH. **detached** ▷ ALOOF, IMPARTIAL, SEPARATE.

detail n aspect, circumstance, complexity, complication, component, element, fact, factor, feature, ingredient, intricacy, item, plur minutiae, nicety, particular, point, refinement, respect, specific, technicality.

detailed adj inf blow-by-blow, complete, complex, comprehensive, descriptive, exact, exhaustive, full, derog fussy, giving all details, derog hair-splitting, intricate, itemized, minute, particularized, specific. Opp GENERAL.

detain vb 1 arrest, capture, confine, gaol, hold, imprison, intern. 2 buttonhole, delay, hinder, hold up, impede, keep, keep waiting, restrain, retard, slow, stop, waylay.

detect *vb* ascertain, become aware of, diagnose, discern, discover, expose, feel, *inf* ferret out, find, hear, identify, locate, note, notice, observe, perceive, *inf* put your finger on, recognize, reveal, scent, see, sense, sight, smell, sniff out, spot, spy, taste, track down, uncover, unearth, unmask.

detective *n* investigator, policeman, policewoman, *inf* private eye, sleuth, *inf* snooper.

detention *n* captivity, confinement, custody, imprisonment, incarceration, internment.

deter *vb* check, daunt, discourage, dismay, dissuade, frighten off, hinder, impede, intimidate, obstruct, prevent, put off, repel, send away, stop, *inf* turn off, warn off. *Opp* ENCOURAGE.

deteriorate *vb* crumble, decay, decline, degenerate, depreciate, disintegrate, fall off, get worse, *inf* go downhill, lapse, relapse, slip, weaken, worsen. *Opp* IMPROVE.

determination *n* *inf* backbone, commitment, courage, dedication, doggedness, drive, firmness, fortitude, *inf* grit, *inf* guts, perseverance, persistence, pertinacity, resoluteness, resolution, resolve, single-mindedness, spirit, steadfastness, *derog* stubbornness, tenacity, willpower.

determine *vb* **1** arbitrate, clinch, conclude, decide, establish, find out, identify, judge, settle. **2** choose, decide on, fix on, resolve, select. **3** *What determined your choice?* affect, condition, dictate, govern, influence, regulate.

determined *adj* adamant, assertive, bent (*on success*), certain, convinced, decided, decisive, definite, dogged, firm, insistent, intent, *derog* obstinate, persistent, pertinacious, purposeful, resolute, resolved, single-minded, steadfast, strong-minded, strong-willed, *derog* stub-

born, sure, tenacious, tough, unwavering. *Opp* IRRESOLUTE.

deterrent *n* barrier, caution, check, curb, difficulty, discouragement, disincentive, dissuasion, hindrance, impediment, obstacle, restraint, threat, *inf* turn-off, warning. *Opp* ENCOURAGEMENT.

detest *vb* abhor, abominate, despise, execrate, loathe. ▷ HATE.

detour *n* deviation, diversion, indirect route, roundabout route. **make a detour** ▷ DEVIATE.

detract *vb* **detract from** diminish, lessen, lower, reduce, take away from.

detrimental *adj* damaging, deleterious, disadvantageous, harmful, hurtful, inimical, injurious, prejudicial, unfavourable. *Opp* ADVANTAGEOUS.

devastate *vb* **1** damage severely, demolish, destroy, flatten, lay waste, level, obliterate, overwhelm, ravage, raze, ruin, sack, waste, wreck. **2** ▷ DISMAY.

develop *vb* **1** advance, age, arise, *inf* blow up, come into existence, evolve, flourish, get better, grow, improve, mature, move on, progress, ripen. *Opp* REGRESS. **2** *develop habits*. acquire, contract, cultivate, evolve, foster, get, pick up. **3** *develop ideas*. amplify, augment, elaborate, enlarge on, expatiate on, unfold, work up. **4** *business developed*. branch out, build up, diversify, enlarge, expand, extend, increase, swell.

development *n* **1** advance, betterment, change, enlargement, evolution, expansion, extension, *inf* forward march, furtherance, gain, growth, improvement, increase, progress, promotion, regeneration, reinforcement, spread. **2** happening, incident, occurrence, outcome, result, upshot. **3** *industrial development*. building, conversion, exploitation, use.

deviate *vb* branch off, depart, digress, diverge, drift, err, go astray, go round, make a detour, stray, swerve, turn aside, turn off, vary, veer, wander.

device n **1** apparatus, appliance, contraption, contrivance, gadget, implement, instrument, invention, machine, tool, utensil. **2** dodge, expedient, gambit, gimmick, manoeuvre, plan, ploy, ruse, scheme, stratagem, stunt, tactic, trick, wile. **3** *heraldic device.* badge, crest, design, figure, logo, motif, shield, sign, symbol, token.

devil n demon, fiend, imp, spirit. **The Devil** the Adversary, Beelzebub, the Evil One, Lucifer, Mephistopheles, *inf* Old Nick, the Prince of Darkness, Satan.

devilish adj demoniac(al), demonic, diabolic(al), fiendish, hellish, impish, infernal, inhuman, Mephisophelian, satanic. ▷ EVIL. *Opp* ANGELIC.

devious adj **1** circuitous, crooked, deviating, indirect, periphrastic, rambling, round-about, sinuous, tortuous, wandering, winding. **2** [*derog*] calculating, cunning, deceitful, evasive, insincere, misleading, scheming, *inf* slippery, sly, sneaky, treacherous, underhand, wily. ▷ DISHONEST. *Opp* DIRECT.

devise vb arrange, conceive, concoct, contrive, *inf* cook up, create, design, engineer, form, formulate, frame, imagine, invent, make up, plan, plot, prepare, project, scheme, think out, think up, work out.

devoted adj committed, dedicated, enthusiastic, faithful, loving, staunch, true, unswerving, wholehearted, zealous. ▷ LOYAL. *Opp* DISLOYAL, HALF-HEARTED.

devotee n *inf* addict, aficionado, *inf* buff, enthusiast, fan, follower, *sl* freak, supporter.

devotion n allegiance, attachment, commitment, dedication, devotedness, enthusiasm, fanaticism, fervour, loyalty, zeal. ▷ LOVE, PIETY.

devour vb consume, demolish, eat up, engulf, swallow up, take in. ▷ DESTROY, EAT.

devout adj God-fearing, godly, holy, religious, sincere, spiritual. ▷ PIOUS. *Opp* IRRELIGIOUS.

dexterous adj adroit, agile, deft, nimble, quick, sharp, skilful. ▷ CLEVER. *Opp* CLUMSY.

diabolical adj evil, fiendish, inhuman, satanic, wicked. ▷ DEVILISH. *Opp* SAINTLY.

diagnose vb detect, determine, distinguish, find, identify, isolate, name, pinpoint, recognize.

diagnosis n analysis, conclusion, explanation, identification, interpretation, opinion, pronouncement, verdict.

diagram n chart, drawing, figure, flow-chart, graph, illustration, outline, picture, plan, representation, sketch, table.

dial n clock, digital display, face, instrument, pointer, speedometer.

dialect n accent, argot, brogue, cant, creole, idiom, jargon, language, patois, phraseology, pronunciation, register, slang, speech, tongue, vernacular.

dialogue n *inf* chat, *inf* chin-wag, colloquy, communication, conference, conversation, debate, discourse, discussion, duologue, exchange, interchange, *old use* intercourse, meeting, oral communication, talk, *inf* tête-à-tête.

diary n annals, appointment book, calendar, chronicle, engagement book, journal, log, record.

dictate vb **1** read aloud, speak slowly. **2** command, decree, direct, enforce, give orders, impose, *inf* lay down the law, make the rules, ordain, order, prescribe, state categorically.

dictator n autocrat, *inf* Big Brother, despot, tyrant. ▷ RULER.

dictatorial adj absolute, arbitrary, authoritarian, autocratic, *inf* bossy, despotic, dogmatic, dominant, domineering, illiberal, imperious, intolerant, omnipotent, oppressive, overbearing, repressive, totalitarian, tyrannical, undemocratic. *Opp* DEMO-CRATIC.

dictionary *n* concordance, glossary, lexicon, thesaurus, vocabulary, word-book.

didactic *adj* instructive, lecturing, pedagogic, pedantic.

die *vb* **1** *inf* bite the dust, *inf* breathe your last, cease to exist, come to the end, decease, depart, expire, fall, *inf* give up the ghost, *sl* kick the bucket, lay down your life, lose your life, pass away, *sl* peg out, perish, *sl* pop off, *sl* snuff it, starve. **2** decline, decrease, die away, disappear, droop, dwindle, ebb, end, fade, fail, fizzle out, go out, languish, lessen, peter out, stop, sub-side, vanish, wane, weaken, wilt, wither.

diet *n* fare, food, intake, nourish-ment, nutriment, nutrition, susten-ance. ● *vb* abstain, *inf* cut down, deny yourself, fast, lose weight, ration yourself, reduce, slim.

differ *vb* **1** be different, be distinct, contrast, deviate, diverge, show dif-ferences, vary. **2** argue, be at odds, be at variance, clash, conflict, contra-dict, disagree, dispute, dissent, fall out, *inf* have a difference, oppose each other, quarrel, take issue with each other. *Opp* AGREE.

difference *n* **1** alteration, change, comparison, contrast, development, deviation, differential, differenti-ation, discrepancy, disparity, dissim-ilarity, distinction, diversity, incompatibility, incongruity, incon-sistency, modification, nuance, unlikeness, variation, variety. *Opp* SIMILARITY. **2** argument, clash, conflict, controversy, debate, disagreement, disharmony, dispute, dissent, quar-rel, strife, tiff, wrangle. *Opp* AGREE-MENT.

different *adj* **1** assorted, clashing, conflicting, contradictory, contrast-ing, deviating, discordant, dis-crepant, disparate, dissimilar, distinguishable, divergent, diverse, heterogeneous, ill-matched, incom-patible, inconsistent, miscellaneous, mixed, multifarious, opposed, oppos-ite, *inf* poles apart, several, sundry, unlike, varied, various. *Opp* SIMILAR. **2** abnormal, altered, anomalous, atypical, bizarre, changed, distinct, distinctive, eccentric, extraordinary, fresh, individual, irregular, new, ori-ginal, particular, peculiar, personal, revolutionary, separate, singular, special, specific, strange, uncommon, unconventional, unique, unortho-dox, unusual. *Opp* CONVENTIONAL.

differentiate *vb* contrast, discrimi-nate, distinguish, tell apart.

difficult *adj* **1** abstruse, advanced, baffling, complex, complicated, deep, *inf* dodgy, enigmatic, hard, in-tractable, intricate, involved, *inf* knotty, *inf* nasty, obscure, perplex-ing, problematical, *inf* thorny, tick-lish, tricky. **2** arduous, awkward, backbreaking, burdensome, chal-lenging, daunting, demanding, exacting, exhausting, formidable, gruelling, heavy, herculean, *inf* killing, laborious, onerous, punish-ing, rigorous, severe, strenuous, tax-ing, tough, uphill. **3** *difficult children.* annoying, disruptive, fussy, head-strong, intractable, obstinate, obstreperous, refractory, stubborn, tiresome, troublesome, trying, unco-operative, unfriendly, unhelpful, unresponsive, unruly. *Opp* COOPER-ATIVE, EASY.

difficulty *n* adversity, challenge, complication, dilemma, embarrass-ment, enigma, *inf* fix, *inf* hang-up, hardship, *inf* hiccup, hindrance, hurdle, impediment, *inf* jam, *inf* mess, obstacle, perplexity, *inf* pickle, pitfall, plight, predicament, problem, puzzle, quandary, snag, *inf* spot, straits, *inf* stumbling-block, tribula-tion, trouble, *inf* vexed question.

diffident *adj* backward, bashful, coy, distrustful, doubtful, fearful, hes-itant, hesitating, inhibited, insecure, introvert, meek, modest, nervous, private, reluctant, reserved, retiring, self-effacing, sheepish, shrinking, shy, tentative, timid, timorous, unad-venturous, unassuming, undercon-

fident, unsure, withdrawn. *Opp* CON-
FIDENT.

diffuse *adj* digressive, discursive,
long-winded, loose, meandering,
rambling, spread out, unstructured,
vague, *inf* waffly, wandering. ▷
WORDY. *Opp* CONCISE. ● *vb* ▷ SPREAD.

dig *vb* **1** burrow, delve, excavate,
gouge, hollow, mine, quarry, scoop,
tunnel. **2** cultivate, fork over, *inf* grub
up, till, trench, turn over. **3** jab,
nudge, poke, prod, punch, shove,
thrust. **dig out** ▷ FIND. **dig up** dis-
inter, exhume.

digest *n* ▷ SUMMARY. ● *vb* **1** absorb,
assimilate, dissolve, ingest, process,
utilize. ▷ EAT. **2** consider, ponder,
study, take in, understand.

digit *n* **1** figure, integer, number,
numeral. **2** finger, toe.

dignified *adj* august, becoming,
calm, courtly, decorous, distinguished, elegant, exalted, formal,
grand, grave, imposing, impressive,
lofty, lordly, majestic, noble, proper,
refined, regal, sedate, serious, sober,
solemn, stately, tasteful, upright.
▷ PROUD. *Opp* UNBECOMING.

dignitary *n inf* high-up, important
person, luminary, notable, official,
inf VIP, worthy.

dignity *n* calmness, courtliness, decorum, elegance, eminence, formality, glory, grandeur, *Lat* gravitas,
gravity, greatness, honour, importance, majesty, nobility, propriety,
regality, respectability, seriousness,
sobriety, solemnity, stateliness. ▷
PRIDE.

digress *vb* depart, deviate, diverge,
drift, get off the subject, *inf* go off at
a tangent, *inf* lose the thread, ramble,
stray, veer, wander.

dilapidated *adj* badly maintained,
broken down, crumbling, decayed,
decrepit, derelict, falling apart,
falling down, in disrepair, in ruins,
neglected, ramshackle, rickety,
ruined, *inf* run-down, shaky, tottering, tumbledown, uncared-for.

dilemma *n inf* catch-22, deadlock,
difficulty, doubt, embarrassment, *inf*

fix, impasse, *inf* jam, *inf* mess, *inf*
pickle, plight, predicament, problem,
quandary, *inf* spot, stalemate.

diligent *adj* assiduous, busy, careful,
conscientious, constant, devoted,
earnest, energetic, hardworking,
indefatigable, industrious, meticulous, painstaking, persevering, persistent, pertinacious, punctilious,
scrupulous, sedulous, studious, thorough, tireless. *Opp* LAZY.

dilute *vb* adulterate, reduce the
strength of, thin, water down,
weaken. *Opp* CONCENTRATE.

dim *adj* **1** bleary, blurred, clouded,
cloudy, dark, dingy, dull, faint,
fogged, foggy, fuzzy, gloomy, grey,
hazy, ill-defined, imperceptible,
indistinct, indistinguishable, misty,
murky, nebulous, obscure, obscured,
pale, shadowy, sombre, unclear,
vague, weak. **2** ▷ STUPID. *Opp* BRIGHT.
● *vb* **1** blacken, cloud, darken, dull,
make dim, mask, obscure, shade,
shroud. **2** become dim, fade, go out,
lose brightness, lower. *Opp* BRIGHTEN.
take a dim view ▷ DISAPPROVE.

dimensions *plur n* capacity, extent,
magnitude, measurements, proportions, scale, scope, size. ▷ MEASURE-
MENT.

diminish *vb* **1** abate, become less,
contract, curtail, decline, decrease,
depreciate, die down, dwindle, ease
off, ebb, fade, lessen, *inf* let up, lower,
peter out, recede, reduce, shorten,
shrink, shrivel, slow down, subside,
wane, *inf* wind down. ▷ CUT. *Opp*
INCREASE. **2** belittle, cheapen, demean,
deprecate, devalue, disparage, minimize, undervalue. *Opp* EXAGGERATE.

diminutive *adj* microscopic, midget,
miniature, minuscule, minute, tiny,
undersized. ▷ SMALL.

din *n* blaring, clamour, clangour,
clatter, commotion, crash, hubbub, hullabaloo, noise, outcry, pandemonium, racket, roar, row, rumpus, shouting, tumult, uproar. ▷
SOUND.

dingy *adj* colourless, dark, depressing, dim, dirty, discoloured, dismal,

drab, dreary, dull, faded, gloomy, grimy, murky, old, seedy, shabby, smoky, soiled, sooty, worn. *Opp* BRIGHT.

dining-room *n* cafeteria, carvery, refectory, restaurant.

dinner *n* banquet, feast. ▷ MEAL.

dip *n* **1** concavity, declivity, dent, depression, fall, hole, hollow, incline, slope. **2** *dip in the sea.* bathe, dive, immersion, plunge, soaking, swim. ● *vb* **1** decline, descend, dive, fall, go down, sag, sink, slope down, slump, subside. **2** douse, drop, duck, dunk, immerse, lower, plunge, submerge. **take a dip** ▷ BATHE.

diplomacy *n* adroitness, delicacy, discretion, finesse, negotiation, skill, tact, tactfulness.

diplomat *n* ambassador, consul, government representative, negotiator, official, peacemaker, politician, representative, tactician.

diplomatic *adj* careful, considerate, delicate, discreet, judicious, polite, politic, prudent, sensitive, subtle, tactful, thoughtful, understanding. *Opp* TACTLESS.

direct *adj* **1** non-stop, shortest, straight, unbroken, undeviating, uninterrupted, unswerving. **2** blunt, candid, categorical, clear, decided, explicit, express, forthright, frank, honest, open, outspoken, plain, point-blank, sincere, straightforward, *derog* tactless, to the point, unambiguous, uncomplicated, *derog* undiplomatic, unequivocal, uninhibited, unqualified, unreserved. **3** *direct experience.* empirical, firsthand, *inf* from the horse's mouth, personal. **4** *direct opposites.* absolute, complete, diametrical, exact, head-on, *inf* out-and-out, utter. *Opp* INDIRECT. ● *vb* **1** address, point, route, send, show the way, tell the way, usher. **2** aim, focus, level, target, train, turn. **3** administer, be in charge of, command, conduct, control, govern, handle, lead, manage, mastermind, oversee, regulate, rule, run, stage-manage, super-

intend, supervise, take charge of. **4** *direct someone to do something.* advise, bid, charge, command, counsel, enjoin, instruct, order, require, tell.

direction *n* aim, approach, (compass) bearing, course, orientation, path, point of the compass, road, route, tack, track, way. **directions** guidance, guidelines, instructions, orders, plans.

director *n* administrator, *inf* boss, executive, governor, manager, managing director, organizer, president, principal. ▷ CHIEF.

directory *n* catalogue, index, list, register.

dirt *n* **1** dust, excrement, filth, garbage, grime, impurity, mess, mire, muck, ooze, ordure, pollution, slime, sludge, smut, soot, stain. ▷ OBSCENITY, RUBBISH. **2** clay, earth, loam, mud, soil.

dirty *adj* **1** befouled, begrimed, besmirched, bespattered, black, dingy, dusty, filthy, foul, grimy, grubby, marked, messy, mucky, muddy, nasty, scruffy, shabby, slatternly, smeary, smudged, soiled, sooty, sordid, spotted, squalid, stained, sullied, tarnished, travel-stained, uncared for, unclean, untidy, unwashed. **2** *dirty water.* cloudy, contaminated, impure, muddy, murky, poisoned, polluted, tainted, untreated. **3** *dirty tactics.* dishonest, dishonourable, illegal, *inf* low-down, mean, rough, treacherous, unfair, ungentlemanly, unscrupulous, unsporting, unsportsmanlike. ▷ CORRUPT. **4** *dirty talk.* coarse, crude, improper, indecent, offensive, rude, smutty, vulgar. ▷ OBSCENE. *Opp* CLEAN. ● *vb* befoul, foul, make dirty, mark, *inf* mess up, smear, smudge, soil, spatter, spot, stain, streak, tarnish. ▷ DEFILE. *Opp* CLEAN.

disability *n* affliction, complaint, defect, disablement, handicap, impairment, incapacity, infirmity, weakness.

disable *vb* cripple, damage, debilitate, enfeeble, *inf* hamstring, handicap, immobilize, impair, incapacitate, injure, lame, maim, make useless, mutilate, paralyse, put out of action, ruin, weaken. **disabled** ▷ HANDICAPPED.

disadvantage *n* drawback, handicap, hardship, hindrance, impediment, inconvenience, liability, *inf* minus, nuisance, privation, snag, trouble, weakness.

disagree *vb* argue, bicker, clash, conflict, contend, differ, dispute, dissent, diverge, fall out, fight, quarrel, squabble, wrangle. **disagree with** ▷ OPPOSE.

disagreeable *adj* disgusting, distasteful, nasty, objectionable, obnoxious, offensive, *inf* off-putting, repellent, sickening, unsavoury. ▷ UNPLEASANT. *Opp* PLEASANT.

disagreement *n* altercation, argument, clash, conflict, contention, controversy, debate, difference, discrepancy, disharmony, disparity, dispute, dissension, dissent, divergence, incompatibility, inconsistency, misunderstanding, opposition, quarrel, squabble, strife, *inf* tiff, variance, wrangle. *Opp* AGREEMENT.

disappear *vb* **1** become invisible, cease to exist, clear, die out, disperse, dissolve, dwindle, ebb, evanesce, evaporate, fade, melt away, recede, vanish, vaporize, wane. ▷ DIE. **2** depart, escape, flee, fly, go, pass out of sight, run away, walk away, withdraw. *Opp* APPEAR.

disappoint *vb* be worse than expected, chagrin, *inf* dash your hopes, disenchant, disillusion, dismay, displease, dissatisfy, fail to satisfy, *inf* let down, upset, vex. ▷ FRUSTRATE. *Opp* SATISFY. **disappointed** disillusioned, frustrated, *inf* let down, unsatisfied. ▷ SAD.

disapproval *n* anger, censure, condemnation, criticism, disapprobation, disfavour, dislike, displeasure, dissatisfaction, hostility, reprimand, reproach. *Opp* APPROVAL.

disapprove *vb* **disapprove of** be displeased by, belittle, blame, censure, condemn, criticize, denounce, deplore, deprecate, dislike, disparage, frown on, jeer at, look askance at, make unwelcome, object to, regret, reject, *inf* take a dim view of, take exception to. *Opp* APPROVE. **disapproving** ▷ CRITICAL.

disarm *vb* **1** demilitarize, demobilize, disband troops, make powerless, take weapons from. **2** charm, mollify, pacify, placate.

disaster *n* accident, act of God, blow, calamity, cataclysm, catastrophe, crash, débâcle, failure, fiasco, *inf* flop, *inf* mess-up, misadventure, mischance, misfortune, mishap, reverse, tragedy, *inf* washout. *Opp* SUCCESS.

disastrous *adj* appalling, awful, calamitous, cataclysmic, catastrophic, crippling, destructive, devastating, dire, dreadful, fatal, ruinous, terrible, tragic. *Opp* SUCCESSFUL.

disbelieve *vb* be sceptical of, discount, discredit, doubt, have no faith in, mistrust, reject, suspect. *Opp* BELIEVE. **disbelieving** ▷ INCREDULOUS.

disc *n* **1** circle, counter, plate, token. **2** album, CD, LP, record, single. **3** [*computing*] CD-ROM, disk, diskette, floppy disk, hard disk.

discard *vb* abandon, cast off, *inf* chuck away, dispense with, dispose of, *inf* ditch, dump, eliminate, get rid of, jettison, junk, reject, scrap, shed, throw away, toss out.

discern *vb* be aware of, be sensitive to, detect, discover, discriminate, distinguish, make out, mark, notice, observe, perceive, recognize, spy. ▷ SEE. **discerning** ▷ PERCEPTIVE.

discernible *adj* detectable, distinguishable, measurable, perceptible. ▷ NOTICEABLE.

discharge *n* **1** release, dismissal. **2** emission, excretion, ooze, pus, secretion, suppuration. ● *vb* **1** belch, eject, emit, expel, exude, give off, give out, pour out, produce, release, secrete, send out, spew, spit out. **2** *discharge guns.* detonate, explode, fire, let off, shoot. **3** *discharge employees.* dismiss, fire, make redundant, remove, sack, throw out. **4** *discharge a prisoner.* absolve, acquit, allow to leave, clear, dismiss, excuse, exonerate, free, let off, liberate, pardon, release. **5** *discharge duties.* accomplish, carry out, execute, fulfil, perform.

disciple *n* acolyte, adherent, admirer, apostle, apprentice, devotee, follower, learner, proselyte, pupil, scholar, student, supporter.

disciplinarian *n* authoritarian, autocrat, despot, dictator, *inf* hardliner, *inf* hard taskmaster, martinet, *inf* slave-driver, *inf* stickler, tyrant.

discipline *n* **1** control, drilling, indoctrination, instruction, management, strictness, system, training. **2** good behaviour, obedience, order, orderliness, routine, self-control, self-restraint. ● *vb* **1** break in, coach, control, drill, educate, govern, indoctrinate, instruct, keep in check, manage, restrain, school, train. **2** castigate, chasten, chastise, correct, penalize, punish, rebuke, reprimand, reprove, scold. **disciplined** ▷ OBEDIENT.

disclaim *vb* deny, disown, forswear, reject, renounce, repudiate. *Opp* ACKNOWLEDGE.

disclose *vb* divulge, expose, let out, make known. ▷ REVEAL.

discolour *vb* bleach, dirty, fade, mark, spoil the colour of, stain, tarnish, tinge.

discomfort *n* ache, care, difficulty, distress, hardship, inconvenience, irritation, soreness, uncomfortableness, uneasiness. ▷ PAIN. *Opp* COMFORT.

disconcert *vb* agitate, bewilder, confuse, discomfit, distract, disturb, fluster, nonplus, perplex, *inf* put off, puzzle, *inf* rattle, ruffle, throw off balance, trouble, unsettle, upset, worry. *Opp* REASSURE.

disconnect *vb* break off, cut off, detach, disengage, divide, part, sever, switch off, take away, turn off,

uncouple, undo, unhitch, unhook, unplug. **disconnected** ▷ INCOHERENT.

discontented *adj* annoyed, disgruntled, displeased, dissatisfied, *inf* fed up, restless, sulky, unhappy, unsettled.

discord *n* **1** argument, conflict, contention, difference of opinion, disagreement, disharmony, dispute, friction, incompatibility, strife. ▷ QUARREL. **2** [*music*] cacophony, clash, jangle. ▷ NOISE. *Opp* HARMONY.

discordant *adj* **1** conflicting, contrary, differing, disagreeing, dissimilar, divergent, incompatible, incongruous, inconsistent, opposed, opposite. ▷ QUARRELSOME. **2** atonal, cacophonous, clashing, dissonant, grating, grinding, harsh, jangling, jarring, shrill, strident, tuneless, unmusical. *Opp* HARMONIOUS.

discount *n* abatement, allowance, concession, cut, deduction, *inf* markdown, rebate, reduction. ● *vb* disbelieve, dismiss, disregard, gloss over, ignore, overlook, reject.

discourage *vb* **1** cow, damp, dampen, daunt, demoralize, depress, disenchant, dishearten, dismay, dispirit, frighten, inhibit, intimidate, overawe, *inf* put down, *inf* put off, scare, *inf* throw cold water on, unman, unnerve. **2** *discourage vandalism.* check, deflect, deter, dissuade, hinder, prevent, put an end to, repress, restrain, slow down, stop, suppress. *Opp* ENCOURAGE.

discouragement *n* constraint, *inf* damper, deterrent, disincentive, hindrance, impediment, obstacle, restraint, setback. *Opp* ENCOURAGEMENT.

discourse *n* **1** ▷ CONVERSATION. **2** dissertation, essay, monograph, paper, speech, thesis, treatise. ▷ WRITING. ● *vb* ▷ SPEAK.

discover *vb* ascertain, bring to light, come across, detect, *inf* dig up, disclose, *inf* dredge up, explore, expose, *inf* ferret out, find, hit on, identify, learn, light upon, locate, notice, observe, perceive, recognize, reveal, search out, spot, *sl* sus out, track down, turn up, uncover, unearth. ▷ INVENT. *Opp* HIDE.

discoverer *n* creator, explorer, finder, initiator, inventor, originator, pioneer, traveller.

discovery *n* breakthrough, conception, detection, disclosure, exploration, *inf* find, innovation, invention, recognition, revelation.

discredit *vb* attack, calumniate, challenge, defame, disbelieve, disgrace, dishonour, disprove, *inf* explode, prove false, raise doubts about, refuse to believe, ruin the reputation of, show up, slander, slur, smear, vilify.

discreet *adj* careful, cautious, chary, circumspect, considerate, delicate, diplomatic, guarded, judicious, low-key, mild, muted, polite, politic, prudent, restrained, sensitive, soft, subdued, tactful, thoughtful, understated, wary. *Opp* INDISCREET.

discrepancy *n* conflict, difference, disparity, dissimilarity, divergence, incompatibility, incongruity, inconsistency, variance. *Opp* SIMILARITY.

discretion *n* circumspection, diplomacy, good sense, judgement, maturity, prudence, responsibility, sensitivity, tact, wisdom. *Opp* TACTLESSNESS.

discriminate *vb* **1** differentiate, distinguish, draw a distinction, separate, tell apart. **2** be biased, be intolerant, be prejudiced, show discrimination. **discriminating** ▷ PERCEPTIVE.

discrimination *n* **1** discernment, good taste, insight, judgement, perceptiveness, refinement, selectivity, subtlety, taste. **2** [*derog*] bias, bigotry, chauvinism, favouritism, intolerance, male chauvinism, prejudice, racialism, racism, sexism, unfairness. *Opp* IMPARTIALITY.

discuss *vb* argue about, confer about, consider, consult about, debate, deliberate, examine, *inf* put heads together, talk about, *inf* weigh up the pros and cons of, write about. ▷ TALK.

discussion *n* argument, colloquy, confabulation, conference, consideration, consultation, conversation, debate, deliberation, dialogue, discourse, examination, exchange of views, *inf* powwow, symposium. ▷ TALK.

disdainful *adj* contemptuous, jeering, mocking, scornful, sneering, supercilious, superior. ▷ PROUD.

disease *n* affliction, ailment, blight, *inf* bug, complaint, *inf* condition, contagion, disorder, infection, infirmity, malady, plague, sickness. ▷ ILLNESS.

diseased *adj* ailing, infirm, sick, unwell. ▷ ILL.

disembark *vb* alight, debark, detrain, get off, go ashore, land. *Opp* EMBARK.

disfigure *vb* blemish, damage, deface, deform, distort, impair, injure, make ugly, mar, mutilate, ruin, scar, spoil. *Opp* BEAUTIFY.

disgrace *n* **1** blot, contumely, degradation, discredit, dishonour, disrepute, embarrassment, humiliation, ignominy, obloquy, odium, opprobrium, scandal, shame, slur, stain, stigma. **2** ▷ OUTRAGE.

disgraceful *adj* contemptible, degrading, dishonourable, embarrassing, humiliating, ignominious, shameful, shaming, wicked. ▷ BAD.

disgruntled *adj* annoyed, cross, disaffected, disappointed, discontented, dissatisfied, *inf* fed up, grumpy, moody, sulky, sullen. ▷ BAD-TEMPERED.

disguise *n* camouflage, cloak, costume, cover, fancy dress, front, *inf* get-up, impersonation, make-up, mask, pretence, smoke-screen. ● *vb* blend into the background, camouflage, conceal, cover up, dress up, falsify, gloss over, hide, make inconspicuous, mask, misrepresent, screen, shroud, veil. **disguise yourself as** ▷ IMPERSONATE.

disgust *n* abhorrence, antipathy, aversion, contempt, detestation, dislike, distaste, hatred, loathing, nausea, outrage, repugnance, repulsion, revulsion, sickness. ● *vb* appal, be

dish

dish   114

distasteful to, displease, horrify, nauseate, offend, outrage, put off, repel, revolt, shock, sicken, *inf* turn your stomach. *Opp* PLEASE. **disgusting** ▷ HATEFUL.

dish *n* **1** basin, bowl, casserole, container, plate, *old use* platter, tureen. **2** concoction, food, item on the menu, recipe. **dish out** ▷ DISTRIBUTE. **dish up** ▷ SERVE.

dishearten *vb* depress, deter, discourage, dismay, put off, sadden. *Opp* ENCOURAGE. **disheartened** ▷ SAD.

dishevelled *adj* bedraggled, disarranged, disordered, knotted, matted, messy, ruffled, rumpled, *inf* scruffy, slovenly, tangled, tousled, uncombed, unkempt, untidy. *Opp* NEAT.

dishonest *adj inf* bent, cheating, corrupt, criminal, crooked, deceitful, deceiving, deceptive, devious, dishonourable, disreputable, false, fraudulent, hypocritical, immoral, insincere, lying, mendacious, misleading, perfidious, *inf* shady, *inf* slippery, specious, swindling, thieving, treacherous, *inf* twofaced, *inf* underhand, unethical, unprincipled, unscrupulous, untrustworthy, untruthful. *Opp* HONEST.

dishonour *n inf* black mark, blot, degradation, discredit, disgrace, humiliation, ignominy, indignity, loss of face, obloquy, opprobrium, reproach, scandal, shame, slander, slur, stain, stigma. *Opp* HONOUR. ● *vb* **1** abuse, affront, debase, defile, degrade, disgrace, offend, profane, shame, slight. **2** ▷ RAPE.

dishonourable *adj* base, blameworthy, compromising, despicable, discreditable, disgraceful, disgusting, dishonest, disloyal, disreputable, ignoble, ignominious, improper, infamous, mean, outrageous, perfidious, reprehensible, scandalous, shabby, shameful, shameless, treacherous, unchivalrous, unethical, unprincipled, unscrupulous, untrustworthy, unworthy, wicked. ▷ CORRUPT. *Opp* HONOURABLE.

disillusion *vb* disabuse, disappoint, disenchant, enlighten, reveal the truth to, undeceive.

disinfect *vb* chlorinate, clean, cleanse, decontaminate, fumigate, purge, purify, sanitize, sterilize.

disinfectant *n* antiseptic, decontaminant, fumigant, germicide.

disinherit *vb* cut off, cut out of a will, deprive someone of his/her birthright, deprive someone of his/her inheritance.

disintegrate *vb* break into pieces, break up, come apart, crack up, crumble, decay, decompose, degenerate, deteriorate, fall apart, lose coherence, moulder, rot, shatter, smash, splinter.

disinterested *adj* detached, dispassionate, impartial, impersonal, neutral, objective, unbiased, uninvolved, unprejudiced. *Opp* BIASED.

disjointed *adj* aimless, broken up, confused, desultory, disconnected, dislocated, disordered, disunited, divided, incoherent, jumbled, loose, mixed up, muddled, rambling, separate, split up, unconnected, uncoordinated, wandering. *Opp* COHERENT.

dislike *n* animus, antagonism, antipathy, aversion, contempt, detestation, disapproval, disfavour, disgust, distaste, hatred, hostility, ill will, loathing, repugnance, revulsion. ● *vb* avoid, despise, detest, disapprove of, feel dislike for, scorn, *inf* take against. ▷ HATE. *Opp* LOVE.

dislocate *vb* disengage, disjoint, displace, misplace, *inf* put out, put out of joint.

disloyal *adj* apostate, faithless, false, insincere, perfidious, recreant, renegade, seditious, subversive, treacherous, treasonable, *inf* two-faced, unfaithful, unreliable, untrue, untrustworthy. *Opp* LOYAL.

disloyalty *n* betrayal, doubledealing, duplicity, faithlessness, falseness, inconstancy, infidelity, perfidy, treachery, treason, unfaithfulness. *Opp* LOYALTY.

dismal *adj* bleak, cheerless, depressing, dreary, dull, funereal, gloomy, grey, grim, joyless, miserable, sombre, wretched. ▷ SAD.

dismantle *vb* demolish, knock down, strike, strip down, take apart, take down. *Opp* ASSEMBLE.

dismay *n* agitation, alarm, anxiety, apprehension, consternation, depression, disappointment, discouragement, distress, dread, gloom, horror, pessimism. ▷ FEAR. ● *vb* alarm, appal, daunt, depress, devastate, disappoint, discompose, discourage, disgust, dishearten, dispirit, distress, horrify, scare, shock, take aback, unnerve. ▷ FRIGHTEN. *Opp* PLEASE.

dismiss *vb* **1** disband, discard, free, let go, *inf* pack off, release, send away, *inf* send packing. **2** belittle, brush aside, discount, disregard, drop, give up, *inf* pooh-pooh, reject, repudiate, set aside, shelve, shrug off, wave aside. **3** *dismiss a worker. inf* axe, banish, cashier, disband, discharge, *inf* fire, get rid of, give notice to, *inf* give someone his/her cards, give the push to, lay off, make redundant, sack.

disobedient *adj* anarchic, contrary, defiant, delinquent, disorderly, disruptive, fractious, headstrong, insubordinate, intractable, mutinous, obdurate, obstinate, obstreperous, perverse, rebellious, recalcitrant, refractory, riotous, selfwilled, stubborn, uncontrollable, undisciplined, ungovernable, unmanageable, unruly, wayward, wild, wilful. ▷ NAUGHTY. *Opp* OBEDIENT.

disobey *vb* **1** be disobedient, mutiny, protest, rebel, revolt, rise up, strike. **2** break, contravene, defy, disregard, flout, ignore, infringe, oppose, rebel against, resist, transgress, violate. *Opp* OBEY.

disorder *n* **1** anarchy, chaos, clamour, confusion, disarray, disorderliness, disorganization, disturbance, fighting, fracas, fuss, jumble, lawlessness, mess, muddle, rumpus, *inf* shambles, tangle, tumult, untidiness, uproar. ▷ COMMOTION. *Opp* ORDER. **2** ▷ ILLNESS.

disorderly *adj* ▷ DISOBEDIENT, DISORGANIZED.

disorganized *adj* aimless, careless, chaotic, confused, disorderly, haphazard, illogical, jumbled, messy, muddled, rambling, scatter-brained, *inf* slapdash, *inf* slipshod, *inf* sloppy, slovenly, straggling, unmethodical, unplanned, unstructured, unsystematic, untidy. *Opp* SYSTEMATIC.

disown *vb* cast off, disclaim knowledge of, renounce, repudiate.

disparage *vb* belittle, demean, depreciate, discredit, insult, *inf* put down, slight, undervalue. ▷ CRITICIZE.

disparaging ▷ UNCOMPLIMENTARY.

dispassionate *adj* calm, composed, cool, equable, even-tempered, level-headed, sober. ▷ IMPARTIAL, UNEMOTIONAL. *Opp* EMOTIONAL.

dispatch *n* bulletin, communiqué, document, letter, message, report. ● *vb* **1** consign, convey, forward, mail, post, send, ship, transmit. **2** ▷ KILL.

dispense *vb* **1** allocate, allot, apportion, assign, deal out, disburse, distribute, dole out, give out, issue, measure out, mete out, parcel out, provide, ration out, share. **2** *dispense medicine.* make up, prepare, supply.

dispense with ▷ OMIT, REMOVE.

disperse *vb* **1** break up, decentralize, devolve, disband, dismiss, dispel, dissipate, distribute, divide up, drive away, send away, send in different directions, separate, spread, stray. *Opp* GATHER. **2** disappear, dissolve, melt away, scatter, spread out, vanish.

displace *vb* **1** disarrange, dislocate, dislodge, disturb, misplace, move, put out of place, shift. **2** crowd out, depose, dispossess, evict, expel, oust, replace, succeed, supersede, supplant, take the place of, unseat, usurp.

display *n* **1** array, demonstration, exhibition, manifestation, pageant, parade, presentation, show, spectacle. **2** ceremony, ostentation, pageantry, pomp, showing off. • vb advertise, air, betray, demonstrate, disclose, exhibit, expose, flaunt, flourish, give evidence of, parade, present, produce, put on show, reveal, set out, show, show off, unfold, unfurl, unveil, vaunt. Opp HIDE.

displease vb anger, offend, inf put out, upset. ▷ ANNOY.

disposable adj **1** at your disposal, available, spendable, usable. **2** biodegradable, expendable, non-returnable, replaceable, inf throw-away.

dispose vb adjust, arrange, array, distribute, group, order, organize, place, position, put, set out, situate. **disposed** ▷ LIABLE. **dispose of** ▷ DESTROY, DISCARD.

disproportionate adj excessive, incommensurate, incongruous, inequitable, inordinate, out of proportion, unbalanced, uneven, unreasonable. Opp PROPORTIONAL.

disprove vb confute, contradict, controvert, demolish, discredit, inf explode, invalidate, negate, rebut, refute, show to be wrong. Opp PROVE.

dispute n ▷ QUARREL. • vb argue against, challenge, contest, contradict, controvert, deny, disagree with, doubt, fault, gainsay, impugn, object to, oppose, inf pick holes in, quarrel with, query, question, raise doubts about, take exception to. ▷ DEBATE. Opp ACCEPT.

disqualify vb bar, debar, declare ineligible, exclude, preclude, prohibit, reject, turn down.

disregard vb brush aside, despise, discount, dismiss, disobey, exclude, inf fly in the face of, forget, ignore, leave out, inf make light of, miss out, neglect, omit, overlook, pass over, pay no attention to, inf pooh-pooh, reject, shrug off, skip, slight, snub, turn a blind eye to. Opp HEED.

disreputable adj dishonest, dishonourable, inf dodgy, dubious, infamous, questionable, raffish, inf shady, suspect, suspicious, unconventional, unreliable, unsound, untrustworthy. Opp REPUTABLE.

disrespectful adj bad-mannered, blasphemous, derisive, discourteous, disparaging, impolite, impudent, inconsiderate, insolent, insulting, irreverent, mocking, scornful, uncivil, uncomplimentary, unmannerly. ▷ RUDE. Opp RESPECTFUL.

disrupt vb agitate, break up, confuse, disconcert, dislocate, disorder, disturb, interfere with, interrupt, intrude on, spoil, throw into disorder, unsettle, upset.

dissatisfaction n annoyance, chagrin, disappointment, discontentment, dismay, displeasure, disquiet, exasperation, frustration, irritation, malaise, mortification, regret, unhappiness. Opp SATISFACTION.

dissatisfied adj disaffected, disappointed, discontented, disgruntled, displeased, fed up, frustrated, unfulfilled, unsatisfied. ▷ UNHAPPY. Opp CONTENTED.

dissident n derog agitator, apostate, dissenter, independent thinker, nonconformer, protester, rebel, recusant, inf refusenik, revolutionary. Opp CONFORMIST.

dissimilar adj antithetical, clashing, conflicting, contrasting, different, disparate, distinct, distinguishable, divergent, diverse, heterogeneous, incompatible, irreconcilable, opposite, unlike, unrelated, various. Opp SIMILAR.

dissipate vb **1** break up, diffuse, disappear, disperse, scatter. **2** distribute, fritter away, spread about, squander, throw away, use up, waste. **dissipated** ▷ IMMORAL.

dissociate vb back away, cut off, detach, disengage, distance, divorce, isolate, segregate. ▷ SEPARATE. Opp ASSOCIATE.

dissolve vb **1** become liquid, decompose, deliquesce, dematerialize, diffuse, disappear, disintegrate, disperse, liquefy, melt away, vanish. **2** dissolve a meeting. adjourn, break up, cancel, disband, dismiss, divorce, end, sever, split up, suspend, terminate, *inf* wind up.

dissuade *vb* **dissuade from** advise against, argue out of, deter from, discourage from, persuade not to, put off, remonstrate against, warn against. *Opp* PERSUADE.

distance *n* **1** breadth, extent, gap, *inf* haul, interval, journey, length, measurement, mileage, range, reach, separation, space, span, stretch, width. **2** aloofness, coolness, haughtiness, isolation, remoteness, separation, *inf* standoffishness, unfriendliness. ● *vb* **distance yourself** be unfriendly, detach yourself, dissociate yourself, keep away, keep your distance, remove yourself, separate yourself, set yourself apart, stay away. *Opp* INVOLVE.

distant *adj* **1** far, far-away, far-flung, *inf* god-forsaken, inaccessible, outlying, out-of-the-way, remote, removed. *Opp* CLOSE. **2** aloof, cool, formal, frigid, haughty, reserved, reticent, stiff, unapproachable, unenthusiastic, unfriendly, withdrawn. *Opp* FRIENDLY.

distasteful *adj* disgusting, displeasing, nasty, nauseating, objectionable, offensive, *inf* off-putting, repugnant, revolting, unpalatable. ▷ UNPLEASANT. *Opp* PLEASANT.

distinct *adj* **1** apparent, clear, clear-cut, definite, evident, noticeable, obvious, palpable, patent, perceptible, plain, precise, recognizable, sharp, unambiguous, unequivocal, unmistakable, visible, well-defined. *Opp* INDISTINCT. **2** contrasting, detached, different, discrete, dissimilar, distinguishable, individual, separate, special, *Lat* sui generis, unconnected, unique.

distinction *n* **1** contrast, difference, differentiation, discrimination, dissimilarity, distinctiveness, dividing line, division, individuality, particularity, peculiarity, separation. *Opp* SIMILARITY. **2** *distinction of being first.* celebrity, credit, eminence, excellence, fame, glory, greatness, honour, importance, merit, prestige, renown, reputation, superiority.

distinctive *adj* characteristic, different, distinguishing, idiosyncratic, individual, inimitable, original, peculiar, personal, singular, special, striking, typical, uncommon, unique. *Opp* COMMON.

distinguish *vb* **1** choose, decide, differentiate, discriminate, judge, make a distinction, separate, tell apart. **2** ascertain, determine, discern, know, make out, perceive, pick out, recognize, see, single out, tell. **distinguished** ▷ FAMOUS.

distort *vb* **1** bend, buckle, contort, deform, misshape, twist, warp, wrench. **2** alter, exaggerate, falsify, garble, misrepresent, pervert, slant, tamper with, twist, violate. **distorted** ▷ GNARLED, FALSE.

distract *vb* bewilder, bother, confound, confuse, deflect, disconcert, distress, divert, harass, mystify, perplex, puzzle, rattle, sidetrack, trouble, worry. **distracted** ▷ DISTRAUGHT, MAD.

distraction *n* **1** disturbance, diversion, interference, interruption, temptation, *inf* upset. **2** agitation, befuddlement, bewilderment, confusion, delirium, frenzy, insanity, madness. **3** ▷ DIVERSION.

distraught *adj* agitated, *inf* beside yourself, distracted, distressed, disturbed, emotional, excited, frantic, hysterical, overcome, overwrought, troubled, upset, worked up. ▷ ANXIOUS. *Opp* CALM.

distress *n* adversity, affliction, angst, anguish, anxiety, danger, desolation, difficulty, discomfort, dismay, fright, grief, heartache, misery, pain, poverty, privation, sadness, sorrow, stress, suffering, torment, tribulation, trouble, unhappiness, woe, worry, wretchedness. ▷ PAIN. ● *vb* afflict, alarm, bother, *inf* cut up, dismay, disturb, frighten, grieve, harass, harrow, hurt, make miserable, oppress, pain, perplex, perturb, plague, sadden, scare, shake, shock,

distribute *vb* allocate, allot, apportion, arrange, assign, circulate, deal out, deliver, *inf* dish out, dispense, disperse, dispose of, disseminate, divide out, *inf* dole out, give out, hand round, issue, mete out, partition, pass round, scatter, share out, spread, strew, take round. *Opp* COLLECT.

district *n* area, community, department, division, locality, neighbourhood, parish, part, partition, precinct, province, quarter, region, sector, territory, vicinity, ward, zone.

distrust *vb* be distrustful of, disbelieve, doubt, have misgivings about, have qualms about, mistrust, question, suspect. *Opp* TRUST.

distrustful *adj* cautious, chary, cynical, disbelieving, distrusting, doubtful, dubious, sceptical, suspicious, uncertain, uneasy, unsure, wary. *Opp* TRUSTFUL.

disturb *vb* **1** agitate, alarm, annoy, bother, discompose, disrupt, distract, distress, excite, fluster, frighten, hassle, interrupt, intrude on, perturb, pester, ruffle, scare, shake, startle, stir up, trouble, unsettle, upset, worry. **2** confuse, disorder, interfere with, jumble up, *inf* mess about with, move, muddle, rearrange, reorganize. **disturbed** ▷ DISTRAUGHT.

disturbance *n* disruption, interference, upheaval, upset. ▷ COMMOTION.

disunited *adj* divided, opposed, polarized, split. *Opp* UNITED.

disunity *n* difference, disagreement, discord, disharmony, disintegration, division, fragmentation, incoherence, opposition, polarization. *Opp* UNITY.

disused *adj* abandoned, archaic, closed, dead, discarded, discontinued, idle, neglected, obsolete, superannuated, unused, withdrawn. ▷ OLD. *Opp* CURRENT.

ditch *n* aqueduct, channel, dike, drain, gully, gutter, moat, trench, watercourse. ● *vb* ▷ ABANDON.

dive *vb* crash-dive, descend, dip, drop, duck, fall, go snorkelling, go under, jump, leap, nosedive, pitch, plummet, plunge, sink, submerge, subside, swoop.

diverge *vb* branch, deviate, divide, fork, go off at a tangent, part, radiate, ramify, separate, split, spread, subdivide. ▷ DIFFER. *Opp* CONVERGE.

diverse *adj* assorted, different, dissimilar, distinct, divergent, diversified, heterogeneous, miscellaneous, mixed, multifarious, varied, various.

diversify *vb* branch out, broaden out, develop, divide, enlarge, expand, extend, spread out, vary.

diversion *n* **1** detour, deviation. **2** amusement, distraction, entertainment, fun, game, hobby, interest, pastime, play, recreation, relaxation, sport.

divert *vb* **1** alter, avert, change direction, deflect, deviate, rechannel, redirect, reroute, shunt, sidetrack, switch, turn aside. **2** amuse, beguile, cheer up, delight, distract, engage, entertain, keep happy, occupy, recreate, regale. **diverting** ▷ FUNNY.

divide *vb* **1** branch, detach, diverge, fork, move apart, part, separate, sunder. **2** allocate, allot, apportion, break up, cut up, deal out, dispense, distribute, dole out, give out, halve, measure out, mete out, parcel out, pass round, share out. **3** *divide a party.* cause disagreement in, disunite, polarize, split. **4** *divide into sets.* arrange, categorize, classify, grade, group, sort out, subdivide. *Opp* GATHER, UNITE.

divine *adj* angelic, celestial, godlike, hallowed, heavenly, holy, immortal, mystical, religious, sacred, saintly, seraphic, spiritual, superhuman, supernatural, transcendental. *Opp* MORTAL. ● *n* ▷ CLERGYMAN. ● *vb* ▷ PROPHESY.

divinity *n* **1** ▷ GOD. **2** religion, religious studies, theology.

division n **1** allocation, allotment, apportionment, cutting up, dividing, partition, segmentation, separation, splitting. **2** disagreement, discord, disunity, feud, quarrel, rupture, schism, split. **3** alcove, compartment, part, recess, section, segment. **4** *division between rooms, lands.* border, borderline, boundary line, demarcation, divider, dividing wall, fence, frontier, margin, partition, screen. **5** *division of a business.* branch, department, section, subdivision, unit.

divorce n annulment, *inf* breakup, decree nisi, dissolution, separation, *inf* split-up. ● vb annul marriage, dissolve marriage, part, separate, *inf* split up.

dizziness n faintness, giddiness, light-headedness, vertigo.

dizzy adj bewildered, confused, dazed, faint, giddy, light-headed, muddled, reeling, shaky, swimming, unsteady, *inf* woozy.

do vb **1** accomplish, achieve, bring about, carry out, cause, commit, complete, effect, execute, finish, fulfil, implement, initiate, instigate, organize, perform, produce, undertake. **2** *do the garden.* arrange, attend to, cope with, deal with, handle, look after, manage, work at. **3** *do sums.* answer, give your mind to, puzzle out, solve, think out, work out. **4** *Will this do?* be acceptable, be enough, be satisfactory, be sufficient, be suitable, satisfy, serve, suffice. **5** *Do as you like.* act, behave, conduct yourself, perform. **do away with** ▷ ABOLISH. **do up** ▷ DECORATE, FASTEN.

docile adj cooperative, domesticated, obedient, submissive, tractable. ▷ TAME.

dock n berth, boatyard, dockyard, dry dock, harbour, haven, jetty, landing-stage, marina, pier, port, quay, slipway, wharf. ● vb **1** anchor, berth, drop anchor, land, moor, put in, tie up. **2** ▷ CUT.

doctor n general practitioner, *inf* GP, *inf* medic, medical officer, medical practitioner, *inf* MO, physician, *derog* quack, surgeon.

doctrine n axiom, belief, conviction, *Lat* credo, creed, dogma, maxim, orthodoxy, postulate, precept, principle, teaching, tenet, theory, thesis.

document n certificate, charter, chronicle, deed, diploma, form, instrument, legal document, licence, manuscript, *inf* MS, paper, parchment, passport, policy, print-out, record, typescript, visa, warrant, will. ● vb ▷ RECORD.

documentary adj **1** authenticated, chronicled, recorded, substantiated, written. **2** factual, historical, nonfiction, real life.

dodge n contrivance, device, knack, manoeuvre, ploy, *sl* racket, ruse, scheme, stratagem, subterfuge, trick, *inf* wheeze. ● vb **1** avoid, duck, elude, escape, evade, fend off, move out of the way, sidestep, swerve, turn away, veer, weave. **2** *dodge work.* shirk, *inf* skive, *inf* wriggle out of. **3** *dodge a question.* equivocate, fudge, hedge, quibble, *inf* waffle.

dog n bitch, *inf* bow-wow, *derog* cur, dingo, hound, mongrel, pedigree, pup, puppy, whelp. ● vb ▷ FOLLOW.

dogma n article of faith, belief, conviction, creed, doctrine, orthodoxy, precept, principle, teaching, tenet, truth.

dogmatic adj arbitrary, assertive, authoritarian, authoritative, categorical, certain, dictatorial, doctrinaire, *inf* hard-line, hidebound, imperious, inflexible, intolerant, legalistic, narrow-minded, obdurate, opinionated, pontifical, positive. ▷ STUBBORN. *Opp* AMENABLE.

dole n [*inf*] benefit, income support, social security, unemployment benefit. **dole out** ▷ DISTRIBUTE. **on the dole** ▷ UNEMPLOYED.

doll n *inf* dolly, figure, marionette, puppet, rag doll.

domestic adj **1** family, household, in the home, private. **2** *domestic air service.* indigenous, inland, internal, national.

domesticated *adj* house-broken, house-trained, tame, tamed, trained. *Opp* WILD.

dominant *adj* **1** biggest, chief, commanding, conspicuous, eyecatching, highest, imposing, largest, main, major, obvious, outstanding, preeminent, prevailing, primary, principal, tallest, uppermost, widespread. **2** ascendant, controlling, dominating, domineering, governing, influential, leading, powerful, predominant, presiding, reigning, ruling, supreme.

dominate *vb* **1** be dominant, be in the majority, control, direct, govern, influence, lead, manage, master, monopolize, outnumber, preponderate, prevail, rule, subjugate, take control, tyrannize. **2** dwarf, look out over, overshadow, tower over.

domineering *adj* authoritarian, autocratic, *inf* bossy, despotic, dictatorial, high-handed, oppressive, overbearing, *inf* pushy, strict, tyrannical. *Opp* SUBMISSIVE.

donate *vb* contribute, give, grant, hand over, make a donation, present, subscribe, supply.

donation *n* alms, contribution, freewill offering, gift, offering, present, subscription.

donor *n* backer, benefactor, contributor, giver, philanthropist, provider, sponsor, supplier, supporter.

doom *n* destiny, end, fate, fortune, karma, kismet, lot.

doomed *adj* **1** condemned, destined, fated, intended, ordained, predestined. **2** *a doomed enterprise*. accursed, bedevilled, cursed, damned, hopeless, ill-fated, ill-starred, luckless, star-crossed, unlucky.

door *n* barrier, doorway, entrance, exit, French window, gate, gateway, opening, portal, postern, revolving door, swing door, way out.

dormant *adj* **1** asleep, comatose, hibernating, inactive, inert, passive, quiescent, quiet, resting, sleeping. **2** *dormant talent*. hidden, latent,

potential, unrevealed, untapped, unused. *Opp* ACTIVE.

dose *n* amount, dosage, measure, portion, prescribed amount, quantity. ● *vb* administer, dispense, prescribe.

dossier *n* file, folder, records, set of documents.

dot *n* decimal point, fleck, full stop, iota, jot, mark, point, speck, spot. ● *vb* fleck, mark with dots, punctuate, speckle, spot, stipple.

dote *vb* dote on adore, idolize, worship. ▷ LOVE.

double *adj* coupled, doubled, dual, duple, duplicated, paired, twin, twofold, two-ply. ● *n* clone, copy, counterpart, *Ger* doppelgänger, duplicate, *inf* look-alike, opposite, *inf* spitting image, twin. ● *vb* duplicate, increase, multiply by two, reduplicate, repeat. **double back** ▷ RETURN. **double up** ▷ COLLAPSE.

double-cross *vb* cheat, deceive, let down, trick. ▷ BETRAY.

doubt *n* **1** agnosticism, anxiety, apprehension, confusion, cynicism, diffidence, disbelief, disquiet, distrust, fear, hesitation, incredulity, indecision, misgiving, mistrust, perplexity, qualm, reservation, scepticism, suspicion, worry. **2** *doubt about meaning*. ambiguity, difficulty, dilemma, problem, query, question, uncertainty. *Opp* CERTAINTY. ● *vb* be dubious, be sceptical about, disbelieve, distrust, fear, feel uncertain about, have doubts about, have misgivings about, have reservations about, hesitate, lack confidence, mistrust, query, question, suspect. *Opp* TRUST.

doubtful *adj* **1** agnostic, cynical, diffident, disbelieving, distrustful, dubious, hesitant, incredulous, sceptical, suspicious, tentative, uncertain, unclear, unconvinced, undecided, unsure. **2** *a doubtful decision*. ambiguous, debatable, dubious, equivocal, *inf* iffy, inconclusive, problematical, questionable, suspect, vague, worrying. **3** *a doubtful ally*. irresolute, uncommitted, unreliable, untrustworthy, vacillating, wavering. *Opp* CERTAIN, DEPENDABLE.

dowdy *adj* colourless, dingy, drab, dull, *inf* frumpish, old-fashioned, shabby, *inf* sloppy, slovenly, *inf* tatty, unattractive, unstylish. *Opp* SMART.

downfall *n* collapse, defeat, overthrow, ruin, undoing.

downhearted *adj* dejected, depressed, discouraged, *inf* down, downcast, miserable, unhappy. ▷ SAD.

downward *adj* declining, descending, downhill, easy, falling, going down. *Opp* UPWARD.

downy *adj* feathery, fleecy, fluffy, furry, fuzzy, soft, velvety, woolly.

drab *adj* cheerless, colourless, dingy, dismal, dowdy, dreary, dull, flat, gloomy, grey, grimy, lacklustre, shabby, sombre, unattractive, uninteresting. *Opp* BRIGHT.

draft *n* 1 first version, notes, outline, plan, rough version, sketch. 2 *bank draft*. cheque, order, postal order. ● *vb* block out, compose, delineate, draw up, outline, plan, prepare, put together, sketch out, work out, write a draft of.

drag *vb* 1 draw, haul, lug, pull, tow, trail, tug. 2 *time drags*. be boring, crawl, creep, go slowly, linger, loiter, lose momentum, move slowly, pass slowly.

drain *n* channel, conduit, culvert, dike, ditch, drainage, drainpipe, duct, gutter, outlet, pipe, sewer, trench, water-course. ● *vb* 1 bleed, clear, draw off, dry out, empty, evacuate, extract, pump out, remove, tap, take off. 2 drip, ebb, leak out, ooze, seep, strain, trickle. 3 *drain resources*. consume, deplete, exhaust, sap, spend, use up.

drama *n* 1 acting, dramatics, dramaturgy, histrionics, improvisation, stagecraft, theatre, theatricals, thespian arts. 2 comedy, dramatization, farce, melodrama, musical, opera, operetta, pantomime, performance, play, production, screenplay, script,

show, stage version, TV version, tragedy. 3 *real-life drama*. action, crisis, excitement, suspense, turmoil.

dramatic *adj* 1 histrionic, stage, theatrical, thespian. 2 *dramatic gestures*. exaggerated, flamboyant, large, overdone, showy. 3 ▷ EXCITING.

dramatist *n* dramaturge, playwright, scriptwriter.

dramatize *vb* 1 adapt, make into a play. 2 exaggerate, make too much of, overdo, overplay, overstate.

drape *n* old use arras, curtain, drapery, hanging, screen, tapestry, valance. ● *vb* cover, decorate, festoon, hang, swathe.

drastic *adj* desperate, dire, draconian, extreme, far-reaching, forceful, harsh, radical, rigorous, severe, strong, vigorous.

draught *n* 1 breeze, current, movement, puff, wind. 2 *draught of ale*. dose, drink, gulp, measure, pull, swallow, *inf* swig.

draw *n* 1 attraction, enticement, lure, *inf* pull. 2 dead-heat, dead-lock, stalemate, tie. 3 competition, lottery, raffle. ● *vb* 1 drag, haul, lug, pull, tow, tug. 2 *draw a crowd*. allure, attract, bring in, coax, entice, invite, lure, persuade, pull in, win over. 3 *draw a sword*. extract, remove, take out, unsheathe, withdraw. 4 *draw lots*. choose, pick, select. 5 *draw a conclusion*. arrive at, come to, deduce, formulate, infer, work out. 6 *draw water*. drain, let (*blood*), pour, pump, syphon, tap. 7 *draw 1-1*. be equal, finish equal, tie. 8 *draw pictures*. depict, map out, mark out, outline, paint, pen, pencil, portray, represent, sketch, trace. **draw out** ▷ EXTEND. **draw up** ▷ DRAFT, HALT.

drawback *n* defect, difficulty, disadvantage, hindrance, hurdle, impediment, obstacle, obstruction, problem, snag, stumbling block.

drawing *n* cartoon, design, graphics, illustration, outline, sketch. ▷ PICTURE.

dread *n* anxiety, apprehension, awe, *inf* cold feet, dismay, fear, *inf* the jitters, nervousness, perturbation, qualm, trepidation, uneasiness, worry. ● *vb* be afraid of, shrink from, view with horror. ▷ FEAR.

dreadful *adj* alarming, appalling, awful, dire, distressing, evil, fearful, frightful, ghastly, grisly, gruesome, harrowing, hideous, horrible, horrifying, indescribable, monstrous, shocking, terrible, tragic, unspeakable, upsetting, wicked. ▷ BAD, FRIGHTENING.

dream *n* **1** daydream, delusion, fantasy, hallucination, illusion, mirage, nightmare, reverie, trance, vision. **2** ambition, aspiration, ideal, pipedream, wish. ● *vb* conjure up, daydream, fancy, fantasize, hallucinate, have a vision, imagine, think. **dream up** ▷ INVENT.

dreary *adj* bleak, boring, cheerless, depressing, dismal, dull, gloomy, joyless, sombre, uninteresting. ▷ MISERABLE.

dregs *n* deposit, grounds (*of coffee*), lees, precipitate, remains, residue, sediment.

drench *vb* douse, drown, flood, inundate, saturate, soak, souse, steep, wet thoroughly.

dress *n* **1** apparel, attire, clothing, costume, garb, garments, *inf* gear, *inf* get-up, outfit, *old use* raiment. ▷ CLOTHES. **2** frock, gown, robe, shift. ● *vb* **1** array, attire, clothe, cover, fit out, provide clothes for, put clothes on, robe. **2** *dress a wound.* attend to, bandage, bind up, care for, put a dressing on, tend, treat. *Opp* UNCOVER.

dressing *n* bandage, compress, plaster, poultice.

dribble *vb* **1** drool, slaver, slobber. **2** drip, flow, leak, ooze, run, seep, trickle.

drift *n* **1** accumulation, bank, dune, heap, mound, pile, ridge. **2** *drift of a speech.* ▷ GIST. ● *vb* **1** be carried, coast, float, meander, move casually, move slowly, ramble, roam, rove, stray, waft, walk aimlessly, wander. **2** *snow drifts.* accumulate, gather, make drifts, pile up.

drill *n* **1** discipline, exercises, instruction, practice, *sl* square-bashing, training. ● *vb* **1** coach, discipline, exercise, indoctrinate, instruct, practise, rehearse, school, teach, train. **2** bore, penetrate, perforate, pierce.

drink *n* **1** beverage, *inf* bevvy, *inf* cuppa, *inf* dram, draught, glass, *inf* gulp, *inf* night-cap, *inf* nip, pint, *joc* potation, sip, swallow, swig, *inf* tipple, tot. **2** alcohol, *inf* booze, *joc* grog, *joc* liquid refreshment, liquor. □ ale, beer, bourbon, brandy, champagne, chartreuse, cider, cocktail, Cognac, crème de menthe, gin, Kirsch, lager, mead, perry, *inf* plonk, port, punch, rum, schnapps, shandy, sherry, vermouth, vodka, whisky, wine. ● *vb* **1** gulp, guzzle, imbibe, *inf* knock back, lap, partake of, *old use* quaff, sip, suck, swallow, swig, *inf* swill. **2** *inf* booze, carouse, get drunk, *inf* indulge, tipple, tope.

drip *n* bead, dribble, drop, leak, splash, spot, tear, trickle. ● *vb* dribble, drizzle, drop, fall in drips, leak, plop, splash, sprinkle, trickle, weep.

drive *n* **1** excursion, jaunt, journey, outing, ride, run, *inf* spin, trip. **2** aggressiveness, ambition, determination, energy, enterprise, enthusiasm, *inf* get-up-and-go, impetus, industry, initiative, keenness, motivation, persistence, *inf* push, vigour, vim, zeal. **3** campaign, crusade, effort. ● *vb* **1** bang, dig, hammer, hit, impel, knock, plunge, prod, push, ram, sink, stab, strike, thrust. **2** coerce, compel, constrain, force, oblige, press, urge. **3** *drive a car.* control, direct, guide, handle, herd, manage, pilot, propel, send, steer. ▷ TRAVEL. **drive out** ▷ EXPEL.

droop *vb* be limp, bend, dangle, fall, flop, hang, sag, slump, wilt, wither.

drop *n* bead, blob, bubble, dab, drip, droplet, globule, pearl, spot, tear. **2** dash, *inf* nip, small quantity, *inf* tot. **3** *a steep drop.* declivity, descent, dive, escarpment, fall, incline, plunge, precipice, scarp. **4** *a drop in price.* cut, decrease, reduction, slump. *Opp* RISE. ● *vb* **1** collapse, descend, dip, dive, fall, go down, jump down, lower, nosedive, plummet, *inf* plump, plunge, sink, slump, subside, swoop, tumble. **2** *drop from a team*. eliminate, exclude, leave out, omit. **3** *drop a friend*. abandon, desert, discard, *inf* dump, forsake, give up, jilt, leave, reject, scrap, shed. **drop behind** ▷ LAG. **drop in on** ▷ VISIT. **drop off** ▷ SLEEP.

drown *vb* **1** engulf, flood, immerse, submerge, swamp. ▷ KILL. **2** *noise drowned my voice*. be louder than, overpower, overwhelm, silence.

drowsy *adj* dozing, dozy, heavyeyed, listless, *inf* nodding off, sleepy, sluggish, somnolent, soporific, tired, weary. *Opp* LIVELY.

drudgery *n* chore, donkey-work, *inf* grind, labour, slavery, *inf* slog, toil, travail. ▷ WORK.

drug *n* **1** cure, medicament, medication, medicine, *old use* physic, remedy, treatment. **2** *inf* dope, narcotic, opiate. □ analgesic, antidepressant, barbiturate, hallucinogen, pain-killer, sedative, stimulant, tonic, tranquillizer. □ caffeine, cannabis, cocaine, digitalis, hashish, heroin, insulin, laudanum, marijuana, morphia, nicotine, opium, phenobarbitone, quinine. ● *vb* anaesthetize, *inf* dope, dose, give a drug to, *inf* knock out, medicate, poison, sedate, stupefy, tranquillize, treat.

drum *n* **1** ▷ BARREL. **2** □ bass-drum, bongo-drum, kettledrum, side-drum, snare-drum, tambour, tenor-drum, plur timpani, tom-tom.

drunk *adj* delirious, fuddled, incapable, inebriate, inebriated, intoxicated, maudlin, [*slang*] blotto, bombed, boozed-up, canned, high, legless, merry, paralytic, pickled, pie-eyed, pissed, plastered, sloshed, soused, sozzled, stoned, tanked, tiddly, tight, tipsy. *Opp* SOBER.

drunkard *n* alcoholic, *inf* boozer, *sl* dipso, dipsomaniac, drunk, *inf* sot, tippler, toper, *sl* wino. *Opp* TEETOTALLER.

dry *adj* **1** arid, baked, barren, dead, dehydrated, desiccated, moistureless, parched, scorched, shrivelled, sterile, thirsty, waterless. *Opp* WET. **2** *a dry book*. boring, dreary, dull, flat, prosaic, stale, tedious, tiresome, uninspired, uninteresting. *Opp* LIVELY. **3** *dry humour*. *inf* dead-pan, droll, expressionless, laconic, lugubrious, unsmiling. ● *vb* become dry, dehumidify, dehydrate, desiccate, go hard, make dry, parch, shrivel, wilt, wither.

dual *adj* binary, coupled, double, duplicate, linked, paired, twin.

dubious *adj* **1** ▷ DOUBTFUL. **2** *a dubious character*. *inf* fishy, *inf* shady, suspect, suspicious, unreliable, untrustworthy.

duck *vb* **1** avoid, bend, bob down, crouch, dip down, dodge, evade, sidestep, stoop, swerve, take evasive action. **2** immerse, plunge, push under, submerge.

due *adj* **1** in arrears, outstanding, owed, owing, payable, unpaid. **2** *due consideration*. adequate, appropriate, decent, deserved, expected, fitting, just, mature, merited, proper, requisite, right, rightful, scheduled, sufficient, suitable, wellearned. ● *n* deserts, entitlement, merits, reward, rights. **dues** ▷ DUTY.

dull *adj* **1** dim, dingy, dowdy, drab, dreary, faded, flat, gloomy, lacklustre, lifeless, matt, plain, shabby, sombre, subdued. **2** *a dull sky*. cloudy, dismal, grey, heavy, leaden, murky, overcast, sullen, sunless. **3** *a dull sound*. deadened, indistinct, muffled, muted. **4** *a dull student*. dense, dim, dim-witted, obtuse, slow, *inf* thick, unimaginative, unintelligent, unresponsive. ▷ STUPID. **5** *a dull edge*. blunt, blunted, unsharpened. **6** *dull talk*. boring, commonplace, dry, monotonous, prosaic, stodgy, tame, tedious, unexciting, uninteresting. *Opp* BRIGHT, SHARP.

dumb *adj* inarticulate, *inf* mum, mute, silent, speechless, tongue-tied, unable to speak.

dummy *n* **1** copy, counterfeit, duplicate, imitation, mock-up, model, reproduction, sample, sham, simulation, substitute, toy. **2** doll, figure, manikin, puppet.

dump *n* **1** junkyard, rubbish-heap, tip. **2** *arms dump.* arsenal, cache, depot, hoard, store. ● *vb* deposit, discard, dispose of, *inf* ditch, drop, empty out, get rid of, jettison, offload, *inf* park, place, put down, reject, scrap, throw away, throw down, tip, unload.

dune *n* drift, hillock, hummock, mound, sand-dune.

dungeon *n* old use donjon, gaol, keep, lock-up, oubliette, pit, prison, vault.

duplicate *adj* alternative, copied, corresponding, identical, matching, second, twin. ● *n* carbon copy, clone, copy, double, facsimile, imitation, likeness, *inf* look-alike, match, photocopy, photostat, replica, reproduction, twin, Xerox. ● *vb* copy, do again, double up on, photocopy, print, repeat, reproduce, Xerox.

durable *adj* enduring, hard-wearing, heavy-duty, indestructible, long-lasting, permanent, resilient, stout, strong, substantial, thick, tough. *Opp* IMPERMANENT, WEAK.

dusk *n* evening, gloaming, gloom, sundown, sunset, twilight.

dust *n* dirt, grime, grit, particles, powder.

dusty *adj* **1** chalky, crumbly, dry, fine, friable, gritty, powdery, sandy,

sooty. **2** *a dusty room.* dirty, filthy, grimy, grubby, mucky, uncleaned, unswept.

dutiful *adj* attentive, careful, compliant, conscientious, devoted, diligent, faithful, hard-working, loyal, obedient, obliging, punctilious, reliable, responsible, scrupulous, thorough, trustworthy, willing. *Opp* IRRESPONSIBLE.

duty *n* **1** allegiance, faithfulness, loyalty, obedience, obligation, onus, responsibility, service. **2** assignment, business, charge, chore, function, job, office, role, stint, task, work. **3** charge, customs, dues, fee, impost, levy, tariff, tax, toll.

dwarf *adj* ▷ SMALL. ● *n* midget, pigmy. ● *vb* dominate, look bigger than, overshadow, tower over.

dwell *vb* abide, be accommodated, live, lodge, reside, stay. **dwell in** ▷ INHABIT.

dwelling *n* abode, domicile, habitation, home, lodging, quarters, residence. ▷ HOUSE.

dying *adj* declining, expiring, fading, failing, moribund, obsolescent. *Opp* ALIVE.

dynamic *adj* active, committed, driving, eager, energetic, enterprising, enthusiastic, forceful, *inf* go-ahead, *derog* go-getting, high-powered, lively, motivated, powerful, pushful, *derog* pushy, spirited, vigorous, zealous. *Opp* APATHETIC.

E

eager *adj* agog, animated, anxious (*to please*), ardent, avid, bursting, committed, craving, desirous, earnest, enthusiastic, excited, fervent, fervid, hungry, impatient, intent, interested, *inf* itching, keen, *inf* keyed up, longing, motivated, passionate, *inf* raring (*to go*), voracious, yearning, zealous. *Opp* APATHETIC.

eagerness *n* alacrity, anxiety, appetite, ardour, avidity, commitment, desire, earnestness, enthusiasm, excitement, fervour, hunger, impatience, intentness, interest, keenness, longing, motivation, passion, thirst, zeal. *Opp* APATHY.

early *adj* 1 advance, ahead of time, before time, first, forward, premature. *Opp* LATE. 2 ancient, antiquated, initial, original, primeval, primitive. ▷ OLD. *Opp* RECENT.

earn *vb* 1 be paid, *inf* bring in, *inf* clear, draw, fetch in, gain, get, *inf* gross, make, make a profit of, net, obtain, pocket, realize, receive, *inf* take home, work for, yield. 2 attain, be worthy of, deserve, merit, qualify for, warrant, win.

earnest *adj* 1 assiduous, committed, conscientious, dedicated, determined, devoted, diligent, eager, hardworking, industrious, involved, purposeful, resolved, zealous. *Opp* CASUAL. 2 grave, heartfelt, impassioned, serious, sincere, sober, solemn, thoughtful, well-meant.

earnings *plur n* income, salary, stipend, wages. ▷ PAY.

earth *n* clay, dirt, ground, humus, land, loam, soil, topsoil.

earthenware *n* ceramics, china, crockery, *inf* crocks, porcelain, pots, pottery.

earthly *adj* corporeal, human, material, materialistic, mortal, mundane, physical, secular, temporal, terrestrial, worldly. *Opp* SPIRITUAL.

earthquake *n* quake, shock, tremor, upheaval.

earthy *adj* bawdy, coarse, crude, down to earth, frank, lusty, ribald, uninhibited. ▷ OBSCENE.

ease *n* 1 aplomb, calmness, comfort, composure, contentment, enjoyment, happiness, leisure, luxury, peace, quiet, relaxation, repose, rest, serenity, tranquillity. 2 dexterity, easiness, effortlessness, facility, nonchalance, simplicity, skill, speed, straightforwardness. *Opp* DIFFICULTY. ● *vb* 1 allay, alleviate, assuage, calm, comfort, decrease, lessen, lighten, mitigate, moderate, pacify, quell, quieten, reduce, relax, relieve, slacken, soothe, tranquillize. 2 edge, guide, inch, manoeuvre, move gradually, slide, slip, steer.

easy *adj* 1 carefree, comfortable, contented, cosy, *inf* cushy, effortless, leisurely, light, painless, peaceful, pleasant, relaxed, relaxing, restful, serene, soft, tranquil, undemanding, unexacting, unhurried, untroubled. 2 clear, elementary, facile, foolproof, *inf* idiot-proof, manageable, plain, simple, straightforward, uncomplicated, understandable, user-friendly. 3 ▷ EASYGOING. *Opp* DIFFICULT.

easygoing *adj* accommodating, affable, amenable, calm, carefree, casual, cheerful, docile, even-tempered, flexible, forbearing, *inf* free and easy, friendly, genial, *inf* happy-go-lucky, indulgent, informal, *inf* laid-back, *derog* lax, lenient, liberal, mellow, natural, nonchalant, open, patient, permissive, placid, relaxed, tolerant, unexcitable, unruffled, *derog* weak. *Opp* STRICT.

eat *vb* consume, devour, digest, feed on, ingest, live on, *old use* partake of, swallow. □ bite, bolt, champ, chew, crunch, gnaw, gobble, gorge, gormandize, graze, grind, gulp, guzzle, *inf* make a pig of yourself, masticate, munch, nibble, overeat, peck, *inf* scoff, *inf* slurp, *inf* stuff (yourself), taste, *inf* tuck in, *inf* wolf. □ banquet, breakfast, dine, feast, lunch, snack, *old use* sup. **eat away**, **eat into** ▷ ERODE.

eatable *adj* digestible, edible, fit to eat, good, palatable, safe to eat, wholesome. ▷ TASTY. *Opp* INEDIBLE.

ebb *vb* fall, flow back, go down, recede, retreat, subside. ▷ DECLINE.

eccentric *adj* **1** aberrant, abnormal, anomalous, atypical, bizarre, cranky, curious, freakish, grotesque, idiosyncratic, *sl* kinky, odd, outlandish, out of the ordinary, peculiar, preposterous, quaint, queer, quirky, singular, strange, unconventional, unusual, *sl* wacky, *inf* way-out, *inf* weird, *inf* zany. ▷ ABSURD, MAD. **2** *eccentric circles.* irregular, off-centre. ● *n* *inf* character, *inf* crackpot, crank, *inf* freak, individualist, nonconformist, *inf* oddball, oddity, *inf* weirdie, *inf* weirdo.

echo *vb* **1** resound, reverberate, ring, sound again. **2** ape, copy, duplicate, emulate, imitate, mimic, mirror, reiterate, repeat, reproduce, say again.

eclipse *vb* **1** block out, blot out, cloud, darken, dim, extinguish, obscure, veil. ▷ COVER. **2** excel, outdo, outshine, overshadow, *inf* put in the shade, surpass, top.

economic *adj* budgetary, business, financial, fiscal, monetary, money-making, trading.

economical *adj* **1** careful, cheese-paring, frugal, parsimonious, provident, prudent, sparing, thrifty. ▷ MISERLY. *Opp* WASTEFUL. **2** *an economical meal.* cheap, cost-effective, inexpensive, lowpriced, money-saving, reasonable, *inf* value-for-money. *Opp* EXPENSIVE.

economize *vb* be economical, cut back, retrench, save, *inf* scrimp, skimp, spend less, *inf* tighten your belt. *Opp* SQUANDER.

economy *n* **1** frugality, *derog* meanness, *derog* miserliness, parsimony, providence, prudence, saving, thrift. *Opp* WASTE. **2** *the national economy.* budget, economic affairs, wealth. **3** ▷ BREVITY.

ecstasy *n* bliss, delight, delirium, elation, enthusiasm, euphoria, exaltation, fervour, frenzy, gratification, happiness, joy, rapture, thrill, trance, *old use* transport.

ecstatic *adj* blissful, delighted, delirious, elated, enraptured, enthusiastic, euphoric, exhilarated, exultant, fervent, frenzied, gleeful, joyful, orgasmic, overjoyed, *inf* over the moon, rapturous, transported. ▷ HAPPY.

eddy *n* circular movement, maelstrom, swirl, vortex, whirl, whirlpool, whirlwind. ● *vb* move in circles, spin, swirl, turn, whirl.

edge *n* **1** border, boundary, brim, brink, circumference, frame, kerb, limit, lip, margin, outline, perimeter, periphery, rim, side, verge. **2** *edge of town.* outlying parts, outskirts, suburbs. **3** *edge on a knife.* acuteness, keenness, sharpness. **4** *edge of a curtain.* edging, fringe, hem, selvage. ● *vb* **1** bind, border, fringe, hem, make an edge for, trim. **2** *edge away.* crawl, creep, inch, move stealthily, sidle, slink, steal, work your way, worm.

edible *adj* digestible, eatable, fit to eat, palatable, safe to eat, wholesome. ▷ TASTY. *Opp* INEDIBLE.

edit *vb* adapt, alter, amend, arrange, assemble, compile, get ready, modify, organize, prepare, put together, select, supervise the production of. □ abridge, annotate, bowdlerize, censor, clean up, condense, copy-edit, correct, cut, dub, emend, expurgate, format, polish, proof-read, rearrange, rephrase, revise, rewrite, select, shorten, splice (film).

edition n **1** copy, issue, number. **2** impression, printing, print-run, publication, version.

educate vb bring up, civilize, coach, counsel, cultivate, discipline, drill, edify, enlighten, guide, improve, inculcate, indoctrinate, inform, instruct, lecture, nurture, rear, school, teach, train, tutor.

educated adj cultured, enlightened, erudite, knowledgeable, learned, literate, numerate, sophisticated, trained, well-bred, well-read.

education n coaching, curriculum, enlightenment, guidance, indoctrination, instruction, schooling, syllabus, teaching, training, tuition. □ academy, college, conservatory, polytechnic, sixth-form college, tertiary college, university. ▷ SCHOOL, TEACHING.

eerie adj inf creepy, frightening, ghostly, mysterious, inf scary, spectral, inf spooky, strange, uncanny, unearthly, unnatural, weird.

effect n **1** aftermath, conclusion, consequence, impact, influence, issue, outcome, repercussion, result, sequel, upshot. **2** feeling, illusion, impression, sensation, sense. ● vb accomplish, achieve, bring about, bring in, carry out, cause, create, effectuate, enforce, execute, implement, initiate, make, produce, put into effect, secure.

effective adj **1** able, capable, competent, effectual, efficacious, functional, impressive, potent, powerful, productive, proficient, real, serviceable, strong, successful, useful, worthwhile. ▷ EFFICIENT. **2** an effective argument. cogent, compelling, convincing, meaningful, persuasive, striking, telling. Opp INEFFECTIVE.

effeminate adj camp, effete, girlish, inf pansy, inf sissy, unmanly, weak, womanish. Opp MANLY.

effervesce vb bubble, ferment, fizz, foam, froth, sparkle.

effervescent adj bubbling, bubbly, carbonated, fizzy, foaming, frothy, gassy, sparkling.

efficient adj businesslike, cost-effective, economic, productive, streamlined, thrifty. ▷ EFFECTIVE. Opp INEFFICIENT.

effort n **1** application, diligence, inf elbow grease, endeavour, exertion, industry, labour, pains, strain, stress, striving, struggle, toil, old use travail, trouble, work. **2** a brave effort. attempt, endeavour, go, try, venture. **3** a successful effort. accomplishment, achievement, exploit, feat, job, outcome, product, production, result.

effusive adj demonstrative, ebullient, enthusiastic, exuberant, fulsome, gushing, lavish, inf over the top, profuse, voluble. Opp RETICENT.

egoism n egocentricity, egotism, narcissism, pride, self-centredness, self-importance, self-interest, selfishness, self-love, self-regard, vanity.

egotistical adj egocentric, self-admiring, self-centred, selfish. ▷ CONCEITED.

eject vb **1** banish, inf boot out, inf bundle out, deport, discharge, dismiss, drive out, evict, exile, expel, get rid of, inf kick out, oust, push out, put out, remove, sack, send out, shoot out, inf shove out, throw out, turn out. **2** ▷ EMIT.

elaborate adj **1** complex, complicated, detailed, exhaustive, intricate, involved, meticulous, minute, painstaking, thorough, well worked out. **2** elaborate décor. baroque, busy, Byzantine, decorative, fancy, fantastic, fussy, grotesque, intricate, ornamental, ornamented, ornate, rococo, showy. Opp SIMPLE. ● vb add to, adorn, amplify, complicate, decorate, develop, embellish, enlarge on, enrich, expand, expatiate on, fill out, flesh out, give details of, improve on, ornament. Opp SIMPLIFY.

elapse vb go by, lapse, pass, slip by.

elastic adj bendy, bouncy, ductile, expandable, flexible, plastic, pliable, pliant, resilient, rubbery, inf springy, stretchable, inf stretchy, yielding. Opp RIGID.

elderly *adj* ageing, *inf* getting on, oldish. ▷ OLD.

elect *adj* [goes after noun] president elect. [synonyms used after noun] designate, to be; [synonyms before noun] chosen, elected, prospective, selected. ● *vb* adopt, appoint, choose, name, nominate, opt for, pick, select, vote for.

election *n* ballot, choice, plebiscite, poll, referendum, selection, vote, voting.

electioneer *vb* campaign, canvass.

electorate *n* constituents, electors, voters.

electric *adj* **1** battery-operated, electrical, mains-operated. **2** *electric atmosphere*. electrifying. ▷ EXCITING.

electricity *n* current, energy, power, power supply.

elegant *adj* artistic, beautiful, chic, courtly, cultivated, dapper, debonair, dignified, exquisite, fashionable, fine, genteel, graceful, gracious, handsome, luxurious, modish, noble, pleasing, *inf* plush, *inf* posh, refined, smart, soigné(e), sophisticated, splendid, stately, stylish, suave, tasteful, urbane, well-bred. *Opp* INELEGANT.

elegy *n* dirge, lament, requiem.

element *n* **1** component, constituent, detail, essential, factor, feature, fragment, hint, ingredient, part, piece, small amount, trace, unit. **2** *in your element*. domain, environment, habitat, medium, sphere, territory. **elements** ▷ RUDIMENTS, WEATHER.

elementary *adj* basic, early, first, fundamental, initial, introductory, primary, principal, rudimentary, simple, straightforward, uncomplicated, understandable. ▷ EASY. *Opp* ADVANCED.

elevate *vb* exalt, hold up, lift, make higher, promote, rear. ▷ RAISE. **elevated** ▷ HIGH, NOBLE.

elicit *vb* bring out, call forth, derive, draw out, evoke, extort, extract, get, obtain, wrest, wring.

eligible *adj* acceptable, allowed, appropriate, authorized, available, competent, equipped, fit, fitting, proper, qualified, suitable, worthy. *Opp* INELIGIBLE.

eliminate *vb* **1** abolish, annihilate, delete, destroy, dispense with, do away with, eject, end, eradicate, exterminate, extinguish, finish off, get rid of, put an end to, remove, stamp out. ▷ KILL. **2** cut out, drop, exclude, knock out, leave out, omit, reject.

élite *n* aristocracy, best, *inf* cream, first-class people, flower, meritocracy, nobility, top people, *inf* upper crust.

eloquent *adj* articulate, expressive, fluent, forceful, *derog* glib, moving, persuasive, plausible, powerful, unfaltering. *Opp* INARTICULATE.

elude *vb* avoid, circumvent, dodge, *inf* duck, escape, evade, foil, get away from, *inf* give (someone) the slip, shake off, slip away from.

elusive *adj* **1** *inf* always on the move, evasive, fugitive, hard to find, slippery. **2** *elusive meaning*. ambiguous, baffling, deceptive, hard to pin down, indefinable, intangible, puzzling, shifting.

emaciated *adj* anorectic, atrophied, bony, cadaverous, gaunt, haggard, shrivelled, skeletal, skinny, starved, underfed, undernourished, wasted away, wizened. ▷ THIN.

emancipate *vb* deliver, discharge, enfranchise, free, give rights to, let go, liberate, loose, manumit, release, set free, unchain. *Opp* ENSLAVE.

embankment *n* bank, causeway, dam, earthwork, mound, rampart.

embark *vb* board, depart, go aboard, leave, set out. *Opp* DISEMBARK. **embark on** ▷ BEGIN.

embarrass *vb* abash, chagrin, confuse, discomfit, discompose, disconcert, discountenance, disgrace, distress, fluster, humiliate, *inf* make you blush, mortify, *inf* put you on the spot, shame, *inf* show up, upset.

embarrassed ▷ ASHAMED. **embarrassing** ▷ AWKWARD, SHAMEFUL.

embellish vb adorn, beautify, deck, decorate, embroider, garnish, ornament, sl tart up, inf titivate. ▷ ELABORATE.

embezzle vb appropriate, misapply, misappropriate, peculate, inf put your hand in the till, take fraudulently. ▷ STEAL.

embezzlement n fraud, misappropriation, misuse of funds, peculation, stealing, theft.

embittered adj acid, bitter, disillusioned, envious, rancorous, resentful, sour. ▷ ANGRY.

emblem n badge, crest, device, image, insignia, mark, regalia, seal, sign, symbol, token.

embody vb **1** exemplify, express, incarnate, manifest, personify, reify, represent, stand for, symbolize. **2** bring together, combine, comprise, embrace, enclose, gather together, include, incorporate, integrate, involve, take in, unite.

embrace vb **1** clasp, cling to, cuddle, enfold, fondle, grasp, hold, hug, kiss, snuggle up to. **2** embrace new ideas. accept, espouse, receive, take on, welcome. **3** ▷ EMBODY.

embryonic adj early, immature, just beginning, rudimentary, underdeveloped, undeveloped, unformed. Opp MATURE.

emerge vb appear, arise, be revealed, come out, come to light, come to notice, emanate, old use issue forth, leak out, inf pop up, proceed, surface, transpire, inf turn out.

emergency n crisis, danger, difficulty, exigency, predicament, serious situation.

emigrate vb depart, go abroad, leave, quit, relocate, resettle, set out.

eminent adj august, celebrated, conspicuous, distinguished, elevated, esteemed, exalted, familiar, famous, great, high-ranking, honoured, illustrious, important, notable, noted, noteworthy, outstanding, pre-eminent, prominent, renowned, well-known. Opp LOWLY.

emit vb belch, discharge, disgorge, ejaculate, eject, exhale, expel, exude, give off, give out, issue, radiate, send out, spew out, spout, transmit, vent, vomit.

emotion n agitation, excitement, feeling, fervour, passion, sentiment, warmth. ▷ ANGER, LOVE, etc.

emotional adj **1** ardent, demonstrative, enthusiastic, excited, fervent, fiery, heated, hot-headed, impassioned, intense, irrational, moved, passionate, romantic, stirred, touched, warm-hearted, inf worked up. ▷ ANGRY, LOVING, etc. **2** emotional language. affecting, biased, emotive, heartfelt, heart-rending, inflammatory, loaded, moving, pathetic, poignant, prejudiced, provocative, sentimental, stirring, subjective, tear-jerking, tender, touching. Opp UNEMOTIONAL.

emphasis n accent, attention, force, gravity, importance, intensity, priority, prominence, strength, stress, urgency, weight.

emphasize vb accent, accentuate, bring out, dwell on, focus on, foreground, give emphasis to, highlight, impress, insist on, make obvious, inf play up, point up, inf press home, inf rub it in, show clearly, spotlight, stress, underline, underscore.

emphatic adj affirmative, assertive, categorical, confident, dogmatic, definite, firm, forceful, insistent, positive, pronounced, resolute, strong, uncompromising, unequivocal. Opp TENTATIVE.

empirical adj experiential, experimental, observed, practical, pragmatic. Opp THEORETICAL.

employ vb **1** commission, engage, enlist, have on the payroll, hire, pay, sign up, take on, use the services of. **2** apply, use, utilize.

employed adj active, busy, earning, engaged, hired, involved, in work, occupied, practising, working. ▷ BUSY. Opp UNEMPLOYED.

employee n old use hand, inf underling, worker. **employees** staff, workforce.

employer n boss, chief, inf gaffer, inf governor, head, manager, owner, proprietor, taskmaster.

employment n business, calling, craft, job, line, livelihood, living, métier, occupation, profession, pursuit, trade, vocation, work.

empty adj 1 bare, blank, clean, clear, deserted, desolate, forsaken, hollow, unfilled, unfurnished, uninhabited, unladen, unoccupied, unused, vacant, void. Opp FULL. 2 empty threats. futile, idle, impotent, ineffective, insincere, meaningless, pointless, purposeless, senseless, silly, unreal, worthless. ● vb clear, discharge, drain, eject, evacuate, exhaust, pour out, remove, take out, unload, vacate, void. Opp FILL.

enable vb aid, allow, approve, assist, authorize, charter, empower, entitle, equip, facilitate, franchise, help, license, make it possible, permit, provide the means, qualify, sanction. Opp PREVENT.

enchant vb allure, beguile, bewitch, captivate, cast a spell on, charm, delight, enrapture, enthral, entrance, fascinate, hypnotize, mesmerize, spellbind. **enchanting** ▷ ATTRACTIVE.

enchantment n charm, conjuration, magic, sorcery, spell, witchcraft, wizardry. ▷ DELIGHT.

enclose vb bound, box, cage, case, cocoon, conceal, confine, contain, cover, encase, encircle, encompass, enfold, envelop, fence in, hedge in, hem in, immure, insert, limit, package, parcel up, pen, restrict, ring, secure, sheathe, shut in, shut up, surround, wall in, wall up, wrap. ▷ IMPRISON.

enclosure n 1 arena, cage, compound, coop, corral, court, courtyard, farmyard, field, fold, paddock, pen, pound, ring, run, sheepfold, stockade, sty, yard. 2 enclosure in an envelope. contents, inclusion, insertion.

encounter n 1 confrontation, meeting. 2 [military] battle, brush, clash, dispute, skirmish, struggle. ▷ FIGHT. ● vb chance upon, clash with, come upon, confront, contend with, inf cross swords with, face, grapple with, happen upon, have an encounter with, meet, inf run into.

encourage vb 1 abet, advocate, animate, applaud, cheer, inf egg on, embolden, give hope to, hearten, incite, inspire, invite, persuade, prompt, rally, reassure, rouse, spur on, support, urge. 2 encourage sales. aid, be an incentive to, be conducive to, boost, engender, foster, further, generate, help, increase, induce, promote, stimulate. Opp DISCOURAGE.

encouragement n applause, approval, boost, cheer, exhortation, incentive, incitement, inspiration, reassurance, inf shot in the arm, stimulation, stimulus, support. Opp DISCOURAGEMENT.

encouraging adj comforting, heartening, hopeful, inspiring, optimistic, positive, promising, reassuring. ▷ FAVOURABLE.

encroach vb enter, impinge, infringe, intrude, invade, make inroads, trespass, violate.

end n 1 boundary, edge, extreme, extremity, limit, pole, tip. 2 cessation, close, coda, completion, conclusion, culmination, curtain (of play), denouement (of plot), ending, expiration, expiry, finale, finish, inf pay-off, resolution. 3 journey's end. destination, home, termination, terminus. 4 end of a queue. back, rear, tail. 5 end of your life. destiny, destruction, doom, extinction, fate, passing, ruin. ▷ DEATH. 6 an end in view. aim, aspiration, consequence, design, effect, intention, objective, outcome, plan, purpose, result, upshot. Opp BEGINNING. ● vb 1 abolish, break off, bring to an end, complete, conclude, cut off, destroy, discontinue, inf drop, eliminate, exterminate, finalize, inf get rid of, halt, phase out, inf put an end to, inf round off, ruin, scotch, terminate, inf wind up. 2 break up, cease, close, come to an end, culminate, die, disappear, expire, fade away, finish, *inf* pack up, reach a climax, stop. *Opp* BEGIN.

endanger *vb* expose to risk, imperil, jeopardize, put at risk, threaten. *Opp* PROTECT.

endearing *adj* appealing, attractive, captivating, charming, disarming, enchanting, engaging, likable, lovable, sweet, winning, winsome. *Opp* REPULSIVE.

endeavour *vb* aim, aspire, attempt, do your best, exert yourself, strive, try.

endless *adj* **1** boundless, immeasurable, inexhaustible, infinite, limitless, measureless, unbounded, unfailing, unlimited. **2** abiding, ceaseless, constant, continual, continuous, enduring, eternal, everlasting, immortal, incessant, interminable, never-ending, nonstop, perpetual, persistent, unbroken, undying, unending, uninterrupted.

endorse *vb* **1** advocate, agree with, approve, authorize, *inf* back, condone, confirm, *inf* OK, sanction, set your seal of approval to, subscribe to, support. **2** *endorse a cheque*. countersign, sign.

endurance *n* determination, fortitude, patience, perseverance, persistence, pertinacity, resolution, stamina, staying-power, strength, tenacity.

endure *vb* **1** carry on, continue, exist, last, live on, persevere, persist, prevail, remain, stay, survive. **2** bear, cope with, experience, go through, *inf* put up with, stand, *inf* stick, *inf* stomach, submit to, suffer, *sl* sweat it out, tolerate, undergo, weather, withstand. **enduring** ▷ ENDLESS.

enemy *n* adversary, antagonist, assailant, attacker, competitor, foe, opponent, opposition, the other side, rival, *inf* them. *Opp* FRIEND.

energetic *adj* active, animated, brisk, dynamic, enthusiastic, fast, forceful, hard-working, high-powered, indefatigable, lively, powerful, quick-moving, spirited, strenuous, tireless, unflagging, vigorous, zestful. *Opp* LETHARGIC.

energy *n* **1** animation, ardour, *inf* dash, drive, dynamism, élan, enthusiasm, exertion, fire, force, forcefulness, *inf* get-up-and-go, *inf* go, life, liveliness, might, *inf* pep, spirit, stamina, strength, verve, vigour, *inf* vim, vitality, vivacity, zeal, zest. *Opp* LETHARGY. **2** fuel, power.

enforce *vb* administer, apply, carry out, compel, execute, implement, impose, inflict, insist on, prosecute, put into effect, require, stress. *Opp* WAIVE.

engage *vb* **1** contract with, employ, enlist, hire, recruit, sign up, take on. **2** *cogs engage*. bite, fit together, interlock. **3** *engage to do something*. ▷ PROMISE. **4** *engaged me in gossip*. ▷ OCCUPY. **5** *engage in sport*. ▷ PARTICIPATE.

engaged *adj* **1** affianced, betrothed, *old use* plighted, *old use* promised, *old use* spoken for. **2** ▷ BUSY.

engagement *n* **1** betrothal, promise to marry, *old use* troth. **2** *social engagements*. appointment, arrangement, commitment, date, fixture, meeting, obligation, rendezvous. **3** ▷ BATTLE.

engine *n* **1** machine, motor. □ diesel, electric, internalcombustion, jet, outboard, petrol, steam, turbine, turbo-jet, turbo-prop. **2** locomotive.

engineer *n* mechanic, technician. ● *vb* ▷ CONSTRUCT, DEVISE.

engrave *vb* carve, chisel, etch, inscribe. ▷ CUT.

enigma *n* conundrum, mystery, *inf* poser, problem, puzzle, riddle.

enjoy *vb* **1** admire, appreciate, bask in, be happy in, delight in, *inf* go in for, indulge in, *inf* lap up, luxuriate in, rejoice in, relish, revel in, savour, take pleasure from, take pleasure in. ▷ LIKE. **2** benefit from, experience, have, take advantage of, use. **enjoy yourself** celebrate, *inf* gad about, *inf* have a fling, have a good time, make merry.

enjoyable *adj* agreeable, amusing, delicious, delightful, diverting, entertaining, gratifying, likeable, *inf* nice, pleasurable, rewarding, satisfying. ▷ PLEASANT. *Opp* UNPLEASANT.

enlarge *vb* amplify, augment, blow up, broaden, build up, develop, dilate, distend, diversify, elongate, expand, extend, fill out, grow, increase, inflate, lengthen, magnify, multiply, spread, stretch, supplement, swell, wax, widen. *Opp* DECREASE. **enlarge on** ▷ ELABORATE.

enlighten *vb* edify, illuminate, inform, make aware. ▷ TEACH.

enlist *vb* **1** conscript, engage, enrol, impress, muster, recruit, sign up. **2** *enlist in the army.* enrol, enter, join up, register, sign on, volunteer. **3** *enlist help.* ▷ OBTAIN.

enliven *vb* animate, arouse, brighten, cheer up, energize, inspire, *inf* pep up, quicken, rouse, stimulate, vitalize, wake up.

enormous *adj* Brobdingnagian, colossal, elephantine, gargantuan, giant, gigantic, gross, huge, hulking, immense, *inf* jumbo, mammoth, massive, mighty, monstrous, mountainous, prodigious, stupendous, titanic, towering, tremendous, vast. ▷ BIG. *Opp* SMALL.

enough *adj* adequate, ample, as much as necessary, sufficient.

enquire *vb* ask, beg, demand, entreat, implore, inquire, query, question, quiz, request. **enquire about** ▷ INVESTIGATE.

enrage *vb* incense, inflame, infuriate, madden, provoke. ▷ ANGER.

enslave *vb* disenfranchise, dominate, make slaves of, subject, subjugate, take away the rights of. *Opp* EMANCIPATE.

ensure *vb* confirm, guarantee, make certain, make sure, secure.

entail *vb* call for, demand, give rise to, involve, lead to, necessitate, require.

enter *vb* **1** arrive, come in, get in, go in, infiltrate, invade, move in, step in.

Opp DEPART. **2** dig into, penetrate, pierce, puncture, push into. **3** *enter a contest.* engage in, enlist in, enrol in, *inf* go in for, join, participate in, sign up for, take part in, take up, volunteer for. **4** *enter names on a list.* add, inscribe, insert, note down, put down, record, register, set down, sign, write. *Opp* REMOVE. **enter into** ▷ BEGIN.

enterprise *n* **1** adventure, effort, endeavour, operation, programme, project, undertaking, venture. **2** adventurousness, ambition, boldness, courage, daring, determination, drive, energy, *inf* get-up-and-go, initiative, *inf* push. **3** business, company, concern, firm, organization.

enterprising *adj* adventurous, ambitious, bold, courageous, daring, determined, eager, energetic, enthusiastic, *inf* go-ahead, *derog* go-getting, hard-working, imaginative, indefatigable, industrious, intrepid, keen, purposeful, *inf* pushful, *derog* pushy, resourceful, spirited, venturesome, vigorous, zealous. *Opp* UNADVENTUROUS.

entertain *vb* **1** amuse, cheer up, delight, divert, keep amused, make laugh, occupy, please, regale, *inf* tickle. *Opp* BORE. **2** *entertain friends.* accommodate, be host to, be hostess to, cater for, give hospitality to, *inf* put up, receive, treat, welcome. **3** *entertain an idea.* accept, agree to, approve, consent to, consider, contemplate, harbour, support, take seriously. *Opp* IGNORE. **entertaining** ▷ INTERESTING.

entertainer *n* artist, artiste, performer. □ acrobat, *actor, actress, ballerina, broadcaster, busker, clown, comedian, comic, compère, conjurer, dancer, disc jockey, DJ, impersonator, jester, juggler, lion-tamer, magician, matador, mime artist, minstrel, singer, stunt man, toreador, trapeze artist, trouper, ventriloquist.* ▷ MUSICIAN.

entertainment *n* **1** amusement, distraction, diversion, enjoyment, fun, night-life, pastime, play, pleasure, recreation, sport. **2** divertissement, exhibition, extravaganza, performance, presentation, production, show, spectacle. □ *ballet, bullfight, cabaret, casino, ceilidh, cinema, circus, concert, dance, disco, discothèque, fair, firework display, flower show, gymkhana, motor show, nightclub, pageant, pantomime, play, radio, recital, recitation, revue, rodeo, son et lumière, tattoo, television, variety show, waxworks, zoo.* ▷ DANCE, DRAMA, MUSIC, SPORT.

enthusiasm *n* **1** ambition, ardour, avidity, commitment, drive, eagerness, excitement, exuberance, *derog* fanaticism, fervour, gusto, keenness, panache, passion, relish, spirit, verve, zeal, zest. *Opp* APATHY. **2** craze, diversion, *inf* fad, hobby, interest, passion, pastime.

enthusiast *n* addict, adherent, admirer, aficionado, *inf* buff, champion, devotee, fan, fanatic, *sl* fiend, *sl* freak, lover, supporter, zealot.

enthusiastic *adj* ambitious, ardent, avid, committed, *inf* crazy, delighted, devoted, eager, earnest, ebullient, energetic, excited, exuberant, fervent, fervid, hearty, impassioned, interested, involved, irrepressible, keen, lively, *inf* mad (about), *inf* mad keen, motivated, optimistic, passionate, positive, rapturous, raring (to go), spirited, unqualified, unstinting, vigorous, wholehearted, zealous. *Opp* APATHETIC. **be enthusiastic** enthuse, get excited, *inf* go into raptures, *inf* go overboard, rave.

entice *vb* allure, attract, cajole, coax, decoy, inveigle, lead on, lure, persuade, seduce, tempt, trap, wheedle.

entire *adj* complete, full, intact, sound, total, unbroken, undivided, uninterrupted, whole.

entitle *vb* **1** call, christen, designate, dub, name, style, term, title. **2** *A licence entitles you to drive.* allow, authorize, empower, enable, justify, license, permit, qualify, warrant.

entitlement *n* claim, ownership, prerogative, right, title.

entity *n* article, being, object, organism, thing, whole.

entrails *plur n* bowels, guts, *inf* innards, inner organs, *inf* insides, intestines, viscera.

entrance *n* **1** access, admission, admittance. **2** appearance, arrival, coming, entry. **3** door, doorway, gate, gateway, ingress, opening, portal, turnstile, way in. **4** ante-room, entrance hall, foyer, lobby, passage, passageway, porch, vestibule. *Opp* EXIT.

entrant *n* applicant, candidate, competitor, contender, contestant, entry, participant, player, rival.

entreat *vb* ask, beg, beseech, implore, importune, petition, sue, supplicate. ▷ REQUEST.

entry *n* **1** insertion, item, jotting, listing, note, record. **2** ▷ ENTRANCE. **3** ▷ ENTRANT.

envelop *vb* cloak, cover, enclose, enfold, enshroud, enwrap, shroud, swathe, veil, wrap. ▷ HIDE.

envelope *n* cover, sheath, wrapper, wrapping.

enviable *adj* attractive, covetable, desirable, favourable, sought-after.

envious *adj* begrudging, bitter, covetous, dissatisfied, *inf* greeneyed, *inf* green with envy, grudging, jaundiced, jealous, resentful.

environment *n* circumstances, conditions, context, ecosystem, environs, habitat, location, milieu, setting, situation, surroundings, territory.

envisage *vb* anticipate, contemplate, dream of, envision, fancy, forecast, foresee, imagine, picture, predict, visualize.

envy *n* bitterness, covetousness, cupidity, desire, discontent, dissatisfaction, ill-will, jealousy, longing, resentment. ● *vb* begrudge, grudge, resent.

ephemeral *adj* brief, evanescent, fleeting, fugitive, impermanent, momentary, passing, short-lived, temporary, transient, transitory. *Opp* PERMANENT.

epidemic adj general, pandemic, prevalent, spreading, universal, widespread. ● n outbreak, pestilence, plague, rash, upsurge.

episode n 1 affair, event, happening, incident, matter, occurrence. 2 chapter, instalment, part, passage, scene, section.

epitome n 1 archetype, embodiment, essence, exemplar, incarnation, personification, quintessence, representation, type. 2 ▷ SUMMARY.

equal adj balanced, coextensive, commensurate, congruent, correspondent, egalitarian, even, fair, identical, indistinguishable, interchangeable, level, like, matched, matching, proportionate, regular, the same, symmetrical, uniform. ▷ EQUIVALENT. Opp UNEQUAL. ● n clone, compeer, counterpart, equivalent, fellow, peer, twin. ● vb 1 balance, correspond to, draw with, tie with. 2 No one equals Caruso. be in the same class as, compare with, match, parallel, resemble, rival, vie with.

equality n 1 balance, congruence, correspondence, equivalence, identity, similarity, uniformity. Opp BIAS. 2 social equality. egalitarianism, even-handedness, fairness, justice, parity. Opp INEQUALITY.

equalize vb balance, catch up, compensate, even up, level, make equal, match, regularize, inf square, standardize.

equate vb assume to be equal, compare, juxtapose, liken, match, parallel, set side by side.

equilibrium n balance, equanimity, equipoise, evenness, poise, stability, steadiness, symmetry.

equip vb accoutre, arm, array, attire, caparison, clothe, dress, fit out, fit up, furnish, inf kit out, outfit, provide, stock, supply.

equipment n accoutrements, apparatus, appurtenances, sl clobber, furnishings, inf gear, inf hardware, implements, instruments, kit, machinery, materials, outfit, paraphernalia, plant, inf rig, inf stuff, supplies, tackle, inf things, tools, trappings. ▷ CLOTHES.

equivalent adj alike, analogous, comparable, corresponding, fair, interchangeable, parallel, proportionate, Lat pro rata, similar, synonymous. ▷ EQUAL.

equivocal adj ambiguous, circumlocutory, equivocating, evasive, noncommittal, oblique, periphrastic, questionable, suspect.

equivocate vb inf beat about the bush, be equivocal, dodge the issue, fence, inf have it both ways, hedge, prevaricate, quibble, waffle.

era n age, date, day, epoch, period, time.

eradicate vb eliminate, erase, get rid of, root out, uproot. ▷ DESTROY.

erase vb cancel, cross out, delete, efface, eradicate, expunge, obliterate, rub out, wipe away, wipe off. ▷ REMOVE.

erect adj perpendicular, rigid, standing, straight, upright, vertical. ● vb build, construct, elevate, establish, lift up, make upright, pitch (a tent), put up, raise, set up.

erode vb abrade, corrode, eat away, eat into, gnaw away, grind down, wash away, wear away.

erotic adj amatory, amorous, aphrodisiac, arousing, lubricious, lustful, sl randy, sl raunchy, seductive, sensual, venereal, voluptuous. ▷ SEXY.

err vb be mistaken, be naughty, sl boob, inf get it wrong, go astray, go wrong, misbehave, miscalculate, sin, inf slip up, transgress.

errand n assignment, commission, duty, job, journey, mission, task, trip.

erratic adj 1 aberrant, capricious, changeable, fickle, fitful, fluctuating, inconsistent, irregular, shifting, spasmodic, sporadic, uneven, unpredictable, unreliable, unstable, unsteady, variable, wayward. Opp REGULAR. 2 aimless, directionless, haphazard, meandering, wandering.

error n inf bloomer, blunder, sl boob, Lat corrigendum, Lat erratum, fallacy, falsehood, fault, flaw, gaffe, *inf* howler, inaccuracy, inconsistency, inexactitude, lapse, misapprehension, miscalculation, misconception, misprint, mistake, misunderstanding, omission, oversight, sin, *inf* slip-up, solecism, transgression, *old use* trespass, wrongdoing. ▷ WRONG.

erupt *vb* be discharged, be emitted, belch, break out, burst out, explode, gush, issue, pour out, shoot out, spew, spout, spurt, vomit.

eruption *n* burst, discharge, emission, explosion, outbreak, outburst, rash.

escapade *n* adventure, exploit, *inf* lark, mischief, practical joke, prank, scrape, stunt.

escape *n* **1** bolt, breakout, departure, flight, flit, getaway, jail-break, retreat, running away. **2** discharge, emission, leak, leakage, seepage. **3** *escape from reality.* avoidance, distraction, diversion, escapism, evasion, relaxation, relief. ● *vb* **1** abscond, *inf* beat it, bolt, break free, break out, *inf* cut and run, decamp, disappear, *sl* do a bunk, elope, flee, fly, get away, *inf* give someone the slip, run away, *sl* scarper, slip away, *inf* slip the net, *inf* take to your heels, *inf* turn tail. **2** discharge, drain, leak, ooze, pour out, run out, seep. **3** *escape the nasty jobs.* avoid, dodge, duck, elude, evade, get away from, shirk, *sl* skive off.

escapism *n* day-dreaming, fantasy, pretence, unreality, wishful thinking.

escort *n* **1** bodyguard, convoy, guard, guide, pilot, protection, protector, safe-conduct. **2** *royal escort.* attendant, entourage, retinue, train. **3** *escort at a dance.* chaperon, companion, *inf* date, partner. ● *vb* accompany, attend, chaperon, conduct, guard, *inf* keep an eye on, *inf* keep tabs on, look after, protect, shepherd, stay with, usher, watch.

essence *n* **1** centre, character, core, cornerstone, crux, essential quality, heart, kernel, life, meaning, nature, pith, quiddity, quintessence, soul, spirit, substance. **2** concentrate, decoction, elixir, extract, flavouring, fragrance, perfume, scent, tincture.

essential *adj* basic, characteristic, chief, crucial, elementary, fundamental, important, indispensable, inherent, innate, intrinsic, irreplaceable, key, leading, main, necessary, primary, principal, quintessential, requisite, vital. *Opp* INESSENTIAL.

establish *vb* **1** base, begin, constitute, construct, create, decree, found, form, inaugurate, initiate, institute, introduce, organize, originate, set up, start. **2** *establish yourself in a job.* confirm, ensconce, entrench, install, lodge, secure, settle, station. **3** *establish facts.* accept, agree, authenticate, certify, confirm, corroborate, decide, demonstrate, fix, prove, ratify, recognize, show to be true, substantiate, verify.

established *adj* deep-rooted, deep-seated, indelible, ineradicable, ingrained, long-lasting, long-standing, permanent, proven, reliable, respected, rooted, secure, traditional, well-known, well-tried. *Opp* NEW.

establishment *n* **1** composition, constitution, creation, formation, foundation, inauguration, inception, institution, introduction, setting up. **2** *a well-run establishment.* business, company, concern, enterprise, factory, household, institution, office, organization, shop.

estate *n* **1** area, development, domain, land. **2** assets, belongings, capital, chattels, effects, fortune, goods, inheritance, lands, possessions, property, wealth.

esteem *n* admiration, credit, estimation, favour, honour, regard, respect, reverence, veneration. ● *vb* ▷ RESPECT.

estimate *n* appraisal, approximation, assessment, calculation, conjecture, estimation, evaluation, guess, *inf* guesstimate, judgement, opinion, price, quotation, reckoning, specification, valuation. ● *vb* appraise, assess, calculate, compute, conjecture, consider, count up, evaluate, gauge, guess, judge, project, reckon, surmise, think out, weigh up, work out.

estimation n appraisal, appreciation, assessment, calculation, computation, consideration, estimate, evaluation, judgement, opinion, rating, view.

estuary n creek, Scot firth, fjord, inlet, Scot loch, river mouth.

eternal adj ceaseless, deathless, endless, everlasting, heavenly, immeasurable, immortal, infinite, lasting, limitless, measureless, never-ending, permanent, perpetual, timeless, unchanging, undying, unending, unlimited. ▷ CONTINUAL. Opp OCCASIONAL, TRANSIENT.

eternity n afterlife, eternal life, immortality, infinity, perpetuity.

ethical adj decent, fair, good, honest, just, moral, noble, principled, righteous, upright, virtuous. Opp IMMORAL.

ethnic adj cultural, folk, national, racial, traditional, tribal.

etiquette n ceremony, civility, code of behaviour, conventions, courtesy, decency, decorum, form, formalities, manners, politeness, propriety, protocol, rules of behaviour, standards of behaviour.

evacuate vb 1 clear, deplete, drain, move out, remove, send away, void. 2 abandon, decamp from, desert, empty, forsake, leave, pull out of, quit, relinquish, vacate, withdraw from.

evade vb 1 avoid, inf chicken out of, circumvent, dodge, duck, elude, escape from, fend off, flinch from, get away from, shirk, shrink from, shun, sidestep, inf skive, steer clear of, turn your back on. 2 evade a question. fudge, hedge, parry. ▷ EQUIVOCATE. Opp CONFRONT.

evaluate vb appraise, assess, calculate the value of, estimate, judge, value, weigh up.

evaporate vb dehydrate, desiccate, disappear, disperse, dissipate, dissolve, dry up, evanesce, melt away, vanish, vaporize.

evasive adj ambiguous, inf cagey, circumlocutory, deceptive, devious, disingenuous, equivocal, equivocating, inconclusive, indecisive, indirect, inf jesuitical, misleading, noncommittal, oblique, prevaricating, roundabout, inf shifty, sophistical, uninformative. Opp DIRECT.

even adj 1 flat, flush, horizontal, level, plane, smooth, straight, true. 2 even pulse. consistent, constant, equalized, measured, metrical, monotonous, proportional, regular, rhythmical, symmetrical, unbroken, uniform, unvarying. 3 even scores. balanced, equal, identical, level, matching, the same. 4 ▷ EVEN-TEMPERED. Opp IRREGULAR. **even out** ▷ FLATTEN. **even up** ▷ EQUALIZE. **get even** ▷ RETALIATE.

evening n dusk, poet eventide, poet gloaming, nightfall, sundown, sunset, twilight.

event n 1 affair, business, chance, circumstance, contingency, episode, eventuality, experience, happening, incident, occurrence. 2 conclusion, consequence, effect, issue, outcome, result, upshot. 3 activity, ceremony, entertainment, function, occasion. 4 sporting event. bout, championship, competition, contest, engagement, fixture, game, match, meeting, tournament.

even-tempered adj balanced, calm, composed, cool, equable, even, impassive, imperturbable, pacific, peaceable, peaceful, placid, poised, reliable, self-possessed, serene, stable, steady, tranquil, unemotional, unexcitable, unruffled. Opp EXCITABLE.

eventual adj concluding, consequent, destined, due, ensuing, expected, final, last, overall, probable, resultant, resulting, ultimate.

everlasting adj ceaseless, deathless, endless, eternal, immortal, incorruptible, infinite, lasting, limitless, measureless, never-ending, permanent, perpetual, persistent, timeless, unchanging, undying, unending. *Opp* TRANSIENT.

evermore *adv* always, eternally, for ever, unceasingly.

evict *vb* dislodge, dispossess, eject, expel, *sl* give (someone) the boot, *inf* kick out, oust, put out, remove, throw out, *inf* turf out, turn out.

evidence *n* attestation, certification, confirmation, corroboration, data, demonstration, deposition, documentation, facts, grounds, information, proof, sign, statement, statistics, substantiation, testimony. **give evidence** ▷ TESTIFY.

evident *adj* apparent, certain, clear, discernible, manifest, noticeable, obvious, palpable, patent, perceptible, plain, self-explanatory, unambiguous, undeniable, unmistakable, visible. *Opp* UNCERTAIN.

evil *adj* **1** amoral, atrocious, base, black-hearted, blasphemous, corrupt, criminal, cruel, depraved, devilish, diabolical, dishonest, fiendish, foul, harmful, hateful, heinous, hellish, immoral, impious, infamous, iniquitous, irreligious, machiavellian, malevolent, malicious, malignant, nefarious, pernicious, perverted, reprobate, satanic, sinful, sinister, treacherous, ungodly, unprincipled, unrighteous, vicious, vile, villainous, wicked, wrong. ▷ BAD. *Opp* GOOD. **2** *evil smell.* foul, nasty, pestilential, poisonous, troublesome, unspeakable, vile. ▷ UNPLEASANT. *Opp* PLEASANT. ● *n* **1** amorality, blasphemy, corruption, criminality, cruelty, depravity, dishonesty, fiendishness, heinousness, immorality, impiety, iniquity, *old use* knavery, malevolence, malice, mischief, pain, sin, sinfulness, suffering, treachery, turpitude, ungodliness, unrighteousness, vice, viciousness, villainy, wickedness, wrongdoing. ▷ CRIME. **2** *Poverty is an evil.* affliction, bane, calamity, catastrophe, curse, disaster, enormity, hardship, harm, ill, misfortune, wrong.

evocative *adj* atmospheric, convincing, descriptive, emotive, graphic, imaginative, provoking, realistic, stimulating, suggestive, vivid.

evoke *vb* arouse, awaken, call up, conjure up, elicit, excite, inspire, invoke, kindle, produce, provoke, raise, rouse, stimulate, stir up, suggest, summon up.

evolution *n* advance, development, emergence, formation, growth, improvement, maturation, maturing, progress, unfolding.

evolve *vb* derive, descend, develop, emerge, grow, improve, mature, modify gradually, progress, unfold.

exact *adj* **1** accurate, correct, dead (*centre*), detailed, faithful, faultless, flawless, meticulous, painstaking, precise, punctilious, right, rigorous, scrupulous, specific, *inf* spot-on, strict, true, truthful, veracious. *Opp* IMPRECISE. **2** *exact copy.* identical, indistinguishable, literal, perfect. ● *vb* claim, compel, demand, enforce, extort, extract, get, impose, insist on, obtain, require. **exacting** ▷ DIFFICULT.

exaggerate *vb* **1** amplify, embellish, embroider, enlarge, inflate, *inf* lay it on thick, magnify, make too much of, maximize, overdo, overemphasize, overestimate, overstate, *inf* pile it on, *inf* play up. *Opp* MINIMIZE. **2** ▷ CARICATURE. **exaggerated** ▷ EXCESSIVE.

exalt *vb* boost, elevate, lift, promote, raise, uplift. ▷ PRAISE. **exalted** ▷ HIGH.

examination *n* **1** analysis, appraisal, assessment, audit, catechism, *inf* exam, inspection, investigation, *inf* oral, paper, post-mortem, review, scrutiny, study, survey, test, *inf* viva, *Lat* viva voce. **2** [*medical*] *inf* check-up, scan. **3** *police examination.* cross-examination, enquiry, inquiry, inquisition, interrogation, probe, questioning, trial.

examine *vb* **1** analyse, appraise, audit (*accounts*), check, *inf* check out, explore, inquire into, inspect, investigate, peruse, probe, research, scan, scrutinize, sift, sort out, study, *sl* sus out, test, vet, weigh up. **2** *examine a*

example 138

witness. catechize, cross-examine, cross-question, *inf* grill, interrogate, *inf* pump, question, sound out, try.

example *n* **1** case, illustration, instance, occurrence, sample, specimen. **2** *example to follow*. ideal, lesson, model, paragon, pattern, prototype. **make an example of** ▷ PUNISH.

exasperate *vb inf* aggravate, drive mad, gall, infuriate, irk, irritate, *inf* needle, pique, provoke, rile, vex. ▷ ANNOY.

excavate *vb* burrow, dig, gouge out, hollow out, mine, scoop out, unearth.

exceed *vb* beat, be more than, do more than, go beyond, go over, outnumber, outshine, outstrip, overstep, overtake, pass, transcend. ▷ EXCEL.

exceedingly *adv* amazingly, especially, exceptionally, excessively, extraordinarily, extremely, outstandingly, specially, unusually, very.

excel *vb* beat, be excellent, better, do best, eclipse, outclass, outdo, outshine, shine, stand out, surpass, top. ▷ EXCEED.

excellent *adj inf* ace, admirable, *inf* brilliant, *old use* capital, champion, choice, consummate, *sl* cracking, distinguished, esteemed, estimable, exceptional, exemplary, extraordinary, *inf* fabulous, *inf* fantastic, fine, first-class, first-rate, flawless, gorgeous, great, high-class, ideal, impressive, magnificent, marvellous, model, notable, outstanding, perfect, *inf* phenomenal, remarkable, *inf* smashing, splendid, sterling, *inf* stunning, *inf* super, superb, superlative, supreme, surpassing, *inf* terrific, *inf* tip-top, *old use* top-hole, *inf* top-notch, top-ranking, *inf* tremendous, unequalled, wonderful. *Opp* BAD.

except *vb* exclude, leave out, omit.

exception *n* **1** exclusion, omission, rejection. **2** abnormality, anomaly, departure, deviation, eccentricity, freak, irregularity, oddity, peculiarity, quirk, rarity. **take exception** ▷ OBJECT.

exceptional *adj* **1** aberrant, abnormal, anomalous, atypical, curious, deviant, eccentric, extraordinary, extreme, isolated, memorable, notable, odd, out-of-the-ordinary, peculiar, phenomenal, quirky, rare, remarkable, singular, solitary, special, strange, surprising, uncommon, unconventional, unexpected, unheard-of, unique, unparalleled, unprecedented, unpredictable, untypical, unusual. **2** ▷ EXCELLENT. *Opp* ORDINARY.

excerpt *n* citation, clip, extract, fragment, highlight, part, passage, quotation, section, selection.

excess *n* **1** abundance, glut, overabundance, overflow, *inf* overkill, profit, redundancy, superabundance, superfluity, surfeit, surplus. *Opp* SCARCITY. **2** debauchery, dissipation, extravagance, intemperance, overindulgence, profligacy, wastefulness. *Opp* MODERATION.

excessive *adj* **1** disproportionate, exaggerated, extravagant, extreme, fanatical, immoderate, inordinate, intemperate, needless, overdone, prodigal, profligate, profuse, superfluous, undue, unnecessary, unneeded, wasteful. ▷ HUGE. *Opp* INADEQUATE. **2** *excessive prices*. exorbitant, extortionate, unjustifiable, unrealistic, unreasonable. *Opp* MODERATE.

exchange *n* deal, interchange, reciprocity, replacement, substitution, *inf* swap, switch. ● *vb* bargain, barter, change, convert (*currency*), interchange, reciprocate, replace, substitute, *inf* swap, switch, *inf* swop, trade, trade in, traffic. **exchange words** ▷ TALK.

excitable *adj inf* bubbly, chattery, edgy, emotional, explosive, fidgety, fiery, highly-strung, hot-tempered, irrepressible, jumpy, lively, mercurial, nervous, passionate, quick-tempered, restive, temperamental, unstable, volatile. *Opp* CALM.

excite *vb* **1** agitate, amaze, animate, arouse, awaken, discompose, disturb, elate, electrify, enthral, exhilarate, fluster, *inf* get going, incite, inflame, interest, intoxicate, make excited, move, perturb, provoke, rouse, stimulate, stir up, thrill, titillate, *inf* turn on, upset, urge, *inf* wind up, *inf* work up. **2** *excite interest.* activate, cause, elicit, encourage, engender, evoke, fire, generate, kindle, motivate, produce, set off, whet. *Opp* CALM.

excited *adj* agitated, boisterous, delirious, eager, enthusiastic, excitable, exuberant, feverish, frantic, frenzied, heated, *inf* het up, hysterical, impassioned, intoxicated, lively, moved, nervous, overwrought, restless, spirited, vivacious, wild. *Opp* APATHETIC.

excitement *n* action, activity, adventure, agitation, animation, commotion, delirium, drama, eagerness, enthusiasm, furore, fuss, heat, intensity, *inf* kicks, passion, stimulation, suspense, tension, thrill, unrest.

exciting *adj* cliff-hanging, dramatic, electric, electrifying, eventful, fastmoving, galvanizing, gripping, heady, hair-raising, inspiring, intoxicating, *inf* nailbiting, provocative, riveting, rousing, sensational, spectacular, spine-tingling, stimulating, stirring, suspenseful, tense, thrilling. ▷ AMAZING. *Opp* BORING.

exclaim *vb* bawl, bellow, blurt out, call, cry out, *old use* ejaculate, shout, utter, vociferate, yell. ▷ SAY.

exclamation *n* bellow, call, cry, *old use* ejaculation, expletive, interjection, oath, shout, swear-word, utterance, vociferation, yell.

exclude *vb* ban, banish, bar, blacklist, debar, disallow, disown, eject, except, excommunicate, expel, forbid, interdict, keep out, leave out, lock out, omit, ostracize, oust, outlaw, prohibit, proscribe, put an embargo on, refuse, reject, repudiate, rule out, shut out, veto. ▷ REMOVE. *Opp* INCLUDE.

exclusive *adj* **1** limiting, restricted, sole, unique, unshared. **2** *an exclusive club.* clannish, classy, closed, fashionable, *sl* posh, private, restrictive, select, selective, snobbish, *inf* upmarket.

excreta *plur n* droppings, dung, excrement, faeces, manure, sewage, waste matter.

excrete *vb* defecate, evacuate the bowels, go to the lavatory, relieve yourself.

excursion *n* cruise, expedition, jaunt, journey, outing, ramble, tour, trip, voyage. ▷ TRAVEL.

excuse *n* alibi, apology, defence, explanation, extenuation, justification, mitigation, palliation, plea, pretext, rationalization, reason, vindication. ● *vb* **1** apologize for, condone, disregard, explain away, forgive, ignore, justify, mitigate, overlook, pardon, pass over, sanction, tolerate, vindicate, warrant. **2** absolve, acquit, clear, discharge, exculpate, exempt, exonerate, free, let off, *inf* let off the hook, liberate, release. *Opp* BLAME.

execute *vb* **1** accomplish, achieve, bring off, carry out, complete, discharge, do, effect, enact, finish, implement, perform, *inf* pull off. **2** kill, put to death. □ *behead, burn, crucify, decapitate, electrocute, garrotte, gas, guillotine, hang, lynch, shoot, stone.*

executive *n* administrator, *inf* boss, director, manager, officer. ▷ CHIEF.

exemplary *adj* admirable, commendable, faultless, flawless, ideal, model, perfect, praiseworthy, unexceptionable.

exemplify *vb* demonstrate, depict, embody, illustrate, personify, represent, show, symbolize, typify.

exempt *vb* except, exclude, excuse, free, let off, *inf* let off the hook, liberate, release, spare.

exercise *n* **1** action, activity, aerobics, callisthenics, effort, exertion, games, gymnastics, PE, sport, *inf* warm-up, *inf* work-out. **2** *military exercises.* discipline, drill, manoeuvres, operation, practice, training. ● *vb* **1** apply, bring to bear, display, effect, employ, execute, exert, expend, implement, put to use, show, use, utilize, wield. **2** *exercise your body.* discipline, drill, exert, jog, keep fit, practise, train, *inf* work out. **3** ▷ WORRY.

exertion *n* action, effort, endeavour, strain, striving, struggle. ▷ WORK.

exhaust *n* discharge, effluent, emission, fumes, gases, smoke. ● *vb* **1** consume, deplete, dissipate, drain, dry up, empty, expend, finish off, *inf* run through, sap, spend, use up, void. **2** debilitate, enervate, *inf* fag, fatigue, prostrate, tax, tire, wear out, weary. **exhausted** ▷ BREATHLESS, WEARY.

exhausting *adj* arduous, backbreaking, crippling, debilitating, demanding, difficult, enervating, fatiguing, gruelling, hard, laborious, punishing, severe, strenuous, taxing, tiring, wearying.

exhaustion *n* debility, fatigue, lassitude, tiredness, weakness, weariness.

exhaustive *adj inf* all-out, careful, comprehensive, full-scale, intensive, meticulous, thorough. *Opp* INCOMPLETE.

exhibit *vb* **1** arrange, display, offer, present, put up, set up, show. **2** *exhibit knowledge.* air, betray, brandish, demonstrate, disclose, evidence, express, *derog* flaunt, indicate, manifest, *derog* parade, reveal, *derog* show off. *Opp* HIDE.

exhibition *n* demonstration, display, *inf* expo, exposition, presentation, show.

exhilarating *adj* bracing, cheering, enlivening, exciting, invigorating, refreshing, rejuvenating, stimulating, tonic, uplifting. ▷ HAPPY.

exhort *vb* advise, encourage, harangue, *inf* give a pep talk to, lecture, sermonize, urge.

exile *n* **1** banishment, deportation, expatriation, expulsion, transportation. **2** deportee, displaced person, émigré, expatriate, outcast, refugee, wanderer. ● *vb* ban, banish, bar, deport, drive out, eject, evict, expatriate, expel, oust, send away, transport.

exist *vb* **1** be, be found, be in existence, be real, happen, occur. **2** abide, continue, endure, hold out, keep going, last, live, remain alive, subsist, survive. **existing** ▷ ACTUAL, CURRENT, LIVING.

existence *n* actuality, being, continuance, life, living, persistence, reality, survival.

exit *n* **1** barrier, door, doorway, egress, gate, gateway, opening, portal, way out. **2** *a hurried exit.* departure, escape, evacuation, exodus, flight, leave-taking, retreat, withdrawal. ● *vb* ▷ DEPART.

exorbitant *adj* disproportionate, excessive, extortionate, extravagant, high, inordinate, outrageous, profiteering, prohibitive, *inf* sky-high, *inf* steep, *inf* stiff, *inf* swingeing, top, unjustifiable, unrealistic, unreasonable, unwarranted. ▷ EXPENSIVE. *Opp* REASONABLE.

exotic *adj* **1** alien, faraway, foreign, remote, romantic, unfamiliar, wonderful. **2** bizarre, colourful, different, exciting, extraordinary, foreign-looking, novel, odd, outlandish, peculiar, rare, singular, strange, striking, unfamiliar, unusual, weird. *Opp* ORDINARY.

expand *vb* **1** amplify, augment, broaden, build up, develop, diversify, elaborate, enlarge, extend, fill out, heighten, increase, make bigger, make longer, prolong. **2** become bigger, dilate, distend, grow, increase, lengthen, open out, stretch, swell, thicken, widen. *Opp* CONTRACT.

expanse *n* area, breadth, extent, range, sheet, space, spread, stretch, sweep, surface, tract.

expansive *adj* **1** affable, amiable, communicative, effusive, extrovert, friendly, genial, open, outgoing, sociable, well-disposed. ▷ TALKATIVE. *Opp* TACITURN. **2** ▷ BROAD. *Opp* NARROW.

expect *vb* **1** anticipate, await, bank on, bargain for, be prepared for, contemplate, count on, envisage, forecast, foresee, have faith in, hope for, imagine, look forward to, plan for, predict, prophesy, reckon on, wait for. **2** *expect obedience.* consider necessary, demand, insist on, look for, rely on, require, want. **3** *I expect he'll come.* assume, believe, conjecture, guess, imagine, judge, presume, presuppose, suppose, surmise, think. **expected** ▷ PREDICTABLE.

expectant *adj* **1** eager, hopeful, *inf* keyed up, *inf* on tenterhooks, optimistic, ready. **2** *inf* expecting, pregnant.

expedient *adj* advantageous, advisable, appropriate, apropos, beneficial, convenient, desirable, helpful, judicious, opportune, politic, practical, pragmatic, profitable, propitious, prudent, right, sensible, suitable, to your advantage, useful, worthwhile. ● *n* contrivance, device, *inf* dodge, manoeuvre, means, measure, method, *inf* ploy, recourse, resort, ruse, scheme, stratagem, tactics.

expedition *n* crusade, excursion, exploration, journey, mission, pilgrimage, quest, raid, safari, tour, trek, trip, undertaking, voyage.

expel *vb* **1** ban, banish, cast out, *inf* chuck out, dismiss, drive out, eject, evict, exile, exorcise, *inf* fire, *inf* kick out, oust, remove, *inf* sack, send away, throw out, turn out, *inf* turf out. **2** *expel fumes.* belch, discharge, emit, exhale, give out, push out, send out, spew out.

expend *vb* consume, disburse, *sl* dish out, employ, pay out, spend, use.

expendable *adj* disposable, inessential, insignificant, replaceable, *inf* throw-away, unimportant.

expense *n* charge, cost, disbursement, expenditure, fee, outgoings, outlay, overheads, payment, price, rate, spending.

expensive *adj* costly, dear, generous, high-priced, over-priced, precious, *inf* pricey, *inf* steep, *inf* up-market, valuable. ▷ EXORBITANT. *Opp* CHEAP.

experience *n* **1** familiarity, involvement, observation, participation, practice, taking part. **2** background, expertise, *inf* know-how, knowledge, *Fr* savoir faire, skill, understanding, wisdom. **3** *a nasty experience.* adventure, circumstance, episode, event, happening, incident, occurrence, ordeal, trial. ● *vb* encounter, endure, face, go through, have a taste of, know, meet, practise, sample, suffer, test out, try, undergo. **experienced** ▷ EXPERT.

experiment *n* demonstration, investigation, *inf* practical, proof, research, test, trial, try-out. ● *vb* do experiments, examine, investigate, make tests, probe, research, test, try out.

experimental *adj* **1** exploratory, on trial, pilot, provisional, tentative, trial. **2** *experimental evidence.* empirical, experiential, proved, tested.

expert *adj* able, *inf* ace, *inf* brilliant, capable, competent, *inf* crack, experienced, knowing, knowledgeable, master, masterly, practised, professional, proficient, qualified, skilful, skilled, sophisticated, specialized, trained, wellversed, worldly-wise. ▷ CLEVER. *Opp* UNSKILFUL. ● *n inf* ace, authority, connoisseur, *inf* dab hand, genius, *derog* know-all, master, *inf* old hand, professional, pundit, specialist, veteran, virtuoso, *derog* wiseacre, *inf* wizard. *Opp* AMATEUR.

expertise *n* adroitness, dexterity, expertness, judgement, *inf* know-how, knowledge, *Fr* savoir faire, skill.

expire *vb* become invalid, cease, come to an end, discontinue, finish, *inf* run out, terminate. ▷ DIE.

explain *vb* **1** clarify, clear up, decipher, decode, define, demonstrate, describe, disentangle, elucidate, expound, *inf* get across, *inf* get over, gloss, illustrate, interpret, make clear, make plain, provide an explanation, resolve, shed light on, simplify, solve, *inf* sort out, spell out, teach, translate, unravel. **2** *explain a mistake.* account for, excuse, give reasons for, justify, legitimatize, legitimize, make excuses for, rationalize, vindicate.

explanation n **1** account, analysis, clarification, definition, demonstration, description, elucidation, exegesis, explication, exposition, gloss, illustration, interpretation, key, meaning, rubric, significance, solution, translation. **2** cause, excuse, justification, motivation, motive, rationalization, reason, vindication.

explanatory adj descriptive, expository, helpful, illuminating, illustrative, interpretive, revelatory.

explicit adj categorical, clear, definite, detailed, direct, exact, express, frank, graphic, manifest, open, outspoken, patent, plain, positive, precise, put into words, said, specific, inf spelt out, spoken, stated, straightforward, unambiguous, unconcealed, unequivocal, unhidden, unreserved, well-defined. Opp IMPLICIT.

explode vb **1** backfire, blast, blow up, burst, detonate, erupt, go off, make an explosion, set off, shatter. **2** explode a theory. debunk, destroy, discredit, disprove, put an end to, rebut, refute, reject.

exploit n achievement, adventure, attainment, deed, enterprise, feat. ● vb **1** build on, capitalize on, inf cash in on, develop, make capital out of, make use of, profit by, profit from, trade on, use, utilize, work on. **2** exploit people. inf bleed, enslave, illtreat, impose on, keep down, manipulate, inf milk, misuse, oppress, inf rip off, inf squeeze dry, take advantage of, treat unfairly, withhold rights from.

explore vb **1** break new ground, probe, prospect, reconnoitre, scout, search, survey, tour, travel through. **2** explore a problem. analyse, examine, inspect, investigate, look into, probe, research, scrutinize, study.

explosion n **1** bang, blast, boom, burst, clap, crack, detonation, discharge, eruption, firing, report. **2** explosion of anger. fit, outbreak, outburst, inf paddy, paroxysm, spasm.

explosive adj dangerous, highlycharged, liable to explode, sensitive, unstable, volatile. Opp STABLE. ● n cordite, dynamite, gelignite, gunpowder, TNT.

exponent n **1** executant, interpreter, performer, player. **2** advocate, champion, defender, expounder, presenter, propagandist, proponent, supporter, upholder.

expose vb bare, betray, dig up, disclose, display, exhibit, lay bare, reveal, show (up), uncover, unearth, unmask. ▷ REVEAL. Opp HIDE.

express vb air, articulate, disclose, give vent to, make known, phrase, put into words, release, vent, ventilate, voice, word. ▷ COMMUNICATE.

expression n **1** cliché, formula, phrase, phraseology, remark, statement, term, turn of phrase, usage, utterance, wording. ▷ SAYING. **2** articulation, confession, declaration, disclosure, revelation, statement. **3** expression in your voice. accent, depth, emotion, expressiveness, feeling, intensity, intonation, nuance, pathos, sensibility, sensitivity, sympathy, tone, understanding. **4** expression on your face. air, appearance, aspect, countenance, face, look, mien. □ beam, frown, glare, glower, grimace, grin, laugh, leer, long face, lour, lower, poker-face, pout, scowl, smile, smirk, sneer, wince, yawn.

expressionless adj **1** blank, inf dead-pan, emotionless, empty, glassy, impassive, inscrutable, pokerfaced, straight-faced, uncommunicative, wooden. **2** boring, dull, flat, monotonous, uninspiring, unmodulated, unvarying. Opp EXPRESSIVE.

expressive adj **1** indicative, meaningful, mobile, revealing, sensitive, significant, striking, suggestive, telling. **2** articulate, eloquent, lively, modulated, varied. Opp EXPRESSIONLESS.

exquisite adj delicate, elegant, fine, intricate, refined, skilful, wellcrafted. ▷ BEAUTIFUL. Opp CRUDE.

extend vb **1** add to, broaden, build up, develop, draw out, enlarge, expand, increase, keep going, lengthen, make longer, open up, pad out, perpetuate, prolong, protract, *inf* spin out, spread, stretch, widen. **2** *extend a deadline.* defer, delay, postpone, put back, put off. **3** *extend your hand.* give, hold out, offer, outstretch, present, proffer, put out, raise, reach out, stick out, stretch out. **4** *The garden extends to the fence.* continue, range, reach.

extensive *adj* broad, comprehensive, expansive, far-ranging, far-reaching, sweeping, vast, wide, wide-spread. ▷ LARGE.

extent *n* amount, area, bounds, breadth, compass, degree, dimensions, distance, expanse, length, limit, magnitude, measure, measurement, proportions, quantity, range, reach, scale, scope, size, space, spread, sweep, width.

exterior *adj* external, outer, outside, outward, superficial. ● *n* coating, covering, façade, front, outside, shell, skin, surface. *Opp* INTERIOR.

exterminate *vb* annihilate, destroy, eliminate, eradicate, extirpate, get rid of, obliterate, put an end to, root out, terminate. ▷ KILL.

external *adj* exterior, outer, outside, outward, superficial. *Opp* INTERNAL.

extinct *adj* burnt out, dead, defunct, died out, exterminated, extinguished, gone, inactive, vanished. ▷ OLD. *Opp* LIVING.

extinguish *vb* blow out, damp down, douse, put out, quench, slake, smother, snuff out, switch off. ▷ DESTROY. *Opp* KINDLE.

extort *vb* blackmail, bully, coerce, exact, extract, force, obtain by force.

extra *adj* accessory, added, additional, ancillary, auxiliary, excess, further, left-over, more, other, reserve, spare, superfluous, supernumerary, supplementary, surplus, temporary, unneeded, unused, unwanted.

extract *n* **1** concentrate, concentration, decoction, distillation, essence, quintessence. **2** abstract, citation, *inf* clip, clipping, cutting, excerpt, passage, quotation, selection. ● *vb*

1 draw out, extricate, pull out, remove, take out, withdraw. **2** *extract a confession.* extort, force out, *inf* winkle out, *inf* worm out, wrench, wrest, wring. **3** *extract what you need.* choose, cull, derive, distil, gather, glean, quote, select. ▷ OBTAIN.

extraordinary *adj* abnormal, amazing, astonishing, astounding, awe-inspiring, bizarre, breathtaking, curious, exceptional, extreme, fantastic, *inf* funny, incredible, marvellous, miraculous, mysterious, mystical, notable, noteworthy, odd, outstanding, peculiar, *inf* phenomenal, prodigious, queer, rare, remarkable, *inf* sensational, signal, singular, special, staggering, strange, striking, stunning, stupendous, surprising, *inf* unbelievable, uncommon, unheard-of, unimaginable, unique, unprecedented, unusual, *inf* weird, wonderful. *Opp* ORDINARY.

extravagance *n* excess, immoderation, improvidence, lavish-ness, overindulgence, overspending, prodigality, profligacy, self-indulgence, wastefulness. *Opp* ECONOMY.

extravagant *adj* exaggerated, excessive, flamboyant, grandiose, immoderate, improvident, lavish, outrageous, overblown, overdone, pretentious, prodigal, profligate, profuse, reckless, self-indulgent, *inf* showy, spendthrift, uneconomical, unreasonable, unthrifty, wasteful. ▷ EXPENSIVE. *Opp* ECONOMICAL.

extreme *adj* **1** acute, drastic, excessive, greatest, intensest, maximum, severest, *inf* terrific, utmost. ▷ EXTRAORDINARY. **2** distant, endmost, farthest, furthest, furthermost, last, outermost, remotest, ultimate, uttermost. **3** *extreme opinions.* absolute, avant-garde, exaggerated, extravagant, extremist, fanatical, *inf* hardline, immoderate, intemperate, intransigent, left-wing, militant, obsessive, outrageous, radical, right-wing, uncompromising, *inf* way-out, zealous. ● *n* bottom, bounds, edge, end, extremity, left wing, limit, maximum, minimum, opposite, pole, right wing, top, ultimate.

extroverted *adj* active, confident, exhibitionist, outgoing, positive. ▷ SOCIABLE. *Opp* INTROVERTED.

exuberant *adj* **1** animated, boisterous, *inf* bubbly, buoyant, eager, ebullient, effervescent, energetic, enthusiastic, excited, exhilarated, exultant, high-spirited, irrepressible, lively, spirited, sprightly, vivacious. ▷ CHEERFUL. **2** *exuberant decoration.* baroque, exaggerated, highly-decorated, ornate, overdone, rich, rococo. **3** *exuberant growth.* abundant, copi-

ous, lush, luxuriant, overflowing, profuse, rank, teeming. *Opp* AUSTERE.

exultant *adj* delighted, ecstatic, elated, joyful, jubilant, *inf* on top of the world, overjoyed, rejoicing. ▷ EXUBERANT.

eye *n* **1** eyeball, *inf* peeper. **2** discernment, perception, sight, vision. ● *vb* contemplate, examine, inspect, look at, observe, regard, scrutinize, study, watch. ▷ SEE.

eye-witness *n* bystander, looker-on, observer, onlooker, passer-by, spectator, watcher, witness.

F

fabric *n* **1** material, stuff, textile. ▷ CLOTH. **2** *fabric of a building.* constitution, construction, framework, make-up, structure, substance.

fabulous *adj* **1** fabled, fairy-tale, fanciful, fictitious, imaginary, legendary, mythical, story-book. **2** ▷ EXCELLENT.

face *n* **1** appearance, countenance, features, lineaments, look, *sl* mug, *old use* physiognomy, visage. ▷ EXPRESSION. **2** *face of building.* aspect, covering, exterior, façade, facet, front, outside, side, surface. ● *vb* **1** be opposite, front, look towards, overlook. **2** *face danger.* appear before, brave, come to terms with, confront, cope with, defy, encounter, experience, face up to, meet, oppose, square up to, stand up to, tackle. **3** *face a wall with plaster.* clad, coat, cover, dress, finish, overlay, sheathe, veneer.

facetious *adj* cheeky, flippant, impudent, irreverent. ▷ FUNNY.

facile *adj* **1** cheap, easy, effortless, hasty, obvious, quick, simple, superficial, unconsidered. **2** *facile talker.* fluent, glib, insincere, plausible, ready, shallow, slick, *inf* smooth.

facility *n* **1** adroitness, alacrity, ease, expertise, fluency, *derog* glibness, skill, smoothness. **2** *a useful facility.* amenity, convenience, help, provision, resource, service.

fact *n* actuality, certainty, *Fr* fait accompli, reality, truth. *Opp* FICTION.
the facts circumstances, data, details, evidence, information, *sl* the lowdown, particulars, statistics.

factor *n* aspect, cause, circumstance, component, consideration, constituent, contingency, detail, determinant, element, fact, influence, ingredient, item, parameter, part, particular.

factory *n* assembly line, forge, foundry, manufacturing plant, mill, plant, refinery, shop-floor, works, workshop.

factual *adj* **1** accurate, *Lat* bona fide, circumstantial, correct, demonstrable, empirical, faithful, genuine, matter-of-fact, objective, plain, prosaic, provable, realistic, straightforward, true, unadorned, unbiased, undistorted, unemotional, unimaginative, unvarnished, valid, verifiable, well-documented. *Opp* FALSE. **2** *a factual film.* biographical, documentary, historical, real-life. *Opp* FICTIONAL.

faculty *n* ability, aptitude, capability, capacity, flair, genius, gift, knack, power, talent.

fade *vb* **1** blanch, bleach, darken, dim, discolour, dull, etiolate, grow pale, whiten. *Opp* BRIGHTEN. **2** become less, decline, decrease, diminish, disappear, dwindle, evanesce, fail, melt away, vanish, wane, weaken. **3** *flowers fade.* droop, flag, perish, shrivel, wilt, wither.

fail *vb* **1** abort, be a failure, be unsuccessful, break down, close down, come to an end, *inf* come to grief, come to nothing, *sl* conk out, *inf* crash, cut out, fall through, *inf* fizzle out, *inf* flop, *inf* fold, fold up, founder, give up, go bankrupt, *inf* go bust, go out of business, meet with disaster, miscarry, misfire, *inf* miss out, peter out, stop working. **2** *fail in health.* decay, decline, deteriorate, diminish, disappear, dwindle, ebb, fade, get worse, give out, melt away, vanish, wane, weaken. **3** *fail to do something.* forget, neglect, omit. **4** *fail someone.* abandon, disappoint, *inf* let down. *Opp* IMPROVE, SUCCEED.

failing n blemish, defect, fault, flaw, foible, imperfection, shortcoming, weakness, weak spot.

failure n 1 abandonment, defeat, disappointment, disaster, downfall, fiasco, inf flop, loss, miscarriage, inf wash-out, wreck. 2 breakdown, collapse, crash, stoppage. 3 failure to do your duty. dereliction, neglect, omission, remissness. Opp SUCCESS.

faint adj 1 blurred, blurry, dim, faded, feeble, hazy, ill-defined, indistinct, misty, muzzy, pale, pastel (colours), shadowy, unclear, vague. 2 faint smell. delicate, slight. 3 faint sounds. distant, hushed, low, muffled, muted, soft, stifled, subdued, thin, weak. 4 faint in the head. dizzy, exhausted, feeble, giddy, light-headed, unsteady, vertiginous, weak, inf woozy. Opp CLEAR, STRONG. ● vb become unconscious, black out, collapse, inf flake out, inf keel over, pass out, swoon.

fair adj 1 blond, blonde, flaxen, golden, light, yellow. 2 fair weather. bright, clear, clement, cloudless, dry, favourable, fine, pleasant, sunny. Opp DARK. 3 a fair decision. disinterested, evenhanded, fair-minded, honest, honourable, impartial, just, lawful, legitimate, nonpartisan, open-minded, proper, right, unbiased, unprejudiced, upright. Opp UNJUST. 4 a fair standard. acceptable, adequate, average, indifferent, mediocre, middling, moderate, ordinary, passable, reasonable, respectable, satisfactory, inf so-so, tolerable. Opp UNACCEPTABLE. 5 ▷ BEAUTIFUL. ● n 1 amusement-park, fair-ground, fun-fair. 2 bazaar, carnival, exhibition, festival, fête, gala, market, sale, show.

fairly adv moderately, pretty, quite, rather, reasonably, somewhat, tolerably, up to a point.

faith n 1 assurance, belief, certitude, confidence, credence, reliance, sureness, trust. Opp DOUBT. 2 conviction, creed, devotion, doctrine, dogma, persuasion, religion.

faithful adj 1 constant, dependable, devoted, dutiful, honest, loyal, reli-

able, staunch, steadfast, trusted, trusty, trustworthy, unswerving. 2 a faithful account. accurate, close, consistent, exact, factual, literal, precise. ▷ TRUE. Opp FALSE.

fake adj artificial, bogus, concocted, counterfeit, ersatz, factitious, false, fictitious, forged, fraudulent, imitation, invented, made-up, mock, sl phoney, pretended, sham, simulated, spurious, synthetic, trumped-up, unfounded, unreal. Opp GENUINE. ● n 1 copy, counterfeit, duplicate, forgery, hoax, imitation, replica, reproduction, sham, simulation. 2 charlatan, cheat, fraud, hoaxer, humbug, impostor, mountebank, sl phoney, quack. ● vb affect, copy, counterfeit, dissemble, falsify, feign, forge, fudge, imitate, make believe, mock up, pretend, put on, reproduce, sham, simulate.

fall n 1 collapse, crash, decline, decrease, depreciation, descent, dip, dive, downswing, downturn, drop, lowering, nosedive, plunge, reduction, slant, slump, tumble. 2 fall of a fortress. capitulation, capture, defeat, overthrow, seizure, submission, surrender. ● vb 1 collapse, inf come a cropper, crash down, dive, drop down, founder, go down, keel over, overbalance, pitch, plummet, plunge, sink, slump, spiral, stumble, topple, trip over, tumble. 2 become less, become lower, decline, decrease, diminish, dwindle, ebb, lessen, subside. 3 descend, drop, fall away, slope down. 4 curtains fell in folds. be suspended, cascade, dangle, dip down, hang. 5 silence fell. come, come about, happen, occur, settle. 6 ▷ DIE. 7 ▷ SURRENDER. **fall apart** ▷ DISINTEGRATE. **fall back** ▷ RETREAT. **fall behind** ▷ LAG. **fall down, fall in** ▷ COLLAPSE. **fall off** ▷ DECLINE. **fall out** ▷ QUARREL. **fall through** ▷ FAIL.

fallacy n delusion, error, flaw, miscalculation, misconception, mistake, solecism.

fallible adj erring, frail, human, imperfect, liable to make mistakes, uncertain, unpredictable, unreliable, weak. *Opp* INFALLIBLE.

fallow *adj* dormant, resting, uncultivated, unplanted, unsown, unused.

false *adj* **1** deceptive, distorted, erroneous, fabricated, fallacious, faulty, fictitious, flawed, imprecise, inaccurate, incorrect, inexact, invalid, misleading, mistaken, spurious, unfactual, unsound, untrue, wrong. ▷ FAKE. **2** *false friends*. deceitful, dishonest, disloyal, double-dealing, double-faced, faithless, lying, treacherous, unfaithful, unreliable, untrustworthy. *Opp* TRUE. **false name** ▷ PSEUDONYM.

falsehood *n* fabrication, *inf* fib, fiction, lie, prevarication, *inf* story, untruth, *sl* whopper.

falsify *vb* alter, *inf* cook (*the books*), counterfeit, distort, exaggerate, fake, forge, *inf* fudge, imitate, misrepresent, mock up, oversimplify, pervert, simulate, slant, tamper with, tell lies about, twist.

falter *vb* **1** become weaker, flag, flinch, hesitate, hold back, lose confidence, pause, quail, stagger, stumble, totter, vacillate, waver. *Opp* PERSIST. **2** stammer, stutter. **faltering** ▷ HESITANT.

fame *n* acclaim, celebrity, distinction, eminence, glory, honour, illustriousness, importance, *inf* kudos, name, *derog* notoriety, pre-eminence, prestige, prominence, public esteem, renown, reputation, repute, *inf* stardom.

familiar *adj* **1** accustomed, common, conventional, current, customary, everyday, frequent, habitual, mundane, normal, ordinary, predictable, regular, routine, stock, traditional, usual, well-known. *Opp* STRANGE. **2** *familiar language*. *inf* chatty, close, confidential, *derog* forward, *inf* free-and-easy, *derog* impudent, informal, intimate, near, *derog* presumptuous, relaxed, sociable, unceremonious. ▷ FRIENDLY. *Opp* FORMAL.
familiar with acquainted with, *inf* at home with, aware of, conscious of,

expert in, informed about, knowledgeable about, trained in, versed in.

family *n* **1** brood, children, *inf* flesh and blood, generation, issue, kindred, *old use* kith and kin, litter, *inf* nearest and dearest, offspring, progeny, relations, relatives, *inf* tribe. **2** ancestry, blood, clan, dynasty, extraction, forebears, genealogy, house, line, lineage, pedigree, race, strain, tribe. □ *ancestor, descendant.* □ *aunt, brother, child, cousin, daughter, father, fiancé(e), forefather, foster-child, foster-parent, godchild, godparent, grandchild, grandparent, guardian, husband,* Amer *junior, kinsman, kinswoman, mother, nephew, next-of-kin, niece, parent, sibling, sister, son, step-child, stepparent, uncle, ward, widow, widower, wife.*

famine *n* dearth, hunger, lack, malnutrition, scarcity, shortage, starvation, want. *Opp* PLENTY.

famished *adj* craving, famishing, hungry, *inf* peckish, ravenous, starved, starving.

famous *adj* acclaimed, big, celebrated, distinguished, eminent, exalted, famed, glorious, great, historic, honoured, illustrious, important, legendary, lionized, notable, noted, *derog* notorious, outstanding, popular, prominent, proverbial, renowned, revered, time-honoured, venerable, well-known, world-famous. *Opp* UNKNOWN.

fan *n* **1** blower, extractor, propeller, ventilator. **2** *a soccer fan*. addict, admirer, aficionado, *inf* buff, devotee, enthusiast, fanatic, *inf* fiend, follower, *inf* freak, lover, supporter. ▷ FANATIC.

fanatic *n* activist, adherent, bigot, extremist, fiend, freak, maniac, militant, zealot.

fanatical *adj* bigoted, excessive, extreme, fervent, fervid, immoderate, irrational, maniacal, militant, obsessive, overenthusiastic, passionate, rabid, single-minded, zealous. *Opp* MODERATE.

fanciful adj capricious, chimerical, fancy, fantastic, illusory, imaginary, imagined, make-believe, unrealistic, whimsical.

fancy adj decorative, elaborate, embellished, embroidered, intricate, ornamented, ornate. ▷ FANCIFUL. ● n ▷ IMAGINATION, WHIM. ● vb **1** conjure up, dream of, envisage, imagine, picture, visualize. ▷ THINK. **2** be attracted to, crave, inf have a yen for, like, long for, prefer, want, wish for. ▷ DESIRE.

fantastic adj **1** absurd, amazing, elaborate, exaggerated, extraordinary, extravagant, fabulous, fanciful, far-fetched, grotesque, imaginative, implausible, incredible, odd, quaint, remarkable, rococo, strange, surreal, unbelievable, unlikely, unrealistic, weird. **2** ▷ EXCELLENT. Opp ORDINARY.

fantasy n chimera, day-dream, delusion, dream, fancy, hallucination, illusion, imagination, invention, make-believe, mirage, pipe-dream, reverie, vision. Opp REALITY.

far adj distant, far-away, far-off, outlying, remote. Opp NEAR.

farcical adj absurd, foolish, ludicrous, preposterous, ridiculous, silly. ▷ FUNNY.

fare n **1** charge, cost, fee, payment, price, ticket. **2** festive fare. ▷ FOOD.

farewell adj goodbye, last, leaving, parting, valedictory. ● n departure, leave-taking, inf send-off, valediction. ▷ GOODBYE.

farm n farmhouse, farmstead, old use grange. □ arable farm, croft, dairy farm, fish farm, fruit farm, livestock farm, organic farm, plantation, poultry farm, ranch, smallholding.

farming n agriculture, agronomy, crofting, cultivation, foodproduction, husbandry.

fascinate vb allure, attract, beguile, bewitch, captivate, charm, delight, enchant, engross, enthral, entice, entrance, hypnotize, interest, mesmerize, rivet, spellbind. **fascinating** ▷ ATTRACTIVE.

fashion n **1** convention, manner, method, mode, way. **2** craze, cut, inf fad, line, look, pattern, rage, style, taste, trend, vogue.

fashionable adj Fr [à] la mode, chic, contemporary, current, elegant, inf in, in vogue, the latest, modern, modish, popular, smart, inf snazzy, sophisticated, stylish, tasteful, inf trendy, up-to-date, inf with it. Opp UNFASHIONABLE.

fast adv at full tilt, briskly, in no time, post-haste, quickly, rapidly, swiftly. ● adj **1** breakneck, brisk, expeditious, express, hasty, headlong, high-speed, hurried, lively, inf nippy, precipitate, quick, rapid, smart, inf spanking, speedy, supersonic, swift, unhesitating. Opp SLOW. **2** fast on the rocks. attached, bound, fastened, firm, fixed, immobile, immovable, secure, tight. **3** fast colours. indelible, lasting, permanent, stable. **4** fast living. ▷ IMMORAL. ● vb abstain, deny yourself, diet, go hungry, go without food, starve. Opp INDULGE.

fasten vb affix, anchor, attach, batten, bind, bolt, buckle, button, chain, clamp, clasp, cling, close, connect, couple, do up, fix, grip, hitch, hook, knot, join, lace, lash, latch on, link, lock, make fast, moor, nail, padlock, paste, peg, pin, rivet, rope, screw down, seal, secure, solder, staple, strap, tack, tape, tether, tie, unite, weld. ▷ STICK. Opp UNDO.

fastener n bond, connection, connector, coupling, fastening, link, linkage. □ anchor, bolt, buckle, button, catch, chain, clamp, clasp, clip, dowel, dowel-pin, drawing-pin, glue, gum, hasp, hook, knot, lace, latch, lock, mooring, nail, padlock, painter, paste, peg, pin, rivet, rope, safety-pin, screw, seal, Sellotape, solder, staple, strap, string, tack, tape, tether, tie, toggle, Velcro, wedge, zip.

fastidious adj choosy, dainty, delicate, discriminating, finical, finicky, fussy, hard to please, nice, particular, inf pernickety, inf picky, selective, squeamish.

fat adj **1** bloated, inf broad in the beam, bulky, chubby, corpulent, dumpy, flabby, fleshy, gross, heavy, massive, obese, overweight, paunchy, plump, podgy, portly, pot-bellied, pudgy, rotund, round, solid, squat, stocky, stout, thick, tubby, weighty, well-fed. ▷ BIG. **2** fat meat. fatty, greasy, oily. Opp LEAN. ● n □ adipose tissue, blubber, butter, dripping, grease, lard, margarine, oil, suet.

fatal adj **1** deadly, final, incurable, lethal, malignant, mortal, terminal. **2** ▷ DISASTROUS.

fatality n casualty, death, loss.

fate n **1** chance, destiny, doom, fortune, karma, kismet, lot, luck, nemesis, inf powers above, predestination, providence, the stars. **2** death, demise, destruction, disaster, downfall, end, ruin.

fated adj certain, cursed, damned, decreed, destined, doomed, foreordained, inescapable, inevitable, intended, predestined, predetermined, preordained, sure.

father n begetter, inf dad, inf daddy, inf pa, inf papa, parent, old use pater, inf pop, sire.

fatigue n debility, exhaustion, feebleness, languor, lassitude, lethargy, tiredness, weakness, weariness. ● vb debilitate, drain, enervate, exhaust, tire, weaken, weary. **fatigued** ▷ WEARY.

fault n **1** blemish, defect, deficiency, demerit, failing, failure, fallacy, flaw, foible, frailty, imperfection, inaccuracy, malfunction, snag, weakness. **2** blunder, inf boob, error, failing, Fr faux pas, gaffe, inf howler, indiscretion, lapse, miscalculation, misconduct, misdeed, mistake, negligence, offence, omission, oversight, peccadillo, shortcoming, sin, slip, transgression, old use trespass, vice, wrongdoing. **3** It was my fault. accountability, blame, culpability, guilt, liability, responsibility. ● vb ▷ CRITICIZE.

faultless adj accurate, correct, exemplary, flawless, ideal, in mint condition, irreproachable, sinless, unimpeachable. ▷ PERFECT. Opp FAULTY.

faulty adj broken, damaged, defective, deficient, flawed, illogical, imperfect, inaccurate, incomplete, incorrect, inoperative, invalid, not working, out of order, shop-soiled, unusable, useless. Opp FAULTLESS.

favour n **1** acceptance, approbation, approval, bias, favouritism, friendliness, goodwill, grace, liking, partiality, preference, support. **2** Do me a favour. benefit, courtesy, gift, good deed, good turn, indulgence, kindness, service. ● vb **1** approve of, be in sympathy with, champion, choose, commend, esteem, inf fancy, inf go for, like, opt for, prefer, show favour to, think well of, value. Opp DISLIKE. **2** abet, advance, back, be advantageous to, befriend, forward, promote, support. ▷ HELP. Opp HINDER.

favourable adj **1** advantageous, appropriate, auspicious, beneficial, benign, convenient, following (wind), friendly, generous, helpful, kind, opportune, positive, promising, propitious, reassuring, suitable, supportive, sympathetic, understanding, well-disposed. **2** a favourable review. approving, commendatory, complimentary, congratulatory, encouraging, enthusiastic, laudatory. **3** a favourable reputation. agreeable, desirable, enviable, good, pleasing, satisfactory. Opp UNFAVOURABLE.

favourite adj beloved, best, choice, chosen, dearest, esteemed, ideal, liked, loved, popular, preferred, selected, well-liked. ● n **1** choice, pick, preference. **2** inf apple of your eye, darling, idol, pet.

fear n alarm, anxiety, apprehension, apprehensiveness, awe, concern, consternation, cowardice, cravenness, diffidence, dismay, doubt, dread, faint-heartedness, foreboding, fright, inf funk, horror, misgiving, nervousness, panic, phobia, qualm, suspicion, terror, timidity, trepidation, uneasiness, worry. ▷ PHOBIA. Opp COURAGE. ● vb be afraid of, dread, quail at, shrink from, suspect, tremble at, worry about.

fearful adj **1** alarmed, apprehensive, frightened, nervous, panic-stricken, scared, terrified, timid. ▷ AFRAID. Opp FEARLESS. **2** ▷ FEARSOME.

fearless adj bold, brave, dauntless, intrepid, resolute, stoical, unafraid, unconcerned, undaunted, valiant, valorous. ▷ COURAGEOUS. Opp FEARFUL.

fearsome adj appalling, aweinspiring, awesome, daunting, dreadful, fearful, frightful, intimidating, terrible, terrifying. ▷ FRIGHTENING.

feasible adj **1** achievable, attainable, easy, possible, practicable, practical, realizable, viable, workable. Opp IMPRACTICAL. **2** a feasible scenario. credible, likely, plausible, reasonable. Opp IMPLAUSIBLE.

feast n banquet, sl blow-out, dinner, inf spread. ▷ MEAL. ● vb dine, gorge, gormandize, inf wine and dine. ▷ EAT.

feat n accomplishment, achievement, act, action, attainment, deed, exploit, performance.

feather n plume, quill. **feathers** down, plumage.

feathery adj downy, fluffy, light, wispy.

feature n **1** aspect, attribute, characteristic, circumstance, detail, facet, hall mark, idiosyncrasy, mark, peculiarity, point, property, quality, trait. **2** newspaper feature. article, column, item, piece, report, story. ● vb **1** emphasize, focus on, give prominence to, highlight, inf play up, present, promote, show up, inf spotlight, inf star, stress. **2** feature in a film. act, appear, figure, participate, perform, play a role, star, take a part. **features** ▷ FACE.

fee n bill, charge, cost, dues, emolument, fare, payment, price, remuneration, subscription, sum, tariff, terms, toll, wage.

feeble adj **1** ailing, debilitated, decrepit, delicate, enfeebled, exhausted, faint, fragile, frail, helpless, ill, impotent, inadequate, ineffective,

infirm, languid, listless, poorly, powerless, puny, sickly, slight, useless, weak. Opp STRONG. **2** effete, feckless, hesitant, incompetent, indecisive, ineffectual, irresolute, inf namby-pamby, spineless, vacillating, weedy, wimpish, inf wishy-washy. **3** feeble excuses. flimsy, insubstantial, lame, paltry, poor, tame, thin, unconvincing.

feed vb **1** cater for, give food to, nourish, nurture, provender, provide for, provision, strengthen, suckle, support, sustain, inf wine and dine. **2** dine, eat, fare, graze, pasture. **feed on** ▷ EAT.

feel vb **1** caress, finger, fondle, handle, hold, manipulate, maul, inf paw, pet, stroke, touch. **2** feel your way. explore, fumble, grope. **3** feel the cold. be aware of, be conscious of, detect, discern, experience, know, notice, perceive, sense, suffer, undergo. **4** It feels cold. appear, give a feeling of, seem. **5** feel something's true. believe, consider, deem, guess, inf have a feeling, inf have a hunch, intuit, judge, think.

feeling n **1** sensation, sense of touch, sensitivity. **2** ardour, emotion, fervour, passion, sentiment, warmth. **3** religious feelings. attitude, belief, consciousness, guess, hunch, idea, impression, instinct, intuition, notion, opinion, perception, thought, view. **4** a feeling for music. fondness, responsiveness, sensibility, sympathy, understanding. **5** [inf] a party feeling. atmosphere, aura, mood, tone, inf vibrations.

fell vb bring down, chop down, cut down, flatten, inf floor, knock down, mow down, prostrate. ▷ KILL.

female adj ▷ FEMININE. Opp MALE. ● n □ aunt, old use damsel, daughter, old use débutante, fiancé, girl, girlfriend, grandmother, lady, inf lass, lesbian, old use maid, old use maiden, old use mistress, mother, niece, sister, spinster, old use or sexist wench, wife, woman. □ bitch, cow, doe, ewe, hen, lioness, mare, nanny-goat, sow, tigress, vixen.

feminine adj derog of men effeminate, female, derog girlish, ladylike, womanly. Opp MASCULINE.

fen n bog, lowland, marsh, morass, quagmire, slough, swamp.

fence n barricade, barrier, fencing, hedge, hurdle, obstacle, paling, palisade, railing, rampart, stockade, wall, wire. ● vb 1 bound, circumscribe, confine, coop up, encircle, enclose, hedge in, immure, pen, restrict, surround, wall in. 2 ▷ FIGHT.

fend vb fend for yourself care for yourself, do for yourself, inf get along, inf get by, look after yourself, inf scrape along, support yourself, survive. fend off ▷ REPEL.

ferment n ▷ COMMOTION. ● vb 1 boil, bubble, effervesce, inf fizz, foam, froth, rise, seethe, work. 2 agitate, excite, foment, incite, instigate, provoke, rouse, stir up.

ferocious adj bestial, bloodthirsty, brutal, cruel, feral, fiendish, fierce, harsh, inhuman, merciless, murderous, pitiless, sadistic, savage, vicious, wild. Opp GENTLE.

ferry n ▷ VESSEL. ● vb carry, export, fetch, import, shift, ship, shuttle, take across, taxi, transport. ▷ CONVEY.

fertile adj abundant, fecund, fertilized, flourishing, fruitful, lush, luxuriant, productive, prolific, rich, teeming, well-manured. Opp STERILE.

fertilize vb 1 impregnate, inseminate, pollinate. 2 cultivate, dress, enrich, feed, make fertile, manure, mulch, nourish, top-dress.

fertilizer n compost, dressing, dung, manure, mulch, nutrient.

fervent adj animated, ardent, avid, burning, committed, devout, eager, earnest, emotional, enthusiastic, excited, fanatical, fervid, fiery, frenzied, heated, impassioned, intense, keen, passionate, rapturous, spirited, vehement, vigorous, warm, wholehearted, zealous. Opp COOL.

fervour n ardour, eagerness, energy, enthusiasm, excitement, fervency, fire, heat, intensity, keenness, passion, sparkle, spirit, vehemence, vigour, warmth, zeal.

fester vb become infected, become inflamed, become poisoned, decay, discharge, gather, go bad, go septic, mortify, ooze, putrefy, rot, run, suppurate, ulcerate.

festival n anniversary, carnival, celebration, commemoration, fair, feast, fête, fiesta, gala, holiday, jamboree, jubilee. ▷ FESTIVITY.

festive adj celebratory, cheerful, cheery, convivial, gay, gleeful, jolly, jovial, joyful, joyous, light-hearted, merry, uproarious. ▷ HAPPY.

festivity n celebration, conviviality, entertainment, feasting, festive occasion, inf jollification, jollity, jubilation, merrymaking, merriment, mirth, rejoicing, revelry, revels. ▷ PARTY.

fetch vb 1 bear, bring, call for, carry, collect, convey, get, import, obtain, pick up, retrieve, transfer, transport. 2 fetch a good price. be bought for, bring in, earn, go for, make, produce, raise, realize, sell for. fetching ▷ ATTRACTIVE.

feud n animosity, antagonism, inf bad blood, conflict, dispute, enmity, grudge, hostility, rivalry, strife, vendetta. ▷ QUARREL.

fever n delirium, feverishness, high temperature.

feverish adj 1 burning, febrile, fevered, flushed, hot, inflamed, trembling. Opp COOL. 2 feverish activity. agitated, excited, frantic, frenetic, frenzied, hectic, hurried, impatient, passionate, restless.

few adj inf few and far between, hardly any, inadequate, infrequent, rare, scarce, sparse, sporadic, inf thin on the ground, uncommon. Opp MANY.

fibre n 1 filament, hair, strand, thread. 2 moral fibre. backbone, character, determination, spirit, tenacity, toughness. ▷ COURAGE.

fickle adj capricious, changeable, changing, disloyal, erratic, faithless, flighty, inconsistent, inconstant, mercurial, mutable, treacherous, undependable, unfaithful, unpredictable, unreliable, unstable, unsteady, *inf* up and down, vacillating, variable, volatile. *Opp* CONSTANT.

fiction *n* concoction, deception, fabrication, fantasy, figment of the imagination, flight of fancy, invention, lies, story-telling, *inf* tall story. ▷ WRITING. *Opp* FACT.

fictional *adj* fabulous, fanciful, imaginary, invented, legendary, made-up, make-believe, mythical, story-book. *Opp* FACTUAL.

fictitious *adj* apocryphal, assumed, fabricated, deceitful, fraudulent, imagined, invented, made-up, spurious, unreal, untrue. ▷ FALSE. *Opp* GENUINE.

fiddle *vb* interfere, meddle, play about, tamper. ▷ FIDGET. **fiddling** ▷ TRIVIAL.

fidget *vb* be restless, *inf* fiddle about, fret, frisk about, fuss, jerk about, *inf* jiggle, *inf* mess about, move restlessly, *inf* play about, shuffle, squirm, twitch, worry, wriggle about.

fidgety *adj* agitated, frisky, impatient, jittery, jumpy, nervous, on edge, restive, restless, *inf* twitchy, uneasy. *Opp* CALM.

field *n* **1** arable land, clearing, enclosure, grassland, *poet* glebe, green, *old use* mead, meadow, paddock, pasture. **2** *a games field.* arena, ground, pitch, playing-field, recreation ground, stadium. **3** *field of activity.* area, *inf* department, domain, province, sphere, subject, territory.

fiend *n* **1** demon, devil, evil spirit, goblin, hobgoblin, imp, Satan, spirit. **2** ▷ FANATIC.

fierce *adj* **1** angry, barbaric, barbarous, bloodthirsty, bloody, brutal, cold-blooded, cruel, dangerous, fearsome, ferocious, fiendish, fiery, homicidal, inhuman, merciless, murderous, pitiless, ruthless, sadistic, savage, untamed, vicious, violent, wild. **2** *fierce opposition.* active, aggressive, competitive, eager, furious, heated, intense, keen, passionate, relentless, strong, unrelenting. *Opp* GENTLE.

fiery *adj* **1** ablaze, afire, aflame, aglow, blazing, burning, fierce, flaming, glowing, heated, hot, incandescent, raging, red, red-hot. **2** *a fiery temper.* angry, ardent, choleric, excitable, fervent, furious, hotheaded, intense, irascible, irritable, livid, mad, passionate, touchy, violent. *Opp* COOL.

fight *n* action, affray, attack, battle, bout, brawl, *inf* brush, *inf* bust-up, clash, combat, competition, conflict, confrontation, contest, counterattack, dispute, dogfight, duel, *inf* dustup, encounter, engagement, feud, *old use* fisticuffs, fracas, fray, *inf* free-for-all, hostilities, joust, match, mêlée, *inf* punch-up, raid, riot, rivalry, row, scramble, scrap, scrimmage, scuffle, *inf* set-to, skirmish, squabble, strife, tussle, war, wrangle. ▷ QUARREL. ● *vb* **1** attack, battle, box, brawl, *inf* brush, clash, compete, conflict, contend, do battle, duel, engage, exchange blows, fence, feud, grapple, have a fight, joust, quarrel, row, scrap, scuffle, skirmish, spar, squabble, stand up (to), strive, struggle, *old use* tilt, tussle, wage war, wrestle. **2** *fight a decision.* campaign against, contest, defy, oppose, protest against, resist, take a stand against.

fighter *n* aggressor, antagonist, attacker, belligerent, campaigner, combatant, contender, contestant, defender. □ *archer, boxer, inf brawler, champion, duellist, freedom fighter, gladiator, guerrilla, gunman, knight, marine, marksman, mercenary, partisan, prize-fighter, pugilist, sniper, swordsman, terrorist, warrior, wrestler.* ▷ SOLDIER.

figure *n* **1** amount, cipher, digit, integer, number, numeral, sum, symbol, value. **2** diagram, drawing, graph, illustration, outline, picture, plate, representation. **3** *plump figure.* body, build, form, outline, physique, shape, silhouette. **4** *bronze figure.* ▷ SCULPTURE. **5** *well-known figure.* ▷ PERSON. ● *vb*

▷ FEATURE. **figure out** ▷ CALCULATE, UNDERSTAND. **figures** ▷ STATISTICS.

file n **1** binder, box-file, case, cover, documentation, document-case, dossier, folder, portfolio, ring-binder. **2** single file. column, line, procession, queue, rank, row, stream, string, train. ● vb **1** arrange, categorize, classify, enter, pigeon-hole, organize, put away, record, register, store, systematize. **2** file through a door. march, parade, proceed in a line, stream, troop.

fill vb **1** be full of, block, inf bung up, caulk, clog, close up, cram, crowd, flood, inflate, jam, load, obstruct, pack, plug, refill, replenish, seal, stock up, stop up, inf stuff, inf top up. Opp EMPTY. **2** fill a need. answer, fulfil, furnish, meet, provide, satisfy, supply. **3** fill a post. execute, hold, occupy, take over, take up. **fill out** ▷ SWELL.

filling n contents, inf innards, insides, padding, stuffing, wadding.

film n **1** coat, coating, cover, covering, haze, layer, membrane, mist, overlay, screen, sheet, skin, slick, tissue, veil. **2** cartoon, old use flick, motion picture, movie, picture, video, video-tape.

filter n colander, gauze, membrane, mesh, riddle, screen, sieve, strainer. ● vb clarify, filtrate, percolate, purify, refine, screen, sieve, sift, strain.

filth n decay, dirt, effluent, garbage, grime, inf gunge, impurity, muck, mud, ordure, pollution, putrescence, refuse, rubbish, scum, sewage, slime, sludge, trash. ▷ EXCRETA.

filthy adj **1** begrimed, caked, defiled, dirty, disgusting, dusty, foul, grimy, grubby, impure, messy, mucky, muddy, nasty, polluted, scummy, slimy, smelly, soiled, sooty, sordid, squalid, stinking, tainted, uncleaned, unkempt, unwashed, vile. **2** ▷ OBSCENE. Opp CLEAN.

final adj clinching, closing, concluding, conclusive, decisive, dying, end, eventual, finishing, last, settled, terminal, terminating, ultimate. Opp INITIAL.

finalize vb clinch, complete, conclude, settle, inf sew up, inf wrap up.

finance n accounting, banking, business, commerce, economics, investment, stocks and shares. ● vb back, fund, guarantee, invest in, pay for, provide money for, subsidize, support, underwrite. **finances** assets, bank account, budget, capital, cash, funds, holdings, income, money, resources, wealth, inf the wherewithal.

financial adj economic, fiscal, monetary, pecuniary.

find vb **1** acquire, arrive at, become aware of, inf bump into, chance upon, come across, come upon, detect, diagnose, dig out, dig up, discover, encounter, espy, expose, inf ferret out, happen on, hit on, identify, learn, light on, locate, meet, note, notice, observe, inf put your finger on, reach, recognize, reveal, spot, stumble on, uncover, unearth. **2** find lost property. get back, recover, rediscover, regain, repossess, retrieve, trace, track down. **3** found me a job. give, pass on, procure, provide, supply. Opp LOSE.

finding n conclusion, decision, decree, judgement, pronouncement, verdict.

fine adj **1** admirable, beautiful, choice, classic, commendable, excellent, first-class, handsome, noble, select, superior, worthy. ▷ GOOD. **2** fine workmanship. consummate, craftsmanlike, meticulous, skilful, skilled. **3** fine sand. minute, powdery, soft. **4** fine fabric. dainty, delicate, exquisite, flimsy, fragile, silky. **5** a fine point. acute, keen, narrow, sharp, slender, slim, thin. **6** a fine distinction. fine-drawn, discriminating, hair-splitting, nice, precise, subtle. **7** fine weather. bright, clear, cloudless, dry, fair, nice, pleasant, sunny. ● n charge, forfeit, penalty.

finish n **1** cessation, close, completion, conclusion, culmination, end, ending, finale, resolution, result, termination. **2** *finish on furniture.* appearance, completeness, gloss, lustre, patina, perfection, polish, shine, smoothness, surface, texture. ● *vb* **1** accomplish, achieve, break off, bring to an end, cease, clinch, complete, conclude, discontinue, end, finalize, fulfil, halt, pack up, perfect, phase out, reach the end, round off, say goodbye, sign off, stop, take your leave, terminate, *inf* wind up, *inf* wrap up. **2** consume, drink up, eat up, empty, exhaust, expend, get through, *inf* polish off, *inf* say goodbye to, use up. **finish off** ▷ KILL.

finite *adj* bounded, calculable, controlled, countable, definable, defined, determinate, fixed, known, limited, measurable, numbered, rationed, restricted. *Opp* INFINITE.

fire *n* **1** blaze, burning, combustion, conflagration, flames, holocaust, inferno, pyre. **2** fireplace, grate, hearth. □ boiler, bonfire, brazier, convector, *electric fire*, forge, furnace, *gas fire*, *immersion-heater*, incinerator, kiln, oven, radiator, stove. **3** *fire in your veins.* ▷ PASSION. ● *vb* **1** bake, burn, heat, ignite, kindle, light, put a light to, set alight, set fire to, spark off. **2** animate, awaken, enkindle, enliven, excite, incite, inflame, inspire, motivate, rouse, stimulate, stir. **3** *fire a gun or missile.* catapult, detonate, discharge, explode, launch, let off, propel, set off, shoot, trigger off. **4** *fire a worker.* dismiss, make redundant, sack, throw out. **fire at** ▷ BOMBARD. **hang fire** ▷ DELAY.

fireproof *adj* flameproof, incombustible, non-flammable. *Opp* INFLAMMABLE.

fire-raiser *n* arsonist, pyromaniac.

firm *adj* **1** compact, compressed, congealed, dense, hard, inelastic, inflexible, rigid, set, solid, stable, stiff, unyielding. **2** *firm on the rocks.* anchored, embedded, fast, fastened, fixed, immovable, secure, steady, tight. **3** *firm convictions.* adamant, decided, determined, dogged, obstinate, persistent, resolute, unshake-able, unwavering. **4** *a firm price.* agreed, settled, unchangeable. **5** *firm friends.* constant, dependable, devoted, faithful, loyal, reliable. ● *n* business, company, concern, corporation, establishment, organization, partnership.

first *adj* **1** cardinal, chief, dominant, foremost, head, highest, key, leading, main, outstanding, paramount, predominant, primary, prime, principal, top, uppermost. **2** *first steps.* basic, elementary, fundamental, initial, introductory, preliminary, rudimentary. **3** *first inhabitants.* aboriginal, archetypal, earliest, eldest, embryonic, oldest, original, primeval. **first-class**, **first-rate** ▷ EXCELLENT.

fish *n* □ brill, brisling, carp, catfish, chub, cod, coelacanth, conger, cuttlefish, dab, dace, eel, flounder, goldfish, grayling, gudgeon, haddock, hake, halibut, herring, jellyfish, lamprey, ling, mackerel, minnow, mullet, perch, pike, pilchard, piranha, plaice, roach, salmon, sardine, sawfish, shark, skate, sole, sprat, squid, starfish, stickleback, sturgeon, swordfish, *inf* tiddler, trout, tuna, turbot, whitebait, whiting. ● *vb* angle, go fishing, trawl.

fisher *n* angler, fisherman, trawlerman.

fit *adj* **1** adapted, adequate, applicable, apposite, appropriate, apropos, apt, becoming, befitting, correct, decent, equipped, fitting, good enough, proper, right, satisfactory, seemly, sound, suitable, suited, timely. **2** able, capable, competent, in good form, on form, prepared, ready, strong, well enough. ▷ HEALTHY. *Opp* UNFIT. ● *n* attack, bout, convulsion, eruption, explosion, outbreak, outburst, paroxysm, seizure, spasm, spell. ● *vb* **1** accord with, become, be fitting for, conform with, correspond to, correspond with, go with, harmonize with, suit. **2** *fit things into place.* arrange, assemble, build, construct, dovetail, install, interlock, join, match, position, put in place, put together. **fit out**, **fit up** ▷ EQUIP.

fix n inf catch-22, corner, difficulty, dilemma, inf hole, inf jam, mess, inf pickle, plight, predicament, problem, quandary. ● vb **1** attach, bind, connect, embed, implant, install, join, link, make firm, plant, position, secure, stabilize, stick. ▷ FASTEN. **2** fix a price. agree, appoint, arrange, arrive at, conclude, confirm, decide, define, establish, finalize, name, ordain, set, settle, sort out, specify. **3** fix a broken window. correct, make good, mend, put right, rectify, remedy, repair.

fixture n date, engagement, event, game, match, meeting.

fizz vb bubble, effervesce, fizzle, foam, froth, hiss, sizzle, sparkle, sputter.

fizzy adj bubbly, effervescent, foaming, sparkling.

flag n banner, bunting, colours, ensign, jack, pennant, pennon, standard, streamer. ● vb **1** ▷ SIGNAL. **2** enthusiasm flagged. ▷ DECLINE.

flake n bit, chip, leaf, scale, scurf, shaving, slice, sliver, splinter, wafer.

flame n blaze, light, tongue. ▷ FIRE. ● vb ▷ FLARE.

flap vb beat, flutter, oscillate, slap, sway, swing, thrash about, thresh about, wag, waggle, wave about.

flare vb **1** blaze, brighten, burst out, erupt, flame, shine. ▷ BURN. **2** ▷ WIDEN.

flash vb coruscate, dazzle, flicker, glare, glint, glitter, light up, reflect, scintillate, shine, spark, sparkle, twinkle. ▷ BURN.

flat adj **1** calm, even, horizontal, level, smooth, unbroken, unruffled. **2** outstretched, prone, prostrate, recumbent, spread-eagled, spread out, supine. **3** a flat voice. bland, boring, dead, dry, dull, featureless, insipid, lacklustre, lifeless, monotonous, spiritless, stale, tedious, tired, unexciting, uninteresting, unmodulated, unvarying. **4** a flat tyre. blown out, burst, deflated, punctured. ● n apartment, bedsitter, flatlet, maisonette, penthouse, rooms, suite.

flatten vb **1** compress, even out, iron out, level out, press, roll, smooth, straighten. **2** crush, demolish, devastate, level, raze, run over, squash, trample. ▷ DESTROY. **3** flatten an opponent. fell, floor, knock down, prostrate. ▷ DEFEAT.

flatter vb be flattering to, inf butter up, compliment, court, curry favour with, fawn on, humour, inf play up to, praise, sl suck up to, inf toady to. Opp INSULT. **flattering** ▷ COMPLIMENTARY, OBSEQUIOUS.

flatterer n inf crawler, inf creep, groveller, lackey, sycophant, time-server, inf toady, inf yes-man.

flattery n adulation, blandishments, inf blarney, inf boot-licking, cajolery, fawning, inf flannel, insincerity, obsequiousness, servility, inf soft soap, sycophancy, unctuousness.

flavour n **1** savour, taste. ▷ FLAVOURING. **2** air, ambience, atmosphere, aura, character, characteristic, feel, feeling, property, quality, spirit, stamp, style. ● vb add flavour to, add taste to, season, spice.

flavouring n additive, essence, extract, seasoning.

flaw n break, defect, error, fallacy, fault, imperfection, inaccuracy, loophole, mistake, shortcoming, slip, split, weakness. ▷ BLEMISH. **flawed** ▷ IMPERFECT.

flawless adj accurate, clean, faultless, immaculate, mint, pristine, sound, spotless, undamaged, unmarked. ▷ PERFECT. Opp IMPERFECT.

flee vb abscond, inf beat a retreat, sl beat it, bolt, clear off, cut and run, decamp, disappear, escape, fly, get away, hurry off, inf make a run for it, make off, retreat, run away, sl scarper, take flight, inf take to your heels, vanish, withdraw.

fleet n armada, convoy, flotilla, navy, squadron, task force.

fleeting adj brief, ephemeral, evanescent, fugitive, impermanent, momentary, mutable, passing, short, short-lived, temporary, transient, transitory. Opp PERMANENT.

flesh n carrion, fat, meat, muscle, tissue.

flex n cable, cord, extension, lead, wire. • vb ▷ BEND.

flexible adj **1** bendable, inf bendy, elastic, flexile, floppy, giving, limp, lithe, plastic, pliable, pliant, rubbery, soft, springy, stretchy, supple, whippy, willowy, yielding. **2** adjustable, alterable, fluid, mutable, open, provisional, variable. **3** a flexible person. accommodating, adaptable, amenable, compliant, conformable, co-operative, docile, easygoing, malleable, open-minded, responsive, tractable, willing. Opp RIGID.

flicker vb blink, flap, flutter, glimmer, gutter, quiver, shake, shimmer, sparkle, tremble, twinkle, vibrate, waver.

flight n **1** journey, trajectory. **2** ▷ ESCAPE.

flimsy adj **1** breakable, brittle, delicate, fine, fragile, frail, insubstantial, light, loose, slight, thin, weak. **2** a flimsy building. decrepit, dilapidated, gimcrack, jerry-built, makeshift, rickety, shaky, tottering, wobbly. **3** a flimsy argument. feeble, implausible, inadequate, superficial, trivial, unbelievable, unconvincing, unsatisfactory. Opp STRONG.

flinch vb blench, cower, cringe, dodge, draw back, duck, falter, jerk away, jump, quail, quake, recoil, shrink back, shy away, start, swerve, wince. **flinch from** ▷ EVADE.

fling vb bowl, inf bung, cast, inf chuck, heave, hurl, launch, lob, pelt, pitch, propel, send, inf shy, inf sling, throw, toss.

flippant adj cheeky, facetious, facile, inf flip, frivolous, light-hearted, shallow, superficial, thoughtless, unserious. Opp SERIOUS.

flirt n female coquette, male philanderer, inf tease. • vb sl chat someone up, lead someone on, make love, philander, toy with someone's affections.

flirtatious adj amorous, coquettish, flirty, derog philandering, playful, derog promiscuous, teasing.

float vb **1** be poised, be suspended, bob, drift, glide, hang, hover, sail, swim, waft. **2** float a ship. launch. Opp SINK.

flock n assembly, congregation, crowd, drove, gathering, herd, horde, multitude, swarm. ▷ GROUP. • vb ▷ GATHER.

flog vb beat, birch, cane, chastise, flagellate, flay, lash, scourge, thrash, whip. ▷ HIT.

flood n **1** cataract, deluge, downpour, flash-flood, inundation, overflow, rush, spate, stream, tidal wave, tide, torrent. **2** abundance, excess, glut, plethora, quantity, superfluity, surfeit, surge. • vb cover, deluge, drown, engulf, fill up, immerse, inundate, overflow, overwhelm, saturate, sink, submerge, swamp.

floor n **1** floorboards, flooring. **2** deck, level, storey, tier.

flop vb **1** collapse, dangle, droop, drop, fall, flag, flap about, hang down, sag, slump, topple, tumble, wilt. **2** ▷ FAIL.

floppy adj dangling, droopy, flabby, hanging, loose, limp, pliable, soft. ▷ FLEXIBLE. Opp RIGID.

flounder vb **1** blunder, flail, fumble, grope, move clumsily, plunge about, stagger, struggle, stumble, tumble, wallow. **2** falter, get confused, make mistakes, talk aimlessly.

flourish n ▷ GESTURE. • vb **1** be fruitful, be successful, bloom, blossom, boom, burgeon, develop, do well, flower, grow, increase, inf perk up, progress, prosper, strengthen, succeed, thrive. **2** flourish an umbrella. brandish, flaunt, gesture with, shake, swing, twirl, wag, wave, wield.

flow n cascade, course, current, drift, ebb, effusion, flood, gush, outpouring, spate, spurt, stream, tide, trickle. • vb bleed, cascade, course, dribble, drift, drip, ebb, flood, flush, glide, gush, issue, leak, move in a stream, ooze, overflow, pour, purl, ripple, roll, run, seep, spill, spring, spurt, squirt, stream, swirl, trickle, well, well up.

flower *n* **1** bloom, blossom, bud, floret, petal. □ begonia, bluebell, buttercup, campanula, campion, candytuft, carnation, catkin, celandine, chrysanthemum, coltsfoot, columbine, cornflower, cowslip, crocus, crowfoot, cyclamen, daffodil, dahlia, daisy, dandelion, forget-me-not, foxglove, freesia, geranium, gladiolus, gypsophila, harebell, hollyhock, hyacinth, iris, jonquil, kingcup, lilac, lily, lupin, marguerite, marigold, montbretia, nasturtium, orchid, pansy, pelargonium, peony, periwinkle, petunia, phlox, pink, polyanthus, poppy, primrose, rhododendron, rose, saxifrage, scabious, scarlet pimpernel, snowdrop, speedwell, sunflower, tulip, violet, wallflower, water-lily. ● *vb* bloom, blossom, *poet* blow, bud, burgeon, come out, have flowers, open out, unfold. ▷ FLOURISH. **bunch of flowers** arrangement, bouquet, corsage, garland, posy, spray, wreath.

fluctuate *vb* alternate, be unsteady, change, go up and down, oscillate, seesaw, shift, swing, vacillate, vary, waver.

fluent *adj* articulate, effortless, eloquent, expressive, *derog* facile, felicitous, flowing, *derog* glib, natural, polished, ready, smooth, voluble, unhesitating. *Opp* HESITANT.

fluff *n* down, dust, feathers, floss, fuzz, thistledown.

fluffy *adj* downy, feathery, fibrous, fleecy, furry, fuzzy, hairy, light, silky, soft, velvety, wispy, woolly.

fluid *adj* **1** aqueous, flowing, gaseous, liquefied, liquid, melted, molten, running, *inf* runny, sloppy, watery. *Opp* SOLID. **2** *a fluid situation.* adjustable, alterable, changing, flexible, mutable, open, variable, undefined. ● *n* gas, liquid, liquor, plasma, vapour.

fluke *n* accident, chance, serendipity, stroke of good luck, twist of fate.

flush *vb* **1** blush, colour, glow, go red, redden. **2** *flush a lavatory.* clean out, cleanse, flood, *inf* pull the plug, rinse

out, wash out. **3** *flush from a hiding-place.* chase out, drive out, expel, send up.

fluster *vb* agitate, bewilder, bother, distract, flurry, perplex, put off, put out, *inf* rattle, *inf* throw, upset. ▷ CONFUSE.

flutter *vb* bat (*eyelid*), flap, flicker, flit, fluctuate, move agitatedly, oscillate, palpitate, quiver, shake, tremble, twitch, vacillate, vibrate, wave.

fly *vb* **1** ascend, flit, glide, hover, rise, sail, soar, swoop, take flight, take wing. **2** *fly a plane.* aviate, pilot, take off in. **3** *fly a flag.* display, flap, flutter, hang up, hoist, raise, show, wave. **4** *fly from danger.* flee, hurry, move quickly, run. ▷ ESCAPE. **fly at** ▷ ATTACK. **fly in the face of** ▷ DISREGARD.

flying *n* aeronautics, air-travel, aviation, flight, *inf* jetting.

foam *n* **1** bubbles, effervescence, froth, head (*on beer*), lather, scum, spume, suds. **2** sponge. ● *vb* boil, bubble, effervesce, fizz, froth, lather, make foam.

focus *n* **1** clarity, correct adjustment, sharpness. **2** centre, core, focal point, heart, hub, pivot, target. ● *vb* aim, centre, concentrate, direct attention, fix attention, home in, spotlight.

fog *n* bad visibility, cloud, haze, miasma, mist, smog, vapour.

foggy *adj* blurred, blurry, clouded, cloudy, dim, hazy, indistinct, misty, murky, obscure. *Opp* CLEAR.

foil *vb* baffle, block, check, circumvent, frustrate, halt, hamper, hinder, obstruct, outwit, prevent, stop, thwart. ▷ DEFEAT.

foist *vb* *inf* fob off, get rid of, impose, offload, palm off.

fold *n* **1** bend, corrugation, crease, crinkle, furrow, gather, hollow, knife-edge, line, pleat, pucker, wrinkle. **2** *fold for sheep.* ▷ ENCLOSURE. ● *vb* **1** bend, crease, crimp, crinkle, double over, jack-knife, overlap, pleat, ply, pucker, tuck in, turn over. **2** close, collapse, let down, put down, shut. **3** *fold in your arms.* clasp, clip, embrace, enclose, enfold, entwine, envelop, hold, hug, wrap. **4** *business folded.* ▷ FAIL.

folk *n* clan, nation, people, the population, the public, race, society, tribe.

follow *vb* **1** accompany, chase, come after, dog, escort, go after, hound, hunt, keep pace with, pursue, replace, shadow, stalk, succeed, supersede, supplant, *inf* tag along with, tail, take the place of, track, trail. **2** *follow a path.* keep to, trace. **3** *follow rules.* abide by, adhere to, attend to, comply with, conform to, heed, honour, obey, observe, pay attention to, stick to, submit to, take notice of. **4** *follow my example.* adopt, be guided by, conform to, copy, imitate, mimic, mirror. **5** *follow an argument.* appreciate, comprehend, grasp, keep up with, take in, understand. **6** *follow football.* admire, be a fan of, keep abreast of, know about, take an interest in, support. **7** *It doesn't follow.* be inevitable, be logical, come about, ensue, happen, have the consequence, mean, result. **following** ▷ SUBSEQUENT.

folly *n* foolishness, insanity, lunacy, madness. ▷ STUPIDITY.

foment *vb* arouse, incite, instigate, kindle, provoke, rouse, stir up. ▷ STIMULATE.

fond *adj* **1** adoring, affectionate, caring, loving, tender, warm. **2** *a fond hope.* ▷ FOOLISH. **be fond of** ▷ LOVE.

fondle *vb* caress, cuddle, handle, pat, pet, snuggle, squeeze, touch.

food *n* aliment, *old use* bread, *old use* comestibles, cooking, cuisine, delicacies, diet, *inf* eatables, *inf* eats, fare, feed, fodder, foodstuff, forage, *inf* grub, *inf* junk food, *old use* meat, *sl* nosh, nourishment, nutriments, provender, provisions, rations, recipe, refreshments, sustenance, swill, *old use* tuck, *old use* viands, *old use* victuals. ▷ MEAL.

fool *n* **1** [*most synonyms inf*] ass, blockhead, booby, buffoon, dim-wit, dope, dunce, dunderhead, dupe, fat-head, half-wit, ignoramus, mug, muggins, mutt, ninny, nit, nitwit, simpleton, sucker, twerp, wally. ▷ IDIOT. **2** clown, comedian, comic, coxcomb, entertainer, jester. ● *vb inf* bamboozle, bluff, cheat, *inf* con, cozen, deceive, defraud, delude, dupe, fleece, gull, *inf* have on, hoax, hoodwink, *inf* kid, mislead, *inf* string along, swindle, take in, tease, trick. **fool about** ▷ MISBEHAVE.

foolish *adj* absurd, asinine, brainless, childish, crazy, daft, *inf* dopey, *inf* dotty, fatuous, feather-brained, feeble-minded, *old use* fond, frivolous, *inf* half-baked, hare-brained, idiotic, illogical, immature, inane, infantile, irrational, *inf* jokey, laughable, light-hearted, ludicrous, mad, meaningless, mindless, misguided, naïve, nonsensical, playful, pointless, preposterous, ridiculous, scatter-brained, *inf* scatty, senseless, shallow, silly, simple, simpleminded, simplistic, *inf* soppy, stupid, thoughtless, unintelligent, unreasonable, unsound, unwise, witless. *Opp* WISE.

foot *n* **1** claw, hoof, paw, trotter. **2** ▷ BASE.

footprint *n* footmark, spoor, track.

forbid *vb* ban, bar, debar, deny, deter, disallow, exclude, interdict, make illegal, outlaw, preclude, prevent, prohibit, proscribe, refuse, rule out, say no to, stop, veto. *Opp* ALLOW.

forbidden *adj* **1** against the law, taboo, unlawful, wrong. **2** *a forbidden area.* closed, out of bounds, restricted, secret.

forbidding *adj* gloomy, grim, menacing, ominous, stern, threatening, uninviting, unwelcoming. ▷ UNFRIENDLY. *Opp* FRIENDLY.

force *n* **1** aggression, *inf* armtwisting, coercion, compulsion, constraint, drive, duress, effort, might, power, pressure, strength, vehemence, vigour, violence. **2** effect, energy, impact, intensity, momentum, shock. **3** *a military force.* army, body, group, troops. **4** *force of an argument.* cogency, effectiveness, per-

forgiveness

suasiveness, rightness, thrust, validity, weight. ● *vb* **1** *inf* bulldoze, coerce, compel, constrain, drive, impel, impose on, make, oblige, order, press-gang, pressurize. **2** *force a door.* break open, burst open, prise open, smash, use force on, wrench. **3** *force something on someone.* impose, inflict.

foreboding *n* anxiety, apprehension, dread, fear, feeling, foreshadowing, forewarning, intimation, intuition, misgiving, omen, portent, premonition, presentiment, suspicion, warning, worry.

forecast *n* augury, expectation, outlook, prediction, prognosis, prognostication, projection, prophecy. ● *vb* ▷ FORESEE.

forefront *n* avant-garde, front, lead, vanguard.

foreign *adj* **1** distant, exotic, faraway, outlandish, remote, strange, unfamiliar, unknown. **2** alien, external, immigrant, imported, incoming, international, outside, overseas, visiting. **3** *foreign ideas.* extraneous, odd, uncharacteristic, unnatural, untypical, unusual, unwanted. *Opp* NATIVE.

foreigner *n* alien, immigrant, newcomer, outsider, overseas visitor, stranger. *Opp* NATIVE.

foremost *adj* first, leading, main, primary, supreme. ▷ CHIEF.

forerunner *n* advance messenger, harbinger, herald, precursor, predecessor. ▷ ANCESTOR.

foresee *vb* anticipate, envisage, expect, forecast, picture. ▷ FORETELL.

foresight *n* anticipation, caution, far-sightedness, forethought, looking ahead, perspicacity, planning, preparation, prudence, readiness, vision.

forest *n* coppice, copse, jungle, plantation, trees, woodland, woods.

foretaste *n* advance warning, augury, example, foreknowledge, forewarning, indication, omen, premonition, preview, sample, specimen, *inf* tip-off, trailer, *inf* try-out.

foretell *vb* augur, *old use* bode, forebode, foreshadow, forewarn, give a foretaste of, herald, portend, predict, presage, prognosticate, prophesy, signify. ▷ FORESEE.

forethought *n* anticipation, caution, far-sightedness, foresight, looking ahead, perspicacity, planning, preparation, prudence, readiness, vision.

forewarning *n* advance warning, augury, omen, premonition, *inf* tip-off. ▷ FORETASTE.

forfeit *n* confiscation, damages, fee, fine, penalty, sequestration. ● *vb* abandon, give up, let go, lose, pay up, relinquish, renounce, surrender.

forge *n* furnace, smithy, workshop. ● *vb* **1** beat into shape, cast, construct, hammer out, manufacture, mould, shape, work. **2** coin, copy, counterfeit, fake, falsify, imitate, make illegally, reproduce. **forge ahead** ▷ ADVANCE.

forgery *n* copy, counterfeit, *inf* dud, fake, fraud, imitation, *inf* phoney, replica, reproduction.

forget *vb* **1** be forgetful, dismiss from your mind, disregard, fail to remember, ignore, leave out, lose track (of), miss out, neglect, omit, overlook, skip, suffer from amnesia, unlearn. **2** be without, leave behind, lose. *Opp* REMEMBER.

forgetful *adj* absent-minded, amnesiac, careless, distracted, inattentive, neglectful, negligent, oblivious, preoccupied, unconscious, unmindful, unreliable, vague, *inf* woolly-minded.

forgivable *adj* allowable, excusable, justifiable, negligible, pardonable, petty, understandable, venial. *Opp* UNFORGIVABLE.

forgive *vb* **1** absolve, acquit, clear, exculpate, excuse, exonerate, indulge, *inf* let off, pardon, spare. **2** *forgive a crime.* condone, ignore, make allowances for, overlook, pass over.

forgiveness *n* absolution, amnesty, clemency, compassion, exculpation, exoneration, grace, indulgence, leniency, mercy, pardon, reprieve, tolerance. *Opp* RETRIBUTION.

forgiving *adj* clement, compassionate, forbearing, generous, magnanimous, merciful, tolerant, understanding. ▷ KIND. *Opp* VENGEFUL.

forgo *vb* abandon, abstain from, do without, forswear, give up, go without, omit, pass up, relinquish, renounce, sacrifice, turn down, waive.

forked *adj* branched, cleft, divergent, divided, fork-like, pronged, split, V-shaped.

forlorn *adj* abandoned, alone, bereft, deserted, forsaken, friendless, lonely, outcast, solitary, unloved. ▷ SAD.

form *n* **1** appearance, arrangement, cast, character, configuration, design, format, framework, genre, guise, kind, manifestation, manner, model, mould, nature, pattern, plan, semblance, sort, species, structure, style, system, type, variety. **2** *human form*. anatomy, body, build, figure, frame, outline, physique, shape, silhouette. **3** *your form in school*. class, grade, group, level, set, stream, tutor-group. **4** *good form*. behaviour, convention, custom, etiquette, fashion, manners, practice. **5** *an application form*. document, paper. **6** *in good form*. condition, *inf* fettle, fitness, health, performance, spirits. **7** ▷ SEAT.
● *vb* **1** bring into existence, cast, constitute, construct, create, design, establish, forge, found, give form to, make, model, mould, organize, produce, shape. **2** appear, arise, come into existence, develop, grow, materialize, take shape. **3** *form a team*. act as, compose, comprise, make up, serve as. **4** *form a habit*. acquire, cultivate, develop, get.

formal *adj* **1** aloof, ceremonial, ceremonious, conventional, cool, correct, customary, dignified, *inf* dressed-up, orthodox, *inf* posh, *derog* pretentious, proper, punctilious, ritualistic, solemn, sophisticated, stately, *inf* starchy, stiff, stiffnecked, unbending, unfriendly. **2** *formal language*. academic, impersonal, official, precise, reserved, specialist, stilted, technical, unemotional. **3** *a formal agreement*. binding, contractual, enforceable, legal, *inf* signed and sealed. **4** *a formal design*. calculated, geometrical, orderly, organized, regular, rigid, symmetrical. *Opp* INFORMAL.

format *n* appearance, design, layout, plan, shape, size, style.

former *adj* bygone, departed, ex-, last, late, old, one-time, past, previous, prior, recent. **the former** earlier, first, first-mentioned. *Opp* LATTER.

formidable *adj* awe-inspiring, awesome, challenging, daunting, difficult, dreadful, fearful, frightening, intimidating, large-scale, *inf* mind-boggling, onerous, overwhelming, prodigious, taxing. *Opp* EASY.

formula *n* **1** form of words, ritual, rubric, spell, wording. **2** *formula for success*. blueprint, method, prescription, procedure, recipe, rule, technique, way.

formulate *vb* **1** articulate, codify, define, express clearly, set out in detail, specify, systematize. **2** concoct, create, devise, evolve, form, invent, map out, originate, plan, work out.

forsake *vb* abandon, break off from, desert, forgo, forswear, give up, jettison, jilt, leave, quit, renounce, repudiate, surrender, throw over, *inf* turn your back on, vacate.

fort *n* camp, castle, citadel, fortification, fortress, garrison, stronghold, tower.

forthright *adj* blunt, candid, decisive, direct, outspoken, plainspeaking, straightforward, unequivocal, unhesitating, uninhibited. ▷ FRANK. *Opp* EVASIVE.

fortify *vb* **1** buttress, defend, garrison, protect, reinforce, secure against attack, shore up. **2** bolster, boost, brace, buoy up, cheer, embolden, encourage, hearten, invigorate, lift the morale of, reassure, stiffen the resolve of, strengthen, support, sustain. *Opp* WEAKEN.

fortitude n backbone, bravery, courage, determination, endurance, firmness, heroism, patience, resolution, stoicism, tenacity, valour, will-power. ▷ COURAGE. *Opp* COWARDICE.

fortunate adj auspicious, blessed, favourable, lucky, opportune, propitious, prosperous, providential, timely. ▷ HAPPY.

fortune n **1** accident, chance, destiny, fate, fortuity, karma, kismet, luck, providence. **2** affluence, assets, estate, holdings, inheritance, means, *inf* millions, money, opulence, *inf* pile, possessions, property, prosperity, riches, treasure, wealth.

fortune-teller n clairvoyant, crystal-gazer, futurologist, oracle, palmist, prophet, seer, soothsayer, star-gazer, sybil.

forward adj **1** advancing, front, frontal, head-first, leading, onward, progressive. **2** *forward planning.* advance, early, forward-looking, future, well-advanced. **3** *a forward child.* advanced, assertive, bold, brazen, cheeky, confident, familiar, *inf* fresh, impertinent, impudent, insolent, over-confident, precocious, presumptuous, pushful, *inf* pushy, shameless, uninhibited. *Opp* BACKWARD. ● vb **1** dispatch, expedite, freight, post on, re-address, send, send on, ship, transmit, transport. **2** *forward your career.* accelerate, advance, encourage, facilitate, foster, further, hasten, help along, *inf* lend a helping hand to, promote, speed up, support. ▷ HELP. *Opp* HINDER.

foster vb **1** advance, cultivate, encourage, further, nurture, promote, stimulate. ▷ HELP. **2** *foster a child.* adopt, bring up, care for, look after, maintain, nourish, nurse, raise, rear, take care of.

foul adj **1** bad, contaminated, disagreeable, disgusting, fetid, filthy, hateful, impure, infected, loathsome, nasty, nauseating, nauseous, noisome, obnoxious, offensive, polluted, putrid, repellent, repugnant, repulsive, revolting, rotten, sickening, smelly, squalid, stinking, vile. ▷ DIRTY, SMELLING. **2** *foul crimes.* abhorrent, abominable, atrocious, beastly, cruel, evil, ignominious, monstrous, scandalous, shameful, vicious, villainous, violent, wicked. **3** *foul language.* abusive, bawdy, blasphemous, coarse, common, crude, impolite, improper, indecent, insulting, licentious, offensive, rude, uncouth, vulgar. ▷ OBSCENE. **4** *foul weather.* foggy, rainy, rough, stormy, violent, windy. ▷ UNPLEASANT. **5** *foul play.* against the rules, dishonest, forbidden, illegal, invalid, prohibited, unfair, unsportsmanlike. *Opp* CLEAN, FAIR. ● n infringement, violation. ● vb ▷ DIRTY. **foul up** ▷ MUDDLE.

found vb **1** begin, bring about, create, endow, establish, fund, *inf* get going, inaugurate, initiate, institute, organize, originate, provide money for, raise, set up, start. **2** base, build, construct, erect, ground, rest, set.

foundation n **1** beginning, endowment, establishment, founding, inauguration, initiation, institution, organizing, setting up, starting. **2** base, basement, basis, bottom, cornerstone, foot, footing, substructure, underpinning. **3** *foundations of science.* basic principle, element, essential, fundamental, origin, *plur* rudiments.

founder vb abort, be wrecked, *inf* come to grief, fail, fall through, go down, miscarry, sink.

fountain n font, fount, fountainhead, jet, source, spout, spray, spring, well, well-spring.

foyer n ante-room, entrance, entrance hall, hall, lobby, reception.

fraction n division, part, portion, section, subdivision.

fracture n break, breakage, chip, cleavage, cleft, crack, fissure, gap, opening, rent, rift, rupture, split. ● vb breach, break, cause a fracture in, chip, cleave, crack, rupture, separate, split, suffer a fracture in.

fragile adj ▷ FRAIL.

fragment n atom, bit, chip, crumb, *plur* debris, morsel, part, particle, piece, portion, remnant, scrap, shard, shiver, shred, sliver, *plur* smithereens, snippet, speck. ● *vb* ▷ BREAK.

fragmentary *adj inf* bitty, broken, disconnected, disintegrated, disjointed, fragmented, imperfect, in bits, incoherent, incomplete, in fragments, partial, scattered, scrappy, sketchy, uncoordinated. *Opp* COMPLETE.

fragrance *n* aroma, bouquet, nose (*of wine*), odour, perfume, redolence, scent, smell.

fragrant *adj* aromatic, odorous, perfumed, redolent, scented, sweet-smelling.

frail *adj* breakable, brittle, dainty, delicate, easily damaged, feeble, flimsy, fragile, insubstantial, light, *derog* puny, rickety, slight, thin, unsound, unsteady, vulnerable, weak, *derog* weedy. ▷ ILL. *Opp* STRONG.

frame *n* **1** bodywork, chassis, construction, scaffolding, structure. ▷ FRAMEWORK. **2** *photo frame.* border, case, casing, edge, edging, mount, mounting. ● *vb* **1** box in, enclose, mount, set off, surround. **2** ▷ COMPOSE. **frame of mind** ▷ ATTITUDE.

framework *n* bare bones, frame, outline, plan, shell, skeleton, support, trellis.

frank *adj* blunt, candid, direct, downright, explicit, forthright, genuine, *inf* heart-to-heart, honest, ingenuous, *inf* no-nonsense, open, outright, outspoken, plain, plain-spoken, revealing, serious, sincere, straightforward, straight from the heart, to the point, trustworthy, truthful, unconcealed, undisguised, unreserved. *Opp* INSINCERE.

frantic *adj* agitated, anxious, berserk, *inf* beside yourself, crazy, delirious, demented, deranged, desperate, distraught, excitable, feverish, *inf* fraught, frenetic, frenzied, furious, hectic, hurried, hysterical, mad, overwrought, panicky, rabid, uncontrollable, violent, wild, worked up. *Opp* CALM.

fraud *n* **1** cheating, chicanery, *inf* con-trick, counterfeit, deceit, deception, dishonesty, double-dealing, duplicity, fake, forgery, hoax, imposture, pretence, *inf* put-up job, ruse, sham, *inf* sharp practice, swindle, trick, trickery. **2** charlatan, cheat, *inf* con-man, hoaxer, humbug, impostor, mountebank, *sl* phoney, *inf* quack, rogue, scoundrel, swindler.

fraudulent *adj inf* bent, bogus, cheating, corrupt, counterfeit, criminal, *inf* crooked, deceitful, devious, *inf* dirty, dishonest, double-dealing, duplicitous, fake, false, forged, illegal, lying, *sl* phoney, sham, specious, swindling, underhand, unscrupulous. *Opp* HONEST.

fray *n* brawl, commotion, conflict, disturbance, fracas, mêlée, quarrel, rumpus. ▷ FIGHT.

frayed *adj* chafed, rough-edged, tattered, threadbare, unravelled, worn. ▷ RAGGED.

freak *adj* aberrant, abnormal, anomalous, atypical, bizarre, exceptional, extraordinary, freakish, odd, peculiar, queer, rare, unaccountable, unforeseeable, unpredictable, unusual, weird. *Opp* NORMAL. ● *n* **1** aberration, abnormality, abortion, anomaly, curiosity, deformity, irregularity, monster, monstrosity, mutant, oddity, *inf* one-off, quirk, rarity, sport, variant. **2** ▷ FANATIC.

free *adj* **1** able, allowed, at leisure, at liberty, idle, independent, loose, not working, uncommitted, unconfined, unconstrained, unencumbered, unfixed, unrestrained, untrammelled. **2** *free from slavery.* emancipated, freeborn, let go, liberated, released, unchained, unfettered, unshackled. **3** *a free country.* autonomous, democratic, independent, self-governing, sovereign. **4** *free access.* accessible, clear, open, permitted, unhindered, unimpeded, unrestricted. **5** *free gifts.* complimentary, gratis, *sl* on the house, unasked-for, unsolicited, without charge. **6** *free space.* available, empty, uninhabited, unoccupied, vacant. **7** *free with money.* bounteous, casual, charitable, generous, lavish, liberal, munificent, ready, unstinting, willing. ● vb **1** absolve, acquit, clear, deliver, discharge, disenthral, emancipate, enfranchise, exculpate, exonerate, let go, let off, let out, liberate, loose, make free, manumit, pardon, parole, ransom, release, reprieve, rescue, save, set free, spare, turn loose, unchain, unfetter, unleash, unlock, unloose. *Opp* CONFINE. **2** *free tangled ropes*. clear, disengage, disentangle, extricate, loose, unbind, undo, unknot, untie. *Opp* TANGLE. **free and easy** ▷ INFORMAL.

freedom *n* **1** autonomy, independence, liberty, self-determination, self-government, sovereignty. *Opp* CAPTIVITY. **2** deliverance, emancipation, exemption, immunity, liberation, release. **3** *freedom to choose*. ability, Fr carte blanche, discretion, free hand, latitude, leeway, leisure, licence, opportunity, permission, power, privilege, right, scope.

freeze *vb* **1** become ice, become solid, congeal, harden, ice over, ice up, solidify, stiffen. **2** chill, cool, make cold, numb. **3** *freeze food*. chill, deep-freeze, dry-freeze, ice, refrigerate. **4** *freeze the frame*. fix, hold, immobilize, keep still, paralyse, peg, petrify, stand still, stick, stop. **freezing** ▷ COLD.

freight *n* cargo, consignment, goods, haul, load, merchandise, payload, shipment.

frenzy *n* agitation, delirium, derangement, excitement, fever, fit, fury, hysteria, insanity, lunacy, madness, mania, outburst, paroxysm, passion, turmoil.

frequent *adj* common, constant, continual, countless, customary, everyday, familiar, habitual, incessant, innumerable, many, normal, numerous, ordinary, persistent, recurrent, recurring, regular, reiterative, repeated, usual. *Opp* INFREQUENT. ● *vb* ▷ HAUNT.

fresh *adj* **1** additional, alternative, different, extra, just arrived, new, recent, supplementary, unfamiliar, up-to-date. **2** alert, energetic, healthy, invigorated, lively, *inf* perky, rested, revived, sprightly, spry, tingling, vigorous, vital. **3** *a fresh recruit*. callow, *inf* green, inexperienced, naïve, raw, unsophisticated, untried, *inf* wet behind the ears. **4** *fresh water*. clear, drinkable, potable, pure, refreshing, sweet, uncontaminated. **5** *fresh air*. airy, circulating, cool, unpolluted, ventilated. **6** *a fresh wind*. bracing, breezy, invigorating, moderate, sharp, stiff, strongish. **7** *fresh food*. healthy, natural, newly gathered, unprocessed, untreated, wholesome. **8** *fresh sheets*. clean, crisp, laundered, untouched, unused, washed-and-ironed. **9** *fresh colours*. bright, clean, glowing, just painted, renewed, restored, sparkling, unfaded, vivid. *Opp* OLD, STALE.

fret *vb* **1** agonize, be anxious, brood, lose sleep, worry. **2** ▷ ANNOY.

fretful *adj* anxious, distressed, disturbed, edgy, irritable, irritated, jittery, peevish, petulant, restless, testy, touchy, worried. ▷ BAD-TEMPERED. *Opp* CALM.

friction *n* **1** abrading, abrasion, attrition, chafing, fretting, grating, resistance, rubbing, scraping. **2** ▷ CONFLICT.

friend *n* acquaintance, associate, *inf* buddy, *inf* chum, companion, comrade, confidant(e), *inf* crony, intimate, *inf* mate, *inf* pal, partner, pen-friend, playfellow, playmate, supporter, well-wisher. ▷ ALLY, LOVER. *Opp* ENEMY. **be friends** ▷ ASSOCIATE. **make friends with** ▷ BEFRIEND.

friendless *adj* abandoned, alienated, alone, deserted, estranged, forlorn, forsaken, isolated, lonely, ostracized, shunned, shut out, solitary, unattached, unloved.

friendliness *n* benevolence, camaraderie, conviviality, devotion, esteem, familiarity, goodwill, helpfulness, hospitality, kindness, neighbourliness, regard, sociability, warmth. *Opp* HOSTILITY.

friendly *adj* accessible, affable, affectionate, agreeable, amiable, amicable, approachable, attached, benevolent, benign, *inf* chummy, civil, close, clubbable, companionable, compatible, comradely, conciliatory, congenial, convivial, cordial, demonstrative, expansive, favourable, genial, good-natured, gracious, helpful, hospitable, intimate, kind, kind-hearted, kindly, likeable, *inf* matey, neighbourly, outgoing, *inf* pally, sympathetic, tender, *inf* thick, warm, welcoming, well-disposed. ▷ FAMILIAR, LOVING, SOCIABLE. *Opp* UNFRIENDLY.

friendship *n* affection, alliance, amity, association, attachment, closeness, comradeship, fellowship, fondness, harmony, intimacy, rapport, relationship. ▷ FRIENDLINESS, LOVE. *Opp* HOSTILITY.

fright *n* **1** jolt, scare, shock, surprise. **2** alarm, apprehension, consternation, dismay, dread, fear, horror, panic, terror, trepidation.

frighten *vb* agitate, alarm, appal, browbeat, bully, cow, *inf* curdle your blood, daunt, dismay, distress, harrow, horrify, intimidate, make afraid, *inf* make your blood run cold, make your hair stand on end, menace, panic, persecute, *inf* petrify, *inf* put the wind up, scare, *inf* scare stiff, shake, shock, startle, terrify, terrorize, threaten, traumatize, tyrannize, unnerve, upset. ▷ DISCOURAGE. *Opp* REASSURE.

frightened *adj* afraid, aghast, alarmed, anxious, appalled, apprehensive, *inf* chicken, cowardly, craven, daunted, fearful, harrowed, horrified, horror-struck, panicky, panic-stricken, petrified, scared, shocked, terrified, terrorstricken, trembling, unnerved, upset, *inf* windy.

frightening *adj* alarming, appalling, blood-curdling, *inf* creepy, daunting, dire, dreadful, eerie, fearful, fearsome, formidable, ghostly, grim, hair-raising, horrifying, intimidating, petrifying, scary, sinister, spine-chilling, *inf* spooky, terrifying, traumatic, uncanny, unnerving, upsetting, weird, worrying. ▷ FRIGHTFUL.

frightful *adj* **1** awful, ghastly, grisly, gruesome, harrowing, hideous, horrible, horrid, horrific, macabre, shocking, terrible. ▷ FRIGHTENING. **2** ▷ BAD.

fringe *n* **1** borders, boundary, edge, limits, marches, margin, outskirts, perimeter, periphery. **2** border, edging, flounce, frill, gathering, ruffle, trimming, valance.

frisky *adj* active, animated, coltish, frolicsome, high-spirited, jaunty, lively, perky, playful, skittish, spirited, sprightly.

frivolity *n* childishness, facetiousness, flippancy, levity, light-heartedness, nonsense, playing about, silliness, triviality. ▷ FUN.

frivolous *adj* casual, childish, facetious, flighty, *inf* flip, flippant, foolish, inconsequential, insignificant, irresponsible, jocular, joking, minor, nugatory, paltry, petty, pointless, puerile, ridiculous, shallow, silly, stupid, superficial, trifling, trivial, trumpery, unimportant, unserious, vacuous, worthless. *Opp* SERIOUS.

frock *n* dress, gown, robe.

frolic *vb* caper, cavort, curvet, dance, frisk about, gambol, have fun, hop about, *inf* horse about, jump about, lark around, leap about, *inf* make whoopee, play about, prance, revel, rollick, romp, skip, skylark, sport.

front *adj* facing, first, foremost, leading, most advanced. ● *n* **1** anterior, bow (*of ship*), façade, face, facing, forefront, foreground, frontage, head, nose, obverse, van, vanguard. **2** battle area, danger zone, front line. **3** *a brave front.* appearance, aspect, bearing, blind, *inf* cover-up, demeanour, disguise, expression, look, mask, pretence, show. *Opp* BACK.

frontal *adj* direct, facing, head-on, oncoming, straight.

frontier *n* border, borderline, boundary, bounds, limit, marches, pale.

froth n bubbles, effervescence, foam, head (on beer), lather, scum, spume, suds.

frown vb inf give a dirty look, glare, glower, grimace, knit your brows, look sullen, lour, lower, scowl. **frown on** ▷ DISAPPROVE.

fruit n □ apple, apricot, avocado, banana, berry, bilberry, blackberry, cherry, coconut, crabapple, cranberry, currant, damson, date, fig, gooseberry, grape, grapefruit, greengage, guava, hip, kiwi fruit, lemon, lichee, lime, litchi, loganberry, lychee, mango, medlar, melon, mulberry, nectarine, olive, orange, papaw, pawpaw, peach, pear, pineapple, plum, pomegranate, prune, quince, raisin, raspberry, satsuma, sloe, strawberry, sultana, tangerine, tomato, ugli.

fruitful adj **1** abundant, bounteous, bountiful, copious, fecund, fertile, flourishing, lush, luxurious, plenteous, productive, profuse, prolific, rich. **2** advantageous, beneficial, effective, gainful, profitable, rewarding, successful, useful, well-spent, worthwhile. Opp FRUITLESS.

fruitless adj **1** barren, sterile, unfruitful, unproductive. **2** abortive, bootless, disappointing, futile, ineffective, ineffectual, pointless, profitless, unavailing, unprofitable, unrewarding, unsuccessful, useless, vain. Opp FRUITFUL.

frustrate vb baffle, balk, baulk, block, check, disappoint, discourage, foil, halt, hamstring, hinder, impede, inhibit, nullify, prevent, inf scotch, stop, stymie, thwart. ▷ DEFEAT. Opp ENCOURAGE.

frustrated adj disappointed, embittered, loveless, lovesick, resentful, thwarted, unfulfilled, unsatisfied.

fuel n □ anthracite, butane, charcoal, coal, coke, derv, diesel, electricity, gas, gasoline, kindling, logs, methylated spirit, nuclear fuel, oil, paraffin, peat, petrol, propane, tinder, wood. ● vb encourage, feed, inflame, keep going, nourish, put fuel on, stoke up, supply with fuel.

fugitive adj ▷ TRANSIENT. ● n deserter, escapee, escaper, refugee, renegade, runaway.

fulfil vb **1** accomplish, achieve, bring about, bring off, carry off, carry out, complete, consummate, discharge, do, effect, effectuate, execute, implement, make come true, perform, realize. **2** fulfil a need. answer, comply with, conform to, meet, obey, respond to, satisfy.

full adj **1** brimming, bursting, inf chock-a-block, inf chock-full, congested, crammed, crowded, filled, jammed, inf jam-packed, loaded, overflowing, packed, replete, solid, stuffed, topped-up, well-filled, well-stocked, well-supplied. **2** a full stomach. gorged, sated, satiated, well-fed. **3** the full story. complete, comprehensive, detailed, entire, exhaustive, plenary, thorough, total, unabridged, uncensored, uncut, unedited, unexpurgated, whole. **4** full speed. extreme, greatest, highest, maximum, top, utmost. **5** a full figure. ample, broad, buxom, fat, large, plump, rounded, voluptuous, well-built. **6** a full skirt. baggy, generous, voluminous, wide. Opp EMPTY, INCOMPLETE, -SMALL.

full-grown adj adult, grown-up, mature, ready, ripe.

fumble vb grope at, feel, handle awkwardly, mishandle, stumble, touch clumsily.

fume vb emit fumes, smoke, smoulder. **fuming** ▷ ANGRY.

fumes plur n exhaust, fog, gases, pollution, smog, smoke, vapour.

fun n amusement, clowning, diversion, enjoyment, entertainment, festivity, inf fooling around, frolic, inf fun-and-games, gaiety, games, inf high jinks, high spirits, horseplay, jocularity, jokes, joking, joc jollification, jollity, laughter, merriment, merrymaking, mirth, pastimes, play, playfulness, pleasure, pranks, recreation, romp, inf skylarking, sport, teasing, tomfoolery. ▷ FRIVOLITY. **make fun of** ▷ MOCK.

function *n* **1** aim, purpose, *Fr* raison d'être, use. ▷ JOB. **2** *an official function*. affair, ceremony, *inf* do, event, occasion, party, reception. ● *vb* act, behave, go, operate, perform, run, work.

functional *adj* functioning, practical, serviceable, useful, utilitarian, working. *Opp* DECORATIVE.

fund *n* cache, hoard, *inf* kitty, mine, pool, reserve, reservoir, stock, store, supply, treasurehouse. **funds** capital, endowments, investments, reserves, resources, riches, savings, wealth. ▷ MONEY.

fundamental *adj* axiomatic, basic, cardinal, central, crucial, elementary, essential, important, key, main, necessary, primary, prime, principal, quintessential, rudimentary, underlying. *Opp* INESSENTIAL.

funeral *n* burial, cremation, entombment, exequies, interment, obsequies, Requiem Mass, wake.

funereal *adj* dark, depressing, dismal, gloomy, grave, mournful, sepulchral, solemn, sombre. ▷ SAD. *Opp* CHEERFUL.

funnel *n* chimney, smoke-stack. ● *vb* channel, direct, filter, pour.

funny *adj* **1** absurd, amusing, comic, comical, crazy, *inf* daft, diverting, droll, eccentric, entertaining, facetious, farcical, foolish, grotesque, hilarious, humorous, *inf* hysterical, ironic, jocose, jocular, *inf* killing, laughable, ludicrous, mad, merry, nonsensical, preposterous, *inf* priceless, *inf* rich, ridiculous, risible, sarcastic, sardonic, satirical, *inf* side-splitting, silly, slapstick, uproarious, waggish, witty, zany. *Opp* SERIOUS. **2** ▷ PECULIAR.

fur *n* bristles, coat, down, fleece, hair, hide, pelt, skin, wool.

furious *adj* **1** boiling, enraged, fuming, incensed, infuriated, irate, livid, mad, raging, savage, wrathful. ▷ ANGRY. **2** *furious activity*. agitated, fierce, frantic, frenzied, intense, tempestuous, tumultuous, turbulent, violent, wild. *Opp* CALM.

furnish *vb* **1** decorate, equip, fit out, fit up, *inf* kit out. **2** *furnish information*. afford, give, grant, provide, supply.

furniture *n* antiques, chattels, effects, equipment, fitments, fittings, fixtures, furnishings, household goods, *inf* movables, possessions. □ armchair, bed, bench, bookcase, bunk, bureau, cabinet, chair, chesterfield, chest of drawers, chiffonier, commode, cot, couch, cradle, cupboard, cushion, desk, divan, drawer, dresser, dressing-table, easel, fender, filing-cabinet, fireplace, mantelpiece, ottoman, overmantel, pelmet, pew, pouffe, rocking-chair, seat, settee, sideboard, sofa, stool, suite, table, trestle-table, wardrobe, workbench.

furrow *n* channel, corrugation, crease, cut, ditch, drill, fissure, fluting, gash, groove, hollow, line, rut, score, scratch, track, trench, wrinkle.

furrowed *adj* **1** creased, crinkled, corrugated, fluted, grooved, ploughed, ribbed, ridged, rutted, scored. **2** *furrowed brow*. frowning, lined, worried, wrinkled. *Opp* SMOOTH.

furry *adj* bristly, downy, feathery, fleecy, fuzzy, hairy, woolly.

further *adj* accessory, additional, another, auxiliary, extra, fresh, more, new, other, spare, supplementary.

furthermore *adv* additionally, also, besides, moreover, too.

furtive *adj* clandestine, concealed, conspiratorial, covert, deceitful, disguised, hidden, mysterious, private, secret, secretive, shifty, sly, *inf* sneaky, stealthy, surreptitious, underhand, untrustworthy. ▷ CRAFTY. *Opp* BLATANT.

fury *n* ferocity, fierceness, force, intensity, madness, power, rage, savagery, tempestuousness, turbulence, vehemence, violence, wrath. ▷ ANGER.

fuse *vb* amalgamate, blend, coalesce, combine, commingle, compound, consolidate, join, meld, melt, merge, mix, solder, unite, weld.

fusillade *n* barrage, burst, firing, outburst, salvo, volley.

fuss *n* ▷ COMMOTION. ● *vb* agitate, bother, complain, *inf* create, fidget, *inf* flap, *inf* get worked up, grumble, make a commotion, worry.

fussy *adj* **1** carping, choosy, difficult, discriminating, *inf* faddy, fastidious, *inf* finicky, hard to please, niggling, *inf* nit-picking, particular, *inf* pernickety, scrupulous, squeamish. **2** *fussy decorations*. Byzantine, complicated, detailed, elaborate, fancy, ornate, overdone, rococo.

futile *adj* abortive, absurd, barren, bootless, empty, foolish, forlorn, fruitless, hollow, impotent, ineffective, ineffectual, pointless, profitless, silly, sterile, unavailing, unproductive, unprofitable, unsuccessful, useless, vain, wasted, worthless. *Opp* FRUITFUL.

future *adj* approaching, awaited, coming, destined, expected, forthcoming, impending, intended, planned, prospective, subsequent, unborn. ● *n* expectations, outlook, prospects, time to come, tomorrow. *Opp* PAST.

fuzz *n* down, floss, fluff, hair.

fuzzy *adj* **1** downy, feathery, fleecy, fluffy, frizzy, furry, linty, woolly. **2** bleary, blurred, cloudy, dim, faint, hazy, ill-defined, indistinct, misty, obscure, out of focus, shadowy, unclear, unfocused, vague. *Opp* CLEAR.

G

gadget *n* apparatus, appliance, contraption, contrivance, device, implement, instrument, invention, machine, tool, utensil.

gag *n* ▷ JOKE. ● *vb* check, curb, keep quiet, muffle, muzzle, prevent from speaking, quiet, silence, stifle, still, suppress.

gaiety *n* brightness, cheerfulness, colourfulness, delight, exhilaration, felicity, glee, happiness, high spirits, hilarity, jollity, joyfulness, joyousness, light-heartedness, liveliness, merriment, merrymaking, mirth.

gain *n* achievement, acquisition, advantage, asset, attainment, benefit, dividend, earnings, income, increase, proceeds, profit, return, revenue, winnings, yield. *Opp* LOSS. ● *vb* 1 acquire, bring in, capture, collect, earn, garner, gather in, get, harvest, make, net, obtain, pick up, procure, profit, realize, reap, receive, win. *Opp* LOSE. 2 *gain your objective.* achieve, arrive at, attain, get to, reach, secure. *Opp* MISS. **gain on** approach, catch up with, close the gap, close with, go faster than, leave behind, overhaul, overtake.

gainful *adj* advantageous, beneficial, fruitful, lucrative, paid, productive, profitable, remunerative, rewarding, useful, worthwhile.

gala *n* carnival, celebration, fair, festival, festivity, fête, *inf* jamboree, party.

gale *n* blast, cyclone, hurricane, outburst, storm, tempest, tornado, typhoon, wind.

gallant *adj* attentive, chivalrous, courageous, courteous, courtly, dashing, fearless, gentlemanly, gracious, heroic, honourable, intrepid, magnanimous, noble, polite, valiant, well-bred. ▷ BRAVE. *Opp* VILLAINOUS.

gallows *plur n* gibbet, scaffold.

gamble *vb* back, bet, chance, draw lots, game, *inf* have a flutter, hazard, lay bets, risk money, speculate, stake money, *inf* take a chance, take risks, *inf* try your luck, venture, wager.

game *adj* ▷ BRAVE, WILLING. ● *n* 1 amusement, diversion, entertainment, frolic, fun, jest, joke, *inf* lark, *inf* messing about, pastime, play, playing, recreation, romp, sport. 2 competition, contest, match, round, tournament. ▷ SPORT. 3 animals, game-birds, prey, quarry. **give the game away** ▷ REVEAL.

gang *n* band, crew, crowd, mob, pack, ring, team. ▷ GROUP. **gang together**, **gang up** ▷ COMBINE.

gangster *n* bandit, brigand, criminal, *inf* crook, desperado, gunman, hoodlum, hooligan, mafioso, mugger, racketeer, robber, ruffian, thug, tough.

gaol *n* borstal, cell, custody, dungeon, guardhouse, jail, *Amer* penitentiary, prison. ● *vb* confine, detain, imprison, incarcerate, intern, *inf* send down, send to prison, *inf* shut away, shut up.

gaoler *n* guard, jailer, prison officer, *sl* screw, warder.

gap *n* 1 aperture, breach, break, cavity, chink, cleft, crack, cranny, crevice, gulf, hole, opening, rent, rift, rip, space, void. 2 breathing-space, discontinuity, hiatus, interlude, intermission, interruption, interval, lacuna, lapse, lull, pause, recess, respite, rest, suspension, wait. 3 *gap between political parties.* difference, disagreement, discrepancy, disparity, distance, divergence, division, incompatibility, inconsistency.

gape vb **1** open, part, split, yawn. **2** inf gawp, gaze, inf goggle, stare.

garbage n debris, detritus, junk, litter, muck, refuse, scrap, trash, waste. ▷ RUBBISH.

garble vb corrupt, distort, falsify, misconstrue, misquote, misrepresent, mutilate, pervert, slant, twist, warp. ▷ CONFUSE.

garden n allotment, patch, plot, yard. □ arbour, bed, border, herbaceous border, lawn, orchard, patio, pergola, rock garden, rose garden, shrubbery, terrace, vegetable garden, walled garden, water garden, window-box. **gardens** grounds, park.

gardening n cultivation, horticulture.

garish adj bright, Brummagem, cheap, crude, flamboyant, flashy, gaudy, harsh, loud, lurid, meretricious, ostentatious, raffish, showy, startling, tasteless, tawdry, vivid, vulgar. Opp DRAB, TASTEFUL.

garment n apparel, attire, clothing, costume, dress, garb, habit, outfit. ▷ CLOTHES.

garrison n **1** contingent, detachment, force, unit. **2** barracks, camp, citadel, fort, fortification, fortress, station, stronghold.

gas n exhalation, exhaust, fumes, miasma, vapour.

gash vb chop, cleave, cut, incise, lacerate, score, slash, slit, split, wound.

gasp vb blow, breathe with difficulty, choke, fight for breath, gulp, inf huff and puff, pant, puff, snort, wheeze. **gasping** ▷ BREATHLESS, THIRSTY.

gate n access, barrier, door, entrance, entry, exit, gateway, kissing-gate, opening, passage, poet portal, portcullis, turnstile, way in, way out, wicket, wicket-gate.

gather vb **1** accumulate, amass, assemble, bring together, build up, cluster, collect, come together, concentrate, congregate, convene, crowd, flock, forgather, get together, group, grow, heap up, herd, hoard, huddle together, marshal, mass, meet, mobilize, muster, pick up, pile up, rally, round up, stockpile, store up, swarm, throng. Opp DISPERSE. **2** gather flowers. cull, garner, glean, harvest, pick, pluck, reap. **3** I gather he's ill. assume, be led to believe, conclude, deduce, guess, infer, learn, surmise, understand.

gathering n assembly, conclave, congress, convention, convocation, function, inf get-together, meeting, party, rally, social. ▷ GROUP.

gaudy adj bright, Brummagem, cheap, crude, flamboyant, flashy, garish, harsh, loud, lurid, meretricious, ostentatious, raffish, showy, startling, tasteless, tawdry, vivid, vulgar. Opp DRAB, TASTEFUL.

gauge n **1** bench-mark, criterion, guide-line, measurement, norm, standard, test, yardstick. **2** capacity, dimensions, extent, measure, size, span, thickness, width. ● vb ▷ ESTIMATE, MEASURE.

gaunt adj **1** bony, cadaverous, emaciated, haggard, hollow-eyed, lanky, lean, pinched, raw-boned, scraggy, scrawny, skeletal, starving, underweight, wasted away. ▷ THIN. Opp PLUMP. **2** a gaunt ruin. bare, bleak, desolate, dreary, forbidding, grim, stark, stern, unfriendly. Opp ATTRACTIVE.

gawky adj awkward, blundering, clumsy, gangling, gauche, inept, lumbering, maladroit, uncoordinated, ungainly, ungraceful, unskilful. Opp GRACEFUL.

gay adj **1** animated, bright, carefree, cheerful, colourful, festive, funloving, jolly, jovial, joyful, lighthearted, lively, merry, sparkling, sunny, vivacious. ▷ HAPPY. **2** ▷ HOMOSEXUAL.

gaze vb contemplate, gape, look, regard, stare, view, wonder (at).

gear n accessories, accoutrements, apparatus, appliances, baggage, belongings, equipment, inf get-up, harness, implements, instruments, kit, luggage, materials, paraphernalia, rig, stuff, tackle, things, tools, trappings. ▷ CLOTHES.

gem n gemstone, jewel, precious stone, sl sparkler.

general adj 1 accepted, accustomed, collective, common, communal, conventional, customary, everyday, familiar, habitual, normal, ordinary, popular, prevailing, prevalent, public, regular, inf run-of-the-mill, shared, typical, usual. 2 general discussion. across-the-board, all-embracing, blanket, broad-based, catholic, comprehensive, diversified, encyclopaedic, extensive, far-ranging, far-reaching, global, heterogeneous, hybrid, inclusive, sweeping, universal, wholesale, wide-ranging, widespread, worldwide. 3 a general idea. approximate, broad, ill-defined, imprecise, indefinite, inexact, in outline, loose, simplified, superficial, unclear, undefined, unspecific, vague. Opp SPECIFIC.

generally adv as a rule, broadly, chiefly, commonly, in the main, mainly, mostly, normally, on the whole, predominantly, principally, usually.

generate vb beget, breed, bring about, cause, create, engender, father, give rise to, make, originate, procreate, produce, propagate, sire, spawn, inf whip up.

generosity n bounty, largesse, liberality, munificence, philanthropy.

generous adj 1 benevolent, big-hearted, bounteous, bountiful, charitable, disinterested, forgiving, inf free, impartial, kind, liberal, magnanimous, munificent, noble, open, open-handed, philanthropic, public-spirited, unmercenary, unprejudiced, unselfish, unsparing, unstinting. 2 generous gifts. handsome, princely, undeserved, unearned, valuable. ▷ EXPENSIVE. 3 generous portions. abundant, ample, copious, lavish, plentiful, sizeable, substantial. ▷ BIG. Opp MEAN, SELFISH.

genial adj affable, agreeable, amiable, cheerful, convivial, cordial, easygoing, good-natured, happy,

jolly, jovial, kindly, pleasant, relaxed, sociable, sunny, warm, warm-hearted. ▷ FRIENDLY. Opp UNFRIENDLY.

genitals plur n genitalia, inf private parts, pudenda, sex organs.

genius n 1 ability, aptitude, bent, brains, brilliance, capability, flair, gift, intellect, intelligence, knack, talent, wit. 2 academic, inf egghead, expert, intellectual, derog know-all, mastermind, thinker, virtuoso.

genteel adj derog affected, chivalrous, courtly, gentlemanly, ladylike, mannered, overpolite, patrician, inf posh, refined, stylish, inf upper-crust. ▷ POLITE.

gentle adj 1 amiable, biddable, compassionate, docile, easygoing, good-tempered, harmless, humane, kind, kindly, lenient, loving, meek, merciful, mild, moderate, obedient, pacific, passive, peace-loving, pleasant, quiet, soft-hearted, sweet-tempered, sympathetic, tame, tender. 2 gentle music. low, muted, peaceful, reassuring, relaxing, soft, soothing. 3 gentle wind. balmy, delicate, faint, light, soft, warm. 4 a gentle hint. indirect, polite, subtle, tactful. 5 a gentle hill. easy, gradual, imperceptible, moderate, slight, steady. Opp HARSH, SEVERE.

genuine adj 1 actual, authentic, authenticated, Lat bona fide, legitimate, original, proper, sl pukka, real, sterling, veritable. 2 genuine feelings. candid, devout, earnest, frank, heartfelt, honest, sincere, true, unaffected, unfeigned. Opp FALSE.

germ n 1 basis, beginning, embryo, genesis, cause, nucleus, origin, root, seed, source, start. 2 bacterium, inf bug, microbe, micro-organism, virus.

germinate vb begin to grow, bud, develop, grow, root, shoot, spring up, sprout, start growing, take root.

gesture n action, flourish, gesticulation, indication, motion, movement, sign, signal. ● vb gesticulate, indicate, motion, sign, signal. □ beckon, bow, nod, point, salute, shake your head, shrug, smile, wave, wink.

get *vb* **1** acquire, be given, bring, buy, come by, come in possession of, earn, fetch, gain, get hold of, inherit, *inf* land, *inf* lay hands on, obtain, pick up, procure, purchase, receive, retrieve, secure, take, win. **2** *get her by phone*. contact, get in touch with, reach, speak to. **3** *get a cold*. catch, come down with, contract, develop, fall ill with, suffer from. **4** *get a criminal*. apprehend, arrest, capture, catch, *inf* collar, *inf* nab, *sl* pinch, seize. **5** *get him to help*. cajole, cause, induce, influence, persuade, prevail on, *inf* twist someone's arm, wheedle. **6** *get tea*. cook, make ready, prepare. **7** *get what he means*. absorb, appreciate, apprehend, comprehend, fathom, follow, glean, grasp, know, take in, understand, work out. **8** *get what he says*. catch, distinguish, hear, make out. **9** *get somewhere*. arrive, come, go, journey, reach, travel. **10** *get cold*. become, grow, turn. **get across** ▷ COMMUNICATE. **get ahead** ▷ PROSPER. **get at** ▷ CRITICIZE. **get away** ▷ ESCAPE. **get down** ▷ DESCEND. **get in** ▷ ENTER. **get off** ▷ DESCEND. **get on** ▷ PROSPER. **get out** ▷ LEAVE. **get together** ▷ GATHER.

getaway *n* escape, flight, retreat.

ghastly *adj* appalling, awful, deathlike, dreadful, frightening, frightful, grim, grisly, gruesome, hideous, horrible, macabre, nasty, shocking, terrible, upsetting. ▷ UNPLEASANT.

ghost *n* apparition, banshee, *inf* bogey, *Ger* doppelgänger, ghoul, hallucination, illusion, phantasm, phantom, poltergeist, shade, shadow, spectre, spirit, *inf* spook, vision, visitant, wraith. **give up the ghost** ▷ DIE.

ghostly *adj* creepy, disembodied, eerie, frightening, illusory, phantasmal, scary, sinister, spectral, *inf* spooky, supernatural, uncanny, unearthly, weird, wraith-like.

giant *adj* ▷ GIGANTIC. ● *n* colossus, Goliath, leviathan, monster, ogre, superhuman, titan, *inf* whopper.

giddiness *n* dizziness, faintness, unsteadiness, vertigo.

giddy *adj* dizzy, faint, light-headed, reeling, silly, spinning, unbalanced, unsteady, vertiginous.

gift *n* **1** benefaction, bonus, bounty, charity, contribution, donation, favour, *inf* give-away, grant, gratuity, *inf* hand-out, honorarium, largesse, offering, present, tip. **2** ability, aptitude, bent, capability, capacity, facility, flair, genius, knack, power, strength, talent.

gifted *adj* able, capable, expert, skilful, skilled, talented. ▷ CLEVER.

gigantic *adj* Brobdingnagian, colossal, elephantine, enormous, gargantuan, giant, herculean, huge, immense, *inf* jumbo, *inf* king-size, mammoth, massive, mighty, monstrous, prodigious, titanic, towering, vast. ▷ BIG. *Opp* SMALL.

giggle *vb* snicker, snigger, titter. ▷ LAUGH.

gimcrack *adj* cheap, *inf* cheap and nasty, flimsy, rubbishy, shoddy, tawdry, trashy, trumpery, useless, worthless.

gimmick *n* device, ploy, ruse, stratagem, stunt, subterfuge, trick.

girder *n* bar, beam, joist, rafter.

girdle *n* band, belt, corset, waistband. ● *vb* ▷ SURROUND.

girl *n* *sl* bird, *old use* damsel, daughter, débutante, fiancée, girlfriend, hoyden, lass, *old use* maiden, *inf* miss, schoolgirl, tomboy, virgin, *old use or sexist* wench. ▷ WOMAN.

girth *n* circumference, measurement round, perimeter.

gist *n* core, direction, drift, essence, general sense, main idea, meaning, nub, pith, point, quintessence, significance.

give *vb* **1** accord, allocate, allot, allow, apportion, assign, award, bestow, confer, contribute, deal out, *inf* dish out, distribute, *inf* dole out, donate, endow, entrust, *inf* fork out, furnish, give away, give out, grant, hand over, lend, let (someone) have, offer, pass over, pay, present, provide, ration out, render, share out, supply. **2** *give information*. deliver, display, express, impart, issue, notify, publish, put across, put into words, reveal, set out, show, tell, transmit. **3** *give a shout*. emit, let out, utter, voice. **4** *give medicine*. administer, dispense, dose with, impose, inflict, mete out, prescribe. **5** *give a party*. arrange, organize, provide, put on, run, set up. **6** *give trouble*. cause, create, engender, occasion. **7** *give under pressure*. be flexible, bend, buckle, collapse, distort, fail, fall apart, give way, warp, yield. *Opp* RECEIVE, TAKE. **give away** ▷ BETRAY. **give in** ▷ SURRENDER. **give off**, **give out** ▷ EMIT. **give up** ▷ ABANDON, SURRENDER.

glad *adj* **1** content, delighted, gratified, joyful, overjoyed, pleased. ▷ HAPPY. *Opp* GLOOMY. **2** *glad to help*. disposed, eager, inclined, keen, ready, willing. *Opp* RELUCTANT.

glamorize *vb* idealize, romanticize.

glamorous *adj* alluring, appealing, colourful, dazzling, enviable, exciting, exotic, fascinating, glittering, prestigious, romantic, smart, spectacular, wealthy. ▷ BEAUTIFUL.

glamour *n* allure, appeal, attraction, brilliance, charm, excitement, fascination, glitter, high-life, lustre, magic, romance. ▷ BEAUTY.

glance *vb* glimpse, have a quick look, peek, peep, scan, skim, *sl* take a dekko. ▷ LOOK.

glare *vb* **1** frown, *inf* give a nasty look, glower, *inf* look daggers, lour, lower, scowl, stare angrily. **2** blaze, dazzle, flare, reflect, shine. ▷ LIGHT. **glaring** ▷ BRIGHT.

glass *n* **1** crystal, glassware. **2** glazing, pane, plate-glass, window. **3** looking-glass, mirror, reflector. **4** beaker, drinking-glass, goblet, tumbler, wine-glass. **5** optical instrument. □ binoculars, field-glasses, goggles, magnifying glass, microscope, opera-glasses, telescope, spyglass. **glasses** *inf* specs, spectacles. □ bifocals, contact-lenses, eyeglass, lorgnette, monocle, pince-nez, reading glasses, sun-glasses, trifocals.

glasshouse *n* conservatory, greenhouse, hothouse, orangery, vinery.

glassy *adj* **1** glazed, gleaming, glossy, icy, polished, shining, shiny, smooth, vitreous. **2** *glassy stare*. ▷ EXPRESSIONLESS.

glaze *vb* burnish, enamel, gloss, lacquer, polish, shellac, shine, varnish.

gleam *vb* flash, glimmer, glint, glisten, glow, reflect, shine. ▷ LIGHT. **gleaming** ▷ BRIGHT.

gleeful *adj* cheerful, delighted, ecstatic, exuberant, exultant, gay, jovial, joyful, jubilant, overjoyed, pleased, rapturous, triumphant. ▷ HAPPY. *Opp* SAD.

glib *adj* articulate, facile, fast-talking, fluent, insincere, plausible, quick, ready, shallow, slick, smooth, smooth-tongued, suave, superficial, unctuous. ▷ TALKATIVE. *Opp* INARTICULATE, SINCERE.

glide *vb* coast, drift, float, fly, freewheel, glissade, hang, hover, move smoothly, sail, skate, ski, skid, skim, slide, slip, soar, stream.

glimpse *n* glance, look, peep, sight, *inf* squint, view. ● *vb* discern, distinguish, espy, get a glimpse of, make out, notice, observe, see briefly, sight, spot, spy.

glisten *vb* flash, gleam, glimmer, glint, glitter, reflect, shine. ▷ LIGHT.

glitter *vb* coruscate, flash, scintillate, spark, sparkle, twinkle. ▷ LIGHT. **glittering** ▷ BRIGHT.

gloat *vb* boast, brag, *inf* crow, exult, glory, rejoice, *inf* rub it in, show off, triumph.

global *adj* broad, far-reaching, international, pandemic, total, universal, wide-ranging, worldwide. *Opp* LOCAL.

globe *n* **1** ball, globule, orb, sphere. **2** earth, planet, world.

gloom *n* blackness, cloudiness, darkness, dimness, dullness, dusk, murk, murkiness, obscurity, semi-darkness, shade, shadow, twilight. ▷ DEPRESSION.

gloomy *adj* **1** cheerless, cloudy, dark, depressing, dim, dingy, dismal, dreary, dull, glum, grim, heavy, joyless, murky, obscure, overcast, shadowy, shady, sombre. **2** *a gloomy mood*. depressed, downhearted, lugubrious, mournful, pessimistic, saturnine. ▷ SAD. *Opp* CHEERFUL.

glorious *adj* **1** celebrated, distinguished, eminent, famed, famous, heroic, illustrious, noble, noted, renowned, triumphant. **2** *glorious weather*. beautiful, bright, brilliant, dazzling, delightful, excellent, fine, gorgeous, grand, impressive, lovely, magnificent, majestic, marvellous, outstanding, pleasurable, resplendent, spectacular, splendid, *inf* super, superb, wonderful. *Opp* ORDINARY.

glory *n* **1** credit, distinction, eminence, fame, honour, *inf* kudos, praise, prestige, renown, repute, reputation, success, triumph. **2** *glory to God*. adoration, exaltation, glorification, gratitude, homage, praise, thanksgiving, veneration, worship **3** *glory of sunrise*. brightness, brilliance, grandeur, magnificence, majesty, radiance, splendour, wonder. ▷ BEAUTY.

gloss *n* **1** brightness, brilliance, burnish, finish, glaze, gleam, lustre, polish, sheen, shine, varnish. **2** annotation, comment, definition, elucidation, exegesis, explanation, footnote, marginal note, note, paraphrase. ● *vb* annotate, comment on, define, elucidate, explain, interpret, paraphrase. **gloss over** ▷ CONCEAL.

glossary *n* dictionary, phrasebook, vocabulary, word-list.

glossy *adj* bright, burnished, glassy, glazed, gleaming, glistening, lustrous, polished, reflective, shiny, silky, sleek, smooth, waxed. *Opp* DULL.

glove *n* gauntlet, mitt, mitten.

glow *n* **1** burning, fieriness, heat, incandescence, luminosity, lustre, phosphorescence, radiation, red-heat, redness. **2** ardour, blush, enthusiasm, fervour, flush, passion, rosiness, warmth. ● *vb* blush, flush, gleam, incandesce, light up, phosphoresce,

radiate heat, redden, smoulder, warm up. ▷ LIGHT.

glower *vb* frown, glare, lour, lower, scowl, stare angrily.

glowing *adj* **1** aglow, bright, hot, incandescent, lambent, luminous, phosphorescent, radiant, red, red-hot, white-hot. **2** *glowing praise*. complimentary, enthusiastic, fervent, passionate, warm.

glue *n* adhesive, cement, fixative, gum, paste, sealant, size, wallpaper-paste. ● *vb* affix, bond, cement, fasten, fix, gum, paste, seal, stick.

glum *adj* cheerless, displeased, gloomy, grim, heavy, joyless, lugubrious, moody, mournful, *inf* out of sorts, saturnine, sullen. ▷ SAD. *Opp* CHEERFUL.

glut *n* abundance, excess, overabundance, overflow, overprovision, plenty, superfluity, surfeit, surplus. *Opp* SCARCITY.

glutton *n joc* good trencherman, gormandizer, gourmand, *inf* greedy-guts, guzzler, *inf* pig.

gluttonous *adj* gormandizing, greedy, *inf* hoggish, *inf* piggish, insatiable, ravenous, voracious.

gnarled *adj* bent, bumpy, contorted, crooked, distorted, knobbly, knotted, knotty, lumpy, rough, rugged, twisted, warped.

gnaw *vb* bite, chew, erode, wear away. ▷ EAT.

go *n* attempt, chance, *inf* crack, opportunity; *inf* shot, *inf* stab, try, turn. ● *vb* **1** advance, begin, be off, commence, decamp, depart, disappear, embark, escape, get away, get going, get moving, get out, get under way, leave, make off, move, *inf* nip along, pass along, pass on, proceed, retire, retreat, run, set off, set out, *inf* shove off, start, take off, take your leave, vanish, *old use* wend your way, withdraw. ▷ RUN, TRAVEL, WALK. **2** die, fade, fail, give way. **3** extend, lead, reach, stretch. **4** *car won't go*. act, function, operate, perform, run, work. **5** *bomb went bang*. give off, make, produce, sound. **6** *Time goes slowly*.

elapse, lapse, pass. **7** *go sour.* become, grow, turn. **8** *Milk goes in the fridge.* belong, feel at home, have a proper place, live. **go away** ▷ DEPART. **go down** ▷ DESCEND, SINK. **go in for** ▷ LIKE. **go into** ▷ INVESTIGATE. **go off** ▷ EXPLODE. **go on** ▷ CONTINUE. **go through** ▷ SUFFER. **go to** ▷ VISIT. **go together** ▷ MATCH. **go with** ▷ ACCOMPANY. **go without** ▷ ABSTAIN.

goad *vb* badger, *inf* chivvy, egg on, *inf* hassle, needle, prick, prod, prompt, spur, urge. ▷ STIMULATE.

go-ahead *adj* ambitious, enterprising, forward-looking, progressive, resourceful. ● *n* approval, *inf* green light, permission, sanction, *inf* say-so, *inf* thumbs-up.

goal *n* aim, ambition, aspiration, design, end, ideal, intention, object, objective, purpose, target.

gobble *vb* bolt, devour, gulp, guzzle. ▷ EAT.

go-between *n* agent, broker, envoy, intermediary, liaison, mediator, messenger, middleman, negotiator. **act as go-between** ▷ MEDIATE.

god,

goddess *ns* deity, divinity, godhead, spirit. **God** the Almighty, the Creator, the supreme being. **the gods** the immortals, the pantheon, the powers above.

godsend *n inf* bit of good luck, blessing, boon, gift, miracle, *inf* stroke of good fortune, windfall.

golden *adj* **1** aureate, gilded, gilt. **2** *golden hair.* blond, blonde, flaxen, yellow.

good *adj* **1** acceptable, admirable, agreeable, appropriate, approved of, commendable, delightful, enjoyable, esteemed, *inf* fabulous, fair, *inf* fantastic, fine, gratifying, happy, *inf* incredible, lovely, marvellous, nice, perfect, *inf* phenomenal, pleasant, pleasing, praiseworthy, proper, remarkable, right, satisfactory, *inf* sensational, sound, splendid, suitable, *inf* super, superb, useful, valid, valuable, wonderful, worthy. ▷ EXCELLENT. **2** *a good person.* angelic, benevolent,

caring, charitable, chaste, considerate, decent, dependable, dutiful, ethical, friendly, helpful, holy, honest, honourable, humane, incorruptible, innocent, just, law-abiding, loyal, merciful, moral, noble, obedient, personable, pure, reliable, religious, righteous, saintly, sound, *inf* straight, thoughtful, true, trustworthy, upright, virtuous, well-behaved, well-mannered, worthy. ▷ KIND. **3** *a good worker.* able, accomplished, capable, conscientious, efficient, gifted, proficient, skilful, skilled, talented. ▷ CLEVER. **4** *good work.* careful, competent, correct, creditable, efficient, meritorious, neat, orderly, presentable, professional, thorough, well-done. **5** *good food.* beneficial, delicious, eatable, healthy, nourishing, nutritious, tasty, well-cooked, wholesome. **6** *a good book.* classic, exciting, great, interesting, readable, well-written. *Opp* BAD. **good-humoured** ▷ GOOD-TEMPERED. **good-looking** ▷ HANDSOME. **good-natured** ▷ GOOD-TEMPERED. **good person** *inf* angel, *inf* jewel, philanthropist, *inf* saint, Samaritan, worthy. **goods 1** belongings, chattels, effects, possessions, property. **2** commodities, freight, load, merchandise, produce, stock, wares.

goodbye *n* farewell, departure, leave-taking, parting words, send-off, valediction. □ *adieu, adios, arrivederci, auf Wiedersehen, au revoir, bon voyage, cheerio, ciao, so long.*

good-tempered *adj* accommodating, amenable, amiable, benevolent, benign, cheerful, cheery, considerate, cooperative, cordial, friendly, genial, good-humoured, good-natured, helpful, in a good mood, obliging, patient, pleasant, relaxed, smiling, sympathetic, thoughtful, willing. ▷ KIND. *Opp* BAD-TEMPERED.

gorge *vb* be greedy, fill up, gormandize, guzzle, indulge yourself, *inf* make a pig of yourself, overeat, *inf* stuff yourself. ▷ EAT.

gorgeous *adj* colourful, dazzling, glorious, magnificent, resplendent,

grain

showy, splendid, sumptuous. ▷ BEAU-TIFUL.

gory *adj* blood-stained, bloody, grisly, gruesome, sanguinary, savage.

gospel *n* creed, doctrine, good news, good tidings, message, religion, revelation, teaching, testament.

gossip *n* **1** casual talk, chatter, *inf* the grapevine, hearsay, prattle, rumour, scandal, small talk, *inf* tattle, *inf* tittle-tattle. **2** *inf* blab, busybody, chatterbox, *inf* Nosey Parker, rumourmonger, scandalmonger, telltale. ● *vb inf* blab, chat, chatter, *inf* natter, prattle, spread scandal, *inf* tattle, tell tales, *inf* tittle-tattle. ▷ TALK.

gouge *vb* chisel, dig, gash, hollow, incise, scoop. ▷ CUT.

gourmet *n Fr* bon viveur, connoisseur, epicure, gastronome, *derog* gourmand.

govern *vb* **1** administer, be in charge of, command, conduct affairs, control, direct, guide, head, lead, look after, manage, oversee, preside over, reign, rule, run, steer, superintend, supervise. **2** *govern your anger.* bridle, check, control, curb, discipline, keep in check, keep under control, master, regulate, restrain, tame.

government *n* administration, authority, bureaucracy, conduct of state affairs, constitution, control, direction, domination, management, oversight, regime, regulation, rule, sovereignty, supervision, surveillance, sway. □ commonwealth, democracy, dictatorship, empire, federation, kingdom, monarchy, oligarchy, republic.

gown *n* dress, frock. ▷ CLOTHES.

grab *vb* appropriate, arrogate, *inf* bag, capture, catch, clutch, *inf* collar, commandeer, expropriate, get hold of, grasp, hold, *inf* nab, pluck, seize, snap up, snatch, usurp.

grace *n* **1** attractiveness, beauty, charm, ease, elegance, fluidity, gracefulness, loveliness, poise, refinement, softness, tastefulness. **2** *God's grace.* beneficence, benevolence, compassion, favour, forgiveness, goodness,

graciousness, kindness, love, mercy. **3** *grace before meals.* blessing, prayer, thanksgiving.

graceful *adj* **1** agile, balletic, deft, dignified, easy, elegant, flowing, fluid, natural, nimble, pliant, slender, slim, smooth, supple, willowy. ▷ BEAUTIFUL. **2** *graceful compliments.* courteous, courtly, delicate, kind, polite, refined, suave, tactful, urbane. *Opp* GRACELESS.

graceless *adj* **1** awkward, clumsy, gangling, gawky, inelegant, maladroit, uncoordinated, ungainly. ▷ CLUMSY. *Opp* GRACEFUL. **2** *graceless manners.* boorish, gauche, inept, tactless, uncouth. ▷ RUDE.

gracious *adj* **1** affable, agreeable, civilized, cordial, courteous, dignified, elegant, friendly, good-natured, pleasant, polite, with grace. ▷ KIND. **2** clement, compassionate, forgiving, generous, indulgent, lenient, magnanimous, pitying, sympathetic. ▷ MERCIFUL. **3** *gracious living.* affluent, expensive, lavish, luxurious, opulent, selfindulgent, sumptuous.

grade *n* category, class, condition, degree, echelon, estate, level, mark, notch, point, position, quality, rank, rung, situation, standard, standing, status, step. ● *vb* **1** arrange, categorize, classify, differentiate, group, organize, range, size, sort. **2** *grade students' work.* assess, evaluate, mark, rank, rate.

gradient *n* ascent, bank, declivity, hill, incline, rise, slope.

gradual *adj* continuous, easy, even, gentle, leisurely, moderate, regular, slow, steady, unhurried, unspectacular. *Opp* SUDDEN.

graduate *vb* **1** become a graduate, be successful, get a degree, pass, qualify. **2** *graduate a measuring-rod.* calibrate, divide into graded sections, gradate, mark off, mark with a scale.

graft *vb* implant, insert, join, splice.

grain *n* **1** atom, bit, crumb, fleck, fragment, granule, iota, jot, mite, molecule, morsel, mote, particle, scrap, seed, speck, trace. **2** ▷ CEREAL.

grand adj 1 aristocratic, august, dignified, eminent, glorious, great, important, imposing, impressive, lordly, magnificent, majestic, noble, opulent, palatial, regal, royal, splendid, stately, sumptuous, superb. ▷ BIG. 2 [derog] haughty, inf high-and-mighty, lofty, patronizing, pompous, posh, inf upper crust. ▷ GRANDIOSE. Opp MODEST.

grandiloquent adj bombastic, elaborate, florid, flowery, fustian, high-flown, inflated, melodramatic, ornate, poetic, pompous, rhetorical, turgid. ▷ GRANDIOSE. Opp SIMPLE.

grandiose adj affected, ambitious, exaggerated, extravagant, flamboyant, inf flashy, grand, highfalutin, ostentatious, overdone, inf over the top, pretentious, showy. ▷ GRANDILOQUENT. Opp MODEST.

grant n allocation, allowance, annuity, award, benefaction, bursary, concession, contribution, donation, endowment, expenses, gift, honorarium, investment, loan, pension, scholarship, sponsorship, subsidy, subvention. ● vb 1 allocate, allot, allow, assign, award, bestow, confer, donate, give, pay, provide, supply. 2 grant that I'm right. accede, accept, acknowledge, admit, agree, concede, consent, vouchsafe.

graph n chart, column-graph, diagram, grid, pie chart, table.

graphic adj clear, descriptive, detailed, lifelike, lucid, photographic, plain, realistic, representational, vivid, well-drawn.

grapple vb clutch (at), grab, seize, tackle, wrestle. ▷ GRASP, FIGHT. **grapple with** grapple with a problem. attend to, come to grips with, contend with, cope with, deal with, engage with, get involved with, handle, inf have a go at, manage, try to solve.

grasp vb 1 catch, clasp, clutch, get hold of, inf get your hands on, grab, grapple with, grip, hang on to, hold, inf nab, seize, snatch, take hold of. 2 grasp an idea. appreciate, apprehend, comprehend, inf cotton on to, follow, inf get the drift of, get the hang of, get the point of, learn, master, realize, take in, understand. **grasping** ▷ GREEDY.

grass n downland, field, grassland, green, lawn, meadow, pasture, playing-field, prairie, savannah, steppe, poet sward, turf, veld. ● vb ▷ INFORM.

grate n fireplace, hearth. ● vb cut, grind, rasp, shred, triturate. **grate on** ▷ ANNOY. **grating** ▷ ANNOYING, HARSH.

grateful adj appreciative, beholden, gratified, indebted, obliged, thankful. Opp UNGRATEFUL.

gratify vb delight, fulfil, indulge, pander to, please, satisfy.

gratis adj complimentary, free, free of charge, gratuitous, without charge.

gratitude n appreciation, gratefulness, thankfulness, thanks.

gratuitous adj 1 ▷ GRATIS. 2 gratuitous insults. baseless, groundless, inappropriate, needless, unasked-for, uncalled-for, undeserved, unjustifiable, unmerited, unnecessary, unprovoked, unsolicited, unwarranted. Opp JUSTIFIABLE.

gratuity n bonus, inf perk, Fr pourboire, present, recompense, reward, tip.

grave adj 1 acute, critical, crucial, dangerous, important, inf life and death, major, momentous, perilous, pressing, serious, severe, significant, terminal (illness), threatening, urgent, vital, weighty, worrying. 2 a grave offence. criminal, indictable, punishable. 3 a grave look. dignified, earnest, grim, long-faced, pensive, sedate, serious, severe, sober, solemn, sombre, subdued, thoughtful, unsmiling. ▷ SAD. Opp CHEERFUL, TRIVIAL. ● n barrow, burial-place, crypt, inf last resting-place, mausoleum, sepulchre, tomb, tumulus, vault. ▷ GRAVESTONE.

gravel n grit, pebbles, shingle, stones.

gravestone n headstone, memorial, monument, tombstone.

graveyard n burial-ground, cemetery, churchyard, necropolis.

gravity n 1 acuteness, danger, importance, magnitude, momentousness, seriousness, severity, significance, weightiness. 2 *behave with gravity*. ceremony, dignity, earnestness, *Lat* gravitas, pomp, reserve, sedateness, sobriety, solemnity. 3 *force of gravity*. attraction, gravitation, heaviness, ponderousness, pull, weight.

graze n abrasion, laceration, raw spot, scrape, scratch. ▷ WOUND.

grease n fat, lubrication, oil.

greasy adj 1 buttery, fatty, oily, slippery, slithery, smeary, waxy. 2 *greasy manner*. fawning, flattering, fulsome, grovelling, ingratiating, slick, *inf* smarmy, sycophantic, toadying, unctuous.

great adj 1 colossal, enormous, extensive, giant, gigantic, grand, huge, immense, large, massive, prodigious, *inf* tremendous, vast. ▷ BIG. 2 *great pain*. acute, considerable, excessive, extreme, intense, marked, pronounced. ▷ SEVERE. 3 *great events*. grand, imposing, large-scale, momentous, serious, significant, spectacular, weighty. ▷ IMPORTANT. 4 *great music*. brilliant, classic, *inf* fabulous, famous, *inf* fantastic, fine, first-rate, outstanding, wonderful. ▷ EXCELLENT. 5 *a great athlete*. able, celebrated, distinguished, eminent, gifted, notable, noted, prominent, renowned, talented, well-known. ▷ FAMOUS. 6 *a great friend*. chief, close, dedicated, devoted, faithful, fast, loyal, main, true, valued. 7 *a great reader*. active, ardent, assiduous, eager, enthusiastic, frequent, habitual, keen, passionate, zealous. 8 ▷ GOOD. *Opp* SMALL, UNIMPORTANT.

greed n 1 appetite, craving, gluttony, gormandizing, hunger, insatiability, intemperance, overeating, ravenousness, selfindulgence, voraciousness, voracity. 2 *greed for wealth*. acquis-itiveness, avarice, covetousness, cupidity, desire, rapacity, self-interest. ▷ SELFISHNESS.

greedy adj 1 famished, gluttonous, gormandizing, *inf* hoggish, hungry, insatiable, intemperate, omnivorous, *inf* piggish, ravenous, self-indulgent, starving, voracious. *Opp* ABSTEMIOUS. 2 *greedy for wealth*. acquisitive, avaricious, avid, covetous, desirous, eager, grasping, materialistic, mean, mercenary, miserly, *inf* moneygrubbing, rapacious, selfish. *Opp* UNSELFISH. **be greedy** ▷ GORGE. **greedy person** ▷ GLUTTON.

green adj 1 grassy, greenish, leafy, verdant. □ emerald, grass-green, jade, khaki, lime, olive, pea-green, turquoise. 2 ▷ IMMATURE.

greenery n foliage, leaves, plants, vegetation.

greet vb accost, acknowledge, address, give a greeting to, hail, receive, salute, *inf* say hello to, usher in, welcome.

greeting n salutation, reception, welcome. **greetings** compliments, congratulations, felicitations, good wishes, regards.

grey adj ashen, blackish, colourless, greying, grizzled, grizzly, hoary, leaden, livid, pearly, silver, silvery, slate-grey, smoky, sooty, whitish. ▷ GLOOMY.

grid n framework, grating, grille, lattice, network.

grief n affliction, anguish, dejection, depression, desolation, despondency, distress, heartache, heartbreak, melancholy, misery, mourning, pain, regret, remorse, sadness, sorrow, suffering, tragedy, unhappiness, woe, wretchedness. ▷ PAIN. *Opp* HAPPINESS. **come to grief** ▷ FAIL.

grievance n 1 calamity, damage, hardship, harm, indignity, injury, injustice. 2 allegation, *inf* bone to pick, charge, complaint, *inf* gripe, objection.

grieve vb 1 afflict, cause grief, depress, dismay, distress, hurt, pain, sadden, upset, wound. *Opp* PLEASE.

2 be in mourning, feel grief, *inf* eat your heart out, fret, lament, mope, mourn, suffer, wail, weep. *Opp* RE-JOICE.

grim *adj* alarming, appalling, awful, cruel, dire, dour, dreadful, fearsome, fierce, forbidding, formidable, frightening, frightful, frowning, ghastly, grisly, gruesome, harsh, hideous, horrible, *inf* horrid, inexorable, inflexible, joyless, louring, menacing, merciless, ominous, pitiless, relentless, ruthless, savage, severe, sinister, stark, stern, sullen, surly, terrible, threatening, unattractive, uncompromising, unfriendly, unpleasant, unrelenting, unsmiling, unyielding. ▷ GLOOMY. *Opp* CHEERFUL.

grime *n* dirt, dust, filth, grit, muck, scum, soot.

grind *vb* **1** abrade, comminute, crumble, crush, erode, granulate, grate, mill, pound, powder, pulverize, rasp, triturate. **2** file, polish, sand, sandpaper, scrape, sharpen, smooth, wear away, whet. **3** *grind your teeth*. gnash, grate, grit, rub together. **grind away** ▷ WORK. **grind down** ▷ OPPRESS.

grip *n* clasp, clutch, grasp, handclasp, hold, purchase, stranglehold. ▷ CONTROL. ● *vb* **1** clasp, clutch, get a grip of, grab, grasp, hold, seize, take hold of. **2** *grip the imagination*. absorb, compel, engage, engross, enthral, entrance, fascinate, hypnotize, mesmerize, rivet, spellbind. **come to grips with** ▷ TACKLE.

grisly *adj* appalling, awful, bloody, disgusting, dreadful, fearful, frightful, ghastly, ghoulish, gory, grim, gruesome, hair-raising, hideous, horrible, *inf* horrid, horrifying, macabre, nauseating, repellent, repulsive, revolting, sickening, terrible.

gristly *adj* leathery, rubbery, tough, uneatable.

gritty *adj* abrasive, dusty, grainy, granular, gravelly, harsh, rasping, rough, sandy.

groan *vb* **1** cry out, lament, moan, sigh, wail, whimper, whine. **2** ▷ COMPLAIN.

groom *n* **1** ostler, stable-lad, stable-man. **2** bridegroom, husband. ● *vb* **1** brush, clean, make neat, neaten, preen, smarten up, spruce up, tidy, *inf* titivate. **2** *groom someone for a job*. coach, drill, educate, get ready, prepare, prime, train up, tutor.

groove *n* channel, cut, fluting, furrow, gouge, gutter, hollow, indentation, rut, score, scratch, slot, striation, track.

grope *vb* cast about, feel about, fish, flounder, fumble, search blindly.

gross *adj* **1** bloated, massive, obese, overweight, repellent, repulsive, revolting. ▷ FAT. **2** churlish, coarse, crude, rude, unrefined, unsophisticated, vulgar. **3** *gross injustice*. blatant, flagrant, glaring, manifest, monstrous, obvious, outrageous, shameful. **4** *gross income*. before tax, inclusive, overall, total, whole.

grotesque *adj* absurd, bizarre, curious, deformed, distorted, fantastic, freakish, gnarled, incongruous, ludicrous, macabre, malformed, misshapen, monstrous, outlandish, preposterous, queer, ridiculous, strange, surreal, twisted, ugly, unnatural, weird.

ground *n* **1** clay, dirt, earth, loam, mud, soil. **2** area, land, property, surroundings, terrain. **3** campus, estate, garden, park. **4** *sports ground*. arena, court, field, pitch, playground, playing-field, recreation ground, stadium. **5** *grounds for complaint*. argument, base, basis, case, cause, excuse, evidence, foundation, justification, motive, proof, rationale, reason. ● *vb* **1** base, establish, found, set, settle. **2** coach, educate, instruct, prepare, teach, train, tutor. **3** beach, run ashore, shipwreck, strand, wreck.

groundless *adj* baseless, chimerical, false, gratuitous, hypothetical, illusory, imaginary, irrational, motiveless, needless, speculative, suppositional, uncalled for, unfounded, unjustifiable, unjustified, unproven, unreasonable, unsound, unsubstantiated, unsupported, unwarranted.

group n 1 [people] alliance, assemblage, assembly, association, band, bevy, body, brotherhood, inf bunch, cadre, cartel, caste, caucus, circle, clan, class, derog clique, club, cohort, colony, committee, community, company, conclave, congregation, consortium, contingent, corps, coterie, coven, crew, crowd, delegation, faction, family, federation, force, fraternity, gang, gathering, guild, horde, host, knot, league, meeting, derog mob, multitude, number, organization, party, phalanx, picket, platoon, posse, derog rabble, ring, sect, derog shower, sisterhood, society, squad, squadron, swarm, syndicate, team, throng, troop, troupe, union, unit. 2 [things, animals] accumulation, agglomeration, assemblage, assortment, batch, battery (guns), brood (chicks), bunch, bundle, category, class, clump, cluster, clutch (eggs), collection, combination, conglomeration, constellation, convoy, covey (birds), fleet, flock, gaggle (geese), galaxy, grouping, heap, herd, hoard, host, litter, mass, pack, pile, pride (lions), school, set, shoal (fish), species. 3 ▷ MUSICIAN. ● vb 1 arrange, assemble, assort, bracket together, bring together, categorize, classify, collect, deploy, gather, herd, marshal, order, organize, put together, set out, sort. 2 associate, band, cluster, come together, congregate, crowd, flock, gather, get together, herd, make groups, swarm, team up, throng.

grovel vb abase yourself, be humble, cower, inf crawl, inf creep, cringe, demean yourself, fawn, flatter, ingratiate yourself, inf kowtow, inf lick someone's boots, prostrate yourself, snivel, inf suck up, inf toady. **grovelling** ▷ OBSEQUIOUS.

grow vb 1 augment, become bigger, broaden, build up, burgeon, come to life, develop, emerge, enlarge, evolve, expand, extend, fill out, flourish, flower, germinate, improve, increase, lengthen, live, make progress, mature, multiply, mushroom, progress, proliferate, prosper, put on growth, ripen, rise, shoot up, spread, spring up, sprout, survive, swell, thicken, thrive. 2 grow roses. cultivate, farm, help along, nurture, produce, propagate, raise. 3 grow older. become, get, turn.

grown-up adj adult, fully-grown, mature, well-developed.

growth n 1 accretion, advance, augmentation, broadening, burgeoning, development, enlargement, evolution, expansion, extension, flowering, getting bigger, growing, improvement, increase, maturation, maturing, progress, proliferation, prosperity, spread, success. 2 crop, harvest, plants, produce, vegetation, yield. 3 cancer, cyst, excrescence, lump, swelling, tumour.

grub n 1 caterpillar, larva, maggot. 2 ▷ FOOD. ● vb ▷ DIG.

grudge n ▷ RESENTMENT. ● vb begrudge, covet, envy, resent.

grudging adj cautious, envious, guarded, half-hearted, hesitant, jealous, reluctant, resentful, secret, unenthusiastic, ungracious, unkind, unwilling. Opp ENTHUSIASTIC.

gruelling adj arduous, backbreaking, crippling, demanding, exhausting, fatiguing, laborious, punishing, severe, stiff, strenuous, taxing, tiring, tough, uphill, wearying. ▷ DIFFICULT. Opp EASY.

gruesome adj appalling, awful, bloody, disgusting, dreadful, fearful, fearsome, frightful, ghastly, ghoulish, gory, grim, grisly, hair-raising, hideous, horrible, inf horrid, horrific, horrifying, macabre, repellent, repugnant, revolting, shocking, sickening, terrible.

gruff adj 1 guttural, harsh, hoarse, husky, rasping, rough, throaty. 2 ▷ BAD-TEMPERED.

grumble vb inf beef, fuss, inf gripe, inf grouch, grouse, make a fuss, inf moan, object, protest, *inf* whinge. ▷ COMPLAIN.

guarantee *n* assurance, bond, oath, obligation, pledge, promise, surety, undertaking, warranty, word of honour. ● *vb* **1** assure, certify, give a guarantee, pledge, promise, swear, undertake, vouch, vow. **2** ensure, make sure of, reserve, secure, stake a claim to.

guard *n* bodyguard, *inf* bouncer, custodian, escort, guardian, *sl* heavy, lookout, *sl* minder, patrol, picket, *sl* screw, security-guard, sentinel, sentry, warder, watchman. ● *vb* be on guard over, care for, defend, keep safe, keep watch on, look after, mind, oversee, patrol, police, preserve, prevent from escaping, protect, safeguard, secure, shelter, shield, stand guard over, supervise, tend, watch, watch over. **on your guard** ▷ ALERT.

guardian *n* **1** adoptive parent, foster-parent. **2** champion, custodian, defender, keeper, preserver, protector, trustee, warden. ▷ GUARD.

guess *n* assumption, conjecture, estimate, feeling, *sl* guesstimate, guesswork, hunch, hypothesis, intuition, opinion, prediction, *inf* shot in the dark, speculation, supposition, surmise, suspicion, theory. ● *vb* assume, conclude, conjecture, divine, estimate, expect, fancy, feel, have a hunch, have a theory, *inf* hazard a guess, hypothesize, imagine, intuit, judge, make a guess, postulate, predict, *inf* reckon, speculate, suppose, surmise, suspect, think likely, work out.

guest *n* **1** caller, company, visitor. **2** *hotel guests*. boarder, customer, lodger, patron, resident, tenant.

guidance *n* advice, briefing, counselling, direction, guidelines, guiding, help, instruction, leadership, management, *inf* spoon-feeding, *inf* taking by the hand, teaching, tips.

guide *n* **1** courier, escort, leader, navigator, pilot. **2** adviser, counsellor, director, guru, mentor. **3** atlas, direct-ory, gazetteer, guidebook, handbook, *Lat* vade mecum. ● *vb* **1** conduct, direct, escort, lead, manoeuvre, navigate, pilot, shepherd, show the way, steer, supervise, usher. **2** advise, brief, control, counsel, educate, give guidance to, govern, help along, influence, instruct, regulate, *inf* take by the hand, teach, train, tutor. *Opp* MISLEAD.

guilt *n* **1** blame, blameworthiness, criminality, culpability, fault, guiltiness, liability, responsibility, sinfulness, wickedness, wrongdoing. **2** *a look of guilt*. bad conscience, contriteness, contrition, dishonour, guilty feelings, penitence, regret, remorse, self-accusation, self-reproach, shame, sorrow. *Opp* INNOCENCE.

guiltless *adj* above suspicion, blameless, clear, faultless, free, honourable, immaculate, innocent, in the right, irreproachable, pure, sinless, untarnished, untroubled, virtuous. *Opp* GUILTY.

guilty *adj* **1** at fault, blameable, blameworthy, culpable, in the wrong, liable, reprehensible, responsible. **2** *a guilty look*. apologetic, ashamed, conscience-stricken, contrite, penitent, *inf* red-faced, regretful, remorseful, repentant, rueful, shamefaced, sheepish, sorry. *Opp* GUILTLESS, SHAMELESS.

gullible *adj* credulous, easily taken in, *inf* green, impressionable, inexperienced, innocent, naïve, suggestible, trusting, unsophisticated, unsuspecting, unwary. *Opp* WARY.

gulp *n* mouthful, swallow, *inf* swig. ● *vb* **1** bolt down, gobble, swallow, *inf* wolf. ▷ EAT. **2** *inf* knock back, quaff, *inf* swig. ▷ DRINK. **3** *gulp back tears*. check, choke back, stifle, suppress.

gumption *n* cleverness, *inf* common sense, enterprise, initiative, judgement, *inf* nous, resourcefulness, sense, wisdom.

gun *n plur* artillery, firearm. □ airgun, automatic, blunderbuss, cannon, machine-gun, mortar, musket, pistol, revolver, rifle, shot-gun, *plur small* arms, sub-

machine-gun, *tommy-gun*. **gun down** ▷ SHOOT.

gunfire *n* cannonade, cross-fire, firing, gunshots, salvo.

gunman *n* assassin, bandit, criminal, desperado, fighter, gangster, killer, murderer, sniper, terrorist.

gurgle *vb* babble, bubble, burble, ripple, purl, splash.

gush *n* burst, cascade, eruption, flood, flow, jet, outpouring, overflow, rush, spout, spurt, squirt, stream, tide, torrent. ● *vb* **1** come in a gush, cascade, flood, flow freely, overflow, pour, run, rush, spout, spurt, squirt, stream, well up. **2** be enthusiastic, be sentimental, bubble over, fuss, *inf* go on, prattle on, talk on. **gushing** ▷ EFFUSIVE, SENTIMENTAL.

gusto *n* appetite, delight, enjoyment, enthusiasm, excitement, liveliness, pleasure, relish, satisfaction, spirit, verve, vigour, zest.

gut *vb* **1** clean, disembowel, draw, eviscerate, remove the guts of. **2** *gut a building*. clear, despoil, empty, loot, pillage, plunder, ransack, ravage, remove the contents of, sack, strip.

guts *plur n* **1** alimentary canal, belly, bowels, entrails, *inf* innards, insides, intestines, stomach, viscera. **2** ▷ COURAGE.

gutter *n* channel, conduit, ditch, drain, duct, guttering, sewer, sluice, trench, trough.

gypsy *n* nomad, Romany, traveller, wanderer.

gyrate *vb* circle, pirouette, revolve, rotate, spin, spiral, swivel, turn, twirl, wheel, whirl.

H

habit *n* **1** convention, custom, pattern, policy, practice, routine, rule, usage, *old use* wont. **2** attitude, bent, disposition, inclination, manner, mannerism, penchant, predisposition, proclivity, propensity, quirk, tendency, way. **3** *bad habit.* addiction, compulsion, craving, dependence, fixation, obsession, vice.

habitable *adj* in good repair, inhabitable, liveable, usable. *Opp* UNINHABITABLE.

habitual *adj* **1** accustomed, common, conventional, customary, established, expected, familiar, fixed, frequent, natural, normal, ordinary, predictable, regular, ritual, routine, set, settled, standard, traditional, typical, usual, *old use* wonted. **2** addictive, besetting, chronic, established, ineradicable, ingrained, obsessive, persistent, recurrent. **3** *habitual smokers.* addicted, conditioned, confirmed, dependent, hardened, *inf* hooked, inveterate, persistent.

hack *vb* carve, chop, gash, hew, mangle, mutilate, slash. ▷ CUT.

hackneyed *adj* banal, clichéd, cliché-ridden, commonplace, conventional, *inf* corny, familiar, feeble, obvious, overused, pedestrian, platitudinous, predictable, stale, stereotyped, stock, threadbare, tired, trite, uninspired, unoriginal. *Opp* NEW.

haggard *adj inf* all skin and bone, careworn, drawn, emaciated, exhausted, gaunt, hollow-cheeked, hollow-eyed, pinched, run-down, scraggy, scrawny, shrunken, thin, tired out, ugly, unhealthy, wasted, weary, withered, worn out, *inf* worried to death. *Opp* HEALTHY.

haggle *vb* argue, bargain, barter, discuss terms, negotiate, quibble, wrangle. ▷ QUARREL.

hail *vb* **1** accost, address, call to, greet, signal to. **2** ▷ ACCLAIM.

hair *n* **1** beard, bristles, curls, fleece, fur, hank, locks, mane, *inf* mop, moustache, shock, tresses, whiskers. **2** coiffure, cut, haircut, *inf* hair-do, hairstyle, style. □ bob, braid, bun, crew-cut, dreadlocks, fringe, Mohican, *inf* perm, permanent wave, pigtail, plait, pony-tail, quiff, ringlets, short back and sides, sideboards, sideburns, tonsure, top-knot. **3** *false hair.* hair-piece, toupee, wig.

hairdresser *n* barber, coiffeur, coiffeuse, hair-stylist.

hairless *adj* bald, bare, cleanshaven, naked, shaved, shaven, smooth. *Opp* HAIRY.

hairy *adj* bearded, bristly, downy, feathery, fleecy, furry, fuzzy, hirsute, long-haired, shaggy, stubbly, woolly. *Opp* HAIRLESS.

half-hearted *adj* apathetic, cool, easily distracted, feeble, indifferent, ineffective, lackadaisical, listless, lukewarm, nonchalant, passive, perfunctory, phlegmatic, uncaring, uncommitted, unconcerned, unenthusiastic, unreliable, wavering, weak, *inf* wishywashy. *Opp* ENTHUSIASTIC.

hall *n* **1** auditorium, concert-hall, lecture room, theatre. **2** corridor, entrance-hall, foyer, hallway, lobby, passage, passageway, vestibule.

hallowed *adj* blessed, consecrated, dedicated, holy, honoured, revered, reverenced, sacred, sacrosanct, worshipped.

hallucinate vb day-dream, dream, fantasize, inf have a trip, have hallucinations, inf see things, see visions.

hallucination n apparition, chimera, day-dream, delusion, dream, fantasy, figment of the imagination, illusion, mirage, vision. ▷ GHOST.

halt n break, cessation, close, end, interruption, pause, standstill, stop, stoppage, termination. ● vb **1** arrest, block, break off, cease, check, curb, end, impede, obstruct, stop, terminate. **2** come to a halt, come to rest, desist, discontinue, draw up, pull up, quit, stop, wait. Opp START. **halting** ▷ HESITANT, IRREGULAR.

halve vb bisect, cut by half, cut in half, decrease, divide into halves, lessen, reduce by half, share equally, split in two.

hammer n mallet, sledge-hammer. ● vb inf bash, batter, beat, drive, knock, pound, smash, strike. ▷ DEFEAT, HIT.

hamper vb baulk, block, curb, curtail, delay, encumber, entangle, fetter, foil, frustrate, handicap, hinder, hold back, hold up, impede, inhibit, interfere with, obstruct, prevent, restrain, restrict, retard, shackle, slow down, thwart, trammel. Opp HELP.

hand n **1** fist, sl mitt, palm, inf paw. **2** hand on a dial. index, indicator, pointer. **3** [old use] factory hands. ▷ WORKER. ● vb convey, deliver, give, offer, pass, present, submit. **at hand** ▷ HANDY. **give a hand** ▷ HELP. **hand down** ▷ BEQUEATH. **hand over** ▷ SURRENDER. **hand round** ▷ DISTRIBUTE. **lend a hand** ▷ HELP. **to hand** ▷ HANDY.

handicap n **1** barrier, burden, disadvantage, difficulty, drawback, encumbrance, hindrance, impediment, inconvenience, limitation, inf minus, nuisance, obstacle, problem, restraint, restriction, shortcoming, stumbling-block. Opp ADVANTAGE. **2** defect, disability, impairment. ● vb be a handicap to, burden, check, curb, disable, disadvantage, encumber, hamper, hinder, hold back,

impede, limit, restrain, restrict, retard, trammel. Opp HELP.

handicapped adj [Some synonyms may cause offence] autistic, bedridden, blind, crippled, deaf, disabled, disadvantaged, dumb, dyslexic, incapacitated, invalid, lame, limbless, maimed, mute, paralysed, paraplegic, retarded, slow, spastic, unsighted. ▷ ILL.

handiwork n achievement, creation, doing, invention, production, responsibility, work.

handle n grip, haft, handgrip, helve, hilt, knob, stock (of rifle). ● vb **1** caress, feel, finger, fondle, grasp, hold, inf maul, pat, inf paw, stroke, touch, treat. **2** handle situations, people. conduct, contend with, control, cope with, deal with, direct, guide, look after, manage, manipulate, tackle, treat. ▷ ORGANIZE. **3** car handles well. manoeuvre, operate, respond, steer, work. **4** handle goods. deal in, do trade in, market, sell, stock, touch, traffic in.

handsome adj **1** admirable, attractive, beautiful, comely, elegant, fair, fine-looking, good-looking, personable, tasteful. Opp UGLY. **2** handsome gift. big, bountiful, generous, goodly, gracious, large, liberal, magnanimous, munificent, sizeable, unselfish, valuable. Opp MEAN.

handy adj **1** convenient, easy to use, helpful, manageable, practical, serviceable, useful, well-designed, worth having. **2** handy with tools. adept, capable, clever, competent, practical, proficient, skilful. **3** keep tools handy. accessible, at hand, available, close at hand, easy to reach, get-at-able, nearby, reachable, ready, to hand. Opp AWKWARD, INACCESSIBLE.

hang vb **1** be suspended, dangle, depend, droop, flap, flop, sway, swing, trail down. **2** hang washing. attach, drape, fasten, fix, peg up, pin up, stick up, suspend. **3** hang in the air. drift, float, hover. **hang about** ▷ DAWDLE. **hang back** ▷ HESITATE. **hanging** ▷ PENDENT. **hangings** ▷ DRAPE. **hang on** ▷ WAIT. **hang on to** ▷ KEEP.

hank *n* coil, length, loop, piece, skein.

hanker *vb* ache, covet, crave, desire, fancy, *inf* have a yen, hunger, itch, long, pine, thirst, want, wish, yearn.

haphazard *adj* accidental, adventitious, arbitrary, casual, chance, chaotic, confusing, disorderly, disorganized, fortuitous, *inf* higgledy-piggledy, *inf* hit-or-miss, illogical, irrational, random, serendipitous, unforeseen, unplanned, unstructured, unsystematic. *Opp* ORDERLY.

happen *vb* arise, befall, *old use* betide, chance, come about, crop up, emerge, follow, materialize, occur, result, take place, *inf* transpire, *inf* turn out. **happen on** ▷ FIND.

happening *n* accident, affair, chance, circumstance, episode, event, incident, occasion, occurrence, phenomenon.

happiness *n* bliss, cheer, cheerfulness, contentment, delight, ecstasy, elation, enjoyment, euphoria, exhilaration, exuberance, felicity, gaiety, gladness, glee, *inf* heaven, high spirits, joy, joyfulness, joyousness, jubilation, light-heartedness, merriment, pleasure, pride, rapture, well-being. *Opp* SADNESS.

happy *adj* **1** beatific, blessed, blissful, *poet* blithe, buoyant, cheerful, cheery, contented, delighted, ecstatic, elated, enraptured, euphoric, exhilarated, exuberant, exultant, felicitous, festive, gay, glad, gleeful, good-humoured, gratified, grinning, halcyon (*days*), *inf* heavenly, high-spirited, idyllic, jocose, jocular, jocund, joking, jolly, jovial, joyful, joyous, jubilant, laughing, light-hearted, lively, merry, *inf* on top of the world, overjoyed, *inf* over the moon, pleased, proud, radiant, rapturous, rejoicing, relaxed, satisfied, smiling, *inf* starry-eyed, sunny, thrilled, triumphant. *Opp* SAD. **2** *a happy accident.* advantageous, appropriate, apt, auspicious, beneficial, convenient, favourable, felicitous, fortuitous, fortunate, lucky, opportune, propitious, timely, welcome, well-timed.

harangue *n* diatribe, exhortation, lecture, *inf* pep talk, tirade. ▷ SPEECH. ● *vb* chivvy, encourage, exhort, lecture, pontificate, preach, sermonize. ▷ SPEAK, TALK.

harass *vb* annoy, attack, badger, bait, bother, chivvy, disturb, harry, *inf* hassle, hound, irritate, molest, nag, persecute, pester, *inf* pick on, *inf* plague, torment, trouble, vex, worry.

harassed *adj inf* at the end of your tether, careworn, distraught, distressed, exhausted, frayed, pressured, strained, stressed, tired, weary, worn out.

harbour *n* anchorage, dock, haven, jetty, landing-stage, marina, mooring, pier, port, quay, safe haven, shelter, wharf. ● *vb* **1** conceal, give asylum to, give refuge to, give sanctuary to, hide, protect, shelter, shield. **2** *harbour a grudge.* cherish, cling on to, hold on to, keep in mind, maintain, nurse, nurture, retain.

hard *adj* **1** adamantine, compact, compressed, dense, firm, flinty, frozen, hardened, impenetrable, impervious, inflexible, rigid, rocky, solid, solidified, steely, stiff, stony, unbreakable, unyielding. **2** *hard labour.* arduous, back-breaking, exhausting, fatiguing, formidable, gruelling, harsh, heavy, laborious, onerous, rigorous, severe, stiff, strenuous, taxing, tiring, tough, uphill, wearying. **3** *a hard problem.* baffling, complex, complicated, confusing, difficult, enigmatic, insoluble, intricate, involved, knotty, perplexing, puzzling, tangled, *inf* thorny. **4** *a hard heart.* callous, cold, cruel, *inf* hard-boiled, hard-hearted, harsh, heartless, hostile, inflexible, intolerant, merciless, obdurate, pitiless, ruthless, severe, stern, strict, unbending, unfeeling, unfriendly, unkind. **5** *a hard blow.* forceful, heavy, powerful, strong, violent. **6** *hard times.* austere, bad, calamitous, disagreeable, distressing, grim, intolerable, painful, unhappy, unpleasant. **7** *a hard worker.* assiduous, conscientious, devoted, indefatigable, industrious, keen, persistent, unflagging, untiring, zealous. *Opp* EASY, SOFT. **hard-headed** ▷ BUSINESSLIKE. **hard-hearted** ▷ CRUEL. **hard up** ▷ POOR. **hard-wearing** ▷ DURABLE.

harden *vb* bake, cake, clot, coagulate, congeal, freeze, gel, jell, ossify, petrify, reinforce, set, solidify, stiffen, strengthen, toughen. *Opp* SOFTEN.

hardly *adv* barely, faintly, only just, rarely, scarcely, seldom, with difficulty.

hardship *n* adversity, affliction, austerity, bad luck, deprivation, destitution, difficulty, distress, misery, misfortune, need, privation, suffering, *inf* trials and tribulations, trouble, unhappiness, want.

hardware *n* equipment, implements, instruments, ironmongery, machinery, tools.

hardy *adj* **1** durable, fit, healthy, hearty, resilient, robust, rugged, strong, sturdy, tough, vigorous. *Opp* TENDER. **2** ▷ BOLD.

harm *n* abuse, damage, detriment, disadvantage, disservice, havoc, hurt, inconvenience, injury, loss, mischief, misfortune, pain, unhappiness, *inf* upset, wrong. ▷ EVIL. ● *vb* abuse, be harmful to, damage, hurt, ill-treat, impair, injure, maltreat, misuse, ruin, spoil, wound. *Opp* BENEFIT.

harmful *adj* addictive, bad, baleful, damaging, dangerous, deadly, deleterious, destructive, detrimental, disadvantageous, evil, fatal, hurtful, injurious, lethal, malign, negative, noxious, pernicious, poisonous, prejudicial, ruinous, unfavourable, unhealthy, unpleasant, unwholesome. *Opp* BENEFICIAL, HARMLESS.

harmless *adj* acceptable, benign, gentle, innocent, innocuous, inoffensive, mild, non-addictive, non-toxic, safe, tame, unobjectionable. *Opp* HARMFUL.

harmonious *adj* **1** concordant, consonant, *inf* easy on the ear, euphonious, harmonizing, melodious, musical, sweet-sounding, tonal, tuneful. *Opp* DISCORDANT. **2** *a harmonious meeting.* agreeable, amicable, compatible, congenial, congruous, cooperative, friendly, integrated, like-minded, sympathetic.

harmonize *vb* agree, balance, be in harmony, blend, cooperate, coordinate, correspond, go together, match, suit each other, tally, tone in.

harmony *n* **1** assonance, concord, consonance, euphony, tunefulness. **2** accord, agreement, amity, balance, compatibility, conformity, congruence, cooperation, friendliness, goodwill, like-mindedness, peace, rapport, sympathy, togetherness, understanding. *Opp* DISCORD.

harness *n* equipment, *inf* gear, straps, tackle. ● *vb* control, domesticate, exploit, keep under control, make use of, mobilize, tame, use, utilize.

harsh *adj* **1** abrasive, bristly, coarse, hairy, rough, scratchy. **2** *harsh sounds.* cacophonous, croaking, croaky, disagreeable, discordant, dissonant, grating, gravelly, grinding, gruff, guttural, hoarse, husky, irritating, jarring, rasping, raucous, rough, screeching, shrill, squawking, stertorous, strident, unpleasant. **3** *harsh colours, light.* bright, brilliant, dazzling, gaudy, glaring, lurid. **4** *harsh smell.* acrid, bitter, sour, unpleasant. **5** *harsh conditions.* arduous, austere, comfortless, difficult, hard, severe, stressful, tough. **6** *harsh criticism, treatment.* abusive, acerbic, bitter, blunt, brutal, cruel, Draconian, frank, hard-hearted, hurtful, impolite, merciless, outspoken, pitiless, severe, sharp, stern, strict, uncivil, unforgiving, unkind, unrelenting, unsympathetic, untempered. *Opp* GENTLE.

harvest *n* crop, gathering-in, produce, reaping, return, yield. ● *vb* bring in, collect, garner, gather, glean, mow, pick, reap, take in.

hash *n* **1** goulash, stew. **2** *inf* botch, confusion, farrago, *inf* hotchpotch, jumble, mess, *inf* mishmash, mixture. **make a hash of** ▷ BUNGLE.

hassle n altercation, argument, bother, confusion, difficulty, disagreement, disturbance, fighting, fuss, harassment, inconvenience, making difficulties, nuisance, persecution, problem, struggle, trouble, upset. ● vb ▷ HARASS, QUARREL.

haste n dispatch, hurry, impetuosity, precipitateness, quickness, rashness, recklessness, rush, urgency. ▷ SPEED.

hasty adj 1 abrupt, fast, foolhardy, headlong, hot-headed, hurried, illconsidered, immediate, impetuous, impulsive, incautious, instantaneous, inf pell-mell, precipitate, quick, rapid, rash, reckless, speedy, sudden, summary (justice), swift. 2 hasty work. brief, careless, cursory, hurried, illconsidered, perfunctory, rushed, short, slapdash, superficial, thoughtless, unthinking. Opp CAREFUL, SLOW.

hat n head-dress. □ Balaclava, bearskin, beret, biretta, boater, bonnet, bowler, busby, cap, coronet, crash-helmet, crown, deerstalker, diadem, fez, fillet, headband, helmet, hood, mitre, skullcap, sombrero, sou'wester, stetson, sun-hat, tiara, top hat, toque, trilby, turban, wig, wimple, yarmulke.

hatch vb 1 brood, incubate. 2 conceive, concoct, contrive, inf cook up, design, devise, inf dream up, formulate, invent, plan, plot, scheme, think up.

hate n 1 ▷ HATRED. 2 a pet hate. abomination, aversion, Fr bête noire, dislike, loathing. ● vb abhor, abominate, be averse to, be hostile to, be revolted by, inf can't bear, inf can't stand, deplore, despise, detest, dislike, execrate, fear, find intolerable, loathe, object to, recoil from, resent, scorn, shudder at. Opp LIKE, LOVE.

hateful adj abhorred, abhorrent, abominable, accursed, awful, contemptible, cursed, inf damnable, despicable, detestable, disgusting, distasteful, execrable, foul, hated, heinous, horrible, inf horrid, loathsome, nasty, nauseating, obnoxious, odious, offensive, repellent, repugnant, repulsive, revolting, vile. ▷ EVIL. Opp LOVABLE.

hatred n abhorrence, animosity, antagonism, antipathy, aversion, contempt, detestation, dislike, enmity, execration, hate, hostility, ill-will, intolerance, loathing, misanthropy, odium, repugnance, revulsion. Opp LOVE.

haughty adj arrogant, boastful, bumptious, cavalier, inf cocky, conceited, condescending, disdainful, egotistical, inf highand-mighty, inf hoity-toity, imperious, lofty, lordly, offhand, patronizing, pompous, presumptuous, pretentious, proud, selfadmiring, self-important, smug, snobbish, inf snooty, inf stuck-up, supercilious, superior, inf uppish, vain. Opp MODEST.

haul vb carry, cart, convey, drag, draw, heave, inf lug, move, pull, tow, trail, transport, tug.

haunt vb 1 frequent, inf hang around, keep returning to, loiter about, patronize, spend time at, visit regularly. 2 haunt the mind. beset, linger in, obsess, plague, prey on, torment.

have vb 1 be in possession of, keep, maintain, own, possess, use, utilize. 2 house has six rooms. comprise, consist of, contain, embody, hold, include, incorporate, involve. 3 have fun, illness. be subject to, endure, enjoy, experience, feel, go through, know, live through, put up with, suffer, tolerate, undergo. 4 have presents. accept, acquire, be given, gain, get, obtain, procure, receive. 5 thieves had the lot. inf get away with, remove, retain, secure, steal, take. 6 have a snack. consume, eat, drink, partake of, swallow. 7 have a party. arrange, hold, organize, prepare, set up. 8 have guests. be host to, cater for, entertain, put up. **have on** ▷ HOAX. **have to** be compelled to, be forced to, have an obligation to, must, need to, ought to, should. **have up** ▷ ARREST.

haven n asylum, refuge, retreat, safety, sanctuary, shelter. ▷ HARBOUR.

havoc n carnage, chaos, confusion, damage, desolation, destruction, devastation, disorder, disruption, inf mayhem, inf rack and ruin, ruin, inf shambles, upset, waste, wreckage.

hazard n chance, danger, jeopardy, peril, risk, threat. • vb dare, gamble, jeopardize, risk, stake, take a chance with, venture.

hazardous adj chancy, dangerous, inf dicey, fraught with danger, parlous, perilous, precarious, risky, inf ticklish, inf tricky, uncertain, unpredictable, unsafe. Opp SAFE.

haze n cloud, film, fog, mist, steam, vapour.

hazy adj 1 blurred, blurry, clouded, cloudy, dim, faint, foggy, fuzzy, indefinite, milky, misty, obscure, unclear. 2 ▷ VAGUE. Opp CLEAR.

head adj ▷ CHIEF. • n 1 brain, cranium, skull. 2 head for figures. ability, brains, capacity, imagination, intelligence, intellect, mind, understanding. 3 head of a mountain. apex, crown, highest point, peak, summit, top, vertex. 4 boss, director, employer, leader, manager, ruler. ▷ CHIEF. 5 head of a school. headmaster, headmistress, head teacher, principal. 6 head of a river. ▷ SOURCE. • vb 1 be in charge of, command, control, direct, govern, guide, lead, manage, rule, run, superintend, supervise. 2 head for home. aim, go, make, inf make a beeline, point, set out, start, steer, turn. **head off** ▷ DEFLECT. **lose your head** ▷ PANIC. **off your head** ▷ MAD.

heading n caption, headline, rubric, title.

headquarters n administration, base, depot, head office, inf HQ, main office, inf nerve-centre.

heal vb 1 become healthy, get better, improve, knit, mend, recover, recuperate, unite. 2 cure, make better, minister to, nurse, rejuvenate, remedy, renew, restore, revitalize, tend, treat. 3 heal differences. patch up, put right, reconcile, repair, settle.

health n 1 condition, constitution, fettle, form, shape, trim. 2 the picture of health. fitness, robustness, soundness, strength, vigour, well-being.

healthy adj 1 active, blooming, fine, fit, flourishing, good, inf hale-and-hearty, hearty, inf in fine fettle, in good shape, lively, perky, robust, sound, strong, sturdy, vigorous, well. 2 bracing, health-giving, hygienic, invigorating, salubrious, sanitary, wholesome. Opp ILL, UNHEALTHY.

heap n accumulation, assemblage, bank, collection, hill, hoard, mass, mound, mountain, pile, stack. • vb accumulate, amass, bank up, collect, gather, hoard, mass, pile, stack, stockpile, store. **heaps** ▷ PLENTY.

hear vb 1 attend to, catch, old use hearken to, heed, listen to, overhear, pay attention to, pick up. 2 hear evidence. examine, investigate, judge, try. 3 hear news. be told, discover, find out, gather, get, inf get wind of, learn, receive.

hearing n case, inquest, inquiry, trial.

heart n 1 sl ticker. 2 centre, core, crux, essence, focus, hub, inside, kernel, marrow, middle, sl nitty-gritty, nub, nucleus, pith. 3 affection, compassion, concern, courage, feeling, goodness, humanity, kindness, love, pity, sensitivity, sympathy, tenderness, understanding, warmth.

heartbreaking adj bitter, distressing, grievous, heart-rending, pitiful, tragic.

heartbroken adj broken-hearted, dejected, desolate, despairing, dispirited, grieved, inconsolable, miserable, inf shattered. ▷ SAD.

hearten vb boost, cheer up, encourage, strengthen, uplift.

heartless adj callous, cold, icy, inhuman, pitiless, ruthless, steely, stony, unconcerned, unemotional, unkind, unsympathetic. ▷ CRUEL.

hearty adj 1 enthusiastic, exuberant, friendly, genuine, healthy, heartfelt, lively, positive, robust, sincere, spirited, strong, vigorous, warm. *Opp* HALF-HEARTED. **2** *a hearty dinner.* ▷ BIG.

heat *n* **1** calorific value, fever, fieriness, glow, hotness, incandescence, warmth. **2** closeness, heat-wave, high temperature, hot weather, humidity, sultriness, torridity, warmth. **3** *heat of the moment.* anger, ardour, eagerness, enthusiasm, excitement, fervour, feverishness, fury, impetuosity, violence. ▷ PASSION. *Opp* COLD. ● *vb* bake, blister, boil, burn, cook, *inf* frizzle, fry, grill, inflame, make hot, melt, reheat, roast, scald, scorch, simmer, sizzle, smoulder, steam, stew, swelter, toast, warm. *Opp* COOL. **heated** ▷ FERVENT, HOT.

heath *n* common land, moor, moorland, open country, waste land, wilderness.

heathen *adj* atheistic, barbaric, godless, idolatrous, infidel, irreligious, pagan, philistine, savage, unenlightened. ● *n* atheist, barbarian, heretic, idolater, infidel, pagan, philistine, savage, sceptic, unbeliever.

heave *vb* **1** drag, draw, haul, hoist, lift, lug, move, pull, raise, tow, tug. **2** ▷ THROW. **heave into sight** ▷ APPEAR. **heave up** ▷ VOMIT.

heaven *n* **1** after-life, Elysium, eternal rest, the hereafter, the next world, nirvana, paradise. **2** bliss, contentment, delight, ecstasy, felicity, happiness, joy, perfection, pleasure, rapture, Utopia. *Opp* HELL.

heavenly *adj* angelic, beatific, beautiful, blissful, celestial, delightful, divine, exquisite, glorious, lovely, other-worldly, *inf* out of this world, saintly, spiritual, sublime, unearthly, wonderful.

heavy *adj* **1** bulky, burdensome, compact, concentrated, dense, hefty, immovable, large, leaden, massive, ponderous, unwieldy, weighty. ▷ BIG, FAT. **2** *heavy work.* arduous, demanding, difficult, hard, exhausting, laborious, onerous, strenuous, tough. **3** *heavy rain.* penetrating, pervasive, severe, torrential. **4** *a heavy crop.* abundant, copious, laden, loaded, profuse, thick. **5** *a heavy heart.* burdened, depressed, gloomy, miserable, sorrowful. ▷ SAD. **6** *[inf]* *a heavy lecture.* deep, dull, intellectual, intense, serious, tedious, wearisome. *Opp* LIGHT. **heavy-handed** ▷ CLUMSY. **heavy-hearted** ▷ SAD.

hectic *adj* animated, boisterous, brisk, bustling, busy, chaotic, excited, feverish, frantic, frenetic, frenzied, hurried, hyperactive, lively, mad, overactive, restless, riotous, rumbustious, *inf* rushed off your feet, turbulent, wild. *Opp* LEISURELY.

hedge *n* barrier, fence, hedgerow, screen. ● *vb inf* beat about the bush, be evasive, equivocate, *inf* hum and haw, quibble, stall, temporize, waffle. **hedge in** ▷ ENCLOSE.

hedonistic *adj* epicurean, extravagant, intemperate, luxurious, pleasure-loving, self-indulgent, sensual, sybaritic, voluptuous. *Opp* PURITANICAL.

heed *vb* attend to, bear in mind, concern yourself about, consider, follow, keep to, listen to, mark, mind, note, notice, obey, observe, pay attention to, regard, take notice of. *Opp* DISREGARD.

heedful *adj* attentive, careful, concerned, considerate, mindful, observant, sympathetic, taking notice, vigilant, watchful. *Opp* HEEDLESS.

heedless *adj* blind, careless, deaf, inattentive, inconsiderate, neglectful, oblivious, reckless, regardless, thoughtless, uncaring, unconcerned, unmindful, unobservant, unsympathetic. *Opp* HEEDFUL.

heel *vb* careen, incline, lean, list, tilt, tip.

hefty *adj* beefy, brawny, bulky, burly, heavy, heavyweight, hulking, husky, large, massive, mighty, muscular, powerful, robust, rugged, solid, substantial, *inf* strapping, strong, tough. ▷ BIG. *Opp* SLIGHT.

height *n* **1** altitude, elevation, level, tallness, vertical measurement. **2** crag, fell, hill, mound, mountain, peak, prominence, ridge, summit, top. **3** *height of your career.* acme, apogee, climax, crest, culmination, extreme, high point, maximum, peak, pinnacle, zenith.

heighten vb add to, amplify, augment, boost, build up, elevate, enhance, improve, increase, intensify, lift up, magnify, make higher, maximize, raise, reinforce, sharpen, strengthen, supplement. Opp LOWER, REDUCE.

hell n **1** eternal punishment, Hades, infernal regions, lower regions, nether world, sl the other place, underworld. **2** ▷ MISERY. Opp HEAVEN.

help n advice, aid, assistance, avail, backing, benefit, boost, collaboration, contribution, cooperation, encouragement, friendship, guidance, moral support, patronage, relief, remedy, succour, support. Opp HINDRANCE. ● vb **1** abet, advise, aid, aid and abet, assist, back, befriend, be helpful, boost, collaborate, contribute, co-operate, encourage, facilitate, forward, further the interests of, inf give a hand, inf lend a hand, profit, promote, prop up, inf rally round, serve, side with, derog spoonfeed, stand by, subsidize, succour, support, take pity on. Opp HINDER. **2** linctus helps a cough. alleviate, benefit, cure, ease, improve, lessen, make easier, relieve, remedy. **3** can't help it. ▷ AVOID, PREVENT.

helper n abettor, accessory, accomplice, ally, assistant, associate, collaborator, colleague, confederate, deputy, helpmate, inf henchman, partner, inf right-hand man, second, supporter, inf willing hands.

helpful adj **1** accommodating, benevolent, caring, considerate, constructive, cooperative, favourable, friendly, helping, kind, neighbourly, obliging, practical, supportive, sympathetic, thoughtful, willing. **2** a helpful comment. advantageous, beneficial, informative, instructive, profitable, useful, valuable, worthwhile. **3** a helpful tool. convenient, easy to use, handy, manageable, practical, serviceable, useful, well designed, worth having. Opp UNHELPFUL, USELESS.

helping adj ▷ HELPFUL. ● n amount, inf dollop, plateful, portion, ration, serving, share.

helpless adj abandoned, crippled, defenceless, dependent, deserted, destitute, disabled, exposed, feeble, handicapped, impotent, incapable, in difficulties, infirm, lame, marooned, powerless, stranded, unprotected, vulnerable. Opp INDEPENDENT.

herald n **1** announcer, courier, messenger, town crier. **2** herald of spring. forerunner, harbinger, omen, precursor, sign. ● vb advertise, announce, indicate, make known, proclaim, promise, publicize. ▷ FORETELL.

herd n bunch, flock, mob, pack, swarm, throng. ▷ GROUP. ● vb assemble, collect, congregate, drive, gather, group together, round up, shepherd.

hereditary adj **1** ancestral, bequeathed, family, handed down, inherited, passed down, passed on, willed. **2** congenital, constitutional, genetic, inborn, inbred, inherent, inheritable, innate, native, natural, transmissible, transmittable.

heresy n blasphemy, dissent, idolatry, nonconformity, rebellion, inf stepping out of line, unorthodox ideas.

heretic n apostate, blasphemer, dissenter, free-thinker, iconoclast, nonconformist, rebel, renegade, unorthodox thinker. Opp BELIEVER.

heretical adj apostate, atheistic, blasphemous, dissenting, freethinking, heathen, iconoclastic, idolatrous, impious, irreligious, nonconformist, pagan, rebellious, unorthodox. Opp ORTHODOX.

heritage n birthright, culture, history, inheritance, legacy, past, tradition.

hermit n anchoress, anchorite, eremite, monk, recluse, solitary.

hero, heroine ns champion, conqueror, daredevil, exemplar, ideal, idol, luminary, protagonist, star, superman, *inf* superstar, super-woman, victor, winner.

heroic *adj* adventurous, audacious, bold, brave, chivalrous, courageous, daring, dauntless, doughty, epic, fearless, gallant, herculean, intrepid, lion-hearted, noble, selfless, staunch, steadfast, stout-hearted, super-human, unafraid, valiant, valorous. *Opp* COWARDLY.

hesitant *adj* cautious, diffident, dithering, faltering, halfhearted, halting, hesitating, indecisive, irresolute, nervous, *inf* shillyshallying, shy, stammering, stumbling, stuttering, tentative, timid, uncertain, uncommitted, undecided, underconfident, unsure, vacillating, wary, wavering. *Opp* DECISIVE, FLUENT.

hesitate *vb* **1** be hesitant, be indecisive, *inf* be in two minds, delay, demur, *inf* dilly-dally, dither, equivocate, falter, halt, hang back, haver, *inf* hum and haw, pause, put it off, *inf* shilly-shally, shrink back, teeter, temporize, think twice, vacillate, wait, waver. **2** stammer, stumble, stutter.

hesitation *n* caution, delay, diffidence, dithering, doubt, indecision, irresolution, nervousness, reluctance, *inf* shilly-shallying, uncertainty, vacillation, wavering.

hidden *adj* **1** camouflaged, concealed, covered, disguised, enclosed, invisible, obscured, out of sight, private, shrouded, *inf* under wraps, undetectable, unnoticeable, unseen, veiled. *Opp* VISIBLE. **2** *hidden meaning.* abstruse, arcane, coded, covert, cryptic, dark, esoteric, implicit, mysterious, mystical, obscure, occult, recondite, secret, unclear. *Opp* OBVIOUS.

hide *n* fur, leather, pelt, skin. ● *vb* **1** blot out, bury, camouflage, cloak, conceal, cover, curtain, disguise, eclipse, enclose, mantle, mask, obscure, put away, put out of sight, screen, secrete, shelter, shroud, veil, wrap up. **2** *go into hiding. inf* go to ground, *inf* hole up, keep hidden, *inf* lie low, lurk, shut yourself away, take

cover. **3** *hide facts.* censor, *inf* hush up, repress, silence, suppress, withhold.

hideous *adj* appalling, beastly, disgusting, dreadful, frightful, ghastly, grim, grisly, grotesque, gruesome, macabre, nauseous, odious, repellent, repulsive, revolting, shocking, sickening, terrible. ▷ UGLY. *Opp* BEAUTIFUL.

hiding-place *n* den, haven, hide, hideaway, *inf* hide-out, *inf* hideyhole, lair, refuge, retreat, sanctuary.

hierarchy *n* grading, ladder, *inf* pecking-order, ranking, scale, sequence, series, social order, system.

high *adj* **1** elevated, extending upwards, high-rise, lofty, raised, soaring, tall, towering. **2** aristocratic, chief, distinguished, eminent, exalted, important, leading, powerful, prominent, royal, top, upper. **3** *high prices.* dear, excessive, exorbitant, expensive, extravagant, outrageous, *inf* steep, unreasonable. **4** *high winds.* exceptional, extreme, great, intense, *inf* stiff, stormy, strong. **5** *a high reputation.* favourable, good, noble, respected, virtuous. **6** *high sounds.* acute, high-pitched, penetrating, piercing, sharp, shrill, soprano, squeaky, treble. *Opp* LOW.**high-and-mighty** ▷ ARROGANT. **high-class** ▷ EXCELLENT. **high-handed** ▷ ARROGANT. **high-minded** ▷ MORAL. **high-powered** ▷ POWERFUL. **high-speed** ▷ FAST. **high-spirited** ▷ LIVELY.

highbrow *adj* **1** academic, bookish, brainy, cultured, intellectual, *derog* pretentious, sophisticated. **2** *highbrow books.* classical, cultural, deep, difficult, educational, improving, serious. *Opp* LOWBROW.

highlight *n* best moment, climax, high spot, peak, top point.

hilarious *adj* boisterous, cheerful, cheering, entertaining, jolly, jovial, lively, merry, mirthful, rollicking, side-splitting, uproarious. ▷ FUNNY.

hill *n* **1** elevation, eminence, foothill, height, hillock, hillside, hummock, knoll, mound, mount, mountain, peak, prominence, ridge, summit. □ *brae, down, fell, pike, stack, tor, wold.* **2** acclivity, ascent, declivity, drop, gradient, incline, ramp, rise, slope.

hinder *vb* arrest, bar, be a hindrance to, check, curb, delay, deter, endanger, frustrate, get in the way of, hamper, handicap, hit, hold back, hold up, impede, keep back, limit, obstruct, oppose, prevent, restrain, restrict, retard, sabotage, slow down, slow up, stand in the way of, stop, thwart. *Opp* HELP.

hindrance *n* bar, barrier, burden, check, curb, deterrent, difficulty, disadvantage, *inf* drag, drawback, encumbrance, handicap, hitch, impediment, inconvenience, limitation, obstacle, obstruction, restraint, restriction, snag, stumbling-block. *Opp* HELP.

hinge *n* articulation, joint, pivot. ● *vb* depend, hang, rest, revolve, turn.

hint *n* **1** allusion, clue, idea, implication, indication, inkling, innuendo, insinuation, pointer, shadow, sign, suggestion, tip, *inf* tip-off. **2** *a hint of herbs.* dash, taste, tinge, touch, trace, undertone, whiff. ● *vb* allude, give a hint, imply, indicate, insinuate, intimate, mention, suggest, tip off.

hire *vb* book, charter, employ, engage, lease, pay for the use of, rent, sign on, take on. **hire out** lease out, let, rent out, take payment for.

hiss *vb* buzz, fizz, purr, rustle, sizzle, whir, whizz.

historic *adj* celebrated, eminent, epoch-making, famed, famous, important, momentous, notable, outstanding, remarkable, renowned, significant, well-known. *Opp* INSIGNIFICANT.

historical *adj* actual, authentic, documented, factual, real, real-life, recorded, true, verifiable. *Opp* FICTITIOUS.

history *n* **1** antiquity, bygone days, heritage, historical events, the old days, the past. **2** annals, biography, chronicles, diaries, narratives, records.

histrionic *adj* actorish, dramatic, theatrical.

hit *n* **1** blow, bull's eye, collision, impact, shot, stroke. **2** success, triumph, *inf* winner. ● *vb* **1** bang, bash, baste, batter, beat, belt, biff, birch, box, bludgeon, buffet, bump, butt, cane, cannon into, clap, clip, clobber, clock, clonk, clout, club, collide with, cosh, crack, crash into, cudgel, cuff, dash, deliver a blow, drive, elbow, flagellate, flail, flick, flip, flog, hammer, head, head-butt, impact, jab, jar, jog, kick, knee, knock, lam, lambaste, lash, nudge, pat, poke, pound, prod, pummel, punch, punt, putt, ram, rap, run into, scourge, slam, slap, slog, slosh, slug, smack, smash, smite, sock, spank, stab, strike, stub, swat, swipe, tan, tap, thrash, thump, thwack, wallop, whack, wham, whip. **2** *The slump hit sales.* affect, attack, bring disaster to, check, damage, do harm to, harm, have an effect on, hinder, hurt, make suffer, ruin. **hit back** ▷ RETALIATE. **hit on** ▷ DISCOVER.

hoard *n* accumulation, cache, collection, fund, heap, pile, reserve, stockpile, store, supply, treasure-trove. ● *vb* accumulate, amass, assemble, collect, gather, keep, lay in, lay up, mass, pile up, put away, put by, save, stockpile, store, treasure. *Opp* SQUANDER, USE.

hoarse *adj* croaking, grating, gravelly, growling, gruff, harsh, husky, rasping, raucous, rough, throaty.

hoax *n* cheat, *inf* con, confidence trick, deception, fake, fraud, humbug, imposture, joke, *inf* leg-pull, practical joke, spoof, swindle, trick. ● *vb* bluff, cheat, *inf* con, cozen, deceive, defraud, delude, dupe, fool, gull, *inf* have on, hoodwink, lead on, mislead, *inf* pull someone's leg, swindle, *inf* take for a ride, take in, trick. ▷ TEASE.

hoaxer *n inf* con-man, impostor, joker, practical joker, trickster. ▷ CHEAT.

hobble *vb* dodder, falter, limp, shuffle, stagger, stumble, totter. ▷ WALK.

hobby *n* amateur interest, avocation, diversion, interest, pastime, pursuit, recreation, relaxation, sideline.

hoist *n* block-and-tackle, crane, davit, jack, lift, pulley, tackle, winch, windlass. ● *vb* elevate, heave, lift, pull up, raise, winch up.

hold *n* **1** clasp, clutch, foothold, grasp, grip, purchase, toehold. **2** *a hold over someone.* ascendancy, authority, control, dominance, influence, leverage, mastery, power, sway. ● *vb* **1** bear, carry, catch, clasp, clench, cling to, clutch, cradle, embrace, enfold, grasp, grip, hang on to, have, hug, keep, possess, retain, seize, support, take. **2** *hold a suspect.* arrest, confine, coop up, detain, imprison, keep in custody, restrain. **3** *hold an opinion.* believe in, stick to, subscribe to, swear to. **4** *hold a pose.* continue, keep up, maintain, occupy, preserve, retain, sustain. **5** *hold a party.* celebrate, conduct, convene, have, organize. **6** *jug holds a litre.* contain, enclose, have a capacity of, include. **7** *My offer holds.* be unaltered, carry on, continue, endure, hold out, keep on, last, persist, remain unchanged, stay. **hold back** ▷ RESTRAIN. **hold forth** ▷ SPEAK, TALK. **hold out** ▷ OFFER, PERSIST. **hold over, hold up** ▷ DELAY. **hold-up** ▷ ROBBERY.

hole *n* **1** abyss, burrow, cave, cavern, cavity, chamber, chasm, crater, dent, depression, excavation, fault, fissure, hollow, indentation, niche, pit, pocket, pot-hole, recess, shaft, tunnel. **2** aperture, breach, break, chink, crack, cut, eyelet, fissure, gap, gash, leak, opening, orifice, perforation, puncture, rip, slit, slot, split, tear, vent.

holiday *n* bank holiday, break, day off, furlough, half-term, leave, recess, respite, rest, sabbatical, time off, vacation.

holiness *n* devotion, divinity, faith, godliness, piety, *derog* religiosity, sacredness, saintliness, *derog* sanctimoniousness, sanctity, venerability.

hollow *adj* **1** empty, unfilled, vacant, void. **2** cavernous, concave, deep, depressed, dimpled, indented, recessed, sunken. **3** *a hollow laugh, victory.* cynical, false, futile, insincere, insubstantial, meaningless, pointless, valueless, worthless. ● *n* bowl, cave, cavern, cavity, concavity, crater, dent, depression, dimple, dint, dip, dish, excavation, furrow, hole, indentation, pit, trough. ▷ VALLEY. **hollow out** ▷ EXCAVATE.

holocaust *n* **1** conflagration, firestorm, inferno. **2** annihilation, bloodbath, destruction, devastation, extermination, genocide, massacre, pogrom.

holy *adj* **1** blessed, consecrated, dedicated, devoted, divine, hallowed, heavenly, revered, sacred, sacrosanct, venerable. **2** *holy pilgrims.* devout, faithful, God-fearing, godly, immaculate, *derog* pietistic, pious, prayerful, pure, religious, reverent, reverential, righteous, saintly, *derog* sanctimonious, sinless, unsullied. *Opp* IRRELIGIOUS.

home *n* **1** abode, accommodation, base, domicile, dwelling, dwelling-place, habitation, household, lodging, quarters, residence. ▷ HOUSE. **2** birthplace, native land. **3** *derog* institution. □ old use *almshouse*, *convalescent home*, *hospice*, *nursing-home*, old use *poorhouse*, *rest home*, *retirement home*, *retreat*, *shelter*.

homeless *adj* abandoned, destitute, dispossessed, down-and-out, evicted, exiled, forsaken, itinerant, nomadic, outcast, rootless, unhoused, vagrant, wandering. ● *plur n* beggars, refugees, tramps, vagabonds, vagrants.

homely *adj* comfortable, congenial, cosy, easygoing, friendly, informal, intimate, modest, natural, relaxed, simple, unaffected, unassuming, unpretentious, unsophisticated. ▷ FAMILIAR. *Opp* FORMAL, SOPHISTICATED.

homogeneous *adj* akin, alike, comparable, compatible, consistent, identical, indistinguishable, matching,

similar, uniform, unvarying. *Opp* DIF-
FERENT.

homosexual *adj inf* camp, gay, lesbian, *derog* queer.

honest *adj* above-board, blunt, candid, conscientious, direct, equitable,
fair, forthright, frank, genuine, good,
honourable, impartial, incorruptible,
just, law-abiding, legal, legitimate,
moral, *inf* on the level, open, outspoken, plain, principled, pure, reliable, respectable, scrupulous,
sincere, square (*deal*), straight,
straightforward, trustworthy, trusty,
truthful, unbiased, unequivocal,
unprejudiced, upright, veracious, virtuous. *Opp* DISHONEST.

honesty *n* **1** fairness, goodness,
honour, integrity, morality, probity,
rectitude, reliability, scrupulousness,
sense of justice, trustworthiness,
truthfulness, uprightness, veracity,
virtue. *Opp* DECEIT. **2** bluntness,
candour, directness, frankness, out-
spokenness, plainness, sincerity,
straightforwardness.

honorary *adj* nominal, titular, unofficial, unpaid.

honour *n* **1** acclaim, accolade, compliment, credit, esteem, fame, good
name, *inf* kudos, regard, renown,
reputation, repute, respect, reverence, veneration. **2** distinction, duty,
importance, pleasure, privilege. **3** *a
sense of honour*. decency, dignity, honesty, integrity, loyalty, morality,
nobility, principle, rectitude, righteousness, sincerity, uprightness,
virtue. ● *vb* acclaim, admire, applaud,
celebrate, commemorate, commend,
dignify, esteem, give credit to,
glorify, pay homage to, pay respects
to, pay tribute to, praise, remember,
respect, revere, reverence, show
respect to, sing the praises of, value,
venerate, worship.

honourable *adj* admirable, chivalrous, creditable, decent, estimable,
ethical, fair, good, high-minded, irreproachable, just, law-abiding, loyal,
moral, noble, principled, proper,
reputable, respectable, respected,
righteous, sincere, *inf* straight, trust-

worthy, trusty, upright, venerable,
virtuous, worthy. ▷ HONEST. *Opp* DIS-
HONOURABLE.

hoodwink *vb* bluff, cheat, *inf* con,
cozen, deceive, defraud, delude,
dupe, fool, gull, *inf* have on, hoax,
lead on, mislead, *inf* pull the wool
over someone's eyes, swindle, *inf*
take for a ride, take in, trick.

hook *n* barb, crook, peg. ▷ FASTENER.
● *vb* **1** ▷ FASTEN. **2** *hook a fish*. capture,
catch, take.

hooligan *n* bully, delinquent, hoodlum, lout, mugger, rough, ruffian,
inf tearaway, thug, tough, troublemaker, vandal, *inf* yob. ▷ CRIMINAL.

hoop *n* band, circle, girdle, loop, ring.

hop *vb* bound, caper, dance, jump,
leap, limp, prance, skip, spring, vault.

hope *n* **1** ambition, aspiration, craving, day-dream, desire, dream, longing, wish, yearning. **2** *hope of better
weather*. assumption, conviction,
expectation, faith, likelihood, optimism, promise, prospect. ● *vb inf*
anticipate, aspire, be hopeful,
believe, contemplate, count on,
desire, expect, foresee, have faith,
have hope, look forward (to), trust,
wish. *Opp* DESPAIR.

hopeful *adj* **1** assured, confident,
expectant, optimistic, positive, sanguine. **2** *hopeful signs*. auspicious,
cheering, encouraging, favourable,
heartening, promising, propitious,
reassuring. *Opp* HOPELESS.

hopefully *adv* **1** confidently, ex-
pectantly, optimistically, with hope.
2 [*inf*] *Hopefully I'll be better tomorrow*.
all being well, most likely, probably.
[Many think this use of *hopefully* is
wrong]

hopeless *adj* **1** defeatist, demoral-
ized, despairing, desperate, disconsolate, fatalist, negative, pessimistic,
resigned, wretched. **2** *a hopeless situation*. daunting, depressing, impossible, incurable, irremediable,
irreparable, irreversible. **3** [*inf*] *He's
hopeless!* feeble, inadequate, incompetent, inefficient, poor, useless,
weak, worthless. *Opp* HOPEFUL.

horde n band, crowd, gang, mob, swarm, throng, tribe. ▷ GROUP.

horizontal adj even, flat, level, lying down, prone, prostrate, supine. Opp VERTICAL.

horrible adj awful, beastly, disagreeable, dreadful, ghastly, hateful, horrid, loathsome, macabre, nasty, objectionable, odious, offensive, revolting, terrible, unkind. ▷ HORRIFIC, UNPLEASANT. Opp PLEASANT.

horrific adj appalling, atrocious, blood-curdling, disgusting, dreadful, frightening, frightful, grisly, gruesome, hair-raising, harrowing, horrendous, horrifying, nauseating, shocking, sickening, spine-chilling, unacceptable, unnerving, unthinkable.

horrify vb alarm, appal, disgust, frighten, harrow, nauseate, outrage, scare, shock, sicken, stun, terrify, unnerve. **horrifying** ▷ HORRIFIC.

horror n **1** abhorrence, antipathy, aversion, detestation, disgust, dislike, dismay, distaste, dread, fear, hatred, loathing, panic, repugnance, revulsion, terror. **2** awfulness, frightfulness, ghastliness, gruesomeness, hideousness.

horse n bronco, carthorse, old use charger, cob, colt, filly, foal, childish gee-gee, gelding, hack, hunter, old use jade, mare, mount, mule, mustang, inf nag, old use palfrey, piebald, pony, race-horse, roan, skewbald, stallion, steed, warhorse.

horseman, horsewoman ns cavalryman, equestrian, jockey, rider.

hospitable adj cordial, courteous, generous, gracious, receptive, sociable, welcoming. ▷ FRIENDLY. Opp INHOSPITABLE.

hospital n clinic, convalescent home, dispensary, health centre, hospice, infirmary, medical centre, nursing home, sanatorium, sick bay.

hospitality n **1** accommodation, catering, entertainment. **2** cordiality, courtesy, friendliness, generosity, sociability, warmth, welcome.

host n **1** army, crowd, mob, multitude, swarm, throng, troop. ▷ GROUP. **2** ▷ COMPÈRE.

hostage n captive, pawn, prisoner, surety.

hostile adj **1** aggressive, antagonistic, antipathetic, attacking, averse, bellicose, belligerent, combative, confrontational, ill-disposed, inhospitable, inimical, malevolent, militant, opposed, oppressive, pugnacious, resentful, rival, unfriendly, unsympathetic, unwelcoming, warlike, warring. ▷ ANGRY. Opp FRIENDLY. **2** hostile conditions. adverse, contrary, opposing, unfavourable, unhelpful, unpropitious. ▷ BAD. Opp FAVOURABLE.

hostility n aggression, animosity, animus, antagonism, bad feeling, belligerence, confrontation, dissension, enmity, estrangement, friction, incompatibility, malevolence, malice, opposition, pugnacity, rancour, resentment, strife, unfriendliness. ▷ HATRED. Opp FRIENDSHIP. **hostilities** ▷ WAR.

hot adj **1** baking, blistering, boiling, burning, close, fiery, flaming, humid, oppressive, inf piping, red-hot, roasting, scalding, scorching, searing, sizzling, steamy, stifling, sultry, summery, sweltering, thermal, torrid, tropical, warm, white-hot. **2** hot temper. ardent, eager, emotional, excited, fervent, fervid, feverish, fierce, heated, hotheaded, impatient, impetuous, inflamed, intense, passionate, violent. **3** hot taste. acrid, biting, gingery, peppery, piquant, pungent, spicy, strong. Opp COLD, COOL. **hot-tempered** ▷ BAD-TEMPERED. **hot under the collar** ▷ ANGRY.

hotel n guest house, hostel, joc hostelry, inn, lodge, motel, pension. ▷ ACCOMMODATION.

hound n ▷ DOG. ● vb annoy, badger, chase, harass, harry, hunt, nag, persecute, pester, pursue.

house n old use abode, domicile, dwelling, dwelling-place, habitation, home, homestead, house-hold, place, residence. □ *apartment*, inf *back-to-back*, *bungalow*, *chalet*, *cottage*, *council house*, *croft*, *detached house*, *farmhouse*, *flat*, *grange*, *hovel*, *homestead*, *hut*, *igloo*, *lodge*, *maisonette*, *manor*, *manse*, *mansion*, *penthouse*, inf *prefab*, *public house*, *rectory*, inf *semi*, *semi-detached house*, *shack*, *shanty*, *terraced house*, *thatched house*, inf *two-up two-down*, *vicarage*, *villa*. ● *vb* accommodate, billet, board, domicile, harbour, keep, lodge, place, inf put up, quarter, shelter, take in.

household *n* establishment, family, home, ménage, inf set-up.

hovel *n* cottage, inf dump, hole, hut, shack, shanty, shed.

hover *vb* **1** be suspended, drift, float, flutter, fly, hang, poise. **2** be indecisive, dally, dither, inf hang about, hang around, hesitate, linger, loiter, pause, vacillate, wait about, waver.

howl *vb* bay, bellow, cry, roar, shout, ululate, wail, yowl.

hub *n* axis, centre, core, focal point, focus, heart, middle, nucleus, pivot.

huddle *n* ▷ GROUP. ● *vb* **1** cluster, converge, crowd, flock, gather, group, heap, herd, jam, jumble, pile, press, squeeze, swarm, throng. **2** cuddle, curl up, hug, nestle, snuggle.

hue *n* cast, complexion, dye, nuance, shade, tincture, tinge, tint, tone. ▷ COLOUR. **hue and cry** ▷ OUTCRY.

hug *vb* clasp, cling to, crush, cuddle, embrace, enfold, fold in your arms, hold close, huddle together, nestle together, nurse, snuggle against, squeeze.

huge *adj* **1** Brobdingnagian, colossal, elephantine, enormous, gargantuan, giant, gigantic, inf hulking, immense, imposing, impressive, inf jumbo, majestic, mammoth, massive, mighty, inf monster, monstrous, monumental, mountainous, prodigious, stupendous, titanic, towering, inf tremendous, vast, weighty, inf whopping. ▷ BIG. **2** *huge number.* ▷ INFINITE. *Opp* SMALL.

hulk *n* **1** body, carcass, frame, hull, shell, wreck. **2** *a clumsy hulk.* lout, lump, oaf.

hulking *adj* awkward, bulky, cumbersome, heavy, ungainly, unwieldy. ▷ BIG, CLUMSY.

hull *n* body, framework, structure.

hum *vb* buzz, drone, murmur, purr, sing, thrum, vibrate, whirr. **hum and haw** ▷ HESITATE.

human *adj* **1** anthropoid, hominid, hominoid, mortal. **2** *human feeling.* kind, rational, reasonable, sensible, sensitive, sympathetic, thoughtful. ▷ HUMANE. *Opp* INHUMAN. **human beings** folk, humanity, mankind, men and women, mortals, people.

humane *adj* altruistic, benevolent, charitable, civilized, compassionate, feeling, forgiving, good, human, humanitarian, kind-hearted, loving, magnanimous, merciful, philanthropic, pitying, refined, sympathetic, tender, understanding, unselfish, warm-hearted. ▷ KIND. *Opp* INHUMANE.

humble *adj* **1** deferential, docile, meek, modest, *derog* obsequious, polite, reserved, respectful, self-effacing, *derog* servile, submissive, subservient, *derog* sycophantic, unassertive, unassuming, unostentatious, unpresuming, unpretentious. *Opp* PROUD. **2** *humble birth.* base, commonplace, ignoble, inferior, insignificant, low, lowly, mean, obscure, ordinary, plebeian, poor, simple, undistinguished, unimportant, unprepossessing, unremarkable. ● *vb* ▷ HUMILIATE.

humid *adj* clammy, damp, dank, moist, muggy, steamy, sticky, sultry, sweaty.

humiliate *vb* abase, abash, break, break someone's spirit, bring someone down, chagrin, chasten, crush, deflate, degrade, demean, discredit, disgrace, embarrass, humble, make someone ashamed, inf make someone eat humble pie, inf make someone feel small, mortify, inf put someone down, inf put someone in his/her place, shame, inf show someone up, inf take someone down a peg. **humiliating** ▷ SHAMEFUL.

humiliation

humiliation *n* abasement, chagrin, degradation, discredit, disgrace, dishonour, embarrassment, ignominy, indignity, loss of face, mortification, obloquy, shame.

humility *n* deference, humbleness, lowliness, meekness, modesty, self-abasement, self-effacement, *derog* servility, shyness, unpretentiousness. *Opp* PRIDE.

humorous *adj* absurd, amusing, comic, comical, diverting, droll, entertaining, facetious, farcical, funny, hilarious, *inf* hysterical, ironic, jocose, jocular, *inf* killing, laughable, merry, *inf* priceless, risible, sarcastic, sardonic, satirical, *inf* side-splitting, slapstick, uproarious, waggish, whimsical, witty, zany. *Opp* SERIOUS.

humour *n* **1** absurdity, badinage, banter, comedy, drollness, facetiousness, fun, incongruity, irony, jesting, jocularity, jokes, joking, merriment, quips, raillery, repartee, satire, *inf* sense of fun, waggishness, wit, witticism, wittiness. **2** *in a good humour.* disposition, frame of mind, mood, spirits, state of mind, temper.

hump *n* **1** bulge, bump, curve, growth, hunch, knob, lump, node, projection, protrusion, protuberance, swelling, tumescence. **2** *hump in the ground.* barrow, hillock, hummock, mound, rise, tumulus. ● *vb* **1** arch, bend, crook, curl, curve, hunch, raise. **2** *hump a load.* drag, heave, hoist, lift, lug, raise, shoulder.

hunch *n* **1** ▷ HUMP. **2** feeling, guess, idea, impression, inkling, intuition, premonition, presentiment, suspicion. ● *vb* arch, bend, crook, curl, curve, huddle, hump, raise, shrug.

hunger *n* **1** appetite, craving, greed, ravenousness, voracity. **2** deprivation, famine, lack of food, malnutrition, starvation, want. ● *vb* ▷ DESIRE.

hungry *adj* aching, avid, covetous, craving, eager, emaciated, famished, famishing, greedy, longing, *inf* peckish, ravenous, starved, starving, underfed, undernourished, voracious.

hunt *n* chase, pursuit, quest, search. ▷ HUNTING. ● *vb* **1** chase, course, dog, ferret, hound, poach, pursue, stalk, track, trail. **2** *hunt for lost property.* *inf* check out, enquire after, ferret out, look for, rummage, search for, seek, trace, track down.

hunter *n* huntsman, huntswoman, predator, stalker, trapper.

hunting *n* blood-sports, coursing, poaching, stalking, trapping.

hurdle *n* **1** barricade, barrier, fence, hedge, jump, obstacle, wall. **2** bar, check, complication, difficulty, handicap, hindrance, impediment, obstruction, problem, restraint, snag, stumbling block.

hurl *vb* cast, catapult, chuck, dash, fire, fling, heave, launch, *inf* let fly, pelt, pitch, project, propel, send, shy, sling, throw, toss.

hurricane *n* cyclone, storm, tempest, tornado, typhoon, whirlwind.

hurry *n* ▷ HASTE. ● *vb* **1** *inf* belt, *inf* buck up, chase, dash, dispatch, *inf* fly, *inf* get a move on, hasten, hurtle, hustle, make haste, move quickly, rush, *inf* shift, speed, *inf* step on it, work faster. **2** *hurry a process.* accelerate, expedite, press on with, quicken, speed up. *Opp* DELAY. **hurried** ▷ HASTY.

hurt *vb* **1** ache, be painful, burn, pinch, smart, sting, suffer pain, throb, tingle. **2** *hurt physically.* abuse, afflict, agonize, bruise, cause pain to, cripple, cut, disable, injure, maim, misuse, mutilate, torture, wound. **3** *hurt mentally.* affect, aggrieve, be hurtful to, *inf* cut to the quick, depress, distress, grieve, humiliate, insult, offend, pain, sadden, torment, upset. **4** *hurt things.* damage, harm, impair, mar, ruin, sabotage, spoil.

hurtful *adj* biting, cruel, cutting, damaging, derogatory, detrimental, distressing, hard to bear, harmful, injurious, malicious, nasty, painful, sarcastic, scathing, spiteful, uncharitable, unkind, upsetting, vicious, wounding. *Opp* KIND.

hurtle *vb* charge, chase, dash, fly, plunge, race, rush, shoot, speed, tear.

hush *int* be quiet! be silent! *inf* hold your tongue! *sl* pipe down! *inf* shut up! ● *vb* ▷ SILENCE. **hush up** ▷ SUP-PRESS.

hustle *vb* **1** bustle, hasten, hurry, jostle, rush, scamper, scurry. **2** *hustled me away.* coerce, compel, force, push, shove, thrust.

hut *n* cabin, den, hovel, lean-to, shack, shanty, shed, shelter.

hybrid *n* amalgam, combination, composite, compound, cross, cross-breed, half-breed, mixture, mongrel.

hygiene *n* cleanliness, health, sanit-ariness, sanitation, wholesomeness.

hygienic *adj* aseptic, clean, disin-fected, germ-free, healthy, pure, salu-brious, sanitary, sterile, sterilized, unpolluted, wholesome. *Opp* UN-HEALTHY.

hypnotic *adj* fascinating, irresistible, magnetic, mesmeric, mesmerizing, sleep-inducing, soothing, soporific, spellbinding.

hypnotize *vb* bewitch, captivate, cast a spell over, dominate, enchant, entrance, fascinate, gain power over, magnetize, mesmerize, *inf* put to sleep, spellbind, *inf* stupefy.

hypocrisy *n* cant, deceit, deception, double-dealing, double standards, double-talk, double-think, duplicity, falsity, *inf* humbug, inconsistency, insincerity.

hypocritical *adj* deceptive, double-dealing, double-faced, duplicitous, false, inconsistent, insincere, Phar-isaical, *inf* phoney, self-deceiving, self-righteous, *inf* two-faced.

hypothesis *n* conjecture, guess, pos-tulate, premise, proposition, specu-lation, supposition, theory, thesis.

hypothetical *adj* academic, alleged, assumed, conjectural, groundless, imaginary, presumed, putative, specu-lative, supposed, suppositional, theo-retical, unreal.

hysteria *n* frenzy, hysterics, mad-ness, mania, panic.

hysterical *adj* berserk, beside your-self, crazed, delirious, demented, dis-traught, frantic, frenzied, irrational, mad, overemotional, rabid, raving, uncontrollable, wild.

I

ice *n* black ice, floe, frost, glacier, iceberg, icicle, rime.

icy *adj* **1** arctic, chilling, freezing, frosty, frozen, glacial, polar, Siberian. ▷ COLD. **2** *icy roads.* glassy, slippery, *inf* slippy, slithery.

idea *n* **1** abstraction, attitude, belief, concept, conception, conjecture, construct, conviction, doctrine, hypothesis, notion, opinion, philosophy, principle, sentiment, teaching, tenet, theory, thought, view. **2** *a bright idea.* brainwave, design, fancy, guess, inspiration, plan, proposal, scheme, suggestion. **3** *idea of a poem.* intention, meaning, point. **4** *idea of what to expect.* clue, guidelines, impression, inkling, intimation, model, pattern, perception, suspicion, vision.

ideal *adj* **1** best, classic, complete, excellent, faultless, model, optimum, perfect, supreme, unsurpassable. **2** *an ideal world.* chimerical, dream, hypothetical, illusory, imaginary, unattainable, unreal, Utopian, visionary. ● *n* **1** acme, criterion, epitome, exemplar, model, paragon, pattern, standard. **2** ▷ PRINCIPLE.

idealistic *adj* high-minded, impractical, over-optimistic, quixotic, romantic, starry-eyed, unrealistic. *Opp* REALISTIC.

idealize *vb* apotheosize, deify, exalt, glamorize, glorify, *inf* put on a pedestal, romanticize. ▷ IDOLIZE.

identical *adj* alike, comparable, congruent, corresponding, duplicate, equal, equivalent, indistinguishable, interchangeable, like, matching, the same, similar, twin. *Opp* DIFFERENT.

identifiable *adj* detectable, discernible, distinctive, distinguishable, familiar, known, named, noticeable, perceptible, recognizable, unmistakable. *Opp* UNIDENTIFIABLE.

identify *vb* **1** distinguish, label, mark, name, pick out, pinpoint, *inf* put a name to, recognize, single out, specify, spot. **2** *identify an illness.* detect, diagnose, discover. **identify with** empathize with, feel for, *inf* put yourself in the shoes of, relate to, sympathize with.

identity *n* **1** *inf* ID, name. **2** character, distinctiveness, individuality, nature, particularity, personality, selfhood, singularity, uniqueness.

ideology *n* assumptions, beliefs, creed, convictions, ideas, philosophy, principles, tenets, theories, underlying attitudes.

idiom *n* argot, cant, choice of words, dialect, expression, jargon, language, manner of speaking, parlance, phrase, phraseology, phrasing, turn of phrase, usage.

idiomatic *adj* colloquial, natural, vernacular, well-phrased.

idiosyncrasy *n* characteristic, eccentricity, feature, habit, individuality, mannerism, oddity, peculiarity, quirk, trait.

idiosyncratic *adj* characteristic, distinctive, eccentric, individual, odd, peculiar, personal, quirky, singular, unique. *Opp* COMMON.

idiot *n* [*most synonyms inf*] ass, blockhead, bonehead, booby, chump, clot, cretin, dim-wit, dolt, dope, duffer, dumb-bell, dummy, dunce, dunderhead, fat-head, fool, half-wit, ignoramus, imbecile, moron, nincompoop, ninny, nitwit, simpleton, twerp, twit.

idiotic *adj* absurd, asinine, crazy, foolish, half-witted, imbecile, insane, irrational, mad, moronic, nonsensical, ridiculous, senseless. ▷ STUPID. Opp SENSIBLE.

idle adj **1** dormant, inactive, inoperative, in retirement, not working, redundant, retired, unemployed, unoccupied, unproductive, unused. **2** apathetic, good-for-nothing, indolent, lackadaisical, lazy, shiftless, slothful, slow, sluggish, torpid, uncommitted, work-shy. **3** idle speculation. casual, frivolous, futile, pointless, worthless. Opp BUSY. ● vb be lazy, dawdle, do nothing, inf hang about, inf kill time, laze, loaf, loll, lounge about, inf mess about, potter, slack, stagnate, take it easy, vegetate. Opp WORK.

idler n inf good-for-nothing, inf layabout, inf lazybones, loafer, malingerer, shirker, inf skiver, slacker, sluggard, wastrel.

idol n **1** deity, effigy, fetish, god, graven image, icon, statue. **2** pop idol. celebrity, inf darling, favourite, hero, inf pin-up, star, inf superstar.

idolize vb adore, adulate, hero-worship, lionize, look up to, revere, reverence, venerate, worship. ▷ IDEALIZE.

idyllic adj Arcadian, bucolic, charming, delightful, happy, idealized, lovely, pastoral, peaceful, perfect, picturesque, rustic, unspoiled.

ignite vb burn, catch fire, fire, kindle, light, set alight, set on fire, spark off, touch off.

ignoble adj base, churlish, cowardly, despicable, disgraceful, dishonourable, infamous, low, mean, selfish, shabby, uncharitable, unchivalrous, unworthy. Opp NOBLE.

ignorance n inexperience, innocence, unawareness, unconsciousness, unfamiliarity. ▷ STUPIDITY. Opp KNOWLEDGE.

ignorant adj **1** ill-informed, innocent, lacking knowledge, oblivious, unacquainted, unaware, unconscious, unfamiliar (with), uninformed, unwitting. **2** benighted, inf clueless, illiterate, uncouth, uncultivated, uneducated, unenlightened, unlettered, unscholarly, unsophist-

icated. ▷ IMPOLITE, STUPID. Opp CLEVER, KNOWLEDGEABLE.

ignore vb disobey, disregard, leave out, miss out, neglect, omit, overlook, pass over, reject, inf shut your eyes to, skip, slight, snub, take no notice of, inf turn a blind eye to.

ill adj **1** ailing, bad, bedridden, bilious, inf dicky, diseased, feeble, frail, inf funny, inf groggy, indisposed, infected, infirm, invalid, nauseated, nauseous, inf off-colour, inf out of sorts, pasty, poorly, queasy, queer, inf seedy, sick, sickly, suffering, inf under the weather, unhealthy, unwell, valetudinarian, weak. Opp HEALTHY. **2** ill effects. bad, damaging, detrimental, evil, harmful, injurious, unfavourable, unfortunate, unlucky. Opp GOOD. ● plur n the infirm, invalids, patients, the sick, sufferers, victims. **be ill** ail, languish, sicken. **ill-advised** ▷ MISGUIDED. **ill-bred** ▷ RUDE. **ill-fated** ▷ UNLUCKY. **ill-humoured** ▷ BAD-TEMPERED. **ill-mannered** ▷ RUDE. **ill-natured** ▷ UNKIND. **ill-omened** ▷ UNLUCKY. **ill-tempered** ▷ BAD-TEMPERED. **ill-treat** ▷ MISTREAT.

illegal adj actionable, against the law, banned, black-market, criminal, felonious, forbidden, illicit, invalid, irregular, outlawed, prohibited, proscribed, unauthorized, unconstitutional, unlawful, unlicensed, wrong, wrongful. ▷ ILLEGITIMATE. Opp LEGAL.

illegible adj indecipherable, indistinct, obscure, unclear, unreadable. Opp LEGIBLE.

illegitimate adj **1** against the rules, improper, inadmissible, incorrect, invalid, irregular, spurious, unauthorized, unjustifiable, unreasonable, unwarranted. ▷ ILLEGAL. **2** bastard, born out of wedlock, natural. Opp LEGITIMATE.

illiterate adj unable to read, uneducated, unlettered. ▷ IGNORANT. Opp LITERATE.

illness n abnormality, affliction, ailment, allergy, attack, blight, inf bug, complaint, condition, contagion, disability, disease, disorder, epidemic, fever, fit, health problem, indisposition, infection, infirmity, malady, malaise, pestilence, plague, sickness, *inf* trouble, *inf* turn, *inf* upset, weakness. ▷ WOUND.

illogical *adj* absurd, fallacious, inconsequential, inconsistent, invalid, irrational, senseless, unreasonable, unsound. ▷ SILLY. *Opp* LOGICAL.

illuminate *vb* **1** brighten, decorate with lights, light up, make brighter, reveal. **2** clarify, clear up, elucidate, enlighten, explain, explicate, throw light on.

illusion *n* **1** apparition, conjuring trick, day-dream, deception, delusion, dream, fancy, fantasy, figment of the imagination, hallucination, mirage. **2** *under an illusion*. error, false impression, misapprehension, misconception, mistake.

illusory *adj* chimerical, deceptive, deluding, delusive, fallacious, false, illusive, imagined, misleading, mistaken, sham, unreal, untrue. ▷ IMAGINARY. *Opp* REAL.

illustrate *vb* **1** demonstrate, elucidate, exemplify, explain, instance, show. **2** adorn, decorate, embellish, illuminate, ornament. **3** depict, draw pictures of, picture, portray.

illustration *n* **1** case in point, demonstration, example, exemplar, instance, sample, specimen. **2** decoration, depiction, diagram, drawing, figure, photograph, picture, sketch. ▷ IMAGE.

image *n* **1** imitation, likeness, projection, reflection, representation. ▷ PICTURE. **2** carving, effigy, figure, icon, idol, statue. **3** *the image of her mother*. counterpart, double, likeness, spitting-image, twin.

imaginary *adj* fabulous, fanciful, fictional, fictitious, hypothetical, imagined, insubstantial, invented, legendary, made-up, mythical, mythological, non-existent, supposed, unreal, visionary. ▷ ILLUSORY. *Opp* REAL.

imagination *n* artistry, creativity, fancy, ingenuity, insight, inspiration, inventiveness, *inf* mind's eye, originality, resourcefulness, sensitivity, thought, vision.

imaginative *adj* artistic, attractive, beautiful, clever, creative, fanciful, ingenious, innovative, inspired, inspiring, inventive, original, poetic, resourceful, sensitive, thoughtful, unusual, visionary, vivid. *Opp* UNIMAGINATIVE.

imagine *vb* **1** conceive, conjure up, *inf* cook up, create, dream up, envisage, fancy, fantasize, invent, make believe, make up, picture, pretend, see, think of, think up, visualize. **2** assume, believe, conjecture, guess, infer, judge, presume, suppose, surmise, suspect, think.

imitate *vb* **1** ape, burlesque, caricature, counterfeit, duplicate, echo, guy, mimic, parody, parrot, portray, reproduce, satirize, send up, simulate, *inf* take off, travesty. ▷ IMPERSONATE. **2** copy, emulate, follow, match, model yourself on.

imitation *adj* artificial, copied, counterfeit, dummy, ersatz, man-made, mock, model, *inf* phoney, reproduction, sham, simulated, synthetic. *Opp* REAL. ● *n* **1** copying, duplication, emulation, mimicry, repetition. **2** *inf* clone, copy, counterfeit, dummy, duplicate, fake, forgery, impersonation, impression, likeness, *inf* mockup, model, parody, reflection, replica, reproduction, sham, simulation, *inf* take-off, toy, travesty.

immature *adj* adolescent, babyish, backward, callow, childish, *inf* green, inexperienced, infantile, juvenile, new, puerile, undeveloped, unripe, young, youthful. *Opp* MATURE.

immediate *adj* **1** instant, instantaneous, prompt, quick, speedy, sudden, swift, unhesitating, unthinking. **2** *immediate need*. current, present, pressing, top-priority, urgent. **3** *immediate neighbours*. adjacent, close, closest, direct, near, nearest, neighbouring, next.

immediately *adv* at once, directly, forthwith, instantly, now, promptly, *inf* right away, straight away, unhesitatingly.

immense *adj* Brobdingnagian, colossal, elephantine, enormous, gargantuan, giant, gigantic, great, huge, *inf* hulking, immeasurable, imposing, impressive, incalculable, *inf* jumbo, large, mammoth, massive, mighty, *inf* monster, monstrous, monumental, mountainous, prodigious, stupendous, titanic, towering, *inf* tremendous, vast, *inf* whopping. ▷ BIG. *Opp* SMALL.

immerse *vb* bathe, dip, drench, drown, duck, dunk, inundate, lower, plunge, sink, submerge. **immersed** ▷ BUSY, INTERESTED.

immersion *n* baptism, dipping, ducking, plunge, submersion.

immigrant *n* alien, arrival, incomer, newcomer, outsider, settler.

imminent *adj* about to happen, approaching, close, coming, foreseeable, forthcoming, impending, looming, menacing, near, threatening.

immobile *adj* **1** ▷ IMMOVABLE. **2** frozen, inexpressive, inflexible, rigid. *Opp* MOBILE.

immobilize *vb* cripple, damage, disable, make immobile, paralyse, put out of action, sabotage, stop.

immoral *adj* abandoned, base, conscienceless, corrupt, debauched, degenerate, depraved, dishonest, dissipated, dissolute, evil, *inf* fast, impure, indecent, irresponsible, licentious, loose, low, profligate, promiscuous, *inf* rotten, sinful, unchaste, unethical, unprincipled, unscrupulous, vicious, villainous, wanton, wrong. ▷ WICKED. *Opp* MORAL. **immoral person** blackguard, cheat, degenerate, liar, libertine, profligate, rake, reprobate, scoundrel, sinner, villain, wrongdoer.

immortal *adj* **1** ageless, ceaseless, deathless, endless, eternal, everlasting, incorruptible, indestructible, never-ending, perpetual, sempiternal, timeless, unchanging, undying, unending, unfading. **2** *immortal beings*. divine, godlike, legendary, mythical. *Opp* MORTAL.

immortalize *vb* apotheosize, beatify, canonize, commemorate, deify, enshrine, keep alive, make immortal, make permanent, memorialize, perpetuate.

immovable *adj* **1** anchored, fast, firm, fixed, immobile, immobilized, motionless, paralysed, riveted, rooted, secure, set, settled, solid, static, stationary, still, stuck, unmoving. **2** ▷ IMMUTABLE.

immune *adj* exempt, free, immunized, inoculated, invulnerable, protected, resistant, safe, unaffected, vaccinated. *Opp* VULNERABLE.

immunize *vb* inoculate, vaccinate.

immutable *adj* constant, dependable, enduring, eternal, fixed, invariable, lasting, obdurate, permanent, perpetual, reliable, settled, stable, steadfast, unalterable, unchangeable, unswerving, unvarying. ▷ RESOLUTE. *Opp* CHANGEABLE.

impact *n* **1** bang, blow, bump, collision, concussion, contact, crash, knock, smash. **2** bearing, consequence, effect, force, impression, influence, repercussions, reverberations, shock, thrust. ● *vb* ▷ HIT.

impair *vb* cripple, damage, harm, injure, mar, ruin, spoil, weaken.

impale *vb* pierce, run through, skewer, spear, spike, spit, stab, stick, transfix.

impartial *adj* balanced, detached, disinterested, dispassionate, equitable, even-handed, fair, fair-minded, just, neutral, non-partisan, objective, open-minded, unbiased, uninvolved, unprejudiced. *Opp* BIASED.

impartiality *n* balance, detachment, disinterest, fairness, justice, neutrality, objectivity, open-mindedness. *Opp* BIAS.

impassable *adj* blocked, closed, obstructed, unusable.

impatient *adj* **1** anxious, eager, keen, impetuous, precipitate, *inf* raring. **2** agitated, chafing, edgy, fidgety, fretful, irritable, nervous, restive, restless, uneasy. **3** *an impatient manner.* abrupt, brusque, curt, hasty, intolerant, irascible, irritable, quick-tempered, short-tempered, snappish, snappy, testy. *Opp* APATHETIC, PATIENT.

impede *vb* arrest, bar, be an impediment to, check, curb, delay, deter, frustrate, get in the way of, hamper, handicap, hinder. *inf* hit, hold back, hold up, keep back, limit, obstruct, oppose, prevent, restrain, restrict, retard, sabotage, slow down, slow up, stand in the way of, stop, thwart. *Opp* HELP.

impediment *n* **1** bar, barrier, burden, check, curb, deterrent, difficulty, disadvantage, *inf* drag, drawback, encumbrance, hindrance, inconvenience, limitation, obstacle, obstruction, restraint, restriction, snag, stumbling-block. **2** ▷ HANDICAP.

impending *adj* about to happen, approaching, close, coming, foreseeable, forthcoming, imminent, looming, menacing, near, *inf* on the horizon, threatening.

impenetrable *adj* **1** dense, hard, resilient, solid, strong. ▷ IMPERVIOUS. **2** impregnable, invincible, inviolable, invulnerable, safe, secure, unassailable, unconquerable. *Opp* VULNERABLE. **3** *impenetrable language.* inaccessible, incomprehensible, inscrutable, unfathomable, *inf* unget-at-able. *Opp* ACCESSIBLE.

imperceptible *adj* faint, gradual, inappreciable, inaudible, indistinguishable, infinitesimal, insignificant, invisible, microscopic, minute, negligible, slight, small, subtle, tiny, unclear, undetectable, unnoticeable, vague. ▷ SMALL. *Opp* PERCEPTIBLE.

imperceptive *adj* impercipient, inattentive, slow, uncritical, undiscriminating, unobservant, unresponsive. ▷ STUPID. *Opp* PERCEPTIVE.

imperfect *adj* blemished, broken, chipped, cracked, damaged, defective, deficient, faulty, flawed, incomplete, incorrect, marred, partial, patchy, shop-soiled, spoilt, unfinished, wanting. *Opp* PERFECT.

imperfection *n* blemish, damage, defect, deficiency, error, failing, fault, flaw, foible, frailty, inadequacy, infirmity, peccadillo, shortcoming, weakness. *Opp* PERFECTION.

impermanent *adj* changing, destructible, ephemeral, evanescent, fleeting, momentary, passing, shifting, short-lived, temporary, transient, transitory, unstable. ▷ CHANGEABLE. *Opp* PERMANENT.

impersonal *adj* aloof, businesslike, cold, cool, correct, detached, disinterested, dispassionate, distant, formal, hard, inhuman, mechanical, objective, official, remote, stiff, unapproachable, unemotional, unfriendly, unprejudiced, unsympathetic, without emotion, wooden. *Opp* FRIENDLY.

impersonate *vb* disguise yourself as, do impressions of, dress up as, masquerade as, mimic, pass yourself off as, portray, pose as, pretend to be, *inf* take off. ▷ IMITATE.

impertinent *adj* bold, brazen, cheeky, *inf* cocky, *inf* cool, discourteous, disrespectful, forward, fresh, impolite, impudent, insolent, insubordinate, insulting, irreverent, pert, saucy. ▷ RUDE. *Opp* RESPECTFUL.

impervious *adj* **1** hermetic, impenetrable, impermeable, non-porous, solid, waterproof, water-repellent, watertight. *Opp* POROUS. **2** ▷ RESISTANT.

impetuous *adj* abrupt, careless, eager, hasty, headlong, hot-headed, impulsive, incautious, offhand, precipitate, quick, rash, reckless, speedy, spontaneous, *inf* spur-of-the-moment, *inf* tearing, thoughtless, unplanned, unpremeditated, unthinking, violent. *Opp* CAUTIOUS.

impetus *n* boost, drive, encouragement, energy, fillip, force, impulse, incentive, inspiration, momentum, motivation, power, push, spur, stimulation, stimulus, thrust.

impiety *n* blasphemy, godlessness, irreverence, profanity, sacrilege, sinfulness, ungodliness, unrighteousness, wickedness. *Opp* PIETY.

impious *adj* blasphemous, godless, irreligious, irreverent, profane, sacrilegious, sinful, unholy. ▷ WICKED. *Opp* PIOUS.

implausible *adj* doubtful, dubious, far-fetched, feeble, improbable, questionable, suspect, unconvincing, unlikely, unreasonable, weak. *Opp* PLAUSIBLE.

implement *n* apparatus, appliance, contrivance, device, gadget, instrument, mechanism, tool, utensil. ● *vb* accomplish, achieve, bring about, carry out, effect, enforce, execute, fulfil, perform, put into effect, put into practice, realize, try out.

implicate *vb* associate, concern, connect, embroil, enmesh, ensnare, entangle, entrap, include, incriminate, inculpate, involve, show involvement in.

implication *n* **1** hidden meaning, hint, innuendo, insinua-tion, overtone, purport, significance. **2** *implication in crime.* association, connection, embroilment, entanglement, inclusion, involvement.

implicit *adj* **1** hinted at, implied, indirect, inherent, insinuated, tacit, understood, undeclared, unexpressed, unsaid, unspoken, unstated, unvoiced. *Opp* EXPLICIT. **2** *implicit faith.* ▷ ABSOLUTE.

imply *vb* **1** hint, indicate, insinuate, intimate, mean, point to, suggest. **2** ▷ SIGNIFY.

impolite *adj* discourteous, disrespectful, ill-bred, ill-mannered, uncivil, vulgar. ▷ RUDE. *Opp* POLITE.

import *vb* bring in, buy in, introduce, ship in. ▷ CONVEY.

important *adj* **1** basic, big, cardinal, central, chief, consequential, critical, epoch-making, essential, foremost, fundamental, grave, historic, key, main, major, momentous, newsworthy, noteworthy, once in a lifetime, outstanding, pressing, primary, principal, rare, salient, serious, signal, significant, strategic, substantial, urgent, valuable, vital, weighty. **2** celebrated, distinguished, eminent, famous, great, high-ranking, influential, known, leading, notable, noted, powerful, pre-eminent, prominent, renowned, top-level, well-known. *Opp* UNIMPORTANT. **be important** ▷ MATTER.

importunate *adj* demanding, impatient, insistent, persistent, pressing, relentless, urgent, unremitting.

importune *vb* badger, harass, hound, pester, plague, plead with, press, solicit, urge. ▷ ASK.

impose *vb* charge with, decree, dictate, enforce, exact, fix, foist, force, inflict, insist on, introduce, lay, levy, prescribe, set. **impose on** ▷ BURDEN, EXPLOIT. **imposing** ▷ IMPRESSIVE.

impossible *adj* hopeless, impracticable, impractical, inconceivable, insoluble, insuperable, insurmountable, *inf* not on, out of the question, unachievable, unattainable, unimaginable, unobtainable, unthinkable, unviable, unworkable. *Opp* POSSIBLE.

impotent *adj* debilitated, decrepit, emasculated, enervated, helpless, inadequate, incapable, incompetent, ineffective, ineffectual, inept, infirm, powerless, unable. ▷ WEAK. *Opp* POTENT.

impracticable *adj* not feasible, unachievable, unworkable, useless. ▷ IMPOSSIBLE. *Opp* PRACTICABLE.

impractical *adj* academic, idealistic, quixotic, romantic, theoretical, unrealistic, visionary. *Opp* PRACTICAL.

imprecise *adj* ambiguous, approximate, careless, estimated, fuzzy, guessed, hazy, ill-defined, inaccurate, inexact, inexplicit, loose, *inf* sloppy, undefined, unscientific, vague, *inf* waffly, *inf* woolly. *Opp* PRECISE.

impregnable *adj* impenetrable, invincible, inviolable, invulnerable, safe, secure, strong, unassailable, unconquerable. *Opp* VULNERABLE.

impress *vb* **1** affect, be memorable to, excite, influence, inspire, leave its mark on, move, persuade, *inf* stick in the mind of, stir, touch. **2** *impress* *a mark.* emboss, engrave, imprint, mark, print, stamp.

impression n **1** effect, impact, influence, mark. **2** belief, consciousness, fancy, feeling, hunch, idea, memory, notion, opinion, recollection, sense, suspicion, view. **3** dent, hollow, imprint, indentation, mark, print, stamp. **4** imitation, impersonation, mimicry, parody, *inf* take-off. **5** *impression of a book.* edition, printing, reprint.

impressionable adj easily influenced, gullible, inexperienced, naïve, persuadable, receptive, responsive, suggestible, susceptible.

impressive adj affecting, august, awe-inspiring, awesome, commanding, distinguished, evocative, exciting, formidable, grand, *derog* grandiose, great, imposing, magnificent, majestic, memorable, moving, powerful, redoubtable, remarkable, splendid, stately, stirring, striking, touching. ▷ BIG. *Opp* INSIGNIFICANT.

imprison vb cage, commit to prison, confine, detain, gaol, immure, incarcerate, intern, jail, keep in custody, keep under house arrest, *inf* keep under lock and key, lock away, lock up, *inf* put away, remand, *inf* send down, shut in, shut up. *Opp* FREE.

imprisonment n confinement, custody, detention, duress, gaol, house arrest, incarceration, internment, jail, remand, restraint.

improbable adj absurd, doubtful, dubious, far-fetched, *inf* hard to believe, implausible, incredible, preposterous, questionable, unbelievable, unconvincing, unexpected, unlikely. *Opp* PROBABLE.

impromptu adj *inf* ad-lib, extempore, extemporized, improvised, impulsive, made-up, offhand, *inf* off the cuff, *inf* off the top of your head, *inf* on the spur of the moment, spontaneous, unplanned, unpremeditated, unprepared, unrehearsed, unscripted. ▷ IMPULSIVE. *Opp* REHEARSED.

improper adj **1** ill-judged, ill-timed, inappropriate, incorrect, infelicitous, inopportune, irregular, mistaken, out of place, uncalled-for, unfit, unseemly, unsuitable, unwarranted. ▷ WRONG. **2** ▷ INDECENT. *Opp* PROPER.

impropriety n inappropriateness, incorrectness, indecency, indelicacy, infelicity, insensitivity, irregularity, rudeness, unseemliness. ▷ OBSCENITY. *Opp* PROPRIETY.

improve vb **1** advance, develop, get better, grow, increase, *inf* look up, move on, progress, *inf* take a turn for the better. **2** *improve after illness.* convalesce, *inf* pick up, rally, recover, recuperate, revive, strengthen, *inf* turn the corner. **3** *improve your ways.* ameliorate, amend, better, correct, enhance, enrich, make better, mend, polish (up), rectify, refine, reform, revise. **4** *improve a home.* decorate, extend, modernize, rebuild, recondition, refurbish, renovate, repair, touch up, update, upgrade. *Opp* WORSEN.

improvement n **1** advance, amelioration, betterment, correction, development, enhancement, gain, increase, progress, rally, recovery, reformation, upswing, upturn. **2** *home improvements.* alteration, extension, *inf* face-lift, modernization, modification, renovation.

improvise vb **1** *inf* ad-lib, concoct, contrive, devise, invent, make do, make up, *inf* throw together. **2** extemporize, perform impromptu, play by ear, vamp.

impudent adj audacious, bold, *inf* cheeky, disrespectful, forward, *inf* fresh, impertinent, insolent, pert, presumptuous, saucy. ▷ RUDE. *Opp* RESPECTFUL.

impulse n **1** drive, force, impetus, motive, pressure, push, stimulus, thrust. **2** caprice, desire, instinct, urge, whim.

impulsive adj automatic, emotional, hare-brained, hasty, headlong, hot-headed, impetuous, instinctive, intuitive, involuntary, madcap, precipitate, rash, reckless, *inf* snap, spontaneous, *inf* spur-of-the-moment, sudden, thoughtless, unconscious, unplanned, unpremeditated, unthinking, wild. ▷ IMPROMPTU. *Opp* DELIBERATE.

impure *adj* **1** adulterated, contaminated, defiled, foul, infected, polluted, tainted, unclean, unwholesome. ▷ DIRTY. **2** ▷ INDECENT.

impurity *n* contamination, defilement, infection, pollution, taint. ▷ DIRT.

inaccessible *adj* cut off, deserted, desolate, godforsaken, impassable, impenetrable, inconvenient, isolated, lonely, *inf* off the beaten track, outlying, out of reach, out-of-the-way, private, remote, solitary, unavailable, unfrequented, *inf* unget-at-able, unobtainable, unreachable, unusable. *Opp* ACCESSIBLE.

inaccurate *adj* erroneous, fallacious, false, faulty, flawed, imperfect, imprecise, incorrect, inexact, misleading, mistaken, unfaithful, unreliable, unsound, untrue, vague, wrong. *Opp* ACCURATE.

inactive *adj* asleep, dormant, hibernating, idle, immobile, inanimate, indolent, inert, languid, lazy, lethargic, out of action, passive, quiescent, quiet, sedentary, sleepy, slothful, slow, sluggish, somnolent, torpid, unemployed, unoccupied, vegetating. *Opp* ACTIVE.

inadequate *adj* deficient, disappointing, faulty, imperfect, incompetent, incomplete, ineffective, insufficient, limited, meagre, mean, niggardly, *inf* pathetic, scanty, scarce, *inf* skimpy, sparse, unacceptable, unsatisfactory, unsuitable. *Opp* ADEQUATE.

inadvisable *adj* foolish, illadvised, imprudent, misguided, unwise. ▷ SILLY. *Opp* WISE.

inanimate *adj* cold, dead, dormant, immobile, inactive, insentient, lifeless, motionless, spiritless, unconscious. *Opp* ANIMATE.

inappropriate *adj* ill-judged, illsuited, ill-timed, improper, inapplicable, inapposite, incompatible, incongruous, incorrect, inept, inopportune, irrelevant, out of place, tactless, tasteless, unbecoming, unbefitting, unfit, unseasonable, unseemly, unsuitable, unsuited, untimely, wrong. *Opp* APPROPRIATE.

inarticulate *adj* dumb, faltering, halting, hesitant, mumbling, mute, shy, silent, speechless, stammering, stuttering, tongue-tied, voiceless. ▷ INCOHERENT. *Opp* ARTICULATE.

inattentive *adj* absent-minded, abstracted, careless, day-dreaming, distracted, dreaming, drifting, heedless, *inf* in a world of your own, lacking concentration, negligent, preoccupied, rambling, remiss, slack, unobservant, vague, wandering, wool-gathering. *Opp* ATTENTIVE.

inaudible *adj* imperceptible, mumbled, quiet, silenced, silent, stifled, undetectable, undistinguishable, unheard. ▷ FAINT. *Opp* AUDIBLE.

incapable *adj* **1** clumsy, helpless, impotent, inadequate, incompetent, ineffective, ineffectual, inept, powerless, stupid, unable, unfit, unqualified, useless, weak. *Opp* CAPABLE. **2** ▷ DRUNK.

incentive *n* bait, *inf* carrot, encouragement, enticement, impetus, incitement, inducement, lure, motivation, reward, stimulus, *inf* sweetener.

incessant *adj* ceaseless, chronic, constant, continual, continuous, endless, eternal, everlasting, interminable, never-ending, non-stop, perennial, permanent, perpetual, persistent, relentless, unbroken, unceasing, unending, unremitting. *Opp* INTERMITTENT, TEMPORARY.

incident *n* **1** affair, circumstance, episode, event, fact, happening, occasion, occurrence, proceeding. **2** *a nasty incident.* accident, confrontation, disturbance, fight, scene, upset. ▷ COMMOTION.

incidental *adj* accidental, adventitious, attendant, casual, chance, fortuitous, inessential, minor, odd, random, secondary, serendipitous, subordinate, subsidiary, unplanned. *Opp* ESSENTIAL.

incipient *adj* beginning, developing, early, embryonic, growing, new, rudimentary, starting.

incisive *adj* acute, clear, concise, cutting, decisive, direct, penetrating, percipient, precise, sharp, telling, trenchant. *Opp* VAGUE.

incite *vb* awaken, encourage, excite, fire, foment, inflame, inspire, prompt, provoke, rouse, spur on, stimulate, stir, urge, whip up, work up.

inclination *n* affection, bent, bias, disposition, fondness, habit, instinct, leaning, liking, partiality, penchant, predilection, predisposition, preference, proclivity, propensity, readiness, tendency, trend, willingness. ▷ DESIRE.

incline *n* acclivity, ascent, declivity, descent, drop, grade, gradient, hill, pitch, ramp, rise, slope. ● *vb* angle, ascend, bank, bend, bow, descend, drop, gravitate, lean, rise, slant, slope, tend, tilt, tip, veer. **inclined (to)** ▷ LIABLE.

include *vb* 1 add in, blend in, combine, comprehend, comprise, consist of, contain, embody, embrace, encompass, incorporate, involve, make room for, mix, subsume, take in. 2 *The price includes tea.* allow for, cover, take into account. *Opp* EXCLUDE.

incoherent *adj* confused, disconnected, disjointed, disordered, disorganized, garbled, illogical, incomprehensible, inconsistent, irrational, jumbled, mixed up, muddled, rambling, scrambled, unclear, unconnected, unstructured, unsystematic. ▷ INARTICULATE. *Opp* COHERENT.

incombustible *adj* fireproof, fire-resistant, flameproof, nonflammable. *Opp* COMBUSTIBLE.

income *n* earnings, gain, interest, pay, pension, proceeds, profits, receipts, return, revenue, salary, takings, wages. *Opp* EXPENSE.

incoming *adj* 1 approaching, arriving, entering, coming, landing, new,

next, returning. 2 *incoming tide.* flowing, rising. *Opp* OUTGOING.

incompatible *adj* antipathetic, at variance, clashing, conflicting, contradictory, contrasting, different, discordant, discrepant, incongruous, inconsistent, irreconcilable, mismatched, opposed, unsuited. *Opp* COMPATIBLE.

incompetent *adj* 1 bungling, clumsy, feckless, gauche, helpless, *inf* hopeless, incapable, ineffective, ineffectual, inefficient, inexperienced, maladroit, unfit, unqualified, unskilled, untrained. 2 bungled, inadequate, inexpert, unacceptable, unsatisfactory, unskilful, useless. *Opp* COMPETENT.

incomplete *adj* abbreviated, abridged, *inf* bitty, deficient, edited, expurgated, faulty, fragmentary, imperfect, insufficient, partial, selective, shortened, sketchy, unfinished, unpolished, wanting. *Opp* COMPLETE.

incomprehensible *adj* abstruse, arcane, baffling, beyond comprehension, cryptic, deep, enigmatic, esoteric, illegible, impenetrable, indecipherable, meaningless, mysterious, mystifying, obscure, opaque, *inf* over my head, perplexing, puzzling, recondite, strange, too difficult, unclear, unfathomable, unintelligible. *Opp* COMPREHENSIBLE.

inconceivable *adj* implausible, impossible to understand, incredible, *inf* mind-boggling, staggering, unbelievable, undreamed-of, unimaginable, unthinkable. *Opp* CREDIBLE.

inconclusive *adj* ambiguous, equivocal, indecisive, indefinite, interrogative, open, open-ended, questionable, uncertain, unconvincing, unresolved, *inf* up in the air. *Opp* CONCLUSIVE.

incongruous *adj* clashing, conflicting, contrasting, discordant, ill-matched, ill-suited, inappropriate, incompatible, inconsistent, irreconcilable, odd, out of keeping, out of place, surprising, uncoordinated, unsuited. ▷ ABSURD. *Opp* COMPATIBLE.

inconsiderate adj careless, cruel, heedless, insensitive, intolerant, negligent, rude, self-centred, selfish, tactless, thoughtless, uncaring, unconcerned, unfriendly, ungracious, unhelpful, unkind, unsympathetic, unthinking. Opp CONSIDERATE.

inconsistent adj capricious, changeable, erratic, fickle, inconstant, patchy, unpredictable, unreliable, unstable, inf up-and-down, variable. ▷ INCOMPATIBLE. Opp CONSISTENT.

inconspicuous adj camouflaged, concealed, discreet, hidden, insignificant, in the background, invisible, modest, ordinary, out of sight, plain, restrained, retiring, self-effacing, small, unassuming, unobtrusive, unostentatious. Opp CONSPICUOUS.

inconvenience n annoyance, bother, discomfort, disruption, drawback, encumbrance, hindrance, impediment, irritation, nuisance, trouble. ● vb annoy, bother, discommode, disturb, incommode, irk, irritate, inf put out, trouble.

inconvenient adj annoying, awkward, bothersome, cumbersome, difficult, embarrassing, ill-timed, inopportune, irksome, irritating, tiresome, troublesome, unsuitable, untimely, untoward, unwieldy. Opp CONVENIENT.

incorporate vb admit, combine, comprehend, comprise, consist of, contain, embody, embrace, encompass, include, involve, mix in, subsume, take in, take into account, unite. Opp EXCLUDE.

incorrect adj erroneous, fallacious, false, faulty, imprecise, improper, inaccurate, inexact, mendacious, misinformed, misleading, mistaken, specious, untrue. Opp CORRECT.

incorrigible adj confirmed, inf dyed-in-the-wool, habitual, hardened, inf hopeless, impenitent, incurable, inveterate, irredeemable, obdurate, shameless, unalterable, unreformable, unrepentant. ▷ WICKED.

incorruptible adj 1 honest, honourable, just, moral, sound, inf straight, true, trustworthy, unbribable, upright. Opp CORRUPT. 2 ▷ EVERLASTING.

increase n addition, amplification, augmentation, boost, build-up, crescendo, development, enlargement, escalation, expansion, extension, gain, growth, increment, inflation, intensification, proliferation, rise, spread, upsurge, upturn. ● vb 1 add to, advance, amplify, augment, boost, broaden, build up, develop, enlarge, expand, extend, improve, lengthen, magnify, make bigger, maximize, multiply, prolong, put up, raise, inf step up, strengthen, stretch, swell, widen. 2 escalate, gain, get bigger, grow, intensify, proliferate, inf snowball, spread, wax. Opp DECREASE.

incredible adj beyond belief, far-fetched, implausible, impossible, improbable, inconceivable, miraculous, surprising, unbelievable, unconvincing, unimaginable, unlikely, untenable, unthinkable. ▷ EXTRAORDINARY. Opp CREDIBLE.

incredulous adj disbelieving, distrustful, doubtful, dubious, mistrustful, questioning, sceptical, suspicious, unbelieving, uncertain, unconvinced. Opp CREDULOUS.

incriminate vb accuse, blame, charge, embroil, implicate, inculpate, indict, involve, inf point the finger at. Opp EXCUSE.

incur vb earn, expose yourself to, get, lay yourself open to, provoke, run up, suffer.

incurable adj 1 fatal, hopeless, inoperable, irremediable, irreparable, terminal, untreatable. Opp CURABLE. 2 ▷ INCORRIGIBLE.

indebted adj old use beholden, bound, grateful, obliged, thankful, under an obligation.

indecent adj inf blue, coarse, crude, dirty, immodest, impolite, improper, impure, indelicate, insensitive, naughty, obscene, offensive, risqué, rude, *inf* sexy, *inf* smutty, suggestive, titillating, unprintable, unrepeatable, unsuitable, vulgar. ▷ INDECOROUS. *Opp* DECENT.

indecisive *adj* doubtful, equivocal, evasive, *inf* in two minds, irresolute, undecided. ▷ HESITANT, INDEFINITE. *Opp* DECISIVE. **be indecisive** ▷ HESITATE.

indecorous *adj* churlish, ill-bred, inappropriate, *inf* in bad taste, tasteless, unbecoming, uncouth, undignified, unseemly, vulgar. ▷ INDECENT. *Opp* DECOROUS.

indefensible *adj* incredible, insupportable, unjustifiable, unpardonable, unreasonable, unsound, untenable, vulnerable, weak. ▷ WRONG.

indefinite *adj* ambiguous, blurred, confused, dim, general, ill-defined, imprecise, indeterminate, inexact, inexplicit, *inf* leaving it open, neutral, obscure, uncertain, unclear, unsettled, unspecific, unspecified, unsure, vague. ▷ INDECISIVE. *Opp* DEFINITE.

indelible *adj* fast, fixed, indestructible, ineffaceable, ineradicable, ingrained, lasting, unfading, unforgettable. ▷ PERMANENT.

indentation *n* cut, dent, depression, dimple, dip, furrow, groove, hollow, indent, mark, nick, notch, pit, recess, score, serration, toothmark, zigzag.

independence *n* 1 autonomy, freedom, individualism, liberty, nonconformity, self-confidence, self-reliance, self-sufficiency. 2 autarchy, home rule, self-determination, self-government, self-rule, sovereignty.

independent *adj* 1 carefree, *inf* footloose, free, freethinking, individualistic, nonconformist, non-partisan, open-minded, private, self-confident, selfreliant, separate, spontaneous, unbeholden, unbiased, uncommitted, unconventional, unprejudiced, untrammelled, without ties. 2 autonomous, liberated, neutral, nonaligned, self-determining, self-governing, sovereign.

indescribable *adj* beyond words, indefinable, inexpressible, stunning, unspeakable, unutterable.

indestructible *adj* durable, enduring, eternal, everlasting, immortal, imperishable, ineradicable, lasting, permanent, shatter-proof, solid, strong, tough, toughened, unbreakable.

index *n* 1 catalogue, directory, guide, key, register, table (*of contents*). 2 ▷ INDICATOR.

indicate *vb* announce, betoken, communicate, convey, denote, describe, designate, display, evidence, express, give an indication (*of*), give notice of, imply, intimate, make known, manifest, mean, notify, point out, register, reveal, say, show, signal, signify, specify, spell, stand for, suggest, symbolize, warn.

indication *n* augury, clue, evidence, forewarning, hint, inkling, intimation, omen, portent, sign, signal, suggestion, symptom, token, warning.

indicator *n* clock, dial, display, gauge, index, instrument, marker, meter, needle, pointer, screen, sign, signal.

indifferent *adj* 1 aloof, apathetic, blasé, bored, casual, cold, cool, detached, disinterested, dispassionate, distant, half-hearted, impassive, incurious, insouciant, neutral, nonchalant, not bothered, uncaring, unconcerned, unemotional, unenthusiastic, unexcited, unimpressed, uninterested, uninvolved, unmoved. ▷ IMPARTIAL. *Opp* ENTHUSIASTIC. 2 commonplace, fair, mediocre, middling, moderate, *inf* nothing to write home about, *inf* poorish, undistinguished, unexciting. ▷ ORDINARY. *Opp* EXCELLENT.

indigestion *n* dyspepsia, flatulence, heartburn.

indignant *adj* *inf* aerated, annoyed, cross, disgruntled, exasperated, furious, heated, infuriated, *inf* in high dudgeon, irate, irked, irritated, livid, mad, *inf* miffed, *inf* peeved, piqued, provoked, *inf* put out, riled, sore, upset, vexed. ▷ ANGRY.

indirect *adj* **1** *inf* all round the houses, ambagious, bendy, circuitous, devious, erratic, long, meandering, oblique, rambling, roundabout, roving, tortuous, twisting, winding, zigzag. **2** *an indirect insult.* ambiguous, backhanded, circumlocutory, disguised, equivocal, euphemistic, evasive, implicit, implied, oblique. *Opp* DIRECT.

indiscreet *adj* careless, foolish, ill-advised, ill-considered, ill-judged, impolite, impolitic, incautious, injudicious, insensitive, tactless, undiplomatic, unguarded, unthinking, unwise. *Opp* DISCREET.

indiscriminate *adj* aimless, careless, casual, confused, desultory, general, haphazard, *inf* hit or miss, imperceptive, miscellaneous, mixed, promiscuous, random, uncritical, undifferentiated, undiscerning, undiscriminating, uninformed, unplanned, unselective, unsystematic, wholesale. *Opp* SELECTIVE.

indispensable *adj* basic, central, compulsory, crucial, essential, imperative, important, key, mandatory, necessary, needed, obligatory, required, requisite, vital. *Opp* UNNECESSARY.

indisputable *adj* absolute, accepted, acknowledged, axiomatic, beyond doubt, certain, clear, definite, evident, incontestable, incontrovertible, indubitable, irrefutable, positive, proved, proven, self-evident, sure, unanswerable, unarguable, undeniable, undisputed, undoubted, unimpeachable, unquestionable. *Opp* DEBATABLE.

indistinct *adj* **1** bleary, blurred, confused, dim, dull, faint, fuzzy, hazy, ill-defined, indefinite, misty, obscure, shadowy, unclear, vague. **2** deadened, muffled, mumbled, muted, slurred, unintelligible, woolly. *Opp* DISTINCT.

indistinguishable *adj* alike, identical, interchangeable, the same, twin, undifferentiated. *Opp* DIFFERENT.

individual *adj* characteristic, different, distinct, distinctive, exclusive, idiosyncratic, individualistic, particular, peculiar, personal, private, separate, singular, special, specific, unique. *Opp* COLLECTIVE, GENERAL. ● *n* ▷ PERSON.

indoctrinate *vb* brainwash, implant, instruct, re-educate, train. ▷ TEACH.

induce *vb* **1** coax, encourage, incite, influence, inspire, motivate, persuade, press, prevail on, stimulate, sway, *inf* talk into, tempt, urge. *Opp* DISCOURAGE. **2** *induce a fever.* bring on, cause, effect, engender, generate, give rise to, lead to, occasion, produce, provoke.

inducement *n* attraction, bait, bribe, encouragement, enticement, incentive, spur, stimulus, *inf* sweetener.

indulge *vb* be indulgent to, cosset, favour, give in to, gratify, humour, mollycoddle, pamper, pander to, spoil, *inf* spoonfeed, treat. *Opp* DEPRIVE. **indulge in** ▷ ENJOY. **indulge yourself** be self-indulgent, drink too much, eat too much, give in to temptation, overdo it, overeat, spoil yourself, succumb, yield.

indulgent *adj* compliant, easygoing, fond, forbearing, forgiving, genial, kind, lenient, liberal, overgenerous, patient, permissive, tolerant. *Opp* STRICT.

industrious *adj* assiduous, busy, conscientious, diligent, dynamic, earnest, energetic, enterprising, hard-working, involved, keen, laborious, persistent, pertinacious, productive, sedulous, tireless, unflagging, untiring, zealous. *Opp* LAZY.

industry *n* **1** business, commerce, manufacturing, production, trade. **2** activity, application, commitment, determination, diligence, dynamism, effort, energy, enterprise, industriousness, keenness, labour, perseverance, persistence, sedulousness, tirelessness, toil, zeal. ▷ WORK. *Opp* LAZINESS.

inedible *adj* bad for you, harmful, indigestible, nauseating, *inf* off, poisonous, rotten, tough, uneatable, unpalatable, unwholesome. *Opp* EDIBLE.

ineffective *adj* **1** fruitless, futile, *inf* hopeless, inept, unconvincing, unproductive, unsuccessful, useless, vain, worthless. **2** disorganized, feckless, feeble, idle, impotent, inadequate, incapable, incompetent, ineffectual, inefficient, powerless, shiftless, unenterprising, weak. *Opp* EFFECTIVE.

inefficient *adj* **1** extravagant, prodigal, uneconomic, wasteful. **2** ▷ INEFFECTIVE. *Opp* EFFICIENT.

inelegant *adj* awkward, clumsy, crude, gauche, graceless, inartistic, rough, uncouth, ungainly, unpolished, unskilful, unsophisticated, unstylish. ▷ UGLY. *Opp* ELEGANT.

ineligible *adj* disqualified, inappropriate, *inf* out of the running, *inf* ruled out, unacceptable, unauthorized, unfit, unqualified, unsuitable, unworthy. *Opp* ELIGIBLE.

inept *adj* **1** awkward, bumbling, bungling, clumsy, gauche, incompetent, inexpert, maladroit, unskilful, unskilled. **2** ▷ INAPPROPRIATE.

inequality *n* contrast, difference, discrepancy, disparity, dissimilarity, imbalance, incongruity, prejudice. *Opp* EQUALITY.

inert *adj* apathetic, dormant, idle, immobile, inactive, inanimate, lifeless, passive, quiescent, quiet, slow, sluggish, static, stationary, still, supine, torpid. *Opp* LIVELY.

inertia *n* apathy, deadness, idleness, immobility, inactivity, indolence, lassitude, laziness, lethargy, listlessness, numbness, passivity, sluggishness, torpor. *Opp* LIVELINESS.

inessential *adj* dispensable, expendable, minor, needless, non-essential, optional, ornamental, secondary, spare, superfluous, unimportant, unnecessary. *Opp* ESSENTIAL.

inevitable *adj* assured, *inf* bound to happen, certain, destined, fated, ineluctable, inescapable, inexorable, ordained, predictable, sure, unavoidable. ▷ RELENTLESS.

inexcusable *adj* ▷ UNFORGIVABLE.

inexpensive *adj* ▷ CHEAP.

inexperienced *adj* *inf* born yesterday, callow, *inf* green, immature, inexpert, innocent, naïve, new, probationary, raw, unaccustomed, unfledged, uninitiated, unskilled, unsophisticated, untried, *inf* wet behind the ears, young. *Opp* EXPERT.

inexplicable *adj* baffling, bewildering, confusing, enigmatic, incomprehensible, inscrutable, insoluble, mysterious, mystifying, perplexing, puzzling, strange, unaccountable, unexplainable, unfathomable, unsolvable. *Opp* STRAIGHTFORWARD.

infallible *adj* certain, dependable, faultless, foolproof, impeccable, perfect, reliable, sound, sure, trustworthy, unbeatable, unerring, unfailing. *Opp* FALLIBLE.

infamous *adj* disgraceful, disreputable, ill-famed, notorious, outrageous, well-known. ▷ WICKED.

infant *n* baby, *inf* toddler, *inf* tot. ▷ CHILD.

infantile *adj* [*derog*] adolescent, babyish, childish, immature, juvenile, puerile. ▷ SILLY. *Opp* MATURE.

infatuated *adj* besotted, charmed, enchanted, *inf* head over heels, in love, obsessed, *inf* smitten.

infatuation *n* *inf* crush, obsession, passion. ▷ LOVE.

infect *vb* **1** blight, contaminate, defile, poison, pollute, spoil, taint. **2** affect, influence, inspire, touch. **infected** ▷ SEPTIC.

infection *n* blight, contagion, contamination, epidemic, pestilence, pollution, virus. ▷ ILLNESS.

infectious *adj* catching, communicable, contagious, spreading, transmissible, transmittable.

informal

infer *vb* assume, conclude, deduce, derive, draw a conclusion, extrapolate, gather, guess, reach the conclusion, surmise, understand, work out.

inferior *adj* **1** humble, junior, lesser, lower, lowly, mean, menial, secondary, second-class, servile, subordinate, subsidiary, unimportant. **2** cheap, indifferent, mediocre, poor, shoddy, tawdry, *inf* tinny. *Opp* SUPERIOR. ● *n* ▷ SUBORDINATE.

infertile *adj* barren, sterile, unfruitful, unproductive.

infest *vb* infiltrate, overrun, pervade, plague. **infested** alive, crawling, swarming, teeming, verminous.

infidelity *n* **1** adultery, unfaithfulness. **2** ▷ DISLOYALTY.

infiltrate *vb* enter secretly, insinuate, intrude, penetrate, spy on.

infinite *adj* astronomical, big, boundless, countless, endless, eternal, everlasting, immeasurable, immense, incalculable, indeterminate, inestimable, inexhaustible, innumerable, interminable, limitless, multitudinous, never-ending, numberless, perpetual, uncountable, undefined, unending, unfathomable, unlimited, unnumbered, untold. ▷ HUGE. *Opp* FINITE.

infinity *n* endlessness, eternity, infinite distance, infinite quantity, infinitude, perpetuity, space.

infirm *adj* bedridden, crippled, elderly, feeble, frail, lame, old, poorly, senile, sickly, unwell. ▷ ILL, WEAK. *Opp* HEALTHY.

inflame *vb* arouse, encourage, excite, fire, foment, goad, ignite, incense, incite, kindle, madden, provoke, rouse, stimulate, stir up, work up. ▷ ANGER. *Opp* COOL. **inflamed** ▷ PASSIONATE, SEPTIC.

inflammable *adj* burnable, combustible, flammable, volatile. *Opp* INCOMBUSTIBLE.

inflammation *n* abscess, boil, infection, irritation, redness, sore, soreness, swelling.

inflate *vb* **1** blow up, dilate, distend, enlarge, puff up, pump up, swell. **2** ▷ EXAGGERATE.

inflexible *adj* **1** adamantine, firm, hard, hardened, immovable, rigid, solid, stiff, unbending, unyielding. **2** adamant, entrenched, fixed, immutable, inexorable, intractable, intransigent, obdurate, obstinate, *inf* pig-headed, refractory, resolute, rigorous, strict, stubborn, unalterable, unchangeable, uncompromising, unhelpful. *Opp* FLEXIBLE.

inflict *vb* administer, apply, deal out, enforce, force, impose, mete out, perpetrate, wreak.

influence *n* ascendancy, authority, control, direction, dominance, effect, guidance, hold, impact, leverage, power, pressure, pull, sway, weight. ● *vb* **1** affect, bias, change, control, direct, dominate, exert influence on, guide, impinge on, impress, manipulate, modify, motivate, move, persuade, prejudice, prompt, put pressure on, stir, sway. **2** *influence a judge*. bribe, corrupt, lead astray, suborn, tempt.

influential *adj* authoritative, compelling, controlling, convincing, dominant, effective, far-reaching, forceful, guiding, important, inspiring, leading, moving, persuasive, potent, powerful, prestigious, significant, strong, telling, weighty. *Opp* UNIMPORTANT.

influx *n* flood, flow, inflow, inundation, invasion, rush, stream.

inform *vb* **1** advise, apprise, brief, communicate to, enlighten, *inf* fill in, give information to, instruct, leak, notify, *inf* put in the picture, teach, tell, *inf* tip off. **2** *inf* blab, give information, *sl* grass, *sl* peach, *sl* rat, *inf* sneak, *inf* split on, *inf* tell, *inf* tell tales. **inform against** ▷ BETRAY. **informed** ▷ KNOWLEDGEABLE.

informal *adj* **1** approachable, casual, comfortable, cosy, easy, easygoing, everyday, familiar, free and easy, friendly, homely, natural, ordinary, relaxed, simple, unceremonious, unofficial, unpretentious, unsophisticated. **2** *informal language*. chatty, colloquial, personal, slangy, vernacular. **3** *an informal design*. asymmetrical, flexible, fluid, intuitive, irregular, spontaneous. *Opp* FORMAL.

information *n* **1** announcement, briefing, bulletin, communication, enlightenment, instruction, message, news, report, statement, *old use* tidings, *inf* tip-off, word. **2** data, database, dossier, evidence, facts, intelligence, knowledge, statistics.

informative *adj* communicative, edifying, educational, enlightening, factual, giving information, helpful, illuminating, instructive, meaningful, revealing, useful. *Opp* MEANINGLESS.

informer *n sl* grass, informant, spy, *sl* stool-pigeon, *inf* tell-tale, traitor.

infrequent *adj* exceptional, intermittent, irregular, occasional, *inf* once in a blue moon, rare, spasmodic, uncommon, unusual. *Opp* FREQUENT.

infringe *vb* breach, break, contravene, defy, disobey, disregard, flout, ignore, overstep, sin against, transgress, violate.

ingenious *adj* adroit, artful, astute, brilliant, clever, complex, crafty, creative, cunning, deft, imaginative, inspired, intelligent, intricate, inventive, neat, original, resourceful, shrewd, skilful, *inf* smart, subtle, talented. *Opp* UNIMAGINATIVE.

ingenuous *adj* artless, childlike, frank, guileless, honest, innocent, naïve, open, plain, simple, sincere, trusting, unaffected, uncomplicated, unsophisticated. *Opp* SOPHISTICATED.

ingredient *n* component, constituent, element, factor, *plur* makings, part.

inhabit *vb old use* abide in, colonize, dwell in, live in, make your home in, occupy, people, populate, possess, reside in, settle in, set up home in.

inhabitable *adj* habitable, in good repair, liveable, usable. *Opp* UNINHABITABLE.

inhabitant *n* citizen, *old use* denizen, dweller, inmate, native, occupant, occupier, *plur* population, resident, settler, tenant, *plur* townsfolk, *plur* townspeople.

inherent *adj* built-in, congenital, essential, fundamental, hereditary, immanent, inborn, inbred, indwelling, ingrained, intrinsic, native, natural.

inherit *vb* be the inheritor of, be left, *inf* come into, receive as an inheritance, succeed to. **inherited** ▷ HEREDITARY.

inheritance *n* bequest, birthright, estate, fortune, heritage, legacy, patrimony.

inhibit *vb* bridle, check, control, curb, discourage, frustrate, hinder, hold back, prevent, quell, repress, restrain. **inhibited** ▷ REPRESSED, SHY.

inhibition *n* **1** bar, barrier, check, constraint, curb, impediment, interference, restraint, stricture. **2** blockage, diffidence, *inf* hang-up, repression, reserve, self-consciousness, shyness.

inhospitable *adj* antisocial, reclusive, reserved, solitary, standoffish, unkind, unsociable, unwelcoming. ▷ UNFRIENDLY. **2** bleak, cold, comfortless, desolate, grim, hostile, lonely. *Opp* HOSPITABLE.

inhuman *adj* animal, barbaric, barbarous, bestial, bloodthirsty, brutish, diabolical, fiendish, merciless, pitiless, ruthless, savage, unnatural, vicious. ▷ INHUMANE. *Opp* HUMAN.

inhumane *adj* cold-hearted, cruel, hard, hard-hearted, heartless, inconsiderate, insensitive, uncaring, uncharitable, uncivilized, unfeeling, unkind, unsympathetic. ▷ INHUMAN. *Opp* HUMANE.

initial *adj* beginning, commencing, earliest, first, inaugural, incipient, introductory, opening, original, primary, starting. *Opp* FINAL.

initiate *vb* activate, actuate, begin, commence, enter upon, get going, get under way, inaugurate, instigate, institute, introduce, launch, originate, set going, set in motion, set up, start, take the initiative, trigger.

initiative *n* ambition, drive, dynamism, enterprise, *inf* get-up-and-go, inventiveness, lead, leadership, originality, resourcefulness. **take the initiative** ▷ INITIATE.

injection *n* *inf* fix, inoculation, *inf* jab, vaccination.

injure *vb* break, crush, cut, damage, deface, disfigure, harm, hurt, ill-treat, impair, mar, ruin, spoil, vandalize. ▷ WOUND.

injurious *adj* **1** damaging, deleterious, destructive, detrimental, harmful, insalubrious, painful, ruinous. **2** ▷ ABUSIVE.

injury *n* damage, harm, hurt, mischief. ▷ WOUND.

injustice *n* bias, bigotry, discrimination, dishonesty, favouritism, illegality, inequality, inequity, one-sidedness, oppression, partiality, partisanship, prejudice, unfairness, unlawfulness, wrong, wrongness. *Opp* JUSTICE.

inn *n* old use hostelry, hotel, *inf* local, pub, tavern.

inner *adj* central, concealed, hidden, innermost, inside, interior, internal, intimate, inward, mental, middle, private, secret. *Opp* OUTER.

innocence *n* **1** goodness, honesty, incorruptibility, purity, righteousness, sinlessness, virtue. **2** [*derog*] gullibility, inexperience, naïvety, simple-mindedness.

innocent *adj* **1** above suspicion, angelic, blameless, chaste, childlike, faultless, free from blame, guiltless, harmless, honest, immaculate, incorrupt, inoffensive, pure, righteous, sinless, spotless, untainted, virginal, virtuous. *Opp* CORRUPT, GUILTY. **2** artless, childlike, credulous, *inf* green, guileless, gullible, inexperienced, ingenuous, naïve, simple, simple-minded, trusting, unsophisticated.

innovation *n* change, departure, invention, new feature, novelty, reform, revolution.

innovator *n* discoverer, experimenter, inventor, pioneer, reformer, revolutionary.

innumerable *adj* countless, many, numberless, uncountable, untold. ▷ INFINITE.

inquest *n* hearing. ▷ INQUIRY.

inquire *vb* ask, explore, investigate, seek information, *inf* probe, search, survey. ▷ ENQUIRE.

inquiry *n* cross-examination, examination, inquest, inquisition, interrogation, investigation, poll, *inf* post-mortem, *inf* probe, referendum, review, study, survey.

inquisitive *adj* curious, impertinent, indiscreet, inquiring, interfering, intrusive, investigative, meddlesome, meddling, *inf* nosy, probing, prying, questioning, sceptical, searching, *inf* snooping, spying. **be inquisitive** ▷ PRY.

insane *adj* *inf* crazy, deranged, lunatic, *inf* mental, psychotic, unbalanced, unhinged. ▷ MAD. *Opp* SANE.

inscription *n* dedication, engraving, epigraph, superscription, writing.

insect *n* *inf* bug, *inf* creepy-crawly. □ ant, aphid, bee, beetle, blackfly, butterfly, cicada, cockchafer, cockroach, cranefly, cricket, daddy-long-legs, damselfly, dragonfly, earwig, firefly, fly, glow-worm, gnat, grasshopper, hornet, ladybird, locust, mantis, mayfly, midge, mosquito, moth, sawfly, termite, tsetse (fly), wasp, weevil.

insecure *adj* **1** dangerous, flimsy, loose, precarious, rickety, rocky, shaky, unsafe, unsound, unstable, unsteady, unsupported, weak, wobbly. **2** an insecure feeling. anxious, apprehensive, defenceless, exposed, open, uncertain, underconfident, unprotected, vulnerable, worried. *Opp* SECURE.

insensible *adj* anaesthetized, benumbed, *inf* dead to the world, inert, insensate, insentient, knocked out, numb, *inf* out, senseless, unaware, unconscious. *Opp* CONSCIOUS.

insensitive adj **1** anaesthetized, dead, numb, unresponsive. **2** boorish, callous, crass, cruel, imperceptive, obtuse, tactless, inf thick-skinned, thoughtless, uncaring, unfeeling, unsympathetic. Opp SENSITIVE.

inseparable adj always together, attached, indissoluble, indivisible, integral.

insert vb drive in, embed, implant, intercalate, interject, interleave, interpolate, interpose, introduce, place in, inf pop in, push in, put in, stick in, tuck in.

inside adj central, indoor, inner, innermost, interior, internal. ● n bowels, centre, contents, core, heart, indoors, interior, lining, middle. Opp OUTSIDE. **insides** ▷ ENTRAILS.

insidious adj creeping, deceptive, furtive, pervasive, secretive, stealthy, subtle, surreptitious, treacherous, underhand. ▷ CRAFTY.

insignificant adj forgettable, inconsiderable, irrelevant, insubstantial, lightweight, meaningless, minor, negligible, paltry, small, trifling, trivial, undistinguished, unimportant, unimpressive, valueless, worthless. Opp SIGNIFICANT.

insincere adj artful, crafty, deceitful, deceptive, devious, dishonest, disingenuous, dissembling, false, feigned, flattering, inf foxy, hollow, hypocritical, lying, inf mealy-mouthed, mendacious, perfidious, inf phoney, pretended, inf put on, inf smarmy, sycophantic, treacherous, inf two-faced, untrue, untruthful, wily. Opp SINCERE.

insist vb **1** assert, asseverate, aver, avow, declare, emphasize, hold, maintain, state, stress, swear, take an oath, vow. **2** assert yourself, be assertive, command, persist, inf put your foot down, stand firm, inf stick to your guns. **insist on** ▷ DEMAND.

insistent adj assertive, demanding, dogged, emphatic, firm, forceful, importunate, inexorable, obstinate, peremptory, persistent, relentless, repeated, resolute, stubborn, unrelenting, unremitting, urgent.

insolence n arrogance, boldness, inf cheek, defiance, disrespect, effrontery, impertinence, impudence, incivility, insubordination, inf lip, presumptuousness, rudeness, inf sauce.

insolent adj arrogant, audacious, bold, brazen, inf cheeky, contemptuous, defiant, disdainful, disrespectful, forward, inf fresh, impertinent, impolite, impudent, insubordinate, insulting, offensive, pert, presumptuous, saucy, shameless, sneering, uncivil. ▷ RUDE. Opp POLITE.

insoluble adj baffling, enigmatic, incomprehensible, inexplicable, mystifying, puzzling, strange, unaccountable, unanswerable, unfathomable, unsolvable. Opp SOLUBLE.

insolvent adj bankrupt, inf bust, failed, ruined. ▷ POOR.

inspect vb check, examine, sl give it the once over, investigate, peruse, pore over, scan, scrutinize, study, survey, vet.

inspection n check, check-up, examination, inf going-over, investigation, review, scrutiny, survey.

inspector n controller, examiner, investigator, official, scrutineer, superintendent, supervisor, tester.

inspiration n **1** creativity, genius, imagination, muse. **2** enthusiasm, impulse, incitement, influence, motivation, prompting, spur, stimulation, stimulus. **3** a sudden inspiration. brainwave, idea, insight, revelation, thought.

inspire vb activate, animate, arouse, awaken, inf egg on, encourage, energize, enthuse, fire, galvanize, influence, inspirit, instigate, kindle, motivate, prompt, provoke, quicken, reassure, set off, spark off, spur, stimulate, stir, support.

instability n capriciousness, change, changeableness, fickleness, fluctuation, flux, impermanence, inconstancy, insecurity, mutability, precariousness, shakiness, transience, uncertainty, unpredictability, unreliability, unsteadiness, *inf* ups-and-downs, vacillation, variability, variations, weakness. *Opp* STABILITY.

install *vb* ensconce, establish, fit, fix, instate, introduce, place, plant, position, put in, settle, set up, situate, station. *Opp* REMOVE:

instalment *n* **1** payment, rent, rental. **2** chapter, episode, part.

instance *n* case, example, exemplar, illustration, occurrence, precedent, sample.

instant *adj* direct, fast, immediate, instantaneous, on-the-spot, prompt, quick, rapid, speedy, split-second, swift, unhesitating, urgent. ● *n* flash, *inf* jiffy, moment, point of time, second, split second, *inf* tick, *inf* trice, *inf* twinkling.

instigate *vb* activate, begin, be the instigator of, bring about, cause, encourage, foment, generate, incite, initiate, inspire, kindle, prompt, provoke, set up, start, stimulate, stir up, urge, *inf* whip up.

instigator *n* agitator, fomenter, inciter, initiator, inspirer, leader, mischief-maker, provoker, ring-leader, troublemaker.

instil *vb inf* din into, imbue, implant, inculcate, indoctrinate, infuse, ingrain, inject, insinuate, introduce.

instinct *n* bent, faculty, feel, feeling, guesswork, hunch, impulse, inclination, instinctive urge, intuition, presentiment, propensity, sixth-sense, the subconscious, tendency, urge.

instinctive *adj* automatic, congenital, constitutional, *inf* gut, impulsive, inborn, inbred, inherent, innate, instinctual, intuitive, involuntary, irrational, mechanical, native, natural, reflex, spontaneous, subconscious, unconscious, unreasoning, unthinking, visceral. *Opp* DELIBERATE.

institute *n* ▷ INSTITUTION. ● *vb* begin, create, establish, fix up, found, inaugurate, initiate, introduce, launch, open, organize, originate, pioneer, set up, start.

institution *n* **1** creation, establishing, formation, founding, inauguration, inception, initiation, introduction, launching, opening, setting-up. **2** academy, asylum, college, establishment, foundation, home, hospital, institute, organization, school, *inf* set-up. **3** convention, custom, habit, practice, ritual, routine, rule, tradition.

instruct *vb* **1** coach, drill, educate, indoctrinate, inform, lecture, prepare, school, teach, train, tutor. **2** authorize, brief, charge, command, direct, enjoin, give the order, order, require, tell.

instruction *n* **1** briefing, coaching, demonstration, drill, education, guidance, indoctrination, lecture, lesson, schooling, teaching, training, tuition, tutorial, tutoring. **2** authorization, brief, charge, command, direction, directive, order, requisition.

instructive *adj* didactic, edifying, educational, enlightening, helpful, illuminating, improving, informational, informative, instructional, revealing.

instructor *n* adviser, coach, trainer, tutor. ▷ TEACHER.

instrument *n* apparatus, appliance, contraption, device, equipment, gadget, implement, machine, mechanism, tool, utensil. **musical instrument** □ *accordion, bagpipes, banjo, bassoon, bugle, castanets, celesta, cello, clarinet, clavichord, clavier, concertina, cor anglais, cornet, cymbals, double-bass, drum, dulcimer, euphonium, fiddle, fife, flugelhorn, flute, fortepiano, French horn, glockenspiel, gong, guitar, harmonica, harmonium, harp, harpsichord, horn, hurdy-gurdy, kettledrum, keyboard, lute, lyre, mouth-organ, oboe, organ, piano, piccolo, pipes, recorder, saxophone, sitar, spinet, synthesizer, tambourine, timpani, triangle, trombone, trumpet, tuba, tubular bells, ukulele, viol, viola, violin, virginals, xylophone, zither.*

instrumental *adj* active, advantageous, beneficial, contributory, helpful, influential, supportive, useful, valuable.

insubordinate *adj* defiant, disobedient, insurgent, mutinous, rebellious, riotous, seditious, undisciplined, unruly. ▷ IMPERTINENT. *Opp* OBEDIENT.

insufficient *adj* deficient, disappointing, inadequate, incomplete, little, meagre, mean, niggardly, *inf* pathetic, poor, scanty, scarce, short, skimpy, sparse, unsatisfactory. *Opp* EXCESSIVE, SUFFICIENT.

insular *adj* closed, cut-off, isolated, limited, narrow, narrow-minded, parochial, provincial, remote, separated. *Opp* BROADMINDED, COSMOPOLITAN.

insulate *vb* **1** cocoon, cover, cushion, enclose, isolate, lag, protect, shield, surround, wrap up. **2** cut off, detach, isolate, keep apart, quarantine, segregate, separate.

insult *n* abuse, affront, aspersion, *inf* cheek, contumely, defamation, impudence, indignity, insulting behaviour, libel, *inf* put-down, rudeness, slander, slight, slur, snub. ● *vb* abuse, affront, be rude to, *inf* call names, *inf* cock a snook at, defame, dishonour, disparage, libel, mock, offend, outrage, patronize, revile, slander, slang, slight, sneer at, snub, *inf* thumb your nose at, vilify. *Opp* COMPLIMENT. **insulting** ▷ RUDE.

insuperable *adj* insurmountable, overwhelming, unconquerable. ▷ IMPOSSIBLE.

insurance *n* assurance, cover, indemnification, indemnity, policy, protection, security.

insure *vb* cover yourself, indemnify, protect, take out insurance.

intact *adj* complete, entire, integral, solid, sound, unbroken, undamaged, whole. ▷ PERFECT.

intangible *adj* abstract, airy, disembodied, elusive, ethereal, evanescent, fleeting, impalpable, imperceptible, imponderable, incorporeal, indefinite, insubstantial, invisible, shadowy, unreal, vague. *Opp* TANGIBLE.

integral *adj* **1** basic, constituent, essential, fundamental, indispensable, intrinsic, irreplaceable, necessary, requisite. *Opp* INESSENTIAL. **2** *an integral unit*. attached, complete, full, indivisible, whole. *Opp* SEPARATE.

integrate *vb* amalgamate, assemble, blend, bring together, coalesce, combine, consolidate, desegregate, fuse, harmonize, join, knit, merge, mix, put together, unify, unite, weld. *Opp* SEPARATE.

integrity *n* **1** decency, fidelity, goodness, fidelity, honour, incorruptibility, loyalty, morality, principle, probity, rectitude, reliability, righteousness, sincerity, trustworthiness, uprightness, veracity, virtue. **2** ▷ UNITY.

intellect *n inf* brains, cleverness, genius, mind, rationality, reason, sense, understanding, wisdom, *old use* wit. ▷ INTELLIGENCE.

intellectual *adj* **1** academic, *inf* bookish, cerebral, cultured, educated, scholarly, studious, thinking, thoughtful. ▷ INTELLIGENT. **2** cultural, deep, difficult, educational, highbrow, improving, thought-provoking. ● *n* academic, *inf* egghead, genius, highbrow, intellectual person, *inf* mastermind, *inf* one of the intelligentsia, savant, thinker.

intelligence *n* **1** ability, acumen, alertness, astuteness, brainpower, *inf* brains, brightness, brilliance, capacity, cleverness, discernment, genius, *inf* grey matter, insight, intellect, judgement, keenness, mind, *inf* nous, perceptiveness, perspicaciousness, perspicacity, quickness, reason, sagacity, sense, sharpness, shrewdness, understanding, wisdom, wit, wits. **2** data, facts, information, knowledge, *inf* low-down, news, notification, report, *inf* tip-off, warning. **3** espionage, secret service, spying.

intelligent *adj* able, acute, alert, astute, brainy, bright, brilliant, *inf* canny, clever, discerning, educated, intellectual, knowing, penetrating, perceptive, percipient, perspicacious, profound, quick, ratiocinative, ra-

interim

tional, reasonable, sagacious, sensible, sharp, shrewd, *inf* smart, thinking, thoughtful, trenchant, wise, *inf* with it, witty. *Opp* STUPID.

intelligible *adj* clear, comprehensible, decipherable, fathomable, legible, logical, lucid, meaningful, plain, straightforward, unambiguous, understandable. *Opp* INCOMPREHENSIBLE.

intend *vb* aim, aspire, contemplate, design, determine, have in mind, mean, plan, plot, propose, purpose, resolve, scheme.

intense *adj* **1** ardent, burning, consuming, deep, eager, earnest, emotional, fanatical, fervent, fervid, impassioned, passionate, powerful, profound, serious, strong, towering, vehement, violent, zealous. *Opp* COOL, HALF-HEARTED. **2** *intense pain.* acute, agonizing, excruciating, extreme, fierce, great, harsh, keen, severe, sharp. *Opp* SLIGHT.

intensify *vb* add to, aggravate, augment, become greater, boost, build up, deepen, emphasize, escalate, fire, focus, fuel, heighten, *inf* hot up, increase, magnify, make greater, quicken, raise, redouble, reinforce, sharpen, *inf* step up, strengthen, whet. *Opp* REDUCE.

intensive *adj* *inf* all-out, comprehensive, concentrated, detailed, exhaustive, high-powered, thorough, unremitting.

intent *adj* absorbed, attentive, bent, committed, concentrated, concentrating, determined, eager, engrossed, enthusiastic, firm, focused, keen, occupied, preoccupied, resolute, set, steadfast, watchful, zealous. *Opp* CASUAL. ● *n* ▷ INTENTION.

intention *n* aim, ambition, design, end, goal, intent, object, objective, plan, point, purpose, target.

intentional *adj* calculated, conscious, contrived, deliberate, designed, intended, knowing, planned, pre-arranged, preconceived, premeditated, prepared, studied, wilful. *Opp* ACCIDENTAL.

intercept *vb* ambush, arrest, block, catch, check, cut off, deflect, head off, impede, interrupt, obstruct, stop, thwart, trap.

intercourse *n* **1** communication, conversation, dealings, interaction, traffic. **2** *sexual intercourse.* carnal knowledge, coition, coitus, congress, copulation, intimacy, love-making, mating, rape, sex, union.

interest *n* **1** attention, attentiveness, care, commitment, concern, curiosity, involvement, notice, regard, scrutiny. **2** *of no interest.* consequence, importance, moment, note, significance, value. **3** *leisure interests.* activity, diversion, hobby, pastime, preoccupation, pursuit, relaxation. ● *vb* absorb, appeal to, arouse the curiosity of, attract, capture the imagination of, captivate, concern, divert, enchant, engage, engross, entertain, enthral, fascinate, intrigue, involve, occupy, preoccupy, stimulate, *inf* turn on. ▷ EXCITE. *Opp* BORE.

interested *adj* **1** absorbed, attentive, curious, engrossed, enthusiastic, immersed, intent, involved, keen, occupied, preoccupied, rapt, responsive, riveted. *Opp* UNINTERESTED. **2** concerned, involved, partial. ▷ BIASED. *Opp* DISINTERESTED.

interesting *adj* absorbing, appealing, attractive, challenging, compelling, curious, engaging, engrossing, entertaining, enthralling, fascinating, gripping, imaginative, important, intriguing, inviting, original, piquant, *often ironic* riveting, spellbinding, unpredictable, unusual, varied. *Opp* BORING.

interfere *vb* be a busybody, butt in, interrupt, intervene, intrude, meddle, obtrude, *inf* poke your nose in, pry, snoop, *inf* stick your oar in, tamper. **interfere with** ▷ OBSTRUCT. **interfering** ▷ NOSY.

interim *adj* half-time, halfway, provisional, stopgap, temporary.

interior *adj* ▷ INTERNAL. ● *n* centre, core, depths, heart, inside, middle, nucleus.

interlude *n* entr'acte, intermezzo, intermission. ▷ INTERVAL.

intermediary *n* agent, ambassador, arbiter, arbitrator, broker, go-between, mediator, middleman, negotiator, referee, spokesperson, umpire.

intermediate *adj* average, *inf* betwixt and between, halfway, intermediary, intervening, mean, medial, median, middle, midway, *inf* neither one thing nor the other, neutral, *inf* sitting on the fence, transitional.

intermittent *adj* broken, discontinuous, erratic, fitful, irregular, occasional, *inf* on and off, periodic, random, recurrent, spasmodic, sporadic. *Opp* CONTINUOUS.

internal *adj* **1** inner, inside, interior. *Opp* EXTERNAL. **2** confidential, hidden, intimate, inward, personal, private, secret, undisclosed.

international *adj* cosmopolitan, global, intercontinental, universal, worldwide.

interpret *vb* clarify, clear up, construe, decipher, decode, define, elucidate, explain, explicate, expound, gloss, make clear, make sense of, paraphrase, render, rephrase, reword, simplify, sort out, translate, understand, unravel, work out.

interpretation *n* clarification, definition, elucidation, explanation, gloss, paraphrase, reading, rendering, translation, understanding, version.

interrogation *n* cross-examination, debriefing, examination, grilling, inquisition, questioning, *inf* third degree.

interrogative *adj* asking, inquiring, inquisitive, interrogatory, investigatory, questioning.

interrupt *vb* **1** *inf* barge in, break in, butt in, *inf* chime in, *inf* chip in, cut in, disrupt, disturb, heckle, hold up, interfere, intervene, intrude, punctuate, obstruct, spoil. **2** break off, call

a halt to, cut off, cut short, discontinue, halt, stop, suspend, terminate.

interruption *n* break, check, disruption, division, gap, halt, hiatus, interference, intrusion, stop, suspension. ▷ INTERVAL.

intersect *vb* bisect each other, converge, criss-cross, cross, divide, meet, pass across each other.

interval *n* **1** adjournment, break, *inf* breather, breathing-space, delay, distance, gap, hiatus, interruption, lapse, lull, opening, pause, recess, respite, rest, space, void, wait. **2** entr'acte, interlude, intermezzo, intermission.

intervene *vb* **1** come between, elapse, happen, occur, pass. **2** arbitrate, butt in, intercede, interfere, interpose, interrupt, intrude, mediate, *inf* step in.

interview *n* appraisal, audience, duologue, formal discussion, meeting, questioning, selection procedure, vetting. ● *vb* appraise, ask questions, evaluate, examine, interrogate, question, sound out, vet.

interweave *vb* criss-cross, entwine, interlace, intertwine, knit, tangle, weave together.

intestines *plur n* bowels, entrails, innards, insides, offal.

intimate *adj* **1** affectionate, close, familiar, informal, loving, sexual. ▷ FRIENDLY. **2** *intimate details.* confidential, detailed, exhaustive, personal, private, secret. ● *n* ▷ FRIEND. ● *vb* ▷ INDICATE.

intimidate *vb* alarm, browbeat, bully, coerce, cow, daunt, dismay, frighten, hector, make afraid, menace, overawe, persecute, petrify, scare, terrify, terrorize, threaten, tyrannize.

intolerable *adj* excruciating, impossible, insufferable, insupportable, unacceptable, unbearable, unendurable. *Opp* TOLERABLE.

intolerant *adj* biased, bigoted, chauvinistic, classist, discriminatory, dogmatic, illiberal, narrow-minded, one-sided, opinionated, prejudiced, racist, sexist, uncharitable, unsympathetic, xenophobic. *Opp* TOLERANT.

intonation *n* accent, delivery, inflection, modulation, pronunciation, sound, speech pattern, tone.

intoxicate *vb* addle, inebriate, make drunk, stupefy. **intoxicated** ▷ DRUNK, EXCITED. **intoxicating** ▷ ALCOHOLIC, EXCITING.

intricate *adj* complex, complicated, convoluted, delicate, detailed, elaborate, entangled, fancy, *inf* fiddly, involved, *inf* knotty, labyrinthine, ornate, sophisticated, tangled, tortuous. *Opp* SIMPLE.

intrigue *n* ▷ PLOT. ● *vb* **1** appeal to, arouse the curiosity of, attract, beguile, captivate, capture the interest of, engage, engross, excite the curiosity of, fascinate, interest, stimulate, *inf* turn on. *Opp* BORE.

intrinsic *adj* basic, essential, fundamental, immanent, inborn, inbred, in-built, inherent, native, natural, proper, real.

introduce *vb* **1** acquaint, make known, present. **2** announce, give an introduction to, lead into, preface. **3** add, advance, bring in, bring out, broach, create, establish, inaugurate, initiate, inject, insert, interpose, launch, make available, offer, phase in, pioneer, put forward, set up, start, suggest, usher in. ▷ BEGIN.

introduction *n* foreword, *inf* intro, *inf* lead-in, opening, overture, preamble, preface, prelude, prologue. ▷ BEGINNING.

introductory *adj* basic, early, first, fundamental, inaugural, initial, opening, prefatory, preliminary, preparatory, starting. *Opp* FINAL.

introverted *adj* contemplative, introspective, inward-looking, meditative, pensive, quiet, reserved, retiring, self-contained, shy, thoughtful, unsociable, withdrawn. *Opp* EXTROVERTED.

intrude *vb* break in, butt in, eavesdrop, encroach, gatecrash, interfere, interpose, interrupt, intervene, join uninvited, obtrude, *inf* snoop.

intruder *n* **1** eavesdropper, gatecrasher, infiltrator, interloper, *inf* uninvited guest. **2** burglar, housebreaker, invader, prowler, raider, robber, *inf* snooper, thief, trespasser.

intuition *n* insight, perceptiveness, percipience. ▷ INSTINCT.

invade *vb* descend on, encroach on, enter, impinge on, infest, infringe, march into, occupy, overrun, penetrate, raid, subdue, violate. ▷ ATTACK.

invalid *adj* **1** null and void, out-of-date, unacceptable, unusable, void, worthless. **2** fallacious, false, illogical, incorrect, irrational, spurious, unconvincing, unfounded, unreasonable, unscientific, unsound, untenable, untrue, wrong. *Opp* VALID. **3** ▷ ILL. ● *n* cripple, incurable, patient, sufferer, valetudinarian.

invaluable *adj* incalculable, inestimable, irreplaceable, precious, priceless, useful. ▷ VALUABLE. *Opp* WORTHLESS.

invariable *adj* certain, changeless, constant, eternal, even, immutable, inflexible, permanent, predictable, regular, reliable, rigid, solid, stable, steady, unalterable, unchangeable, unchanging, unfailing, uniform, unvarying, unwavering. *Opp* VARIABLE.

invasion *n* **1** encroachment, incursion, infiltration, inroad, intrusion, onslaught, raid, violation. ▷ ATTACK. **2** colony, flood, horde, infestation, spate, stream, swarm, throng.

invasive *adj* burgeoning, increasing, mushrooming, profuse, proliferating, relentless, unstoppable.

invent *vb* coin, conceive, concoct, construct, contrive, *inf* cook up, create, design, devise, discover, *inf* dream up, fabricate, formulate, *inf* hit upon, imagine, improvise, make up, originate, plan, put together, think up, trump up.

invention *n* **1** brainchild, coinage, contrivance, creation, design, discovery. **2** contraption, device, gadget. **3** deceit, fabrication, falsehood, fantasy, fiction, figment, lie. **4** ▷ INVENTIVENESS.

inventive adj clever, creative, enterprising, fertile, imaginative, ingenious, innovative, inspired, original, resourceful. Opp BANAL.

inventiveness n creativity, genius, imagination, ingenuity, inspiration, invention, originality, resourcefulness.

inventor n architect, author, inf boffin, creator, designer, discoverer, maker, originator.

inverse adj opposite, reversed, transposed.

invert vb capsize, overturn, reverse, transpose, turn upside down, upset.

invest vb 1 buy stocks and shares, play the market, speculate. 2 lay out, put to work, inf sink, use profitably, venture. **invest in** ▷ BUY.

investigate vb analyse, consider, enquire about, examine, explore, follow up, gather evidence about, inf go into, inquire into, look into, probe, research, scrutinize, sift (evidence), study, inf suss out, weigh up.

investigation n enquiry, examination, inquiry, inquisition, inspection, inf post-mortem, inf probe, quest, research, review, scrutiny, search, study, survey.

invidious adj discriminatory, objectionable, offensive, undesirable, unfair, unjust, unwarranted.

invigorating adj bracing, enlivening, exhilarating, fresh, healthful, health-giving, healthy, refreshing, rejuvenating, revitalizing, salubrious, stimulating, tonic, vitalizing. Opp EXHAUSTING.

invincible adj impregnable, indestructible, indomitable, insuperable, invulnerable, strong, unassailable, unbeatable, unconquerable, unstoppable.

invisible adj camouflaged, concealed, covered, disguised, hidden, imperceptible, inconspicuous, obscured, out of sight, secret, undetectable, unnoticeable, unnoticed, unseen. Opp VISIBLE.

invite vb 1 ask, encourage, request, summon, urge. 2 attract, entice, solicit, tempt. **inviting** ▷ ATTRACTIVE.

invoice n account, bill, list, statement.

invoke vb appeal to, call for, cry out for, entreat, implore, pray for, solicit, supplicate.

involuntary adj automatic, conditioned, impulsive, instinctive, mechanical, reflex, spontaneous, unconscious, uncontrollable, unintentional, unthinking, unwitting. Opp DELIBERATE.

involve vb 1 comprise, contain, embrace, entail, hold, include, incorporate, take in. 2 affect, concern, interest, touch. 3 involve in crime. embroil, implicate, include, incriminate, inculpate, inf mix up. **involved** ▷ BUSY, COMPLEX.

involvement n 1 activity, interest, participation. 2 association, complicity, entanglement, partnership.

ironic adj derisive, double-edged, ironical, mocking, sarcastic, satirical, wry.

irony n double meaning, mockery, paradox, sarcasm, satire.

irrational adj absurd, arbitrary, biased, crazy, emotional, emotive, illogical, insane, mad, nonsensical, prejudiced, senseless, subjective, surreal, unconvincing, unintelligent, unreasonable, unreasoning, unsound, unthinking, wild. ▷ SILLY. Opp RATIONAL.

irregular adj 1 erratic, fitful, fluctuating, halting, haphazard, intermittent, occasional, random, spasmodic, sporadic, unequal, unpredictable, unpunctual, variable, varying, wavering. 2 abnormal, anomalous, eccentric, exceptional, extraordinary, illegal, improper, odd, peculiar, quirky, unconventional, unofficial, unplanned, unscheduled, unusual. 3 irregular surface. broken, bumpy, jagged, lumpy, patchy, pitted, ragged, rough, uneven, up and down. Opp REGULAR.

irrelevant adj inf beside the point, extraneous, immaterial, impertinent, inapplicable, inapposite, inappropriate, inessential, malapropos, *inf* neither here nor there, pointless, unconnected, unnecessary, unrelated. *Opp* RELEVANT.

irreligious *adj* agnostic, atheistic, godless, heathen, humanist, impious, irreverent, pagan, sinful, uncommitted, unconverted, ungodly, unrighteous, wicked. *Opp* RELIGIOUS.

irreparable *adj* hopeless, incurable, irrecoverable, irremediable, irretrievable, irreversible, lasting, permanent, unalterable.

irreplaceable *adj* inimitable, priceless, unique. ▷ RARE.

irrepressible *adj* boisterous, bouncy, *inf* bubbling, buoyant, ebullient, resilient, uncontrollable, ungovernable, uninhibited, unmanageable, unrestrainable, unstoppable, vigorous. ▷ LIVELY. *Opp* LETHARGIC.

irresistible *adj* compelling, inescapable, inexorable, irrepressible, not to be denied, overpowering, overriding, overwhelming, persuasive, powerful, relentless, seductive, strong, unavoidable, uncontrollable. *Opp* WEAK.

irresolute *adj* doubtful, fickle, flexible, *inf* hedging your bets, indecisive, open to compromise, tentative, uncertain, undecided, vacillating, wavering, weak, weak-willed. ▷ HESITANT. *Opp* RESOLUTE.

irresponsible *adj* antisocial, careless, conscienceless, devilmay-care, feckless, immature, immoral, inconsiderate, negligent, rash, reckless, selfish, shiftless, thoughtless, unethical, unreliable, unthinking, untrustworthy, wild. *Opp* RESPONSIBLE.

irreverent *adj* blasphemous, disrespectful, impious, irreligious, profane, sacrilegious, ungodly, unholy. ▷ RUDE. *Opp* REVERENT.

irrevocable *adj* binding, final, fixed, hard and fast, immutable, irreparable, irretrievable, irreversible, permanent, settled, unalterable, unchangeable.

irrigate *vb* flood, inundate, supply water to, water.

irritable *adj* bad-tempered, cantankerous, choleric, crabby, cross, crotchety, crusty, curmudgeonly, dyspeptic, easily annoyed, edgy, fractious, grumpy, ill-humoured, ill-tempered, impatient, irascible, oversensitive, peevish, pettish, petulant, *inf* prickly, querulous, *inf* ratty, short-tempered, snappy, testy, tetchy, touchy, waspish. ▷ ANGRY. *Opp* EVEN-TEMPERED.

irritate *vb* 1 cause irritation, itch, rub, tickle, tingle. 2 ▷ ANNOY.

island *n plur* archipelago, atoll, coral reef, isle, islet.

isolate *vb* cloister, cordon off, cut off, detach, exclude, insulate, keep apart, place apart, quarantine, seclude, segregate, separate, sequester, set apart, shut off, shut out, single out. **isolated** ▷ SOLITARY.

issue *n* 1 affair, argument, controversy, dispute, matter, point, problem, question, subject, topic. 2 conclusion, consequence, effect, end, impact, outcome, *inf* payoff, repercussions, result, upshot. 3 *issue of a magazine.* copy, edition, instalment, number, printing, publication, version. ● *vb* 1 appear, come out, emerge, erupt, flow out, gush, leak, rise, spring. 2 announce, bring out, broadcast, circulate, declare, disseminate, distribute, give out, make public, print, produce, promulgate, publicize, publish, put out, release, send out, supply.

itch *n* 1 irritation, prickling, tickle, tingling. 2 ache, craving, desire, hankering, hunger, impatience, impulse, longing, need, restlessness, thirst, urge, wish, yearning, *inf* yen. ● *vb* 1 be irritated, prickle, tickle, tingle. 2 ▷ DESIRE.

item *n* 1 article, bit, component, contribution, entry, ingredient, lot, matter, object, particular, thing. 2 *item in a newspaper.* account, article, feature, notice, piece, report.

J

jab *vb* dig, elbow, nudge, poke, prod, stab, thrust. ▷ HIT.

jacket *n* casing, cover, covering, envelope, folder, sheath, skin, wrapper, wrapping. ▷ COAT.

jaded *adj* **1** ▷ WEARY. **2** bored, *inf* fed up, gorged, listless, sated, satiated, *inf* sick and tired, surfeited. *Opp* LIVELY.

jagged *adj* angular, barbed, broken, chipped, denticulate, indented, irregular, notched, ragged, rough, serrated, sharp, snagged, spiky, toothed, uneven, zigzag. *Opp* SMOOTH.

jail, jailer *ns* ▷ GAOL, GAOLER.

jam *n* **1** blockage, bottleneck, congestion, crush, obstruction, press, squeeze, stoppage, throng. ▷ CROWD. **2** difficulty, dilemma, embarrassment, *inf* fix, *inf* hole, *inf* hot water, *inf* pickle, plight, predicament, quandary, tight corner, trouble. **3** conserve, jelly, marmalade, preserve. ● *vb* **1** block, *inf* bung up, clog, congest, cram, crowd, crush, fill, force, pack, obstruct, overcrowd, ram, squash, squeeze, stop up, stuff. **2** prop, stick, wedge.

jar *n* amphora, carafe, container, crock, ewer, glass, jug, mug, pitcher, pot, receptacle, urn, vessel. ▷ BOTTLE. *vb* **1** jerk, jog, jolt, *inf* rattle, shake, shock, upset. **2** *That noise jars on me.* grate, grind, *inf* jangle. ▷ ANNOY. **jarring** ▷ HARSH.

jargon *n* argot, cant, creole, dialect, idiom, language, patois, slang, vernacular.

jaunt *n* excursion, expedition, outing, tour, trip. ▷ JOURNEY.

jaunty *adj* alert, breezy, bright, brisk, buoyant, carefree, *inf* cheeky, debonair, frisky, lively, perky, spirited, sprightly. ▷ HAPPY.

jazzy *adj* **1** animated, rhythmic, spirited, swinging, syncopated, vivacious. ▷ LIVELY. *Opp* SEDATE. **2** *jazzy colours.* bold, clashing, contrasting, flashy, gaudy, loud.

jealous *adj* **1** bitter, covetous, envious, *inf* green-eyed, *inf* green with envy, grudging, jaundiced, resentful. **2** *jealous of your reputation.* careful, possessive, protective, vigilant, watchful.

jeer *vb* barrack, boo, chaff, deride, disapprove, gibe, heckle, hiss, *inf* knock, laugh, make fun (of), mock, scoff, sneer, taunt, *inf* twit. ▷ RIDICULE. *Opp* CHEER.

jeopardize *vb* endanger, gamble, imperil, menace, put at risk, risk, threaten, venture.

jerk *vb* jar, jiggle, jog, jolt, lurch, move jerkily, move suddenly, pluck, pull, *inf* rattle, shake, tug, tweak, twist, twitch, wrench, *inf* yank.

jerky *adj* bouncy, bumpy, convulsive, erratic, fitful, jolting, jumpy, rough, shaky, spasmodic, *inf* stopping and starting, twitchy, uncontrolled, uneven. *Opp* STEADY.

jest *n*, *vb* ▷ JOKE.

jester *n* buffoon, clown, comedian, comic, fool, joker.

jet *adj* ▷ BLACK. ● *n* **1** flow, fountain, gush, rush, spout, spray, spurt, squirt, stream. **2** nozzle, sprinkler.

jetty *n* breakwater, groyne, landing-stage, mole, pier, quay, wharf.

jewel *n* brilliant, gem, gemstone, ornament, precious stone, *inf* rock, *inf* sparkler. ▷ JEWELLERY. □ amber, cairngorm, carnelian, coral, diamond, emerald, garnet, ivory, jade, jasper, jet, lapis lazuli, moonstone, onyx, opal, pearl, *rhinestone, ruby, sapphire, topaz, turquoise.*

jeweller n goldsmith, silversmith.

jewellery n gems, jewels, ornaments, treasure, *inf* sparklers. □ *bangle, beads, bracelet, brooch, chain, charm, clasp, cuff-links, earring, locket, necklace, pendant, pin, ring, signet ring, tie-pin, watch, watch-chain.*

jilt vb abandon, break with, desert, *inf* ditch, drop, *inf* dump, forsake, *inf* give someone the brush-off, leave behind, *inf* leave in the lurch, renounce, repudiate, *inf* throw over, *inf* wash your hands of.

jingle n **1** doggerel, rhyme, song, tune, verse. **2** chinking, clinking, jangling, ringing, tinkling, tintinnabulation. ● vb chime, chink, clink, jangle, ring, tinkle. ▷ SOUND.

job n **1** activity, assignment, charge, chore, duty, errand, function, housework, mission, operation, project, pursuit, responsibility, role, stint, task, undertaking, work. **2** appointment, business, calling, career, craft, employment, livelihood, living, métier, occupation, position, post, profession, sinecure, trade, vocation.

jobless adj out of work, redundant, unemployed, unwaged.

jocular adj cheerful, gay, glad, gleeful, happy, jocund, jokey, joking, jolly, jovial, joyous, jubilant, merry, overjoyed, rejoicing. Opp SAD, SERIOUS.

jog vb **1** bounce, jar, jerk, joggle, jolt, knock, nudge, shake. ▷ HIT. **2** *jog the memory.* activate, arouse, prompt, refresh, remind, set off, stimulate, stir. **3** *jog round the park.* exercise, lope, run, trot.

join n connection, joint, knot, link, mend, seam. ● vb **1** add, amalgamate, attach, combine, connect, couple, dock, dovetail, fit, fix, juxtapose, knit, link, marry, merge, put together, splice, tack on, unite, yoke. ▷ FASTEN. Opp SEPARATE. **2** abut, adjoin, border on, come together, converge, meet, touch, verge on. **3** *join a crowd.* accompany, associate with, follow, go with, *inf* latch on to, tag along

with, team up with. **4** *join a club.* affiliate with, become a member of, enlist in, enrol in, participate in, register for, sign up for, subscribe to, volunteer for. Opp LEAVE.

joint adj collaborative, collective, combined, common, communal, concerted, cooperative, corporate, general, mutual, shared, united. Opp SEPARATE. ● n articulation, connection, hinge, junction, union.

joist n beam, girder, rafter.

joke n *inf* crack, funny story, *inf* gag, old use jape, jest, laugh, *inf* one-liner, pleasantry, pun, quip, wisecrack, witticism. ● vb banter, be facetious, clown, fool about, have a laugh, jest, make jokes, quip, tease.

jolly adj cheerful, delighted, gay, glad, gleeful, grinning, high-spirited, jocose, jocular, jocund, joking, jovial, joyful, joyous, jubilant, laughing, merry, playful, rejoicing, rosy-faced, smiling, sportive. ▷ HAPPY. Opp SAD.

jolt vb **1** bounce, bump, jar, jerk, jog, shake, twitch. ▷ HIT. **2** *jolt me into action.* astonish, disturb, nonplus, shake up, shock, startle, stun, surprise.

jostle vb crowd in on, hustle, press, push, shove.

jot vb **jot down** note, scribble, take down. ▷ WRITE.

journal n **1** gazette, magazine, monthly, newsletter, newspaper, paper, periodical, publication, review, weekly. **2** account, annals, chronicle, diary, dossier, history, log, memoir, record, scrapbook.

journalist n broadcaster, columnist, contributor, correspondent, *derog* hack, *inf* newshound, newspaperman, newspaperwoman, pressman, reporter, writer.

journey n excursion, expedition, itinerary, jaunt, mission, odyssey, outing, peregrination, progress, route, tour, transition, travelling, trip, wandering. □ *cruise, drive, flight, hike, joyride, pilgrimage, ramble, ride, run, safari, sail, sea crossing, sea passage, trek, voyage, walk.* ● vb ▷ TRAVEL.

joy *n* bliss, cheer, cheerfulness, delight, ecstasy, elation, euphoria, exaltation, exhilaration, exultation, felicity, gaiety, gladness, glee, gratification, happiness, high spirits, hilarity, jocularity, joviality, joyfulness, joyousness, jubilation, light-heartedness, merriment, mirth, pleasure, rapture, rejoicing, triumph. *Opp* SORROW.

joyful *adj* buoyant, cheerful, delighted, ecstatic, elated, euphoric, exhilarated, exultant, gay, glad, gleeful, jocund, jolly, jovial, joyous, jubilant, light-hearted, merry, overjoyed, pleased, rapturous, rejoicing, triumphant. ▷ HAPPY. *Opp* SAD.

jubilee *n* anniversary, celebration, commemoration, festival.

judge *n* **1** *sl* beak, justice, magistrate. **2** adjudicator, arbiter, arbitrator, moderator, referee, umpire. **3** *judge of wine*. authority, connoisseur, critic, expert, reviewer. ● *vb* **1** condemn, convict, examine, pass judgement on, pronounce judgement on, punish, sentence, try. **2** adjudicate, mediate, moderate, referee, umpire. **3** believe, conclude, consider, decide, decree, deem, determine, estimate, gauge, guess, reckon, rule, suppose. **4** *judge others*. appraise, assess, criticize, evaluate, give your opinion of, rate, rebuke, scold, sit in judgement on, size up, weigh.

judgement *n* **1** arbitration, award, conclusion, conviction, decision, decree, *old use* doom, finding, outcome, penalty, punishment, result, ruling, verdict. **2** *use your judgement*. acumen, common sense, discernment, discretion, discrimination, expertise, good sense, reason, wisdom. ▷ INTELLIGENCE. **3** *in my judgement*. assessment, belief, estimation, evaluation, idea, impression, mind, notion, opinion, point of view, valuation.

judicial *adj* **1** forensic, legal, official. **2** ▷ JUDICIOUS.

judicious *adj* appropriate, astute, careful, circumspect, considered, diplomatic, discerning, discreet, discriminating, enlightened, expedient, judicial, politic, prudent, sage, sensible, shrewd, sober, thoughtful, well-advised, well-judged. ▷ WISE.

jug *n* bottle, carafe, container, decanter, ewer, flagon, flask, jar, pitcher, vessel.

juggle *vb* alter, *inf* cook, *inf* doctor, falsify, *inf* fix, manipulate, misrepresent, move about, rearrange, rig, tamper.

juice *n* drink, extract, fluid, liquid, sap.

juicy *adj* lush, moist, soft, *inf* squelchy, succulent, wet. *Opp* DRY.

jumble *n* chaos, clutter, confusion, disarray, disorder, farrago, hotchpotch, mess, muddle, tangle. ● *vb* confuse, disarrange, disorganize, *inf* mess up, mingle, mix up, muddle, shuffle, tangle. *Opp* ARRANGE.

jump *n* **1** bounce, bound, hop, leap, pounce, skip, spring, vault. **2** ditch, fence, gap, gate, hurdle, obstacle. **3** *a jump in prices*. ▷ RISE. ● *vb* **1** bounce, bound, caper, dance, frisk, frolic, gambol, hop, leap, pounce, prance, skip, spring. **2** *jump a fence*. clear, hurdle, vault. **3** *jump in surprise*. flinch, recoil, start, wince. **jump on** ▷ ATTACK. **make someone jump** ▷ STARTLE.

junction *n* confluence, connection, corner, crossroads, interchange, intersection, joining, juncture, *inf* link-up, meeting, points, T-junction, union.

jungle *n* forest, rain-forest, tangle, undergrowth, woods.

junior *adj* inferior, lesser, lower, minor, secondary, subordinate, subsidiary, younger. *Opp* SENIOR.

junk *n* clutter, debris, flotsam and jetsam, garbage, litter, lumber, oddments, odds and ends, refuse, rubbish, rummage, scrap, trash, waste. ● *vb* ▷ DISCARD.

just *adj* apt, deserved, equitable, ethical, even-handed, fair, fair-minded, honest, impartial, justified, lawful, legal, legitimate, merited, neutral, proper, reasonable, rightful, right-minded, unbiased, unprejudiced, upright. ▷ MORAL. *Opp* UNJUST.

justice *n* **1** equity, even-handedness, fair-mindedness, fair play, impartiality, integrity, legality, neutrality, objectivity, right. ▷ MORALITY. **2** the law, legal proceedings, the police, punishment, retribution, vengeance.

justifiable *adj* acceptable, allowable, defensible, excusable, forgivable, justified, lawful, legitimate, pardonable, permissible, reasonable, understandable, warranted. *Opp* UNJUSTIFIABLE.

justify *vb* condone, defend, exculpate, excuse, exonerate, explain, explain away, forgive, legitimate, legitimize, pardon, rationalize, substantiate, support, sustain, uphold, validate, vindicate, warrant.

jut *vb* beetle, extend, overhang, poke out, project, protrude, stick out. *Opp* RECEDE.

juvenile *adj* **1** babyish, childish, immature, infantile, puerile, unsophisticated. **2** adolescent, *inf* teenage, underage, young, youthful. *Opp* MATURE.

K

keen *adj* **1** active, ambitious, anxious, ardent, assiduous, avid, bright, clever, committed, dedicated, devoted, diligent, eager, enthusiastic, fervent, fervid, industrious, intelligent, intense, intent, interested, motivated, passionate, quick, zealous. **2** *a keen knife*. knife-edged, piercing, razorsharp, sharp, sharpened. **3** *a keen wit*. acerbic, acid, acute, biting, clever, cutting, discerning, incisive, lively, mordant, observant, pungent, rapier-like, sarcastic, satirical, scathing, shrewd, sophisticated, stinging. **4** *keen eyesight*. acute, clear, fine, perceptive, sensitive. **5** *a keen wind*. bitter, cold, extreme, icy, intense, penetrating, severe. **6** *keen prices*. competitive, low, rock-bottom. *Opp* APATHETIC, DULL.

keep *vb* **1** accumulate, amass, conserve, guard, hang on to, hoard, hold, maintain, preserve, protect, put aside, put away, retain, safeguard, save, store, stow away, withhold. **2** *keep going*. carry on, continue, do again and again, do for a long time, keep on, persevere in, persist in. **3** *keep left*. remain, stay. **4** *keep a family*. be responsible for, care for, cherish, feed, finance, foster, guard, have charge of, look after, maintain, manage, mind, own, pay for, protect, provide for, subsidize, support, take charge of, tend, watch over. **5** *keep a birthday*. celebrate, commemorate, mark, observe, solemnize. **6** *food keeps in the fridge*. be preserved, be usable, last, survive, stay fresh, stay good. **7** *won't keep you*. block, check, confine, curb, delay, detain, deter, get in the way of, hamper, hinder, hold up, impede, imprison, obstruct, prevent, restrain, retard. **keep still**

▷ STAY. **keep to** ▷ FOLLOW, OBEY. **keep up** ▷ PROLONG, SUSTAIN.

keeper *n* caretaker, curator, custodian, gaoler, guard, guardian, *inf* minder, warden, warder.

kernel *n* centre, core, essence, heart, middle, nub, pith.

key *n* **1** answer, clarification, clue, explanation, indicator, pointer, secret, solution. **2** *key to a map*. glossary, guide, index, legend.

keyboard *n* □ accordion, celesta, clavichord, clavier, fortepiano, harmonium, harpsichord, organ, piano, old use pianoforte, spinet, synthesizer, virginals.

kick *vb* boot, heel, punt. ▷ HIT.

kidnap *vb* abduct, capture, carry off, run away with, seize, snatch.

kill *vb* annihilate, assassinate, be the killer of, *sl* bump off, butcher, cull, decimate, destroy, *inf* dispatch, *inf* do away with, *sl* do in, execute, exterminate, *inf* finish off, *inf* knock off, liquidate, martyr, massacre, murder, put down, put to death, put to sleep, slaughter, slay, *inf* snuff out, take life, *Amer sl* waste. □ behead, brain, choke, crucify, decapitate, disembowel, drown, electrocute, eviscerate, garrotte, gas, guillotine, hang, knife, lynch, poison, pole-axe, shoot, smother, stab, starve, stifle, stone, strangle, suffocate, throttle.

killer *n* assassin, butcher, cutthroat, destroyer, executioner, exterminator, gunman, *sl* hit man, murderer, slayer.

killing *n* annihilation, assassination, bloodbath, bloodshed, butchery, carnage, decimation, destruction, elimination, eradication, euthanasia, execution, extermination, extinction, fratricide, genocide, homicide, infanticide, liquidation, manslaughter, martyrdom, massacre, matricide, murder, parricide, patricide, pogrom, regicide, slaughter, sororicide, suicide, unlawful killing, uxoricide.

kin n clan, family, *inf* folks, kindred, kith and kin, relations, relatives.

kind adj accommodating, affable, affectionate, agreeable, altruistic, amenable, amiable, amicable, approachable, attentive, avuncular, beneficent, benevolent, benign, bountiful, brotherly, caring, charitable, comforting, compassionate, congenial, considerate, cordial, courteous, encouraging, fatherly, favourable, friendly, generous, genial, gentle, good-natured, good-tempered, gracious, helpful, hospitable, humane, humanitarian, indulgent, kind-hearted, kindly, lenient, loving, merciful, mild, motherly, neighbourly, nice, obliging, patient, philanthropic, pleasant, polite, public-spirited, sensitive, sisterly, soft-hearted, sweet, sympathetic, tactful, tender, tender-hearted, thoughtful, tolerant, understanding, unselfish, warm, warm-hearted, well-intentioned, well-meaning, well-meant. *Opp* UNKIND. ● n brand, breed, category, class, description, family, form, genre, genus, make, manner, nature, persuasion, race, set, sort, species, style, type, variety.

kindle vb 1 burn, fire, ignite, light, set alight, set fire to, spark off. 2 ▷ AROUSE.

king n 1 crowned head, His Majesty, monarch, ruler, sovereign. 2 ▷ CHIEF.

kingdom n country, empire, land, monarchy, realm.

kink n 1 bend, coil, crimp, crinkle, curl, knot, loop, tangle, twist, wave. 2 ▷ QUIRK.

kiosk n booth, stall. □ *bookstall, newsstand, telephone-box.*

kiss vb caress, embrace, *sl* neck, osculate, *old use* spoon. ▷ TOUCH.

kit n accoutrements, apparatus, appurtenances, baggage, effects, equipment, gear, *joc* impedimenta, implements, luggage, outfit, paraphernalia, rig, supplies, tackle, tools, tools of the trade, utensils.

kitchen n cookhouse, galley, kitchenette, scullery.

knack n ability, adroitness, aptitude, art, bent, dexterity, expertise, facility, flair, genius, gift, habit, intuition, *inf* know-how, skill, talent, trick, *inf* way.

knapsack n backpack, haversack, rucksack.

knead vb manipulate, massage, pound, press, pummel, squeeze, work.

kneel vb bend, bow, crouch, fall to your knees, genuflect, stoop.

knickers plur n old use bloomers, boxer-shorts, briefs, drawers, panties, pants, shorts, trunks, underpants.

knife n blade. □ *butter-knife, carving-knife, clasp-knife, cleaver, dagger, flick-knife, machete, penknife, pocket-knife, scalpel, sheath knife.* ● vb cut, pierce, slash, stab. ▷ KILL, WOUND.

knit vb 1 crochet, weave. 2 bind, combine, connect, fasten, heal, interlace, interweave, join, knot, link, marry, mend, tie, unite. **knit your brow** ▷ FROWN.

knob n boss, bulge, bump, handle, lump, projection, protrusion, protuberance, stud, swelling.

knock vb 1 bang, *inf* bash, buffet, bump, pound, rap, smack, *old use* smite, strike, tap, thump. ▷ HIT. 2 ▷ CRITICIZE. **knock down** ▷ DEMOLISH. **knock off** ▷ CEASE. **knock out** ▷ STUN.

knot n 1 bond, bow, ligature, tangle, tie. 2 ▷ GROUP. ● vb bind, do up, entangle, entwine, join, knit, lash, link, tether, tie, unite. ▷ FASTEN. *Opp* UNTIE.

know vb 1 be certain, have confidence, have no doubt. 2 *know facts.* be cognizant of, be familiar with, be knowledgeable about, comprehend, discern, have experience of, have in mind, realize, remember, understand. 3 *know a person.* be acquainted with, be a friend of, be friends with.

4 differentiate, distinguish, identify, make out, perceive, recognize, see.

know-all *n* expert, pundit, *inf* show-off, wiseacre.

knowing *adj* astute, clever, conspiratorial, cunning, discerning, experienced, expressive, meaningful, perceptive, shrewd. ▷ CUNNING, KNOWLEDGEABLE. *Opp* INNOCENT.

knowledge *n* **1** data, facts, information, intelligence, *sl* low-down. **2** acquaintance, awareness, background, cognition, competence, consciousness, education, erudition, experience, expertise, familiarity, grasp, insight, *inf* know-how, learning, lore, memory, science, scholarship, skill, sophistication, technique, training. *Opp* IGNORANCE.

knowledgeable *adj* *Fr* au fait, aware, cognizant, conversant, educated, enlightened, erudite, experienced, expert, familiar (with), *sl* genned up, informed, *inf* in the know, learned, scholarly, versed (in), well-informed. *Opp* IGNORANT.

L

label n brand, docket, hallmark, identification, imprint, logo, marker, sticker, tag, ticket, trademark. ● vb brand, call, categorize, class, classify, define, describe, docket, identify, mark, name, pigeon-hole, stamp, tag.

laborious adj **1** arduous, back-breaking, difficult, exhausting, fatiguing, gruelling, hard, heavy, herculean, onerous, stiff, strenuous, taxing, tiresome, tough, uphill, wearisome, wearying. Opp EASY. **2** a laborious style. artificial, contrived, forced, heavy, laboured, overdone, overworked, pedestrian, ponderous, strained, unnatural. Opp FLUENT.

labour n **1** inf donkey-work, drudgery, effort, exertion, industry, navvying, inf pains, slavery, strain, inf sweat, toil, work. **2** employees, old use hands, wage-earners, workers, workforce. **3** childbirth, contractions, delivery, labour pains, parturition, old use travail. ● vb drudge, exert yourself, navvy, inf slave, strain, strive, struggle, inf sweat, toil, travail. ▷ WORK. **laboured** ▷ LABORIOUS.

labourer n blue-collar worker, employee, old use hand, manual worker, inf navvy, wage-earner, worker.

labour-saving adj convenient, handy, helpful, time-saving.

labyrinth n complex, jungle, maze, network, tangle.

lace n **1** filigree, mesh, net, netting, openwork, tatting, web. **2** bootlace, cord, shoelace, string, thong. ● vb ▷ FASTEN.

lacerate vb claw, cut, gash, graze, mangle, rip, scrape, scratch, slash, tear. ▷ WOUND.

lack n absence, dearth, deficiency, deprivation, famine, insufficiency, need, paucity, privation, scarcity, shortage, want. Opp PLENTY. ● vb be lacking in, be short of, be without, miss, need, require, want.

lacking adj defective, deficient, inadequate, insufficient, short, unsatisfactory, weak. ▷ STUPID.

laden adj burdened, inf chock-full, fraught, full, hampered, loaded, oppressed, piled high, weighed down.

lady n **1** wife, woman. ▷ FEMALE. **2** aristocrat, peeress. ▷ TITLE.

ladylike adj aristocratic, courtly, cultured, dainty, decorous, elegant, genteel, modest, noble, polished, posh, prim and proper, derog prissy, refined, respectable, well-born, well-bred. ▷ POLITE.

lag vb **1** be slow, inf bring up the rear, come last, dally, dawdle, delay, drop behind, fall behind, go too slow, hang about, hang back, idle, linger, loiter, saunter, straggle, trail. **2** lag pipes. insulate, wrap up.

lair n den, hide-out, hiding-place, refuge, resting-place, retreat, shelter.

lake n boating-lake, lagoon, lido, Scot loch, mere, pool, pond, reservoir, sea, tarn, water.

lame adj **1** crippled, disabled, halting, handicapped, hobbled, hobbling, incapacitated, limping, maimed, spavined. **2** a lame leg. dragging, game, inf gammy, injured, stiff. **3** a lame excuse. feeble, flimsy, inadequate, poor, tame, thin, unconvincing, weak. ● vb cripple, disable, hobble, incapacitate, maim. **be lame** ▷ LIMP.

lament *n* dirge, elegy, lamentation, moaning, monody, mourning, requiem, threnody. ● *vb* bemoan, bewail, complain, cry, deplore, express your sorrow, grieve, keen, mourn, regret, shed tears, sorrow, wail, weep.

lamentable *adj* deplorable, regrettable, unfortunate, unhappy. ▷ SAD.

lamentation *n* complaints, crying, grief, grieving, lamenting, moaning, mourning, regrets, sobbing, tears, wailing, weeping.

lamp *n* bulb, fluorescent lamp, headlamp, lantern, standard lamp, street light, torch. ▷ LIGHT.

land *n* **1** coast, ground, landfall, shore, *joc* terra firma. **2** *lie of the land.* geography, landscape, terrain, topography. **3** country, fatherland, homeland, motherland, nation, region, state, territory. **4** earth, farmland, soil. **5** *land you own.* estate, grounds, property. ● *vb* **1** alight, arrive, berth, come ashore, come to rest, disembark, dismount, dock, end a journey, get down, go ashore, light, reach landfall, settle, touch down. **2** *land yourself a job.* ▷ GET.

landing *n* **1** docking, re-entry, return, splashdown, touchdown. **2** alighting, arrival, deplaning, disembarkation. **3** ▷ LANDING-STAGE.

landing-stage *n* berth, dock, harbour, jetty, landing, pier, quay, wharf.

landlady,

landlord *ns* **1** host, hostess, hotelier, *old use* innkeeper, licensee, publican, restaurateur. **2** landowner, lessor, letter, manager, manageress, owner, proprietor.

landmark *n* **1** feature, guidepost, high point, identification, visible feature. **2** milestone, new era, turning-point, watershed.

landscape *n* aspect, countryside, outlook, panorama, prospect, rural scene, scene, scenery, view, vista.

language *n* **1** parlance, speech, tongue. □ *argot, cant, colloquialism,* *dialect, formal language, idiolect, idiom, informal language, jargon, journalese, lingua franca, inf lingo, patois, register, slang, vernacular.* **2** linguistics. □ *etymology, lexicography, orthography, philology, phonetics, psycholinguistics, semantics, semiotics, sociolinguistics.* **3** *computer language.* code, system of signs.

languid *adj* apathetic, *inf* droopy, feeble, inactive, inert, lackadaisical, lazy, lethargic, slow, sluggish, torpid, unenthusiastic, weak. *Opp* ENERGETIC.

languish *vb* decline, flag, lose momentum, mope, pine, slow down, stagnate, suffer, sulk, waste away, weaken, wither. *Opp* FLOURISH.

lank *adj* **1** drooping, lifeless, limp, long, straight, thin. **2** ▷ LANKY.

lanky *adj* angular, awkward, bony, gangling, gaunt, lank, lean, long, scraggy, scrawny, skinny, tall, thin, ungraceful, weedy. *Opp* GRACEFUL, STURDY.

lap *n* **1** knees, thighs. **2** circle, circuit, course, orbit, revolution. ● *vb* ▷ DRINK.

lapse *n* **1** backsliding, blunder, decline, error, failing, fault, flaw, mistake, omission, relapse, shortcoming, slip, *inf* slip-up, temporary failure, weakness. **2** *lapse of time.* break, gap, hiatus, *inf* hold-up, intermission, interruption, interval, lacuna, lull, pause. ● *vb* **1** decline, deteriorate, diminish, drop, fall, sink, slide, slip, slump, subside. **2** *My membership lapsed.* become invalid, expire, finish, run out, stop, terminate.

large *adj* above average, abundant, ample, big, bold, broad, bulky, burly, capacious, colossal, commodious, considerable, copious, elephantine, enormous, extensive, fat, formidable, gargantuan, generous, giant, gigantic, grand, great, heavy, hefty, high, huge, *inf* hulking, immense, immeasurable, impressive, incalculable, infinite, *inf* jumbo, *inf* king-sized, largish, lofty, long, mammoth, massive, mighty, monstrous, monumental, mountainous, outsize, overgrown, oversized, prodigious, *inf* roomy, sizeable, spacious, substantial, swingeing (*increase*), tall, thick, *inf* thumping, *inf* tidy (*sum*), titanic, towering, *inf* tremendous, vast, voluminous, weighty, *inf* whacking, *inf* whopping, wide. *Opp* SMALL.

larva *n* caterpillar, grub, maggot.

lash *n* ▷ WHIP. ● *vb* **1** beat, birch, cane, flail, flog, scourge, strike, thrash, whip. ▷ HIT. **2** ▷ CRITICIZE.

last *adj* closing, concluding, final, furthest, hindmost, latest, most recent, rearmost, terminal, terminating, ultimate. *Opp* FIRST. ● *vb* carry on, continue, endure, hold, hold out, keep on, linger, live, persist, remain, stay, survive, *inf* wear well. *Opp* DIE, FINISH. **lasting** ▷ PERMANENT.

late *adj* **1** behindhand, belated, delayed, dilatory, overdue, slow, tardy, unpunctual. **2** *a late edition.* current, last, new, recent, up-to-date. **3** *the late king.* dead, deceased, departed, ex-, former, past, previous.

latent *adj* dormant, hidden, invisible, potential, undeveloped, undiscovered.

latitude *n inf* elbow-room, freedom, leeway, liberty, room, scope, space.

latter *adj* closing, concluding, last, last-mentioned, later, recent, second. *Opp* FORMER.

lattice *n* criss-cross, framework, grid, mesh, trellis.

laugh *vb* beam, be amused, burst into laughter, chortle, chuckle, *sl* fall about, giggle, grin, guffaw, roar with laughter, simper, smile, smirk, sneer, snicker, snigger, *inf* split your sides, titter. **laugh at** ▷ RIDICULE.

laughable *adj* absurd, derisory, ludicrous, preposterous, ridiculous. ▷ FUNNY.

laughing-stock *n* butt, figure of fun, victim.

laughter *n* chuckling, giggling, guffawing, hilarity, *inf* hysterics, laughing, laughs, merriment, mirth, snickering, sniggering, tittering. ▷ RIDICULE.

launch *vb* **1** begin, embark on, establish, float, found, inaugurate, initiate, open, organize, set in motion, set off, set up, start. **2** blast off, catapult, dispatch, fire, propel, send off, set off, shoot.

lavatory *n* bathroom, cloakroom, convenience, *inf* Gents, *inf* Ladies, latrine, *inf* loo, *inf* men's room, *childish* potty, *old use* privy, public convenience, toilet, urinal, water-closet, WC, *inf* women's room.

lavish *adj* **1** abundant, bountiful, copious, exuberant, free, generous, liberal, luxuriant, luxurious, munificent, opulent, plentiful, profuse, sumptuous, unselfish, unsparing, unstinting. **2** excessive, extravagant, improvident, prodigal, self-indulgent, wasteful. *Opp* ECONOMICAL.

law *n* **1** act, bill [= *draft law*], bylaw, commandment, decree, directive, edict, injunction, mandate, measure, order, ordinance, pronouncement, regulation, rule, statute. **2** *laws of science.* axiom, formula, postulate, principle, proposition, theory. **3** *laws of decency.* code, convention, practice. **4** *court of law.* justice, litigation.

law-abiding *adj* compliant, decent, disciplined, good, honest, obedient, orderly, peaceable, peaceful, respectable, well-behaved. *Opp* LAWLESS.

lawful *adj* allowable, allowed, authorized, constitutional, documented, just, justifiable, legal, legitimate, permissible, permitted, prescribed, proper, recognized, regular, right, rightful, valid. *Opp* ILLEGAL.

lawless *adj* anarchic, anarchical, badly-behaved, chaotic, disobedient, disorderly, illdisciplined, insubordinate, mutinous, rebellious, riotous, rowdy, seditious, turbulent, uncontrolled, undisciplined, ungoverned, unregulated, unrestrained, unruly, wild. ▷ WICKED. *Opp* LAW-ABIDING.

lawlessness n anarchy, chaos, disobedience, disorder, mob-rule, rebellion, rioting. *Opp* ORDER.

lawyer n advocate, barrister, counsel, legal representative, member of the bar, solicitor.

lax adj careless, casual, easygoing, flexible, indulgent, lenient, loose, neglectful, negligent, permissive, relaxed, remiss, slack, slipshod, unreliable, vague. *Opp* STRICT.

laxative n aperient, enema, purgative.

lay vb 1 apply, arrange, deposit, leave, place, position, put down, rest, set down, set out, spread. 2 *lay foundations*. build, construct, establish. 3 *lay the blame on someone*. ascribe, assign, attribute, burden, charge, impose, plant, *inf* saddle. 4 *lay plans*. concoct, create, design, organize, plan, set up. **lay bare** ▷ REVEAL. **lay bets** ▷ GAMBLE. **lay by** ▷ STORE. **lay down the law** ▷ DICTATE. **lay in** ▷ STORE. **lay into** ▷ ATTACK. **lay low** ▷ DEFEAT. **lay off something** ▷ CEASE. **lay someone off** ▷ DISMISS. **lay to rest** ▷ BURY. **lay up** ▷ STORE. **lay waste** ▷ DESTROY.

layer n 1 coat, coating, covering, film, sheet, skin, surface, thickness. 2 *layer of rock*. seam, stratum, substratum. **in layers** laminated, layered, sandwiched, stratified.

layman n 1 amateur, nonspecialist, untrained person. *Opp* PROFESSIONAL. 2 [church] layperson, member of the congregation, parishioner, unordained person. *Opp* CLERGYMAN.

laze vb be lazy, do nothing, idle, lie about, loaf, lounge, relax, sit about, unwind.

laziness n dilatoriness, idleness, inactivity, indolence, lethargy, loafing, lounging about, shiftlessness, slackness, sloth, slowness, sluggishness, torpor. *Opp* INDUSTRY.

lazy adj 1 dilatory, easily pleased, easygoing, idle, inactive, indolent, languid, lethargic, listless, shiftless, *inf* skiving, slack, slothful, slow, sluggish, torpid, unenterprising, workshy. 2 peaceful, quiet, relaxing. *Opp* ENERGETIC, INDUSTRIOUS. **be lazy** ▷ LAZE. **lazy person** ▷ SLACKER.

lead n 1 direction, example, guidance, leadership, model, pattern, precedent. 2 *lead on a crime*. clue, hint, line, tip, tip-off. 3 *lead in a race*. first place, front, spearhead, van, vanguard. 4 *lead in a play*. chief part, hero, heroine, principal, protagonist, starring role, title role. 5 cable, flex, wire. 6 *dog's lead*. chain, leash, strap. ● vb 1 conduct, draw, escort, guide, influence, pilot, prompt, show the way, steer, usher. 2 be in charge of, captain, command, direct, govern, head, manage, preside over, rule, *inf* skipper, superintend, supervise. 3 be first, be in front, be in the lead, go first, head the field. 4 *lead the field*. beat, defeat, excel, outdo, outstrip, precede, surpass, vanquish. *Opp* FOLLOW. **lead astray** ▷ MISLEAD. **leading** ▷ CHIEF, INFLUENTIAL. **lead off** ▷ BEGIN.

leader n 1 ayatollah, boss, captain, chieftain, commander, conductor, courier, demagogue, director, figurehead, godfather, guide, head, patriarch, premier, prime minister, principal, ringleader, superior, *inf* supremo. ▷ CHIEF, RULER. 2 *leader in a newspaper*. editorial, leading article.

leaf n 1 blade, foliage, frond, greenery. 2 folio, page, sheet.

leaflet n advertisement, bill, booklet, brochure, circular, flyer, folder, handbill, handout, notice, pamphlet.

league n alliance, association, coalition, confederation, *derog* conspiracy, federation, fraternity, guild, society, union. ▷ GROUP. **be in league with** ▷ CONSPIRE.

leak n 1 discharge, drip, emission, escape, exudation, leakage, oozing, seepage, trickle. 2 aperture, break, chink, crack, crevice, cut, fissure, flaw, hole, opening, perforation, puncture, rent, split, tear. 3 *security leak*. disclosure, revelation. ● vb 1 discharge, drip, escape, exude, ooze, percolate, seep, spill, trickle. 2 *leak secrets*. disclose, divulge, give away, let out, let slip, *inf* let the cat out of the bag about, make known, pass on, reveal, inf spill the beans about.

leaky adj cracked, dripping, holed, perforated, punctured.

lean adj angular, bony, emaciated, gangling, gaunt, hungry-looking, lanky, long, rangy, scraggy, scrawny, skinny, slender, slim, spare, thin, weedy, wiry. Opp FAT. ● vb **1** bank, careen, heel over, incline, keel over, list, slant, slope, tilt, tip. **2** loll, prop yourself up, recline, rest, support yourself.

leaning n bent, bias, favouritism, inclination, instinct, liking, partiality, penchant, predilection, preference, propensity, readiness, taste, tendency, trend.

leap vb **1** bound, clear (a fence), hop over, hurdle, jump, leapfrog, skip over, spring, vault. **2** caper, cavort, dance, frisk, frolic, gambol, hop, prance, romp. **3** leap on someone. ambush, attack, pounce.

learn vb acquire, ascertain, assimilate, become aware of, become proficient in, be taught, inf catch on, commit to memory, discover, find out, gain, grasp, master, memorize, inf mug up, pick up, remember, study, inf swot up. **learned** ▷ ACADEMIC, EDUCATED.

learner n apprentice, beginner, cadet, initiate, L-driver, novice, pupil, scholar, starter, student, trainee, tiro.

learning n culture, education, erudition, information, knowledge, lore, scholarship, wisdom.

lease n agreement, contract. ● vb charter, hire out, let, rent out, sublet.

least adj fewest, lowest, minimum, negligible, poorest, slightest, smallest, tiniest.

leather n chamois, hide, skin, suede.

leave n **1** authorization, consent, dispensation, liberty, licence, permission, sanction. **2** leave from work. absence, free time, furlough, holiday, recess, sabbatical, time off, vacation. ● vb **1** inf be off, inf check out,

decamp, depart, disappear, sl do a bunk, escape, exeunt [they go out], exit [he/she goes out], get away, get out, go away, go out, sl hop it, inf pull out, sl push off, retire, retreat, run away, say goodbye, set off, inf take off, take your leave, withdraw. **2** abandon, desert, evacuate, forsake, vacate. **3** leave your job. inf chuck in, inf drop out of, give up, quit, relinquish, renounce, resign from, retire from, inf walk out of, inf wash your hands of. **4** leave it there. allow to stay, inf let alone, let be. **5** left it here. deposit, place, position, put down, set down. **6** left it somewhere. forget, lose, mislay. **7** leave it to you. assign, cede, consign, entrust, refer, relinquish. **8** leave in a will. bequeath, hand down, will. **leave off** ▷ STOP. **leave out** ▷ OMIT.

lecture n **1** address, discourse, disquisition, instruction, lesson, paper, speech, talk, treatise. **2** lecture on bad manners. diatribe, harangue, sermon. ▷ REPRIMAND. ● vb **1** be a lecturer, teach. **2** discourse, give a lecture, harangue, inf hold forth, pontificate, preach, sermonize, speak, talk formally. **3** ▷ REPRIMAND.

lecturer n don, fellow, instructor, professor, speaker, teacher, tutor.

ledge n mantel, overhang, projection, ridge, shelf, sill, step, windowsill.

left adj, n **1** left-hand, port [= left facing bow of ship], sinistral. **2** left wing in politics. communist, Labour, leftist, liberal, Marxist, progressive, radical, derog red, revolutionary, socialist. Opp RIGHT.

leg n **1** limb, member, inf peg, inf pin, shank. □ ankle, calf, foot, hock, knee, shin, thigh. **2** brace, column, pillar, prop, support, upright. **3** leg of a journey. lap, length, part, section, stage, stretch. **pull someone's leg** ▷ HOAX.

legacy n bequest, endowment, estate, inheritance.

legal adj **1** above-board, acceptable, admissible, allowable, allowed, authorized, constitutional, just, lawful, legalized, legitimate, licensed, licit,

legalize

permitted, permissible, proper, regular, right, rightful, valid. *Opp* ILLEGAL. **2** *legal proceedings*. forensic, judicial, judiciary.

legalize *vb* allow, authorize, legitimate, legitimize, license, make legal, normalize, permit, regularize, validate. *Opp* BAN.

legend *n* epic, folk-tale, myth, saga, tradition. ▷ STORY.

legendary *adj* **1** apocryphal, epic, fabled, fabulous, fictional, fictitious, imaginary, invented, made-up, mythical, non-existent, story-book, traditional. **2** *a legendary name*. ▷ FAMOUS.

legible *adj* clear, decipherable, distinct, intelligible, neat, plain, readable, understandable. *Opp* ILLEGIBLE.

legitimate *adj* **1** authentic, genuine, proper, real, regular, true. ▷ LEGAL. **2** *a legitimate deception*. ethical, just, justifiable, moral, proper, reasonable, right. *Opp* ILLEGITIMATE. ● *vb* ▷ LEGALIZE.

leisure *n* breathing-space, ease, holiday, liberty, opportunity, quiet, recreation, relaxation, relief, repose, respite, rest, spare time, time off.

leisurely *adj* easy, gentle, lingering, peaceful, relaxed, relaxing, restful, unhurried. ▷ SLOW. *Opp* BRISK.

lend *vb* advance, loan. *Opp* BORROW.

length *n* **1** distance, extent, footage, measure, measurement, mileage, reach, size, span, stretch. **2** duration, period, stretch, term.

lengthen *vb* continue, drag out, draw out, elongate, enlarge, expand, extend, get longer, increase, make longer, *inf* pad out, prolong, protract, pull out, stretch. *Opp* SHORTEN.

lenient *adj* charitable, easygoing, forbearing, forgiving, gentle, humane, indulgent, merciful, mild, permissive, soft, soft-hearted, sparing, tolerant. ▷ KIND. *Opp* STRICT.

less *adj* fewer, reduced, shorter, smaller. *Opp* MORE.

lessen *vb* **1** assuage, cut, deaden, decrease, ease, lighten, lower, make less, minimize, mitigate, reduce,

relieve, tone down. **2** abate, become less, decline, decrease, die away, diminish, dwindle, ease off, let up, moderate, slacken, subside, tail off, weaken. *Opp* INCREASE.

lesson *n* **1** class, drill, instruction, laboratory, lecture, practical, seminar, session, task, teaching, tutorial, workshop. **2** *a moral lesson*. admonition, example, moral, warning.

let *vb* **1** agree to, allow to, authorize to, consent to, enable to, give permission to, license to, permit to, sanction to. **2** *let a house*. charter, contract out, hire, lease, rent. **let alone**, **let be** ▷ LEAVE. **let go**, **let loose** ▷ LIBERATE. **let off** ▷ FIRE. **let out** ▷ LIBERATE. **let someone off** ▷ ACQUIT. **let up** ▷ LESSEN.

letdown *n* anti-climax, disappointment, disillusionment, *inf* wash-out.

lethal *adj* deadly, fatal, mortal, poisonous.

lethargic *adj* apathetic, comatose, dull, heavy, inactive, indifferent, indolent, languid, lazy, listless, phlegmatic, sleepy, slow, slothful, sluggish, torpid. ▷ WEARY. *Opp* ENERGETIC.

lethargy *n* apathy, idleness, inactivity, indolence, inertia, laziness, listlessness, slothfulness, slowness, sluggishness, torpor, weariness. *Opp* ENERGY.

letter *n* **1** character, consonant, sign, symbol, vowel. **2** *old use* billet-doux, card, communication, dispatch, epistle, message, missive, note, postcard. **letters** correspondence, junk mail, mail, post.

level *adj* **1** even, flat, flush, horizontal, plane, regular, smooth, straight, true, uniform. **2** horizontal. **3** *level scores*. balanced, even, equal, matching, *inf* neck-and-neck, the same. *Opp* UNEVEN. ● *n* **1** altitude, depth, elevation, height, value. **2** degree, echelon, grade, plane, position, rank, *inf* rung on the ladder, stage, standard, standing, status. **3** *level in a building*. floor, storey. ● *vb* **1** even out, flatten, rake, smooth.

2 bulldoze, demolish, destroy, devastate, knock down, lay low, raze, tear down, wreck. **level-headed** ▷ SENSIBLE.

lever vb force, prise, wrench.

liable adj **1** accountable, answerable, blameworthy, responsible. **2** *liable to fall over.* apt, disposed, inclined, in the habit of, likely, minded, predisposed, prone, ready, susceptible, tempted, vulnerable, willing.

liaison n **1** communication, contact, cooperation, liaising, linkage, links, mediation, relationship, tie. **2** ▷ AFFAIR.

liar n deceiver, false witness, *inf* fibber, perjurer, *inf* story-teller.

libel n calumny, defamation, denigration, insult, lie, misrepresentation, obloquy, scandal, slander, slur, smear, vilification. ● vb blacken the name of, calumniate, defame, denigrate, disparage, malign, misrepresent, slander, slur, smear, write lies about, traduce, vilify.

libellous adj calumnious, cruel, damaging, defamatory, disparaging, false, hurtful, insulting, lying, malicious, mendacious, scurrilous, slanderous, untrue, vicious.

liberal adj **1** abundant, ample, bounteous, bountiful, copious, free, generous, lavish, munificent, open-handed, plentiful, unstinting. **2** *liberal attitudes.* big-hearted, broadminded, charitable, easygoing, enlightened, fair-minded, humanitarian, indulgent, impartial, latitudinarian, lenient, magnanimous, open-minded, permissive, philanthropic, tolerant, unbiased, unbigoted, unopinionated, unprejudiced, unselfish. *Opp* NARROW-MINDED. **3** *liberal politics.* progressive, radical, reformist. *Opp* CONSERVATIVE.

liberalize vb broaden, ease, enlarge, make more liberal, moderate, open up, relax, soften, widen.

liberate vb deliver, discharge, disenthral, emancipate, enfranchise, free, let go, let loose, let out, loose, manumit, ransom, release, rescue, save, set free, untie. *Opp* CAPTURE, SUBJUGATE.

liberty n autonomy, emancipation, independence, liberation, release, self-determination, self-rule. ▷ FREEDOM. **at liberty** ▷ FREE.

licence n **1** certificate, credentials, document, papers, permit, warrant. **2** ▷ FREEDOM.

license vb **1** allow, approve, authorize, certify, commission, empower, entitle, give a licence to, permit, sanction, validate. **2** buy a licence for, make legal.

lid n cap, cover, covering, top.

lie n deceit, dishonesty, disinformation, fabrication, falsehood, falsification, *inf* fib, fiction, invention, misrepresentation, prevarication, untruth, *inf* whopper. *Opp* TRUTH. ● vb **1** *inf* be economical with the truth, bluff, commit perjury, deceive, falsify the facts, *inf* fib, perjure yourself, prevaricate, tell lies. **2** be horizontal, be prone, be prostrate, be recumbent, be supine, lean back, lounge, recline, repose, rest, sprawl, stretch out. **3** *The house lies in a valley.* be, be found, be located, be situated, exist. **lie low** ▷ HIDE.

life n **1** being, existence, living. **2** activity, animation, dash, élan, energy, enthusiasm, exuberance, *inf* go, liveliness, soul, sparkle, spirit, sprightliness, verve, vigour, vitality, vivacity, zest. **3** autobiography, biography, memoir, story.

lifeless adj **1** comatose, dead, deceased, inanimate, inert, insensate, insensible, killed, motionless, unconscious. **2** *lifeless desert.* arid, bare, barren, desolate, empty, sterile, uninhabited, waste. **3** *a lifeless performance.* apathetic, boring, dull, flat, heavy, lacklustre, lethargic, slow, torpid, unexciting, wooden. *Opp* LIVELY, LIVING.

lifelike adj authentic, convincing, faithful, graphic, natural, photographic, realistic, true-to-life, vivid. *Opp* UNREALISTIC.

lift n elevator, hoist. ● vb **1** buoy up, carry, elevate, heave up, hoist, jack

up, pick up, pull up, raise, rear.
2 ascend, fly, lift off, rise, soar.
3 boost, cheer, enhance, improve,
promote. **4** ▷ STEAL.

light *adj* **1** lightweight, portable,
underweight, weightless. *Opp* HEAVY.
2 bright, illuminated, lit-up, well-lit.
Opp DARK. **3** *light work.* ▷ EASY. **4** *a light
wind.* ▷ GENTLE. **5** *a light touch.* ▷ DELIC-
ATE. **6** *light colours.* ▷ PALE. **7** *a light
heart.* ▷ CHEERFUL. **8** *light traffic.* ▷
SPARSE. ● *n* **1** beam, blaze, brightness,
brilliance, effulgence, flare, flash, flu-
orescence, glare, gleam, glint, glitter,
glow, halo, illumination, incandescence, luminosity, lustre, phosphorescence, radiance, ray, reflection,
scintillation, shine, sparkle, twinkle.
□ *candlelight, daylight, firelight, gaslight,
moonlight, starlight, sunlight, torchlight,
twilight.* □ *arc light, beacon, bulb, can-
delabra, candle, chandelier, electric light,
flare, floodlight, fluorescent lamp, headlamp, headlight, lamp, lantern, laser,
lighthouse, lightship, neon light, pilot
light, searchlight, spotlight, standard
lamp, street light, strobe, stroboscope,
taper, torch, traffic lights.* ● *vb* **1** fire,
ignite, kindle, put a match to, set
alight, set fire to, switch on. *Opp*
EXTINGUISH. **2** ▷ LIGHTEN. **bring to light**
▷ DISCOVER. **give light, reflect light**
be bright, be luminous, be phosphorescent, blaze, blink, burn, coruscate,
dazzle, flash, flicker, glare, gleam,
glimmer, glint, glisten, glitter, glow,
radiate, reflect, scintillate, shimmer,
shine, spark, sparkle, twinkle. **light-
headed** ▷ DIZZY. **light-hearted** ▷
CHEERFUL. **light up** ▷ LIGHTEN. **shed
light on** ▷ EXPLAIN.

lighten *vb* **1** cast light on, floodlight,
illuminate, irradiate, light up, shed
light on, shine on. **2** *The sky lightened.*
become lighter, brighten, cheer up,
clear. **3** ▷ LESSEN.

lighthouse *n* beacon, light, lightship, warning-light.

like *adj* akin to, analogous to, close
to, cognate with, comparable to, congruent with, corresponding to, equal
to, equivalent to, identical to, parallel to, similar to. ● *n* liking, partiality,
predilection, preference. ● *vb* admire,
approve of, appreciate, be attracted
to, be fond of, be interested in, be
keen on, be partial to, be pleased by,
delight in, enjoy, find pleasant, *sl* go
for, *inf* go in for, have a high regard
for, *inf* have a weakness for, prefer,
relish, revel in, take pleasure in, *inf*
take to, welcome. ▷ LOVE. *Opp* HATE.

likeable *adj* admirable, attractive,
charming, congenial, endearing,
interesting, lovable, nice, personable,
pleasant, pleasing. ▷ FRIENDLY. *Opp*
HATEFUL.

likelihood *n* chance, hope, possibility, probability, prospect.

likely *adj* **1** anticipated, expected,
feasible, foreseeable, plausible, possible, predictable, probable, reasonable, unsurprising. **2** *a likely candidate.* able, acceptable, appropriate,
convincing, credible, favourite, fitting, hopeful, promising, qualified,
suitable, *inf* tipped to win. **3** *likely to
come.* apt, disposed, inclined, liable,
prone, ready, tempted, willing. *Opp*
UNLIKELY.

liken *vb* compare, equate, juxtapose,
match.

likeness *n* **1** affinity, analogy, compatibility, congruity, correspondence,
resemblance, similarity. *Opp* DIFFER-
ENCE. **2** copy, depiction, drawing,
duplicate, facsimile, image, model,
picture, portrait, replica, representation, reproduction, study.

liking *n* affection, affinity, appetite,
eye, fondness, inclination, partiality,
penchant, predilection, predisposition, preference, propensity, *inf* soft
spot, taste, weakness. ▷ LOVE. *Opp*
HATRED.

limb *n* appendage, member, offshoot,
projection. □ *arm, bough, branch, flip-
per, foreleg, forelimb, leg, wing.*

limber *vb* **limber up** exercise, get
ready, loosen up, prepare, warm up.

limbo *n* **in limbo** abandoned, forgotten, in abeyance, left out, neglected,
neither one thing nor the other, *inf*
on hold, *inf* on the back burner, unattached.

literal

limit *n* **1** border, boundary, bounds, brink, confines, demarcation line, edge, end, extent, extreme point, frontier, perimeter. **2** ceiling, check, curb, cut-off point, deadline, inhibition, limitation, maximum, restraint, restriction, stop, threshold. ● *vb* bridle, check, circumscribe, confine, control, curb, define, fix, hold in check, put a limit on, ration, restrain, restrict. **limited** ▷ FINITE, INADEQUATE.

limitation *n* **1** ▷ LIMIT. **2** defect, deficiency, fault, inadequacy, shortcoming, weakness.

limitless *adj* boundless, countless, endless, everlasting, immeasurable, incalculable, inexhaustible, infinite, innumerable, never-ending, numberless, perpetual, renewable, unbounded, unconfined, unending, unimaginable, unlimited, unrestricted. ▷ VAST. *Opp* FINITE.

limp *adj inf* bendy, drooping, flabby, flaccid, flexible, *inf* floppy, lax, loose, pliable, sagging, slack, soft, weak, wilting, yielding. ▷ WEARY. *Opp* RIGID. ● *vb* be lame, falter, hobble, hop, stagger, totter.

line *n* **1** band, borderline, boundary, contour, contour line, dash, mark, streak, striation, strip, stripe, stroke, trail. **2** corrugation, crease, *inf* crow's feet, fold, furrow, groove, score, wrinkle. **3** cable, cord, flex, hawser, lead, rope, string, thread, wire. **4** chain, column, cordon, crocodile, file, procession, queue, rank, row, series. **5** *railway line.* branch, main line, route, service, track. ● *vb* **1** mark with lines, rule, score, streak, striate, underline. **2** *line the street.* border, edge, fringe. **3** *line a garment.* cover the inside, insert a lining, pad, reinforce. **line up** ▷ ALIGN, QUEUE.

linger *vb* continue, dally, dawdle, delay, dither, endure, hang about, hover, idle, lag, last, loiter, pause, persist, procrastinate, remain, *inf* shilly-shally, stay, stay behind, *inf* stick around, survive, temporize, wait about. *Opp* HURRY.

lining *n* inner coat, inner layer, interfacing, liner, padding.

link *n* **1** bond, connection, connector, coupling, join, joint, linkage, tie, yoke. ▷ FASTENER. **2** affiliation, alliance, association, communication, interdependence, liaison, partnership, relationship, *inf* tie-up, twinning, union. ● *vb* **1** amalgamate, associate, attach, compare, concatenate, connect, couple, interlink, join, juxtapose, make a link, merge, network, relate, see a link, twin, unite, yoke. ▷ FASTEN.

lip *n* brim, brink, edge, rim.

liquefy *vb* become liquid, dissolve, liquidize, melt, run, thaw. *Opp* SOLIDIFY.

liquid *adj* aqueous, flowing, fluid, liquefied, melted, molten, running, *inf* runny, sloppy, *inf* sloshy, thin, watery, wet. *Opp* SOLID. ● *n* fluid, juice, liquor, solution, stock.

liquidate *vb* annihilate, destroy, *inf* do away with, *inf* get rid of, remove, silence, wipe out. ▷ KILL.

liquor *n* **1** alcohol, *sl* booze, *sl* hard stuff, intoxicants, *sl* shorts, spirits, strong drink. **2** ▷ LIQUID.

list *n* catalogue, column, directory, file, index, inventory, listing, register, roll, roster, rota, schedule, shopping-list, table. ● *vb* **1** catalogue, enumerate, file, index, itemize, make a list of, note, record, register, tabulate, write down. **2** bank, careen, heel, incline, keel over, lean, slant, slope, tilt, tip.

listen *vb* attend, concentrate, eavesdrop, *old use* hark, hear, heed, *inf* keep your ears open, lend an ear, overhear, pay attention, take notice.

listless *adj* apathetic, enervated, feeble, heavy, languid, lazy, lethargic, lifeless, phlegmatic, sluggish, tired, torpid, unenthusiastic, uninterested, weak. ▷ WEARY. *Opp* LIVELY.

literal *adj* close, exact, faithful, matter of fact, plain, prosaic, strict, unimaginative, verbatim, word for word.

literary adj **1** cultured, educated, erudite, imaginative, learned, refined, scholarly, well-read, widely-read. **2** literary style. ornate, derog pedantic, poetic, polished, rhetorical, derog self-conscious, sophisticated, stylish.

literate adj **1** educated, wellread. **2** accurate, correct, readable, well-written.

literature n books, brochures, circulars, creative writing, handbills, handouts, leaflets, pamphlets, papers, writings. □ autobiography, biography, comedy, crime fiction, criticism, drama, epic, essay, fantasy, fiction, folk-tale, journalism, myth and legend, novels, parody, poetry, propaganda, prose, romance, satire, science fiction, tragedy. ▷ WRITING.

lithe adj agile, flexible, limber, lissom, loose-jointed, pliable, pliant, supple. Opp STIFF.

litter n bits and pieces, clutter, debris, fragments, garbage, jumble, junk, mess, odds and ends, refuse, rubbish, trash, waste. ● vb clutter, fill with litter, make untidy, inf mess up, scatter, strew.

little adj **1** inf baby, bantam, compact, concise, diminutive, inf dinky, dwarf, exiguous, fine, fractional, infinitesimal, lean, lilliputian, microscopic, midget, inf mini, miniature, minuscule, minute, narrow, petite (woman), inf pint-sized, inf pocketsized, inf poky, portable, pygmy, short, slender, slight, small, inf teeny, thin, tiny, toy, undergrown, undersized, inf wee, inf weeny. Opp BIG. **2** little food. inadequate, insufficient, meagre, mean, inf measly, miserly, modest, niggardly, parsimonious, inf piddling, scanty, skimpy, stingy, ungenerous, unsatisfactory. **3** of little importance. inconsequential, insignificant, minor, negligible, nugatory, slim (chance), slight, trifling, trivial, unimportant.

live adj **1** ▷ LIVING. **2** a live fire. ▷ ALIGHT. **3** a live issue. contemporary, current, important, pressing, relevant, topical, vital. Opp DEAD. ● vb

1 breathe, continue, endure, exist, flourish, function, last, persist, remain, stay alive, survive. Opp DIE. **2** be accommodated, dwell, lodge, reside, room, stay. **3** live on £20 a week. fare, inf get along, keep going, make a living, pay the bills, subsist. **live in** ▷ INHABIT. **live on** ▷ EAT.

liveliness n activity, animation, boisterousness, bustle, dynamism, energy, enthusiasm, exuberance, inf go, gusto, high spirits, spirit, sprightliness, verve, vigour, vitality, vivacity, zeal. Opp APATHY.

lively adj active, agile, alert, animated, boisterous, bubbly, bustling, busy, cheerful, colourful, dashing, eager, energetic, enthusiastic, exciting, expressive, exuberant, frisky, gay, high-spirited, irrepressible, jaunty, jazzy, jolly, merry, nimble, inf perky, playful, quick, spirited, sprightly, stimulating, strong, vigorous, vital, vivacious, vivid, inf zippy. ▷ HAPPY. Opp APATHETIC.

livestock n cattle, farm animals.

living adj active, actual, alive, animate, breathing, existing, extant, flourishing, functioning, live, old use quick, sentient, surviving, vigorous, vital. ▷ LIVELY. Opp DEAD, EXTINCT. ● n income, livelihood, occupation, subsistence, way of life.

load n **1** burden, cargo, consignment, freight, lading, lorry-load, shipment, van-load. **2** load of responsibility. inf albatross, anxiety, care, inf cross, encumbrance, inf millstone, onus, trouble, weight, worry. ● vb **1** burden, encumber, fill, heap, overwhelm, pack, pile, ply, saddle, stack, stow, weigh down. **2** load a gun. charge, prime. **loaded** ▷ BIASED, LADEN, WEALTHY.

loafer n idler, inf good-fornothing, layabout, inf lazybones, lounger, shirker, sl skiver, vagrant, wastrel.

loan n advance, credit, mortgage. ● vb advance, allow, credit, lend.

loathe vb abhor, abominate, be averse to, be revolted by, despise, detest, dislike, execrate, find intol-

look

erable, hate, object to, recoil from, resent, scorn, shudder at. *Opp* LOVE.

lobby *n* **1** ante-room, corridor, entrance hall, entry, foyer, hall, hallway, porch, reception, vestibule. **2** *environmental lobby.* campaign, campaigners, pressure-group, supporters. ● *vb* persuade, petition, pressurize, try to influence, urge.

local *adj* **1** adjacent, adjoining, nearby, neighbouring, serving the locality. **2** *local politics.* community, limited, narrow, neighbourhood, parochial, particular, provincial, regional. *Opp* GENERAL, NATIONAL. ● *n* **1** inhabitant, resident, townsman, townswoman. **2** ▷ PUB.

locality *n* area, catchment area, community, district, location, neighbourhood, parish, region, residential area, town, vicinity, zone.

localize *vb* concentrate, confine, contain, enclose, keep within bounds, limit, narrow down, pin down, restrict. *Opp* SPREAD.

locate *vb* **1** come across, detect, discover, find, identify, *inf* lay your hands on, *inf* run to earth, search out, track down, unearth. **2** build, establish, find a place for, found, place, position, put, set up, site, situate, station.

location *n* **1** locale, locality, place, point, position, setting, site, situation, spot, venue, whereabouts. **2** *film locations.* background, scene, setting.

lock *n* bar, bolt, catch, clasp, fastening, hasp, latch, padlock. ● *vb* bolt, close, fasten, padlock, seal, secure, shut. **lock away** ▷ IMPRISON. **lock out** ▷ EXCLUDE. **lock up** ▷ IMPRISON.

lodge *n* ▷ HOUSE. ● *vb* **1** accommodate, billet, board, house, *inf* put up. **2** abide, dwell, live, *inf* put up, reside, stay, stop. **3** *lodge a complaint.* enter, file, make formally, put on record, record, register, submit.

lodger *n* boarder, guest, inmate, paying guest, resident, tenant.

lodgings *n* accommodation, apartment, billet, boarding-house, *inf* digs,

lodging-house, *sl* pad, quarters, rooms, shelter, *sl* squat, temporary home.

lofty *adj* **1** elevated, high, imposing, majestic, noble, soaring, tall, towering. **2** ▷ ARROGANT.

log *n* **1** timber, wood. **2** account, diary, journal, record.

logic *n* clarity, deduction, intelligence, logical thinking, ratiocination, rationality, reasonableness, reasoning, sense, validity.

logical *adj* clear, cogent, coherent, consistent, deductive, intelligent, methodical, rational, reasonable, sensible, sound, *inf* step-by-step, structured, systematic, valid, well-reasoned, well-thought-out, wise. *Opp* ILLOGICAL.

loiter *vb* be slow, dally, dawdle, hang back, linger, *inf* loaf about, *inf* mess about, skulk, *inf* stand about, straggle.

lone *adj* isolated, separate, single, solitary, solo, unaccompanied. ▷ LONELY.

lonely *adj* **1** abandoned, alone, forlorn, forsaken, friendless, lonesome, loveless, neglected, outcast, reclusive, retiring, solitary, unsociable, withdrawn. ▷ SAD. **2** *inf* cut off, deserted, desolate, distant, far-away, isolated, *inf* off the beaten track, out of the way, remote, secluded, unfrequented, uninhabited.

long *adj* big, drawn out, elongated, endless, extended, extensive, great, interminable, large, lasting, lengthy, longish, prolonged, protracted, slow, stretched, sustained, time-consuming, unending. ● *vb* crave, hanker, have a longing (for), hunger, *inf* itch, pine, thirst, wish, yearn. **long for** ▷ DESIRE. **long-lasting, long-lived** ▷ PERMANENT. **long-standing** ▷ OLD. **long-suffering** ▷ PATIENT. **long-winded** ▷ TEDIOUS.

longing *n* appetite, craving, desire, hankering, hunger, *inf* itch, need, thirst, urge, wish, yearning, *inf* yen.

look *n* **1** gaze, glance, glimpse, observation, peek, peep, sight, *inf* squint, view. **2** air, appearance, aspect, attractiveness, bearing, beauty, complexion, countenance, demeanour, expression, face, looks, manner, mien. ● *vb* **1** behold, *inf* cast your eye, consider, contemplate, examine, eye, gape, *inf* gawp, gaze, glance, glimpse, goggle, have a look, inspect, observe, ogle, pay attention (to), peek, peep, peer, read, regard, scan, scrutinize, see, skim through, squint, stare, study, survey, *sl* take a dekko, take note (of), view, watch. **2** *The house looks south.* face, overlook. **3** *look pleased.* appear, seem. **look after** ▷ TEND. **look down on** ▷ DESPISE. **look for** ▷ SEEK. **look into** ▷ INVESTIGATE. **look out** ▷ BEWARE. **look up to** ▷ ADMIRE.

look-out *n* guard, sentinel, sentry, watchman.

loom *vb* appear, arise, dominate, emerge, hover, impend, materialize, menace, rise, stand out, stick up, take shape, threaten, tower.

loop *n* bend, bow, circle, coil, curl, eye, hoop, kink, noose, ring, turn, twist, whorl. ● *vb* bend, coil, curl, entwine, make a loop, turn, twist, wind.

loophole *n* escape, *inf* get-out, *inf* let-out, outlet, way out.

loose *adj* **1** detachable, detached, disconnected, independent, insecure, loosened, movable, moving, scattered, shaky, unattached, unconnected, unfastened, unsteady, wobbly. **2** *loose animals.* at large, at liberty, escaped, free, free-range, released, roaming, uncaged, unconfined, unfettered, unrestricted, untied. **3** *loose hair.* dangling, hanging, spread out, straggling, trailing. **4** *loose clothing.* baggy, *inf* floppy, loose-fitting, slack, unbuttoned. **5** *loose thinking.* broad, careless, casual, diffuse, general, ill-defined, illogical, imprecise, inexact, informal, lax, rambling, rough, *inf* sloppy, unscientific, unstructured, vague. *Opp* PRECISE, SECURE, TIGHT. **6** ▷ IMMORAL. ● *vb* ▷ FREE, LOOSEN.

loosen *vb* **1** ease off, free, let go, loose, make loose, relax, release, separate, slacken, unfasten, unloose, untie. ▷ UNDO. **2** become loose, come adrift, open up. *Opp* TIGHTEN.

loot *n* booty, contraband, haul, *inf* ill-gotten gains, plunder, prize, spoils, *inf* swag, takings. ● *vb* despoil, pillage, plunder, raid, ransack, ravage, rifle, rob, sack, steal from.

lopsided *adj* askew, asymmetrical, awry, *inf* cockeyed, crooked, one-sided, tilting, unbalanced, unequal, uneven.

lord *n* aristocrat, noble, peer. □ *baron, count, duke, earl,* old use *thane, viscount.* ▷ RULER.

lose *vb* **1** be deprived of, cease to have, drop, find yourself without, forfeit, forget, leave (somewhere), mislay, misplace, miss, part with, stray from. *Opp* FIND. **2** admit defeat, be defeated, capitulate, *inf* come to grief, fail, get beaten, get thrashed, succumb, suffer defeat. *Opp* WIN. **3** *lose your chance.* fritter, let slip, squander, waste. **4** *lose pursuers.* escape from, evade, get rid of, give the slip, leave behind, outrun, shake off, throw off. **losing** ▷ UNSUCCESSFUL.

loser *n* the defeated, runner-up, the vanquished. *Opp* WINNER.

loss *n* bereavement, damage, defeat, deficit, depletion, deprivation, destruction, diminution, disappearance, erosion, failure, forfeiture, impairment, privation, reduction, sacrifice. *Opp* GAIN. **losses** casualties, deaths, death toll, fatalities.

lost *adj* **1** abandoned, departed, destroyed, disappeared, extinct, forgotten, gone, irrecoverable, irretrievable, left behind, mislaid, misplaced, missing, strayed, untraceable, vanished. **2** absorbed, daydreaming, dreamy, distracted, engrossed, preoccupied, rapt. **3** corrupt, damned, fallen. ▷ WICKED.

lot *n a lot in a sale.* ▷ ITEM. **a lot of, lots of** ▷ PLENTY. **draw lots** ▷ GAMBLE. **the lot** all (of), everything, the whole thing, *inf* the works.

lotion *n* balm, cream, embrocation, liniment, ointment, pomade, salve, unguent.

lottery *n* **1** raffle, sweepstake. **2** gamble, speculation, venture.

loud *adj* **1** audible, blaring, booming, clamorous, clarion (*call*), deafening, ear-splitting, echoing, fortissimo, high, noisy, penetrating, piercing, raucous, resounding, reverberant, reverberating, roaring, rowdy, shrieking, shrill, sonorous, stentorian, strident, thundering, thunderous, vociferous. **2** *loud colours.* ▷ GAUDY. *Opp* QUIET.

lounge *n* drawing-room, front room, living-room, parlour, salon, sitting-room. ● *vb* be idle, be lazy, dawdle, hang about, idle, *inf* kill time, laze, loaf, lie around, loiter, *inf* loll about, *inf* mess about, *inf* mooch about, relax, *inf* skive, slouch, slump, sprawl, stand about, take it easy, vegetate, waste time.

lout *n* boor, churl, rude person, oaf, *inf* yob.

lovable *adj* adorable, appealing, attractive, charming, cuddly, *inf* cute, *inf* darling, dear, enchanting, endearing, engaging, fetching, likeable, lovely, pleasing, taking, winning, winsome. *Opp* HATEFUL.

love *n* **1** admiration, adoration, adulation, affection, ardour, attachment, attraction, desire, devotion, fancy, fervour, fondness, infatuation, liking, passion, regard, tenderness, warmth. ▷ FRIENDSHIP. **2** beloved, darling, dear, dearest, loved one. ▷ LOVER. ● *vb* **1** admire, adore, be charmed by, be fond of, be infatuated by, be in love with, care for, cherish, desire, dote on, fancy, *inf* have a crush on, have a passion for, idolize, lose your heart to, lust after, treasure, value, want, worship. ▷ LIKE. *Opp* HATE. **in love** besotted, devoted, enamoured, fond, *inf* head over heels, infatuated. **love affair** affair, amour, courtship, intrigue, liaison, relationship, romance. **make love** be intimate, *inf* canoodle, caress, copulate, court, cuddle, embrace, flirt, fornicate, have

intercourse, have sex, kiss, mate, *sl* neck, *inf* pet, philander, *old use* spoon, woo. ▷ SEX.

loved *adj* beloved, cherished, darling, dear, dearest, esteemed, favourite, precious, treasured, valued, wanted.

loveless *adj* cold, frigid, heartless, passionless, undemonstrative, unfeeling, unloving, unresponsive. *Opp* LOVING. ▷ UNLOVED.

lovely *adj* appealing, attractive, charming, delightful, enjoyable, fine, good, nice, pleasant, pretty, sweet. ▷ BEAUTIFUL. *Opp* NASTY.

lover *n* admirer, boyfriend, companion, concubine, fiancé(e), *old use* follower, friend, gigolo, girlfriend, *inf* intended, mate, mistress, *old use* paramour, suitor, sweetheart, *sl* toy boy, valentine.

lovesick *adj* frustrated, languishing, lovelorn, pining.

loving *adj* admiring, adoring, affectionate, amorous, ardent, attached, brotherly, caring, close, concerned, dear, demonstrative, devoted, doting, fatherly, fond, friendly, inseparable, kind, maternal, motherly, passionate, paternal, protective, sisterly, tender, warm. ▷ FRIENDLY, SEXY. *Opp* LOVELESS.

low *adj* **1** flat, low-lying, sunken. **2** *low trees.* little, short, squat, stumpy, stunted. **3** *low status.* abject, base, degraded, humble, inferior, junior, lesser, lower, lowly, menial, miserable, modest, servile. **4** *low behaviour.* churlish, coarse, common, cowardly, crude, *old use* dastardly, disreputable, ignoble, mean, nasty, vulgar, wicked. ▷ IMMORAL. **5** *low sounds.* gentle, indistinct, muffled, murmurous, muted, pianissimo, quiet, soft, subdued, whispered. **6** *low notes.* bass, deep, reverberant. *Opp* HIGH. **in low spirits** ▷ SAD. **low point** ▷ NADIR.

lowbrow *adj* accessible, easy, ordinary, pop, popular, *derog* rubbishy, simple, straightforward, *derog* trashy, *derog* uncultured, undemanding, unpretentious, unsophisticated. *Opp* HIGHBROW.

lower *vb* **1** dip, drop, haul down, let down, take down. **2** *lower prices*. bring down, cut, decrease, discount, lessen, mark down, reduce, *inf* slash. **3** *lower the volume*. abate, diminish, quieten, tone down, turn down. **4** *lower yourself*. abase, belittle, debase, degrade, demean, discredit, disgrace, humble, humiliate, stoop. *Opp* RAISE.

lowly *adj* base, humble, insignificant, little-known, low, low-born, meek, modest, obscure, unimportant. ▷ ORDINARY. *Opp* EMINENT.

loyal *adj* committed, constant, dedicated, dependable, devoted, dutiful, faithful, honest, patriotic, reliable, sincere, stable, staunch, steadfast, steady, true, trustworthy, trusty, unswerving, unwavering. *Opp* DISLOYAL.

loyalty *n* allegiance, constancy, dedication, dependability, devotion, duty, faithfulness, fealty, fidelity, honesty, patriotism, reliability, staunchness, steadfastness, trustworthiness. *Opp* DISLOYALTY.

lubricate *vb* grease, oil.

luck *n* **1** accident, chance, coincidence, destiny, fate, *inf* fluke, fortune, serendipity. **2** *wished her luck*. *inf* break, good fortune, happiness, prosperity, success.

lucky *adj* **1** accidental, appropriate, chance, *inf* fluky, fortuitous, opportune, providential, timely, unintentional, unplanned, welcome. **2** blessed, favoured, fortunate, successful. ▷ HAPPY. **3** *lucky number*. advantageous, auspicious. *Opp* UNLUCKY.

luggage *n* baggage, belongings, *inf* gear, impedimenta, paraphernalia, *inf* things. □ bag, basket, box, brief-case, case, chest, hamper, handbag, hand luggage, haversack, holdall, knapsack, pannier, old use portmanteau, purse, rucksack, satchel, suitcase, trunk, wallet.

lukewarm *adj* **1** room temperature, tepid, warm. **2** apathetic, cool, half-hearted, indifferent, unenthusiastic.

lull *n* break, calm, delay, gap, halt, hiatus, interlude, interruption, interval, lapse, *inf* let-up, pause, respite, rest, silence. ● *vb* calm, hush, pacify, quell, quieten, soothe, subdue, tranquillize.

lumber *n* **1** beams, boards, planks, timber, wood. **2** bits and pieces, clutter, jumble, junk, litter, odds and ends, rubbish, trash, *inf* white elephants. ● *vb* **1** blunder, move clumsily, shamble, trudge. **2** ▷ BURDEN.

luminous *adj* bright, glowing, luminescent, lustrous, phosphorescent, radiant, refulgent, shining. ▷ LIGHT.

lump *n* **1** ball, bar, bit, block, cake, chunk, clod, clot, cube, *inf* dollop, gob, gobbet, hunk, ingot, mass, nugget, piece, slab, wad, wedge, *inf* wodge. **2** boil, bulge, bump, carbuncle, cyst, excrescence, growth, hump, knob, node, nodule, protrusion, protuberance, spot, swelling, tumescence, tumour. ● *vb* **lump together** ▷ COMBINE.

lunacy *n* delirium, dementia, derangement, frenzy, hysteria, illogicality, insanity, madness, mania, psychosis, unreason. ▷ STUPIDITY.

lunatic *adj* ▷ MAD. ● *n inf* crackpot, *inf* crank, *inf* loony, madman, madwoman, maniac, *inf* mental case, *inf* nutcase, *inf* nutter, psychopath, psychotic.

lunge *vb* **1** jab, stab, strike, thrust. **2** charge, dash, dive, lurch, plunge, pounce, rush, spring, throw yourself.

lurch *vb* heave, lean, list, lunge, pitch, plunge, reel, roll, stagger, stumble, sway, totter, wallow. **leave in the lurch** ▷ ABANDON.

lure *vb* allure, attract, bait, charm, coax, decoy, draw, entice, induce, inveigle, invite, lead on, persuade, seduce, tempt.

lurid *adj* **1** bright, gaudy, glaring, glowing, striking, vivid. **2** ▷ SENSATIONAL.

lurk *vb* crouch, hide, lie in wait, lie low, prowl, skulk, steal.

luscious *adj* appetizing, delectable, delicious, juicy, mouth-watering, rich, succulent, sweet, tasty.

lust *n* **1** carnality, concupiscence, desire, lasciviousness, lechery, libido, licentiousness, passion, sensuality, sexuality. **2** appetite, craving, greed, hunger, itch, longing.

lustful *adj* carnal, concupiscent, erotic, lascivious, lecherous, lewd, libidinous, licentious, on heat, passionate, *sl* randy, salacious, sensual, *sl* turned on. ▷ SEXY.

lustrous *adj* burnished, glazed, gleaming, glossy, metallic, polished, reflective, sheeny, shiny.

luxuriant *adj* **1** abundant, ample, copious, dense, exuberant, fertile, flourishing, green, lush, opulent, plenteous, plentiful, profuse, prolific, rank, rich, teeming, thick, thriving, verdant. **2** ▷ ORNATE. *Opp* SPARSE.

luxurious *adj* comfortable, costly, expensive, extravagant, grand, hedonistic, lavish, lush, magnificent, opulent, pampered, *inf* plush, *inf* posh, rich, *inf* ritzy, self-indulgent, splendid, sumptuous, sybaritic, voluptuous. *Opp* SPARTAN.

luxury *n* affluence, comfort, ease, enjoyment, extravagance, grandeur, hedonism, high living, indulgence, magnificence, opulence, pleasure, relaxation, self-indulgence, splendour, sumptuousness, voluptuousness.

lying *adj* crooked, deceitful, deceptive, dishonest, double-dealing, duplicitous, false, hypocritical, inaccurate, insincere, mendacious, misleading, perfidious, unreliable, untrustworthy, untruthful. *Opp* TRUTHFUL. ● *n* deceit, deception, dishonesty, duplicity, falsehood, *inf* fibbing, hypocrisy, mendacity, perfidy, perjury, prevarication.

lyrical *adj* emotional, expressive, impassioned, inspired, melodious, musical, poetic, rapturous, rhapsodic, song-like, sweet, tuneful. *Opp* PROSAIC.

M

macabre *adj* eerie, fearsome, frightful, ghoulish, grim, grisly, grotesque, gruesome, morbid, *inf* sick, unhealthy, weird.

machine *n* appliance, contraption, contrivance, device, engine, gadget, implement, instrument, mechanism, motor, robot, tool. ▷ MACHINERY.

machinery *n* **1** apparatus, equipment, gear, machines, plant. **2** constitution, method, organization, procedure, structure, system.

mackintosh *n* anorak, cape, mac, sou'wester, waterproof. ▷ COAT.

mad *adj* **1** *inf* batty, berserk, *inf* bonkers, *inf* certified, *inf* crackers, crazed, crazy, *inf* daft, delirious, demented, deranged, disordered, distracted, *inf* dotty, eccentric, fanatical, frantic, frenzied, hysterical, insane, irrational, *inf* loony, lunatic, maniacal, manic, *inf* mental, moonstruck, *Lat* non compos mentis, *inf* nutty, *inf* off your head, *inf* off your rocker, *inf* out of your mind, possessed, *inf* potty, psychotic, *inf* queer in the head, *inf* round the bend, *inf* round the twist, *inf* screwy, *inf* touched, unbalanced, unhinged, unstable, *inf* up the pole, wild. *Opp* SANE. **2** *a mad comedy.* ▷ ABSURD. **3** ▷ ANGRY. **4** ▷ ENTHUSIASTIC.

madden *vb* anger, craze, derange, *inf* drive crazy, enrage, exasperate, excite, incense, inflame, infuriate, irritate, make you mad, *inf* make your blood boil, *inf* make you see red, provoke, *inf* send you round the bend, unhinge, vex.

madman,

madwoman *ns inf* crackpot, *inf* crank, eccentric, *inf* loony, lunatic, maniac, *inf* mental case, *inf* nutcase, *inf* nutter, psychopath, psychotic.

madness *n* delirium, dementia, derangement, eccentricity, folly, frenzy, hysteria, illogicality, insanity, lunacy, mania, mental illness, psychosis, unreason. ▷ STUPIDITY.

magazine *n* **1** comic, journal, monthly, newspaper, pamphlet, paper, periodical, publication, quarterly, weekly. **2** *magazine of weapons.* ammunition dump, armoury, arsenal, storehouse.

magic *adj* **1** conjuring, miraculous, mystic, necromantic, supernatural. **2** bewitching, charming, enchanting, entrancing, magical, spellbinding. ● *n* **1** black magic, charm, enchantment, hocus-pocus, incantation, *inf* mumbo-jumbo, necromancy, occultism, sorcery, spell, voodoo, witchcraft, witchery, wizardry. **2** conjuring, illusion, legerdemain, sleight of hand, trickery, tricks.

magician *n* conjuror, enchanter, enchantress, illusionist, magus, necromancer, sorcerer, *old use* warlock, witch, witch-doctor, wizard.

magnetic *adj* alluring, attractive, bewitching, captivating, charismatic, charming, compelling, engaging, enthralling, entrancing, fascinating, hypnotic, inviting, irresistible, seductive, spellbinding. *Opp* REPULSIVE.

magnetism *n* allure, appeal, attractiveness, charisma, charm, drawing power, fascination, irresistibility, lure, power, pull, seductiveness.

magnificent *adj* awe-inspiring, beautiful, distinguished, excellent, fine, glorious, gorgeous, grand, grandiose, great, imposing, impressive, majestic, marvellous, noble, opulent, *inf* posh, regal, resplendent, rich, spectacular, splendid, stately, sumptuous, superb, wonderful. *Opp* ORDINARY.

magnify *vb* **1** amplify, augment, *inf* blow up, enlarge, expand, increase, intensify, make larger. *Opp* SHRINK. **2** *magnify difficulties*. *inf* blow up out of proportion, dramatize, exaggerate, heighten, inflate, make too much of, maximize, overdo, overestimate, overstate. *Opp* MINIMIZE.

magnitude *n* bigness, enormousness, extent, greatness, immensity, importance, size.

mail *n* correspondence, letters, parcels, post. ● *vb* dispatch, forward, post, send.

maim *vb* cripple, disable, hamstring, handicap, incapacitate, lame, mutilate. ▷ WOUND.

main *adj* basic, biggest, cardinal, central, chief, critical, crucial, dominant, dominating, essential, first, foremost, fundamental, greatest, largest, leading, major, most important, outstanding, paramount, predominant, pre-eminent, prevailing, primary, prime, principal, special, strongest, supreme, top, vital. *Opp* MINOR.

mainly *adv* above all, as a rule, chiefly, especially, essentially, first and foremost, generally, in the main, largely, mostly, normally, on the whole, predominantly, primarily, principally, usually.

maintain *vb* **1** carry on, continue, hold to, keep going, keep up, perpetuate, persevere in, persist in, preserve, retain, stick to, sustain. **2** *maintain a car*. care for, keep in good condition, look after, service, take care of. **3** *maintain a family*. feed, keep, pay for, provide for, stand by, support. **4** *maintain your innocence*. affirm, allege, argue, assert, aver, claim, contend, declare, defend, insist, proclaim, profess, state, uphold.

maintenance *n* **1** care, conservation, looking after, preservation, repairs, servicing, upkeep. **2** alimony, allowance, contribution, subsistence, support.

majestic *adj* august, awe-inspiring, awesome, dignified, distinguished, elevated, exalted, glorious, grand, grandiose, imperial, imposing, impressive, kingly, lofty, lordly, magisterial, magnificent, monumental, noble, pompous, princely, queenly, regal, royal, splendid, stately, striking, sublime.

majesty *n* awesomeness, dignity, glory, grandeur, kingliness, loftiness, magnificence, nobility, pomp, royalty, splendour, stateliness, sublimity.

major *adj* bigger, chief, considerable, extensive, greater, important, key, larger, leading, outstanding, principal, serious, significant. ▷ MAIN. *Opp* MINOR.

majority *n* **1** *inf* best part, *inf* better part, bulk, greater number, mass, preponderance. **2** adulthood, coming of age, manhood, maturity, womanhood. **be in the majority** ▷ DOMINATE.

make *n* brand, kind, model, sort, type, variety. ● *vb* **1** assemble, beget, bring about, build, compose, constitute, construct, contrive, craft, create, devise, do, engender, erect, execute, fabricate, fashion, forge, form, frame, generate, invent, make up, manufacture, mass-produce, originate, produce, put together, think up. **2** *make dinner*. concoct, cook, *inf* fix, prepare. **3** *make clothes*. knit, *inf* run up, sew, weave. **4** *make an effigy*. carve, cast, model, mould, sculpt, shape. **5** *make a speech*. deliver, pronounce, utter. ▷ SPEAK. **6** *made her chairperson*. appoint, elect, nominate, ordain. **7** *make P into B*. alter, change, convert, modify, transform, turn. **8** *make a fortune*. earn, gain, get, obtain, receive. **9** *make a good employee*. become, change into, grow into, turn into. **10** *make your objective*. accomplish, achieve, arrive at, attain, catch, get to, reach, win. **11** *2 + 2 makes 4*. add up to, amount to, come to, total. **12** *make rules*. agree, arrange, codify, decide on, draw up, establish, fix, write. **13** *make her happy*. cause to become, render.

14 *make trouble.* bring about, carry out, cause, give rise to, provoke, result in. **15** *make them obey.* coerce, compel, constrain, force, induce, oblige, order, pressurize, prevail on, require. **make amends** ▷ COMPENSATE. **make believe** ▷ IMAGINE. **make fun of** ▷ RIDICULE. **make good** ▷ PROSPER. **make love** ▷ LOVE. **make off** ▷ DEPART. **make off with** ▷ STEAL. **make out** ▷ UNDERSTAND. **make up** ▷ INVENT. **make up for** ▷ COMPENSATE. **make up your mind** ▷ DECIDE.

make-believe *adj* fanciful, feigned, imaginary, made-up, mock, *inf* pretend, pretended, sham, simulated, unreal. ● *n* dream, fantasy, playacting, pretence, self-deception, unreality.

maker *n* architect, author, builder, creator, director, manufacturer, originator, producer.

makeshift *adj* emergency, improvised, provisional, stopgap, temporary.

maladjusted *adj* disturbed, muddled, neurotic, unbalanced.

male *adj* manly, masculine, virile. ● *n* □ bachelor, *inf* bloke, boy, boyfriend, *inf* bridegroom, brother, chap, *inf* codger, father, fellow, gentleman, groom, *inf* guy, husband, lad, lover, man, son, *inf* squire, uncle, widower. □ buck, bull, cock, dog, ram, stallion, tom(cat). *Opp* FEMALE.

malefactor *n* delinquent, lawbreaker, offender, villain, wrongdoer. ▷ CRIMINAL.

malice *n* animosity, *inf* bitchiness, bitterness, *inf* cattiness, enmity, hatred, hostility, ill-will, malevolence, maliciousness, malignity, nastiness, rancour, spite, spitefulness, vengefulness, venom, viciousness, vindictiveness.

malicious *adj inf* bitchy, bitter, *inf* catty, evil, evil-minded, hateful, ill-natured, malevolent, malignant, mischievous, nasty, rancorous, revengeful, sly, spiteful, vengeful, venomous, vicious, villainous, vindictive, wicked. *Opp* KIND.

malignant *adj* dangerous, deadly, destructive, fatal, harmful, injurious, life-threatening, poisonous, *inf* terminal, uncontrollable, virulent. ▷ MALICIOUS.

malleable *adj* ductile, plastic, pliable, soft, tractable, workable. *Opp* BRITTLE.

malnutrition *n* famine, hunger, starvation, undernourishment.

man *n* **1** [either sex] ▷ MANKIND. **2** ▷ MALE. ● *vb* cover, crew, provide staff for, staff.

manage *vb* **1** administer, be in charge of, be manager of, command, conduct, control, direct, dominate, govern, head, lead, look after, mastermind, operate, organize, oversee, preside over, regulate, rule, run, superintend, supervise, take care of, take control of, take over. **2** *manage your jobs.* accomplish, achieve, bring about, carry out, contend with, cope with, deal with, do, finish, get through, handle, manipulate, muddle through, perform, sort out, succeed in, undertake. **3** *Can you manage?* cope, fend for yourself, *inf* make it, scrape by, shift for yourself, succeed, survive. **4** *can manage £10.* afford, spare.

manageable *adj* **1** acceptable, convenient, easy to manage, handy, neat, reasonable. *Opp* AWKWARD. **2** amenable, compliant, controllable, disciplined, docile, governable, submissive, tame, tractable. ▷ OBEDIENT. *Opp* DISOBEDIENT.

manager,

manageress *ns* administrator, *inf* boss, chief, controller, director, executive, foreman, forewoman, governor, head, organizer, overseer, proprietor, ruler, superintendent, supervisor. ▷ CHIEF.

mandatory *adj* compulsory, essential, necessary, needed, obligatory, required, requisite.

mangle *vb* butcher, cripple, crush, cut, damage, deform, disfigure, hack, injure, lacerate, maim, maul, mutilate, ruin, spoil, squash, tear, wound.

mangy *adj* dirty, filthy, motheaten, nasty, scabby, scruffy, shabby, slovenly, squalid, *inf* tatty, unkempt, wretched.

manhandle *vb* **1** carry, haul, heave, hump, lift, manoeuvre, move, pull, push. **2** abuse, batter, *inf* beat up, ill-treat, knock about, maltreat, mistreat, misuse, *inf* rough up, treat roughly.

mania *n* craving, craze, enthusiasm, fad, fetish, frenzy, infatuation, obsession, passion, preoccupation, rage. ▷ MADNESS.

maniac *n* lunatic, psychopath, psychotic. ▷ MADMAN.

manifest *adj* apparent, blatant, clear, conspicuous, discernible, evident, explicit, glaring, noticeable, obvious, patent, plain, recognizable, undisguised, visible. ● *vb* ▷ SHOW.

manifesto *n* declaration, policy statement.

manipulate *vb* **1** feel, massage, rub, stimulate. **2** *manipulate people.* control, direct, engineer, exploit, guide, handle, influence, manage, manoeuvre, orchestrate, steer.

mankind *n* *Lat* homo sapiens, human beings, humanity, humankind, the human race, man, men and women, mortals, people.

manly *adj* chivalrous, gallant, heroic, *inf* macho, male, mannish, masculine, strong, swashbuckling, vigorous, virile. ▷ BRAVE. *Opp* EFFEMINATE.

man-made *adj* artificial, imitation, manufactured, massproduced, processed, simulated, synthetic, unnatural. *Opp* NATURAL.

manner *n* **1** approach, fashion, means, method, mode, procedure, process, style, technique, way. **2** air, aspect, attitude, bearing, behaviour, character, conduct, demeanour, deportment, disposition, look, mien. **3** *all manner of things.* genre, kind, sort, type, variety.

manners *plur n* behaviour, breeding, civility, conduct, courtesy, decorum, etiquette, gentility, politeness, protocol, refinement, social graces.

mannerism *n* characteristic, habit, idiosyncrasy, peculiarity, quirk, trait.

manoeuvre *n* device, dodge, gambit, intrigue, move, operation, plan, plot, ploy, ruse, scheme, stratagem, strategy, tactics, trick. ● *vb* contrive, engineer, guide, jockey, manipulate, move, navigate, negotiate, pilot, steer.

manoeuvres *plur n* army exercise, operation, training.

mansion *n* castle, château, manor, manor-house, palace, stately home, villa. ▷ HOUSE.

mantle *n* cape, cloak, covering, hood, shawl, shroud, wrap. ● *vb* ▷ COVER.

manufacture *vb* assemble, build, construct, create, fabricate, make, mass-produce, prefabricate, process, put together, *inf* turn out. **manufactured** ▷ MAN-MADE.

manufacturer *n* factory-owner, industrialist, maker, producer.

manure *n* compost, dung, fertilizer, *inf* muck.

manuscript *n* document, papers, script. ▷ BOOK.

many *adj* abundant, assorted, copious, countless, diverse, frequent, innumerable, multifarious, myriad, numberless, numerous, profuse, *inf* umpteen, uncountable, untold, varied, various. *Opp* FEW.

map *n* chart, diagram, plan.

mar *vb* blight, blot, damage, deface, disfigure, harm, hurt, impair, ruin, spoil, stain, taint, tarnish, wreck.

marauder *n* bandit, buccaneer, invader, pirate, plunderer, raider.

march *n* cortège, demonstration, march-past, parade, procession, progress. ● *vb* file, pace, parade, step, stride, troop. ▷ WALK.

margin *n* **1** border, boundary, brink, edge, frieze, perimeter, periphery, rim, side, verge. **2** allowance, latitude, leeway, room, scope, space.

marginal *adj* borderline, doubtful, insignificant, minimal, negligible, peripheral, slight, small, unimportant.

marital *adj* conjugal, matrimonial, nuptial.

mark *n* **1** blemish, blot, blotch, dent, dot, fingermark, *plur* graffiti, impression, line, marking, pockmark, print, scar, scratch, scribble, smear, smudge, smut, *inf* splotch, spot, stain, *plur* stigmata, streak, trace, vestige. **2** *mark of breeding.* characteristic, feature, indication, indicator, marker, token. **3** *identifying mark.* badge, brand, device, emblem, fingerprint, hallmark, label, seal, sign, stamp, standard, symbol, trademark. ● *vb* **1** blemish, blot, brand, bruise, cut, damage, deface, dent, dirty, disfigure, draw on, make a mark on, mar, scar, scratch, scrawl over, scribble on, smudge, spot, stain, stamp, streak, tattoo, write on. **2** *mark pupils' work.* appraise, assess, correct, evaluate, grade, tick. **3** *mark my words.* attend to, heed, listen to, mind, note, notice, observe, pay attention to, take note of, take seriously, *inf* take to heart, watch.

market *n* auction, bazaar, exchange, fair, marketplace, sale. ▷ SHOP. ● *vb* advertise, deal in, make available, merchandise, peddle, promote, put on the market, retail, sell, *inf* tout, trade, trade in, try to sell, vend.

marksman *n* crack shot, gunman, sharpshooter, sniper.

maroon *vb* abandon, cast away, desert, forsake, isolate, leave, put ashore, strand.

marriage *n* **1** matrimony, partnership, union, wedlock. **2** nuptials, union, wedding. □ *bigamy, monogamy, polygamy.*

marriageable *adj* adult, mature, nubile.

marry *vb* espouse, *inf* get hitched, *inf* get spliced, join in matrimony, *inf* tie the knot, unite, wed.

marsh *n* bog, fen, marshland, morass, mud, mudflats, quagmire, quicksands, saltings, saltmarsh, *old use* slough, swamp, wetland.

marshal *vb* arrange, assemble, collect, deploy, draw up, gather, group, line up, muster, organize, set out.

martial *adj* aggressive, bellicose, belligerent, militant, military, pugnacious, soldierly, warlike. *Opp* PEACEABLE.

marvel *n* miracle, phenomenon, wonder. ● *vb* **marvel at** admire, applaud, be amazed by, be astonished by, be surprised by, gape at, praise, wonder at.

marvellous *adj* admirable, amazing, astonishing, astounding, breathtaking, excellent, exceptional, extraordinary, *inf* fabulous, *inf* fantastic, glorious, impressive, incredible, magnificent, miraculous, out of the ordinary, *inf* out of this world, phenomenal, praiseworthy, prodigious, remarkable, *inf* sensational, spectacular, splendid, staggering, stunning, stupendous, *inf* super, superb, surprising, *inf* terrific, unbelievable, wonderful, wondrous. *Opp* ORDINARY.

masculine *adj* boyish, *inf* butch, gentlemanly, heroic, *inf* macho, male, manly, mannish, muscular, powerful, strong, vigorous, virile. *Opp* FEMININE.

mash *vb* beat, crush, grind, mangle, pound, pulp, pulverize, smash, squash.

mask *n* camouflage, cloak, cover, cover-up, disguise, façade, front, guise, screen, shield, veil, visor. ● *vb* blot out, camouflage, cloak, conceal, cover, disguise, hide, obscure, screen, shield, shroud, veil.

masonry *n* bricks, brickwork, stone, stonework.

mass *adj* comprehensive, general, large-scale, popular, universal, wholesale, widespread. ● *n* **1** accumulation, agglomeration, aggregation, body, bulk, *inf* chunk, collection, concretion, conglomeration, *inf* dollop, heap, hoard, *inf* hunk, *inf* load, lot, lump, mound, mountain, pile, profusion, quantity, stack, volume. **2** ▷ GROUP. ● *vb* accumulate, aggregate, amass, assemble, collect, congregate, convene, flock together, gather, marshal, meet, mobilize, muster, pile up, rally.

massacre *vb* annihilate, slaughter. ▷ KILL.

massage *vb* knead, manipulate, rub.

mast *n* aerial, flagpole, maypole, pylon, transmitter.

master *n* **1** *inf* boss, employer, governor, keeper, lord, overseer, owner, person in charge, proprietor, ruler, taskmaster. ▷ CHIEF. **2** captain, skipper. **3** *master of an art. inf* ace, authority, expert, genius, maestro, mastermind, virtuoso. **4** ▷ TEACHER. ● *vb* **1** become expert in, *inf* get off by heart, *inf* get the hang of, grasp, know, learn, understand. **2** break in, bridle, check, conquer, control, curb, defeat, dominate, *inf* get the better of, govern, manage, overcome, overpower, quell, regulate, repress, rule, subdue, subjugate, suppress, tame, triumph over, vanquish.

masterly *adj* accomplished, adroit, consummate, dexterous, excellent, expert, masterful, matchless, practised, proficient, skilful, skilled, unsurpassable.

mastermind *n* architect, brains, conceiver, contriver, creator, engineer, expert, genius, intellectual, inventor, manager, originator, planner, prime mover. ● *vb* carry through, conceive, contrive, devise, direct, engineer, execute, manage, organize, originate, plan, plot. ▷ MANAGE.

masterpiece *n* best work, *Fr* chef-d'oeuvre, classic, *inf* hit, *Lat* magnum opus, masterwork, *Fr* pièce de résistance.

match *n* **1** bout, competition, contest, duel, game, test match, tie, tournament, tourney. **2** *met my match.* complement, counterpart, double, equal, equivalent, twin. **3** *a good match.* combination, fit, pair, similarity. **4** *a love match.* alliance, friend-ship, marriage, partnership, relationship, union. ● *vb* **1** agree, accord, be compatible, be equivalent, be the same, be similar, blend, coincide, combine, compare, coordinate, correspond, fit, *inf* go together, harmonize, suit, tally, tie in, tone in. *Opp* CONTRAST. **2** ally, combine, fit, join, link up, marry, mate, pair off, pair up, put together, team up. *Opp* SPLIT. **matching** ▷ SIMILAR.

mate *n* **1** *inf* better half, companion, consort, helpmeet, husband, partner, spouse, wife. ▷ FRIEND. **2** assistant, associate, collaborator, colleague, helper. ● *vb* become partners, copulate, couple, have intercourse, *inf* have sex, join, marry, *inf* pair up, unite, wed.

material *adj* concrete, corporeal, palpable, physical, solid, substantial, tangible. ● *n* **1** fabric, stuff, textile. ▷ CLOTH. **2** components, constituents, content, data, facts, ideas, information, matter, notes, resources, statistics, stuff, subject matter, substance, supplies, things.

materialize *vb* appear, become visible, emerge, occur, take shape, *inf* turn up.

mathematics *plur n* mathematical science, *inf* maths, number work. □ *addition, algebra, arithmetic, calculus, division, geometry, multiplication, operational research, statistics, subtraction, trigonometry.*

matted *adj* knotted, tangled, uncombed, unkempt. ▷ DISHEVELLED.

matter *n* **1** body, material, stuff, substance. **2** discharge, pus, suppuration. **3** *a matter of life and death.* affair, business, concern, episode, event, fact, incident, issue, occurrence, question, situation, subject, thing, topic. **4** *What's the matter?* difficulty, problem, trouble, upset, worry. ● *vb* be important, be of consequence, be significant, count, make a difference, mean something, signify. **matter-of-fact** ▷ PROSAIC.

mature *adj* **1** adult, advanced, experienced, full-grown, grown-up, nubile, of age, perfect, sophisticated, well-developed. **2** mellow, ready, ripe, seasoned. *Opp* IMMATURE. ● *vb* age, come to fruition, develop, grow up, mellow, reach maturity, ripen.

maturity *n* adulthood, completion, majority, mellowness, perfection, readiness, ripeness.

maul *vb* claw, injure, *inf* knock about, lacerate, mangle, manhandle, mutilate, paw, savage, treat roughly, wound.

maximize *vb* **1** add to, augment, build up, increase, make the most of. **2** inflate, magnify, overdo, overstate. ▷ EXAGGERATE. *Opp* MINIMIZE.

maximum *adj* biggest, extreme, full, fullest, greatest, highest, largest, maximal, most, peak, supreme, top, topmost, utmost, uttermost. ● *n* apex, ceiling, climax, extreme, highest point, peak, pinnacle, top, upper limit, zenith. *Opp* MINIMUM.

maybe *adv* conceivably, perhaps, possibly.

maze *n* complex, confusion, convolution, labyrinth, network, tangle, web.

meadow *n* field, *old use* mead, paddock, pasture.

meagre *adj* deficient, inadequate, insufficient, lean, mean, paltry, poor, puny, scanty, skimpy, slight, sparse, thin, unsatisfying. ▷ SMALL. *Opp* GENEROUS.

meal *n inf* blow-out, *old use* collation, repast, *inf* spread. □ banquet, barbecue, breakfast, buffet, dinner, *inf elevenses*, feast, high tea, lunch, luncheon, picnic, snack, supper, take-away, tea, tea-break, old use tiffin.

mean *adj* **1** beggarly, *inf* cheese-paring, close, close-fisted, illiberal, *inf* mingy, miserly, niggardly, parsimonious, *inf* penny-pinching, selfish, sparing, stingy, *inf* tight, tight-fisted, ungenerous. **2** *a mean disposition.* callous, churlish, contemptible, cruel, despicable, hard-hearted, ignoble, ill-tempered, malicious, nasty, shabby, shameful, small-minded, *inf* sneaky, spiteful, uncharitable, unkind,

vicious. **3** *a mean dwelling.* base, common, humble, inferior, insignificant, low, lowly, miserable, poor, shabby, squalid, wretched. *Opp* GENEROUS, VALUABLE. ● *vb* **1** augur, betoken, communicate, connote, convey, denote, *inf* drive at, express, foretell, *inf* get over, herald, hint at, imply, indicate, intimate, portend, presage, refer to, represent, say, show, signal, signify, specify, spell out, stand for, suggest, symbolize. **2** *I mean to succeed.* aim, desire, have in mind, hope, intend, plan, propose, purpose, want, wish. **3** *The job means long hours.* entail, involve, necessitate.

meander *vb* ramble, rove, snake, twist and turn, wander, wind, zigzag. **meandering** ▷ TWISTY.

meaning *n* connotation, content, definition, denotation, drift, explanation, force, gist, idea, implication, import, importance, interpretation, message, point, purport, purpose, relevance, sense, significance, signification, substance, thrust, value.

meaningful *adj* deep, eloquent, expressive, meaning, pointed, positive, pregnant, relevant, serious, significant, suggestive, telling, tell-tale, weighty, worthwhile. *Opp* MEANINGLESS.

meaningless *adj* **1** absurd, coded, incomprehensible, incoherent, inconsequential, irrelevant, nonsensical, pointless, senseless. **2** *meaningless compliments.* empty, flattering, hollow, insincere, shallow, silly, sycophantic, vacuous, worthless. *Opp* MEANINGFUL.

means *n* **1** ability, capacity, channel, course, fashion, machinery, manner, medium, method, mode, process, way. **2** *private means.* ▷ WEALTH.

measurable *adj* appreciable, considerable, perceptible, quantifiable, reasonable, significant. *Opp* NEGLIGIBLE.

measure *n* **1** allocation, allowance, amount, amplitude, extent, magnitude, portion, quantity, quota, range, ration, scope, size, unit. ▷ MEASURE-

MENT. **2** criterion, *inf* litmus test, standard, test, touchstone, yardstick. **3** *measures to curb crime.* act, action, bill, control, course of action, expedient, law, means, procedure, step. ● *vb* assess, calculate, calibrate, compute, count, determine, estimate, gauge, judge, mark out, meter, plumb (*depth*), quantify, rank, rate, reckon, survey, take measurements of, weigh. **measure out** ▷ DISPENSE.

measurement *n* amount, calculation, dimensions, extent, figure, mensuration, size. ▷ MEASURE. □ area, breadth, bulk, capacity, depth, distance, height, length, mass, speed, time, volume, weight, width. □ acreage, footage, mileage, tonnage.

meat *n* flesh. ▷ FOOD. □ bacon, beef, chicken, game, gammon, ham, lamb, mutton, pork, poultry, turkey, veal, venison. □ brawn, breast, burger, brisket, chine, chops, chuck, cutlet, fillet, flank, hamburger, leg, loin, mince, offal, paté, potted meat, rib, rissole, rump, sausage, scrag, shoulder, silverside, sirloin, sparerib, steak, topside, tripe.

mechanic *n* engineer, technician.

mechanical *adj* **1** automated, automatic, machine-driven, technological. **2** cold, habitual, impersonal, inhuman, instinctive, lifeless, matter-of-fact, perfunctory, reflex, routine, soulless, unconscious, unemotional, unfeeling, unimaginative, uninspired, unthinking. *Opp* HUMAN.

mechanize *vb* automate, bring up to date, computerize, equip with machines, modernize.

medal *n* award, decoration, honour, medallion, prize, reward, trophy.

medallist *n* champion, victor, winner.

meddle *vb inf* be a busybody, butt in, interfere, *inf* poke your nose in, pry, snoop, tamper.

mediate *vb* act as go-between, act as mediator, arbitrate, intercede, liaise, negotiate.

mediator *n* arbiter, arbitrator, broker, conciliator, go-between, intercessor, intermediary, judge, liaison officer, middleman, moderator, negotiator, peacemaker, referee, umpire.

medicinal *adj* curative, healing, medical, remedial, restorative, therapeutic.

medicine *n* **1** healing, surgery, therapeutics, therapy, treatment. **2** cure, dose, drug, medicament, medication, nostrum, panacea, *old use* physic, prescription, remedy, treatment. □ anaesthetic, antibiotic, antidote, antiseptic, aspirin, capsule, gargle, herbal remedy, iodine, inhaler, linctus, lotion, lozenge, narcotic, ointment, painkiller, pastille, penicillin, pill, sedative, suppository, tablet, tonic, tranquillizer.

mediocre *adj* amateurish, average, *inf* common-or-garden, commonplace, everyday, fair, indifferent, inferior, medium, middling, moderate, ordinary, passable, pedestrian, poorish, *inf* run-of-the-mill, second-rate, *inf* so-so, undistinguished, unexceptional, unexciting, uninspired, unremarkable, weakish. *Opp* OUTSTANDING.

meditate *vb* be lost in thought, brood, cerebrate, chew over, cogitate, consider, contemplate, deliberate, mull things over, muse, ponder, pray, reflect, ruminate, think, turn over.

meditation *n* cerebration, contemplation, deliberation, musing, prayer, reflection, rumination, thought, yoga.

meditative *adj* brooding, contemplative, pensive, prayerful, rapt, reflective, ruminative, thoughtful.

medium *adj* average, intermediate, mean, medial, median, mid, middle, middling, mid-sized, midway, moderate, normal, ordinary, standard, usual. ● *n* **1** average, centre, compromise, mean, middle, midpoint, norm. **2** agency, approach, channel, form, means, method, mode, vehicle, way. **3** clairvoyant, seer, spiritualist. **the media, mass media** ▷ COMMUNICATION.

meek *adj* acquiescent, compliant, deferential, docile, forbearing, gentle, humble, long-suffering, lowly, mild, modest, non-militant, obedient, patient, peaceable, quiet, resigned, retiring, self-effacing, shy, soft, spineless, submissive, tame, timid, tractable, unambitious, unassuming, unprotesting, weak, *inf* wimpish. *Opp* AGGRESSIVE.

meet *vb* **1** *inf* bump into, chance upon, collide with, come across, confront, contact, encounter, face, happen on, have a meeting with, run across, run into, see. **2** be introduced to, make the acquaintance of. **3** come and fetch, greet, *inf* pick up, rendezvous with, welcome. **4** assemble, collect, come together, congregate, convene, forgather, gather, have a meeting, muster, rally, rendezvous. **5** *The ends don't meet.* abut, adjoin, come together, connect, converge, cross, intersect, join, link up, merge, touch, unite. **6** *meet a request.* acquiesce in, agree to, answer, comply with, deal with, fulfil, *inf* measure up to, observe, pay, satisfy, settle, take care of. **7** *meet difficulties.* encounter, endure, experience, go through, suffer, undergo.

meeting *n* **1** assembly, gathering, *inf* get-together, *inf* powwow. □ *audience, board, briefing, cabinet, caucus, committee, conclave, conference, congregation, congress, convention, council, discussion group, forum, prayer meeting, rally, seminar, service, synod.* **2** appointment, assignation, date, engagement, *inf* get-together, rendezvous, *old use* tryst. **3** *chance meeting.* confrontation, contact, encounter. **4** *meeting of lines, roads.* confluence (*of rivers*), convergence, crossing, crossroads, intersection, joining, junction, T-junction, union.

melancholy *adj* cheerless, dejected, depressed, depressing, despondent, disconsolate, dismal, dispirited, dispiriting, *inf* down, down-hearted, forlorn, gloomy, glum, joyless, lifeless, low, lugubrious, melancholic, miserable, moody, morose, mournful, sombre, sorrowful, unhappy, woebegone, woeful. ▷ SAD. *Opp* CHEERFUL. ● *n* ▷ SADNESS.

mellow *adj* **1** mature, rich, ripe, smooth, sweet. **2** *mellow mood.* agreeable, amiable, comforting, cordial, genial, gentle, happy, kindly, peaceful, pleasant, reassuring, soft, subdued, warm. *Opp* HARSH. ● *vb* age, develop, improve with age, mature, ripen, soften, sweeten.

melodious *adj* dulcet, *inf* easy on the ear, euphonious, harmonious, lyrical, mellifluous, melodic, sweet, tuneful.

melodramatic *adj* emotional, exaggerated, *inf* hammy, histrionic, overdone, overdrawn, *inf* over the top, sensationalized, sentimental, theatrical.

melody *n* air, song, strain, subject, theme, tune.

melt *vb* deliquesce, dissolve, liquefy, soften, thaw, unfreeze. **melt away** ▷ DISAPPEAR.

member *n* associate, colleague, fellow, life-member, paid-up member.

memorable *adj* catchy (*tune*), distinguished, extraordinary, haunting, historic, impressive, indelible, ineradicable, never-to-beforgotten, notable, outstanding, remarkable, striking, unforgettable.

memorial *n* cairn, cenotaph, gravestone, headstone, monument, plaque, reminder, statue, tablet, tomb.

memorize *vb* commit to memory, *inf* get off by heart, learn, learn by rote, learn parrot-fashion, remember, retain.

memory *n* **1** ability to remember, recall, retention. **2** impression, recollection, reminder, reminiscence, souvenir. **3** *memory of the dead.* fame, honour, name, remembrance, reputation, respect.

menace *n* danger, peril, threat, warning. ● *vb* alarm, bully, cow, intimidate, terrify, terrorize, threaten. ▷ FRIGHTEN.

mend vb **1** fix, patch up, put right, rectify, remedy, renew, renovate, repair, restore. □ *beat out, darn, patch, replace parts, sew up, solder, stitch up, touch up, weld.* **2** *mend your ways.* ameliorate, amend, correct, cure, improve, make better, reform, revise. **3** *mend after illness.* convalesce, get better, heal, improve, recover, recuperate.

menial adj base, boring, common, degrading, demeaning, humble, inferior, insignificant, low, lowly, servile, slavish, subservient, unskilled, unworthy. ● n inf dogsbody, lackey, minion, slave, underling. ▷ SERVANT.

mental adj **1** abstract, cerebral, cognitive, conceptual, intellectual, rational, theoretical. **2** *mental illness.* emotional, psychological, subjective, temperamental. ▷ MAD.

mentality n attitude, bent, character, disposition, frame of mind, inclination, inf make-up, outlook, personality, predisposition, propensity, psychology, set, temperament, way of thinking.

mention vb acknowledge, allude to, animadvert on, bring up, broach, cite, comment on, disclose, draw attention to, enumerate, hint at, inf let drop, let out, make known, make mention, name, note, observe, pay tribute to, point out, quote, recognize, refer to, remark, report, reveal, say, speak about, touch on, write about.

mercenary adj acquisitive, avaricious, covetous, grasping, greedy, inf money-mad, venal. ● n ▷ FIGHTER.

merchandise n commodities, goods, items for sale, produce, products, stock. ● vb ▷ ADVERTISE.

merchant n broker, dealer, distributor, retailer, salesman, seller, shopkeeper, stockist, supplier, trader, tradesman, tradeswoman, vendor, wholesaler.

merciful adj beneficent, benevolent, charitable, clement, compassionate, forbearing, forgiving, generous, gracious, humane, humanitarian, indulgent, kind, kind-hearted, kindly, lenient, liberal, magnanimous, mild, pitying, inf soft, soft-hearted, sympathetic, tender-hearted, tolerant. Opp MERCILESS.

merciless adj barbaric, barbarous, brutal, callous, cold, cruel, cutthroat, hard, hard-hearted, harsh, heartless, indifferent, inexorable, inflexible, inhuman, inhumane, intolerant, malevolent, pitiless, relentless, remorseless, rigorous, ruthless, savage, severe, stern, stonyhearted, strict, tyrannical, unbending, unfeeling, unforgiving, unkind, unmerciful, unrelenting, unremitting, vicious. Opp MERCIFUL.

mercy n beneficence, benignity, charity, clemency, compassion, feeling, forbearance, forgiveness, generosity, grace, humaneness, humanity, indulgence, kind-heartedness, kindness, leniency, love, pity, quarter, sympathy, understanding.

merge vb **1** amalgamate, blend, coalesce, combine, come together, confederate, consolidate, fuse, integrate, join together, link up, mingle, mix, pool, put together, unite. **2** *motorways merge.* converge, join, meet. Opp SEPARATE.

merit n credit, distinction, excellence, good, goodness, importance, quality, strength, talent, value, virtue, worth, worthiness. ● vb be entitled to, be worthy of, deserve, earn, have a right to, incur, justify, rate, warrant.

meritorious adj admirable, commendable, estimable, exemplary, honourable, laudable, praiseworthy, worthy.

merriment n amusement, cheerfulness, conviviality, exuberance, gaiety, glee, good cheer, high spirits, hilarity, jocularity, joking, jollity, joviality, inf larking about, laughter, levity, light-heartedness, liveliness, mirth, vivacity. ▷ MERRYMAKING.

merry adj bright, inf bubbly, carefree, cheerful, cheery, inf chirpy, convivial, festive, fun-loving, gay, glad, hilarious, jocular, jolly, jovial, joyful, joyous, light-hearted, lively, mirthful, rollicking, spirited, vivacious. ▷ HAPPY. Opp SERIOUS.

merrymaking n carousing, celebration, conviviality, festivity, frolic, fun, inf fun and games, inf jollification, inf junketing, merriment, revelry, roistering, sociability, old use wassailing. ▷ PARTY.

mesh n grid, lace, lacework, lattice, lattice-work, net, netting, network, reticulation, screen, sieve, tangle, tracery, trellis, web, webbing.

mess n 1 chaos, clutter, confusion, dirt, disarray, disorder, hotchpotch, jumble, litter, inf mishmash, muddle, inf shambles, tangle, untidiness. ▷ CONFUSION, DIRT. 2 made a mess of it. inf botch, failure, inf hash, inf mix-up. 3 got into a mess. difficulty, dilemma, inf fix, inf jam, inf pickle, plight, predicament, problem, trouble. ● vb **mess about** amuse yourself, loaf, loiter, lounge about, inf monkey about, inf muck about, inf play about. **make a mess of** ▷ BUNGLE, MUDDLE. **mess up** ▷ MUDDLE. **mess up a job** ▷ BUNGLE.

message n announcement, bulletin, cable, communication, communiqué, dispatch, information, intelligence, letter, memo, memorandum, missive, news, note, notice, report, statement, old use tidings.

messenger n bearer, carrier, courier, dispatch-rider, emissary, envoy, errand-boy, errand-girl, go-between, harbinger, herald, intermediary, legate, Mercury, messenger-boy, messenger-girl, nuncio, postman, runner.

messy adj blowzy, careless, chaotic, cluttered, dirty, dishevelled, disorderly, filthy, grubby, mucky, muddled, inf shambolic, slapdash, sloppy, slovenly, unkempt, untidy. Opp NEAT.

metallic adj 1 gleaming, lustrous, shiny. 2 clanking, clinking, ringing.

metaphorical adj allegorical, figurative, non-literal, symbolic. Opp LITERAL.

method n 1 approach, fashion, inf knack, manner, means, methodology, mode, Lat modus operandi, plan, procedure, process, programme, recipe, scheme, style, technique, trick, way. 2 arrangement, design, discipline, neatness, order, orderliness, organization, pattern, routine, structure, system.

methodical adj businesslike, careful, deliberate, disciplined, logical, meticulous, neat, ordered, orderly, organized, painstaking, precise, rational, regular, routine, structured, systematic, tidy. Opp DISORGANIZED.

meticulous adj accurate, exact, exacting, fastidious, inf finicky, painstaking, particular, perfectionist, precise, punctilious, scrupulous, thorough. Opp CARELESS.

microbe n bacillus, bacterium, inf bug, germ, micro-organism, virus.

middle adj central, centre, halfway, inner, inside, intermediate, intervening, mean, medial, median, mid, middle-of-the-road, midway, neutral. ● n bull's eye, centre, core, crown (of road), focus, half-way point, heart, hub, inside, middle position, midpoint, midst, nucleus.

middling adj average, fair, inf fair to middling, indifferent, mediocre, moderate, modest, inf nothing to write home about, ordinary, passable, run-of-the-mill, inf so-so, unremarkable. Opp OUTSTANDING.

might n capability, capacity, energy, force, muscle, potency, power, strength, superiority, vigour.

mighty adj brawny, dominant, doughty, energetic, enormous, forceful, great, hefty, muscular, potent, powerful, robust, inf strapping, strong, sturdy, vigorous, weighty. ▷ BIG. Opp WEAK.

migrate vb emigrate, go, immigrate, move, relocate, resettle, settle, travel.

mild adj 1 affable, amiable, conciliatory, docile, easygoing, equable, forbearing, forgiving, gentle, good-tempered, harmless, indulgent, inoffensive, kind, kindly, lenient, meek, merciful, modest, non-violent, pacific, peaceable, placid, quiet, inf soft, soft-hearted, submissive, sympathetic, tractable, unassuming, understanding, yielding. **2** mild weather. balmy, calm, clement, fair, peaceful, pleasant, serene, temperate, warm. **3** a mild illness. insignificant, minor, modest, slight, trivial, unimportant. **4** mild flavour. bland, delicate, faint, mellow, soothing, subtle. Opp SEVERE, STRONG.

mildness n affability, amiability, clemency, docility, forbearance, gentleness, kindness, leniency, moderation, placidity, softness, sympathy, tenderness. Opp ASPERITY.

militant adj active, aggressive, assertive, attacking, combative, fierce, hostile, positive, pugnacious. Opp PASSIVE. ● n activist, extremist, inf hawk, partisan.

militaristic adj bellicose, belligerent, combative, fond of fighting, hawkish, hostile, pugnacious, warlike. Opp PEACEABLE.

military adj armed, belligerent, combatant, enlisted, fighting, martial, uniformed, warlike. Opp CIVIL.

militate vb **militate against** cancel out, counter, counteract, countervail, discourage, hinder, oppose, prevent, resist.

milk vb bleed, drain, exploit, extract, tap, wring.

milky adj chalky, cloudy, misty, opaque, whitish. Opp CLEAR.

mill n **1** factory, foundry, plant, shop, works, workshop. **2** crusher, grinder, quern, watermill, windmill. ● vb crush, granulate, grate, grind, pound, powder, pulverize. **mill about** move aimlessly, seethe, swarm, throng, wander.

mimic n caricaturist, imitator, impersonator, impressionist. ● vb ape, caricature, copy, do impressions of, echo, imitate, impersonate, lampoon, look like, inf make fun of, mirror, mock, parody, parrot, pretend to be, reproduce, ridicule, satirize, simulate, sound like, inf take off.

mind n **1** astuteness, brain, brainpower, brains, cleverness, inf grey matter, head, insight, intellect, intelligence, judgement, memory, mental power, perception, psyche, rationality, reason, reasoning, remembrance, sagacity, sapience, sense, shrewdness, thinking, understanding, wisdom, wit, wits. **2** attitude, belief, bias, disposition, humour, inclination, intention, opinion, outlook, persuasion, plan, point of view, position, view, viewpoint, way of thinking, wishes. ● vb **1** attend to, care for, guard, keep an eye on, look after, take care of, take charge of, watch. **2** mind the warning. be careful about, beware of, heed, listen to, look out for, mark, note, obey, pay attention to, remember, take notice of, watch out for. **3** won't mind if he's late. be annoyed, be bothered, be offended, be resentful, bother, care, complain, disapprove, grumble, object, take offence, worry. **be in two minds** ▷ HESITATE. **make up your mind** ▷ DECIDE. **out of your mind** ▷ MAD.

mindful adj alert, attentive, aware, conscious, heedful, inf on the lookout, vigilant, watchful. ▷ CAREFUL. Opp CARELESS.

mindless adj brainless, fatuous, idiotic, obtuse, senseless, thick, thoughtless, unintelligent, unthinking, witless. ▷ STUPID. Opp INTELLIGENT.

mine n **1** coalfield, colliery, excavation, opencast mine, pit, quarry, shaft, tunnel, working. **2** mine of information. fund, repository, source, store, storehouse, supply, treasury, vein, wealth. ● vb dig, excavate, extract, quarry, remove, scoop out, unearth.

mineral n metal, ore, rock.

mingle vb amalgamate, associate, blend, circulate, combine, commingle, fraternize, get together, inf hobnob, intermingle, intermix, join, merge, mix, move about, *inf* rub shoulders, socialize, unite.

miniature *adj* baby, diminutive, dwarf, pocket, pygmy, reduced, scaled-down, small-scale, tiny, toy. ▷ SMALL.

minimal *adj* least, minimum, negligible, nominal, slightest, smallest, token.

minimize *vb* **1** cut down, decrease, diminish, lessen, pare, prune, reduce. **2** *minimize problems.* belittle, decry, depreciate, devalue, gloss over, make light of, play down, underestimate, undervalue. *Opp* MAXIMIZE.

minimum *adj* bottom, least, littlest, lowest, minimal, minutest, nominal, *inf* rock-bottom, slightest, smallest. ● *n* least, lowest, minimum amount, minimum quantity, nadir. *Opp* MAXIMUM.

minister *n* ▷ CLERGYMAN, OFFICIAL. ● *vb* **minister to** aid, assist, attend to, care for, help, look after, nurse, see to, support, wait on.

minor *adj* inconsequential, inferior, insignificant, lesser, little, negligible, petty, secondary, smaller, subordinate, subsidiary, trivial, unimportant. ▷ SMALL. *Opp* MAJOR. ● *n* ▷ ADOLESCENT, CHILD.

minstrel *n* balladeer, bard, entertainer, jongleur, musician, singer, troubadour.

mint *adj* brand-new, first-class, fresh, immaculate, new, perfect, unblemished, unmarked, unused. ● *n* fortune, heap, *inf* packet, pile, stack, unlimited supply, vast amount. ● *vb* cast, coin, forge, make, manufacture, produce, stamp out, strike.

minute *adj* diminutive, dwarf, infinitesimal, insignificant, lilliputian, microscopic, *inf* mini, miniature, minuscule, *inf* pint-sized, pocket, pygmy, tiny. ▷ SMALL.

minutes *plur n* log, notes, proceedings, record, résumé, summary, transactions.

miracle *n* marvel, miraculous event, mystery, wonder.

miraculous *adj* abnormal, extraordinary, incredible, inexplicable, magic, magical, mysterious, paranormal, phenomenal, preternatural, remarkable, supernatural, unaccountable, unbelievable, unexplainable. ▷ MARVELLOUS.

mirage *n* delusion, hallucination, illusion, vision.

mire *n* bog, fen, marsh, morass, mud, ooze, quagmire, quicksand, slime, *old use* slough, swamp. ▷ DIRT.

mirror *n* glass, looking-glass, reflector, speculum. ● *vb* echo, reflect, repeat, send back.

misadventure *n* accident, calamity, catastrophe, disaster, ill fortune, mischance, misfortune, mishap.

misanthropic *adj* anti-social, cynical, mean, nasty, surly, unfriendly, unpleasant, unsociable. *Opp* PHILANTHROPIC.

misappropriate *vb* defalcate, embezzle, expropriate, peculate. ▷ STEAL.

misbehave *vb* be a nuisance, be bad, behave badly, be mischievous, *inf* blot your copybook, *inf* carry on, commit an offence, default, disobey, do wrong, err, fool about, make mischief, *inf* mess about, *inf* muck about, offend, *inf* play about, play up, *inf* raise Cain, sin, transgress.

misbehaviour *n* badness, delinquency, disobedience, disorderliness, horseplay, indiscipline, insubordination, mischief, mischief-making, misconduct, misdemeanour, naughtiness, rowdyism, rudeness, sin, vandalism, wrongdoing.

miscalculate *vb inf* boob, err, *inf* get it wrong, go wrong, make a mistake, miscount, misjudge, misread, overestimate, overrate, overvalue, *inf* slip up, underestimate, underrate.

miscarriage *n miscarriage of justice.* breakdown, collapse, defeat, error, failure, perversion.

miscarry vb **1** abort, inf lose a baby, suffer a miscarriage. **2** break down, inf come to grief, come to nothing, fail, fall through, founder, go wrong, misfire. Opp SUCCEED.

miscellaneous adj assorted, different, old use divers, diverse, heterogeneous, manifold, mixed, motley, multifarious, sundry, varied, various.

miscellany n assortment, diversity, gallimaufry, hotchpotch, jumble, medley, mélange, inf mixed bag, mixture, pot-pourri, inf ragbag, variety.

mischief n **1** devilment, devilry, escapade, impishness, misbehaviour, misconduct, inf monkey business, naughtiness, playfulness, prank, rascality, roguishness, scrape, inf shenanigans, trouble. **2** damage, difficulty, evil, harm, hurt, injury, misfortune, trouble.

mischievous adj annoying, badly behaved, boisterous, disobedient, elvish, fractious, frolicsome, full of mischief, impish, lively, naughty, playful, inf puckish, rascally, roguish, sportive, uncontrollable, inf up to no good. ▷ WICKED. Opp WELL-BEHAVED.

miser n hoarder, miserly person, niggard, inf Scrooge, inf skinflint. Opp SPENDTHRIFT.

miserable adj **1** broken-hearted, crestfallen, inf cut up, dejected, depressed, desolate, despairing, despondent, disappointed, disconsolate, dismayed, dispirited, distressed, doleful, inf down, downcast, downhearted, forlorn, friendless, gloomy, glum, grief-stricken, heartbroken, hopeless, in low spirits, inf in the doldrums, inf in the dumps, joyless, lachrymose, languishing, lonely, low, melancholy, moping, mournful, sad, sorrowful, suicidal, tearful, uneasy, unfortunate, unhappy, unlucky, woebegone, woeful, wretched. **2** churlish, cross, disagreeable, discontented, inf grumpy, ill-natured, mean, miserly, morose, pessimistic, sour, sulky, sullen, surly, taciturn, unfriendly, unhelpful, unsociable. **3** miserable living conditions. abject,

awful, bad, deplorable, destitute, disgraceful, distressing, heart-breaking, hopeless, impoverished, inadequate, inhuman, lamentable, pathetic, pitiable, pitiful, poor, shameful, sordid, soul-destroying, squalid, vile, uncivilized, uncomfortable, vile, worthless, wretched. **4** miserable weather. cheerless, damp, depressing, dismal, dreary, grey, inclement, sunless, unpleasant, wet. Opp HAPPY, PLEASANT.

miserly adj avaricious, inf cheeseparing, inf close, inf close-fisted, covetous, economical, grasping, greedy, mean, mercenary, mingy, niggardly, parsimonious, penny-pinching, penurious, sparing, stingy, inf tight, inf tight-fisted. Opp GENEROUS.

misery n **1** angst, anguish, anxiety, bitterness, dejection, depression, despair, desperation, despondency, discomfort, distress, dolour, gloom, grief, heartache, heartbreak, inf hell, hopelessness, melancholy, sadness, sorrow, suffering, unhappiness, woe, wretchedness. Opp HAPPINESS. **2** adversity, affliction, deprivation, destitution, hardship, indigence, misfortune, need, oppression, penury, poverty, privation, squalor, suffering, inf trials and tribulations, tribulation, trouble, want, wretchedness.

misfire vb abort, fail, fall through, inf flop, founder, go wrong, miscarry. Opp SUCCEED.

misfortune n accident, adversity, affliction, bad luck, blow, calamity, catastrophe, contretemps, curse, disappointment, disaster, evil, hard luck, hardship, ill-luck, misadventure, mischance, mishap, reverse, setback, tragedy, trouble, vicissitude.

misguided adj erroneous, foolish, ill-advised, ill-judged, inappropriate, incorrect, inexact, misinformed, misjudged, misled, mistaken, unfounded, unjust, unsound, unwise. ▷ WRONG.

misjudge vb get wrong, guess wrongly, inf jump to the wrong conclusion, make a mistake, misinterpret, overestimate, overvalue, underestimate, undervalue. ▷ MISCALCULATE.

mislay vb lose, mislocate, misplace, put in the wrong place.

mislead vb bluff, confuse, delude, fool, give misleading information to, give a wrong impression to, lead astray, inf lead up the garden path, lie to, misdirect, misguide, misinform, outwit, inf take for a ride, take in, inf throw off the scent, trick. ▷ DECEIVE. **misleading** ▷ DECEPTIVE, PUZZLING.

miss vb **1** absent yourself from, avoid, be absent from, be too late for, dodge, escape, evade, fail to keep, forget, forgo, let go, lose, play truant from, inf skip, inf skive off. **2** miss a target. be wide of, fail to hit, fall short of. **3** miss absent friends. feel nostalgia for, grieve for, lament, long for, need, pine for, want, yearn for. **miss out** ▷ OMIT.

misshapen adj awry, bent, contorted, corkscrew, crippled, crooked, crumpled, deformed, disfigured, distorted, gnarled, grotesque, knotted, malformed, monstrous, screwed up, tangled, twisted, twisty, ugly, warped. Opp PERFECT.

missile n projectile. □ arrow, ballistic missile, bomb, boomerang, brickbat, bullet, dart, grenade, guided missile, rocket, shell, shot, torpedo. ▷ WEAPON.

missing adj absent, disappeared, lost, mislaid, inf skiving, straying, truant, unaccounted-for. Opp PRESENT.

mission n **1** delegation, deputation, expedition, exploration, journey, sortie, task-force, voyage. **2** mission in life. aim, assignment, calling, commitment, duty, function, goal, job, life's work, métier, objective, occupation, profession, purpose, quest, undertaking, vocation. **3** evangelical mission. campaign, crusade, holy war.

missionary n campaigner, crusader, evangelist, minister, preacher, proselytizer.

mist n **1** cloud, drizzle, fog, haze, smog, vapour. **2** condensation, film, steam.

mistake n inf bloomer, blunder, inf boob, inf botch, inf clanger, erratum, error, false step, fault, Fr faux pas, gaffe, inf howler, inaccuracy, indiscretion, lapse, misapprehension, miscalculation, misconception, misjudgement, misprint, misspelling, misunderstanding, omission, oversight, slip, slip-up, solecism, wrong move. ● vb confuse, inf get the wrong end of the stick, get wrong, misconstrue, misinterpret, misjudge, misread, misunderstand, mix up, inf take the wrong way.

mistaken adj erroneous, distorted, false, faulty, ill-judged, inaccurate, inappropriate, incorrect, inexact, misguided, misinformed, unfounded, unjust, unsound. ▷ WRONG. Opp CORRECT.

mistimed adj badly timed, early, inconvenient, inopportune, late, unseasonable, untimely. Opp OPPORTUNE.

mistreat vb abuse, batter, damage, harm, hurt, ill-treat, ill-use, injure, inf knock about, maltreat, manhandle, misuse, molest, treat roughly.

mistress n [mostly old use] **1** chief, head, keeper, owner, person in charge, proprietor. **2** ▷ TEACHER. **3** ▷ LOVER.

mistrust n apprehension, inf chariness, distrust, doubt, misgiving, reservation, scepticism, suspicion, uncertainty, unsureness, wariness. ● vb be sceptical about, be suspicious of, be wary of, disbelieve, distrust, doubt, fear, have doubts about, have misgivings about, have reservations about, question, suspect. Opp TRUST.

misty adj bleary, blurred, blurry, clouded, cloudy, dim, faint, foggy, fuzzy, hazy, indistinct, murky, obscure, opaque, shadowy, smoky, steamy, unclear, vague. Opp CLEAR.

misunderstand vb inf get the wrong end of the stick, get wrong, misapprehend, miscalculate, misconceive, misconstrue, mishear, misinterpret, misjudge, misread, miss the point of, mistake, mistranslate. *Opp* UNDERSTAND.

misunderstanding *n* **1** error, failure of understanding, false impression, misapprehension, miscalculation, misconception, misconstruction, misinterpretation, misjudgement, misreading, mistake, *inf* mix up, wrong idea. **2** argument, *inf* contretemps, controversy, difference of opinion, disagreement, discord, dispute. ▷ QUARREL.

misuse *n* abuse, careless use, corruption, ill-treatment, ill-use, maltreatment, misapplication, misappropriation, mishandling, mistreatment, perversion. ● *vb* **1** damage, harm, mishandle, treat carelessly. **2** *misuse an animal.* abuse, batter, damage, harm, hurt, ill-treat, ill-use, injure, *inf* knock about, maltreat, manhandle, mistreat, molest, treat roughly. **3** *misuse funds.* fritter away, misappropriate, squander, use wrongly, waste.

mitigate *vb* abate, allay, alleviate, decrease, ease, extenuate, lessen, lighten, make milder, moderate, palliate, qualify, reduce, relieve, soften, *inf* take the edge off, temper, tone down. *Opp* AGGRAVATE.

mix *n* amalgam, assortment, blend, combination, compound, range, variety. ● *vb* **1** alloy, amalgamate, blend, coalesce, combine, commingle, compound, confuse, diffuse, emulsify, fuse, homogenize, integrate, intermingle, join, jumble up, make a mixture, meld, merge, mingle, mix up, muddle, put together, shuffle, stir together, unite. *Opp* SEPARATE. **2** *mix with people.* ▷ SOCIALIZE.

mixed *adj* **1** assorted, different, diverse, heterogeneous, miscellaneous, varied, various. **2** *mixed with other things.* adulterated, alloyed, diluted, impure. **3** *mixed ingredients.* amalgamated, combined, composite, hybrid, integrated, joint, mongrel, united. **4** *mixed feelings.* ambiguous, ambivalent, confused, equivocal, muddled, uncertain.

mixture *n* **1** alloy, amalgam, amalgamation, association, assortment, blend, collection, combination, composite, compound, concoction, conglomeration, emulsion, farrago, fusion, gallimaufry, *inf* hotchpotch, intermingling, jumble, medley, mélange, merger, mess, mingling, miscellany, *inf* mishmash, mix, *inf* motley collection, pastiche, potpourri, selection, suspension, synthesis, variety. **2** cross-breed, half-caste, hybrid, mongrel.

moan *n* complaint, grievance, lament, lamentation. ● *vb* **1** complain, grieve, *inf* grouse, grumble, lament. **2** cry, groan, keen, sigh, ululate, wail, weep, whimper, whine. ▷ SOUND.

mob *n* *inf* bunch, crowd, gang, herd, horde, host, multitude, pack, press, rabble, riot, *inf* shower, swarm, throng. ▷ GROUP. ● *vb* besiege, crowd round, hem in, jostle, surround, swarm round, throng round.

mobile *adj* **1** itinerant, motorized, movable, portable, transportable, travelling, unfixed. **2** able to move, active, agile, independent, moving, nimble, *inf* on the go, *inf* up and about. **3** *mobile features.* animated, changeable, changing, expressive, flexible, fluid, plastic, shifting. *Opp* IMMOVABLE.

mobilize *vb* activate, assemble, call up, conscript, enlist, enrol, gather, get together, levy, marshal, muster, organize, rally, stir up, summon.

mock *adj* artificial, counterfeit, ersatz, fake, false, imitation, make-believe, man-made, *inf* pretend, sham, simulated, substitute. ● *vb* decry, deride, disparage, flout, gibe at, insult, jeer at, lampoon, laugh at, make fun of, make sport of, parody, poke fun at, ridicule, satirize, scoff at, scorn, *inf* send up, sneer at, tantalize, taunt, tease, travesty. ▷ MIMIC.

mockery *n* derision, insults, jeering, laughter, ridicule, scorn. □ *burlesque*, *caricature, lampoon, parody, sarcasm, satire, inf send-up, inf spoof, inf take-off, travesty.*

mocking adj contemptuous, derisive, disparaging, disrespectful, insulting, irreverent, jeering, rude, sarcastic, satirical, scornful, taunting, teasing, uncomplimentary, unkind. *Opp* RESPECTFUL.

mode n **1** approach, configuration, manner, medium, method, *Lat* modus operandi, procedure, set-up, system, technique, way. **2** ▷ FASHION.

model adj **1** imitation, miniature, scaled-down, toy. **2** *model pupil*. exemplary, ideal, perfect, unequalled. ● n **1** archetype, copy, dummy, effigy, facsimile, image, imitation, likeness, miniature, *inf* mock-up, paradigm, prototype, replica, representation, scale model, toy. **2** *model of excellence*. byword, epitome, example, exemplar, ideal, nonpareil, paragon, pattern, standard, yardstick. **3** *artist's model*. poser, sitter, subject. **4** *latest model*. brand, design, kind, mark, type, version. **5** *fashion model*. mannequin. ● vb carve, fashion, form, make, mould, sculpt, shape. **model yourself on** ▷ IMITATE.

moderate adj **1** average, balanced, calm, cautious, commonsensical, cool, deliberate, fair, judicious, medium, middle, *inf* middle-of-the-road, middling, modest, normal, ordinary, rational, reasonable, respectable, sensible, sober, steady, temperate, unexceptional, usual. *Opp* EXTREME. **2** *moderate winds*. gentle, light, mild. ● vb **1** abate, become less extreme, decline, decrease, die down, ease off, subside. **2** blunt, calm, check, curb, dull, ease, keep down, lessen, make less extreme, mitigate, modify, modulate, mollify, reduce, regulate, restrain, slacken, subdue, temper, tone down.

moderately adv comparatively, fairly, passably, *inf* pretty, quite, rather, reasonably, somewhat, to some extent.

moderation n balance, caution, common sense, fairness, reasonableness, restraint, reticence, sobriety, temperance.

modern adj advanced, avant-garde, contemporary, current, fashionable, forward-looking, fresh, futuristic, in vogue, latest, modish, new, newfangled, novel, present, present-day, progressive, recent, stylish, *inf* trendy, up-to-date, up-to-the-minute, *inf* with it. *Opp* OLD.

modernize vb bring up-to-date, *inf* do up, improve, make modern, rebuild, redesign, redo, refurbish, regenerate, rejuvenate, renovate, revamp, update.

modest adj **1** diffident, humble, inconspicuous, lowly, meek, plain, quiet, reserved, restrained, reticent, retiring, self-effacing, simple, unassuming, unobtrusive, unostentatious, unpretentious. *Opp* CONCEITED. **2** bashful, chaste, coy, decent, demure, discreet, proper, seemly, self-conscious, shamefaced, shy, simple. **3** *a modest income*. limited, medium, middling, moderate, normal, ordinary, reasonable, unexceptional. *Opp* EXCESSIVE.

modesty n **1** humbleness, humility, lowliness, meekness, reserve, restraint, reticence, self-effacement, simplicity. *Opp* OSTENTATION. **2** *modesty about undressing*. bashfulness, coyness, decency, demureness, discretion, propriety, seemliness, self-consciousness, shame, shyness.

modify vb adapt, adjust, alter, amend, change, convert, improve, reconstruct, redesign, remake, remodel, reorganize, revise, reword, rework, transform, vary. ▷ MODERATE.

modulate vb adjust, balance, change key, change the tone, lower the tone, moderate, regulate, soften, tone down.

moist adj affected by moisture, clammy, damp, dank, dewy, humid, misty, *inf* muggy, rainy, *inf* runny, steamy, watery, wettish. ▷ WET. *Opp* DRY.

moisten vb damp, dampen, humidify, make moist, moisturize, soak,

monumental

spray, wet. *Opp* DRY.

moisture *n* condensation, damp, dampness, dankness, dew, humidity, liquid, precipitation, spray, steam, vapour, water, wet, wetness.

molest *vb* abuse, accost, annoy, assault, attack, badger, bother, disturb, harass, harry, hassle, hector, ill-treat, interfere with, irk, irritate, manhandle, mistreat, *inf* needle, persecute, pester, plague, set on, tease, torment, vex, worry.

molten *adj* fluid, liquefied, liquid, melted, soft.

moment *n* **1** flash, instant, *inf* jiffy, minute, second, split second, *inf* tick, *inf* trice, *inf* twinkling of an eye, *inf* two shakes. **2** *a historic moment.* hour, juncture, occasion, opportunity, point in time, stage, time.

momentary *adj* brief, ephemeral, evanescent, fleeting, fugitive, hasty, passing, quick, short, short-lived, temporary, transient, transitory. *Opp* PERMANENT.

momentous *adj* consequential, critical, crucial, decisive, epoch-making, fateful, grave, historic, important, portentous, serious, significant, weighty. *Opp* UNIMPORTANT.

monarch *n* crowned head, emperor, empress, king, potentate, queen, ruler, tsar.

monarchy *n* domain, empire, kingdom, realm.

money *n* affluence, arrears, assets, bank-notes, *inf* bread, capital, cash, change, cheque, coin, copper, credit card, credit transfer, currency, damages, debt, dividend, *inf* dough, dowry, earnings, endowment, estate, expenditure, finance, fortune, fund, grant, income, interest, investment, legal tender, loan, *inf* lolly, *old use* lucre, mortgage, *inf* nest-egg, notes, outgoings, patrimony, pay, penny, pension, pocket-money, proceeds, profit, *inf* the ready, remittance, resources, revenue, riches, salary, savings, silver, sterling, takings, tax, traveller's cheque, wage, wealth, *inf* the wherewithal, winnings.

mongrel *n* cross-breed, cur, half-breed, hybrid, mixed breed.

monitor *n* **1** detector, guardian, prefect, supervisor, watchdog. **2** *TV monitor.* screen, set, television, TV, VDU, visual display unit. ● *vb* audit, check, examine, *inf* keep an eye on, oversee, record, supervise, trace, track, watch.

monk *n* brother, friar, hermit.

monkey *n* ape, primate, simian. □ *baboon, chimpanzee, gibbon, gorilla, marmoset, orang-utan.*

monopolize *vb* control, *inf* corner the market in, dominate, have a monopoly of, *inf* hog, keep for yourself, own, shut others out of, take over. *Opp* SHARE.

monotonous *adj* boring, colourless, dreary, dull, featureless, flat, level, repetitious, repetitive, soporific, tedious, tiresome, tiring, toneless, unchanging, uneventful, unexciting, uniform, uninteresting, unvarying, wearisome. *Opp* INTERESTING.

monster *n* abortion, beast, bogeyman, brute, demon, devil, fiend, freak, giant, horror, monstrosity, monstrous creature, mutant, ogre, troll.

monstrous *adj* **1** colossal, elephantine, enormous, gargantuan, giant, gigantic, great, huge, hulking, immense, *inf* jumbo, mammoth, mighty, prodigious, titanic, towering, tremendous, vast. ▷ BIG. **2** *a monstrous crime.* abhorrent, atrocious, awful, beastly, brutal, cruel, devilish, disgusting, dreadful, evil, ghoulish, grisly, gross, gruesome, heinous, hideous, *inf* horrendous, horrible, horrific, horrifying, inhuman, nightmarish, obscene, outrageous, repulsive, shocking, terrible, ugly, villainous, wicked. ▷ EVIL.

monument *n* cairn, cenotaph, cross, gravestone, headstone, mausoleum, memorial, obelisk, pillar, prehistoric remains, relic, reminder, shrine, tomb, tombstone.

monumental *adj* **1** aweinspiring, awesome, classic, enduring, epoch-making, grand, historic, impressive, large-scale, lasting, major, memorable, unforgettable. ▷ BIG. **2** *a monumental plaque.* commemorative, memorial.

mood *n* **1** attitude, disposition, frame of mind, humour, inclination, nature, spirit, state of mind, temper, vein. **2** atmosphere, feeling, tone. ▷ ANGRY, HAPPY, SAD, etc. **in the mood** ▷ READY.

moody *adj* abrupt, bad-tempered, cantankerous, capricious, changeable, crabby, cross, crotchety, depressed, depressive, disgruntled, erratic, fickle, gloomy, grumpy, *inf* huffy, ill-humoured, inconstant, irritable, melancholy, mercurial, miserable, morose, peevish, petulant, *inf* short, short-tempered, snappy, sulky, sullen, temperamental, testy, *inf* touchy, unpredictable, unreliable, unstable, volatile. ▷ SAD.

moor *n* fell, heath, moorland, wasteland. ● *vb* anchor, berth, dock, make fast, secure, tie up. ▷ FASTEN.

mope *vb* be sad, brood, despair, grieve, languish, *inf* moon, pine, sulk.

moral *adj* **1** blameless, chaste, decent, ethical, good, highminded, honest, honourable, incorruptible, innocent, irreproachable, just, law-abiding, noble, principled, proper, pure, respectable, responsible, right, righteous, sinless, trustworthy, truthful, upright, upstanding, virtuous. **2** *a moral tale.* allegorical, cautionary, didactic, moralistic, moralizing. *Opp* IMMORAL. ● *n* lesson, maxim, meaning, message, point, precept, principle, teaching. **morals** ▷ MORALITY. **moral tale** allegory, cautionary tale, fable, parable.

morale *n* attitude, cheerfulness, confidence, *Fr* esprit de corps, *inf* heart, mood, self-confidence, self-esteem, spirit, state of mind.

morality *n* behaviour, conduct, decency, ethics, ethos, fairness, goodness, honesty, ideals, integrity, justice, morals, principles, propriety, rectitude, righteousness, rightness,

scruples, standards, uprightness, virtue.

moralize *vb* lecture, philosophize, pontificate, preach, sermonize.

morbid *adj* black (*humour*), brooding, dejected, depressed, ghoulish, gloomy, grim, grotesque, gruesome, lugubrious, macabre, melancholy, monstrous, morose, pathological, pessimistic, *inf* sick, sombre, unhappy, unhealthy, unpleasant, unwholesome. *Opp* CHEERFUL.

more *adj* added, additional, extra, further, increased, longer, new, other, renewed, supplementary. *Opp* LESS.

moreover *adv* also, as well, besides, further, furthermore, in addition, *old use* to boot, too.

morose *adj* bad-tempered, churlish, depressed, gloomy, glum, grim, humourless, ill-natured, melancholy, moody, mournful, pessimistic, saturnine, sour, sulky, sullen, surly, taciturn, unhappy, unsociable. ▷ SAD. *Opp* CHEERFUL.

morsel *n* bite, crumb, fragment, gobbet, mouthful, nibble, piece, sample, scrap, small amount, soupçon, spoonful, taste, titbit. ▷ BIT.

mortal *adj* **1** ephemeral, human, passing, temporal, transient. *Opp* IMMORTAL. **2** *mortal sickness.* deadly, fatal, lethal, terminal. **3** *mortal enemies.* deadly, implacable, irreconcilable, remorseless, sworn, unrelenting. ● *n* creature, human being, man, person, soul, woman.

mortality *n* **1** corruptibility, humanity, impermanence, transience. **2** *infant mortality.* death-rate, dying, fatalities, loss of life.

mortify *vb* abash, chagrin, chasten, *inf* crush, deflate, embarrass, humble, humiliate, *inf* put down, shame.

mostly *adv* chiefly, commonly, generally, largely, mainly, normally, predominantly, primarily, principally, typically, usually.

moth-eaten *adj* antiquated, decrepit, holey, mangy, ragged, shabby, *inf* tatty. ▷ OLD.

mother *n old use* dam, *inf* ma, *inf* mamma, *old use* mater, *inf* mum, *inf* mummy, parent. ● *vb* care for, cherish, coddle, comfort, cuddle, fuss over, indulge, look after, love, nourish, nurse, nurture, pamper, protect, spoil, take care of.

motherly *adj* caring, kind, maternal, protective. ▷ LOVING.

motif *n* decoration, design, device, figure, idea, leitmotif, ornament, pattern, symbol, theme.

motion *n* action, activity, agitation, change, commotion, development, evolution, move, movement, progress, rise and fall, shift, stir, stirring, to and fro, travel, travelling, trend. ● *vb* ▷ GESTURE.

motionless *adj* at rest, calm, frozen, immobile, inanimate, inert, lifeless, paralysed, peaceful, resting, stagnant, static, stationary, still, stock-still, unmoving. *Opp* MOVING.

motivate *vb* activate, actuate, arouse, cause, drive, egg on, encourage, excite, galvanize, goad, incite, induce, influence, inspire, instigate, move, occasion, persuade, prompt, provoke, push, rouse, spur, stimulate, stir, urge.

motive *n* aim, ambition, cause, drive, encouragement, end, enticement, grounds, impulse, incentive, incitement, inducement, inspiration, instigation, intention, lure, motivation, object, provocation, purpose, push, rationale, reason, spur, stimulation, stimulus, thinking.

motor *n* ▷ ENGINE, VEHICLE. ● *vb* drive, go by car. ▷ TRAVEL.

mottled *adj* blotchy, brindled, dappled, flecked, freckled, marbled, patchy, spattered, speckled, spotted, spotty, streaked, streaky, variegated.

motto *n* adage, aphorism, catchphrase, maxim, precept, proverb, rule, saw, saying, slogan.

mould *n* blight, fungus, growth, mildew. ● *vb* cast, fashion, forge, form, model, *inf* sculpt, shape, stamp, work.

mouldy *adj* carious, damp, decaying, decomposing, fusty, mildewed, mouldering, musty, putrefying, rotten, stale.

mound *n* bank, dune, elevation, heap, hill, hillock, hummock, hump, knoll, pile, stack, tumulus.

mount *n* ▷ MOUNTAIN. ● *vb* **1** ascend, clamber up, climb, fly up, go up, rise, rocket upwards, scale, shoot up, soar. *Opp* DESCEND. **2** *mount a horse.* get astride, get on, jump onto. **3** *savings mount.* accumulate, build up, escalate, expand, get bigger, grow, increase, intensify, multiply, pile up, swell. *Opp* DECREASE. **4** *mount a picture.* display, exhibit, frame, install, prepare, put in place, put on, set up.

mountain *n* alp, arête, *Scot* ben, elevation, eminence, height, hill, mound, mount, peak, prominence, range, ridge, sierra, summit, tor, volcano.

mountainous *adj* alpine, craggy, daunting, formidable, high, hilly, precipitous, rocky, rugged, steep, towering. ▷ BIG.

mourn *vb* bemoan, bewail, fret, go into mourning, grieve, keen, lament, mope, pine, regret, wail, weep. *Opp* REJOICE.

mournful *adj* dismal, distressed, distressing, doleful, funereal, gloomy, grief-stricken, grieving, heartbreaking, heartbroken, lamenting, lugubrious, melancholy, plaintive, plangent, sad, sorrowful, tearful, tragic, unhappy, woeful. *Opp* CHEERFUL.

mouth *n* **1** *inf* chops, *sl* gob, jaws, *sl* kisser, lips, maw, muzzle, palate. **2** *mouth of cave.* aperture, door, doorway, entrance, exit, gate, gateway, inlet, opening, orifice, outlet, vent, way in. **3** *mouth of a river.* delta, estuary, outflow. ● *vb* articulate, enunciate, form, pronounce. ▷ SAY.

mouthful *n* bite, gobbet, gulp, morsel, sip, spoonful, swallow, taste.

movable *adj* adjustable, changeable, detachable, floating, mobile, portable, transferable, transportable, unfixed, variable. *Opp* IMMOVABLE.

move *n* **1** act, action, deed, device, dodge, gambit, manoeuvre, measure, movement, ploy, ruse, step, stratagem, *inf* tack, tactic. **2** *a career move*. change, changeover, relocation, shift, transfer. **3** *your move*. chance, go, opportunity, turn. ● *vb* **1** *move about*. be agitated, be astir, budge, change places, change position, fidget, flap, roll, shake, shift, stir, swing, toss, tremble, turn, twist, twitch, wag, *inf* waggle, wave, *inf* wiggle. **2** *move along*. cruise, fly, jog, journey, make headway, make progress, march, pass, proceed, travel, walk. **3** *move quickly*. bolt, *inf* bowl along, canter, career, dash, dart, flit, flounce, fly, gallop, hasten, hurry, hurtle, hustle, *inf* nip, race, run, rush, shoot, speed, stampede, streak, sweep along, sweep past, *inf* tear, *inf* zip, *inf* zoom. **4** *move slowly*. amble, crawl, dawdle, drift, stroll. **5** *move gracefully*. dance, flow, glide, skate, skim, slide, slip, sweep. **6** *move awkwardly*. dodder, falter, flounder, lumber, lurch, pitch, shuffle, stagger, stumble, sway, totter, trip, trundle. **7** *move stealthily*. crawl, creep, edge, slink, slither. **8** *move things*. carry, export, import, relocate, shift, ship, transfer, transplant, transport, transpose. **9** *moved him to act*. encourage, impel, influence, inspire, persuade, prompt, stimulate, urge. **10** *move the crowd's feelings*. affect, arouse, enrage, fire, impassion, rouse, stir, touch. **11** *moved to improve the situation*. act, do something, make a move, take action. **move away** ▷ DEPART. **move back** ▷ RETREAT. **move down** ▷ DESCEND. **move in** ▷ ENTER. **move round** ▷ CIRCULATE, ROTATE. **move towards** ▷ APPROACH. **move up** ▷ ASCEND.

movement *n* **1** action, activity, migration, motion, shifting, stirring. ▷ GESTURE, MOVE. **2** *movement towards green issues*. change, development, drift, evolution, progress, shift,

swing, tendency, trend. **3** *a political movement*. campaign, crusade, drive, faction, group, organization, party. **4** *military movements*. exercise, operation.

movie *n* film, *inf* flick, motion picture.

moving *adj* **1** active, alive, astir, dynamic, flowing, going, in motion, mobile, movable, on the move, travelling, under way. *Opp* MOTIONLESS. **2** *a moving tale*. affecting, emotional, emotive, exciting, heart-rending, heart-warming, inspirational, inspiring, pathetic, poignant, spine-tingling, stirring, *inf* tear-jerking, thrilling, touching.

mow *vb* clip, cut, scythe, shear, trim.

muck *n* dirt, droppings, dung, excrement, faeces, filth, grime, *inf* gunge, manure, mess, mire, mud, ooze, ordure, rubbish, scum, sewage, slime, sludge.

mucky *adj* dirty, filthy, foul, grimy, grubby, messy, muddy, scummy, slimy, soiled, sordid, squalid. *Opp* CLEAN.

mud *n* clay, dirt, mire, muck, ooze, silt, slime, sludge, slurry, soil.

muddle *n* chaos, clutter, confusion, disorder, *inf* hotchpotch, jumble, mess, *inf* mishmash, *inf* mix up, *inf* shambles, tangle, untidiness. ● *vb* **1** bemuse, bewilder, confound, confuse, disorient, disorientate, mislead, perplex, puzzle. *Opp* CLARIFY. **2** disarrange, disorder, disorganize, entangle, *inf* foul up, jumble, make a mess of, *inf* mess up, mix up, scramble, shuffle, tangle. *Opp* TIDY.

muddy *adj* **1** caked, dirty, filthy, messy, mucky, soiled. **2** *muddy water*. cloudy, impure, misty, opaque. **3** *muddy ground*. boggy, marshy, sloppy, sodden, soft, spongy, waterlogged, wet. *Opp* CLEAN, FIRM.

muffle *vb* **1** cloak, conceal, cover, enclose, enfold, envelop, shroud, swathe, wrap up. **2** *muffle noise*. damp, dampen, deaden, disguise, dull, hush, mask, mute, quieten, silence, soften, stifle, still, suppress, tone down.

muffled *adj* damped, deadened, dull, fuzzy, indistinct, muted, silenced, stifled, suppressed, unclear, woolly. *Opp* CLEAR.

mug *n* beaker, cup, *old use* flagon, pot, tankard. ● *vb* assault, beat up, jump on, molest, rob, set on, steal from. ▷ ATTACK. **mug up** ▷ LEARN.

mugger *n* attacker, hooligan, robber, ruffian, thief, thug. ▷ CRIMINAL.

mugging *n* attack, robbery, street crime. ▷ CRIME.

muggy *adj* clammy, close, damp, humid, moist, oppressive, steamy, sticky, stuffy, sultry, warm.

multiple *adj* complex, compound, double, many, numerous, plural, quadruple, quintuple, triple.

multiplicity *n* abundance, array, complex, diversity, number, plurality, profusion, variety.

multiply *vb* **1** double, quadruple, quintuple, *inf* times, triple. **2** become numerous, breed, increase, proliferate, propagate, reproduce, spread.

multitude *n* crowd, host, large number, legion, lots, mass, myriad, swarm, throng. ▷ GROUP.

mumble *vb* be inarticulate, murmur, mutter, speak indistinctly, swallow your words.

munch *vb* bite, chew, champ, chomp, crunch, eat, gnaw, masticate.

mundane *adj* banal, common, commonplace, down-to-earth, dull, everyday, familiar, human, material, physical, practical, quotidian, routine, temporal, worldly. ▷ ORDINARY. *Opp* EXTRAORDINARY, SPIRITUAL.

municipal *adj* borough, city, civic, community, district, local, public, town, urban.

murder *n* assassination, fratricide, genocide, homicide, infanticide, killing, manslaughter, matricide, parricide, patricide, regicide, sororicide, unlawful killing, uxoricide. ● *vb* ▷ KILL.

murderer *n* assassin, *inf* butcher, cutthroat, gunman, homicide, killer, slayer.

murderous *adj* barbarous, bloodthirsty, bloody, brutal, cruel, dangerous, deadly, fell, ferocious, fierce, homicidal, inhuman, pitiless, ruthless, savage, vicious, violent.

murky *adj* clouded, cloudy, dark, dim, dismal, dreary, dull, foggy, funereal, gloomy, grey, misty, muddy, obscure, overcast, shadowy, sombre. *Opp* CLEAR.

murmur *n* background noise, buzz, drone, grumble, hum, mutter, rumble, susurration, undertone, whisper. ● *vb* drone, hum, moan, mumble, mutter, rumble, speak in an undertone, whisper. ▷ GRUMBLE, TALK.

muscular *adj* athletic, *inf* beefy, brawny, broad-shouldered, burly, hefty, *inf* hulking, husky, powerful, powerfully built, robust, sinewy, *inf* strapping, strong, sturdy, tough, well-built, well-developed, wiry. *Opp* WEAK.

muse *vb* cogitate, consider, contemplate, deliberate, meditate, mull over, ponder, reflect, ruminate, study, think.

mushy *adj* pulpy, spongy, squashy. ▷ SOFT.

music *n* harmony. □ *blues, chamber music, choral music, classical music, dance music, disco music, folk, instrumental music, jazz, orchestral music, plain-song, pop, ragtime, reggae, rock, soul, swing.* □ *anthem, ballad, cadenza, calypso, canon, cantata, canticle, carol, chant, concerto, dance, dirge, duet, étude, fanfare, fugue, hymn, improvisation, intermezzo, lullaby, march, musical, nocturne, nonet, octet, opera, operetta, oratorio, overture, prelude, quartet, quintet, rhapsody, rondo, scherzo, sea shanty, septet, sextet, sonata, song, spiritual, symphony, toccata, trio.*

musical *adj* euphonious, harmonious, lyrical, melodious, pleasant, sweet-sounding, tuneful. **musical instrument** ▷ INSTRUMENT.

musician *n* composer, music-maker, performer, player, singer. □ *accompanist, bass, bugler, cellist, clarinettist, conductor, contralto, drummer, fiddler, flautist, guitarist, harpist, instrumentalist, maestro, minstrel, oboist, organist, percussionist, pianist, piper, soloist, soprano, tenor, timpanist, treble, trombonist, trumpeter, violinist, virtuoso, vocalist.* **musicians** □ *band, choir, chorus, consort, duet, duo, ensemble, group, nonet, octet, orchestra, quartet, quintet, septet, sextet, trio.*

muster *vb* assemble, call together, collect, come together, convene, convoke, gather, get together, group, marshal, mobilize, rally, round up, summon.

musty *adj* airless, damp, dank, fusty, mildewed, mildewy, mouldy, smelly, stale, stuffy, unventilated.

mutant *n* abortion, anomaly, deviant, freak, monster, monstrosity, sport, variant.

mutation *n* alteration, deviance, evolution, metamorphosis, modification, transfiguration, transformation, transmutation, variation. ▷ CHANGE.

mute *adj* dumb, quiet, silent, speechless, tacit, taciturn, tight-lipped, tongue-tied, voiceless. ● *vb* damp, dampen, deaden, dull, hush, make quieter, mask, muffle, quieten, silence, soften, stifle, still, suppress, tone down.

mutilate *vb* cripple, damage, deface, disable, disfigure, dismember, injure, lame, maim, mangle, mar, spoil, vandalize, wound.

mutinous *adj* contumacious, defiant, disobedient, insubordinate, insurgent, insurrectionary, rebellious, refractory, revolutionary, seditious, subversive, ungovernable, unmanageable, unruly. *Opp* OBEDIENT.

mutiny *n* defiance, disobedience, insubordination, insurgency, insurrection, rebellion, revolt, revolution, sedition, subversion, unruliness, uprising. ● *vb* agitate, be mutinous, disobey, rebel, revolt, rise up, strike.

mutter *vb* drone, grumble, mumble, murmur, speak in an undertone, whisper. ▷ GRUMBLE, TALK.

mutual *adj* common, interactive, joint, reciprocal, reciprocated, requited, shared.

muzzle *n* jaws, mouth, nose, snout. ● *vb* censor, gag, restrain, silence, stifle, suppress.

mysterious *adj* arcane, baffling, bewildering, bizarre, confusing, cryptic, curious, dark, enigmatic, incomprehensible, inexplicable, inscrutable, insoluble, magical, miraculous, mystical, mystifying, obscure, perplexing, puzzling, recondite, secret, strange, uncanny, unexplained, unfathomable, unknown, weird. *Opp* STRAIGHTFORWARD.

mystery *n* conundrum, enigma, miracle, problem, puzzle, question, riddle, secret.

mystical *adj* abnormal, arcane, cabalistic, ineffable, metaphysical, mysterious, occult, other-worldly, preternatural, religious, spiritual, supernatural. *Opp* MUNDANE.

mystify *vb* baffle, *inf* bamboozle, *inf* beat, bewilder, confound, confuse, *inf* flummox, fool, hoax, perplex, puzzle, *inf* stump.

myth *n* **1** allegory, fable, legend, mythology, symbolism. **2** fabrication, falsehood, fiction, invention, make-believe, pretence, untruth.

mythical *adj* **1** allegorical, fabled, fabulous, legendary, mythic, mythological, poetic, symbolic. **2** false, fanciful, fictional, imaginary, invented, make-believe, non-existent, pretended, unreal. *Opp* REAL.

N

nadir *n* bottom, depths, low point, zero. *Opp* ZENITH.

nag *n* ▷ HORSE. ● *vb* annoy, badger, chivvy, find fault with, goad, *inf* go on at, harass, hector, *inf* henpeck, keep complaining, pester, *inf* plague, scold, worry.

nail *n* pin, spike, stud, tack. ● *vb* ▷ FASTEN.

naïve *adj* artless, *inf* born yesterday, candid, childlike, credulous, *inf* green, guileless, gullible, inexperienced, ingenuous, innocent, open, simple, simple-minded, stupid, trustful, trusting, unsophisticated, unsuspecting, unwary. *Opp* ARTFUL.

naked *adj* bare, denuded, disrobed, exposed, in the nude, nude, stark-naked, stripped, unclothed, unconcealed, uncovered, undraped, undressed.

name *n* 1 alias, appellation, Christian name, first name, forename, given name, *inf* handle, identity, nickname, nom de plume, pen name, personal name, pseudonym, sobriquet, surname, title. 2 denomination, designation, epithet, term. ● *vb* 1 baptize, call, christen, dub, style. 2 *name a book.* entitle, label. 3 *named him man of the match.* appoint, choose, commission, delegate, designate, elect, nominate, select, single out, specify. **named** ▷ SPECIFIC.

nameless *adj* 1 anonymous, incognito, unheard-of, unidentified, unnamed, unsung. 2 *nameless horrors.* dreadful, horrible, indescribable, inexpressible, shocking, unmentionable, unspeakable, unutterable.

nap *n* catnap, doze, *inf* forty winks, rest, *inf* shut-eye, siesta, sleep, snooze.

narrate *vb* chronicle, describe, detail, recount, rehearse, relate, repeat, report, retail, tell, unfold.

narration *n* commentary, reading, recital, recitation, relation, story-telling, telling, voiceover.

narrative *n* account, chronicle, description, history, report, story, tale, *inf* yarn.

narrator *n* author, chronicler, raconteur, reporter, storyteller.

narrow *adj* attenuated, close, confined, constricted, constricting, cramped, enclosed, fine, limited, restricted, slender, slim, thin, tight. *Opp* WIDE.

narrow-minded *adj* biased, bigoted, conservative, conventional, hidebound, illiberal, inflexible, insular, intolerant, narrow, old-fashioned, parochial, petty, prejudiced, prim, prudish, puritanical, reactionary, rigid, small-minded, straitlaced, *inf* stuffy. *Opp* BROAD-MINDED.

nasty *adj* [*Nasty* refers to anything you do not like. The range of synonyms is almost limitless: we give only a selection here.] bad, beastly, dangerous, difficult, dirty, disagreeable, disgusting, distasteful, foul, hateful, horrible, loathsome, *sl* lousy, objectionable, obnoxious, *inf* off-putting, repulsive, revolting, severe, sickening, unkind, unpleasant. *Opp* NICE.

nation *n* civilization, community, country, domain, land, people, population, power, race, realm, society, state, superpower.

national *adj* 1 ethnic, popular, racial. 2 *a national emergency.* countrywide, general, nationwide, state, widespread. ● n citizen, inhabitant, native, resident, subject.

nationalism n chauvinism, jingoism, loyalty, patriotism, xenophobia.

native adj 1 aboriginal, indigenous, local, original. 2 native wit. congenital, hereditary, inborn, inbred, inherent, inherited, innate, mother (wit), natural. ● n aborigine, life-long resident.

natural adj 1 common, everyday, habitual, normal, ordinary, predictable, regular, routine, standard, typical, usual. 2 natural feelings. healthy, hereditary, human, inborn, inherited, innate, instinctive, intuitive, kind, maternal, native, paternal, proper, right. 3 a natural smile. artless, authentic, candid, genuine, guileless, sincere, spontaneous, unaffected, unpretentious, unselfconscious, unstudied. 4 natural resources. crude (oil), raw, unadulterated, unprocessed, unrefined. 5 a natural leader. born, congenital, untaught. Opp UNNATURAL.

nature n 1 countryside, creation, ecology, environment, natural history, scenery, wildlife. 2 attributes, character, complexion, constitution, disposition, essence, humour, makeup, manner, personality, properties, quality, temperament, traits. 3 category, description, kind, sort, species, type, variety.

naughty adj 1 bad, badly-behaved, bad-mannered, boisterous, contrary, defiant, delinquent, disobedient, disorderly, disruptive, fractious, headstrong, impish, impolite, incorrigible, insubordinate, intractable, misbehaved, mischievous, obstinate, obstreperous, perverse, playful, puckish, rascally, rebellious, refractory, roguish, rude, self-willed, stubborn, troublesome, uncontrollable, undisciplined, ungovernable, unmanageable, unruly, wayward, wicked, wild, wilful. 2 [inf] cheeky, improper, ribald, risqué, shocking, inf smutty, vulgar. ▷ OBSCENE. Opp POLITE, WELL BEHAVED.

nauseate vb disgust, offend, repel, revolt, sicken.

nauseous adj disgusting, foul, loathsome, nauseating, offensive, repulsive, revolting, sickening, stomach-turning.

nautical adj marine, maritime, naval, seafaring, seagoing, yachting.

navigate vb captain, direct, drive, guide, handle, manoeuvre, map-read, pilot, sail, skipper, steer.

navy n armada, convoy, fleet, flotilla.

near adj 1 abutting, adjacent, adjoining, bordering, close, connected, contiguous, immediate, nearby, neighbouring, next-door. 2 Christmas is near. approaching, coming, forthcoming, imminent, impending, looming, inf round the corner. 3 near friends. close, dear, familiar, intimate, related. Opp DISTANT.

nearly adv about, all but, almost, approaching, approximately, around, as good as, close to, just about, not quite, practically, roughly, virtually.

neat adj 1 adroit, clean, dainty, deft, dexterous, elegant, inf natty, orderly, organized, pretty, inf shipshape, smart, inf spick and span, spruce, straight, systematic, tidy, trim, uncluttered, well-kept. 2 accurate, expert, methodical, meticulous, precise, skilful. 3 neat alcohol. pure, inf straight, unadulterated, undiluted. Opp CLUMSY, UNTIDY.

necessary adj compulsory, destined, essential, fated, imperative, important, indispensable, ineluctable, inescapable, inevitable, inexorable, mandatory, needed, needful, obligatory, predestined, required, requisite, unavoidable, vital. Opp UNNECESSARY.

necessity n 1 compulsion, essential, inevitability, inf must, need, obligation, prerequisite, requirement, requisite, Lat sine qua non. 2 beggary, destitution, hardship, indigence, need, penury, poverty, privation, shortage, suffering, want.

need n call, demand, lack, requirement, want. ▷ NECESSITY. ● vb be short of, call for, crave, demand, depend on, lack, miss, rely on, require, want.

needless adj excessive, gratuitous, pointless, redundant, superfluous, unnecessary.

needy adj badly off, destitute, inf hard up, impecunious, impoverished, indigent, necessitous, penurious, poverty-stricken, underpaid. ▷ POOR.

negate vb annul, cancel out, deny, gainsay, invalidate, nullify, oppose.

negative adj adversarial, antagonistic, inf anti, contradictory, destructive, disagreeing, dissenting, grudging, nullifying, obstructive, opposing, pessimistic, uncooperative, unenthusiastic, unresponsive, unwilling. ● n denial, no, refusal, rejection, veto. Opp POSITIVE.

neglect n carelessness, dereliction of duty, disregard, inadvertence, inattention, indifference, negligence, oversight, slackness. ● vb abandon, be remiss about, disregard, forget, ignore, leave alone, let slide, lose sight of, miss, omit, overlook, pay no attention to, shirk, skip. **neglected** ▷ DERELICT.

negligent adj careless, forgetful, heedless, inattentive, inconsiderate, indifferent, irresponsible, lax, offhand, reckless, remiss, slack, sloppy, slovenly, thoughtless, uncaring, unthinking. Opp CAREFUL.

negligible adj imperceptible, inconsequential, inconsiderable, insignificant, minor, nugatory, paltry, petty, slight, small, tiny, trifling, trivial, unimportant. Opp CONSIDERABLE.

negotiate vb arbitrate, bargain, come to terms, confer, deal, discuss terms, haggle, intercede, make arrangements, mediate, parley, transact.

negotiation n arbitration, bargaining, conciliation, debate, diplomacy, discussion, mediation, parleying, transaction.

negotiator n agent, ambassador, arbitrator, broker, conciliator, diplomat, go-between, intercessor, intermediary, mediator, middleman.

neighbourhood n area, community, district, environs, locality, place, purlieus, quarter, region, surroundings, vicinity, zone.

neighbouring adj adjacent, adjoining, attached, bordering, close, closest, connecting, contiguous, near, nearby, nearest, next-door, surrounding.

neighbourly adj civil, considerate, friendly, helpful, kind, sociable, thoughtful, well-disposed.

nerve n coolness, determination, firmness, fortitude, resolution, resolve, will-power. ▷ COURAGE.

nervous adj afraid, agitated, anxious, apprehensive, disturbed, edgy, excitable, fearful, fidgety, flustered, fretful, highly-strung, ill-at-ease, inf in a tizzy, insecure, inf jittery, inf jumpy, inf nervy, neurotic, on edge, inf on tenterhooks, inf rattled, restive, restless, ruffled, shaky, shy, strained, tense, timid, inf touchy, inf twitchy, uneasy, unnerved, unsettled, inf uptight, worried. ▷ FRIGHTENED. Opp CALM.

nestle vb cuddle, curl up, huddle, nuzzle, snuggle.

net n lace, lattice-work, mesh, netting, network, web. ● vb 1 capture, catch, enmesh, ensnare, trammel, trap. 2 net £200 a week. accumulate, bring in, clear, earn, get, make, realize, receive, inf take home.

network n 1 inf criss-cross, grid, labyrinth, lattice, maze, mesh, net, netting, tangle, tracery, web. 2 complex, organization, system.

neurosis n abnormality, anxiety, depression, mental condition, obsession, phobia.

neurotic adj anxious, distraught, disturbed, irrational, maladjusted, nervous, obsessive, overwrought, unbalanced, unstable.

neuter adj ambiguous, ambivalent, asexual, indeterminate, uncertain. ● vb castrate, inf doctor, emasculate, geld, spay, sterilize.

neutral adj 1 detached, disinterested, dispassionate, fair, impartial, indifferent, non-aligned, non-belligerent, non-partisan, objective, unaffiliated, unaligned, unbiased, uncommitted, uninvolved, unprejudiced. Opp BIASED. 2 neutral colours. characterless, colourless, drab, dull, indefinite, indeterminate, intermediate, neither one thing nor the other, pale, vague. Opp DISTINCTIVE.

neutralize vb annul, cancel out, compensate for, counteract, counterbalance, invalidate, make ineffective, make up for, negate, nullify, offset, wipe out.

new adj 1 brand-new, clean, different, fresh, mint, strange, unfamiliar, unheard of, untried, unused. 2 new ideas. advanced, contemporary, current, different, fashionable, latest, modern, modernistic, newfangled, novel, original, recent, revolutionary, inf trendy, up-to-date. 3 new data. added, additional, changed, extra, further, just arrived, supplementary, unexpected, unknown. Opp OLD.

newcomer n alien, arrival, immigrant, new boy, new girl, outsider, settler, stranger.

news n account, advice, announcement, bulletin, communication, communiqué, dispatch, headlines, information, intelligence, inf the latest, message, newscast, newsflash, newsletter, notice, pressrelease, proclamation, report, rumour, statement, old use tidings, word.

newspaper n inf daily, gazette, journal, paper, periodical, inf rag, tabloid.

next adj 1 adjacent, adjoining, closest, nearest, neighbouring, next-door. 2 the next moment. following, soonest, subsequent, succeeding.

nice adj 1 accurate, careful, delicate, discriminating, exact, fine, hair-splitting, meticulous, precise, punctilious, scrupulous, subtle. 2 nice manners. dainty, elegant, fastidious, fussy, particular, inf pernickety, pol-

ished, refined, well-mannered. 3 [inf: In this sense, nice refers to anything which you like. The range of synonyms is almost limitless: we give only a selection here.] acceptable, agreeable, amiable, attractive, beautiful, delicious, delightful, friendly, good, gratifying, kind, likeable, pleasant, satisfactory, welcome. Opp NASTY.

niche n alcove, corner, hollow, nook, recess.

nickname n alias, sobriquet.

niggardly adj mean, miserly, parsimonious, stingy.

nimble adj acrobatic, active, adroit, agile, brisk, deft, dextrous, limber, lithe, lively, inf nippy, quick-moving, sprightly, spry, swift. Opp CLUMSY.

nip vb bite, clip, pinch, snag, snap at, squeeze.

nobility n 1 dignity, glory, grandeur, greatness, high-mindedness, integrity, magnanimity, morality, nobleness, uprightness, virtue, worthiness. 2 the nobility. aristocracy, élite, gentry, nobles, peerage, the ruling classes, inf the upper crust.

noble adj 1 aristocratic, inf blue-blooded, courtly, distinguished, élite, gentle, high-born, high-ranking, patrician, princely, royal, thoroughbred, titled, upper-class. 2 noble deeds. brave, chivalrous, courageous, gallant, glorious, heroic. 3 noble thoughts. elevated, high-flown, honourable, lofty, magnanimous, moral, upright, virtuous, worthy. 4 noble music. dignified, elegant, grand, great, imposing, impressive, magnificent, majestic, splendid, stately. Opp BASE, COMMON. ● n aristocrat, gentleman, gentlewoman, grandee, lady, lord, nobleman, noblewoman, patrician, peer, peeress.

nod vb bend, bob, bow. **nod off** ▷ SLEEP.

noise n inf babel, bawling, bedlam, blare, cacophony, inf caterwauling, clamour, clangour, clatter, commotion, din, discord, inf fracas, hubbub, inf hullabaloo, outcry, pandemonium, inf racket, row, inf rumpus, screaming, screeching, shouting, shrieking, tumult, uproar, yelling. ▷ SOUND. *Opp* SILENCE.

noiseless *adj* inaudible, mute, muted, quiet, silent, soft, soundless, still. *Opp* NOISY.

noisy *adj* blaring, boisterous, booming, cacophonous, chattering, clamorous, deafening, discordant, dissonant, ear-splitting, fortissimo, harsh, loud, raucous, resounding, reverberating, rowdy, screaming, screeching, shrieking, shrill, strident, talkative, thunderous, tumultuous, unmusical, uproarious, vociferous. *Opp* NOISELESS.

nomadic *adj* itinerant, peripatetic, roving, travelling, vagrant, wandering, wayfaring.

nominal *adj* **1** formal, in name only, ostensible, self-styled, *inf* so-called, supposed, theoretical, titular. **2** *a nominal sum.* insignificant, minimal, minor, small, token.

nominate *vb* appoint, choose, designate, elect, name, propose, put forward, *inf* put up, recommend, select, specify.

non-existent *adj* chimerical, fictional, fictitious, hypothetical, imaginary, imagined, legendary, made-up, mythical, unreal. *Opp* REAL.

nonplus *vb* amaze, baffle, confound, disconcert, dumbfound, flummox, perplex, puzzle, render speechless.

nonsense *n* **1** [Most synonyms *inf*] balderdash, bilge, boloney, bosh, bunk, bunkum, claptrap, codswallop, double-Dutch, drivel, eyewash, fiddlesticks, foolishness, gibberish, gobbledegook, mumbo jumbo, piffle, poppycock, rot, rubbish, silliness, stuff and nonsense, stupidity, tommy-rot, trash, tripe, twaddle. **2** *The plan was a nonsense.* absurdity, inanity, mistake, nonsensical idea.

nonsensical *adj* absurd, asinine, crazy, *inf* daft, fatuous, foolish, idiotic, illogical, impractical, inane, incomprehensible, irrational, laughable, ludicrous, mad, meaningless, preposterous, ridiculous, senseless, stupid, unreasonable. ▷ SILLY. *Opp* SENSIBLE.

non-stop *adj* ceaseless, constant, continual, continuous, endless, eternal, incessant, interminable, perpetual, persistent, *inf* round-the-clock, steady, unbroken, unending, uninterrupted, unremitting.

norm *n* criterion, measure, model, pattern, rule, standard, type, yardstick.

normal *adj* **1** accepted, accustomed, average, common, commonplace, conventional, customary, established, everyday, familiar, general, habitual, natural, ordinary, orthodox, predictable, prosaic, quotidian, regular, routine, *inf* run-of-the-mill, standard, typical, universal, unsurprising, usual. **2** *a normal person.* balanced, healthy, rational, reasonable, sane, stable, *inf* straight, well-adjusted. *Opp* ABNORMAL.

normalize *vb* legalize, regularize, regulate, return to normal.

nose *n* **1** nostrils, proboscis, snout. **2** *nose of a boat.* bow, front, prow. ● *vb* enter cautiously, insinuate yourself, intrude, nudge your way, penetrate, probe, push, shove. **nose about** ▷ PRY.

nostalgia *n* longing, memory, pining, regret, reminiscence, sentiment, sentimentality, yearning.

nostalgic *adj* emotional, maudlin, regretful, romantic, sentimental, wistful, yearning.

nosy *adj* curious, eavesdropping, inquisitive, interfering, meddlesome, prying.

notable *adj* celebrated, conspicuous, distinctive, distinguished, eminent, evident, extraordinary, famous, illustrious, important, impressive, memorable, noted, noteworthy, noticeable, obvious, outstanding, pre-eminent, prominent, rare, remarkable, renowned, singular, striking, uncommon, unforgettable, unusual, well-known. *Opp* ORDINARY.

note *n* **1** billet-doux, chit, communication, correspondence, epistle, jotting, letter, *inf* memo, memorandum, message, postcard. **2** annotation, comment, cross-reference, explanation, footnote, gloss, jotting, marginal note. **3** *a note in your voice.* feeling, quality, sound, tone. **4** *a £5 note.* banknote, bill, currency, draft. ● *vb* **1** enter, jot down, record, scribble, write down. **2** *note mentally.* detect, discern, discover, feel, find, heed, mark, mind, notice, observe, pay attention to, remark, register, see, spy, take note of. **noted** ▷ FAMOUS.

noteworthy *adj* exceptional, extraordinary, rare, remarkable, uncommon, unique, unusual. *Opp* ORDINARY.

nothing *n cricket* duck, *tennis* love, *old use* naught, *football* nil, nought, zero, *sl* zilch.

notice *n* **1** advertisement, announcement, handbill, handout, intimation, leaflet, message, note, notification, placard, poster, sign, warning. **2** attention, awareness, cognizance, consciousness, heed, note, regard. ● *vb* be aware, detect, discern, discover, feel, find, heed, make out, mark, mind, note, observe, pay attention to, perceive, register, remark, see, spy, take note. **give notice** ▷ NOTIFY, WARN.

noticeable *adj* appreciable, audible, clear, clear-cut, considerable, conspicuous, detectable, discernible, distinct, distinguishable, manifest, marked, measurable, notable, observable, obtrusive, obvious, overt, palpable, perceivable, perceptible, plain, prominent, pronounced, salient, significant, striking, unconcealed, unmistakable, visible. *Opp* IMPERCEPTIBLE.

notify *vb* acquaint, advise, alert, announce, apprise, give notice, inform, make known, proclaim, publish, report, tell, warn.

notion *n* apprehension, belief, concept, conception, fancy, hypothesis, idea, impression, *inf* inkling, opinion, sentiment, theory, thought, understanding, view.

notorious *adj* disgraceful, disreputable, flagrant, ill-famed, infamous, outrageous, overt, patent, scandalous, shocking, talked about, undisguised, undisputed, well-known. ▷ FAMOUS, WICKED.

nourish *vb* feed, maintain, nurse, nurture, provide for, strengthen, support, sustain. **nourishing** ▷ NUTRITIOUS.

nourishment *n* diet, food, goodness, nutrient, nutriment, nutrition, sustenance, *old use* victuals.

novel *adj* different, fresh, imaginative, innovative, new, odd, original, rare, singular, startling, strange, surprising, uncommon, unconventional, unfamiliar, untested, unusual. *Opp* FAMILIAR. ● *n* best-seller, *inf* blockbuster, fiction, novelette, novella, romance, story. ▷ WRITING.

novelty *n* **1** freshness, newness, oddity, originality, strangeness, surprise, unfamiliarity, uniqueness. **2** bauble, curiosity, gimmick, knick-knack, ornament, souvenir, trifle, trinket.

novice *n* amateur, apprentice, beginner, *inf* greenhorn, inexperienced person, initiate, learner, probationer, tiro, trainee.

now *adv* at once, at present, here and now, immediately, instantly, just now, nowadays, promptly, *inf* right now, straight away, today.

noxious *adj* corrosive, foul, harmful, nasty, noisome, objectionable, poisonous, polluting, sulphureous, sulphurous, unwholesome.

nub *n* centre, core, crux, essence, gist, heart, kernel, nucleus, pith, point.

nucleus *n* centre, core, heart, kernel, middle.

nude *adj* bare, disrobed, exposed, in the nude, naked, stark-naked, stripped, unclothed, uncovered, undressed.

nudge *vb* bump, dig, elbow, hit, jab, jog, jolt, poke, prod, push, shove, touch.

nuisance *n* annoyance, bother, burden, inconvenience, irritant, irritation, *inf* pain, pest, plague, trouble, vexation, worry.

nullify *vb* abolish, annul, cancel, do away with, invalidate, negate, neutralize, quash, repeal, rescind, revoke, stultify.

numb *adj* anaesthetized, *inf* asleep, benumbed, cold, dead, deadened, frozen, immobile, insensible, insensitive, paralysed, senseless, suffering from pins and needles. *Opp* SENSITIVE. ● *vb* anaesthetize, benumb, deaden, desensitize, drug, dull, freeze, immobilize, make numb, paralyse, stun, stupefy.

number *n* **1** digit, figure, integer, numeral, unit. **2** aggregate, amount, *inf* bunch, collection, crowd, multitude, quantity, sum, total. ▷ GROUP. **3** *musical number.* item, piece, song. **4** *a number of a magazine.* copy, edition, impression, issue, printing, publication. ● *vb* add up to, total, work out at. ▷ COUNT.

numerous *adj* abundant, copious, countless, endless, incalculable, infinite, innumerable, many, multitudinous, myriad, numberless, plentiful, several, uncountable, untold. *Opp* FEW.

nun *n* abbess, mother-superior, novice, prioress, sister.

nurse *n* **1** district-nurse, *old use* matron, sister. **2** nanny, nursemaid. ● *vb* **1** care for, look after, minister to, nurture, tend, treat. **2** breast-feed, feed, suckle, wet-nurse. **3** cherish, coddle, cradle, cuddle, dandle, hold, hug, mother, pamper.

nursery *n* **1** crèche, kindergarten, nursery school. **2** garden centre, market garden.

nurture *vb* bring up, cultivate, educate, feed, look after, nourish, nurse, rear, tend, train.

nut *n* kernel. □ *almond, brazil, cashew, chestnut, cob-nut, coconut, filbert, hazel, peanut, pecan, pistachio, walnut.*

nutrient *n* fertilizer, goodness, nourishment.

nutriment *n* food, goodness, nourishment, nutrition, sustenance.

nutritious *adj* alimentary, beneficial, good for you, health-giving, healthy, nourishing, sustaining, wholesome.

O

oasis n **1** spring, watering-hole, well. **2** asylum, haven, refuge, resort, retreat, safe harbour, sanctuary.

oath n **1** assurance, avowal, guarantee, pledge, promise, undertaking, vow, word of honour. **2** blasphemy, curse, exclamation, expletive, *inf* four-letter word, imprecation, malediction, obscenity, profanity, swearword.

obedient *adj* acquiescent, amenable, biddable, compliant, conformable, deferential, disciplined, docile, duteous, dutiful, law-abiding, manageable, submissive, subservient, tamed, tractable, well-behaved, well-trained. *Opp* DISOBEDIENT.

obese *adj* corpulent, gross, overweight. ▷ FAT.

obey *vb* abide by, accept, acquiesce in, act in accordance with, adhere to, agree to, be obedient to, be ruled by, bow to, carry out, comply with, conform to, defer to, do what you are told, execute, follow, fulfil, give in to, heed, honour, implement, keep to, mind, observe, perform, *inf* stick to, submit to, take orders from. *Opp* DISOBEY.

object n **1** article, body, entity, item, thing. **2** aim, end, goal, intent, intention, objective, point, purpose, reason. **3** *object of ridicule.* butt, destination, target. ● *vb* argue, be opposed, carp, cavil, complain, demur, disapprove, dispute, dissent, expostulate, *sl* grouse, grumble, make an objection, *inf* mind, *inf* moan, oppose, protest, quibble, raise objections, raise questions, remonstrate, take a stand, take exception. *Opp* ACCEPT, AGREE.

objection n argument, cavil, challenge, complaint, demur, demurral, disapproval, exception, opposition, outcry, protest, query, question, quibble, refusal, remonstration.

objectionable *adj* abhorrent, detestable, disagreeable, disgusting, dislikeable, displeasing, distasteful, foul, hateful, insufferable, intolerable, loathsome, nasty, nauseating, noisome, obnoxious, odious, offensive, *inf* off-putting, repellent, repugnant, repulsive, revolting, sickening, unacceptable, undesirable, unwanted. ▷ UNPLEASANT. *Opp* ACCEPTABLE.

objective *adj* **1** detached, disinterested, dispassionate, factual, impartial, impersonal, neutral, open-minded, outward-looking, rational, scientific, unbiased, uncoloured, unemotional, unprejudiced. **2** *objective evidence.* empirical, existing, observable, real. *Opp* SUBJECTIVE. ● n aim, ambition, aspiration, design, destination, end, goal, hope, intent, intention, object, point, purpose, target.

obligation n commitment, compulsion, constraint, contract, duty, liability, need, requirement, responsibility. ▷ PROMISE. *Opp* OPTION.

obligatory *adj* binding, compulsory, essential, mandatory, necessary, required, requisite, unavoidable. *Opp* OPTIONAL.

oblige *vb* **1** coerce, compel, constrain, force, make, require. **2** *Please oblige me.* accommodate, gratify, indulge, please. **obliged** ▷ BOUND, GRATEFUL. **obliging** ▷ HELPFUL, POLITE.

oblique *adj* **1** angled, askew, aslant, canted, declining, diagonal, inclined, leaning, listing, raked, rising, skewed, slanted, slanting, slantwise, sloping, tilted. **2** *an oblique insult.* backhanded, circuitous, circumlocutory, devious, implicit, implied, indirect, roundabout. ▷ EVASIVE. *Opp* DIRECT.

obliterate *vb* blot out, cancel, cover over, delete, destroy, efface, eliminate, eradicate, erase, expunge, extirpate, leave no trace of, rub out, wipe out.

oblivion *n* **1** anonymity, darkness, disregard, extinction, limbo, neglect, obscurity. **2** amnesia, coma, forgetfulness, ignorance, insensibility, obliviousness, unawareness, unconsciousness.

oblivious *adj* forgetful, heedless, ignorant, insensible, insensitive, unacquainted, unaware, unconscious, unfeeling, uninformed, unmindful, unresponsive. *Opp* AWARE.

obscene *adj* abominable, bawdy, *inf* blue, coarse, corrupting, crude, debauched, degenerate, depraved, dirty, disgusting, distasteful, filthy, foul, foul-mouthed, gross, immodest, immoral, improper, impure, indecent, indecorous, indelicate, *inf* kinky, lecherous, lewd, loathsome, nasty, *inf* off-colour, offensive, outrageous, perverted, pornographic, prurient, repulsive, ribald, risqué, rude, salacious, scatological, scurrilous, shameful, shameless, shocking, *inf* sick, smutty, suggestive, unchaste, vile, vulgar. ▷ OBJECTIONABLE, SEXY. *Opp* DECENT.

obscenity *n* abomination, blasphemy, coarseness, dirtiness, evil, filth, foulness, grossness, immorality, impropriety, indecency, lewdness, licentiousness, offensiveness, outrage, perversion, pornography, profanity, scurrility, vileness. ▷ SWEARWORD.

obscure *adj* **1** blurred, clouded, concealed, covered, dark, dim, faint, foggy, hazy, hidden, inconspicuous, indefinite, indistinct, masked, misty, murky, nebulous, secret, shadowy, shady, shrouded, unclear, unlit, unrecognizable, vague, veiled. *Opp* CLEAR. **2** *an obscure joke.* arcane, baffling, complex, cryptic, delphic, enigmatic, esoteric, incomprehensible,

mystifying, perplexing, puzzling, recherché, recondite, strange. *Opp* OBVIOUS. **3** *an obscure poet.* forgotten, minor, undistinguished, unfamiliar, unheard of, unimportant, unknown, unnoticed. *Opp* FAMOUS. ● *vb* block out, blur, cloak, cloud, conceal, cover, darken, disguise, eclipse, envelop, hide, make obscure, mask, obfuscate, overshadow, screen, shade, shroud, veil. *Opp* CLARIFY.

obsequious *adj* abject, *inf* bootlicking, crawling, cringing, deferential, effusive, fawning, flattering, fulsome, *inf* greasy, grovelling, ingratiating, insincere, mealy-mouthed, menial, *inf* oily, servile, *inf* smarmy, submissive, subservient, sycophantic, unctuous. **be obsequious** ▷ GROVEL.

observant *adj* alert, astute, attentive, aware, careful, eagle-eyed, heedful, mindful, on the lookout, *inf* on the qui vive, perceptive, percipient, quick, sharp-eyed, shrewd, vigilant, watchful, with eyes peeled. *Opp* INATTENTIVE.

observation *n* **1** attention (to), examination, inspection, monitoring, scrutiny, study, surveillance, viewing, watching. **2** comment, note, opinion, reaction, reflection, remark, response, sentiment, statement, thought, utterance.

observe *vb* **1** consider, contemplate, detect, discern, examine, *inf* keep an eye on, look at, monitor, note, notice, perceive, regard, scrutinize, see, spot, spy, stare at, study, view, watch, witness. **2** *observe rules.* abide by, adhere to, comply with, conform to, follow, heed, honour, keep, obey, pay attention to, respect. **3** *observe Easter.* celebrate, commemorate, keep, mark, recognize, remember, solemnize. **4** *observed that it was badly acted.* animadvert (on), comment, declare, explain, make an observation, mention, reflect, remark, say, state.

observer *n* beholder, bystander, commentator, eyewitness, looker-on, onlooker, spectator, viewer, watcher, witness.

obsess *vb* become an obsession with, bedevil, consume, control, dominate, grip, haunt, monopolize, plague, possess, preoccupy, rule, take hold of.

obsession *n* addiction, *inf* bee in your bonnet, conviction, fetish, fixation, *inf* hang-up, *inf* hobby-horse, *Fr* idée fixe, infatuation, mania, passion, phobia, preoccupation, *sl* thing.

obsessive *adj* addictive, compulsive, consuming, controlling, dominating, haunting, passionate.

obsolescent *adj* ageing, aging, declining, dying out, fading, going out of use, losing popularity, moribund, *inf* on the way out, waning.

obsolete *adj* anachronistic, antiquated, antique, archaic, dated, dead, discarded, disused, extinct, old-fashioned, *inf* old hat, out-dated, out-of-date, outmoded, passé, primitive, superannuated, superseded, unfashionable. ▷ OLD. *Opp* CURRENT.

obstacle *n* bar, barricade, barrier, block, blockage, catch, check, difficulty, hindrance, hurdle, impediment, obstruction, problem, restriction, snag, *inf* stumbling-block.

obstinate *adj* adamant, *sl* bloody-minded, defiant, determined, dogged, firm, headstrong, immovable, inflexible, intractable, intransigent, *inf* mulish, obdurate, persistent, pertinacious, perverse, *inf* pig-headed, refractory, resolute, rigid, self-willed, single-minded, *inf* stiff-necked, stubborn, tenacious, uncooperative, unreasonable, unyielding, wilful, wrong-headed. *Opp* AMENABLE.

obstreperous *adj* awkward, boisterous, disorderly, irrepressible, naughty, rough, rowdy, *inf* stroppy, turbulent, uncontrollable, undisciplined, unmanageable, unruly, vociferous, wild. ▷ NOISY. *Opp* WELL-BEHAVED.

obstruct *vb* arrest, bar, block, bring to a standstill, check, curb, delay, deter, frustrate, halt, hamper, hinder, hold up, impede, inhibit, interfere with, interrupt, occlude, prevent, restrict, retard, slow down, stand in the way of, *inf* stonewall, stop, *inf* stymie, thwart. *Opp* HELP.

obtain *vb* **1** acquire, attain, be given, bring, buy, capture, come by, come into possession of, earn, elicit, enlist (help), extort, extract, find, gain, get, get hold of, *inf* lay your hands on, *inf* pick up, procure, purchase, receive, secure, seize, take possession of, win. **2** *rules still obtain.* apply, be in force, be in use, be relevant, be valid, exist, prevail, stand.

obtrusive *adj* blatant, conspicuous, forward, importunate, inescapable, interfering, intrusive, meddling, meddlesome, noticeable, out of place, prominent, unwanted, unwelcome. ▷ OBVIOUS. *Opp* INCONSPICUOUS.

obtuse *adj* dense, dull, imperceptive, slow, slow-witted. ▷ STUPID. *Opp* CLEVER.

obviate *vb* avert, forestall, make unnecessary, preclude, prevent, remove, take away.

obvious *adj* apparent, bald, blatant, clear, clear-cut, conspicuous, distinct, evident, eye-catching, flagrant, glaring, gross, inescapable, intrusive, manifest, notable, noticeable, obtrusive, open, overt, palpable, patent, perceptible, plain, prominent, pronounced, recognizable, self-evident, self-explanatory, straightforward, unconcealed, undisguised, undisputed, unmistakable, visible. *Opp* HIDDEN, OBSCURE.

occasion *n* **1** chance, circumstance, moment, occurrence, opportunity, time. **2** *no occasion for rudeness.* call, cause, excuse, grounds, justification, need, reason. **3** *a happy occasion.* affair, celebration, ceremony, event, function, *inf* get-together, happening, incident, occurrence, party.

occasional *adj* casual, desultory, fitful, infrequent, intermittent, irregular, odd, *inf* once in a while, periodic, random, rare, scattered, spasmodic, sporadic, uncommon, unpredictable. *Opp* FREQUENT, REGULAR.

occult *adj* ▷ SUPERNATURAL. ● *n* black arts, black magic, cabbalism, diabolism, occultism, sorcery, the supernatural, witchcraft.

occupant *n* denizen, householder, incumbent, inhabitant, lessee, lodger, occupier, owner, resident, tenant.

occupation *n* 1 incumbency, lease, occupancy, possession, residency, tenancy, tenure, use. 2 appropriation, colonization, conquest, invasion, oppression, seizure, subjection, subjugation, suzerainty, *inf* takeover, usurpation. 3 appointment, business, calling, career, employment, job, *inf* line, métier, position, post, profession, situation, trade, vocation, work. 4 *leisure occupation*. activity, diversion, entertainment, hobby, interest, pastime, pursuit, recreation.

occupy *vb* 1 dwell in, inhabit, live in, move into, reside in, take up residence in, tenant. 2 *occupy space*. fill, take up, use, utilize. 3 capture, colonize, conquer, garrison, invade, overrun, possess, subjugate, take over, take possession of. 4 *occupy your time*. absorb, busy, divert, engage, engross, involve, preoccupy. **occupied** ▷ BUSY.

occur *vb* appear, arise, befall, be found, chance, come about, come into being, *old use* come to pass, *inf* crop up, develop, exist, happen, manifest itself, materialize, *inf* show up, take place, *inf* transpire, *inf* turn out, *inf* turn up.

occurrence *n* affair, case, circumstance, development, event, happening, incident, manifestation, matter, occasion, phenomenon, proceeding.

odd *adj* 1 *odd numbers*. uneven. *Opp* EVEN. 2 *an odd sock*. extra, left over, *inf* one-off, remaining, single, spare, superfluous, surplus, unmatched, unused. 3 *odd jobs*. casual, irregular, miscellaneous, occasional, part-time, random, sundry, varied, various. 4 *odd behaviour*. abnormal, anom-

alous, atypical, bizarre, *inf* cranky, curious, deviant, different, eccentric, exceptional, extraordinary, freak, funny, idiosyncratic, incongruous, inexplicable, *inf* kinky, outlandish, out of the ordinary, peculiar, puzzling, queer, rare, singular, strange, uncharacteristic, uncommon, unconventional, unexpected, unusual, weird. *Opp* NORMAL.

oddments *plur n* bits, bits and pieces, fragments, *inf* junk, leftovers, litter, odds and ends, offcuts, remnants, scraps, shreds, unwanted pieces.

odious *adj* detestable, execrable, loathsome, offensive, repugnant, repulsive. ▷ HATEFUL.

odorous *adj* fragrant, odoriferous, perfumed, scented. ▷ SMELLING.

odour *n* aroma, bouquet, fragrance, nose, redolence, scent, smell, stench, *inf* stink.

odourless *adj* deodorized, unscented. *Opp* ODOROUS.

offence *n* 1 breach, crime, fault, felony, infringement, lapse, malefaction, misdeed, misdemeanour, outrage, peccadillo, sin, transgression, trespass, violation, wrong, wrongdoing. 2 anger, annoyance, disgust, displeasure, hard feelings, indignation, irritation, pique, resentment, *inf* upset. **give offence** ▷ OFFEND.

offend *vb* 1 affront, anger, annoy, cause offence, chagrin, disgust, displease, embarrass, give offence, hurt your feelings, insult, irritate, make angry, *inf* miff, outrage, pain, provoke, *inf* put your back up, revolt, rile, sicken, slight, snub, upset, vex. 2 *offend against the law*. do wrong, transgress, violate. **be offended** be annoyed, *inf* take umbrage.

offender *n* criminal, culprit, delinquent, evil-doer, guilty party, lawbreaker, malefactor, miscreant, outlaw, sinner, transgressor, wrongdoer.

offensive *adj* 1 abusive, annoying, antisocial, coarse, detestable, disagreeable, disgusting, displeasing, disrespectful, embarrassing, foul, impolite, improper, indecent, insulting, loathsome, nasty, nauseating, nauseous, noxious, objectionable, obnoxious, *inf* off-putting, repugnant, revolting, rude, sickening, unpleasant, unsavoury, vile, vulgar. ▷ OBSCENE. *Opp* PLEASANT. **2** *offensive action.* aggressive, antagonistic, attacking, belligerent, hostile, threatening, warlike. *Opp* PEACEABLE. ● *n* ▷ ATTACK.

offer *n* bid, proposal, proposition, suggestion, tender. ● *vb* **1** bid, extend, give the opportunity of, hold out, make an offer of, make available, proffer, put forward, put up, suggest. **2** *offer to help.* come forward, propose, *inf* show willing, volunteer.

offering *n* contribution, donation, gift, oblation, offertory, present, sacrifice.

offhand *adj* **1** abrupt, aloof, careless, cavalier, cool, curt, off-handed, perfunctory, unceremonious, uncooperative, uninterested. ▷ CASUAL. **2** ▷ IMPROMPTU.

office *n* **1** bureau, room, workplace, workroom. **2** appointment, assignment, commission, duty, function, job, occupation, place, position, post, responsibility, role, situation, work.

officer *n* **1** adjutant, aide-de-camp, CO, commandant, commanding officer. **2** *police officer.* constable, PC, policeman, policewoman, WPC. **3** ▷ OFFICIAL.

official *adj* accredited, approved, authentic, authoritative, authorized, bona fide, certified, formal, lawful, legal, legitimate, licensed, organized, proper, recognized, true, trustworthy, valid. ▷ FORMAL. ● *n* administrator, agent, appointee, authorized person, bureaucrat, dignitary, executive, functionary, mandarin, officer, organizer, representative, responsible person. □ *bailiff, captain, chief, clerk of court, commander, commissioner, consul, customs officer, director, elder* (of church), *equerry, governor, manager, marshal, mayor, mayoress, minister, monitor, ombudsman, overseer, prefect,*

president, principal, proctor, proprietor, registrar, sheriff, steward, superintendent, supervisor, usher.

officiate *vb* adjudicate, be in charge, be responsible, chair (*a meeting*), conduct, have authority, manage, preside, referee, *inf* run (*a meeting*), umpire.

officious *adj inf* bossy, bumptious, *inf* cocky, dictatorial, forward, impertinent, interfering, meddlesome, meddling, overzealous, *inf* pushy, self-appointed, self-important.

offset *vb* cancel out, compensate for, counteract, counterbalance, make amends for, make good, make up for, redress. ▷ BALANCE.

offshoot *n* branch, by-product, derivative, development, *inf* spin-off, subsidiary product.

offspring *n* [*sing*] baby, child, descendant, heir, successor. [*plur*] brood, family, fry, issue, litter, progeny, *old use* seed, spawn, young.

often *adv* again and again, *inf* all the time, commonly, constantly, continually, frequently, generally, habitually, many times, regularly, repeatedly, time after time, time and again, usually.

oil *vb* grease, lubricate.

oily *adj* **1** buttery, fat, fatty, greasy, oleaginous. **2** *an oily manner.* ▷ OBSEQUIOUS.

ointment *n* balm, cream, embrocation, emollient, liniment, lotion, paste, salve, unguent.

old *adj* **1** ancient, antediluvian, antiquated, antique, crumbling, decayed, decaying, decrepit, dilapidated, early, historic, medieval, obsolete, primitive, quaint, ruined, superannuated, time-worn, venerable, veteran, vintage. ▷ OLD-FASHIONED. **2** *old times.* bygone, classical, forgotten, former, (*time*) immemorial, *old use* olden, past, prehistoric, previous, primeval, primitive, primordial, remote. **3** *old people.* advanced in years, aged, *inf* doddery, elderly, geriatric, *inf* getting on, grey-haired, hoary, *inf* in your dotage, long-lived, oldish, *inf* past it, senile. **4** *old customs.* age-old, enduring, established, lasting, long-standing, time-honoured, traditional, well-established. **5** *old clothes.* moth-eaten, ragged, scruffy, shabby, threadbare, worn, worn-out. **6** *old bread.* dry, stale. **7** *old tickets.* cancelled, expired, invalid, used. **8** *an old hand.* experienced, expert, familiar, mature, practised, skilled, veteran. *Opp* NEW, YOUNG. **old age** *inf* declining years, decrepitude, *inf* dotage, senility. **old person** centenarian, *inf* fogey, *inf* fogy, nonagenarian, octogenarian, pensioner, septuagenarian.

old-fashioned *adj* anachronistic, antiquated, archaic, backward-looking, conventional, dated, fusty, hackneyed, narrow-minded, obsolete, old, *inf* old hat, out of date, out of touch, outdated, outmoded, passé, pedantic, prim, proper, prudish, reactionary, time-honoured, traditional, unfashionable. *Opp* MODERN. **old-fashioned person** *inf* fogey, *inf* fogy, *inf* fuddy-duddy, pedant, reactionary, *inf* square.

omen *n* augury, auspice, foreboding, forewarning, harbinger, indication, portent, premonition, presage, prognostication, sign, token, warning, *inf* writing on the wall.

ominous *adj* baleful, dire, fateful, forbidding, foreboding, grim, ill-omened, ill-starred, inauspicious, lowering, menacing, portentous, prophetic, sinister, threatening, unfavourable, unlucky, unpromising, unpropitious, warning. *Opp* AUSPICIOUS.

omission *n* **1** deletion, elimination, exception, excision, exclusion. **2** failure, gap, neglect, negligence, oversight, shortcoming.

omit *vb* **1** cross out, cut, dispense with, drop, edit out, eliminate, erase, except, exclude, ignore, jump, leave out, miss out, overlook, pass over, reject, skip, strike out. **2** fail, forget, neglect.

omnipotent *adj* all-powerful, almighty, invincible, supreme, unconquerable.

oncoming *adj* advancing, approaching, facing, looming, nearing.

onerous *adj* burdensome, demanding, heavy, laborious, taxing. ▷ DIFFICULT.

one-sided *adj* **1** biased, bigoted, partial, partisan, prejudiced. **2** *one-sided game.* ill-matched, unbalanced, unequal, uneven.

onlooker *n* bystander, eyewitness, looker-on, observer, spectator, watcher, witness.

only *adj* lone, one, single, sole, solitary, unique. ● *adv* barely, exclusively, just, merely, simply, solely.

ooze *vb* bleed, discharge, emit, exude, leak, secrete, seep, weep.

opaque *adj* cloudy, dark, dim, dull, filmy, hazy, impenetrable, muddy, murky, obscure, turbid, unclear. *Opp* CLEAR.

open *adj* **1** agape, ajar, gaping, unbolted, unfastened, unlocked, unsealed, unwrapped, wide, wide-open, yawning. **2** accessible, available, exposed, free, public, revealed, unenclosed, unprotected, unrestricted. **3** *open space.* bare, broad, clear, empty, extensive, spacious, treeless, uncrowded, undefended, unfenced, unobstructed, vacant. **4** *open arms.* extended, outstretched, spread out, unfolded. **5** *open nature.* artless, candid, communicative, flexible, frank, generous, guileless, honest, innocent, magnanimous, open-minded, responsive, sincere, straightforward, transparent, uninhibited. **6** *open defiance.* apparent, barefaced, blatant, conspicuous, downright, evident, flagrant, obvious, outspoken, overt, plain, unconcealed, undisguised, visible. **7** *an open question.* arguable, debatable, moot, problematical, unanswered, undecided, unresolved, unsettled. *Opp* CLOSED, HIDDEN. ● *vb* **1** unbar, unblock, unbolt, unclose, uncork, undo, unfasten, unfold, unfurl, unlatch, unlock, unroll, unseal, untie, unwrap. **2** become open, gape, yawn. **3** *open proceedings.* activate, begin, commence, establish, *inf* get going, inaugurate, initiate, *inf* kick off, launch, set in motion, set up, start. *Opp* CLOSE.

opening *adj* first, inaugural, initial, introductory. *Opp* FINAL. ● *n* **1** aperture, breach, break, chink, cleft, crack, crevice, cut, door, doorway, fissure, gap, gash, gate, gateway, hatch, hole, leak, mouth, orifice, outlet, rent, rift, slit, slot, space, split, tear, vent. **2** beginning, birth, commencement, dawn, inauguration, inception, initiation, launch, outset, start. **3** *a business opening. inf* break, chance, opportunity, way in.

operate *vb* **1** act, function, go, perform, run, work. **2** *operate a machine.* control, deal with, drive, handle, manage, use, work. **3** *operate on a patient.* do an operation, perform surgery.

operation *n* **1** control, direction, function, functioning, management, operating, performance, running, working. **2** action, activity, business, campaign, effort, enterprise, exercise, manoeuvre, movement, procedure, proceeding, process, project, transaction, undertaking, venture. **3** [*medical*] biopsy, surgery, transplant.

operational *adj* functioning, going, in operation, in use, in working order, operating, operative, running, *inf* up and running, usable, working.

operative *adj* **1** ▷ OPERATIONAL. **2** *the operative word.* crucial, important, key, principal, relevant, significant. ● *n* ▷ WORKER.

opinion *n* assessment, attitude, belief, comment, conclusion, conjecture, conviction, estimate, feeling, guess, idea, impression, judgement, notion, perception, point of view, sentiment, theory, thought, view, viewpoint, way of thinking.

opponent *n* adversary, antagonist, challenger, competitor, contender, contestant, enemy, foe, opposer, opposition, rival. *Opp* ALLY.

opportune *adj* advantageous, appropriate, auspicious, beneficial, convenient, favourable, felicitous, fortunate, good, happy, lucky, propitious, right, suitable, timely, welltimed. *Opp* INCONVENIENT.

opportunity *n inf* break, chance, moment, occasion, opening, possibility, time.

oppose *vb* argue with, attack, be at variance with, be opposed to, challenge, combat, compete against, confront, contend with, contest, contradict, controvert, counter, counterattack, defy, disagree with, disapprove of, dissent from, face, fight, object to, obstruct, *inf* pit your wits against, quarrel with, resist, rival, stand up to, *inf* take a stand against, take issue with, withstand. *Opp* SUPPORT. **opposed** ▷ HOSTILE, OPPOSITE.

opposite *adj* **1** antithetical, conflicting, contradictory, contrasting, converse, different, hostile, incompatible, inconsistent, opposed, opposing, rival. **2** contrary, reverse. **3** *your opposite number.* corresponding, equivalent, facing, matching, similar. ● *n* antithesis, contrary, converse, reverse.

opposition *n* antagonism, antipathy, competition, defiance, disapproval, enmity, hostility, objection, resistance, scepticism, unfriendliness. ▷ OPPONENT. *Opp* SUPPORT.

oppress *vb* abuse, afflict, burden, crush, depress, encumber, enslave, exploit, grind down, harass, intimidate, keep under, maltreat, overburden, persecute, pressurize, *inf* ride roughshod over, subdue, subjugate, terrorize, *inf* trample on, tyrannize, weigh down.

oppressed *adj* browbeaten, downtrodden, enslaved, exploited, misused, persecuted, subjugated, tyrannized.

oppression *n* abuse, despotism, enslavement, exploitation, harassment, injustice, maltreatment, persecution, pressure, subjection, subjugation, suppression, tyranny.

oppressive adj **1** brutal, cruel, despotic, harsh, repressive, tyrannical, undemocratic, unjust. **2** airless, close, heavy, hot, humid, muggy, stifling, stuffy, suffocating, sultry.

optimism n buoyancy, cheerfulness, confidence, hope, idealism, positiveness. *Opp* PESSIMISM.

optimistic adj buoyant, cheerful, confident, expectant, hopeful, idealistic, *inf* looking on the bright side, positive, sanguine. *Opp* PESSIMISTIC.

optimum adj best, finest, firstclass, first-rate, highest, ideal, maximum, most favourable, perfect, prime, superlative, top.

option n alternative, chance, choice, election, possibility, selection.

optional adj avoidable, discretionary, dispensable, elective, inessential, possible, unforced, unnecessary, voluntary. *Opp* COMPULSORY.

oral adj by mouth, said, spoken, unwritten, uttered, verbal, vocal, voiced.

oratory n declamation, eloquence, enunciation, fluency, *inf* gift of the gab, grandiloquence, magniloquence, rhetoric, speaking, speech making.

orbit n circuit, course, path, revolution, trajectory. ● vb circle, encircle, go round, travel round.

orbital adj circular, encircling.

orchestrate vb **1** arrange, compose. **2** ▷ ORGANIZE.

ordeal n affliction, anguish, difficulty, distress, hardship, misery, *inf* nightmare, pain, suffering, test, torture, trial, tribulation, trouble.

order n **1** arrangement, array, classification, codification, disposition, lay-out, *inf* line-up, neatness, organization, pattern, progression, sequence, series, succession, system, tidiness. **2** calm, control, discipline, good behaviour, government, harmony, law and order, obedience, orderliness, peace, peacefulness, quiet, rule. **3** *social orders.* caste, category, class, degree, group, hierarchy, kind, level, rank, sort, status. **4** *in good order.* condition, repair, state. **5** *orders to be obeyed.* command, decree, direction, directive, edict, fiat, injunction, instruction, law, mandate, ordinance, regulation, requirement, rule. **6** *an order for goods.* application, booking, commission, demand, mandate, request, requisition, reservation. **7** *religious orders.* association, brotherhood, community, fraternity, group, guild, lodge, sect, sisterhood, society, sodality, sorority. *Opp* DISORDER. ● vb **1** arrange, categorize, classify, codify, lay out, organize, put in order, sort out, tidy up. **2** *old use* bid, charge, command, compel, decree, demand, direct, enjoin, instruct, ordain, require, tell. **3** apply for, ask for, book, reserve, requisition, send away for.

orderly adj **1** careful, methodical, neat, organized, regular, symmetrical, systematic, tidy, well-arranged, well-organized, well-prepared. *Opp* CONFUSED, DISORGANIZED. **2** civilized, controlled, decorous, disciplined, law-abiding, peaceable, polite, restrained, well-behaved, well-mannered. *Opp* UNDISCIPLINED.

ordinary adj accustomed, average, common, *inf* common or garden, commonplace, conventional, customary, established, everyday, fair, familiar, habitual, humble, *inf* humdrum, indifferent, mediocre, medium, middling, moderate, modest, mundane, nondescript, normal, orthodox, passable, pedestrian, plain, prosaic, quotidian, reasonable, regular, routine, *inf* run-of-the-mill, satisfactory, simple, *inf* so-so, standard, stock, traditional, typical, undistinguished, unexceptional, unexciting, unimpressive, uninspired, uninteresting, unpretentious, unremarkable, unsurprising, usual, well-known, workaday. *Opp* EXTRA-ORDINARY.

organic adj **1** animate, biological, growing, live, living, natural. **2** *an organic whole.* coherent, coordinated, evolving, integral, integrated, methodical, organized, structured, systematic.

organism *n* animal, being, cell, creature, living thing, plant.

organization *n* **1** arrangement, categorization, classification, codification, composition, coordination, logistics, organizing, planning, regimentation, *inf* running, structuring. **2** *a business organization*. alliance, association, body, business, club, combine, company, concern, confederation, conglomerate, consortium, corporation, federation, firm, group, institute, institution, league, network, *inf* outfit, party, society, syndicate, union.

organize *vb* **1** arrange, catalogue, categorize, classify, codify, compose, coordinate, group, order, *inf* pigeonhole, put in order, rearrange, regiment, *inf* run, sort, sort out, structure, systematize, tabulate, tidy up. *Opp* JUMBLE. **2** build, coordinate, create, deal with, establish, make arrangements for, manage, mobilize, orchestrate, plan, put together, run, *inf* see to, set up, take care of. **organized** ▷ OFFICIAL, SYSTEMATIC.

orgy *n* Bacchanalia, *inf* binge, debauch, *inf* fling, party, *inf* rave-up, revel, revelry, Saturnalia, *inf* spree.

orient *vb* acclimatize, accommodate, accustom, adapt, adjust, condition, familiarize, orientate, position.

oriental *adj* Asiatic, eastern, far-eastern.

origin *n* **1** base, basis, beginning, birth, cause, commencement, cradle, creation, dawn, derivation, foundation, fount, fountainhead, genesis, inauguration, inception, launch, outset, provenance, root, source, start, well-spring. *Opp* END. **2** *humble origins*. ancestry, background, descent, extraction, family, genealogy, heritage, lineage, parentage, pedigree, start in life, stock.

original *adj* **1** aboriginal, archetypal, earliest, first, initial, native, primal, primitive, primordial. **2** *original antiques*. actual, authentic, genuine,

real, true, unique. **3** *original ideas*. creative, first-hand, fresh, imaginative, ingenious, innovative, inspired, inventive, new, novel, resourceful, thoughtful, unconventional, unfamiliar, unique, unusual. *Opp* HACKNEYED.

originate *vb* **1** arise, be born, be derived, be descended, begin, come, commence, crop up, derive, emanate, emerge, issue, proceed, spring up, start, stem. **2** beget, be the inventor of, bring about, coin, conceive, create, design, discover, engender, found, give birth to, inaugurate, initiate, inspire, institute, introduce, invent, launch, mastermind, pioneer, produce, think up.

ornament *n* accessory, adornment, bauble, beautification, decoration, embellishment, embroidery, enhancement, filigree, frill, frippery, garnish, gewgaw, ornamentation, tracery, trimming, trinket. ▷ JEWELLERY. ● *vb* adorn, beautify, deck, decorate, dress up, elaborate, embellish, emblazon, emboss, embroider, enhance, festoon, garnish, prettify, trim.

ornamental *adj* attractive, decorative, fancy, flashy, pretty, showy.

ornate *adj* arabesque, baroque, *inf* busy, decorated, elaborate, fancy, flamboyant, florid, flowery, fussy, luxuriant, ornamented, overdone, pretentious, rococo. *Opp* PLAIN.

orphan *n* foundling, stray, waif.

orthodox *adj* accepted, accustomed, approved, authorized, common, conformist, conservative, conventional, customary, established, mainstream, normal, official, ordinary, prevailing, recognized, regular, standard, traditional, usual, well-established. *Opp* UNCONVENTIONAL.

ostensible *adj* alleged, apparent, outward, pretended, professed, *inf* put-on, reputed, specious, supposed, visible. *Opp* REAL.

ostentation *n* affectation, display, exhibitionism, flamboyance, *inf* flashiness, flaunting, parade, pretention, pretentiousness, self-advertisement, show, showing-off, *inf* swank. *Opp* MODESTY.

ostentatious *adj* flamboyant, *inf* flashy, pretentious, showy, *inf* swanky, vainglorious. ▷ BOASTFUL. *Opp* MODEST.

ostracize *vb* avoid, banish, *inf* black, blackball, blacklist, boycott, cast out, cold-shoulder, *inf* cut, *inf* cut dead, exclude, excommunicate, expel, isolate, reject, *inf* send to Coventry, shun, shut out, snub. *Opp* BEFRIEND.

oust *vb* banish, drive out, eject, expel, *inf* kick out, remove, replace, *inf* sack, supplant, take over from, unseat.

outbreak *n* epidemic, *inf* flare-up, plague, rash, upsurge.

outburst *n* attack, effusion, eruption, explosion, fit, flood, outbreak, outpouring, paroxysm, rush, spasm, surge, upsurge.

outcast *n* castaway, displaced person, exile, leper, outlaw, outsider, pariah, refugee, reject, untouchable.

outcome *n* conclusion, consequence, effect, end-product, result, sequel, upshot.

outcry *n* cry of disapproval, dissent, hue and cry, objection, opposition, protest, protestation, remonstrance.

outdo *vb* beat, defeat, exceed, excel, *inf* get the better of, outbid, outdistance, outrun, outshine, outstrip, outweigh, overcome, surpass, top, trump.

outdoor *adj* alfresco, open-air, out of doors, outside.

outer *adj* **1** exterior, external, outside, outward, superficial, surface. **2** distant, further, outlying, peripheral, remote. *Opp* INNER.

outfit *n* **1** accoutrements, attire, costume, ensemble, equipment, garb, *inf* gear, *inf* get-up, *inf* rig, suit, trappings, *inf* turn-out. **2** ▷ ORGANIZATION.

outgoing *adj* **1** *outgoing president.* departing, emeritus, ex-, former, last, leaving, past, retiring. **2** *outgoing tide.* ebbing, falling, retreating. **3** ▷ SOCI-ABLE. *Opp* INCOMING. **outgoings** ▷ EXPENSE.

outing *n* excursion, expedition, jaunt, picnic, ride, tour, trip.

outlast *vb* outlive, survive.

outlaw *n* bandit, brigand, criminal, deserter, desperado, fugitive, highwayman, marauder, outcast, renegade, robber. ● *vb* ban, exclude, forbid, prohibit, proscribe. ▷ BANISH.

outlet *n* **1** channel, discharge, duct, egress, escape route, exit, mouth, opening, orifice, safety valve, vent, way out. **2** ▷ SHOP.

outline *n* **1** abstract, *inf* bare bones, diagram, digest, draft, framework, plan, précis, résumé, *inf* rough idea, *inf* rundown, scenario, skeleton, sketch, summary, synopsis, thumbnail sketch. **2** contour, figure, form, profile, shadow, shape, silhouette. ● *vb* delineate, draft, give the gist of, give the outline, plan out, précis, rough out, sketch out, summarize.

outlook *n* **1** aspect, panorama, scene, sight, vantage point, view, vista. **2** *your mental outlook.* angle, attitude, frame of mind, opinion, perspective, point of view, position, slant, standpoint, viewpoint. **3** *the weather outlook.* expectations, forecast, *inf* look-out, prediction, prognosis, prospect.

outlying *adj* distant, far-away, far-flung, far-off, outer, outermost, remote. *Opp* CENTRAL.

output *n* achievement, crop, harvest, production, productivity, result, yield.

outrage *n* **1** atrocity, crime, *inf* disgrace, enormity, indignity, outrageous act, scandal, *inf* sensation, violation. **2** anger, bitterness, disgust, fury, horror, indignation, resentment, revulsion, shock, wrath. ● *vb* ▷ ANGER.

outrageous *adj* **1** abominable, atrocious, barbaric, beastly, bestial, criminal, cruel, disgraceful, disgusting, execrable, infamous, iniquitous, monstrous, nefarious, notorious, offensive, preposterous, revolting, scandalous, shocking, unspeakable, unthinkable, vile, villainous, wicked. **2** *outrageous prices.* excessive, extortionate, extravagant, immoderate, unreasonable. *Opp* REASONABLE.

outside *adj* **1** exterior, external, facing, outer, outward, superficial, surface, visible. **2** *outside interference.* alien, extraneous, foreign. **3** *outside chance.* ▷ REMOTE. ● *n* appearance, case, casing, exterior, façade, face, front, look, shell, skin, surface.

outsider *n* alien, foreigner, *inf* gatecrasher, guest, immigrant, interloper, intruder, newcomer, non-member, non-resident, outcast, stranger, trespasser, visitor.

outskirts *plur n* borders, edge, environs, fringe, margin, outer areas, periphery, purlieus, suburbs. *Opp* CENTRE.

outspoken *adj* blunt, candid, direct, explicit, forthright, frank, plainspoken, tactless, unambiguous, undiplomatic, unequivocal, unreserved. ▷ HONEST. *Opp* EVASIVE.

outstanding *adj* **1** above the rest, celebrated, conspicuous, distinguished, dominant, eminent, excellent, exceptional, extraordinary, first-class, first-rate, great, important, impressive, memorable, notable, noteworthy, noticeable, predominant, pre-eminent, prominent, remarkable, singular, special, striking, superior, top rank, unrivalled. ▷ FAMOUS. *Opp* ORDINARY. **2** ▷ OVERDUE.

outward *adj* apparent, evident, exterior, external, manifest, noticeable, observable, obvious, ostensible, outer, outside, superficial, surface, visible.

outwit *vb* deceive, dupe, fool, *inf* get the better of, gull, hoax, hoodwink, make a fool of, outfox, outmanoeuvre, *inf* outsmart, *inf* put one over on, *inf* take in, trick. ▷ CHEAT.

oval *adj* egg-shaped, ellipsoidal, elliptical, oviform, ovoid.

ovation *n* acclaim, acclamation, applause, cheering, plaudits, praise.

overcast *adj* black, clouded, cloudy, dark, dismal, dull, gloomy, grey, leaden, lowering, murky, sombre, starless, stormy, sunless, threatening. *Opp* CLOUDLESS.

overcoat *n* greatcoat, mackintosh, top-coat, trench-coat.

overcome *adj* at a loss, beaten, *inf* bowled over, *inf* done in, exhausted, overwhelmed, prostrate, speechless. ● *vb* ▷ OVERTHROW.

overcrowded *adj* congested, crammed, crawling, filled to capacity, full, jammed, *inf* jampacked, overloaded, packed.

overdue *adj* **1** belated, delayed, late, slow, tardy, unpunctual. *Opp* EARLY. **2** *overdue bills.* due, outstanding, owing, unpaid, unresolved, unsettled.

overeat *vb* be greedy, eat too much, feast, gorge, gormandize, *inf* guzzle, indulge yourself, *inf* make a pig of yourself, overindulge, *inf* stuff yourself.

overflow *vb* brim over, flood, pour over, run over, spill, well up.

overgrown *adj* **1** outsize, oversized. ▷ BIG. **2** *overgrown garden.* overrun, rank, tangled, uncut, unkempt, untidy, untrimmed, unweeded, weedy, wild.

overhang *vb* beetle, bulge, jut, project, protrude, stick out.

overhaul *vb* **1** check over, examine, *inf* fix, inspect, mend, rebuild, recondition, refurbish, renovate, repair, restore, service. **2** ▷ OVERTAKE.

overhead *adj* aerial, elevated, high, overhanging, raised, upper.

overlook *vb* **1** fail to notice, forget, leave out, miss, neglect, omit. **2** condone, disregard, excuse, gloss over, ignore, let pass, make allowances for, pardon, pass over, pay no attention to, *inf* shut your eyes to, *inf* turn a blind eye to, *inf* write off. **3** *overlook a lake.* face, front, have a view of, look at, look down on, look on to.

overpower *vb* ▷ OVERTHROW.

overpowering *adj* compelling, consuming, inescapable, insupportable, irrepressible, irresistible, overriding, overwhelming, powerful, strong, unbearable, uncontrollable, unendurable.

oversee *vb* administer, be in charge of, control, direct, invigilate, *inf* keep an eye on, preside over, superintend, supervise, watch over.

oversight *n* **1** carelessness, dereliction of duty, error, failure, fault, mistake, omission. **2** *oversight of a job.* administration, control, direction, management, supervision, surveillance.

overstate *vb* *inf* blow up out of proportion, embroider, exaggerate, magnify, make too much of, maximize, overemphasize, overstress.

overt *adj* apparent, blatant, clear, evident, manifest, obvious, open, patent, plain, unconcealed, undisguised, visible. *Opp* SECRET.

overtake *vb* catch up with, gain on, leave behind, outdistance, outpace, outstrip, overhaul, pass.

overthrow *n* conquest, defeat, destruction, mastery, rout, subjugation, suppression, unseating. ● *vb* beat, bring down, conquer, crush, deal with, defeat, depose, dethrone, get the better of, *inf* lick, master, oust, overcome, overpower, overturn, overwhelm, rout, *inf* send packing, subdue, *inf* topple, triumph over, unseat, vanquish, win against.

overtone *n* association, connotation, hint, implication, innuendo, reverberation, suggestion, undertone.

overturn *vb* **1** capsize, flip, invert, keel over, knock over, spill, tip over, topple, turn over, *inf* turn turtle, turn upside down, up-end, upset. **2** ▷ OVERTHROW.

overwhelm *vb* **1** engulf, flood, immerse, inundate, submerge, swamp. **2** ▷ OVERTHROW. **overwhelming** ▷ OVERPOWERING.

owe *vb* be in debt, have debts.

owing *adj* due, outstanding, overdue, owed, payable, unpaid, unsettled. **owing to** because of, caused by, on account of, resulting from, thanks to, through.

own *vb* be the owner of, have, hold, possess. **own up** ▷ CONFESS.

owner *n* freeholder, holder, landlady, landlord, possessor, proprietor.

P

pace n **1** step, stride. **2** *a fast pace.* gait, *inf* lick, movement, quickness, rate, speed, tempo, velocity. ● vb ▷ WALK.

pacify vb appease, assuage, calm, conciliate, humour, mollify, placate, quell, quieten, soothe, subdue, tame, tranquillize. *Opp* ANGER.

pack n **1** bale, box, bundle, package, packet, parcel. **2** backpack, duffel bag, haversack, kitbag, knapsack, rucksack. **3** ▷ GROUP. ● vb **1** bundle (up), fill, load, package, parcel up, put, put together, store, stow, wrap up. **2** compress, cram, crowd, jam, overcrowd, press, ram, squeeze, stuff, tamp down, wedge. **pack off** ▷ DISMISS. **pack up** ▷ FINISH.

pact n agreement, alliance, armistice, arrangement, bargain, compact, concord, concordat, contract, covenant, deal, *Fr* entente, league, peace, settlement, treaty, truce, understanding.

pad n **1** cushion, filler, hassock, kneeler, padding, pillow, stuffing, wad. **2** jotter, memo pad, notebook, stationery, writing pad. ● vb cushion, fill, line, pack, protect, stuff, upholster, wad. **pad out** ▷ EXTEND.

padding n **1** filling, protection, upholstery, stuffing, wadding. **2** prolixity, verbiage, verbosity, *inf* waffle, wordiness.

paddle n oar, scull. ● vb **1** propel, row, scull. **2** dabble, splash about, wade.

paddock n enclosure, field, meadow, pasture.

pagan adj atheistic, godless, heathen, idolatrous, infidel, irreligious, polytheistic, unchristian. ● n atheist, heathen, infidel, savage, unbeliever.

page n **1** folio, leaf, recto, sheet, side, verso. **2** errand-boy, messenger, page-boy.

pageant n ceremony, display, extravaganza, parade, procession, show, spectacle, tableau.

pageantry n ceremony, display, formality, grandeur, magnificence, pomp, ritual, show, spectacle, splendour.

pain n ache, aching, affliction, agony, anguish, cramp, crick, discomfort, distress, headache, hurt, irritation, ordeal, pang, smart, smarting, soreness, spasm, stab, sting, suffering, tenderness, throb, throes, toothache, torment, torture, twinge. ● vb ▷ HURT.

painful adj **1** aching, *inf* achy, agonizing, burning, cruel, excruciating, *old use* grievous, hard to bear, hurting, inflamed, piercing, raw, severe, sharp, smarting, sore, *inf* splitting (*head*), stabbing, stinging, tender, throbbing. **2** distressing, harrowing, hurtful, laborious, *inf* traumatic, trying, unpleasant, upsetting, vexing. **3** *a painful decision.* difficult, hard, troublesome, uncongenial. *Opp* PAINLESS. **be painful** ▷ HURT.

painkiller n anaesthetic, analgesic, anodyne, palliative, sedative.

painless adj comfortable, easy, effortless, pain-free, simple, trouble-free, undemanding. *Opp* PAINFUL.

paint n colour, colouring, dye, pigment, stain, tint. □ distemper, emulsion, enamel, gloss paint, lacquer, matt paint, oil-colour, oil-paint, oils, pastel, primer, tempera, undercoat, varnish, water-colour, whitewash. ● vb **1** apply paint to, coat, colour, cover, daub, decorate, dye, enamel, gild, lacquer, redecorate, stain, tint, touch up, varnish, whitewash. **2** delineate, depict, describe, picture, portray, represent.

painter *n* artist, decorator, illustrator, miniaturist.

painting *n* fresco, landscape, miniature, mural, oil-painting, portrait, still-life, water-colour.

pair *n* brace, couple, duet, duo, mates, partners, partnership, set of two, twins, twosome. ● *vb* **pair off**, **pair up** couple, double up, find a partner, get together, join up, *inf* make a twosome, match up, *inf* pal up, team up.

palace *n* castle, château, mansion, official residence, stately home. ▷ HOUSE.

palatable *adj* acceptable, agreeable, appetizing, easy to take, eatable, edible, nice to eat, pleasant, tasty. *Opp* UNPALATABLE.

palatial *adj* aristocratic, grand, large-scale, luxurious, majestic, opulent, *inf* posh, splendid, stately, upmarket.

pale *adj* **1** anaemic, ashen, blanched, bloodless, cadaverous, colourless, corpse-like, *inf* deathly, drained, etiolated, ghastly, ghostly, ill-looking, pallid, pasty, *inf* peaky, sallow, sickly, unhealthy, wan, *inf* washed-out, *inf* whey-faced, white, whitish. **2** *pale colours.* bleached, dim, faded, faint, light, pastel, subtle, weak. *Opp* BRIGHT. ● *vb* become pale, blanch, blench, dim, etiolate, fade, lighten, lose colour, whiten.

pall *n* cloth, mantle, shroud, veil. ▷ COVERING. ● *vb* become boring, become uninteresting, cloy, irritate, jade, sate, satiate, weary.

palliative *adj* alleviating, calming, reassuring, sedative, soothing. ● *n* painkiller, sedative, tranquillizer.

palpable *adj* apparent, corporeal, evident, manifest, obvious, patent, physical, real, solid, substantial, tangible, touchable, visible. *Opp* INTANGIBLE.

palpitate *vb* beat, flutter, pound, pulsate, quiver, shiver, throb, tremble, vibrate.

paltry *adj* contemptible, inconsequential, insignificant, petty, *inf* piddling, pitiable, puny, trifling, unimportant, worthless. ▷ SMALL. *Opp* IMPORTANT.

pamper *vb* coddle, cosset, humour, indulge, mollycoddle, overindulge, pet, spoil, spoonfeed.

pamphlet *n* booklet, brochure, bulletin, catalogue, circular, flyer, folder, handbill, handout, leaflet, notice, tract.

pan *n* container, utensil. □ *billycan, casserole, frying-pan, pot, saucepan, skillet.* ● *vb* ▷ CRITICIZE.

panache *n* animation, brio, confidence, dash, élan, energy, enthusiasm, flair, flamboyance, flourish, savoirfaire, self-assurance, spirit, style, swagger, verve, zest.

pandemonium *n* babel, bedlam, chaos, confusion, hubbub, noise, rumpus, turmoil, uproar. ▷ COMMOTION.

pander *n* go-between, *inf* pimp, procurer. ● *vb* **pander to** bow to, cater for, fulfil, gratify, humour, indulge, please, provide, satisfy.

pane *n* glass, light, panel, sheet of glass, window.

panel *n* **1** insert, pane, panelling, rectangle, *plur* wainscot. **2** committee, group, jury, team.

panic *n* alarm, consternation, *inf* flap, horror, hysteria, stampede, terror. ● *vb* become panic-stricken, *inf* fall apart, *inf* flap, *inf* go to pieces, *inf* lose your head, *inf* lose your nerve, overreact, stampede. ▷ FEAR.

panic-stricken *adj* alarmed, *inf* beside yourself, disorientated, frantic, frenzied, horrified, hysterical, *inf* in a cold sweat, *inf* in a tizzy, jumpy, overexcited, panicky, panic-struck, terror-stricken, undisciplined, unnerved, worked-up. ▷ FRIGHTENED. *Opp* CALM.

panorama n landscape, perspective, prospect, scene, view, vista.

panoramic adj commanding, extensive, scenic, sweeping, wide.

pant vb blow, breathe quickly, gasp, inf huff and puff, puff, wheeze. **panting** ▷ BREATHLESS.

pants n 1 old use bloomers, boxer shorts, briefs, camiknickers, drawers, knickers, panties, pantihose, shorts, inf smalls, trunks, underpants, inf undies, Y-fronts. 2 ▷ TROUSERS.

paper n 1 folio, leaf, sheet. □ A4 (A1, A2, etc), card, cardboard, cartridge paper, foolscap, manila, notepaper, papyrus, parchment, postcard, quarto, stationery, tissue-paper, toilet paper, tracing-paper, vellum, wallpaper, wrapping-paper, writing-paper. 2 certificate, credentials, deed, document, form, inf ID, identification, licence, record. 3 the daily paper. inf daily, journal, newspaper, inf rag, tabloid. 4 an academic paper. article, discourse, dissertation, essay, monograph, thesis, treatise.

parable n allegory, exemplum, fable, moral tale. ▷ WRITING.

parade n cavalcade, ceremony, column, cortège, display, file, march-past, motorcade, pageant, procession, review, show, spectacle. ● vb 1 assemble, file past, form up, line up, make a procession, march past, present yourself, process. ▷ WALK. 2 ▷ DISPLAY.

paradise n Eden, Elysium, heaven, Shangri-La, Utopia.

paradox n absurdity, anomaly, contradiction, incongruity, inconsistency, self-contradiction.

paradoxical adj absurd, anomalous, conflicting, contradictory, illogical, improbable, incongruous, self-contradictory.

parallel adj 1 equidistant. 2 parallel events. analogous, cognate, contemporary, corresponding, equivalent, like, matching, similar. ● n 1 analogue, counterpart, equal, likeness, match. 2 analogy, comparison, correspondence, equivalence, kinship, resemblance, similarity. ● vb be parallel to, be parallel with, compare with, correspond to, duplicate, echo, equate with, keep pace with, match, remind you of, run alongside.

paralyse vb anaesthetize, cripple, deactivate, deaden, desensitize, disable, freeze, halt, immobilize, incapacitate, lame, numb, petrify, stop, stun.

paralysed adj crippled, dead, desensitized, disabled, handicapped, immobile, immovable, incapacitated, lame, numb, palsied, paralytic, paraplegic, rigid, unusable, useless.

paralysis n deadness, immobility, numbness, palsy, paraplegia.

paraphernalia plur n accessories, apparatus, baggage, belongings, chattels, inf clobber, effects, equipment, gear, impedimenta, materials, inf odds and ends, possessions, property, inf rig, stuff, tackle, things, trappings.

paraphrase vb explain, interpret, put into other words, rephrase, restate, reword, rewrite, translate.

parcel n bale, box, bundle, carton, case, pack, package, packet. **parcel out** ▷ DIVIDE. **parcel up** ▷ PACK.

parch vb bake, burn, dehydrate, desiccate, dry, scorch, shrivel, wither. **parched** ▷ DRY, THIRSTY.

pardon n absolution, amnesty, condonation, discharge, exculpation, exoneration, forgiveness, indulgence, mercy, release, reprieve. ● vb absolve, condone, exculpate, excuse, exonerate, forgive, free, grant pardon, let off, overlook, release, remit, reprieve, set free, spare.

pardonable adj allowable, condonable, excusable, forgivable, justifiable, minor, negligible, petty, understandable, venial (sin). Opp UNFORGIVABLE.

parent n begetter, father, guardian, mother, procreator, progenitor.

parentage *n* ancestry, birth, descent, extraction, family, line, lineage, pedigree, stock.

park *n* common, gardens, green, recreation ground. □ *amusement park, arboretum, botanical gardens, car-park, estate, national park, nature reserve, parkland, reserve, theme park.* ● *vb* deposit, leave, place, position, put, station, store. **park yourself** ▷ SETTLE.

parliament *n* assembly, conclave, congress, convocation, council, diet, government, legislature, lower house, senate, upper house.

parody *n* burlesque, caricature, distortion, imitation, lampoon, mimicry, satire, *inf* send-up, *inf* spoof, *inf* take-off, travesty. ● *vb* ape, burlesque, caricature, guy, imitate, lampoon, mimic, satirize, *inf* send up, *inf* take off, travesty. ▷ RIDICULE.

parry *vb* avert, block, deflect, evade, fend off, push away, repel, repulse, stave off, ward off.

part *n* **1** bit, branch, component, constituent, department, division, element, fraction, fragment, ingredient, parcel, particle, percentage, piece, portion, ramification, scrap, section, sector, segment, shard, share, single item, subdivision, unit. **2** department, faction, party, section, subdivision, unit. **3** *part of a book.* chapter, episode. **4** *part of a town.* area, district, neighbourhood, quarter, region, sector, vicinity. **5** *part of the body.* limb, member, organ. **6** *part in a play.* cameo, character, role. ● *vb* **1** cut off, detach, disconnect, divide, pull apart, separate, sever, split, sunder. *Opp* JOIN. **2** break away, depart, go away, leave, part company, quit, say goodbye, separate, split up, take leave, withdraw. *Opp* MEET. **part with** ▷ RELINQUISH. **take part** ▷ PARTICIPATE.

partial *adj* **1** imperfect, incomplete, limited, qualified, unfinished. *Opp* COMPLETE. **2** *partial judge.* biased, one-sided, partisan, prejudiced, unfair. *Opp* IMPARTIAL. **be partial to** ▷ LIKE.

participate *vb* assist, be active, be involved, contribute, cooperate, engage, enter, help, join in, partake, share, take part.

participation *n* activity, assistance, complicity, contribution, cooperation, engagement, involvement, partnership, sharing.

particle *n* **1** bit, crumb, dot, drop, fragment, grain, hint, iota, jot, mite, morsel, *old use* mote, piece, scintilla, scrap, shred, sliver, *inf* smidgen, speck, trace. **2** atom, electron, molecule, neutron.

particular *adj* **1** distinct, idiosyncratic, individual, peculiar, personal, singular, specific, uncommon, unique, unmistakable. **2** *particular with detail.* exact, nice, painstaking, precise, rigorous, scrupulous, thorough. **3** *gave particular pleasure.* especial, exceptional, important, marked, notable, noteworthy, outstanding, significant, special, unusual. **4** *particular about food.* choosy, critical, discriminating, fastidious, finical, finicky, fussy, meticulous, nice, *inf* pernickety, selective. *Opp* GENERAL, EASYGOING. **particulars** circumstances, details, facts, information, *sl* lowdown.

parting *n* departure, farewell, going away, leave-taking, leaving, saying goodbye, separation, splitting up, valediction.

partisan *adj* biased, bigoted, blinkered, devoted, factional, fanatical, narrow-minded, one-sided, partial, prejudiced, sectarian, unfair. *Opp* IMPARTIAL. ● *n* adherent, devotee, fanatic, follower, freedom fighter, guerrilla, resistance fighter, supporter, underground fighter, zealot.

partition *n* **1** break-up, division, separation, splitting up. **2** barrier, panel, room-divider, screen, wall. ● *vb* cut up, divide, parcel out, separate off, share out, split up, subdivide.

partner *n* **1** accessory, accomplice, ally, assistant, associate, *inf* bedfellow, collaborator, colleague, companion, comrade, confederate, helper, *inf* mate, *sl* sidekick. **2** consort, husband, mate, spouse, wife.

partnership n **1** affiliation, alliance, association, combination, company, confederation, cooperative, syndicate. **2** collaboration, complicity, cooperation. **3** marriage, relationship, union.

party n **1** celebration, inf do, festivity, function, gathering, inf get-together, inf jollification, inf knees-up, merrymaking, inf rave-up, inf shindig, social gathering. □ ball, banquet, barbecue, ceilidh, dance, inf disco, discothèque, feast, inf hen-party, house-warming, orgy, picnic, reception, reunion, inf stag-party, tea-party, wedding. **2** a political party. alliance, association, bloc, cabal, inf camp, caucus, clique, coalition, faction, junta, league, sect, side. ▷ GROUP.

pass n **1** canyon, col, cut, defile, gap, gorge, gully, opening, passage, ravine, valley, way through. **2** identity pass. authority, authorization, clearance, inf ID, licence, passport, permission, permit, safe-conduct, ticket, warrant. ● vb **1** go beyond, go by, move on, move past, outstrip, overhaul, overtake, proceed, progress, inf thread your way. **2** time passes. disappear, elapse, fade, go away, lapse, tick by, vanish. **3** pass drinks. circulate, deal out, deliver, give, hand over, offer, present, share, submit, supply, transfer. **4** pass a resolution. agree, approve, authorize, confirm, decree, enact, establish, ordain, pronounce, ratify, validate. **5** I pass! inf give in, opt out, say nothing, waive your rights. **pass away** ▷ DIE. **pass on** ▷ TRANSFER. **pass out** ▷ FAINT. **pass over** ▷ IGNORE.

passable adj **1** acceptable, adequate, admissible, allowable, all right, fair, indifferent, mediocre, middling, moderate, not bad, ordinary, satisfactory, inf so-so, tolerable. Opp UNACCEPTABLE. **2** clear, navigable, open, traversable, unblocked, unobstructed, usable. Opp IMPASSABLE.

passage n **1** corridor, entrance, hall, hallway, lobby, passageway, vestibule. **2** passage of time. advance, flow, lapse, march, movement, moving on, passing, progress, progression, transition. **3** sea passage. crossing, cruise, voyage. ▷ JOURNEY. **4** through passage. pass, route, thoroughfare, tunnel, way through. ▷ OPENING. **5** passage from a book. citation, episode, excerpt, extract, paragraph, part, piece, portion, quotation, scene, section, selection.

passenger n commuter, rider, traveller, voyager.

passer-by n bystander, onlooker, witness.

passion n appetite, ardour, avidity, avidness, commitment, craving, craze, desire, drive, eagerness, emotion, enthusiasm, fanaticism, fervency, fervour, fire, flame, frenzy, greed, heat, hunger, infatuation, intensity, keenness, love, lust, mania, obsession, strong feeling, suffering, thirst, urge, urgency, vehemence, zeal, zest.

passionate adj ardent, aroused, avid, burning, committed, eager, emotional, enthusiastic, excited, fanatical, fervent, fiery, frenzied, greedy, heated, hot, hungry, impassioned, infatuated, inflamed, intense, lustful, manic, obsessive, roused, sexy, strong, urgent, vehement, violent, worked up, zealous. Opp APATHETIC.

passive adj apathetic, complaisant, compliant, deferential, docile, impassive, inert, inactive, long-suffering, malleable, non-violent, patient, phlegmatic, pliable, quiescent, receptive, resigned, sheepish, submissive, supine, tame, tractable, unassertive, unmoved, unresisting, yielding. ▷ CALM. Opp ACTIVE.

past adj bygone, dead, inf dead and buried, earlier, ended, finished, forgotten, former, gone, historical, late, olden (days), inf over and done with, previous, recent, sometime. ● n antiquity, days gone by, former times, history, old days, olden days, past times. Opp FUTURE.

paste n **1** adhesive, fixative, glue, gum. **2** pâté, spread. ● vb fix, glue, stick. ▷ FASTEN.

pastiche n blend, composite, compound, inf hotchpotch, mess, miscellany, mixture, inf motley collection, patchwork, selection.

pastime n activity, amusement, avocation, distraction, diversion, entertainment, fun, game, hobby, leisure activity, occupation, play, recreation, relaxation, sport.

pastoral adj **1** agrarian, agricultural, Arcadian, bucolic, country, farming, idyllic, outdoor, provincial, rural, rustic. ▷ PEACEFUL. Opp URBAN. **2** pastoral duties. clerical, ecclesiastical, ministerial, parochial, priestly.

pasture n field, grassland, grazing, mead, meadow, paddock, pasturage.

pat vb caress, dab, slap, stroke, tap. ▷ TOUCH.

patch n darn, mend, piece, reinforcement, repair. ● vb cover, darn, fix, mend, reinforce, repair, sew up, stitch up.

patchy adj inf bitty, blotchy, changing, dappled, erratic, inconsistent, irregular, speckled, spotty, uneven, unpredictable, variable, varied, varying. Opp UNIFORM.

patent adj apparent, blatant, clear, conspicuous, evident, flagrant, manifest, obvious, open, plain, self-evident, transparent, undisguised, visible.

path n **1** alley, bridle-path, bridleway, esplanade, footpath, footway, pathway, pavement, Amer sidewalk, towpath, track, trail, walk, walkway, way. ▷ ROAD. **2** approach, course, direction, flight path, orbit, route, trajectory, way.

pathetic adj **1** affecting, distressing, emotional, emotive, heartbreaking, heart-rending, lamentable, moving, piteous, pitiable, pitiful, plaintive, poignant, stirring, touching, tragic. ▷ SAD. **2** ▷ INADEQUATE.

pathos n emotion, feeling, pity, poignancy, sadness, tragedy.

patience n **1** calmness, composure, endurance, equanimity, forbearance, fortitude, leniency, long-suffering, resignation, restraint, self-control, serenity, stoicism, toleration, inf unflappability. **2** work with patience. assiduity, determination, diligence, doggedness, endurance, firmness, perseverance, persistence, pertinacity, inf stickability, tenacity.

patient adj **1** accommodating, acquiescent, calm, compliant, composed, docile, easygoing, even-tempered, forbearing, forgiving, lenient, long-suffering, mild, philosophical, quiet, resigned, self-possessed, serene, stoical, submissive, tolerant, uncomplaining. **2** a patient worker. assiduous, determined, diligent, dogged, persevering, persistent, steady, tenacious, unhurried, untiring. Opp IMPATIENT. ● n case, invalid, outpatient, sufferer.

patriot n derog chauvinist, loyalist, nationalist, derog xenophobe.

patriotic adj derog chauvinistic, derog jingoistic, loyal, nationalistic, derog xenophobic.

patriotism n derog chauvinism, derog jingoism, loyalty, nationalism, derog xenophobia.

patrol n **1** beat, guard, policing, sentry-duty, surveillance, vigilance, watch. **2** guard, lookout, patrolman, sentinel, sentry, watchman. ● vb be on patrol, defend, guard, inspect, keep a lookout, make the rounds, police, protect, stand guard, tour, walk the beat, watch over.

patron n **1** advocate, inf angel, backer, benefactor, champion, defender, helper, philanthropist, promoter, sponsor, subscriber, supporter. **2** patron of a shop. client, customer, frequenter, inf regular, shopper.

patronage n backing, business, custom, help, sponsorship, support, trade.

patronize vb **1** back, be a patron of, bring trade to, buy from, deal with, encourage, frequent, give patronage to, shop at, support. **2** *be patronizing towards.* humiliate, *inf* look down on, *inf* look down your nose at, *inf* put down, talk down to. **patronizing** ▷ SUPERIOR.

pattern *n* **1** arrangement, decoration, design, device, figuration, figure, motif, ornamentation, sequence, shape, system, tessellation. **2** archetype, criterion, example, exemplar, guide, ideal, model, norm, original, paragon, precedent, prototype, sample, specimen, standard, yardstick.

pause *n* break, *inf* breather, breathing space, caesura, check, delay, gap, halt, hesitation, hiatus, hold-up, interlude, intermission, interruption, interval, lacuna, lapse, *inf* let-up, lull, moratorium, respite, rest, standstill, stop, stoppage, suspension, wait. ● *vb* break off, delay, falter, halt, hang back, have a pause, hesitate, hold, mark time, rest, stop, *inf* take a break, *inf* take a breather, wait.

pave *vb* asphalt, concrete, cover with paving, flag, *old use* macadamize, *inf* make up, surface, tarmac, tile. **pave the way** ▷ PREPARE.

pavement *n* footpath, *Amer* sidewalk. ▷ PATH.

pay *n* cash in hand, compensation, dividend, earnings, emoluments, fee, gain, honorarium, income, money, payment, profit, recompense, reimbursement, remittance, return, salary, settlement, stipend, take-home pay, wages. ● *vb* **1** *inf* cough up, *inf* fork out, give, grant, hand over, proffer, recompense, remunerate, requite, spend, *inf* stump up. **2** *pay debts.* bear the cost of, clear, compensate, *inf* foot, honour, indemnify, meet, pay back, pay off, pay up, refund, reimburse, repay, settle. **3** *crime doesn't pay.* avail, benefit, be profitable, pay off, produce results, prove worthwhile, yield a return. **4** *pay for mistakes.* be punished, suffer. ▷ ATONE. **pay back** ▷ RETALIATE.

payment *n* advance, alimony, allowance, charge, commission, compensation, contribution, cost, deposit, disbursement, donation, expenditure, fare, fee, figure, fine, instalment, loan, outgoings, outlay, pocket-money, premium, price, ransom, rate, remittance, reward, royalty, *inf* sub, subscription, subsistence, supplement, surcharge, tip, toll, wage. *Opp* INCOME.

peace *n* **1** accord, agreement, amity, conciliation, concord, friendliness, harmony, order. *Opp* CONFLICT. **2** alliance, armistice, cease-fire, pact, treaty, truce. *Opp* WAR. **3** *peace of mind.* calm, calmness, peace and quiet, peacefulness, placidity, quiet, repose, serenity, silence, stillness, tranquillity. *Opp* ANXIETY.

peaceable *adj* amicable, civil, conciliatory, cooperative, friendly, gentle, harmonious, inoffensive, mild, non-violent, pacific, peace-loving, placid, temperate, understanding. *Opp* QUARRELSOME.

peaceful *adj* balmy, calm, easy, gentle, pacific, placid, pleasant, quiet, relaxing, restful, serene, slow-moving, soothing, still, tranquil, undisturbed, unruffled, untroubled. *Opp* NOISY, STORMY.

peacemaker *n* adjudicator, appeaser, arbitrator, conciliator, diplomat, intercessor, intermediary, mediator, reconciler, referee, umpire.

peak *n* **1** apex, brow, cap, crest, crown, eminence, hill, mountain, pinnacle, point, ridge, summit, tip, top. **2** *peak of your career.* acme, apogee, climax, consummation, crisis, crown, culmination, height, highest point, zenith.

peal *n* carillon, chime, chiming, clangour, knell, reverberation, ringing, tintinnabulation, toll. ● *vb* chime, clang, resonate, ring, ring the changes, sound, toll.

peasant *n* [*derog*] boor, bumpkin, churl, oaf, rustic, serf, swain, village idiot, yokel.

pebbles *plur n* cobbles, gravel, stones.

peculiar *adj* **1** aberrant, abnormal, anomalous, atypical, bizarre, curious, deviant, eccentric, exceptional, freakish, funny, odd, offbeat, outlandish, out of the ordinary, quaint, queer, quirky, strange, surprising, uncommon, unconventional, unusual, weird. **2** *your peculiar style.* characteristic, different, distinctive, identifiable, idiosyncratic, individual, natural, particular, personal, private, singular, special, unique, unmistakable. *Opp* COMMON, ORDINARY.

peculiarity *n* abnormality, characteristic, difference, distinctiveness, eccentricity, foible, idiosyncrasy, individuality, mannerism, oddity, outlandishness, quirk, singularity, speciality, trait, uniqueness.

pedantic *adj* **1** academic, bookish, donnish, dry, formal, humourless, learned, old-fashioned, pompous, scholarly, schoolmasterly, stiff, stilted, *inf* stuffy. **2** *inf* by the book, doctrinaire, exact, fastidious, fussy, inflexible, *inf* nit-picking, precise, punctilious, strict, unimaginative. *Opp* INFORMAL, LAX.

peddle *vb inf* flog, hawk, market, *inf* push, sell, traffic in, vend.

pedestrian *adj* **1** pedestrianized, traffic-free. **2** banal, boring, dreary, dull, commonplace, flat-footed, lifeless, mundane, prosaic, run-of-the-mill, tedious, unimaginative, uninteresting. ▷ ORDINARY. ● *n inf* foot-slogger, foot-traveller, stroller, walker.

pedigree *adj* pure-bred, thoroughbred. ● *n* ancestry, blood, descent, extraction, family, family history, genealogy, line, lineage, parentage, roots, stock, strain.

pedlar *n old use* chapman, *inf* cheapjack, *old use* colporteur, door-to-door salesman, hawker, *inf* pusher, seller, street-trader, trafficker, vendor.

peel *n* coating, rind, skin. ● *vb* denude, flay, hull, pare, skin, strip. ▷ UNDRESS.

peep *vb* **1** glance, have a look, peek, squint. ▷ LOOK. **2** ▷ SHOW.

peer *n* aristocrat, grandee, noble, nobleman, noblewoman, patrician, titled person. □ *baron, baroness, countess, duchess, duke, earl, lady, lord, marchioness, marquis, viscount, viscountess.* ● *vb* have a look, look earnestly, spy, squint. ▷ LOOK. **peers 1** aristocracy, nobility, peerage. **2** colleagues, compeers, confrères, equals, fellows, peer-group.

peevish *adj* cantankerous, churlish, crabby, crusty, curmudgeonly, grumpy, illhumoured, irritable, petulant, querulous, testy, touchy, waspish. ▷ BAD-TEMPERED.

peg *n* bolt, dowel, pin, rod, stick, thole-pin. ● *vb* ▷ FASTEN.

pelt *n* coat, fur, hide, skin. ● *vb* assail, bombard, shower, strafe. ▷ THROW.

pen *n* **1** coop, *Amer* corral, enclosure, fold, hutch, pound. **2** ball-point, biro, felt-tip, fountain pen, *old use* quill.

penalize *vb* discipline, fine, impose a penalty on, punish.

penalty *n* fine, forfeit, price. ▷ PUNISHMENT. **pay the penalty** ▷ ATONE.

penance *n* amends, atonement, contrition, penitence, punishment, reparation. **do penance** ▷ ATONE.

pendent *adj* dangling, hanging, loose, pendulous, suspended, swaying, swinging, trailing.

pending *adj* about to happen, forthcoming, *inf* hanging fire, imminent, impending, *inf* in the offing, undecided, waiting.

penetrate *vb* **1** bore through, break through, drill into, enter, get into, get through, infiltrate, lance, make a hole, perforate, pierce, probe, puncture, stab, stick in. **2** *damp penetrates.* filter through, impregnate, percolate through, permeate, pervade, seep into, suffuse.

penitent *adj* apologetic, conscience-stricken, contrite, regretful, remorseful, repentant, rueful, shamefaced, sorry. *Opp* UNREPENTANT.

pennon *n* banner, flag, pennant, standard, streamer.

pension *n* annuity, benefit, old age pension, superannuation.

pensive adj brooding, cogitating, contemplative, day-dreaming, inf far-away, inf in a brown study, lost in thought, meditative, reflective, ruminative, thoughtful.

penury n beggary, destitution, impoverishment, indigence, lack, need, poverty, scarcity, want.

people n **1** folk, human beings, humanity, humans, individuals, ladies and gentlemen, mankind, men and women, mortals, persons. **2** citizenry, citizens, community, electorate, inf grass roots, Gr hoi polloi, nation, inf the plebs, populace, population, the public, society, subjects. **3** your own people. clan, family, kinsmen, kith and kin, nation, race, relations, relatives, tribe. ● vb colonize, fill, inhabit, occupy, overrun, populate, settle.

perceive vb **1** become aware of, catch sight of, descry, detect, discern, discover, distinguish, espy, glimpse, hear, identify, make out, note, notice, observe, recognize, see, spot. **2** appreciate, apprehend, comprehend, deduce, feel, inf figure out, gather, grasp, infer, know, realize, sense, understand.

perceptible adj appreciable, audible, detectable, discernible, distinct, distinguishable, evident, identifiable, manifest, marked, notable, noticeable, observable, obvious, palpable, perceivable, plain, recognizable, unmistakable, visible. Opp IMPERCEPTIBLE.

perception n appreciation, apprehension, awareness, cognition, comprehension, consciousness, discernment, insight, instinct, intuition, knowledge, observation, perspective, realization, recognition, sensation, sense, understanding, view.

perceptive adj acute, alert, astute, attentive, aware, clever, discerning, discriminating, observant, penetrating, percipient, perspicacious, quick, responsive, sensitive, sharp, sharp-eyed, shrewd, sympathetic, understanding. ▷ INTELLIGENT.

perch n rest, resting-place, roost. ● vb balance, rest, roost, settle, sit.

percussion n □ bell, castanets, celesta, chime bar, cymbal, glockenspiel, gong, kettledrum, maracas, rattle, tambourine, timpani, triangle, tubular bells, vibraphone, whip, wood block, xylophone. ▷ DRUM.

perdition n damnation, doom, downfall, hell, hellfire, ruin, ruination.

perfect adj **1** absolute, complete, completed, consummate, excellent, exemplary, faultless, finished, flawless, ideal, immaculate, incomparable, matchless, mint, superlative, unbeatable, undamaged, unexceptionable, unqualified, whole. **2** blameless, irreproachable, pure, sinless, spotless, unimpeachable. **3** accurate, authentic, correct, exact, faithful, immaculate, impeccable, precise, tailor-made, true. Opp IMPERFECT. ● vb bring to fruition, bring to perfection, carry through, complete, consummate, effect, execute, finish, fulfil, make perfect, realize, inf see through.

perfection n **1** beauty, completeness, excellence, faultlessness, flawlessness, ideal, precision, purity, wholeness. Opp IMPERFECTION. **2** the perfection of a plan. accomplishment, achievement, completion, consummation, end, fruition, fulfilment, realization.

perforate vb bore through, drill, penetrate, pierce, prick, punch, puncture, riddle.

perform vb **1** accomplish, achieve, bring about, carry on, carry out, commit, complete, discharge, dispatch, do, effect, execute, finish, fulfil, inf pull off. **2** behave, function, go, operate, run, work. **3** perform on stage. act, appear, dance, feature, figure, take part. **4** perform a play, song. enact, mount, play, present, produce, put on, render, represent, serenade, sing, stage.

performance n **1** accomplishment, achievement, carrying out, comple-

permit

tion, doing, execution, fulfilment.
2 act, behaviour, conduct, deception, exhibition, exploit, feat, play-acting, pretence. **3** *stage performance*. acting, début, impersonation, interpretation, play, playing, portrayal, presentation, production, rendition, representation. □ *concert*, *dress rehearsal*, *first night*, *last night*, *matinée*, *première*, *preview*, *rehearsal*, *show*, *sketch*, *turn*.

performer *n* actor, actress, artist, artiste, player, singer, star, *inf* superstar, thespian, trouper. ▷ ENTERTAINER.

perfume *n* **1** aroma, bouquet, fragrance, odour, scent. ▷ SMELL. **2** aftershave, eau de Cologne, scent, toilet water.

perfunctory *adj* apathetic, automatic, brief, cursory, dutiful, fleeting, half-hearted, hurried, inattentive, indifferent, mechanical, offhand, routine, superficial, uncaring, unenthusiastic, uninterested, uninvolved, unthinking. *Opp* ENTHUSIASTIC.

perhaps *adv* conceivably, maybe, *old use* peradventure, *old use* perchance, possibly.

peril *n* danger, hazard, insecurity, jeopardy, risk, susceptibility, threat, vulnerability.

perilous *adj* dangerous, hazardous, insecure, risky, uncertain, unsafe, vulnerable. *Opp* SAFE.

perimeter *n* border, borderline, boundary, bounds, circumference, confines, edge, fringe, frontier, limit, margin, periphery, verge.

period *n* **1** duration, interval, phase, season, session, span, spell, stage, stint, stretch, term, while. **2** aeon, age, epoch, era. ▷ TIME.

periodic *adj* cyclical, intermittent, occasional, recurrent, repeated, spasmodic, sporadic.

peripheral *adj* **1** distant, on the perimeter, outer, outermost, outlying. **2** borderline, incidental, inessential, irrelevant, marginal, minor, nonessential, secondary, tangential, unimportant, unnecessary. *Opp* CENTRAL.

perish *vb* **1** be destroyed, be killed, die, expire, fall, lose your life, meet your death, pass away. **2** crumble away, decay, decompose, disintegrate, go bad, rot.

perishable *adj* biodegradable, destructible, liable to perish, unstable. *Opp* PERMANENT.

perjury *n* bearing false witness, lying, mendacity.

permanent *adj* abiding, ceaseless, changeless, chronic, constant, continual, continuous, durable, endless, enduring, eternal, everlasting, fixed, immutable, incessant, incurable, indestructible, indissoluble, ineradicable, interminable, invariable, irreparable, irreversible, lasting, lifelong, long-lasting, never-ending, nonstop, ongoing, perennial, perpetual, persistent, stable, steady, unalterable, unceasing, unchanging, undying, unending. *Opp* TEMPORARY.

permeate *vb* diffuse, filter through, flow through, impregnate, infiltrate, penetrate, percolate, pervade, saturate, soak through, spread through.

permissible *adj* acceptable, admissible, allowable, allowed, excusable, lawful, legal, legitimate, licit, permitted, proper, right, sanctioned, tolerable, valid, venial (*sin*). *Opp* UNACCEPTABLE.

permission *n* agreement, approbation, approval, acquiescence, assent, authority, authorization, consent, dispensation, franchise, *inf* go-ahead, *inf* green light, leave, licence, *inf* rubber stamp, sanction, seal of approval, stamp of approval, support. ▷ PERMIT.

permissive *adj* acquiescent, consenting, easygoing, indulgent, latitudinarian, lenient, liberal, libertarian, tolerant.

permit *n* authority, authorization, certification, charter, licence, order, pass, passport, ticket, visa, warrant.
● *vb* admit, agree to, allow, approve of, authorize, consent to, endorse,

enfranchise, give an opportunity for, give permission for, give your blessing to, legalize, license, make possible, sanction, *old use* suffer, support, tolerate.

perpendicular *adj* at right angles, erect, plumb, straight up and down, upright, vertical.

perpetual *adj* abiding, ageless, ceaseless, chronic, constant, continual, continuous, endless, enduring, eternal, everlasting, frequent, immortal, immutable, incessant, incurable, indestructible, ineradicable, interminable, invariable, lasting, long-lasting, never-ending, non-stop, ongoing, perennial, permanent, persistent, protracted, recurrent, recurring, repeated, *old use* sempiternal, timeless, unceasing, unchanging, undying, unending, unfailing, unremitting. *Opp* TEMPORARY.

perpetuate *vb* continue, eternalize, eternize, extend, immortalize, keep going, maintain, make permanent, preserve.

perplex *vb* baffle, *inf* bamboozle, befuddle, bewilder, confound, confuse, disconcert, distract, dumbfound, muddle, mystify, nonplus, puzzle, *inf* stump, *inf* throw, worry.

perquisite *n* benefit, bonus, *inf* consideration, emolument, extra, fringe benefit, gratuity, *inf* perk, tip.

persecute *vb* abuse, afflict, annoy, badger, bother, bully, discriminate against, harass, hector, hound, illtreat, intimidate, maltreat, martyr, molest, oppress, pester, *inf* put the screws on, suppress, terrorize, torment, torture, trouble, tyrannize, victimize, worry.

persist *vb* be diligent, be steadfast, carry on, continue, endure, go on, *inf* hang on, hold out, *inf* keep at it, keep going, *inf* keep it up, keep on, last, linger, persevere, *inf* plug away, remain, *inf* soldier on, stand firm, stay, *inf* stick at it. *Opp* CEASE.

persistent *adj* **1** ceaseless, chronic, constant, continual, continuous, endless, eternal, everlasting, incessant, interminable, lasting, long-lasting, never-ending, obstinate, permanent, perpetual, persisting, recurrent, recurring, remaining, repeated, unending, unrelenting, unrelieved, unremitting. *Opp* BRIEF, INTERMITTENT. **2** assiduous, determined, dogged, hard-working, indefatigable, patient, persevering, pertinacious, relentless, resolute, steadfast, steady, stubborn, tenacious, tireless, unflagging, untiring, unwavering, zealous. *Opp* LAZY.

person *n* adolescent, adult, baby, being, *inf* body, character, child, *inf* customer, figure, human, human being, individual, infant, mortal, personage, soul, *inf* type, woman. ▷ MAN, PEOPLE, WOMAN.

persona *n* character, exterior, façade, guise, identity, image, part, personality, role, self-image.

personal *adj* **1** distinct, distinctive, exclusive, idiosyncratic, individual, inimitable, particular, peculiar, private, special, unique, your own. *Opp* GENERAL. **2** *a personal appearance.* actual, in person, in the flesh, live, physical. **3** *personal letters.* confidential, friendly, individual, informal, intimate, private, secret. *Opp* PUBLIC. **4** *personal friends.* bosom, close, dear, familiar, intimate, known. **5** *personal remarks.* belittling, critical, derogatory, disparaging, insulting, offensive, pejorative, rude, slighting, unfriendly. **6** *personal knowledge.* direct, empirical, experiential, firsthand.

personality *n* **1** attractiveness, character, charisma, charm, disposition, identity, individuality, magnetism, *inf* make-up, nature, persona, psyche, temperament. **2** *inf* big name, celebrity, idol, luminary, name, public figure, star, superstar.

personification *n* allegorical representation, embodiment, epitome, human likeness, incarnation, living image, manifestation.

personify *vb* allegorize, embody, epitomize, exemplify, give human shape to, incarnate, manifest, personalize, represent, stand for, symbolize, typify.

personnel n employees, manpower, people, staff, workers, workforce.

perspective n angle, approach, attitude, outlook, point of view, position, prospect, slant, standpoint, view, viewpoint.

persuade vb bring round, cajole, coax, convert, convince, entice, exhort, importune, induce, influence, inveigle, press, prevail upon, prompt, talk into, tempt, urge, use persuasion, wheedle (into), win over. Opp DISSUADE.

persuasion n 1 argument, blandishment, brainwashing, cajolery, coaxing, conditioning, enticement, exhortation, inducement, persuading, propaganda, reasoning. 2 affiliation, belief, conviction, creed, denomination, faith, religion, sect.

persuasive adj cogent, compelling, conclusive, convincing, credible, effective, efficacious, eloquent, forceful, influential, logical, plausible, potent, reasonable, sound, strong, telling, unarguable, valid, watertight. Opp UNCONVINCING.

pertain vb appertain, apply, be relevant, have bearing, have reference, have relevance, refer. **pertain to** affect, concern.

pertinent adj apposite, appropriate, apropos, apt, fitting, germane, relevant, suitable. Opp IRRELEVANT.

perturb vb agitate, alarm, bother, confuse, discomfit, discompose, disconcert, disquiet, distress, disturb, fluster, frighten, make anxious, ruffle, scare, shake, trouble, unnerve, unsettle, upset, vex, worry. Opp REASSURE.

peruse vb examine, inspect, look over, read, run your eye over, scan, scrutinize, study.

pervade vb affect, diffuse, fill, filter through, flow through, impregnate, penetrate, percolate, permeate, saturate, spread through, suffuse.

pervasive adj general, inescapable, insidious, omnipresent, penetrating, permeating, pervading, prevalent, rife, ubiquitous, universal, widespread.

perverse adj adamant, contradictory, contrary, disobedient, fractious, headstrong, illogical, inappropriate, inflexible, intractable, intransigent, obdurate, obstinate, peevish, inf pigheaded, rebellious, refractory, selfwilled, stubborn, tiresome, uncooperative, unhelpful, unreasonable, wayward, wilful, wrong-headed. Opp REASONABLE.

perversion n 1 corruption, distortion, falsification, misrepresentation, misuse, twisting. 2 aberration, abnormality, depravity, deviance, deviation, immorality, impropriety, inf kinkiness, perversity, unnaturalness, vice, wickedness.

pervert n debauchee, degenerate, deviant, perverted person, profligate. ● vb 1 bend, deflect, distort, divert, falsify, misrepresent, perjure, subvert, twist, undermine. 2 pervert a witness. bribe, corrupt, lead astray.

perverted adj abnormal, amoral, bad, corrupt, debauched, degenerate, depraved, deviant, dissolute, eccentric, evil, immoral, improper, inf kinky, profligate, sick, twisted, unnatural, unprincipled, warped, wicked, wrong. ▷ OBSCENE. Opp NATURAL.

pessimism n cynicism, despair, despondency, fatalism, gloom, hopelessness, negativeness, resignation, unhappiness. Opp OPTIMISM.

pessimistic adj bleak, cynical, defeatist, despairing, despondent, fatalistic, gloomy, hopeless, melancholy, morbid, negative, resigned, unhappy. ▷ SAD. Opp OPTIMISTIC.

pest n 1 annoyance, bane, bother, curse, irritation, nuisance, inf pain in the neck, inf thorn in your flesh, trial, vexation. 2 inf bug, inf creepy-crawly, insect, parasite, plur vermin.

pester vb annoy, badger, bait, besiege, bother, inf get under someone's skin, harass, harry, *inf* hassle, irritate, molest, nag, nettle, plague, provoke, torment, trouble, worry.

pestilence *n* blight, curse, epidemic, pandemic, plague, scourge. ▷ ILLNESS.

pet *n inf* apple of your eye, darling, favourite, idol. ● *vb* caress, cuddle, fondle, kiss, nuzzle, pat, stroke. ▷ TOUCH.

petition *n* appeal, application, entreaty, list of signatures, plea, request, solicitation, suit, supplication. ● *vb* appeal to, call upon, deliver a petition to, entreat, importune, solicit, sue, supplicate. ▷ ASK.

petty *adj* **1** inconsequential, insignificant, minor, niggling, small, trivial, trifling. ▷ UNIMPORTANT. *Opp* IMPORTANT. **2** *petty complaints.* grudging, mean, nit-picking, small-minded, ungenerous. *Opp* GENEROUS.

phase *n* development, period, season, spell, stage, state, step. ▷ TIME. **phase in** ▷ INTRODUCE. **phase out** ▷ FINISH.

phenomenal *adj* amazing, astonishing, astounding, exceptional, extraordinary, *inf* fantastic, incredible, marvellous, *inf* mind-boggling, miraculous, notable, outstanding, prodigious, rare, remarkable, *inf* sensational, singular, staggering, stunning, unbelievable, unorthodox, unusual, *inf* wonderful. *Opp* ORDINARY.

phenomenon *n* **1** circumstance, event, experience, fact, happening, incident, occasion, occurrence, sight. **2** *an unusual phenomenon.* curiosity, marvel, miracle, phenomenal person, phenomenal thing, prodigy, rarity, sensation, spectacle, wonder.

philanthropic *adj* altruistic, beneficent, benevolent, bountiful, caring, charitable, generous, humane, humanitarian, magnanimous, munificent, public-spirited, ungrudging. ▷ KIND. *Opp* MISANTHROPIC.

philanthropist *n* altruist, benefactor, donor, giver, *inf* Good Samaritan, humanitarian, patron, provider, sponsor.

philistine *adj* boorish, ignorant, lowbrow, materialistic, uncivilized, uncultivated, uncultured, unenlightened, unlettered, vulgar.

philosopher *n* sage, student of philosophy, thinker.

philosophical *adj* **1** abstract, academic, analytical, erudite, esoteric, ideological, impractical, intellectual, learned, logical, metaphysical, rational, reasoned, scholarly, theoretical, thoughtful, wise. **2** calm, collected, composed, detached, equable, imperturbable, judicious, patient, reasonable, resigned, serene, sober, stoical, unemotional, unruffled. *Opp* EMOTIONAL.

philosophize *vb* analyse, moralize, pontificate, preach, rationalize, reason, sermonize, theorize, think things out.

philosophy *n* **1** epistemology, ideology, logic, metaphysics, rationalism, thinking. **2** *philosophy of life.* attitude, convictions, outlook, set of beliefs, tenets, values, viewpoint, wisdom.

phlegmatic *adj* apathetic, cold, cool, frigid, impassive, imperturbable, indifferent, lethargic, passive, placid, slow, sluggish, stoical, stolid, torpid, undemonstrative, unemotional, unenthusiastic, unfeeling, uninvolved, unresponsive. *Opp* EXCITABLE.

phobia *n* anxiety, aversion, dislike, dread, *inf* hang-up, hatred, horror, loathing, neurosis, obsession, repugnance, revulsion. ▷ FEAR. □ *agoraphobia* (open space), *arachnophobia* (spiders), *claustrophobia* (enclosed space), *xenophobia* (foreigners).

phone *vb* call, dial, *inf* give a buzz, ring, telephone.

phoney *adj* affected, artificial, assumed, bogus, cheating, contrived, counterfeit, deceitful, ersatz, factitious, fake, faked, false, fictitious, fraudulent, hypocritical, imitation, insincere, mock, pretended, *inf* pseudo, *inf* put-on, *inf* put-up, sham, spurious, synthetic, trick, unreal. *Opp* REAL.

pierce

photocopy *vb* copy, duplicate, photostat, print off, reproduce, *inf* run off.

photograph *n* enlargement, exposure, negative, *inf* photo, picture, plate, positive, print, shot, slide, *inf* snap, snapshot, transparency. ● *vb* film, shoot, snap, take a photograph of.

photographic *adj* **1** accurate, exact, faithful, graphic, lifelike, naturalistic, realistic, representational, true to life. **2** *photographic memory.* pictorial, retentive, visual.

phrase *n* clause, expression. ▷ SAYING. ● *vb* ▷ SAY.

phraseology *n* diction, expression, idiom, language, parlance, phrasing, style, turn of phrase, wording.

physical *adj* actual, bodily, carnal, concrete, corporal, corporeal, earthly, fleshly, incarnate, material, mortal, palpable, physiological, real, solid, substantial, tangible. *Opp* INTANGIBLE, SPIRITUAL.

physician *n* consultant, doctor, general practitioner, *inf* GP, *inf* medic, medical practitioner, specialist.

physiological *adj* anatomical, bodily, physical. *Opp* PSYCHOLOGICAL.

physique *n* body, build, figure, form, frame, muscles, physical condition, shape.

pick *n* **1** choice, election, option, preference, selection. **2** best, cream, élite, favourite, flower, pride. ● *vb* **1** cast (*actor*), choose, decide on, elect, fix on, make a choice of, name, nominate, opt for, prefer, select, settle on, single out, vote for. **2** *pick flowers.* collect, cull, cut, gather, harvest, pluck, pull off, take. **pick on** ▷ BULLY. **pick up** ▷ GET, IMPROVE.

pictorial *adj* diagrammatic, graphic, illustrated, realistic, representational, vivid.

picture *n* **1** delineation, depiction, image, likeness, outline, portrayal, profile, representation. □ *abstract, cameo, caricature, cartoon, collage, design, doodle, drawing, engraving, etch-*ing, fresco, plur graffiti, plur graphics, icon, identikit, illustration, landscape, montage, mosaic, mural, oil-painting, old master, painting, photofit, photograph, pin-up, plate, portrait, print, reproduction, self-portrait, silhouette, sketch, slide, inf snap, snapshot, still life, transfer, transparency, triptych, Fr trompe l'oeil, video, vignette. **2** film, movie, moving picture, video. ▷ FILM. ● *vb* **1** caricature, delineate, depict, display, doodle, draw, engrave, etch, evoke, film, illustrate, outline, paint, photograph, portray, print, represent, show, sketch, video. **2** *picture the future.* conceive, describe, dream up, envisage, envision, fancy, imagine, see in your mind's eye, think up, visualize.

picturesque *adj* **1** attractive, charming, colourful, idyllic, lovely, pleasant, pretty, quaint, scenic, *inf* story-book. ▷ BEAUTIFUL. *Opp* UNATTRACTIVE. **2** *picturesque language.* colourful, descriptive, expressive, graphic, imaginative, poetic, vivid. *Opp* PROSAIC.

pie *n* flan, pasty, patty, quiche, tart, tartlet, turnover, vol-au-vent.

piece *n* **1** bar, bit, bite, block, chip, chunk, crumb, division, *inf* dollop, fraction, fragment, grain, helping, hunk, length, lump, morsel, part, particle, portion, quantity, remnant, sample, scrap, section, segment, shard, share, shred, slab, slice, sliver, snippet, speck, stick, tablet, *inf* titbit, wedge. **2** component, constituent, element, spare part, unit. **3** *piece of music, work.* article, composition, example, instance, item, number, passage, specimen, work. ▷ MUSIC, WRITING. **piece together** ▷ ASSEMBLE.

pied *adj* dappled, flecked, mottled, particoloured, patchy, piebald, spotted, variegated.

pier *n* **1** breakwater, jetty, landing-stage, quay, wharf. ▷ DOCK. **2** buttress, column, pile, pillar, post, support, upright.

pierce *vb* bayonet, bore through, cut, drill, enter, go through, impale, jab, lance, make a hole in, penetrate, perforate, poke through, prick, punch, puncture, riddle, skewer, spear, spike, spit, stab, stick into, thrust into, transfix, tunnel through, wound. **piercing** ▷ SHARP.

piety n dedication, devotedness, devotion, devoutness, faith, godliness, holiness, piousness, religion, *derog* religiosity, saintliness, sanctity. *Opp* IMPIETY.

pig n boar, hog, *inf* piggy, piglet, runt, sow, swine.

pile n **1** abundance, accumulation, agglomeration, collection, concentration, conglomeration, deposit, heap, hoard, *inf* load, mass, mound, *inf* mountain, plethora, quantity, stack, stockpile, supply, *inf* tons. **2** column, pier, post, support, upright. ● vb accumulate, amass, assemble, bring together, build up, collect, concentrate, deposit, gather, heap, hoard, load, mass, stack up, stockpile, store.

pilfer vb *inf* filch, *inf* pinch, rob, shoplift. ▷ STEAL.

pilgrim n crusader, *old use* palmer. ▷ TRAVELLER.

pill n bolus, capsule, lozenge, pastille, pellet, pilule, tablet. ▷ MEDICINE.

pillage n buccaneering, depredation, despoliation, devastation, looting, marauding, piracy, plunder, plundering, ransacking, rape, rapine, robbery, robbing, sacking, stealing, stripping. ● vb despoil, devastate, loot, maraud, plunder, raid, ransack, ravage, raze, rob, sack, steal, strip, vandalize.

pillar n baluster, caryatid, column, pier, pilaster, pile, post, prop, shaft, stanchion, support, upright.

pilot n **1** airman, *old use* aviator, captain, flier. **2** coxswain, helmsman, navigator, steersman. ● vb conduct, convey, direct, drive, fly, guide, lead, navigate, shepherd, steer.

pimple n blackhead, boil, eruption, pustule, spot, swelling, *sl* zit. **pimples** acne, rash.

pin n *old use* bodkin, bolt, brooch, clip, dowel, drawing-pin, hatpin, nail, peg, rivet, safety-pin, spike, staple, thole, tiepin. ● vb clip, nail, pierce, staple, tack, transfix. ▷ FASTEN.

pinch vb **1** crush, grip, hurt, nip, press, squeeze, tweak. **2** ▷ STEAL.

pine vb mope, mourn, sicken, waste away. **pine for** ▷ WANT.

pinnacle n **1** acme, apex, cap, climax, consummation, crest, crown, crowning point, height, highest point, peak, summit, top, zenith. **2** *pinnacle on a roof.* spire, steeple, turret.

pioneer n **1** colonist, discoverer, explorer, frontiersman, frontierswoman, pathfinder, settler, trailblazer. **2** innovator, inventor, originator, pace-maker, trend-setter. ● vb begin, *inf* bring out, create, develop, discover, establish, experiment with, found, inaugurate, initiate, institute, introduce, invent, launch, open up, originate, set up, start.

pious adj **1** dedicated, devoted, devout, faithful, god-fearing, godly, good, holy, moral, religious, reverent, reverential, saintly, sincere, spiritual, virtuous. *Opp* IMPIOUS. **2** [derog] *inf* goody-goody, *inf* holier-than-thou, hypocritical, insincere, mealy-mouthed, Pharisaical, pietistic, sanctimonious, self-righteous, self-satisfied, *inf* smarmy, unctuous. *Opp* SINCERE.

pip n **1** pit, seed, stone. **2** mark, spot, star. **3** bleep, blip, sound, stroke.

pipe n conduit, channel, duct, hose, hydrant, line, main, pipeline, piping, tube. ● vb **1** carry along a pipe, carry along a wire, channel, convey, deliver, supply, transmit. **2** *pipe a tune.* blow, play, sound, *inf* tootle, whistle. **pipe up** ▷ SPEAK. **piping** ▷ HOT, SHRILL.

piquant adj **1** appetizing, pungent, salty, sharp, spicy, tangy, tart, tasty. *Opp* BLAND. **2** *a piquant notion.* arresting, exciting, interesting, provocative, stimulating. *Opp* BANAL.

pirate n buccaneer, old use corsair, marauder, privateer, sea rover. ▷ THIEF. ● vb ▷ PLAGIARIZE.

pit n 1 abyss, chasm, crater, depression, ditch, excavation, hole, hollow, pothole, rut, trench, well. 2 coalmine, colliery, mine, mineshaft, quarry, shaft, working.

pitch n 1 bitumen, tar. 2 pitch of a roof. angle, gradient, incline, slope, steepness, tilt. 3 musical pitch. frequency, tuning. 4 soccer pitch. arena, ground, playing-field, stadium. ● vb 1 erect, put up, raise, set up. 2 pitch stones. bowl, inf bung, cast, inf chuck, fire, fling, heave, hurl, launch, lob, sling, throw, toss. 3 pitch into the water. dive, drop, fall headlong, plummet, plunge, inf take a nose-dive, topple. **pitch about** ▷ TOSS. **pitch in** ▷ COOPERATE. **pitch into** ▷ ATTACK.

piteous adj affecting, distressing, heartbreaking, heart-rending, lamentable, miserable, moving, pathetic, pitiable, pitiful, plaintive, poignant, touching, woeful, wretched. ▷ SAD.

pitfall n catch, danger, difficulty, hazard, peril, snag, trap.

pitiful adj 1 abject, contemptible, deplorable, hopeless, inadequate, incompetent, insignificant, laughable, mean, inf miserable, inf pathetic, pitiable, ridiculous, sorry, trifling, unimportant, useless, worthless. Opp ADMIRABLE. 2 ▷ PITEOUS.

pitiless adj bloodthirsty, brutal, callous, cruel, ferocious, hard, heartless, inexorable, inhuman, merciless, relentless, ruthless, sadistic, unfeeling, unrelenting, unrelieved, unremitting, unsympathetic. Opp MERCIFUL.

pitted adj dented, eaten away, eroded, inf holey, marked, pock-marked, rough, scarred, uneven. Opp SMOOTH.

pity n charity, clemency, commiseration, compassion, condolence, feeling, forbearance, forgiveness, grace, humanity, kindness, leniency, love, mercy, regret, old use ruth, softness, sympathy, tenderness, understanding, warmth. Opp CRUELTY. ● vb inf bleed for, commiserate with, inf feel for, feel sorry for, show pity for, sympathize with, weep for.

pivot n axis, axle, centre, fulcrum, gudgeon, hinge, hub, pin, point of balance, spindle, swivel. ● vb hinge, revolve, rotate, spin, swivel, turn, twirl, whirl.

placard n advert, advertisement, bill, notice, poster, sign.

placate vb appease, calm, conciliate, humour, mollify, pacify, soothe.

place n 1 area, country, district, locale, locality, location, locus, neighbourhood, part, point, position, quarter, region, scene, setting, site, situation, inf spot, town, venue, vicinity, inf whereabouts. 2 a place in society. condition, degree, estate, function, grade, job, mission, niche, office, position, rank, role, standing, station, status. 3 a place to live. ▷ HOUSE. 4 a place to sit. ▷ SEAT. ● vb 1 deposit, dispose, inf dump, lay, leave, locate, pinpoint, plant, position, put down, rest, set down, set out, settle, situate, stand, station, inf stick. 2 arrange, categorize, class, classify, grade, order, position, put in order, rank, sort. 3 can't place it. identify, put a name to, put into context, recognize, remember.

placid adj 1 collected, composed, cool, equable, even-tempered, imperturbable, level-headed, mild, phlegmatic, restful, sensible, stable, steady, unexcitable. 2 calm, motionless, peaceful, quiet, tranquil, unruffled, untroubled. Opp EXCITABLE, STORMY.

plagiarize vb appropriate, borrow, copy, inf imitate, infringe copyright, inf lift, pirate, purloin, reproduce. ▷ STEAL.

plague n 1 affliction, bane, blight, calamity, contagion, epidemic, infection, outbreak, pandemic, pestilence. ▷ ILLNESS. 2 infestation, invasion, nuisance, scourge, swarm, visitation. ● vb afflict, annoy, be a nuisance to, bother, distress, disturb, harass, harry, hound, irritate, molest, *inf* nag, persecute, pester, torment, torture, trouble, vex, worry.

plain *adj* **1** apparent, audible, certain, clear, comprehensible, definite, distinct, evident, intelligible, legible, lucid, manifest, obvious, patent, simple, transparent, unambiguous, understandable, unmistakable, visible, well-defined. *Opp* OBSCURE. **2** *plain speech*. basic, blunt, candid, direct, downright, explicit, forthright, frank, honest, informative, outspoken, plain-spoken, prosaic, sincere, straightforward, unequivocal, unvarnished. **3** *plain living*. austere, drab, everyday, frugal, homely, modest, ordinary, simple, Spartan, stark, unadorned, unattractive, undecorated, unexciting, unprepossessing, unpretentious, unremarkable, workaday. *Opp* SOPHISTICATED. ● *n* grassland, pampas, pasture, prairie, savannah, steppe, tundra, veld.

plaintive *adj* doleful, melancholy, mournful, plangent, sorrowful, wistful. ▷ SAD.

plan *n* **1** *inf* bird's-eye view, blueprint, chart, design, diagram, drawing, layout, map, representation, sketchmap. **2** *a plan of action*. aim, course of action, design, formula, idea, intention, method, plot, policy, procedure, programme, project, proposal, proposition, *inf* scenario, scheme, strategy, system. ● *vb* **1** arrange, concoct, contrive, design, devise, draw up a plan, formulate, invent, map out, *inf* mastermind, organize, outline, plot, prepare, scheme, think out, work out. **2** *I plan to go away*. aim, conspire, contemplate, envisage, expect, intend, mean, propose, think of. **planned** ▷ DELIBERATE.

plane *adj* even, flat, flush, level, smooth, uniform. ● *n* **1** flat surface, level, surface. **2** ▷ AIRCRAFT.

planet *n* globe, orb, satellite, sphere, world. □ *Earth, Jupiter, Mars, Mercury, Neptune, Pluto, Saturn, Uranus, Venus*.

plank *n* beam, board, planking, timber.

planning *n* arrangement, design, drafting, forethought, organization, preparation, setting up, thinking out.

plant *n* greenery, growth, undergrowth, vegetation. □ *annual, bulb, cactus, cereal, climber, fern, flower, fungus, grass, herb, lichen, moss, perennial, shrub, tree, vegetable, vine, water-plant, weed*. ▷ FLOWER, TREE, VEGETABLE. **2** *a manufacturing plant*. factory, foundry, mill, shop, works, workshop. **3** *industrial plant*. apparatus, equipment, machinery, machines. ● *vb* **1** bed out, set out, sow, transplant. **2** locate, place, position, put, situate, station.

plaster *n* **1** mortar, stucco. **2** dressing, sticking-plaster. ● *vb* apply, bedaub, coat, cover, daub, smear, spread.

plastic *adj* ductile, flexible, malleable, pliable, shapable, soft, supple, workable. □ *bakelite, celluloid, polystyrene, polythene, polyurethane, polyvinyl, PVC, vinyl*.

plate *n* **1** *old use* charger, dinnerplate, dish, platter, salver, side-plate, soup-plate, *old use* trencher. **2** lamina, lamination, layer, leaf, pane, panel, sheet, slab, stratum. **3** *plates in a book*. illustration, *inf* photo, photograph, picture, print. **4** *a dental plate*. dentures, false teeth. ● *vb* anodize, coat, cover, electroplate, galvanize (*with* zinc), gild (*with* gold).

platform *n* **1** dais, podium, rostrum, stage, stand. **2** *political platform*. ▷ POLICY.

platitude *n* banality, cliché, commonplace, truism.

plausible *adj* **1** acceptable, believable, conceivable, credible, imaginable, likely, logical, persuasive, possible, probable, rational, reasonable, sensible, tenable, thinkable. *Opp* IMPLAUSIBLE. **2** deceptive, glib, meretricious, misleading, specious, smooth, sophistical.

play *n* **1** amusement, diversion, entertainment, frivolity, fun, *inf* fun and games, *inf* horseplay, joking, make-believe, merrymaking, playing, pretending, recreation, revelry, *inf*

plentiful

skylarking, sport. **2** *play in moving parts.* flexibility, freedom, freedom of movement, *inf* give, latitude, leeway, looseness, movement, tolerance. **3** ▷ DRAMA. ● *vb* **1** amuse yourself, caper, cavort, disport yourself, enjoy yourself, fool about, frisk, frolic, gambol, *inf* have a good time, have fun, *inf* mess about, romp, sport. **2** *play a game.* join in, participate, take part. **3** *play an opponent.* challenge, compete against, oppose, rival, take on, vie with. **4** *play a role.* act, depict, impersonate, perform, portray, pretend to be, represent, take the part of. **5** *play an instrument.* make music on, perform on, strum. **6** *play the radio.* have on, listen to, operate, put on, switch on. play about ▷ MISBEHAVE. play along, play ball ▷ COOPERATE. play down ▷ MINIMIZE. play for time ▷ DELAY. play it by ear ▷ IMPROVISE. play up ▷ MISBEHAVE. play up to ▷ FLATTER.

player *n* **1** athlete, competitor, contestant, participant, sportsman, sportswoman. **2** actor, actress, artiste, entertainer, instrumentalist, musician, performer, soloist, Thespian, trouper. ▷ ENTERTAINER, MUSICIAN.

playful *adj* active, cheerful, coltish, facetious, flirtatious, frisky, frolicsome, fun-loving, good-natured, high-spirited, humorous, impish, jesting, *inf* jokey, joking, kittenish, light-hearted, lively, mischievous, puckish, roguish, skittish, spirited, sportive, sprightly, teasing, *inf* tongue-in-cheek, vivacious, waggish. *Opp* SERIOUS.

plea *n* **1** appeal, entreaty, invocation, petition, prayer, request, solicitation, suit, supplication. **2** argument, excuse, explanation, justification, pretext, reason.

plead *vb* **1** appeal, ask, beg, beseech, cry out, demand, entreat, implore, importune, petition, request, seek, solicit, supplicate. **2** allege, argue, assert, aver, declare, maintain, reason, swear.

pleasant *adj* acceptable, affable, agreeable, amiable, approachable, attractive, balmy, beautiful, charming, cheerful, congenial, decent, delicious, delightful, enjoyable, entertaining, excellent, fine, friendly, genial, gentle, good, gratifying, *inf* heavenly, hospitable, kind, likeable, lovely, mellow, mild, nice, palatable, peaceful, pleasing, pleasurable, pretty, reassuring, relaxed, satisfying, soothing, sympathetic, warm, welcome, welcoming. *Opp* ANNOYING, UNPLEASANT.

please *vb* **1** amuse, cheer up, content, delight, divert, entertain, give pleasure to, gladden, gratify, humour, make happy, satisfy, suit. **2** *Do what you please.* ▷ WANT. **pleasing** ▷ PLEASANT.

pleased *adj inf* chuffed, *derog* complacent, contented, delighted, elated, euphoric, glad, grateful, gratified, *sl* over the moon, satisfied, thankful, thrilled. ▷ HAPPY. *Opp* ANNOYED.

pleasure *n* **1** bliss, comfort, contentment, delight, ecstasy, enjoyment, euphoria, fulfilment, gladness, gratification, happiness, joy, rapture, satisfaction, solace. **2** amusement, diversion, entertainment, fun, luxury, recreation, self-indulgence.

pleat *n* crease, flute, fold, gather, tuck.

plebiscite *n* ballot, poll, referendum, vote.

pledge *n* **1** assurance, covenant, guarantee, oath, pact, promise, undertaking, vow, warranty, word. **2** *a pledge left at a pawnbroker's.* bail, bond, collateral, deposit, pawn, security, surety. ● *vb* agree, commit yourself, contract, give your word, guarantee, promise, swear, undertake, vouch, vouchsafe, vow.

plenary *adj* full, general, open.

plentiful *adj* abounding, abundant, ample, bounteous, bountiful, bristling, bumper (*crop*), copious, generous, inexhaustible, lavish, liberal, overflowing, plenteous, profuse, prolific. *Opp* SCARCE. **be plentiful** ▷ ABOUND.

plenty n abundance, adequacy, affluence, cornucopia, excess, fertility, flood, fruitfulness, glut, *inf* heaps, *inf* lashings, *inf* loads, a lot, *inf* lots, *inf* masses, more than enough, much, *inf* oceans, *inf* oodles, *inf* piles, plentitude, plentifulness, plethora, prodigality, profusion, prosperity, quantities, *inf* stacks, sufficiency, superabundance, surfeit, surplus, *inf* tons, wealth. *Opp* SCARCITY.

pliable adj 1 bendable, *inf* bendy, ductile, flexible, plastic, pliant, springy, supple. 2 *a pliable character.* adaptable, compliant, docile, easily influenced, easily led, easily persuaded, impressionable, manageable, persuadable, receptive, responsive, susceptible, suggestible, tractable, yielding.

plod vb 1 slog, tramp, trudge. ▷ WALK. 2 drudge, grind on, labour, *inf* peg away, persevere, *inf* plug away, toil. ▷ WORK.

plot n 1 acreage, allotment, area, estate, garden, lot, parcel, patch, smallholding, tract. 2 *a plot of a novel.* chain of events, narrative, organization, outline, scenario, story, story-line, thread. 3 *a subversive plot.* cabal, conspiracy, intrigue, machination, plan, scheme. ● vb 1 chart, compute, draw, map out, mark, outline, plan, project. 2 *plot to rob a bank.* collude, conspire, have designs, intrigue, machinate, scheme. 3 *plot a crime.* arrange, *inf* brew, conceive, concoct, *inf* cook up, design, devise, dream up, hatch.

pluck n ▷ COURAGE. vb 1 collect, gather, harvest, pick, pull off, remove. 2 grab, jerk, pull, seize, snatch, tear away, tweak, yank. 3 *pluck a chicken.* denude, remove feathers from, strip. 4 *pluck a violin.* play pizzicato, strum, twang.

plug n 1 bung, cork, stopper. 2 ▷ ADVERTISEMENT. ● vb 1 block up, *inf* bung up, close, cork, fill, jam, seal, stop up, stuff up. 2 advertise, commend, mention frequently, promote, publicize, puff, recommend. **plug away** ▷ WORK.

plumb adv 1 accurately, *inf* dead, exactly, precisely, *inf* slap. 2 perpendicularly, vertically. ● vb fathom, measure, penetrate, probe, sound.

plumbing n heating system, pipes, water-supply.

plume n feather, *plur* plumage, quill.

plump adj ample, buxom, chubby, dumpy, overweight, podgy, portly, pudgy, *inf* roly-poly, rotund, round, squat, stout, tubby, *inf* well-upholstered. ▷ FAT. *Opp* THIN. **plump for** ▷ CHOOSE.

plunder n booty, contraband, loot, pickings, pillage, prize, spoils, swag, takings. ● vb capture, despoil, devastate, lay waste, loot, maraud, pillage, raid, ransack, ravage, rifle, rob, sack, seize, spoil, steal from, strip, vandalize.

plunge vb 1 descend, dip, dive, drop, engulf, fall, fall headlong, hurtle, immerse, jump, leap, lower, nose-dive, pitch, plummet, sink, submerge, swoop, tumble. 2 force, push, stick, thrust.

poach vb 1 hunt, steal. 2 ▷ COOK.

pocket n bag, container, pouch, receptacle. ● vb ▷ TAKE.

pod n case, hull, shell.

poem n *inf* ditty, *inf* jingle, piece of poetry, rhyme, verse. □ ballad, ballade, doggerel, eclogue, elegy, epic, epithalamium, haiku, idyll, lay, limerick, lyric, nursery-rhyme, pastoral, ode, sonnet, vers libre. ▷ VERSE.

poet n bard, lyricist, minstrel, poetaster, rhymer, rhymester, sonneteer, versifier. ▷ WRITER.

poetic adj emotive, *derog* flowery, imaginative, lyrical, metrical, musical, poetical. *Opp* PROSAIC.

poignant adj affecting, distressing, heartbreaking, heartfelt, heart-rending, moving, painful, pathetic, piquant, piteous, pitiful, stirring, tender, touching, upsetting. ▷ SAD.

point n 1 apex, peak, prong, sharp end, spike, spur, tine, tip. 2 *a point in space.* location, place, position, site, situation, spot. 3 *a point in time.*

instant, juncture, moment, second, stage, time. **4** *decimal point*. dot, full stop, mark, speck, spot. **5** *the point of an argument*. aim, burden, crux, drift, end, essence, gist, goal, heart, import, intention, meaning, motive, nub, object, objective, pith, purpose, quiddity, relevance, significance, subject, substance, theme, thrust, use, usefulness. **6** *points to raise*. aspect, detail, idea, item, matter, particular, question, thought, topic. **7** *good points in her character*. attribute, characteristic, facet, feature, peculiarity, property, quality, trait. ● *vb* **1** call attention to, direct attention to, draw attention to, indicate, point out, show, signal. **2** aim, direct, guide, lead, steer. **pointed** ▷ SHARP. **to the point** ▷ RELEVANT.

pointer *n* arrow, hand (*of clock*), indicator.

pointless *adj* aimless, fatuous, fruitless, futile, inane, ineffective, senseless, silly, unproductive, useless, vain, worthless. ▷ STUPID.

poise *n* aplomb, assurance, balance, calmness, composure, coolness, dignity, equanimity, equilibrium, equipoise, imperturbability, presence, sang-froid, self-confidence, self-control, self-possession, serenity, steadiness. ● *vb* balance, be poised, hover, keep in balance, support, suspend.

poised *adj* **1** balanced, hovering, in equilibrium, standing, steady, teetering, wavering. **2** *poised to begin*. keyed up, prepared, ready, set, standing by, waiting. **3** *a poised performer*. assured, calm, composed, cool, coolheaded, dignified, self-confident, self-possessed, serene, suave, *inf* unflappable, unruffled, urbane.

poison *n* bane, toxin, venom. ● *vb* **1** adulterate, contaminate, infect, pollute, taint. ▷ KILL. **2** *poison the mind*. corrupt, defile, deprave, envenom, pervert, prejudice, subvert, warp. **poisoned** ▷ DIRTY, POISONOUS.

poisonous *adj* deadly, fatal, infectious, lethal, mephitic, miasmic, mortal, noxious, poisoned, septic, toxic, venomous, virulent.

poke *vb* butt, dig, elbow, goad, jab, jog, nudge, prod, stab, stick, thrust. ▷ HIT. **poke about** ▷ SEARCH. **poke fun at** ▷ RIDICULE. **poke out** ▷ PROTRUDE.

poky *adj* confined, cramped, inconvenient, restrictive, uncomfortable. ▷ SMALL. *Opp* SPACIOUS.

polar *adj* antarctic, arctic, freezing, glacial, icy, Siberian. ▷ COLD.

polarize *vb* diverge, divide, move to opposite positions, separate, split.

pole *n* **1** bar, beanpole, column, flagpole, mast, post, rod, shaft, spar, staff, stake, standard, stick, stilt, upright. **2** *opposite poles*. end, extreme, limit. **poles apart** ▷ DIFFERENT.

police *n sl* the Bill, constabulary, *sl* the fuzz, *inf* the law, police force, policemen. ● *vb* control, guard, keep in order, keep the peace, monitor, oversee, patrol, protect, provide a police presence, supervise, watch over.

policeman, policewoman *ns inf* bobby, constable, *sl* cop, *sl* copper, detective, *Fr* gendarme, inspector, officer, PC, police constable, *sl* rozzer, woman police constable, WPC.

policy *n* **1** approach, code of conduct, custom, guidelines, *inf* line, method, practice, principles, procedure, protocol, regulations, rules, stance, strategy, tactics. **2** intentions, manifesto, plan of action, platform, programme, proposals.

polish *n* **1** brightness, brilliance, finish, glaze, gleam, gloss, lustre, sheen, shine, smoothness, sparkle. **2** beeswax, French polish, oil, shellac, varnish, wax. **3** *His manners show polish*. *inf* class, elegance, finesse, grace, refinement, sophistication, style, suavity, urbanity. ● *vb* brighten, brush up, buff up, burnish, Frenchpolish, gloss, rub down, rub up, shine, smooth, wax. **polish off** ▷ FINISH. **polish up** ▷ IMPROVE.

polished adj 1 bright, burnished, glassy, gleaming, glossy, lustrous, shining, shiny. 2 polished manners. civilized, inf classy, cultivated, cultured, debonair, elegant, expert, faultless, fine, finished, flawless, genteel, gracious, impeccable, perfect, perfected, polite, inf posh, refined, soigné(e), sophisticated, suave, urbane. Opp ROUGH.

polite adj agreeable, attentive, chivalrous, civil, considerate, correct, courteous, courtly, cultivated, deferential, diplomatic, discreet, euphemistic, formal, gallant, genteel, gentlemanly, gracious, ladylike, obliging, polished, proper, respectful, tactful, thoughtful, well-bred, well-mannered, well-spoken. Opp RUDE.

political adj 1 administrative, civil, diplomatic, governmental, legislative, parliamentary, state. 2 activist, factional, militant, partisan, party-political. □ anarchist, capitalist, communist, conservative, democrat, fascist, Labour, leftist, left-wing, liberal, Marxist, moderate, monarchist, nationalist, Nazi, parliamentarian, radical, republican, revolutionary, rightist, right-wing, socialist, Tory, old use Whig.

politics n diplomacy, government, political affairs, political science, public affairs, statecraft, statesmanship. □ anarchy, capitalism, communism, democracy, dictatorship, martial law, monarchy, oligarchy, republic.

poll n 1 ballot, election, vote. 2 canvass, census, plebiscite, referendum, survey. ● vb ballot, canvass, question, sample, survey.

pollute vb adulterate, befoul, blight, contaminate, corrupt, defile, dirty, foul, infect, poison, soil, taint.

pomp n brilliance, ceremonial, ceremony, display, formality, glory, grandeur, magnificence, ostentation, pageantry, ritual, show, solemnity, spectacle, splendour.

pompous adj affected, arrogant, bombastic, conceited, grandiloquent, grandiose, haughty, inf highfalutin, imperious, long-winded, magisterial, ornate, ostentatious, overbearing, pedantic, pontifical, posh, pretentious, self-important, sententious, showy, smug, snobbish, inf snooty, inf stuck-up, inf stuffy, supercilious, turgid, vain, vainglorious. ▷ PROUD. Opp MODEST.

ponderous adj 1 awkward, bulky, burdensome, cumbersome, heavy, hefty, huge, massive, unwieldy, weighty. Opp LIGHT. 2 a ponderous style. dreary, dull, elephantine, heavy-handed, humourless, inflated, laboured, lifeless, long-winded, overdone, pedestrian, plodding, prolix, slow, stilted, stodgy, tedious, tiresome, verbose, inf windy. Opp LIVELY.

pool n lagoon, lake, mere, oasis, paddling-pool, pond, puddle, swimming-pool, tarn. ● vb ▷ COMBINE.

poor adj 1 badly off, bankrupt, beggarly, inf broke, deprived, destitute, disadvantaged, inf down-and-out, inf hard up, homeless, impecunious, impoverished, in debt, indigent, insolvent, necessitous, needy, inf on your uppers, penniless, penurious, poverty-stricken, sl skint, straitened, underpaid, underprivileged. 2 poor soil. barren, exhausted, infertile, sterile, unfruitful, unproductive. 3 a poor salary. inadequate, insufficient, low, meagre, mean, scanty, small, sparse, unprofitable, unrewarding. 4 poor in health. inf below par, poorly. ▷ ILL. 5 poor quality. amateurish, bad, cheap, defective, deficient, disappointing, faulty, imperfect, inferior, low-grade, mediocre, paltry, second-rate, shoddy, substandard, unacceptable, unsatisfactory, useless, worthless. 6 poor child! forlorn, hapless, ill-fated, luckless, miserable, pathetic, pitiable, sad, unfortunate, unhappy, unlucky, wretched. Opp GOOD, LARGE, LUCKY, RICH. ● plur n beggars, the destitute, down-and-outs, the homeless, paupers, tramps, the underprivileged, vagrants, wretches.

populace n commonalty, derog Gk hoi polloi, masses, people, public, derog rabble, derog riff-raff.

position

popular *adj* **1** accepted, acclaimed, *inf* all the rage, approved, celebrated, famous, fashionable, favoured, favourite, *inf* in, in demand, liked, lionized, loved, renowned, sought-after, *inf* trendy, well-known, well-liked, well-received. *Opp* UNPOPULAR. **2** *popular opinion.* average, common, conventional, current, democratic, general, of the people, ordinary, predominant, prevailing, representative, standard, universal.

popularize *vb* **1** make popular, promote, spread. **2** *popularize classics.* make easy, simplify, *derog* tart up.

populate *vb* colonize, dwell in, fill, inhabit, live in, occupy, overrun, people, reside in, settle.

population *n* citizenry, citizens, community, denizens, folk, inhabitants, natives, occupants, people, populace, public, residents.

populous *adj* crowded, full, heavily populated, jammed, overcrowded, overpopulated, packed, swarming, teeming.

porch *n* doorway, entrance, lobby, portico.

pore *vb* **pore over** examine, go over, peruse, read, scrutinize, study.

pornographic *adj* arousing, *inf* blue, erotic, explicit, explicitly, sexual, sexy, titillating. ▷ OBSCENE.

porous *adj* absorbent, cellular, holey, penetrable, permeable, pervious, spongy. *Opp* IMPERVIOUS.

port *n* anchorage, dock, dockyard, harbour, haven, marina, mooring, sea-port.

portable *adj* compact, convenient, easy to carry, handy, light, lightweight, manageable, mobile, movable, pocket, pocket-sized, small, transportable. *Opp* UNWIELDY.

porter *n* **1** caretaker, concierge, doorkeeper, doorman, gatekeeper, janitor, security-guard, watchman. **2** baggage-handler, bearer, carrier.

portion *n* allocation, allowance, bit, chunk, division, fraction, fragment, helping, hunk, measure, part, percentage, piece, quantity, quota, ration, scrap, section, segment, serving, share, slice, sliver, subdivision, wedge. **portion out** ▷ SHARE.

portrait *n* depiction, image, likeness, picture, portrayal, profile, representation, self-portrait. ▷ PICTURE.

portray *vb* **1** delineate, depict, describe, evoke, illustrate, paint, picture, represent, show. **2** ▷ IMPERSONATE.

pose *n* **1** attitude, position, posture, stance. **2** act, affectation, attitudinizing, façade, masquerade, pretence. ● *vb* **1** keep still, model, sit, strike a pose. **2** attitudinize, *inf* be a poser, be a poseur, posture, *inf* put on airs, show off. **3** *pose a question.* advance, ask, broach, posit, postulate, present, put forward, submit, suggest. **pose as** ▷ IMPERSONATE.

poser *n* **1** dilemma, enigma, problem, puzzle, question, riddle. **2** ▷ POSEUR.

poseur *n* attitudinizer, exhibitionist, fraud, impostor, masquerader, *inf* phoney, *inf* poser, pretender, *inf* show-off.

posh *adj inf* classy, elegant, fashionable, formal, grand, lavish, luxurious, ostentatious, rich, showy, smart, snobbish, stylish, sumptuous, *inf* swanky, *inf* swish.

position *n* **1** locality, location, locus, place, placement, point, reference, site, situation, spot, whereabouts. **2** *an awkward position.* circumstances, condition, predicament, situation, state. **3** *position of the body.* angle, pose, posture, stance. **4** *intellectual position.* assertion, attitude, contention, hypothesis, opinion, outlook, perspective, principle, proposition, standpoint, thesis, view, viewpoint. **5** *position in a firm.* appointment, degree, employment, function, grade, job, level, niche, occupation, place, post, rank, role, standing, station, status, title. ● *vb* arrange, deploy, dispose, fix, locate, place, put, settle, site, situate, stand, station.

positive adj **1** affirmative, assured, categorical, certain, clear, conclusive, confident, convinced, decided, definite, emphatic, explicit, firm, incontestable, incontrovertible, irrefutable, real, sure, undeniable, unequivocal. **2** *positive advice*. beneficial, constructive, helpful, optimistic, practical, useful, worthwhile. *Opp* NEGATIVE.

possess vb **1** be in possession of, enjoy, have, hold, own. **2** be gifted with, embody, embrace, include. **3** *possess territory*. acquire, control, dominate, govern, invade, occupy, rule, seize, take over. **4** *possess a person*. bewitch, captivate, cast a spell over, charm, enthral, haunt, hypnotize, obsess.

possessions plur n assets, belongings, chattels, effects, estate, fortune, goods, property, riches, things, wealth, worldly goods.

possessive adj clinging, dominating, domineering, jealous, overbearing, proprietorial, protective, selfish. ▷ GREEDY.

possibility n capability, chance, danger, feasibility, likelihood, odds, opportunity, plausibility, potential, potentiality, practicality, probability, risk.

possible adj achievable, admissible, attainable, conceivable, credible, *inf* doable, feasible, imaginable, likely, obtainable, *inf* on, plausible, potential, practicable, practical, probable, prospective, realizable, reasonable, tenable, thinkable, viable, workable. *Opp* IMPOSSIBLE.

possibly adv God willing, *inf* hopefully, if possible, maybe, *old use* peradventure, *old use* perchance, perhaps.

post n **1** baluster, bollard, brace, capstan, column, gate-post, leg, newel, pale, paling, picket, pier, pile, pillar, pole, prop, pylon, shaft, stake, stanchion, standard, starting-post, strut, support, upright, winning-post. **2** *a sentry's post*. location, place, point, position, station. **3** *post in a firm*.

appointment, assignment, employment, function, job, occupation, office, place, position, situation, task, work. **4** airmail, cards, delivery, junk mail, letters, mail, packets, parcels, postcards. ● vb **1** advertise, announce, display, pin up, proclaim, promulgate, publicize, publish, put up, stick up. **2** *post a letter*. dispatch, mail, send, transmit. **3** *post a sentry*. appoint, assign, locate, place, position, set, situate, station.

poster n advertisement, announcement, bill, broadsheet, circular, display, flyer, notice, placard, sign.

posterity n descendants, future generations, heirs, issue, offspring, progeny, successors.

postpone vb adjourn, defer, delay, extend, hold over, keep in abeyance, lay aside, put back, put off, *inf* put on ice, *inf* put on the back burner, *inf* shelve, stay, suspend, temporize.

postscript n addendum, addition, afterthought, codicil (*to will*), epilogue, *inf* PS.

postulate vb assume, hypothesize, posit, propose, suppose, theorize.

posture n **1** appearance, bearing, carriage, deportment, pose, position, stance. **2** ▷ ATTITUDE.

posy n bouquet, bunch of flowers, buttonhole, corsage, nosegay, spray.

pot n basin, bowl, casserole, cauldron, container, crock, crucible, dish, jar, pan, saucepan, stewpot, teapot, urn, vessel.

potent adj **1** effective, forceful, formidable, influential, intoxicating (*drink*), mighty, overpowering, overwhelming, powerful, puissant, strong, vigorous. ▷ STRONG. **2** *a potent argument*. ▷ PERSUASIVE. *Opp* WEAK.

potential adj **1** aspiring, budding, embryonic, future, *inf* hopeful, intending, latent, likely, possible, probable, promising, prospective, *inf* would-be. **2** *potential disaster*. imminent, impending, looming, threatening. ● n aptitude, capability, capacity, possibility, resources.

potion n brew, concoction, decoction, dose, draught, drink, drug, elixir, liquid, medicine, mixture, philtre, potation, tonic.

potter vb dabble, do odd jobs, fiddle about, loiter, mess about, tinker, work.

pottery n ceramics, china, crockery, crocks, earthenware, porcelain, stoneware, terracotta.

pouch n bag, pocket, purse, reticule, sack, wallet.

poultry n □ bantam, chicken, duck, fowl, goose, guinea-fowl, hen, pullet, turkey.

pounce vb ambush, attack, drop on, jump on, leap on, seize, snatch, spring at, strike, swoop down on, take by surprise.

pound n compound, corral, enclosure, pen. ● vb batter, beat, crush, grind, hammer, knead, mash, powder, pulp, pulverize, smash. ▷ HIT.

pour vb 1 cascade, course, discharge, disgorge, flood, flow, gush, run, spew, spill, spout, spurt, stream. 2 pour wine. decant, empty, serve, tip.

poverty n 1 beggary, bankruptcy, debt, destitution, hardship, impecuniousness, indigence, insolvency, necessity, need, penury, privation, want. 2 a poverty of talent. absence, dearth, insufficiency, lack, paucity, scarcity, shortage. Opp WEALTH.

powder n dust, particles, talc. ● vb 1 atomize, comminute, crush, granulate, grind, pound, pulverize, reduce to powder. 2 besprinkle, coat, cover with powder, dredge, dust, sprinkle.

powdered adj 1 ▷ POWDERY. 2 dehydrated, dried, freeze-dried.

powdery adj chalky, crumbly, crushed, disintegrating, dry, dusty, fine, friable, granular, granulated, ground, loose, powdered, pulverized, sandy. Opp SOLID, WET.

power n 1 ability, capability, capacity, competence, drive, energy, faculty, force, might, muscle, potential, skill, talent, vigour. 2 power to arrest. authority, privilege, right. 3 power of

a tyrant. ascendancy, inf clout, command, control, dominance, domination, dominion, influence, mastery, omnipotence, oppression, potency, rule, sovereignty, supremacy, sway. ▷ STRENGTH. Opp WEAKNESS.

powerful adj authoritative, cogent, commanding, compelling, consuming, convincing, dominant, dynamic, effective, effectual, energetic, forceful, high-powered, influential, invincible, irresistible, mighty, muscular, omnipotent, overpowering, overwhelming, persuasive, potent, sovereign, vigorous, weighty. ▷ STRONG. Opp POWERLESS.

powerless adj defenceless, disabled, feeble, helpless, impotent, incapable, incapacitated, ineffective, ineffectual, paralysed, unable, unfit. ▷ WEAK. Opp POWERFUL.

practicable adj achievable, attainable, inf doable, feasible, performable, possible, practical, realistic, sensible, viable, workable. Opp IMPRACTICABLE.

practical adj 1 applied, empirical, experimental. 2 businesslike, capable, competent, down-to-earth, efficient, expert, hard-headed, matter-of-fact, inf no-nonsense, pragmatic, proficient, realistic, sensible, skilled. 3 a practical tool. convenient, functional, handy, usable, useful, utilitarian. 4 ▷ PRACTICABLE. Opp IMPRACTICAL, THEORETICAL. **practical joke** ▷ TRICK.

practically adv almost, close to, just about, nearly, to all intents and purposes, virtually.

practice n 1 action, actuality, application, doing, effect, operation, reality, use. 2 inf dummy-run, exercise, practising, preparation, rehearsal, inf run-through, training, inf try-out, inf work-out. 3 common practice. convention, custom, habit, modus operandi, routine, tradition, way, wont. 4 a doctor's practice. business, office, work.

practise vb 1 do exercises, drill, exercise, prepare, rehearse, train, warm up, inf work out. 2 practise what *you preach.* apply, carry out, do, engage in, follow, make a practice of, perform, put into practice.

praise n **1** acclaim, acclamation, accolade, admiration, adulation, applause, approbation, approval, commendation, compliment, congratulation, encomium, eulogy, homage, honour, ovation, panegyric, plaudits, testimonial, thanks, tribute. **2** *praise to God.* adoration, devotion, glorification, worship. ● *vb* **1** acclaim, admire, applaud, cheer, clap, commend, compliment, congratulate, *inf* crack up, eulogize, extol, give a good review of, marvel at, offer praise to, pay tribute to, *inf* rave about, recommend, *inf* say nice things about, show approval of. *Opp* CRITICIZE. **2** *praise God.* adore, exalt, glorify, honour, laud, magnify, worship. *Opp* CURSE.

praiseworthy *adj* admirable, commendable, creditable, deserving, laudable, meritorious, worthy. ▷ GOOD. *Opp* BAD.

pram n baby-carriage, *old use* perambulator, push-chair.

prance *vb* bound, caper, cavort, dance, frisk, frolic, gambol, hop, jig about, jump, leap, play, romp, skip, spring.

prattle *vb* babble, blather, chatter, gabble, maunder, *inf* rattle on, *inf* witter on.

pray *vb* beseech, call upon, invoke, say prayers, supplicate. ▷ ASK.

prayer n collect, devotion, entreaty, invocation, litany, meditation, petition, praise, supplication.

prayer-book n breviary, missal.

preach *vb* **1** deliver a sermon, evangelize, expound, proselytize, spread the Gospel. **2** expatiate, give moral advice, harangue, *inf* lay down the law, lecture, moralize, pontificate, sermonize.

preacher n cleric, crusader, divine, ecclesiastic, evangelist, minister, missionary, moralist, pastor, revivalist. ▷ CLERGYMAN.

prearranged *adj* arranged beforehand, fixed, planned, predetermined, prepared, rehearsed, thought out. *Opp* SPONTANEOUS.

precarious *adj* dangerous, *inf* dicey, *inf* dodgy, dubious, hazardous, insecure, perilous, risky, rocky, shaky, slippery, treacherous, uncertain, unreliable, unsafe, unstable, unsteady, vulnerable, wobbly. *Opp* SAFE.

precaution n anticipation, defence, insurance, preventive measure, protection, provision, safeguard, safety measure.

precede *vb* be in front of, come before, go ahead, go before, go in front, herald, introduce, lead, lead into, pave the way for, preface, prefix, start, usher in. *Opp* FOLLOW.

precious *adj* **1** costly, expensive, invaluable, irreplaceable, priceless, valuable. *Opp* WORTHLESS. **2** adored, beloved, darling, dear, loved, prized, treasured, valued, venerated.

precipice n bluff, cliff, crag, drop, escarpment, precipitous face, rock.

precipitate *adj* breakneck, hasty, headlong, meteoric, premature. ▷ QUICK. ● *vb* accelerate, advance, bring on, cause, encourage, expedite, further, hasten, hurry, incite, induce, instigate, occasion, provoke, spark off, trigger off.

precipitation n □ dew, downpour, drizzle, hail, rain, rainfall, shower, sleet, snow, snowfall.

precipitous *adj* abrupt, perpendicular, sharp, sheer, steep, vertical.

precise *adj* **1** accurate, clear-cut, correct, defined, definite, distinct, exact, explicit, fixed, measured, right, specific, unambiguous, unequivocal, well-defined. *Opp* IMPRECISE. **2** *precise work.* careful, critical, exacting, fastidious, faultless, finicky, flawless, meticulous, nice, perfect, punctilious, rigorous, scrupulous. *Opp* CARELESS.

preclude *vb* avert, avoid, bar, debar, exclude, forestall, frustrate, impede, make impossible, obviate, pre-empt, prevent, prohibit, rule out, thwart.

prejudiced

precocious *adj* advanced, forward, gifted, mature, quick. ▷ CLEVER. *Opp* BACKWARD.

preconception *n* assumption, bias, expectation, preconceived idea, predisposition, prejudgement, prejudice, presupposition.

predatory *adj* acquisitive, avaricious, covetous, extortionate, greedy, hunting, marauding, pillaging, plundering, preying, rapacious, ravenous, voracious.

predecessor *n* ancestor, antecedent, forebear, forefather, forerunner, precursor.

predetermined *adj* **1** fated, destined, doomed, ordained, predestined. **2** agreed, prearranged, pre-planned, recognized, *inf* set up.

predicament *n* crisis, difficulty, dilemma, embarrassment, emergency, *inf* fix, impasse, *inf* jam, *inf* mess, *inf* pickle, plight, problem, quandary, situation, state.

predict *vb* augur, forebode, forecast, foresee, foreshadow, foretell, foretoken, forewarn, hint, intimate, presage, prognosticate, prophesy, tell fortunes.

predictable *adj* anticipated, certain, expected, foreseeable, foreseen, likely, *inf* on the cards, probable, sure, unsurprising. *Opp* UNPREDICTABLE.

predominant *adj* ascendant, chief, dominating, leading, main, preponderant, prevailing, prevalent, primary, ruling, sovereign.

predominate *vb* be in the majority, control, dominate, *inf* have the upper hand, hold sway, lead, outnumber, outweigh, preponderate, prevail, reign, rule.

pre-eminent *adj* distinguished, eminent, excellent, incomparable, matchless, outstanding, peerless, supreme, unrivalled, unsurpassed.

pre-empt *vb* anticipate, appropriate, arrogate, expropriate, forestall, seize, take over.

preface *n* exordium, foreword, introduction, *inf* lead-in, overture, preamble, prelude, proem, prolegomenon, prologue. ● *vb* begin, introduce, lead into, open, precede, prefix, start.

prefer *vb* advocate, *inf* back, be partial to, choose, fancy, favour, *inf* go for, incline towards, like, like better, opt for, pick out, *inf* plump for, *inf* put your money on, recommend, select, single out, think preferable, vote for, want.

preferable *adj* advantageous, better, better-liked, chosen, desirable, favoured, likely, nicer, preferred, recommended, wanted. *Opp* OBJECTIONABLE.

preference *n* **1** choice, fancy, favourite, liking, option, pick, selection, wish. **2** favouritism, inclination, partiality, predilection, prejudice, proclivity.

preferential *adj* advantageous, better, biased, favourable, favoured, privileged, showing favouritism, special, superior.

pregnant *adj* **1** carrying a child, expectant, *inf* expecting, gestating, gravid, parturient, *old use* with child. **2** *pregnant remark.* ▷ MEANINGFUL.

prejudice *n* bias, bigotry, chauvinism, discrimination, dogmatism, fanaticism, favouritism, intolerance, jingoism, leaning, narrowmindedness, partiality, partisanship, predilection, predisposition, prejudgement, racialism, racism, sexism, unfairness, xenophobia. *Opp* TOLERANCE. ● *vb* **1** bias, colour, incline, influence, interfere with, make prejudiced, predispose, sway. **2** *prejudice your chances.* damage, harm, injure, ruin, spoil, undermine.

prejudiced *adj* biased, bigoted, chauvinist, discriminatory, illiberal, intolerant, jaundiced, jingoistic, leading (*question*), loaded, narrowminded, one-sided, parochial, partial, partisan, racist, sexist, tendentious, unfair, xenophobic. *Opp* IMPARTIAL.
prejudiced person bigot, chauvinist, fanatic, racist, sexist, zealot.

prejudicial adj damaging, deleterious, detrimental, disadvantageous, harmful, inimical, injurious, unfavourable.

preliminary adj advance, earliest, early, experimental, exploratory, first, inaugural, initial, introductory, opening, prefatory, preparatory, qualifying, tentative, trial. ● n ▷ PRELUDE.

prelude n beginning, inf curtain-raiser, exordium, introduction, opener, opening, overture, preamble, precursor, preface, preliminary, preparation, proem, prolegomenon, prologue, start, starter, inf warm-up. Opp CONCLUSION, POSTSCRIPT.

premature adj abortive, before time, early, hasty, ill-timed, precipitate, inf previous, too early, too soon, undeveloped, untimely. Opp LATE.

premeditated adj calculated, conscious, considered, contrived, deliberate, intended, intentional, planned, prearranged, preconceived, predetermined, preplanned, studied, wilful. Opp SPONTANEOUS.

premiss n assertion, assumption, basis, grounds, hypothesis, proposition, supposition, thesis.

premonition n anxiety, fear, foreboding, forewarning, inf funny feeling, inf hunch, indication, intuition, misgiving, omen, portent, presentiment, suspicion, warning, worry.

preoccupied adj **1** absorbed, engaged, engrossed, immersed, interested, involved, obsessed, sunk, taken up, wrapped up. **2** absent-minded, abstracted, day-dreaming, distracted, faraway, inattentive, lost in thought, musing, pensive, pondering, rapt, reflecting, thoughtful.

preparation n arrangements, briefing, inf gearing up, getting ready, groundwork, making provision, measures, organization, plans, practice, preparing, setting up, spadework, training.

prepare vb **1** arrange, cook, devise, inf do what's necessary, inf fix up, get ready, make arrangements, make ready, organize, pave the way, plan, process, set up. ▷ MAKE. **2** prepare for exams. inf cram, practise, revise, study, inf swot. **3** prepare pupils for exams. brief, coach, educate, equip, instruct, rehearse, teach, train, tutor. **prepared** ▷ PRE-ARRANGED, READY. **prepare yourself** be prepared, be ready, brace yourself, discipline yourself, fortify yourself, steel yourself.

preposterous adj bizarre, excessive, extreme, grotesque, monstrous, outrageous, surreal, unreasonable, unthinkable. ▷ ABSURD.

prerequisite adj compulsory, essential, indispensable, mandatory, necessary, obligatory, prescribed, required, requisite, specified, stipulated. Opp OPTIONAL. ● n condition, essential, necessity, precondition, proviso, qualification, requirement, requisite, Lat sine qua non, stipulation.

prescribe vb advise, assign, command, demand, dictate, direct, fix, impose, instruct, lay down, ordain, order, recommend, require, specify, stipulate, suggest.

presence n **1** attendance, closeness, companionship, company, nearness, propinquity, proximity, society. **2** air, appearance, aura, bearing, comportment, demeanour, impressiveness, mien, personality, poise, self-assurance, self-possession.

present adj **1** adjacent, at hand, close, here, in attendance, nearby. **2** contemporary, current, existing, extant, present-day, up-to-date. ● n **1** inf here and now, today. **2** alms, bonus, bounty, charity, contribution, donation, endowment, gift, grant, gratuity, handout, offering, tip. ● vb **1** award, bestow, confer, dispense, distribute, donate, give, hand over, offer. **2** present evidence. adduce, bring forward, demonstrate, display, exhibit, furnish, proffer, put forward, reveal, set out, show, submit. **3** present a guest. announce, introduce, make known. **4** present a play. act, bring out, perform, put on, stage. **present yourself** ▷ ATTEND, REPORT.

presentable *adj* acceptable, adequate, all right, clean, decent, decorous, fit to be seen, good enough, neat, passable, proper, respectable, satisfactory, suitable, tidy, tolerable, *inf* up to scratch, worthy.

presently *adv old use* anon, before long, by and by, *inf* in a jiffy, shortly, soon.

preserve *n* **1** conserve, jam, jelly, marmalade. **2** *wildlife preserve*. reservation, reserve, sanctuary. • *vb* **1** care for, conserve, defend, guard, keep, lay up, look after, maintain, perpetuate, protect, retain, safeguard, save, secure, stockpile, store, support, sustain, uphold, watch over. *Opp* DESTROY. **2** *preserve food*. bottle, can, chill, cure, dehydrate, dry, freeze, freeze-dry, irradiate, jam, pickle, refrigerate, salt, tin. **3** *preserve a corpse*. embalm, mummify.

preside *vb* be in charge, chair, officiate, take charge, take the chair. **preside over** ▷ GOVERN.

press *n* magazines, the media, newspapers. • *vb* **1** apply pressure to, compress, condense, cram, crowd, crush, depress, force, gather, *inf* jam, push, shove, squash, squeeze, subject to pressure. **2** *press laundry*. flatten, iron, smooth. **3** *press someone to stay*. ask, beg, bully, coerce, constrain, dragoon, entreat, exhort, implore, importune, induce, *inf* lean on, persuade, pressure, pressurize, put pressure on, request, require, urge. **pressing** ▷ URGENT.

pressure *n* **1** burden, compression, force, heaviness, load, might, power, stress, weight. **2** *pressure of modern life*. adversity, affliction, constraints, demands, difficulties, exigencies, *inf* hassle, hurry, oppression, problems, strain, stress, urgency. • *vb* ask, beg, bully, coerce, constrain, dragoon, entreat, exhort, implore, importune, induce, *inf* lean on, persuade, press, pressurize, put pressure on, request, require, urge.

prestige *n* cachet, celebrity, credit, distinction, eminence, esteem, fame, glory, good name, honour, importance, influence, *inf* kudos, regard, renown, reputation, respect, standing, stature, status.

prestigious *adj* acclaimed, august, celebrated, creditable, distinguished, eminent, esteemed, estimable, famed, famous, highly-regarded, high-ranking, honourable, honoured, important, influential, pre-eminent, renowned, reputable, respected, significant, wellknown. *Opp* INSIGNIFICANT.

presume *vb* **1** assume, believe, conjecture, gather, guess, hypothesize, imagine, infer, postulate, suppose, surmise, suspect, *inf* take for granted, *inf* take it, think. **2** *He presumed to correct me*. be presumptuous enough, dare, have the effrontery, make bold, take the liberty, venture.

presumptuous *adj* arrogant, bold, brazen, *inf* cheeky, conceited, forward, impertinent, impudent, insolent, over-confident, *inf* pushy, shameless, unauthorized, unwarranted. ▷ PROUD.

pretence *n* act, acting, affectation, appearance, artifice, camouflage, charade, counterfeiting, deception, disguise, display, dissembling, dissimulation, excuse, façade, falsification, feigning, feint, fiction, front, guise, hoax, *inf* humbug, hypocrisy, insincerity, invention, lying, make-believe, masquerade, pose, posing, posturing, pretext, ruse, sham, show, simulation, subterfuge, trickery, wile. ▷ DECEIT.

pretend *vb* **1** act, affect, allege, behave insincerely, bluff, counterfeit, deceive, disguise, dissemble, dissimulate, fake, feign, fool, hoax, hoodwink, imitate, impersonate, *inf* kid, lie, *inf* make out, mislead, perform, play a part, play-act, pose, posture, profess, purport, put on an act, sham, simulate, take someone in, trick. **2** ▷ IMAGINE. **3** ▷ CLAIM.

pretender *n* aspirant, claimant, rival, suitor.

pretentious *adj* affected, *inf* arty, conceited, exaggerated, extravagant, grandiose, *inf* highfalutin, inflated, ostentatious, overblown, *inf* over the top, pompous, showy, *inf* snobbish, superficial. *Opp* UNPRETENTIOUS.

pretext *n* cloak, cover, disguise, excuse, pretence.

pretty *adj* appealing, attractive, *inf* bonny, charming, *inf* cute, dainty, delicate, *inf* easy on the eye, fetching, good-looking, lovely, nice, pleasing, *derog* pretty-pretty, winsome. ▷ BEAUTIFUL. *Opp* UGLY. ● *adv* fairly, moderately, quite, rather, reasonably, somewhat, tolerably. *Opp* VERY.

prevail *vb* be prevalent, hold sway, predominate, preponderate, succeed, triumph, *inf* win the day. ▷ WIN. **prevailing** ▷ PREVALENT.

prevalent *adj* accepted, ascendant, chief, common, commonest, current, customary, dominant, dominating, effectual, established, extensive, familiar, fashionable, general, governing, influential, main, mainstream, normal, ordinary, orthodox, pervasive, popular, powerful, predominant, prevailing, principal, ruling, ubiquitous, universal, usual, widespread. *Opp* UNUSUAL.

prevaricate *vb inf* beat about the bush, be evasive, cavil, deceive, equivocate, *inf* fib, hedge, lie, mislead, quibble, temporize.

prevent *vb* anticipate, avert, avoid, baffle, bar, block, check, control, curb, deter, fend off, foil, forestall, frustrate, hamper, *inf* head off, *inf* help (*can't help it*), hinder, impede, inhibit, inoculate against, intercept, *inf* nip in the bud, obstruct, obviate, preclude, pre-empt, prohibit, *inf* put a stop to, restrain, save, stave off, stop, take precautions against, thwart, ward off. ▷ FORBID. *Opp* ENCOURAGE.

preventive *adj* anticipatory, counteractive, deterrent, obstructive, precautionary, pre-emptive, preventative.

previous *adj* **1** above-mentioned, aforementioned, aforesaid, antecedent, earlier, erstwhile, foregoing, former, past, preceding, prior. *Opp* SUBSEQUENT. **2** ▷ PREMATURE.

prey *n* kill, quarry, victim. ● *vb* **prey on** eat, feed on, hunt, kill, live off. ▷ EXPLOIT.

price *n* **1** amount, charge, cost, *inf* damage, expenditure, expense, fare, fee, figure, outlay, payment, rate, sum, terms, toll, value, worth. **2** *Give me a price.* estimate, offer, quotation, valuation. ▷ PAYMENT. **pay the price for** ▷ ATONE.

priceless *adj* **1** costly, dear, expensive, incalculable, inestimable, invaluable, irreplaceable, precious, *inf* pricey, rare, valuable. *Opp* WORTHLESS. **2** ▷ FUNNY.

prick *vb* **1** bore into, jab, lance, perforate, pierce, punch, puncture, riddle, stab, sting. **2** ▷ STIMULATE.

prickle *n* **1** barb, bristle, bur, needle, spike, spine, thorn. **2** irritation, itch, pricking, prickling, tingle, tingling. ● *vb* irritate, itch, make your skin crawl, scratch, sting, tingle.

prickly *adj* **1** barbed, bristly, rough, scratchy, sharp, spiky, spiny, stubbly, thorny, unshaven. *Opp* SMOOTH. **2** ▷ IRRITABLE.

pride *n* **1** *Fr* amour propre, gratification, happiness, honour, pleasure, satisfaction, self-respect, self-satisfaction. ▷ DIGNITY. **2** *her pride and joy.* jewel, treasure, treasured possession. **3** *pride before a fall.* arrogance, being proud, *inf* big-headedness, boastfulness, conceit, egotism, haughtiness, hubris, megalomania, narcissism, overconfidence, presumption, self-admiration, self-esteem, self-importance, self-love, smugness, snobbery, snobbishness, vainglory, vanity. *Opp* HUMILITY.

priest *n* confessor, Druid, lama, minister, preacher. ▷ CLERGYMAN.

priggish *adj* conservative, fussy, *inf* goody-goody, haughty, moralistic, prudish, self-righteous, sententious, stiff-necked, *inf* stuffy. ▷ PRIM.

prim *adj* demure, fastidious, formal, inhibited, narrow-minded, precise, *inf* prissy, proper, prudish, *inf* starchy, strait-laced. *Opp* BROADMINDED.

primal *adj* **1** early, earliest, first, original, primeval, primitive, primordial. **2** ▷ PRIMARY.

primarily *adv* basically, chiefly, especially, essentially, firstly, fundamentally, generally, mainly, mostly, particularly, predominantly, pre-eminently, principally.

primary *adj* basic, cardinal, chief, dominant, first, foremost, fundamental, greatest, important, initial, leading, main, major, outstanding, paramount, predominant, pre-eminent, primal, prime, principal, supreme, top.

prime *adj* **1** best, first-class, first-rate, foremost, select, superior, top, top-quality. ▷ EXCELLENT. **2** ▷ PRIMARY. ● *vb* get ready, prepare.

primitive *adj* **1** aboriginal, ancient, barbarian, early, first, prehistoric, primeval, savage, uncivilized, uncultivated. **2** *primitive technology*. antediluvian, backward, basic, *inf* behind the times, crude, elementary, obsolete, rough, rudimentary, simple, simplistic, undeveloped. ▷ OLD. **3** *primitive art*. childlike, crude, naïve, unpolished, unrefined, unsophisticated. *Opp* ADVANCED, SOPHISTICATED.

principal *adj* basic, cardinal, chief, dominant, dominating, first, foremost, fundamental, greatest, highest, important, key, leading, main, major, outstanding, paramount, predominant, pre-eminent, prevailing, primary, prime, starring, supreme, top. ● *n* **1** ▷ CHIEF. **2** *the principal in a play*. diva, hero, heroine, lead, leading role, prima ballerina, protagonist, star.

principle *n* **1** assumption, axiom, belief, creed, criterion, doctrine, dogma, ethic, idea, ideal, maxim, notion, precept, proposition, rule, standard, teaching, tenet, truism, truth, values. **2** *a person of principle*. conscience, high-mindedness, honesty, honour, ideals, integrity, morality, probity, scruples, standards,

uprightness, virtue. **principles** basics, elements, essentials, fundamentals, laws, philosophy, theory.

print *n* **1** impression, imprint, indentation, mark, stamp. **2** characters, fount, lettering, letters, printing, text, type, typeface. **3** copy, duplicate, engraving, etching, facsimile, linocut, lithograph, monoprint, photograph, reproduction, silk screen, woodcut. ▷ PICTURE. ● *vb* **1** copy, impress, imprint, issue, publish, run off, stamp. **2** ▷ WRITE.

prior *adj* earlier, erstwhile, former, late, old, onetime, previous.

priority *n* first place, greater importance, precedence, preference, prerogative, right-of-way, seniority, superiority, urgency.

prise *vb* force, lever, prize, wrench.

prison *n old use* approved school, *old use* Borstal, cell, *sl* clink, custody, detention centre, dungeon, gaol, guardhouse, house of correction, jail, *inf* lock-up, *Amer* penitentiary, oubliette, reformatory, *sl* stir, youth custody centre. ▷ CAPTIVITY.

prisoner *n* captive, convict, detainee, *inf* gaolbird, hostage, inmate, internee, lifer, *inf* old lag, *inf* trusty.

privacy *n* concealment, isolation, monasticism, quietness, retirement, retreat, seclusion, secrecy, solitude.

private *adj* **1** exclusive, individual, particular, personal, privately owned, reserved. **2** classified, confidential, *inf* hush-hush, *inf* off the record, restricted, secret, top secret, undisclosed. **3** *a private meeting*. clandestine, closed, covert, intimate, surreptitious. **4** *a private hideaway*. concealed, hidden, inaccessible, isolated, little-known, quiet, secluded, sequestered, solitary, unknown, withdrawn. *Opp* PUBLIC.

privilege *n* advantage, benefit, concession, entitlement, exemption, freedom, immunity, licence, prerogative, right.

privileged *adj* **1** advantaged, authorized, élite, entitled, favoured, honoured, immune, licensed, powerful, protected, sanctioned, special, superior. **2** ▷ WEALTHY.

prize n accolade, award, jackpot, *inf* purse, reward, trophy, winnings. ● vb **1** appreciate, approve of, cherish, esteem, hold dear, like, rate highly, regard, revere, treasure, value. **2** ▷ PRISE.

probable adj believable, convincing, credible, expected, feasible, likely, *inf* odds-on, plausible, possible, predictable, presumed, undoubted, unquestioned. *Opp* IMPROBABLE.

probationer n apprentice, beginner, inexperienced worker, learner, novice, tiro.

probe n enquiry, examination, exploration, inquiry, investigation, research, scrutiny, study. ● vb **1** delve, dig, penetrate, plumb, poke, prod. **2** *probe a problem.* examine, explore, go into, inquire into, investigate, look into, research into, scrutinize, study.

problem n **1** brain-teaser, conundrum, enigma, mystery, *inf* poser, puzzle, question, riddle. **2** *a worrying problem.* burden, *inf* can of worms, complication, difficulty, dilemma, dispute, *inf* facer, *inf* headache, *inf* hornet's nest, predicament, quandary, set-back, snag, trouble, worry.

problematic adj complicated, controversial, debatable, difficult, disputed, doubtful, enigmatic, hard to deal with, *inf* iffy, intractable, moot (*point*), problematical, puzzling, questionable, sensitive, taxing, *inf* tricky, uncertain, unsettling, worrying. *Opp* STRAIGHTFORWARD.

procedure n approach, conduct, course of action, *inf* drill, formula, method, methodology, *Lat* modus operandi, plan of action, policy, practice, process, routine, scheme, strategy, system, technique, way.

proceed vb **1** advance, carry on, continue, follow, forge ahead, *inf* get going, go ahead, go on, make headway, make progress, move along, move forward, *inf* press on, progress.

2 arise, be derived, begin, develop, emerge, grow, originate, spring up, start. ▷ RESULT.

proceedings plur n **1** events, *inf* goings-on, happenings, things. **2** *legal proceedings.* action, lawsuit, procedure, process. **3** *proceedings of a meeting.* annals, business, dealings, *inf* doings, matters, minutes, records, report, transactions.

proceeds plur n earnings, gain, gate, income, profit, receipts, returns, revenue, takings. ▷ MONEY.

process n **1** function, method, operation, procedure, proceeding, system, technique. **2** *process of ageing.* course, development, evolution, experience, progression. ● vb **1** alter, change, convert, deal with, make usable, manage, modify, organize, prepare, refine, transform, treat. **2** ▷ PARADE.

procession n cavalcade, chain, column, cortège, file, line, march, march-past, motorcade, pageant, parade, sequence, string, succession, train.

proclaim vb **1** announce, advertise, assert, declare, give out, make known, profess, promulgate, pronounce, publish. **2** ▷ DECREE.

procrastinate vb be dilatory, be indecisive, dally, defer a decision, delay, *inf* dilly-dally, dither, *inf* drag your feet, equivocate, evade the issue, hesitate, *inf* hum and haw, pause, *inf* play for time, postpone, put things off, *inf* shilly-shally, stall, temporize, vacillate, waver.

procure vb acquire, buy, come by, find, get, *inf* get hold of, *inf* lay your hands on, obtain, *inf* pick up, purchase, requisition.

prod vb dig, elbow, goad, jab, nudge, poke, push, urge on. ▷ HIT, URGE.

prodigal adj excessive, extravagant, immoderate, improvident, irresponsible, lavish, profligate, reckless, self-indulgent, wasteful. *Opp* THRIFTY.

prodigy n curiosity, freak, genius, marvel, miracle, phenomenon, rarity, sensation, talent, virtuoso, *inf* whizz kid, wonder, *Ger* Wunderkind.

produce *n* crop, harvest, output, yield. ▷ PRODUCT. ● *vb* **1** assemble, bring out, cause, compose, conjure up, construct, create, cultivate, develop, fabricate, form, generate, give rise to, grow, initiate, invent, make, manufacture, originate, provoke, result in, supply, think up, turn out, yield. **2** *produce evidence.* advance, bring out, disclose, display, exhibit, furnish, introduce, offer, present, provide, put forward, reveal, show, supply, throw up. **3** *produce children.* bear, beget, breed, give birth to, raise, rear. **4** *produce a play.* direct, mount, present, put on, stage.

product *n* **1** artefact, by-product, commodity, end-product, goods, merchandise, output, produce, production. **2** consequence, effect, fruit, issue, outcome, result, upshot, yield.

productive *adj* **1** beneficial, busy, constructive, creative, effective, efficient, gainful (*employment*), inventive, profitable, profitmaking, remunerative, rewarding, useful, valuable, worthwhile. **2** *a productive garden.* abundant, bounteous, bountiful, fecund, fertile, fruitful, lush, prolific, vigorous. *Opp* UNPRODUCTIVE.

profess *vb* **1** affirm, announce, assert, asseverate, aver, confess, confirm, declare, maintain, state, vow. **2** *profess to be an expert.* allege, claim, make out, pretend, purport.

profession *n* **1** business, calling, career, craft, employment, job, line of work, métier, occupation, trade, vocation, work. **2** *profession of love.* acknowledgement, affirmation, announcement, assertion, avowal, confession, declaration, statement, testimony.

professional *adj* **1** able, authorized, educated, experienced, expert, knowledgeable, licensed, official, proficient, qualified, skilled, trained. *Opp* AMATEUR. **2** full-time, paid. **3** *professional work.* businesslike, competent, conscientious, efficient, masterly, proper, skilful, thorough, well-done.

Opp UNPROFESSIONAL. ● *n* expert, professional player, professional worker.

proficient *adj* able, accomplished, adept, capable, competent, efficient, expert, gifted, professional, skilled, talented. *Opp* INCOMPETENT.

profile *n* **1** contour, outline, shape, side view, silhouette. **2** *personal profile.* account, biography, *Lat* curriculum vitae, sketch, study.

profit *n* advantage, benefit, excess, gain, interest, proceeds, return, revenue, surplus, yield. ● *vb* **1** advance, avail, benefit, further the interests of, pay, serve. ▷ HELP. **2** *profit from a sale.* capitalize (on), *inf* cash in, *inf* make a killing, make a profit, make money. **profit by, profit from** ▷ EXPLOIT.

profitable *adj* advantageous, beneficial, commercial, enriching, fruitful, gainful, lucrative, money-making, paying, productive, profit-making, remunerative, rewarding, useful, valuable, well-paid, worthwhile. *Opp* UNPROFITABLE.

profiteer *n* black-marketeer, exploiter, extortionist, racketeer. ● *vb* exploit, extort, fleece, overcharge.

profligate *adj* **1** abandoned, debauched, degenerate, depraved, dissolute, immoral, libertine, licentious, loose, perverted, promiscuous, sinful, sybaritic, unprincipled, wanton. ▷ WICKED. **2** extravagant, prodigal, reckless, spendthrift, wasteful.

profound *adj* **1** deep, heartfelt, intense, sincere. **2** *a profound discussion.* abstruse, arcane, erudite, esoteric, imponderable, informed, intellectual, knowledgeable, learned, penetrating, philosophical, recondite, sagacious, scholarly, serious, thoughtful, wise. **3** *profound silence.* absolute, complete, extreme, fundamental, perfect, thorough, total, unqualified. *Opp* SUPERFICIAL.

profuse *adj* abundant, ample, bountiful, copious, extravagant, exuberant, generous, lavish, luxuriant, plentiful, productive, prolific, superabundant, thriving, unsparing, unstinting. *Opp* MEAN, SPARSE.

programme *n* **1** agenda, bill of fare, calendar, curriculum, *inf* line-up, listing, menu, plan, routine, schedule, scheme, syllabus, timetable. **2** *a TV programme*. broadcast, performance, presentation, production, show, transmission.

progress *n* **1** advance, breakthrough, development, evolution, forward movement, furtherance, gain, growth, headway, improvement, march (*of time*), maturation, progression, *inf* step forward. **2** journey, route, travels, way. **3** *progress in a career*. advancement, betterment, elevation, promotion, rise, *inf* step up. ● *vb* advance, *inf* come on, develop, *inf* forge ahead, go forward, go on, make headway, make progress, move forward, press forward, press on, proceed, prosper. ▷ IMPROVE. *Opp* REGRESS, STAGNATE.

progression *n* **1** ▷ PROGRESS. **2** chain, concatenation, course, flow, order, row, sequence, series, string, succession.

progressive *adj* **1** accelerating, advancing, continuing, continuous, developing, escalating, gradual, growing, increasing, ongoing, steady. **2** *progressive ideas*. advanced, avantgarde, contemporary, dynamic, enterprising, forward-looking, *inf* go-ahead, modernistic, radical, reformist, revisionist, revolutionary, up-to-date. *Opp* CONSERVATIVE.

prohibit *vb* ban, bar, block, censor, check, *inf* cut out, debar, disallow, exclude, foil, forbid, hinder, impede, inhibit, interdict, make illegal, outlaw, place an embargo on, preclude, prevent, proscribe, restrict, rule out, shut out, stop, taboo, veto. *Opp* ALLOW.

prohibitive *adj* discouraging, excessive, exorbitant, impossible, *inf* out of reach, out of the question, unreasonable, unthinkable.

project *n* activity, assignment, contract, design, enterprise, idea, job, piece of research, plan, programme, proposal, scheme, task, undertaking, venture. ● *vb* **1** concoct, contrive, design, devise, invent, plan, propose, scheme, think up. **2** beetle, bulge, extend, jut out, overhang, protrude, stand out, stick out. **3** *project into space*. cast, *inf* chuck, fling, hurl, launch, lob, propel, shoot, throw. **4** *project light*. cast, flash, shine, throw out. **5** *project future profits*. estimate, forecast, predict.

proliferate *vb* burgeon, flourish, grow, increase, multiply, mushroom, reproduce, thrive.

prolific *adj* **1** abundant, bounteous, bountiful, copious, fruitful, numerous, plenteous, profuse, rich. **2** *a prolific writer*. creative, fertile, productive. *Opp* UNPRODUCTIVE.

prolong *vb* delay, *inf* drag out, draw out, elongate, extend, increase, keep up, lengthen, make longer, *inf* pad out, protract, *inf* spin out, stretch out. *Opp* SHORTEN.

prominent *adj* **1** conspicuous, discernible, distinguishable, evident, eye-catching, large, notable, noticeable, obtrusive, obvious, pronounced, recognizable, salient, significant, striking. *Opp* INCONSPICUOUS. **2** bulging, jutting out, projecting, protruding, protuberant, sticking out. **3** celebrated, distinguished, eminent, familiar, foremost, illustrious, important, leading, major, much-publicized, noted, outstanding, public, renowned. ▷ FAMOUS. *Opp* UNKNOWN.

promiscuous *adj* casual, haphazard, indiscriminate, irresponsible, non-selective, random, undiscriminating. ▷ IMMORAL. *Opp* MORAL.

promise *n* **1** assurance, commitment, compact, contract, covenant, guarantee, oath, pledge, undertaking, vow, word, word of honour. **2** *actor with promise*. capability, expectation(s), latent ability, potential, promising qualities, talent. ● *vb* **1** agree, assure, commit yourself, consent, contract, engage, give a promise, give your word, guarantee, pledge, swear, take an oath, undertake, vow. **2** *The clouds promise rain.* augur, *old use* betoken, forebode, foretell, hint at, indicate, presage, prophesy, show signs of, suggest.

promising *adj* auspicious, budding, encouraging, favourable, hopeful, likely, optimistic, propitious, talented, *inf* up-and-coming.

promontory *n* cape, foreland, headland, peninsula, point, projection, ridge, spit, spur.

promote *vb* **1** advance, elevate, exalt, give promotion, move up, prefer, raise, upgrade. **2** *promote a product.* advertise, back, boost, champion, encourage, endorse, further, help, make known, market, patronize, *inf* plug, popularize, publicize, *inf* push, recommend, sell, speak for, sponsor, support. ▷ HELP.

promoter *n* backer, champion, patron, sponsor, supporter.

promotion *n* **1** advancement, elevation, preferment, rise, upgrading. **2** *promotion of a product.* advertising, backing, encouragement, furtherance, marketing, publicity, recommendation, selling, sponsorship.

prompt *adj* eager, efficient, expeditious, immediate, instantaneous, on time, punctual, timely, unhesitating, willing. ▷ QUICK. *Opp* UNPUNCTUAL. ● *n* cue, line, reminder. ● *vb* advise, coax, egg on, encourage, exhort, help, incite, influence, inspire, jog the memory, motivate, nudge, persuade, prod, provoke, remind, rouse, spur, stimulate, urge.

prone *adj* **1** face down, flat, horizontal, lying, on your front, prostrate, stretched out. *Opp* SUPINE. **2** *prone to colds.* apt, disposed, given, inclined, liable, likely, predisposed, subject, susceptible, tending, vulnerable. *Opp* IMMUNE.

prong *n* point, spike, spur, tine.

pronounce *vb* **1** articulate, aspirate, enunciate, express, put into words, say, sound, speak, utter, vocalize, voice. **2** *pronounce judgement.* announce, assert, asseverate, declare,

decree, judge, make known, proclaim, state. ▷ SPEAK.

pronounced *adj* clear, conspicuous, decided, definite, distinct, evident, inescapable, marked, noticeable, obvious, prominent, recognizable, striking, unambiguous, undisguised, unmistakable, well-defined.

pronunciation *n* accent, articulation, delivery, diction, elocution, enunciation, inflection, intonation, modulation, speech.

proof *n* **1** authentication, certification, confirmation, corroboration, demonstration, evidence, facts, grounds, substantiation, testimony, validation, verification. **2** *the proof of the pudding.* criterion, judgement, measure, test, trial.

prop *n* brace, buttress, crutch, post, stay, strut, support, truss, upright. ● *vb* **1** bolster, brace, buttress, hold up, reinforce, shore up, support, sustain. **2** lean, rest, stand.

propaganda *n* advertising, brainwashing, disinformation, indoctrination, persuasion, publicity.

propagate *vb* **1** breed, generate, increase, multiply, produce, proliferate, reproduce. **2** *propagate ideas.* circulate, disseminate, pass on, promote, promulgate, publish, spread, transmit. **3** *propagate plants.* grow from seed, layer, sow, take cuttings.

propel *vb* drive, force, impel, launch, move, *inf* pitchfork, push, send, set in motion, shoot, spur, thrust, urge.

propeller *n* rotor, screw, vane.

proper *adj* **1** becoming, conventional, decent, decorous, delicate, dignified, formal, genteel, gentlemanly, grave, in good taste, ladylike, modest, polite, *derog* prim, *derog* prudish, respectable, sedate, seemly, serious, solemn, tactful, tasteful. **2** acceptable, accepted, advisable, apposite, appropriate, apropos, apt, deserved, fair, fitting, just, lawful, legal, normal, orthodox, rational, sensible, suitable, unexceptionable, usual, valid. **3** *the proper time.* accurate, correct, exact, precise, right. **4** *the proper place.* allocated, distinctive, individual, own, particular, reserved, separate, special, unique. *Opp* IMPROPER.

property *n* **1** assets, belongings, capital, chattels, effects, fortune, *inf* gear, goods, holdings, patrimony, possessions, resources, riches, wealth. **2** acreage, buildings, estate, land, premises. **3** attribute, characteristic, feature, hallmark, idiosyncrasy, oddity, peculiarity, quality, quirk, trait.

prophecy *n* augury, crystal-gazing, divination, forecast, foretelling, fortune-telling, oracle, prediction, prognosis, prognostication, vaticination.

prophesy *vb* augur, bode, divine, forecast, foresee, foreshadow, foretell, portend, predict, presage, prognosticate, promise, vaticinate.

prophet *n* clairvoyant, forecaster, fortune-teller, oracle, seer, sibyl, soothsayer.

prophetic *adj* apocalyptic, farseeing, oracular, predictive, prescient, prognostic, prophesying, sibylline.

propitious *adj* advantageous, auspicious, favourable, fortunate, happy, lucky, opportune, promising, providential, rosy, timely, well-timed.

proportion *n* **1** balance, comparison, correlation, correspondence, distribution, equivalence, ratio, statistical relationship. **2** allocation, fraction, part, percentage, piece, quota, ration, section, share. ▷ NUMBER, QUANTITY. **proportions** dimensions, extent, magnitude, measurements, size, volume.

proportional *adj* analogous, balanced, commensurate, comparable, corresponding, equitable, in proportion, just, proportionate, relative, symmetrical. *Opp* DISPROPORTIONATE.

proposal *n* bid, declaration, draft, motion, offer, plan, project, proposition, recommendation, scheme, statement, suggestion, tender.

propose *vb* **1** advance, ask for, *inf* come up with, present, propound, put forward, recommend, submit, suggest. **2** aim, have in mind, intend, mean, offer, plan, purpose. **3** *propose a candidate.* nominate, put forward, put up, sponsor.

propriety *n* appropriateness, aptness, correctness, courtesy, decency, decorum, delicacy, dignity, etiquette, fairness, fitness, formality, gentility, good form, good manners, gravity, justice, modesty, politeness, *derog* prudishness, refinement, respectability, sedateness, seemliness, sensitivity, suitability, tact, tastefulness. *Opp* IMPROPRIETY.

prosaic *adj* **1** clear, direct, down to earth, factual, matter-of-fact, plain, simple, straightforward, to the point, unadorned, understandable, unemotional, unsentimental, unvarnished. **2** [*derog*] characterless, clichéd, commonplace, dry, dull, flat, hackneyed, lifeless, monotonous, mundane, pedestrian, prosy, routine, stereotyped, trite, unfeeling, unimaginative, uninspired, uninspiring, unpoetic, unromantic. ▷ ORDINARY. *Opp* POETIC.

prosecute *vb* **1** accuse, arraign, bring an action against, bring to trial, charge, indict, institute legal proceedings against, prefer charges against, put on trial, sue, take legal proceedings against, take to court. **2** ▷ PURSUE.

prospect *n* **1** aspect, landscape, outlook, panorama, perspective, scene, seascape, sight, spectacle, view, vista. **2** *prospect of fine weather.* anticipation, chance, expectation, hope, likelihood, opportunity, possibility, probability, promise. ● *vb* explore, quest, search, survey.

prospective *adj* anticipated, approaching, awaited, coming, expected, forthcoming, future, imminent, impending, intended, likely, looked-for, negotiable, pending, possible, potential, probable.

prospectus *n* announcement, brochure, catalogue, leaflet, manifesto, pamphlet, programme, scheme, syllabus.

proud

prosper vb become prosperous, be successful, inf boom, burgeon, develop, do well, fare well, flourish, inf get ahead, inf get on, inf go from strength to strength, grow, inf make good, inf make your fortune, profit, progress, strengthen, succeed, thrive. Opp FAIL.

prosperity n affluence, inf bonanza, inf boom, good fortune, growth, opulence, plenty, profitability, riches, success, wealth.

prosperous adj affluent, inf blooming, inf booming, buoyant, expanding, flourishing, fruitful, healthy, moneyed, moneymaking, productive, profitable, prospering, rich, successful, thriving, vigorous, wealthy, inf well-heeled, well-off, well-to-do. Opp UNSUCCESSFUL.

prostitute n old use bawd, call girl, old use camp follower, old use courtesan, old use harlot, inf hooker, streetwalker, old use strumpet, inf tart, toy boy, trollop, whore. ● vb cheapen, debase, degrade, demean, devalue, lower, misuse.

prostrate adj ▷ OVERCOME, PRONE. ● vb prostrate yourself abase yourself, bow, kneel, kowtow, lie flat, submit. ▷ GROVEL.

protagonist n chief actor, contender, contestant, hero, heroine, lead, leading figure, principal, title role.

protect vb care for, cherish, conserve, defend, escort, guard, harbour, insulate, keep, keep safe, look after, mind, preserve, provide cover for, safeguard, screen, secure, shield, stand up for, support, take care of, tend, watch over. Opp ENDANGER, NEGLECT.

protection n 1 care, conservation, custody, defence, guardianship, patronage, preservation, safekeeping, safety, security, tutelage. 2 barrier, buffer, bulwark, cloak, cover, guard, insulation, screen, shelter, shield.

protective adj 1 fireproof, insulating, preservative, protecting, sheltering, shielding, waterproof. 2 protective parents. careful, defensive, heedful, jealous, paternalistic, possessive, solicitous, vigilant, watchful.

protector n benefactor, bodyguard, champion, defender, guard, guardian, sl minder, patron.

protest n 1 complaint, cry of disapproval, demur, demurral, dissent, exception, grievance, inf gripe, inf grouse, grumble, objection, opposition, outcry, protestation, remonstrance. 2 inf demo, demonstration, march, rally. ● vb 1 appeal, argue, challenge a decision, complain, cry out, expostulate, express disapproval, fulminate, inf gripe, inf grouse, grumble, make a protest, inf moan, object, remonstrate, take exception. 2 demonstrate, inf hold a demo, march. 3 protest your innocence. affirm, assert, asseverate, aver, declare, insist on, profess, swear.

protracted adj endless, extended, interminable, long-drawn-out, long-winded, never-ending, prolonged, spun-out. ▷ LONG. Opp SHORT.

protrude vb balloon, bulge, extend, jut out, overhang, poke out, project, stand out, stick out, stick up, swell.

protruding adj bulbous, bulging, distended, gibbous, humped, jutting, overhanging, projecting, prominent, protuberant, swollen, tumescent.

proud adj 1 appreciative, delighted, glad, gratified, happy, honoured, pleased, satisfied. 2 a proud bearing. brave, dignified, independent, self-respecting. 3 a proud history. august, distinguished, glorious, great, honourable, illustrious, noble, reputable, respected, splendid, worthy. 4 [derog] arrogant, inf big-headed, boastful, bumptious, inf cocksure, inf cocky, conceited, disdainful, egocentric, egotistical, grand, haughty, inf high and mighty, immodest, lordly, narcissistic, self-centred, self-important, self-satisfied, smug, snobbish, inf snooty, inf stuck-up, supercilious, inf swollen-headed, inf toffee-nosed, vain, vainglorious. Opp MODEST.

provable adj demonstrable, verifiable. Opp UNPROVABLE.

prove vb ascertain, assay, attest, authenticate, inf bear out, certify, check, confirm, corroborate, demonstrate, establish, explain, justify, show to be true, substantiate, test, verify. Opp DISPROVE.

proven adj accepted, proved, reliable, tried and tested, trustworthy, undoubted, unquestionable, valid, verified. Opp DOUBTFUL, THEORETICAL.

proverb n adage, maxim, old use saw. ▷ SAYING.

proverbial adj aphoristic, axiomatic, clichéd, conventional, customary, famous, legendary, time-honoured, traditional, well-known.

provide vb afford, allot, allow, arrange for, cater, contribute, donate, endow, equip, inf fix up with, inf fork out, furnish, give, grant, lay on, lend, make provision, offer, present, produce, purvey, spare, stock, supply, yield.

providence n destiny, divine intervention, fate, fortune, karma, kismet.

provident adj careful, economical, far-sighted, forward-looking, frugal, judicious, prudent, thrifty.

providential adj felicitous, fortunate, happy, lucky, opportune, timely.

provincial adj 1 local, regional. Opp NATIONAL. 2 [derog] backward, boorish, bucolic, insular, narrow-minded, parochial, rural, rustic, small-minded, uncultivated, uncultured, unsophisticated. Opp COSMOPOLITAN.

provisional adj conditional, interim, stopgap, temporary, tentative, transitional. Opp DEFINITIVE, PERMANENT.

provisions plur n food, foodstuff, groceries, provender, rations, requirements, stocks, stores, subsistence, supplies, old use victuals.

proviso n condition, exception, limitation, provision, qualification, requirement, restriction, rider, stipulation.

provocation n inf aggravation, cause, challenge, grievance, grounds, incentive, incitement, inducement, justification, motivation, motive, reason, stimulus, taunts, teasing.

provocative adj 1 alluring, arousing, erotic, pornographic, inf raunchy, seductive, sensual, sensuous, inf sexy, tantalizing, tempting. 2 inf aggravating, annoying, infuriating, irksome, irritating, maddening, provoking, teasing, vexing.

provoke vb 1 activate, arouse, awaken, bring about, call forth, cause, elicit, encourage, excite, foment, generate, give rise to, induce, initiate, inspire, instigate, kindle, motivate, promote, prompt, spark off, start, stimulate, stir up, urge on, work up. 2 inf aggravate, anger, annoy, enrage, exasperate, gall, inf get on your nerves, goad, incense, incite, inflame, infuriate, insult, irk, irritate, madden, offend, outrage, pique, rile, rouse, tease, torment, upset, vex, inf wind up, worry. Opp PACIFY.

prowess n 1 ability, adeptness, adroitness, aptitude, cleverness, competence, dexterity, excellence, expertise, genius, mastery, proficiency, skill, talent. 2 prowess in battle. boldness, bravery, courage, daring, doughtiness, gallantry, heroism, mettle, spirit, valour.

prowl vb creep, lurk, roam, rove, skulk, slink, sneak, steal. ▷ WALK.

proximity n 1 closeness, nearness, propinquity. 2 locality, neighbourhood, vicinity.

prudent adj advisable, careful, cautious, circumspect, discreet, economical, far-sighted, frugal, judicious, politic, proper, provident, reasonable, sagacious, sage, sensible, shrewd, thoughtful, thrifty, vigilant, watchful, wise. Opp UNWISE.

prudish adj decorous, easily shocked, illiberal, intolerant, narrow-minded, old-fashioned, inf old-maidish, priggish, prim, inf prissy, proper, puritanical, rigid, shockable, strait-laced, strict. *Opp* BROAD-MINDED.

prune *vb* clip, cut back, lop, pare down, trim. ▷ CUT.

pry *vb* be curious, be inquisitive, be nosy, delve, *inf* ferret, inquire, interfere, intrude, investigate, meddle, *inf* nose about, peer, poke about, *inf* poke your nose in, search, *inf* snoop, *inf* stick your nose in. **prying** ▷ INQUISITIVE.

pseudonym *n* alias, assumed name, false name, incognito, nickname, *Fr* nom de plume, pen-name, sobriquet, stage name.

psychic *adj* clairvoyant, extrasensory, magical, mental, metaphysical, mystic, occult, preternatural, psychical, spiritual, supernatural, telepathic. ● *n* astrologer, clairvoyant, crystal-gazer, fortune-teller, medium, mind-reader, spiritualist, telepathist.

psychological *adj* cerebral, emotional, mental, subconscious, subjective, subliminal, unconscious. *Opp* PHYSIOLOGICAL.

pub *n old use* alehouse, bar, *sl* boozer, cocktail lounge, *old use* hostelry, inn, *inf* local, public house, saloon, tavern, wine bar.

puberty *n* adolescence, growing-up, juvenescence, pubescence, sexual maturity, *inf* teens.

public *adj* **1** accessible, available, common, familiar, free, known, open, shared, unconcealed, unrestricted, visible, well-known. **2** *public support.* civic, civil, collective, communal, community, democratic, general, majority, national, popular, social, universal. **3** *a public figure.* ▷ PROMINENT. *Opp* PRIVATE. ● *n the public.* citizens, the community, the country, the nation, people, the populace, society, voters.

publication *n* **1** appearance, issuing, printing, production. ▷ BOOK, MAGAZINE. **2** advertising, announcement, broadcasting, declaration, disclosure, dissemination, proclamation, promulgation, publicizing, reporting.

publicity *n* **1** attention, *inf* ballyhoo, fame, *inf* hype, limelight, notoriety. **2** advertising, marketing, promotion. ▷ ADVERTISEMENT.

publicize *vb* advertise, *sl* hype, *inf* plug, promote, *old use* puff. ▷ PUBLISH.

publish *vb* **1** bring out, circulate, issue, make available, print, produce, put on sale, release. **2** *publish secrets.* advertise, announce, break the news about, broadcast, communicate, declare, disclose, disseminate, divulge, issue a statement about, *inf* leak, make known, make public, proclaim, promulgate, publicize, *inf* put about, report, reveal, spread.

pucker *vb* compress, contract, crease, crinkle, draw together, purse, screw up, squeeze, tighten, wrinkle.

puerile *adj* babyish, boyish, childish, immature, infantile, juvenile. ▷ SILLY.

puff *n* **1** blast, blow, breath, draught, flurry, gust, whiff, wind. **2** *a puff of smoke.* cloud, wisp. ● *vb* **1** blow, breathe heavily, gasp, huff, pant, wheeze. **2** *puff at a cigar.* inf drag, draw, inhale, pull, smoke, suck. **3** *sails puffed by the wind.* balloon, billow, distend, enlarge, inflate, rise, swell.

pugnacious *adj* aggressive, antagonistic, argumentative, bellicose, belligerent, combative, contentious, disputatious, excitable, fractious, hostile, hottempered, litigious, militant, unfriendly, warlike. ▷ QUARRELSOME. *Opp* PEACEABLE.

pull *vb* **1** drag, draw, haul, lug, tow, trail. *Opp* PUSH. **2** jerk, pluck, rip, tug, wrench, *inf* yank. **3** *pull a tooth.* extract, pull out, remove, take out. **pull off** ▷ DETACH. **pull out** ▷ WITHDRAW. **pull round** ▷ RECOVER. **pull someone's leg** ▷ TEASE. **pull through** ▷ RECOVER. **pull together** ▷ COOPERATE. **pull up** ▷ HALT.

pulp *n* mash, mush, paste, pap, purée. ● *vb* crush, liquidize, mash, pound, pulverize, purée, smash, squash.

pulsate vb beat, drum, oscillate, palpitate, pound, pulse, quiver, reverberate, throb, tick, vibrate.

pulse n beat, drumming, oscillation, pounding, pulsation, rhythm, throb, ticking, vibration.

pump vb drain, draw off, empty, force, raise, siphon. **pump up** blow up, fill, inflate.

punch vb 1 beat, sl biff, box, inf clout, cuff, jab, poke, prod, pummel, slog, sl slug, sl sock, strike, thump. ▷ HIT. 2 ▷ PIERCE.

punctual adj in good time, inf on the dot, on time, prompt. Opp UNPUNCTUAL.

punctuate vb 1 insert punctuation, point. 2 punctuated by applause. break, interrupt, intersperse, inf pepper.

punctuation n marks, points, stops. □ accent, apostrophe, asterisk, bracket, caret, cedilla, colon, comma, dash, exclamation mark, full stop, hyphen, question mark, quotation marks, speech marks, semicolon.

puncture n blow-out, burst, burst tyre, inf flat, flat tyre, hole, leak, opening, perforation, pin-prick, rupture. ● vb deflate, go through, let down, penetrate, perforate, pierce, prick, rupture.

pungent adj 1 aromatic, hot, peppery, piquant, seasoned, sharp, spicy, strong, tangy. 2 acid, acrid, astringent, caustic, inf chemically, harsh, sour, stinging. 3 pungent criticism. biting, bitter, incisive, mordant, sarcastic, scathing, trenchant.

punish vb castigate, chasten, chastise, correct, discipline, exact retribution from, impose punishment on, inflict punishment on, inf make an example of, pay back, penalize, inf rap over the knuckles, scold, inf teach someone a lesson.

punishment n chastisement, correction, discipline, forfeit, imposition, inf just deserts, penalty, punitive measure, retribution, revenge, sentence. □ banishment, beating, the birch, old use Borstal, the cane, capital punishment, cashiering, confiscation of property, corporal punishment, detention, excommunication, execution, exile, fine, flogging, gaol, inf hiding, imprisonment, jail, keelhauling, lashing, pillory, prison, probation, scourging, spanking, the stocks, torture, whipping.

punitive adj disciplinary, penal, retaliatory, retributive, revengeful, vindictive.

puny adj diminutive, dwarf, feeble, frail, sickly, stunted, underdeveloped, undernourished, undersized. ▷ SMALL. Opp LARGE, STRONG.

pupil n apprentice, beginner, disciple, follower, learner, novice, protégé(e), scholar, schoolboy, schoolchild, schoolgirl, student, tiro.

puppet n doll, dummy, finger-puppet, glove-puppet, hand-puppet, marionette, string-puppet.

purchase n 1 acquisition, inf buy (a good buy), investment. 2 grasp, grip, hold, leverage, support. ● vb acquire, buy, get, invest in, obtain, pay for, procure, secure.

pure adj 1 authentic, genuine, neat, real, solid, sterling, straight, unadulterated, unalloyed, undiluted. 2 pure food. eatable, germ-free, hygienic, natural, pasteurized, uncontaminated, untainted, wholesome. 3 pure water. clean, clear, distilled, drinkable, fresh, potable, sterile, unpolluted. 4 pure in morals. blameless, chaste, decent, good, impeccable, innocent, irreproachable, maidenly, modest, moral, proper, sinless, stainless, virginal, virtuous. 5 pure genius. absolute, complete, downright, inf out-and-out, perfect, sheer, thorough, total, true, unmitigated, unqualified, utter. 6 pure science. abstract, academic, conjectural, conceptual, hypothetical, speculative, theoretical. Opp IMPURE, PRACTICAL.

purgative n aperient, cathartic, enema, laxative, purge.

purge vb 1 clean out, cleanse, clear, depurate, empty, purify, wash out. 2 purge your opponents. eject, eliminate, eradicate, expel, get rid of, liquidate, oust, remove, root out.

purify *vb* clarify, clean, cleanse, decontaminate, depurate, disinfect, distil, filter, fumigate, make pure, purge, refine, sanitize, sterilize.

puritan *n* fanatic, *derog* killjoy, moralist, *derog* prude, zealot.

puritanical *adj* ascetic, austere, moralistic, narrow-minded, pietistic, prim, proper, prudish, rigid, self-denying, self-disciplined, severe, stern, stiff-necked, strait-laced, strict, temperate, unbending, uncompromising. *Opp* HEDONISTIC.

purpose *n* **1** aim, ambition, aspiration, design, end, goal, hope, intent, intention, motivation, motive, object, objective, outcome, plan, point, rationale, result, target, wish. **2** determination, devotion, drive, firmness, persistence, resolution, resolve, steadfastness, tenacity, will, zeal. **3** *purpose of a tool*. advantage, application, benefit, good (*what's the good of it?*), point, practicality, use, usefulness, utility, value. ● *vb* ▷ INTEND.

purposeful *adj* calculated, decided, decisive, deliberate, determined, devoted, firm, persistent, positive, resolute, steadfast, *derog* stubborn, tenacious, unwavering, wilful, zealous. ▷ INTENTIONAL. *Opp* HESITANT.

purposeless *adj* aimless, bootless, empty, gratuitous, meaningless, pointless, senseless, unnecessary, useless, vacuous, wanton. *Opp* MEANINGFUL, USEFUL.

purposely *adv* consciously, deliberately, intentionally, knowingly, on purpose, wilfully.

purse *n* bag, handbag, moneybag, pocketbook, pouch, wallet.

pursue *vb* **1** chase, follow, go after, go in pursuit of, harry, hound, hunt, keep up with, run after, shadow, stalk, *inf* tail, trace, track down, trail. **2** aim for, aspire to, be committed to, carry on, conduct, continue, dedicate yourself to, engage in, follow up, *inf* go for, persevere in, persist in, proceed with, prosecute, *inf* stick with, strive for, try for. **3** *pursue truth*. inquire into, investigate, quest after, search for, seek.

pursuit *n* **1** chase, chasing, following, harrying, *inf* hue and cry, hunt, hunting, pursuing, shadowing, stalking, tracking down, trail. **2** *leisure pursuits*. activity, employment, enthusiasm, hobby, interest, obsession, occupation, pastime, pleasure, speciality, specialization.

push *vb* **1** advance, drive, force, hustle, impel, jostle, move, nudge, poke, press, prod, propel, set in motion, shove, thrust. **2** *push a button*. depress, press. **3** *push into a space*. compress, cram, crowd, crush, insert, jam, pack, put, ram, squash, squeeze. **4** *push someone to act*. browbeat, bully, coerce, compel, constrain, dragoon, encourage, force, hurry, importune, incite, induce, influence, *inf* lean on, motivate, nag, persuade, pressurize, prompt, put pressure on, spur, stimulate, urge. **5** *push a new product*. advertise, boost, make known, market, *inf* plug, promote, publicize. *Opp* PULL. **push around** ▷ BULLY. **push off** ▷ DEPART. **push on** ▷ ADVANCE.

put *vb* **1** arrange, assign, commit, consign, deploy, deposit, dispose, fix, hang, lay, leave, locate, park, place, *inf* plonk, position, rest, set down, settle, situate, stand, station. **2** *put a question*. express, formulate, frame, phrase, say, state, utter, voice, word, write. **3** *put a proposal*. advance, bring forward, offer, outline, present, propose, submit, suggest, tender. **4** *put blame on someone*. attach, attribute, cast, fix, impose, inflict, lay, *inf* pin. **put across** ▷ COMMUNICATE. **put back** ▷ RETURN. **put by** ▷ SAVE. **put down** ▷ KILL, SUPPRESS. **put in** ▷ INSERT, INSTALL. **put off** ▷ POSTPONE. **put out** ▷ EJECT, EXTINGUISH. **put over** ▷ COMMUNICATE. **put right** ▷ REPAIR. **put someone up** ▷ ACCOMMODATE. **put up** ▷ RAISE. **put your foot down** ▷ INSIST. **put your foot in it** ▷ BLUNDER.

putative *adj* alleged, assumed, conjectural, presumed, reputed, rumoured, supposed, supposititious.

putrefy vb decay, decompose, go bad, go off, moulder, rot, spoil.

putrid adj bad, corrupt, decaying, decomposing, fetid, foul, mouldy, putrefying, rotting, spoilt.

puzzle n inf brain-teaser, conundrum, difficulty, dilemma, enigma, mystery, paradox, inf poser, problem, quandary, question, riddle. ● vb baffle, bewilder, confound, confuse, inf floor, inf flummox, mystify, nonplus, perplex, set thinking, inf stump, inf stymie, worry. **puzzle out** ▷ SOLVE. **puzzle over** ▷ CONSIDER.

puzzling adj ambiguous, baffling, bewildering, confusing, cryptic, enigmatic, impenetrable, inexplicable, insoluble, inf mind-boggling, mysterious, mystifying, perplexing, strange, unaccountable, unanswerable, unfathomable, worrying. Opp STRAIGHTFORWARD.

pygmy adj dwarf, lilliputian, midget, tiny. ▷ SMALL.

Q

quadrangle *n* cloisters, courtyard, enclosure, *inf* quad, yard.

quagmire *n* bog, fen, marsh, mire, morass, mud, quicksand, *old use* slough, swamp.

quail *vb* back away, be apprehensive, blench, cower, cringe, falter, flinch, quake, recoil, show fear, shrink, tremble, wince.

quaint *adj* antiquated, antique, charming, curious, eccentric, fanciful, fantastic, odd, offbeat, old-fashioned, old-world, outlandish, peculiar, picturesque, strange, *inf* twee, unconventional, unexpected, unfamiliar, unusual, whimsical.

quake *vb* convulse, heave, move, quaver, quiver, rock, shake, shiver, shudder, stagger, sway, tremble, vibrate, wobble.

qualification *n* **1** ability, aptitude, capability, capacity, certification, competence, eligibility, experience, fitness, *inf* know-how, knowledge, proficiency, quality, skill, suitability, training. **2** certificate, degree, diploma, doctorate, first degree, Master's degree, matriculation. **3** *agree without qualification.* caveat, condition, exception, limitation, modification, proviso, reservation, restriction.

qualified *adj* **1** able, capable, certificated, competent, equipped, experienced, expert, fit, practised, professional, proficient, skilled, trained, well-informed. *Opp* UNSKILLED. **2** *qualified applicants.* appropriate, eligible, suitable. **3** *qualified praise.* cautious, conditional, equivocal, guarded, half-hearted, limited, modified, provisional, reserved, restricted. *Opp* UNCONDITIONAL.

qualify *vb* **1** authorize, empower, entitle, equip, fit, make eligible, permit, sanction. **2** become eligible, get through, *inf* make the grade, meet requirements, pass. **3** *qualify your praise.* abate, lessen, limit, mitigate, moderate, modulate, restrain, restrict, soften, temper, weaken.

quality *n* **1** calibre, class, condition, excellence, grade, rank, sort, standard, status, value, worth. **2** *personal qualities.* attribute, characteristic, distinction, feature, mark, peculiarity, property, trait.

quandary *n inf* catch-22, *inf* cleft stick, confusion, difficulty, dilemma, perplexity, plight, predicament, uncertainty.

quantity *n* aggregate, amount, bulk, consignment, dosage, dose, expanse, extent, length, load, lot, magnitude, mass, measurement, number, part, portion, proportion, quantum, sum, total, volume, weight. ▷ MEASURE.

quarrel *n* altercation, argument, bickering, clash, conflict, confrontation, contention, controversy, debate, difference, disagreement, discord, disharmony, dispute, dissension, division, feud, *inf* hassle, misunderstanding, row, *inf* ructions, rupture, *inf* scene, schism, *inf* slanging match, split, squabble, strife, *inf* tiff, vendetta, wrangle. ● *vb* argue, *inf* be at loggerheads, *inf* be at odds, bicker, clash, conflict, contend, *inf* cross swords, differ, disagree, dispute, dissent, *inf* fall out, feud, haggle, misunderstand one another, *inf* row, squabble, wrangle. ▷ FIGHT. **quarrel with** ▷ DISPUTE.

quarrelsome *adj* aggressive, angry, argumentative, bad-tempered, cantankerous, choleric, contentious, contrary, cross, defiant, disagreeable, dyspeptic, explosive, fractious, impatient, irascible, irritable, peevish, petulant, querulous, quick-tempered, *inf* stroppy, testy, truculent, unfriendly, volatile ▷ PUGNACIOUS. *Opp* PEACEABLE.

quarry *n* 1 game, kill, object, prey, victim. 2 excavation, mine, pit, working. ● *vb* dig out, excavate, extract, mine.

quarter *n* area, district, division, locality, neighbourhood, part, region, section, sector, territory, vicinity, zone. ● *vb* accommodate, billet, board, house, lodge, *inf* put up, shelter, station. **quarters** abode, accommodation, barracks, billet, domicile, dwelling-place, home, housing, living quarters, lodgings, residence, rooms, shelter.

quash *vb* 1 abolish, annul, cancel, invalidate, overrule, overthrow, reject, rescind, reverse, revoke. 2 ▷ QUELL.

quaver *vb* falter, fluctuate, oscillate, pulsate, quake, quiver, shake, shiver, shudder, tremble, vibrate, waver.

quay *n* berth, dock, harbour, jetty, landing-stage, pier, wharf.

queasy *adj* bilious, *inf* green, *inf* groggy, nauseated, nauseous, *inf* poorly, *inf* queer, sick, unwell. ▷ ILL.

queer *adj* 1 aberrant, abnormal, anomalous, atypical, bizarre, curious, different, eerie, exceptional, extraordinary, *inf* fishy, freakish, *inf* funny, incongruous, inexplicable, irrational, mysterious, odd, offbeat, outlandish, peculiar, puzzling, quaint, remarkable, *inf* rum, singular, strange, unaccountable, uncanny, uncommon, unconventional, unexpected, unnatural, unorthodox, unusual, weird. 2 *inf* cranky, deviant, eccentric, questionable, *inf* shady (*customer*), *inf* shifty, suspect, suspicious. ▷ MAD. *Opp* NORMAL. 3 ▷ ILL. 4 ▷ HOMOSEXUAL.

quell *vb* 1 crush, overcome, put down, quash, repress, subdue, suppress. 2 *quell fears*. allay, alleviate, calm, mitigate, moderate, mollify, pacify, soothe, tranquillize.

quench *vb* 1 allay, appease, cool, sate, satisfy, slake. 2 *quench a fire*. damp down, douse, extinguish, put out, smother, snuff out, stifle, suppress.

quest *n* crusade, expedition, exploration, hunt, mission, pilgrimage, pursuit, search, voyage of discovery. ● *vb* **quest after** ▷ SEEK.

question *n* 1 *inf* brain-teaser, conundrum, demand, enquiry, inquiry, *inf* poser, query, request, riddle. 2 *an unresolved question*. argument, controversy, debate, difficulty, dispute, doubt, misgiving, mystery, objection, problem, puzzle, uncertainty. ● *vb* 1 ask, catechize, cross-examine, crossquestion, debrief, enquire of, examine, *inf* grill, inquire of, interrogate, interview, probe, *inf* pump, quiz. 2 *question a decision*. argue over, be sceptical about, call into question, cast doubt upon, challenge, dispute, doubt, enquire about, impugn, inquire about, object to, oppose, quarrel with, query.

questionable *adj* arguable, borderline, debatable, disputable, doubtful, dubious, *inf* iffy, moot, problematical, *inf* shady (*customer*), suspect, suspicious, uncertain, unclear, unprovable, unreliable.

questionnaire *n* catechism, opinion poll, question sheet, quiz, survey, test.

queue *n* chain, column, concatenation, *inf* crocodile, file, line, line-up, procession, row, string, succession, tail-back, train. ● *vb* fall in, form a queue, line up, wait in a queue.

quibble *n* ▷ OBJECTION. ● *vb inf* bandy words, be evasive, carp, cavil, equivocate, *inf* nit-pick, object, pettifog, *inf* split hairs, wrangle.

quick *adj* 1 breakneck, brisk, expeditious, express, fast, *old use* fleet, headlong, high-speed, *inf* nippy, precipitate, rapid, *inf* smart (*pace*), *inf* spanking, speedy, swift. 2 *a quick reaction*. adroit, agile, animated, brisk, deft, dexterous, energetic, lively, nimble, spirited, spry, vigorous. **3** *a quick response.* abrupt, early, hasty, hurried, immediate, instant, instantaneous, perfunctory, precipitate, prompt, punctual, ready, sudden, summary, unhesitating. **4** *a quick mind.* acute, alert, apt, astute, bright, clever, intelligent, perceptive, quick-witted, sharp, shrewd, smart. *Opp* SLOW. **5** *a quick rest.* brief, fleeting, momentary, passing, perfunctory, short, short-lived, temporary, transitory. **6** *[old use] the quick and the dead.* ▷ ALIVE. *Opp* SLOW.

quicken *vb* **1** accelerate, expedite, go faster, hasten, hurry, speed up. **2** ▷ AROUSE.

quiet *adj* **1** inaudible, noiseless, silent, soundless. **2** *quiet music.* hushed, low, pianissimo, soft, *It* sotto voce. **3** *a quiet person.* composed, contemplative, contented, gentle, introverted, meditative, meek, mild, modest, peaceable, reserved, retiring, shy, taciturn, thoughtful, uncommunicative, unforthcoming, unsociable, withdrawn. **4** *a quiet life.* cloistered, sheltered, tranquil, unadventurous, unexciting, untroubled. **5** *a quiet place.* isolated, lonely, peaceful, private, secluded, sequestered, undisturbed, unfrequented. **6** *quiet weather.* calm, motionless, placid, restful, serene, still. *Opp* BUSY, NOISY, RESTLESS.

quieten *vb* **1** calm, compose, hush, lull, pacify, sedate, soothe, subdue, tranquillize. **2** deaden, dull, muffle, mute, reduce the volume of, silence, soften, stifle, suppress, tone down.

quirk *n* aberration, caprice, crotchet, eccentricity, idiosyncrasy, kink, oddity, peculiarity, trick, whim.

quit *vb* **1** abandon, decamp from, depart from, desert, exit from, forsake, go away from, leave, walk out (on), withdraw. **2** abdicate, discontinue, drop, give up, leave, *inf* pack it in, relinquish, renounce, repudiate, resign from, retire from, withdraw from. **3** *[inf] Quit pushing!* cease, desist from, discontinue, leave off, stop.

quite *adv* [NB: the two senses are almost opposite.] **1** *Yes, I've quite finished.* absolutely, altogether, completely, entirely, perfectly, thoroughly, totally, unreservedly, utterly, wholly. **2** *quite good, but not perfect.* comparatively, fairly, moderately, *inf* pretty, rather, relatively, somewhat, to some extent.

quits *adj* equal, even, level, repaid, revenged, square.

quiver *vb* flicker, fluctuate, flutter, oscillate, palpitate, pulsate, quake, quaver, shake, shiver, shudder, tremble, vibrate, wobble.

quixotic *adj* fanciful, foolhardy, idealistic, impracticable, impractical, romantic, *inf* starry-eyed, unrealistic, unrealizable, unselfish, Utopian, visionary. *Opp* REALISTIC.

quiz *n* competition, exam, examination, questioning, questionnaire, quiz-game, test. ● *vb* ▷ QUESTION.

quizzical *adj* amused, comical, curious, intrigued, perplexed, puzzled, queer, questioning.

quota *n* allocation, allowance, apportionment, assignment, *inf* cut, part, portion, proportion, ration, share.

quotation *n* **1** allusion, citation, *inf* clip, cutting, excerpt, extract, passage, piece, reference, selection. **2** estimate, price, tender, valuation.

quote *vb* **1** cite, instance, mention, produce a quotation from, refer to, repeat, reproduce. **2** *quote a price.* estimate, tender.

R

rabble n crowd, gang, herd, *Gk* hoi polloi, horde, mob, *inf* riffraff, swarm, throng. ▷ GROUP.

race n **1** breed, clan, ethnic group, family, folk, genus, kind, lineage, nation, people, species, stock, tribe, variety. **2** chase, competition, contention, contest, heat, rivalry. □ *cross-country, greyhound race, horse-race, hurdles, marathon, motor-race, regatta, relay, road-race, rowing, scramble, speedway, sprint, steeple-chase, stock-car race, swimming, track event.* ● vb **1** *I'll race you!* compete with, contest with, have a race with, try to beat. **2** *race along.* career, dash, *inf* fly, gallop, hasten, hurry, move fast, run, rush, speed, sprint, *inf* tear, *inf* zip, *inf* zoom.

racetrack n cinder-track, circuit, dog-track, lap, racecourse.

racial adj ethnic, folk, genetic, national, tribal.

racism n bias, bigotry, chauvinism, discrimination, intolerance, prejudice, racialism, xenophobia. □ *anti-Semitism, apartheid.*

racist adj biased, bigoted, chauvinist, discriminatory, intolerant, prejudiced, racialist, xenophobic. □ *anti-Semitic.*

rack n frame, framework, holder, scaffold, scaffolding, shelf, stand, support. ● vb ▷ TORTURE.

radiant adj **1** beaming, bright, brilliant, effulgent, gleaming, glorious, glowing, incandescent, luminous, phosphorescent, refulgent, shining. **2** *The bride was radiant.* ▷ HAPPY.

radiate vb beam, diffuse, emanate, emit, give off, gleam, glow, send out, shed, shine, spread, transmit.

radical adj **1** basic, cardinal, deep-seated, elementary, essential, fundamental, primary, principal, profound. **2** complete, comprehensive, drastic, entire, exhaustive, thorough, thoroughgoing. **3** *radical politics.* extreme, extremist, fanatical, far-reaching, revolutionary, *derog* subversive. *Opp* MODERATE, SUPERFICIAL.

radio n CB, *sl* ghettoblaster, portable, receiver, set, *inf* transistor, transmitter, walkie-talkie, *old use* wireless. ● vb broadcast, send out, transmit.

rafter n beam, girder, joist.

rage n ▷ ANGER. ● vb be angry, boil, fume, go berserk, lose control, rave, *inf* see red, seethe, storm.

ragged adj **1** chafed, frayed, in ribbons, old, patched, patchy, ravelled, rent, ripped, rough, rough-edged, shabby, shaggy, tattered, tatty, threadbare, torn, unkempt, unravelled, untidy, worn out. **2** *ragged line.* denticulated, disorganized, erratic, irregular, jagged, serrated, uneven, zigzag.

rags plur n bits and pieces, cloths, fragments, old clothes, remnants, ribbons, scraps, shreds, tatters.

raid n assault, attack, blitz, foray, incursion, inroad, invasion, onslaught, sally, sortie, strike, surprise attack, swoop. ● vb **1** assault, attack, descend on, invade, pounce on, rush, storm, swoop down on. **2** loot, maraud, pillage, plunder, ransack, rifle, rob, sack, steal from, strip.

raider n attacker, brigand, invader, looter, marauder, outlaw, pillager, pirate, plunderer, ransacker, robber, rustler, thief.

railway n line, permanent way, *Amer* railroad, rails, track. □ *branch line,* *cable railway, funicular, light railway, main line, metro, mineral line, monorail, mountain railway, narrow gauge, rack-and-pinion, rapid transit system, siding, standard gauge, tramway, tube, underground.* ▷ TRAIN.

rain n cloudburst, deluge, downpour, drizzle, precipitation, raindrops, rainfall, rainstorm, shower, squall. ● vb inf bucket down, drizzle, pelt, pour, inf rain cats and dogs, spit, teem.

rainy adj damp, drizzly, showery, wet.

raise vb 1 elevate, heave up, hoist, hold up, jack up, lift, loft, pick up, put up, rear. 2 *raise prices.* augment, boost, increase, inflate, put up, inf up. 3 *raise to a higher rank.* exalt, prefer, promote, upgrade. 4 *raise a monument.* build, construct, create, erect, set up. 5 *raise hopes.* activate, arouse, awaken, build up, buoy up, encourage, engender, enlarge, excite, foment, foster, heighten, incite, kindle, motivate, provoke, rouse, stimulate, uplift. 6 *raise animals, children, crops.* breed, bring up, care for, cultivate, educate, farm, grow, look after, nurture, produce, propagate, rear. 7 *raise money.* amass, collect, get, make, receive, solicit. 8 *raise questions.* advance, bring up, broach, express, instigate, introduce, mention, moot, originate, pose, present, put forward, suggest. *Opp* LOWER, REDUCE. **raise from the dead** ▷ RESURRECT. **raise the alarm** ▷ WARN.

rally n 1 assembly, inf demo, demonstration, gathering, march, mass meeting, protest. 2 ▷ COMPETITION. ● vb 1 assemble, convene, get together, marshal, muster, organize, round up, summon. 2 come together, reassemble, reform, regroup. 3 *rally after illness.* ▷ RECOVER.

ram vb 1 bump, butt, collide with, crash into, slam into, smash into, strike. ▷ HIT. 2 compress, cram, crowd, crush, drive, force, jam, pack, press, push, squash, squeeze, tamp down, wedge.

ramble n hike, tramp, trek, walk. ● vb 1 hike, range, roam, rove, tramp, trek, stroll, wander. ▷ WALK. 2 digress, drift, inf lose the thread, maunder, inf rabbit on, inf rattle on, talk aimlessly, wander, inf witter on.

rambling adj 1 circuitous, indirect, labyrinthine, meandering, roundabout, tortuous, twisting, wandering, winding, zigzag. *Opp* DIRECT. 2 aimless, circumlocutory, confused, diffuse, digressive, disconnected, discursive, disjointed, illogical, incoherent, jumbled, muddled, periphrastic, unstructured, verbose, wordy. *Opp* COHERENT. 3 *a rambling house.* asymmetrical, extensive, irregular, large, sprawling, straggling, straggly. *Opp* COMPACT.

ramification n branch, byproduct, complication, consequence, division, effect, extension, implication, offshoot, result, subdivision, upshot.

ramp n acclivity, gradient, incline, rise, slope.

rampage n frenzy, riot, tumult, uproar, vandalism, violence. ● vb behave violently, go berserk, go wild, lose control, race about, run amok, run riot, rush about, storm about. **on the rampage** ▷ WILD.

ramshackle adj broken-down, crumbling, decrepit, derelict, dilapidated, flimsy, jerry-built, rickety, ruined, run-down, shaky, tottering, tumbledown, unsafe, unstable, unsteady. *Opp* SOLID.

random adj accidental, adventitious, aimless, arbitrary, casual, chance, fortuitous, haphazard, inf hit-or-miss, indiscriminate, irregular, serendipitous, stray, unconsidered, unplanned, unpremeditated, unspecific, unsystematic. *Opp* DELIBERATE, SYSTEMATIC.

range n 1 area, compass, distance, extent, field, gamut, limit, orbit, radius, reach, scope, span, spectrum, sphere, spread, sweep. 2 *a wide range of goods.* diversity, selection, variety. 3 *range of mountains.* chain, file, line, rank, row, series, string, tier. ● vb

1 differ, extend, fluctuate, go, reach, run the gamut, spread, stretch, vary. **2** ▷ RANK. **3** ▷ ROAM.

rank adj **1** *rank growth*. ▷ ABUNDANT. **2** *rank smell*. ▷ SMELLING. ● n **1** column, file, formation, line, order, queue, row, series, tier. **2** birth, blood, caste, class, condition, degree, echelon, estate, grade, level, position, standing, station, status, stratum, title. ● vb arrange, array, assort, categorize, class, classify, grade, graduate, line up, order, organize, range, rate, set out in order, sort.

ransack vb **1** comb, explore, go through, rake through, rummage through, scour, search, *inf* turn upside down. **2** *ransack a shop*. despoil, loot, pillage, plunder, raid, ravage, rob, sack, strip, wreck.

ransom n payment, *inf* payoff, price, redemption. ● vb buy the release of, deliver, redeem.

rap vb **1** knock, strike, tap. ▷ HIT. **2** ▷ CRITICIZE.

rape n **1** assault, sexual attack. **2** ▷ PILLAGE. ● vb assault, defile, deflower, dishonour, force yourself on, *inf* have your way with, *old use* ravish, violate.

rapid adj alacritous, breakneck, brisk, expeditious, express, fast, *old use* fleet, hasty, headlong, high-speed, hurried, immediate, impetuous, instant, instantaneous, *inf* lightning, *inf* nippy, precipitate, prompt, quick, smooth, speedy, swift, unchecked, uninterrupted. *Opp* SLOW.

rapids plur n cataract, current, waterfall, white water.

rapture n bliss, delight, ecstasy, elation, euphoria, exaltation, happiness, joy, pleasure, thrill, transport.

rare adj abnormal, atypical, curious, exceptional, extraordinary, *inf* few and far between, infrequent, irreplaceable, limited, occasional, odd, out of the ordinary, peculiar, scarce, singular, special, strange, surprising, uncommon, unfamiliar, unusual. *Opp* COMMON.

rascal n blackguard, *old use* bounder, devil, good-fornothing, imp, knave,

mischiefmaker, miscreant, ne'er-do-well, rapscallion, rogue, *inf* scallywag, scamp, scoundrel, troublemaker, villain, wastrel. ▷ CRIMINAL.

rash adj careless, foolhardy, harebrained, hasty, headlong, headstrong, heedless, hotheaded, hurried, ill-advised, ill-considered, impetuous, imprudent, impulsive, incautious, indiscreet, injudicious, madcap, precipitate, reckless, risky, thoughtless, unthinking, wild. *Opp* CAREFUL. ● n **1** efflorescence, eruption, spots. **2** *a rash of thefts*. ▷ OUTBREAK.

rasp vb **1** abrade, file, grate, rub, scrape. **2** *rasp orders*. croak, screech, speak hoarsely. ▷ SPEAK. **rasping** ▷ HARSH.

rate n **1** gait, pace, speed, tempo, velocity. **2** amount, charge, cost, fare, fee, figure, payment, price, scale, tariff, wage. ● vb **1** appraise, assess, class, classify, compute, consider, estimate, evaluate, gauge, grade, judge, measure, prize, put a price on, rank, reckon, regard, value, weigh. **2** *rate a prize*. be worthy of, deserve, merit. **3** ▷ REPRIMAND.

rather adv **1** fairly, moderately, *inf* pretty, quite, relatively, slightly, somewhat. **2** *would rather have tea than coffee*. more willingly, preferably, sooner.

ratify vb approve, authorize, confirm, endorse, sanction, sign, validate, verify.

rating n classification, evaluation, grade, grading, mark, order, placing, ranking.

ratio n balance, correlation, correspondence, fraction, percentage, proportion, relationship.

ration n allocation, allotment, allowance, amount, helping, measure, percentage, portion, quota, share. ● vb allocate, allot, apportion, conserve, control, distribute fairly, dole out, give out, limit, parcel out, restrict, share equally. **rations** food, necessaries, necessities, provisions, stores, supplies.

rational adj balanced, clear-headed, commonsense, enlightened, intelligent, judicious, logical, lucid, normal, ratiocinative, reasonable, reasoned, reasoning, sane, sensible, sound, thoughtful, wise. Opp IRRATIONAL.

rationale n argument, case, cause, excuse, explanation, grounds, justification, logical basis, principle, reason, reasoning, theory, vindication.

rationalize vb 1 account for, be rational about, elucidate, excuse, explain, justify, make rational, provide a rationale for, ratiocinate, think through, vindicate. 2 ▷ REORGANIZE.

rattle vb 1 clatter, vibrate. 2 agitate, jar, inf jiggle about, joggle, jolt, shake about. 3 [inf] rattled him by booing. alarm, discomfit, discompose, disconcert, disturb, fluster, frighten, make nervous, put off, unnerve, upset, worry. **rattle off** ▷ RECITE. **rattle on** ▷ RAMBLE, TALK.

raucous adj ear-splitting, harsh, husky, grating, jarring, noisy, rasping, rough, screeching, shrill, squawking, strident.

ravage vb damage, despoil, destroy, devastate, lay waste, loot, pillage, plunder, raid, ransack, ruin, sack, spoil, wreak havoc on, wreck.

rave vb 1 be angry, fulminate, fume, rage, rant, roar, storm, thunder. 2 be enthusiastic, enthuse, inf go into raptures, inf gush, rhapsodize.

ravenous adj famished, hungry, insatiable, ravening, starved, starving, voracious. ▷ GREEDY.

ravish vb 1 bewitch, captivate, capture, charm, delight, enchant, entrance, spellbind, transport. 2 ▷ RAPE. **ravishing** ▷ BEAUTIFUL.

raw adj 1 fresh, rare (steak), uncooked, underdone, unpre-pared, wet (fish). 2 raw materials. crude, natural, unprocessed, unrefined, untreated. 3 raw recruits. inf green, ignorant, immature, inexperienced, innocent, new, unseasoned, untrained, untried.

4 raw skin. bloody, chafed, grazed, inflamed, painful, red, rough, scraped, scratched, sensitive, sore, tender, vulnerable. 5 raw wind. ▷ COLD.

ray n 1 bar, beam, laser, pencil, shaft, streak, stream. 2 a ray of hope. flicker, gleam, glimmer, hint, indication, scintilla, sign, trace.

raze vb bulldoze, demolish, destroy, flatten, level, tear down.

razor n □ cut-throat razor, disposable razor, electric razor, safety razor.

reach n compass, distance, orbit, range, scope, sphere. ● vb 1 achieve, arrive at, attain, come to, get hold of, get to, go as far as, grasp, inf make, take, touch. 2 reach for the salt. put out your hand, stretch, try to get. 3 reach me by phone. communicate with, contact, get in touch with. **reach out** ▷ EXTEND.

react vb act, answer, behave, conduct yourself, reciprocate, reply, respond, retaliate, retort, take revenge. **react to** ▷ COUNTER.

reaction n answer, backlash, inf come-back, counter, countermove, effect, feedback, parry, reciprocation, reflex, rejoinder, reply, reprisal, response, retaliation, retort, revenge, riposte.

reactionary adj conservative, die-hard, old-fashioned, rightist, right-wing, inf stick-in-the-mud, traditionalist, unprogressive. Opp PROGRESSIVE.

read vb 1 devour, inf dip into, glance at, interpret, look over, peruse, pore over, review, scan, skim, study. 2 can't read the handwriting. decipher, decode, interpret, make out, understand.

readable adj 1 absorbing, compulsive, easy, engaging, enjoyable, entertaining, gripping, interesting, stimulating, well-written. Opp BORING. 2 clear, comprehensible, decipherable, distinct, intelligible, legible, neat, plain, understandable. Opp ILLEGIBLE.

readily adv cheerfully, eagerly, easily, effortlessly, freely, gladly, happily, promptly, quickly, ungrudgingly, unhesitatingly, voluntarily, willingly.

ready adj 1 accessible, inf all set, arranged, at hand, available, complete, convenient, done, finalized, finished, fit, obtainable, prepared, primed, ripe, set, set up, waiting. 2 ready to help. agreeable, consenting, content, disposed, eager, equipped, inf game, glad, inclined, in the mood, keen, inf keyed up, liable, likely, minded, of a mind, open, organized, pleased, poised, predisposed, primed, inf psyched up, raring (to go), trained, willing. 3 ready wit. acute, adroit, alert, apt, facile, immediate, prompt, quick, quick-witted, rapid, sharp, smart, speedy. Opp SLOW, UNPREPARED.

real adj 1 actual, authentic, certain, corporeal, everyday, existing, factual, genuine, material, natural, ordinary, palpable, physical, pure, realistic, tangible, visible. 2 authenticated, Lat bona fide, legal, legitimate, official, valid, verifiable. 3 real friends. dependable, positive, reliable, sound, true, trustworthy, worthy. 4 real grief. earnest, heartfelt, honest, sincere, truthful, unaffected, undoubted, unfeigned, unquestionable. Opp FALSE.

realism n 1 authenticity, fidelity, naturalism, verisimilitude. 2 realism in business. clear-sightedness, common sense, objectivity, practicality, pragmatism.

realistic adj 1 businesslike, clear-sighted, commonsense, down-to-earth, feasible, hardheaded, inf hard-nosed, levelheaded, logical, matter-of-fact, inf no-nonsense, objective, possible, practicable, practical, pragmatic, rational, sensible, tough, unemotional, unsentimental, viable, workable. 2 realistic pictures. authentic, convincing, faithful, graphic, lifelike, natural, recognizable, representational, true-to-life, truthful, vivid. 3 realistic prices. acceptable, adequate, fair, genuine, justifiable, moderate, reasonable. Opp UNREALISTIC.

reality n actuality, authenticity, certainty, empirical knowledge, experience, fact, life, inf nittygritty, real life, the real world, truth, verity. Opp FANTASY.

realize vb 1 accept, appreciate, apprehend, be aware of, become conscious of, inf catch on to, comprehend, conceive of, inf cotton on to, grasp, know, perceive, recognize, see, sense, inf twig, understand, inf wake up to. 2 realize an ambition. accomplish, achieve, bring about, complete, effect, effectuate, fulfil, implement, make a reality of, obtain, perform, put into effect. 3 realize a price. inf bring in, inf clear, earn, fetch, make, net, obtain, produce.

realm n country, domain, empire, kingdom, monarchy, principality.

reap vb 1 cut, garner, gather in, glean, harvest, mow. 2 reap a reward. acquire, bring in, collect, get, obtain, receive, win.

rear adj back, end, hind, hinder, hindmost, last, rearmost. Opp FRONT. ● n 1 back, end, stern (of ship), tail-end. 2 ▷ BUTTOCKS. ● vb 1 breed, bring up, care for, cultivate, educate, feed, look after, nurse, nurture, produce, raise, train. 2 rear your head. elevate, hold up, lift, raise, uplift. 3 ▷ BUILD.

rearrange vb change round, regroup, reorganize, switch round, swop round, transpose. ▷ CHANGE.

rearrangement n anagram, reorganization, transposition. ▷ CHANGE.

reason n 1 apology, argument, case, cause, defence, excuse, explanation, grounds, incentive, justification, motive, occasion, pretext, rationale, vindication. 2 brains, common sense, inf gumption, intelligence, judgement, logic, mind, inf nous, perspicacity, rationality, reasonableness, sanity, sense, understanding, wisdom, wit. ▷ REASONING. 3 reason for living. aim, goal, intention, motivation, motive, object, objective, point, purpose, spur, stimulus. ● vb 1 act rationally, calculate, cerebrate, conclude, consider, deduce, estimate, figure out, hypothesize, infer, intellectualize, judge, *inf* put two and two together, ratiocinate, resolve, theorize, think, use your head, work out. **2** *I reasoned with her.* argue, debate, discuss, expostulate, remonstrate.

reasonable *adj* **1** calm, helpful, honest, intelligent, rational, realistic, sane, sensible, sincere, sober, thinking, thoughtful, unemotional, wise. **2** *reasonable argument.* arguable, believable, credible, defensible, justifiable, logical, plausible, practical, reasoned, sound, tenable, viable, well-thought-out. **3** *reasonable prices.* acceptable, appropriate, average, cheap, competitive, conservative, fair, inexpensive, moderate, ordinary, proper, right, suitable, tolerable, unexceptionable. *Opp* IRRATIONAL.

reasoning *n* analysis, argument, case, *derog* casuistry, cerebration, deduction, dialectic, hypothesis, line of thought, logic, proof, rationalization, *derog* sophistry, theorizing, thinking.

reassure *vb* assure, bolster, buoy up, calm, cheer, comfort, encourage, give confidence to, hearten, *inf* set someone's mind at rest, support, uplift. *Opp* ALARM, THREATEN. **reassuring** ▷ SOOTHING, SUPPORTIVE.

rebel *adj* ▷ REBELLIOUS. ● *n* anarchist, apostate, dissenter, freedom fighter, heretic, iconoclast, insurgent, malcontent, maverick, mutineer, nonconformist, recusant, resistance fighter, revolutionary, schismatic. ● *vb* be a rebel, disobey, dissent, fight, *inf* kick over the traces, mutiny, refuse to obey, revolt, rise up, *inf* run riot, *inf* take a stand. *Opp* CONFORM. **rebel against** ▷ DEFY.

rebellion *n* contumacy, defiance, disobedience, insubordination, insurgency, insurrection, mutiny, rebelliousness, resistance, revolt, revolution, rising, schism, sedition, uprising.

rebellious *adj inf* bolshie, breakaway, contumacious, defiant, difficult, disaffected, disloyal, disobedient, incorrigible, insubordinate, insur-

gent, intractable, malcontent, mutinous, obstinate, quarrelsome, rebel, recalcitrant, refractory, resistant, revolting, revolutionary, seditious, uncontrollable, ungovernable, unmanageable, unruly, wild. *Opp* OBEDIENT.

rebirth *n* reawakening, regeneration, renaissance, renewal, resurgence, resurrection, return, revival.

rebound *vb inf* backfire, *inf* boomerang, bounce, misfire, recoil, ricochet, spring back.

rebuff *n inf* brush-off, check, discouragement, refusal, rejection, slight, snub. ● *vb* cold-shoulder, decline, discourage, refuse, reject, repulse, slight, snub, spurn, turn down.

rebuild *n* reassemble, reconstruct, recreate, redevelop, refashion, regenerate, remake. ▷ RECONDITION.

rebuke *vb* admonish, castigate, censure, chide, reprehend, reproach, reprove, scold, upbraid. ▷ REPRIMAND.

recall *vb* **1** bring back, call in, summon, withdraw. **2** ▷ REMEMBER.

recede *vb* abate, decline, dwindle, ebb, fall back, go back, lessen, regress, retire, retreat, return, shrink back, sink, slacken, subside, wane, withdraw.

receipt *n* **1** account, acknowledgement, bill, proof of purchase, sales slip, ticket. **2** *receipt of goods.* acceptance, delivery, reception. **receipts** gains, gate, income, proceeds, profits, return, takings.

receive *vb* **1** accept, acquire, be given, be paid, be sent, collect, come by, come into, derive, earn, gain, get, gross, inherit, make, net, obtain, take. **2** *receive an injury.* bear, be subjected to, endure, experience, meet with, suffer, sustain, undergo. **3** *receive visitors.* accommodate, admit, entertain, greet, let in, meet, show in, welcome. *Opp* GIVE.

recent *adj* brand-new, contemporary, current, fresh, just out, latest, modern, new, novel, present-day, up-to-date, young. *Opp* OLD.

reception n **1** greeting, response, welcome. **2** ▷ PARTY.

receptive adj amenable, favourable, flexible, interested, open, open-minded, responsive, susceptible, sympathetic, tractable, welcoming, well-disposed. Opp RESISTANT.

recess n **1** alcove, apse, bay, cavity, corner, cranny, hollow, indentation, niche, nook. **2** adjournment, break, inf breather, breathing-space, interlude, intermission, interval, respite, rest, time off.

recession n decline, depression, downturn, slump.

recipe n directions, formula, instructions, method, plan, prescription, procedure, technique.

reciprocal adj corresponding, exchanged, joint, mutual, requited, returned, shared.

reciprocate vb exchange, give the same in return, match, repay, requite, return.

recital n **1** concert, performance, programme. **2** recital of events. account, description, narration, narrative, recounting, rehearsal, relation, repetition, story, telling. ▷ RECITATION.

recitation n declaiming, declamation, delivery, monologue, narration, performance, presentation, reading, old use rendition, speaking, telling.

recite vb articulate, declaim, deliver, narrate, perform, present, quote, inf rattle off, recount, reel off, rehearse, relate, repeat, speak, tell.

reckless adj **1** brash, careless, inf crazy, daredevil, inf devil-maycare, foolhardy, harebrained, inf harum-scarum, hasty, heedless, impetuous, imprudent, impulsive, inattentive, incautious, indiscreet, injudicious, irresponsible, inf mad, madcap, negligent, rash, thoughtless, unconsidered, unwise, wild. Opp CAREFUL. **2** reckless criminals. dangerous, desperate, hardened, violent.

reckon vb **1** add up, appraise, assess, calculate, compute, count, enumerate, estimate, evaluate, figure out, gauge, number, tally, total, value, work out. **2** ▷ THINK.

reclaim vb **1** get back, inf put in for, recapture, recover, regain. **2** reclaim derelict land. make usable, redeem, regenerate, reinstate, rescue, restore, salvage, save.

recline vb lean back, lie, loll, lounge, repose, rest, sprawl, stretch out.

recluse n anchoress, anchorite, hermit, loner, monk, nun, solitary.

recognizable adj detectable, distinctive, distinguishable, identifiable, known, noticeable, perceptible, undisguised, unmistakable, visible.

recognize vb **1** detect, diagnose, discern, distinguish, identify, know, name, notice, perceive, pick out, place (can't place him), inf put a name to, recall, recollect, remember, see, spot. **2** recognize your faults. accept, acknowledge, admit to, appreciate, be aware of, concede, confess, grant, realize, understand. **3** recognize someone's rights. approve of, inf back, endorse, legitimize, ratify, sanction, support, validate.

recoil vb blench, draw back, falter, flinch, jerk back, jump, quail, shrink, shy away, start, wince. ▷ REBOUND.

recollect vb hark back to, recall, reminisce about, summon up, think back to. ▷ REMEMBER.

recommend vb **1** advise, advocate, counsel, exhort, prescribe, propose, put forward, suggest, urge. **2** applaud, approve of, inf back, commend, favour, inf plug, praise, inf push, inf put in a good word for, speak well of, support, vouch for. ▷ ADVERTISE.

recommendation n advice, advocacy, approbation, approval, inf backing, commendation, counsel, favourable mention, reference, seal of approval, support, testimonial.

reconcile vb bring together, old use conciliate, harmonize, make friendly again, placate, reunite, settle differences between. **be reconciled to**

accept, adjust to, resign yourself to, submit to.

recondition vb make good, overhaul, rebuild, renew, renovate, repair, restore.

reconnaissance n examination, exploration, inspection, investigation, observation, inf recce, reconnoitring, scouting, spying, survey.

reconnoitre vb inf case, inf check out, examine, explore, gather intelligence (about), inspect, investigate, patrol, scout, scrutinize, spy, survey, sl suss out.

reconsider vb be converted, change your mind, come round, reappraise, reassess, re-examine, rethink, review your position, think better of.

reconstruct vb act out, mock up, recreate, rerun. ▷ REBUILD.

record n 1 account, annals, archives, catalogue, chronicle, diary, documentation, dossier, file, journal, log, memorandum, minutes, narrative, note, register, report, transactions. 2 best performance, best time. 3 ▷ RECORDING. ● vb 1 chronicle, document, enter, inscribe, list, log, minute, note, put down, register, set down, take down, transcribe, write down. 2 record on tape. keep, preserve, tape, tape-record, video.

recording n performance, release. □ album, audio-tape, cassette, CD, compact disc, digital recording, disc, long-playing record, LP, mono recording, record, single, stereo recording, tape, tape-recording, tele-recording, video, video-cassette, video disc, videotape.

record-player n CD player, gramophone, midi system, old use phonograph, record deck, turntable.

recount vb communicate, describe, detail, impart, narrate, recite, relate, report, tell, unfold.

recover vb 1 find, get back, get compensation for, make good, make up for, recapture, reclaim, recoup, regain, repossess, restore, retrieve, salvage, trace, track down, win back. 2 inf be on the mend, come round, convalesce, inf get back on your feet,

get better, heal, improve, mend, inf pull round, inf pull through, rally, recuperate, regain your strength, revive, survive, inf take a turn for the better.

recovery n 1 recapture, reclamation, repossession, restoration, retrieval, salvage, salvaging. 2 recovery from illness. advance, convalescence, cure, deliverance, healing, improvement, progress, rally, recuperation, revival, upturn.

recreation n amusement, distraction, diversion, enjoyment, entertainment, fun, games, hobby, leisure, pastime, play, pleasure, refreshment, relaxation, sport.

recrimination n accusation, inf come-back, counter-attack, counter-charge, reprisal, retaliation, retort.

recruit n apprentice, beginner, conscript, inf greenhorn, initiate, learner, neophyte, inf new boy, new girl, novice, tiro, trainee. Opp VETERAN. ● vb advertise for, conscript, draft in, engage, enlist, enrol, old use impress, mobilize, muster, register, sign on, sign up, take on.

rectify vb amend, correct, cure, inf fix, make good, put right, repair, revise.

recumbent adj flat, flat on your back, horizontal, lying down, prone, reclining, stretched out, supine. Opp UPRIGHT.

recuperate vb convalesce, get better, heal, improve, mend, rally, regain strength, revive. ▷ RECOVER.

recur vb be repeated, come back again, happen again, persist, reappear, repeat, return.

recurrent adj chronic, cyclical, frequent, intermittent, iterative, periodic, persistent, recurring, regular, repeated, repetitive, returning. ▷ CONTINUAL.

recycle vb reclaim, recover, retrieve, reuse, salvage, use again.

red adj bloodshot, blushing, embarrassed, fiery, flaming, florid, flushed, glowing, inflamed, rosy, rubicund, ruddy. □ auburn, blood-red, brick-red, cardinal, carmine, carroty, cerise, cherry, chestnut, crimson, damask, flame-coloured, foxy, magenta, maroon, orange, pink, rose, roseate, ruby, scarlet, titian, vermilion, wine-coloured. **red herring** ▷ DECOY.

redden vb blush, colour, flush, glow.

redeem vb buy back, cash in, exchange for cash, reclaim, recover, re-purchase, trade in, win back. ▷ LIBERATE. **redeem yourself** ▷ ATONE.

redolent adj 1 aromatic, fragrant, perfumed, scented, smelling. 2 redolent of the past. reminiscent, suggestive.

reduce vb 1 abate, abbreviate, abridge, clip, compress, curtail, cut, cut back, cut down, decimate, decrease, detract from, devalue, dilute, diminish, inf dock (wages), inf ease up on, halve, impair, lessen, limit, lower, make less, minimize, moderate, narrow, prune, shorten, shrink, simplify, inf slash, slim down, tone down, trim, truncate, weaken, whittle. 2 become less, contract, dwindle, shrink. 3 reduce a liquid. concentrate, condense, thicken. 4 reduce to rubble. break up, destroy, grind, pulp, pulverize, triturate. 5 reduce to poverty. degrade, demote, downgrade, humble, impoverish, move down, put down, ruin. Opp INCREASE, RAISE.

reduction n 1 contraction, curtailment, inf cutback, deceleration (of speed), decimation, decline, decrease, diminution, drop, impairment, lessening, limitation, loss, moderation, narrowing, remission, shortening, shrinkage, weakening. 2 reduction in price. concession, cut, depreciation, devaluation, discount, rebate, refund. Opp INCREASE.

redundant adj excessive, inessential, non-essential, superfluous, supernumerary, surplus, too many, unnecessary, unneeded, unwanted. Opp NECESSARY.

reek n stench, stink. ▷ SMELL.

reel n bobbin, spool. ● vb falter, lurch, pitch, rock, roll, spin, stagger, stumble, sway, totter, waver, whirl, wobble. **reel off** ▷ RECITE.

refer vb refer to 1 allude to, bring up, cite, comment on, draw attention to, make reference to, mention, name, point to, quote, speak of, specify, touch on. 2 refer one person to another. direct to, guide to, hand over to, pass on to, recommend to, send to. 3 refer to the dictionary. consult, go to, look up, resort to, study, turn to.

referee n adjudicator, arbiter, arbitrator, judge, mediator, umpire.

reference n 1 allusion, citation, example, illustration, instance, intimation, mention, note, quotation, referral, remark. 2 endorsement, recommendation, testimonial.

refill vb fill up, refuel, renew, replenish, top up.

refine vb 1 clarify, cleanse, clear, decontaminate, distil, process, purify, treat. 2 refine manners. civilize, cultivate, improve, perfect, polish.

refined adj 1 aristocratic, civilized, courteous, courtly, cultivated, cultured, delicate, dignified, discerning, discriminating, educated, elegant, fastidious, genteel, gentlemanly, gracious, ladylike, nice, polished, polite, inf posh, precise, derog pretentious, derog prissy, sensitive, sophisticated, stylish, subtle, tasteful, inf uppercrust, urbane, well-bred, well brought-up. Opp RUDE. 2 refined oil. clarified, distilled, processed, purified, treated. Opp CRUDE.

refinement n 1 breeding, inf class, courtesy, cultivation, delicacy, discernment, discrimination, elegance, finesse, gentility, graciousness, polish, derog pretentiousness, sensitivity, sophistication, style, subtlety, taste, urbanity. 2 refinements in design. alteration, change, enhancement, improvement, modification, perfection.

reflect vb 1 echo, mirror, return, send back, shine back, throw back. 2 brood, cerebrate, inf chew things over, consider, contemplate, deliberate, meditate, ponder, remind your-

self, reminisce, ruminate. ▷ THINK.
3 *Her success reflects her hard work.* bear
witness to, correspond to, demon-
strate, evidence, exhibit, illustrate,
indicate, match, point to, reveal,
show.

reflection n **1** echo, image, likeness.
2 *reflection of hard work.* demonstration, evidence, indication, manifestation, result. **3** *no reflection on you.*
aspersion, censure, criticism, discredit, imputation, reproach, shame,
slur. **4** *time for reflection.* cerebration,
cogitation, contemplation, deliberation, meditation, pondering, rumination, self-examination, study,
thinking, thought.

reflective adj **1** glittering, lustrous,
reflecting, shiny, silvery. **2** ▷
THOUGHTFUL.

reform vb **1** ameliorate, amend,
become better, better, change, convert, correct, improve, make better,
mend, put right, reconstruct, rectify,
remodel, reorganize, save. **2** *reform a
system.* purge, reconstitute, regenerate, revolutionize.

refrain vb **refrain from** abstain from,
avoid, cease, desist from, do without, eschew, forbear, leave off, *inf*
quit, renounce, stop.

refresh vb **1** cool, energize, enliven,
fortify, freshen, invigorate, *inf* perk
up, quench the thirst of, reanimate,
rejuvenate, renew, restore, resuscitate, revitalize, revive, slake (*thirst*).
2 *refresh the memory.* activate, awaken,
jog, prod, prompt, remind, stimulate.

refreshing adj **1** bracing, cool,
enlivening, exhilarating, inspiriting,
invigorating, restorative, reviving,
stimulating, thirst-quenching, tingling, tonic. *Opp* EXHAUSTING. **2** *a
refreshing change.* different, fresh,
interesting, new, novel, original,
unexpected, unfamiliar, unforeseen,
unpredictable, welcome. *Opp* BORING.

refreshments plur n drinks, eatables, *inf* eats, *inf* nibbles, snack.
▷ DRINK, FOOD.

refrigerate vb chill, cool, freeze, ice,
keep cold.

refuge n asylum, *inf* bolt-hole, cover,
harbour, haven, *inf* hideaway, hide-
out, *inf* hidey-hole, hiding-place, protection, retreat, safety, sanctuary,
security, shelter, stronghold.

refugee n displaced person, émigré,
exile, fugitive, outcast, runaway.

refund n rebate, repayment. ● vb give
back, pay back, recoup, reimburse,
repay, return.

refusal n *inf* brush-off, denial, disagreement, disapproval, rebuff, rejection, veto. *Opp* ACCEPTANCE.

refuse n detritus, dirt, garbage, junk,
litter, rubbish, trash, waste. ● vb
baulk at, decline, deny, disallow, *inf*
jib at, *inf* pass up, rebuff, reject, repudiate, say no to, spurn, turn down,
veto, withhold. *Opp* ACCEPT, GRANT.

refute vb counter, discredit, disprove,
negate, prove wrong, rebut.

regain vb be reunited with, find, get
back, recapture, reclaim, recoup,
recover, repossess, retake, retrieve,
return to, win back.

regal adj *derog* haughty, imperial,
kingly, lordly, majestic, noble, palatial, *derog* pompous, princely,
queenly, royal, stately. ▷ SPLENDID.

regard n **1** gaze, look, scrutiny, stare.
2 attention, care, concern, consideration, deference, heed, notice, reference, respect, sympathy, thought.
3 admiration, affection, appreciation,
approbation, approval, deference,
esteem, favour, honour, love, respect,
reverence, veneration. ● vb **1** behold,
contemplate, eye, gaze at, keep an
eye on, look at, note, observe,
scrutinize, stare at, view, watch.
2 *regarded me as a liability.* account,
consider, deem, esteem, judge, look
upon, perceive, rate, reckon, respect,
think of, value, view, weigh up.

regarding prep about, apropos, concerning, connected with, involving,
on the subject of, pertaining to, *inf*
re, respecting, with reference to,
with regard to.

regardless adj **regardless of** careless about, despite, heedless of,
indifferent to, neglectful of, notwith-

standing, unconcerned about, unmindful of.

regime n administration, control, discipline, government, leadership, management, order, reign, rule, system.

regiment vb arrange, control, discipline, organize, regulate, systematize.

region n area, country, department, district, division, expanse, land, locality, neighbourhood, part, place, province, quarter, sector, territory, tract, vicinity, zone.

register n archives, catalogue, chronicle, diary, directory, file, index, inventory, journal, ledger, list, record, roll, tally. ● vb 1 enlist, enrol, enter your name, join, sign on. 2 *register a complaint*. catalogue, enter, list, log, make official, minute, present, record, set down, submit, write down. 3 *register emotion*. betray, display, divulge, express, indicate, manifest, reflect, reveal, show. 4 *register in a hotel*. inf check in, sign in. 5 *register what someone says*. keep in mind, make a note of, mark, notice, take account of.

regress vb backslide, degenerate, deteriorate, fall back, go back, move backwards, retreat, retrogress, revert, slip back. *Opp* PROGRESS.

regret n 1 bad conscience, compunction, contrition, guilt, penitence, pricking of conscience, remorse, repentance, self-accusation, self-condemnation, self-reproach, shame. 2 disappointment, grief, sadness, sorrow, sympathy. ● vb accuse yourself, bemoan, be regretful, be sad, bewail, deplore, deprecate, feel remorse, grieve (about), lament, mourn, repent (of), reproach yourself, rue, weep (over).

regretful adj apologetic, ashamed, conscience-stricken, contrite, disappointed, guilty, penitent, remorseful, repentant, rueful, sorry. ▷ SAD. *Opp* UNREPENTANT.

regrettable adj deplorable, disappointing, distressing, lamentable,

reprehensible, sad, shameful, undesirable, unfortunate, unhappy, unlucky, unwanted, upsetting, woeful, wrong.

regular adj 1 consistent, constant, equal, even, fixed, measured, ordered, predictable, recurring, repeated, rhythmic, steady, symmetrical, systematic, uniform, unvarying. □ *daily, hourly, monthly, weekly, yearly*. 2 *a regular procedure*. accustomed, common, commonplace, conventional, customary, established, everyday, familiar, frequent, habitual, known, normal, official, ordinary, orthodox, prevailing, proper, routine, scheduled, standard, traditional, typical, usual. 3 *a regular supporter*. dependable, faithful, reliable. *Opp* IRREGULAR. ● n inf faithful, frequenter, habitué, regular customer, patron.

regulate vb 1 administer, conduct, control, direct, govern, manage, monitor, order, organize, oversee, restrict, supervise. 2 *regulate temperature*. adjust, alter, balance, change, get right, moderate, modify, set, vary.

regulation n by-law, commandment, decree, dictate, directive, edict, law, order, ordinance, requirement, restriction, rule, ruling, statute.

rehearsal n dress rehearsal, inf dry run, exercise, practice, preparation, inf read-through, inf runthrough, inf try-out.

rehearse vb drill, go over, practise, prepare, inf run over, inf run through, try out.

rehearsed adj calculated, practised, pre-arranged, premeditated, prepared, scripted, studied, thought out. *Opp* IMPROMPTU.

reign n administration, ascendancy, command, empire, government, jurisdiction, kingdom, monarchy, power, rule, sovereignty. ● vb be king, be on the throne, be queen, command, govern, have power, hold sway, rule, inf wear the crown.

reincarnation n rebirth, return to life, transmigration.

reinforce vb **1** back up, bolster, buttress, fortify, give strength to, hold up, prop up, stay, stiffen, strengthen, support, toughen. **2** *reinforce an army.* add to, assist, augment, help, increase the size of, provide reinforcements for, supplement.

reinforcements plur n additional troops, auxiliaries, back-up, help, reserves, support.

reinstate vb recall, rehabilitate, restore, take back, welcome back. Opp DISMISS.

reject vb **1** cast off, discard, discount, dismiss, eliminate, exclude, jettison, inf junk, put aside, scrap, send back, throw away, throw out. **2** *reject friends.* disown, inf drop, inf give someone the cold shoulder, jilt, rebuff, renounce, repel, repudiate, repulse, inf send packing, shun, spurn, turn your back on. **3** *reject an invitation.* brush aside, decline, refuse, say no to, turn down, veto. Opp ACCEPT, ADOPT.

rejoice vb be happy, celebrate, delight, exult, glory, revel, triumph. Opp GRIEVE.

relapse n degeneration, deterioration, recurrence (*of illness*), regression, reversion, inf set-back, worsening. ● vb backslide, degenerate, deteriorate, fall back, have a relapse, lapse, regress, retreat, revert, sink back, slip back, weaken.

relate vb **1** communicate, describe, detail, divulge, impart, make known, narrate, present, recite, recount, rehearse, report, reveal, tell. **2** ally, associate, compare, connect, consider together, coordinate, correlate, couple, join, link. **relate to 1** appertain to, apply to, bear upon, be relevant to, concern, inf go with, pertain to, refer to. **2** *relate to other people.* be friends with, empathize with, fraternize with, handle, have a relationship with, identify with, socialize with, understand.

related adj affiliated, akin, allied, associated, cognate, comparable, connected, consanguineous, interconnected, interdependent, interrelated, joined, joint, linked, mutual, parallel, reciprocal, relative, similar, twin. ▷ RELEVANT. Opp UNRELATED.

relation n **1** old use kinsman, old use kinswoman, plur kith and kin, member of the family, relative. ▷ FAMILY. **2** *relation of a story.* ▷ NARRATION.

relationship n **1** affiliation, affinity, association, attachment, bond, closeness, connection, consanguinity, correlation, correspondence, interconnection, interdependence, kinship, link, parallel, pertinence, rapport, ratio, tie, understanding. ▷ SIMILARITY. Opp CONTRAST. **2** affair, inf intrigue, inf liaison, love affair, romance, sexual relations. ▷ FRIENDSHIP.

relative adj ▷ RELATED, RELEVANT. **relative to** commensurate (with), comparative, proportional, proportionate. Opp UNRELATED. ● n ▷ RELATION.

relax vb **1** be easy, be relaxed, calm down, cool down, feel at home, inf let go, inf put your feet up, rest, inf slow down, inf take it easy, unbend, unwind. Opp TENSION. **2** *relax your vigilance.* abate, curb, decrease, diminish, ease off, lessen, loosen, mitigate, moderate, reduce, release, relieve, slacken, soften, temper, inf tone down, unclench, unfasten, weaken. Opp INCREASE.

relaxation n **1** ease, informality, loosening up, relaxing, repose, rest, unwinding. ▷ RECREATION. Opp TENSION. **2** abatement, alleviation, diminution, lessening, inf let-up, mitigation, moderation, remission, slackening, weakening. Opp INCREASE.

relaxed adj derog blasé, calm, carefree, casual, comfortable, contented, cool, cosy, easygoing, inf free and easy, friendly, good-humoured, happy, inf happy-golucky, informal, insouciant, inf laid-back, derog lax, leisurely, light-hearted, nonchalant, peaceful, reassuring, restful, serene, *derog* slack, tranquil, unconcerned, unhurried, untroubled. *Opp* TENSE.

relay *n* **1** shift, turn. **2** *live relay*. broadcast, programme, transmission. ● *vb* broadcast, communicate, pass on, send out, spread, televise, transmit.

release *vb* **1** acquit, allow out, deliver, discharge, dismiss, emancipate, excuse, exonerate, free, let go, let loose, let off, liberate, loose, pardon, rescue, save, set free, set loose, unchain, unfasten, unfetter, unleash, unshackle, untie. *Opp* DETAIN. **2** fire off, launch, let fly, let off, send off. **3** *release information*. circulate, disseminate, distribute, issue, make available, present, publish, put out, send out, unveil.

relegate *vb* **1** consign to a lower position, demote, downgrade, put down. **2** banish, dispatch, exile.

relent *vb* acquiesce, become more lenient, be merciful, capitulate, give in, give way, relax, show pity, soften, weaken, yield.

relentless *adj* **1** dogged, fierce, hard-hearted, implacable, incessant, inexorable, intransigent, merciless, obdurate, obstinate, pitiless, remorseless, ruthless, uncompromising, unfeeling, unforgiving, unmerciful, unyielding. ▷ CRUEL. **2** unceasing, unrelieved, unstoppable, unyielding. ▷ CONTINUOUS.

relevant *adj* appertaining, applicable, apposite, appropriate, apropos, apt, connected, essential, fitting, germane, linked, material, pertinent, proper, related, relative, significant, suitable, suited, to the point. *Opp* IRRELEVANT.

reliable *adj* certain, conscientious, consistent, constant, dependable, devoted, efficient, faithful, honest, infallible, loyal, predictable, proven, punctilious, regular, reputable, responsible, safe, solid, sound, stable, staunch, steady, sure, trusted, trustworthy, trusty, unchanging, unfailing. *Opp* UNRELIABLE.

relic *n* heirloom, heritage, inheritance, keepsake, memento, remains, reminder, remnant, souvenir, survival, token, vestige.

relief *n* abatement, aid, alleviation, assistance, assuagement, comfort, cure, deliverance, diversion, ease, help, *inf* let-up, mitigation, palliation, relaxation, release, remedy, remission, respite, rest.

relieve *vb* abate, alleviate, anaesthetize, assuage, bring relief to, calm, comfort, console, cure, diminish, disburden, disencumber, dull, ease, lessen, lift, lighten, make less, mitigate, moderate, palliate, reduce, relax, release, rescue, soften, soothe, unburden. ▷ HELP. *Opp* INTENSIFY.

religion *n* **1** belief, creed, divinity, doctrine, dogma, *derog* pietism, theology. **2** creed, cult, denomination, faith, persuasion, sect. □ *Buddhism, Christianity, Hinduism, Islam, Judaism, Sikhism, Taoism, Zen.*

religious *adj* **1** devotional, divine, holy, sacramental, sacred, scriptural, theological. *Opp* SECULAR. **2** churchgoing, committed, dedicated, devout, God-fearing, godly, *derog* pietistic, pious, *derog* religiose, reverent, righteous, saintly, *derog* sanctimonious, spiritual. *Opp* IRRELIGIOUS. **3** *religious wars*. bigoted, doctrinal, fanatical, sectarian, schismatic.

relinquish *vb* concede, give in, hand over, part with, submit, surrender, yield.

relish *n* **1** appetite, delight, enjoyment, enthusiasm, gusto, pleasure, zest. **2** flavour, piquancy, savour, tang, taste. ● *vb* appreciate, delight in, enjoy, like, love, revel in, savour, take pleasure in.

reluctant *adj* averse, disinclined, grudging, hesitant, loath, unenthusiastic, unwilling. *Opp* EAGER.

rely *vb* **rely on** *inf* bank on, count on, depend on, have confidence in, lean on, put your faith in, *inf* swear by, trust.

remain *vb* old use abide, be left, carry on, continue, endure, keep on, linger, live on, persevere, persist, stay, *inf* stay put, survive, tarry, wait. **remaining** ▷ RESIDUAL.

remainder *n* balance, excess, extra, remnant, residue, residuum, rest, surplus. ▷ REMAINS.

remains *plur n* **1** crumbs, debris, detritus, dregs, fragments, *inf* leftovers, oddments, *inf* odds and ends, offcuts, remainder, remnants, residue, rubble, ruins, scraps, traces, vestiges, wreckage. **2** *historic remains.* heirloom, heritage, inheritance, keepsake, memento, monument, relic, reminder, souvenir, survival. **3** *human remains.* ashes, body, bones, carcass, corpse.

remake *vb* piece together, rebuild, reconstitute, reconstruct, redo. ▷ RENEW.

remark *n* comment, mention, observation, opinion, reflection, statement, thought, utterance, word. ● *vb* **1** assert, comment, declare, mention, note, observe, pass comment, reflect, say, state. **2** heed, mark, notice, observe, perceive, see, take note of.

remarkable *adj* amazing, astonishing, astounding, conspicuous, curious, different, distinguished, exceptional, extraordinary, important, impressive, marvellous, memorable, notable, noteworthy, odd, out-of-the-ordinary, outstanding, peculiar, phenomenal, prominent, signal, significant, singular, special, strange, striking, surprising, *inf* terrific, *inf* tremendous, uncommon, unforgettable, unusual, wonderful. *Opp* ORDINARY.

remedy *n inf* answer, antidote, corrective, countermeasure, cure, cure-all, drug, elixir, medicament, medication, medicine, nostrum, palliative, panacea, prescription, redress, relief, restorative, solution, therapy, treatment. ● *vb* alleviate, *inf* ameliorate, answer, control, correct, counteract, *inf* fix, heal, help, mend, mitigate, palliate, put right, rectify, redress, relieve, repair, solve, treat. ▷ CURE.

remember *vb* **1** be mindful of, have a memory of, have in mind, keep in mind, recognize. **2** learn, memorize, retain. **3** *remember old times.* be nostalgic about, hark back to, recall, recollect, reminisce about, review, summon up, tell stories about, think back to. **4** *remember Christmas.* celebrate, commemorate, observe. *Opp* FORGET.

remind *vb* give a reminder to, jog the memory of, nudge, prompt.

reminder *n* **1** aide-mémoire, cue, hint, *inf* memo, memorandum, mnemonic, note, *inf* nudge, prompt, *inf* shopping list. **2** heirloom, inheritance, keepsake, memento, relic, souvenir, survival.

reminisce *vb* be nostalgic, hark back, look back, recall, remember, review, tell stories, think back.

reminiscence *n* account, anecdote, memoir, memory, recollection, remembrance.

reminiscent *adj* evocative, nostalgic, recalling, redolent, suggestive.

remiss *adj* careless, dilatory, forgetful, irresponsible, lax, negligent, slack, thoughtless. *Opp* CAREFUL.

remit *vb* **1** *remit a debt.* cancel, let off, settle. **2** abate, decrease, ease off, lessen, relax, slacken. **3** dispatch, forward, send, transmit. ▷ PAY.

remittance *n* allowance, fee, payment.

remnants *plur n* bits, fragments, *inf* leftovers, oddments, offcuts, residue, scraps, traces, vestiges. ▷ REMAINS.

remodel *vb* ▷ RENEW.

remorse *n* bad conscience, compunction, contrition, grief, guilt, mortification, pangs of conscience, penitence, pricking of conscience, regret, repentance, sadness, self-accusation, self-reproach, shame, sorrow.

remorseful *adj* ashamed, conscience-stricken, contrite, grief-stricken, guilt-ridden, guilty, penitent, regretful, repentant, rueful, sorry. *Opp* UNREPENTANT.

remorseless *adj* dogged, implacable, inexorable, intransigent, merciless, obdurate, pitiless, relentless, ruthless, uncompromising, unforgiving, unkind, unmerciful, unremitting. ▷ CRUEL.

remote *adj* **1** alien, cut off, desolate, distant, far-away, foreign, God-forsaken, hard to find, inaccessible, isolated, lonely, outlying, out of reach, out of the way, secluded, solitary, unfamiliar, unfrequented, *inf* unget-at-able, unreachable. *Opp* CLOSE. **2** *a remote chance*. doubtful, implausible, improbable, negligible, outside, poor, slender, slight, small, unlikely. *Opp* SURE. **3** *a remote manner*. abstracted, aloof, cold, cool, detached, haughty, preoccupied, reserved, standoffish, uninvolved, withdrawn. *Opp* FRIENDLY.

removal *n* **1** relocation, removing, taking away, transfer, transportation. **2** elimination, eradication, extermination, liquidation, purge, purging. ▷ KILLING. **3** *removal from a job*. deposition, dethronement, dislodgement, dismissal, displacement, ejection, expulsion, *inf* firing, making redundant, ousting, redundancy, *inf* sacking, transference, unseating. **4** *removal of teeth*. drawing, extraction, pulling, taking out, withdrawal.

remove *vb* abolish, abstract, amputate (*limb*), banish, clear away, cut off, cut out, delete, depose, detach, disconnect, dismiss, dispense with, displace, dispose of, do away with, eject, eliminate, eradicate, erase, evict, excise, exile, expel, expunge, *inf* fire, *inf* get rid of, *inf* kick out, kill, oust, purge, root out, rub out, *inf* sack, send away, separate, strike out, sweep away, take out, throw out, turn out, undo, unfasten, uproot, wash off, wipe (*tape-recording*), wipe out. **2** *remove furniture*. carry away, convey, move, take away, transfer, transport. **3** *remove a tooth*. draw out, extract, pull out, take out. **4** *remove clothes*. doff (*a hat*), peel off, strip off, take off.

rend *vb* cleave, lacerate, pull apart, rip, rupture, shred, split, tear.

render *vb* **1** cede, deliver, furnish, give, hand over, offer, present, proffer, provide, surrender, tender, yield. **2** *render a song*. execute, interpret, perform, play, produce, sing. **3** *rendered me speechless*. cause to be, make.

rendezvous *n* appointment, assignation, date, engagement, meeting, meeting-place, *old use* tryst.

renegade *n* apostate, backslider, defector, deserter, fugitive, heretic, mutineer, outlaw, rebel, runaway, traitor, turncoat.

renege *vb* **renege on** abjure, abrogate, *inf* back out of, break, default on, fail to keep, go back on, *sl* rat on, repudiate, *sl* welsh on.

renew *vb* **1** bring up to date, *inf* do up, *inf* give a face-lift to, improve, mend, modernize, overhaul, recondition, reconstitute, recreate, redecorate, redesign, redevelop, redo, refit, refresh, refurbish, regenerate, reintroduce, rejuvenate, remake, remodel, renovate, repaint, repair, replace, replenish, restore, resume, resurrect, revamp, revitalize, revive, touch up, transform, update. **2** *renew an activity*. come back to, pick up again, recommence, restart, resume, return to. **3** *renew vows*. confirm, reaffirm, reiterate, repeat, restate.

renounce *vb* **1** abandon, abjure, abstain from, declare your opposition to, deny, desert, discard, disown, eschew, forgo, forsake, forswear, give up, reject, repudiate, spurn. **2** *renounce the throne*. abdicate, *inf* quit, relinquish, resign, surrender.

renovate *vb* ▷ RENEW.

renovation *n* improvement, modernization, overhaul, reconditioning, redevelopment, refit, refurbishment, renewal, repair, restoration, transformation, updating.

renowned *adj* celebrated, distinguished, eminent, illustrious, noted, prominent, well-known. ▷ FAMOUS.

rent *n* **1** fee, hire, instalment, payment, rental. **2** *a rent in a garment*. ▷ SPLIT. ● *vb* charter, farm out, hire, lease, let.

reorganize *vb* rationalize, re-arrange, re-deploy, reshuffle, restructure.

repair *vb* **1** *inf* fix, mend, overhaul, patch up, put right, rectify, refit, restore, service. ▷ RENEW. **2** darn, patch, sew up.

repay *vb* **1** compensate, give back, pay back, recompense, refund, reimburse, remunerate, settle. **2** avenge, get even, *inf* get your own back, reciprocate, requite, retaliate, return, revenge.

repeal *vb* abolish, abrogate, annul, cancel, invalidate, nullify, rescind, reverse, revoke.

repeat *vb* **1** do again, duplicate, redo, rehearse, replay, replicate, reproduce, re-run, show again. **2** echo, quote, recapitulate, re-echo, regurgitate, reiterate, restate, retell, say again.

repel *vb* **1** check, drive away, fend off, fight off, hold off, *inf* keep at bay, parry, push away, rebuff, repulse, resist, ward off, withstand. **2** *repel water*. be impermeable to, exclude, keep out, reject. **3** *cruelty repels us*. alienate, be repellent to, disgust, nauseate, offend, *inf* put off, revolt, sicken, *inf* turn off. *Opp* ATTRACT.

repellent *adj* **1** impermeable, impervious, resistant, unsusceptible. **2** ▷ REPULSIVE.

repent *vb* bemoan, be repentant about, bewail, feel repentance for, lament, regret, reproach yourself for, rue.

repentance *n* contrition, guilt, penitence, regret, remorse, self-accusation, self-reproach, shame, sorrow.

repentant *adj* apologetic, ashamed, conscience-stricken, contrite, grief-stricken, guilt-ridden, guilty, penitent, regretful, remorseful, rueful, sorry. *Opp* UNREPENTANT.

repertory *n* collection, repertoire, repository, reserve, stock, store, supply.

repetitive *adj* boring, incessant, iterative, monotonous, recurrent, repeated, repeating, repetitious, tautologous, tedious, unchanging, unvaried. ▷ CONTINUAL.

replace *vb* **1** make good, put back, reinstate, restore, return. **2** be a replacement for, come after, follow, oust, succeed, supersede, supplant, take over from, take the place of. ▷ DEPUTIZE. **3** *replace worn parts*. change, renew, substitute.

replacement *n* *inf* fill-in, proxy, stand-in, substitute, successor, understudy.

replenish *vb* fill up, refill, renew, restock, top up.

replete *adj* *inf* bursting, crammed, gorged, *inf* jam-packed, overloaded, sated, stuffed. ▷ FULL.

replica *n* *inf* carbon copy, clone, copy, duplicate, facsimile, imitation, likeness, model, reconstruction, reproduction.

reply *n* acknowledgement, answer, *inf* come-back, reaction, rejoinder, response, retort, riposte. ● *vb* answer, give a reply, react, rejoin, respond. **reply to** ▷ ACKNOWLEDGE, COUNTER.

report *n* **1** account, announcement, article, communication, communiqué, description, dispatch, narrative, news, record, statement, story, *inf* write-up. **2** backfire, bang, blast, boom, crack, detonation, discharge, explosion, noise. ● *vb* **1** announce, broadcast, circulate, communicate, declare, describe, disclose, divulge, document, give an account of, notify, present a report on, proclaim, publish, put out, record, recount, reveal, state, tell. **2** *report for duty*. present yourself, check in, clock in, introduce yourself, make yourself known, present yourself, sign in. **3** *report someone to the police*. complain about, denounce, inform against, *inf* tell on.

reporter *n* columnist, commentator, correspondent, journalist, newscaster, newsman, newspaperman, newspaperwoman, news presenter, newswoman, photojournalist.

repose *n* calm, calmness, comfort, ease, inactivity, peace, peacefulness, poise, quiescence, quiet, quietness, relaxation, respite, rest, serenity, stasis, stillness, tranquillity. ▷ SLEEP. *Opp* ACTIVITY.

reprehensible *adj* blameworthy, culpable, deplorable, disgraceful, immoral, objectionable, regrettable, remiss, shameful, unworthy, wicked. ▷ GUILTY. *Opp* INNOCENT.

represent *vb* **1** act out, assume the guise of, be an example of, embody, enact, epitomize, exemplify, exhibit, express, illustrate, impersonate, incarnate, masquerade as, personify, pose as, present, pretend to be, stand for, symbolize, typify. **2** characterize, define, delineate, depict, describe, draw, paint, picture, portray, reflect, show, sketch. **3** act for, speak for, stand up for.

representation *n* depiction, figure, icon, image, imitation, likeness, model, picture, portrait, portrayal, resemblance, semblance, statue.

representative *adj* **1** archetypal, average, characteristic, illustrative, normal, typical. *Opp* ABNORMAL. **2** *representative government*. chosen, democratic, elected, elective, popular. *Opp* TOTALITARIAN. ● *n* **1** delegate, deputy, proxy, spokesman, spokeswoman, stand-in, substitute. **2** agent, *inf* rep, salesman, salesperson, saleswoman, *inf* traveller. **3** ambassador, consul, diplomat, emissary, envoy, legate. **4** *Amer* congressman, councillor, Member of Parliament, MP, ombudsman.

repress *vb* **1** control, crush, curb, keep down, limit, oppress, overcome, put down, quell, restrain, subdue, subjugate. **2** *repress emotion*. *inf* bottle up, frustrate, inhibit, stifle, suppress.

repressed *adj* **1** cold, frigid, frustrated, inhibited, neurotic, *inf* prim and proper, tense, unbalanced, undemonstrative, *inf* uptight. *Opp* UNINHIBITED. **2** *repressed emotion*. *inf* bottled up, hidden, latent, subconscious, suppressed, unconscious, unfulfilled.

repression *n* **1** authoritarianism, censorship, coercion, control, despotism, dictatorship, oppression, restraint, subjugation, totalitarianism, tyranny. **2** *repression of emotion*. *inf* bottling up, frustration, inhibition, suffocation, suppression.

repressive *adj* authoritarian, autocratic, brutal, coercive, cruel, despotic, dictatorial, fascist, harsh, illiberal, oppressive, restricting, severe, totalitarian, tyrannical, undemocratic, unenlightened. *Opp* LIBERAL.

reprieve *n* amnesty, pardon, postponement, respite, stay of execution. ● *vb* commute a sentence, forgive, let off, pardon, postpone execution, set free, spare.

reprimand *n* admonition, castigation, censure, condemnation, criticism, *inf* dressing-down, *inf* going-over, *inf* lecture, lesson, *inf* rap on the knuckles, rebuke, remonstration, reproach, reproof, scolding, *inf* slap on the wrist, *inf* slating, *inf* talking-to, *inf* telling-off, *inf* ticking-off, upbraiding, *inf* wigging. ● *vb* admonish, berate, blame, *inf* carpet, castigate, censure, chide, condemn, correct, criticize, disapprove of, *inf* dress down, find fault with, *inf* haul over the coals, *inf* lecture, *inf* rap, rate, *inf* read the riot act to, rebuke, reprehend, reproach, reprove, scold, *inf* slate, *inf* take to task, *inf* teach a lesson, *inf* tell off, *inf* tick off, upbraid. *Opp* PRAISE.

reprisal *n* counter-attack, getting even, redress, repayment, retaliation, retribution, revenge, vengeance.

reproach *n* blame, disapproval, disgrace, scorn. ● *vb* censure, criticize, scold, show disapproval of, upbraid. ▷ REPRIMAND. *Opp* PRAISE.

reproachful *adj* admonitory, censorious, condemnatory, critical, disapproving, disparaging, reproving, scornful, withering.

reproduce *vb* **1** copy, counterfeit, duplicate, forge, imitate, mimic, photocopy, print, redo, reissue, reprint, simulate. ▷ REPEAT. **2** beget young, breed, increase, multiply, procreate, produce offspring, propagate, regenerate, spawn.

reproduction *n* **1** breeding, cloning, increase, multiplying, procreation, proliferation, propagation, spawning. **2** *inf* carbon copy, clone, copy, duplicate, facsimile, fake, forgery, imitation, likeness, print, replica.

repudiate *vb* **1** deny, disagree with, dispute, rebuff, refute, reject, scorn, turn down. *Opp* ACKNOWLEDGE. **2** *repudiate an agreement*. abrogate, discard, disown, go back on, recant, renounce, rescind, retract, reverse, revoke.

repugnant *adj* ▷ REPULSIVE.

repulsive *adj* abhorrent, abominable, beastly, disagreeable, disgusting, distasteful, distressing, foul, gross, hateful, hideous, loathsome, nasty, nauseating, nauseous, objectionable, obnoxious, odious, offensive, *inf* off-putting, repellent, repugnant, revolting, *inf* sick, sickening, unattractive, unpalatable, unpleasant, unsavoury, unsightly, vile. ▷ UGLY. *Opp* ATTRACTIVE.

reputable *adj* creditable, dependable, esteemed, famous, good, highly regarded, honourable, honoured, prestigious, reliable, respectable, respected, trustworthy, unimpeachable, *inf* up-market, well-thought-of, worthy. *Opp* DISREPUTABLE.

reputation *n* character, fame, name, prestige, recognition, renown, repute, standing, stature, status.

reputed *adj* alleged, assumed, believed, considered, deemed, famed, judged, purported, reckoned, regarded, rumoured, said, supposed, thought.

request *n* appeal, application, call, demand, entreaty, petition, plea, prayer, question, requisition, solicitation, suit, supplication. ● *vb* adjure, appeal, apply (for), ask, beg, beseech, call for, claim, demand, desire, entreat, implore, importune, invite, petition, pray for, require, requisition, seek, solicit, supplicate.

require *vb* **1** be missing, be short of, depend on, lack, need, want. **2** *require a response*. call for, coerce, command, compel, direct, force, insist, instruct, make, oblige, order, put pressure on. ▷ REQUEST. **required** ▷ REQUISITE.

requirement *n* condition, demand, essential, necessity, need, precondition, prerequisite, provision, proviso, qualification, *Lat* sine qua non, stipulation.

requisite *adj* compulsory, essential, imperative, indispensable, mandatory, necessary, needed, obligatory, prescribed, required, set, stipulated. *Opp* OPTIONAL.

requisition *n* application, authorization, demand, mandate, order, request, voucher. ● *vb* **1** demand, order, *inf* put in for, request. **2** appropriate, commandeer, confiscate, expropriate, occupy, seize, take over, take possession of.

rescue *n* deliverance, emancipation, freeing, liberation, recovery, release, relief, salvage. ● *vb* **1** deliver, emancipate, extricate, free, let go, liberate, loose, ransom, release, save, set free. **2** get back, recover, retrieve, salvage.

research *n* analysis, enquiry, examination, experimentation, exploration, fact-finding, inquiry, investigation, *inf* probe, scrutiny, searching, study. ● *vb* *inf* check out, *inf* delve into, experiment, investigate, *inf* probe, search, study.

resemblance *n* affinity, closeness, coincidence, comparability, comparison, conformity, congruity, correspondence, equivalence, likeness, similarity, similitude.

resemble *vb* approximate to, bear resemblance to, be similar to, compare with, look like, mirror, sound like, *inf* take after.

resent *vb* begrudge, be resentful about, dislike, envy, feel bitter about, grudge, grumble at, object to, *inf* take exception to, *inf* take umbrage at.

resentful adj aggrieved, annoyed, begrudging, bitter, disgruntled, displeased, embittered, envious, grudging, hurt, indignant, irked, jaundiced, jealous, malicious, offended, inf peeved, inf put out, spiteful, unfriendly, ungenerous, upset, vexed, vindictive. ▷ ANGRY.

resentment n animosity, bitterness, discontent, envy, grudge, hatred, hurt, ill-will, indignation, irritation, jealousy, malevolence, malice, pique, rancour, spite, unfriendliness, vexation, vindictiveness. ▷ ANGER.

reservation n 1 condition, doubt, hedging, hesitation, misgiving, proviso, qualification, qualm, reluctance, reticence, scepticism, scruple. 2 *hotel reservation.* appointment, booking. 3 *a wildlife reservation.* ▷ RESERVE.

reserve n 1 cache, fund, hoard, inf nest-egg, reservoir, savings, stock, stockpile, store, supply. 2 inf backup, deputy, plur reinforcements, replacement, stand-by, inf stand-in, substitute, understudy. 3 *a wildlife reserve.* enclave, game park, preserve, protected area, reservation, safaripark, sanctuary. 4 aloofness, caution, modesty, quietness, reluctance, reticence, self-consciousness, self-effacement, shyness, derog standoffishness, taciturnity, timidity. ● vb 1 earmark, hoard, hold back, keep, keep back, preserve, put aside, retain, save, set aside, stockpile, store up. 2 *reserve seats.* inf bag, book, order, pay for. **reserved** ▷ RETICENT.

reside vb **reside in** dwell in, inhabit, live in, lodge in, occupy, settle in.

residence n old use abode, address, domicile, dwelling, dwelling-place, habitation, home, quarters, seat. ▷ HOUSE.

resident adj in residence, living in, permanent, remaining, staying. ● n citizen, denizen, dweller, householder, houseowner, inhabitant, inf local, native.

residual adj abiding, continuing, left over, outstanding, persisting, remaining, surviving, unconsumed, unused.

resign vb abandon, abdicate, sl chuck in, forsake, give up, leave, quit, relinquish, renounce, retire, stand down, step down, surrender, vacate. **resigned** ▷ PATIENT. **resign yourself to** ▷ ACCEPT.

resilient adj 1 bouncy, elastic, firm, plastic, pliable, rubbery, springy, supple. Opp BRITTLE. 2 *a resilient person.* adaptable, buoyant, irrepressible, strong, tough, unstoppable. Opp VULNERABLE.

resist vb avoid, be resistant to, check, confront, counteract, defy, face up to, hinder, inf hold out against, inf hold your ground against, impede, inhibit, keep at bay, oppose, prevent, rebuff, refuse, stand up to, withstand. ▷ FIGHT. Opp ASSIST, YIELD.

resistant adj defiant, hostile, intransigent, invulnerable, obstinate, opposed, refractory, stubborn, uncooperative, unresponsive, unyielding. **resistant to** against, impervious to, invulnerable to, opposed to, proof against, repellent of, unaffected by, unsusceptible to, unyielding to. Opp SUSCEPTIBLE.

resolute adj adamant, bold, committed, constant, courageous, decided, decisive, determined, dogged, firm, immovable, immutable, indefatigable, derog inflexible, derog obstinate, persevering, persistent, pertinacious, relentless, resolved, single-minded, staunch, steadfast, strong-minded, strong-willed, derog stubborn, tireless, unbending, undaunted, unflinching, unshakable, unswerving, untiring, unwavering. Opp IRRESOLUTE.

resolution n 1 boldness, commitment, constancy, determination, devotion, doggedness, firmness, derog obstinacy, perseverance, persistence, pertinacity, purposefulness, resolve, single-mindedness, staunchness, steadfastness, derog stubbornness, tenacity, will-power. ▷ COURAGE. 2 commitment, oath, pledge, promise, undertaking, vow. 3 *resolu-*

tion at a meeting. decision, motion, proposal, proposition, statement. **4** *resolution of a problem.* answer, denouement, disentangling, resolving, settlement, solution, sorting out.

resolve n ▷ RESOLUTION. ● vb **1** agree, conclude, decide formally, determine, elect, fix, make a decision, make up your mind, opt, pass a resolution, settle, undertake, vote. **2** *resolve a problem.* answer, clear up, disentangle, figure out, settle, solve, sort out, work out.

resonant adj booming, echoing, full, pulsating, resounding, reverberant, reverberating, rich, ringing, sonorous, thunderous, vibrant, vibrating.

resort n **1** alternative, course of action, expedient, option, recourse, refuge, remedy, reserve. **2** *a seaside resort.* holiday town, retreat, spa, *old use* wateringplace. ● vb **resort to 1** adopt, *inf* fall back on, have recourse to, make use of, turn to, use. **2** frequent, go to, *inf* hang out in, haunt, invade, patronize, visit.

resound vb boom, echo, pulsate, resonate, reverberate, ring, rumble, thunder, vibrate. **resounding** ▷ RESONANT.

resourceful adj clever, creative, enterprising, imaginative, ingenious, innovative, inspired, inventive, original, skilful, *inf* smart, talented. Opp SHIFTLESS.

resources plur n **1** assets, capital, funds, possessions, property, reserves, riches, wealth. ▷ MONEY. **2** *natural resources.* materials, raw materials.

respect n **1** admiration, appreciation, awe, consideration, courtesy, deference, esteem, homage, honour, liking, love, politeness, regard, reverence, tribute, veneration. **2** *perfect in every respect.* aspect, attribute, characteristic, detail, element, facet, feature, particular, point, property, quality, trait, way. ● vb admire, appreciate, be polite to, defer to, esteem, have high regard for, hon-

our, look up to, pay homage to, revere, reverence, show respect to, think well of, value, venerate. Opp DESPISE.

respectable adj **1** decent, genteel, honest, honourable, law-abiding, refined, respected, unimpeachable, upright, worthy. **2** *respectable clothes.* chaste, clean, decorous, dignified, modest, presentable, proper, seemly. Opp DISREPUTABLE. **3** *a respectable sum.* ▷ CONSIDERABLE.

respectful adj admiring, civil, considerate, cordial, courteous, deferential, dutiful, gentlemanly, gracious, humble, ladylike, obliging, polite, proper, reverent, reverential, *derog* servile, subservient, thoughtful, well-mannered. Opp DISRESPECTFUL.

respective adj individual, own, particular, personal, relevant, separate, several, special, specific.

respite n break, *inf* breather, delay, hiatus, holiday, intermission, interruption, interval, *inf* let-up, lull, pause, recess, relaxation, relief, remission, rest, time off, time out, vacation.

resplendent adj brilliant, dazzling, glittering, shining, splendid. ▷ BRIGHT.

respond vb **respond to 1** acknowledge, answer, counter, give a response to, react to, reciprocate, reply to. **2** *respond to need.* ▷ SYMPATHIZE.

response n acknowledgement, answer, *inf* comeback, counter, counterblast, feedback, reaction, rejoinder, reply, retort, riposte.

responsible adj **1** at fault, culpable, guilty, liable, to blame. **2** *a responsible person.* accountable, answerable, concerned, conscientious, creditable, dependable, diligent, dutiful, ethical, honest, in charge, law-abiding, loyal, mature, moral, reliable, sensible, sober, steady, thinking, thoughtful, trustworthy, unselfish. Opp IRRESPONSIBLE. **3** *a responsible job.* burdensome, decision-making, executive, *inf* frontline, important, managerial, *inf* top. *Opp* MENIAL.

responsive *adj* alert, alive, aware, impressionable, interested, open, perceptive, receptive, sensitive, sharp, sympathetic, warm-hearted, wideawake, willing. *Opp* UNINTERESTED.

rest *n* **1** break, *inf* breather, breathing-space, comfort, ease, hiatus, idleness, inactivity, indolence, interlude, intermission, interval, leisure, *inf* let-up, *inf* lie-down, *inf* loafing, lull, nap, pause, quiet, recess, relaxation, relief, remission, repose, respite, siesta, tea-break, time off, vacation. ▷ SLEEP. **2** base, brace, bracket, holder, prop, stand, support, trestle, tripod. **3** ▷ REMAINDER. ● *vb* **1** be still, doze, have a rest, idle, laze, lie back, lie down, lounge, nod off, *inf* put your feet up, recline, relax, snooze, *inf* take a nap, *inf* take it easy, unwind. ▷ SLEEP. **2** lean, place, position, prop, set, stand, support. **3** *It all rests on the weather.* depend, hang, hinge, rely, turn. **come to rest** ▷ HALT.

restaurant *n* eating-place. □ *bistro, brasserie, buffet, café, cafeteria, canteen, carvery, diner, dining-room, grill, refectory, snack-bar, steak-house.*

restful *adj* calm, calming, comfortable, leisurely, peaceful, quiet, relaxed, relaxing, reposeful, soothing, still, tranquil, undisturbed, unhurried, untroubled. *Opp* EXHAUSTING.

restless *adj* **1** agitated, anxious, edgy, excitable, fidgety, highly-strung, impatient, *inf* jittery, jumpy, nervous, *inf* on tenterhooks, restive, skittish, uneasy, worked up, worried. ▷ ACTIVE. **2** *a restless night.* disturbed, interrupted, sleepless, *inf* tossing and turning, troubled, uncomfortable, unsettled. *Opp* RESTFUL.

restore *vb* **1** bring back, give back, make restitution, put back, reinstate, replace, return. **2** *restore antiques.* clean, *inf* do up, fix, *inf* make good, mend, rebuild, recondition, reconstruct, refurbish, renew, renovate, repair, touch up. **3** *restore good rela-*

tions. re-establish, rehabilitate, reinstate, reintroduce, rekindle, revive. **4** *restore to health.* cure, nurse, rejuvenate, resuscitate, revitalize.

restrain *vb* **1** check, control, curb, govern, hold back, inhibit, keep back, keep under control, limit, regulate, rein in, repress, restrict, stifle, stop, strait-jacket, subdue, suppress. **2** arrest, bridle, confine, detain, fetter, handcuff, harness, imprison, incarcerate, jail, *inf* keep under lock and key, lock up, manacle, muzzle, pinion, tie up. **restrained** ▷ CALM, DISCREET.

restrict *vb* circumscribe, confine, control, cramp, delimit, enclose, impede, imprison, inhibit, keep within bounds, limit, regulate, shut. ▷ RESTRAIN. *Opp* FREE.

restriction *n* ban, check, constraint, control, curb, curfew, inhibition, limit, limitation, proviso, qualification, regulation, restraint, rule, stipulation.

result *n* **1** conclusion, consequence, effect, end-product, fruit, issue, outcome, repercussion, sequel, upshot. **2** *result of a trial.* decision, judgement, verdict. **3** *result of a sum.* answer, product, score, total. ● *vb* arise, be produced, come about, develop, emanate, emerge, ensue, eventuate, follow, happen, issue, occur, proceed, spring, stem, take place, turn out. **result in** ▷ CAUSE.

resume *vb* begin again, carry on, continue, *inf* pick up the threads, proceed, recommence, reconvene, re-open, restart.

resumption *n* continuation, recommencement, re-opening, *inf* restart.

resurrect *vb* breathe new life into, bring back, raise (from the dead), reawaken, restore, resuscitate, revitalize, revive. ▷ RENEW.

retain *vb* **1** *inf* hang on to, hold, hold back, keep, keep control of, maintain, preserve, reserve, save. *Opp* LOSE. **2** *retain moisture.* absorb, soak up. **3** *retain facts.* keep in mind, learn, memorize, remember. *Opp* FORGET.

retaliate vb avenge yourself, be revenged, counter-attack, exact retribution, inf get even, inf get your own back, inf give tit for tat, hit back, pay back, repay, revenge yourself, seek retribution, inf settle a score, strike back, inf take an eye for an eye, take revenge, wreak vengeance.

retaliation n counter-attack, reprisal, retribution, revenge, vengeance.

retard vb check, handicap, hinder, hold back, hold up, impede, obstruct, postpone, put back, set back, slow down. ▷ DELAY. **retarded** ▷ BACKWARD.

reticent adj aloof, derog antisocial, bashful, cautious, derog cold, cool, demure, diffident, discreet, distant, modest, quiet, remote, reserved, restrained, retiring, secretive, self-conscious, self-effacing, shy, silent, derog standoffish, taciturn, timid, uncommunicative, undemonstrative, unemotional, unforthcoming, unresponsive, unsociable, withdrawn. Opp DEMONSTRATIVE.

retinue n attendants, company, entourage, followers, inf hangers-on, servants, suite, train.

retire vb 1 give up, leave, quit, resign. 2 retire from society. become reclusive, cloister yourself, go away, go into retreat, retreat from the world, sequester yourself, withdraw. 3 aestivate, go to bed, hibernate, sl hit the hay. ▷ SLEEP.

retort n answer, inf comeback, rebuttal, rejoinder, reply, response, retaliation, riposte. ● vb answer, counter, react, rejoin, reply, respond, retaliate, return.

retract vb 1 draw in, pull back, pull in. 2 abandon, cancel, disclaim, disown, forswear, inf have second thoughts about, recant, renounce, repeal, repudiate, rescind, reverse, revoke, withdraw.

retreat n 1 departure, escape, evacuation, exit, flight, retirement, withdrawal. 2 a secluded retreat. asylum, den, haven, inf hideaway, hideout, hiding-place, refuge, resort, sanctuary, shelter. ● vb 1 back away, back down, climb down, decamp, depart, evacuate, fall back, flee, give ground, go away, leave, move back, pull back, retire, inf run away, take flight, inf take to your heels, inf turn tail, withdraw. 2 the floods retreated. ebb, flow back, recede, shrink back. Opp ADVANCE.

retribution n compensation, Lat quid pro quo, recompense, redress, reprisal, retaliation, revenge, old use satisfaction, vengeance. Opp FORGIVENESS.

retrieve vb bring back, come back with, fetch back, find, get back, make up for, recapture, reclaim, recoup, recover, regain, repossess, rescue, restore, return, salvage, save, take back, trace, track down.

retrograde adj backward, negative, regressive, retreating, retrogressive, reverse.

retrospective adj backward-looking, looking back, looking behind, nostalgic, with hindsight.

return n 1 advent, arrival, homecoming, reappearance, re-entry. 2 return to normality. re-establishment (of), regression, reversion. 3 return of a problem recrudescence, recurrence, re-emergence, repetition. 4 return of stolen goods. replacing, restitution, restoration, retrieval. 5 return on an investment. benefit, earnings, gain, income, interest, proceeds, profit, yield. ● vb 1 backtrack, come back, do a U-turn, double back, go back, reassemble, reconvene, re-enter, regress, retrace your steps, revert, turn back. 2 put back, readdress, repatriate, replace, restore, send back. 3 return money. exchange, give back, refund, reimburse, repay. 4 return a verdict. inf come up with, deliver, give, proffer, report. 5 The problem returned. inf crop up again, happen again, reappear, recur, resurface.

reveal vb announce, bare, betray, bring to light, communicate, confess, declare, denude, dig up, disclose, display, divulge, exhibit, expose, inf give the game away, lay bare, leak, *inf* let on, *inf* let out, *inf* let slip, make known, open, proclaim, produce, publish, show, show up, *inf* spill the beans about, *inf* take the wraps off, tell, uncover, undress, unearth, unfold, unmask, unveil. *Opp* HIDE.

revel n carnival, festival, fête, *inf* jamboree, *inf* rave-up, *inf* spree. ▷ REVELRY. ● *vb* carouse, celebrate, *inf* have a spree, have fun, indulge in revelry, *inf* live it up, make merry, *inf* paint the town red. **revel in** ▷ ENJOY.

revelation n admission, announcement, communiqué, confession, declaration, disclosure, discovery, exposé, exposure, information, *inf* leak, news, proclamation, publication, revealing, unmasking, unveiling.

revelry n carousing, celebration, conviviality, debauchery, festivity, fun, gaiety, *inf* high jinks, jollification, jollity, *inf* junketing, *inf* living it up, merry-making, revelling, revels, roistering, *inf* spree. ▷ PARTY.

revenge n reprisal, retaliation, retribution, spitefulness, vengeance, vindictiveness. ● *vb* avenge, repay. **be revenged** ▷ RETALIATE.

revenue n gain, income, interest, money, proceeds, profits, receipts, returns, takings, yield.

reverberate vb boom, echo, pulsate, resonate, resound, ring, rumble, throb, thunder, vibrate.

revere vb admire, adore, adulate, beatify, esteem, feel reverence for, glorify, honour, idolize, pay homage to, praise, respect, reverence, value, venerate, worship. *Opp* DESPISE.

reverence n admiration, adoration, adulation, awe, deference, devotion, esteem, glorification, homage, honour, idolization, praise, respect, veneration, worship.

reverent adj adoring, awed, awestruck, deferential, devoted, devout, pious, prayerful, religious, respectful, reverential, solemn, worshipful. *Opp* IRREVERENT.

reverie n *inf* brown study, daydream, dream, fantasy, meditation.

reverse adj back, back-to-front, backward, contrary, converse, inverse, inverted, opposite, rear. ● n **1** antithesis, contrary, converse, opposite. **2** back, rear, underside, verso, wrong side. **3** defeat, difficulty, disaster, failure, misfortune, mishap, problem, reversal, setback, *inf* upset, vicissitude. ● *vb* **1** change, invert, overturn, transpose, turn round, turn upsidedown. **2** *reverse a car.* back, drive backwards, go into reverse. **3** *reverse a decision.* abandon, annul, cancel, countermand, invalidate, negate, nullify, overturn, quash, recant, repeal, rescind, retract, revoke, undo.

review n **1** examination, *inf* look back, *inf* post-mortem, reappraisal, reassessment, recapitulation, reconsideration, re-examination, report, retrospective, study, survey. **2** *book review.* appreciation, assessment, commentary, criticism, critique, evaluation, judgement, notice, *inf* write-up. ● *vb* **1** appraise, assess, consider, evaluate, examine, *inf* go over, inspect, reassess, recapitulate, reconsider, re-examine, scrutinize, study, survey, take stock of, *inf* weigh up. **2** *review a book.* criticize, write a review of.

revise vb **1** adapt, alter, change, correct, edit, emend, improve, modify, overhaul, *inf* polish up, reconsider, rectify, *inf* redo, *inf* rehash, rephrase, revamp, reword, rework, rewrite, update. **2** *revise for exams.* brush up, *inf* cram, learn, study, *inf* swot.

revival n advance, progress, quickening, reanimation, reawakening, rebirth, recovery, renaissance, renewal, restoration, resurgence, resurrection, resuscitation, return, revitalization, upsurge.

revive vb **1** awaken, come back to life, *inf* come round, *inf* come to, quicken, rally, reawaken, recover, resurrect, rouse, waken. *Opp* RELAPSE. **2** bring back to life, *inf* cheer up, freshen, invigorate, refresh, renew, restore, resuscitate, revitalize, strengthen. *Opp* WEARY.

revolt n civil war, coup, coup d'état, insurrection, mutiny, putsch, rebellion, reformation, revolution, rising, *inf* take-over, uprising. ● *vb* **1** disobey, dissent, mutiny, rebel, riot, rise up. **2** appal, disgust, nauseate, offend, outrage, repel, sicken, upset. **revolting** ▷ OFFENSIVE.

revolution n **1** ▷ REVOLT. **2** circuit, cycle, gyration, orbit, rotation, spin, turn. **3** change, reorganization, reorientation, shift, transformation, *inf* turn-about, upheaval, *inf* upset, *inf* U-turn.

revolutionary adj **1** insurgent, mutinous, rebel, rebellious, seditious, subversive. **2** *revolutionary ideas*. avant-garde, challenging, creative, different, experimental, extremist, innovative, new, novel, progressive, radical, *inf* unheard-of, upsetting. *Opp* CONSERVATIVE. ● n anarchist, extremist, freedom fighter, insurgent, mutineer, rebel, terrorist.

revolve vb circle, go round, gyrate, orbit, pirouette, pivot, reel, rotate, spin, swivel, turn, twirl, wheel, whirl.

revulsion n abhorrence, aversion, disgust, hatred, loathing, nausea, outrage, repugnance.

reward n award, bonus, bounty, compensation, decoration, favour, honour, medal, payment, prize, recompense, remuneration, requital, return, tribute. *Opp* PUNISHMENT. ● vb compensate, decorate, give a reward to, honour, recompense, remunerate, repay. *Opp* PENALIZE, PUNISH. **rewarding** ▷ PROFITABLE, WORTHWHILE.

rhapsodize vb be expansive, effuse, enthuse, *inf* go into raptures.

rhetoric n *derog* bombast, eloquence, expressiveness, *inf* gift of the gab, grandiloquence, magniloquence, oratory, rhetorical language, *derog* speechifying.

rhetorical adj [*most synonyms derog*] artifical, bombastic, florid, *inf* flowery, fustian, grandiloquent, grandiose, highflown, insincere, oratorical, ornate, pretentious, verbose, wordy.

rhyme n doggerel, jingle, poem. ▷ VERSE.

rhythm n accent, beat, measure, metre, movement, pattern, pulse, stress, tempo, throb, time.

rhythmic adj beating, measured, metrical, predictable, pulsing, regular, repeated, steady, throbbing. *Opp* IRREGULAR.

ribald adj bawdy, coarse, disrespectful, earthy, naughty, racy, rude, scurrilous, *inf* smutty, vulgar. ▷ OBSCENE.

ribbon n band, braid, line, strip, stripe, tape, trimming. **in ribbons** ▷ RAGGED.

rich adj **1** affluent, *inf* flush, *inf* loaded, moneyed, opulent, plutocratic, prosperous, wealthy, *inf* well-heeled, well-off, well-to-do. *Opp* POOR. **2** *rich furnishings*. costly, elaborate, expensive, lavish, luxurious, precious, priceless, splendid, sumptuous, valuable. **3** *rich land*. fecund, fertile, fruitful, lush, productive. **4** *a rich harvest*. abundant, ample, bountiful, copious, plenteous, plentiful, profuse, prolific, teeming. **5** *rich colours*. deep, full, intense, strong, vibrant, vivid, warm. **6** *rich food*. cloying, creamy, fat, fattening, fatty, full-flavoured, heavy, highly-flavoured, luscious, sumptuous, sweet. **rich person** billionaire, capitalist, millionaire, plutocrat, tycoon.

riches plur n affluence, fortune, means, money, opulence, plenty, possessions, prosperity, resources, wealth.

rickety adj dilapidated, flimsy, frail, insecure, ramshackle, shaky, tottering, tumbledown, unsteady, wobbly. ▷ WEAK.

rid vb clear, deliver (from), free, purge, rescue, save. **get rid of** ▷ DESTROY, REMOVE.

riddle n **1** *inf* brain-teaser, conundrum, enigma, mystery, *inf* poser, problem, puzzle, question. **2** filter, screen, sieve. ● vb **1** filter, screen, sieve, sift, strain. **2** *riddle with holes*.

honeycomb, *inf* pepper, perforate, pierce, puncture.

ride *n* ▷ JOURNEY. ● *vb* **1** *ride a bike*. control, handle, manage, sit on, steer. **2** *ride on a bike*. be carried, freewheel, pedal. **3** *ride on a horse*. amble, canter, gallop, trot. ▷ TRAVEL.

ridge *n* arête, bank, crest, edge, embankment, escarpment. ▷ HILL.

ridicule *n* badinage, banter, burlesque, caricature, contumely, derision, invective, jeering, jibing, lampoon, laughter, mockery, parody, raillery, *inf* ribbing, sarcasm, satire, scorn, sneers, taunts, teasing. ● *vb* be sarcastic, be satirical about, burlesque, caricature, chaff, deride, gibe at, guy, hold up to ridicule, jeer at, jibe at, joke about, lampoon, laugh at, make fun of, make jokes about, mimic, mock, parody, pillory, *inf* poke fun at, *inf* rib, satirize, scoff at, *inf* send up, sneer at, subject to ridicule, *inf* take the mickey, taunt, tease, travesty.

ridiculous *adj* absurd, amusing, comic, comical, *inf* crazy, *inf* daft, eccentric, farcical, foolish, grotesque, hilarious, illogical, irrational, laughable, ludicrous, mad, nonsensical, preposterous, senseless, silly, unbelievable, unreasonable, weird, *inf* zany. ▷ FUNNY, STUPID. *Opp* SENSIBLE.

rife *adj* abundant, common, endemic, prevalent, widespread.

rift *n* **1** breach, break, chink, cleft, crack, fracture, gap, gulf, opening, split. **2** *a rift between friends*. alienation, conflict, difference, disagreement, disruption, division, opposition, schism, separation.

rig *n* **1** ▷ RIGGING. **2** *oil rig*. platform. **3** [*inf*] *sporting rig*. apparatus, clothes, equipment, gear, kit, outfit, stuff, tackle. ● *vb* **rig out** equip, fit out, kit out, outfit, provision, set up, supply.

rigging *n* rig, tackle. □ *halyards, ropes and pulleys, sails*.

right *adj* **1** decent, ethical, fair, good, honest, honourable, just, law-abiding, lawful, moral, principled, responsible, righteous, right-minded, upright, virtuous. **2** *right answers*. accurate, apposite, appropriate, apt, correct, exact, factual, faultless, fitting, genuine, perfect, precise, proper, sound, suitable, true, truthful, valid, veracious. **3** *the right way*. advantageous, beneficial, best, convenient, good, normal, preferable, preferred, recommended, sensible, usual. **4** *your right side*. right-hand, starboard [= *right facing bow of ship*]. **5** *right wing in politics*. conservative, fascist, reactionary, Tory. *Opp* LEFT, WRONG. ● *n* **1** decency, equity, ethics, fairness, goodness, honesty, integrity, justice, morality, propriety, reason, truth, virtue. **2** *right to free speech*. entitlement, facility, freedom, liberty, prerogative, privilege. **3** *right to give orders*. authority, commission, franchise, licence, position, power, title. ● *vb* **1** amend, correct, make amends for, put right, rectify, redress, remedy, repair, set right. **2** pick up, set upright, stand upright, straighten up.

righteous *adj* blameless, ethical, God-fearing, good, guiltless, *derog* holier-than-thou, honest, just, law-abiding, moral, pure, *derog* sanctimonious, upright, upstanding, virtuous. *Opp* SINFUL.

rightful *adj* authorized, *Lat* bona fide, correct, just, lawful, legal, legitimate, licensed, licit, proper, real, true, valid. *Opp* ILLEGAL.

rigid *adj* **1** adamantine, firm, hard, inelastic, inflexible, set, solid, steely, stiff, strong, unbending, wooden. **2** *rigid discipline*. harsh, intransigent, punctilious, stern, strict, uncompromising, unkind, unrelenting, unyielding. ▷ OBSTINATE, RIGOROUS. *Opp* FLEXIBLE.

rigorous *adj* **1** conscientious, demanding, exact, exacting, meticulous, painstaking, precise, punctilious, rigid, scrupulous, strict, stringent, structured, thorough, tough, uncompromising, undeviating, unsparing, unswerving. *Opp* LAX. **2** *rigorous climate*. extreme, hard, harsh, inclement, inhospitable,

river

severe, unfriendly, unpleasant. ▷
COLD. *Opp* MILD.

rim *n* brim, brink, circumference,
edge, lip, perimeter, periphery.

rind *n* crust, husk, outer layer, peel,
skin.

ring *n* **1** annulus, band, bracelet,
circle, circlet, collar, corona, eyelet,
girdle, halo, hoop, loop, O, ringlet.
2 *boxing ring.* arena, enclosure, rink.
3 *drugs ring.* association, band, gang,
mob, organization, syndicate. ▷
GROUP. **4** *the ring of a bell.* boom, buzz,
chime, clang, clink, *inf* ding-a-ling,
jangle, jingle, knell, peal, ping,
resonance, reverberation, tinkle,
tintinnabulation, tolling. **5** *give me a
ring sometime.* inf bell, *inf* buzz, call,
inf tinkle. ● *vb* **1** bind, circle,
embrace, encircle, enclose, encompass, gird, surround. **2** boom, buzz,
chime, clang, clink, jangle, jingle,
peal, ping, resonate, resound, reverberate, sound (the knell), tinkle, toll.
3 call, *inf* give a buzz, phone, ring
up, telephone.

rinse *vb* bathe, clean, cleanse,
drench, flush, sluice, swill, wash.

riot *n* affray, anarchy, brawl, chaos,
commotion, demonstration, disor-
der, disturbance, fracas, fray,
hubbub, imbroglio, insurrection,
lawlessness, mass protest, mêlée,
mutiny, pandemonium, *inf* punch-
up, revolt, rioting, riotous behaviour,
rising, row, *inf* rumpus, *inf* shindy,
strife, tumult, turmoil, unrest,
uproar, violence. ● *vb* brawl, create a
riot, *inf* go on the rampage, *inf* go
wild, mutiny, rampage, rebel, revolt,
rise up, run riot, *inf* take to the
streets. ▷ FIGHT.

riotous *adj* anarchic, boisterous,
chaotic, disorderly, lawless, mutinous, noisy, obstreperous,
rampageous, rebellious, rowdy,
tumultuous, uncivilized, uncontrollable, undisciplined, ungovernable,
unrestrained, unruly, uproarious,
violent, wild. *Opp* ORDERLY.

rip *vb* gash, lacerate, pull apart, rend,
rupture, shred, slit, split, tear.

ripe *adj* mature, mellow, ready to
use.

ripen *vb* age, become riper, come to
maturity, develop, mature, mellow.

ripple *n* ▷ WAVE. ● *vb* agitate, disturb,
make waves, purl, ruffle, stir.

rise *n* **1** acclivity, ascent, bank, camber, climb, elevation, hill, hump,
incline, ramp, ridge, slope. **2** *a rise in
prices.* escalation, gain, increase,
increment, jump, leap, upsurge,
upswing, upturn, upward move-
ment. ● *vb* **1** arise, ascend, climb, fly
up, go up, jump, leap, levitate, lift,
lift off, mount, soar, spring, take off.
2 get to your feet, get up, stand up.
3 *prices rise each year.* escalate, grow,
increase, spiral. **4** *cliffs rise above us.*
loom, stand out, stick up, tower. **rise
up** ▷ REBEL.

risk *n* **1** chance, likelihood, possibility. **2** danger, gamble, hazard, peril,
speculation, uncertainty, venture.
● *vb* **1** chance, dare, endanger,
hazard, imperil, jeopardize. **2** *risk
money.* gamble, speculate, venture.

risky *adj* inf chancy, *inf* dicey, hazardous, *inf* iffy, perilous, precarious,
unsafe. ▷ DANGEROUS. *Opp* SAFE.

ritual *n* ceremonial, ceremony, custom, formality, liturgy, observance,
practice, rite, routine, sacrament,
service, set procedure, solemnity,
tradition.

rival *n* adversary, antagonist, challenger, competitor, contender,
contestant, enemy, opponent, opposition. ● *vb* **1** challenge, compete
with, contend with, contest, emulate, oppose, struggle with, undercut, vie with. *Opp* COOPERATE. **2** be as
good as, compare with, equal, match,
measure up to.

rivalry *n* antagonism, competition,
competitiveness, conflict, contention, feuding, opposition, strife. *Opp*
COOPERATION.

river *n* brook, rivulet, stream, watercourse, waterway. □ *channel, confluence, delta, estuary, lower reaches, mouth,
source, tributary, upper reaches.*

road n roadway, route, way. □ alley, arterial road, avenue, boulevard, bridle-path, bridle-way, bypass, byroad, byway, cart-track, causeway, clearway, crescent, cul-de-sac, drive, driveway, dual carriageway, Amer freeway, highway, lane, motorway, one-way street, path, pathway, ring road, service road, side-road, side-street, slip-road, street, thoroughfare, tow-path, track, trail, trunk road, old use turnpike.

roam vb amble, drift, meander, prowl, ramble, range, rove, saunter, stray, stroll, travel, walk, wander.

roar vb bellow, cry out, growl, howl, shout, snarl, thunder, yell, yowl. ▷ SOUND.

rob vb burgle, inf con, defraud, hold up, loot, inf mug, old use mulct, pick pockets, pilfer from, pillage, plunder, ransack, rifle, steal from. ▷ STEAL.

robber n bandit, brigand, burglar, cat burglar, inf con-man, defrauder, embezzler, old use highwayman, housebreaker, looter, inf mugger, pickpocket, pirate, shoplifter, swindler, thief.

robbery n breaking and entering, burglary, inf con, confidence trick, embezzlement, fraud, hijacking, inf hold-up, larceny, looting, inf mugging, pilfering, pillage, plunder, sacking, inf scrumping, shoplifting, stealing, inf stick-up, theft, thieving.

robe n cloak, dress, frock, gown. □ bathrobe, caftan, cassock, dressing-gown, habit, housecoat, kimono, peignoir, surplice, vestment. ● vb ▷ DRESS.

robot n android, automated machine, automaton, bionic man, bionic woman, computerized machine, mechanical man.

robust adj 1 athletic, brawny, fit, inf hale and hearty, hardy, healthy, hearty, muscular, powerful, rugged, sound, strong, sturdy, tough, vigorous. 2 durable, serviceable, strongly-made, well-made. Opp WEAK.

rock n boulder, crag, ore, outcrop, scree, stone. □ igneous, metamorphic, sedimentary. □ basalt, chalk, clay, flint, gneiss, granite, gravel, lava, limestone, marble, obsidian, pumice, quartz, sandstone, schist, shale, slate, tufa, tuff. ● vb 1 lurch, move to and fro, pitch, reel, roll, shake, sway, swing, toss, totter, wobble. 2 ▷ SHOCK.

rocky adj 1 barren, inhospitable, pebbly, rough, rugged, stony. 2 ▷ UNSTEADY.

rod n bar, baton, cane, dowel, pole, rail, shaft, spoke, staff, stick, strut, wand.

rogue n blackguard, charlatan, cheat, inf con-man, fraud, old use knave, mischief-maker, inf quack, rapscallion, rascal, ruffian, scoundrel, swindler, trickster, villain, wastrel, wretch. ▷ CRIMINAL.

role n 1 character, impersonation, lines, part, portrayal. 2 role in a business. contribution, duty, function, job, position, post, task.

roll n 1 cylinder, drum, reel, scroll, spool, tube. 2 catalogue, directory, index, inventory, list, listing, record, register. ● vb 1 go round, gyrate, move round, revolve, rotate, run, somersault, spin, tumble, turn, twirl, whirl. 2 coil, curl, furl, make into a roll, twist, wind, wrap. 3 roll the lawn. flatten, level off, level out, smooth. 4 ship rolled in the storm. lumber, lurch, pitch, reel, rock, stagger, sway, toss, totter, wallow, welter. **rolling** ▷ WAVY. **roll in, roll up** ▷ ARRIVE.

romance n 1 idyll, love story, novel. ▷ WRITING. 2 adventure, colour, excitement, fascination, glamour, mystery. 3 affair, amour, attachment, intrigue, liaison, love affair, relationship.

romantic adj 1 colourful, dream-like, exotic, fabulous, fairy-tale, glamorous, idyllic, nostalgic, picturesque. 2 romantic feelings. affectionate, amorous, emotional, erotic, loving, passionate, inf sexy, inf soppy, tender. 3 romantic fiction. emotional, escapist, heart-warming, nostalgic, reassuring, sentimental, derog sloppy, tender, unrealistic. 4 romantic ideals.

chimerical, *inf* head in the clouds, idealistic, illusory, impractical, improbable, quixotic, starry-eyed, unworkable, Utopian, visionary. *Opp* REALISTIC.

room *n* **1** *inf* elbow-room, freedom, latitude, leeway, margin, scope, space, territory. **2** *a room in a house.* apartment, cell, *old use* chamber. □ *ante-room, attic, audience chamber, bathroom, bedroom, boudoir, cell, cellar, chapel, classroom, cloakroom, conservatory, corridor, dining-room, dormitory, drawing-room, dressing-room, gallery, guest-room, hall, kitchen, kitchenette, laboratory, landing, larder, laundry, lavatory, library, living-room, loft, lounge, music-room, nursery, office, pantry, parlour, passage, play-room, porch, salon, saloon, scullery, sick-room, sitting-room, spare room, stateroom, store-room, studio, study, toilet, utility room, waiting-room, ward, washroom, WC, workroom, workshop.*

roomy *adj* capacious, commodious, large, sizeable, spacious, voluminous. ▷ BIG. *Opp* SMALL.

root *n* **1** radicle, rhizome, rootlet, tap root, tuber. **2** *the root of a problem.* base, basis, bottom, cause, foundation, fount, origin, seat, source, starting-point. ● *vb* **root out** ▷ REMOVE.

rope *n* cable, cord, line, strand, string. □ *halyard, hawser, lanyard, lariat, lasso, tether.* ● *vb* bind, hitch, lash, moor, tether, tie. ▷ FASTEN.

rot *n* **1** corrosion, corruption, decay, decomposition, deterioration, disintegration, dry rot, mould, mouldiness, putrefaction, wet rot. **2** *What rot!* ▷ NONSENSE. ● *vb* become rotten, corrode, crumble, decay, decompose, degenerate, deteriorate, disintegrate, fester, go bad, *inf* go off, perish, putrefy, rust, spoil.

rota *n* list, roster, schedule, timetable.

rotary *adj* gyrating, revolving, rotating, rotatory, spinning, turning, twirling, twisting, whirling.

rotate *vb* **1** go round, gyrate, have a rotary movement, move round,

pirouette, pivot, reel, revolve, roll, spin, swivel, turn, turn anticlockwise, turn clockwise, twiddle, twirl, twist, wheel, whirl. **2** *rotate duties.* alternate, pass round, share out, take in turn, take turns.

rotten *adj* **1** bad, corroded, crumbling, decayed, decaying, decomposed, disintegrating, foul, mouldering, mouldy, *inf* off, overripe, perished, putrid, rusty, smelly, tainted, unfit for consumption, unsound. *Opp* SOUND. **2** ▷ IMMORAL.

rough *adj* **1** broken, bumpy, coarse, craggy, irregular, jagged, knobbly, lumpy, pitted, rocky, rugged, rutted, stony, uneven. **2** *rough skin.* bristly, callused, chapped, coarse, hairy, harsh, leathery, ragged, scratchy, shaggy, unshaven, wrinkled. **3** *a rough sea.* agitated, choppy, stormy, tempestuous, turbulent, violent, wild. **4** *a rough voice.* cacophonous, discordant, grating, gruff, harsh, hoarse, husky, rasping, raucous, strident, unmusical, unpleasant. *Opp* SMOOTH. **5** *rough manners, a rough fellow.* badly-behaved, bluff, blunt, brusque, churlish, ill-bred, impolite, loutish, rowdy, rude, surly, *inf* ugly, uncivil, uncivilized, undisciplined, unfriendly. **6** *rough treatment.* brutal, cruel, painful, ruffianly, thuggish, violent. **7** *rough work.* amateurish, careless, clumsy, crude, hasty, imperfect, inept, *inf* rough and ready, unfinished, unpolished, unskilful. **8** *a rough estimate.* approximate, general, hasty, imprecise, inexact, sketchy, vague. *Opp* EXACT, GENTLE, SMOOTH.

roughly *adv* about, approximately, around, close to, nearly.

round *adj* **1** [*two-dimensional*] annular, circular, curved, discshaped, hoop-shaped, orbicular, ring-shaped. **2** [*three-dimensional*] ball-shaped, bulbous, cylindrical, globelike, globoid, globular, orb-shaped, spherical, spheroid. **3** *a round figure.* ample, full, plump, rotund, rounded, well-padded. ▷ FAT. ● *n* bout, contest, game, heat, stage. ● *vb* skirt, travel round, turn. **round off** ▷ COMPLETE. **round on** ▷ ATTACK. **round the bend** ▷ MAD. **round the clock** ▷ CONTINUOUS. **round up** ▷ ASSEMBLE.

roundabout *adj* circuitous, circular, devious, indirect, long, meandering, oblique, rambling, tortuous, twisting, winding. *Opp* DIRECT. ● *n* **1** carousel, merry-go-round, *old use* whirligig. **2** traffic island.

round-shouldered *adj* hunchbacked, humpbacked, stooping.

rouse *vb* **1** arise, arouse, awaken, call, get up, wake up. **2** *rouse to a frenzy.* agitate, animate, electrify, excite, galvanize, goad, incite, inflame, provoke, spur on, stimulate, stir up, *inf* wind up, work up.

rout *vb* conquer, crush, overpower, overwhelm, put to flight, *inf* send packing. ▷ DEFEAT.

route *n* course, direction, itinerary, journey, path, road, way.

routine *adj* accustomed, commonplace, customary, everyday, familiar, habitual, normal, ordinary, perfunctory, planned, run-of-the-mill, scheduled, uneventful, wellrehearsed. ● *n* **1** course of action, custom, *inf* drill, habit, method, pattern, plan, practice, procedure, schedule, system, way. **2** *comedy routine.* act, number, performance, programme, set piece.

row *n* **1** [rhyme with *crow*] chain, column, cordon, file, line, queue, rank, sequence, series, string, tier. **2** [rhyme with *cow*] ado, commotion, fuss, hubbub, hullabaloo, *inf* racket, rumpus, tumult, uproar. ▷ NOISE. **3** altercation, argument, controversy, disagreement, dispute, fight, fracas, *inf* ructions, *inf* slanging match, squabble. ▷ QUARREL. ● *vb* **1** [rhyme with *crow*] *row a boat.* move, propel, scull. **2** [rhyme with *cow*] ▷ QUARREL.

rowdy *adj* badly-behaved, boisterous, disorderly, ill-disciplined, irrepressible, lawless, obstreperous, riotous, rough, turbulent, undisciplined, unruly, violent, wild. ▷ NOISY. *Opp* QUIET.

royal *adj* imperial, kingly, majestic, princely, queenly, regal, stately. ● *n* [*inf*] member of royal family. □ *consort, Her/His Majesty, Her/His Royal Highness, king, monarch, prince, princess, queen, queen mother, regent, sovereign.* ▷ NOBLE.

rub *vb* **1** caress, knead, massage, smooth, stroke. **2** abrade, chafe, graze, scrape, wear away. **3** *rub clean.* buff, burnish, polish, scour, scrub, shine, wipe. **rub it in** ▷ EMPHASIZE. **rub out** ▷ ERASE. **rub up the wrong way** ▷ ANNOY.

rubbish *n* **1** debris, detritus, dregs, dross, filth, flotsam and jetsam, garbage, junk, leavings, *inf* left-overs, litter, lumber, muck, *inf* odds and ends, offal, offcuts, refuse, rejects, rubble, scrap, slops, sweepings, trash, waste. **2** ▷ NONSENSE.

rubble *n* broken bricks, debris, fragments, remains, ruins, wreckage.

ruddy *adj* flushed, fresh, glowing, healthy, red, sunburnt.

rude *adj* **1** abrupt, abusive, badmannered, bad-tempered, blasphemous, blunt, boorish, brusque, cheeky, churlish, coarse, common, condescending, contemptuous, discourteous, disparaging, disrespectful, foul, graceless, gross, ignorant, illbred, ill-mannered, impertinent, impolite, improper, impudent, in bad taste, inconsiderate, indecent, insolent, insulting, loutish, mocking, naughty, oafish, offensive, offhand, patronizing, peremptory, personal (*remarks*), saucy, scurrilous, shameless, tactless, unchivalrous, uncivil, uncomplimentary, uncouth, ungracious, *old use* unmannerly, unprintable, vulgar. ▷ OBSCENE. *Opp* POLITE. **2** *rude workmanship.* awkward, basic, bumbling, clumsy, crude, inartistic, primitive, rough, rough-hewn, simple, unpolished, unskilful, unsophisticated, unsubtle. *Opp* SOPHISTICATED. **be rude to** ▷ INSULT.

rudeness *n* abuse, *inf* backchat, bad manners, boorishness, *inf* cheek, churlishness, condescension, contempt, discourtesy, disrespect, ill-breeding, impertinence, impudence, incivility, insolence, insults, oafishness, tactlessness, uncouthness, vulgarity.

rudiments *plur n* basic principles, basics, elements, essentials, first principles, foundations, fundamentals.

rudimentary *adj* basic, crude, elementary, embryonic, immature, initial, introductory, preliminary, primitive, provisional, undeveloped. *Opp* ADVANCED.

ruffian *n inf* brute, bully, desperado, gangster, hoodlum, hooligan, lout, mugger, rogue, scoundrel, thug, *inf* tough, villain, *inf* yob.

ruffle *vb* 1 agitate, disturb, ripple, stir. 2 *ruffle your hair*. derange, disarrange, dishevel, disorder, *inf* mess up, rumple, tangle, tousle. 3 *ruffle your composure*. annoy, confuse, disconcert, disquiet, fluster, irritate, *inf* nettle, *inf* rattle, *inf* throw, unnerve, unsettle, upset, vex, worry. *Opp* SMOOTH.

rug *n* blanket, coverlet, mat, matting.

rugged *adj* 1 bumpy, craggy, irregular, jagged, pitted, rocky, rough, stony, uneven. 2 *rugged conditions*. arduous, difficult, hard, harsh, onerous, rough, severe, tough. 3 *rugged good looks*. burly, hardy, husky, muscular, robust, rough, strong, sturdy, ungraceful, unpolished, weatherbeaten.

ruin *n* bankruptcy, breakdown, collapse, *inf* crash, destruction, downfall, end, failure, fall, ruination, undoing, wreck. ● *vb* damage, demolish, destroy, devastate, flatten, overthrow, shatter, spoil, wreck. **ruins** debris, havoc, remains, rubble, wreckage.

ruined *adj* crumbling, derelict, dilapidated, fallen down, in ruins, ramshackle, ruinous, tumbledown, uninhabitable, unsafe, wrecked.

ruinous *adj* 1 apocalyptic, calamitous, cataclysmic, catastrophic, crushing, destructive, devastating, dire, disastrous, fatal, harmful, injurious, pernicious, shattering. 2 ▷ RUINED.

rule *n* 1 axiom, code, decree, *plur* guidelines, law, ordinance, practice, precept, principle, regulation, ruling, statute. 2 administration, ascendancy, authority, command, control, domination, dominion, empire, government, influence, jurisdiction, management, mastery, oversight, power, regime, reign, sovereignty, supervision, supremacy, sway. 3 *as a general rule*. convention, custom, norm, routine, standard. ● *vb* 1 administer, be the ruler of, command, control, direct, dominate, govern, guide, hold sway, lead, manage, predominate, reign, run, superintend. 2 adjudicate, decide, decree, deem, determine, find, judge, pronounce, resolve. **rule out** ▷ EXCLUDE.

ruler *n* administrator, *inf* Big Brother, law-maker, leader, manager. □ autocrat, Caesar, demagogue, despot, dictator, doge, emir, emperor, empress, governor, kaiser, king, lord, monarch, potentate, president, prince, princess, queen, rajah, regent, satrap, sovereign, sultan, suzerain, triumvirate [= three ruling jointly], tyrant, tsar, viceroy. ▷ CHIEF.

rumour *n* chat, *inf* chit-chat, gossip, hearsay, *inf* low-down, news, prattle, report, scandal, *inf* tittletattle, whisper.

run *n* 1 canter, dash, gallop, jog, marathon, race, sprint, trot. 2 *a run in the car*. drive, excursion, jaunt, journey, joyride, ride, *inf* spin, trip. 3 *run of bad luck*. chain, sequence, series, stretch. 4 *chicken run*. compound, coop, enclosure, pen. ● *vb* 1 bolt, canter, career, dash, gallop, hare, hurry, jog, race, rush, scamper, scoot, scurry, scuttle, speed, sprint, tear, trot. 2 *buses run hourly*. go, operate, ply, provide a service, travel. 3 *car runs well*. behave, function, perform, work. 4 *water runs downhill*. cascade, dribble, flow, gush, leak, pour, spill, stream, trickle. 5 *Who runs the country?* administer, conduct, control, direct, govern, look after, maintain,

manage, rule, supervise. **run across**
▷ MEET. **run after** ▷ PURSUE. **run away**
▷ ESCAPE. **run into** ▷ MEET.

runner n **1** athlete, competitor,
entrant, hurdler, jogger, participant,
sprinter. **2** courier, dispatch-rider,
errand-boy, errand-girl, messenger.
3 *plant sends out runners.* offshoot,
shoot, sprout, sucker, tendril.

runny adj fluid, free-flowing, liquid,
running, thin, watery. *Opp* SOLID, VIS-
COUS.

rupture n **1** breach, break, burst,
cleavage, fracture, puncture, rift,
split. **2** *rupture between friends.* break-
up, disunity, schism, separation.
3 [*medical*] hernia. ● vb break, burst,
fracture, part, separate, split.

rural adj agrarian, agricultural, Arcadian, bucolic, countrified, pastoral,
rustic, sylvan. *Opp* URBAN.

rush n **1** bustle, dash, haste, hurry,
panic, pressure, race, scramble,
speed, turmoil, urgency. **2** *rush of
water.* cataract, flood, gush, spate,
surge. **3** *rush of people.* charge,
onslaught, stampede. ● vb bolt, burst,
bustle, canter, career, charge, dash,
fly, gallop, *inf* get a move on, hare,
hasten, hurry, jog, make haste, move
fast, race, run, scamper, *inf* scoot,
scramble, scurry, scuttle, shoot,
speed, sprint, stampede, *inf* step on
it, *inf* tear, trot, *inf* zoom.

rust vb become rusty, corrode, crumble away, oxidize, rot.

rustic adj **1** ▷ RURAL. **2** *rustic simplicity.* artless, clumsy, crude, naïve,
derog oafish, plain, rough, simple,
uncomplicated, uncultured, unpolished, unsophisticated.

rusty adj **1** corroded, oxidized, rotten, tarnished. **2** [*inf*] *My French is
rusty.* dated, forgotten, out of practice, unused.

rut n **1** channel, furrow, groove,
indentation, pothole, track, trough,
wheel-mark. **2** *in a rut.* dead end,
habit, pattern, routine, treadmill.

ruthless adj bloodthirsty, brutal, callous, cruel, dangerous, ferocious,
fierce, hard, heartless, inexorable,
inhuman, merciless, pitiless, relentless, sadistic, unfeeling, unrelenting,
unsympathetic, vicious, violent. *Opp*
MERCIFUL.

S

sabotage n disruption, vandalism, wilful damage, wrecking. ● vb cripple, damage, destroy, disable, disrupt, incapacitate, put out of action, inf throw a spanner in the works (of), vandalize, wreck.

sack n 1 bag, pouch. 2 inf the boot, inf the chop, dismissal, firing, redundancy, inf your cards. ● vb 1 inf axe, discharge, dismiss, inf fire, give someone notice, inf give someone the boot, inf give someone the chop, inf give someone the sack, lay off, make redundant. 2 ▷ DESTROY, PLUNDER. **get the sack** be dismissed, be sacked, inf get your cards, get your marching orders, lose your job.

sacred adj blessed, blest, consecrated, dedicated, divine, godly, hallowed, holy, religious, revered, sacrosanct, sanctified, venerable, venerated. Opp SECULAR.

sacrifice n immolation, oblation, offering, propitiation, votive offering. ● vb 1 immolate, kill, offer up, slaughter, yield up. 2 abandon, forfeit, forgo, give up, let go, lose, relinquish, renounce, surrender.

sacrilege n blasphemy, desecration, disrespect, heresy, impiety, irreverence, profanation.

sacrilegious adj atheistic, blasphemous, disrespectful, heretical, impious, irreligious, irreverent, profane, ungodly. ▷ WICKED. Opp REVERENT.

sacrosanct adj inviolable, inviolate, protected, respected, secure, untouchable. ▷ SACRED.

sad adj 1 abject, inf blue, brokenhearted, careworn, cheerless, crestfallen, dejected, depressed, desolate, despairing, desperate, despondent, disappointed, disconsolate, discontented, discouraged, disgruntled, dis-

heartened, disillusioned, dismal, dispirited, dissatisfied, distressed, doleful, dolorous, inf down, downcast, downhearted, dreary, forlorn, friendless, funereal, gloomy, glum, grave, grief-stricken, grieving, grim, guilty, heartbroken, inf heavy, heavy-hearted, homesick, hopeless, in low spirits, inf in the doldrums, joyless, lachrymose, lonely, inf long-faced, inf low, lugubrious, melancholy, miserable, moody, moping, morose, mournful, funereal, gloomy, penitent, pessimistic, piteous, pitiable, pitiful, plaintive, poignant, regretful, rueful, saddened, serious, sober, sombre, sorrowful, sorry, tearful, troubled, unhappy, unsatisfied, upset, wistful, woebegone, woeful, wretched. 2 sad news. calamitous, deplorable, depressing, disastrous, discouraging, dispiriting, distressing, grievous, heartbreaking, heart-rending, lamentable, morbid, moving, painful, regrettable, inf tear-jerking, touching, tragic, unfortunate, unsatisfactory, unwelcome, upsetting. 3 a sad state of disrepair. ▷ UNSATISFACTORY. Opp HAPPY.

sadden vb aggrieve, inf break someone's heart, deject, depress, disappoint, discourage, dishearten, dismay, dispirit, distress, grieve, make sad, upset. Opp CHEER.

sadistic adj barbarous, beastly, brutal, inhuman, monstrous, perverted, pitiless, ruthless, vicious. ▷ CRUEL.

sadness n bleakness, care, dejection, depression, desolation, despair, despondency, disappointment, disillusionment, dissatisfaction, distress, dolour, gloom, glumness, grief, heartbreak, heaviness, homesickness, hopelessness, joylessness, loneliness, melancholy, misery, moping, moroseness, mournfulness, pessimism, poignancy, regret, ruefulness, seriousness, soberness, sombreness, sorrow, tearfulness, trouble, unhappiness, wistfulness, woe. *Opp* HAPPINESS.

safe *adj* **1** defended, foolproof, guarded, immune, impregnable, invulnerable, protected, secured, shielded. ▷ SECURE. *Opp* VULNERABLE. **2** *inf* alive and well, *inf* all right, *inf* in one piece, intact, sound, undamaged, unharmed, unhurt, uninjured, unscathed, well, whole. **3** *safe drivers*. cautious, circumspect, dependable, reliable, trustworthy. **4** *safe pets*. docile, friendly, harmless, innocuous, tame. **5** *safe to drink*. decontaminated, drinkable, eatable, fit for human consumption, fresh, good, non-poisonous, non-toxic, pasteurized, potable, pure, purified, uncontaminated, unpolluted, wholesome. **6** *safe vehicle*. airworthy, roadworthy, seaworthy, tried and tested. *Opp* DANGEROUS. **make safe** ▷ SECURE. **safe keeping** care, charge, custody, guardianship, keeping, protection.

safeguard *vb* care for, defend, keep safe, look after, protect, shelter, shield.

safety *n* **1** cover, immunity, invulnerability, protection, refuge, sanctuary, security, shelter. **2** *safety of air travel*. dependability, harmlessness, reliability.

sag *vb* be limp, bend, dip, droop, fall, flop, hang down, sink, slump. ▷ DROP.

sail *n* **1** canvas. □ *foresail, gaffsail, jib, lateen sail, lugsail, mainsail, mizzen, spinnaker, spritsail, topsail*. **2** cruise, sea-passage, voyage. ▷ JOURNEY. ● *vb* **1** captain, navigate, paddle, pilot, punt, row, skipper, steer. **2** cruise, go sailing, put to sea, set sail, steam. ▷ TRAVEL.

sailor *n* mariner, *old use* sea dog, seafarer, seaman. □ *able seaman, bargee, boatman, boatswain, bosun, captain, cox, coxswain, plur crew, deck-hand, helmsman, mate, midshipman, navigator, pilot, rating, rower, skipper, yachtsman, yachtswoman*.

saintly *adj* angelic, blessed, blest, chaste, godly, holy, innocent, moral, pious, pure, religious, righteous, seraphic, sinless, virginal, virtuous. ▷ GOOD. *Opp* SATANIC.

sake *n* account, advantage, behalf, benefit, gain, good, interest, welfare.

salary *n* compensation, earnings, emolument, income, pay, payment, remuneration, stipend, wages.

sale *n* marketing, selling, trade, traffic, transaction, vending. □ *auction, bazaar, closing-down sale, fair, jumble sale, market, rummage sale, spring sale*.

salesperson *n* assistant, auctioneer, representative, salesman, saleswoman, shop-boy, shop-girl, shopkeeper.

saliva *n* *inf* dribble, *inf* spit, spittle, sputum.

sallow *adj* anaemic, bloodless, colourless, etiolated, pale, pallid, pasty, unhealthy, wan, yellowish.

salt *adj* brackish, briny, saline, salted, salty, savoury. *Opp* FRESH.

salubrious *adj* health-giving, healthy, hygienic, invigorating, nice, pleasant, refreshing, sanitary, wholesome. *Opp* UNHEALTHY.

salute *n* acknowledgement, gesture, greeting, salutation, wave. ● *vb* accost, acknowledge, address, greet, hail, honour, pay respects to, recognize. ▷ GESTURE.

salvage *n* **1** reclamation, recovery, rescue, retrieval, salvation, saving. **2** recyclable material, waste. ● *vb* conserve, preserve, reclaim, recover, recycle, redeem, rescue, retrieve, reuse, save, use again.

salvation *n* deliverance, escape, help, preservation, redemption, rescue, saving, way out. *Opp* DAMNATION.

salve *n* balm, cream, demulcent, embrocation, emolient, liniment, lotion, ointment, unguent. ● *vb* alleviate, appease, assuage, comfort, ease, mitigate, mollify, soothe.

same *adj* **1** actual, identical, selfsame. **2** *two women wearing the same jacket*. analogous, comparable, consistent, corresponding, duplicate, equal, equivalent, indistinguishable, interchangeable, matching, parallel, similar, synonymous [= *having same meaning*], twin, unaltered, unchanged, uniform, unvaried. *Opp* DIFFERENT.

sample *n* bit, demonstration, example, foretaste, free sample, illustration, indication, instance, model, pattern, representative piece, selection, snippet, specimen, taste, trailer (*of film*), trial offer. ● *vb* experience, inspect, take a sample of, taste, test, try.

sanatorium *n* clinic, convalescent home, hospital, nursing home, rest-home.

sanctify *vb* beatify, bless, canonize, consecrate, hallow, justify, purify.

sanctimonious *adj* canting, holier-than-thou, hypocritical, insincere, moralizing, pharisaical, *sl* pi, pietistic, pious, self-righteous, sententious, *inf* smarmy, smug, superior, unctuous.

sanction *n* agreement, approval, authorization, *inf* blessing, confirmation, consent, encouragement, endorsement, legalization, licence, permission, ratification, support, validation. ● *vb* agree to, allow, approve, authorize, confirm, consent to, endorse, *inf* give your blessing to, give permission for, legalize, legitimize, licence, permit, ratify, support, validate.

sanctity *n* divinity, godliness, grace, holiness, piety, sacredness, saintliness.

sanctuary *n* **1** asylum, haven, protection, refuge, retreat, safety, shelter. **2** *wildlife sanctuary*. conservation area, park, preserve, reservation, reserve. **3** *a holy sanctuary*. chapel, church, holy of holies, holy place, sanctum, shrine, temple.

sands *plur n* beach, seaside, shore, *poet* strand.

sane *adj inf* all there, balanced, *Lat* compos mentis, *inf* in your right mind, level-headed, lucid, normal, of sound mind, rational, reasonable, sensible, sound, stable, well-balanced. *Opp* MAD.

sanguine *adj* buoyant, cheerful, confident, expectant, hopeful, *inf* looking on the bright side, optimistic, positive. *Opp* PESSIMISTIC.

sanitary *adj* aseptic, bacteria-free, clean, disinfected, germfree, healthy, hygienic, pure, salubrious, sterile, sterilized, uncontaminated, unpolluted, wholesome. *Opp* UNHEALTHY.

sanitation *n* drainage, drains, lavatories, sanitary arrangements, sewage disposal, sewers.

sap *n* fluid, life-blood, moisture, vigour, vitality, vital juices. ● *vb* bleed, drain. ▷ EXHAUST.

sarcasm *n* acerbity, asperity, contumely, derision, irony, malice, mockery, ridicule, satire, scorn.

sarcastic *adj* acerbic, acidulous, biting, caustic, contemptuous, cutting, demeaning, derisive, disparaging, hurtful, ironic, ironical, mocking, satirical, scathing, sharp, sneering, spiteful, taunting, trenchant, venomous, vitriolic, withering, wounding. ▷ HUMOROUS.

sardonic *adj* bitter, black, cruel, cynical, grim, heartless, malicious, mordant, wry. ▷ HUMOROUS.

sash *n* band, belt, cummerbund, girdle, waistband.

satanic *adj* demonic, devilish, diabolical, fiendish, hellish, infernal, Mephistophelian. ▷ WICKED. *Opp* SAINTLY.

satchel *n* bag, pouch, school-bag, shoulder-bag.

satellite *n* **1** moon, planet. **2** *man-made satellite*. spacecraft, sputnik.

satire *n* burlesque, caricature, derision, invective, irony, lampoon, mockery, parody, ridicule, satirical comedy, scorn, *inf* send-up, *inf* spoof, *inf* take-off, travesty. ▷ WRITING.

satirical *adj* critical, derisive, disparaging, disrespectful, ironic, irreverent, mocking, scornful. ▷ HUMOROUS, SARCASTIC.

satirize vb be satirical about, burlesque, caricature, criticize, deride, hold up to ridicule, lampoon, laugh at, make fun of, mimic, mock, parody, pillory, inf send up, inf take off, travesty. ▷ RIDICULE.

satisfaction n comfort, content, contentment, delight, enjoyment, fulfilment, gratification, happiness, joy, pleasure, pride, self-satisfaction. Opp DISSATISFACTION.

satisfactory adj acceptable, adequate, inf all right, competent, fair, inf good enough, inf not bad, passable, pleasing, satisfying, sufficient, suitable, tolerable, inf up to scratch. Opp UNSATISFACTORY.

satisfy vb appease, assuage, comfort, comply with, content, fill, fulfil, gratify, make happy, meet, pacify, placate, please, put an end to, quench, sate, satiate, serve (a need), settle, slake (thirst), solve, supply. Opp FRUSTRATE. **satisfied** ▷ CONTENT.

saturate vb drench, fill, impregnate, permeate, soak, souse, steep, suffuse, waterlog, wet.

sauce n 1 condiment, gravy, ketchup, relish. 2 ▷ INSOLENCE.

saucepan n cauldron, pan, pot, skillet, stockpot.

savage adj 1 barbarian, barbaric, cannibal, heathen, pagan, primitive, uncivilized, uncultivated, uneducated. Opp CIVILIZED. 2 savage beasts. feral, fierce, undomesticated, untamed, wild. 3 savage attack. angry, atrocious, barbarous, beastly, bestial, blistering, bloodthirsty, bloody, brutal, callous, cold-blooded, cruel, demonic, diabolical, ferocious, fierce, heartless, inhuman, merciless, murderous, pitiless, ruthless, sadistic, unfeeling, vicious, violent. Opp TAME. ● n barbarian, beast, brute, cannibal, fiend, savage person. ● vb attack, bite, claw, lacerate, maul, mutilate.

save vb 1 be sparing with, collect, conserve, economize, hoard, hold back, hold on to, invest, keep, inf lay aside, inf put by, put in a safe place, reserve, retain, scrape together, set aside, inf stash away, store up, take care of, use wisely. Opp WASTE. 2 save from captivity. bail out, deliver, free, liberate, ransom, redeem, release, rescue, set free. 3 save from destruction. recover, retrieve, salvage. 4 save from danger. defend, deliver, guard, keep safe, preserve, protect, safeguard, screen, shelter, shield. 5 saved me from looking a fool. check, deter, preclude, prevent, spare, stop. Opp ABANDON.

saving n 1 economizing, frugality, parsimony, prudence, inf scrimping and scraping, thrift. 2 cut, discount, economy, reduction.

savings n capital, funds, investments, inf nest-egg, reserves, resources, riches, wealth.

saviour n 1 champion, defender, deliverer, inf friend in need, guardian, liberator, rescuer. 2 [theological] Christ, Our Lord, The Messiah, The Redeemer.

savour n flavour, piquancy, relish, smell, tang, taste, zest. ● vb appreciate, delight in, enjoy, relish, smell, taste.

savoury adj appetizing, delicious, flavoursome, piquant, salty. ▷ TASTY. Opp SWEET.

saw n 1 □ chain-saw, hack-saw, jigsaw, ripsaw. 2 [old use] just an old saw. ▷ SAYING. ● vb ▷ CUT.

say vb affirm, allege, announce, answer, articulate, assert, asseverate, aver, old use bruit abroad, inf come out with, comment, communicate, convey, declare, disclose, divulge, ejaculate, enunciate, exclaim, express, intimate, maintain, mention, mouth, phrase, pronounce, inf put it about, read out, recite, rejoin, remark, repeat, reply, report, respond, retort, reveal, signify, state, suggest, tell, utter. ▷ SPEAK, TALK, TELL.

saying n adage, aphorism, apophthegm, axiom, catch-phrase, catchword, cliché, dictum, epigram, expression, formula, maxim, motto, phrase, precept, proverb, quotation, remark, *old use* saw, slogan, statement, tag, truism, watchword.

scab *n* clot of blood, crust, sore.

scale *n* **1** dandruff, flake, plate, scurf. **2** *remove scale from teeth*. caking, coating, crust, deposit, encrustation, *inf* fur, plaque, tartar. **3** *the scale on a thermometer*. calibration, gradation, graduation. **4** *the social scale*. hierarchy, ladder, order, ranking, spectrum. **5** *small/large scale*. proportion, ratio. ▷ SIZE. **6** *musical scale*. sequence, series. □ *chromatic scale, diatonic scale, major scale, minor scale*. ● *vb* ascend, clamber up, climb, go up, mount. **scales** balance, weighing-machine.

scamper *vb* dash, frisk, frolic, gambol, hasten, hurry, play, romp, run, rush, scuttle.

scan *vb* **1** check, examine, explore, eye, gaze at, investigate, look at, pore over, scrutinize, search, stare at, study, survey, view, watch. **2** *scan the papers*. flip through, glance at, read quickly, skim, thumb through.

scandal *n* **1** discredit, disgrace, dishonour, disrepute, embarrassment, ignominy, infamy, notoriety, obloquy, outrage, reproach, sensation, shame. **2** calumny, defamation, gossip, innuendo, libel, rumour, slander, slur, *inf* smear, *inf* tittle-tattle.

scandalize *vb* affront, appal, disgust, horrify, offend, outrage, shock, upset.

scandalous *adj* **1** disgraceful, disgusting, dishonourable, disreputable, ignominious, immodest, immoral, improper, indecent, indecorous, infamous, licentious, notorious, outrageous, shameful, shocking, sinful, sordid, unmentionable, unspeakable, wicked. **2** *a scandalous lie*. calumnious, defamatory, libellous, scurrilous, slanderous, untrue.

scansion *n* metre, prosody, rhythm. ▷ VERSE.

scanty *adj* **1** inadequate, insufficient, meagre, mean, *sl* measly, *inf* mingy, minimal, scant, scarce, *inf* skimpy, sparing, sparse, stingy. ▷

SMALL. *Opp* PLENTIFUL. **2** *scanty clothes*. indecent, revealing, *inf* see-through, thin.

scapegoat *n* dupe, *sl* fall guy, *inf* front, victim, whipping-boy.

scar *n* blemish, brand, burn, cicatrice, cicatrix, cut, disfigurement, injury, mark, scab, scratch. ▷ WOUND. ● *vb* blemish, brand, burn, damage, deface, disfigure, injure, leave a scar on, mark, scratch, spoil.

scarce *adj* *inf* few and far between, *inf* hard to come by, *inf* hard to find, inadequate, infrequent, in short supply, insufficient, lacking, meagre, rare, scant, scanty, sparse, *inf* thin on the ground, uncommon, unusual. *Opp* PLENTIFUL.

scarcely *adv* barely, hardly, only just.

scarcity *n* dearth, famine, inadequacy, insufficiency, lack, need, paucity, poverty, rarity, shortage, want. *Opp* PLENTY.

scare *n* alarm, jolt, shock, start. ▷ FRIGHT. ● *vb* **1** alarm, dismay, intimidate, make someone afraid, *inf* make someone jump, menace, panic, shake, shock, startle, terrorize, threaten, unnerve. ▷ FRIGHTEN. *Opp* REASSURE.

scarf *n* headscarf, muffler, shawl, stole.

scary *adj* [*inf*] creepy, eerie, hair-raising, horrible, scaring, unnerving. ▷ FRIGHTENING.

scathing *adj* biting, caustic, critical, humiliating, mordant, satirical, savage, scornful, tart, withering. *Opp* COMPLIMENTARY.

scatter *vb* **1** break up, disband, disintegrate, dispel, disperse, divide, send in all directions, separate. **2** *scatter seeds*. broadcast, disseminate, intersperse, shed, shower, sow, spread, sprinkle, strew, throw about. *Opp* GATHER.

scatterbrained *adj* absent-minded, careless, crazy, disorganized, forgetful, frivolous, hare-brained, inattentive, muddled, *inf* not with it, *inf* scatty, thoughtless, unreliable, unsystematic, vague. ▷ SILLY.

scavenge *vb* forage, rummage, scrounge, search.

scenario *n* design, framework, layout, outline, plan, scheme, storyline, structure, summary.

scene *n* **1** area, background, context, locale, locality, location, place, position, setting, site, situation, spot, whereabouts. **2** *a beautiful scene.* picture, sight, spectacle. ▷ SCENERY. **3** *scene from a film.* act, chapter, *inf* clip, episode, part, section, sequence. **4** *a nasty scene.* altercation, argument, *inf* carry-on, commotion, disturbance, furore, fuss, quarrel, row, tantrum, *inf* to-do, *inf* upset.

scenery *n* **1** landscape, outlook, panorama, prospect, scene, terrain, view, vista. **2** *stage scenery.* backdrop, flats, set, setting.

scenic *adj* attractive, beautiful, breathtaking, grand, impressive, lovely, panoramic, picturesque, pretty, spectacular.

scent *n* **1** aroma, bouquet, fragrance, nose, odour, perfume, redolence, smell. **2** after-shave, eau de cologne, lavender water, perfume. **3** *an animal's scent.* spoor, track, trail. ● *vb* ▷ SMELL. **scented** ▷ SMELLING.

sceptic *n* agnostic, cynic, doubter, *inf* doubting Thomas, disbeliever, scoffer, unbeliever. *Opp* BELIEVER.

sceptical *adj* agnostic, cynical, disbelieving, distrustful, doubting, dubious, incredulous, mistrustful, questioning, scoffing, suspicious, uncertain, unconvinced, unsure. *Opp* CONFIDENT.

scepticism *n* agnosticism, cynicism, disbelief, distrust, doubt, dubiety, incredulity, lack of confidence, mistrust, suspicion. *Opp* FAITH.

schedule *n* agenda, calendar, diary, itinerary, list, plan, programme, register, scheme, timetable. ● *vb* appoint, arrange, assign, book, earmark, fix a time, organize, outline, plan, programme, time, timetable.

scheme *n* **1** approach, blueprint, design, draft, idea, method, plan, procedure, programme, project, proposal, scenario, strategy, system. **2** *a dishonest scheme.* conspiracy, *inf* dodge, intrigue, machinations, manoeuvre, plot, *inf* ploy, *inf* racket, ruse, stratagem, subterfuge, tactic. **3** *colour scheme.* arrangement, design. ● *vb* collude, connive, conspire, *inf* cook something up, *inf* hatch a plot, intrigue, machinate, manoeuvre, plan, plot.

scholar *n* academic, *inf* egghead, expert, highbrow, intellectual, professor, pundit, savant. ▷ PUPIL.

scholarly *adj* **1** academic, bookish, *inf* brainy, *inf* deep, erudite, highbrow, intellectual, knowledgeable, learned, lettered, widely-read. **2** *scholarly treatise.* documented, researched, rigorous, scientific, well-argued, well-informed.

scholarship *n* **1** academic achievement, education, erudition, intellectual attainment, knowledge, learning, research, schooling, scientific rigour, wisdom. **2** *a scholarship to Oxford.* award, bursary, endowment, exhibition, fellowship, grant.

school *n* **1** educational institution. □ *academy, boarding-school, coeducational school, college, comprehensive (school), first school, grammar school, high school, infant school, junior school, kindergarten, nursery school, playgroup, preparatory school, primary school, public school, secondary school, seminary.* **2** *a school of whales.* shoal. ▷ GROUP. ● *vb* ▷ EDUCATE.

science *n* organized knowledge, systematic study. □ *acoustics, aeronautics, agricultural science, anatomy, anthropology, artifical intelligence, astronomy, astrophysics, behavioural science, biochemistry, biology, biophysics, botany, chemistry, climatology, computer science, cybernetics, dietetics, domestic science, dynamics, earth science, ecology, economics, electronics, engineering, entomology, environmental science, food science, genetics, geographical science, geology, geophysics, hydraulics, informa-*

tion technology, life science, linguistics, materials science, mathematics, mechanics, medical science, metallurgy, meteorology, microbiology, mineralogy, ornithology, pathology, pharmacology, physics, physiology, political science, psychology, robotics, sociology, space technology, telecommunications, thermodynamics, toxicology, veterinary science, zoology.

scientific adj analytical, methodical, meticulous, orderly, organized, precise, rational, regulated, rigorous, systematic.

scientist n inf boffin, researcher, scientific expert, technologist.

scintillating adj brilliant, clever, coruscating, dazzling, effervescent, flashing, glittering, lively, sparkling, vivacious, witty. Opp DULL.

scoff vb 1 belittle, be sarcastic, be scornful, deride, disparage, gibe, jeer, jibe, laugh, mock, inf poke fun, ridicule, sneer, taunt, tease. 2 ▷ EAT.

scold vb admonish, berate, blame, inf carpet, castigate, censure, chide, criticize, disapprove of, find fault with, inf jump down someone's throat, inf lecture, inf nag, rate, rebuke, reprehend, reprimand, reproach, reprove, inf slate, inf tell off, inf tick off, upbraid.

scoop n 1 bailer, ladle, shovel, spoon. 2 news scoop. exclusive, inside story, inf latest, revelation. ● vb dig, excavate, gouge, hollow, scrape, shovel, spoon.

scope n 1 ambit, area, breadth, compass, competence, extent, field, limit, range, reach, span, sphere, terms of reference. 2 scope for expansion. capacity, chance, inf elbow-room, freedom, latitude, leeway, liberty, opportunity, outlet, room, space, spread.

scorch vb blacken, brand, burn, char, heat, roast, sear, singe.

score n 1 account, amount, count, marks, points, reckoning, result, sum, tally, total. 2 score on furniture. cut, groove, incision, line, mark, nick, scrape, scratch, slash. ● vb 1 account for, achieve, add up, inf chalk up, earn, gain, inf knock up, make, tally, win. 2 score a groove. cut, engrave, gouge, incise, mark, scrape, scratch, slash. 3 score music. orchestrate, write out. **settle a score** ▷ RETALIATE.

scorn n contempt, contumely, derision, detestation, disdain, disgust, dislike, dismissal, disparagement, disrespect, jeering, mockery, rejection, ridicule, scoffing, sneering, taunt-ing. Opp ADMIRATION. ● vb be scornful about, contemn, deride, despise, disapprove of, disdain, dislike, dismiss, disparage, hate, insult, jeer at, laugh at, look down on, make fun of, mock, reject, ridicule, inf scoff at, sneer at, spurn, taunt, inf turn up your nose at. Opp ADMIRE.

scornful adj condescending, contemptuous, contumelious, deprecative, derisive, disdainful, dismissive, disparaging, disrespectful, haughty, insulting, jeering, mocking, patronizing, sarcastic, satirical, scathing, scoffing, sneering, inf snide, inf snooty, supercilious, superior, taunting, withering. Opp RESPECTFUL.

scoundrel n blackguard, blighter, bounder, cad, good-for-nothing, heel, knave, miscreant, rascal, rogue, ruffian, scallywag, scamp, villain, wretch.

scour vb 1 abrade, buff up, burnish, clean, cleanse, polish, rub, scrape, scrub, shine, wash. 2 scour the house. comb, forage through, hunt through, rake through, ransack, rummage through, search, inf turn upside down.

scourge n 1 affliction, bane, curse, evil, misery, misfortune, plague, torment, woe. 2 ▷ WHIP. ● vb beat, belt, flagellate, flog, horsewhip, lash, whip.

scout n lookout, spy. ● vb explore, get information, hunt around, investigate, look about, reconnoitre, search, inf snoop, spy.

scowl vb frown, glower, grimace, inf look daggers, lower.

scraggy *adj* bony, emaciated, gaunt, lanky, lean, scrawny, skinny, starved, thin, underfed. *Opp* PLUMP.

scramble *n* commotion, confusion, *inf* free-for-all, haste, hurry, mêlée, race, rush, scrimmage, struggle. • *vb* **1** clamber, climb, crawl, grope, move awkwardly, scrabble. **2** *scramble for gold.* compete, contend, dash, fight, hasten, hurry, jostle, push, run, rush, scuffle, strive, struggle, tussle, vie. **3** *scramble a message.* confuse, jumble, mix up.

scrap *n* **1** atom, bit, crumb, fraction, fragment, grain, hint, iota, jot, mite, molecule, morsel, particle, piece, rag, scintilla, shard, shred, sliver, snippet, speck, trace. **2** *inf* junk, leavings, litter, odds and ends, offcuts, refuse, rejects, remains, remnants, residue, rubbish, salvage, waste. **3** *a friendly scrap.* argument, quarrel, scuffle, *inf* set-to, squabble, tiff, tussle, wrangle. ▷ FIGHT. • *vb* **1** abandon, cancel, discard, *inf* ditch, drop, give up, jettison, throw away, write off. **2** *scrap over trifles.* argue, bicker, flare up, quarrel, spar, squabble, tussle, wrangle. ▷ FIGHT.

scrape *n* **1** abrasion, graze, injury, laceration, scratch, scuff, wound. **2** *an awkward scrape.* difficulty, escapade, *inf* kettle of fish, piece of mischief, plight, prank, predicament, trouble. • *vb* **1** abrade, bark, bruise, damage, graze, injure, lacerate, scratch, scuff, skin, wound. **2** *scrape clean.* clean, file, rasp, rub, scour, scrub. **scrape together** ▷ COLLECT.

scrappy *adj* bitty, careless, disjointed, fragmentary, hurriedly done, imperfect, incomplete, inconclusive, sketchy, slipshod, unfinished, unpolished, unsatisfactory. *Opp* PERFECT.

scratch *n* abrasion, damage, dent, gash, gouge, graze, groove, indentation, injury, laceration, line, mark, score, scoring, scrape, scuff, wound. • *vb* abrade, claw at, cut, damage the surface of, dent, gash, gouge, graze, groove, incise, injure, lacerate, mark, rub, scarify, score, scrape, scuff, wound. **up to scratch** ▷ SATISFACTORY.

scrawl *vb* doodle, scribble, write hurriedly. ▷ WRITE.

scream *n & vb* bawl, caterwaul, cry, howl, roar, screech, shout, shriek, squeal, wail, yell, yowl.

screen *n* **1** blind, curtain, divider, partition. **2** camouflage, concealment, cover, disguise, protection, shelter, shield, smokescreen. **3** *sift through a screen.* filter, mesh, riddle, sieve, strainer. • *vb* **1** divide, partition off, subdivide, wall off. **2** camouflage, cloak, conceal, cover, disguise, guard, hide, mask, protect, safeguard, shade, shelter, shield, shroud, veil. **3** *screen employees for security.* *inf* check out, examine, investigate, process, sift out, vet.

screw *n* **1** bolt, screw-bolt. **2** rotation, spiral, turn, twist. • *vb* rotate, turn, twist. **screw down** ▷ FASTEN. **screw up** ▷ BUNGLE, TWIST.

scribble *vb* ▷ SCRAWL.

scribe *n* amanuensis, clerk, copyist, secretary, transcriber, writer.

script *n* **1** calligraphy, handwriting, penmanship. **2** *script of a play.* libretto, screenplay, text, words.

scripture *n* bible, holy writ, sacred writings, Word of God. □ *Bhagavad-Gita,* inf *the Good Book, the Gospel, Holy Bible, Koran, Upanishad.*

scrounge *vb* beg, cadge, importune.

scrub *vb* **1** brush, clean, rub, scour, wash. **2** ▷ CANCEL.

scruffy *adj* bedraggled, dirty, dishevelled, disordered, dowdy, frowsy, messy, ragged, scrappy, shabby, slatternly, slovenly, tatty, ungroomed, unkempt, untidy, worn out. *Opp* SMART.

scruple *n* compunction, conscience, doubt, hesitation, misgiving, qualm, reluctance, *inf* second thought. • *vb* [*usu neg*] be reluctant, have a conscience (about), have scruples (about), hesitate, hold back (from), *inf* think twice (about).

scrupulous *adj* **1** careful, cautious, conscientious, diligent, exacting, fastidious, *inf* finicky, meticulous, minute, neat, painstaking, precise, punctilious, rigid, rigorous, strict, systematic, thorough. **2** *scrupulous honesty.* ethical, fair-minded, honest, honourable, just, moral, principled, proper, upright, upstanding. *Opp* UNSCRUPULOUS.

scrutinize *vb* analyse, check, examine, *inf* go over with a toothcomb, inspect, investigate, look closely at, *inf* probe, sift, study.

scrutiny *n* analysis, examination, inspection, investigation, probing, search, study.

sculpture *n* three-dimensional art. □ *bas-relief, bronze, bust, carving, caryatid, cast, effigy, figure, figurine, maquette, marble, moulding, plaster cast, relief, statue, statuette.* ● *vb* carve, cast, chisel, fashion, form, hew, model, mould, *inf* sculpt, shape.

scum *n* dirt, film, foam, froth, impurities, suds.

scurrilous *adj* abusive, calumnious, coarse, defamatory, derogatory, disparaging, foul, indecent, insulting, libellous, low, obscene, offensive, opprobrious, scabrous, shameful, slanderous, vile, vulgar.

sea *adj* aquatic, marine, maritime, nautical, naval, ocean-going, oceanic, salt-water, seafaring, seagoing. ● *n inf* briny, *poet* deep, lake, *old use* main, ocean.

seal *n* **1** sea-lion, walrus. **2** *royal seal.* badge, coat of arms, crest, emblem, escutcheon, impression, imprint, mark, monogram, sign, stamp, symbol, token. ● *vb* **1** close, fasten, lock, make airtight, make watertight, plug, secure, shut, stick down, stop up. **2** *seal an agreement.* affirm, authenticate, *inf* clinch, conclude, confirm, corroborate, decide, endorse, finalize, guarantee, ratify, settle, sign, validate, verify.

seam *n* **1** join, stitching. **2** *seam of coal.* bed, layer, lode, stratum, thickness, vein.

seamy *adj* disreputable, distasteful, nasty, repulsive, shameful, sordid, squalid, unattractive, unpleasant, unsavoury, unwholesome.

search *n* check, enquiry, examination, hunt, inspection, investigation, look, *inf* probe, pursuit, quest, scrutiny. ● *vb* **1** cast about, explore, ferret about, hunt, investigate, *inf* leave no stone unturned, look, nose about, poke about, prospect, pry, seek. **2** *search suspects.* check, examine, *inf* frisk, inspect, scrutinize. **3** *search a house.* comb, go through, ransack, rifle, rummage through, scour. **searching** ▷ INQUISITIVE, THOROUGH.

seaside *n* beach, coast, coastal resort, sands, sea-coast, sea-shore, shore.

season *n* period, phase, time. ● *vb* **1** add seasoning to, flavour, *inf* pep up, salt, spice. **2** *season wood.* age, harden, mature, ripen.

seasonable *adj* appropriate, apt, convenient, favourable, fitting, normal, opportune, propitious, suitable, timely, well-timed.

seasoning *n* additives, condiments, flavouring, relish, zest. □ *dressing, herbs, mustard, pepper, salt, sauce, spice, vinegar.*

seat *n* **1** place, sitting-place. □ *armchair, bench, carver, chair, chaise longue, couch, deck-chair, dining-chair, easy chair, Fr fauteuil, form, pew, pillion, pouffe, reclining chair, rocking-chair, saddle, settee, settle, sofa, squab, stall, stool, throne, window seat.* **2** *a country seat.* ▷ RESIDENCE. **3** ▷ BUTTOCKS. **seat yourself** ▷ SIT.

secateurs *plur n* clippers, cutters, pruning shears.

secluded *adj* cloistered, concealed, cut off, hidden, inaccessible, isolated, lonely, monastic, *inf* off the beaten track, private, remote, retired, screened, sequestered, sheltered, shut away, solitary, unfrequented, unvisited. *Opp* PUBLIC.

seclusion *n* concealment, hiding, isolation, loneliness, privacy, remoteness, retirement, separation, shelter, solitariness.

second *adj* added, additional, alternative, another, complementary, duplicate, extra, following, further, later, matching, next, other, repeated, subsequent, twin. ● *n* **1** flash, instant, *inf* jiffy, moment, *inf* tick, *inf* twinkling, *inf* wink. **2** *second in a fight.* assistant, deputy, helper, *inf* number two, *inf* right-hand man, right-hand woman, second-in-command, *inf* stand-in, subordinate, supporter, understudy, vice-. ● *vb* **1** aid, assist, back, encourage, give approval to, help, promote, side with, sponsor, support. **2** *second to another job.* move, reassign, relocate, shift, transfer.

secondary *adj* **1** alternative, ancillary, auxiliary, *inf* backup, extra, inessential, inferior, lesser, lower, minor, nonessential, reinforcing, reserve, second, second-rate, spare, subordinate, subsidiary, supplementary, supporting, supportive, unimportant. **2** *secondary sources.* copied, derivative, second-hand, unoriginal.

second-hand *adj* **1** *inf* hand-me-down, old, used, worn. *Opp* NEW. **2** *second-hand experience.* indirect, secondary, vicarious. *Opp* DIRECT.

second-rate *adj* commonplace, indifferent, inferior, low-grade, mediocre, middling, ordinary, poor, second-best, second-class, undistinguished, unexciting, uninspiring.

secret *adj* **1** clandestine, concealed, covert, disguised, hidden, *inf* hushed up, *inf* hush-hush, invisible, private, secluded, shrouded, stealthy, undercover, underground, unknown. ▷ SECRETIVE. **2** *secret papers.* classified, confidential, inaccessible, intimate, personal, restricted, sensitive, top-secret, undisclosed, unpublished. **3** *secret meanings.* arcane, cryptic, encoded, esoteric, incomprehensible, mysterious, occult, recondite. **4** *secret about his private life.* ▷ SECRETIVE. *Opp* OPEN, PUBLIC.

secretary *n* amanuensis, clerk, filing-clerk, personal assistant, scribe, shorthand-typist, stenographer, typist, word-processor operator.

secrete *vb* **1** cloak, conceal, cover up, disguise, enshroud, hide, mask, put away, put into hiding. **2** *secrete fluid.* discharge, emit, excrete, exude, give off, leak, ooze, produce, release.

secretion *n* discharge, emission, escape, excretion, leakage, release.

secretive *adj* close-lipped, enigmatic, furtive, mysterious, quiet, reserved, reticent, secret, shifty, silent, taciturn, tight-lipped, uncommunicative, unforthcoming, withdrawn. *Opp* COMMUNICATIVE.

sect *n* cult, denomination, faction, order, party, persuasion. ▷ GROUP.

sectarian *adj* bigoted, clannish, cliquish, cultic, denominational, dogmatic, exclusive, factional, fanatical, inflexible, narrow, narrow-minded, partial, partisan, prejudiced, rigid, schismatic.

section *n* bit, branch, chapter, compartment, component, department, division, element, fraction, fragment, group, instalment, leg (*of journey*), part, passage, piece, portion, quarter, sample, sector, segment, slice, stage, subdivision, subsection.

sector *n* area, district, division, part, quarter, region, zone. ▷ SECTION.

secular *adj* civil, earthly, lay, material, mundane, non-religious, temporal, terrestrial, worldly. *Opp* RELIGIOUS.

secure *adj* **1** cosy, defended, guarded, immune, impregnable, invulnerable, protected, safe, sheltered, shielded, snug, unharmed, unhurt, unscathed. **2** *secure doors.* bolted, burglarproof, closed, fast, fastened, fixed, foolproof, immovable, locked, shut, solid, tight, unyielding. **3** *secure faith.* certain, confident, firm, stable, steady, strong, sure, unquestioning. ● *vb* **1** defend, guard, make safe, preserve, protect, shelter, shield. **2** anchor, attach, bolt, close, fix, lock, make fast, screw down, tie down. ▷ FASTEN. **3** *secure a loan.* acquire, be promised, come by, gain, get, obtain, procure, win.

sedate *adj* calm, collected, composed, controlled, conventional, cool, decorous, deliberate, dignified, equable, even-tempered, formal, grave, imperturbable, level-headed, peaceful, *derog* prim, proper, quiet, sensible, serene, serious, slow, sober, solemn, staid, strait-laced, tranquil, unruffled. *Opp* LIVELY. ● *vb* calm, put to sleep, tranquillize, treat with sedatives.

sedative *adj* anodyne, calming, lenitive, narcotic, relaxing, soothing, soporific, tranquillizing. ● *n* anodyne, barbiturate, calmative, depressant, narcotic, opiate, sleeping-pill, soporific, tranquillizer.

sedentary *adj* desk-bound, immobile, inactive, seated, sitting down. *Opp* ACTIVE.

sediment *n* deposit, dregs, grounds, lees, precipitate, remains, residue, *inf* sludge.

sedition *n* agitation, incitement, insurrection, mutiny, rabblerousing, revolt, treachery, treason. ▷ REBELLION.

seduce *vb* **1** allure, beguile, charm, corrupt, deceive, decoy, deprave, ensnare, entice, inveigle, lead astray, lure, mislead, tempt. **2** debauch, deflower, dishonour, rape, ravish, *old use* ruin, violate.

seduction *n* **1** allurement, attraction, charm, temptation. **2** rape, ravishing. ▷ SEX.

seductive *adj* alluring, appealing, attractive, bewitching, captivating, charming, coquettish, enchanting, enticing, flirtatious, inviting, irresistible, persuasive, provocative, *inf* sexy, tantalizing, tempting. *Opp* REPULSIVE.

see *vb* **1** behold, catch sight of, descry, discern, discover, distinguish, espy, glimpse, identify, look at, make out, mark, note, notice, observe, perceive, recognize, regard, sight, spot, spy, view, watch, witness. **2** *see what someone means.* appreciate, apprehend, comprehend, fathom, follow, *inf* get the hang of, grasp, know, perceive, realize, take in, understand. **3** *see problems ahead.* anticipate, conceive, envisage, foresee, foretell, imagine, picture, visualize. **4** *see what can be done.* consider, decide, discover, investigate, mull over, reflect on, think about, weigh up. **5** *see a play.* attend, be a spectator at, watch. **6** *seeing him tonight.* court, go out with, *inf* have a date with, meet, socialize with, visit, woo. **7** *see you home.* accompany, conduct, escort. **8** *saw fighting in the war.* endure, experience, go through, suffer, survive, undergo. **9** *Guess who I saw today!* encounter, face, meet, run into, talk to, visit. **see to** ▷ ORGANIZE.

seed *n* **1** egg, embryo, germ, ovule, ovum, semen, spawn, sperm, spore. **2** *seed in fruit.* pip, pit, stone. ● *vb* ▷ SOW.

seek *vb* aim at, apply for, ask for, aspire to, beg for, demand, desire, go after, hope for, hunt for, inquire after, look for, pursue, quest after, request, search for, solicit, strive after, try for, want, wish for.

seem *vb* appear, feel, give an impression of being, have an appearance of being, look, pretend to be, sound.

seep *vb* dribble, drip, exude, flow, leak, ooze, percolate, run, soak, trickle.

seer *n* clairvoyant, fortune-teller, oracle, prophet, prophetess, psychic, sibyl, soothsayer, vaticinator.

seethe *vb* be agitated, be angry, boil, bubble, erupt, foam, froth up, rise, simmer, stew, surge.

segment *n* bit, compartment, department, division, element, fraction, fragment, part, piece, portion, quarter, section, sector, slice, subdivision, subsection, wedge.

segregate *vb* compartmentalize, cut off, exclude, isolate, keep apart, put apart, separate, sequester, set apart, shut out.

segregation *n* **1** apartheid, discrimination. **2** isolation, quarantine, seclusion, separation.

seize *vb* **1** abduct, apprehend, arrest, capture, catch, clutch, *inf* collar, detain, grab, grasp, grip, hold, *inf* nab, pluck, possess, snatch, take, take into custody, take prisoner. **2** *seize a country.* annex, invade. **3** *seize property.* appropriate, commandeer, confiscate, hijack, impound, steal, take away. *Opp* RELEASE. **seize up** ▷ STICK.

seizure *n* **1** abduction, annexation, appropriation, arrest, capture, confiscation, hijacking, invasion, sequestration, theft, usurpation. **2** [*medical*] apoplexy, attack, convulsion, epileptic fit, fit, paroxysm, spasm, stroke.

seldom *adv* infrequently, occasionally, rarely.

select *adj* best, choice, chosen, élite, excellent, exceptional, exclusive, favoured, finest, first-class, first-rate, *inf* hand-picked, preferred, prime, privileged, rare, selected, special, top-quality. *Opp* ORDINARY. ● *vb* appoint, cast (*actor for role*), choose, decide on, elect, nominate, opt for, pick, prefer, settle on, single out, vote for.

selection *n* **1** choice, option, pick, preference. **2** *a selection of goods.* assortment, range, variety. **3** *selection from the classics.* excerpts, extracts, passages, quotations.

selective *adj* careful, *inf* choosy, discerning, discriminating, particular, specialized. *Opp* COMPREHENSIVE, IMPERCEPTIVE.

self-confident *adj* assertive, assured, collected, cool, fearless, independent, outgoing, poised, positive, self-assured, self-possessed, self-reliant, sure of yourself. ▷ BOLD. *Opp* SELF-CONSCIOUS.

self-conscious *adj* awkward, bashful, blushing, coy, diffident, embarrassed, ill at ease, insecure, nervous, reserved, self-effacing, sheepish, shy, uncomfortable, unnatural. ▷ TIMID. *Opp* SELF-CONFIDENT.

self-contained *adj* **1** complete, independent, separate. **2** aloof, cold, reserved, self-reliant, uncommu-

nicative, undemonstrative, unemotional.

self-control *n* calmness, composure, coolness, patience, resolve, restraint, self-command, self-denial, self-discipline, self-possession, self-restraint, will-power.

self-denial *n* abstemiousness, fasting, moderation, self-abnegation, self-sacrifice, temperance, unselfishness. *Opp* SELFINDULGENCE.

self-employed *adj* freelance, independent.

self-esteem *n* **1** ▷ SELF-RESPECT. **2** arrogance, *inf* big-headedness, conceit, egotism, overconfidence, self-admiration, self-importance, self-love, smugness, vanity.

self-explanatory *adj* apparent, axiomatic, blatant, clear, conspicuous, eye-catching, flagrant, glaring, inescapable, manifest, obvious, patent, plain, recognizable, self-evident, understandable, unmistakable, visible.

self-governing *adj* autonomous, free, independent, sovereign.

self-important *adj* arrogant, bombastic, conceited, grandiloquent, haughty, magisterial, ostentatious, pompous, pontifical, pretentious, self-centred, sententious, smug, *inf* snooty, *inf* stuckup, supercilious, vainglorious.

self-indulgence *n* extravagance, gluttony, greed, hedonism, pleasure, profligacy, self-gratification. ▷ SELFISHNESS. *Opp* SELF-DENIAL.

self-indulgent *adj* dissipated, epicurean, extravagant, gluttonous, gourmandizing, greedy, hedonistic, immoderate, intemperate, pleasure-loving, profligate, sybaritic. ▷ SELFISH. *Opp* ABSTEMIOUS.

selfish *adj* acquisitive, avaricious, covetous, demanding, egocentric, egotistic, grasping, greedy, inconsiderate, mean, mercenary, miserly, self-absorbed, self-centred, self-indulgent, self-interested, self-seeking, self-serving, *inf* stingy, thoughtless, uncaring, ungenerous, unhelpful,

unsympathetic, worldly. *Opp*
UNSELFISH.

selfishness *n* acquisitiveness, avarice, covetousness, egotism, greed, meanness, miserliness, niggardliness, possessiveness, self-indulgence, self-interest, selflove, self-regard, *inf* stinginess, thoughtlessness.

self-reliant *adj* autonomous, independent, self-contained, self-sufficient, self-supporting.

self-respect *n Fr* amour propre, dignity, honour, integrity, morale, pride, self-confidence, self-esteem.

self-righteous *adj* complacent, *inf* goody-goody, *inf* holier-than-thou, mealy-mouthed, pharisaical, pietistic, pious, pompous, priggish, proud, sanctimonious, self-important, self-satisfied, sleek, smug, superior, vain.

self-sufficient *adj* autonomous, independent, self-reliant, self-supporting.

self-willed *adj* determined, dogged, forceful, headstrong, inflexible, intractable, intransigent, *inf* mulish, obstinate, *inf* pigheaded, single-minded, *inf* stiffnecked, stubborn, uncontrollable, uncooperative, wilful.

sell *vb* **1** auction, barter, deal in, exchange, give in part-exchange, handle, hawk, *inf* keep, *inf* knock down, offer for sale, peddle, *inf* put under the hammer, retail, sell off, stock, tout, trade, *inf* trade in (*traded in my car*), traffic in, vend. **2** *sell hard*. advertise, market, merchandise, package, promote, *inf* push.

seller *n* dealer, merchant, stockist, supplier, trader, vendor. □ agent, barrow-boy, broker, old use *colporteur*, costermonger, old use *hawker*, market-trader, pedlar, inf *rep*, representative, retailer, salesman, salesperson, saleswoman, *shop assistant*, shopkeeper, storekeeper, street trader, tradesman, traveller, wholesaler. ▷ SHOP.

seminal *adj* basic, constructive, creative, fertile, formative, imaginative, important, influential, innovative, new, original, primary, productive.

send *vb* **1** address, consign, convey, deliver, direct, dispatch, fax, forward, mail, post, remit, ship, transmit. **2** *send a rocket to the moon*. fire, launch, project, propel, release, shoot. **send away** ▷ DISMISS. **send down** ▷ IMPRISON. **send for** ▷ SUMMON. **send-off** *n* ▷ GOODBYE. **send out** ▷ EMIT. **send round** ▷ CIRCULATE. **send up** ▷ PARODY.

senile *adj* declining, doddery, *inf* in your dotage, old, *derog* past it.

senior *adj* chief, elder, higher, high-ranking, major, older, principal, revered, superior, well-established. *Opp* JUNIOR.

sensation *n* **1** awareness, feeling, perception, sense. **2** *affair caused a sensation*. commotion, excitement, furore, outrage, scandal, stir, thrill.

sensational *adj* **1** blood-curdling, hair-raising, lurid, melodramatic, overwritten, scandal-mongering, shocking, startling, stimulating, violent. **2** [*inf*] *a sensational result*. amazing, astonishing, astounding, breathtaking, electrifying, exciting, extraordinary, *inf* fabulous, *inf* fantastic, *inf* great, incredible, marvellous, remarkable, spectacular, spine-tingling, stirring, superb, surprising, thrilling, unbelievable, unexpected, wonderful.

sense *n* **1** awareness, consciousness, faculty, feeling, sensation. □ hearing, sight, smell, taste, touch. **2** brains, cleverness, gumption, intellect, intelligence, intuition, judgement, logic, *inf* nous, perception, reason, reasoning, understanding, wisdom, wit. **3** *the sense of a message*. coherence, connotations, denotation, *inf* drift, gist, import, intelligibility, interpretation, meaning, message, point, purport, significance, signification, substance. ● *vb* be aware (of), detect, discern, divine, feel, guess, *inf* have a hunch, intuit, notice, perceive, *inf* pick up vibes, realize, respond to, suspect, understand. ▷ FEEL, HEAR, SEE, SMELL, TASTE. **make sense of** ▷ UNDERSTAND.

senseless *adj* **1** anaesthetized, asleep, comatose, insensate, insensible, knocked out, numb, *inf* out like a light, stunned, unconscious. **2** absurd, crazy, fatuous, meaningless, pointless, purposeless, silly. ▷ STUPID.

sensible *adj* **1** calm, common-sense, commonsensical, cool, discreet, discriminating, intelligent, judicious, level-headed, logical, prudent, rational, realistic, reasonable, reasoned, sage, sane, serious-minded, sound, straightforward, thoughtful, wise. *Opp* STUPID. **2** *sensible phenomena.* corporeal, existent, material, palpable, perceptible, physical, real, tangible, visible. **3** *sensible clothes.* comfortable, functional, *inf* no-nonsense, practical, useful. *Opp* FASHIONABLE, IMPRACTICAL. **sensible of** acquainted with, alert to, alive to, appreciative of, aware of, cognizant of, in touch with, mindful of, responsive to, *inf* wise to.

sensitive *adj* **1** considerate, perceptive, reactive, receptive, responsive, susceptible, sympathetic, tactful, thoughtful, understanding. **2** *a sensitive temperament.* emotional, hypersensitive, impressionable, temperamental, thin-skinned, touchy, volatile, vulnerable. **3** *sensitive skin.* delicate, fine, fragile, painful, soft, sore, tender. **4** *a sensitive topic.* confidential, controversial, delicate, *inf* tricky. *Opp* INSENSITIVE. **sensitive to** affected by, attuned to, aware of, considerate of, perceptive about, receptive to, responsive to, understanding about.

sensual *adj* animal, bodily, carnal, fleshly, physical, pleasure-loving, self-indulgent, voluptuous, worldly. ▷ SEXY. *Opp* ASCETIC.

sensuous *adj* beautiful, emotional, gratifying, lush, luxurious, rich, richly embellished.

sentence *n* **1** exclamation, question, statement, thought, utterance. **2** decision, judgement, pronouncement, punishment, ruling. ● *vb* condemn, pass judgement on, pronounce sentence on.

sentiment *n* **1** attitude, belief, idea, judgement, opinion, outlook, thought, view. **2** *sentiment of a poem.* emotion, feeling, sensibility.

sentimental *adj* **1** compassionate, emotional, nostalgic, romantic, soft-hearted, sympathetic, tearful, tender, warm-hearted, *inf* weepy. **2** [*derog*] gushing, *inf* gushy, indulgent, insincere, maudlin, mawkish, *inf* mushy, overdone, over-emotional, *inf* sloppy, *inf* soppy, *inf* sugary, tear-jerking, *inf* treacly, unrealistic, *sl* yucky. *Opp* CYNICAL.

sentimentality *n* bathos, emotionalism, insincerity, *inf* kitsch, mawkishness, nostalgia, *inf* slush.

sentry *n* guard, lookout, patrol, picket, sentinel, watch, watchman.

separable *adj* detachable, distinguishable, fissile, removable.

separate *adj* apart, autonomous, cloistered, cut off, detached, different, discrete, disjoined, distinct, divided, divorced, fenced off, free-standing, independent, individual, isolated, particular, peculiar, secluded, segregated, separated, shut off, solitary, unattached, unconnected, unique, unrelated, unshared, withdrawn. ● *vb* **1** break up, cut off, detach, disconnect, disengage, disentangle, disjoin, dismember, dissociate, divide, fence off, fragment, hive off, isolate, keep apart, part, pull apart, segregate, sever, split, sunder, take apart, uncouple, unfasten, unhook, unravel, unyoke. **2** *The paths separate here.* bifurcate, branch, diverge, fork. **3** *separated the grain from the chaff.* abstract, distinguish, filter out, remove, set apart, sift out, winnow. **4** *He separated from his partner.* become estranged, disband, divorce, part company, *inf* split up. *Opp* COMBINE, UNITE.

separation *n* **1** amputation, cutting off, detachment, disconnection, dismemberment, dissociation, division, fission, fragmentation, parting, rift,

service

severance, splitting. *Opp* CONNECTION.
2 *separation of partners*. break, *inf*
break-up, divorce, estrangement, rift,
split. *Opp* UNION.

septic *adj* diseased, festering,
infected, inflamed, poisoned, puru-
lent, putrefying, putrid, suppurating.

sequel *n* consequence, continuation,
development, *inf* follow-up, issue,
outcome, result, upshot.

sequence *n* **1** arrangement, chain,
concatenation, course, cycle, line,
order, procession, programme, progression, range, row, run, series, set,
string, succession, train. **2** *a sequence
from a film*. inf clip, episode, excerpt,
extract, scene, section.

serene *adj* **1** calm, idyllic, peaceful,
placid, pleasing, quiet, restful, still,
tranquil, unclouded, undisturbed,
unperturbed, unruffled, untroubled.
2 *serene temperament*. collected, composed, contented, cool, easy-going,
equable, even-tempered, imperturbable, pacific, peaceable, poised,
self-possessed, *inf* unflappable. *Opp*
BOISTEROUS, EXCITABLE.

series *n* **1** arrangement, chain, concatenation, course, cycle, line, order,
procession, programme, progression,
range, row, run, sequence, set,
string, succession, train. **2** *TV series*.
mini-series, serial, *inf* soap, soap-
opera.

serious *adj* **1** dignified, grave, grim,
humourless, long-faced, pensive,
poker-faced, sedate, sober, solemn,
sombre, staid, stern, straight-faced,
thoughtful, unsmiling. *Opp* CHEERFUL.
2 *serious discussion*. deep, earnest,
heavy, honest, important, intellectual, momentous, profound, signifi-
cant, sincere, weighty. **3** *serious illness*.
acute, appalling, awful, calamitous,
critical, dangerous, dreadful, frightful, ghastly, grievous, hideous, horrible, *inf* life-and-death, nasty, severe,
shocking, terrible, unfortunate,
unpleasant, urgent, violent. *Opp*
TRIVIAL. **4** *serious worker*. careful,
committed, conscientious, diligent,
hard-working.

sermon *n* address, discourse,
homily, lecture, lesson, talk.

serpentine *adj* labyrinthine, meandering, roundabout, sinuous,
snaking, tortuous, twisting, vermic-
ular, winding. *Opp* STRAIGHT.

serrated *adj* cogged, crenellated,
denticulate, indented, jagged,
notched, saw-like, toothed, zigzag.
Opp STRAIGHT.

servant *n* assistant, attendant, *derog*
dogsbody, *inf* domestic, *derog* drudge,
helper, *derog* hireling, *derog* menial,
old use servitor, *inf* skivvy, slave, *old
use* vassal. □ au pair, barmaid, barman,
batman, inf boots, butler, chamber-maid,
inf char, charwoman, chauffeur, chef,
cleaner, old use coachman, commission-
aire, cook, inf daily, errand boy, fac-
totum, derog flunkey, footman, govern-
ness, groom, home help, houseboy, house-
maid, housekeeper, kitchenmaid, derog
lackey, lady-in-waiting, maid, maidserv-
ant, major-domo, manservant, nanny,
page, parlour-maid, old use postilion,
old use retainer, plur retinue, scout,
scullery maid, old use scullion, old use
seneschal, slave, steward, stewardess,
valet, waiter, waitress.

serve *vb* **1** accommodate, aid, assist,
attend, *inf* be at someone's beck and
call, further, help, look after, minister to, wait upon, work for. **2** *serve in
the forces*. be employed, do your duty,
enlist, fight, sign on. **3** *serve goods*.
deal out, distribute, dole out, give
out, make available, provide, sell,
supply. **4** *serve at table*. carve, *inf* dish
up, officiate, wait. **5** *serve a sentence*.
complete, endure, go through, pass,
spend, survive.

service *n* **1** aid, assistance, benefit,
favour, help, kindness, office. **2** *service
of the community*. attendance (on),
employment (by), ministering (to),
work (for). **3** *a bus service*. business,
organization, provision, system,
timetable. **4** *give the car a service*.
check-over, maintenance, overhaul,
repair, servicing. **5** *church service*.
ceremony, liturgy, meeting, rite,
ritual, worship. □ baptism, christening,
communion, compline, evensong, fu-

neral, marriage, Mass, matins, Requiem Mass, vespers. ● *vb service a vehicle.* check, maintain, mend, overhaul, repair, tune.

serviceable *adj* dependable, durable, functional, hard-wearing, lasting, practical, strong, tough, usable.

servile *adj* abject, acquiescent, base, *inf* boot-licking, craven, cringing, deferential, fawning, flattering, grovelling, humble, ingratiating, low, menial, obsequious, slavish, submissive, subservient, sycophantic, *inf* time-serving, toadying, unctuous. *Opp* BOSSY. **be servile** ▷ GROVEL.

serving *n* helping, plateful, portion, ration.

session *n* **1** assembly, conference, discussion, hearing, meeting, sitting. **2** *a session at the baths.* period, term, time.

set *adj* **1** *set price.* advertised, agreed, arranged, defined, definite, fixed, prearranged, predetermined, prepared, scheduled, standard. **2** *set in your ways.* established, invariable, predictable, regular, stable, unchanging, unvarying. ● *n* **1** batch, bunch, category, class, clique, collection, combination, kind, series, sort. ▷ GROUP. **2** *a TV set.* apparatus, receiver. **3** *set for a play.* scene, scenery, setting, stage. ● *vb* **1** arrange, assign, deploy, deposit, dispose, lay, leave, locate, lodge, park, place, plant, *inf* plonk, put, position, rest, set down, set out, settle, situate, stand, station. **2** *set a clock.* adjust, correct, put right, rectify, regulate. **3** *set a post in concrete.* embed, fasten, fix. **4** *set like concrete.* become firm, congeal, *inf* gel, harden, *inf* jell, stiffen, take shape. **5** *set a problem.* ask, express, formulate, frame, phrase, pose, present, put forward, suggest, write. **6** *set a target.* allocate, allot, appoint, decide, designate, determine, establish, identify, name, ordain, prescribe, settle. **set about** ▷ ATTACK, BEGIN. **set free** ▷ LIBERATE. **set off** ▷ DEPART, EXPLODE. **set on** ▷ ATTACK. **set on fire** ▷ IGNITE. **set out** ▷ DEPART. **set up** ▷ ESTABLISH.

set-back *n inf* blow, check, complication, defeat, delay, difficulty, disappointment, hindrance, *inf* hitch, hold-up, impediment, misfortune, obstacle, problem, relapse, reverse, snag, upset.

settee *n* chaise longue, couch, sofa.

setting *n* **1** background, context, environment, environs, frame, habitat, locale, location, place, position, site, surroundings. **2** *setting for a play.* backcloth, backdrop, scene, scenery, set.

settle *vb* **1** arrange, conclude, deal with, decide, organize, put in order, straighten out. **2** alight, come to rest, land, light, *inf* make yourself comfortable, *inf* park yourself, pause, rest, roost, sit down. **3** *settle things in place.* assign, deploy, deposit, dispose, lay, locate, lodge, park, place, plant, position, put, rest, set, set down, situate, stand, station. **4** *the dust settled.* calm down, clear, compact, go down, sink, subside. **5** *settle what to do.* agree, choose, decide, establish, fix. **6** *settle differences.* end, negotiate, put an end to, reconcile, resolve, sort out, square. **7** *settle debts.* clear, discharge, pay, pay off. **8** *settle new territory.* become established in, colonize, immigrate, make your home in, occupy, people, set up home in, stay in.

settlement *n* **1** camp, colony, community, encampment, kibbutz, outpost, post, town, village. **2** agreement, arbitration, arrangement, contract, payment.

settler *n* colonist, frontiersman, immigrant, newcomer, pioneer, squatter.

sever *vb* **1** amputate, break, cut off, detach, disconnect, disjoin, part, remove, separate, split, terminate. ▷ CUT. **2** *sever a relationship.* abandon, break off, discontinue, end, put an end to, suspend, terminate.

several *adj* assorted, certain, different, divers, a few, a handful of, many, miscellaneous, a number of, some, sundry, a variety of, various.

severe *adj* **1** aloof, brutal, cold, cold-hearted, cruel, disapproving, dour, exacting, forbidding, glowering, grave, grim, hard, harsh, inexorable, merciless, obdurate, pitiless, relentless, rigorous, stern, stony, strict, unbending, uncompromising, unkind, unsmiling, unsympathetic, unyielding. **2** *severe illness.* acute, critical, dangerous, drastic, fatal, great, intense, keen, life-threatening, mortal, nasty, serious, sharp, terminal, troublesome. **3** *severe penalties.* draconian, extreme, maximum, oppressive, punitive, stringent. **4** *severe weather.* adverse, bad, inclement, violent, *inf* wicked. ▷ COLD, STORMY. **5** *a severe challenge.* arduous, demanding, difficult, onerous, punishing, taxing, tough. **6** *severe style.* austere, bare, chaste, plain, simple, spartan, stark, unadorned. *Opp* FRIENDLY, MILD, ORNATE.

sew *vb* baste, darn, hem, mend, repair, stitch, tack.

sewage *n* effluent, waste.

sewer *n* drain, drainage, sanitation, septic tank, soak-away.

sewing *n* dressmaking, embroidery, mending, needlepoint, needlework, tapestry.

sex *n* **1** gender, sexuality. **2** carnal knowledge, coition, coitus, congress, consummation of marriage, copulation, coupling, fornication, *inf* going to bed, incest, intercourse, intimacy, love-making, masturbation, mating, orgasm, perversion, rape, seduction, sexual intercourse, sexual relations, union. **have sex (with)** be intimate (with), consummate marriage, copulate (with), couple (with), fornicate (with), have sexual intercourse (with), make love (to), mate (with), rape, ravish, *sl* screw, seduce, unite (with).

sexism *n inf* chauvinism, discrimination, prejudice.

sexual *adj* **1** genital, procreative, progenitive, reproductive. **2** ▷ SEXY.

sexuality *n* gender. □ *bisexuality, hermaphroditism, heterosexuality, homosexuality.*

sexy *adj* **1** amorous, carnal, concupiscent, erotic, lascivious, lecherous, *derog* lewd, libidinous, *derog* lubricious, lustful, passionate, provocative, *derog* prurient, *inf* randy, seductive, sensual, sexual, *inf* sultry, venereal, voluptuous. **2** attractive, *inf* beddable, desirable, *sl* dishy, flirtatious. **3** *sexy books.* aphrodisiac, arousing, pornographic, *sl* raunchy, salacious, *inf* steamy, suggestive, titillating, *inf* torrid. ▷ OBSCENE.

shabby *adj* **1** bedraggled, dilapidated, dingy, dirty, dowdy, drab, faded, frayed, *inf* grubby, mangy, *inf* moth-eaten, ragged, run-down, *inf* scruffy, seedy, tattered, *inf* tatty, threadbare, unattractive, worn, worn-out. *Opp* SMART. **2** *shabby behaviour.* base, contemptible, despicable, disagreeable, discreditable, dishonest, dishonourable, disreputable, ignoble, *inf* low-down, mean, nasty, shameful, shoddy, unfair, unfriendly, ungenerous, unkind, unworthy. *Opp* HONOURABLE.

shack *n* cabin, hovel, hut, lean-to, shanty, shed.

shade *n* **1** ▷ SHADOW. **2** awning, blind, canopy, covering, curtain, parasol, screen, shelter, shield, umbrella, Venetian blind. **3** *a shade of blue.* colour, hue, intensity, tinge, tint, tone. **4** *shades of meaning.* degree, difference, nicety, nuance, variation. ● *vb* **1** camouflage, conceal, cover, hide, mask, obscure, protect, screen, shield, shroud, veil. **2** *shade with pencil.* black out, block in, cross-hatch, darken, fill in, make dark.

shadow *n* **1** darkness, dimness, dusk, gloom, obscurity, penumbra, semi-darkness, shade, umbra. **2** *The sun casts shadows.* outline, shape, silhouette. **3** *a shadow of doubt.* ▷ HINT. ● *vb* dog, follow, hunt, *inf* keep tabs on, keep watch on, pursue, stalk, *inf* tag onto, tail, track, trail, watch.

shadowy *adj* **1** dark, dim, faint, hazy, ill-defined, indefinite, indistinct, nebulous, obscure, unclear, unrecognizable, vague. ▷ GHOSTLY. **2** ▷ SHADY.

shady adj **1** poet bosky, cool, dark, dim, dusky, gloomy, leafy, shaded, shadowy, sheltered, sunless. Opp SUNNY. **2** a shady character. devious, dishonest, disreputable, dubious, inf fishy, questionable, shifty, suspicious, unreliable, untrustworthy. Opp HONEST.

shaft n **1** arrow, column, handle, helve, pillar, pole, post, rod, shank, stanchion, stem, stick, upright. **2** duct, mine, pit, tunnel, well, working. **3** shaft of light. beam, gleam, laser, pencil, ray, streak.

shaggy adj bushy, dishevelled, fibrous, fleecy, hairy, hirsute, matted, rough, tousled, unkempt, unshorn, untidy, woolly. Opp SMOOTH.

shake vb **1** convulse, heave, jump, quake, quiver, rattle, rock, shiver, shudder, sway, throb, totter, tremble, vibrate, waver, wobble. **2** shake your umbrella. agitate, brandish, flourish, gyrate, jar, jerk, inf jiggle, inf joggle, jolt, oscillate, sway, swing, twirl, twitch, vibrate, wag, inf waggle, wave, inf wiggle. **3** The bad news shook us. alarm, distress, disturb, frighten, perturb, inf rattle, shock, startle, inf throw, unnerve, unsettle, upset. ▷ SURPRISE.

shaky adj **1** decrepit, dilapidated, feeble, flimsy, frail, insecure, precarious, ramshackle, rickety, rocky, shaking, unreliable, unsound, unsteady, weak, wobbly. **2** a shaky voice. faltering, quavering, quivering, trembling, tremulous. **3** a shaky start. nervous, tentative, uncertain, underconfident, unimpressive, unpromising. Opp STEADY, STRONG.

shallow adj **1** shallow water. [There are no apt synonyms for this sense.] **2** shallow argument. empty, facile, foolish, frivolous, glib, insincere, puerile, silly, simple, inf skin-deep, slight, superficial, trivial, unconvincing, unscholarly, unthinking. Opp DEEP.

sham adj artificial, bogus, counterfeit, ersatz, fake, false, fictitious, fraudulent, imitation, make-believe, mock, inf pretend, pretended, simulated, synthetic. ● n counterfeit, fake, fiction, fraud, hoax, imitation, make-believe, pretence, inf put-up job, simulation. ● vb counterfeit, fake, feign, imitate, make believe, pretend, simulate.

shambles plur n **1** battlefield, scene of carnage, slaughterhouse. **2** [inf] chaos, confusion, devastation, disorder, mess, muddle, inf pigsty, inf tip.

shame n **1** chagrin, degradation, discredit, disgrace, dishonour, distress, embarrassment, guilt, humiliation, ignominy, infamy, loss of face, mortification, obloquy, opprobrium, remorse, stain, stigma, vilification. **2** a shame to mistreat him so. outrage, pity, scandal, wickedness. ● vb abash, chagrin, chasten, discomfit, disconcert, discountenance, disgrace, embarrass, humble, humiliate, make someone ashamed, mortify, inf put someone in his/her place, inf show someone up.

shamefaced adj **1** abashed, ashamed, chagrined, inf hang-dog, humiliated, mortified, penitent, inf red-faced, remorseful, repentant, sorry. **2** bashful, coy, embarrassed, modest, self-conscious, sheepish, shy, timid. Opp SHAMELESS.

shameful adj **1** a shameful crime. base, contemptible, deplorable, disgraceful, ignoble, infamous, low, mean, outrageous, reprehensible, scandalous, unworthy. ▷ WICKED. **2** shameful to be found out. compromising, degrading, demeaning, discreditable, dishonourable, embarrassing, humiliating, ignominious, sl infra dig, inglorious, lowering, mortifying, undignified. Opp HONOURABLE.

shameless adj **1** barefaced, bold, brazen, cheeky, cool, defiant, flagrant, hardened, impenitent, impudent, incorrigible, insolent, unabashed, unashamed, unrepent-

shed

ant. **2** *shameless nudity.* frank, honest, immodest, improper, indecorous, open, rude, shocking, unblushing, unconcealed, undisguised, unselfconscious. *Opp* SHAMEFACED.

shape *n* **1** body, build, figure, physique, profile, silhouette. **2** *geometrical shape.* configuration, figure, form, format, model, mould, outline, pattern. □ [two-dimensional] *circle, diamond, ellipse, heptagon, hexagon, lozenge, oblong, octagon, oval, parallelogram, pentagon, polygon, quadrant, quadrilateral, rectangle, rhomboid, rhombus, ring, semicircle, square, trapezium, trapezoid, triangle.* [three-dimensional] *cone, cube, cylinder, decahedron, hemisphere, hexahedron, octahedron, polyhedron, prism, pyramid, sphere.* ● *vb* adapt, adjust, carve, cast, cut, fashion, form, frame, give shape to, model, mould, *inf* sculpt, sculpture, whittle.

shapeless *adj* **1** amorphous, formless, indeterminate, irregular, nebulous, undefined, unformed, unstructured, vague. **2** *a shapeless figure.* deformed, distorted, *inf* dumpy, flat, misshapen, twisted, unattractive, unshapely. *Opp* SHAPELY.

shapely *adj* attractive, comely, *inf* curvaceous, elegant, good-looking, graceful, neat, trim, *inf* voluptuous, well-proportioned. *Opp* SHAPELESS.

share *n* allocation, allotment, allowance, bit, cut, division, due, fraction, helping, part, percentage, piece, portion, proportion, quota, ration, serving, *sl* whack. ● *vb* **1** allocate, allot, apportion, deal out, distribute, divide, dole out, *inf* go halves or shares (with), halve, partake of, portion out, ration out, share out, split. **2** *share work.* be involved, cooperate, join, participate, take part. **shared** ▷ JOINT.

sharp *adj* **1** acute, arrow-shaped, cutting, fine, jagged, keen, knife-edged, needle-sharp, pointed, razor-sharp, sharpened, spiky, tapering. **2** *sharp bend, drop.* abrupt, acute, angular, hairpin, marked, precipitous, sheer, steep, sudden, surprising, unex-

pected, vertical. **3** *sharp focus.* clear, defined, distinct, focused, well-defined. **4** *a sharp storm.* extreme, heavy, intense, serious, severe, sudden, violent. **5** *sharp frost.* biting, bitter, keen, nippy. ▷ COLD. **6** *sharp pain.* acute, excruciating, painful, stabbing, stinging. **7** *sharp rejoinder.* acerbic, acid, acidulous, barbed, biting, caustic, critical, cutting, hurtful, incisive, malicious, mocking, mordant, sarcastic, sardonic, scathing, spiteful, tart, trenchant, unkind, venomous, vitriolic. **8** *sharp mind.* acute, agile, alert, artful, astute, bright, clever, crafty, *inf* cute, discerning, incisive, intelligent, observant, penetrating, perceptive, probing, quick-witted, searching, shrewd, *inf* smart. **9** *sharp eyes.* attentive, eagle-eyed, observant, *inf* peeled (*keep your eyes peeled*), quick, watchful, wide-open. **10** *sharp taste, smell.* acid, acrid, bitter, caustic, hot, piquant, pungent, sour, spicy, tangy, tart. **11** *sharp sound.* clear, detached, ear-splitting, high, high-pitched, penetrating, piercing, shrieking, shrill, staccato, strident. *Opp* BLUNT, DULL, SLIGHT.

sharpen *vb* file, grind, hone, make sharp, strop, whet. *Opp* BLUNT.

sharpener *n* file, grindstone, hone, pencil-sharpener, strop, whetstone.

shatter *vb* blast, break, break up, burst, crack, crush, dash to pieces, demolish, destroy, disintegrate, explode, pulverize, shiver, smash, *inf* smash to smithereens, splinter, split, wreck. **shattered** ▷ SURPRISED, WEARY.

sheaf *n* bunch, bundle, file, ream.

shear *vb* clip, strip, trim. ▷ CUT.

sheath *n* casing, covering, scabbard, sleeve.

sheathe *vb* cocoon, cover, encase, enclose, put away, put in a sheath, wrap.

shed *n* hut, hutch, lean-to, outhouse, penthouse, potting-shed, shack, shelter, storehouse. ● *vb* abandon, cast off, discard, drop, let fall, moult, pour off, scatter, shower, spill, spread, throw off. **shed light** ▷ SHINE.

sheen n brightness, burnish, glaze, gleam, glint, gloss, lustre, patina, polish, radiance, reflection, shimmer, shine.

sheep n ewe, lamb, mutton, ram, wether.

sheepish adj abashed, ashamed, bashful, coy, docile, embarrassed, guilty, meek, mortified, reticent, self-conscious, self-effacing, shamefaced, shy, timid. Opp SHAMELESS.

sheer adj 1 absolute, arrant, complete, downright, out-and-out, plain, pure, simple, thoroughgoing, total, unadulterated, unalloyed, unmitigated, unmixed, unqualified, utter. 2 a sheer cliff. abrupt, perpendicular, precipitous, steep, vertical. 3 sheer silk. diaphanous, filmy, fine, flimsy, gauzy, gossamer, inf see-through, thin, translucent, transparent.

sheet n 1 bedsheet, duvet cover. 2 [paper] folio, leaf, page. 3 [glass, etc] pane, panel, plate. 4 [ice, etc] blanket, coating, covering, film, lamina, layer, membrane, skin, veneer. 5 [water] area, expanse, surface.

shelf n ledge, shelving.

shell n 1 carapace (of tortoise), case, casing, covering, crust, exterior, façade, hull, husk, outside, pod. 2 fired shells at them. cartridge, projectile. ● vb attack with gunfire, barrage, bomb, bombard, fire at, shoot at, strafe.

shellfish n bivalve, crustacean, mollusc. □ barnacle, clam, cockle, conch, crab, crayfish, cuttlefish, limpet, lobster, mussel, oyster, prawn, scallop, shrimp, whelk, winkle.

shelter n 1 asylum, cover, haven, lee, protection, refuge, safety, sanctuary, security. 2 barrier, concealment, cover, fence, hut, roof, screen, shield. 3 seek shelter for the night. accommodation, home, housing, lodging, resting-place. ▷ HOUSE. 4 air-raid shelter. bunker. ● vb 1 defend, enclose, guard, keep safe, protect, safeguard, screen, secure, shade,

shield. 2 shelter a runaway. accommodate, give shelter to, harbour, hide, inf put up. **sheltered** ▷ QUIET.

shelve vb 1 defer, hold in abeyance, lay aside, postpone, put off, put on ice. 2 ▷ SLOPE.

shield n 1 barrier, bulwark, defence, guard, protection, safeguard, screen, shelter. 2 a warrior's shield. buckler, heraldry escutcheon. ● vb cover, defend, guard, keep safe, protect, safeguard, screen, shade, shelter.

shift n 1 adjustment, alteration, change, move, switch, transfer, transposition. 2 night shift. crew, gang, group, period, inf stint, team, workforce. ● vb adjust, alter, budge, change, displace, reposition, switch, transfer, transpose. ▷ MOVE. **shift for yourself** ▷ MANAGE.

shiftless adj idle, indolent, ineffective, inefficient, inept, irresponsible, lazy, unambitious, unenterprising. Opp RESOURCEFUL.

shifty adj artful, canny, crafty, cunning, deceitful, designing, devious, dishonest, evasive, inf foxy, furtive, scheming, secretive, inf shady, inf slippery, sly, treacherous, tricky, untrustworthy, wily. Opp STRAIGHTFORWARD.

shimmer vb flicker, glimmer, glisten, ripple. ▷ SHINE.

shine n brightness, burnish, coruscation, glaze, gleam, glint, gloss, glow, luminosity, lustre, patina, phosphorescence, polish, radiance, reflection, sheen, shimmer, sparkle, varnish. ● vb 1 beam, be luminous, blaze, coruscate, dazzle, emit light, flare, flash, glare, gleam, glint, glisten, glitter, glow, phosphoresce, radiate, reflect, scintillate, shed light, shimmer, sparkle, twinkle. 2 used to shine at maths. be brilliant, be clever, do well, excel, inf make your mark, stand out. 3 shine your shoes. brush, buff up, burnish, clean, polish, rub up. **shining** ▷ BRIGHT, CONSPICUOUS.

shingle n 1 gravel, pebbles, stones. 2 roofing shingle. tile.

shiny *adj* bright, brilliant, burnished, gleaming, glistening, glossy, glowing, luminous, lustrous, phosphorescent, polished, reflective, rubbed, shimmering, shining, sleek, smooth. *Opp* DULL.

ship *n* boat. ▷ VESSEL. ● *vb* carry, *inf* cart, convey, deliver, ferry, freight, move, send, transport.

shirk *vb* avoid, dodge, duck, evade, get out of, neglect, shun. **shirk work** be lazy, malinger, *inf* skive, slack.

shiver *n* flutter, frisson, quiver, rattle, shake, shudder, thrill, tremor, vibration. ● *vb* chatter, flap, flutter, quake, quaver, quiver, rattle, shake, shudder, tremble, twitch, vibrate.

shock *n* **1** blow, collision, concussion, impact, jolt, thud. **2** *came as a shock. inf* bombshell, surprise, *inf* thunderbolt. **3** *state of shock.* dismay, distress, fright, trauma, upset. ● *vb* **1** alarm, amaze, astonish, astound, confound, daze, dismay, distress, dumbfound, frighten, *inf* give someone a turn, jar, jolt, numb, paralyse, petrify, rock, scare, shake, stagger, startle, stun, stupefy, surprise, *inf* throw, traumatize, unnerve. **2** *Sadism shocks us.* appal, disgust, horrify, nauseate, offend, outrage, repel, revolt, scandalize, sicken.

shoddy *adj* **1** cheap, flimsy, *inf* gimcrack, inferior, jerry-built, meretricious, nasty, poor quality, *inf* rubbishy, second-rate, shabby, *sl* tacky, *inf* tatty, tawdry, *inf* trashy. **2** *shoddy work.* careless, messy, negligent, slipshod, *inf* sloppy, slovenly, untidy. *Opp* SUPERIOR.

shoe *n* plur footwear. □ boot, bootee, brogue, clog, espadrille, inf flip-flop, galosh, gum-boot, inf lace-up, moccasin, plimsoll, pump, sabot, sandal, inf slip-on, slipper, trainer, wader, wellington.

shoemaker *n* bootmaker, cobbler.

shoot *n* branch, bud, new growth, offshoot, sprout, sucker, twig. ● *vb* **1** *shoot a gun.* aim, discharge, fire. **2** *shoot the enemy.* aim at, bombard, fire at, gun down, hit, hunt, kill, *inf* let fly at, open fire on, *inf* pick off,

shell, snipe at, strafe, *inf* take potshots at. **3** *shoot from your chair.* bolt, dart, dash, fly, hurtle, leap, move quickly, race, run, rush, speed, spring, streak. **4** *plants shoot in the spring.* bud, burgeon, develop, flourish, grow, put out shoots, spring up, sprout.

shop *n* boutique, cash-and-carry, department store, *old use* emporium, establishment, market, outlet, retailer, seller, store, wholesaler. □ baker, betting shop, bookshop, butcher, chandler, chemist, confectioner, couturier, creamery, dairy, delicatessen, draper, fishmonger, florist, garden-centre, greengrocer, grocer, haberdasher, herbalist, hypermarket, ironmonger, jeweller, launderette, minimarket, newsagent, off-licence, outfitter, pawnbroker, pharmacy, post office, poulterer, stationer, supermarket, tailor, take-away, tobacconist, toyshop, video shop, vintner, watchmaker.

shopkeeper *n* dealer, merchant, retailer, salesgirl, salesman, saleswoman, stockist, storekeeper, supplier, trader, tradesman.

shopper *n* buyer, customer, patron.

shopping *n* **1** buying, *inf* spending-spree. **2** goods, purchases.

shopping-centre *n* arcade, complex, hypermarket, mall, precinct.

shore *n* bank, beach, coast, edge, foreshore, sands, seashore, seaside, shingle, strand. ● *vb* **shore up** ▷ SUPPORT.

short *adj* **1** diminutive, *inf* dumpy, dwarfish, little, midget, *fem* petite, *derog* pint-sized, slight, small, squat, *inf* stubby, *inf* stumpy, stunted, tiny, *inf* wee, undergrown. **2** *a short visit.* brief, cursory, curtailed, ephemeral, fleeting, momentary, passing, quick, short-lived, temporary, transient, transitory. **3** *a short book.* abbreviated, abridged, compact, concise, cut, pocket, shortened, succinct. **4** *in short supply.* deficient, inadequate, insufficient, lacking, limited, low, meagre, scanty, scarce, sparse, wanting. **5** *a short manner.* abrupt, bad-tempered, blunt, brusque, cross, curt, gruff, grumpy, impolite, irritable, laconic, sharp, snappy, taciturn, terse, testy, uncivil, unfriendly, unkind, unsympathetic. *Opp* EXPANSIVE, LONG, PLENTIFUL, TALL. **cut short** ▷ SHORTEN.

shortage *n* absence, dearth, deficiency, deficit, insufficiency, lack, paucity, poverty, scarcity, shortfall, want. *Opp* PLENTY.

shortcoming *n* bad habit, defect, deficiency, drawback, failing, failure, fault, flaw, foible, imperfection, limitation, vice, weakness, weak point.

shorten *vb* abbreviate, abridge, compress, condense, curtail, cut, cut down, cut short, diminish, dock, lop, précis, prune, reduce, shrink, summarize, take up (*clothes*), telescope, trim, truncate. *Opp* LENGTHEN.

shortly *adv* old use anon, before long, by and by, directly, presently, soon.

short-sighted *adj* **1** myopic, nearsighted. **2** unadventurous, unimaginative, without vision.

short-tempered *adj* abrupt, acerbic, brusque, crabby, cross, crusty, curt, gruff, irascible, irritable, peevish, peremptory, shrewish, snappy, testy, touchy, waspish. *Opp* GOOD-TEMPERED.

shot *n* **1** ball, bullet, discharge, missile, pellet, projectile, round, *inf* slug. **2** *heard a shot.* bang, blast, crack, explosion, report. **3** *a first-class shot.* marksman, markswoman, sharpshooter. **4** *give it a shot.* attempt, chance, *inf* crack, effort, endeavour, *inf* go, hit, kick, *inf* stab, stroke, try. **5** *photographic shot.* angle, photograph, picture, scene, sequence, snap, snapshot.

shout *vb* bawl, bellow, *inf* belt, call, cheer, clamour, cry out, exclaim, howl, rant, roar, scream, screech, shriek, talk loudly, vociferate, whoop, yell, yelp, yowl. *Opp* WHISPER.

shove *vb* ˙*inf* barge, crowd, drive, elbow, hustle, impel, jostle, nudge, press, prod, push, shoulder, thrust.

shovel *vb* clear, dig, scoop, shift.

show *n* **1** drama, performance, play, presentation, production. ▷ ENTERTAINMENT. **2** *flower show.* competition, demonstration, display, exhibition, *inf* expo, exposition, fair, presentation. **3** *show of strength.* appearance, demonstration, façade, illusion, impression, pose, pretence, threat. **4** *just for show.* affectation, exhibitionism, flamboyance, ostentation, pretentiousness, showing off. ● *vb* **1** bare, betray, demonstrate, display, divulge, exhibit, expose, make public, make visible, manifest, open up, present, produce, reveal, uncover. **2** *Let your feelings show.* appear, be seen, be visible, catch the eye, come out, emerge, make an appearance, materialize, *inf* peep through, stand out, stick out. **3** *show the way.* conduct, direct, escort, guide, indicate, lead, point out, steer, usher. **4** *show kindness.* accord, bestow, confer, grant, treat with. **5** *This photo shows us at work.* depict, give a picture of, illustrate, picture, portray, represent, symbolize. **6** *Show me how.* clarify, describe, elucidate, explain, instruct, make clear, teach, tell. **7** *Tests show I was right.* attest, bear out, confirm, corroborate, demonstrate, evince, exemplify, manifest, prove, substantiate, verify, witness. **show off** ▷ BOAST. **show up** ▷ ARRIVE, HUMILIATE.

showdown *n* confrontation, crisis, *inf* decider, decisive encounter, *inf* moment of truth.

shower *n* **1** drizzle, sprinkling. ▷ RAIN. **2** douche, shower-bath. ● *vb* **1** deluge, drop, rain, spatter, splash, spray, sprinkle. **2** *shower with gifts.* heap, inundate, load, overwhelm.

show-off *n* *inf* big-head, boaster, braggart, conceited person, egotist, exhibitionist, *inf* poser, poseur, *inf* showman, swaggerer.

showy *adj* bright, conspicuous, elaborate, fancy, flamboyant, flashy, florid, fussy, garish, gaudy, lavish, *inf* loud, lurid, ornate, ostentatious, *inf* over the top, pretentious, striking, trumpery, vulgar. *Opp* DISCREET.

shred *n* atom, bit, fragment, grain, hint, iota, jot, piece, scintilla, scrap, sliver, snippet, speck, trace. ● *vb* cut to shreds, destroy, grate, rip up, scrap, tear. **shreds** rags, ribbons, strips, tatters.

shrewd *adj* acute, artful, astute, calculating, *inf* canny, clever, crafty, cunning, discerning, discriminating, *inf* foxy, ingenious, intelligent, knowing, observant, perceptive, percipient, perspicacious, quick-witted, sage, sharp, sly, smart, wily, wise. *Opp* STUPID.

shriek *vb* cry, scream, screech, squawk, squeal.

shrill *adj* ear-splitting, high, high-pitched, jarring, penetrating, piercing, piping, screaming, screeching, screechy, sharp, shrieking, strident, treble, whistling. *Opp* GENTLE, SONOROUS.

shrine *n* altar, chapel, holy of holies, holy place, place of worship, reliquary, sanctum, tomb. ▷ CHURCH.

shrink *vb* **1** become smaller, contract, decrease, diminish, dwindle, lessen, make smaller, narrow, reduce, shorten. ▷ SHRIVEL. *Opp* EXPAND. **2** *shrink with fear.* back off, cower, cringe, flinch, hang back, quail, recoil, retire, shy away, wince, withdraw. *Opp* ADVANCE.

shrivel *vb* become parched, become wizened, curl, dehydrate, desiccate, droop, dry out, dry up, pucker up, wilt, wither, wrinkle. ▷ SHRINK.

shroud *n* blanket, cloak, cloud, cover, mantle, mask, pall, veil, winding-sheet. ● *vb* camouflage, cloak, conceal, cover, disguise, enshroud, envelop, hide, mask, screen, swathe, veil, wrap up.

shrub *n* bush, tree. □ *berberis, blackthorn, broom, bryony, buckthorn, buddleia, camellia, daphne, forsythia, gorse, heather, hydrangea, japonica, jasmine, lavender, lilac, myrtle, privet, rhododendron, rosemary, rue, viburnum.*

shudder *vb* be horrified, convulse, jerk, quake, quiver, rattle, shake, shiver, squirm, tremble, vibrate.

shuffle *vb* **1** confuse, disorganize, intermix, intersperse, jumble, mix, mix up, rearrange, reorganize. **2** *shuffle along.* drag your feet, scrape, shamble, slide. ▷ WALK.

shun *vb* avoid, disdain, eschew, flee, *inf* give the cold shoulder to, keep clear of, rebuff, reject, shy away from, spurn, steer clear of, turn away from. *Opp* SEEK.

shut *vb* bolt, close, fasten, latch, lock, push to, replace, seal, secure, slam. **shut in** ▷ CONFINE, IMPRISON. **shut off** ▷ ISOLATE. **shut out** ▷ EXCLUDE. **shut up** ▷ CONFINE, IMPRISON, SILENCE.

shutter *n* blind, louvre, screen.

shy *adj* apprehensive, backward, bashful, cautious, chary, coy, diffident, hesitant, inhibited, introverted, modest, *inf* mousy, nervous, reserved, reticent, retiring, self-conscious, self-effacing, sheepish, timid, timorous, underconfident, wary, withdrawn. *Opp* ASSERTIVE, UNINHIBITED. ● *vb* ▷ THROW.

sibling *n* brother, sister, twin. ▷ FAMILY.

sick *adj* **1** afflicted, ailing, bedridden, diseased, ill, indisposed, infirm, *inf* laid up, *inf* poorly, *inf* queer, sickly, *inf* under the weather, unhealthy, unwell. ▷ ILL. **2** airsick, bilious, carsick, likely to vomit, nauseated, nauseous, queasy, seasick, squeamish. **3** *sick of rudeness.* annoyed (by), bored (with), disgusted (by), distressed (by), *inf* fed up (with), glutted (with), nauseated (by), sated (with), sickened (by), tired, troubled (by), upset (by), weary. **4** [*inf*] *a sick joke.* ▷ MORBID. **be sick** ▷ VOMIT.

sicken *vb* **1** *inf* catch a bug, fail, fall ill, take sick, weaken. **2** appal, be sickening to, disgust, make someone sick, nauseate, offend, repel, revolt, *inf* turn someone off, *inf* turn someone's stomach. **sickening** ▷ REPULSIVE.

sickly *adj* **1** ailing, anaemic, delicate, drawn, feeble, frail, ill, pale, pallid, *inf* peaky, unhealthy, wan, weak. ▷ ILL. *Opp* HEALTHY. **2** *sickly sentiment.* cloying, maudlin, mawkish, *inf* mushy, nasty, nauseating, obnoxious, *inf* off-putting, syrupy, treacly, unpleasant. *Opp* REFRESHING.

sickness *n* biliousness, nausea, queasiness, vomiting. ▷ ILLNESS.

side *n* **1** *sides of a cube.* elevation, face, facet, flank, surface. **2** *side of the road.* border, boundary, brim, brink, edge, fringe, limit, margin, perimeter, rim, verge. **3** *sides in a debate.* angle, aspect, attitude, perspective, point of view, position, school of thought, slant, standpoint, view, viewpoint. **4** *sides in a quarrel.* army, camp, faction, interest, party, sect, team. ● *vb* **side with** ally with, favour, form an alliance with, *inf* go along with, join up with, partner, prefer, support, team up with. ▷ HELP.

sidestep *vb* avoid, circumvent, dodge, *inf* duck, evade, skirt round.

sidetrack *vb* deflect, distract, divert.

sideways *adj* **1** crabwise, indirect, lateral, oblique. **2** *a sideways glance.* covert, sidelong, sly, *inf* sneaky, unobtrusive.

siege *n* blockade. ● *vb* ▷ BESIEGE.

sieve *n* colander, riddle, screen, strainer. ● *vb* ▷ SIFT.

sift *vb* **1** filter, riddle, screen, separate, sieve, strain. **2** *sift evidence.* analyse, examine, investigate, pick out, review, scrutinize, select, sort out, weed out, winnow.

sigh *n* breath, exhalation, murmur, suspiration. ▷ SOUND.

sight *n* **1** eyesight, seeing, vision, visual perception. **2** *within sight.* field of vision, gaze, range, view, visibility. **3** *a brief sight of it.* glimpse, look. **4** *an impressive sight.* display, exhibition, scene, show, show-piece, spectacle. ● *vb* behold, descry, discern, distinguish, espy, glimpse, make out, notice, observe, perceive, recognize, see, spot. **catch sight of** ▷ SEE.

sightseer *n* globe-trotter, holiday-maker, tourist, tripper, visitor.

sign *n* **1** augury, forewarning, hint, indication, indicator, intimation,

omen, pointer, portent, presage, warning. ▷ SIGNAL. **2** *sign that someone was here.* clue, *inf* giveaway, indication, manifestation, marker, proof, reminder, spoor *(of animal)*, suggestion, symptom, token, trace, vestige. **3** *put up a sign.* advertisement, notice, placard, poster, publicity, signboard. **4** *identifying sign.* badge, brand, cipher, device, emblem, flag, hieroglyph, ideogram, ideograph, insignia, logo, mark, monogram, rebus, symbol, trademark. ● *vb* **1** autograph, countersign, endorse, inscribe, write. **2** ▷ SIGNAL. **sign off** ▷ FINISH. **sign on** ▷ ENLIST. **sign over** ▷ TRANSFER.

signal *n* **1** communication, cue, gesticulation, gesture, *inf* goahead, indication, motion, sign, signal, *inf* tip-off, token, warning. □ *alarm-bell, beacon, bell, burglar-alarm, buzzer, flag, flare, gong, green light, indicator, password, red light, reveille, rocket, semaphore signal, siren, smoke-signal, tocsin, old use trafficator, traffic-lights, warning-light, whistle, winker.* **2** *radio signal.* broadcast, emission, output, transmission, waves. ● *vb* beckon, communicate, flag, gesticulate, give or send a signal, indicate, motion, notify, sign, wave. ▷ GESTURE.

signature *n* autograph, endorsement, mark, name.

signet *n* seal, stamp.

significance *n* denotation, force, idea, implication, import, importance, message, point, purport, relevance, sense, signification, usefulness, value, weight. ▷ MEANING.

significant *adj* **1** eloquent, expressive, indicative, informative, knowing, meaningful, pregnant, revealing, suggestive, symbolic, *inf* tell-tale. **2** *significant event.* big, consequential, considerable, historic, important, influential, memorable, newsworthy, noteworthy, relevant, salient, serious, sizeable, valuable, vital, worthwhile. *Opp* INSIGNIFICANT.

signify *vb* **1** announce, be a sign of, betoken, communicate, connote, convey, denote, express, foretell, impart, imply, indicate, intimate, make known, reflect, reveal, signal, suggest, symbolize, tell, transmit. **2** *It doesn't signify.* be significant, count, matter, merit consideration.

signpost *n* finger-post, pointer, road-sign, sign.

silence *n* **1** calm, calmness, hush, noiselessness, peace, quiet, quietness, quietude, soundlessness, stillness, tranquillity. *Opp* NOISE. **2** *Her silence puzzled us.* dumbness, muteness, reticence, speechlessness, taciturnity, uncommunicativeness. ● *vb* **1** gag, hush, keep quiet, make silent, muzzle, repress, shut up, suppress. **2** *silence engine noise.* damp, deaden, muffle, mute, quieten, smother, stifle. **Silence!** Be quiet! Be silent! *inf* Hold your tongue! Hush! Keep quiet! *inf* Pipe down! Shut up! Stop talking!

silent *adj* **1** hushed, inaudible, muffled, muted, noiseless, quiet, soundless. **2** dumb, laconic, *inf* mum, reserved, reticent, speechless, taciturn, tight-lipped, tongue-tied, uncommunicative, unforthcoming, voiceless. **3** *silent listeners.* attentive, rapt, restrained, still. **4** *silent agreement.* implicit, implied, mute, tacit, understood, unexpressed, unspoken, unuttered. *Opp* EXPLICIT, NOISY, TALK-ATIVE. **be silent** keep quiet, *inf* pipe down, say nothing, *inf* shut up.

silhouette *n* contour, form, outline, profile, shadow, shape.

silky *adj* delicate, fine, glossy, lustrous, satiny, sleek, smooth, soft, velvety.

silly *adj* **1** absurd, asinine, brainless, childish, crazy, daft, *inf* dopey, *inf* dotty, fatuous, feather-brained, feeble-minded, flighty, *old use* fond, foolish, frivolous, grotesque, *inf* half-baked, hare-brained, idiotic, ill-advised, illogical, immature, impractical, imprudent, inadvisable, inane, infantile, irrational, *inf* jokey, laughable, light-hearted, ludicrous, mad, meaningless, mindless, misguided, naïve, nonsensical, playful, pointless, preposterous, ridiculous, scatter-brained, *inf* scatty, senseless,

shallow, simple, simple-minded, simplistic, *inf* soppy, stupid, thoughtless, unintelligent, unreasonable, unsound, unwise, wild, witless. *Opp* SERIOUS, WISE. **2** *[inf] knocked silly.* ▷ UNCONSCIOUS.

silt *n* alluvium, deposit, mud, ooze, sediment, slime, sludge.

silvan *adj* arboreal, leafy, tree-covered, wooded.

similar *adj* akin, alike, analogous, comparable, compatible, congruous, co-ordinating, corresponding, equal, equivalent, harmonious, homogeneous, identical, indistinguishable, like, matching, parallel, related, resembling, the same, toning, twin, uniform, well-matched. *Opp* DIFFERENT.

similarity *n* affinity, closeness, congruity, correspondence, equivalence, homogeneity, kinship, likeness, match, parallelism, relationship, resemblance, sameness, similitude, uniformity. *Opp* DIFFERENCE.

simmer *vb* boil, bubble, cook, seethe, stew.

simple *adj* **1** artless, basic, candid, childlike, elementary, frank, fundamental, guileless, homely, honest, humble, ingenuous, innocent, lowly, modest, *derog* naïve, natural, *derog* silly, simple-minded, sincere, unaffected, unassuming, unpretentious, unsophisticated. *Opp* SOPHISTICATED. **2** *simple instructions.* clear, comprehensible, direct, easy, fool-proof, intelligible, lucid, straightforward, uncomplicated, understandable. *Opp* COMPLEX. **3** *a simple dress.* austere, classical, plain, severe, stark, unadorned, unembellished. *Opp* ORNATE.

simplify *vb* clarify, explain, make simple, paraphrase, prune, *inf* put in words of one syllable, streamline, unravel, untangle. *Opp* COMPLICATE.

simplistic *adj* [*always derog*] facile, inadequate, naïve, oversimple, oversimplified, shallow, silly, superficial.

simulate *vb* act, counterfeit, dissimulate, enact, fake, feign, imitate, *inf* mock up, play-act, pretend, reproduce, sham.

simultaneous *adj* coinciding, concurrent, contemporaneous, parallel, synchronized, synchronous.

sin *n* blasphemy, corruption, depravity, desecration, devilry, error, evil, fault, guilt, immorality, impiety, iniquity, irreverence, misdeed, offence, peccadillo, profanation, sacrilege, sinfulness, transgression, *old use* trespass, ungodliness, unrighteousness, vice, wickedness, wrong, wrongdoing. ● *vb* be guilty of sin, blaspheme, do wrong, err, fall from grace, go astray, lapse, misbehave, offend, stray, transgress.

sincere *adj* candid, direct, earnest, frank, genuine, guileless, heartfelt, honest, open, real, serious, simple, *inf* straight, straightforward, true, truthful, unaffected, unfeigned, upright, wholehearted. *Opp* INSINCERE.

sincerity *n* candour, directness, earnestness, frankness, genuineness, honesty, honour, integrity, openness, straightforwardness, trustworthiness, truthfulness, uprightness.

sinewy *adj* brawny, muscular, strapping, tough, wiry. ▷ STRONG.

sinful *adj* bad, blasphemous, corrupt, damnable, depraved, erring, evil, fallen, guilty, immoral, impious, iniquitous, irreligious, irreverent, profane, sacrilegious, ungodly, unholy, unrighteous, vile, wicked, wrong, wrongful. *Opp* RIGHTEOUS.

sing *vb* carol, chant, chirp, chorus, croon, descant, hum, intone, serenade, trill, vocalize, warble, whistle, yodel.

singe *vb* blacken, burn, char, scorch, sear.

singer *n* songster, vocalist. □ *alto, balladeer, baritone, bass, carol-singer, castrato, plur choir, choirboy, choirgirl, chorister, plur chorus, coloratura, contralto, counter-tenor, crooner, It diva, folk singer, minstrel, opera singer, pop star, precentor, It prima donna, soloist, soprano, tenor, treble, troubadour.*

single *adj* **1** exclusive, individual, isolated, lone, odd, one, only, personal, separate, singular, sole, solitary, unique, unparalleled. **2** *a single person.* celibate, *inf* free, unattached, unmarried. ● *vb* **single out** ▷ CHOOSE.

single-handed *adj* alone, independent, solitary, unaided, unassisted, without help.

single-minded *adj* dedicated, determined, devoted, dogged, *derog* fanatical, *derog* obsessive, persevering, resolute, steadfast, tireless, unswerving, unwavering.

singular *adj* **1** ▷ SINGLE. **2** abnormal, curious, different, distinct, eccentric, exceptional, extraordinary, odd, outstanding, peculiar, rare, remarkable, strange, unusual. ▷ DISTINCTIVE. *Opp* COMMON.

sinister *adj* **1** dark, disquieting, disturbing, evil, forbidding, foreboding, frightening, gloomy, inauspicious, malevolent, malignant, menacing, minatory, ominous, threatening, upsetting. **2** *sinister motives.* bad, corrupt, criminal, dishonest, furtive, illegal, nefarious, questionable, *inf* shady, suspect, treacherous, unworthy, villainous.

sink *n* basin, stoup, washbowl. ● *vb* **1** collapse, decline, descend, diminish, disappear, droop, drop, dwindle, ebb, fade, fail, fall, go down, go lower, plunge, set (*sun sets*), slip down, subside, vanish, weaken. **2** be engulfed, be submerged, founder, go down, go under. **3** *sink a ship.* scupper, scuttle. **4** *sink a borehole.* bore, dig, drill, excavate.

sinner *n* evil-doer, malefactor, miscreant, offender, reprobate, transgressor, wrongdoer.

sip *vb* drink, lap, sample, taste.

sit *vb* **1** be seated, perch, rest, seat (yourself), settle, squat, take a seat, *inf* take the weight off your feet. **2** *sit for a portrait.* pose. **3** *sit an exam.* be a candidate in, *inf* go in for, take, write. **4** *Parliament sat for 12 hours.* assemble, be in session, convene, gather, get together, meet.

site n area, campus, ground, location, place, plot, position, setting, situation, spot. ● vb ▷ SITUATE.

sitting-room n drawing-room, living-room, lounge.

situate vb build, establish, found, install, locate, place, position, put, set up, site, station.

situation n 1 area, locale, locality, location, place, position, setting, site, spot. 2 an awkward situation. case, circumstances, condition, inf kettle of fish, plight, position, predicament, state of affairs. 3 situations vacant. employment, job, place, position, post.

size n amount, area, bigness, breadth, bulk, capacity, depth, dimensions, extent, gauge, height, immensity, largeness, length, magnitude, mass, measurement, proportions, scale, scope, volume, weight, width. ▷ MEASURE. ● vb **size up** ▷ ASSESS.

sizeable adj considerable, decent, generous, largish, significant, worthwhile. ▷ BIG.

skate vb glide, skim, slide.

skeleton n bones, frame, framework, structure.

sketch n 1 description, design, diagram, draft, drawing, outline, picture, plan, inf rough, skeleton, vignette. 2 comic sketch. performance, playlet, scene, skit, turn. ● vb depict, draw, indicate, outline, portray, represent. **sketch out** ▷ OUTLINE.

sketchy adj bitty, crude, cursory, hasty, hurried, imperfect, incomplete, inexact, perfunctory, rough, scrappy, undeveloped, unfinished, unpolished. Opp DETAILED, PERFECT.

skid vb aquaplane, glide, go out of control, slide, slip.

skilful adj able, accomplished, adept, adroit, apt, artful, capable, competent, consummate, crafty, cunning, deft, dexterous, experienced, expert, gifted, handy, ingenious, masterful, masterly, practised, professional, proficient, qualified, shrewd, smart, talented, trained, versatile, versed, workmanlike. ▷ CLEVER. Opp UNSKILFUL.

skill n ability, accomplishment, adroitness, aptitude, art, artistry, capability, cleverness, competence, craft, cunning, deftness, dexterity, experience, expertise, facility, flair, gift, handicraft, ingenuity, knack, mastery, professionalism, proficiency, prowess, shrewdness, talent, technique, training, versatility, workmanship.

skilled adj experienced, expert, qualified, trained, versed. ▷ SKILFUL.

skim vb 1 aquaplane, coast, fly, glide, move lightly, plane, sail, skate, ski, skid, slide, slip. 2 skim a book. dip into, leaf through, look through, read quickly, scan, skip, thumb through.

skin n casing, coat, coating, complexion, covering, epidermis, exterior, film, fur, hide, husk, integument, membrane, outside, peel, pelt, rind, shell, surface. ● vb excoriate, flay, pare, peel, shell, strip.

skin-deep adj insubstantial, shallow, superficial, trivial, unimportant.

skinny adj bony, emaciated, gaunt, half-starved, lanky, scraggy, wasted. ▷ THIN.

skip vb 1 bound, caper, cavort, dance, frisk, gambol, hop, jump, leap, prance, romp, spring. 2 skip the boring bits. avoid, forget, ignore, leave out, miss out, neglect, omit, overlook, pass over, skim through. 3 skip lessons. be absent from, cut, miss, play truant from.

skirmish n brush, fight, fray, scrimmage, inf set-to, tussle. ● vb ▷ FIGHT.

skirt vb avoid, border, bypass, circle, encircle, go round, pass round, inf steer clear of, surround.

skit n burlesque, parody, satire, sketch, spoof, inf take-off.

sky n air, atmosphere, poet blue, poet empyrean, poet firmament, poet heavens, space, stratosphere, poet welkin.

slab n block, chunk, hunk, lump, piece, slice, wedge, inf wodge.

slack adj 1 drooping, limp, loose, sagging, soft. Opp TIGHT. 2 slack attitude. careless, dilatory, disorganized, easy-going, flaccid, idle, inattentive, indolent, lax, lazy, listless, neglectful, negligent, permissive, relaxed, remiss, slothful, unbusinesslike, uncaring, undisciplined. Opp RIGOROUS. 3 slack trade. inactive, quiet, slow, slow-moving, sluggish. Opp BUSY. ● vb be lazy, idle, malinger, neglect your duty, shirk, inf skive.

slacken vb 1 ease off, loosen, relax, release. 2 slacken speed. abate, decrease, ease, lessen, lower, moderate, reduce, slow down.

slacker n inf good-for-nothing, idler, lazy person, malingerer, sl skiver, sluggard.

slake vb allay, assuage, cool, ease, quench, relieve, satisfy.

slam vb 1 bang, shut. 2 [inf] ▷ CRITICIZE.

slander n backbiting, calumny, defamation, denigration, insult, libel, lie, misrepresentation, obloquy, scandal, slur, smear, vilification. ● vb blacken the name of, calumniate, defame, denigrate, disparage, libel, malign, misrepresent, slur, smear, spread tales about, tell lies about, traduce, vilify.

slanderous adj abusive, calumnious, cruel, damaging, defamatory, disparaging, false, hurtful, insulting, libellous, lying, malicious, mendacious, scurrilous, untrue, vicious.

slang n argot, cant, jargon. ● vb ▷ INSULT. **slanging match** ▷ QUARREL.

slant n 1 angle, bevel, camber, cant, diagonal, gradient, incline, list, pitch, rake, ramp, slope, tilt. 2 slant on a problem. approach, attitude, perspective, point of view, standpoint, view, viewpoint. 3 slant to the news. bias, distortion, emphasis, imbalance, one-sidedness, prejudice. ● vb 1 be at an angle, be skewed, incline, lean, shelve, slope, tilt. 2 slant the news. bias, colour, distort, prejudice, twist, weight. **slanting** ▷ OBLIQUE.

slap vb smack, spank. ▷ HIT.

slash vb gash, slit. ▷ CUT.

slaughter n bloodshed, butchery, carnage, killing, massacre, murder. ● vb annihilate, butcher, massacre, murder, slay. ▷ KILL.

slaughterhouse n abattoir, shambles.

slave n old use bondslave, drudge, serf, thrall, vassal. ▷ SERVANT. ● vb drudge, exert yourself, grind away, labour, inf sweat, toil, inf work your fingers to the bone. ▷ WORK.

slave-driver n despot, hard taskmaster, tyrant.

slaver vb dribble, drool, foam at the mouth, salivate, slobber, spit.

slavery n bondage, captivity, enslavement, serfdom, servitude, subjugation, thraldom, vassalage. Opp FREEDOM.

slavish adj 1 abject, cringing, fawning, grovelling, humiliating, menial, obsequious, servile, submissive. 2 slavish imitation. close, flattering, strict, sycophantic, unimaginative, unoriginal. Opp INDEPENDENT.

slay vb assassinate, bump off, butcher, destroy, dispatch, execute, exterminate, inf finish off, martyr, massacre, murder, put down, put to death, slaughter. ▷ KILL.

sleazy adj cheap, contemptible, dirty, disreputable, low-class, mean, mucky, run-down, seedy, slovenly, sordid, squalid, unprepossessing.

sledge n bob-sleigh, sled, sleigh, toboggan.

sleek adj 1 brushed, glossy, graceful, lustrous, shining, shiny, silken, silky, smooth, soft, trim, velvety, well-groomed. Opp UNTIDY. 2 a sleek look. complacent, contented, fawning, self-satisfied, inf slimy, inf smarmy, smug, suave, thriving, unctuous, well-fed.

sleep n inf beauty sleep, catnap, coma, dormancy, doze, inf forty winks, hibernation, sl kip, inf nap, repose, rest, *inf* shut-eye, siesta, slumber, snooze, torpor, unconsciousness. ● *vb* aestivate, be sleeping, be unconscious, catnap, *inf* doss down, doze, *inf* drop off, drowse, fall asleep, go to bed, *inf* have forty winks, hibernate, *sl* kip, *inf* nod off, rest, slumber, snooze, *inf* take a nap.

sleeping ▷ ASLEEP.

sleepiness *n* drowsiness, lassitude, lethargy, somnolence, tiredness, torpor.

sleepless *adj* awake, conscious, disturbed, insomniac, restless, *inf* tossing and turning, wakeful, watchful, wide awake. *Opp* ASLEEP.

sleepwalker *n* noctambulist, somnambulist.

sleepy *adj* 1 comatose, *inf* dopey, drowsy, heavy, lethargic, ready to sleep, sluggish, somnolent, soporific, tired, torpid, weary. 2 *a sleepy village.* boring, dull, inactive, quiet, restful, slowmoving, unexciting. *Opp* LIVELY.

slender *adj* 1 fine, graceful, lean, narrow, slight, svelte, sylphlike, trim. ▷ THIN. 2 *slender thread.* feeble, fragile, tenuous. 3 *slender means.* inadequate, meagre, scanty, small. *Opp* FAT, LARGE.

slice *n* carving, layer, piece, rasher, shaving, sliver, wedge. ● *vb* carve, shave off. ▷ CUT.

slick *adj* 1 adroit, artful, clever, cunning, deft, dextrous, efficient, quick, skilful, smart. 2 *a slick talker.* glib, meretricious, plausible, *inf* smarmy, smooth, smug, specious, suave, superficial, *inf* tricky, unctuous, untrustworthy, urbane, wily. 3 *slick hair.* glossy, oiled, plastered down, shiny, sleek, smooth.

slide *n* 1 avalanche, landslide, landslip. 2 *photographic slide.* transparency. ● *vb* aquaplane, coast, glide, glissade, plane, skate, ski, skid, skim, slip, slither, toboggan.

slight *adj* 1 imperceptible, inadequate, inconsequential, inconsiderable, insignificant, insufficient, little, minor, negligible, scanty, slim (*chance*), small, superficial, trifling, trivial, unimportant. 2 *slight build.*

delicate, diminutive, flimsy, fragile, frail, petite, sickly, slender, slim, svelte, sylphlike, thin, tiny, weak. *Opp* BIG. ● *n*, *vb* ▷ INSULT.

slightly *adv* hardly, moderately, only just, scarcely. *Opp* VERY.

slim *adj* 1 fine, graceful, lean, narrow, slender, svelte, sylphlike, trim. ▷ THIN. 2 *a slim chance.* little, negligible, remote, slight, unlikely. ● *vb* become slimmer, diet, lose weight, reduce.

slime *n* muck, mucus, mud, ooze, sludge.

slimy *adj* clammy, greasy, mucous, muddy, oily, oozy, slippery, *inf* slippy, slithery, *inf* squidgy, *inf* squishy, wet.

sling *vb* cast, *inf* chuck, fling, heave, hurl, launch, *inf* let fly, lob, pelt, pitch, propel, shoot, shy, throw, toss.

slink *vb* creep, edge, move guiltily, prowl, skulk, slither, sneak, steal.

slinky *adj* [*inf*] *a slinky dress.* clinging, close-fitting, graceful, *inf* sexy, sinuous, sleek.

slip *n* 1 accident, *inf* bloomer, blunder, error, fault, *Fr* faux pas, impropriety, inaccuracy, indiscretion, lapse, miscalculation, mistake, oversight, *inf* slip of the pen, slip of the tongue, *inf* slip-up. 2 *slip of paper.* note, piece, sheet, strip. ● *vb* 1 aquaplane, coast, glide, glissade, move out of control, skate, ski, skid, skim, slide, slither, stumble, trip. 2 *slipped into the room.* creep, edge, move quietly, slink, sneak, steal. **give someone the slip** ▷ ESCAPE. **let slip** ▷ REVEAL. **slip away, slip the net** ▷ ESCAPE. **slip up** ▷ BLUNDER.

slippery *adj* 1 glassy, greasy, icy, lubricated, oily, slimy, *inf* slippy, slithery, smooth, wet. 2 *a slippery customer.* crafty, cunning, devious, evasive, *inf* hard to pin down, shifty, sly, *inf* smarmy, smooth, sneaky, specious, *inf* tricky, unreliable, untrustworthy, wily.

slipshod *adj* careless, disorganized, lax, messy, slapdash, *inf* sloppy, slovenly, untidy.

slit n aperture, breach, break, chink, cleft, crack, cut, fissure, gap, gash, hole, incision, opening, rift, slot, split, tear, vent. ● vb cut, gash, slice, split, tear.

slither vb creep, glide, inf skitter, slide, slink, slip, snake, worm.

sliver n chip, flake, shard, shaving, snippet, splinter, strip. ▷ PIECE.

slobber vb dribble, drool, salivate, slaver.

slogan n battle-cry, catch-phrase, catchword, jingle, motto, war-cry, watchword. ▷ SAYING.

slope n angle, bank, bevel, camber, cant, gradient, hill, incline, pitch, rake, ramp, scarp, slant, tilt. □ [upwards] acclivity, ascent, rise. □ [downwards] decline, declivity, descent, dip, drop, fall. ● vb ascend, bank, decline, descend, dip, fall, incline, lean, pitch, rise, shelve, slant, tilt, tip. **sloping** ▷ OBLIQUE.

sloppy adj 1 liquid, messy, runny, inf sloshy, slushy, inf splashing about, squelchy, watery, wet. 2 sloppy work. careless, dirty, disorganized, lax, messy, slapdash, slipshod, slovenly, unsystematic, untidy. 3 ▷ SENTIMENTAL.

slot n 1 aperture, breach, break, channel, chink, cleft, crack, cut, fissure, gap, gash, groove, hole, incision, opening, rift, slit, split, vent. 2 slot on a schedule. place, position, space, spot, time.

sloth n apathy, idleness, indolence, inertia, laziness, lethargy, sluggishness, torpor.

slouch vb droop, hunch, loaf, loll, lounge, sag, shamble, slump, stoop.

slovenly adj careless, inf couldn't-care-less, disorganized, lax, messy, shoddy, slapdash, slatternly, inf sloppy, thoughtless, unmethodical, untidy. Opp CAREFUL.

slow adj 1 careful, cautious, crawling, dawdling, delayed, deliberate, dilatory, gradual, lagging, late, lazy, leisurely, lingering, loitering, measured, moderate, painstaking, plodding, protracted, slow-moving, sluggardly, sluggish, steady, tardy, torpid, unhurried, unpunctual. 2 slow learner. backward, dense, dim, dull, obtuse, inf thick. ▷ STUPID. 3 slow worker. phlegmatic, reluctant, unenthusiastic, unwilling. ▷ SLUGGISH. Opp FAST. ● vb **slow down** brake, decelerate, inf ease up, go slower, hold back, reduce speed. **be slow** ▷ DAWDLE, DELAY.

sludge n mire, muck, mud, ooze, precipitate, sediment, silt, slime, slurry, slush.

sluggish adj apathetic, dull, idle, inactive, indolent, inert, lazy, lethargic, lifeless, listless, phlegmatic, slothful, torpid, unresponsive. ▷ SLOW. Opp LIVELY.

sluice vb flush, rinse, swill, wash.

slumber n, vb ▷ SLEEP.

slump n collapse, crash, decline, depression, dip, downturn, drop, fall, falling-off, plunge, recession, trough. Opp BOOM. ● vb 1 collapse, crash, decline, dive, drop, fall off, plummet, plunge, recede, sink, slip, inf take a nosedive, worsen. Opp PROSPER. 2 slump in a chair. be limp, collapse, droop, flop, hunch, loll, lounge, sag, slouch, subside.

slur n affront, aspersion, calumny, imputation, innuendo, insinuation, insult, libel, slander, smear, stigma. ● vb garble, lisp, mumble.

slurry n mud, ooze, slime.

sly adj artful, inf canny, inf catty, conniving, crafty, cunning, deceitful, designing, devious, disingenuous, inf foxy, furtive, guileful, insidious, knowing, scheming, secretive, inf shifty, shrewd, inf sneaky, inf snide, stealthy, surreptitious, treacherous, tricky, underhand, wily. Opp CANDID, OPEN.

smack vb pat, slap, spank. ▷ HIT.

small adj 1 inf baby, bantam, compact, concise, cramped, diminutive, inf dinky, dwarf, exiguous, fine, fractional, infinitesimal, lean, lilliputian, little, microscopic, midget, inf mini, miniature, minuscule, minute, narrow, petite, *inf* pint-sized, *inf* pocket-sized, *inf* poky, portable, pygmy, short, slender, slight, *inf* teeny, thin, tiny, toy, undergrown, undersized, *inf* wee, *inf* weeny. **2** *small helpings.* inadequate, insufficient, meagre, mean, *inf* measly, miserly, modest, niggardly, parsimonious, *inf* piddling, scanty, skimpy, stingy, ungenerous, unsatisfactory. **3** *a small problem.* inconsequential, insignificant, minor, negligible, nugatory, slim (*chance*), slight, trifling, trivial, unimportant. *Opp* BIG. **small arms** ▷ WEAPON.

small-minded *adj* bigoted, grudging, hidebound, illiberal, intolerant, narrow, narrowminded, old-fashioned, parochial, petty, prejudiced, rigid, selfish, trivial, unimaginative. ▷ MEAN. *Opp* BROAD-MINDED.

smart *adj* **1** acute, adept, artful, astute, bright, clever, crafty, *inf* cute, discerning, ingenious, intelligent, perceptive, perspicacious, quick, quickwitted, shrewd, *sl* streetwise. *Opp* DULL. **2** *smart appearance.* bright, chic, clean, dapper, *inf* dashing, elegant, fashionable, fresh, modish, *inf* natty, neat, *inf* posh, *inf* snazzy, *Fr* soigné, spruce, stylish, tidy, trim, well-dressed, well-groomed, well-looked-after. *Opp* SCRUFFY. **3** *a smart pace.* brisk, *inf* cracking, fast, forceful, quick, rapid, *inf* rattling, speedy, swift. **4** *a smart blow.* painful, sharp, stinging, vigorous. ● *vb* ▷ HURT.

smash *vb* **1** *smash to pieces.* crumple, crush, demolish, destroy, shatter, squash, wreck. ▷ BREAK. **2** *smash into a wall.* bang, bash, batter, bump, collide, crash, hammer, knock, pound, ram, slam, strike, thump, wallop. ▷ HIT.

smear *n* **1** blot, daub, mark, smudge, stain, streak. **2** *a smear on your name.* aspersion, calumny, defamation, imputation, innuendo, insinuation, libel, slander, slur, stigma, vilification. ● *vb* **1** dab, daub, plaster, rub, smudge, spread, wipe. **2** *smear a reputation.* attack, besmirch, blacken, calumniate, defame, discredit, libel,

malign, slander, stigmatize, tarnish, vilify.

smell *n* odour, redolence. □ [pleasant] *aroma, bouquet, fragrance, incense, nose, perfume, scent.* □ [unpleasant] *fetor, mephitis, miasma, inf pong, pungency, reek, stench, stink, whiff.* ● *vb* **1** *inf* get a whiff of, scent, sniff. **2** *onions smell. inf* hum, *inf* pong, reek, stink, whiff.

smelling *adj* [*Smelling* is usually used in combination: sweet-smelling, etc.] **1** *pleasant-smelling.* aromatic, fragrant, musky, odoriferous, odorous, perfumed, redolent, scented, spicy. **2** *unpleasantsmelling.* fetid, foul, gamy, *inf* high, malodorous, mephitic, miasmic, musty, noisome, *inf* off, *sl* pongy, pungent, putrid, rank, reeking, rotten, smelly, stinking, *inf* whiffy. *Opp* ODOURLESS.

smelly *adj* ▷ SMELLING.

smile *n, vb* beam, grin, leer, simper, smirk, sneer.

smoke *n* **1** air pollution, exhaust, fog, fumes, gas, smog, steam, vapour. **2** cigar, cigarette, cheroot, *inf* fag, pipe, tobacco. ● *vb* **1** emit smoke, fume, reek, smoulder. **2** *smoke cigars.* inhale, puff at.

smoky *adj* clouded, dirty, foggy, grimy, hazy, sooty. *Opp* CLEAR.

smooth *adj* **1** even, flat, horizontal, level, plane, regular, unbroken, unruffled. **2** *smooth sea.* calm, peaceful, placid, quiet, restful. **3** *a smooth finish.* burnished, glassy, glossy, polished, satiny, shiny, silken, silky, sleek, soft, velvety. **4** *smooth progress.* comfortable, easy, effortless, fluent, steady, uncluttered, uneventful, uninterrupted, unobstructed. **5** *a smooth taste.* agreeable, bland, mellow, mild, pleasant, soft, soothing. **6** *a smooth mixture.* creamy, flowing, runny. **7** *a smooth talker.* convincing, facile, glib, insincere, plausible, polite, self-assured, self-satisfied, slick, smug, sophisticated, suave, untrustworthy, urbane. *Opp* ROUGH. ● *vb* buff up, burnish, even out, file, flatten, iron, level, level off, plane, polish, press, roll out, sand down, sandpaper.

smother *vb* **1** asphyxiate, choke, cover, kill, snuff out, stifle, strangle, suffocate, throttle. **2** ▷ SUPPRESS.

smoulder *vb* burn, smoke. **smouldering** ▷ ANGRY.

smudge *vb* blot, blur, dirty, mark, smear, stain, streak.

smug *adj* complacent, conceited, *inf* holier-than-thou, pleased, priggish, self-important, selfrighteous, self-satisfied, sleek, superior. *Opp* HUMBLE.

snack *n* bite, *inf* elevenses, *inf* nibble, refreshments. ▷ MEAL.

snack-bar *n* buffet, café, cafeteria, fast-food restaurant, transport café.

snag *n* catch, complication, difficulty, drawback, hindrance, hitch, impediment, obstacle, obstruction, problem, set-back, *inf* stumbling-block. ● *vb* catch, jag, rip, tear.

snake *n* ophidian, serpent. □ *adder, anaconda, boa constrictor, cobra, copperhead, flying-snake, grass snake, mamba, python, rattlesnake, sand snake, sea snake, sidewinder, tree snake, viper.* ● *vb* crawl, creep, meander, twist and turn, wander, worm, zigzag. **snaking** ▷ TWISTY.

snap *adj* ▷ SUDDEN. ● *vb* **1** break, crack, fracture, give way, part, split. **2** *snap your fingers.* click, crack, pop. **3** *dog snapped at me.* bite, gnash, nip, snatch. **4** *snap orders.* bark, growl, *inf* jump down someone's throat, snarl, speak angrily.

snare *n* ambush, booby-trap, *old use* gin, noose, springe, trap. ● *vb* capture, catch, decoy, ensnare, entrap, net, trap.

snarl *vb* **1** bare the teeth, growl. **2** *snarl up rope.* confuse, entangle, jam, knot, tangle, twist.

snatch *vb* **1** catch, clutch, grab, grasp, lay hold of, pluck, seize, take, wrench away, wrest away. **2** abduct, kidnap, remove, steal.

sneak *vb* **1** creep, move stealthily, prowl, skulk, slink, stalk, steal. **2** [*inf*] *sneak on someone. sl* grass, inform

(against), report, *sl* snitch, *inf* tell tales (about).

sneaking *adj* furtive, half-formed, intuitive, lurking, nagging, *inf* niggling, persistent, private, secret, uncomfortable, unconfessed, undisclosed, unproved, worrying.

sneaky *adj* cheating, contemptible, crafty, deceitful, despicable, devious, dishonest, furtive, *inf* low-down, mean, nasty, shady, *inf* shifty, sly, treacherous, underhand, unorthodox, unscrupulous, untrustworthy. *Opp* STRAIGHTFORWARD.

sneer *vb* be contemptuous, be scornful, boo, curl your lip, hiss, hoot, jeer, laugh, mock, scoff, sniff. **sneer at** ▷ DENIGRATE, RIDICULE.

sniff *vb* **1** *inf* get a whiff of, scent, smell. **2** ▷ SNIVEL. **3** ▷ SNEER.

snigger *vb* chuckle, giggle, laugh, snicker, titter.

snip *vb* clip, dock, nick, nip. ▷ CUT.

snipe *vb* fire, shoot, *inf* take pot-shots. **snipe at** ▷ CRITICIZE.

snippet *n* fragment, morsel, particle, scrap, shred, snatch. ▷ PIECE.

snivel *vb* blubber, cry, grizzle, mewl, sob, sniff, sniffle, snuffle, whimper, whine, *inf* whinge. ▷ WEEP.

snobbish *adj* affected, condescending, disdainful, élitist, haughty, high-falutin, *inf* hoitytoity, lofty, lordly, patronizing, pompous, *inf* posh, presumptuous, pretentious, *inf* putting on airs, self-important, smug, *inf* snooty, *inf* stuck-up, supercilious, superior, *inf* toffee-nosed. ▷ CONCEITED. *Opp* UNPRETENTIOUS.

snoop *vb* be inquisitive, butt in, do detective work, interfere, intrude, investigate, meddle, *inf* nose about, pry, sneak, spy, *inf* stick your nose in.

snooper *n* busybody, detective, investigator, meddler, sneak, spy.

snout *n* face, muzzle, nose, nozzle, proboscis, trunk.

snub *vb* be rude to, brush off, cold-shoulder, disdain, humiliate, insult, offend, *inf* put someone down, rebuff, reject, scorn, *inf* squash.

snuff *vb* extinguish, put out. **snuff it**
▷ DIE. **snuff out** ▷ KILL.

snug *adj* **1** comfortable, *inf* comfy,
cosy, enclosed, friendly, intimate,
protected, reassuring, relaxed, relaxing, restful, safe, secure, sheltered,
soft, warm. **2** *a snug fit.* close-fitting,
exact, well-tailored.

soak *vb* bathe, drench, *inf* dunk,
immerse, marinate, penetrate, permeate, pickle, saturate, souse, steep,
submerge, wet thoroughly. **soaked,
soaking** ▷ WET. **soak up** ▷ ABSORB.

soar *vb* **1** ascend, climb, float, fly,
glide, hang, hover, rise, tower.
2 *prices soared.* escalate, increase, rise,
rocket, shoot up, spiral.

sob *vb* blubber, cry, gasp, snivel, *inf*
sob your heart out, whimper. ▷ WEEP.

sober *adj* **1** calm, clear-headed, composed, dignified, grave, in control,
level-headed, lucid, peaceful, quiet,
rational, sedate, sensible, serene,
serious, solemn, steady, subdued,
tranquil, unexciting. *Opp* SILLY. **2** *sober
habits.* abstemious, moderate, *inf* on
the wagon, restrained, self-con-
trolled, staid, teetotal, temperate.
Opp DRUNK. **3** *sober dress.* colourless,
drab, dull, plain, sombre.

sociable *adj* affable, approachable,
old use clubbable, companionable,
convivial, extroverted, friendly,
gregarious, hospitable, neighbourly,
outgoing, warm, welcoming. ▷
SOCIAL. *Opp* UNFRIENDLY, WITHDRAWN.

social *adj* **1** civilized, collaborative,
gregarious, organized. **2** *social events.*
collective, communal, community,
general, group, popular, public. ▷
SOCIABLE. *Opp* SOLITARY. ● *n* dance, disco,
inf do, gathering, *inf* get-together,
party, reception, reunion, soirée. ▷
PARTY.

socialize *vb* associate, be sociable,
entertain, fraternize, get together,
inf go out together, join in, keep company, mix, relate.

society *n* **1** civilization, the community, culture, the human family,
mankind, nation, people, the public.
2 *the society of our friends.* cama-

raderie, companionship, company,
fellowship, friendship, togetherness.
3 *a secret society, etc.* academy,
alliance, association, brotherhood,
circle, club, confraternity, fraternity,
group, guild, league, organization,
sisterhood, sodality, sorority, union.

sofa *n* chaise longue, couch, settee,
sofa bed. ▷ SEAT.

soft *adj* **1** compressible, crumbly,
cushiony, elastic, flabby, flexible,
floppy, limp, malleable, mushy, plastic, pliable, pliant, pulpy, spongy,
springy, squashable, squashy,
squeezable, supple, tender, yielding.
2 *soft ground.* boggy, marshy, muddy,
sodden, waterlogged. **3** *a soft bed.*
comfortable, cosy. **4** *soft texture.*
downy, feathery, fleecy, fluffy, furry,
satiny, silky, sleek, smooth, velvety.
5 *soft music.* dim, faint, low, mellifluous, muted, peaceful, quiet, relaxing, restful, soothing, subdued. **6** *soft
breeze.* balmy, delicate, gentle, light,
mild, pleasant, warm. **7** *[inf] a soft
option.* easy, undemanding. **8** *soft feelings.* ▷ SOFT-HEARTED. *Opp* HARD, HARSH,
VIOLENT.

soften *vb* **1** abate, alleviate, buffer,
cushion, deaden, decrease, deflect,
diminish, lower, make softer, mellow, mitigate, moderate, muffle,
pacify, palliate, quell, quieten, reduce
the impact of, subdue, temper, tone
down, turn down. **2** dissolve, fluff
up, lighten, liquefy, make softer,
melt. **3** *soften in attitude.* become
softer, concur, ease up, give in, give
way, *inf* let up, relax, succumb,
weaken, yield. *Opp* HARDEN, INTENSIFY.

soft-hearted *adj* benign, compassionate, conciliatory, easygoing, generous, indulgent, kind-hearted, *derog*
lax, lenient, merciful, permissive,
sentimental, *inf* soft, sympathetic,
tender, tender-hearted, tolerant,
understanding. ▷ KIND. *Opp* CRUEL.

soggy *adj* drenched, dripping, heavy
(*soil*), saturated, soaked, sodden, *inf*
sopping, wet through. ▷ WET. *Opp* DRY.

soil *n* clay, dirt, earth, ground,
humus, land, loam, marl, topsoil.
● *vb* befoul, besmirch, blacken, con-

taminate, defile, dirty, make dirty, muddy, pollute, smear, stain, sully, tarnish.

solace n comfort, consolation, reassurance, relief. ● vb ▷ CONSOLE.

soldier n fighter, fighting man, fighting woman, *old use* man at arms, serviceman, servicewoman, warrior. □ cadet, cavalryman, centurion, commando, conscript, guardsman, gunner, infantryman, lancer, *marine*, *mercenary*, NCO, officer, paratrooper, private, recruit, regular, rifleman, sapper, sentry, trooper, plur troops, warrior. ▷ FIGHTER, RANK. ● vb **soldier on** ▷ PERSIST.

sole adj exclusive, individual, lone, one, only, single, singular, solitary, unique.

solemn adj 1 earnest, gloomy, glum, grave, grim, long-faced, reserved, sedate, serious, sober, sombre, staid, straight-faced, thoughtful, unsmiling. Opp CHEERFUL. 2 *a solemn occasion*. august, awe-inspiring, awesome, ceremonial, ceremonious, dignified, ecclesiastical, formal, grand, holy, important, imposing, impressive, liturgical, momentous, pompous, religious, ritualistic, stately. Opp FRIVOLOUS.

solicit vb appeal for, ask for, beg, entreat, importune, petition, seek.

solicitous adj 1 attentive, caring, concerned, considerate, sympathetic. 2 ▷ ANXIOUS.

solid adj 1 concrete, hard, impenetrable, impermeable, rigid, unmoving. 2 *a solid crowd*. compact, crowded, dense, jammed, packed. 3 *solid gold*. authentic, genuine, pure, real, unadulterated, unalloyed, unmixed. 4 *a solid hour*. continual, continuous, entire, unbroken, uninterrupted, unrelieved, whole. 5 *solid foundations*. firm, fixed, immovable, robust, sound, stable, steady, stout, strong, sturdy, substantial, unbending, unyielding, well-made. 6 *a solid shape*. cubic, rounded, spherical, thick, three-dimensional. 7 *solid evidence*. authoritative, cogent, coherent, convincing, genuine, in-

controvertible, indisputable, irrefutable, provable, proven, real, sound, tangible, weighty. 8 *solid support*. complete, dependable, effective, like-minded, reliable, stalwart, strong, trustworthy, unanimous, undivided, united, unwavering, vigorous. Opp FLUID, FRAGMENTARY, WEAK.

solidarity n accord, agreement, coherence, cohesion, concord, harmony, like-mindedness, unanimity, unity. Opp DISUNITY.

solidify vb cake, clot, coagulate, congeal, crystallize, freeze, harden, jell, set, thicken. Opp LIQUEFY.

soliloquy n monologue, speech.

solitary adj 1 alone, antisocial, cloistered, companionless, friendless, isolated, lonely, lonesome, reclusive, unsociable, withdrawn. 2 *a solitary survivor*. individual, one, only, single, sole. 3 *a solitary place*. desolate, distant, hidden, inaccessible, isolated, out-of-the-way, private, remote, secluded, sequestered, unfrequented, unknown. Opp NUMEROUS, PUBLIC, SOCIAL. ● n anchorite, hermit, inf loner, recluse.

solitude n aloneness, friendlessness, isolation, loneliness, privacy, remoteness, retirement, seclusion.

solo adv alone, individually, on your own, unaccompanied.

soloist n performer, player, singer. ▷ MUSICIAN.

soluble adj 1 explicable, manageable, solvable, tractable, understandable. 2 *soluble in water*. dispersing, dissolving, melting. Opp INSOLUBLE.

solution n 1 answer, clarification, conclusion, denouement, elucidation, explanation, explication, key, outcome, resolution, solving, unravelling, working out. 2 *a chemical solution*. blend, compound, emulsion, infusion, mixture, suspension.

solve vb answer, clear up, inf crack, decipher, elucidate, explain, explicate, figure out, find the solution to, interpret, puzzle out, resolve, unravel, work out.

solvent adj creditworthy, in credit, profitable, reliable, self-supporting, solid, sound, viable. Opp BANKRUPT.

sombre adj black, bleak, cheerless, dark, dim, dismal, doleful, drab, dreary, dull, funereal, gloomy, grave, grey, joyless, lowering, lugubrious, melancholy, morose, mournful, serious, sober. ▷ SAD. Opp CHEERFUL.

somewhat adv fairly, moderately, inf pretty, quite, rather, inf sort of.

song n air, inf ditty, inf hit, lyric, number, tune. □ anthem, aria, ballad, blues, calypso, cantata, canticle, carol, chant, chorus, descant, folk-song, hymn, jingle, Ger lied [plur lieder], lullaby, madrigal, nursery rhyme, plainsong, pop song, psalm, reggae, rock, serenade, shanty, soul, spiritual, wassail.

sonorous adj deep, full, loud, powerful, resonant, resounding, reverberant, rich, ringing. Opp SHRILL.

soon adv old use anon, inf any minute now, before long, inf in a minute, presently, quickly, shortly, straight away.

sooner adv **1** before, earlier. **2** sooner have tea than coffee. preferably, rather.

soot n dirt, grime.

soothe vb allay, appease, assuage, calm, comfort, compose, ease, mollify, pacify, quiet, relieve, salve, settle, still, tranquillize.

soothing adj **1** balmy, balsamic, comforting, demulcent, emollient, healing, lenitive, mild, palliative. **2** soothing music. calming, gentle, peaceful, pleasant, reassuring, relaxing, restful, serene.

sophisticated adj **1** adult, sl cool, cosmopolitan, cultivated, cultured, elegant, fashionable, inf grown-up, mature, polished, inf posh, derog pretentious, refined, stylish, urbane, worldly. Opp UNSOPHISTICATED. **2** sophisticated ideas. advanced, clever, complex, complicated, elaborate, hard to understand, ingenious, intricate, involved, subtle. Opp PRIMITIVE, SIMPLE.

soporific adj boring, deadening, hypnotic, sedative, sleep-inducing, sleepy, somnolent. Opp LIVELY.

sorcerer n conjuror, enchanter, enchantress, magician, magus, medicine man, necromancer, sorceress, old use warlock, witch, witch-doctor, wizard.

sorcery n black magic, charms, conjuring, diabolism, incantations, magic, inf mumbo jumbo, necromancy, the occult, spells, voodoo, witchcraft, wizardry.

sordid adj **1** dingy, dirty, disreputable, filthy, foul, miserable, inf mucky, nasty, offensive, polluted, putrid, ramshackle, seamy, seedy, inf sleazy, inf slummy, squalid, ugly, unclean, undignified, unpleasant, unsanitary, wretched. Opp CLEAN. **2** sordid dealings. avaricious, base, corrupt, covetous, degenerate, despicable, dishonourable, ignoble, ignominious, immoral, mean, mercenary, rapacious, selfish, inf shabby, shameful, unethical, unscrupulous. Opp HONOURABLE.

sore adj **1** aching, burning, chafing, delicate, hurting, inflamed, painful, raw, red, sensitive, smarting, stinging, tender. **2** aggrieved, hurt, irked, inf peeved, inf put out, resentful, upset, vexed. ▷ ANNOYED. ● n abrasion, abscess, boil, bruise, burn, carbuncle, gall, gathering, graze, infection, inflammation, injury, laceration, pimple, rawness, redness, scrape, spot, swelling, ulcer. ▷ WOUND. **make sore** abrade, bruise, burn, chafe, chap, gall, graze, hurt, inflame, lacerate, redden, rub.

sorrow n **1** affliction, anguish, dejection, depression, desolation, despair, desperation, despondency, disappointment, discontent, disgruntlement, dissatisfaction, distress, dolour, gloom, glumness, grief, heartache, heartbreak, heaviness, homesickness, hopelessness, loneliness, melancholy, misery, misfortune, mourning, sad feelings, sadness, suffering, tearfulness, tribulation, trouble, unhappiness, wistfulness, woe, wretchedness. *Opp* HAP-PINESS. **2** *sorrow for wrongdoing.* apologies, guilt, penitence, regret, remorse, repentance. ● *vb* agonize, be sorrowful, be sympathetic, bewail, grieve, lament, mourn, weep. *Opp* REJOICE.

sorrowful *adj* broken-hearted, conscience-stricken, contrite, guilt-ridden, penitent, regretful, remorseful, repentant, shamefaced. **2** *sorry for the homeless.* compassionate, concerned, merciful, pitying, sympathetic, understanding.

sorry *adj* apologetic, ashamed, conscience-stricken, contrite, guilt-ridden, penitent, regretful, remorseful, repentant, shamefaced. **2** *sorry for the homeless.* compassionate, concerned, merciful, pitying, sympathetic, understanding.

sort *n* **1** brand, category, class, classification, description, form, genre, group, kind, make, mark, nature, quality, set, type, variety. **2** breed, class, family, genus, race, species, strain, stock, variety. ● *vb* arrange, assort, catalogue, categorize, classify, divide, file, grade, group, order, organize, put in order, rank, systematize, tidy. *Opp* MIX. **sort out 1** choose, *inf* put on one side, segregate, select, separate, set aside. **2** *sort out a problem.* attend to, clear up, cope with, deal with, find an answer to, grapple with, handle, manage, organize, put right, resolve, solve, straighten out, tackle.

soul *n* **1** psyche, spirit. **2** [*inf*] *poor soul!* ▷ PERSON.

soulful *adj* deeply felt, eloquent, emotional, expressive, fervent, heartfelt, inspiring, moving, passionate, profound, sincere, spiritual, stirring, uplifting, warm. *Opp* SOULLESS.

soulless *adj* cold, inhuman, insincere, mechanical, perfunctory, routine, spiritless, superficial, trite, unemotional, unfeeling, uninspiring, unsympathetic. *Opp* SOULFUL.

sound *adj* **1** durable, fit, healthy, hearty, *inf* in good shape, robust, secure, solid, strong, sturdy, tough, undamaged, uninjured, unscathed, vigorous, well, whole. **2** *sound food.* eatable, edible, fit for human consumption, good, wholesome. **3** *sound ideas.* balanced, coherent, commonsense, convincing, correct, judicious, logical, orthodox, prudent, rational, reasonable, reasoned, sane, sensible, well-founded, wise. **4** *a sound business.* dependable, established, profitable, recognized, reliable, reputable, safe, secure, trustworthy, viable. *Opp* BAD, WEAK. ● *n* din, noise, resonance, timbre, tone. □ [Most of these words can be used as either *nouns* or *verbs.*] *bang, bark, bawl, bay, bellow, blare, blast, bleat, bleep, boo, boom, bray, buzz, cackle, caw, chime, chink, chirp, chirrup, chug, clack, clamour, clang, clank, clap, clash, clatter, click, clink, cluck, coo, crack, crackle, crash, creak, croak, croon, crow, crunch, cry, drone, echo, explosion, fizz, grate, grizzle, groan, growl, grunt, gurgle, hiccup, hiss, honk, hoot, howl, hum, jabber, jangle, jeer, jingle, lisp, low, miaow, moan, moo, murmur, neigh, patter, peal, ping, pip, plop, pop, purr, quack, rattle, report, reverberation, ring, roar, rumble, rustle, scream, screech, shout, shriek, sigh, sizzle, skirl, slam, slurp, smack, snap, snarl, sniff, snore, snort, sob, splutter, squawk, squeak, squeal, squelch, swish, throb, thud, thump, thunder, tick, ting, tinkle, toot, trumpet, twang, tweet, twitter, wail, warble, whimper, whine, whinny, whir, whistle, whiz, whoop, woof, yap, yell, yelp, yodel, yowl.* ▷ NOISE. ● *vb* **1** become audible, be heard, echo, make a noise, resonate, resound, reverberate. **2** *sound a signal.* activate, cause, create, make, make audible, produce, pronounce, set off, utter. **sound out** check, examine, inquire into, investigate, measure, plumb, probe, research, survey, test, try.

soup *n* broth, consommé, stock.

sour *adj* **1** acid, acidic, acidulous, bitter, citrus, lemony, pungent, sharp, tangy, tart, unripe, vinegary. **2** *sour milk.* bad, curdled, *inf* off, rancid, stale, turned. **3** *sour remarks.* acerbic, bad-tempered, bitter, caustic, cross, crusty, curmudgeonly, cynical, disaffected, disagreeable, grudging, grumpy, ill-natured, irritable, jaundiced, peevish, petulant, snappy, testy, unpleasant.

source *n* **1** author, begetter, cause, creator, derivation, informant, initiator, originator, root, starting-point. **2** *source of river.* head, origin, spring, start, well-head, well-spring. ▷ BEGINNING.

souvenir *n* heirloom, keepsake, memento, relic, reminder.

sovereign *adj* **1** absolute, all-powerful, dominant, highest, royal, supreme, unlimited. **2** *sovereign state.* autonomous, independent, self-governing. ● *n* emperor, empress, king, monarch, prince, princess, queen. ▷ RULER.

sow *vb* broadcast, disseminate, plant, scatter, seed, spread.

space *adj* extraterrestrial, interplanetary, interstellar, orbiting. ● *n* **1** emptiness, endlessness, infinity, ionosphere, stratosphere, the universe. **2** *space to move about.* inf elbow-room, expanse, freedom, latitude, leeway, margin, room, scope, spaciousness. **3** *an empty space.* area, blank, break, chasm, concourse, distance, duration, gap, hiatus, hole, intermission, interval, lacuna, lapse, opening, place, spell, stretch, time, vacuum, wait. ● *vb space things out.* ▷ ARRANGE.

spacious *adj* ample, broad, capacious, commodious, extensive, large, open, roomy, sizeable, vast, wide. ▷ BIG. *Opp* SMALL.

span *n* breadth, compass, distance, duration, extent, interval, length, period, reach, scope, stretch, term, width. ● *vb* arch over, bridge, cross, extend across, go over, pass over, reach over, straddle, stretch over, traverse.

spank *vb* slap, slipper, smack. ▷ HIT, PUNISH.

spar *vb* box, exchange blows, scrap, shadow-box. ▷ FIGHT.

spare *adj* **1** additional, auxiliary, extra, free, inessential, in reserve, leftover, odd, remaining, superfluous, supernumerary, supplementary, surplus, unnecessary, unneeded, unused, unwanted. *Opp* NECESSARY. **2** *a spare figure.* ▷ THIN. ● *vb* **1** be merciful to, deliver, forgive, free, have mercy on, let go, let off, liberate, pardon, redeem, release, reprieve, save. **2** *spare money, time, etc.* afford, allow, donate, give, give up, manage, part with, provide, sacrifice. **sparing** ▷ ECONOMICAL, MISERLY.

spark *n* flash, flicker, gleam, glint, scintilla, sparkle. ● *vb* **spark off** ignite, kindle. ▷ PROVOKE.

sparkle *vb* burn, coruscate, flash, flicker, gleam, glint, glitter, reflect, scintillate, shine, spark, twinkle, wink. ▷ LIGHTEN.

sparkling *adj* **1** brilliant, flashing, glinting, glittering, scintillating, shining, shiny, twinkling. ▷ BRIGHT. *Opp* DULL. **2** *sparkling drinks.* aerated, bubbling, bubbly, carbonated, effervescent, fizzy, foaming.

sparse *adj* inf few and far between, inadequate, light, little, meagre, scanty, scarce, scattered, sparing, spread out, thin, inf thin on the ground. *Opp* PLENTIFUL.

spartan *adj* abstemious, ascetic, austere, bare, bleak, disciplined, frugal, hard, harsh, plain, rigid, rigorous, severe, simple, stern, strict. *Opp* LUXURIOUS.

spasm *n* attack, contraction, convulsion, eruption, fit, jerk, outburst, paroxysm, seizure, *plur* throes, twitch.

spasmodic *adj* inf by fits and starts, erratic, fitful, intermittent, interrupted, irregular, jerky, occasional, inf on and off, periodic, sporadic. *Opp* CONTINUOUS, REGULAR.

spate *n* cataract, flood, flow, gush, inundation, onrush, outpouring, rush, torrent.

spatter vb bespatter, besprinkle, daub, pepper, scatter, shower, slop, speckle, splash, splatter, spray, sprinkle.

speak vb answer, argue, articulate, ask, communicate, complain, converse, declaim, declare, deliver a speech, discourse, ejaculate, enunciate, exclaim, express yourself, fulminate, harangue, hold a conversation, hold forth, object, inf pipe up, plead, pronounce words, read aloud, recite, say something, soliloquize, inf speechify, talk, tell, use your voice, utter, verbalize, vocalize, voice. ▷ SAY, TALK. **speak about** ▷ MENTION. **speak to** ▷ ADDRESS. **speak your mind** be honest, say what you think, speak honestly, speak out, state your opinion, voice your thoughts.

speaker n lecturer, mouthpiece, orator, public speaker, spokesperson.

spear n assegai, harpoon, javelin, lance, pike.

special adj 1 different, distinguished, exceptional, extraordinary, important, infrequent, momentous, notable, noteworthy, odd, inf out-of-the-ordinary, rare, red-letter (day), remarkable, significant, strange, uncommon, unconventional, unorthodox, unusual. Opp ORDINARY. 2 Petrol has a special smell. characteristic, distinctive, idiosyncratic, memorable, peculiar, singular, unique, unmistakable. 3 my special chair. especial, individual, particular, personal. 4 a special tool for the job. bespoke, proper, specialized, specific.

specialist n 1 authority, connoisseur, expert, fancier (pigeon fancier), master, professional, inf pundit, researcher. 2 [medical] consultant. ▷ MEDICINE.

speciality n inf claim to fame, expertise, field, forte, genius, inf line, specialization, special knowledge, special skill, strength, strong point, talent.

specialize vb **specialize in** be a specialist in, be best at, concentrate on, devote yourself to, have a reputation for.

specialized adj esoteric, expert, specialist, unfamiliar.

species n breed, class, genus, kind, race, sort, type, variety.

specific adj clear-cut, defined, definite, detailed, exact, explicit, express, fixed, identi-fied, individual, itemized, known, named, particular, peculiar, precise, predetermined, special, specified, unequivocal. Opp GENERAL.

specify vb be specific about, define, denominate, detail, enumerate, establish, identify, itemize, list, name, particularize, inf set out, spell out, stipulate.

specimen n example, exemplar, illustration, instance, model, pattern, representative, sample.

specious adj casuistic, deceptive, misleading, plausible, seductive.

speck n bit, crumb, dot, fleck, grain, mark, mite, old use mote, particle, speckle, spot, trace.

speckled adj blotchy, brindled, dappled, dotted, flecked, freckled, mottled, patchy, spattered (with), spotted, spotty, sprinkled (with), stippled.

spectacle n ceremonial, ceremony, colourfulness, display, exhibition, extravaganza, grandeur, magnificence, ostentation, pageantry, parade, pomp, show, sight, spectacular effects, splendour. **spectacles** ▷ GLASS.

spectacular adj beautiful, breathtaking, colourful, dramatic, elaborate, eye-catching, impressive, magnificent, derog ostentatious, sensational, showy, splendid, stunning.

spectator n plur audience, beholder, bystander, plur crowd, eyewitness, looker-on, observer, onlooker, passer-by, viewer, watcher, witness.

spectre n apparition, ghost, phantom, presentiment, vision, wraith. ▷ SPIRIT.

spectrum n compass, extent, gamut, orbit, range, scope, series, span, spread, sweep, variety.

speculate vb **1** conjecture, consider, hypothesize, make guesses, meditate, ponder, reflect, ruminate, surmise, theorize, weigh up, wonder. ▷ THINK. **2** speculate in shares. gamble, invest speculatively, inf play the market, take a chance, wager.

speculative adj **1** abstract, based on guesswork, conjectural, doubtful, inf gossipy, hypothetical, notional, suppositional, suppositious, theoretical, unfounded, uninformed, unproven, untested. Opp PROVEN. **2** speculative investments. inf chancy, inf dicey, inf dodgy, hazardous, inf iffy, risky, uncertain, unpredictable, unreliable, unsafe. Opp SAFE.

speech n **1** articulation, communication, declamation, delivery, diction, elocution, enunciation, expression, pronunciation, speaking, talking, using words, utterance. **2** dialect, idiolect, idiom, jargon, language, parlance, register, tongue. **3** a public speech. address, discourse, disquisition, harangue, homily, lecture, oration, paper, presentation, sermon, inf spiel, talk, tirade. **4** speech in a play. dialogue, lines, monologue, soliloquy.

speechless adj dumb, dumbfounded, dumbstruck, inarticulate, inf mum, mute, nonplussed, silent, thunderstruck, tongue-tied, voiceless. Opp TALKATIVE.

speed n **1** pace, rate, tempo, velocity. **2** alacrity, briskness, celerity, dispatch, expeditiousness, fleetness, haste, hurry, quickness, rapidity, speediness, swiftness. ● vb **1** inf belt, inf bolt, inf bowl along, canter, career, dart, dash, flash, flit, fly, gallop, inf go like the wind, hasten, hurry, hurtle, make haste, move quickly, inf nip, inf put your foot down, race, run, rush, shoot, sprint, stampede, streak, tear, inf zoom. **2** speed on the road. break the speed limit, go too fast. **speed up** ▷ ACCELERATE.

speedy adj **1** expeditious, fast, old use fleet, nimble, quick, rapid, swift. **2** a speedy exit. hasty, hurried, immediate, precipitate, prompt, unhesitating. Opp SLOW.

spell n **1** bewitchment, charm, conjuration, conjuring, enchantment, incantation, magic formula, sorcery, witchcraft, witchery. **2** the spell of the theatre. allure, captivation, charm, enthralment, fascination, glamour, magic. **3** a spell of rain. interval, period, phase, season. **4** a spell at the wheel. session, stint, stretch, term, time, tour of duty, turn, watch. ● vb augur, bode, foretell, indicate, mean, portend, presage, signal, signify, suggest. **spell out** ▷ CLARIFY.

spellbound adj bewitched, captivated, charmed, enchanted, enthralled, entranced, fascinated, hypnotized, mesmerized, overcome, overpowered, transported.

spend vb **1** inf blue, consume, inf cough up, disburse, exhaust, expend, inf fork out, fritter, inf get through, invest, inf lash out, pay out, inf shell out, inf splash out, inf splurge, squander. **2** spend time. devote, fill, occupy, pass, use up, waste.

spendthrift n inf big spender, prodigal, profligate, wasteful person, wastrel. Opp MISER.

sphere n **1** ball, globe, globule, orb, spheroid. **2** sphere of influence. area, department, discipline, domain, field, province, range, scope, speciality, subject, territory. **3** social sphere. caste, class, domain, milieu, position, rank, society, station, stratum, walk of life.

spherical adj ball-shaped, globe-shaped, globular, rotund, round, spheric, spheroidal.

spice n **1** flavouring, piquancy, relish, seasoning. □ allspice, bayleaf, capsicum, cardamom, cassia, cayenne, chilli, cinnamon, cloves, coriander, curry powder, ginger, grains of paradise, juniper, mace, nutmeg, paprika, pepper, pimento, poppy seed, saffron, sesame, turmeric. **2** add spice to life. colour, excitement, gusto, interest, *inf* lift, *inf* pep, sharpness, stimulation, vigour, zest.

spicy *adj* aromatic, fragrant, gingery, highly flavoured, hot, peppery, piquant, pungent, seasoned, spiced, tangy, zestful. *Opp* BLAND.

spike *n* barb, nail, pin, point, projection, prong, skewer, spine, stake, tine. ● *vb* impale, perforate, pierce, skewer, spear, spit, stab, stick.

spill *vb* **1** overturn, slop, splash about, tip over, upset. **2** brim, flow, overflow, pour, run. **3** *lorry spilled its load.* discharge, drop, scatter, shed, tip.

spin *vb* **1** gyrate, pirouette, revolve, rotate, swirl, turn, twirl, twist, wheel, whirl. **2** *head was spinning.* be giddy, reel, suffer vertigo, swim. **spin out** ▷ PROLONG.

spindle *n* axis, axle, pin, rod, shaft.

spine *n* **1** backbone, spinal column, vertebrae. **2** *hedgehog's spines.* barb, bristle, needle, point, prickle, prong, quill, spike, spur, thorn.

spineless *adj* cowardly, craven, faint-hearted, feeble, helpless, irresolute, *inf* lily-livered, pusillanimous, *inf* soft, timid, unheroic, weedy, *inf* wimpish. ▷ WEAK. *Opp* BRAVE.

spiral *adj* cochlear, coiled, corkscrew, turning, whorled. ● *n* coil, curl, helix, screw, whorl. ● *vb* **1** turn, twist. **2** *spiralling prices.* ▷ FALL, RISE.

spire *n* flèche, pinnacle, steeple.

spirit *n* **1** *Lat* anima, breath, mind, psyche, soul. **2** *supernatural spirits.* apparition, *inf* bogy, demon, devil, genie, ghost, ghoul, gremlin, hobgoblin, imp, incubus, nymph, phantasm, phantom, poltergeist, *poet* shade, shadow, spectre, *inf* spook, sprite, sylph, vision, visitant, wraith, zombie. **3** *spirit of a poem.* aim, atmosphere, essence, feeling, heart, intention, meaning, mood, purpose, sense. **4** *fighting spirit.* animation, bravery, cheerfulness, confidence, courage, daring, determination, dynamism, energy, enthusiasm, fire, fortitude, *inf* get-up-and-go, *inf* go, *inf* guts, heroism, liveliness, mettle, morale,

motivation, optimism, pluck, resolve, valour, verve, vivacity, will-power, zest. **5** ▷ ALCOHOL.

spirited *adj* active, animated, assertive, brave, brisk, buoyant, courageous, daring, determined, dynamic, energetic, enterprising, enthusiastic, frisky, gallant, *inf* gutsy, intrepid, lively, mettlesome, plucky, positive, resolute, sparkling, sprightly, vigorous, vivacious. *Opp* SPIRITLESS.

spiritless *adj* apathetic, cowardly, defeatist, despondent, dispirited, dull, irresolute, lacklustre, languid, lethargic, lifeless, listless, melancholy, negative, passive, slow, unenterprising, unenthusiastic. *Opp* SPIRITED.

spiritual *adj* devotional, divine, eternal, heavenly, holy, incorporeal, inspired, other-worldly, religious, sacred, unworldly, visionary. *Opp* TEMPORAL.

spit *n* **1** dribble, saliva, spittle, sputum. ● *vb* dribble, expectorate, salivate, splutter. **spit out** ▷ DISCHARGE. **spitting image** ▷ TWIN.

spite *n* animosity, animus, antagonism, *inf* bitchiness, bitterness, *inf* cattiness, gall, grudge, hate, hatred, hostility, ill-feeling, ill will, malevolence, malice, maliciousness, malignity, rancour, resentment, spleen, venom, vindictiveness. ● *vb* ▷ ANNOY.

spiteful *adj* acid, acrimonious, *inf* bitchy, bitter, *inf* catty, cruel, cutting, hateful, hostile, hurtful, ill-natured, invidious, malevolent, malicious, nasty, poisonous, punitive, rancorous, resentful, revengeful, sharp, *inf* snide, sour, unforgiving, venomous, vicious, vindictive. *Opp* KIND.

splash *vb* **1** bespatter, besprinkle, shower, slop, *inf* slosh, spatter, spill, splatter, spray, sprinkle, squirt, wash. **2** *splash about in water.* bathe, dabble, paddle, wade. **3** *splash news across the front page.* blazon, display, exhibit, flaunt, *inf* plaster, publicize, show, spread. **splash out** ▷ SPEND.

splay vb make a V-shape, slant, spread.

splendid adj admirable, aweinspiring, beautiful, brilliant, costly, dazzling, dignified, elegant, fine, first-class, glittering, glorious, gorgeous, grand, great, handsome, imposing, impressive, lavish, luxurious, magnificent, majestic, marvellous, noble, ornate, *derog* ostentatious, palatial, *inf* posh, refulgent, regal, resplendent, rich, royal, *derog* showy, spectacular, *inf* splendiferous, stately, sublime, sumptuous, *inf* super, superb, supreme, wonderful. ▷ EXCELLENT.

splendour n beauty, brilliance, ceremony, costliness, display, elegance, *inf* glitter, glory, grandeur, luxury, magnificence, majesty, nobility, ostentation, pomp, pomp and circumstance, refulgence, richness, show, spectacle, stateliness, sumptuousness.

splice vb bind, conjoin, entwine, join, knit, marry, tie together, unite.

splinter n chip, flake, fragment, shard, shaving, shiver, sliver. ● vb chip, crack, fracture, shatter, shiver, smash, split. ▷ BREAK.

split n **1** break, chink, cleavage, cleft, crack, cranny, crevice, fissure, furrow, gash, groove, leak, opening, rent, rift, rip, rupture, slash, slit, tear. **2** breach, dichotomy, difference, dissension, divergence of opinion, division, divorce, estrangement, schism, separation. ▷ QUARREL. ● vb **1** break up, disintegrate, divide, divorce, go separate ways, move apart, separate. **2** *split logs*. burst, chop, cleave, crack, rend, rip apart, rip open, slash, slice, slit, splinter, tear. ▷ CUT. **3** *split profits*. allocate, allot, apportion, distribute, divide, halve, share. **4** *road splits*. bifurcate, branch, diverge, fork.

split on ▷ INFORM.

spoil vb **1** blight, blot, blotch, bungle, damage, deface, destroy, disfigure, *inf* dish, harm, injure, *inf* make a mess of, mar, *inf* mess up, ruin, stain, undermine, undo, upset, vitiate, worsen, wreck. Opp IMPROVE. **2** *food spoiled in the heat*. become useless, curdle, decay, decompose, go bad, *inf* go off, moulder, perish, putrefy, rot, *inf* turn. **3** *spoil children*. coddle, cosset, dote on, indulge, make a fuss of, mollycoddle, over-indulge, pamper.

spoken adj oral, unwritten, verbal, *Lat* viva voce. Opp WRITTEN.

spokesperson n mouthpiece, representative, spokesman, spokeswoman.

sponge vb **1** clean, cleanse, mop, rinse, sluice, swill, wash, wipe. **2** *[inf] sponge on friends*. be dependent (on), cadge (from), scrounge (from).

spongy adj absorbent, compressible, elastic, giving, porous, soft, springy, yielding. Opp SOLID.

sponsor n *inf* angel, backer, benefactor, donor, patron, promoter, supporter. ● vb back, be a sponsor of, finance, fund, help, patronize, promote, subsidize, support, underwrite.

sponsorship n aegis, auspices, backing, benefaction, funding, guarantee, patronage, promotion, support.

spontaneous adj **1** *inf* ad lib, extempore, impromptu, impulsive, *inf* off-the-cuff, unplanned, unpremeditated, unprepared, unrehearsed, voluntary. **2** *a spontaneous reaction*. automatic, instinctive, instinctual, involuntary, mechanical, natural, reflex, unconscious, unconstrained, unforced, unthinking. Opp PREMEDITATED.

spooky adj creepy, eerie, frightening, ghostly, haunted, mysterious, scary, uncanny, unearthly, weird.

spool n bobbin, reel.

spoon n dessert-spoon, ladle, tablespoon, teaspoon.

spoon-feed vb cosset, help, indulge, mollycoddle, pamper, spoil.

spoor n footprints, scent, traces, track.

sporadic adj erratic, fitful, intermittent, irregular, occasional, periodic, scattered, separate, unpredictable.

sport n 1 activity, amusement, diversion, enjoyment, entertainment, exercise, fun, games, pastime, play, pleasure, recreation. □ *aerobics, angling, archery, athletics, badminton, base-ball, basketball, billiards, blood sports, bobsleigh, bowls, boxing, canoeing, climbing, cricket, croquet, cross-country, curling, darts, decathlon, discus, fishing, football, gliding, golf, gymnastics, hockey, hunting, hurdling, ice-hockey, javelin, jogging, keep-fit, lacrosse, marathon, martial arts, mountaineering, netball, orienteering, pentathlon, inf ping-pong, polo, pool, pot-holing, quoits, racing, rock-climbing, roller-skating, rounders, rowing, Rugby, running, sailing, shooting, shot, show-jumping, skating, skiing, skin-diving, sky-diving, snooker, soccer, squash, street-hockey, surfing, surf-riding, swimming, table-tennis, tennis, tobogganing, trampolining, volley-ball, water-polo, water-skiing, wind-surfing, winter sports, wrestling, yachting.* ▷ ATHLETICS, RACE. 2 badinage, banter, humour, jesting, joking, merriment, raillery, teasing. ● vb 1 caper, cavort, divert yourself, frisk about, frolic, gambol, lark about, rollick, romp, skip about. 2 *sport new clothes*. display, exhibit, flaunt, show off, wear.

sporting adj considerate, fair, generous, good-humoured, honourable, sportsmanlike.

sportive adj coltish, frisky, kittenish, light-hearted, playful, waggish. ▷ SPRIGHTLY.

sportsperson n contestant, participant, player, sportsman, sportswoman.

sporty adj 1 active, athletic, energetic, fit, vigorous. 2 *sporty clothes*. casual, informal, inf loud, rakish, showy, inf snazzy.

spot n 1 blemish, blot, blotch, discoloration, dot, fleck, mark, patch, smudge, speck, speckle, stain, stigma. 2 *spot on the skin*. birthmark, boil, freckle, plur impetigo, mole, naevus, pimple, pock, pock-mark, plur rash, sty, whitlow, sl zit. 3 *spots of rain*. bead, blob, drop. 4 *spot for a*

picnic. locale, locality, location, neighbourhood, place, point, position, scene, setting, site, situation. 5 *an awkward spot*. difficulty, dilemma, embarrassment, mess, predicament, quandary, situation. 6 *spot of bother*. bit, small amount, inf smidgen. ● vb 1 blot, discolour, fleck, mark, mottle, smudge, spatter, speckle, splash, spray, stain. 2 ▷ SEE.

spotless adj 1 clean, fresh, immaculate, laundered, unmarked, unspotted, white. 2 *spotless reputation*. blameless, faultless, flawless, immaculate, innocent, irreproachable, pure, unblemished, unsullied, untarnished, inf whiter than white.

spotty adj blotchy, dappled, flecked, freckled, mottled, pimply, pock-marked, pocky, spattered, speckled, speckly, inf splodgy, spotted.

spouse n better half, old use helpmate, husband, partner, wife.

spout n duct, fountain, gargoyle, geyser, jet, lip, nozzle, outlet, rose (of *watering-can*), spray, waterspout. ● vb 1 discharge, emit, erupt, flow, gush, jet, pour, shoot, spew, spit, spurt, squirt, stream. 2 ▷ TALK.

sprawl vb 1 flop, lean back, lie, loll, lounge, recline, relax, slouch, slump, spread out, stretch out. 2 be scattered, branch out, spread, straggle.

spray n 1 drizzle, droplets, fountain, mist, shower, splash, sprinkling. 2 *spray of flowers*. arrangement, bouquet, branch, bunch, corsage, posy, sprig. 3 *spray for paint*. aerosol, atomizer, spray-gun, sprinkler, vaporizer. ● vb diffuse, disperse, scatter, shower, spatter, splash, spread in droplets, sprinkle.

spread n 1 broadcasting, broadening, development, diffusion, dispensing, dispersal, dissemination, distribution, expansion, extension, growth, increase, passing on, proliferation, promotion, promulgation. 2 *spread of a bird's wings*. breadth, compass, extent, size, span, stretch, sweep. 3 ▷ MEAL. ● vb 1 arrange, display, lay out, open out, unfold, unfurl, unroll. **2** broaden, enlarge, expand, extend, fan out, get bigger, get longer, get wider, lengthen, *inf* mushroom, proliferate, straggle, widen. **3** *spread news.* advertise, broadcast, circulate, diffuse, dispense, disperse, disseminate, distribute, divulge, give out, make known, pass on, pass round, proclaim, promote, promulgate, publicize, publish, scatter, sow, transmit. **4** *spread butter.* apply, cover a surface with, smear.

spree *n inf* binge, debauch, escapade, *inf* fling, frolic, *inf* orgy, outing, revel. ▷ REVELRY.

sprightly *adj* active, agile, animated, brisk, *inf* chipper, energetic, jaunty, lively, nimble, *inf* perky, playful, quickmoving, spirited, sportive, spry, vivacious. *Opp* LETHARGIC.

spring *n* **1** bounce, buoyancy, elasticity, give, liveliness, resilience. **2** *clock spring.* coil, mainspring. **3** *spring of water.* fount, fountain, geyser, source (*of river*), spa, well, well-spring. ● *vb* bounce, bound, hop, jump, leap, pounce, vault. **spring from** come from, derive from, proceed from, stem from. **spring up** appear, arise, burst forth, come up, develop, emerge, germinate, grow, shoot up, sprout.

springy *adj* bendy, elastic, flexible, pliable, resilient, spongy, stretchy, supple. *Opp* RIGID.

sprinkle *vb* drip, dust, pepper, scatter, shower, spatter, splash, spray, strew.

sprint *vb* dash, *inf* hare, race, speed, *inf* tear. ▷ RUN.

sprout *n* bud, shoot. ● *vb* bud, come up, develop, emerge, germinate, grow, shoot up, spring up.

spruce *adj* clean, dapper, elegant, groomed, *inf* natty, neat, *inf* posh, smart, tidy, trim, well-dressed, well-groomed, *inf* well-turned-out. *Opp* SCRUFFY. ● *vb* **spruce up** ▷ TIDY.

spur *n* **1** encouragement, goad, impetus, incentive, incitement, inducement, motivation, motive, prod, prompting, stimulus, urging. **2** *motorway spur.* branch, projection. ● *vb* animate, egg on, encourage, impel, incite, motivate, pressure, pressurize, prick, prod, prompt, provide an incentive, stimulate, urge.

spurn *vb* disown, give (someone) the cold shoulder, jilt, rebuff, reject, renounce, repel, repudiate, repulse, shun, snub, turn your back on.

spy *n* contact, double agent, fifth columnist, *sl* grass, infiltrator, informant, informer, *inf* mole, private detective, secret agent, snooper, stool-pigeon, undercover agent. ● *vb* **1** be a spy, be engaged in spying, eavesdrop, gather intelligence, inform, *inf* snoop. **2** ▷ SEE. **spy on** keep under surveillance, *inf* tail, trail, watch.

spying *n* counter-espionage, detective work, eavesdropping, espionage, intelligence, snooping, surveillance.

squabble *vb* argue, bicker, clash, *inf* row, wrangle. ▷ QUARREL.

squalid *adj* **1** dingy, dirty, disgusting, filthy, foul, insalubrious, mean, mucky, nasty, poverty-stricken, repulsive, run-down, *inf* sleazy, slummy, sordid, ugly, uncared-for, unpleasant, wretched. *Opp* CLEAN. **2** *squalid behaviour.* corrupt, degrading, dishonest, dishonourable, disreputable, immoral, scandalous, *inf* shabby, shameful, unethical, unworthy. *Opp* HONOURABLE.

squander *vb inf* blow, *inf* blue, dissipate, *inf* fritter, misuse, spend unwisely, *inf* splurge, use up, waste. *Opp* SAVE.

square *adj* **1** perpendicular, rectangular, right-angled. **2** *a square deal.* *inf* above-board, decent, equitable, ethical, fair, honest, honourable, proper, *inf* right and proper, *inf* straight. ● *n* **1** piazza, plaza. **2** [*inf*] *an old-fashioned square.* bourgeois, conformist, conservative, conventional person, die-hard, *inf* fuddy-duddy, *inf* old fogy, *inf* stick-in-the-mud, traditionalist. ● *vb* *square an account.* ▷

SETTLE. **squared** chequered, criss-crossed, marked in squares.

squash vb **1** compress, crumple, crush, flatten, mangle, mash, pound, press, pulp, smash, stamp on, tamp down, tread on. **2** *squash into a room.* cram, crowd, pack, push, ram, shove, squeeze, stuff, thrust, wedge. **3** *squash an uprising.* control, put down, quash, quell, repress, suppress. **4** *squash with a look.* humiliate, *inf* put down, silence, snub.

squashy adj mashed up, mushy, pulpy, shapeless, soft, spongy, squelchy, yielding. *Opp* FIRM.

squat adj burly, dumpy, plump, podgy, short, stocky, thick, thickset. *Opp* TALL. ● vb crouch, sit.

squeamish adj inf choosy, dainty, fastidious, finicky, over-scrupulous, particular, *inf* pernickety, prim, *inf* prissy, prudish, scrupulous.

squeeze vb **1** clasp, compress, crush, embrace, enfold, exert pressure on, flatten, grip, hug, mangle, pinch, press, squash, stamp on, tread on, wring. **2** cram, crowd, pack, push, ram, shove, squash, stuff, tamp, thrust, wedge. **squeeze out** expel, extrude, force out.

squirm vb twist, wriggle, writhe.

squirt vb ejaculate, eject, gush, jet, send out, shoot, spit, splash, spout, spray, spurt.

stab n **1** blow, cut, jab, prick, puncture, thrust, wound, wounding. **2** *stab of pain.* ▷ PAIN. ● vb bayonet, cut, injure, jab, lance, perforate, pierce, puncture, skewer, spike, stick, thrust, transfix, wound. **have a stab at** ▷ TRY.

stability n balance, constancy, durability, equilibrium, firmness, immutability, permanence, reliability, solidity, soundness, steadiness, strength. *Opp* INSTABILITY.

stabilize vb balance, become stable, give stability to, keep upright, make stable, settle. *Opp* UPSET.

stable adj **1** balanced, firm, fixed, solid, sound, steady, strong, sturdy.

2 constant, continuing, durable, established, immutable, lasting, long-lasting, permanent, predictable, resolute, steadfast, unchanging, unwavering. **3** *a stable personality.* balanced, even-tempered, reasonable, sane, sensible. *Opp* UNSTABLE.

stack n **1** accumulation, heap, hill, hoard, mound, mountain, pile, quantity, stock, stockpile, store. **2** chimney, pillar, smokestack. **3** *stack of hay.* old use cock, haycock, haystack, rick, stook. ● vb accumulate, amass, assemble, build up, collect, gather, heap, load, mass, pile, *inf* stash away, stockpile.

stadium n amphitheatre, arena, ground, sports-ground.

staff n **1** baton, cane, crook, crosier, flagstaff, pike, pole, rod, sceptre, shaft, stake, standard, stave, stick, token, wand. **2** *staff of a business.* assistants, crew, employees, *old use* hands, personnel, officers, team, workers, workforce. ● vb man, provide with staff, run.

stage n **1** apron, dais, performing area, platform, podium, proscenium, rostrum. **2** *stage of a journey.* juncture, leg, phase, period, point, time. ● vb arrange, *inf* get up, mount, organize, perform, present, produce, *inf* put on, set up, stage-manage.

stagger vb **1** falter, lurch, pitch, reel, rock, stumble, sway, teeter, totter, walk unsteadily, waver, wobble. **2** *price staggered us.* alarm, amaze, astonish, astound, confuse, dismay, dumbfound, flabbergast, shake, shock, startle, stun, stupefy, surprise, worry.

stagnant adj motionless, sluggish, stale, standing, static, still, without movement. *Opp* MOVING.

stagnate vb achieve nothing, become stale, be stagnant, degenerate, deteriorate, idle, languish, stand still, stay still, vegetate. *Opp* PROGRESS.

stain n **1** blemish, blot, blotch, discoloration, mark, smear, smudge, speck, spot. **2** *a wood stain.* colouring, dye, paint, pigment, tinge, tint, varnish. ● vb **1** blacken, blemish, blot, contaminate, dirty, discolour, make dirty, mark, smudge, soil, tarnish. **2** *stain your reputation.* besmirch, damage, defile, disgrace, shame, spoil, sully, taint. **3** *stain wood.* colour, dye, paint, tinge, tint, varnish.

stair n riser, step, tread. **stairs** escalator, flight of stairs, staircase, stairway, steps.

stake n **1** paling, palisade, pike, pile, pillar, pole, post, rod, sceptre, shaft, standard, stave, stick, upright. **2** *a gambler's stake.* bet, pledge, wager. ● vb **1** fasten, hitch, secure, tether, tie up. **2** *stake a claim.* establish, put on record, state. **3** *stake my life on it.* bet, chance, gamble, hazard, risk, venture, wager. **stake out** define, delimit, demarcate, enclose, fence in, mark off, outline.

stale adj **1** dry, hard, limp, mouldy, musty, *inf* off, old, *inf* past its best, tasteless. **2** *stale ideas.* banal, clichéd, familiar, hackneyed, old-fashioned, out-of-date, overused, stock, threadbare, *inf* tired, trite, uninteresting, unoriginal, worn out. *Opp* FRESH.

stalemate n deadlock, impasse, standstill.

stalk n branch, shaft, shoot, stem, trunk, twig. ● vb **1** chase, dog, follow, haunt, hound, hunt, pursue, shadow, tail, track, trail. **2** *stalk about.* prowl, rove, stride, strut. ▷ WALK.

stall n booth, compartment, kiosk, stand, table. ● vb be obstructive, delay, hang back, haver, hesitate, pause, *inf* play for time, postpone, prevaricate, procrastinate, put off, stonewall, stop, temporize, waste time.

stalwart adj courageous, dependable, determined, faithful, indomitable, intrepid, redoubtable, reliable, resolute, robust, staunch, steadfast, sturdy, tough, trustworthy, valiant. ▷ BRAVE, STRONG. *Opp* WEAK.

stamina n endurance, energy, *inf* grit, indomitability, resilience, staunchness, staying power, *inf* stickability.

stammer vb falter, hesitate, hem and haw, splutter, stumble, stutter. ▷ TALK.

stamp n **1** brand, die, hallmark, impression, imprint, print, punch, seal. **2** *stamp of genius.* characteristic, mark, sign. **3** *stamp on a letter.* franking, postage stamp. ● vb **1** bring down, strike, thump. **2** *stamp a mark.* brand, emboss, engrave, impress, imprint, label, mark, print, punch. **stamp on** ▷ SUPPRESS. **stamp out** ▷ ELIMINATE.

stampede n charge, dash, flight, panic, rout, rush, sprint. ● vb **1** bolt, career, charge, dash, gallop, panic, run, rush, sprint, *inf* take to your heels, tear. **2** *stampede cattle.* frighten, panic, rout, scatter.

stand n **1** base, pedestal, rack, support, tripod, trivet. **2** booth, kiosk, stall. **3** grandstand, terraces. ● vb **1** arise, get to your feet, get up, rise. **2** *Stand it on the floor.* arrange, deposit, erect, locate, place, position, put up, set up, situate, station, upend. **3** *Trees stand along the avenue.* be, be situated, exist. **4** *My offer stands.* be unchanged, continue, remain valid, stay. **5** *Can't stand onions.* abide, bear, endure, put up with, suffer, tolerate, *inf* wear. **stand by** ▷ SUPPORT. **stand for** ▷ SYMBOLIZE. **stand in for** ▷ DEPUTIZE. **stand out** ▷ SHOW. **stand up for** ▷ PROTECT, SUPPORT. **stand up to** ▷ RESIST.

standard adj accepted, accustomed, approved, average, basic, classic, common, conventional, customary, definitive, established, everyday, familiar, habitual, normal, official, ordinary, orthodox, popular, prevailing, prevalent, recognized, regular, routine, set, staple (*diet*), stock, traditional, typical, universal, usual. *Opp* UNUSUAL. ● n **1** archetype, benchmark, criterion, example, exemplar, gauge, grade, guide, guideline, ideal, level of achievement, measure, measurement, model, paradigm, pattern, requirement, rule, sample, specification, touchstone, yardstick. **2** average, level, mean, norm. **3** *standard of* *a regiment.* banner, colours, ensign, flag, pennant. **4** *lamp standard.* column, pillar, pole, post, support, upright. **standards** ▷ MORALITY.

standardize *vb* average out, conform to a standard, equalize, homogenize, normalize, regiment, stereotype, systematize.

standoffish *adj* aloof, antisocial, cold, cool, distant, frosty, haughty, remote, reserved, reticent, retiring, secretive, self-conscious, *inf* snooty, taciturn, unapproachable, uncommunicative, unforthcoming, unfriendly, unsociable, withdrawn. *Opp* FRIENDLY.

standpoint *n* angle, attitude, belief, opinion, perspective, point of view, position, stance, vantage point, view, viewpoint.

standstill *n inf* dead end, deadlock, halt, *inf* hold-up, impasse, jam, stalemate, stop, stoppage.

staple *adj* basic, chief, important, main, principal. ▷ STANDARD.

star *n* **1** celestial body, sun. □ *asteroid, comet, evening star, falling star, lodestar, morning star, nova, shooting star, supernova.* **2** asterisk, pentagram. **3** *TV star.* attraction, big name, celebrity, It diva, *inf* draw, idol, leading lady, leading man, personage, It prima donna, starlet, superstar. ▷ PERFORMER.

starchy *adj* aloof, conventional, formal, prim, stiff. ▷ UNFRIENDLY.

stare *vb* gape, *inf* gawp, gaze, glare, goggle, look fixedly, peer. **stare at** contemplate, examine, eye, scrutinize, study, watch.

stark *adj* **1** austere, bare, bleak, depressing, desolate, dreary, gloomy, grim. **2** *stark contrast.* absolute, clear, complete, obvious, perfect, plain, sharp, sheer, thoroughgoing, total, unqualified, utter.

start *n* **1** beginning, birth, commencement, creation, dawn, establishment, founding, fount, inauguration, inception, initiation, institution, introduction, launch, onset, opening, origin, outset, point of departure, setting out, spring,

springboard. *Opp* FINISH. **2** *an unfair start.* advantage, edge, head-start, opportunity. **3** *bankloan gave me a start.* assistance, backing, financing, help, *inf* leg-up, *inf* send-off, sponsorship. **4** *a nasty start.* jump, shock, surprise. ● *vb* **1** depart, embark, *inf* get going, *inf* get under way, *sl* hit the road, *inf* kick off, leave, move off, proceed, set off, set out. **2** *start something.* activate, beget, begin, commence, create, embark on, engender, establish, found, *inf* get cracking on, *inf* get off the ground, *inf* get the ball rolling, give birth to, inaugurate, initiate, instigate, institute, introduce, launch, open, originate, pioneer, set in motion, set up. *Opp* FINISH. **3** *start at sudden noise.* blench, draw back, flinch, jerk, jump, quail, recoil, shy, spring up, twitch, wince. **make someone start** ▷ STARTLE.

startle *vb* agitate, alarm, catch unawares, disturb, frighten, give you a start, jolt, make you jump, make you start, scare, shake, shock, surprise, take aback, take by surprise, upset. **startling** ▷ SURPRISING.

starvation *n* deprivation, famine, hunger, malnutrition, undernourishment, want.

starve *vb* die of starvation, go hungry, go without, perish. **starve yourself** diet, fast, go on hunger strike, refuse food. **starving** ▷ HUNGRY.

state *n* **1** *plur* circumstances, condition, fitness, health, mood, *inf* shape, situation. **2** agitation, excitement, *inf* flap, panic, plight, predicament, *inf* tizzy. **3** *a sovereign state.* land, nation. ▷ COUNTRY. ● *vb* affirm, announce, assert, asseverate, aver, communicate, declare, express, formulate, proclaim, put into words, report, specify, submit, testify, voice. ▷ SAY, SPEAK, TALK.

stately *adj* august, dignified, distinguished, elegant, formal, grand, imperial, imposing, impressive, lofty, majestic, noble, pompous, regal, royal, solemn, splendid, striking. *Opp* INFORMAL. **stately home** ▷ MANSION.

steal

statement n account, affirmation, announcement, annunciation, assertion, bulletin, comment, communication, communiqué, declaration, disclosure, explanation, message, notice, proclamation, proposition, report, testament, testimony, utterance.

statesman n diplomat, politician.

static adj constant, fixed, immobile, immovable, inert, invariable, motionless, passive, stable, stagnant, stationary, steady, still, unchanging, unmoving. Opp MOBILE, VARIABLE.

station n 1 calling, caste, class, degree, employment, level, location, occupation, place, position, post, rank, situation, standing, status. 2 *fire station*. base, depot, headquarters, office. 3 *radio station*. channel, company, transmitter, wavelength. 4 *railway station*. halt, platform, stopping-place, terminus, train station. ● vb assign, garrison, locate, place, position, put, site, situate, spot, stand.

stationary adj at a standstill, at rest, halted, immobile, immovable, motionless, parked, pausing, standing, static, still, stock-still, unmoving. Opp MOVING.

stationery n paper, office supplies, writing materials.

statistics n data, figures, information, numbers.

statue n carving, figure, statuette. ▷ SCULPTURE.

statuesque adj dignified, elegant, imposing, impressive, poised, stately, upright.

stature n 1 build, height, size, tallness. 2 *artist of international stature*. esteem, greatness, recognition. ▷ STATUS.

status n class, degree, eminence, grade, importance, level, position, prestige, prominence, rank, reputation, significance, standing, station, stature, title.

staunch adj ▷ STEADFAST.

stay n 1 holiday, *old use* sojourn, stop, stop-over, visit. 2 *stay of execution*. ▷ DELAY. 3 ▷ SUPPORT. ● vb 1 *old use* bide, carry on, continue, endure, *inf* hang about, hold out, keep on, last, linger, live on, loiter, persist, remain, survive, *old use* tarry, wait. 2 *stay in a hotel. old use* abide, be accommodated, be a guest, be housed, board, dwell, live, lodge, reside, settle, *old use* sojourn, stop, visit. 3 *stay judgement*. ▷ DELAY.

steadfast adj committed, constant, dedicated, dependable, determined, devoted, faithful, firm, loyal, patient, persevering, reliable, resolute, resolved, single-minded, sound, stalwart, staunch, steady, true, trustworthy, trusty, unchanging, unfaltering, unflinching, unswerving, unwavering. ▷ STRONG. Opp UNRELIABLE.

steady adj 1 balanced, confident, fast, firm, immovable, poised, safe, secure, settled, solid, stable, substantial. 2 *a steady flow*. ceaseless, changeless, consistent, constant, continuous, dependable, endless, even, incessant, invariable, never-ending, nonstop, perpetual, persistent, regular, reliable, repeated, rhythmic, *inf* round-the-clock, unbroken, unchanging, undeviating, unfaltering, unhurried, uniform, uninterrupted, unrelieved, unremitting, unvarying. Opp UNSTEADY. 3 ▷ STEADFAST. ● vb 1 balance, brace, hold steady, keep still, make steady, secure, stabilize, support. 2 *steady your nerves*. calm, control, soothe, tranquillize.

steal vb 1 annex, appropriate, arrogate, burgle, commandeer, confiscate, embezzle, expropriate, *inf* filch, hijack, *inf* knock off, *inf* lift, loot, *inf* make off with, misappropriate, *inf* nick, peculate, pick pockets, pilfer, pillage, *inf* pinch, pirate, plagiarize, plunder, poach, purloin, *inf* rip you off, rob, seize, shop-lift, *inf* sneak, *inf* snitch, *inf* swipe, take, thieve, usurp, walk off with. 2 *steal quietly upstairs*.

creep, move stealthily, slink, slip, sneak, tiptoe.

stealing n robbery, theft, thieving. □ break-in, burglary, embezzlement, fraud, hijacking, housebreaking, larceny, looting, misappropriation, mugging, peculation, pilfering, pillage, piracy, plagiarism, plundering, poaching, purloining, scrumping, shop-lifting.

stealthy adj clandestine, concealed, covert, disguised, furtive, imperceptible, inconspicuous, quiet, secret, secretive, inf shifty, sly, inf sneaky, surreptitious, underhand, unobtrusive. Opp BLATANT.

steam n condensation, haze, mist, smoke, vapour.

steamy adj 1 blurred, clouded, cloudy, fogged over, foggy, hazy, misted over, misty. 2 a steamy atmosphere. close, damp, humid, moist, muggy, inf sticky, sultry, sweaty, sweltering. 3 [inf] steamy sex scenes. ▷ SEXY.

steep adj 1 abrupt, bluff, headlong, perpendicular, precipitous, sharp, sheer, sudden, vertical. Opp GRADUAL. 2 steep prices. ▷ EXPENSIVE. ● vb ▷ SOAK.

steeple n pinnacle, point, spire.

steer vb be at the wheel, control, direct, drive, guide, navigate, pilot. **steer clear of** ▷ AVOID.

stem n peduncle, shoot, stalk, stock, trunk, twig. ● vb arise, come, derive, develop, emanate, flow, issue, originate, proceed, result, spring, sprout. 2 to stem the flow. ▷ CHECK.

stench n mephitis, inf pong, reek, stink. ▷ SMELL.

step n 1 footfall, footstep, pace, stride, tread. 2 doorstep, rung, stair, tread. 3 a step forward. advance, move, movement, progress, progression. 4 step in a process. action, initiative, manoeuvre, measure, phase, procedure, stage. ● vb put your foot, stamp, stride, trample, tread. ▷ WALK. **steps** ladder, stairs, staircase, stairway, stepladder. **step down** ▷ RESIGN. **step in** ▷ ENTER, INTERVENE. **step on it** ▷ HURRY. **step up** ▷ INCREASE. **take steps** ▷ BEGIN.

stereoscopic adj solid-looking, three-dimensional, inf 3-D.

stereotype n formula, model, pattern, stereotyped idea.

stereotyped adj clichéd, conventional, formalized, hackneyed, predictable, standard, standardized, stock, typecast, unoriginal.

sterile adj 1 arid, barren, childless, dry, fruitless, infertile, lifeless, unfruitful, unproductive. 2 sterile bandage. antiseptic, aseptic, clean, disinfected, germ-free, hygienic, pure, sanitary, sterilized, uncontaminated, uninfected, unpolluted. 3 a sterile attempt. abortive, fruitless, hopeless, pointless, unprofitable, useless. Opp FERTILE, FRUITFUL, SEPTIC.

sterilize vb 1 clean, cleanse, decontaminate, depurate, disinfect, fumigate, make sterile, pasteurize, purify. 2 sterilize animals. caponize, castrate, emasculate, geld, neuter, perform a vasectomy on, spay, vasectomize.

stern adj adamant, austere, authoritarian, critical, dour, forbidding, frowning, grim, hard, harsh, inflexible, obdurate, resolute, rigid, rigorous, severe, strict, stringent, tough, unbending, uncompromising, unrelenting, unremitting. ▷ SERIOUS. Opp SOFT-HEARTED. ● n stern of ship. aft, back, rear end.

stew n casserole, goulash, hash, hotpot, ragout. ● vb boil, braise, casserole, simmer. ▷ COOK.

steward, stewardess ns 1 attendant, waiter. ▷ SERVANT. 2 marshal, officer, official.

stick n branch, stalk, twig. □ bar, baton, cane, club, hockey-stick, pike, pole, rod, staff, stake, walking-stick, wand. ● vb 1 bore, dig, impale, jab, penetrate, pierce, pin, poke, prick, prod, punch, puncture, run through, spear, spike, spit, stab, thrust, transfix. 2 stick with glue. adhere, affix, agglutinate, bind, bond, cement, cling, coagulate, fuse together, glue, gum, paste, solder, weld. ▷ FASTEN. 3 stick in your mind. be fixed, continue, endure, keep on, last, linger, persist, remain, stay. **4** *stick in mud.* become trapped, get bogged down, seize up, jam, wedge. **5** ▷ TOLERATE. **stick at** ▷ PERSIST. **stick in** ▷ PENETRATE. **stick out** ▷ PROTRUDE. **stick together** ▷ UNITE. **stick up** ▷ PROTRUDE. **stick up for** ▷ DEFEND. **stick with** ▷ SUPPORT.

sticky *adj* **1** adhesive, glued, gummed, self-adhesive. **2** *sticky paint.* gluey, glutinous, *inf* gooey, gummy, tacky, viscous. **3** *sticky weather.* clammy, close, damp, dank, humid, moist, muggy, steamy, sultry, sweaty. *Opp* DRY.

stiff *adj* **1** compact, dense, firm, hard, heavy, inelastic, inflexible, rigid, semi-solid, solid, solidified, thick, tough, unbending, unyielding, viscous. **2** *stiff joints.* arthritic, immovable, painful, paralysed, rheumatic, taut, tight. **3** *a stiff task.* arduous, challenging, difficult, exacting, exhausting, hard, laborious, tiring, tough, uphill. **4** *stiff opposition.* determined, dogged, obstinate, powerful, resolute, stubborn, unyielding, vigorous. **5** *a stiff manner.* artificial, awkward, clumsy, cold, forced, formal, graceless, haughty, inelegant, laboured, mannered, pedantic, self-conscious, standoffish, starchy, stilted, *inf* stuffy, tense, turgid, ungainly, unnatural, wooden. **6** *stiff penalties.* cruel, drastic, excessive, harsh, hurtful, merciless, pitiless, punishing, punitive, relentless, rigorous, severe, strict. **7** *stiff wind.* brisk, fresh, strong. **8** *stiff drink.* alcoholic, potent, strong. *Opp* EASY, RELAXED, SOFT.

stiffen *vb* become stiff, clot, coagulate, congeal, dry out, harden, jell, set, solidify, thicken, tighten, toughen.

stifle *vb* **1** asphyxiate, choke, smother, strangle, suffocate, throttle. **2** *stifle laughter.* check, control, curb, dampen, deaden, keep back, muffle, restrain, suppress, withhold. **3** *stifle free speech.* crush, destroy, extinguish, kill off, quash, repress, silence, stamp out, stop.

stigma *n* blot, brand, disgrace, dishonour, mark, reproach, shame, slur, stain, taint.

stigmatize *vb* brand, condemn, defame, denounce, disparage, label, mark, pillory, slander, vilify.

still *adj* at rest, calm, even, flat, hushed, immobile, inert, lifeless, motionless, noiseless, pacific, peaceful, placid, quiet, restful, serene, silent, smooth, soundless, stagnant, static, stationary, tranquil, unmoving, unruffled, untroubled, windless. *Opp* ACTIVE, NOISY. ● *vb* allay, appease, assuage, calm, lull, make still, pacify, quieten, settle, silence, soothe, subdue, suppress, tranquillize. *Opp* AGITATE.

stimulant *n* antidepressant, drug, *inf* pick-me-up, restorative, *inf* reviver, *inf* shot in the arm, tonic. ▷ STIMULUS.

stimulate *vb* activate, arouse, awaken, cause, encourage, excite, fan, fire, foment, galvanize, goad, incite, inflame, inspire, instigate, invigorate, kindle, motivate, prick, prompt, provoke, quicken, rouse, set off, spur, stir up, titillate, urge, whet. *Opp* DISCOURAGE.

stimulating *adj* arousing, challenging, exciting, exhilarating, inspirational, inspiring, interesting, intoxicating, invigorating, provocative, provoking, rousing, stirring, thought-provoking, titillating. *Opp* UNINTERESTING.

stimulus *n* challenge, encouragement, fillip, goad, incentive, inducement, inspiration, prompting, provocation, spur, stimulant. *Opp* DISCOURAGEMENT.

sting *n* bite, prick, stab. ▷ PAIN. ● *vb* **1** bite, nip, prick, wound. **2** smart, tingle. ▷ HURT.

stingy *adj* **1** avaricious, cheeseparing, close, close-fisted, covetous, mean, mingy, miserly, niggardly, parsimonious, penny-pinching, tight-fisted, ungenerous. **2** *stingy helpings.* inadequate, insufficient, meagre, *inf* measly, scanty. ▷ SMALL. *Opp* GENEROUS.

stink *n*, *vb* ▷ SMELL.

stipulate *vb* demand, insist on, make a stipulation, require, specify.

stipulation *n* condition, demand, prerequisite, proviso, requirement, specification.

stir *n* ▷ COMMOTION. ● *vb* **1** agitate, beat, blend, churn, mingle, mix, move about, scramble, whisk. **2** *stir from sleep*. arise, bestir yourself, *inf* get a move on, *inf* get going, get up, move, rise, *inf* show signs of life, *inf* stir your stumps. **3** *stir emotions*. activate, affect, arouse, awaken, challenge, disturb, electrify, excite, exhilarate, fire, impress, inspire, kindle, move, resuscitate, revive, rouse, stimulate, touch, upset.

stirring *adj* affecting, arousing, challenging, dramatic, electrifying, emotional, emotion-charged, emotive, exciting, exhilarating, heady, impassioned, inspirational, inspiring, interesting, intoxicating, invigorating, moving, provocative, provoking, rousing, spirited, stimulating, thought-provoking, thrilling, titillating, touching. *Opp* UNEXCITING.

stitch *vb* darn, mend, repair, sew, tack.

stock *adj* accustomed, banal, clichéd, common, commonplace, conventional, customary, expected, hackneyed, ordinary, predictable, regular, routine, run-of-the-mill, set, standard, staple, stereotyped, *inf* tired, traditional, trite, unoriginal, usual. *Opp* UNEXPECTED. ● *n* **1** cache, hoard, reserve, reservoir, stockpile, store, supply. **2** *stock of a shop*. commodities, goods, merchandise, range, wares. **3** *farm stock*. animals, beasts, cattle, flocks, herds, livestock. **4** *ancient stock*. ancestry, blood, breed, descent, dynasty, extraction, family, forebears, genealogy, line, lineage, parentage, pedigree. **5** *meat stock*. broth, soup. ● *vb* carry, deal in, handle, have available, *inf* keep, keep in stock, market, offer, provide,

sell, supply, trade in. **out of stock** sold out, unavailable. **take stock** ▷ REVIEW.

stockade *n* fence, paling, palisade, wall.

stockings *n* nylons, panti-hose, socks, tights.

stockist *n* merchant, retailer, seller, shopkeeper, supplier.

stocky *adj* burly, compact, dumpy, heavy-set, short, solid, squat, stubby, sturdy, thickset. *Opp* THIN.

stodgy *adj* **1** filling, heavy, indigestible, lumpy, soggy, solid, starchy. *Opp* SUCCULENT. **2** *a stodgy lecture*. boring, dull, ponderous, *inf* stuffy, tedious, tiresome, turgid, unexciting, unimaginative, uninteresting. *Opp* LIVELY.

stoical *adj* calm, cool, disciplined, impassive, imperturbable, long-suffering, patient, philosophical, phlegmatic, resigned, stolid, uncomplaining, unemotional, unexcitable, *inf* unflappable. *Opp* EXCITABLE.

stoke *vb* fuel, keep burning, mend, put fuel on, tend.

stole *n* cape, shawl, wrap.

stolid *adj* bovine, dull, heavy, immovable, impassive, lumpish, phlegmatic, unemotional, unexciting, unimaginative, wooden. ▷ STOICAL. *Opp* LIVELY.

stomach *n* abdomen, belly, *inf* guts, *inf* insides, *derog* paunch, *derog* pot, *inf* tummy. ● *vb* ▷ TOLERATE.

stomach-ache *n* colic, *inf* collywobbles, *inf* gripes, *inf* tummy-ache.

stone *n* **1** boulder, cobble, *plur* gravel, pebble, rock, *plur* scree. ▷ ROCK. **2** block, flagstone, sett, slab. **3** *a memorial stone*. gravestone, headstone, memorial, monolith, obelisk, tablet. **4** *precious stone*. ▷ JEWEL. **5** *stone in fruit*. pip, pit, seed.

stony *adj* **1** pebbly, rocky, rough, shingly. **2** *stony silence*. adamant, chilly, cold, coldhearted, expressionless, frigid, hard, *inf* hardboiled, heartless, hostile, icy, indifferent, insensitive, merciless, pitiless, steely, stony-hearted, uncaring, unemotional, unfeeling, unforgiving, unfriendly, unresponsive, unsympathetic.

stooge n butt, dupe, inf fall-guy, lackey, puppet.

stoop vb **1** bend, bow, crouch, duck, hunch your shoulders, kneel, lean, squat. **2** condescend, degrade yourself, deign, humble yourself, lower yourself, sink.

stop n **1** ban, cessation, close, conclusion, end, finish, halt, shut-down, standstill, stoppage, termination. **2** a stop for refreshments. break, destination, pause, resting-place, stage, station, stopover, terminus. **3** a stop at a hotel. holiday, old use sojourn, stay, vacation, visit. ● vb **1** break off, call a halt to, cease, conclude, cut off, desist from, discontinue, end, finish, halt, inf knock off, leave off, inf pack in, pause, quit, refrain from, rest from, suspend, terminate. **2** stop the flow. bar, block, check, curb, cut off, delay, frustrate, halt, hamper, hinder, immobilize, impede, intercept, interrupt, inf nip in the bud, obstruct, put a stop to, stanch, staunch, stem, suppress, thwart. **3** stop in a hotel. be a guest, have a holiday, old use sojourn, spend time, stay, visit. **4** stop a gap. inf bung up, close, fill in, plug, seal. **5** stop a thief. arrest, capture, catch, detain, hold, seize. **6** the rain stopped. be over, cease, come to an end, finish, peter out. **7** the bus stopped. come to rest, draw up, halt, pull up.

stopper n bung, cork, plug.

store n **1** accumulation, cache, fund, hoard, quantity, reserve, reservoir, stock, stockpile, supply. ▷ STOREHOUSE. **2** a grocery store. outlet, retail business, retailers, supermarket. ▷ SHOP. ● vb accumulate, aggregate, deposit, hoard, keep, lay by, lay in, lay up, preserve, put away, reserve, save, set aside, inf stash away, stockpile, stock up, stow away.

storehouse n depository, repository, storage, store, store-room. □ armoury, arsenal, barn, cellar, cold-storage, depot, granary, larder, pantry, safe, silo, stock-room, strong-room, treasury, vault, warehouse.

storey n deck, floor, level, stage, tier.

storm n **1** disturbance, onslaught, outbreak, outburst, stormy weather, tempest, tumult, turbulence. □ blizzard, cloudburst, cyclone, deluge, dust-storm, electrical storm, gale, hailstorm, hurricane, mistral, monsoon, rainstorm, sandstorm, simoom, sirocco, snowstorm, squall, thunderstorm, tornado, typhoon, whirlwind. **2** storm of protest. ▷ CLAMOUR. ● vb ▷ ATTACK.

stormy adj angry, blustery, choppy, fierce, furious, gusty, raging, rough, squally, tempestuous, thundery, tumultuous, turbulent, vehement, violent, wild, windy. Opp CALM.

story n **1** account, anecdote, chronicle, fiction, history, narration, narrative, plot, recital, record, scenario, tale, yarn. □ allegory, children's story, crime story, detective story, epic, fable, fairy-tale, fantasy, folk-tale, legend, mystery, myth, novel, parable, romance, saga, science fiction, SF, thriller, inf whodunit. **2** story in newspaper. article, dispatch, exclusive, feature, news item, piece, report, scoop. **3** falsehood, inf fib, lie, tall story, untruth.

storyteller n author, biographer, narrator, raconteur, teller.

stout adj **1** inf beefy, big, bulky, burly, inf chubby, corpulent, fleshy, heavy, inf hulking, overweight, plump, portly, solid, stocky, inf strapping, thick-set, inf tubby, well-built. ▷ FAT. Opp THIN. **2** stout rope. durable, reliable, robust, sound, strong, sturdy, substantial, thick, tough. **3** stout fighter. bold, brave, courageous, fearless, gallant, heroic, intrepid, plucky, resolute, spirited, valiant. Opp WEAK.

stove n boiler, cooker, fire, furnace, heater, oven, range.

stow vb load, pack, put away, inf stash away, store.

straggle vb be dispersed, be scattered, dangle, dawdle, drift, fall behind, lag, loiter, meander, ramble, scatter, spread out, stray, string out, trail, wander. **straggling** ▷ DISORGANIZED, LOOSE.

straight adj 1 aligned, direct, flat, linear, regular, smooth, true, unbending, undeviating, unswerving. 2 neat, orderly, organized, right, inf shipshape, sorted out, spruce, tidy. 3 a straight sequence. consecutive, continuous, non-stop, perfect, sustained, unbroken, uninterrupted, unrelieved. 4 ▷ STRAIGHTFORWARD. Opp CROOKED, INDIRECT, UNTIDY. **straight away** at once, directly, immediately, instantly, now, without delay.

straighten vb disentangle, make straight, put straight, rearrange, sort out, tidy, unbend, uncurl, unravel, untangle, untwist.

straightforward adj blunt, candid, direct, easy, forthright, frank, genuine, honest, intelligible, lucid, open, plain, simple, sincere, straight, truthful, uncomplicated. Opp DEVIOUS.

strain n 1 anxiety, difficulty, effort, exertion, hardship, pressure, stress, tension, worry. 2 genetic strain. ▷ ANCESTRY. ● vb 1 haul, heave, make taut, pull, stretch, tighten, tug. 2 strain to succeed. attempt, endeavour, exert yourself, labour, make an effort, strive, struggle, toil, try. 3 strain yourself. exercise, exhaust, overtax, inf push to the limit, stretch, tax, tire out, weaken, wear out, weary. 4 strain a muscle. damage, hurt, injure, overwork, pull, rick, sprain, tear, twist, wrench. 5 strain liquid. clear, drain, draw off, filter, percolate, purify, riddle, screen, separate, sieve, sift.

strained adj 1 artificial, constrained, distrustful, embarrassed, false, forced, insincere, self-conscious, stiff, tense, uncomfortable, uneasy, unnatural. 2 strained look. drawn, tired, weary. 3 strained interpretation. farfetched, incredible, laboured, unlikely, unreasonable. Opp NATURAL, RELAXED.

strainer n colander, filter, riddle, sieve.

strand n fibre, filament, string, thread, wire. ● vb 1 abandon, desert, forsake, leave stranded, lose, maroon. 2 strand a ship. beach, ground, run aground, wreck. **stranded** ▷ AGROUND, HELPLESS.

strange adj 1 abnormal, astonishing, atypical, bizarre, curious, eerie, exceptional, extraordinary, fantastic, inf funny, grotesque, irregular, odd, out-of-the-ordinary, outré, peculiar, quaint, queer, rare, remarkable, singular, surprising, surreal, uncommon, unexpected, unheard-of, unique, unnatural, untypical, unusual. 2 strange neighbours. inf cranky, eccentric, sinister, unconventional, weird, inf zany. 3 a strange problem. baffling, bewildering, inexplicable, insoluble, mysterious, mystifying, perplexing, puzzling, unaccountable. 4 strange places. alien, exotic, foreign, little-known, off the beaten track, outlandish, out-of-the-way, remote, unexplored, unmapped. 5 strange experience. different, fresh, new, novel, unaccustomed, unfamiliar. Opp FAMILIAR, ORDINARY.

strangeness n abnormality, bizarreness, eccentricity, eeriness, extraordinariness, irregularity, mysteriousness, novelty, oddity, oddness, outlandishness, peculiarity, quaintness, queerness, rarity, singularity, unconventionality, unfamiliarity.

stranger n alien, foreigner, guest, newcomer, outsider, visitor.

strangle vb 1 asphyxiate, choke, garrotte, smother, stifle, suffocate, throttle. 2 strangle a cry. ▷ SUPPRESS.

strangulate vb bind, compress, constrict, squeeze.

strangulation n asphyxiation, garrotting, suffocation.

strap n band, belt, strop, tawse, thong, webbing. ● vb ▷ FASTEN.

stratagem n artifice, device, inf dodge, manoeuvre, plan, ploy, ruse, scheme, subterfuge, tactic, trick.

strategic adj advantageous, critical, crucial, deliberate, key, planned, politic, tactical, vital.

strategy n approach, design, manoeuvre, method, plan, plot, policy, procedure, programme, inf scenario, scheme, tactics.

stratum n layer, seam, table, thickness, vein.

straw n corn, stalks, stubble.

stray adj 1 abandoned, homeless, lost, roaming, roving, wandering. 2 stray bullets. accidental, casual, chance, haphazard, isolated, lone, occasional, odd, random, single. ● vb 1 get lost, get separated, go astray, meander, move about aimlessly, ramble, range, roam, rove, straggle, wander. 2 stray from the point. deviate, digress, diverge, drift, get off the subject, inf go off at a tangent, veer.

streak n 1 band, bar, dash, line, mark, score, smear, stain, stria, striation, strip, stripe, stroke, vein. 2 a selfish streak. component, element, strain, touch, trace. 3 streak of good luck. period, run, series, spate, spell, stretch, time. ● vb 1 mark with streaks, smear, smudge, stain, striate. 2 streak past. dart, dash, flash, fly, gallop, hurtle, move at speed, rush, inf scoot, speed, sprint, tear, inf whip, zoom.

streaky adj barred, lined, smeary, smudged, streaked, striated, stripy, veined.

stream n 1 beck, brook, brooklet, burn, channel, freshet, poet rill, river, rivulet, streamlet, watercourse. 2 cascade, cataract, current, deluge, effluence, flood, flow, fountain, gush, jet, outpouring, rush, spate, spurt, surge, tide, torrent. ● vb cascade, course, deluge, flood, flow, gush, issue, pour, run, spill, spout, spurt, squirt, surge, well.

streamer n banner, flag, pennant, pennon, ribbon.

streamlined adj 1 aerodynamic, elegant, graceful, hydrodynamic, sleek, smooth. 2 ▷ EFFICIENT.

street n avenue, roadway, terrace. ▷ ROAD.

strength n 1 brawn, capacity, condition, energy, fitness, force, health, might, muscle, power, resilience, robustness, sinew, stamina, stoutness, sturdiness, toughness, vigour. 2 strength of purpose. inf backbone, commitment, courage, determination, firmness, inf grit, perseverance, persistence, resolution, resolve, spirit, tenacity. Opp WEAKNESS.

strengthen vb 1 bolster, boost, brace, build up, buttress, encourage, fortify, harden, hearten, increase, make stronger, prop up, reinforce, stiffen, support, tone up, toughen. 2 strengthen an argument. back up, consolidate, corroborate, enhance, justify, substantiate. Opp WEAKEN.

strenuous adj 1 arduous, backbreaking, burdensome, demanding, difficult, exhausting, gruelling, hard, laborious, punishing, stiff, taxing, tough, uphill. Opp EASY. 2 strenuous efforts. active, committed, determined, dogged, dynamic, eager, energetic, herculean, indefatigable, laborious, pertinacious, resolute, spirited, strong, tenacious, tireless, unremitting, vigorous, zealous. Opp CASUAL.

stress n 1 anxiety, difficulty, distress, hardship, pressure, strain, tenseness, tension, trauma, worry. 2 accent, accentuation, beat, emphasis, importance, significance, underlining, urgency, weight. ● vb 1 accent, accentuate, assert, draw attention to, emphasize, feature, highlight, insist on, lay stress on, mark, put stress on, repeat, spotlight, underline, underscore. 2 stressed by work. burden, distress, overstretch, pressure, pressurize, push to the limit, tax, weigh down.

stressful adj anxious, difficult, taxing, tense, tiring, traumatic, worrying. Opp RELAXED.

stretch n 1 period, spell, stint, term, time, tour of duty. 2 stretch of country. area, distance, expanse, length, span, spread, sweep, tract. ● vb 1 broaden, crane (your neck), dilate, distend, draw out, elongate, enlarge, expand, extend, flatten out, inflate, lengthen, open out, pull out, spread out, swell, tauten, tighten, widen. **2** *stretch into the distance.* be unbroken, continue, disappear, extend, go, reach out, spread. **3** *stretch resources.* overextend, overtax, *inf* push to the limit, strain, tax.

strew *vb* disperse, distribute, scatter, spread, sprinkle.

strict *adj* **1** austere, authoritarian, autocratic, firm, harsh, merciless, *inf* no-nonsense, rigorous, severe, stern, stringent, tyrannical, uncompromising. *Opp* EASYGOING. **2** *strict rules.* absolute, binding, defined, *inf* hard and fast, inflexible, invariable, precise, rigid, stringent, tight, unchangeable. *Opp* FLEXIBLE. **3** *strict truthfulness.* accurate, complete, correct, exact, meticulous, perfect, precise, right, scrupulous.

stride *n* pace, step. ● *vb* ▷ WALK.

strident *adj* clamorous, discordant, grating, harsh, jarring, loud, noisy, raucous, screeching, shrill, unmusical. *Opp* SOFT.

strife *n* animosity, arguing, bickering, competition, conflict, discord, disharmony, dissension, enmity, friction, hostility, quarrelling, rivalry, unfriendliness. ▷ FIGHT. *Opp* COOPERATION.

strike *n* **1** go-slow, industrial action, stoppage, walk-out, withdrawal of labour. **2** assault, attack, bombardment. ● *vb* **1** bang against, bang into, beat, collide with, hammer, impel, knock, rap, run into, smack, smash into, *inf* thump, *inf* whack. ▷ ATTACK, HIT. **2** *strike a match.* ignite, light. **3** *tragedy struck us forcibly.* affect, afflict, *inf* come home to, impress, influence. **4** *clock struck one.* chime, ring, sound. **5** *strike for more pay. inf* come out, *inf* down tools, stop work, take industrial action, withdraw labour, work to rule. **6** *strike a flag, tent.* dismantle, lower, pull down, remove, take down.

striking *adj* affecting, amazing, arresting, conspicuous, distinctive, extraordinary, glaring, imposing, impressive, memorable, noticeable, obvious, out-of-the-ordinary, outstanding, prominent, showy, stunning, telling, unmistakable, unusual. *Opp* INCONSPICUOUS.

string *n* **1** cable, cord, fibre, line, rope, twine. **2** chain, file, line, procession, progression, queue, row, sequence, series, stream, succession, train. ● *vb string together* connect, join, line up, link, thread. **stringed instruments** strings. □ banjo, cello, clavichord, double-bass, *inf* fiddle, guitar, harp, harpsichord, lute, lyre, piano, sitar, spinet, ukulele, viola, violin, zither.

stringy *adj* chewy, fibrous, gristly, sinewy, tough. *Opp* TENDER.

strip *n* band, belt, fillet, lath, line, narrow piece, ribbon, shred, slat, sliver, stripe, swathe. ● *vb* **1** bare, clear, decorticate, defoliate, denude, divest, *old use* doff, excoriate, flay, lay bare, peel, remove the covering, remove the paint, remove the skin, skin, uncover. *Opp* COVER. **2** *strip to the waist.* bare yourself, disrobe, expose yourself, get undressed, uncover yourself. *Opp* DRESS. **strip down** ▷ DISMANTLE. **strip off** ▷ UNDRESS.

stripe *n* band, bar, chevron, line, ribbon, streak, striation, strip, stroke, swathe.

striped *adj* banded, barred, lined, streaky, striated, stripy.

strive *vb* attempt, *inf* do your best, endeavour, make an effort, strain, struggle, try. ▷ FIGHT.

stroke *n* **1** action, blow, effort, knock, move, swipe. ▷ HIT. **2** *a stroke of the pen.* flourish, gesture, line, mark, movement, sweep. **3** [medical] apoplexy, attack, embolism, fit, seizure, spasm, thrombosis. ● *vb* caress, fondle, massage, pass your hand over, pat, pet, rub, soothe, touch.

stroll *n, vb* amble, meander, saunter, wander. ▷ WALK.

strong *adj* **1** durable, hard, hardwearing, heavy-duty, impregnable, indestructible, permanent, reinforced, resilient, robust, sound, stout, substantial, thick, unbreakable, well-made. **2** *strong physique*. athletic, *inf* beefy, *inf* brawny, burly, fit, *inf* hale and hearty, hardy, *inf* hefty, *inf* husky, mighty, muscular, powerful, robust, sinewy, stalwart, *inf* strapping, sturdy, tough, well-built, wiry. **3** *strong personality*. assertive, committed, determined, domineering, dynamic, energetic, forceful, independent, reliable, resolute, stalwart, steadfast, *inf* stout, strong-minded, strong-willed, tenacious, vigorous. ▷ STUBBORN. **4** *strong commitment*. active, assiduous, deep-rooted, deep-seated, *derog* doctrinaire, *derog* dogmatic, eager, earnest, enthusiastic, fervent, fierce, firm, genuine, intense, keen, loyal, passionate, positive, rabid, sedulous, staunch, true, vehement, zealous. **5** *strong government*. decisive, dependable, *derog* dictatorial, fearless, *derog* tyrannical, unswerving, unwavering. **6** *strong measures*. aggressive, draconian, drastic, extreme, harsh, high-handed, ruthless, severe, tough, unflinching, violent. **7** *a strong army*. formidable, invincible, large, numerous, powerful, unconquerable, well-armed, well-equipped, well-trained. **8** *strong colour, light*. bright, brilliant, clear, dazzling, garish, glaring, vivid. **9** *strong taste, smell*. concentrated, highly-flavoured, hot, intense, noticeable, obvious, overpowering, prominent, pronounced, pungent, sharp, spicy, unmistakable. **10** *strong evidence*. clear-cut, cogent, compelling, convincing, evident, influential, persuasive, plain, solid, telling, undisputed. **11** *strong drink*. alcoholic, concentrated, intoxicating, potent, undiluted. *Opp* WEAK.

stronghold *n* bastion, bulwark, castle, citadel, *old use* fastness, fort, fortification, fortress, garrison.

structure *n* **1** arrangement, composition, configuration, constitution, design, form, formation, *inf* make-up, order, organization, plan, shape, system. **2** complex, construction, edifice, erection, fabric, framework, pile, superstructure. ▷ BUILDING.
● *vb* arrange, build, construct,

design, form, frame, give structure to, organize, shape, systematize.

struggle *n* **1** challenge, difficulty, effort, endeavour, exertion, labour, problem. **2** ▷ FIGHT. ● *vb* **1** endeavour, exert yourself, labour, make an effort, move violently, strain, strive, toil, try, work hard, wrestle, wriggle about, writhe about. **2** *struggle through mud*. flail, flounder, stumble, wallow. **3** ▷ FIGHT.

stub *n* butt, end, remains, remnant, stump. ● *vb* ▷ HIT.

stubble *n* **1** stalks, straw. **2** beard, bristles, *inf* five-o'clock shadow, hair, roughness.

stubbly *adj* bristly, prickly, rough, unshaven.

stubborn *adj* defiant, determined, difficult, disobedient, dogged, dogmatic, headstrong, inflexible, intractable, intransigent, mulish, obdurate, obstinate, opinionated, persistent, pertinacious, *inf* pig-headed, recalcitrant, refractory, rigid, self-willed, tenacious, uncompromising, uncontrollable, uncooperative, unmanageable, unreasonable, unyielding, wayward, wilful. *Opp* AMENABLE.

stuck *adj* **1** bogged down, cemented, fast, fastened, firm, fixed, glued, immovable. **2** *stuck on a problem*. baffled, beaten, held up, *inf* stumped, *inf* stymied.

stuck-up *adj* arrogant, *inf* big-headed, bumptious, *inf* cocky, conceited, condescending, *inf* high-and-mighty, patronizing, proud, self-important, snobbish, *inf* snooty, supercilious, *inf* toffee-nosed. *Opp* MODEST.

student *n* apprentice, disciple, learner, postgraduate, pupil, scholar, schoolchild, trainee, undergraduate.

studied *adj* calculated, conscious, contrived, deliberate, intentional, planned, premeditated.

studious *adj* academic, assiduous, attentive, bookish, brainy, earnest, hard-working, intellectual, scholarly, serious-minded, thoughtful.

study vb **1** analyse, consider, contemplate, enquire into, examine, give attention to, investigate, learn about, look closely at, peruse, ponder, pore over, read carefully, research, scrutinize, survey, think about, weigh. **2** *study for exams. inf* cram, learn, *inf* mug up, read, *inf* swot, work.

stuff n **1** ingredients, matter, substance. **2** fabric, material, textile. ▷ CLOTH. **3** *all sorts of stuff.* accoutrements, articles, belongings, *inf* bits and pieces, *inf* clobber, effects, *inf* gear, impedimenta, junk, objects, *inf* paraphernalia, possessions, *inf* tackle, things. ● vb **1** compress, cram, crowd, force, jam, pack, press, push, ram, shove, squeeze, stow, thrust, tuck. **2** *stuff a cushion.* fill, line, pad. **stuff yourself** ▷ EAT.

stuffing n **1** filling, lining, padding, quilting, wadding. **2** *stuffing in poultry.* forcemeat, seasoning.

stuffy adj **1** airless, close, fetid, fuggy, fusty, heavy, humid, muggy, musty, oppressive, stale, steamy, stifling, suffocating, sultry, unventilated, warm. *Opp* AIRY. **2** [*inf*] *a stuffy old bore.* boring, conventional, dreary, dull, formal, humourless, narrow-minded, old-fashioned, pompous, prim, staid, *inf* stodgy, strait-laced. *Opp* LIVELY.

stumble vb **1** blunder, flounder, lurch, miss your footing, reel, slip, stagger, totter, trip, tumble. ▷ WALK. **2** *stumble in speech.* become tongue-tied, falter, hesitate, pause, stammer, stutter.

stumbling-block n bar, difficulty, hindrance, hurdle, impediment, obstacle, snag.

stump vb baffle, bewilder, *inf* catch out, confound, confuse, defeat, *inf* flummox, mystify, outwit, perplex, puzzle, *inf* stymie. **stump up** ▷ PAY.

stun vb **1** daze, knock out, knock senseless, make unconscious. **2** amaze, astonish, astound, bewilder, confound, confuse, dumbfound, flabbergast, numb, shock, stagger,

stupefy. **stunning** ▷ BEAUTIFUL, STUPENDOUS.

stunt n *inf* dare, exploit, feat, trick. ● vb stunt growth. ▷ CHECK.

stupendous adj amazing, colossal, enormous, exceptional, extraordinary, huge, incredible, marvellous, miraculous, notable, phenomenal, prodigious, remarkable, *inf* sensational, singular, special, staggering, stunning, tremendous, unbelievable, wonderful. *Opp* ORDINARY.

stupid adj [*Most synonyms derog*] **1** addled, bird-brained, bone-headed, bovine, brainless, clueless, cretinous, dense, dim, doltish, dopey, drippy, dull, dumb, empty-headed, featherbrained, feeble-minded, foolish, gormless, half-witted, idiotic, ignorant, imbecilic, imperceptive, ineducable, lacking, lumpish, mindless, moronic, naïve, obtuse, puerile, senseless, silly, simple, simpleminded, slow, slow in the uptake, slowwitted, subnormal, thick, thickheaded, thick-skulled, thickwitted, unintelligent, unthinking, unwise, vacuous, weak in the head, witless. **2** *a stupid thing to do.* absurd, asinine, barmy, crack-brained, crass, crazy, fatuous, feeble, futile, half-baked, hare-brained, ill-advised, inane, irrational, irrelevant, irresponsible, laughable, ludicrous, lunatic, mad, nonsensical, pointless, rash, reckless, ridiculous, risible, scatterbrained, thoughtless, unjustifiable. **3** *stupid after a knock on the head.* dazed, in a stupor, semi-conscious, sluggish, stunned, stupefied. *Opp* INTELLIGENT. **stupid person** ▷ FOOL.

stupidity n absurdity, crassness, denseness, dullness, *inf* dumbness, fatuity, fatuousness, folly, foolishness, futility, idiocy, ignorance, imbecility, inanity, lack of intelligence, lunacy, madness, mindlessness, naïvety, pointlessness, recklessness, silliness, slowness, thoughtlessness. *Opp* INTELLIGENCE.

stupor n coma, daze, inertia, lassitude, lethargy, numbness, shock, state of insensibility, torpor, trance, unconsciousness.

sturdy adj **1** athletic, brawny, burly, hardy, healthy, hefty, husky, muscular, powerful, robust, stalwart, stocky, inf strapping, vigorous, well-built. **2** sturdy shoes, etc. durable, solid, sound, substantial, tough, well-made. **3** sturdy opposition. determined, firm, indomitable, resolute, staunch, steadfast, uncompromising, vigorous. ▷ STRONG. Opp WEAK.

stutter vb stammer, stumble. ▷ TALK.

style n **1** dash, elegance, flair, flamboyance, panache, polish, refinement, smartness, sophistication, stylishness, taste. **2** not my style. approach, character, custom, habit, idiosyncrasy, manner, method, way. **3** style in writing. diction, mode, phraseology, phrasing, register, sentence structure, tenor, tone, wording. **4** style in clothes. chic, cut, design, dress-sense, fashion, look, mode, pattern, shape, tailoring, type, vogue.

stylish adj Fr à la mode, chic, inf classy, contemporary, inf dapper, elegant, fashionable, modern, modish, inf natty, inf posh, smart, inf snazzy, sophisticated, inf trendy, up-to-date. Opp OLD-FASHIONED.

subconscious adj deep-rooted, hidden, inner, intuitive, latent, repressed, subliminal, suppressed, unacknowledged, unconscious. Opp CONSCIOUS.

subdue vb check, curb, hold back, keep under, moderate, quieten, repress, restrain, suppress, temper. ▷ SUBJUGATE.

subdued adj **1** chastened, crestfallen, depressed, downcast, grave, reflective, repressed, restrained, serious, silent, sober, solemn, thoughtful. ▷ SAD. Opp EXCITED. **2** subdued music. calm, hushed, low, mellow, muted, peaceful, placid, quiet, soft, soothing, toned down, tranquil, unobtrusive.

subject adj **1** captive, dependent, enslaved, oppressed, ruled, subjugated. **2** subject to interference. exposed, liable, prone, susceptible, vulnerable. Opp FREE. ● n **1** citizen, dependant, national, passport-holder, taxpayer, voter. **2** subject for discussion. affair, business, issue, matter, point, proposition, question, theme, thesis, topic. **3** subject of study. area, branch of knowledge, course, discipline, field. □ anatomy, archaeology, architecture, art, astronomy, biology, business, chemistry, computing, craft, design, divinity, domestic science, drama, economics, education, electronics, engineering, English, environmental science, ethnology, etymology, geography, geology, heraldry, history, languages, Latin, law, linguistics, literature, mathematics, mechanics, medicine, metallurgy, metaphysics, meteorology, music, natural history, oceanography, ornithology, penology, pharmacology, pharmacy, philology, philosophy, photography, physics, physiology, politics, psychology, religious studies, science, scripture, social work, sociology, sport, surveying, technology, theology, topology, zoology. ● vb **1** subject a thing to scrutiny. expose, lay open, submit. **2** ▷ SUBJUGATE.

subjective adj biased, emotional, inf gut (reaction), idiosyncratic, individual, instinctive, intuitive, personal, prejudiced, self-centred. Opp OBJECTIVE.

subjugate vb beat, conquer, control, crush, defeat, dominate, enslave, enthral, inf get the better of, master, oppress, overcome, overpower, overrun, put down, quash, quell, subdue, subject, tame, triumph over, vanquish.

sublimate vb channel, convert, divert, idealize, purify, redirect, refine.

sublime adj ecstatic, elated, elevated, exalted, great, heavenly, high, high-minded, lofty, noble, spiritual, transcendent. Opp BASE.

submerge vb **1** cover with water, dip, drench, drown, inf dunk, engulf, flood, immerse, inundate, overwhelm, soak, swamp. **2** dive, go down, go under, plummet, sink, subside.

submission n 1 acquiescence, capitulation, compliance, giving in, surrender, yielding. ▷ SUBMISSIVENESS. 2 contribution, entry, offering, presentation, tender. 3 *a legal submission.* argument, claim, contention, idea, proposal, suggestion, theory.

submissive adj accommodating, acquiescent, amenable, biddable, *derog* boot-licking, compliant, deferential, docile, humble, meek, obedient, obsequious, passive, pliant, resigned, servile, slavish, supine, sycophantic, tame, tractable, unassertive, uncomplaining, unresisting, weak, yielding. *Opp* ASSERTIVE.

submissiveness n acquiescence, assent, compliance, deference, docility, humility, meekness, obedience, obsequiousness, passivity, resignation, servility, submission, subservience, tameness.

submit vb 1 accede, bow, capitulate, concede, give in, *inf* knuckle under, succumb, surrender, yield. 2 *submit a proposal.* advance, enter, give in, hand in, offer, present, proffer, propose, propound, put forward, state, suggest. **submit to** ▷ ACCEPT, OBEY.

subordinate adj inferior, junior, lesser, lower, menial, minor, secondary, subservient, subsidiary. ● n aide, assistant, dependant, employee, inferior, junior, menial, *inf* underling. ▷ SERVANT.

subscribe vb **subscribe to** 1 contribute to, covenant to, donate to, give to, patronize, sponsor, support. 2 *subscribe to a magazine.* be a subscriber to, buy regularly, pay a subscription to. 3 *subscribe to a theory.* advocate, agree with, approve of, *inf* back, believe in, condone, consent to, endorse, *inf* give your blessing to.

subscriber n patron, regular customer, sponsor, supporter.

subscription n due, fee, payment, regular contribution, remittance.

subsequent adj coming, consequent, ensuing, following, future, later, next, resultant, resulting, succeeding, successive. *Opp* PREVIOUS.

subside vb 1 abate, calm down, decline, decrease, die down, diminish, dwindle, ebb, fall, go down, lessen, melt away, moderate, quieten, recede, shrink, slacken, wear off. 2 *subside into a chair.* collapse, descend, lower yourself, settle, sink. *Opp* RISE.

subsidiary adj additional, ancillary, auxiliary, complementary, contributory, inferior, lesser, minor, secondary, subordinate, supporting.

subsidize vb aid, back, finance, fund, give subsidy to, maintain, promote, sponsor, support, underwrite.

subsidy n aid, backing, financial help, funding, grant, maintenance, sponsorship, subvention, support.

substance n 1 actuality, body, concreteness, corporeality, reality, solidity. 2 chemical, fabric, make-up, material, matter, stuff. 3 *substance of an argument.* core, essence, gist, import, meaning, significance, subject-matter, theme. 4 *[old use] a person of substance.* ▷ WEALTH.

substandard adj *inf* below par, disappointing, inadequate, inferior, poor, shoddy, unworthy.

substantial adj 1 durable, hefty, massive, solid, sound, stout, strong, sturdy, well-built, well-made. 2 big, consequential, considerable, generous, great, large, significant, sizeable, worthwhile. *Opp* FLIMSY, SMALL.

substitute adj 1 acting, deputy, relief, reserve, stand-by, surrogate, temporary. 2 alternative, ersatz, imitation. ● n alternative, deputy, locum, proxy, relief, replacement, reserve, stand-in, stopgap, substitution, supply, surrogate, understudy. ● vb 1 change, exchange, interchange, replace, *inf* swop, *inf* switch. 2 *substitute for an absentee.* act as a substitute, cover, deputize, double, stand in, supplant, take the place of, take over the role of, understudy.

subtle adj 1 delicate, elusive, faint, fine, gentle, mild, slight, unobtrusive. 2 *subtle argument.* arcane, clever, indirect, ingenious, mysterious, recondite, refined, shrewd, sophisticated, tactful, understated. ▷ CUNNING. *Opp* OBVIOUS.

subtract *vb* debit, deduct, remove, take away, take off. *Opp* ADD.

suburban *adj* outer, outlying, residential.

suburbs *n* fringes, outer areas, outskirts, residential areas, suburbia.

subversive *adj* challenging, disruptive, insurrectionary, questioning, radical, seditious, traitorous, treacherous, treasonous, undermining, unsettling. ▷ REVOLUTIONARY. *Opp* CONSERVATIVE, ORTHODOX.

subvert *vb* challenge, corrupt, destroy, disrupt, overthrow, overturn, pervert, ruin, undermine, upset, wreck.

subway *n* tunnel, underpass.

succeed *vb* **1** accomplish your objective, *inf* arrive, be a success, do well, flourish, *inf* get on, *inf* get to the top, *inf* make it, prosper, thrive. **2** be effective, *inf* catch on, produce results, work. **3** be successor to, come after, follow, inherit from, replace, take over from. *Opp* FAIL. **succeeding** ▷ SUBSEQUENT.

success *n* **1** fame, good fortune, prosperity, wealth. **2** *success of a plan.* accomplishment, achievement, attainment, completion, effectiveness, successful outcome. **3** *a great success.* *inf* hit, *inf* sensation, triumph, victory, *inf* winner. *Opp* FAILURE.

successful *adj* **1** booming, effective, effectual, flourishing, fruitful, lucrative, money-making, productive, profitable, profit-making, prosperous, rewarding, thriving, useful, well-off. **2** best-selling, celebrated, famed, famous, high-earning, leading, popular, top, unbeaten, victorious, well-known, winning. *Opp* UNSUCCESSFUL.

succession *n* chain, flow, line, procession, progression, run, sequence, series, string.

successive *adj* consecutive, continuous, in succession, succeeding, unbroken, uninterrupted.

successor *n* heir, inheritor, replacement.

succinct *adj* brief, compact, concise, condensed, epigrammatic, pithy, short, terse, to the point. *Opp* WORDY.

succulent *adj* fleshy, juicy, luscious, moist, mouthwatering, palatable, rich.

succumb *vb* accede, be overcome, capitulate, give in, give up, give way, submit, surrender, yield. *Opp* SURVIVE.

suck *vb* **suck up** absorb, draw up, pull up, soak up. **suck up to** ▷ FLATTER.

sudden *adj* **1** abrupt, brisk, hasty, hurried, impetuous, impulsive, precipitate, quick, rash, *inf* snap, swift, unconsidered, unplanned, unpremeditated. *Opp* SLOW. **2** *a sudden shock.* acute, sharp, startling, surprising, unannounced, unexpected, unforeseeable, unforeseen, unlooked-for. *Opp* PREDICTABLE.

suds *n* bubbles, foam, froth, lather, soapsuds.

sue *vb* **1** indict, institute legal proceedings against, proceed against, prosecute, summons, take legal action against. **2** *sue for peace.* ▷ ENTREAT.

suffer *vb* **1** bear, cope with, endure, experience, feel, go through, live through, *inf* put up with, stand, tolerate, undergo, withstand. **2** *suffer from a wound.* ache, agonize, feel pain, hurt, smart. **3** *suffer for a crime.* atone, be punished, make amends, pay.

suffice *vb* answer, be sufficient, *inf* do, satisfy, serve.

sufficient *adj* adequate, enough, satisfactory. *Opp* INSUFFICIENT.

suffocate *vb* asphyxiate, choke, smother, stifle, stop breathing, strangle, throttle.

sugar *n* □ *brown sugar, cane sugar, caster sugar, demerara, glucose, granulated sugar, icing sugar, lump sugar, molasses, sucrose, sweets, syrup, treacle.* ● *vb* sweeten.

sugary adj **1** glazed, iced, sugared, sweetened. ▷ SWEET. **2** sugary sentiments. cloying, honeyed, sickly. ▷ SENTIMENTAL.

suggest vb **1** advise, advocate, counsel, moot, move, propose, propound, put forward, raise, recommend, urge. **2** call to mind, communicate, hint, imply, indicate, insinuate, intimate, make you think (of), mean, signal.

suggestion n **1** advice, counsel, offer, plan, prompting, proposal, recommendation, urging. **2** breath, hint, idea, indication, intimation, notion, suspicion, touch, trace.

suggestive adj **1** evocative, expressive, indicative, reminiscent, thought-provoking. **2** ▷ INDECENT.

suicidal adj **1** hopeless, inf kamikaze, self-destructive. **2** ▷ DESOLATE.

suit n outfit. ▷ CLOTHES. ● vb **1** accommodate, be suitable for, conform to, fill your needs, fit in with, gratify, harmonize with, match, please, satisfy, tally with. Opp DISPLEASE. **2** That colour suits you. become, fit, look good on.

suitable adj acceptable, applicable, apposite, appropriate, apt, becoming, befitting, congenial, convenient, correct, decent, decorous, fit, fitting, handy, old use meet, opportune, pertinent, proper, relevant, right, satisfactory, seemly, tasteful, timely, well-chosen, well-judged, well-timed. Opp UNSUITABLE.

sulk vb be sullen, brood, mope, pout.

sullen adj **1** antisocial, bad-tempered, brooding, churlish, crabby, cross, disgruntled, dour, glum, grim, grudging, ill-humoured, lugubrious, moody, morose, inf out of sorts, petulant, pouting, resentful, silent, sour, stubborn, sulking, sulky, surly, uncommunicative, unforgiving, unfriendly, unhappy, unsociable. ▷ SAD. **2** a sullen sky. cheerless, dark, dismal, dull, gloomy, grey, leaden, sombre. Opp CHEERFUL.

sultry adj **1** close, hot, humid, inf muggy, oppressive, steamy, stifling, stuffy, warm. Opp COLD. **2** sultry beauty. erotic, mysterious, passionate, provocative, seductive, sensual, sexy, voluptuous.

sum n aggregate, amount, number, quantity, reckoning, result, score, tally, total, whole. ● vb **sum up** ▷ SUMMARIZE.

summarize vb abridge, condense, digest, encapsulate, give the gist, make a summary, outline, précis, inf recap, recapitulate, reduce, review, shorten, simplify, sum up. Opp ELABORATE.

summary n abridgement, abstract, condensation, digest, epitome, gist, outline, précis, recapitulation, reduction, résumé, review, summation, summing-up, synopsis.

summery adj bright, sunny, tropical, warm. ▷ HOT. Opp WINTRY.

summit n **1** apex, crown, head, height, peak, pinnacle, point, top. Opp BASE. **2** summit of success. acme, apogee, climax, culmination, high point, zenith. Opp NADIR.

summon vb **1** command, demand, invite, order, send for, subpoena. **2** assemble, call, convene, convoke, gather together, muster, rally.

sunbathe vb bake, bask, inf get a tan, sun yourself, tan.

sunburnt adj blistered, bronzed, brown, peeling, tanned, weatherbeaten.

sundry adj assorted, different, old use divers, miscellaneous, mixed, various.

sunken adj **1** submerged, underwater, wrecked. **2** sunken cheeks. concave, depressed, drawn, hollow, hollowed.

sunless adj cheerless, cloudy, dark, dismal, dreary, dull, gloomy, grey, overcast, sombre. Opp SUNNY.

sunlight n daylight, sun, sunbeams, sunshine.

sunny adj **1** bright, clear, cloudless, fair, fine, summery, sunlit, sunshiny, unclouded. Opp SUNLESS. **2** ▷ CHEERFUL.

sunrise n dawn, daybreak.

sunset n dusk, evening, gloaming, nightfall, sundown, twilight.

sunshade n awning, canopy, parasol.

superannuated adj **1** discharged, inf pensioned off, inf put out to grass, old, retired. **2** discarded, disused, obsolete, thrown out, worn out. ▷ OLD.

superannuation n annuity, pension.

superb adj admirable, excellent, fine, first-class, first-rate, grand, impressive, marvellous, superior. ▷ SPLENDID. Opp INFERIOR.

superficial adj **1** cosmetic, external, exterior, on the surface, outward, shallow, skin-deep, slight, surface, unimportant. **2** careless, casual, cursory, desultory, facile, frivolous, hasty, hurried, inattentive, lightweight, inf nodding (*acquaintance*), oversimplified, passing, perfunctory, simple-minded, simplistic, sweeping (*generalization*), trivial, unconvincing, uncritical, undiscriminating, unquestioning, unscholarly, unsophisticated. Opp ANALYTICAL, DEEP.

superfluous adj excess, excessive, extra, needless, redundant, spare, superabundant, surplus, unnecessary, unneeded, unwanted. Opp NECESSARY.

superhuman adj **1** god-like, herculean, heroic, phenomenal, prodigious. **2** *superhuman powers.* divine, higher, metaphysical, supernatural.

superimpose vb overlay, place on top of.

superintend vb administer, be in charge of, be the supervisor of, conduct, control, direct, look after, manage, organize, oversee, preside over, run, supervise, watch over.

superior adj **1** better, inf classier, greater, higher, higher-born, loftier, more important, more impressive, nobler, senior, inf up-market. **2** *superior quality.* choice, exclusive, fine, first-class, first-rate, select, top, unrivalled. **3** *superior attitude.* arrogant, condescending, contemptuous, disdainful, élitist, haughty, inf high-and-mighty, lofty, paternalistic, patronizing, self-important, smug, snobbish, inf snooty, stuck-up, supercilious. Opp INFERIOR.

superlative adj best, choicest, consummate, excellent, finest, first-rate, incomparable, matchless, peerless, inf tip-top, inf top-notch, unrivalled, unsurpassed. ▷ SUPREME.

supernatural adj abnormal, ghostly, inexplicable, magical, metaphysical, miraculous, mysterious, mystic, occult, other-worldly, paranormal, preternatural, psychic, spiritual, uncanny, unearthly, unnatural, weird.

superstition n delusion, illusion, myth, inf old wives' tale, superstitious belief.

superstitious adj credulous, groundless, illusory, irrational, mythical, traditional, unfounded, unprovable.

supervise vb administer, be in charge of, be the supervisor of, conduct, control, direct, govern, invigilate (*an exam*), inf keep an eye on, lead, look after, manage, organize, oversee, preside over, run, superintend, watch over.

supervision n administration, conduct, control, direction, government, invigilation, management, organization, oversight, running, surveillance.

supervisor n administrator, chief, controller, director, executive, foreman, inf gaffer, head, inspector, invigilator, leader, manager, organizer, overseer, superintendent, timekeeper.

supine adj **1** face upwards, flat on your back, prostrate, recumbent. Opp PRONE. **2** ▷ PASSIVE.

supplant vb displace, dispossess, eject, expel, oust, replace, inf step into the shoes of, supersede, inf topple, unseat.

supple adj bending, inf bendy, elastic, flexible, flexile, graceful, limber, lithe, plastic, pliable, pliant, resilient, soft. *Opp* RIGID.

supplement *n* **1** additional payment, excess, surcharge. **2** *a newspaper supplement, etc.* addendum, addition, annexe, appendix, codicil, continuation, endpiece, extra, insert, postscript, sequel. • *vb* add to, augment, boost, complement, extend, reinforce, *inf* top up.

supplementary *adj* accompanying, added, additional, ancillary, auxiliary, complementary, excess, extra, new, supportive.

supplication *n* appeal, entreaty, petition, plea, prayer, request, solicitation.

supplier *n* dealer, provider, purveyor, retailer, seller, shopkeeper, vendor, wholesaler.

supply *n* **1** cache, hoard, quantity, reserve, reservoir, stock, stockpile, store. **2** equipment, food, necessities, provisions, rations, shopping. **3** *a regular supply.* delivery, distribution, provision, provisioning. • *vb* cater to, contribute, deliver, distribute, donate, endow, equip, feed, furnish, give, hand over, pass on, produce, provide, purvey, sell, stock.

support *n* **1** aid, approval, assistance, backing, back-up, bolstering, contribution, cooperation, donation, encouragement, fortifying, friendship, help, interest, loyalty, patronage, protection, reassurance, reinforcement, sponsorship, succour. **2** brace, bracket, buttress, crutch, foundation, frame, pillar, post, prop, sling, stanchion, stay, strut, substructure, trestle, truss, underpinning. **3** *financial support.* expenses, funding, keep, maintenance, subsistence, upkeep. • *vb* **1** bear, bolster, buoy up, buttress, carry, give strength to, hold up, keep up, prop up, provide a support for, reinforce, shore up, strengthen, underlie, underpin. **2** *support someone in trouble.* aid, assist, back, be faithful to, champion, comfort, defend, encourage, favour, fight for, give support to, help, rally round, reassure, side with,

speak up for, stand by, stand up for, stay with, *inf* stick up for, *inf* stick with, take someone's part. **3** *support a family.* bring up, feed, finance, fund, keep, look after, maintain, nourish, provide for, sustain. **4** *support a charity.* be a supporter of, be interested in, contribute to, espouse (*a cause*), follow, give to, patronize, pay money to, sponsor, subsidize, work for. **5** *support a point of view.* accept, adhere to, advocate, agree with, allow, approve, argue for, confirm, corroborate, defend, endorse, explain, justify, promote, ratify, substantiate, uphold, validate, verify. *Opp* SUBVERT, WEAKEN. **support yourself** lean, rest.

supporter *n* **1** adherent, admirer, advocate, aficionado, apologist, champion, defender, devotee, enthusiast, *inf* fan, fanatic, follower, seconder, upholder, voter. **2** ally, assistant, collaborator, helper, henchman, second.

supportive *adj* caring, concerned, encouraging, favourable, heartening, helpful, interested, kind, loyal, positive, reassuring, sustaining, sympathetic, understanding. *Opp* SUBVERSIVE.

suppose *vb* **1** accept, assume, believe, conclude, conjecture, expect, guess, infer, judge, postulate, presume, presuppose, speculate, surmise, suspect, take for granted, think. **2** daydream, fancy, fantasize, hypothesize, imagine, maintain, postulate, pretend, theorize. **supposed** ▷ HYPOTHETICAL, PUTATIVE. **supposed to** due to, expected to, having a duty to, meant to, required to.

supposition *n* assumption, belief, conjecture, fancy, guess, *inf* guesstimate, hypothesis, inference, notion, opinion, presumption, speculation, surmise, theory, thought.

suppress *vb* **1** conquer, *inf* crack down on, crush, end, finish off, halt, overcome, overthrow, put an end to, put down, quash, quell, stamp out, stop, subdue. **2** *suppress emotion.* bottle up, censor, choke back, conceal, cover up, hide, hush up, keep quiet about, keep secret, muffle, mute, obstruct, prohibit, repress, restrain, silence, smother, stamp on, stifle, strangle.

supremacy n ascendancy, dominance, domination, dominion, lead, mastery, predominance, preeminence, sovereignty, superiority.

supreme adj best, choicest, consummate, crowning, culminating, excellent, finest, first-rate, greatest, highest, incomparable, matchless, outstanding, paramount, peerless, predominant, pre-eminent, prime, principal, superlative, surpassing, inf tip-top, top, inf top-notch, ultimate, unbeatable, unbeaten, unparalleled, unrivalled, unsurpassable, unsurpassed.

sure adj **1** assured, certain, confident, convinced, decided, definite, persuaded, positive. **2** sure to come. bound, certain, compelled, obliged, required. **3** a sure fact. accurate, clear, convincing, guaranteed, indisputable, inescapable, inevitable, infallible, proven, reliable, true, unchallenged, undeniable, undisputed, undoubted, verifiable. **4** a sure ally. dependable, effective, established, faithful, firm, infallible, loyal, reliable, resolute, safe, secure, solid, steadfast, steady, trustworthy, trusty, undeviating, unerring, unfailing, unfaltering, unflinching, unswerving, unwavering. Opp UNCERTAIN.

surface n **1** coat, coating, covering, crust, exterior, façade, integument, interface, outside, shell, skin, veneer. **2** cube has six surfaces. face, facet, plane, side. **3** a working surface. bench, table, top, worktop. ● vb **1** appear, arise, inf come to light, come up, inf crop up, emerge, materialize, inf pop up, rise. **2** coat, cover, laminate, veneer.

surfeit n excess, flood, glut, overabundance, overindulgence, oversupply, plethora, superfluity, surplus.

surge n burst, gush, increase, onrush, onset, outpouring, rush, upsurge. ▷ WAVE. ● vb billow, eddy,

flow, gush, heave, make waves, move irresistibly, push, roll, rush, stampede, stream, sweep, swirl, well up.

surgery n **1** biopsy, operation. **2** a doctor's surgery. clinic, consulting room, health centre, infirmary, medical centre, sick-bay.

surly adj bad-tempered, boorish, cantankerous, churlish, crabby, cross, crotchety, inf crusty, curmudgeonly, dyspeptic, gruff, inf grumpy, illnatured, illtempered, irascible, miserable, morose, peevish, rough, rude, sulky, sullen, testy, touchy, uncivil, unfriendly, ungracious, unpleasant. Opp FRIENDLY.

surmise vb assume, believe, conjecture, expect, fancy, gather, guess, hypothesize, imagine, infer, judge, postulate, presume, presuppose, sense, speculate, suppose, suspect, take for granted, think.

surpass vb beat, better, do better than, eclipse, exceed, excel, go beyond, leave behind, inf leave standing, outclass, outdistance, outdo, outperform, outshine, outstrip, overshadow, top, transcend, worst.

surplus n balance, excess, extra, glut, oversupply, remainder, residue, superfluity, surfeit.

surprise n **1** alarm, amazement, astonishment, consternation, dismay, incredulity, stupefaction, wonder. **2** a complete surprise. blow, inf bolt from the blue, inf bombshell, inf eye-opener, jolt, shock. ● vb **1** alarm, amaze, astonish, astound, disconcert, dismay, dumbfound, flabbergast, nonplus, rock, shock, stagger, startle, stun, stupefy, inf take aback, take by surprise, inf throw. **2** surprise someone doing wrong. capture, catch out, inf catch red-handed, come upon, detect, discover, take unawares.

surprised adj alarmed, amazed, astonished, astounded, disconcerted, dismayed, dumbfounded, flabbergasted, incredulous, inf knocked for six, nonplussed, inf shattered, shocked, speechless, staggered, startled, struck dumb, stunned, taken aback, taken by surprise, *inf* thrown, thunderstruck.

surprising *adj* alarming, amazing, astonishing, astounding, disconcerting, extraordinary, frightening, incredible, *inf* off-putting, shocking, staggering, startling, stunning, sudden, unexpected, unforeseen, unlooked-for, unplanned, unpredictable, upsetting. *Opp* PREDICTABLE.

surrender *n* capitulation, giving in, resignation, submission. ● *vb* **1** acquiesce, capitulate, *inf* cave in, collapse, concede, fall, *inf* give in, give up, give way, give yourself up, resign, submit, succumb, *inf* throw in the towel, *inf* throw up the sponge, yield. **2** *surrender your ticket*. deliver up, give up, hand over, part with, relinquish. **3** *surrender your rights*. abandon, cede, renounce, waive.

surreptitious *adj* clandestine, concealed, covert, crafty, disguised, furtive, hidden, private, secret, secretive, shifty, sly, *inf* sneaky, stealthy, underhand. *Opp* BLATANT.

surround *vb* beset, besiege, cocoon, cordon off, encircle, enclose, encompass, engulf, environ, girdle, hedge in, hem in, ring, skirt, trap, wrap.

surrounding *adj* adjacent, adjoining, bordering, local, nearby, neighbouring.

surroundings *plur n* ambience, area, background, context, environment, location, milieu, neighbourhood, setting, vicinity.

surveillance *n* check, observation, reconnaissance, scrutiny, supervision, vigilance, watch.

survey *n* appraisal, assessment, census, count, evaluation, examination, inquiry, inspection, investigation, review, scrutiny, study, triangulation. ● *vb* **1** appraise, assess, estimate, evaluate, examine, inspect, investigate, look over, review, scrutinize, study, view, weigh up. **2** do a survey of, map out, measure, plan out, plot, reconnoitre, triangulate.

survival *n* continuance, continued existence, persistence.

survive *vb* **1** *inf* bear up, carry on, continue, endure, keep going, last, live, persist, remain. **2** *survive disaster*. come through, live through, outlast, outlive, pull through, weather, withstand. *Opp* SUCCUMB.

susceptible *adj* affected (by), disposed, given, inclined, liable, open, predisposed, prone, responsive, sensitive, vulnerable. *Opp* RESISTANT.

suspect *adj* doubtful, dubious, inadequate, questionable, *inf* shady, suspected, suspicious, unconvincing, unreliable, unsatisfactory, untrustworthy. ● *vb* **1** call into question, disbelieve, distrust, doubt, have suspicions about, mistrust. **2** *suspect that she's lying*. believe, conjecture, consider, guess, imagine, infer, presume, speculate, suppose, surmise, think.

suspend *vb* **1** dangle, hang, swing. **2** *suspend work*. adjourn, break off, defer, delay, discontinue, freeze, hold in abeyance, hold up, interrupt, postpone, put off, *inf* put on ice, shelve. **3** *suspend from duty*. debar, dismiss, exclude, expel, lay off, lock out, send down.

suspense *n* anticipation, anxiety, apprehension, doubt, drama, excitement, expectancy, expectation, insecurity, irresolution, nervousness, not knowing, tension, uncertainty, waiting.

suspicion *n* **1** apprehension, apprehensiveness, caution, distrust, doubt, dubiety, dubiousness, *inf* funny feeling, guess, hesitation, *inf* hunch, impression, misgiving, mistrust, presentiment, qualm, scepticism, uncertainty, wariness. **2** *suspicion of a smile*. glimmer, hint, inkling, shadow, suggestion, tinge, touch, trace.

suspicious *adj* **1** apprehensive, *inf* chary, disbelieving, distrustful, doubtful, dubious, incredulous, in doubt, mistrustful, sceptical, uncertain, unconvinced, uneasy, wary. *Opp* TRUSTFUL. **2** *suspicious character*. disreputable, dubious, *inf* fishy, peculiar, questionable, *inf* shady, suspect, suspected, unreliable, untrustworthy. *Opp* TRUSTWORTHY.

sustain *vb* **1** continue, develop, elongate, extend, keep alive, keep going, keep up, maintain, prolong. **2** ▷ SUPPORT.

sustenance *n* eatables, edibles, food, foodstuffs, nourishment, nutriment, provender, provisions, rations, *old use* victuals.

swag *n* booty, loot, plunder, takings.

swagger *vb* parade, strut. ▷ WALK.

swallow *vb* consume, *inf* down, gulp down, guzzle, ingest, take down. ▷ DRINK, EAT. **swallow up** absorb, assimilate, enclose, enfold, make disappear. ▷ SWAMP.

swamp *n* bog, fen, marsh, marshland, morass, mud, mud-flats, quagmire, quicksand, salt-marsh, *old use* slough, wetlands. ● *vb* deluge, drench, engulf, envelop, flood, immerse, inundate, overcome, overwhelm, sink, submerge, swallow up.

swampy *adj* boggy, marshy, muddy, soft, soggy, unstable, waterlogged, wet. *Opp* DRY, FIRM.

swarm *n* cloud, crowd, hive, horde, host, multitude. ▷ GROUP. ● *vb* cluster, congregate, crowd, flock, gather, mass, move in a swarm, throng. **swarm up** ▷ CLIMB. **swarm with** ▷ TEEM.

swarthy *adj* brown, dark, darkcomplexioned, dark-skinned, dusky, tanned.

swashbuckling *adj* adventurous, aggressive, bold, daredevil, daring, dashing, *inf* macho, manly, swaggering. *Opp* TIMID.

sway *vb* **1** bend, fluctuate, lean from side to side, oscillate, rock, roll, swing, undulate, wave. **2** *sway opinions.* affect, bias, bring round, change (someone's mind), convert, convince, govern, influence, persuade, win over. **3** *sway from a chosen path.* divert, go off course, swerve, veer, waver.

swear *vb* **1** affirm, asseverate, attest, aver, avow, declare, give your word, insist, pledge, promise, state on oath, take an oath, testify, vouchsafe, vow. **2** blaspheme, curse, execrate, imprecate, use swearwords, utter profanities.

swear-word *n inf* bad language, blasphemy, curse, execration, expletive, *inf* four-letter word, imprecation, oath, obscenity, profanity, swearing.

sweat *vb* **1** *inf* glow, perspire, swelter. **2** ▷ WORK.

sweaty *adj* clammy, damp, moist, perspiring, sticky, sweating.

sweep *vb* brush, clean, clear, dust, tidy up. **sweep along** ▷ MOVE. **sweep away** ▷ REMOVE. **sweeping** ▷ GENERAL, SUPERFICIAL.

sweet *adj* **1** aromatic, fragrant, honeyed, luscious, mellow, perfumed, sweetened, sweetscented, sweetsmelling. **2** [*derog*] *sickly sweet.* cloying, saccharine, sentimental, sickening, sickly, sugary, syrupy, treacly. **3** *sweet sounds.* dulcet, euphonious, harmonious, heavenly, mellifluous, melodious, musical, pleasant, silvery, soothing, tuneful. **4** *a sweet nature.* affectionate, amiable, attractive, charming, dear, endearing, engaging, friendly, genial, gentle, gracious, lovable, lovely, nice, pretty, unselfish, winning. *Opp* ACID, BITTER, NASTY, SAVOURY. ● *n* **1** *inf* afters, dessert, pudding. **2** [*usu plur*] *old use* bon-bons, *Amer* candy, confectionery, *inf* sweeties, *old use* sweetmeats. □ *acid drop, barley sugar, boiled sweet, bull's-eye, butterscotch, candy, candyfloss, caramel, chewing-gum, chocolate, fondant, fruit pastille, fudge, humbug, liquorice, lollipop, marshmallow, marzipan, mint, nougat, peppermint, rock, toffee, Turkish delight.*

sweeten *vb* **1** make sweeter, sugar. **2** *sweeten your temper.* appease, assuage, calm, mellow, mollify, pacify, soothe.

sweetener *n* □ *artificial sweetener, honey, saccharine, sugar, sweetening, syrup.*

swell *vb* **1** balloon, become bigger, belly, billow, blow up, bulge, dilate, distend, enlarge, expand, fatten, fill out, grow, increase, inflate, mushroom, puff up, rise. **2** *swell numbers.* augment, boost, build up, extend, increase, make bigger, raise, step up. *Opp* SHRINK.

swelling *n* blister, boil, bulge, bump, distension, enlargement, excrescence, hump, inflammation, knob, lump, node, nodule, prominence, protrusion, protuberance, tumescence, tumour.

sweltering *adj* humid, muggy, oppressive, steamy, sticky, stifling, sultry, torrid, tropical. ▷ HOT.

swerve *vb* career, change direction, deviate, diverge, dodge about, sheer off, swing, take avoiding action, turn aside, veer, wheel.

swift *adj* agile, brisk, expeditious, fast, *old use* fleet, fleet-footed, hasty, hurried, nimble, *inf* nippy, prompt, quick, rapid, speedy, sudden. *Opp* SLOW.

swill *vb* **1** bathe, clean, rinse, sponge down, wash. **2** ▷ DRINK.

swim *vb* bathe, dive in, float, go swimming, *inf* take a dip.

swimming-bath *n* baths, leisure-pool, lido, swimming-pool.

swim-suit *n* bathing-costume, bathing-dress, bathing-suit, bikini, swimwear, trunks.

swindle *n* cheat, chicanery, *inf* con, confidence trick, deception, double-dealing, fraud, knavery, *inf* racket, *inf* rip-off, *inf* sharp practice, *inf* swizz, trickery. ● *vb inf* bamboozle, cheat, *inf* con, cozen, deceive, defraud, *inf* diddle, *inf* do, double-cross, dupe, exploit, *inf* fiddle, *inf* fleece, fool, gull, hoax, hoodwink, mulct, *inf* pull a fast one on you, *inf* rook, *inf* take you for a ride, trick, *inf* welsh (*on a bet*).

swindler *n* charlatan, cheat, cheater, *inf* con man, counterfeiter, double-crosser, extortioner, forger, fraud, hoaxer, impostor, knave, mountebank, quack, racketeer, scoundrel, *inf* shark, trickster, *inf* twister.

swing *n* change, fluctuation, movement, oscillation, shift, variation. ● *vb* **1** be suspended, dangle, flap, fluctuate, hang loose, move from side to side, move to and fro, oscillate, revolve, rock, roll, sway, swivel, turn, twirl, wave about. **2** *swing opinion.* affect, bias, bring round, change (*someone's mind*), convert, convince, govern, influence, persuade, win over. **3** *support swung to the opposition.* change, move across, shift, transfer, vary. **4** *swing from a path.* deviate, divert, go off course, swerve, veer, waver, zigzag.

swipe *vb* **1** lash out at, strike, swing at. ▷ HIT. **2** ▷ STEAL.

swirl *vb* boil, churn, circulate, curl, eddy, move in circles, seethe, spin, surge, twirl, twist, whirl.

switch *n* circuit-breaker, lightswitch, power-point. ● *vb* change, divert, exchange, redirect, replace, reverse, shift, substitute, *inf* swap, transfer, turn.

swivel *vb* gyrate, pirouette, pivot, revolve, rotate, spin, swing, turn, twirl, wheel.

swoop *vb* descend, dive, drop, fall, fly down, lunge, plunge, pounce. **swoop on** ▷ RAID.

sword *n* blade, broadsword, cutlass, dagger, foil, kris, rapier, sabre, scimitar.

sycophantic *adj* flattering, servile, *inf* smarmy, toadyish, unctuous.

syllabus *n* course, curriculum, outline, programme of study.

symbol *n* mark, sign, token. □ *badge, brand, character, cipher, coat of arms, crest, emblem, figure, hieroglyph, ideogram, ideograph, image, insignia, letter, logo, logotype, monogram, motif, number, numeral, pictogram, pictograph, trademark.*

symbolic *adj* allegorical, emblematic, figurative, meaningful, metaphorical, representative, significant, suggestive, symptomatic, token (*gesture*).

symbolize *vb* be a sign of, betoken, communicate, connote, denote, epitomize, imply, indicate, mean, represent, signify, stand for, suggest.

symmetrical *adj* balanced, even, proportional, regular. *Opp* ASYMMETRICAL.

sympathetic *adj* benevolent, caring, charitable, comforting, commiserating, compassionate, concerned, consoling, empathetic, friendly, humane, interested, kind-hearted, kindly, merciful, pitying, soft-hearted, solicitous, sorry, supportive, tender, tolerant, understanding, warm. *Opp* UNSYMPATHETIC.

sympathize *vb inf* be on the same wavelength, be sorry, be sympathetic, comfort, commiserate, condole, console, empathize, feel, grieve, have sympathy, identify (with), mourn, pity, respond, show sympathy, understand.

sympathy *n* affinity, commiseration, compassion, concern, condolence, consideration, empathy, feeling, fellow-feeling, kindness, mercy, pity, rapport, solicitousness, tenderness, understanding.

symptom *n* characteristic, evidence, feature, indication, manifestation, mark, marker, sign, warning, warning-sign.

symptomatic *adj* characteristic, indicative, representative, suggestive, typical.

synthesis *n* amalgamation, blend, coalescence, combination, composite, compound, fusion, integration, union. *Opp* ANALYSIS.

synthetic *adj* artificial, bogus, concocted, counterfeit, ersatz, fabricated, fake, *inf* made-up, man-made, manufactured, mock, *inf* phoney, simulated, spurious, unnatural. *Opp* GENUINE, NATURAL.

syringe *n* hypodermic, needle.

system *n* **1** network, organization, *inf* set-up, structure. **2** approach, arrangement, logic, method, methodology, *Lat* modus operandi, order, plan, practice, procedure, process, routine, rules, scheme, technique. **3** *system of government*. constitution, regime. **4** *system of knowledge*. categorization, classification, code, discipline, philosophy, science, set of principles, theory.

systematic *adj* according to plan, businesslike, categorized, classified, codified, constitutional, coordinated, logical, methodical, neat, ordered, orderly, organized, planned, rational, regimented, routine, scientific, structured, tidy, well-arranged, well-organized, well-rehearsed, well-run. *Opp* UNSYSTEMATIC.

systematize *vb* arrange, catalogue, categorize, classify, codify, make systematic, organize, rationalize, regiment, standardize, tabulate.

T

table *n* **1** bench, board, counter, desk, gate-leg table, kitchen table, worktop. **2** *table of information.* agenda, catalogue, chart, diagram, graph, index, inventory, list, register, schedule, tabulation, timetable. ● *vb* bring forward, lay on the table, offer, proffer, propose, submit.

tablet *n* **1** capsule, drop, lozenge, medicine, pastille, pellet, pill. **2** *tablet of soap.* bar, block, chunk, piece, slab. **3** *tablet of stone.* gravestone, headstone, memorial, plaque, plate, tombstone.

taboo *adj* banned, censored, disapproved of, forbidden, interdicted, prohibited, proscribed, unacceptable, unlawful, unmentionable, unnamable. ▷ RUDE. ● *n* anathema, ban, curse, interdiction, prohibition, proscription, taboo subject.

tabulate *vb* arrange as a table, catalogue, index, list, pigeon-hole, set out in columns, systematize.

tacit *adj* implicit, implied, silent, undeclared, understood, unexpressed, unsaid, unspoken, unvoiced.

taciturn *adj* mute, quiet, reserved, reticent, silent, tight-lipped, uncommunicative, unforthcoming. *Opp* TALKATIVE.

tack *n* **1** drawing-pin, nail, pin, tin-tack. **2** *the wrong tack.* approach, bearing, course, direction, heading, line, policy, procedure, technique. ● *vb* **1** nail, pin. ▷ FASTEN. **2** sew, stitch. **3** *tack in a yacht.* beat against the wind, change course, go about, zigzag. **tack on** ▷ ADD.

tackle *n* **1** accoutrements, apparatus, *inf* clobber, equipment, fittings, gear, implements, kit, outfit, paraphernalia, rig, rigging, tools. **2** *a football tackle.* attack, block, challenge, interception, intervention. ● *vb* **1** address (yourself to), apply yourself to, attempt, attend to, combat, *inf* come to grips with, concentrate on, confront, cope with, deal with, engage in, face up to, focus on, get involved in, grapple with, handle, *inf* have a go at, manage, set about, settle down to, sort out, take on, undertake. **2** *tackle an opponent.* attack, challenge, intercept, stop, take on.

tacky *adj* adhesive, gluey, *inf* gooey, gummy, sticky, viscous, wet. *Opp* DRY.

tact *n* adroitness, consideration, delicacy, diplomacy, discernment, discretion, finesse, judgement, perceptiveness, politeness, savoir-faire, sensitivity, tactfulness, thoughtfulness, understanding. *Opp* TACTLESSNESS.

tactful *adj* adroit, appropriate, considerate, courteous, delicate, diplomatic, discreet, judicious, perceptive, polite, politic, sensitive, thoughtful, understanding. *Opp* TACTLESS.

tactical *adj* artful, calculated, clever, deliberate, planned, politic, prudent, shrewd, skilful, strategic.

tactics *plur n* approach, campaign, course of action, design, device, manoeuvre, manoeuvring, plan, ploy, policy, procedure, ruse, scheme, stratagem, strategy.

tactless *adj* blundering, blunt, boorish, bungling, clumsy, discourteous, gauche, heavyhanded, hurtful, impolite, impolitic, inappropriate, inconsiderate, indelicate, indiscreet, inept, insensitive, maladroit, misjudged, thoughtless, uncivil, uncouth, undiplomatic, unkind. ▷ RUDE. *Opp* TACTFUL.

tactlessness *n* boorishness, clumsiness, gaucherie, indelicacy, indiscretion, ineptitude, insensitivity, lack of diplomacy, misjudgement, thoughtlessness, uncouthness. ▷ RUDENESS. *Opp* TACT.

tag *n* **1** docket, label, marker, name tag, price tag, slip, sticker, tab, ticket. **2** *a Latin tag.* ▷ SAYING. ● *vb* identify, label, mark, ticket. **tag along with** ▷ FOLLOW.

tail *n* appendage, back, brush (*of fox*), buttocks, end, extremity, rear, rump, scut (*of rabbit*), tail-end. ● *vb* dog, follow, hunt, pursue, shadow, stalk, track, trail. **tail off** ▷ DECLINE.

taint *vb* **1** adulterate, contaminate, defile, dirty, infect, poison, pollute, soil. **2** *taint a reputation.* besmirch, blacken, blemish, damage, dishonour, harm, ruin, slander, smear, spoil, stain, sully, tarnish.

take *vb* **1** acquire, bring, carry away, *inf* cart off, catch, clasp, clutch, fetch, gain, get, grab, grasp, grip, hold, pick up, pluck, remove, secure, seize, snatch, transfer. **2** *take prisoners.* abduct, arrest, capture, catch, corner, detain, ensnare, entrap, secure. **3** *take property.* appropriate, get away with, pocket. ▷ STEAL. **4** *take 2 from 4.* deduct, eliminate, subtract, take away. **5** *take passengers.* accommodate, carry, contain, have room for, hold. **6** *take a partner.* accompany, conduct, convey, escort, ferry, guide, lead, transport. **7** *take a taxi.* engage, hire, make use of, travel by, use. **8** *take a subject.* have lessons in, learn about, read, study. **9** *can't take pain.* abide, accept, bear, brook, endure, receive, *inf* stand, *inf* stomach, suffer, tolerate, undergo, withstand. **10** *take food, drink.* consume, drink, eat, have, swallow. **11** *It takes courage to own up.* necessitate, need, require, use up. **12** *take a new name.* adopt, assume, choose, select. **take aback** ▷ SURPRISE. **take after** ▷ RESEMBLE. **take against** ▷ DISLIKE. **take back** ▷ WITHDRAW. **take in** ▷ ACCOMMODATE, DECEIVE, UNDERSTAND. **take life** ▷ KILL. **take off** ▷ IMITATE. **take off, take out** ▷ REMOVE. **take on, take up** ▷ UNDERTAKE. **take over** ▷ USURP. **take part** ▷

PARTICIPATE. **take place** ▷ HAPPEN. **take to task** ▷ REPRIMAND. **take up** ▷ BEGIN, OCCUPY.

take-over *n* amalgamation, combination, incorporation, merger.

takings *plur n* earnings, gains, gate, income, proceeds, profits, receipts, revenue.

tale *n* account, anecdote, chronicle, narration, narrative, relation, report, *sl* spiel, story, yarn. ▷ WRITING.

talent *n* ability, accomplishment, aptitude, brilliance, capacity, expertise, facility, faculty, flair, genius, gift, ingenuity, knack, *inf* know-how, prowess, skill, strength, versatility.

talented *adj* able, accomplished, artistic, brilliant, distinguished, expert, gifted, inspired, proficient, skilful, skilled, versatile. ▷ CLEVER. *Opp* UNSKILFUL.

talisman *n* amulet, charm, fetish, mascot.

talk *n* **1** baby-talk, *inf* blarney, chat, *inf* chin-wag, *inf* chit-chat, confabulation, conference, conversation, dialogue, discourse, discussion, gossip, intercourse, language, palaver, *inf* powwow, *inf* tattle, *inf* tittle-tattle, words. **2** *a public talk.* address, diatribe, exhortation, harangue, lecture, oration, *inf* peptalk, presentation, sermon, speech, tirade. ● *vb* **1** address one another, articulate ideas, commune, communicate, confer, converse, deliver a speech, discourse, discuss, enunciate, exchange views, have a conversation, *inf* hold forth, lecture, negotiate, *inf* pipe up, pontificate, prate, pronounce words, say something, sermonize, speak, tell, use language, use your voice, utter, verbalize, vocalize. □ babble, bawl, bellow, blab, blether, blurt out, breathe, burble, call out, chat, chatter, clamour, croak, cry, drawl, drone, gabble, gas, gibber, gossip, grunt, harp, howl, intone, jabber, jaw, jeer, lisp, maunder, moan, mumble, murmur, mutter, natter, patter, prattle, pray, preach, rabbit on, rant, rasp, rattle on, rave, roar, *scream, screech, shout, shriek, slur, snap, snarl, speak in an undertone, splutter, spout, squeal, stammer, stutter, tattle, vociferate, wail, whimper, whine, whinge, whisper, witter, yell.* **2** *talk French.* communicate in, express yourself in, pronounce, speak. **3** *get someone to talk.* confess, give information, *inf* grass, inform, *inf* let on, *inf* spill the beans, *inf* squeal, *inf* tell tales. ▷ SAY, SPEAK. **talk about** ▷ DISCUSS. **talk to** ▷ ADDRESS.

talkative *adj* articulate, *inf* chatty, communicative, effusive, eloquent, expansive, garrulous, glib, gossipy, long-winded, loquacious, open, prolix, unstoppable, verbose, vocal, voluble, wordy. *Opp* TACITURN. **talkative person** chatter-box, *sl* gas-bag, gossip, *sl* wind-bag.

tall *adj* colossal, giant, gigantic, high, lofty, soaring, towering. ▷ BIG. *Opp* SHORT.

tally *n* addition, count, reckoning, record, sum, total. ● *vb* **1** accord, agree, coincide, concur, correspond, match up, square. **2** *tally up the bill.* add, calculate, compute, count, reckon, total, work out.

tame *adj* **1** amenable, biddable, broken in, compliant, disciplined, docile, domesticated, gentle, manageable, meek, mild, obedient, safe, subdued, submissive, tamed, tractable, trained. **2** *tame animals.* approachable, bold, fearless, friendly, sociable, unafraid. **3** *a tame story.* bland, boring, dull, feeble, flat, insipid, lifeless, tedious, unadventurous, unexciting, uninspiring, uninteresting, vapid, *inf* wishy-washy. *Opp* EXCITING, WILD. ● *vb* break in, conquer, curb, discipline, domesticate, house-train, humble, keep under, make tame, master, mollify, mute, quell, repress, subdue, subjugate, suppress, temper, tone down, train.

tamper *vb* **tamper with** alter, *inf* fiddle about with, interfere with, make adjustments to, meddle with, tinker with.

tan *n* sunburn, suntan. ● *vb* bronze, brown, burn, colour, darken, get tanned.

tang *n* acidity, *inf* bite, *inf* edge, *inf* nip, piquancy, pungency, savour, sharpness, spiciness, zest.

tangible *adj* actual, concrete, corporeal, definite, material, palpable, perceptible, physical, positive, provable, real, solid, substantial, tactile, touchable. *Opp* INTANGIBLE.

tangle *n* coil, complication, confusion, jumble, jungle, knot, labyrinth, mass, maze, mesh, mess, muddle, scramble, twist, web. ● *vb* **1** complicate, confuse, entangle, entwine, *inf* foul up, intertwine, interweave, muddle, ravel, scramble, *inf* snarl up, twist. **2** *tangle fish in a net.* catch, enmesh, ensnare, entrap, trap. *Opp* DISENTANGLE, FREE. **3** *tangle with criminals.* become involved with, confront, cross. **tangled** ▷ DISHEVELLED, INTRICATE.

tangy *adj* acid, appetizing, bitter, fresh, piquant, pungent, refreshing, sharp, spicy, strong, tart. *Opp* BLAND.

tank *n* **1** aquarium, basin, cistern, reservoir. **2** *army tank.* armoured vehicle.

tanned *adj* brown, sunburnt, suntanned, weather-beaten.

tantalize *vb* bait, entice, frustrate, *inf* keep on tenterhooks, lead on, plague, provoke, taunt, tease, tempt, titillate, torment.

tap *n* **1** *Amer* faucet, spigot, stopcock, valve. **2** knock, rap. ● *vb* knock, rap, strike. ▷ HIT.

tape *n* **1** band, belt, binding, braid, fillet, ribbon, strip, stripe. **2** audiotape, cassette, magnetic tape, taperecording, videotape.

taper *n* candle, lighter, spill. ● *vb* attenuate, become narrower, narrow, thin. **taper off** ▷ DECLINE.

target *n* **1** aim, ambition, end, goal, hope, intention, objective, purpose. **2** *target of attack.* butt, object, quarry, victim.

tariff n **1** charges, menu, pricelist, schedule. **2** *tariff on imports.* customs, duty, excise, impost, levy, tax, toll.

tarnish vb **1** blacken, corrode, dirty, discolour, soil, spoil, stain, taint. **2** *tarnish a reputation.* blemish, blot, calumniate, defame, denigrate, disgrace, dishonour, mar, ruin, spoil, stain, sully.

tarry vb dawdle, delay, *inf* hang about, hang back, linger, loiter, pause, procrastinate, temporize, wait.

tart adj **1** acid, acidic, acidulous, astringent, biting, citrus, harsh, lemony, piquant, pungent, sharp, sour, tangy. **2** *a tart rejoinder.* ▷ SHARP. *Opp* BLAND, SWEET. ● n **1** flan, pastry, pasty, patty, pie, quiche, tartlet, turnover. **2** ▷ PROSTITUTE.

task n activity, assignment, burden, business, charge, chore, duty, employment, enterprise, errand, imposition, job, mission, requirement, test, undertaking, work. **take to task** ▷ REPRIMAND.

taste n **1** character, flavour, relish, savour. **2** bit, bite, morsel, mouthful, nibble, piece, sample, titbit. **3** *an acquired taste.* appetite, appreciation, choice, fancy, fondness, inclination, judgement, leaning, liking, partiality, preference. **4** *a person of taste.* breeding, cultivation, culture, discernment, discretion, discrimination, education, elegance, fashion sense, finesse, good judgement, perception, perceptiveness, polish, refinement, sensitivity, style, tastefulness. ● vb nibble, relish, sample, savour, sip, test, try. **in bad taste** ▷ TASTELESS. **in good taste** ▷ TASTEFUL.

tasteful adj aesthetic, artistic, attractive, charming, *Fr* comme il faut, correct, cultivated, decorous, dignified, discerning, discreet, discriminating, elegant, fashionable, in good taste, judicious, *inf* nice, polite, proper, refined, restrained, sensitive, smart, stylish, tactful, well-judged. *Opp* TASTELESS.

tasteless adj **1** cheap, coarse, crude, *inf* flashy, garish, gaudy, graceless, improper, inartistic, in bad taste, indecorous, indelicate, inelegant, injudicious, in poor taste, *inf* kitsch, *inf* loud, meretricious, ugly, unattractive, uncouth, uncultivated, undiscriminating, unfashionable, unimaginative, unpleasant, unrefined, unseemly, unstylish, vulgar. *Opp* TASTEFUL. **2** *tasteless food.* bland, characterless, flavourless, insipid, mild, uninteresting, watered-down, watery, weak, *inf* wishy-washy. *Opp* TASTY.

tasty adj appetizing, delectable, delicious, flavoursome, luscious, *inf* mouth-watering, *inf* nice, palatable, *inf* scrumptious, toothsome, *sl* yummy. □ acid, bitter, creamy, fruity, hot, meaty, peppery, piquant, salty, savoury, sharp, sour, spicy, sugary, sweet, tangy, tart. *Opp* TASTELESS.

tattered adj frayed, ragged, rent, ripped, shredded, tatty, threadbare, torn, worn out. *Opp* SMART.

tatters plur n bits, pieces, rags, ribbons, shreds, torn pieces.

tatty adj **1** frayed, old, patched, ragged, ripped, scruffy, shabby, tattered, torn, threadbare, untidy, worn out. **2** ▷ TAWDRY. *Opp* SMART.

taunt vb annoy, goad, insult, jeer at, reproach, tease, torment. ▷ RIDICULE.

taut adj firm, rigid, stiff, strained, stretched, tense, tight. *Opp* SLACK.

tautological adj long-winded, otiose, pleonastic, prolix, redundant, repetitious, repetitive, superfluous, tautologous, verbose, wordy. *Opp* CONCISE.

tautology n duplication, long-windedness, pleonasm, prolixity, repetition, verbiage, verbosity, wordiness.

tavern n *old use* alehouse, bar, hostelry, inn, *inf* local, pub, public house.

tawdry adj *inf* Brummagem, cheap, common, eye-catching, fancy, *inf* flashy, garish, gaudy, inferior, meretricious, poor quality, showy, tasteless, tatty, tinny, vulgar, worthless. *Opp* TASTEFUL.

tax *n* charge, due, duty, imposition, impost, levy, tariff, *old use* tribute. □ *airport tax, community charge, corporation tax, customs, death duty, estate duty, excise, income tax, poll tax, property tax, rates, old use tithe, toll, value added tax. vb* **1** assess, exact, impose a tax on, levy a tax on. **2** *tax someone's patience.* burden, exhaust, make heavy demands on, overwork, pressure, pressurize, strain, try. ▷ TIRE. **tax with** accuse of, blame for, censure for, charge with, reproach for, reprove for.

taxi *n* cab, *old use* hackney carriage, minicab.

teach *vb* advise, brainwash, coach, counsel, demonstrate to, discipline, drill, edify, educate, enlighten, familiarize with, give lessons in, ground in, impart knowledge to, implant knowledge in, inculcate habits in, indoctrinate, inform, instruct, lecture, school, train, tutor.

teacher *n* adviser, educator, guide. □ *coach, counsellor, demonstrator, don, governess, guru, headteacher, housemaster, housemistress, instructor, lecturer, maharishi, master, mentor, mistress, pedagogue, preacher, preceptor, professor, pundit, schoolmaster, schoolmistress, schoolteacher, trainer, tutor.*

teaching *n* **1** education, guidance, instruction, training. □ *brainwashing, briefing, coaching, computer-aided learning, counselling, demonstration, familiarization, grounding, indoctrination, lecture, lesson, practical, preaching, rote learning, schooling, seminar, tuition, tutorial, work experience, workshop.* **2** *religious teachings.* doctrine, dogma, gospel, precept, principle, tenet.

team *n* club, crew, gang, *inf* line up, side. ▷ GROUP.

tear *n* **1** [rhymes with *fear*] droplet, tear-drop. [*plur*] *inf* blubbering, crying, sobs, weeping. **2** [rhymes with *bear*] cut, fissure, gap, gash, hole, laceration, opening, rent, rip, slit, split. ● *vb* claw, gash, lacerate, mangle, pierce, pull apart, rend, rip, rive, rupture, scratch, sever, shred, slit, snag, split. **shed tears** ▷ WEEP.

tearful *adj inf* blubbering, crying, emotional, in tears, lachrymose, snivelling, sobbing, weeping, *inf* weepy, wet-cheeked, whimpering. ▷ SAD.

tease *vb inf* aggravate, annoy, badger, bait, chaff, goad, harass, irritate, laugh at, make fun of, mock, *inf* needle, *inf* nettle, pester, plague, provoke, *inf* pull someone's leg, *inf* rib, tantalize, taunt, torment, vex, worry. ▷ RIDICULE.

teasing *n* badinage, banter, chaffing, joking, mockery, provocation, raillery, *inf* ribbing, ridicule, taunts.

technical *adj* **1** complicated, detailed, esoteric, expert, professional, specialized. **2** *technical skill.* engineering, industrial, mechanical, technological, scientific.

technician *n* engineer, mechanic, skilled worker, *plur* technical staff.

technique *n* **1** approach, dodge, knack, manner, means, method, mode, procedure, routine, system, trick, way. **2** *an artist's technique.* art, artistry, cleverness, craft, craftsmanship, expertise, facility, *inf* knowhow, proficiency, skill, talent, workmanship.

technological *adj* advanced, automated, computerized, electronic, scientific.

tedious *adj* banal, boring, dreary, *inf* dry-as-dust, dull, endless, *inf* humdrum, irksome, laborious, long-drawn-out, long-winded, monotonous, prolonged, repetitious, slow, soporific, tiresome, tiring, unexciting, uninteresting, vapid, wearing, wearisome, wearying. *Opp* INTERESTING.

tedium *n* boredom, dreariness, dullness, ennui, long-windedness, monotony, repetitiousness, slowness, tediousness.

teem *vb* **1** abound (in), be alive (with), be full (of), be infested, be overrun (by), *inf* bristle, *inf* crawl, proliferate, seethe, swarm with. **2** ▷ RAIN.

teenager n adolescent, boy, girl, juvenile, minor, youngster, youth.

teetotal adj abstemious, abstinent, sl on the wagon, restrained, self-denying, self-disciplined, temperate.

teetotaller n abstainer, non-drinker.

telegram n cable, cablegram, fax, telex, wire.

telepathic adj clairvoyant, psychic.

telephone n inf blower, carphone, handset, phone. ● vb inf buzz, call, dial, inf give someone a buzz, inf give someone a call, inf give someone a tinkle, phone, ring, ring up.

telescope vb abbreviate, collapse, compress, elide, shorten.

telescopic adj adjustable, collapsible, expanding, extending, retractable.

televise vb broadcast, relay, send out, transmit.

television n inf the box, monitor, receiver, inf small screen, inf telly, video.

tell vb 1 acquaint with, advise, announce, assure, communicate, describe, disclose, divulge, explain, impart, inform, make known, narrate, notify, portray, promise, recite, recount, rehearse, relate, reveal, utter. ▷ SPEAK, TALK. 2 tell the difference. calculate, comprehend, decide, discover, discriminate, distinguish, identify, notice, recognize, see. 3 told me what to do. command, direct, instruct, order. **tell off** ▷ REPRIMAND.

teller n 1 author, narrator, raconteur, storyteller. 2 teller in a bank. bank clerk, cashier.

telling adj considerable, effective, influential, potent, powerful, significant, striking, weighty.

temper n 1 attitude, character, disposition, frame of mind, humour, inf make-up, mood, personality, state of mind, temperament. 2 watch your temper. anger, churlishness, fit of anger, fury, hot-headedness, ill-humour, irascibility, irritability, inf paddy, passion, peevishness, petulance, rage, surliness, tantrum, unpredictability, volatility, inf wax, wrath. 3 keep your temper. calmness, composure, sl cool, coolness, equanimity, sang-froid, self-control, self-possession. ● vb 1 assuage, lessen, mitigate, moderate, modify, modulate, reduce, soften, soothe, tone down. 2 temper steel. harden, strengthen, toughen.

temperament n attitude, character, old use complexion, disposition, frame of mind, old use humour, inf make-up, mood, nature, personality, spirit, state of mind, temper.

temperamental adj 1 characteristic, congenital, constitutional, inherent, innate, natural. 2 temperamental moods. capricious, changeable, emotional, erratic, excitable, explosive, fickle, highly-strung, impatient, inconsistent, inconstant, irascible, irritable, mercurial, moody, neurotic, passionate, sensitive, touchy, undependable, unpredictable, unreliable, inf up and down, variable, volatile.

temperance n abstemiousness, continence, moderation, self-discipline, self-restraint, sobriety, teetotalism.

temperate adj calm, controlled, disciplined, moderate, reasonable, restrained, self-possessed, sensible, sober, stable, steady. Opp EXTREME.

tempest n cyclone, gale, hurricane, tornado, tumult, typhoon, whirlwind. ▷ STORM.

tempestuous adj fierce, furious, tumultuous, turbulent, vehement, violent, wild. ▷ STORMY. Opp CALM.

temple n church, house of god, mosque, pagoda, place of worship, shrine, synagogue.

tempo n beat, pace, pulse, rate, rhythm, speed.

temporal adj earthly, fleshly, impermanent, material, materialistic, mortal, mundane, non-religious, passing, secular, sublunary, terrestrial, transient, transitory, worldly. Opp SPIRITUAL.

temporary adj 1 brief, ephemeral, evanescent, fleeting, fugitive, impermanent, interim, makeshift, momentary, passing, provisional, short, short-lived, short-term, stopgap, transient, transitory. **2** *temporary captain.* acting. *Opp* PERMANENT.

tempt *vb* allure, attract, bait, bribe, cajole, captivate, coax, decoy, entice, fascinate, inveigle, lure, offer incentives, persuade, seduce, tantalize, woo. **tempting** ▷ APPETIZING, ATTRACTIVE.

temptation *n* allure, allurement, appeal, attraction, cajolery, coaxing, draw, enticement, fascination, inducement, lure, persuasion, pull, seduction, snare, wooing.

tenable *adj* arguable, believable, conceivable, credible, creditable, defendable, defensible, feasible, justifiable, legitimate, logical, plausible, rational, reasonable, sensible, sound, supportable, understandable, viable. *Opp* INDEFENSIBLE.

tenacious *adj* determined, dogged, firm, intransigent, obdurate, obstinate, persistent, pertinacious, resolute, single-minded, steadfast, strong, stubborn, tight, uncompromising, unfaltering, unshakeable, unswerving, unwavering, unyielding. *Opp* WEAK.

tenant *n* inhabitant, leaseholder, lessee, lodger, occupant, occupier, resident.

tend *vb* **1** attend to, care for, cherish, cultivate, guard, keep, *inf* keep an eye on, look after, manage, mind, minister to, mother, protect, supervise, take care of, watch. **2** *tend the sick.* nurse, treat. **3** *tend to fall asleep.* be biased, be disposed, be inclined, be liable, be prone, have a tendency, incline.

tendency *n* bias, disposition, drift, inclination, instinct, leaning, liability, partiality, penchant, predilection, predisposition, proclivity, proneness, propensity, readiness, susceptibility, trend.

tender *adj* **1** dainty, delicate, fleshy, fragile, frail, green, immature, soft, succulent, vulnerable, weak, young.

2 *tender meat.* chewable, eatable, edible. **3** *a tender wound.* aching, inflamed, painful, sensitive, smarting, sore. **4** *a tender love-song.* emotional, heartfelt, moving, poignant, romantic, sentimental, stirring, touching. **5** *tender care.* affectionate, amorous, caring, compassionate, concerned, considerate, fond, gentle, humane, kind, loving, merciful, pitying, soft-hearted, sympathetic, tender-hearted, warm-hearted. *Opp* TOUGH, UNSYMPATHETIC.

tense *adj* **1** rigid, strained, stretched, taut, tight. **2** *a tense person.* anxious, apprehensive, edgy, excited, fidgety, highly-strung, intense, jittery, jumpy, *inf* keyed-up, nervous, on edge, *inf* on tenterhooks, overwrought, restless, strained, stressed, *inf* strung up, touchy, uneasy, *sl* uptight, worried. **3** *a tense situation.* exciting, fraught, *inf* nail-biting, nerve-racking, stressful, worrying. *Opp* RELAXED.

tension *n* **1** pull, strain, stretching, tautness, tightness. **2** *the tension of waiting.* anxiety, apprehension, edginess, excitement, nervousness, stress, suspense, unease, worry. *Opp* RELAXATION.

tent *n* □ bell tent, big-top, frame tent, marquee, ridge tent, tepee, trailer tent, wigwam.

tentative *adj* cautious, diffident, doubtful, experimental, exploratory, half-hearted, hesitant, inconclusive, indecisive, indefinite, nervous, preliminary, provisional, shy, speculative, timid, uncertain, uncommitted, unsure, *inf* wishywashy. *Opp* DECISIVE.

tenuous *adj* attenuated, fine, flimsy, fragile, insubstantial, slender, slight, weak. ▷ THIN. *Opp* STRONG.

tepid *adj* **1** lukewarm, warm. **2** *a tepid response.* ▷ APATHETIC.

term *n* **1** duration, period, season, span, spell, stretch, time. **2** *a school term. Amer* semester, session. **3** *technical terms.* appellation, designation, epithet, expression, name, phrase, saying, title, word. **terms 1** conditions, particulars, provisions, provisos, specifications, stipulations. **2** *a hotel's terms.* charges, fees, prices, rates, schedule, tariff.

terminal *adj* deadly, fatal, final, incurable, killing, lethal, mortal. ● *n* **1** keyboard, VDU, work-station. **2** *passenger terminal.* airport, terminus. **3** *electric terminal.* connection, connector, coupling.

terminate *vb* bring to an end, cease, come to an end, discontinue, end, finish, *inf* pack in, phase out, stop, *inf* wind up. ▷ END. *Opp* BEGIN.

terminology *n* argot, cant, choice of words, jargon, language, nomenclature, phraseology, special terms, technical language, vocabulary.

terminus *n* destination, last stop, station, terminal, termination.

terrain *n* country, ground, land, landscape, territory, topography.

terrestrial *adj* earthly, mundane, ordinary, sublunary.

terrible *adj* **1** acute, appalling, awful, *inf* beastly, distressing, dreadful, fearful, fearsome, formidable, frightening, frightful, ghastly, grave, gruesome, harrowing, hideous, horrendous, horrible, horrific, horrifying, insupportable, intolerable, loathsome, nasty, nauseating, outrageous, revolting, shocking, terrific, terrifying, unbearable, vile. **2** ▷ BAD.

terrific *adj* *Terrific* may mean *causing terror* (▷ TERRIBLE). It is more often used *informally* of anything which is *extreme* in its own way: *a terrific problem* ▷ EXTREME; *terrific size* ▷ BIG; *a terrific party* ▷ EXCELLENT; *a terrific storm* ▷ VIOLENT.

terrify *vb* appal, dismay, horrify, *inf* make your blood run cold, petrify, shock, terrorize. ▷ FRIGHTEN. **terrified** ▷ FRIGHTENED. **terrifying** ▷ FRIGHTENING.

territory *n* area, colony, *old use* demesne, district, domain, dominion, enclave, jurisdiction, land, neighbourhood, precinct, preserve, province, purlieu, region, sector, sphere, state, terrain, tract, zone. ▷ COUNTRY.

terror *n* alarm, awe, consternation, dismay, dread, fright, *inf* funk, horror, panic, shock, trepidation. ▷ FEAR.

terrorist *n* assassin, bomber, desperado, gunman, hijacker.

terrorize *vb* browbeat, bully, coerce, cow, intimidate, menace, persecute, terrify, threaten, torment, tyrannize. ▷ FRIGHTEN.

terse *adj* abrupt, brief, brusque, compact, concentrated, concise, crisp, curt, epigrammatic, incisive, laconic, pithy, short, *inf* short and sweet, *inf* snappy, succinct, to the point. *Opp* VERBOSE.

test *n* analysis, appraisal, assay, assessment, audition, *inf* check-over, *inf* check-up, evaluation, examination, inspection, interrogation, investigation, probation, quiz, screen-test, trial, *inf* try-out. ● *vb* analyse, appraise, assay, assess, audition, check, evaluate, examine, experiment with, inspect, interrogate, investigate, probe, *inf* put someone through their paces, put to the test, question, quiz, screen, try out.

testify *vb* affirm, attest, aver, bear witness, declare, give evidence, proclaim, state on oath, swear, vouch, witness.

testimonial *n* character reference, commendation, recommendation, reference.

testimony *n* affidavit, assertion, declaration, deposition, evidence, statement, submission.

tether *n* chain, cord, fetter, halter, lead, leash, painter, restraint, rope. ● *vb* chain up, fetter, keep on a tether, leash, restrain, rope, secure, tie up. ▷ FASTEN.

text *n* **1** argument, content, contents, matter, subject matter, wording. **2** *a literary text.* book, textbook, work. ▷ WRITING. **3** *a text from scripture.* line, motif, passage, quotation, sentence, theme, topic, verse.

textile *n* fabric, material, stuff. ▷ CLOTH.

texture *n* appearance, composition, consistency, feel, grain, quality, surface, tactile quality, touch, weave.

thank *vb* acknowledge, express thanks, say thank you, show gratitude.

thankful *adj* appreciative, contented, glad, grateful, happy, indebted, pleased, relieved. *Opp* UNGRATEFUL.

thankless *adj* bootless, futile, profitless, unappreciated, unrecognized, unrewarded, unrewarding. *Opp* PROFITABLE.

thanks *plur n* acknowledgement, appreciation, gratefulness, gratitude, recognition, thanksgiving. **thanks to** as a result of, because of, owing to, through.

thaw *vb* become liquid, defrost, de-ice, heat up, melt, soften, uncongeal, unfreeze, unthaw, warm up. *Opp* FREEZE.

theatre *n* 1 auditorium, hall, opera-house, playhouse. **2** acting, dramaturgy, histrionic arts, show business, thespian arts. □ *ballet, masque, melodrama, mime, musical, music-hall, opera, pantomime, play*. ▷ DRAMA, ENTERTAINMENT, PERFORMANCE.

theatrical *adj* **1** dramatic, histrionic, thespian: **2** [*derog*] *a theatrical exit*. affected, artificial, calculated, demonstrative, exaggerated, forced, *inf* hammy, melodramatic, ostentatious, overacted, overdone, *inf* over the top, pompous, selfimportant, showy, stagy, stilted, unconvincing, unnatural. *Opp* NATURAL.

theft *n* burglary, larceny, pilfering, robbery, thievery. ▷ STEALING.

theme *n* **1** argument, core, essence, gist, idea, issue, keynote, matter, point, subject, text, thesis, thread, topic. **2** *a musical theme*. air, melody, motif, subject, tune.

theology *n* divinity, religion, religious studies.

theoretical *adj* abstract, academic, conjectural, doctrinaire, hypothetical, ideal, notional, pure (*science*), putative, speculative, suppositional,
unproven, untested. *Opp* PRACTICAL, PROVEN.

theorize *vb* conjecture, form a theory, guess, hypothesize, speculate.

theory *n* **1** argument, assumption, belief, conjecture, explanation, guess, hypothesis, idea, notion, speculation, supposition, surmise, thesis, view. **2** *theory of a subject*. laws, principles, rules, science. *Opp* PRACTICE.

therapeutic *adj* beneficial, corrective, curative, healing, healthy, helpful, medicinal, remedial, restorative, salubrious. *Opp* HARMFUL.

therapist *n* counsellor, healer, physiotherapist, psychoanalyst, psychotherapist.

therapy *n* cure, healing, remedy, tonic, treatment. □ *chemotherapy, group therapy, hydrotherapy, hypnotherapy, occupational therapy, physiotherapy, psychotherapy, radiotherapy*. ▷ MEDICINE.

therefore *adv* accordingly, consequently, hence, so, thus.

thesis *n* **1** argument, assertion, contention, hypothesis, idea, opinion, postulate, premise, premiss, proposition, theory, view. **2** *a research thesis*. disquisition, dissertation, essay, monograph, paper, tract, treatise.

thick *adj* **1** broad, *inf* bulky, chunky, stout, sturdy, wide. ▷ FAT. **2** *a thick layer*. deep, heavy, substantial, woolly. **3** *a thick crowd*. compact, dense, impassable, impenetrable, numerous, packed, solid. **4** *thick liquid*. clotted, coagulated, concentrated, condensed, firm, glutinous, heavy, jellied, sticky, stiff, viscid, viscous. **5** *thick growth*. abundant, bushy, luxuriant, plentiful. **6** *thick with visitors*. alive, bristling, *inf* chock-full, choked, covered, crammed, crawling, crowded, filled, full, jammed, swarming, teeming. *Opp* THIN.

thicken *vb* coagulate, clot, concentrate, condense, congeal, firm up, gel, jell, reduce, solidify, stiffen.

thickness n **1** breadth, density, depth, fatness, viscosity, width. **2** *a thickness of paint, rock*. coating, layer, seam, stratum.

thief n bandit, brigand, burglar, cat-burglar, cutpurse, embezzler, foot-pad, highwayman, housebreaker, kleptomaniac, looter, mugger, peculator, pickpocket, pilferer, pirate, plagiarist, poacher, purloiner, robber, safe-cracker, shoplifter, stealer, swindler. ▷ CRIMINAL.

thieving adj dishonest, light-fingered, rapacious. ● n ▷ STEALING.

thin adj **1** anorexic, attenuated, bony, cadaverous, emaciated, fine, flat-chested, gangling, gaunt, lanky, lean, narrow, pinched, rangy, scraggy, scrawny, skeletal, skinny, slender, slight, slim, small, spare, spindly, underfed, undernourished, underweight, wiry. *Opp* FAT. **2** *a thin layer*. delicate, diaphanous, filmy, fine, flimsy, gauzy, insubstantial, light, *inf* see-through, shallow, sheer (*silk*), superficial, translucent, wispy. **3** *a thin crowd*. meagre, scanty, scarce, scattered, sparse. **4** *thin liquid*. dilute, flowing, fluid, runny, sloppy, watery, weak. **5** *thin atmosphere*. rarefied. **6** *a thin excuse*. feeble, implausible, tenuous, transparent, unconvincing. *Opp* DENSE, STRONG, THICK. ● vb dilute, water down, weaken. **thin out 1** become less dense, decrease, diminish, disperse. **2** make less dense, prune, reduce, trim, weed out.

thing n **1** apparatus, artefact, article, body, contrivance, device, entity, gadget, implement, invention, item, object, utensil. **2** affair, circumstance, deed, event, eventuality, happening, incident, occurrence, phenomenon. **3** *a thing on your mind*. concept, detail, fact, factor, feeling, idea, point, statement, thought. **4** *a thing to be done*. act, action, chore, deed, job, responsibility, task. **5** [*inf*] *a thing about snakes*. aversion, fixation, *inf* hang-up, mania, neurosis, obsession, passion, phobia, preoccupation. **things 1** baggage, belongings, clothing, equipment, *inf* gear, luggage,

possessions, *inf* stuff. **2** *How are things?* circumstances, conditions, life.

think vb **1** attend, brood, chew things over, cogitate, concentrate, consider, contemplate, day-dream, deliberate, dream, dwell (on), fantasize, give thought (to), meditate, *inf* mull over, muse, ponder, *inf* rack your brains, reason, reflect, remind yourself of, reminisce, ruminate, use your intelligence, work things out, worry. **2** *Do you think it's true?* accept, admit, assume, be convinced, believe, be under the impression, conclude, deem, estimate, feel, guess, have faith, imagine, judge, presume, reckon, suppose, surmise. **think better of** ▷ RECONSIDER. **thinking** ▷ INTELLIGENT, THOUGHTFUL. **think up** ▷ DEVISE.

thinker n *inf* brain, innovator, intellect, inventor, *inf* mastermind, philosopher, sage, savant, scholar.

thirst n **1** drought, dryness, thirstiness. **2** *thirst for knowledge*. appetite, craving, desire, eagerness, hunger, itch, longing, love (of), lust, passion, urge, wish, yearning, *inf* yen. ● vb be thirsty, crave, have a thirst, hunger, long, strive (after), wish, yearn. **thirst for** ▷ WANT.

thirsty adj **1** arid, dehydrated, dry, *inf* gasping, panting, parched. **2** *thirsty for news*. avid, craving, desirous, eager, greedy, hankering, itching, longing, voracious, yearning.

thorn n barb, bristle, needle, prickle, spike, spine.

thorny adj **1** barbed, bristly, prickly, scratchy, sharp, spiky, spiny. **2** ▷ DIFFICULT.

thorough adj **1** assiduous, attentive, careful, comprehensive, conscientious, deep, detailed, diligent, efficient, exhaustive, extensive, full, *inf* in-depth, methodical, meticulous, minute, observant, orderly, organized, painstaking, particular, penetrating, probing, scrupulous, searching, systematic, thoughtful, watchful. *Opp* SUPERFICIAL. **2** *a thorough rascal*. absolute, arrant, complete, downright, out-and-out, perfect, proper, sheer, thoroughgoing, total, unmitigated, unmixed, unqualified, utter.

thought *n* **1** *inf* brainwork, brooding, *inf* brown study, cerebration, cogitation, concentration, consideration, contemplation, day-dreaming, deliberation, intelligence, introspection, meditation, mental activity, musing, pensiveness, ratiocination, rationality, reason, reasoning, reflection, reverie, rumination, study, thinking, worrying. **2** *a clever thought.* belief, concept, conception, conclusion, conjecture, conviction, idea, notion, observation, opinion. **3** *no thought of gain.* aim, design, dream, expectation, hope, intention, objective, plan, prospect, purpose, vision. **4** *a kind thought.* attention, concern, consideration, kindness, solicitude, thoughtfulness.

thoughtful *adj* **1** absorbed, abstracted, anxious, attentive, brooding, contemplative, dreamy, grave, introspective, meditative, pensive, philosophical, rapt, reflective, serious, solemn, studious, thinking, wary, watchful, worried. **2** *thoughtful work.* careful, conscientious, diligent, exhaustive, intelligent, methodical, meticulous, observant, orderly, organized, painstaking, rational, scrupulous, sensible, systematic, thorough. **3** *a thoughtful kindness.* attentive, caring, compassionate, concerned, considerate, friendly, good-natured, helpful, obliging, public-spirited, solicitous, unselfish. ▷ KIND. *Opp* THOUGHTLESS.

thoughtless *adj* **1** absentminded, careless, forgetful, hasty, heedless, ill-considered, impetuous, inadvertent, inattentive, injudicious, irresponsible, mindless, negligent, rash, reckless, *inf* scatter-brained, unobservant, unthinking. ▷ STUPID. **2** *a thoughtless insult.* cruel, heartless, impolite, inconsiderate, insensitive, rude, selfish, tactless, uncaring, undiplomatic, unfeeling. ▷ UNKIND. *Opp* THOUGHTFUL.

thrash *vb* beat, birch, cane, flay, flog, lash, scourge, whip. ▷ DEFEAT, HIT.

thread *n* **1** fibre, filament, hair, strand. □ *cotton, line, silk, string, thong, twine, wool, yarn.* **2** *thread of a story.* argument, continuity, course, direction, drift, line of thought, plot, story line, tenor, theme. ● *vb* put on a thread, string together. **thread your way** file, pass, pick your way, wind.

threadbare *adj* frayed, old, ragged, scruffy, shabby, tattered, tatty, worn, worn-out.

threat *n* **1** commination, intimidation, menace, warning. **2** *threat of rain.* danger, forewarning, intimation, omen, portent, presage, risk, warning.

threaten *vb* **1** browbeat, bully, cow, intimidate, make threats against, menace, pressurize, terrorize. ▷ FRIGHTEN. *Opp* REASSURE. **2** *clouds threaten rain.* forebode, foreshadow, forewarn of, give warning of, portend, presage, warn of. **3** *the recession threatens jobs.* endanger, imperil, jeopardize, put at risk.

threatening *adj* forbidding, grim, impending, looming, menacing, minatory, ominous, portentous, sinister, stern, *inf* ugly, unfriendly, worrying. *Opp* SUPPORTIVE.

three *n* triad, trio, triplet, triumvirate.

three-dimensional *adj* in the round, rounded, sculptural, solid, stereoscopic.

threshold *n* **1** doorstep, doorway, entrance, sill. **2** *threshold of a new era.* ▷ BEGINNING.

thrifty *adj* careful, *derog* closefisted, economical, frugal, *derog* mean, *derog* niggardly, parsimonious, provident, prudent, skimping, sparing. *Opp* EXTRAVAGANT.

thrill *n* adventure, *inf* buzz, excitement, frisson, *inf* kick, pleasure, sensation, shiver, suspense, tingle, titillation, tremor. ● *vb* arouse, delight, electrify, excite, galvanize, rouse, stimulate, stir, titillate. **thrilling** ▷ EXCITING.

thriller n crime story, detective story, mystery, inf whodunit. ▷ WRITING.

thrive vb be vigorous, bloom, boom, burgeon, inf come on, develop strongly, do well, expand, flourish, grow, increase, inf make strides, prosper, succeed. Opp DIE. **thriving** ▷ PROSPEROUS, VIGOROUS.

throat n gullet, neck, oesophagus, uvula, windpipe.

throaty adj deep, gravelly, gruff, guttural, hoarse, husky, rasping, rough, thick.

throb vb beat, palpitate, pound, pulsate, pulse, vibrate.

throe n convulsion, effort, fit, labour, plur labour-pains, pang, paroxysm, spasm. ▷ PAIN.

thrombosis n blood-clot, embolism.

throng n assembly, crowd, crush, gathering, horde, jam, mass, mob, multitude, swarm. ▷ GROUP.

throttle vb asphyxiate, choke, smother, stifle, strangle, suffocate. ▷ KILL.

throw vb 1 bowl, inf bung, cast, inf chuck, fling, heave, hurl, launch, lob, pelt, pitch, propel, put (the shot), send, inf shy, inf sling, toss. 2 throw light. cast, project, shed. 3 throw a rider. dislodge, floor, shake off, throw down, throw off, unseat, upset. 4 ▷ DISCONCERT. **throw away** ▷ DISCARD. **throw out** ▷ EXPEL. **throw up** ▷ PRODUCE, VOMIT.

throw-away adj 1 cheap, disposable. 2 throw-away remark. casual, offhand, passing, unimportant.

thrust vb butt, drive, elbow, force, impel, jab, lunge, plunge, poke, press, prod, propel, push, ram, send, shoulder, shove, stab, stick, urge.

thug n assassin, inf bully-boy, delinquent, desperado, gangster, inf hoodlum, hooligan, killer, mugger, inf rough, ruffian, inf tough, troublemaker, vandal, inf yob. ▷ CRIMINAL.

thunder n clap, crack, peal, roll, rumble. ▷ SOUND.

thunderous adj booming, deafening, reverberant, reverberating, roaring, rumbling. ▷ LOUD.

thus adv accordingly, consequently, for this reason, hence, so, therefore.

thwart vb baffle, baulk, block, check, foil, frustrate, hinder, impede, obstruct, prevent, stand in the way of, stop, stump.

ticket n 1 coupon, pass, permit, token, voucher. 2 price ticket. docket, label, marker, tab, tag.

ticklish adj 1 inf giggly, responsive to tickling, sensitive. 2 a ticklish problem. awkward, delicate, difficult, risky, inf thorny, touchy, tricky.

tide n current, drift, ebb and flow, movement, rise and fall.

tidiness n meticulousness, neatness, order, orderliness, organization, smartness, system. Opp DISORDER.

tidy adj 1 neat, orderly, presentable, shipshape, smart, inf spick and span, spruce, straight, trim, uncluttered, well-groomed, well-kept. 2 tidy habits. businesslike, careful, house-proud, methodical, meticulous, organized, systematic, well-organized. Opp UNTIDY. ● vb arrange, clean up, groom, make tidy, neaten, put in order, rearrange, reorganize, set straight, smarten, spruce up, straighten, titivate. Opp MUDDLE.

tie vb 1 bind, chain, do up, hitch, interlace, join, knot, lash, moor, rope, secure, splice, tether, truss up. ▷ FASTEN. Opp UNTIE. 2 tie in a race. be equal, be level, be neck and neck, draw.

tier n course (of bricks), layer, level, line, order, range, rank, row, stage, storey, stratum, terrace.

tight adj 1 close, fast, firm, fixed, immovable, secure, snug. 2 a tight lid. airtight, close-fitting, hermetic, impermeable, impervious, leakproof, sealed, waterproof, watertight. 3 tight supervision. harsh, inflexible, precise, rigorous, severe, strict, stringent. 4 tight ropes. rigid, stiff, stretched, taut, tense. 5 a tight space. compact, constricted, crammed, cramped, crowded, dense, inadequate, limited, packed, small. **6** ▷ DRUNK. **7** ▷ MISERLY. *Opp* FREE, LOOSE.

tighten *vb* **1** become tighter, clamp down, close, close up, constrict, harden, make tighter, squeeze, stiffen, tense. ▷ FASTEN. **2** *tighten ropes.* pull tighter, stretch, tauten. **3** *tighten screws.* give another turn to, screw up. *Opp* LOOSEN.

till *vb* cultivate, dig, farm, plough, work.

tilt *vb* **1** angle, bank, cant, careen, heel over, incline, keel over, lean, list, slant, slope, tip. **2** *tilt with lances.* joust, thrust. ▷ FIGHT.

timber *n* beam, board, boarding, deal, lath, log, lumber, plank, planking, post, softwood, tree, tree trunk. ▷ WOOD.

time *n* **1** date, hour, instant, juncture, moment, occasion, opportunity, point. **2** duration, interval, period, phase, season, semester, session, spell, stretch, term, while. □ aeon, century, *day*, decade, eternity, fortnight, hour, lifetime, minute, month, second, week, weekend, year. **3** *time of Nero.* age, days, epoch, era, period. **4** *time in music.* beat, measure, rhythm, tempo. ● *vb* **1** choose a time for, estimate, fix a time for, judge, organize, plan, schedule, timetable. **2** *time a race.* clock, measure the time of.

timeless *adj* ageless, deathless, eternal, everlasting, immortal, immutable, indestructible, permanent, unchanging, undying, unending.

timely *adj* appropriate, apt, fitting, suitable.

timepiece *n* □ *chronometer*, *clock*, *digital clock*, *digital watch*, *hourglass*, *stop-watch*, *sundial*, *timer*, *watch*, *wristwatch*.

timetable *n* agenda, calendar, curriculum, diary, list, programme, roster, rota, schedule.

timid *adj* afraid, apprehensive, bashful, chicken-hearted, cowardly, coy, diffident, fainthearted, fearful, modest, *inf* mousy, nervous, pusillanimous, reserved, retiring, scared, sheepish, shrinking, shy, spineless, tentative, timorous, unadventurous, unheroic, wimpish. ▷ FRIGHTENED. *Opp* BOLD.

tingle *n* **1** itch, itching, pins and needles, prickling, stinging, throb, throbbing, tickle, tickling. **2** *a tingle of excitement.* quiver, sensation, shiver, thrill. ● *vb* itch, prickle, sting, tickle.

tinker *vb* dabble, fiddle, fool about, interfere, meddle, *inf* mess about, *inf* play about, tamper, try to mend, work amateurishly.

tinny *adj* cheap, flimsy, inferior, insubstantial, poor-quality, shoddy, tawdry.

tinsel *n* decoration, glitter, gloss, show, sparkle, tinfoil.

tint *n* colour, colouring, dye, hue, shade, stain, tincture, tinge, tone, wash.

tiny *adj* diminutive, dwarf, imperceptible, infinitesimal, insignificant, lilliputian, microscopic, midget, *inf* mini, miniature, minuscule, minute, negligible, pygmy, *inf* teeny, unimportant, *inf* wee, *inf* weeny. ▷ SMALL. *Opp* BIG.

tip *n* **1** apex, cap, crown, end, extremity, ferrule, finial, head, nib, peak, pinnacle, point, sharp end, summit, top, vertex. **2** *tip for a waiter.* inf baksheesh, gift, gratuity, inducement, money, *inf* perk, present, reward, service-charge, *inf* sweetener. **3** *useful tips.* advice, clue, forecast, hint, information, pointer, prediction, suggestion, tip-off, warning. **4** *rubbish tip.* dump, rubbish-heap. ● *vb* **1** careen, incline, keel, lean, list, slant, slope, tilt. **2** drop off, dump, empty, pour out, spill, unload, upset, **3** *tip a waiter.* give a tip to, remunerate, reward. **tip over** ▷ OVERTURN.

tire *vb* **1** become bored, become tired, flag, grow weary, weaken. **2** debilitate, drain, enervate, exhaust, fatigue, *inf* finish, *sl* knacker, make tired, overtire, sap, *inf* shatter, *inf* take it out of, tax, wear out, weary. *Opp* REFRESH. **tired** ▷ WEARY. **tired of**

bored with, *inf* fed up with, impatient with, sick of. **tiring** ▷ EXHAUSTING.

tiredness *n* drowsiness, exhaustion, fatigue, inertia, jet-lag, lassitude, lethargy, listlessness, sleepiness, weariness.

tireless *adj* determined, diligent, dogged, dynamic, energetic, hardworking, indefatigable, persistent, pertinacious, resolute, sedulous, unceasing, unfaltering, unflagging, untiring, unwavering, vigorous. *Opp* LAZY.

tiresome *adj* **1** boring, dull, monotonous, tedious, tiring, unexciting, uninteresting, wearisome, wearying. *Opp* EXCITING. **2** *tiresome delays*. annoying, bothersome, distracting, exasperating, inconvenient, infuriating, irksome, irritating, maddening, petty, troublesome, trying, unwelcome, upsetting, vexatious, vexing.

tiring *adj* debilitating, demanding, difficult, exhausting, fatiguing, hard, laborious, strenuous, taxing, wearying. *Opp* REFRESHING.

tissue *n* **1** fabric, material, structure, stuff, substance. **2** *tissuepaper*. ▢ lavatory paper, napkin, paper handkerchief, serviette, toilet paper, tracing-paper.

title *n* **1** caption, heading, headline, inscription, name, rubric. **2** appellation, designation, form of address, office, position, rank, status. ▢ *Baron, Baroness, Count, Countess, Dame, Doctor, Dr, Duchess, Duke, Earl, Lady, Lord, Marchioness, Marquis, Master, Miss, Mr, Mrs, Ms, Professor, Rev, Reverend, Sir, Viscount, Viscountess*. ▷ RANK, ROYAL. **3** *title to an inheritance*. claim, deed, entitlement, interest, ownership, possession, prerogative, right. ● *vb* call, designate, entitle, give a title to, label, name, tag.

titled *adj* aristocratic, noble, upper class.

titter *vb* chortle, chuckle, giggle, snicker, snigger. ▷ LAUGH.

titular *adj* formal, nominal, official, putative, *inf* so-called, theoretical, token. *Opp* ACTUAL.

toast *vb* **1** brown, grill. ▷ COOK. **2** *toast a guest*. drink a toast to, drink the health of, drink to, honour, pay tribute to, raise your glass to.

tobacco *n* ▢ cigar, cigarette, pipe tobacco, plug, snuff.

together *adv* all at once, at the same time, collectively, concurrently, consecutively, continuously, cooperatively, hand in hand, in chorus, in unison, jointly, shoulder to shoulder, side by side, simultaneously.

toil *n inf* donkey work, drudgery, effort, exertion, industry, labour, work. ● *vb* drudge, exert yourself, grind away, *inf* keep at it, labour, *inf* plug away, *inf* slave away, struggle, *inf* sweat. ▷ WORK.

toilet *n* **1** convenience, latrine, lavatory, *sl* loo, *old use* privy, urinal, water closet, WC. **2** *[old use] make your toilet*. dressing, grooming, making up, washing.

token *adj* cosmetic, dutiful, emblematic, insincere, nominal, notional, perfunctory, representative, superficial, symbolic. *Opp* GENUINE. ● *n* **1** badge, emblem, evidence, expression, indication, mark, marker, proof, reminder, sign, symbol, testimony. **2** *a token of esteem*. keepsake, memento, reminder, souvenir. **3** *a bus token*. coin, counter, coupon, disc, voucher.

tolerable *adj* **1** acceptable, allowable, bearable, endurable, sufferable, supportable. **2** *tolerable food*. adequate, all right, average, fair, mediocre, middling, *inf* OK, ordinary, passable, satisfactory. *Opp* INTOLERABLE.

tolerance *n* **1** broad-mindedness, charity, fairness, forbearance, forgiveness, lenience, open-mindedness, openness, patience, permissiveness. **2** *tolerance of others*. acceptance, sufferance, sympathy (towards), toleration, understanding. **3** *tolerance in moving parts*. allowance, clearance, deviation, fluctuation, play, variation.

tolerant *adj* big-hearted, broad-minded, charitable, easygoing, fair, forbearing, forgiving, generous, indulgent, *derog* lax, lenient, liberal, magnanimous, open-minded, patient, permissive, *derog* soft, sympathetic, understanding, unprejudiced. *Opp* INTOLERANT.

tolerate *vb* abide, accept, admit, bear, brook, concede, condone, countenance, endure, *inf* lump (*I'll have to lump it!*), make allowances for, permit, *inf* put up with, sanction, *inf* stand, *inf* stick, *inf* stomach, suffer, *inf* take, undergo, *inf* wear, weather.

toll *n* charge, dues, duty, fee, levy, payment, tariff, tax. ● *vb* chime, peal, ring, sound, strike.

tomb *n* burial chamber, burial place, catacomb, crypt, grave, gravestone, last resting-place, mausoleum, memorial, monument, sepulchre, tombstone, vault.

tonality *n* key, tonal centre.

tone *n* **1** accent, colouring, expression, feel, inflection, intonation, manner, modulation, note, phrasing, pitch, quality, sonority, sound, timbre. **2** *tone of a poem, place.* air, atmosphere, character, effect, feeling, mood, spirit, style, temper, vein. **3** *colour tone.* colour, hue, shade, tinge, tint, tonality. **tone down** ▷ SOFTEN. **tone in** ▷ HARMONIZE. **tone up** ▷ STRENGTHEN.

tongue *n* dialect, idiom, language, parlance, patois, speech, talk, vernacular.

tongue-tied *adj* dumb, dumbfounded, inarticulate, *inf* lost for words, mute, silent, speechless.

tonic *n* boost, cordial, dietary supplement, fillip, *inf* pick-me-up, refresher, restorative, stimulant.

tool *n* apparatus, appliance, contraption, contrivance, device, gadget, hardware, implement, instrument, invention, machine, mechanism, utensil, weapon. □ [carpentry] auger, awl, *brace and bit*, bradawl, chisel, clamp, cramp, drill, file, fretsaw, gimlet, glass-paper, hacksaw, hammer, jigsaw, mallet, pincers, plane, pliers, power-drill, rasp, sander, sandpaper, saw, screwdriver, spokeshave, T-square, vice, wrench. □ [gardening] billhook, dibber, fork, grass-rake, hoe, lawnmower, mattock, pruning knife, pruning shears, rake, roller, scythe, secateurs, shears, sickle, spade, Strimmer, trowel. □ [various] axe, bellows, chainsaw, chopper, clippers, crowbar, cutter, hatchet, jack, ladder, lever, penknife, pick, pickaxe, pitchfork, pocket-knife, scissors, shovel, sledgehammer, spanner, tape-measure, tongs, tweezers.

tooth *n* □ canine, eye-tooth, fang, incisor, molar, tusk, wisdom tooth. **false teeth** bridge, denture, dentures, plate.

toothed *adj* cogged, crenellated, denticulate, indented, jagged, serrated. *Opp* SMOOTH.

top *adj inf* ace, best, choicest, finest, first, foremost, greatest, highest, incomparable, leading, maximum, most, peerless, pre-eminent, prime, principal, supreme, topmost, unequalled, winning. *n* **1** acme, apex, apogee, crest, crown, culmination, head, height, high point, peak, pinnacle, summit, tip, vertex, zenith. **2** *top of a table.* surface. **3** *top of a jar.* cap, cover, covering, lid, stopper. *Opp* BOTTOM. ● *vb* **1** complete, cover, decorate, finish off, garnish, surmount. **2** beat, be higher than, better, cap, exceed, excel, outdo, outstrip, surpass, transcend.

topic *n* issue, matter, point, question, subject, talking-point, text, theme, thesis.

topical *adj* contemporary, current, recent, timely, up-to-date.

topography *n* features, geography, *inf* lie of the land.

topple *vb* **1** bring down, fell, knock down, overturn, throw down, tip over, upset. **2** collapse, fall, overbalance, totter, tumble. **3** *topple a rival.* oust, overthrow, unseat. ▷ DEFEAT.

torch *n* bicycle lamp, brand, electric lamp, flashlight, lamp, *old use* link.

torment *n* affliction, agony, anguish, distress, harassment, misery, ordeal, persecution, plague, scourge, suffering, torture, vexation, woe, worry, wretchedness. ▷ PAIN. ● *vb* afflict, annoy, bait, be a torment to, bedevil, bother, bully, distress, harass, inflict pain on, intimidate, *inf* nag, persecute, pester, plague, tease, torture, vex, victimize, worry. ▷ HURT.

torpid *adj* apathetic, dormant, dull, inactive, indolent, inert, lackadaisical, languid, lethargic, lifeless, listless, passive, phlegmatic, slothful, slow, slow-moving, sluggish, somnolent, spiritless. *Opp* LIVELY.

torrent *n* cascade, cataract, deluge, downpour, effusion, flood, flow, gush, inundation, outpouring, overflow, rush, spate, stream, tide.

torrential *adj* copious, heavy, relentless, soaking, teeming, violent.

tortuous *adj* bent, circuitous, complicated, contorted, convoluted, corkscrew, crooked, curling, curvy, devious, indirect, involved, labyrinthine, mazy, meandering, roundabout, serpentine, sinuous, turning, twisted, twisting, twisty, wandering, winding, zigzag. *Opp* DIRECT, STRAIGHT.

torture *n* **1** cruelty, degradation, humiliation, inquisition, persecution, punishment, torment. **2** affliction, agony, anguish, distress, misery, pain, plague, scourge, suffering. ● *vb* **1** be cruel to, brainwash, bully, cause pain to, degrade, dehumanize, humiliate, hurt, inflict pain on, intimidate, persecute, rack, torment, victimize. **2** *tortured by doubts*. afflict, agonize, annoy, bedevil, bother, distress, harass, *inf* nag, pester, plague, tease, vex, worry.

toss *vb* **1** bowl, cast, *inf* chuck, fling, flip, heave, hurl, lob, pitch, shy, sling, throw. **2** *toss about in a storm*. bob, dip, flounder, lurch, move restlessly, pitch, plunge, reel, rock, roll, shake, twist and turn, wallow, welter, writhe, yaw.

total *adj* **1** complete, comprehensive, entire, full, gross, overall, whole. **2** *total disaster*. absolute, downright, out-and-out, outright, perfect, sheer, thorough, thoroughgoing, unalloyed, unmitigated, unqualified, utter. ● *n* aggregate, amount, answer, lot, sum, totality, whole. ● *vb* **1** add up to, amount to, come to, make. **2** add up, calculate, compute, count, find the sum of, find the total of, reckon up, totalize, *inf* tot up, work out.

totalitarian *adj* absolute, arbitrary, authoritarian, autocratic, despotic, dictatorial, fascist, illiberal, one-party, oppressive, tyrannous, undemocratic, unrepresentative. *Opp* DEMOCRATIC.

totter *vb* dodder, falter, reel, rock, stagger, stumble, teeter, topple, tremble, waver, wobble. ▷ WALK.

touch *n* **1** feeling, texture, touching. **2** brush, caress, contact, dab, pat, stroke, tap. **3** *an expert's touch*. ability, capability, experience, expertise, facility, feel, flair, gift, knack, manner, sensitivity, skill, style, technique, understanding, way. **4** *a touch of salt*. bit, dash, drop, hint, intimation, small amount, suggestion, suspicion, taste, tinge, trace. ● *vb* **1** be in contact with, brush, caress, contact, cuddle, dab, embrace, feel, finger, fondle, graze, handle, hit, kiss, lean against, manipulate, massage, nuzzle, pat, paw, pet, push, rub, stroke, tap, tickle. **2** *touch the emotions*. affect, arouse, awaken, concern, disturb, impress, influence, inspire, move, stimulate, stir, upset. **3** *touch 100 m.p.h*. attain, reach, rise to. **4** *I can't touch her skill*. be in the same league as, *inf* come up to, compare with, equal, match, parallel, rival. **touched** ▷ EMOTIONAL, MAD. **touching** ▷ EMOTIONAL. **touch off** ▷ BEGIN, IGNITE. **touch on** ▷ MENTION. **touch up** ▷ IMPROVE.

touchy *adj* edgy, highly strung, hypersensitive, irascible, irritable, jittery, jumpy, nervous, over-sensitive, peevish, querulous, quick-tempered, sensitive, short-tempered, snappy, temperamental, tense, testy, tetchy, thin-skinned, unpredictable, waspish.

tough *adj* **1** durable, hard-wearing, indestructible, lasting, rugged, sound, stout, strong, substantial, unbreakable, well-built, well-made. **2** *tough physique. inf* beefy, brawny, burly, hardy, muscular, robust, stalwart, strong, sturdy. **3** *tough opposition.* invulnerable, merciless, obdurate, obstinate, resilient, resistant, resolute, ruthless, stiff, stubborn, tenacious, unyielding. **4** *a tough taskmaster.* cold, cool, *inf* hardboiled, hardened, *inf* hard-nosed, inhuman, severe, stern, stony, uncaring, unsentimental, unsympathetic. **5** *tough meat.* chewy, hard, gristly, leathery, rubbery, uneatable. **6** *tough work.* arduous, demanding, difficult, exacting, exhausting, gruelling, hard, laborious, stiff, strenuous, taxing, troublesome. **7** *a tough problem.* baffling, intractable, *inf* knotty, mystifying, perplexing, puzzling, *inf* thorny. *Opp* EASY, TENDER, WEAK.

toughen *vb* harden, make tougher, reinforce, strengthen.

tour *n* circular tour, drive, excursion, expedition, jaunt, journey, outing, peregrination, ride, trip. ● *vb* do the rounds of, explore, go round, make a tour of, visit. ▷ TRAVEL.

tourist *n* day-tripper, holidaymaker, sightseer, traveller, tripper, visitor.

tournament *n* championship, competition, contest, event, match, meeting, series.

tow *vb* drag, draw, haul, lug, pull, trail, tug.

tower *n* □ belfry, *campanile*, castle, fort, fortress, *keep*, minaret, *pagoda*, skyscraper, *spire*, steeple, *turret*. ● *vb* ascend, dominate, loom, rear, rise, soar, stand out, stick up.

towering *adj* **1** colossal, gigantic, high, huge, imposing, lofty, mighty, soaring. ▷ TALL. **2** *a towering rage.* extreme, fiery, immoderate, intemperate, intense, mighty, overpowering, passionate, unrestrained, vehement, violent.

town *n* borough, city, community, conurbation, municipality, settlement, township, urban district, village.

toxic *adj* dangerous, deadly, harmful, lethal, noxious, poisonous. *Opp* HARMLESS.

trace *n* **1** clue, evidence, footprint, *inf* give-away, hint, indication, intimation, mark, remains, sign, spoor, token, track, trail, vestige. **2** ▷ BIT. ● *vb* **1** detect, discover, find, get back, recover, retrieve, seek out, track down. ▷ TRACK. **2** *trace an outline.* copy, draw, go over, make a copy of, mark out, sketch. **kick over the traces** ▷ REBEL.

track *n* **1** footmark, footprint, mark, scent, spoor, trace, trail, wake (*of ship*). **2** *a farm track.* bridle-path, bridle-way, cart-track, footpath, path, route, trail, way. ▷ ROAD. **3** *a racing track.* circuit, course, dirt-track, race-track. **4** *railway track.* branch, branch line, line, mineral line, permanent way, rails, railway, route, tramway. ● *vb* chase, dog, follow, hound, hunt, pursue, shadow, stalk, tail, trace, trail. **make tracks** ▷ DEPART. **track down** ▷ TRACE.

trade *n* **1** barter, business, buying and selling, commerce, dealing, exchange, industry, market, marketing, merchandising, trading, traffic, transactions. **2** *a skilled trade.* calling, career, craft, employment, job, *inf* line, occupation, profession, pursuit, work. ● *vb* buy and sell, do business, have dealings, market goods, merchandise, retail, sell, traffic (in). **trade in** ▷ EXCHANGE. **trade on** ▷ EXPLOIT.

trader *n* broker, buyer, dealer, merchant, retailer, roundsman, salesman, seller, shopkeeper, stockist, supplier, tradesman, trafficker (*in illegal goods*), vendor.

tradition *n* **1** convention, custom, habit, institution, practice, rite, ritual, routine, usage. **2** *popular tradition.* belief, folklore.

traditional *adj* **1** accustomed, conventional, customary, established, familiar, habitual, historic, normal, orthodox, regular, time-honoured, typical, usual. *Opp* UNCONVENTIONAL. **2** *traditional stories.* folk, handed down, old, oral, popular, unwritten. *Opp* MODERN.

traffic *n* conveyance, movements, shipping, transport, transportation. ▷ VEHICLE. ● *vb* ▷ TRADE.

tragedy *n* adversity, affliction, *inf* blow, calamity, catastrophe, disaster, misfortune. *Opp* COMEDY.

tragic *adj* **1** appalling, awful, calamitous, catastrophic, depressing, dire, disastrous, dreadful, fatal, fearful, hapless, ill-fated, ill-omened, ill-starred, inauspicious, lamentable, terrible, tragical, unfortunate, unlucky. **2** *a tragic expression.* bereft, distressed, funereal, grief-stricken, hurt, pathetic, piteous, pitiful, sorrowful, woeful, wretched. ▷ SAD. *Opp* COMIC.

trail *n* **1** evidence, footmarks, footprints, marks, scent, signs, spoor, traces, wake (*of ship*). **2** path, pathway, route, track. ▷ ROAD. ● *vb* **1** dangle, drag, draw, haul, pull, tow. **2** chase, follow, hunt, pursue, shadow, stalk, tail, trace, track down. **3** ▷ DAWDLE.

train *n* **1** carriage, coach, diesel, *inf* DMU, electric train, express, intercity, local train, railcar, steam train, stopping train. **2** *train of servants.* cortège, entourage, escort, followers, guard, line, retainers, retinue, staff, suite. **3** *train of events.* ▷ SEQUENCE. ● *vb* **1** coach, discipline, drill, educate, instruct, prepare, school, teach, tutor. **2** do exercises, exercise, *inf* get fit, practise, prepare yourself, rehearse, *inf* work out. **3** ▷ AIM.

trainee *n* apprentice, beginner, cadet, learner, *inf* L-driver, novice, pupil, starter, student, tiro, unqualified person.

trainer *n* coach, instructor, teacher, tutor.

trait *n* attribute, characteristic, feature, idiosyncrasy, peculiarity, property, quality, quirk.

traitor *n* apostate, betrayer, blackleg, collaborator, defector, deserter, double-crosser, fifth columnist, informer, *inf* Judas, quisling, renegade, turncoat.

tramp *n* **1** hike, march, trek, trudge, walk. **2** *a homeless tramp.* beggar, *inf* destitute person, *inf* dosser, *inf* down and out, drifter, homeless person, rover, traveller, vagabond, vagrant, wanderer. ● *vb* *inf* footslog, hike, march, plod, stride, toil, traipse, trek, trudge, *sl* yomp. ▷ WALK.

trample *vb* crush, flatten, squash, *inf* squish, stamp on, step on, tread on, walk over.

trance *n* *inf* brown study, daydream, daze, dream, ecstasy, hypnotic state, rapture, reverie, semi-consciousness, spell, stupor, unconsciousness.

tranquil *adj* **1** calm, halcyon (*days*), peaceful, placid, quiet, restful, serene, still, undisturbed, unruffled. *Opp* STORMY. **2** *a tranquil mood.* collected, composed, dispassionate, *inf* laid-back, sedate, sober, unemotional, unexcited, untroubled. *Opp* EXCITED.

tranquillizer *n* barbiturate, bromide, narcotic, opiate, sedative.

transaction *n* agreement, bargain, business, contract, deal, negotiation, proceeding.

transcend *vb* beat, exceed, excel, outdo, outstrip, rise above, surpass, top.

transcribe *vb* copy out, render, reproduce, take down, translate, transliterate, write out.

transfer *vb* bring, carry, change, convey, deliver, displace, ferry, hand over, make over, move, pass on, pass over, relocate, remove, second, shift, sign over, take, transplant, transport, transpose.

transform *vb* adapt, alter, change, convert, improve, metamorphose, modify, mutate, permute, rebuild, reconstruct, remodel, revolutionize, transfigure, translate, transmogrify, transmute, turn.

transformation

transformation n adaptation, alteration, change, conversion, improvement, metamorphosis, modification, mutation, reconstruction, revolution, transfiguration, transition, translation, transmogrification, transmutation, *inf* turn-about.

transgression n crime, error, fault, lapse, misdeed, misdemeanour, offence, sin, wickedness, wrongdoing.

transient adj brief, ephemeral, evanescent, fleeting, fugitive, impermanent, momentary, passing, *inf* quick, short, short-lived, temporary, transitory. *Opp* PERMANENT.

transit n conveyance, journey, movement, moving, passage, progress, shipment, transfer, transportation, travel.

transition n alteration, change, change-over, conversion, development, evolution, modification, movement, progress, progression, shift, transformation, transit.

translate vb change, convert, decode, elucidate, explain, express, gloss, interpret, make a translation, paraphrase, render, reword, spell out, transcribe. ▷ TRANSFORM.

translation n decoding, gloss, interpretation, paraphrase, rendering, transcription, transliteration, version.

translator n interpreter, linguist.

transmission n 1 broadcasting, communication, diffusion, dissemination, relaying, sending out. 2 *transmission of goods.* carriage, carrying, conveyance, dispatch, sending, shipment, shipping, transfer, transference, transport, transportation.

transmit vb 1 convey, dispatch, disseminate, forward, pass on, post, send, transfer, transport. 2 *transmit a message.* broadcast, cable, communicate, emit, fax, phone, radio, relay, telephone, telex, wire. *Opp* RECEIVE.

transparent adj 1 clear, crystalline, diaphanous, filmy, gauzy, limpid, pellucid, *inf* see-through, sheer,

translucent. 2 *transparent honesty.* ▷ CANDID.

transplant vb displace, move, relocate, reposition, resettle, shift, transfer, uproot.

transport n carrier, conveyance, haulage, removal, shipment, shipping, transportation. □ *aircraft, barge, boat, bus, cable-car, car, chair-lift, coach, cycle, ferry, horse, lorry, Metro, minibus, old use omnibus, ship, space-shuttle, taxi, train, tram, van.* □ *air, canal, railway, road, sea, waterways.* ▷ VEHICLE, VESSEL. ● vb 1 bear, carry, convey, fetch, haul, move, remove, send, shift, ship, take, transfer. 2 ▷ DEPORT.

transpose vb change, exchange, interchange, metathesize, move round, rearrange, reverse, substitute, swap, switch, transfer.

transverse adj crosswise, diagonal, oblique.

trap n ambush, booby-trap, deception, gin, mantrap, net, noose, pitfall, ploy, snare, trick. ● vb ambush, arrest, capture, catch, catch out, corner, deceive, dupe, ensnare, entrap, inveigle, net, snare, trick.

trappings *plur* n accessories, accompaniments, accoutrements, adornments, appointments, decorations, equipment, finery, fittings, furnishings, *inf* gear, ornaments, paraphernalia, *inf* things, trimmings.

trash n 1 debris, garbage, junk, litter, refuse, rubbish, sweepings, waste. 2 ▷ NONSENSE.

travel n globe-trotting, moving around, peregrination, touring, tourism, travelling, wandering. □ *cruise, drive, excursion, expedition, exploration, flight, hike, holiday, journey, march, migration, mission, outing, pilgrimage, ramble, ride, safari, sail, sea-passage, tour, trek, trip, visit, voyage, walk.* ● vb *inf* gad about, *inf* gallivant, journey, make a trip, move, proceed, progress, roam, *poet* rove, voyage, wander. ▷ GO. □ *aviate, circumnavigate (the world), commute, cruise, cycle, drive, emigrate, fly, free-wheel, hike, hitch-hike, march, migrate, motor, navigate,* *paddle, pedal, pilot, punt, ramble, ride, row, sail, shuttle, steam, tour, trek, walk.*

traveller n **1** astronaut, aviator, commuter, cosmonaut, cyclist, driver, flyer, migrant, motorcyclist, motorist, passenger, pedestrian, sailor, voyager, walker. **2** *a company traveller.* inf rep, representative, salesman, saleswoman. **3** *overseas travellers.* explorer, globe-trotter, hiker, hitchhiker, holidaymaker, pilgrim, rambler, stowaway, tourist, tripper, wanderer, wayfarer. **4** *live as travellers.* gypsy, itinerant, nomad, tinker, tramp, vagabond.

travelling adj homeless, itinerant, migrant, migratory, mobile, nomadic, peripatetic, restless, roaming, roving, touring, vagrant, wandering.

treacherous adj **1** deceitful, disloyal, double-crossing, double-dealing, duplicitous, faithless, false, perfidious, sneaky, unfaithful, untrustworthy. **2** *treacherous conditions.* dangerous, deceptive, hazardous, misleading, perilous, risky, shifting, unpredictable, unreliable, unsafe, unstable. Opp LOYAL, RELIABLE.

treachery n betrayal, dishonesty, disloyalty, double-dealing, duplicity, faithlessness, infidelity, perfidy, untrustworthiness. ▷ TREASON. Opp LOYALTY.

tread vb **tread on** crush, squash underfoot, stamp on, step on, trample, walk on. ▷ WALK.

treason n betrayal, high treason, mutiny, rebellion, sedition. ▷ TREACHERY.

treasure n cache, cash, fortune, gold, hoard, jewels, riches, treasure trove, valuables, wealth. ● vb adore, appreciate, cherish, esteem, guard, keep safe, love, prize, rate highly, value, venerate, worship.

treasury n bank, exchequer, hoard, repository, storeroom, treasurehouse, vault.

treat n entertainment, gift, outing, pleasure, surprise. ● vb **1** attend to, behave towards, care for, look after, use. **2** *treat a topic.* consider, deal with, discuss, tackle. **3** *treat a patient, wound.* cure, dress, give treatment to, heal, medicate, nurse, prescribe medicine for, tend. **4** *treat food.* process. **5** *treat a friend to dinner.* entertain, give a treat, pay for, provide for, regale.

treatise n disquisition, dissertation, essay, monograph, pamphlet, paper, thesis, tract. ▷ WRITING.

treatment n **1** care, conduct, dealing (with), handling, management, manipulation, organization, reception, usage, use. **2** *treatment of illness.* cure, first aid, healing, nursing, remedy, therapy. ▷ MEDICINE, THERAPY.

treaty n agreement, alliance, armistice, compact, concordat, contract, covenant, convention, inf deal, entente, pact, peace, protocol, settlement, truce, understanding.

tree n bush, sapling, standard. □ bonsai, conifer, cordon, deciduous tree, espalier, evergreen, pollard, standard. □ ash, banyan, baobab, bay, beech, birch, cacao, cedar, chestnut, cypress, elder, elm, eucalyptus, fir, fruit-tree, gum-tree, hawthorn, hazel, holly, horse-chestnut, larch, lime, maple, oak, olive, palm, pine, plane, poplar, redwood, rowan, sequoia, spruce, sycamore, tamarisk, tulip tree, willow, yew.

tremble vb quail, quake, quaver, quiver, rock, shake, shiver, shudder, vibrate, waver.

tremendous adj alarming, appalling, awful, fearful, fearsome, frightening, frightful, horrifying, shocking, startling, terrible, terrific. ▷ BIG, EXCELLENT, REMARKABLE.

tremor n **1** agitation, hesitation, quavering, quiver, shaking, trembling, vibration. **2** earthquake, seismic disturbance.

tremulous adj **1** agitated, anxious, excited, frightened, jittery, jumpy, nervous, timid, uncertain. Opp CALM. **2** quivering, shaking, shivering, trembling, inf trembly, vibrating. Opp STEADY.

trend n **1** bent, bias, direction, drift, inclination, leaning, movement, shift, tendency. **2** *latest trend.* craze, *inf* fad, fashion, mode, *inf* rage, style, *inf* thing, vogue, way.

trendy adj *inf* all the rage, contemporary, fashionable, *inf* in, latest, modern, stylish, up-to-date, voguish. *Opp* OLD-FASHIONED.

trespass vb encroach, enter illegally, intrude, invade.

trial n **1** case, court martial, enquiry, examination, hearing, inquisition, judicial proceeding, lawsuit, tribunal. **2** attempt, check, *inf* dry run, experiment, rehearsal, test, testing, trial run, *inf* try-out. **3** *a sore trial.* affliction, burden, difficulty, hardship, nuisance, ordeal, *sl* pain in the neck, *inf* pest, problem, tribulation, trouble, worry.

triangular adj three-cornered, three-sided.

tribe n clan, dynasty, family, group, horde, house, nation, pedigree, people, race, stock, strain.

tribute n accolade, appreciation, commendation, compliment, eulogy, glorification, homage, honour, panegyric, praise, recognition, respect, testimony. **pay tribute to** ▷ HONOUR.

trick n **1** illusion, legerdemain, magic, sleight of hand. **2** *deceitful trick.* cheat, *inf* con, deceit, deception, fraud, hoax, imposture, joke, *inf* leg-pull, manoeuvre, ploy, practical joke, prank, pretence, ruse, scheme, stratagem, stunt, subterfuge, swindle, trap, trickery, wile. **3** *clever trick.* art, craft, device, dodge, expertise, gimmick, knack, *inf* know-how, secret, skill, technique. **4** *a trick of speech.* characteristic, habit, idiosyncrasy, mannerism, peculiarity, way. ● vb *inf* bamboozle, bluff, catch out, cheat, *inf* con, cozen, deceive, defraud, *inf* diddle, dupe, fool, hoax, hoodwink, *inf* kid, mislead, outwit, *inf* pull your leg, swindle, *inf* take in.

trickery n bluffing, cheating, chicanery, deceit, deception, dishonesty, double-dealing, duplicity, fraud, *inf* funny business, guile, *inf* hocus-pocus, *inf* jiggerypokery, knavery, *inf* skulduggery, slyness, swindling, trick.

trickle vb dribble, drip, drizzle, drop, exude, flow slowly, leak, ooze, percolate, run, seep. *Opp* GUSH.

trifle vb behave frivolously, dabble, fiddle, fool about, play about. **trifling** ▷ TRIVIAL.

trill vb sing, twitter, warble, whistle.

trim adj compact, neat, orderly, *inf* shipshape, smart, spruce, tidy, well-groomed, well-kept, well-ordered. *Opp* UNTIDY. ● vb **1** clip, crop, cut, dock, pare down, prune, shape, shear, shorten, snip, tidy. **2** ▷ DECORATE.

trip n day out, drive, excursion, expedition, holiday, jaunt, journey, outing, ride, tour, visit, voyage. ● vb **1** blunder, catch your foot, fall, stagger, stumble, totter, tumble. **2** *trip along.* caper, dance, frisk, gambol, run, skip. **make a trip** ▷ TRAVEL.

trite adj banal, commonplace, ordinary, pedestrian, predictable, uninspired, uninteresting.

triumph n **1** accomplishment, achievement, conquest, coup, *inf* hit, knockout, master-stroke, *inf* smash hit, success, victory, *inf* walk-over, win. **2** *return in triumph.* celebration, elation, exultation, joy, jubilation, rapture. ● vb be victorious, carry the day, prevail, succeed, take the honours, win. **triumph over** ▷ DEFEAT.

triumphant adj **1** conquering, dominant, successful, victorious, winning. *Opp* UNSUCCESSFUL. **2** boastful, *inf* cocky, elated, exultant, gleeful, gloating, immodest, joyful, jubilant, proud, triumphal.

trivial adj *inf* fiddling, *inf* footling, frivolous, inconsequential, inconsiderable, inessential, insignificant, little, meaningless, minor, negligible, paltry, pettifogging, petty, *inf* piddling, *inf* piffling, silly, slight, small, superficial, trifling, trite, unimportant, worthless. *Opp* IMPORTANT.

trophy n **1** booty, loot, mementoes, rewards, souvenirs, spoils. **2** *a sport-*

ing trophy. award, cup, laurels, medal, palm, prize.

trouble *n* **1** adversity, affliction, anxiety, burden, difficulty, distress, grief, hardship, illness, inconvenience, misery, misfortune, pain, problem, sadness, sorrow, suffering, trial, tribulation, unhappiness, vexation, worry. **2** *crowd trouble.* bother, commotion, conflict, discontent, discord, disorder, dissatisfaction, disturbance, fighting, fuss, misbehaviour, misconduct, naughtiness, row, strife, turmoil, unpleasantness, unrest, violence. **3** *engine trouble.* breakdown, defect, failure, fault, malfunction. **4** *took the trouble to get it right.* care, concern, effort, exertion, labour, pains, struggle, thought. ● *vb* afflict, agitate, alarm, anguish, annoy, bother, cause trouble to, concern, discommode, distress, disturb, exasperate, grieve, harass, *inf* hassle, hurt, impose on, inconvenience, interfere with, irk, irritate, molest, nag, pain, perturb, pester, plague, *inf* put out, ruffle, threaten, torment, upset, vex, worry. *Opp* REASSURE. **troubled** ▷ WORRIED.

troublemaker *n Fr* agent provocateur, agitator, criminal, culprit, delinquent, hooligan, malcontent, mischief-maker, offender, rabble-rouser, rascal, ringleader, ruffian, scandalmonger, *inf* stirrer, vandal, wrongdoer.

troublesome *adj* annoying, badly-behaved, bothersome, disobedient, disorderly, distressing, inconvenient, irksome, irritating, naughty, *inf* pestiferous, pestilential, rowdy, tiresome, trying, uncooperative, unruly, upsetting, vexatious, vexing, wearisome, worrisome, worrying. *Opp* HELPFUL.

trousers *n inf* bags, breeches, corduroys, culottes, denims, dungarees, jeans, jodhpurs, *old use* knickerbockers, *inf* Levis, overalls, *Amer* pants, plus-fours, shorts, ski-pants, slacks, *Scot* trews, trunks.

truancy *n* absenteeism, desertion, malingering, shirking, *inf* skiving.

truant *n* absentee, deserter, dodger, idler, malingerer, runaway, shirker, *inf* skiver. **play truant** be absent, desert, malinger, *inf* skive, stay away.

truce *n* agreement, armistice, ceasefire, moratorium, pact, peace, suspension of hostilities, treaty.

true *adj* **1** accurate, actual, authentic, confirmed, correct, exact, factual, faithful, faultless, flawless, genuine, literal, proper, real, realistic, right, veracious, verified, veritable. *Opp* FALSE. **2** *a true friend.* constant, dedicated, dependable, devoted, faithful, firm, honest, honourable, loyal, reliable, responsible, sincere, staunch, steadfast, steady, trustworthy, trusty, upright. **3** *the true owner.* authorized, legal, legitimate, rightful, valid. **4** *true aim.* accurate, exact, perfect, precise, *inf* spot-on, unerring, unswerving. *Opp* INACCURATE.

truncheon *n* baton, club, cudgel, staff, stick.

trunk *n* **1** bole, shaft, stalk, stem, stock. **2** *a person's trunk.* body, frame, torso. **3** *an elephant's trunk.* nose, proboscis. **4** *a clothes' trunk.* box, case, casket, chest, coffer, crate, locker, suitcase.

trust *n* **1** assurance, belief, certainty, certitude, confidence, conviction, credence, faith, reliance. **2** *a position of trust.* responsibility, trusteeship. ● *vb* **1** *inf* bank on, believe in, be sure of, confide in, count on, depend on, have confidence in, have faith in, *inf* pin your hopes on, rely on. **2** assume, expect, hope, imagine, presume, suppose, surmise. *Opp* DOUBT.

trustful *adj* confiding, credulous, gullible, innocent, trusting, unquestioning, unsuspecting, unsuspicious, unwary. *Opp* DISTRUSTFUL.

trustworthy *adj* constant, dependable, ethical, faithful, honest, honourable, loyal, moral, on the level, principled, reliable, responsible, *inf* safe, sensible, sincere, steadfast, steady, straightforward, true, *old use* trusty, truthful, upright. *Opp* DECEITFUL.

truth n **1** facts, reality. *Opp* LIE. **2** accuracy, authenticity, correctness, exactness, factuality, genuineness, integrity, reliability, truthfulness, validity, veracity, verity. **3** *an accepted truth*. axiom, fact, maxim, truism.

truthful adj accurate, candid, correct, credible, earnest, factual, faithful, forthright, frank, honest, proper, realistic, reliable, right, sincere, *inf* straight, straightforward, true, trustworthy, valid, veracious, unvarnished. *Opp* DISHONEST.

try n attempt, *inf* bash, *inf* crack, effort, endeavour, experiment, *inf* go, *inf* shot, *inf* stab, test, trial. ● vb **1** aim, attempt, endeavour, essay, exert yourself, make an effort, strain, strive, struggle, venture. **2** *try something new*. appraise, *inf* check out, evaluate, examine, experiment with, *inf* have a go at, *inf* have a stab at, investigate, test, try out, undertake. **trying** ▷ ANNOYING, TIRESOME. **try someone's patience** ▷ ANNOY.

tub n barrel, bath, butt, cask, drum, keg, pot, vat.

tube n capillary, conduit, cylinder, duct, hose, main, pipe, spout, tubing.

tuck vb cram, gather, insert, push, put away, shove, stuff. **tuck in** ▷ EAT.

tuft n bunch, clump, cluster, tuffet, tussock.

tug vb drag, draw, haul, heave, jerk, lug, pluck, pull, tow, twitch, wrench, *inf* yank.

tumble vb **1** collapse, drop, fall, flop, pitch, roll, stumble, topple, trip up. **2** *tumble things into a heap*. disarrange, dump, jumble, mix up, rumple, shove, spill, throw carelessly, toss.

tumbledown adj badly maintained, broken down, crumbling, decrepit, derelict, dilapidated, ramshackle, rickety, ruined, shaky, tottering.

tumult n ado, agitation, chaos, commotion, confusion, disturbance, excitement, ferment, fracas, frenzy, hubbub, hullabaloo, rumpus, storm, tempest, upheaval, uproar, welter.

tumultuous adj agitated, boisterous, confused, excited, frenzied, hectic, passionate, stormy, tempestuous, turbulent, unrestrained, unruly, violent, wild. *Opp* CALM.

tune n air, melody, motif, song, strain, theme. ● vb adjust, calibrate, regulate, set, temper.

tuneful adj *inf* catchy, euphonious, mellifluous, melodic, melodious, musical, pleasant, singable, sweetsounding. *Opp* TUNELESS.

tuneless adj atonal, boring, cacophonous, discordant, dissonant, harsh, monotonous, unmusical. *Opp* TUNEFUL.

tunnel n burrow, gallery, hole, mine, passage, passageway, shaft, subway, underpass. ● vb burrow, dig, excavate, mine, penetrate.

turbulent adj **1** agitated, boisterous, confused, disordered, excited, hectic, passionate, restless, seething, turbid, unrestrained, violent, volatile, wild. **2** *a turbulent crowd*. badly-behaved, disorderly, lawless, obstreperous, riotous, rowdy, undisciplined, unruly. **3** *turbulent weather*. blustery, bumpy, choppy (*sea*), rough, stormy, tempestuous, violent, wild, windy. *Opp* CALM.

turf n grass, grassland, green, lawn, *poet* sward.

turgid adj affected, bombastic, flowery, fulsome, grandiose, highflown, overblown, pompous, pretentious, stilted, wordy. *Opp* ARTICULATE.

turmoil n *inf* bedlam, chaos, commotion, confusion, disorder, disturbance, ferment, *inf* hubbub, *inf* hullabaloo, pandemonium, riot, row, rumpus, tumult, turbulence, unrest, upheaval, uproar, welter. *Opp* CALM.

turn n **1** circle, coil, curve, cycle, loop, pirouette, revolution, roll, rotation, spin, twirl, twist, whirl. **2** angle, bend, change of direction, corner, deviation, *inf* dogleg, hairpin bend, junction, loop, meander, reversal, shift, turning-point, *inf* U-turn, zigzag. **3** *your turn in a game*. chance, *inf* go, innings, opportunity, shot, stint. **4** *a comic turn.* ▷ PERFORMANCE. **5** *a nasty turn.* ▷ ILLNESS. ● *vb* **1** circle, coil, curl, gyrate, hinge, loop, move in a circle, orbit, pivot, revolve, roll, rotate, spin, spiral, swivel, twirl, twist, whirl, wind, yaw. **2** bend, change direction, corner, deviate, divert, go round a corner, negotiate a corner, steer, swerve, veer, wheel. **3** *turn a pumpkin into a coach.* adapt, alter, change, convert, make, modify, remake, remodel, transfigure, transform. **4** *turn to and fro.* squirm, twist, wriggle, writhe. **turn aside** ▷ DEVIATE. **turn down** ▷ REJECT. **turn into** ▷ BECOME. **turn off** ▷ DEVIATE, DISCONNECT, REPEL. **turn on** ▷ ATTRACT, CONNECT. **turn out** ▷ EXPEL, HAPPEN, PRODUCE. **turn over** ▷ CONSIDER, OVERTURN. **turn tail** ▷ ESCAPE. **turn up** ▷ ARRIVE, DISCOVER.

turning-point *n* crisis, crossroads, new direction, revolution, watershed.

turnover *n* business, cash-flow, efficiency, output, production, productivity, profits, revenue, throughput, yield.

twiddle *vb* fiddle with, fidget with, fool with, mess with, twirl, twist.

twig *n* branch, offshoot, shoot, spray, sprig, sprout, stalk, stem, stick, sucker, tendril.

twilight *n* dusk, evening, eventide, gloaming, gloom, halflight, nightfall, sundown, sunset.

twin *adj* balancing, corresponding, double, duplicate, identical, indistinguishable, *inf* look-alike, matching, paired, similar, symmetrical. ● *n* clone, counterpart, double, duplicate, *inf* look-alike, match, pair, *inf* spitting image.

twirl *vb* **1** gyrate, pirouette, revolve, rotate, spin, turn, twist, wheel, whirl, wind. **2** *twirl an umbrella.* brandish, twiddle, wave.

twist *n* **1** bend, coil, curl, kink, knot, loop, tangle, turn, zigzag. **2** *a twist to a story.* revelation, surprise ending. ● *vb* **1** bend, coil, corkscrew, curl, curve, loop, revolve, rotate, screw, spin, spiral, turn, weave, wind, wreathe, wriggle, writhe, zigzag. **2** *twist ropes.* entangle, entwine, intertwine, interweave, tangle. **3** *twist a lid off.* jerk, wrench, wrest. **4** *twist out of shape.* buckle, contort, crinkle, crumple, distort, screw up, warp, wrinkle. **5** *twist meaning.* alter, change, falsify, misquote, misrepresent. **twisted** ▷ CONFUSED, PERVERTED, TWISTY.

twisty *adj* bending, bendy, circuitous, coiled, contorted, crooked, curving, curvy, *inf* in and out, indirect, looped, meandering, misshapen, rambling, roundabout, serpentine, sinuous, snaking, tortuous, twisted, twisting, *inf* twisting and turning, winding, zigzag. *Opp* STRAIGHT.

twitch *n* blink, convulsion, flutter, jerk, jump, spasm, tic, tremor. ● *vb* fidget, flutter, jerk, jump, start, tremble.

two *n* couple, duet, duo, match, pair, twosome.

type *n* **1** category, class, classification, description, designation, form, genre, group, kind, mark, set, sort, species, variety. **2** *He was the very type of evil.* embodiment, epitome, example, model, pattern, personification, standard. **3** *printed in large type.* characters, font, fount, lettering, letters, print, printing, typeface.

typical *adj* **1** characteristic, distinctive, particular, representative, special. **2** *a typical day.* average, conventional, normal, ordinary, orthodox, predictable, standard, stock, unsurprising, usual. *Opp* UNUSUAL.

tyrannical *adj* absolute, authoritarian, autocratic, *inf* bossy, cruel, despotic, dictatorial, domineering, harsh, high-handed, illiberal, imperious, oppressive, overbearing, ruthless, severe, totalitarian, tyrannous, undemocratic, unjust. *Opp* DEMOCRATIC, LIBERAL.

tyrant *n* autocrat, despot, dictator, *inf* hard taskmaster, oppressor, slavedriver. ▷ RULER.

U

ugly *adj* **1** deformed, disfigured, disgusting, dreadful, frightful, ghastly, grim, grisly, grotesque, gruesome, hideous, horrible, *inf* horrid, ill-favoured, loathsome, misshapen, monstrous, nasty, objectionable, odious, offensive, repellent, repulsive, revolting, shocking, sickening, terrible. **2** *ugly furniture.* displeasing, inartistic, inelegant, plain, tasteless, unattractive, unpleasant, unprepossessing, unsightly. **3** *an ugly mood.* angry, cross, dangerous, forbidding, hostile, menacing, ominous, sinister, surly, threatening, unfriendly. *Opp* BEAUTIFUL.

ulterior *adj* concealed, covert, hidden, personal, private, secondary, secret, undeclared, underlying, undisclosed, unexpressed. *Opp* OVERT.

ultimate *adj* **1** closing, concluding, eventual, extreme, final, furthest, last, terminal, terminating. **2** *ultimate truth.* basic, fundamental, primary, root, underlying.

umpire *n* adjudicator, arbiter, arbitrator, judge, linesman, moderator, official, *inf* ref, referee.

unable *adj* impotent, incompetent, powerless, unfit, unprepared, unqualified. *Opp* ABLE.

unacceptable *adj* bad, forbidden, illegal, improper, inadequate, inadmissible, inappropriate, inexcusable, insupportable, intolerable, invalid, taboo, unsatisfactory, unsuitable, wrong. *Opp* ACCEPTABLE.

unaccompanied *adj* alone, lone, single-handed, sole, solo, unaided, unescorted.

unaccountable *adj* ▷ INEXPLICABLE.

unaccustomed *adj* ▷ STRANGE.

unadventurous *adj* **1** cautious, cowardly, spiritless, timid, unimaginative. **2** *an unadventurous life.* cloistered, limited, protected, sheltered, unexciting. *Opp* ADVENTUROUS.

unalterable *adj* ▷ IMMUTABLE.

unambiguous *adj* ▷ DEFINITE.

unanimous *adj* ▷ UNITED.

unasked *adj* ▷ UNINVITED.

unassuming *adj* ▷ MODEST.

unattached *adj* autonomous, *inf* available, free, independent, separate, single, uncommitted, unmarried, *inf* unspoken for.

unattractive *adj* characterless, colourless, displeasing, dull, inartistic, inelegant, nasty, objectionable, *inf* off-putting, plain, repellent, repulsive, tasteless, uninviting, unpleasant, unprepossessing, unsightly. ▷ UGLY. *Opp* ATTRACTIVE.

unauthorized *adj* illegal, illegitimate, illicit, irregular, unapproved, unlawful, unofficial. *Opp* OFFICIAL.

unavoidable *adj* certain, compulsory, destined, fated, fixed, ineluctable, inescapable, inevitable, inexorable, mandatory, necessary, obligatory, predetermined, required, sure, unalterable.

unaware *adj* ▷ IGNORANT.

unbalanced *adj* **1** asymmetrical, irregular, lopsided, off-centre, shaky, uneven, unstable, wobbly. **2** biased, bigoted, one-sided, partial, partisan, prejudiced, unfair, unjust. **3** *unbalanced mind.* ▷ MAD.

unbearable *adj* insufferable, insupportable, intolerable, overpowering, overwhelming, unacceptable, unendurable. *Opp* TOLERABLE.

unbeatable *adj* ▷ INVINCIBLE.

unconscious

unbecoming *adj* dishonourable, improper, inappropriate, indecorous, indelicate, offensive, tasteless, unattractive, unbefitting, undignified, ungentlemanly, unladylike, unseemly, unsuitable. *Opp* DECOROUS.

unbelievable *adj* ▷ INCREDIBLE.

unbelieving *adj* ▷ INCREDULOUS.

unbend *vb* **1** straighten, uncurl, untwist. **2** loosen up, relax, rest, unwind.

unbending *adj* ▷ INFLEXIBLE.

unbiased *adj* balanced, disinterested, enlightened, even-handed, fair, impartial, independent, just, neutral, non-partisan, objective, openminded, reasonable, *inf* straight, unbigoted, undogmatic, unprejudiced. *Opp* BIASED.

unbreakable *adj* ▷ INDESTRUCTIBLE.

unbroken *adj* ▷ CONTINUOUS, WHOLE.

uncalled-for *adj* ▷ UNNECESSARY.

uncared-for *adj* ▷ DERELICT.

uncaring *adj* ▷ CALLOUS.

unceasing *adj* ▷ CONTINUOUS.

uncertain *adj* **1** ambiguous, arguable, *inf* chancy, confusing, conjectural, cryptic, enigmatic, equivocal, hazardous, hazy, *inf* iffy, imprecise, incalculable, inconclusive, indefinite, indeterminate, problematical, puzzling, questionable, risky, speculative, *inf* touch and go, unclear, unconvincing, undecided, undetermined, unforeseeable, unknown, unresolved, woolly. **2** *uncertain what to believe.* agnostic, ambivalent, doubtful, dubious, *inf* hazy, insecure, *inf* in two minds, self-questioning, unconvinced, undecided, unsure, vague, wavering. **3** *an uncertain climate.* changeable, erratic, fitful, inconstant, irregular, precarious, unpredictable, unreliable, unsettled, variable. *Opp* CERTAIN.

unchanging *adj* ▷ CONSTANT.

uncharitable *adj* ▷ UNKIND.

uncivilized *adj* anarchic, antisocial, backward, barbarian, barbaric, barbarous, brutish, crude, disorganized, illiterate, Philistine, primitive, savage, uncultured, uneducated, unenlightened, unsophisticated, wild. *Opp* CIVILIZED.

unclean *adj* ▷ DIRTY.

unclear *adj* ▷ UNCERTAIN.

unclothed *adj* ▷ NAKED.

uncomfortable *adj* **1** bleak, cold, comfortless, cramped, hard, inconvenient, lumpy, painful. **2** *uncomfortable clothes.* formal, restrictive, stiff, tight, tight-fitting. **3** *an uncomfortable silence.* awkward, distressing, embarrassing, nervous, restless, troubled, uneasy, worried. *Opp* COMFORTABLE.

uncommon *adj* ▷ UNUSUAL.

uncommunicative *adj* ▷ TACITURN.

uncomplimentary *adj* censorious, critical, deprecatory, depreciatory, derogatory, disapproving, disparaging, pejorative, scathing, slighting, unfavourable, unflattering. ▷ RUDE. *Opp* COMPLIMENTARY.

uncompromising *adj* ▷ INFLEXIBLE.

unconcealed *adj* ▷ OBVIOUS.

unconditional *adj* absolute, categorical, complete, full, outright, total, unequivocal, unlimited, unqualified, unreserved, unrestricted, wholehearted, *inf* with no strings attached. *Opp* CONDITIONAL.

uncongenial *adj* alien, antipathetic, disagreeable, incompatible, unattractive, unfriendly, unpleasant, unsympathetic. *Opp* CONGENIAL.

unconquerable *adj* ▷ INVINCIBLE.

unconscious *adj* **1** anaesthetized, *inf* blacked-out, comatose, concussed, *inf* dead to the world, insensible, *inf* knocked out, *inf* knocked silly, oblivious, *inf* out for the count, senseless, sleeping. **2** blind, deaf, ignorant, oblivious, unaware. **3** *unconscious humour.* accidental, inadvertent, unintended, unintentional, unwitting. **4** *an unconscious reaction.* automatic, *sl* gut, impulsive, instinctive, involuntary, reflex, spontaneous, unthinking. **5** *an unconscious desire.* repressed, subconscious, subliminal, suppressed. *Opp* CONSCIOUS.

unconsciousness n inf blackout, coma, faint, oblivion, sleep.

uncontrollable adj ▷ UNDISCIPLINED.

unconventional adj abnormal, atypical, inf cranky, eccentric, exotic, futuristic, idiosyncratic, independent, inventive, non-conforming, non-standard, odd, off-beat, original, peculiar, progressive, revolutionary, strange, surprising, unaccustomed, unorthodox, inf way-out, wayward, weird, zany. Opp CONVENTIONAL.

unconvincing adj implausible, improbable, incredible, invalid, spurious, unbelievable, unlikely. Opp PERSUASIVE.

uncooperative adj lazy, obstructive, recalcitrant, selfish, unhelpful, unwilling. Opp COOPERATIVE.

uncover vb bare, come across, detect, dig up, disclose, discover, disrobe, exhume, expose, locate, reveal, show, strip, take the wraps off, undress, unearth, unmask, unveil, unwrap. Opp COVER.

undamaged adj ▷ PERFECT.

undefended adj defenceless, exposed, helpless, insecure, unarmed, unfortified, unguarded, unprotected, vulnerable, weaponless. Opp SECURE.

undemanding adj ▷ EASY.

undemonstrative adj ▷ ALOOF.

underclothes plur n lingerie, inf smalls, underclothing, undergarments, underthings, underwear, inf undies. □ bra, braces, brassière, briefs, camiknickers, corset, drawers, garter, girdle, knickers, panties, pantihose, pants, petticoat, slip, suspenders, tights, trunks, underpants, underskirt, vest.

undercurrent n atmosphere, feeling, hint, sense, suggestion, trace, undertone.

underestimate vb belittle, depreciate, dismiss, disparage, minimize, miscalculate, misjudge, underrate, undervalue. Opp EXAGGERATE.

undergo vb bear, be subjected to, endure, experience, go through, live through, put up with, inf stand, submit yourself to, suffer, withstand.

underground adj 1 buried, hidden, subterranean, sunken. 2 clandestine, revolutionary, secret, subversive, unofficial, unrecognized.

undergrowth n brush, bushes, ground cover, plants, vegetation.

undermine vb burrow under, destroy, dig under, erode, excavate, mine under, ruin, sabotage, sap, subvert, tunnel under, undercut, weaken, wear away.

underprivileged adj deprived, destitute, disadvantaged, downtrodden, impoverished, needy, oppressed. ▷ POOR. Opp PRIVILEGED.

undersea adj subaquatic, submarine, underwater.

understand vb 1 appreciate, apprehend, be conversant with, inf catch on, comprehend, inf cotton on to, decipher, decode, fathom, figure out, follow, gather, inf get, inf get to the bottom of, grasp, interpret, know, learn, make out, make sense of, master, perceive, realize, recognize, see, take in, inf twig. 2 understand animals. be in sympathy with, empathize with, sympathize with.

understanding n 1 ability, acumen, brains, cleverness, discernment, insight, intellect, intelligence, judgement, penetration, perceptiveness, percipience, sense, wisdom. 2 understanding of a problem. appreciation, apprehension, awareness, cognition, comprehension, grasp, knowledge. 3 understanding between people. accord, agreement, compassion, consensus, consent, consideration, empathy, fellow feeling, harmony, kindness, mutuality, sympathy, tolerance. 4 a formal understanding. arrangement, bargain, compact, contract, deal, entente, pact, settlement, treaty.

understate vb belittle, inf make light of, minimize, inf play down, inf soft-pedal. Opp EXAGGERATE.

undertake vb 1 agree, attempt, consent, covenant, guarantee, pledge, promise, try. **2** *undertake a task*. accept responsibility for, address, approach, attend to, begin, commence, commit yourself to, cope with, deal with, embark on, grapple with, handle, manage, tackle, take on, take up.

undertaking *n* **1** affair, business, enterprise, project, task, venture. **2** agreement, assurance, contract, guarantee, pledge, promise, vow.

undervalue *vb* belittle, depreciate, dismiss, disparage, minimize, miscalculate, misjudge, underestimate, underrate.

underwater *adj* subaquatic, submarine, undersea.

undeserved *adj* unearned, unfair, unjustified, unmerited, unwarranted.

undesirable *adj* ▷ OBJECTIONABLE.

undisciplined *adj* anarchic, chaotic, disobedient, disorderly, disorganized, intractable, rebellious, uncontrollable, uncontrolled, ungovernable, unmanageable, unruly, unsystematic, untrained, wild, wilful. *Opp* OBEDIENT.

undiscriminating *adj* ▷ IMPERCEPTIVE.

undisguised *adj* ▷ OBVIOUS.

undistinguished *adj* ▷ ORDINARY.

undo *vb* **1** detach, disconnect, disengage, loose, loosen, open, part, separate, unbind, unbuckle, unbutton, unchain, unclasp, unclip, uncouple, unfasten, unfetter, unhook, unleash, unlock, unpick, unpin, unscrew, unseal, unshackle, unstick, untether, untie, unwrap, unzip. **2** *undo someone's good work*. annul, cancel out, destroy, mar, nullify, quash, reverse, ruin, spoil, undermine, vitiate, wipe out, wreck.

undoubted *adj* ▷ INDISPUTABLE.

undoubtedly *adv* certainly, definitely, doubtless, indubitably, of course, surely, undeniably, unquestionably.

undress *vb* disrobe, divest yourself, *inf* peel off, shed your clothes, strip off, take off your clothes, uncover yourself. **undressed** *adj* ▷ NAKED.

undue *adj* ▷ EXCESSIVE.

undying *adj* ▷ ETERNAL.

uneasy *adj* anxious, apprehensive, awkward, concerned, distressed, distressing, disturbed, edgy, fearful, insecure, jittery, nervous, restive, restless, tense, troubled, uncomfortable, unsettled, upsetting, worried.

uneducated *adj* ▷ IGNORANT.

unemotional *adj* apathetic, clinical, cold, cool, dispassionate, frigid, hard-hearted, heartless, impassive, indifferent, objective, unfeeling, unmoved, unresponsive. *Opp* EMOTIONAL.

unemployed *adj* jobless, laid off, on the dole, out of work, redundant, *inf* resting, unwaged. ▷ IDLE.

unendurable *adj* ▷ UNBEARABLE.

unenthusiastic *adj* ▷ APATHETIC, UNINTERESTED.

unequal *adj* **1** different, differing, disparate, dissimilar, uneven, varying. **2** *unequal treatment*. biased, prejudiced, unjust. **3** *an unequal contest*. ill-matched, one-sided, unbalanced, uneven, unfair. *Opp* EQUAL, FAIR.

unequalled *adj* incomparable, inimitable, matchless, peerless, supreme, surpassing, un-matched, unparalleled, unrivalled, unsurpassed.

unethical *adj* ▷ IMMORAL.

uneven *adj* **1** bent, broken, bumpy, crooked, irregular, jagged, jerky, pitted, rough, rutted, undulating, wavy. **2** *an uneven rhythm*. erratic, fitful, fluctuating, inconsistent, spasmodic, unpredictable, variable, varying. **3** *an uneven load*. asymmetrical, lopsided, unsteady. **4** *uneven contest*. illmatched, one-sided, unbalanced, unequal, unfair. *Opp* EVEN.

uneventful *adj* ▷ UNEXCITING.

unexciting *adj* boring, dreary, dry, dull, humdrum, monotonous, predictable, quiet, repetitive, routine, soporific, straightforward, tedious, trite, uneventful, uninspiring, unin-

teresting, vapid, wearisome. ▷ ORDIN-
ARY. *Opp* EXCITING.

unexpected *adj* accidental, chance,
fortuitous, sudden, surprising,
unforeseen, unhoped-for, unlooked-
for, unplanned, unpredictable,
unusual. *Opp* PREDICTABLE.

unfair *adj* ▷ UNJUST.

unfaithful *adj* deceitful, disloyal,
double-dealing, duplicitous, faithless,
false, fickle, inconstant, perfidious,
traitorous, treacherous, treasonable,
unreliable, untrue, untrustworthy.
Opp FAITHFUL.

unfaithfulness *n* **1** duplicity, perfidy, treachery, treason. **2** adultery,
infidelity.

unfamiliar *adj* ▷ STRANGE.

unfashionable *adj* dated, obsolete,
old-fashioned, *inf* out, outmoded,
passé, superseded, unstylish. *Opp*
FASHIONABLE.

unfasten *vb* ▷ UNDO.

unfavourable *adj* **1** adverse, attacking, contrary, critical, disapproving,
discouraging, hostile, ill-disposed,
inauspicious, negative, opposing,
uncomplimentary, unfriendly, unhelpful, unkind, unpromising, unpropitious, unsympathetic. **2** *an
unfavourable reputation.* bad, undesirable, unenviable, unsatisfactory. *Opp*
FAVOURABLE.

unfeeling *adj* ▷ CALLOUS.

unfinished *adj* imperfect, incomplete, rough, sketchy, uncompleted,
unpolished. *Opp* PERFECT.

unfit *adj* **1** ill-equipped, inadequate,
incapable, incompetent, unsatisfactory, useless. **2** *unfit for family viewing.*
improper, inappropriate, unbecom-
ing, unsuitable, unsuited. **3** *an unfit
athlete.* feeble, flabby, out of condition, unhealthy. ▷ ILL. *Opp* FIT.

unflagging *adj* ▷ TIRELESS.

unflinching *adj* ▷ RESOLUTE.

unforeseen *adj* ▷ UNEXPECTED.

unforgettable *adj* ▷ MEMORABLE.

unforgivable *adj* inexcusable, mortal (*sin*), reprehensible, shameful,

unjustifiable, unpardonable, unwar-
rantable. *Opp* FORGIVABLE.

unfortunate *adj* ▷ UNLUCKY.

unfriendly *adj* aggressive, aloof,
antagonistic, antisocial, cold, cool,
detached, disagreeable, distant, forbidding, frigid, haughty, hostile, ill-
disposed, ill-natured, impersonal,
indifferent, inhospitable, menacing,
nasty, obnoxious, offensive, remote,
reserved, rude, sour, standoffish, *inf*
starchy, stern, supercilious, threatening, unapproachable, uncivil,
uncongenial, unenthusiastic, unforthcoming, unkind, unneigh-
bourly, unresponsive, unsociable,
unsympathetic, unwelcoming. *Opp*
FRIENDLY.

ungainly *adj* ▷ AWKWARD.

ungodly *adj* ▷ IRRELIGIOUS.

ungovernable *adj* ▷ UNDISCIPLINED.

ungrateful *adj* displeased, ill-
mannered, rude, selfish, unappreci-
ative, unthankful. *Opp* GRATEFUL.

unhappy *adj* **1** dejected, depressed,
dispirited, down, downcast, gloomy,
miserable, mournful, sorrowful.
▷ SAD. **2** *unhappy about losing.* bad-
tempered, disaffected, discontented,
disgruntled, disillusioned, displeased,
dissatisfied, *inf* fed up, *inf* grumpy,
morose, sulky, sullen, unsatisfied.
3 *an unhappy choice.* ▷ UNSATISFACTORY.

unhealthy *adj* **1** ailing, debilitated,
delicate, diseased, feeble, frail,
infected, infirm, *inf* poorly, sick,
sickly, suffering, unwell, valetudin-
ary, weak. ▷ ILL. **2** *unhealthy conditions.* deleterious, detrimental, dirty,
harmful, insalubrious, insanitary,
noxious, polluted, unhygienic, unwholesome. *Opp* HEALTHY.

unheard-of *adj* ▷ UNUSUAL.

unhelpful *adj* disobliging, inconsiderate, negative, slow, uncivil, uncooperative, unwilling. *Opp* HELPFUL.

unhygienic *adj* ▷ UNHEALTHY.

unidentifiable *adj* anonymous,
camouflaged, disguised, hidden, undetectable, unidentified, unknown,
unrecognizable. *Opp* IDENTIFIABLE.

united

unidentified adj anonymous, incognito, mysterious, nameless, unfamiliar, unknown, unmarked, unnamed, unrecognized, unspecified. Opp SPECIFIC.

uniform adj consistent, even, homogeneous, identical, indistinguishable, predictable, regular, same, similar, single, standard, unbroken, unvaried, unvarying. Opp DIFFERENT. ● n costume, livery, outfit.

unify vb amalgamate, bring together, coalesce, combine, consolidate, fuse, harmonize, integrate, join, merge, unite, weld together. Opp SEPARATE.

unimaginative adj banal, boring, clichéd, derivative, dull, hackneyed, inartistic, insensitive, obvious, ordinary, prosaic, stale, trite, ugly, uninspired, uninteresting, unoriginal. Opp IMAGINATIVE.

unimportant adj ephemeral, forgettable, immaterial, inconsequential, inconsiderable, inessential, insignificant, irrelevant, lightweight, minor, negligible, peripheral, petty, secondary, slight, trifling, trivial, valueless, worthless. ▷ SMALL. Opp IMPORTANT.

uninhabitable adj condemned, in bad repair, unliveable, unusable. Opp HABITABLE.

uninhabited adj abandoned, deserted, desolate, empty, tenantless, uncolonized, unoccupied, unpeopled, unpopulated, untenanted, vacant.

uninhibited adj abandoned, candid, casual, easygoing, frank, informal, natural, open, outgoing, outspoken, relaxed, spontaneous, unbridled, unconstrained, unrepressed, unreserved, unrestrained, unselfconscious, wild. Opp REPRESSED.

unintelligent adj ▷ STUPID.

unintelligible adj ▷ INCOMPREHENSIBLE.

unintentional adj accidental, fortuitous, inadvertent, involuntary, unconscious, unintended, unplanned, unwitting. Opp INTENTIONAL.

uninterested adj apathetic, bored, incurious, indifferent, lethargic, passive, phlegmatic, unconcerned, unenthusiastic, uninvolved, unresponsive. Opp INTERESTED.

uninteresting adj boring, dreary, dry, dull, flat, monotonous, obvious, predictable, tedious, unexciting, uninspiring, vapid, wearisome. ▷ ORDINARY. Opp INTERESTING.

uninterrupted adj ▷ CONTINUOUS.

uninvited adj 1 unasked, unbidden, unwelcome. 2 an uninvited comment. gratuitous, unsolicited, voluntary.

uninviting adj ▷ UNATTRACTIVE.

union n 1 alliance, amalgamation, association, coalition, confederation, conjunction, federation, integration, joining together, merger, unanimity, unification, unity. 2 amalgam, blend, combination, combining, compound, fusion, grafting, marrying, mixture, synthesis, welding. 3 marriage, matrimony, partnership, wedlock.

unique adj distinctive, incomparable, lone, inf one-off, peculiar, peerless, inf second to none, single, singular, unequalled, unparalleled, unrepeatable, unrivalled.

unit n component, constituent, element, entity, item, module, part, piece, portion, section, segment, whole.

unite vb ally, amalgamate, associate, blend, bring together, coalesce, collaborate, combine, commingle, confederate, connect, consolidate, conspire, cooperate, couple, federate, fuse, go into partnership, harmonize, incorporate, integrate, interlock, join, join forces, link, link up, marry, merge, mingle, mix, stick together, tie up, unify, weld together. ▷ MARRY. Opp SEPARATE.

united adj agreed, allied, coherent, collective, common, concerted, co-ordinated, corporate, harmonious, integrated, joint, like-minded, mutual, inf of one mind, shared, inf solid, unanimous, undivided. Opp DISUNITED. **be united** ▷ AGREE.

unity n accord, agreement, coherence, concord, consensus, harmony, integrity, like-mindedness, oneness, rapport, solidarity, unanimity, wholeness. *Opp* DISUNITY.

universal adj all-embracing, all-round, boundless, common, comprehensive, cosmic, general, global, international, omnipresent, pandemic, prevailing, prevalent, total, ubiquitous, unbounded, unlimited, widespread, worldwide.

universe n cosmos, creation, the heavens, *old use* macrocosm.

unjust adj biased, bigoted, indefensible, inequitable, one-sided, partial, partisan, prejudiced, undeserved, unfair, unjustified, unlawful, unmerited, unreasonable, unwarranted, wrong, wrongful. *Opp* JUST.

unjustifiable adj excessive, immoderate, indefensible, inexcusable, unacceptable, unconscionable, unforgivable, unjust, unreasonable, unwarranted. *Opp* JUSTIFIABLE.

unkind adj abrasive, *inf* beastly, callous, caustic, cold-blooded, discourteous, disobliging, hard, hard-hearted, harsh, heartless, hurtful, ill-natured, impolite, inconsiderate, inhuman, inhumane, insensitive, malevolent, malicious, mean, merciless, nasty, pitiless, relentless, rigid, rough, ruthless, sadistic, savage, selfish, severe, sharp, spiteful, stern, tactless, thoughtless, uncaring, uncharitable, unchristian, unfeeling, unfriendly, unpleasant, unsympathetic, unthoughtful, vicious. ▷ ANGRY, CRITICAL, CRUEL. *Opp* KIND.

unknown adj **1** anonymous, disguised, incognito, mysterious, nameless, strange, unidentified, unnamed, unrecognized, unspecified. **2** *an unknown country.* alien, foreign, uncharted, undiscovered, unexplored, unfamiliar, unmapped. **3** *an unknown actor.* humble, insignificant, little-known, lowly, obscure, undistinguished, unheard-of, unimportant. *Opp* FAMOUS.

unlawful adj ▷ ILLEGAL.

unlikely adj **1** dubious, farfetched, implausible, improbable, incredible, suspect, suspicious, *inf* tall (*story*), unbelievable, unconvincing, unthinkable. **2** *an unlikely possibility.* distant, doubtful, faint, *inf* outside, remote, slight. *Opp* LIKELY.

unlimited adj ▷ BOUNDLESS.

unload vb disburden, discharge, drop off, *inf* dump, empty, offload, take off, unpack. *Opp* LOAD.

unloved adj abandoned, discarded, forsaken, hated, loveless, lovelorn, neglected, rejected, spurned, uncared-for, unvalued, unwanted. *Opp* LOVED.

unlucky adj **1** accidental, calamitous, chance, disastrous, dreadful, tragic, unfortunate, untimely, unwelcome. **2** *an unlucky person. inf* accident-prone, hapless, luckless, unhappy, unsuccessful, wretched. **3** *an unlucky number.* cursed, ill-fated, ill-omened, ill-starred, inauspicious, jinxed, ominous, unfavourable. *Opp* LUCKY.

unmanageable adj ▷ UNDISCIPLINED.

unmarried adj *inf* available, celibate, *inf* free, single, unwed. **unmarried person** bachelor, celibate, spinster.

unmentionable adj ▷ TABOO.

unmistakable adj ▷ DEFINITE, OBVIOUS.

unnamed adj ▷ UNIDENTIFIED.

unnatural adj **1** abnormal, bizarre, eccentric, eerie, extraordinary, fantastic, freak, freakish, inexplicable, magic, magical, odd, outlandish, preternatural, queer, strange, supernatural, unaccountable, uncanny, unusual, weird. **2** *unnatural feelings.* callous, cold-blooded, cruel, hardhearted, heartless, inhuman, inhumane, monstrous, perverse, perverted, sadistic, savage, stonyhearted, unfeeling, unkind. **3** *unnatural behaviour.* actorish, affected, bogus, contrived, fake, feigned, forced, insincere, laboured, mannered, *inf* out of character, overdone, *inf* phoney, pretended, *inf* pseudo, *inf* put on, self-conscious, stagey, stiff, stilted, theatrical, uncharacteristic, unspontaneous. **4** *unnatural materials*. artificial, fabricated, imitation, man-made, manufactured, simulated, synthetic. *Opp* NATURAL.

unnecessary *adj* dispensable, excessive, expendable, extra, inessential, needless, nonessential, redundant, supererogatory, superfluous, surplus, uncalled-for, unjustified, unneeded, unwanted, useless. *Opp* NECESSARY.

unobtrusive *adj* ▷ INCONSPICUOUS.

unofficial *adj* friendly, informal, *inf* off the record, private, secret, unauthorized, unconfirmed, undocumented, unlicensed. *Opp* OFFICIAL.

unorthodox *adj* ▷ UNCONVENTIONAL.

unpaid *adj* **1** due, outstanding, owing, payable, unsettled. **2** *unpaid work*. honorary, unremunerative, unsalaried, voluntary.

unpalatable *adj* disgusting, distasteful, inedible, nasty, nauseating, *inf* off, rancid, sickening, sour, tasteless, unacceptable, unappetizing, uneatable, unpleasant. *Opp* PALATABLE.

unparalleled *adj* ▷ UNEQUALLED.

unpardonable *adj* ▷ UNFORGIVABLE.

unplanned *adj* ▷ SPONTANEOUS.

unpleasant *adj* abhorrent, abominable, antisocial, appalling, atrocious, awful, bad-tempered, beastly, bitter, coarse, crude, despicable, detestable, diabolical, dirty, disagreeable, disgusting, displeasing, distasteful, dreadful, evil, execrable, fearful, fearsome, filthy, foul, frightful, ghastly, grim, grisly, gruesome, harsh, hateful, *inf* hellish, hideous, horrible, horrid, horrifying, improper, indecent, inhuman, irksome, loathsome, *inf* lousy, malevolent, malicious, mucky, nasty, nauseating, objectionable, obnoxious, odious, offensive, *inf* offputting, repellent, repugnant, repulsive, revolting, rude, shocking, sickening, sickly, sordid, sour, spiteful, squalid, terrible, ugly, unat-tractive, uncouth, undesirable, unfriendly, unkind, unpalatable, unsavoury, unwelcome, upsetting, vexing, vicious, vile, vulgar. ▷ BAD. *Opp* PLEASANT.

unpopular *adj* despised, disliked, friendless, hated, ignored, *inf* in bad odour, minority (*interests*), out of favour, rejected, shunned, unfashionable, unloved, unwanted. *Opp* POPULAR.

unpredictable *adj* changeable, surprising, uncertain, unexpected, unforeseeable, variable. *Opp* PREDICTABLE.

unprejudiced *adj* ▷ UNBIASED.

unpremeditated *adj* ▷ SPONTANEOUS.

unprepared *adj inf* caught napping, caught out, ill-equipped, surprised, taken off-guard, unready. *Opp* READY.

unpretentious *adj* humble, modest, plain, simple, straightforward, unaffected, unassuming, unostentatious, unsophisticated. *Opp* PRETENTIOUS.

unproductive *adj* **1** fruitless, futile, ineffective, pointless, unprofitable, unrewarding, useless, valueless, worthless. **2** *an unproductive garden*. arid, barren, infertile, sterile, unfruitful. *Opp* PRODUCTIVE.

unprofessional *adj* amateurish, casual, incompetent, inefficient, inexpert, lax, negligent, shoddy, *inf* sloppy, unethical, unfitting, unprincipled, unseemly, unskilful, unskilled, unworthy. *Opp* PROFESSIONAL.

unprofitable *adj* futile, lossmaking, pointless, uncommercial, uneconomic, ungainful, unproductive, unremunerative, unrewarding, worthless. *Opp* PROFITABLE.

unprovable *adj* doubtful, inconclusive, questionable, undemonstrable, unsubstantiated, unverifiable. *Opp* PROVABLE, PROVEN.

unpunctual *adj* behindhand, belated, delayed, detained, lastminute, late, overdue, tardy, unreliable. *Opp* PUNCTUAL.

unravel *vb* disentangle, free, solve, sort out, straighten out, undo, untangle.

unreal *adj* chimerical, false, fanciful, illusory, imaginary, imagined, make-believe, nonexistent, phantasmal, *inf* pretend, *inf* pseudo, sham. ▷ HYPOTHETICAL. *Opp* REAL.

unrealistic *adj* **1** inaccurate, non-representational, unconvincing, unlifelike, unnatural, unrecognizable. **2** *unrealistic ideas.* delusory, fanciful, idealistic, impossible, impracticable, impractical, over-ambitious, quixotic, romantic, silly, visionary, unreasonable, unworkable. **3** *unrealistic prices.* ▷ EXCESSIVE. *Opp* REALISTIC.

unreasonable *adj* ▷ IRRATIONAL.

unrecognizable *adj* ▷ UNIDENTIFIABLE.

unrelated *adj* **1** different, independent, unconnected, unlike. **2** ▷ IRRELEVANT. *Opp* RELATED.

unreliable *adj* **1** deceptive, false, flimsy, implausible, inaccurate, misleading, suspect, unconvincing. **2** *unreliable friends.* changeable, disreputable, fallible, fickle, inconsistent, irresponsible, treacherous, undependable, unpredictable, unsound, unstable, untrustworthy. *Opp* RELIABLE.

unrepentant *adj* brazen, confirmed, conscienceless, hardened, impenitent, incorrigible, incurable, inveterate, irredeemable, shameless, unapologetic, unashamed, unblushing, unreformable, unregenerate. *Opp* REPENTANT.

unripe *adj* green, immature, sour, unready. *Opp* RIPE.

unrivalled *adj* ▷ UNEQUALLED.

unruly *adj* ▷ UNDISCIPLINED.

unsafe *adj* ▷ DANGEROUS.

unsatisfactory *adj* defective, deficient, disappointing, displeasing, dissatisfying, faulty, frustrating, imperfect, inadequate, incompetent, inefficient, inferior, insufficient, lacking, not good enough, poor, *inf* sad (*state of affairs*), unacceptable, unhappy, unsatisfying, *inf* wretched. *Opp* SATISFACTORY.

unscrupulous *adj* amoral, conscienceless, corrupt, *inf* crooked, cunning, dishonest, dishonourable, immoral, improper, self-interested, shameless, *inf* slippery, sly, unconscionable, unethical, untrustworthy. *Opp* SCRUPULOUS.

unseemly *adj* ▷ UNBECOMING.

unseen *adj* ▷ INVISIBLE.

unselfish *adj* altruistic, caring, charitable, considerate, disinterested, generous, humanitarian, kind, liberal, magnanimous, open-handed, philanthropic, public-spirited, self-effacing, selfless, self-sacrificing, thoughtful, ungrudging, unstinting. *Opp* SELFISH.

unsightly *adj* ▷ UGLY.

unskilful *adj* amateurish, bungled, clumsy, crude, incompetent, inept, inexpert, maladroit, *inf* rough and ready, shoddy, unprofessional. *Opp* SKILFUL.

unskilled *adj* inexperienced, unqualified, untrained. *Opp* SKILLED.

unsociable *adj* ▷ UNFRIENDLY.

unsophisticated *adj* artless, childlike, guileless, ingenuous, innocent, lowbrow, naïve, plain, provincial, simple, simple-minded, straightforward, unaffected, uncomplicated, unostentatious, unpretentious, unrefined, unworldly. *Opp* SOPHISTICATED.

unsound *adj* ▷ WEAK.

unspeakable *adj* dreadful, indescribable, inexpressible, nameless, unutterable.

unspecified *adj* ▷ UNIDENTIFIED.

unstable *adj* capricious, changeable, fickle, inconsistent, inconstant, mercurial, shifting, unpredictable, unsteady, variable, volatile. *Opp* STABLE.

unsteady *adj* **1** flimsy, frail, insecure, precarious, rickety, *inf* rocky, shaky, tottering, unbalanced, unsafe, unstable, wobbly. **2** changeable, erratic, inconstant, intermittent, irregular, variable. **3** *an unsteady light.* flickering, fluctuating, quavering, quivering, trembling, tremulous, wavering. *Opp* STEADY.

unsuccessful *adj* **1** abortive, failed, fruitless, futile, ill-fated, ineffective, ineffectual, loss-making, sterile, unavailing, unlucky, unproductive, unprofitable, unsatisfactory, useless, vain, worthless. **2** *unsuccessful contestants.* beaten, defeated, foiled, hapless, losing, luckless, vanquished. *Opp* SUCCESSFUL.

unsuitable *adj* ill-chosen, ill-judged, ill-timed, inapposite, inappropriate, incongruous, inept, irrelevant, mistaken, unbefitting, unfitting, unhappy, unsatisfactory, unseasonable, unseemly, untimely. *Opp* SUITABLE.

unsure *adj* ▷ UNCERTAIN.

unsurpassed *adj* ▷ UNEQUALLED.

unsuspecting *adj* ▷ CREDULOUS.

unsympathetic *adj* apathetic, cool, cold, dispassionate, hardhearted, heartless, impassive, indifferent, insensitive, neutral, pitiless, reserved, ruthless, stony, stonyhearted, unaffected, uncaring, uncharitable, unconcerned, unfeeling, uninterested, unkind, unmoved, unpitying, unresponsive. *Opp* SYMPATHETIC.

unsystematic *adj* anarchic, chaotic, confused, disorderly, disorganized, haphazard, illogical, jumbled, muddled, *inf* shambolic, *inf* sloppy, unmethodical, unplanned, unstructured, untidy. *Opp* SYSTEMATIC.

unthinkable *adj* ▷ INCONCEIVABLE.

unthinking *adj* ▷ THOUGHTLESS.

untidy *adj* **1** careless, chaotic, cluttered, confused, disorderly, disorganized, haphazard, *inf* higgledy-piggledy, in disarray, jumbled, littered, *inf* messy, muddled, *inf* shambolic, slapdash, *inf* sloppy, slovenly, *inf* topsyturvy, unsystematic, upsidedown. **2** *untidy hair.* bedraggled, blowzy, dishevelled, disordered, rumpled, scruffy, shabby, tangled, tousled, uncared-for,

uncombed, ungroomed, unkempt. *Opp* TIDY.

untie *vb* cast off (*boat*), disentangle, free, loosen, release, unbind, undo, unfasten, unknot, untether.

untried *adj* experimental, innovatory, new, novel, unproved, untested. *Opp* ESTABLISHED.

untroubled *adj* carefree, peaceful, straightforward, undisturbed, uninterrupted, unruffled.

untrue *adj* ▷ FALSE.

untrustworthy *adj* ▷ DISHONEST.

untruthful *adj* ▷ LYING.

unused *adj* blank, clean, fresh, intact, mint (*condition*), new, pristine, unopened, untouched, unworn. *Opp* USED.

unusual *adj* abnormal, atypical, curious, *inf* different, exceptional, extraordinary, *inf* freakish, *inf* funny, irregular, odd, out of the ordinary, peculiar, queer, rare, remarkable, singular, strange, surprising, uncommon, unconventional, unexpected, unfamiliar, *inf* unheard-of, *inf* unique, unnatural, unorthodox, untypical, unwonted. *Opp* USUAL.

unutterable *adj* ▷ INDESCRIBABLE.

unwanted *adj* ▷ UNNECESSARY.

unwarranted *adj* ▷ UNJUSTIFIABLE.

unwary *adj* ▷ CARELESS.

unwavering *adj* ▷ RESOLUTE.

unwelcome *adj* disagreeable, unacceptable, undesirable, uninvited, unpopular, unwanted. *Opp* WELCOME.

unwell *adj* ▷ ILL.

unwholesome *adj* ▷ UNHEALTHY.

unwieldy *adj* awkward, bulky, clumsy, cumbersome, inconvenient, ungainly, unmanageable. *Opp* HANDY, PORTABLE.

unwilling *adj* averse, backward, disinclined, grudging, half-hearted, hesitant, ill-disposed, indisposed, lazy, loath, opposed, reluctant, resistant, slow, uncooperative, unenthusiastic, unhelpful. *Opp* WILLING.

unwise adj inf daft, foolhardy, foolish, ill-advised, ill-judged, illogical, imperceptive, impolitic, imprudent, inadvisable, indiscreet, inexperienced, injudicious, irrational, irresponsible, mistaken, obtuse, perverse, rash, reckless, senseless, short-sighted, silly, stupid, thoughtless, unintelligent, unreasonable. Opp WISE.

unworldly adj ▷ SPIRITUAL.

unworthy adj contemptible, despicable, discreditable, dishonourable, disreputable, ignoble, inappropriate, mediocre, second-rate, shameful, substandard, undeserving, unsuitable. Opp WORTHY.

unwritten adj oral, spoken, verbal, inf word-of-mouth. Opp WRITTEN.

unyielding adj ▷ INFLEXIBLE.

upbringing n breeding, bringing-up, care, education, instruction, nurture, raising, rearing, teaching, training.

update vb amend, bring up to date, correct, modernize, review, revise.

upgrade vb enhance, expand, improve, make better.

upheaval n chaos, commotion, confusion, disorder, disruption, disturbance, revolution, inf to-do, turmoil.

uphill adj arduous, difficult, exhausting, gruelling, hard, laborious, stiff, strenuous, taxing, tough.

uphold vb back, champion, defend, endorse, maintain, preserve, protect, stand by, support, sustain.

upkeep n care, conservation, keep, maintenance, operation, preservation, running, support.

uplifting adj civilizing, edifying, educational, enlightening, ennobling, enriching, humanizing, improving, spiritual. Opp SHAMEFUL.

upper adj elevated, higher, raised, superior, upstairs.

uppermost adj dominant, highest, loftiest, supreme, top, topmost.

upright adj 1 erect, on end, perpendicular, vertical. 2 an upright judge. conscientious, fair, good, high-minded, honest, honourable, incorruptible, just, moral, principled, righteous, inf straight, true, trustworthy, upstanding, virtuous. ● n column, pole, post, vertical.

uproar n inf bedlam, brawling, chaos, clamour, commotion, confusion, din, disorder, disturbance, furore, inf hubbub, inf hullabaloo, inf a madhouse, noise, outburst, outcry, pandemonium, inf racket, riot, row, inf ructions, inf rumpus, tumult, turbulence, turmoil.

uproot vb deracinate, destroy, eliminate, eradicate, extirpate, get rid of, inf grub up, pull up, remove, root out, tear up, weed out.

upset vb 1 capsize, destabilize, overturn, spill, tip over, topple. 2 upset a plan. affect, alter, change, confuse, defeat, disorganize, disrupt, hinder, interfere with, interrupt, jeopardize, overthrow, spoil. 3 upset feelings. agitate, alarm, annoy, disconcert, dismay, distress, disturb, excite, fluster, frighten, grieve, irritate, offend, perturb, inf rub up the wrong way, ruffle, scare, unnerve, worry.

upside-down adj inverted, inf topsy-turvy, upturned, wrong way up.

upstart n Fr nouveau riche, social climber, inf yuppie.

up-to-date adj 1 advanced, current, latest, modern, new, present-day, recent. 2 contemporary, fashionable, inf in, modish, stylish, inf trendy. Opp OLD-FASHIONED.

upward adj ascending, going up, rising, uphill. Opp DOWNWARD.

urban adj built-up, densely populated, metropolitan, suburban. Opp RURAL.

urge n compulsion, craving, desire, drive, eagerness, hunger, impetus, impulse, inclination, instinct, inf itch, longing, pressure, thirst, wish, yearning, inf yen. ● vb accelerate, advise, advocate, appeal to, beg, beseech, inf chivvy, compel, counsel, drive, inf egg on, encourage, entreat, exhort, force, goad, impel, implore, importune, incite, induce, invite,

utter

move on, nag, persuade, plead with, press, prod, prompt, propel, push, recommend, solicit, spur, stimulate. *Opp* DISCOURAGE.

urgent *adj* **1** acute, compelling, compulsive, dire, essential, exigent, high-priority, immediate, imperative, important, inescapable, instant, necessary, pressing, top-priority, unavoidable. **2** *an urgent cry for help.* eager, earnest, forceful, importunate, insistent, persistent, persuasive, solicitous.

usable *adj* acceptable, current, fit to use, functional, functioning, operating, operational, serviceable, valid, working.

use *n* advantage, application, benefit, employment, function, necessity, need, *inf* point, profit, purpose, usefulness, utility, value, worth. ● *vb* **1** administer, apply, deal with, employ, exercise, exploit, handle, make use of, manage, operate, put to use, utilize, wield, work. **2** consume, drink, eat, exhaust, expend, spend, use up, waste, wear out.

used *adj* cast-off, *inf* hand-medown, second-hand, soiled. *Opp* UNUSED.

useful *adj* **1** advantageous, beneficial, constructive, good, helpful, invaluable, positive, profitable, salutary, valuable, worthwhile. **2** *a useful*

tool. convenient, effective, efficient, handy, powerful, practical, productive, utilitarian. **3** *a useful player.* capable, competent, effectual, proficient, skilful, successful, talented. *Opp* USELESS.

useless *adj* **1** fruitless, futile, hopeless, pointless, unavailing, unprofitable, unsuccessful, vain, worthless. **2** *inf* broken down, *inf* clapped out, dead, dud, impractical, ineffective, inefficient, unusable. **3** *a useless player.* incapable, incompetent, ineffectual, lazy, unhelpful, unskilful, unsuccessful, untalented. *Opp* USEFUL.

usual *adj* accepted, accustomed, average, common, conventional, customary, everyday, expected, familiar, general, habitual, natural, normal, official, ordinary, orthodox, predictable, prevalent, recognized, regular, routine, standard, stock, traditional, typical, unexceptional, unsurprising, well-known, widespread, wonted. *Opp* UNUSUAL.

usurp *vb* appropriate, assume, commandeer, seize, steal, take, take over.

utensil *n* appliance, device, gadget, implement, instrument, machine, tool.

utter *vb* articulate, *inf* come out with, express, pronounce, voice. ▷ SPEAK, TALK.

V

vacancy *n* job, opening, place, position, post, situation.

vacant *adj* **1** available, bare, blank, clear, empty, free, hollow, open, unfilled, unused, usable, void. **2** abandoned, deserted, uninhabited, unoccupied, untenanted. **3** *a vacant look*. absent-minded, abstracted, blank, deadpan, dreamy, expressionless, far-away, fatuous, inattentive, vacuous. *Opp* BUSY.

vacate *vb* abandon, depart from, desert, evacuate, get out of, give up, leave, quit, withdraw from.

vacuous *adj* apathetic, blank, empty-headed, expressionless, inane, mindless, uncomprehending, unintelligent, vacant. ▷ STUPID. *Opp* ALERT.

vacuum *n* emptiness, space, void.

vagary *n* caprice, fancy, fluctuation, quirk, uncertainty, unpredictability, *inf* ups and downs, whim.

vagrant *n* beggar, destitute person, *inf* down-and-out, homeless person, itinerant, tramp, traveller, vagabond, wanderer, wayfarer.

vague *adj* **1** ambiguous, ambivalent, broad, confused, diffuse, equivocal, evasive, general, generalized, imprecise, indefinable, indefinite, inexact, loose, nebulous, uncertain, unclear, undefined, unspecific, unsure, *inf* woolly. **2** amorphous, blurred, dim, hazy, ill-defined, indistinct, misty, shadowy, unrecognizable. **3** absent-minded, careless, disorganized, forgetful, inattentive, scatter-brained, thoughtless. *Opp* DEFINITE.

vain *adj* **1** arrogant, *inf* bigheaded, boastful, *inf* cocky, conceited, egotistical, haughty, narcissistic, proud, self-important, self-satisfied, *inf* stuck-up, vainglorious. *Opp* MODEST.

2 *a vain attempt*. abortive, fruitless, futile, ineffective, pointless, senseless, unavailing, unproductive, unrewarding, unsuccessful, useless, worthless. *Opp* SUCCESSFUL.

valiant *adj* bold, brave, courageous, doughty, gallant, heroic, plucky, stalwart, stout-hearted, valorous. *Opp* COWARDLY.

valid *adj* acceptable, allowed, approved, authentic, authorized, *Lat* bona fide, convincing, current, genuine, lawful, legal, legitimate, official, permissible, permitted, proper, ratified, rightful, sound, suitable, usable. *Opp* INVALID.

validate *vb* authenticate, authorize, certify, endorse, legalize, legitimize, make valid, ratify.

valley *n* canyon, chasm, coomb, dale, defile, dell, dingle, glen, gorge, gulch, gully, hollow, pass, ravine, vale.

valour *n* bravery, courage, pluck.

valuable *adj* **1** costly, dear, expensive, generous, irreplaceable, precious, priceless, prized, treasured, valued. **2** *valuable advice*. advantageous, beneficial, constructive, esteemed, helpful, invaluable, positive, profitable, useful, worthwhile. *Opp* WORTHLESS.

value *n* **1** cost, price, worth. **2** advantage, benefit, importance, merit, significance, use, usefulness. ● *vb* **1** assess, estimate the value of, evaluate, price, *inf* put a figure on. **2** appreciate, care for, cherish, esteem, *inf* have a high regard for, *inf* hold dear, love, prize, respect, treasure.

vandal *n* barbarian, delinquent, hooligan, looter, marauder, Philistine, raider, ruffian, savage, thug, trouble-maker.

vanish *vb* clear, clear off, disappear, disperse, dissolve, dwindle, evaporate, fade, go away, melt away, pass. *Opp* APPEAR.

vanity *n* arrogance, *inf* bigheadedness, conceit, egotism, narcissism, pride, self-esteem.

vaporize *vb* dry up, evaporate, turn to vapour.

vapour *n* exhalation, fog, fumes, gas, haze, miasma, mist, smoke, steam.

variable *adj* capricious, changeable, erratic, fickle, fitful, fluctuating, fluid, inconsistent, inconstant, mercurial, mutable, protean, shifting, temperamental, uncertain, unpredictable, unreliable, unstable, unsteady, *inf* up-and-down, vacillating, varying, volatile, wavering. *Opp* INVARIABLE.

variation *n* alteration, change, conversion, deviation, difference, discrepancy, diversification, elaboration, modification, permutation, variant.

variety *n* **1** alteration, change, difference, diversity, unpredictability, variation. **2** array, assortment, blend, collection, combination, jumble, medley, miscellany, mixture, multiplicity. **3** brand, breed, category, class, form, kind, make, sort, species, strain, type.

various *adj* assorted, contrasting, different, differing, dissimilar, diverse, heterogeneous, miscellaneous, mixed, *inf* motley, multifarious, several, sundry, varied, varying. *Opp* SIMILAR.

vary *vb* **1** change, deviate, differ, fluctuate, go up and down, vacillate. **2** *vary your speed.* adapt, adjust, alter, convert, modify, reset, switch, transform, upset. *Opp* STABILIZE. **varied**, **varying** ▷ VARIOUS.

vast *adj* boundless, broad, colossal, enormous, extensive, gigantic, great, huge, immeasurable, immense, infinite, interminable, large, limitless, mammoth, massive, measureless, monumental, never-ending, titanic, tremendous, unbounded, unlimited, voluminous, wide. ▷ BIG. *Opp* SMALL.

vault *n* basement, cavern, cellar, crypt, repository, strongroom, undercroft. ● *vb* bound over, clear, hurdle, jump, leap, leapfrog, spring over.

veer *vb* change direction, dodge, swerve, tack, turn, wheel.

vegetable *adj* growing, organic. ● *n* □ artichoke, asparagus, aubergine, bean, beet, beetroot, broad bean, broccoli, Brussels sprout, butter bean, cabbage, carrot, cauliflower, celeriac, celery, chicory, courgette, cress, cucumber, garlic, kale, kohlrabi, leek, lettuce, marrow, mushroom, onion, parsnip, pea, pepper, potato, pumpkin, radish, runner bean, salsify, shallot, spinach, sugar beet, swede, sweetcorn, tomato, turnip, watercress, zucchini.

vegetate *vb* be inactive, do nothing, *inf* go to seed, idle, lose interest, stagnate.

vegetation *n* foliage, greenery, growing things, growth, plants, undergrowth, weeds.

vehement *adj* animated, ardent, eager, enthusiastic, excited, fervent, fierce, forceful, heated, impassioned, intense, passionate, powerful, strong, urgent, vigorous, violent. *Opp* APATHETIC.

vehicle *n* conveyance. □ ambulance, *inf* buggy, bulldozer, bus, cab, camper, caravan, carriage, cart, old use charabanc, chariot, coach, dump truck, dustcart, estate car, fire-engine, float, gig, go-kart, hearse, horse-box, jeep, juggernaut, lorry, minibus, minicab, *inf* motor, motor car, old use omnibus, pantechnicon, patrol-car, pick-up, removal van, rickshaw, scooter, sedan-chair, side-car, sledge, snowplough, stage-coach, steamroller, tank, tanker, taxi, traction-engine, tractor, trailer, tram, transporter, trap, trolley-bus, truck, tumbrel, van, wagon, sl wheels. ▷ CAR, CYCLE, TRAIN, VESSEL.

veil *vb* camouflage, cloak, conceal, cover, disguise, hide, mask, shroud.

vein *n* **1** artery, blood vessel, capillary. **2** *mineral vein.* bed, course, deposit, line, lode, seam, stratum. **3** ▷ MOOD.

veneer n coating, covering, finish, gloss, layer, surface. ● vb ▷ COVER.

venerable adj aged, ancient, august, dignified, esteemed, estimable, honourable, honoured, old, respectable, respected, revered, reverenced, sedate, venerated, worshipped, worthy of respect.

venerate vb adore, esteem, heroworship, honour, idolize, look up to, pay homage to, respect, revere, reverence, worship.

vengeance n reprisal, retaliation, retribution, revenge, inf tit for tat.

vengeful adj avenging, bitter, rancorous, revengeful, spiteful, unforgiving, vindictive. Opp FORGIVING.

venom n poison, toxin.

venomous adj deadly, lethal, poisonous, toxic.

vent n aperture, cut, duct, gap, hole, opening, orifice, outlet, passage, slit, slot, split. ● vb articulate, express, give vent to, let go, make known, release, utter, ventilate, voice. ▷ SPEAK.

ventilate vb aerate, air, freshen, oxygenate.

venture n enterprise, experiment, gamble, risk, speculation, undertaking. ● vb **1** bet, chance, dare, gamble, put forward, risk, speculate, stake, wager. **2** venture out. dare to go, risk going.

venturesome adj adventurous, bold, courageous, daring, doughty, fearless, intrepid.

venue n location, meeting-place, rendezvous.

verbal adj **1** lexical, linguistic. **2** a verbal message. oral, said, spoken, unwritten, vocal, wordof-mouth. Opp WRITTEN.

verbatim adj exact, faithful, literal, precise, word for word.

verbose adj diffuse, garrulous, longwinded, loquacious, prolix, rambling, repetitious, talkative, voluble. ▷ WORDY. Opp CONCISE.

verbosity n inf beating about the bush, circumlocution, diffuseness, garrulity, long-windedness, loquacity, periphrasis, prolixity, repetition, verbiage, wordiness.

verdict n adjudication, assessment, conclusion, decision, finding, judgement, opinion, sentence.

verge n bank, boundary, brim, brink, edge, hard shoulder, kerb, lip, margin, roadside, shoulder, side, threshold, wayside.

verifiable adj demonstrable, provable.

verify vb affirm, ascertain, attest to, authenticate, bear witness to, check out, confirm, corroborate, demonstrate the truth of, establish, prove, show the truth of, substantiate, support, uphold, validate, vouch for.

verisimilitude n authenticity, realism.

vermin plur n parasites, pests.

vernacular adj common, everyday, indigenous, local, native, ordinary, popular, vulgar.

versatile adj adaptable, allpurpose, all-round, flexible, gifted, multipurpose, resourceful, skilful, talented.

verse n lines, metre, rhyme, stanza. □ blank verse, Chaucerian stanza, clerihew, couplet, free verse, haiku, hexameter, limerick, ottava rima, pentameter, quatrain, rhyme royal, sestina, sonnet, Spenserian stanza, terza rima, triolet, triplet, vers libre, villanelle. ▷ POEM.

versed adj accomplished, competent, experienced, expert, knowledgeable, practised, proficient, skilled, taught, trained.

version n **1** account, description, portrayal, reading, rendition, report, story. **2** adaptation, interpretation, paraphrase, rendering, translation. **3** design, form, kind, mark, model, style, type, variant.

vertical adj erect, perpendicular, precipitous, sheer, upright. Opp HORIZONTAL.

vertigo *n* dizziness, giddiness, light-headedness.

very *adv* acutely, enormously, especially, exceedingly, extremely, greatly, highly, *inf* jolly, most, noticeably, outstandingly, particularly, really, remarkably, *inf* terribly, truly, uncommonly, unusually.

vessel *n* **1** ▷ CONTAINER. **2** bark, boat, craft, ship. □ *aircraftcarrier, barge, bathysphere, battleship, brigantine, cabin cruiser, canoe, catamaran, clipper, coaster, collier, coracle, corvette, cruise-liner, cruiser, cutter, destroyer, dhow, dinghy, dredger, dugout, ferry, freighter, frigate, galleon, galley, gondola, gunboat, houseboat, hovercraft, hydrofoil, hydroplane, ice-breaker, junk, kayak, ketch, landing-craft, launch, lifeboat, lighter, lightship, liner, longboat, lugger, man-of-war, merchant ship, minesweeper, motor boat, narrow-boat, oil-tanker, packet-ship, paddle-steamer, pontoon, power-boat, pram, privateer, punt, quinquereme, raft, rowing-boat, sailing-boat, sampan, schooner, skiff, sloop, smack, speed-boat, steamer, steamship, submarine, tanker, tender, torpedo boat, tramp steamer, trawler, trireme, troopship, tug, warship, whaler, wind-jammer, yacht, yawl.*

vet *vb inf* check out, examine, investigate, review, scrutinize.

veteran *adj* experienced, mature, old, practised. ● *n* experienced soldier, ex-serviceman, ex-servicewoman, old hand, old soldier, survivor.

veto *n* ban, block, embargo, prohibition, proscription, refusal, rejection, *inf* thumbs down. ● *vb* ban, bar, blackball, block, disallow, dismiss, forbid, prohibit, proscribe, quash, refuse, reject, rule out, say no to, turn down, vote against. *Opp* APPROVE.

vex *vb inf* aggravate, annoy, bother, displease, exasperate, harass, irritate, provoke, *inf* put out, trouble, upset, worry. ▷ ANGER.

viable *adj* achievable, feasible, operable, possible, practicable, practical, realistic, reasonable, supportable, sustainable, usable, workable. *Opp* IMPRACTICAL.

vibrant *adj* alert, alive, dynamic, electric, energetic, lively, living, pulsating, quivering, resonant, thrilling, throbbing, trembling, vibrating, vivacious. *Opp* LIFELESS.

vibrate *vb* fluctuate, judder, oscillate, pulsate, quake, quiver, rattle, resonate, reverberate, shake, shiver, shudder, throb, tremble, wobble.

vibration *n* juddering, oscillation, pulsation, quivering, rattling, resonance, reverberation, shaking, shivering, shuddering, throbbing, trembling, tremor.

vicarious *adj* delegated, deputed, indirect, second-hand, surrogate.

vice *n* **1** badness, corruption, degeneracy, degradation, depravity, evil, evil-doing, immorality, iniquity, lechery, profligacy, promiscuity, sin, venality, villainy, wickedness, wrongdoing. **2** bad habit, blemish, defect, failing, fault, flaw, foible, imperfection, shortcoming, weakness.

vicinity *n* area, district, environs, locale, locality, neighbourhood, outskirts, precincts, proximity, purlieus, region, sector, territory, zone.

vicious *adj* **1** atrocious, barbaric, barbarous, beastly, bloodthirsty, brutal, callous, cruel, diabolical, fiendish, heinous, hurtful, inhuman, merciless, monstrous, murderous, pitiless, ruthless, sadistic, savage, unfeeling, vile, violent. **2** *a vicious character.* bad, *inf* bitchy, *inf* catty, depraved, evil, heartless, immoral, malicious, mean, perverted, rancorous, sinful, spiteful, venomous, villainous, vindictive, vitriolic, wicked. **3** *vicious animals.* aggressive, bad-tempered, dangerous, ferocious, fierce, snappy, untamed, wild. **4** *a vicious wind.* cutting, nasty, severe, sharp, unpleasant. *Opp* GENTLE.

vicissitude *n* alteration, change, flux, instability, mutability, mutation, shift, uncertainty, unpredictability, variability.

victim n 1 casualty, fatality, injured person, patient, sufferer, wounded person. 2 *sacrificial victim*. martyr, offering, prey, sacrifice.

victimize vb bully, cheat, discriminate against, exploit, intimidate, oppress, persecute, *inf* pick on, prey on, take advantage of, terrorize, torment, treat unfairly, *inf* use. ▷ CHEAT.

victor n champion, conqueror, prizewinner, winner. *Opp* LOSER.

victorious adj champion, conquering, first, leading, prevailing, successful, top, top-scoring, triumphant, unbeaten, undefeated, winning. *Opp* UNSUCCESSFUL.

victory n achievement, conquest, knockout, mastery, success, superiority, supremacy, triumph, *inf* walkover, win. *Opp* DEFEAT.

vie vb compete, contend, strive, struggle.

view n 1 aspect, landscape, outlook, panorama, perspective, picture, prospect, scene, scenery, seascape, spectacle, townscape, vista. 2 angle, look, perspective, sight, vision. 3 *political views*. attitude, belief, conviction, idea, judgement, notion, opinion, perception, position, thought. ● vb 1 behold, consider, contemplate, examine, eye, gaze at, inspect, observe, perceive, regard, scan, stare at, survey, witness. 2 *view TV*. look at, see, watch.

viewer n *plur* audience, observer, onlooker, spectator, watcher, witness.

viewpoint n angle, perspective, point of view, position, slant, standpoint.

vigilant adj alert, attentive, awake, careful, circumspect, eagle-eyed, observant, on the watch, on your guard, *inf* on your toes, sharp, wakeful, wary, watchful, wideawake. *Opp* NEGLIGENT.

vigorous adj active, alive, animated, brisk, dynamic, energetic, fit, flourishing, forceful, full-blooded, *inf* full of beans, growing, hale and hearty, healthy, lively, lusty, potent, prosperous, red-blooded, robust, spirited, strenuous, strong, thriving, virile, vital, vivacious, zestful. *Opp* FEEBLE.

vigour n animation, dynamism, energy, fitness, force, forcefulness, gusto, health, life, liveliness, might, potency, power, robustness, spirit, stamina, strength, verve, *inf* vim, virility, vitality, vivacity, zeal, zest.

vile adj bad, base, contemptible, degenerate, depraved, despicable, disgusting, evil, execrable, filthy, foul, hateful, horrible, immoral, loathsome, low, nasty, nauseating, obnoxious, odious, offensive, perverted, repellent, repugnant, repulsive, revolting, sickening, sinful, ugly, vicious, wicked.

vilify vb abuse, calumniate, defame, denigrate, deprecate, disparage, revile, *inf* run down, slander, *inf* smear, speak evil of, traduce, vituperate.

villain n blackguard, criminal, evildoer, malefactor, mischiefmaker, miscreant, reprobate, rogue, scoundrel, sinner, wretch. ▷ CRIMINAL.

villainous adj bad, corrupt, criminal, dishonest, evil, sinful, treacherous, vile. ▷ WICKED.

vindictive adj avenging, malicious, nasty, punitive, rancorous, revengeful, spiteful, unforgiving, vengeful, vicious. *Opp* FORGIVING.

vintage adj choice, classic, fine, good, high-quality, mature, mellowed, old, seasoned, venerable.

violate vb 1 breach, break, contravene, defy, disobey, disregard, flout, ignore, infringe, overstep, sin against, transgress. 2 *violate someone's privacy*. abuse, desecrate, disturb, invade, profane. 3 *[of men]* *violate a woman*. assault, attack, debauch, dishonour, force yourself on, rape, ravish.

violation n breach, contravention, defiance, flouting, infringement, invasion, offence (against), transgression.

violent *adj* **1** acute, damaging, dangerous, destructive, devastating, explosive, ferocious, fierce, forceful, furious, hard, harmful, intense, powerful, rough, ruinous, savage, severe, strong, swingeing, tempestuous, turbulent, uncontrollable, vehement, wild. **2** *violent behaviour.* barbaric, berserk, bloodthirsty, brutal, cruel, desperate, frenzied, headstrong, homicidal, murderous, riotous, rowdy, ruthless, uncontrolled, unruly, vehement, vicious, wild. *Opp* GENTLE.

VIP *n* celebrity, dignitary, important person.

virile *adj derog* macho, manly, masculine, potent, vigorous.

virtue *n* **1** decency, fairness, goodness, high-mindedness, honesty, honour, integrity, justice, morality, nobility, principle, rectitude, respectability, righteousness, right-mindedness, sincerity, uprightness, worthiness. **2** advantage, asset, good point, merit, quality, *inf* redeeming feature, strength. **3** *sexual virtue.* abstinence, chastity, honour, innocence, purity, virginity. *Opp* VICE.

virtuoso *n* expert, genius, maestro, prodigy, showman, *inf* wizard. ▷ MUSICIAN.

virtuous *adj* blameless, chaste, decent, ethical, exemplary, fair, God-fearing, good, *derog* goodygoody, high-minded, high-principled, honest, honourable, innocent, irreproachable, just, law-abiding, moral, noble, praiseworthy, principled, pure, respectable, right, righteous, right-minded, sincere, *derog* smug, spotless, trustworthy, uncorrupted, unimpeachable, unsullied, upright, virginal, worthy. *Opp* WICKED.

virulent *adj* **1** dangerous, deadly, lethal, life-threatening, noxious, pernicious, poisonous, toxic, venomous. **2** *virulent abuse.* acrimonious, bitter, hostile, malicious, malign, malignant, mordant, nasty, spiteful, splenetic, vicious, vitriolic.

viscous *adj* gluey, sticky, syrupy, thick, viscid. *Opp* RUNNY.

visible *adj* apparent, clear, conspicuous, detectable, discernible, distinct, evident, manifest, noticeable, observable, obvious, open, perceivable, perceptible, plain, recognizable, unconcealed, undisguised, unmistakable. *Opp* INVISIBLE.

vision *n* **1** eyesight, perception, sight. **2** apparition, chimera, day-dream, delusion, fantasy, ghost, hallucination, illusion, mirage, phantasm, phantom, spectre, spirit, wraith. **3** *a man of vision.* far-sightedness, foresight, imagination, insight, spirituality, understanding.

visionary *adj* dreamy, fanciful, far-sighted, futuristic, idealistic, imaginative, impractical, mystical, prophetic, quixotic, romantic, speculative, transcendental, unrealistic, Utopian. ● *n* dreamer, idealist, mystic, poet, prophet, romantic, seer.

visit *n* **1** call, *old use* sojourn, stay, stop, visitation. **2** day out, excursion, outing, trip. ● *vb* call on, come to see, *inf* descend on, *inf* drop in on, go to see, *inf* look up, make a visit to, pay a call on, *inf* pop in on, stay with. **visit regularly** ▷ HAUNT.

visitor *n* **1** caller, *plur* company, guest. **2** holiday-maker, sightseer, tourist, traveller, tripper. **3** *a visitor from abroad.* alien, foreigner, migrant, visitant.

visor *n* protector, shield, sun-shield.

vista *n* landscape, outlook, panorama, prospect, scene, scenery, seascape, view.

visualize *vb* conceive, dream up, envisage, imagine, picture.

vital *adj* **1** alive, animate, animated, dynamic, energetic, exuberant, life-giving, live, lively, living, sparkling, spirited, sprightly, vigorous, vivacious, zestful. *Opp* LIFELESS. **2** *vital information.* compulsory, current, crucial, essential, fundamental, imperative, important, indispensable, mandatory, necessary, needed, relevant, requisite. *Opp* INESSENTIAL.

vitality n animation, dynamism, energy, exuberance, inf go, life, liveliness, inf sparkle, spirit, sprightliness, stamina, strength, vigour, inf vim, vivacity, zest.

vitriolic adj abusive, acid, biting, bitter, caustic, cruel, destructive, hostile, hurtful, malicious, savage, scathing, vicious, vindictive, virulent.

vituperate vb abuse, berate, calumniate, censure, defame, denigrate, deprecate, disparage, reproach, revile, inf run down, slander, upbraid, vilify.

vivacious adj animated, bubbly, cheerful, ebullient, energetic, high-spirited, light-hearted, lively, merry, positive, spirited, sprightly. Opp LETHARGIC.

vivid adj 1 bright, brilliant, colourful, dazzling, fresh, derog gaudy, gay, gleaming, glowing, intense, rich, shining, showy, strong, vibrant. 2 a vivid description. clear, detailed, graphic, imaginative, lifelike, lively, memorable, powerful, realistic, striking. Opp LIFELESS.

vocabulary n 1 diction, lexis, words. 2 dictionary, glossary, lexicon, phrase book, word-list.

vocal adj 1 oral, said, spoken, sung, voiced. 2 vocal in discussion. communicative, forthcoming, loquacious, outspoken, talkative, vociferous. Opp TACITURN.

vocation n calling, career, employment, job, life's work, occupation, profession, trade.

vogue n craze, fad, fashion, inf latest thing, mode, rage, style, taste, trend. **in vogue** ▷ FASHIONABLE.

voice n accent, articulation, expression, idiolect, inflexion, intonation, singing, sound, speaking, speech, tone, utterance. ● vb ▷ SPEAK.

void adj 1 blank, empty, unoccupied, vacant. 2 a void contract. annulled, cancelled, inoperative, invalid, not binding, unenforceable, useless. ● n blank, emptiness, nothingness, space, vacancy, vacuum.

volatile adj 1 explosive, sensitive, unstable. 2 volatile moods. changeable, erratic, fickle, flighty, inconstant, lively, mercurial, temperamental, unpredictable, inf up and down, variable. Opp STABLE.

volley n barrage, bombardment, burst, cannonade, fusillade, salvo, shower.

voluble adj chatty, fluent, garrulous, glib, loquacious, talkative. ▷ WORDY.

volume n 1 old use tome. ▷ BOOK. 2 volume of a container. aggregate, amount, bulk, capacity, dimensions, mass, measure, quantity, size.

voluminous adj ample, billowing, bulky, capacious, cavernous, enormous, extensive, gigantic, great, huge, immense, large, mammoth, massive, roomy, spacious, vast. ▷ BIG. Opp SMALL.

voluntary adj 1 elective, free, gratuitous, optional, spontaneous, unpaid, willing. Opp COMPULSORY. 2 a voluntary act. conscious, deliberate, intended, intentional, planned, premeditated, wilful. Opp INVOLUNTARY.

volunteer vb 1 be willing, offer, propose, put yourself forward. 2 ▷ ENLIST.

voluptuous adj 1 hedonistic, luxurious, pleasure-loving, self-indulgent, sensual, sybaritic, 2 voluptuous figure. attractive, buxom, inf curvaceous, desirable, erotic, sensual, inf sexy, shapely, inf well-endowed.

vomit vb be sick, inf bring up, disgorge, inf heave up, inf puke, regurgitate, retch, inf spew up, inf throw up.

voracious adj avid, eager, fervid, gluttonous, greedy, hungry, insatiable, keen, ravenous, thirsty.

vortex n eddy, spiral, whirlpool, whirlwind.

vote n ballot, election, plebiscite, poll, referendum, show of hands. ● vb ballot, cast your vote. **vote for** choose, elect, nominate, opt for, pick, return, select, settle on.

vouch *vb* **vouch for** answer for, back, certify, endorse, guarantee, speak for, sponsor, support.

voucher *n* coupon, ticket, token.

vow *n* assurance, guarantee, oath, pledge, promise, undertaking, word of honour. ● *vb* declare, give an assurance, give your word, guarantee, pledge, promise, swear, take an oath.

voyage *n* cruise, journey, passage. ● *vb* circumnavigate, cruise, sail. ▷ TRAVEL.

vulgar *adj* **1** churlish, coarse, common, crude, foul, gross, ill-bred, impolite, improper, indecent, indecorous, low, offensive, rude, uncouth, ungentlemanly, unladylike. ▷ OBSCENE. *Opp* POLITE. **2** *vulgar colour scheme.* crude, gaudy, inartistic, in bad taste, inelegant, insensitive, lowbrow, plebeian, tasteless, tawdry, unrefined, unsophisticated. *Opp* TASTEFUL.

vulnerable *adj* **1** at risk, defenceless, exposed, helpless, unguarded, unprotected, weak, wide open. **2** easily hurt, sensitive, thin-skinned, touchy. *Opp* RESILIENT.

W

wad *n* bundle, lump, mass, pack, pad, plug, roll.

wadding *n* filling, lining, packing, padding, stuffing.

wade *vb* ford, paddle, splash. ▷ WALK.

waffle *n* evasiveness, padding, prevarication, prolixity, verbiage, wordiness. ● *vb inf* beat about the bush, *inf* blather on, hedge, prattle, prevaricate.

waft *vb* **1** be borne, drift, float, travel. **2** bear, carry, convey, puff, transmit, transport.

wag *vb* bob, flap, move to and fro, nod, oscillate, rock, shake, sway, undulate, *inf* waggle, wave, *inf* wiggle.

wage *n* compensation, earnings, emolument, honorarium, income, pay, pay packet, recompense, remuneration, reward, salary, stipend. ● *vb* carry on, conduct, engage in, fight, prosecute, pursue, undertake.

wager *vb* bet, gamble.

wail *vb* caterwaul, complain, cry, howl, lament, moan, shriek, waul, weep, *inf* yowl.

waist *n* middle, waistline.

waistband *n* belt, cummerbund, girdle.

wait *n* delay, halt, hesitation, hiatus, *inf* hold-up, intermission, interval, pause, postponement, rest, stay, stop, stoppage. ● *vb* **1** *old use* bide, delay, halt, *inf* hang about, *inf* hang on, hesitate, hold back, keep still, linger, mark time, pause, remain, rest, *inf* sit tight, stand by, stay, stop, *old use* tarry. **2** *wait at table.* serve.

waive *vb* abandon, cede, disclaim, dispense with, forgo, give up, relinquish, remit, renounce, resign, sign away, surrender.

wake *n* **1** funeral, vigil, watch. **2** *wake of a ship.* path, track, trail, turbulence, wash. ● *vb* **1** arouse, awaken, bring to life, call, disturb, galvanize, rouse, stimulate, stir, waken. **2** become conscious, bestir yourself, *inf* come to life, get up, rise, *inf* stir, wake up. **wake up to** ▷ REALIZE. **waking** ▷ CONSCIOUS.

wakeful *adj* alert, awake, insomniac, *inf* on the qui vive, restless, sleepless.

walk *n* **1** bearing, carriage, gait, stride. **2** constitutional, hike, *old use* promenade, ramble, saunter, stroll, traipse, tramp, trek, trudge, *inf* turn. **3** *a paved walk.* aisle, alley, path, pathway, pavement. ● *vb* **1** be a pedestrian, travel on foot. □ *amble, crawl, creep, dodder,* inf *foot-slog, hike, hobble, limp, lope, lurch, march, mince, sl mooch, pace, pad, paddle, parade, old use perambulate, plod, promenade, prowl, ramble, saunter, scuttle, shamble, shuffle, slink, stagger, stalk, steal, step, inf stomp, stride, stroll, strut, stumble, swagger, tiptoe, inf toddle, totter, traipse, tramp, trample, trek, troop, trot, trudge, waddle, wade.* **2** *don't walk on the flowers.* stamp, step, trample, tread. **walk away with** ▷ WIN. **walk off with** ▷ STEAL. **walk out** ▷ QUIT. **walk out on** ▷ DESERT.

walker *n* hiker, pedestrian, rambler.

wall *n* □ *barricade, barrier, bulkhead, bulwark, dam, dike, divider, embankment, fence, fortification, hedge, obstacle, paling, palisade, parapet, partition, rampart, screen, sea-wall, stockade.* **wall in** ▷ ENCLOSE.

wallet *n* notecase, pocketbook, pouch, purse.

wallow *vb* **1** flounder, lie, pitch about, roll about, stagger about, tumble, wade, welter. **2** *wallow in luxury.* glory, indulge yourself, luxuriate, revel, take delight.

wan *adj* anaemic, ashen, bloodless, colourless, exhausted, faint, feeble, livid, pale, pallid, pasty, sickly, tired, waxen, worn.

wand *n* baton, rod, staff, stick.

wander *vb* **1** drift, go aimlessly, meander, prowl, ramble, range, roam, rove, saunter, stray, stroll, travel about, walk, wind. **2** *wander off course.* curve, deviate, digress, drift, err, go off at a tangent, stray, swerve, turn, twist, veer, zigzag. **wandering** ▷ INATTENTIVE, NOMADIC.

wane *vb* decline, decrease, dim, diminish, dwindle, ebb, fade, fail, *inf* fall off, grow less, lessen, peter out, shrink, subside, taper off, weaken. *Opp* STRENGTHEN.

want *n* **1** demand, desire, need, requirement, wish. **2** *a want of ready cash.* absence, lack, need. **3** *war against want.* dearth, famine, hunger, insufficiency, penury, poverty, privation, scarcity, shortage. ● *vb* **1** aspire to, covet, crave, demand, desire, fancy, hanker after, *inf* have a yen for, hunger for, *inf* itch for, like, long for, miss, pine for, please, prefer, *inf* set your heart on, thirst after, thirst for, wish for, yearn for. **2** *want manners.* be short of, lack, need, require.

war *n* campaign, conflict, crusade, fighting, hostilities, military action, strife, warfare. □ *ambush, assault, attack, battle, blitz, blockade, bombardment, counter-attack, engagement, guerrilla warfare, invasion, manoeuvres, operations, resistance, siege, skirmish.* **wage war** ▷ FIGHT.

ward *n* charge, dependant, minor. ● *vb* **ward off** avert, beat off, block, chase away, check, deflect, fend off, forestall, parry, push away, repel, repulse, stave off, thwart, turn aside.

warder *n* gaoler, guard, jailer, keeper, prison officer.

warehouse *n* depository, depot, store, storehouse.

wares *plur n* commodities, goods, manufactures, merchandise, produce, stock, supplies.

warlike *adj* aggressive, bellicose, belligerent, hawkish, hostile, militant, militaristic, pugnacious, warmongering, warring.

warm *adj* **1** close, hot, lukewarm, subtropical, sultry, summery, temperate, tepid, warmish. **2** *warm clothes.* cosy, thermal, thick, winter, woolly. **3** *a warm welcome.* affable, affectionate, ardent, cordial, emotional, enthusiastic, excited, fervent, friendly, genial, impassioned, kind, loving, passionate, sympathetic, warm-hearted. *Opp* COLD, UNFRIENDLY. ● *vb* heat, make warmer, melt, raise the temperature of, thaw, thaw out. *Opp* COOL.

warn *vb* admonish, advise, alert, caution, counsel, forewarn, give a warning, give notice, inform, notify, raise the alarm, remind, *inf* tip off.

warning *n* **1** advance notice, augury, forewarning, hint, indication, notice, notification, omen, portent, premonition, presage, prophecy, reminder, sign, signal, threat, *inf* tip-off, *inf* word to the wise. □ *alarm, alarm-bell, beacon, bell, fire-alarm, flashing light, fog-horn, gong, hooter, red light, siren, traffic-lights, whistle.* **2** *let off with a warning.* admonition, advice, caution, caveat, reprimand.

warp *vb* become deformed, bend, buckle, contort, curl, curve, deform, distort, kink, twist.

warrant *n* authority, authorization, certification, document, entitlement, guarantee, licence, permit, pledge, sanction, search-warrant, voucher, warranty. ● *vb* ▷ JUSTIFY.

wary *adj* alert, apprehensive, attentive, *inf* cagey, careful, cautious, chary, circumspect, distrustful, heedful, observant, on the lookout, on your guard, suspicious, vigilant, watchful. *Opp* RECKLESS.

wash n old use ablutions, bath, rinse, shampoo, shower. ● vb **1** clean, cleanse, flush, launder, mop, rinse, scrub, shampoo, sluice, soap down, sponge down, swab down, swill, wipe. **2** bath, bathe, old use make your toilet, perform your ablutions, shower. **3** The sea washes against the cliff. break, dash, flow, lap, pound, roll, splash. **wash your hands of** ▷ ABANDON.

washing n cleaning, dirty clothes, laundry, inf the wash.

washout n débâcle, disappointment, disaster, failure, inf flop.

waste adj **1** discarded, extra, superfluous, unprofitable, unusable, unused, unwanted, worthless. **2** waste land. bare, barren, derelict, empty, overgrown, run-down, uncared-for, uncultivated, undeveloped, unproductive, wild. ● n **1** debris, dregs, effluent, excess, garbage, junk, leavings, inf left-overs, litter, offcuts, refuse, remnants, rubbish, scrap, scraps, trash, unusable material, unwanted material, wastage. **2** extravagance, indulgence, overprovision, prodigality, profligacy, self-indulgence. ● vb be wasteful with, dissipate, fritter, misspend, misuse, over provide, sl splurge, squander, use up, use wastefully. Opp CONSERVE. **waste away** become emaciated, become thin, become weaker, mope, pine, weaken.

wasteful adj excessive, expensive, extravagant, improvident, imprudent, lavish, needless, prodigal, profligate, reckless, spendthrift, thriftless, uneconomical, unthrifty. Opp ECONOMICAL. **wasteful person** ▷ SPENDTHRIFT.

watch n chronometer, clock, digital watch, stop-watch, timepiece, timer, wrist-watch. ● vb **1** attend, concentrate, contemplate, eye, gaze, heed, keep an eye open for, keep your eyes on, look at, mark, note, observe, pay attention, regard, see, spy on, stare, take notice, view. **2** watch sheep. care for, chaperon, defend, guard, keep an eye on, keep watch on, look after,

mind, protect, safeguard, shield, superintend, supervise, take charge of, tend. **keep watch** ▷ GUARD. **on the watch** ▷ WATCHFUL. **watch your step** ▷ BEWARE.

watcher n plur audience, inf looker-on, observer, onlooker, spectator, viewer, witness.

watchful adj attentive, eagleeyed, heedful, observant, inf on the lookout, inf on the qui vive, on the watch, quick, sharp-eyed, vigilant. ▷ ALERT. Opp INATTENTIVE.

watchman n caretaker, custodian, guard, lookout, night-watchman, security guard, sentinel, sentry, watch.

water n **1** Adam's ale, bath water, brine, distilled water, drinking water, mineral water, rainwater, sea water, spa water, spring water, tap water. **2** lake, lido, ocean, pond, pool, river, sea. ▷ STREAM. ● vb damp, dampen, douse, drench, flood, hose, inundate, irrigate, moisten, saturate, soak, souse, spray, sprinkle, wet. **water down** ▷ DILUTE.

waterfall n cascade, cataract, chute, rapids, torrent, white water.

waterlogged adj full of water, saturated, soaked.

waterproof adj damp-proof, impermeable, impervious, water-repellent, water-resistant, watertight, weatherproof. Opp LEAKY. ● n cape, ground-sheet, inf mac, mackintosh, sou'wester.

watertight adj hermetic, sealed, sound. ▷ WATERPROOF.

watery adj **1** aqueous, bland, characterless, dilute, diluted, fluid, liquid, inf runny, inf sloppy, tasteless, thin, watered-down, weak, inf wishy-washy. **2** watery eyes. damp, moist, tear-filled, tearful, inf weepy. ▷ WET.

wave n **1** billow, breaker, crest, heave, ridge, ripple, roller, surf, swell, tidal wave, undulation, wavelet, inf white horse. **2** flourish, gesticulation, gesture, sign, signal. **3** a wave of enthusiasm. current, flood, ground swell, outbreak, surge, tide, upsurge. **4** *a new wave*. advance, fashion, tendency, trend. **5** *radio waves*. pulse, vibration. ● *vb* **1** billow, brandish, flail about, flap, flourish, fluctuate, flutter, move to and fro, ripple, shake, sway, swing, twirl, undulate, waft, wag, waggle, wiggle, zigzag. **2** gesticulate, gesture, indicate, sign, signal. **wave aside** ▷ DISMISS.

wavelength *n* channel, station, waveband.

waver *vb inf* be in two minds, be unsteady, change, falter, flicker, hesitate, quake, quaver, quiver, shake, shiver, shudder, sway, teeter, tergiversate, totter, tremble, vacillate, wobble.

wavy *adj* curling, curly, curving, heaving, rippling, rolling, sinuous, undulating, up and down, winding, zigzag. *Opp* FLAT, STRAIGHT.

way *n* **1** advance, direction, headway, journey, movement, progress, route. ▷ ROAD. **2** distance, length, measurement. **3** *a way to do something*. approach, avenue, course, fashion, knack, manner, means, method, mode, *Lat* modus operandi, path, procedure, process, system, technique. **4** *foreign ways*. custom, fashion, habit, *Lat* modus vivendi, practice, routine, style, tradition. **5** *funny ways*. characteristic, eccentricity, idiosyncrasy, oddity, peculiarity. **6** *in some ways*. aspect, circumstance, detail, feature, particular, respect.

waylay *vb* accost, ambush, await, buttonhole, detain, intercept, lie in wait for, pounce on, surprise. ▷ ATTACK.

wayward *adj* disobedient, headstrong, obstinate, self-willed, stubborn, uncontrollable, uncooperative, wilful. ▷ NAUGHTY. *Opp* COOPERATIVE.

weak *adj* **1** breakable, brittle, decrepit, delicate, feeble, flawed, flimsy, fragile, frail, frangible, inadequate, insubstantial, rickety, shaky, slight, substandard, tender, thin, unsafe, unsound, unsteady, unsubstantial. **2** *weak in health*. anaemic, debilitated, delicate, enervated, exhausted, feeble, flabby, frail, helpless, ill, infirm, listless, *inf* low, *inf* poorly, puny, sickly, slight, thin, tired out, wasted, weakly, *derog* weedy. **3** *a weak character*. cowardly, fearful, impotent, indecisive, ineffective, ineffectual, irresolute, poor, powerless, pusillanimous, spineless, timid, timorous, unassertive, weak-minded, wimpish. **4** *a weak position*. defenceless, exposed, unguarded, unprotected, vulnerable. **5** *weak excuses*. hollow, lame, *inf* pathetic, shallow, unbelievable, unconvincing, unsatisfactory. **6** *weak light*. dim, distant, fading, faint, indistinct, pale, poor, unclear, vague. **7** *weak tea*. dilute, diluted, tasteless, thin, watery. *Opp* STRONG.

weaken *vb* **1** debilitate, destroy, dilute, diminish, emasculate, enervate, enfeeble, erode, exhaust, impair, lessen, lower, make weaker, reduce, ruin, sap, soften, thin down, undermine, *inf* water down. **2** abate, become weaker, decline, decrease, dwindle, ebb, fade, flag, give in, give way, sag, wane, yield. *Opp* STRENGTHEN.

weakling *n* coward, *inf* milksop, *inf* pushover, *inf* runt, *inf* softie, weak person, *inf* weed, *inf* wimp.

weakness *n* **1** *inf* Achilles' heel, blemish, defect, error, failing, fault, flaw, flimsiness, foible, fragility, frailty, imperfection, inadequacy, mistake, shortcoming, softness, *inf* weak spot. **2** debility, decrepitude, delicacy, feebleness, impotence, incapacity, infirmity, lassitude, vulnerability. ▷ ILLNESS. **3** *a weakness for wine*. affection, fancy, fondness, inclination, liking, partiality, penchant, predilection, *inf* soft spot, taste. *Opp* STRENGTH.

wealth *n* **1** affluence, assets, capital, fortune, *old use* lucre, means, opulence, possessions, property, prosperity, riches, *old use* substance. ▷ MONEY. *Opp* POVERTY. **2** *a wealth of information*. abundance, bounty, copiousness, cornucopia, mine, plenty, profusion, store, treasury. *Opp* SCARCITY.

wealthy *adj* affluent, *inf* flush, *inf* loaded, moneyed, opulent, *joc* plutocratic, privileged, prosperous, rich, *inf* well-heeled, well-off, well-to-do. *Opp* POOR. **wealthy person** billionaire, capitalist, millionaire, plutocrat, tycoon.

weapon *n* bomb, gun, missile. □ *airgun, arrow, atom bomb, ballistic missile, battering-ram, battleaxe, bayonet, bazooka, blowpipe, blunderbuss, boomerang, bow and arrow, bren-gun, cannon, carbine, catapult, claymore, cosh, crossbow, CS gas, cudgel, cutlass, dagger, depth-charge, dirk, flame-thrower, foils, grenade, old use halberd, harpoon, H-bomb, howitzer, incendiary bomb, javelin, knuckleduster, lance, land-mine, laser beam, longbow, machete, machine-gun, mine, mortar, musket, mustard gas, napalm bomb, pike, pistol, pole-axe, rapier, revolver, rifle, rocket, sabre, scimitar, shotgun, inf six-shooter, sling, spear, sten-gun, stiletto, sub-machine-gun, sword, tank, tear-gas, time-bomb, tomahawk, tommy-gun, torpedo, truncheon, warhead, water-cannon.* **weapons** armaments, armoury, arms, arsenal, magazine, munitions, ordnance, weaponry. □ *artillery, automatic weapons, biological weapons, chemical weapons, firearms, missiles, nuclear weapons, small arms, strategic weapons, tactical weapons.*

wear *vb* 1 be dressed in, clothe yourself in, don, dress in, have on, present yourself in, put on, wrap up in. 2 *wear a smile.* adopt, assume, display, exhibit, show. 3 *wears the carpet.* damage, fray, injure, mark, scuff, weaken, wear away. 4 *wear well.* endure, last, *inf* stand the test of time, survive. **wear away** ▷ ERODE. **wear off** ▷ SUBSIDE. **wear out** ▷ WEARY.

wearisome *adj* boring, dreary, exhausting, monotonous, repetitive, tedious, tiring, wearying. ▷ TROUBLESOME. *Opp* STIMULATING.

weary *adj* bone-weary, *inf* dead beat, *inf* dog-tired, *inf* done in, drained,

drawn, drowsy, enervated, exhausted, *inf* fagged, fatigued, fed up, flagging, foot-sore, impatient, jaded, *inf* jetlagged, *sl* knackered, listless, prostrate, *inf* shattered, *inf* sick (of), sleepy, spent, tired out, travel-weary, wearied, *inf* whacked, worn out. *Opp* FRESH, LIVELY. ● *vb* 1 debilit-ate, drain, enervate, exhaust, fatigue, *inf* finish, make tired, *sl* knacker, overtire, sap, *inf* shatter, *inf* take it out of, tax, tire, wear out. *Opp* REFRESH. 2 become bored, become tired, flag, grow weary, weaken.

weather *n* climate, the elements, meteorological conditions. □ *blizzard, breeze, cloud, cyclone, deluge, dew, downpour, drizzle, drought, fog, frost, gale, hail, haze, heatwave, hoar-frost, hurricane, ice, lightning, mist, rain, rainbow, shower, sleet, slush, snow, snowstorm, squall, storm, sunshine, tempest, thaw, thunder, tornado, typhoon, whirlwind, wind.* ● *vb* ▷ SURVIVE. **under the weather** ▷ ILL.

weave *vb* 1 braid, criss-cross, entwine, interlace, intertwine, interweave, knit, plait, sew. 2 *weave a story.* compose, create, make, plot, put together. 3 *weave through a crowd.* dodge, make your way, tack, *inf* twist and turn, wind, zigzag.

web *n* criss-cross, lattice, mesh, net, network.

wedding *n* marriage, nuptials, union.

wedge *vb* cram, force, jam, pack, squeeze, stick.

weep *vb* bawl, *inf* blub, blubber, cry, *inf* grizzle, lament, mewl, moan, shed tears, snivel, sob, wail, whimper, whine.

weigh *vb* 1 measure the weight of. 2 *weigh evidence.* assess, consider, contemplate, evaluate, judge, ponder, reflect on, think about, weigh up. 3 *evidence weighed with the jury.* be important, carry weight, count, *inf* cut ice, have weight, matter. **weigh down** ▷ BURDEN. **weigh up** ▷ EVALUATE.

weighing-machine *n* balance, scales, spring-balance, weighbridge.

whine

weight n 1 avoirdupois, burden, density, heaviness, load, mass, pressure, strain, tonnage. 2 *My voice has some weight.* authority, credibility, emphasis, force, gravity, importance, power, seriousness, significance, substance, value, worth. ● vb ballast, bias, hold down, keep down, load, make heavy, weigh down.

weird adj 1 creepy, eerie, ghostly, mysterious, preternatural, scary, inf spooky, supernatural, unaccountable, uncanny, unearthly, unnatural. 2 *weird behaviour.* abnormal, bizarre, inf cranky, curious, eccentric, inf funny, grotesque, odd, outlandish, peculiar, queer, quirky, strange, unconventional, unusual, inf wayout, inf zany. Opp CONVENTIONAL, NATURAL.

welcome adj acceptable, accepted, agreeable, appreciated, desirable, gratifying, much-needed, inf nice, pleasant, pleasing, pleasurable. Opp UNWELCOME. ● n greeting, hospitality, reception, salutation. ● vb 1 give a welcome to, greet, hail, receive. 2 *They welcome criticism.* accept, appreciate, approve of, delight in, like, want.

weld vb bond, cement, fuse, join, solder, unite. ▷ FASTEN.

welfare n advantage, benefit, felicity, good, happiness, health, interest, prosperity, well-being.

well adj 1 fit, hale, healthy, hearty, inf in fine fettle, lively, robust, sound, strong, thriving, vigorous. 2 *All is well.* all right, fine, inf OK, satisfactory. ● n fountain, shaft, source, spring, waterhole, well-spring. □ artesian well, borehole, gusher, oasis, oil well, wishing-well.

well-behaved adj cooperative, disciplined, docile, dutiful, good, hardworking, law-abiding, manageable, inf nice, polite, quiet, well-trained. ▷ OBEDIENT. Opp NAUGHTY.

well-bred adj courteous, courtly, cultivated, decorous, genteel, polite, proper, refined, sophisticated, urbane, well-brought-up, well-mannered. Opp RUDE.

well-built adj athletic, big, brawny, burly, hefty, muscular, powerful, stocky, inf strapping, strong, sturdy, upstanding. Opp SMALL.

well-known adj celebrated, eminent, familiar, famous, illustrious, noted, derog notorious, prominent, renowned. Opp UNKNOWN.

well-meaning adj good-natured, obliging, sincere, well-intentioned, well-meant. ▷ KIND. Opp UNKIND.

well-off adj affluent, comfortable, moneyed, prosperous, rich, inf well-heeled, well-to-do. Opp POOR.

well-spoken adj articulate, educated, polite, inf posh, refined, inf upper crust.

wet adj 1 awash, bedraggled, clammy, damp, dank, dewy, drenched, dripping, moist, muddy, saturated, sloppy, soaked, soaking, sodden, soggy, sopping, soused, spongy, submerged, waterlogged, watery, wringing. 2 *wet weather.* drizzly, humid, misty, pouring, rainy, showery, teeming. 3 *wet paint.* runny, sticky, tacky. ● n dampness, dew, drizzle, humidity, liquid, moisture, rain. ● vb dampen, douse, drench, irrigate, moisten, saturate, soak, spray, sprinkle, steep, water. Opp DRY.

wheel n circle, disc, hoop, ring. □ bogie, castor, cog-wheel, spinning-wheel, steering-wheel. ● vb change direction, circle, gyrate, move in circles, pivot, spin, swerve, swing round, swivel, turn, veer, whirl.

wheeze vb breathe noisily, cough, gasp, pant, puff.

whereabouts n location, neighbourhood, place, position, site, situation, vicinity.

whiff n breath, hint, puff, smell.

whim n caprice, desire, fancy, impulse, quirk, urge.

whine vb complain, cry, inf grizzle, groan, moan, snivel, wail, weep, whimper, inf whinge.

whip n birch, cane, cat, cat-o'-nine-tails, crop, horsewhip, lash, riding-crop, scourge, switch. ● vb **1** beat, birch, cane, flagellate, flog, horse-whip, lash, scourge, inf tan, thrash. ▷ HIT. **2** beat, stir vigorously, whisk.

whirl vb circle, gyrate, pirouette, reel, revolve, rotate, spin, swivel, turn, twirl, twist, wheel.

whirlpool n eddy, maelstrom, swirl, vortex, whirl.

whirlwind n cyclone, hurricane, tor-nado, typhoon, vortex, waterspout.

whisk n beater, mixer. ● vb beat, mix, stir, whip.

whiskers plur n bristles, hairs, moustache.

whisper n **1** murmur, undertone. **2** a whisper of scandal. gossip, hearsay, rumour. ● vb breathe, hiss, murmur, mutter. ▷ TALK.

whistle n hooter, pipe, pipes, siren. ● vb blow, pipe.

white adj chalky, clean, cream, ivory, milky, off-white, silver, snow-white, snowy, spotless, whitish. ▷ PALE.

whiten vb blanch, bleach, etiolate, fade, lighten, pale.

whole adj coherent, complete, entire, full, healthy, in one piece, intact, integral, integrated, perfect, sound, total, unabbreviated, un-abridged, unbroken, uncut, un-damaged, undivided, unedited, un-expurgated, unharmed, unhurt, uninjured, unscathed. Opp FRAGMENT-ARY, INCOMPLETE.

wholesale adj comprehensive, extensive, general, global, indis-criminate, mass, total, universal, widespread. Opp LIMITED.

wholesome adj beneficial, good, healthful, health-giving, healthy, hygienic, nourishing, nutritious, salubrious, sanitary. Opp UNHEALTHY.

wicked adj abominable, inf awful, bad, base, beastly, corrupt, criminal, depraved, diabolical, dissolute, egre-gious, evil, foul, guilty, heinous, ill-tempered, immoral, impious, incorrigible, indefensible, iniquitous, insupportable, intolerable, irrespons-ible, lawless, lost (soul), machia-vellian, malevolent, malicious, mischievous, murderous, naughty, nefarious, offensive, perverted, ras-cally, scandalous, shameful, sinful, sinister, spiteful, inf terrible, un-godly, unprincipled, unregenerate, unrighteous, unscrupulous, vicious, vile, villainous, violent, wrong. ▷ IRRELIGIOUS, OBSCENE. Opp MORAL.
wicked person ▷ VILLAIN.

wickedness n baseness, depravity, enormity, guilt, heinousness, im-morality, infamy, iniquity, irrespon-sibility, old use knavery, malice, misconduct, naughtiness, sin, sin-fulness, spite, turpitude, ungod-liness, unrighteousness, vileness, villainy, wrong, wrongdoing. ▷ EVIL.

wide adj **1** ample, broad, expansive, extensive, large, panoramic, roomy, spacious, vast, yawning. **2** wide sym-pathies. all-embracing, broad-minded, catholic, comprehensive, eclectic, encyclopedic, inclusive, wide-ranging. **3** arms open wide. extended, open, outspread, outstretched. **4** a wide shot. off-course, off-target. Opp NARROW.

widen vb augment, broaden, dilate, distend, enlarge, expand, extend, flare, increase, make wider, open out, spread, stretch.

widespread adj common, endemic, extensive, far-reaching, general, global, pervasive, prevalent, rife, uni-versal, wholesale. Opp RARE.

width n beam (of ship), breadth, broadness, calibre (of gun), compass, diameter, distance across, extent, girth, range, scope, span, thickness.

wield vb **1** brandish, flourish, handle, hold, manage, ply, wave. **2** wield power. employ, exercise, exert, have, possess, use.

wild adj **1** wild animals. free, undo-mesticated, untamed. **2** a wild moor. deserted, desolate, inf God-forsaken, natural, overgrown, remote, rough, rugged, uncultivated, unenclosed, unfarmed, uninhabited, waste. **3** wild behaviour. aggressive, barbaric, barbarous, berserk, boisterous, disorderly, ferocious, fierce, frantic, hysterical, lawless, mad, noisy, obstreperous, on the rampage, out of control, rabid, rash, reckless, riotous, rowdy, savage, uncivilized, uncontrollable, uncontrolled, undisciplined, ungovernable, unmanageable, unrestrained, unruly, uproarious, violent. **4** *wild weather.* blustery, stormy, tempestuous, turbulent, violent, windy. **5** *wild enthusiasm.* eager, excited, extravagant, uninhibited, unrestrained. **6** *wild notions.* crazy, fantastic, impetuous, irrational, silly, unreasonable. **7** *a wild guess.* inaccurate, random, unthinking. *Opp* CALM, CULTIVATED, TAME.

wilderness *n* desert, jungle, waste, wasteland, wilds.

wile *n* artifice, gambit, *inf* game, machination, manoeuvre, plot, ploy, ruse, stratagem, subterfuge, trick.

wilful *adj* **1** calculated, conscious, deliberate, intended, intentional, premeditated, purposeful, voluntary. *Opp* ACCIDENTAL. **2** *a wilful character.* inf bloody-minded, determined, dogged, headstrong, immovable, intransigent, obdurate, obstinate, perverse, *inf* pigheaded, refractory, self-willed, stubborn, uncompromising, unyielding, wayward. *Opp* AMENABLE.

will *n* aim, commitment, desire, determination, disposition, inclination, intent, intention, longing, purpose, resolution, resolve, volition, will-power, wish. ● *vb* **1** command, encourage, force, influence, inspire, persuade, require, wish. **2** *will a fortune.* bequeath, hand down, leave, pass on, settle on.

willing *adj* acquiescent, agreeable, amenable, assenting, complaisant, compliant, consenting, content, cooperative, disposed, docile, *inf* game, happy, helpful, inclined, pleased, prepared, obliging, ready, well-disposed. ▷ EAGER. *Opp* UNWILLING.

wilt *vb* become limp, droop, fade, fail, flag, flop, languish, sag, shrivel, weaken, wither. *Opp* THRIVE.

wily *adj* artful, astute, canny, clever, crafty, cunning, deceptive, designing, devious, disingenuous, furtive, guileful, ingenious, knowing, scheming, shifty, shrewd, skilful, sly, tricky, underhand. ▷ DISHONEST. *Opp* STRAIGHTFORWARD.

win *vb* **1** be the winner, be victorious, carry the day, come first, conquer, overcome, prevail, succeed, triumph. **2** *win a prize.* achieve, acquire, *inf* carry off, collect, *inf* come away with, deserve, earn, gain, get, obtain, *inf* pick up, receive, secure, *inf* walk away with. *Opp* LOSE.

wind *n* **1** air-current, blast, breath, breeze, current of air, cyclone, draught, gale, gust, hurricane, monsoon, puff, squall, storm, tempest, tornado, whirlwind, *poet* zephyr. **2** *wind in the stomach.* flatulence, gas, heartburn. ● *vb* bend, coil, curl, curve, furl, loop, meander, ramble, reel, roll, slew, snake, spiral, turn, twine, twist, *inf* twist and turn, veer, wreathe, zigzag. **winding** ▷ TORTUOUS. **wind up** ▷ FINISH.

window *n* □ casement, dormer, double-glazed window, embrasure, fanlight, *French window*, light, oriel, pane, sash window, skylight, shop window, stained-glass window, windscreen.

windswept *adj* bare, bleak, desolate, exposed, unprotected. ▷ WINDY.

windy *adj* blowy, blustery, boisterous, breezy, draughty, fresh, gusty, squally, stormy, tempestuous. ▷ WINDSWEPT. *Opp* CALM.

wink *vb* **1** bat (*eyelid*), blink, flutter. **2** *lights winked.* flash, flicker, sparkle, twinkle.

winner *n* inf champ, champion, conquering hero, conqueror, first, medallist, prizewinner, title-holder, victor. *Opp* LOSER.

winning *adj* **1** champion, conquering, first, leading, prevailing, successful, top, top-scoring, triumphant, unbeaten, undefeated, victorious. *Opp* UNSUCCESSFUL. **2** *a winning smile.* ▷ ATTRACTIVE.

wintry *adj* arctic, icy, snowy. ▷ COLD. *Opp* SUMMERY.

wipe *vb* brush, clean, cleanse, dry, dust, mop, polish, rub, scour, sponge, swab, wash. **wipe out** ▷ DESTROY.

wire *n* **1** cable, coaxial cable, flex, lead, wiring. **2** cablegram, telegram. ▷ COMMUNICATION.

wiry *adj* lean, muscular, sinewy, strong, thin, tough.

wisdom *n* astuteness, common sense, discernment, discrimination, good sense, insight, judgement, judiciousness, penetration, perceptiveness, perspicacity, prudence, rationality, reason, sagacity, sapience, sense, understanding. ▷ INTELLIGENCE.

wise *adj* **1** astute, discerning, enlightened, erudite, fair, just, knowledgeable, penetrating, perceptive, perspicacious, philosophical, sagacious, sage, sensible, shrewd, sound, thoughtful, understanding, well-informed. ▷ INTELLIGENT. **2** *a wise decision.* advisable, appropriate, considered, diplomatic, expedient, informed, judicious, politic, proper, prudent, rational, reasonable, right. *Opp* UNWISE. **wise person** philosopher, pundit, sage.

wish *n* aim, ambition, appetite, aspiration, craving, desire, fancy, hankering, hope, inclination, *inf* itch, keenness, longing, objective, request, urge, want, yearning, *inf* yen. ● *vb* ask, choose, crave, desire, hope, want, yearn. **wish for** ▷ WANT.

wisp *n* shred, strand, streak.

wispy *adj* flimsy, fragile, gossamer, insubstantial, light, streaky, thin. *Opp* SUBSTANTIAL.

wistful *adj* disconsolate, forlorn, melancholy, mournful, nostalgic, regretful, yearning. ▷ SAD.

wit *n* **1** banter, cleverness, comedy, facetiousness, humour, ingenuity, jokes, puns, quickness, quips, repartee, witticisms, wordplay. ▷ INTELLIGENCE. **2** comedian, comic, humorist, jester, joker, wag.

witch *n* enchantress, gorgon, hag, sibyl, sorceress, *plur* weird sisters.

witchcraft *n* black magic, charms, enchantment, *inf* hocus-pocus, incantation, magic, *inf* mumbo-jumbo, necromancy, the occult, occultism, sorcery, spells, voodoo, witchery, wizardry.

withdraw *vb* **1** abjure, call back, cancel, *inf* go back on, recall, rescind, retract, take away, take back. **2** *withdraw from the fight.* back away, back down, back out, *inf* chicken out, *inf* cry off, draw back, drop out, fall back, move back, pull back, pull out, *inf* quit, recoil, retire, retreat, run away, *inf* scratch, secede, shrink back. ▷ LEAVE. *Opp* ADVANCE, ENTER. **3** *withdraw teeth.* extract, pull out, remove, take out.

withdrawn *adj* bashful, diffident, distant, introverted, private, quiet, reclusive, remote, reserved, retiring, shy, silent, solitary, taciturn, timid, uncommunicative. *Opp* SOCIABLE.

wither *vb* become dry, become limp, dehydrate, desiccate, droop, dry out, dry up, fail, flag, flop, sag, shrink, shrivel, waste away, wilt. *Opp* THRIVE.

withhold *vb* check, conceal, control, hide, hold back, keep back, keep secret, repress, reserve, retain, suppress. *Opp* GIVE.

withstand *vb* bear, brave, confront, cope with, defy, endure, fight, grapple with, hold out against, last out against, oppose, *inf* put up with, resist, stand up to, *inf* stick, survive, take, tolerate, weather (*storm*). *Opp* SURRENDER.

witness *n* bystander, eyewitness, looker-on, observer, onlooker, spectator, viewer, watcher. ● *vb* attend, behold, be present at, look on, note, notice, observe, see, view, watch. **bear witness** ▷ TESTIFY.

witty *adj* amusing, clever, comic, droll, facetious, funny, humorous, ingenious, intelligent, jocular, quick-witted, sarcastic, sharp-witted, waggish.

wizard *n* enchanter, magician, magus, sorcerer, *old use* warlock, witch-doctor.

wobble *vb* be unsteady, heave, move unsteadily, oscillate, quake, quiver, rock, shake, sway, teeter, totter, tremble, vacillate, vibrate, waver.

wobbly *adj* insecure, loose, rickety, rocky, shaky, teetering, tottering, unbalanced, unsafe, unstable, unsteady. *Opp* STEADY.

woe *n* affliction, anguish, dejection, despair, distress, grief, heartache, melancholy, misery, misfortune, sadness, suffering, trouble, unhappiness, wretchedness. ▷ SORROW. *Opp* HAPPINESS.

woebegone *adj* crestfallen, dejected, downhearted, forlorn, gloomy, melancholy, miserable, *inf* sorry for yourself, woeful, wretched. ▷ SAD. *Opp* CHEERFUL.

woman *n sl* bird, bride, *old use* dame, *old use* damsel, daughter, dowager, female, girl, girlfriend, *derog* hag, *derog* harridan, housewife, hoyden, *derog* hussy, lady, lass, madam, Madame, maid, *old use* maiden, matriarch, matron, mistress, mother, *derog* termagant, *derog* virago, virgin, widow, wife.

wonder *n* **1** admiration, amazement, astonishment, awe, bewilderment, curiosity, fascination, respect, reverence, stupefaction, surprise, wonderment. **2** *a wonder of science.* marvel, miracle, phenomenon, prodigy, *inf* sensation. ● *vb* ask yourself, be curious, be inquisitive, conjecture, marvel, ponder, question yourself, speculate. ▷ THINK. **wonder at** ▷ ADMIRE.

wonderful *adj* amazing, astonishing, astounding, extraordinary, impressive, incredible, marvellous, miraculous, phenomenal, remarkable, surprising, unexpected, *old use* wondrous. *Opp* ORDINARY.

woo *vb* **1** *sl* chat up, court, make love to. **2** *woo custom.* attract, bring in, coax, cultivate, persuade, pursue, seek, try to get.

wood *n* **1** afforestation, coppice, copse, forest, grove, jungle, orchard, plantation, spinney, thicket, trees, woodland, woods. **2** blockboard, chipboard, deal, planks, plywood, timber. □ balsa, beech, cedar, chestnut, ebony, elm, mahogany, oak, pine, rosewood, sandalwood, sapele, teak, walnut.

wooded *adj* afforested, *poet* bosky, forested, silvan, timbered, tree-covered, woody.

wooden *adj* **1** ligneous, timber, wood. **2** *wooden acting.* dead, emotionless, expressionless, hard, inflexible, lifeless, rigid, stiff, stilted, unbending, unemotional, unnatural. *Opp* LIVELY.

woodwind *n* □ bassoon, clarinet, cor anglais, flute, oboe, piccolo, recorder.

woodwork *n* carpentry, joinery.

woody *adj* fibrous, hard, ligneous, tough. ▷ WOODEN.

woolly *adj* **1** wool, woollen. **2** *woolly toy.* cuddly, downy, fleecy, furry, fuzzy, hairy, shaggy, soft. **3** *woolly ideas.* ambiguous, blurry, confused, hazy, ill-defined, indefinite, indistinct, uncertain, unclear, unfocused, vague.

word *n* **1** expression, name, term. **2** ▷ NEWS. **3** ▷ PROMISE. ● *vb* articulate, express, phrase. **word for word** ▷ VERBATIM.

wording *n* choice of words, diction, expression, language, phraseology, phrasing, style, terminology.

wordy *adj* chatty, diffuse, digressive, discursive, garrulous, long-winded, loquacious, pleonastic, prolix, rambling, repetitious, talkative, unstoppable, verbose, voluble, *inf* windy. *Opp* CONCISE.

work *n* **1** *inf* donkey-work, drudgery, effort, exertion, *inf* fag, *inf* graft, *inf* grind, industry, labour, *inf* plod, slavery, *inf* slog, *inf* spadework, strain, struggle, *inf* sweat, toil, *old use* travail. **2** *work to be done.* assignment, chore, commission, duty, errand, homework, housework, job, mission, project, responsibility, task, undertaking. **3** *regular work.* business,

worker

calling, career, employment, job, livelihood, living, métier, occupation, post, profession, situation, trade. ● vb **1** inf beaver away, be busy, drudge, exert yourself, inf fag, inf grind away, inf keep your nose to the grindstone, labour, make efforts, navvy, inf peg away, inf plug away, inf potter about, inf slave, inf slog away, strain, strive, struggle, sweat, toil, travail. **2** act, be effective, function, go, operate, perform, run, succeed, thrive. **3** work slaves hard. drive, exploit, utilize. **working** ▷ EMPLOYED, OPERATIONAL. **work out** ▷ CALCULATE. **work up** ▷ DEVELOP, EXCITE.

worker n artisan, breadwinner, coolie, craftsman, employee, old use hand, labourer, member of staff, navvy, operative, operator, peasant, practitioner, servant, slave, tradesman, wage-earner, working man, working woman, workman.

workforce n employees, staff, workers.

workmanship n art, artistry, competence, craft, craftsmanship, expertise, handicraft, handiwork, skill, technique.

workshop n factory, mill, smithy, studio, workroom.

world n **1** earth, globe, planet. **2** area, circle, domain, field, milieu, sphere.

worldly adj avaricious, covetous, earthly, fleshly, greedy, human, material, materialistic, mundane, physical, profane, secular, selfish, temporal. Opp SPIRITUAL.

worm vb crawl, creep, slither, squirm, wriggle, writhe.

worn adj **1** frayed, moth-eaten, old, ragged, inf scruffy, shabby, tattered, inf tatty, thin, threadbare, worn-out. **2** ▷ WEARY.

worried adj afraid, agitated, agonized, alarmed, anxious, apprehensive, bothered, concerned, distraught, distressed, disturbed, edgy, fearful, inf fraught, fretful, guilt-ridden, insecure, nervous, nervy, neurotic, obsessed (by), on edge, overwrought, perplexed, perturbed, solicitous, tense, troubled, uncertain, uneasy, unhappy, upset, vexed.

worry n **1** agitation, anxiety, apprehension, disquiet, distress, fear, neurosis, perplexity, perturbation, tension, unease, uneasiness. **2** affliction, annoyance, bother, burden, care, concern, misgiving, problem, plur trials and tribulations, trouble, vexation. ● vb **1** agitate, annoy, inf badger, bother, depress, disquiet, distress, disturb, exercise, inf hassle, irritate, molest, nag, perplex, perturb, pester, plague, tease, threaten, torment, trouble, upset, vex. Opp REASSURE. **2** worry about money. agonize, be anxious, be worried, brood, exercise yourself, feel uneasy, fret.

worsen vb **1** aggravate, exacerbate, heighten, increase, intensify, make worse. **2** his health worsened. decline, degenerate, deteriorate, fail, get worse, inf go downhill, weaken. Opp IMPROVE.

worship n adoration, adulation, deification, devotion, glorification, homage, idolatry, love, praise, reverence, veneration. ● vb admire, adore, adulate, be devoted to, deify, dote on, exalt, extol, glorify, heroworship, idolize, kneel before, laud, lionize, look up to, love, magnify, pay homage to, praise, pray to, inf put on a pedestal, revere, reverence, venerate.

worth n benefit, cost, good, importance, merit, quality, significance, use, usefulness, utility, value. **be worth** be priced at, cost, have a value of.

worthless adj old use bootless, dispensable, disposable, frivolous, futile, inf good-for-nothing, hollow, insignificant, meaningless, meretricious, paltry, pointless, poor, inf rubbishy, inf trashy, trifling, trivial, trumpery, unimportant, unproductive, unprofitable, unusable, useless, vain, valueless. Opp WORTHWHILE.

worthwhile adj advantageous, beneficial, considerable, enriching, fruitful, fulfilling, gainful, gratifying, helpful, important, invaluable, meaningful, noticeable, productive, profitable, remunerative, rewarding, satisfying, significant, sizeable, substantial, useful, valuable. ▷ WORTHY. *Opp* WORTHLESS.

worthy *adj* admirable, commendable, creditable, decent, deserving, estimable, good, honest, honourable, laudable, meritorious, praiseworthy, reputable, respectable, worth supporting, worthwhile. *Opp* UNWORTHY.

wound *n* damage, hurt, injury, scar, trauma. □ *amputation, bite, bruise, burn, contusion, cut, fracture, gash, graze, laceration, lesion, mutilation, puncture, scab, scald, scar, scratch, sore, sprain, stab, sting, strain, weal, welt.* ● *vb* cause pain to, damage, harm, hurt, injure, traumatize. □ *amputate, bite, blow up, bruise, burn, claw, cut, fracture, gash, gore, graze, hit, impale, knife, lacerate, maim, make sore, mangle, maul, mutilate, scratch, shoot, sprain, strain, stab, sting, torture. Opp* HEAL, MEND.

wrap *n* cape, cloak, mantle, poncho, shawl, stole. ● *vb* bind, bundle up, cloak, cocoon, conceal, cover, do up, encase, enclose, enfold, enshroud, envelop, hide, insulate, lag, muffle, pack, package, shroud, surround, swaddle, swathe, wind.

wreathe *vb* adorn, decorate, encircle, festoon, intertwine, interweave, twist, weave.

wreck *n* 1 hulk, shipwreck. ▷ WRECKAGE. 2 *the wreck of all my hopes.* demolition, destruction, devastation, loss, obliteration, overthrow, ruin, termination, undoing. ● *vb* 1 annihilate, break up, crumple, crush, dash to pieces, demolish, destroy, devastate, ruin, shatter, smash, spoil, *inf* write off. 2 *wreck a ship.* capsize, founder, ground, scuttle, sink, shipwreck.

wreckage *n* bits, debris, *inf* flotsam and jetsam, fragments, pieces, remains, rubble, ruins.

wrench *vb* force, jerk, lever, prize, pull, rip, strain, tear, tug, twist, wrest, wring, *inf* yank.

wrestle *vb* grapple, strive, struggle, tussle. ▷ FIGHT.

wretch *n* 1 beggar, down-and-out, miserable person, pauper, unfortunate. 2 ▷ VILLAIN.

wretched *adj* 1 dejected, depressed, dispirited, downhearted, hapless, melancholy, miserable, pathetic, pitiable, pitiful, unfortunate. ▷ SAD. 2 ▷ UNSATISFACTORY.

wriggle *vb* crawl, snake, squirm, twist, waggle, wiggle, wobble, worm, writhe, zigzag.

wring *vb* 1 clasp, compress, crush, grip, press, shake, squeeze, twist, wrench, wrest. 2 coerce, exact, extort, extract, force.

wrinkle *n* corrugation, crease, crinkle, *inf* crow's foot, dimple, fold, furrow, gather, line, pleat, pucker, ridge, ripple. ● *vb* corrugate, crease, crinkle, crumple, fold, furrow, gather, make wrinkles, pleat, pucker up, ridge, ripple, ruck up, rumple, screw up.

wrinkled *adj* corrugated, creased, crinkly, crumpled, furrowed, lined, pleated, ridged, ripply, rumpled, screwed up, shrivelled, undulating, wavy, wizened, wrinkly. *Opp* SMOOTH.

write *vb* be a writer, compile, compose, copy, correspond, doodle, draft, draw up, engrave, indite, inscribe, jot, note, pen, print, put in writing, record, scrawl, scribble, set down, take down, transcribe, type. **write off** ▷ CANCEL, DESTROY.

writer *n* 1 amanuensis, clerk, copyist, *derog* pen-pusher, scribe, secretary, typist. 2 author, bard, composer, *derog* hack, littérateur, wordsmith. □ *biographer, columnist, contributor, copy-writer, correspondent, diarist, dramatist, essayist, freelancer, ghost-writer, journalist, leader-writer, librettist, novelist, playwright, poet, reporter, scriptwriter.*

writhe *vb* coil, contort, jerk, squirm, struggle, thrash about, thresh about, twist, wriggle.

writing *n* 1 calligraphy, characters, copperplate, cuneiform, handwriting, hieroglyphics, inscription, italics, letters, longhand, notation, penmanship, printing, runes, scrawl, screed, scribble, script, shorthand. **2** authorship, composition, journalism. **3** hard copy, literature, manuscript, opus, printout, text, typescript, work. □ *article, autobiography, belles-lettres, biography, comedy, copy-writing, correspondence, crime story, criticism, detective story, diary, dissertation, documentary, drama, editorial, epic, epistle, essay, fable, fairy-tale, fantasy, fiction, folk-tale, history, legal document, legend, letter, libretto, lyric, monograph, mystery, myth, newspaper column, nonfiction, novel, parable, parody, philosophy, play, poem, propaganda, prose, reportage, romance, saga, satire, science fiction, scientific writing, scriptwriting, SF, sketch, story, tale, thesis, thriller, tragedy, tragi-comedy, travel writing, treatise, trilogy, TV script, verse, inf whodunit, yarn.*

written *adj* documentary, *inf* in black and white, inscribed, in writing, set down, transcribed, typewritten. *Opp* SPOKEN.

wrong *adj* **1** base, blameworthy, corrupt, criminal, crooked, deceitful, dishonest, dishonourable, evil, felonious, illegal, illegitimate, illicit, immoral, iniquitous, irresponsible, mendacious, misleading, naughty, reprehensible, sinful, specious, unethical, unjustifiable, unlawful, unprincipled, unscrupulous, vicious, villainous, wicked, wrong-headed.

2 *wrong answers.* erroneous, fallacious, false, imprecise, improper, inaccurate, incorrect, inexact, misinformed, mistaken, unfounded, untrue. **3** *a wrong decision.* curious, illadvised, ill-considered, ill-judged, impolitic, imprudent, injudicious, misguided, misjudged, unacceptable, unfair, unjust, unsound, unwise, wrongful. **4** *go the wrong way.* abnormal, contrary, inappropriate, incongruous, inconvenient, misleading, opposite, unconventional, undesirable, unhelpful, unsuitable, worst. **5** *Something's wrong.* amiss, broken down, defective, faulty, out of order, unusable. ▷ BAD. *Opp* RIGHT. ● *vb* abuse, be unfair to, cheat, damage, do an injustice to, harm, hurt, injure, malign, maltreat, misrepresent, mistreat, traduce, treat unfairly. **do wrong** ▷ MISBEHAVE.

wrongdoer *n* convict, criminal, crook, culprit, delinquent, evil-doer, law-breaker, malefactor, mischief-maker, miscreant, offender, sinner, transgressor.

wrongdoing *n* crime, delinquency, disobedience, evil, immorality, indiscipline, iniquity, malpractice, misbehaviour, mischief, naughtiness, offence, sin, sinfulness, wickedness.

wry *adj* **1** askew, aslant, awry, bent, contorted, crooked, deformed, distorted, lopsided, twisted, uneven. **2** *a wry sense of humour.* droll, dry, ironic, mocking, sardonic.

Y

yard *n* court, courtyard, enclosure, garden, *inf* quad, quadrangle.

yarn *n* **1** fibre, strand, thread. **2** account, anecdote, fiction, narrative, story, tale.

yawning *adj* gaping, open, wide.

yearly *adj* annual, perennial, regular.

yearn *vb* ache, feel desire, hanker, have a craving, hunger, itch, long, pine. ▷ WANT.

yellow *adj* □ chrome yellow, cream, gold, golden, orange, tawny.

yield *n* **1** crop, harvest, output, produce, product. **2** earnings, gain, income, interest, proceeds, profit, return, revenue. ● *vb* **1** acquiesce, agree, assent, bow, capitulate, *inf* cave in, cede, comply, concede, defer, give in, give up, give way, *inf* knuckle under, submit, succumb, surrender, *inf* throw in the towel, *inf* throw up the sponge. **2** *yield interest*. bear, earn, generate, pay out, produce, provide, return, supply. **yielding** ▷ FLEXIBLE, SPONGY, SUBMISSIVE.

young *adj* **1** baby, early, growing, immature, new-born, undeveloped, unfledged, youngish. **2** *young people*. adolescent, juvenile, pubescent, teenage, underage, youthful. **3** *young for your age*. babyish, boyish, callow, childish, girlish, *inf* green, immature, inexperienced, infantile, juvenile, naïve, puerile. ● *n* brood, family, issue, litter, offspring, progeny. **young creatures** bullock, calf, chick, colt, cub, cygnet, duckling, fawn, fledgling, foal, gosling, heifer, kid, kitten, lamb, leveret, nestling, pullet, puppy, yearling. **young people** adolescent, baby, boy, *derog* brat, child, girl, infant, juvenile, *inf* kid, lad, lass, *inf* nipper, teenager, toddler, *derog* urchin, youngster, youth.

youth *n* **1** adolescence, babyhood, boyhood, childhood, girlhood, growing up, immaturity, infancy, minority, pubescence, *inf* salad days, *inf* teens. **2** adolescent, boy, juvenile, *inf* kid, *inf* lad, minor, stripling, teenager, youngster.

youthful *adj* fresh, lively, sprightly, vigorous, well-preserved, young-looking. ▷ YOUNG.

Z

zany *adj* absurd, clownish, crazy, eccentric, idiotic, *inf* loony, *inf* mad, madcap, playful, ridiculous, silly, *sl* wacky.

zeal *n derog* bigotry, earnestness, enthusiasm, fanaticism, fervour, partisanship.

zealot *n* bigot, extremist, fanatic, partisan, radical.

zealous *adj* conscientious, diligent, eager, earnest, enthusiastic, fanatical, fervent, keen, militant, obsessive, partisan, passionate. *Opp* APATHETIC.

zenith *n* acme, apex, apogee, climax, height, highest point, meridian, peak, pinnacle, summit, top. *Opp* NADIR.

zero *n cricket* duck, *tennis* love, naught, nil, nothing, nought, *sl* zilch.
zero in on ▷ AIM.

zest *n* appetite, eagerness, energy, enjoyment, enthusiasm, exuberance, hunger, interest, liveliness, pleasure, thirst, zeal.

zigzag *adj* bendy, crooked, *inf* in and out, indirect, meandering, serpentine, twisting, winding. ● *vb* bend, curve, meander, snake, tack, twist, wind.

zone *n* area, belt, district, domain, locality, neighbourhood, province, quarter, region, section, sector, sphere, territory, tract, vicinity.

zoo *n* menagerie, safari park, zoological gardens.

zoom *vb* career, dart, dash, hurry, hurtle, race, rush, shoot, speed, *inf* whiz, *inf* zip. ▷ MOVE.

Spell-it-right guide

Contents

Looking for patterns:

●●●●●● **Looking for patterns** ●●●●●●

The key to a generally more positive approach to spelling is to look constantly for **patterns**. There are two kinds of pattern which are helpful:
- patterns of sound/letter relationship
- patterns of letter/letter relationship

Sound/letter patterns

At first sight looking for correspondences between the sounds and letters of English seems a daunting task. The first sound in the name 'George' can be spelled in eight different ways:

j as in jug	**g** as in gesture
dg as in judge	**gg** as in suggest
dj as in adjust	**de** as in grandeur
di as in soldier	
ch as in sandwich (as pronounced by some speakers)	

Vowels cause even more difficulty. For example, the vowel sound in 'beat' is commonly spelled in seven different ways:

ee as in beet	**ea** as in beat
e as in theme	**ie** as in fief
ei as in receive	**ey** as in key
i as in routine	

In addition it occurs in these words:
    quay   people

Leaving the latter two 'exceptions' on one side, however, it is easy to see patterns of sound/letter correspondence:

beet	**beat**	**fief**	
feed	heap	thief	
feet	leap	piece	etc.

Letter/letter patterns

As we learn to read we come to recognize the combinations of letters that are typical of English. For example given a small amount of time, most people could think of words that contained these letter combinations: –IGH– –UGH–

It is much more difficult to think of words that contain the combination –EGH–. There are some, but they are fairly obscure.

The other way in which we habitually use patterning is in the recognition of word stems, prefixes, and suffixes: once you understand and can spell *psychology* you should not have too much trouble spelling the first part of *psychiatry* and *psychoanalysis* or the endings of *geology* and *histology*.

Developing a personal strategy

If you wish to develop a personal strategy based on this, you need to begin by analysing the nature of the mistakes you make. It is then necessary to attach your problem words to words that you can spell. A typical problem area is the double or single letters that occur in words like accommodation, imitate, and professional. You could try to learn the whole list of problem words by heart. An approach more likely to succeed however is to group the words according to a series of patterns and thus relate problem words to others that have the same pattern:

words with no double letters
    pedal, imitate, etc.
words with one pair of double letters
    accelerate, assist, etc.
words with two pairs of double letters
    accommodation, address, etc.

You could develop a similar approach to problems of sound/letter correspondence. That is what happens in the most famous spelling rule of all:

'I before E except after C, when the sound is long EE'

Finally, and most important, *write it down*. If you wish to remember a visual pattern it is important that you should see it. When you are trying to learn a spelling that causes problems, a well-known method is *look – cover – write – check*:

✔ **Look** at the correct spelling on the printed page so that you 'print' it on your brain. Spell the word out loud.
✔ **Cover** it up.
✔ **Write** it down from memory, spelling it out loud as you do so.
✔ **Check** against the printed version that you have got it right.

With a problem word this process should be repeated at increasing intervals until you are confident that it is fixed in your mind. Also, when in doubt about a spelling, it is always worth writing down its various possible forms on scrap paper to see which looks right.

●●●●● **Rules based on patterns** ●●●●●

Spelling rules and patterns fall into two broad groups:
- those that cover the spelling of certain sounds which can be written in two or three different ways
- those that explain how adding to a word changes the spelling of the original word

Sounds and letters

The rules that follow are not exhaustive, but have been chosen because they are useful and fairly easy to remember.

–ie– and –ei–

i before e *except after* c *when the sound is long* 'ee'
EXAMPLES: thief, receive
EXCEPTIONS: caffeine, codeine, counterfeit, protein, seize, species, (*plus* either, neither, inveigle)

–c– and –s–

c noun *s* verb
(easily remembered because the initial letters are in alphabetical order: C–N–S–V)

EXAMPLES:	NOUN	VERB
	practice	practise
	prophecy	prophesy

-ise, -ize, -yse

This is an area where an old rule and a new one are in conflict. Traditionally there was a group of words derived from Greek which reflected the Greek spelling by ending -ize. Examples include *organize* and *realize*. Today it is permissible to spell almost any word with this sound at the end with -ise, except for capsize which must be spelled with a −z−. In addition, a small number of words of Greek origin end -yse and must be spelled that way (unless you are American and prefer to spell them -yze). They include *analyse* and *paralyse*.

-able, -ible

There *is* a rule, but it requires a fair amount of linguistic knowledge to apply it!

-ible is reserved for words borrowed from Latin and the list of 180 or so words spelled in this way is 'closed'–no new words are being created spelled in this way. More common words spelled in this way are:

accessible	admissible	audible	collapsible
combustible	compatible	comprehensible	contemptible
credible	defensible	destructible	digestible
divisible	edible	fallible	flexible
forcible	gullible	horrible	illegible
implausible	inaccessible	incontrovertible	incredible
indefensible	indelible	inedible	insensible
intelligible	invincible	invisible	illegible
irresistible	irreversible	ostensible	permissible
plausible	possible	responsible	reversible
sensible	susceptible	suggestible	tangible
terrible	visible		

Words derived from Old English words and all new words now created with this ending are spelled -able. So the list includes old words like:

affordable	laughable	washable

and new words (often ugly!) like:

networkable	unclubbable	windsurfable

A quick check, which works most of the time, is that if you remove -able from a word, you are usually still left with a complete word. If you do the same with -ible, generally you are not.

-ar, -er, -or

Tricky, because there is some overlap. In most cases, when a verb is turned into a noun (meaning 'the person who does this') we add -er (or just -r to words ending in -e):

designer, maker, miner

All new nouns made from verbs work in this way. But verbs that end in -ate make nouns ending in -ator. There are a number of other nouns derived from verbs which also end in -or, of which the commonest are:

actor	contractor	contributor	defector
distributor	governor	guarantor	inspector
inventor	investor	persecutor	prosecutor
prospector	reflector	resistor	sailor
supervisor	surveyor	survivor	visitor

There are also a few that add *-ar*, of which the commonest are:
> beggar, burglar, liar

●●●●● **Rules for changing words** ●●●●●

The other group of rules or patterns covers how we spell words when we add bits to them.

Adding -s

We add -s to words for two reasons:
– to make nouns plural
– to form the she/he form of the present tense of verbs

The rules for both are the same, so the plural -s rules are given here, with a few additional rules which apply only to plurals.

1 Normally just add *-s*:
> *papers, hopes*

2 Words that end with any of the following, add *-es*. *-ch, -s, -sh, -x, -z*:
> *branches, masses, bushes, boxes, chintzes*

3 Words that end in *-f* or *-fe*, change the ending to *ves*:
> *wives, calves*

   Exceptions to this:
> *beliefs, chiefs, dwarfs, griefs, gulfs, proofs, roofs*

4 Words that end in *vowel + y*, add *-s*:
> *days, boys*

5 Words that end in *consonant + y*, change the *-y* to *-ies*:
> *babies, spies*

6 Words that end in *-o* normally just add *-s*:
> *pianos, radios*

   There is however a group of common words which add -es:

buffaloes	*cargoes* (can be *cargos*)	*dominoes*
echoes	*goes*	*grottoes*
haloes	*heroes*	*mangoes*
mosquitoes	*mottoes* (can be *mottos*)	*potatoes*
tomatoes	*tornadoes*	*torpedoes*
vetoes	*volcanoes*	

Adding -ing and -ed

When using verbs we often need to add the grammatical suffixes *-ing* and *-ed* to the stem of the verb:

As I was *walking* along the High Street I *bumped* into an old friend.

Unless the verb is covered by one of the rules opposite, you simply add the suffix.

Before adding the suffix

1 Words ending in *consonant + y;* change the *y* to *i* before *-ed*
   cry → *crying* → *cried*
2 Words ending in *vowel + y;* just add the suffix:
   played
   Exceptions:
   said, paid, laid

Adding -ly

Many adjectives can be turned into adverbs by the addition of the suffix *-ly*. Normally this is simply added to the adjective. There are a few exceptions:

1 If the word ends in *-ll*, simply add *y*.
   fully
2 Words of more than one syllable ending in *-y*, remove the *-y* and add *-ily*.
   happily
3 Words ending with a consonant followed by *-le*, remove the final *e* and add *y*.
   terribly
4 Most single syllable words ending in *-y* are regular, except for:
   daily, gaily

Adding -er and -est

The comparative and superlative forms of many adjectives are formed by adding the suffixes *-er* and *-est*:

great, greater, greatest

The suffixes are normally added without further change. There are four groups of exceptions:

1 Words that end in a consonant followed by *-y;* change the *-y* to an *-i* before adding the suffix:
   happier, happiest
2 Words with one syllable which contains a long vowel sound and which end with *-e* (e.g. late); remove the *-e* before adding the suffix:
   later, latest
3 Words of one syllable containing a short vowel sound and ending in a single consonant letter (e.g. *sad*); double the final consonant before adding the suffix:
   sadder, saddest
4 Words ending in *-l* normally just add the suffix, but there is one exception:
   cruel → *crueller* → *cruellest*

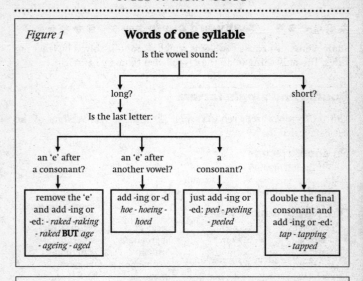

Figure 1 **Words of one syllable**

Is the vowel sound:

long? short?

Is the last letter:

an 'e' after a consonant? | an 'e' after another vowel? | a consonant?

remove the 'e' and add -ing or -ed: - *raked -raking - raked* **BUT** *age - ageing - aged*

add -ing or -d *hoe - hoeing - hoed*

just add -ing or -ed: *peel - peeling - peeled*

double the final consonant and add -ing or -ed: *tap - tapping - tapped*

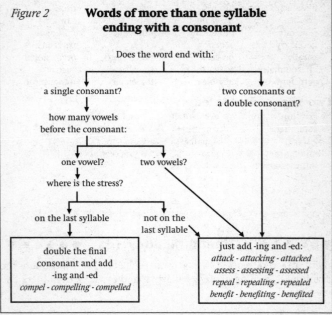

Figure 2 **Words of more than one syllable ending with a consonant**

Does the word end with:

a single consonant? two consonants or a double consonant?

how many vowels before the consonant:

one vowel? two vowels?

where is the stress?

on the last syllable not on the last syllable

double the final consonant and add -ing and -ed *compel - compelling - compelled*

just add -ing and -ed: *attack - attacking - attacked assess - assessing - assessed repeal - repealing - repealed benefit - benefiting - benefited*

●●●●●● **Awkward customers** ●●●●●●

Some words just cause problems which cannot be solved by learning rules. The only thing to do then is to learn them by heart.

Double and single letters

This problem was referred to earlier. These are longer versions of the lists suggested there.

No double letters

fulfil (fulfill in AmE)

imitate	marvel	omit
patrol	pedal	transmit

One pair of double letters

abbreviate	accelerate	accident	accomplish
accurate	allergy	appropriate	approximate
assist	beginning	brilliant	caterpillar
collapse	collect	commemorate	commit
corridor	desiccated	disappear	disappoint
dissatisfied	discuss	exaggerate	excellent
gorilla	happen(ed)	harass	illusion
illustrate	immediate	innuendo	millionaire
necessary	occasion	occur	paraffin
parallel	proceed	procession	professional
questionnaire	scissors	sheriff	succint
sufficient	terrible	tomorrow	tranquillity

Two pairs of double letters

accommodation	accidentally	address
commission	committed	embarrass
guerrilla	happiness	mattress
millennium	possess	successful
unnecessary	woollen	

●●●●●● **Other difficult words** ●●●●●●

There are several words that just cause problems. This list contains the commonest spelling errors regularly found by GCSE examiners and teachers:

abscess
absence
achievement
acknowledgement
acquaintance
acquiesce
acquire
across
adequate
advertisement
aeroplane
always
amateur
analysis
anonymous
anxious
ascent
atmosphere
bargain
basically
beautiful
because
beginning
behaviour
beneficial
biscuit
building
canoe/canoeing
catalogue
cemetery
chaos
character
cigarette
college
column
compulsory
condemn
conspiracy
correspondence
criticism
debt
deceit
deceive
definite
different
disagree
disappear

discipline
enormous
enthusiasm
especially
exaggerate
exceptional
excitement
existence
expense
extremely
extraordinary
favourite
fierce
February
foreign
forty
friends
further
gaol
grammar
guarantee
hypocrisy
immediately
interrupt
intrigue
irrelevant
jealousy
jeopardy
knowledge
language
leisure
liar
library
magnificent
maintenance
manoeuvre
marriage
melancholy
naturally
negotiate
neither
obedient
offered
opinion
opportunity
opposition
ordinary

originally
outrageous
overrule
paid
parliament
particularly
peculiar
perceive
permanent
permission
permitted
persistent
piece
precede
preference
preferred
prejudice
preparation
pretentious
prevalent
privilege
probably
psychiatry
psychology
pursue
questionnaire
receive
reference
refrigerator
regularly
relieved
reminiscence
religious
responsible
rhyme
rhythm
ridiculous
schedule
sentence
separate
severely
silhouette
similar/similarly
simultaneous
sincerely
soliloquy
sponsored

specimen	unconscious	usually
supersede	undoubtedly	vacuum
surprise	unfortunately	vehicle
sympathy	unnecessarily	vicious
tragedy	until	yesterday

One way to use this list is to go through it picking out words that cause you a problem. Write out your own 'problem list' and work through it systematically, learning the correct spellings.

●●●●● Words sometimes confused ●●●●●

☞ accept/except

I *accept* everything you say *except* your claim that you are telling the truth.

☞ access/excess

I could not gain *access* to the building because of an *excess* of security precautions.

☞ adverse/averse

adverse means 'preventing success'
averse means 'strongly opposed to'

☞ affect/effect

– as nouns
affect is a relatively uncommon word and means 'mood, mental state, emotion'
effect means 'the result of an action', or 'personal possession'
– as verbs
affect means 'to alter the state of something, to have an effect on it'
effect means 'to bring something about', as in *effect a change*

☞ all ready/already

'Now are we *all ready?* she asked, *already* beginning to get flustered.

☞ all together/altogether

If you put his mistakes *all together*, his reputation looks *altogether* different.

☞ amend/emend

both words have a similar meaning of 'changing something', but *amend* carries a meaning of 'make improvements to', while *emend* tends to mean 'correct a mistake in'

☞ appraise/apprise

After *appraising* my work, the inspector *apprised* me of his opinion.

☞ ascent/assent

ascent means 'climb'; *assent* means 'agreement'

☞ auger/augur

The student's inability to use a simple *auger* to bore a hole did not *augur* well for his career as a boatbuilder.

☞ aural/oral

In the French examination we had to do a dictation, which tested our *aural* ability, and also give a five minute talk to demonstrate our *oral* skills.

☞ awhile/a while

awhile is an adverb; *a while* is a noun phrase. So:
    'Let's rest *awhile*', she said after *a while*.

☞ bail/bale

After being let out of prison on *bail* he went on a parachuting course. On his first descent he broke his leg landing on a *bale* of straw.

☞ base/bass

In some operas the *bass* singer plays a villain or other *base* characters.

☞ biannual/biennial

If you're lucky you get *biannual* holidays (every six months); if you're unlucky they are *biennial* (every two years).

☞ born/borne

The couple's problems seemed too great to be *borne*, especially after their sixth child was *born*.

☞ buy/by/bye

by is a preposition with a range of meanings; *bye* is a noun with meanings in cricket and other games; either spelling can be used in *by the by(e)* and *by(e)-law*

☞ calendar/colander

I must put a note on the *calendar* in the kitchen to remind me to buy a new *colander* for the vegetables.

☞ callous/callus

'Is that a wart on your finger or just a *callus?*' she asked *callously.*

☞ cannon/canon

The cathedral *canon* wanted to fire a small *cannon* from the tower to scare the pigeons but he was told it was against the *canons* of the church.

☞ canvas/canvass

When he went round the area to *canvass* votes, he carried his election literature in a *canvas* holdall.

☞ censer/censor/censure

A *censer* is a container in which incense is burned

A *censor* is someone who controls the content of books, newspapers, films, and other media.

If you *censure* someone, you criticize or condemn them.

☞ cereal/serial

As he ate his breakfast *cereal* he read the comic strip *serial* in his daily paper.

☞ complement/compliment

A *compliment* is paid to someone you admire. The *complement* is what completes something: the ship's *complement* is its crew, without which it would be incomplete.

☞ complaisant/complacent

Someone who is *complaisant* wishes to please others.

Complacent people are easily pleased and probably pleased with themselves.

☞ contagious/contiguous

A *contagious* disease is one that can be passed on by physical contact.

Two things that are *contiguous* are next to each other and may actually be touching.

☞ council/counsel

At the meeting of the royal *council* the king asked his senior ministers for their *counsel* about what he should do.

☞ crevasse/crevice

From a great height the huge *crevasses* in the ice looked like tiny *crevices* in a sheet of crumpled paper.

☞ curb/kerb

A *curb* is something that restrains someone or something (or *curbs* them).

A *kerb* is the edge of a pavement.

☞ currant/current

A *currant* is a piece of dried fruit.

A *current* is a moving stream of water in the sea.

Current also means 'happening now'.

☞ defuse/diffuse

If you *defuse* something you literally remove its fuse, so more generally it means 'neutralize, remove the danger from'.

If you *diffuse* something you spread it around.

☞ dependant/dependent

His father was not *dependent* on the state, although he had nineteen *dependants*.

☞ deprecate/depreciate

The cricket authorities *deprecated* the batsman's bad behaviour, arguing that it would only cause the reputation of cricket as a sport to *depreciate*.

☞ disassemble/dissemble

The clever nine-year-old said, 'Father, I will not *dissemble*. It was I who *disassembled* your computer.'

☞ dinghy/dingy

A dirty little sailing boat could be described as a *dingy dinghy*.

☞ emigrate/immigrate

As a rule, those who *immigrate* into one country must first have *emigrated* from another.

☞ ensure/insure

Before they went on holiday he *ensured* that the house and contents were fully *insured*.

☞ exalt/exult

If you *exalt* something you raise it up, literally or figuratively.

If you *exult*, you rejoice.

☞ faze/phase

I was completely *fazed* by her behaviour which seemed to mark a new *phase* in our relationship.

☞ flaunt/flout

The streaker *flouted* all the conventions of cricketing society by *flaunting* his body in front of the Test Match crowd.

☞ foreword/forward

In her *foreword* to the book she put *forward* some new arguments.

☞ gild/guild/gilt/guilt

At courses run by the *Guild* of Cake Decorators you can learn how to put gold icing, or *gilt*, on a cake; they call the lesson '*Gilding* the gingerbread'. The slogan 'Naughty but nice' suggests that if you eat cream cakes you should feel a pleasurable *guilt*.

☞ grill/grille

A *grill* is something you cook on.
A *grille* is a barred opening in a wall.

☞ human/humane

Most *human* beings who eat meat expect the treatment of the animals they consume to be *humane;* they do not want them to suffer.

☞ impractical/impracticable

An *impractical* person, who does not have much idea of how things should be done, is likely to suggest *impracticable* (unworkable) solutions to problems.

☞ inapt/inept

An *inapt* solution is one which is not suitable for that particular problem. It may well be suggested by someone who isn't very good at such things, who is, in fact, *inept.*

☞ index/indexes/indices

In everyday usage the plural of *index* is *indexes*. *Indices* is reserved for the mathematical sense of *index*. (As in: The minister referred to a number of different *indices* to show how prices were moving.)

☞ ingenious/ingenuous

Ingenuous means 'Honourably straightforward; open, frank, candid' (OED)–often innocently so.
Ingenious means clever.

☞ interment/internment

Interment means burial.
Internment means imprisonment.

☞ lightening/lightning

During a long and very dull lecture about the effects of thunder and *lightning* on pregnant moles, the only thing that was *lightening* my boredom was the thought that it could not go on for ever.

☞ liqueur/liquor

A *liqueur* is a strong and usually sweet liquor (alcoholic drink) such as Cointreau or Bénédictine. A *liquor* can also be a more general term for a liquid.

☞ loathe/loath

If you *loathe* something, you hate it and are *loath* (unwilling) to have anything to do with it.

☞ lose/loose

These two are sometimes confused (because *lose* rhymes with choose?) You might, for example, *lose* a pet dog if you left it *loose* rather than tied up.

☞ meter/metre

A *meter* is used to measure things. A *metre* is a distance and also the regular pattern of strong and weak syllables in metrical poetry.

☞ militate/mitigate

To *militate* is to conflict with or work against someone or something.
To *mitigate* is to lessen the harmful effects of something or someone.

☞ miner/minor

A *miner* digs underground.
A *minor* is under age.

☞ moral/morale

The *moral* of the story was that when an army's *morale* is low it loses battles.

☞ naval/navel

Naval means concerning the navy.
A *navel* is a belly button.

☞ palate/palette/pallet

The *palate* is part of the mouth.

A *palette* is the range of colours used by an artist or the small tray they are placed on.

A *pallet* is a wooden platform on which goods are stacked for storage or carriage. It is also a straw bed or mattress.

☞ passed/past

These two are sometimes confused.

Passed is the past tense and past participle of the verb to pass:

I have *passed* my exam; all the students in our year *passed*.

Past is an adjective or a preposition:

I have *passed* all my examinations so the time for worrying is *past*.

He walked *past* the house.

☞ peninsula/peninsular

Peninsula is a noun:

Devon and Cornwall form a *peninsula*.

Peninsular is the adjective derived from it:

The *Peninsular* War was fought in Spain against the French.

☞ precede/proceed

As the procession *proceeded* along the Mall, the Royal Carriage *preceded* that of the Prime Minister.

☞ prescribe/proscribe

Prescribe means recommend or advise.

Proscribe means ban or forbid.

☞ principle/principal

Principle is a noun and means what is central to something, a fundamental truth:

Whenever we argued he always insisted on taking things back to first *principles*.

Principal can be either an adjective or a noun. As an adjective it means 'main or chief'; as a noun it means 'the head or leader of a group or organization':

The *principal* rule, or *principle,* on which the college was run was that the *Principal* was always right.

☞ resister/resistor

A *resister* is someone who resists.

A *resistor* is an electronic device which reduces the flow of an electric current.

☞ sceptic/septic

He was always a *sceptic*, so he did not believe me when I told him that the wound had gone *septic*.

☞ sight/site/cite

He argued that tourism was bad for the developing world and *cited* one example where a popular *site* had become an eyesore rather than a *sight* for sore eyes.

☞ stationary/stationery

Stationary is an adjective and means not moving.
Stationery is a noun referring to paper and other office materials.

☞ taught/taut

Subjects are *taught* in schools.
Taut is the opposite of loose or slack.

☞ waiver/waver

She never *wavered* in her determination to get the bank to renounce their legal right to repossess her house. In the end she got the *waiver* she was requesting.

complementary
purple-yellow

+ red, red blue

- yellow, red blue

- yellow green, orange red purple.

orange yellow try
blue
2 primary
complementary
high light.